BARNETT NEWMAN

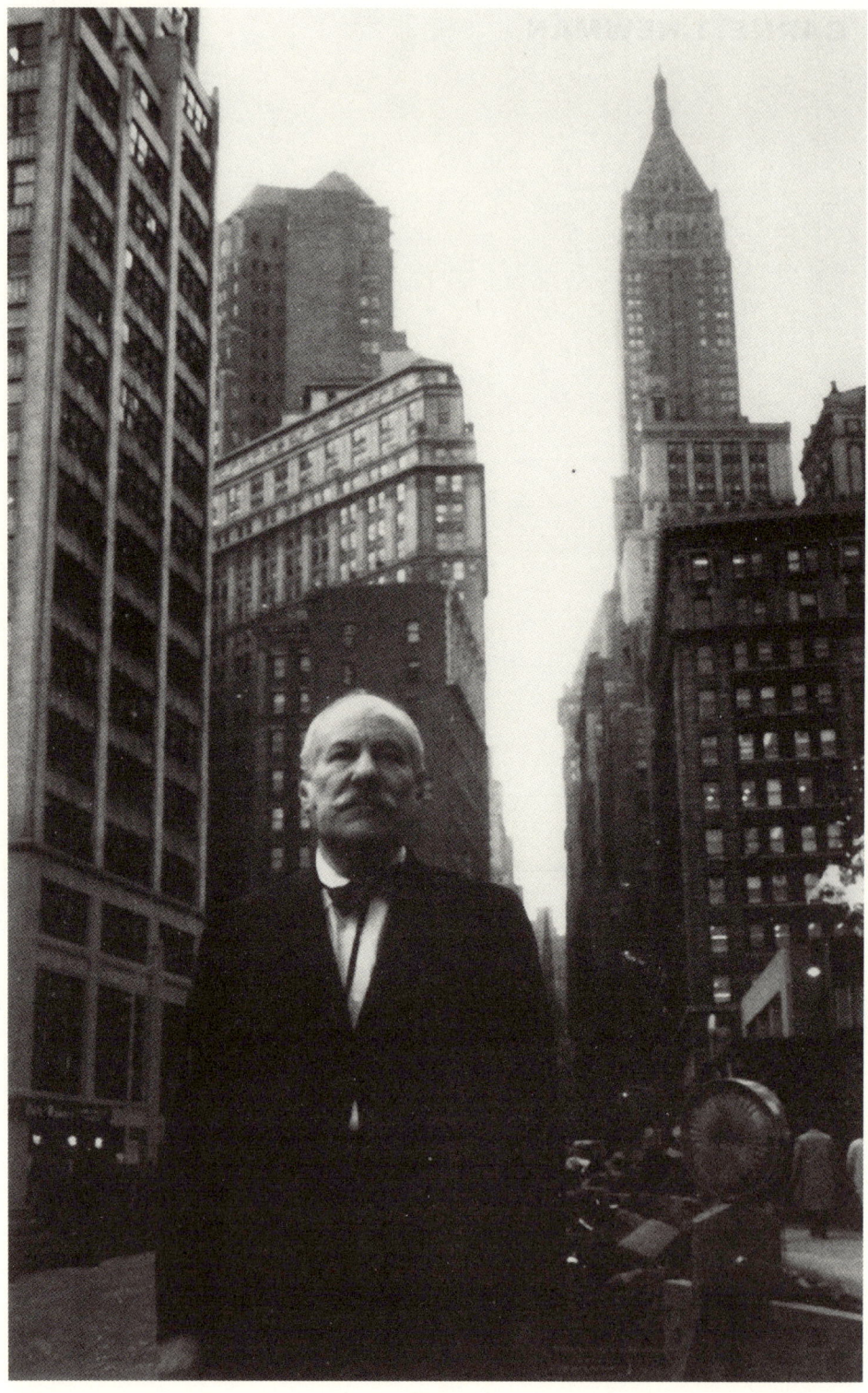

BARNETT
NEWMAN
HERE

AMY
NEWMAN

PRINCETON UNIVERSITY PRESS | PRINCETON AND OXFORD

Published by Princeton University Press, 41 William Street,
Princeton, New Jersey 08540

In the United Kingdom: Princeton University Press, 99 Banbury Road,
Oxford OX2 6JX

press.princeton.edu

GPSR Authorized Representative: Easy Access System Europe - Mustamäe tee
50, 10621 Tallinn, Estonia, gpsr.requests@easproject.com

Frontispiece: Barnett Newman near his Front Street studio, 1963. Photograph
Robert Murray.

Jacket image: Barnett Newman in his studio, standing before *Who's Afraid of
Red, Yellow and Blue III* (detail), photograph by Alexander Liberman. © 2025
The Barnett Newman Foundation / Artists Rights Society (ARS), New York.
Courtesy of *Studio International*. All Rights Reserved

ISBN 9780691249186
ISBN (ebook) 9780691274706

Library of Congress Cataloging-in-Publication Data
Names: Newman, Amy, 1949- author.
Title: Barnett Newman : here / Amy Newman.
Description: Princeton : Princeton University Press, [2025] |
    Includes bibliographical references and index.
Identifiers: LCCN 2024047853 (print) | LCCN 2024047854 (ebook) |
    ISBN 9780691249186 (hardcover) | ISBN 9780691274706 (ebook)
Subjects: LCSH: Newman, Barnett, 1905-1970. |
    Artists—United States—Biography.
Classification: LCC N6537.N48 N49 2025 (print) | LCC N6537.N48 (ebook) |
    DDC 759.13--dc23/eng/20250529
LC record available at https://lccn.loc.gov/2024047853
LC ebook record available at https://lccn.loc.gov/2024047854

British Library Cataloging-in-Publication Data is available

Editorial: Michelle Komie and Annie Miller
Production Editorial: Terri O'Prey
Text Design: Heather Hansen
Jacket/Cover Design: Heather Hansen
Production: Steven Sears
Publicity: Jodi Price

This book has been composed in Adobe Text Pro with Berthold Akzidenz

Printed in the United States of America

1 3 5 7 9 10 8 6 4 2

God tested Abraham, saying to him, "Abraham!"
And he said, "Here I am."
Genesis 22:1

Then I heard the voice of my Lord saying, "Whom
shall I send? Who will go for us?" And I said, "Here
am I; send me."
Isaiah 6:8

Barnett Newman Haftarah portion

CONTENTS

INTRODUCTION. "BARNEY" 1

PART ONE. GENETIC MOMENT: 1905–32 7

1 A guy who cuts classes 9
2 Beginning 22
3 The most intense experiences 31
4 "The fox knows many things" 40

PART TWO. THE VOICE: 1933–47 51

5 The Civil Service Man 53
6 Miss Greenhouse 60
7 The Search 66
8 The Answer 72
9 Marriage 77
10 Merit 85
11 Dignity 93
12 The Stance 105
13 Objector 112
14 Polemics 121
15 What About Isolationist Art? 126
16 What did you do during the war? 135
17 Betty Parsons 149
18 The Breton of American painting 159
19 The Plasmic Image 173
20 The Terror 180
21 Only the pure idea 187
22 The First Man Was an Artist 198

PART THREE. OUTCRY: 1948–58 209

23 Onement 211
24 Embattled 217
25 The Sublime 230
26 Subjects of the Artist 238
27 Man is present 246
28 "A show at the Betty Parsons Gallery" 252
29 "The biggest scandal in N.Y. art world" 261
30 Irascibles 273
31 Compelled 284
32 Ambiguous men 292
33 "Fifteen Americans" 301
34 Aesthetics and ornithology 307
35 L'Errance (The Wandering) 319
36 Indignation 329
37 The blackest period 341
38 "Newman interests us much more" 359
39 Losses 369
40 Turning point 376
41 "Mensch. Times ten" 385

PART FOUR. VIR HEROICUS SUBLIMIS: 1958–70 395

42 "The New American Painting" 397
43 The Lema Sabachthani and the glory 407
44 French & Company 417
45 "A man and his work" 424
46 "Newman standard time" 436
47 Authenticity 448
48 "Mr. Newman, why do you paint?" 454
49 Prometheus Bound 462
50 Priority 468
51 West Coast 477
52 "The Reputation of Barnett Newman" 484

53 Black and white 491
54 Statements 498
55 Europe 507
56 "Questionable historical facts" 516
57 São Paulo 528
58 Stations of the Cross 538
59 Who's Afraid 549
60 "The urge to be exalted" 558
61 *Broken Obelisk* 565
62 "For Impassioned Criticism" 570
63 Knoedler 585
64 "New York Painting and Sculpture: 1940–1970" 596
65 "At Home" 606

Acknowledgments 617
Notes 619
Index 667
Photo Credits 695

Color plates follow page 358.

BARNETT NEWMAN

INTRODUCTION
"BARNEY"

Here. A place in the world. Proof that one exists. Barnett Newman spent a lifetime searching for confirmation of a simple idea.

After World War II, in various places around the world, there occurred a moment when a small number of artists were experimenting with paintings that were startling: more psychologically fraught, more abstract, on bigger canvases marked with signature motifs and gestures. One of the artists looked at an almost entirely uninflected field of paint, inscribed it with one vertical, and realized that it said all he wanted to say. "Here I am." Just at the point when the culture was ready to accept as art something previously unimaginable, Barnett Newman stood poised as the person with the audacity to create it.

For fifty years, his example remained a touchstone for artists. "Barney," as he was universally known, seemed unshakably installed in the most elite room of the pantheon of 20th-century American artists. For much of that time he was "widely thought of," wrote the esteemed critic David Sylvester, "as the greatest painter to have emerged since the Second World War,"[1] and even now, in a radically recast history, scores of artists in each generation that followed his cite him as influential in one way or another—formally or philosophically, as a maker or as a model; an "ideal." His works, often given pride of place in major museums all over the world, democratically deliver a heart-stopping experience to any viewers willing to let down their guards, to abandon preconceptions or defenses or vapid expectations, and give themselves over to the encounter. Though some pieces are among the largest paintings produced in the period in which he worked, even the small ones—as small as an inch and a half wide—can make a viewer feel the same being-penetrating aura that is felt in the presence of a primeval natural vista, a colossal remnant of an ancient civilization, or an individual soul in meditation: a *place* in the world, both a mystery and a metaphysical fact, that inspires in the sympathetic collaborator what the artist called the recognition of "his own totality, of his own separateness, of his own individuality, and at the same time . . . connection." Not every artist feels as exalted a calling. Yet, what higher ambition could an artist have? What other ambition would be worth pursuing?

This was the corner that Newman backed himself into, less by design—psychologically, he had no choice—than by standards, doubts, and superego. That he got where he was headed—eventually—is the story everyone learns at the Museum of Modern Art or the Stedelijk, the National Gallery or the Reina Sofía, Tate, Pompidou, or Metropolitan museums. But how—the particular labyrinth that he navigated—is something else. Often he would tell people, "it's only after man knows *where* he is that he can ask himself 'who am I?' and 'where am I going?'" Newman faced down these questions daily, and answered them. On the journey, he created a "character" with a vitality, style, and charisma that, while belying his turmoil, enabled him to find his way.

Everybody who ever met him in the 1950s and '60s has a Barnett Newman story that is related with delight and a smile, charmed by the opportunity to recall the dapper, avuncular and loquacious, perpetual presence. (Barney would attend the opening of an envelope, said Andy Warhol.) These stories have been passed down with surprising consistency—if not accuracy—to later generations of those inclined to talk knowingly about New York art or artists. He ran for mayor of New York City (how bold). He taught himself Yiddish so he could read the Anarchist newspapers (how committed). He sued fellow artist and friend, Ad Reinhardt (how appalling). He said, "If my painting were properly understood, it would mean the end of state capitalism." He said, "Aesthetics is for the artist as ornithology is for the birds." He stopped painting and "disappeared" after his second, poorly received show. He tried to make a living by playing the horses. He took on the esteemed art historian Erwin Panofsky in a battle over Latin grammar, and *won*. He designed a synagogue in the form of a baseball stadium. He, a Jew, shocked—shocked!—the cultural establishment by redefining a trope as canonical as any representation in history: the Stations of the Cross.

Most of the stories have their source in two biographical monographs that Thomas Hess, the editor of *Art News* magazine, wrote in 1969 and 1970. By that time, Hess, who had been the devil incarnate—"sinister" and "Stalinic"[2]—to Barney in the 1950s, the respected authority who threw every obstacle in his path, had become not just a champion of the artist, but an intimate, a pal, and adorer. And so the assumption is made that whatever appeared in his books had the blessing of Barney, and thus was true in substance and specifics.

And this was perfectly appropriate: Barnett Newman, a haberdasher's son, fanatical about tailoring, insisted on inhabiting a bespoke world, made to his measure. "Barney preconceived Barney Newman," William Rubin, the late scholar and director of the Museum of Modern Art's Department of Painting and Sculpture, said almost twenty years after the painter's death. "That is, the man I knew didn't simply paint these pictures. The pictures were painted by a painter conceived by the man I knew . . . . He conceived what Barney Newman should look like, what Barney Newman should do, and what he should not do."[3] It wasn't sufficient to be the maker of paintings that have come to be acknowledged as almost perfectly embodying and reflecting their time, the art works that, for many, crystallized the statement that in retrospect seemed to be required in America in the 1950s and '60s. Everything about those paintings—the way they could be discussed, described, handled, and sold—and especially the man who made them, was to be expertly fit, sometimes shoe-horned, to his specifications. In this way Newman, with either instinct or prescience, created during his lifetime something that had previously taken centuries to develop: a coherent avatar—the congruent, un-parsable artist-art-mythology. If this wasn't unique during the postwar years—think Pollock or de Kooning—it was uniquely self-conscious, with enduring implications.

Barney was, eponymously, the "new man" (like Henry James's Christopher), a name to which, when he was about 15 or 16, he added a blessing by attaching as his first—or sometimes middle—name "Benedict" (or "Baruch"), possibly under the influence of an infatuation with the godfather of apostate Jewish intellectuals, Spinoza, possibly because in Genesis, God told Abraham he would make his name a blessing. By that age, Barney, born in 1905, could be forgiven for judging himself blessed, having, as a first-generation citizen, experienced in its wondrous immediacy New York's momentum and progress at the beginning of the 20th century—in housing, education, transportation, communication—and, linked to that, the rise of his family's fortunes. In this new world, this "America," he not only understood that anything was possible, he refused to accept that anything was *im*possible. The immigrant's son would run for mayor of the country's largest city; he would challenge, on intellectual terms, a variety of authorities high and low and personally engineer public notice for it; he would correspond with luminaries in fields that ranged wide; and he would conceive of, and become recognized as, the "artist" he always felt himself to be—one of a tiny number of those who invented (in the public's imagination) the most "American," the most *not*-immigrant, art.

But even while he identified with the progressive, he idiosyncratically wore the habit of the conservative—literally: immaculately tailored tweeds and hound's-tooth checks, silk bow ties, brushed fedoras or squire's weekend caps, brigadier's mustaches—and a démodé monocle. Neither passively nor actively would he accept standard operating procedure; customizing was his forte, from his name and his image (the monocle became, in effect, a trademark), to Jesuitical, anomalous interpretations of everyone else's actions or words, or experiences (baseball, for example). He developed uniquely "Newman" definitions of common terms: "color," "subject," "scale," "shape," "series," "variation," "uniqueness," "drawing," "painting." The things and concepts that artists considered daily for hundreds of years were, to Barney's mind, generally misconceived. And he could tell you why.

You could easily understand how a person born at the beginning of a new century, to parents only recently emigrated from the "Old World" to an America that itself was being born as modern society, a world in which almost everything was different and filled with possibility, would feel propellant ambition to create a shining self in that world. But what form would that self take, and in what arena? Ultimately, as the story goes, on his 43rd birthday (the lateness was always to rankle other artists of his generation) he found the work that he was, he often said, "compelled" to do.

"One of the things that Barney Newman basically decided was that you have an image," said Rubin. "Decided" or "compelled" (as Barney would say)? At a particular moment in American art, everything turned on that question: "compelled" was authentic, "decided" was counterfeit, feigned. And then, ten years later, it didn't seem to matter so much. The next generation wanted him, learned from him, claimed him. Was Barney an aesthetic freeloader or a seer? A cynic among his peers, or too advanced for them to see? Was he, as Sylvester thought, "The Ugly Duckling": "the character who appears on the scene when a member of a different species is expected"?

"All the artists of [his] generation talked about 'my image.' And what they meant by 'my image' was the picture that established your style and that people got to know you by . . . . If you repeat the same thing enough, the public and the art public identify that with conviction: that this man must have had a vision because nobody would sit there day after day painting this kind of picture unless it was really part of them in some way. I don't think that Barney's repetition of [the] zips was just a strategy. I think that Barney had a vision. But that the vision was also a function of a strategy. In other words, he might have had other visions. And cancelled them out. Because this one, he felt, was sufficiently him, and that it was possible for him to grow in it. And that it's better not to have too many visions."

Rubin was talking about Barney's vivid presence among artists, and the mythology of an iconic, revelatory, self-contained, and abiding art. But Rubin was on to something even more interesting, something that emerges after piecing together historical evidence that significantly torques the official autobiography. The familiar Barnett Newman, Harold Rosenberg's artist of "Spiritual Grandeur," was not created suddenly out of whole cloth in 1948. He was in no sense a fraud, nothing significant is exactly untrue, and he was by no means cynical about his art or the mid-20th-century notion of art's high purpose. On the contrary, so confirmed was he in the conviction that art-conceiving and -making was nearly sacramental, that he was virtually paralyzed by the calling. And yet, he was certain he had been "called" and spent over half of his adult life consciously incubating, cerebrating, preparing himself for the act. There's no evidence that he was motivated by any crass desire for money or fame. Rather, while he was producing the art that he believed was necessary, he also created a creator that he believed was worthy of that art: a thoughtful, savvy, and disciplined unity in the service of his vision. It was almost in concept Baroque theater, an auteur-encompassing *Gesamtkunstwerk*. He may have had the not entirely rare (among artists) qualities of grandiosity and narcissism, but he imagined them into a cohesive vision of an art and an artist that seemed to be exactly what his culture called for, as much in the early years of his career, when he was underappreciated—when the art community required someone to exist "beyond the pale" to be able to lionize those just inside it—as in the later years when he became the next generation's favorite father figure.

Thomas Hess, Barney's Boswell, certainly had an inkling of his role. Writing an anecdote about a time, in 1959, that Barney visited Meyer Schapiro's famous Columbia seminar on Abstract Expressionism, Hess checked the facts with Schapiro himself. "If that's the way Barney remembers it," Schapiro said with a smile, "that's the way to write it."[4]

Endless words have been written "revising" Barney's contribution from different points of view, every writer selectively dependent on incomplete views: Newman said this, or Newman said that (or, didn't say that). Formalist or expressionist? Kabbalist or existentialist? Minimalist or American romantic? Much has been made by critics of Barney's Anarchism, and it's understandable: *he* made much of his Anarchism, attributing his fluency in Yiddish to his hunger to read Anarchist journals, and writing, toward the end of his life, an introduction to the memoirs of Prince Peter Kropotkin. But although his sympathy was genuine—in *his fashion*—his adherence was belied by the way in which he spent the first half of his life aggressively working *within* the system. Verbally challenging it yes, but not executing an end run around it. (This was something Barney himself winkingly acknowledged: "The glory of knocking the other fellow down [in football] involves too many chances of being knocked down yourself. That is why we always preferred baseball. There, at least, you can slide."[5]) Retrospectively, in 1968, when students the world over were taking to the streets, it was safe for Barney to write, as the foreword to Peter Kropotkin's *Memoirs*, "The True Revolution Is Anarchist!", and satisfying for him to speak to young activists. At the same time, he saw the Broadway production of *Hair* over and over and extolled the Dionysian in so much of the youth culture, but it didn't make him a hippie. Regarding his political pacifism—again, he was true to it in his fashion; life would have been so improved *if* it were possible to live that way. He knew what he believed, but he was too much involved in and too buffeted by real life as it existed to be philosophically faithful. From the internal pressure of this conflict came the outcry, came *lema sabachthani*, came his paintings.

America in the 1960s and '70s enjoyed a good Olympian narrative for its art and artists; and so there is the mythology of Barnett Newman. On the other hand, we have the story of the man's life. And it's not the story of a figure inhabiting the rarefied ether of art-historical Valhalla, but of a vivid human being with a ravenous appetite for experience and agency, embedded in a specific time and place in the world. The art he created, of categorical contraction, was not the antithesis of the life he lived but a response to it: a kind of intense reduction, a black-hole compression, a *demi-glace* concentration, that consolidated, compacted, and consumed the multifariousness of that life in a statement of *presence*: "something, where if you stand in front of it, you know you're there."[6]

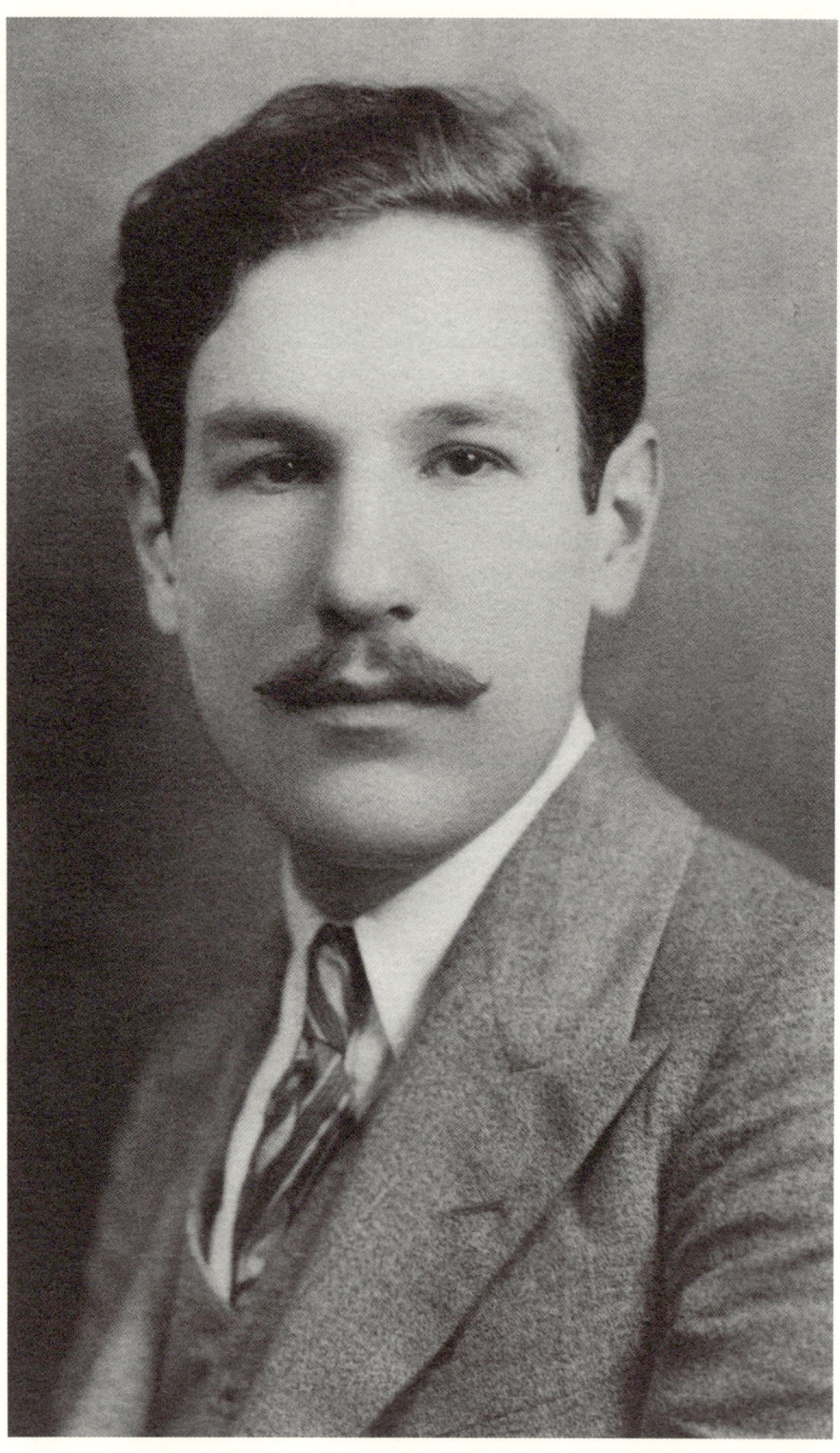

PART ONE

GENETIC MOMENT 1905–32

ONE

A GUY WHO CUTS CLASSES

He was a truant.

One hundred nine days missed at De Witt Clinton High School between January 1920 and January 1922.

Barney himself made the choice to attend Clinton, a long and complicated trek from the bucolic Bronx back into the Manhattan that his family had left behind eight years earlier. His siblings, his cousins, his friends could go to one of the local high schools—Morris or East Bronx or the new Evander Childs. But Barney thought the Bronx was "provincial"[1]: the reputation, the academics, and very particularly the sports at Clinton, better suited his self-image, and a student strike and the tribulations and trial of three teachers accused of "political disloyalty" piqued his scrappy disposition. And so he would walk down the steep hill from his home on Belmont Avenue to catch the elevated local at 174th Street, travel sixty minutes to Fifty-Third Street in "the city," then crawl along at six miles an hour on a "cable trolley" to Tenth Avenue and Fifty-Ninth Street to the school that was acknowledged as the largest and "one of the most perfect in its appointments" in America.[2]

The gables and dormers and high-pitched roofs! The limestone, the elaborately encrusted brick and luxuriously ornate portico! It perfectly fit the aspirations of a 14-year-old who began life in a tenement. The grandiose Flemish Revival building was the physical embodiment of American privilege, almost as exceptional as what was inside. When it was built in 1906 to accommodate the surging number of children of new immigrants it was envisioned as a demonstration model of how to do everything right: fireproof, filled with more light and air than any previous school building, with a two-thousand-seat auditorium, three gymnasia, "natatorium" (swimming pool); a lunch room that could "efficiently" feed four thousand hungry boys, and state-of-the-art science labs. In 1918, when Barney insisted on his maverick choice, Clinton already had a championship football team, track team, skating team, and a rowing club that practiced in the Harlem River. It was the school, in other words, that Barney felt he deserved.

But—not for the last time—things did not go according to his plan. Freshman year he did not, in fact, make it to the Tenth Avenue building, but was placed instead into an annex on Eighty-Seventh Street off Lexington Avenue.[3] He did not make the varsity football team as he had hoped—he was a little small, a little soft—with only the dramatic scar on his right cheek to show for his effort. And there were other scars, those of unabashed anti-Semitism. His grades, never good to begin with, declined over time; he missed more than one day in four, and dallied long enough to be marked late on fifty additional days.

By this time, he was already primed for a certain irreverence toward institutions of formal education, fortified by a bar mitzvah boy's callow arrogance. Fifteen months

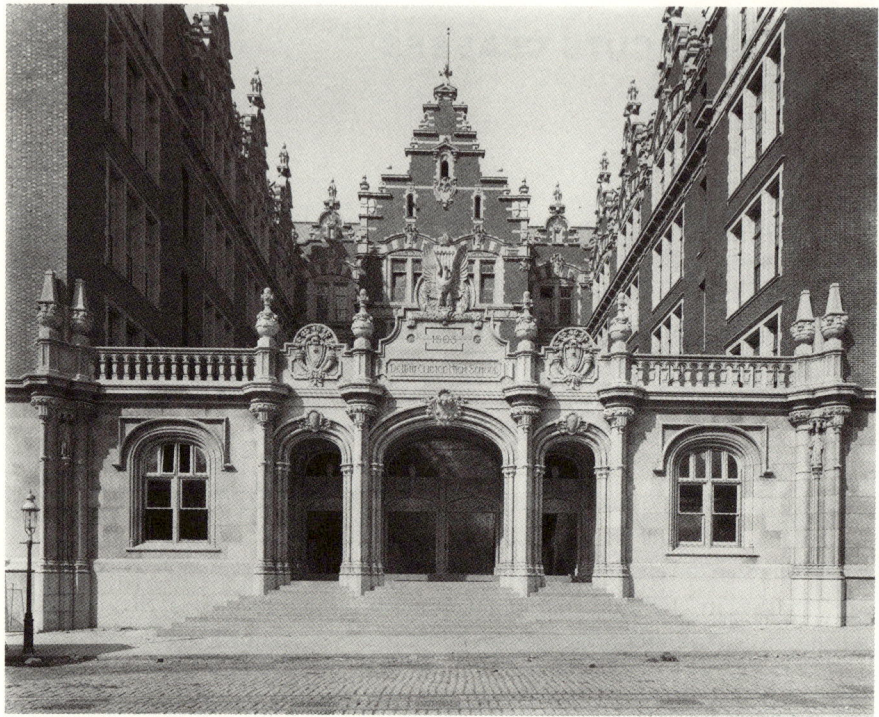

Fig. 1 Aspirational architecture: De Witt Clinton High School, c.1906. Wurts Bros., MNY 233692, Museum of the City of New York

earlier, as he was preparing to be called to publicly read and personally interpret a portion of the Torah, three weeks of well-publicized riots broke out at New York's public schools, including P.S. 44, his own. Atypically, these protesters were not rowdy agitators but the normally compliant, significantly Jewish, students and their parents, like Barney and his family. If political consciousness and social character are formed in early adolescence, one can easily imagine the future Barney—the manifesto writer, the mayoral candidate—on the barricades. He "heard about the controversy and organized a strike of its own for P.S. 44," wrote Thomas Hess, relaying Barney's account. "He offered his followers the irresistible attraction of parading around with signs and cutting classes."[4] Disposed to question authority, already exhibiting the anarchism that he would later extol in Kropotkin, it's not surprising that the teenage Barney decided high school was not for him. "I never paid much respect to institutions," he remarked proudly near the end of his life. "I'm a guy who cuts classes."[5]

As he told the story nearly fifty years later, the siren that seduced him on his daily Manhattan-bound odyssey was the Metropolitan Museum of Art. Specifically, what drew him was something that went "beyond the work," he saw there, something that "had to do with the men who had done them . . . a world of miracles made not by magicians or by an apocalyptic muse but by men, creative men . . . who said clearly that art is a human activity."[6]

From both parents Barney received support to be singular, and encouragement to be exegetical. Abraham and the truant officers were in contact, and when Barney was expelled, his father spoke to the school, then read Barney the riot act. But his mother, Anna, had introduced him to art, and his aunt to the museum.[7] By the time he was 15, he was already entertaining the thought of becoming an artist, making and signing drawings "B.B. Newman."[8] And so to sweeten his school sentence, Anna gave him permission to cut into his high-school day to attend the Art Students League for three months—Antique Drawing, taught by Duncan Smith, six days a week, 1:00 to 4:30—in the fall of 1922.[9] The trips to the Capitol movie theater, on Fifty-Eighth and Broadway, which also cut into the school day, he presumably organized himself.[10]

Barney and his siblings—George (born 1907), Gertrude (1909), and Sarah (1912)—would have two ethics imprinted on them in the apartment on Belmont Avenue: from their father, an intellectual relationship with the texts of Judaism, the emotional residue and generational trauma of Jewish history, and the transmutation of both into a passionate political Zionism; and from their mother, the ultimacy of a spiritual life in art. If in the early years of the 1900s, among striving immigrants who began on the Lower East Side, cultural aspiration was a fashion, *chez* Newman artistic ambition was a cult, his mother notorious in the neighborhood as a "culture freak" and laughed at by the extended family.[11] If children pounding on pianos had "become a craze," as the *Jewish Daily Forward* reported, in the Bronx, a center of piano manufacturing with over fifty factories,[12] Anna would purchase her own "baby grand." The apartment was "lousy with tutors."[13] Brought with the barely five-foot Anna (*nee* Steinberg) from the old country was a diamond ring; this valuable went in and out of pawnshops as she hired private instructors in art, and, as Jewish movie stars achieved celebrity, in elocution and drama. A student of the great Hungarian violinist Leopold Auer introduced Barney to opera. Hebrew teachers—young men from Russia needing work, needing money, were hired by Abraham.[14] All four children had these lessons, but not all received the same encouragement. Relatives were given the definite impression that Gertrude, "quiet and unassuming," was the "least intelligent" in the family,[15] but it was she who was the prodigy on the piano, invited by neighbors to play Chopin when they entertained. Sarah felt the middle children were "terribly neglected"; while she was the adored baby, Barney was undeniably the favorite, her hero and her mentor, since the day he caught her, a small child, reading a "trashy" book. "How can you waste your life on something like this?" he yelled, taking the book and tearing it in half.[16]

On a Tuesday in October 1917, students—tens of thousands of whom were from "emergency class-rooms" and below-par schools[17]—"howled and paraded," beating other students, burning books, and throwing stones, cans, and bottles. Two days later, violent demonstrations broke out in the Bronx, with the student mob growing to more than five thousand, reaching P.S. 44 and, there, Barney, the incipient provocateur.

The riots over the "Gary Plan" in New York City were a microcosm of upheavals in the city's culture, struggling to absorb the tremendous influx of foreign populations.[18] Immigrants counted on traditional academic education to transmit the values of the society, its hopes, and aspirations, and to open doors to professions. For Jews, especially, who had been barred from the professions in the world they left behind, academic education was non-negotiable. But the numbers of new students were so great that, even with a spate of new construction, they could not be accommodated. Of the nearly eight hundred thousand students in New York's system in 1914, half did not go on to seventh grade and only eighty thousand graduated from high school. When the reform administration of Mayor John Purroy Mitchel unseated the corrupt Tammany rule, it decided to act: "the people were tired of seeing the children swarming all over the city the day after graduation looking for work and unfitted to do anything that could support them."[19]

Just a few years earlier, in Gary, Indiana, a young city with an expanding population—the "corporate town" of U.S. Steel—the problem seemed to have been solved with a creative "work–study–play" plan. Fifty minutes of vocational training, sports, and art; sewing, cooking, and manual training were added to traditional subjects; and students were platooned through a tripartite day, allowing academic classrooms to double their capacity.[20] Notwithstanding that the plan was attacked as initiated and "controlled by the Rockefeller and Steel Trusts in order to make our schools an annex to mill and factory,"[21] *this* was the model Mayor Mitchel followed. The first "Gary plan school" opened in Brooklyn with no public debate and no warning to students or parents. Barney's school, with forty classrooms serving sixty-nine classes, was

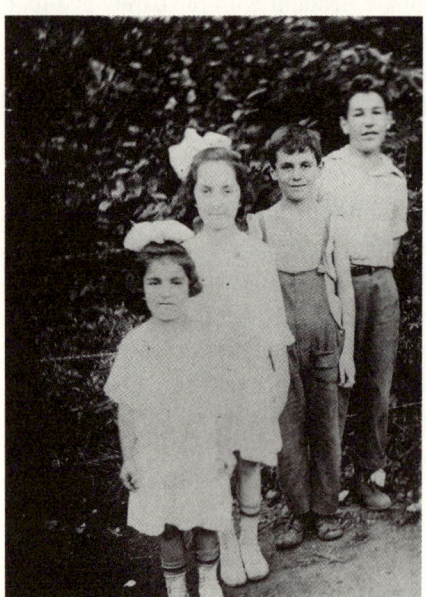

Fig. 2 From top: Barnett, George, Gertrude ("Goldie"), Sarah Newman, c.1917

reorganized to include "pre-vocational training"[22] in February 1916. Eighteen months later, with the plan in thirty-four schools,[23] it had become a political and ideological flashpoint. Mitchel had the support of reform civic, religious, and welfare groups, and academic, popular, and politically radical journals, but in the drummed-up hysteria of the municipal election campaign the Tammany opposition inflamed immigrant—specifically Jewish—parents, who felt they had been manipulated, their aspirations thwarted, and that religion was under attack: the longer school day would cut into extra-curricular religious study.[24] Tammany ward leaders visited homes and "mobilized anti-Gary forces vigorously in Italian and Jewish neighborhoods" with the result that many "non-English-speaking

Yiddish mothers" believed that industrial training under the plan would make their children "slaves" of John D. Rockefeller.[25] At high schools where a third of the student body was partially or entirely self-supporting, strikers also protested the impact on their after-school jobs opened by the labor shortage when the U.S. entered World War I. At De Witt Clinton, things got particularly ugly when several Jewish teachers of Russian ancestry, questioned by a Board of Education committee, were asked, "Don't you believe that the Jewish students, especially the Russians, need to be disciplined out of their individualism?" and three were suspended for "sedition." New York newspapers were filled with arguments pro and con. There was incendiary speechifying on street corners, and "massive demonstrations, student strikes, and school riots"[26] brought mothers and children into hostile confrontation with school officials and police.

Over half the student population in the Bronx did not attend classes the day the demonstrations reached P.S. 44. The next day, a Friday, when police dispersed the crowds, the boys and girls withdrew to regroup at Crotona Park, a block from the Newman home. There were rallies of children all over the Bronx that evening, the atmosphere scented with an air of "scientific" anti-Semitism exhaled by the most respectable cultural guardians.[27] Anna's faith in art proposed a transubstantiation of bitter experience; Abraham's Zionism longed for a concrete foundation on which a mortified Jew could reclaim dignity. If, as a young child on the Lower East Side, Barney experienced uncritically anti-Semitism exploited for political, public, and private purposes, now he would rebel against what he came to recognize as ritualized indignity. This consciousness would bind with his parents' dreams to become the agar on which his character—psychological, social, moral—and his "character"—that is, his persona—grew.

Life in the Tremont section of the Bronx was not typically so filled with agitation. In the memories of those who were children then, the years through the end of World War I can seem like a lower-middle-class, ethnic version of Booth Tarkington's se-pia-toned America. The more developed areas were like a small town, with farms and pasture just a few miles to the north.

By 1886, those members of the Lower East Side Jewish community who had managed to rise into the lower-middle class began to move up geographically as well, into the Bronx. The Third Avenue El, an extension of Manhattan's Second Avenue El, was continued into the Bronx that year, physically and psychologically bringing the district into New York. Construction of apartments for the middle class among large expanses of undeveloped lots, young trees, and exposed electrical lines, became so active that by 1916 the first zoning laws in the country were enacted to exert some control over development.

In 1911, the Newmans—Abraham, who had begun to have some success in the menswear business, Anna, 6-year-old Barney, 4-year-old George and 2-year-old Gertrude (called Goldie)—left not only the congestion and the pollution that so worried Anna,[28] but also the familiarity of the immigrant community, and followed a few other Newman relatives to a Bronx that was still almost rural. They turned their backs on streets they first knew filled with horse-drawn carts but now filled with automobiles, electrified trolleys, and the looming new Manhattan Bridge. They had endured miserable years of construction too close to their tenement at the far end of Cherry Street and, as far as they were concerned, the only impact was bad; the area under the bridge's anchorage became especially dangerous and crime-ridden. In the Bronx, other great public works of the era were more to the family's advantage. Steam-powered trains that ran on elevated trestles from upper Manhattan to Bronx Park were electrified by 1902, and a station was built at the northwest corner of Crotona Park. Two years later, the White Plains Road IRT subway opened a station near the northeast corner. Both were in the shadow of the striking brown and yellow Bronx Borough Hall—designed by one of the most famous architects of his day, George B. Post, as the city hall only thirteen years earlier, when the Bronx was not even a borough of New York City but an "annexed district"[29]—and within a few blocks of 1820 Belmont Avenue, the Newmans' new home. Belmont Avenue was a stretch of five- and six-story brick buildings, trimmed with contrasting stone and ornamented cornices, all of them larger, airier, and altogether more comfortable than the teeming tenements downtown; number 1820 stood out as particularly attractive, with its decorative pattern of leaded glass windows.

Tremont Avenue, the coalescing neighborhood in the South Bronx, had come to life as recently as 1908, when the Van Cortlandt Park IRT El was completed. A commercial street, the stretch near Barney's home was a mix of new banks built in grand historicizing styles and small family-owned businesses: Oscar Rothstein's dry goods, a haberdashery, a butcher, a barber. There was a well-used library, and the Belmont movie theater where children would congregate on Saturdays. Most of the merchants on Tremont lived in the residential area around Crotona Park, a beautifully landscaped, tree-filled neighborhood of two- and three-story private homes and a few apartment buildings. The working-class area of multiple-family dwellings was significantly Jewish, with a small number of Italian and Irish families. The Newmans' neighbors at 1820 Belmont were overwhelmingly from Russia, with a few from Romania, Austria, Poland, Germany—there was a single English family— and most of the employed parents were in the garment industry. The building was filled with children.[30]

When the Newmans arrived, women would be seen on the street in ankle-length dresses or more "modern" shirtwaists; after 1918, the dresses were shorter, and in the winter snug hats appeared and, depending on the economic situation of the wearer, a mink, rabbit, or fox fur piece with a taxidermied head draped over the shoulder. There were still horse-drawn wagons on the street along with the cars[31]—Austins, Fords, Plymouths—that fewer than half the families owned.[32] Nearby, Pelham Parkway had opened in 1911 as a one-lane "highway."[33]

Most of the local traveling in the Bronx of Barney's childhood, though, was by electric trolley. These ran on Tremont, on 180th Street, on Webster Avenue, and

163rd Street. On weekends he could take one or walk the half mile northeast to Bronx Park to see the animals, or east to the West Farms neighborhood, an area that still retained much of its rural character with Revolutionary War-era mansions, and where, in 1916, building began on what would be two years later a world's fair. Walking a few blocks southwest to Claremont Park, he might have run into the future artist William Steig and his gang. Close by, Van Cortlandt Park or Pelham Bay Park were places for picnics, farther away Bear Mountain was for boat rides.[34] There were lively clubs with Saturday afternoon lectures, dancing to 78 rpm records, and informal socializing. Vaudeville and movie theaters, like the Prospect Theater on Prospect Avenue, had exotic, dazzling interiors where a child could fantasize an afternoon away.

There were Victory Gardens and bonfires on Election Day; in the streets girls jumped rope[35] and boys in knickers, like Nathan Libby and his older cousin Barney, always sporting a cap even then when he still had a head of luxurious dark, wavy hair, played punch ball and stickball. Most boys did not own a bicycle but Barney had one, peddling around with Libby on the handlebars talking about "boy things" and sports. Barney was known for his ice-skating prowess in Van Cortlandt Park until severe appendicitis when he was eleven forced a hiatus from sports. The real athlete was his brother, George, a basketball player who became one of the stars of his high school team. When they returned home, they'd be greeted by the aroma from Anna's kosher kitchen of *grivenas*[36] frying in schmaltz for the mashed potatoes and egg that accompanied a plate-sized veal cutlet—followed by stewed prunes.[37] Years later, recipes in Barney's hand for dishes like meat loaf, pot roast, stuffed cabbage, and chopped meat and sauerkraut would fall out of books where he'd tucked them; by then he'd advise companions to have half a grapefruit as the sensible *digestif* after the heavy food.

Many of the Jewish families would spend Friday evenings after dinner at the synagogue, which functioned as a cultural center, and where often there would be lectures by well-known literary and public figures. On the Jewish High Holidays in the fall, children would flood the parks, and then congregate around the synagogue to wait for their parents to emerge to go home for a big dinner.[38] Some parents—like Steig's—would attend Socialist meetings at the Second Assembly District Meeting House, or socialize at *Landsmanshaftn*, benevolent and burial societies of immigrants from the same European town. Abraham Newman was a member of the Order of the Sons of Zion, a fraternal group founded in 1908 to promote Zionism through political activism and education. In 1917, 1350 members in New York met in 91 "camps";[39] the Dr. Leon Pinsker Camp, where Abraham was financial secretary,[40] met on the first and third Sundays of each month. His identity as a Zionist was so significant an aspect of his life that it was emphasized not only in his obituary in 1947, but in Anna's 1965 obituary as well.

For immigrant Jews, the relationship to Judaism—and which aspects and in what way they were transmitted to their children—was complicated. In the old country very little conscious thought was required for Jewish identification; Hasidim, Kabbalists, secular Socialists, political Zionists, Anarchists—as far as the rest of the world was concerned they were *Jews*. In New York, frequently united "only" by history and language, these segments had the freedom to proclaim their differences and refine their distinctions, very often through acutely sensitive and precise Talmudic-style hair-splitting. The framing of concepts and the vocabulary that was used took on the fervor of religion, even when the substance was vehemently secular.

Religious and secular ideologies "in the heated actuality of East European Jewish life [had] a way of becoming intertwined," the critic and historian Irving Howe explained, and "the imagery of religious aspiration [found] a strange hospitality in secular speech."[41] Whether one used Yiddish or Hebrew was a choice at the heart of self-definition. Barney's father's political philosophy was secular Zionism, and he flirted with Haskalah—the Jewish Enlightenment which encouraged Jews to revive Hebrew as a living language; to learn European languages, study secular subjects, and engage with the secular culture; and to remove the Talmud from the center of Jewish education, among other assimilationist efforts. On the other hand, Yiddish, and *Yiddishkeit*, was the emotional and visceral assurance of survival. Yiddish was spoken at home, and Abraham used both Yiddish and Hebrew when he wrote to Barney. Barney grew up in this tradition and remained in it throughout his life. The two languages had their rhetorical uses, and Barney was always a sophisticated practitioner of rhetoric. One of his favorite polemical tactics years later was to slyly evoke a scholarly Jewish reference in arguing *ostensibly* against what he considered a specious Jewish identification. Some victims could be cut off at the knees by it, while others were welcomed into the joke. And the reflexive instinct for the passion, the *gamesmanship*, of Jewish-style disputation would forever be one of Barney's most marked characteristics.

The parsing of an immigrant's intellectual identity will always be fuzzy. Abraham's roots were in a culture, community, and family dedicated to learning. Some residents of Lomza, Poland, including Abraham's maternal uncle, attended the renowned Volozhyn Yeshiva—the first "modern" Jewish religious seminary—about 200 miles away, but Lomza itself had particularly revered rabbis and places of worship and study. It was both home to noted Kabbalists and, at the other end of the spectrum, an early fount of Zionism. About six years before Abraham left, a group of educated young men collected roughly five hundred books in Hebrew, Yiddish, and Russian and established a library. In New York, Jewish immigrants continued that tradition as great buyers of books and Abraham had his own Judaica library in the Bronx. He was deeply grounded and educated in his religion and, at the same time, intellectually motivated to modernize and Americanize his relationship to it. It was a common enough situation that works were written or translated and published pointedly for this market, and such are the ones in Abraham's library.

The five volumes of *Legends of the Talmud, En Jacob: Agada of the Babylonian Talmud by Rabbi Jacob Ibn Chabib*, printed in the United States between 1916 and 1921, had Hebrew text alongside its English translation expressly to counteract assimilation in America.[42] There are two parts to the Talmud, the *Halacha*, which consists of all the laws concerning Jewish life, and the *Agada*, known as "The Homiletics of the Talmud"—narrations, ethics, sociology, astronomy, and medicine. It was from his comfortable familiarity with this text—of which Jewish sages say, "He who wishes to become acquainted with his creator, let him study the Agada"[43]—that Barney was able to scatter pearls of wisdom years later. The eleven-volume translation of *Popular History of the Jews* by Heinrich Graetz, begun in German in 1853, was the first comprehensive attempt to write the history of the Jews as the history of a living people. Graetz's monumental work was not uncontroversial: observant religionists faulted its "excessive and rather naïve rationalism," but because it emphasized everything "understandable and logical" in the history of the Jewish people—"the forces and the ideals which had assured its survival throughout the centuries"—it was exactly what the secular Zionist Abraham admired. Graetz stressed the universalist ethics of Judaism; he despised mystical forces and movements such as Kabbalah and Hasidism, he was not interested in the history of the Jews of Poland, Russia, and Turkey, and "in his attachment to Haskalah expressed contempt bordering on hatred for 'the fossilized Polish talmudists.' " He referred to Yiddish as "a ridiculous gibberish."[44]

This last represented precisely what a Polish Jew, in the Bronx, in 1926, wanted to move beyond, and Graetz was revered. But there was also its supplementary volume of recent events written by Max Raisin and edited by Alexander Harkavy.[45] Harkavy, born in Belorussia, a Vilna resident who was displaced by the 1881 pogroms, was a renowned Yiddish lexicographer who spent his life and international career devoted to the language. Raisin, born in Poland, was a reform-movement rabbi in America who fervently supported Zionism when it was *not* popular to do so in the reform movement. There can be no more perfect crystallization of the ambivalent identity struggle of the new American Jew than the after-the-fact collaboration of these three scholars.[46]

Abraham's books indicate a serious interest in the religion, history, and future of the Jewish people, but, at least among the ones that have survived, none was the sort that a *scholar* of Talmud would require or use.[47] The family legend, relayed by Barney to Hess, that Abraham dazzled the citizens of Lomza with his learned "marriage dissertation," having helped his rabbi uncle "collate an encyclopedia of Talmudic decisions," has little support in his life or surviving library in America. Most likely, these English-language books that promoted Hebrew as a living language—like the 1914 *Students' Hebrew and Chaldee Dictionary to the Old Testament*, with its supplement, "Neo-Hebrew Vocabulary"[48]—were those Abraham felt were important for the education of the next generation of Jewish children, including his own. A children's schoolbook from the Newman household of these years, a Hebrew volume of biblical tales with engraved illustrations after 19th-century academic paintings, is of particular interest because it was also largely an "art" book.

"Are the general principles of literary history and literary research applicable to the Tanach [Old Testament]?" Barney asked in a thousand-word fragment that appears to be from a paper he wrote in college. Titled "The Literature of the Jewish

People," it is a deeply informed, although not scholarly, discussion that provides a window into the significance of these texts to Barney, and his conversance with them:

> Is it possible, in general, to discuss "Biblical literature" and "Biblical literary history"?
>   We wish to assert that today it is possible to give a positive answer . . . There is no question the scriptures not only exert an influence through its content but also through its form and that without its special literary qualities, the Tanach would hardly have had so profound an effect . . . . *One cannot comprehend the Tanach, even as a religious book, if one is not able to appreciate the extraordinary literary art of the Biblical poets and thinkers* [emphasis added].

Written sometime before he was 25, Barney was already thinking about how "art," not dogma, was the persuasive form to embody spiritual meaning.[49]

If not before, then certainly after 1913, when his father established the National Hebrew School of the Bronx a few blocks from the apartment,[50] Barney attended Hebrew school, continuing his studies at least a year or two past 1918 when he became a bar mitzvah.[51] At the original National Hebrew School founded on the Lower East Side in 1910, there was controversy as to what should be taught. Religion? Nationalistic ideology? Should everything be taught in Hebrew? It was a Zionist, secular school,[52] but very quickly it was recognized by prominent Jewish leaders.[53] The affiliate founded by Abraham employed three teachers for 125 boys and 125 girls, who studied four hours on Sunday mornings and three hours weekday afternoons,[54] and served a community of ambiguous richness. Although it was a Labor Zionist school, the chart of weekly Torah portions on Barney's 1918 report card indicates that religion was, in fact, studied. And although the school taught Hebrew, it could not rely on parents knowing that language as a living language; nor could the school assume parents had a reading knowledge of English. The "rules and regulations" were outlined in Yiddish, the common practice of Zionists to recruit and address the populace.

On Saturday, February 2, 1918, with newspapers reporting war news both fortunate for Abraham's business (despite the Army's requirements, there would be no shortage of wool) and demoralizing for the population (wheat would be rationed), Barney became a bar mitzvah.

The portion of the Torah that is read on any day is determined by Jewish law, and the portion of the haftarah—selections from the Prophets—that is linked with it by tradition; it does not vary, no matter who the reader is. One wouldn't want to make too much of the *parsha* assigned to a particular 13-year-old boy. But if we keep in mind that the boy by nature had an unusually healthy self-regard, and the Torah portion included the wondrous occasion of Adonai's revelation of Torah at Mt. Sinai; and if, in addition, that boy was inclined to a visual imagination and the portion describes extraordinary imagery instead of enumerating laws or narrating genealogical or military histories; and if that boy was of the omnivorous intellectual sort who grew into a man who happily saw polemical source material everywhere he turned his mind; *and* if, when it came time to name his own creations the man returned to these very same brief but powerful paragraphs for so many titles—*Covenant, The Name, The Three, The Third, The Voice, The Throne (Cathedra), Here, Not There—Here, The Wandering (L'Errance)* . . . well, some speculating is irresistible. But there is no question that his personal relationship with the text remained vivid. In 1960, when his new friend Meyer Schapiro lent him a copy of Schapiro's dazzlingly erudite essay on Freud's "little book on Leonardo"—in which the scholar marshals theology, the history of visual forms and local church doctrine, Egyptian and Classical Greek and Roman mythology, local *quattrocento* Italian art politics and scientific investigations, and Leonardo's biography and personal, professional, and artistic evolution, among many other references, to reveal the blinkered thinness of Freud's psychoanalytic interpretation—Barney's response was: "I believe I told you that Isaiah's image of the angel touching his lips with burning coals to give him speech and therefore the power of prophecy was my Bar Mitzvah Haftorah."

What Barney read from the Torah on that day was Exodus 18:1–20:23. In addition to containing the ur-description of God giving the Ten Commandments to Moses—pretty heady for a 13-year-old—the portion describes what is certainly the most vivid, literally awe-inspiring, abstract visual imagery of the Old Testament.

The wandering Israelites are encamped in the desert. Moses ascends the mountain and receives instruction from God, himself:

And the Lord said to Moses, "Behold, I am coming to you in the thickness of the cloud, in order that the people hear when I speak to you . . . . And they shall be prepared for the third day, for on the third day, the Lord will descend before the eyes of all the people upon Mount Sinai. And you shall set boundaries for the people around, saying, Beware of ascending the mountain or touching its edge; whoever touches the mountain shall surely be put to death . . . .

It came to pass on the third day when it was morning, that there were thunder claps and lightning flashes, and a thick cloud was upon the mountain, and a very powerful blast of a shofar, and the entire nation that was in the camp shuddered. Moses brought the people out toward God from the camp, and they stood at the bottom of the mountain. And the entire Mount Sinai smoked because the Lord had descended upon it in fire, and its smoke ascended like the smoke of the kiln, and the entire mountain quaked violently.

The sound of the shofar grew increasingly stronger; Moses would speak and God would answer him with a voice . . . . "I am the Lord, your God, Who took you out of the land of Egypt, out of the house of bondage. You shall not have the gods of others in My presence. You shall not make for yourself a graven image or any likeness which is in the heavens above, which is on the earth below, or which is in the water beneath the earth . . . .

And all the people saw the voices and the torches, the sound of the shofar, and the smoking mountain, and the people saw and trembled; so they stood from afar. . . . Moses said to the people, "Fear not, for God has come in order to exalt you, and in order that His awe shall be upon your faces."

The commentary on this portion, which Barney would have been taught as he studied for his public reading, included the following, from Rabbi Abahu:

When a person sees an extraordinary event entirely contrary to the usual way of things, then he talks about it. The more unusual the event, the greater is his amazement, and the more he must express his wonder over the thing that he saw or heard. However, surprise and wonder can reach a point where it is no longer possible to express anything. The means of expression no longer function, and a person is left speechless and dumbfounded.[55]

Barney's haftorah was from Isaiah:

In the year that King Uzziah died, I beheld my Lord seated on a high and lofty throne; and the skirts of His robe filled the Temple. Seraphs stood in attendance on Him . . . . And one would call to the other, "Holy, holy, holy! The Lord of Hosts! His presence fills all the earth!" . . . I cried, "Woe is me; I am lost! For I am a man of unclean lips And I live among a people of unclean lips; Yet my own eyes have beheld The King Lord of Hosts." Then one of the seraphs flew over to me with a live coal, which he had taken from the altar with a pair of tongs. He touched it to my lips and declared, "Now that this has touched your lips, Your guilt shall depart And your sin be purged away." Then I heard the voice of my Lord saying, "Whom shall I send? Who will go for us?" And I said, "Here am I; send me."[56]

"You could denounce religion as superstition and worse, but the Yom Kippur service shook the heart, and the voices of the Talmud lured the mind," is how Irving Howe described the conflict of the generation that reached America. One did not have to be a believer to get the picture as a 13-year-old. Nor does there need to be any implication that this material was the literal subject of future *illustration*, to recognize the awe-filled power, both abstract and sublime, that resonated for the mature Barney, who would derive at least thirteen titles from these texts.

Exhilarated from the intensely focused study and preparation for what was a one-shot performance, Barney then entered his school's Junior Four Minute Men contest.[57] The Four Minute Men, part of the U.S. Government Committee on Public Information, sent monthly bulletins to schools to be used as "text matter from which the pupils prepare four minute speeches or essays." The topic that April was the Third Liberty Loan, and the rhetorical style that was encouraged—declarative, unnuanced, righteously propagandistic—would sit comfortably on a young man feeling his oats. Barney was proud to tell Hess almost sixty years later that he prevailed.

The big excitement of 1918 for the local Tremont residents came that summer, with the opening of the New York International Exposition of Science, Art, and Industries—seventy buildings and an amusement park on 28 acres in the West Farms district. There were military parades, speeches, and what is now called "business development"; but for a 13-year-old, the fun was in the roller coaster and carnival games, the athletic exhibitions, swimming contests, trapeze and tight-rope displays, concerts and dazzling colored-light illuminations well into the night. And then, suddenly, before the exposition's closing on November 1, that sort of mass congregation would become terrifying. The influenza epidemic—which ultimately killed fifty to a hundred million people worldwide—had arrived in the United States.

Already by mid-September there were quarantines and the numbers and fear snowballed: 115 new cases one day, 150 the next, 172 the day after that, then 352, then 999. The Surgeon General recommended that states and municipalities close churches, schools, theaters and

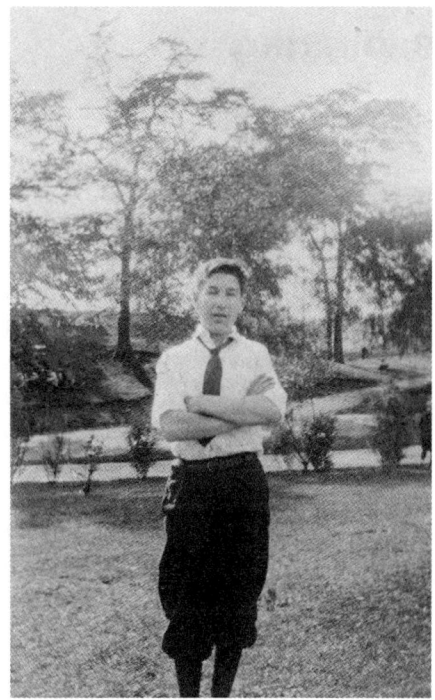

Fig. 3 "Barney," c.1920

public institutions. New York instituted staggered closing times for stores, factories, theaters, and other places of assembly to reduce commuting crowds. Every single aspect of life in the city was impacted: so many operators fell sick that telephone service was significantly curtailed. There were 142,336 cases of influenza and pneumonia, and 21,260 combined deaths through November.[58] And then, as quickly as it had arrived, by the day of the armistice the worst appeared to be over.

The close-knit extended Newman family in New York survived the first wave. But in January 1919, the flu reappeared with a vengeance. Barney's aunt, Abraham's beneficent sister Guta, who had taken in a teenage boy with the sickness because his working parents could not care for him, succumbed.

TWO
BEGINNING

Guta Naimen, one year older than Abraham, and her husband, Moszk-Herszk Ciech-anowicz, were the relatives with whom Abraham and Anna settled when they arrived in New York in September 1900, disembarking from the Holland–America ship *S.S. Statendam*. On the ship's manifest they listed the Ciechanowiczs' 49 Henry Street address as their destination, but Guta and her three children had only arrived in New York less than a week before. Moszk-Herszk, naturalized in August as Morris Sikow-itz, had come five years earlier to "establish" himself, and it was with his brother Elias and his family that Guta's husband was living. Morris eventually purchased tickets for all of Guta's younger siblings (except Abraham, who seems to have paid his own and Anna's way) and all of them listed Elias's address as their destination. For many years afterwards, children never knew when they went to sleep if they might wake up on the floor so that newcomers could take the beds. It was a very crowded apartment.

Abram—before his name was Americanized—had been born in the town of Lomza, in the Gubernia of Lomza, where his parents were temporarily residing, in October 1870.[1] Lomza, in northeast Poland on the bank of the Narev River, had a very old Jewish community; a synagogue and a cemetery existed as early as 1494 but by the end of the 16th century Jews were virtually absent. Over the next 220 years the community rose and fell, existed and ceased to exist, according to the whims of those in power. If the history of Barney's birthright is difficult to follow, it is because it mirrors the arbitrary, precarious, and unpredictable life of a Polish Jewish family. But because, when it came time to establish for posterity the narrative of his own life, Barney determined its importance "so that the man and his work emerge," with "the facts of his life properly respected,"[2] it is worth unraveling.

The Naiman family is first recorded in the Lomza Gubernia in 1806 with the birth of Barney's great-grandfather, Lejzor Naiman, about 30 miles northeast from the town of Lomza in the shtetl of Wasosz, one of 14 Jews in a population of 770.[3] Although in 1807 a ten-year suspension of civil rights was imposed upon Lomza's Jews, there are stories that point to instances of prosperity: it is said that Napoleon, passing through on his way to Russia in 1812, commandeered the largest home in Lomza for his quarters, the residence owned by the Jew Yudl Blomowicz.[4]

Under the reign of Nicholas I, 1825 to 1855, there were over six hundred anti-Jewish decrees in Russian territory—ranging from expulsions from traditionally Jewish villages, to heavy censorship, to conscription of youngsters for up to twenty-five years.[5] Except for select individuals who could prove they had sufficient capital and who had adopted a European style of life, European dress, and fluency in European languages, Lomzan Jews were removed in 1822 to the nearby town of Rybaki.[6] In 1830 this same community *joined* Poles in the November rebellion against the Russian Empire. The suppression of this uprising caused Lomza great suffering, but the byproduct was that serious opposition to a Jewish population died down. A period of even greater reconciliation between the Jewish and Polish populations preceded the 1863 Polish rebellion—during which Jews once again participated in demonstrations, fought, and provided material support—but ended in increased xenophobia. Of the 150 people arrested, over a hundred were Jews, including many of the most assimilated and prosperous, deputies in the Municipal Council among them. Intense Russification followed: rabbis were required to be fluent in the Russian language, and secular subjects had to be taught in the *cheder*. The grand Beit Midrash—the seat of the rabbinical court, and where the elite would pray—was, for a time, closed down.

Lejzer-Herzk Naiman, Abraham's father, was born in Wasosz in 1847, a relatively calm time. By his tenth birthday, the number of Jews in Wasosz had exploded to 453 of a total population of 1389, and circumstances were such that within a few years, Lejzer-Herzk was able to own a small retail store. There he met and married Golda-Leja Lavski, whose parents lived in the town of Lomza, where the Jewish population and opportunities for trade had been growing since residence permits were issued in 1830. Although relations were tense after 1863, the Russians recognized that they needed suppliers and middlemen for the construction of barracks, and Jews were allowed to establish businesses: the sugar plant; soap, chicory, cotton, brick, and roofing-tile factories; seven windmills; several carpentry and metal-working shops. Optimistically, they organized in Lomza the *Pidyon Shvuyim*—Redemption of Prisoners—to purchase the release of Jews who had been conscripted into the Russian Imperial Army. Sometime between the birth of Guta and Abram, Lejzer-Herzk and Golda-Leja moved from Wasosz to this much more cosmopolitan town, with its six thousand inhabitants, of whom nearly half were Jewish.

In the temporarily stable climate, and with the influence of the Haskalah, many Jews were inclined to learn Russian, become involved in political life and—now that the forcible conscription of Jews as young as 12 years old[7] had been reduced from up to twenty-five years to five—actually volunteer for the Russian Army. But when, in 1881, Tsar Alexander II was assassinated by terrorists, Alexander III pursued an aggressively anti-Jewish policy.

Newman/Naiman/Neiman family legend has it that Lejzer-Herzk was a rabbi and a scholar; no evidence to support this appears in Polish or Russian records, but his oldest son, Abram's brother Josef, who emigrated from Lomza to Palestine, became a rabbi distinguished enough to be known, honorifically, as "Der Lomzer," and his headstone bears the inscription "Son of the Rabbi Zvi-Eliezar Nejman of Lomza" (Zvi-Eliezar is a version of Lejzer-Herzk).

The serious learning was on Golda-Leja's side: her father, Samuel-Meir Lavski, appears in Lomza records as a stall owner and a trader in hardware, but also a teacher in the Shas Society. Both he and Golda-Leja's grandfather were scholars who trained their sons in Torah. Golda-Leja's brother Boruch-Szmul Lavski—the relative who studied in the Volozhyn Yeshiva—became a renowned rabbi in Krynki, about 70 miles to the east, in 1883. "You never *said* the name 'Lavski,'" according to a great-grandson, "you *intoned* it with awe," and *if* Abram had indeed been secretary to an important rabbi, it was probably this uncle. Boruch-Szmul was a personage with whom every relative would want to claim association: he was the author of the highly regarded *Minchas Boruch*, a book of questions and discussions on religious law—traditionally known as *responsa*—which brought him offers of rabbinates in Russia, Lithuania, and Poland, and was active as a rabbinic arbitrator in commercial and legal disputes. But Rabbi Lavski left Lomza when Abram was very young.

Lejzer-Herzk and Golda-Leja had nine children, at least seven of whom survived into adulthood. Josef was the first, born in 1866 when Lejzer-Herzk was 19 and Golda-Leja 22. Abram was the third child, after Guta in 1869. There followed three more boys and three more girls, the last, Etke, in 1883. Abram's brother Morris often told his children that Etke's birth had "killed" his mother. Perhaps, in his mind, that is how it seemed. But Etke was nine months old when Golda-Leja died at the age of 39.

Golda-Leja's extraordinary mother, Hinda, 70 at the time with eight children and fifty-five grandchildren and in business running a hardware store, took in Lejzer-Herzk's brood and raised them, while he remarried. Abram and his brothers went to the local yeshiva, the typical education for Jewish young men, religious or not, who had no access to secular colleges in Russian Poland.

The after-effect of the 1863 rebellion that had the most lasting impact on Abram had to do with the beginnings of modern Zionism in Poland. Around the time that Abram was born, academics gathering in Lomza formed "Friends of Zion and Jerusalem," the first of several Zionist groups in the city. The "Daughters of Zion," young women who taught Hebrew language and Jewish history to girls, was a national organization founded in Lomza. In 1891, when Josef immigrated to Palestine, young adults like Abram raised money for the new *Chovevei Tzion beit midrash* (Lovers of Zion study center) to purchase land and support settlers in Palestine. A few years later, a Lomzan society financed an emissary to travel throughout Palestine and report back. When Abram died in 1947 he owned 36 dinars—about 9 acres—in Balfouria, the first Zionist village to be founded in Palestine after the 1917 Balfour Declaration.

Barney would later talk about his father's five years in the Russian Army, during a period that bridged the reigns of "two tsars," how impressed he was "by the elegant gardens and sculptures of Tsarskoyo Selo and the museum of the Hermitage, its walls carpeted with great paintings," when he was "stationed in St. Petersburg as a conscript."[8] Alexander II died in 1881, when Abram—whether born in 1870 or 1873—was still too young for the Russian Army under that tsar in those years; the "two tsars" could only refer to Alexander III (1881–94) and Nicholas II (1894–1917).[9] Abram would have been in his early twenties in that time period—a period that coincided with the term of the infamous war minister, Petr Vannovskii (1881–97)—so his service is certainly possible. But the Hermitage was likely a bit of fancy, inserted by either Abraham or Barney. No surviving relatives ever heard stories of any family member being in the Russian Army.

Fifty years earlier, the particularly punishing conscription under Nicholas I explicitly intended "to bring about their gradual merging with the Christian nationalities and to uproot those superstitious and harmful prejudices which are instilled by the teaching of the Talmud."[10] Alexander II relaxed both the aggressive assimilationist and the aggressive discriminatory practices, but *that* more moderate policy was again reversed by Alexander III and Vannovskii. Earlier the Minister of the Interior considered abolishing the Pale of Settlement, into which Jews were traditionally segregated, but the new policy of the early 1880s involved "coercive urbanization" of Jews, increased segregation, and violent pogroms.[11] In 1888 or '89, when Abram would have begun his service under "two tsars," new regulations restricted the movements of Jews, even those who had served in the military.[12] In 1891, when about twenty thousand Jews were banished from Moscow, was Abram Naiman strolling in St. Petersburg and enjoying the walls of the Hermitage "carpeted with great paintings"? Barney's widow's version, years later, is somewhat more plausible: after his years in a yeshiva, Abram was drafted, "spent some time near St. Petersburg," and saw the Summer Palace (in Pavlovski).[13]

When, exactly, Abraham met or married Anna Steinberg is unknown: on the 1910 U.S. Census—which, considering discrepancies from one report to the next, was only as accurate as Abraham was feeling on that day—1899 is listed as the date of their marriage. They were definitely husband and wife when they arrived in New York in 1900. Ena—as she was known in Poland—was the oldest of six children born between 1879 and 1890 to Mendel Zurkowicz Steinberg from Myszyniec and Yenta Vigdorovna Gronowicz, whose parents moved to Lomza from Czerna. The family may have been well-off "bankers," as Barney would claim, but no documents from either shtetl survived World War II to confirm it, and the record of Barney's grandparents' marriage in 1877 in Lomza indicates no special status. Mendel was listed as "illiterate" on the document recording Anna Steinberg's birth in 1879—possibly as some beneficial ruse—and as a "trader" on that recording her sister's birth two years later. The tale that Abraham won "the daughter of the richest man," because he was the "cream of the crop" intellectually—as Annalee would maintain—is unlikely, whether it originated with Abraham, Anna, or Barney. The family lore as told by Barney's sister Sarah was that Anna, dazzled by his scholarship, "seduced" Abraham, who was going to be a rabbi. "She took these candlesticks . . . which were the only real possession her family had, and she ran away with him to America. He never became a rabbi."[14]

Men make their own history, but not under circumstances chosen by themselves, Marx announced. Those circumstances are encountered, given, and transmitted from the past: "The tradition of all the dead generations weighs like a nightmare on the brain of the living."[15] Abraham "felt himself a heroic character," Barney told Hess.[16] The Talmudic scholar, the Russian military man, the Zionist pioneer *manqué*, the son of "relatively modest businessmen" who was taken into the bosom of the "well-to-do" because of his superior nature—this is what in Yiddish is called *yichus*: an untranslatable concept that has to do with establishing "good blood," a dignified lineage, pedigree. Possibly it is all true. On the other hand, it may be a tale of what *almost* happened—the scholar did not become a rabbi, the soldier's privileges were restricted, the pioneer never saw the state of Israel formed, the Depression thwarted his wife's dreams—but didn't, because of a particular time and place, and terribly arduous circumstance. It may be, in other words, what was in Barney's mind when during his life he repeated that "the father is the tragic figure."

Of the Jews expelled from Moscow in 1891, many went to America, but greater numbers took refuge in Poland. These so-called "Litvaks" (though they were not from Lithuania) were more secular, worldly, and business-minded than their Polish co-religionists, and there were cultural abrasions, more so after a second wave of new refugees arrived, this time actually from Lithuania. Nevertheless, because of these infusions Jewish life in Lomza flourished during the late 1890s. The town organized a shelter for the needy, an infirmary, an elementary school (Talmud Torah), an advanced yeshiva, and an abattoir for the ritual slaughter of animals. The old wooden synagogue, demolished in 1859 and rebuilt in 1881 as a stone building with carvings and impressive windows, "eventually became a 'fortress of the Zionist movement in Lomza.'" Political and religious thought ranged over the spectrum, from Zionism to Kabbalism to Hasidism—virtually all the Hasidic courts and dynasties in Poland of the time were represented. Jews were over half—426 out of 710—of Lomza's tailors, shoemakers, carpenters, metalsmiths, blacksmiths, and leatherworkers and over half the master artisans. The breweries were in Jewish hands.

And then, within a very few years, the tide shifted again. "'Christian, buy only from Christians' became a popular slogan. Catholic farmers formed a cooperative, the members of which were obligated to purchase their equipment and supplies from the cooperative, which in turn bought their crops." When steamship lines, in 1899, advertised transport of Jewish emigrants to America through cards sent to soldiers, Vannovskii determined that all mail received by Jewish soldiers from relatives overseas was enticement to desert. There were new crackdowns.[17]

Perhaps "both Anna and Abraham felt constricted by life in Lomza" as Barney would have it,[18] or maybe they felt threatened. Whatever the cause, it was time to leave.

The crowded apartment on Henry Street that "Abraham" and Anna "Neumann"—as they appear on the S.S. Statendam's manifest—went to on that early September day was duplicated all over the Lower East Side, which was in a sense America's own "pale of settlement": over a quarter of a million Jews living in a little more than a square mile. The turn-of-the-century ethnic experience in that neighborhood, so familiar from the writing of Jacob Riis and Henry Roth and Irving Howe—its filthy streets and pushcarts, teeming tenements with reeking hallways and communal privies, petty crimes, dead horses, protesting workers, and radicalized citizens; but also its theaters, music halls, candy stores, and restaurants unknown in the old country— turned out to be only an eleven-year interregnum for the Newmans. Over the next five years, as four more of Abraham's brothers and sisters moved in, Lejzer-Herzk and Golda-Leja's children remained tightly knit in America. But by 1904 Barney's parents had good reason to want to improve their living situation: Anna had already lost a baby boy, and was pregnant with Barney. Before they decamped for the Bronx, they moved to 462 Cherry Street. It was one in a row of four six-story brick and stone houses with ground floor stores[19] recently constructed under the "New Tenement Law" of 1901—a stunning improvement from wherever they had been living before. Every apartment had running water and a water closet. No longer were there reeking enclosed air shafts; mandated courtyards now provided ventilation through exterior windows in every room. Crucially, construction and egress requirements addressed fire safety.[20]

Among its other enticements, the building on Cherry Street fronted a new, 10-acre park with flower beds, a bandstand for concerts, and "broad walks" where a child could run.[21] Barney, George, and Goldie were born at home,[22] likely delivered by a midwife from the Henry Street Settlement.

But the block retained a disconcertingly mixed character, with two-story wood buildings and several 19th-century saloons. It was not anyone's idea of paradise. Until 1955, when more than 35 acres of landfill were deposited for the East River Park,[23] it really did dead-end into the river.

Fifteen years earlier, the area was "one of the most thickly populated on the east side," a congestion of marble, lumber, coal, and pig-iron yards, factories and stables and rookeries—and homes. In 1895, after six years of condemnation proceedings, just south had been cleared to create Corlears Hook Park while parts of Cherry a few blocks west remained among the poorest streets in the city. In 1905 there were five-, six-, and seven-story tenements of railroad flats, "each building replete with the redolence of a hundred different cooking odors and the resounding of ten different languages. Almost no English was spoken, except for the exotic varieties . . . each supposed to be correct."[24] The census reveals a poignant profile of the community into which Barney was born. In six tenement houses about 675 people were living in three- and four-room apartments, an average of 5.6 people per apartment. Of 118 heads of household, 52 were garment workers of one sort or another, 36 were manual workers (including day laborers and building-trade workers), and 15 were peddlers. Six small businessmen, three rabbis, five "housewives" (widows or deserted wives), and one teacher made up the remainder. Ninety-two boarders lived with the 118 families. Almost everyone had arrived within the previous six years.[25]

In the early 1880s, there were no Jews at all on Cherry Street.[26] And when Jews moved there, their lives were shadowed by fear. The street was a southern "border"; below lived Irish immigrants, and Jewish children knew not to cross over.[27] A few blocks away were opium smokers in Chinatown, and Jewish children were warned to avoid them as well.[28] And west were "the worst hooligans."[29] One boy who lived it would later write:

[We] grew up with our fists—the Jewish boys fighting the Poles, the Poles the Irish, the Irish the Italians, and all of them usually against the Jews. . . . Cherry Street was foreign to the core—a unique ingathering of dress as well as tongue. It was extraordinarily one-world, however, when it came to the brutal simplicity of how a boy went about getting something he wanted. One never asked for a gift or a toy or an apple from a fruit stand. In the accepted norm, one merely stole—and then was away with the petty spoils, sitting by the river, eating the fruits that fast legs made possible, planning another escapade.[30]

There were "horrifying block-fights" during which boys loaded their "stocking hats with glass and stone and charged away." On July Fourth and Election Day the gangs' divisions temporarily disappeared and the boys "teamed up to make six-story-high bonfires. We collected wood for days, foraging around South Street and the warehouses. Anything that could burn. . . . It would take hours and great skill to pile up the stuff. The base of the bonfire would often be 50 feet in length and width, rising a hundred feet to the pyramid's point—and the boy who climbed up to set it off at the top was the hero of the fire."[31]

Even 5- or 6-year-olds ran wild on the streets with gangs.[32] The East River was just another street, where swimming and makeshift boating occasionally ended in accidents and drownings.[33] Barney might have been too young or too supervised to dive off the docks like his cousins did[34]—although his stories of Abraham's swimming lessons may have taken place there—but not too young to appreciate the water's lure. It's not a coincidence that he would later choose Front Street, also one block from the East River (less than a mile south of Cherry) for the studio he occupied for sixteen years.

There was the bustle of commerce on Canal Street, action in the shops on Hester, Stanton, and Rivington; children as young as 5 were already carrying goods, threading needles, and sewing buttons in the smaller garment "shops" inside the tenements.[35] Other aspects of Lower East Side life were less benign. Harry Roskolenko, who was born in 1907 and grew up on Cherry Street, wrote that "great fires were as common as the cold. For heat, most people burned coal [and] great fires used to rage through the tenements during the long winters. The burned bodies would be laid out in the streets, covered with sacking or tarpaulins."[36] In the spring of 1909, when Barney was four, thousands of people ran to the spot, just down the street from the Newmans' home, where a drug factory exploded, killing a man and injuring a boy who lived on the block, "thinking that the factory had been blown up with a bomb."[37]

Rumors of bombs or of medical experiments or vendettas settled by arson in the public schools were not uncommon in the immediate neighborhood, and would be the cause of panic, mobs, and stampedes. Infant mortality was shockingly common; a map at the Bureau of Child Hygiene recorded summer deaths by placing colored tacks on the address where a child had died. Cherry Street a block west of Barney's home was notorious as "the Lung Block"; near the end of July 1909, when Goldie Newman was five months old, the streets adjacent to the Lung Block on the map were so loaded with red tacks—indicating a child under one year—that it was "impossible to stick any more in."[38]

Apartments in the neighborhood were crowded, with a quarter of families sleeping five to a room. Abraham's brother Morris, who lived three blocks away, slept

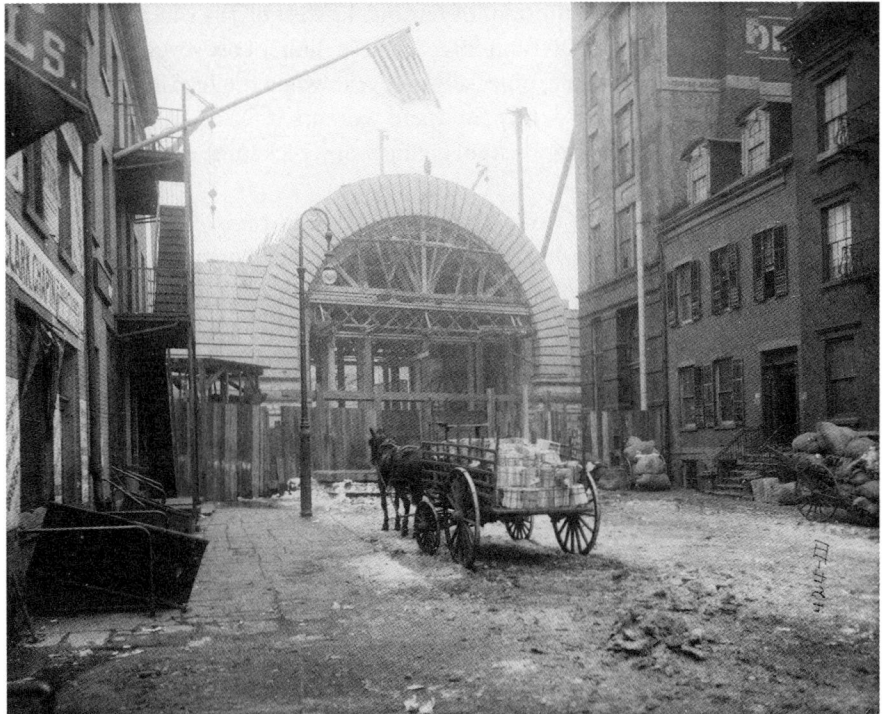

Fig. 4 Cherry Street during the construction of the Manhattan Bridge, 1907. Photograph Eugene de Salignac

on the roof in the summer; others, on fire escapes. In 1910, there were 166 people, including a dozen "roomers," in the 27 units that made up 462 Cherry Street; one apartment had 12 occupants. "Abraam and Annie Neuman," three living children, and Jacob Jaffe, a 26-year-old "roomer" who had arrived from Russia in 1905 and identified himself as a peddler, lived with Barney.[39] The heads of the other households, in their late twenties to late thirties, were tailors, but there were also waiters, factory workers, salesmen, and a couple of grocers. None of the wives claimed to work; several were illiterate, reading neither English, Yiddish, nor Russian. Privacy was virtually unknown.

On a hot summer night it was "awful. The ceaseless and strident noises from the streets, the . . . stenches," reported St. Rose's Home for Incurable Cancer down the block. The nine-bed hospital was appealing for aid to relocate after ten years, because the district was so congested, "so hot and close in summer as to be almost suffocating. The air is filled frequently with many unclean odors,"[40] at least some emanating from Gouverneur Slip, where the kosher ritual killing of chickens took place.

In the density of humanity, mothers lived in fear of tuberculosis, "the white plague"; in 1906 so many Jews on the Lower East Side were afflicted that it came to be known as "a Jewish disease" or "the tailors' disease."[41] In 1908, when the neighborhood was severely impacted by the economic depression, "there were appalling scenes of hunger and destitution." A few blocks west of 462 Cherry, a People's Kitchen was established on Division Street, where dinner cost seven cents.[42] Protests were frequent, and visible, especially that year, when the Jewish trades erupted in strikes. And in July 1910, fifty thousand workers walked out in the historic Cloakmakers Strike, leading to weeks of raging mobs, picketing, and parades in the neighborhood.[43]

Jacob Riis's seminal 1890 work, *How the Other Half Lives*, is filled with both rampant prejudice and vivid description of the desperate tenement lives of recent immigrants. "A friend of mine who manufactures cloth once boasted to me that nowadays, on cheap clothing, New York 'beats the world.' 'To what,' I asked, 'do you attribute it?' 'To the cutter's long knife and the Polish Jew'. . . . Practically the Jew has monopolized the business."[44]

Riis devoted a chapter to "The Sweaters of Jewtown." "The sweater is simply the middleman, the sub-contractor, a workman like his fellows, perhaps with the single distinction from the rest that he knows a little English; perhaps not even that, but with the accidental possession of two or three sewing-machines . . . drums up work among the clothing-houses." Ten years later, in 1900, with over 90 percent of the garment industry controlled by Jews and the eastern European "Moths of Division Street" who acted as their own subcontractors, sewing and finishing pre-cut materials,[45] Abraham Newman entered the business by selling the sewing machines—or "heads"—to the "sweaters" in the smaller workshops located in tenements. He bought one, sold it, bought two with the profit, sold them.[46] By the time Morris arrived in 1910, Abraham was no longer selling sewing machine heads and had become a kind of broker between the producers and the sellers of menswear: he identified himself not as a "sweater," but as a "salesman" in a "clothing house."[47] For the intelligent and entrepreneurial immigrants in his position—those not locked into laborers' positions—the industry presented real opportunity. Some wound up with empires and amassed fortunes. Abraham and Morris were among the ambitious, if not wildly successful, prosperous enough by 1911 for the Newmans to escape the "many unclean odors" and relocate to the Bronx.

THREE
THE MOST INTENSE EXPERIENCES

In 1917, Abraham and Morris established "Newman, Menkes & Tikotsky," at 35 East Broadway,[1] a small, six-story building of clothing manufacturers. By 1905, the street was "the most prosperous thoroughfare on the East Side"[2]—meaning middle class— with jewelers, furriers, leather merchants, and the banks, restaurants, barbers, and drugstores that a bustling community required. It was Abraham's neighborhood in January 1920, when Prohibition brought flourishing speakeasies; in May 1920, when the Anarchist Andrea Salsedo plunged to his death from a nearby fourteenth-floor window where the FBI held him; and in September 1920, when less than a mile away a horse-drawn cart packed with dynamite exploded and killed thirty-eight in front of the Morgan bank. He was there—without Menkes and Tikotsky—in 1924, when the "Johnson Bill," which dramatically, punitively, restricted immigration from eastern and southern Europe, radically changed the nature of the garment trade in New York. And he was still there in March and April 1925, when a series of property-destroying attacks and blackjack- and iron pipe-beatings occurred at the small cloak and suit manufacture on the sixth floor. That shop was non-union, and the suspects were organizers.

The Newmans of Abraham's generation were constitutionally, unquestioningly, supportive of unions. Most were Labor Bundists, not Communists, their sympathies "a sort of mash-up of socialist–anarchist–liberal, in the Russian tradition."[3] "A. Newman," a modest operation centered around the cutting table, seems to have escaped the violence: perhaps it was too small for the goons to bother with, or perhaps the employees were unionized. But in July 1926, a "long, violent and disastrous strike" began, motivated more by factional maneuvering within the Communist Party than by International Ladies' Garment Workers' Union negotiations. "In the whole immigrant Jewish experience there was probably nothing to match the civil war in the garment center for sheer ugliness,"[4] and it's very likely here that the source of Barney's lifelong disdain for Communism and his infatuation with Anarchism can be located. Even small fry were affected as the strike dragged on through mid-December and disruption coursed down the chain. "A. Newman" relocated one block west and across the street from the elevated Chatham Square station to 7 East Broadway, a smaller, four-story structure built as a residence, now shared by five clothing operations, "Gelman Bros. Jewelers" and Abraham's *two* businesses—"Biltwell Clothing Company, Clothiers-Tailors to The CIVIL SERVICE MAN" (likely a subsidiary showroom for the parent Biltwell Company) and "A. Newman Clothing Manufacturer." It was here that from 1927, when he graduated City College, Barney worked for his father and embarked on the earliest of his quixotic ventures.

Abraham was a small man—Morris was 5'2" and bragged that he was the tallest of the siblings—who made a big impact. He was well liked, and the characteristics family and friends saw over the next fifty years in Barney—personal charisma; charm as a storyteller; intellectual capacity, pursuits, and playfulness; wit and humor and progressive politics—are the same ones admired in his father.[5] Other traits that distinguished Barney throughout his life—his strong will, his relentless determination to prevail, his "*doggedness*"—also marked the Newmans of Abraham's generation.[6] When Barney and Abraham came up against each other, Barney was the one to yield.

In late 1922, there was the matter of college. At that time it would not have been a foregone conclusion—only 8 percent of 18- to 21-year-olds in the country opted to attend—but they were not Jews: by 1910, 70 percent of the graduates of City College had Jewish surnames, "nearly all Russian or Polish or Hungarian (as opposed to the earlier German or Sephardic)."[7] Barney talked to his father, told him that he did not want to go to college, that he wanted to spend his time at the Art Students League. "He said that he would read all the books." Abraham "looked at him and said, 'OK, Barney, I know you'll read all the books. But tell me one thing: what should I tell the relatives?'"[8] Barney would go to college.

But in 1922 he still had to finish high school, and that was a problem. De Witt Clinton was not inclined to give him a diploma because he had missed so much class time. He passed his exams, "but they felt there was something about his character." He didn't mind that he wouldn't graduate, but Anna did. She insisted on going to a graduation: he had to get a diploma. "So he went back to school, and they made him go around to each one of his teachers and get the teacher to write a character OK for him. And that was the way he got his diploma."[9] It was a pretty embarrassing, if not humiliating, way to be launched into adulthood.

Over the course of his life, Barney would form vehement attachments with men he found admirable, challenging, and worthy to be his intellectual contestants, who would set him on a particular path and fire his mental passion. Sometime in 1922–23 it became difficult for the reality of college to compete with Adolph Gottlieb and Alex Borodulin.[10]

Gottlieb had attended John Sloan's and Robert Henri's sessions at the Art Students League in 1920, but was not there the fall of 1922 when Barney first came. They may have met earlier, when the Gottlieb family moved to the Grand Concourse in the Bronx in 1921, or they may have met later, through Borodulin, a "mutual friend" who was at City College (CCNY), as Barney recounted in 1964, although Borodulin's son does not believe his father went to CCNY.[11] Either way, Gottlieb was quite an eye-opener for Barney. Only two years older, he had so completely committed himself to life as an artist as to be beholden to no one but himself. He had done more than cut classes at Stuyvesant High School; he had dropped out—objecting parents be damned—and worked his passage to Europe in 1921, when he was 17. For eighteen months he had managed to live in Paris, studying at the Académie de la Grande Chaumière and the Louvre, and to visit museums and galleries in Berlin,

Munich, Dresden, Vienna, and Prague. In 1923, Barney, a freshman at City College, was attending the very popular three-hour evening Life Drawing and Composition class given at the League by William von Schlegell; Cézanne was "*the* great model for the students," and von Schlegell was "a Cézanne man."[12] Plus, the class attracted beautiful girls from Texas. Gottlieb was taking John Sloan's class along with Alexander Calder, John Graham, and the future cartoonist, Otto Soglow, and Barney, who paid for a locker even when not registered for a class, hung around them.

The Art Students League was a truly vital school at that time, "the center of the art world," according to the artist and longtime League teacher Will Barnet,[13] "the most advanced and lively place" for a young artist to be, according to Gottlieb. Sloan and Henri were liberal and "open to all the new ideas . . . even though they didn't practice them."[14] When Barnet arrived as a student a few years later, he was greeted by the superintendent: "Young man, we have a revolution going on here. They want to get rid of Rembrandt." Young would-be painters were exhorted "to be one's self, to be honest with one's self, to do as one thinks, to follow one's own vision," by Allen Tucker, a beloved teacher.[15] Students—who paid month by month—exhibited a wide range of commitment. Some attended classes, some simply took advantage of the lockers and studio space; classes had monitors, but no one kept track of the hours. "You could walk in and walk out; you could walk into a class that wasn't yours."[16] The cafeteria was the place where you declared yourself: years later, teaching a few sessions of Barnet's class, Barney entered the cafeteria with Bob Kane—at that time a student—who pointed out the division between the "bohemian artists, who were the majority, and high-society groups, people from wealthy families, some of whom had studios in Carnegie Hall" across the street. Barney told Kane that when *he* had gone to the League, one had to "look into the cafeteria before you entered. Very often the Communists were there, and you didn't want to sit with *them*."[17]

Although he later claimed to have spent his high-school hours at the Metropolitan Museum, Barney never mentioned seeing the huge and historic loan show of Degas, Courbet, Cézanne, Manet, Monet, Pissarro, Renoir, Gauguin, Matisse, Picasso, and others, which hung from May to September 1921—"degenerate, modernistic works" intended to break down law and order and destroy "our entire social system," according to a pamphlet mailed to newspapers by the anonymous "Committee of Citizens and Supporters of the Museum." Rather, he told Hess that the January 1922 preview of the Kelekian collection sale, the first sale of modern French painting in the United States, including Matisse, Cézanne, Picasso, Renoir, Cassatt, was "the first time I saw how painting could be 'real.' "[18] The regular gallery excursions remembered by Barney, Gottlieb, and Aaron Siskind happened after Gottlieb returned in 1923, and what they saw by Americans generally "consisted of paintings that imitated Cézanne quite literally."[19] Gottlieb was finishing high school in the evenings, working in his father's stationery business days, and attending art classes when he could. In a summer sketch class at the Educational Alliance, Barney joined him.

However it was that Alexander Borodulin, Gottlieb's friend, entered Barney's life, he arrived at a crucial moment. Borodulin was deeply read, a serious thinker with passionate positions, and for at least the next decade he presented an equally compelling alternative to Gottlieb as a model for Barney to fashion his future.

Borodulin, born in Russia, immigrated to New York in 1908 at 4 years old and grew up in eastern Brooklyn at a time "when New Lots Avenue was just that, the new lots without houses." His father, Lazer, was a science writer for the Yiddish newspaper, *Der Tog*. Somehow, the Borodulin family became good friends with the more Americanized Gottliebs, and so did Alex and Adolph.[20] Alex and Barney had a natural affinity: they both came from intensely intellectual, philosophically disputatious homes filled with books; they agreed on the paramount significance of Spinoza.

Although Borodulin "hated all kinds of modernism"—ultimately insurmountable, leading to a permanent rift[21]—through the 1920s and early '30s, he and Barney were especially close, almost like family, encouraging each other to exercise both intellectual and physical muscles. For years, Borodulin was attracted to the emerging "sport" of weightlifting because of its "antiquarian" aspect, "the Greek ideal."[22] With (Jewish) cultural heroes like Harry Houdini, his mother's passion for lessons, and his own drive for self-improvement, Barney was an easy mark. He bought himself the standardized free weights of the Milo Bar-Bell company and their *Strength* magazine, and subscribed to the systematic "progressive" courses of weightlifting.

Borodulin, who would go on to write scientific journalism and several politically left-leaning plays, was already writing poetry that he shared with Barney. Before the end of the decade, Barney, too, made some awkward, youthfully tortured, attempts, and continued to compose for occasions through the 1940s. He made a reading list, a sort of poetry 101 that includes anthologies as well as specific poets worthy of focus: Rupert Brooks, Walter De La Mare, Emily Dickinson, Ford Madox Hueffer (who changed his name to Ford Madox Ford in 1919), Amy Lowell, John Masefield, and W. B. Yeats among them. Multiple reworkings of a number of Barney's poems survive. At the same time, Gottlieb was focusing on poetry, especially T. S. Eliot and Ezra Pound, finding what he thought was an "odd source" for "expressionist" paintings titled after poems he was "fascinated by."

For all his initial resistance, at least part of Barney internalized Abraham's point. As it was for David Levinsky, in Abraham Cahan's eponymous novel, college "was not merely a place in which I was to fit myself for the battle of life, nor merely one in which I was going to acquire knowledge. It was a symbol of spiritual promotion as well. University-bred people were the real nobility of the world. A college diploma was a certificate of moral as well as intellectual aristocracy."[23] Barney was independent enough and sophisticated enough to know that City College "was a place where bright young men educated *themselves*."[24] While the complete college experience might have been dampened by Prohibition, Barney thrived. He wrote poetry, he reviewed music performances for *The Campus* newspaper, he joined clubs to discuss "ideas" and literature and philosophy and art. And he developed a distinctive epistolary and essayistic voice that was very different from his witty and punning personal voice: preternaturally authoritative, with a bludgeon of mathematical–

philosophical Maimonidean logic to silence contradiction. With some refinements, it would characterize his writing for the rest of his life.

Barney approached college the way he had approached everything else before. "They threw him out a couple of times because he was always late for class and cutting a lot. Because he was always a bohemian. He used to stay up late with the fellows and then get up late in the morning."[25] During these years the muses battled for his soul: poetry slipped as he aspired to locate his vocation, longing for the "most intense of all experiences."[26] He was, in his word, a "bug" on music—specifically piano—and he even attempted to compose.[27] Years later, in 1958 in Western Canada, he played a section of a startling, original symphony from this period, which he described as "a little bit of Bartók, a little bit of Tchaikovsky."[28] He "organized a music column" for the college newspaper in order to get free tickets to concerts, later claiming that "for a long period of my life I spent every night in concerts."[29] He skipped every session of one science class, but was offered a passing grade if he taught the instructor to read music. He always felt guilty—not simply for never completing his end of the bargain—but because he knew he "missed something in not knowing about science,"[30] something he made efforts to rectify in the 1930s. In the spring of his sophomore year, as a 19-year-old, he argued with his Latin teacher about an "F." "My dear Mr. Newman," the teacher wrote, "There is no error in the grade assigned you, and your letter to me makes it clear that you ought to repeat the course. If you knew as much Latin as you think you know, you would have known that the paper you submitted was considerably below our requirements. Your percentage on that part of the paper which I myself marked was about 40%."[31] Thirty-seven years later, this particular disappointment and embarrassment haunted his relentless, if slyly witty, engagement with the scholar Erwin Panofsky in an arcane dispute about Latin grammar.

It was during his junior year that he wrote the earliest bit of Newman art commentary that survives: a 1925 review of an exhibition of paintings by, in his words, "one of the world's greatest critics," Roger Fry. "Critic Turned Artist," which appeared in City College's literary magazine, *The Lavender*, is both prescient and ironic. The painful and poignant scenario Barney described was the very one he lived in 1950 and 1951: "The reputation . . . of Mr. Roger Fry as critic has proved unfortunate for Roger Fry the artist, for he was ill received in New York. Mr. Fry, who is famous for his contributions to the science of aesthetics, especially as it concerns painting, for his additions to our knowledge of primitive art, for his opinions of men and schools, and for his work in the modern movement, now finds his attempt at expression in paint treated without mercy by every critic . . . *his judges deplored the fact that a man of such keen critical ability should begin to paint* [emphasis added]." Barney's *defense* of a critic painting—he called Fry "an artist of ability"—while not dependent on the critic's philosophical stance, was made in support of someone whose "science of aesthetics" Barney entirely repudiated once he actually had some lived experience of making art.

Young men naturally develop and refine their identities, passions, and positions in tandem, opposition, and gamesmanship with their peers, and Barney particularly was susceptible to a kind of style- and subject-seduction by others. Even the sophisticated Gottlieb's jaunty moustache was quickly duplicated on Barney's clean-shaven upper lip. It was Barney's inclination, nascent at this time, but characteristic of so much of his later behavior, to seize upon an infatuation and run with it furiously toward the goalpost, like the football player he never quite managed to be. He could clearly *envision* the implications of the trajectory, he could *see* that goal in front of him, but for many years it was a miserable source of frustration. He didn't seem to understand that he lacked—or why he needed—the particular skill-set to get there. He protested the rules, they were an interference; he was impatient to get to the meat, the nut, the heart of the matter. It would take two decades until he did. But at CCNY he only kept catching passes.

Barney sampled subjects: traditional academics, languages, but also seven terms of "public speaking," and four of "military science"—the precursor of ROTC. In the 1920s, philosophy was one of two "most popular" departments per CCNY yearbooks; Barney discovered it in his junior year, favoring Scott Buchanan but stamped for life, as were so many others, by Morris Raphael Cohen, "the culture hero of the City College boys, at least the brighter and tougher ones, who learned not to fear (too much) his probing, combative style"[32] and the "living example of the power of reason."[33] Students were both in awe of, and identified with, him; like many of them he came from a poor, Lower East Side background before attending City College, where his experience, he wrote, was that "what the professors lacked in love of learning, the student body made up."[34] His Yiddish-accented style of teaching was Socratic—in some opinions, even "sadistic"—but impersonally so. He was, he said, after the truth, although he acknowledged that in his youth his natural tendency "to conquer my opponent [was] stronger than reason." The kinds of students that came to Cohen, according to Irving Howe (speaking from personal experience) were the ones who "could have withstood it—Jewish boys with minds honed to dialectic, bearing half-conscious memories of *pilpul* [Talmudic disputation] indifferent to the prescriptions of gentility, intent on a vision of lucidity." And what those students came away with was "a vision of mind, a style of quest," and hundreds of anecdotes about "his scathing rigors of mind."[35] Cohen told Barney to his face that he was "the guy who will *certainly* never get anyplace" and told his friends that "they ought to keep away" from him.[36] (Of the six philosophy courses he took, four were "incomplete.")

A photograph from the period shows Newman, Gottlieb, Borodulin, and Soglow in Central Park, young men as full of joy and pride and purpose as any storybook musketeers. There were other good friends met at City College who presented additional worlds, possibilities, and models: Aaron Siskind, the young poet and future photographer; William Lipkind, whose intellectual passion for Pre-Columbian cultures led to anthropology and award-winning children's books; Leo Yamin, future educator; Max Margulis, leftist writer and future violinist, voice teacher, and founder of Blue Note records; and Jesse Lowenthal, poet and literary-minded upper-class German Jew from the Bronx, who would marry the artist Carmen Herrera. Louis Zukofsky, the Lower East Side-born poet, already in print as a Columbia Univer-

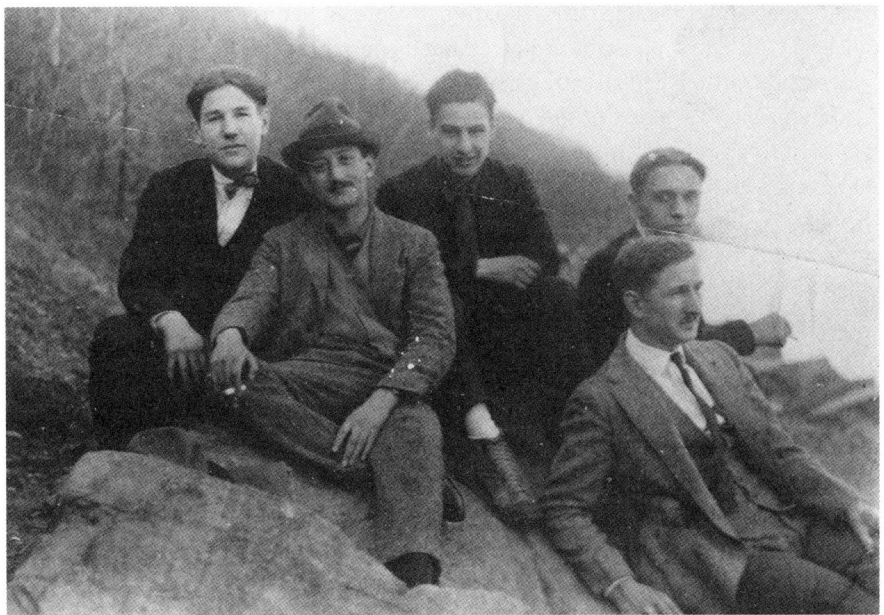

Fig. 5 From left: Barnett Newman, Adolph Gottlieb, Alexander Borodulin, Otto Soglow, unidentified, c.1925

sity student, was a friend of Lowenthal's and as early as February 1931, published Lowenthal in the "objectivist" issue of *Poetry* that he edited.[37] Lowenthal's style of extreme elegance—which, as a legendary English teacher at Stuyvesant High School, always included a beautiful three-piece suit, "gold watch chain looping across his waistcoat front," gold-rimmed spectacles, and "old-world manners"[38]—encouraged Barney's own sartorial flair.

"At City College we had [the Clionian] literary society," Siskind recalled, which met once a week to discuss literature and its members' writing. "And that is where I first knew Barney Newman. But of course he wasn't painting then. We had one painter in the group . . . who used to meet us after the meeting, and that was Adolph Gottlieb. . . . and because they were also interested in painting [we] used to go along once in a while to the shows on 57th Street." In Wildenstein or Agnew galleries they discovered great works by El Greco and Tintoretto. "Frequently" on Saturday nights, they went to the Metropolitan Museum for "concerts and if the concert wasn't especially interesting we'd wander around looking at the paintings and have the whole museum to ourselves."[39] Once, when Barney and Gottlieb saw a *London Gazette* reproduction of a scroll painting in the Boston Museum of Fine Arts—*The Burning of the Sanjo Palace*, although they didn't know it at the time—they were so moved, they decided to make a pilgrimage to see it, staying at the YMCA. The museum had trouble locating it; the young men persisted; dust covers were removed in the storage area. When it was finally found, they felt it was worth all the exertions, so tremendous an impact did the "great painting" make.[40] Similarly, in 1926, when

Barney read about the Barnes Foundation in Merion, Pennsylvania, his instinct was to lead a contingent of aesthetically inflamed youth to see it.

By 1926 Gottlieb had already garnered a press notice as one of the "Leading artists of America"[41]—albeit in the *Jewish Daily Bulletin*. And in 1927 Gottlieb's contribution to an open, self-selected art exhibition in the fashionable Alamac Hotel on Seventy-First Street and Broadway was noted as "one of the best: according to the jury"[42]—albeit in *The Home News*. For Barney, seeing a friend's name appear in print, no matter the venue, was a challenge. It was time for him to look for a bigger voice on a bigger stage.

Alfred Barr was not-yet-director of the not-yet-founded Museum of Modern Art in 1926, but, as an associate professor at Wellesley, he was sufficiently on the radar to have been invited to review *The Art of Painting* by Albert C. Barnes for *The Saturday Review of Literature*. Barney, too, "reviewed" the Barnes dogma that year—on, he said, a paper bag while sitting in a luncheonette—but he focused on the limited and dictatorial viewing policy at the Barnes Foundation, three years old by then, which Barr never mentioned. And yet, since there's no indication that Barney read the book—none of his typical sentence-by-sentence dissection, or quotation—it is likely that Barney was prompted by Barr's discussion and, especially, his tone: both young men, the 24-year-old Barr and the 21-year-old Barney, arguing nearly opposite positions, similarly assume the stance of pompous windbag. "Of all human institutions, teaching has shown itself to be the greatest of failures," Barney's great experience, and two courses at the Art Students League, enabled him to declare in his opening sentence.

He was frustrated: the Barnes Foundation refused to allow him, and the philosophy class from City College he hoped to bring along, to visit, since they were not enrolled as students there. This "gross crime against humanity" drove him to formulate in a pique-filled letter just what he thought the goal of art was and is the earliest record we have of his position.

> Mr. Barnes's actions spring from the passionate desire of our modern age to build up an objective criticism of art and from the belief common to our age that the right way to view art is objectively, which means essentially that all appreciation is the contemplation of form, which is the essence of art . . . . It is evident that all this manifests a nominalistic attitude toward art which makes of art an accidental, almost arbitrary phenomenon, void of significance. All this exemplifies perfectly the rot that is nominalism. Our critics, Mr. Barnes, Mr. [T. S.] Eliot, tell us in true nominalistic style that the artist creates form. This is a falsehood that has created much mischief, to say the least. The artist emphatically does not create form. The artist expresses in a work of art an aesthetic idea which is innate and eternal.[43]

Twenty-eight years later, he was still firm, and still smarting: "My dislike of Barnes Foundation and what Barnes stood for is so intense I could not accept any invitation," he telegraphed to Jackson Pollock in 1954. "My revulsion is my own, it goes back to my teens when it enormously affected my life and thinking." The impact clearly was so strong that he misplaced the event to an earlier age, when the museum did not yet exist and the book had not yet been published, to emphasize its formative influence.

In the early fall of 1929, New York was buzzing about the opening of the Museum of Modern Art. In *Vogue*, the founding director Alfred Barr invoked "the overwhelming interest in modern art developed during the last twenty years" as fundamental to its creation. Barr was referring to interest among the Rockefellers, the Crowninshields, the Sullivans, the Blisses, the Goodyears, the Quinns—an altogether different demographic from the Newmans, the Gottliebs, the Siskinds, and the Borodulins. And yet, with their twenty-something years on earth, the conceptual rationale behind "modern" painting is what the young men passionately discussed. It was a pretty long and a pretty rapid leap.

"The point was not to be right, it was to assert ourselves!" wrote Robert Musil about youth's need to stake out territory. "A young man needs to shine, far more than he needs to see something in the light."[44]

FOUR

"THE FOX KNOWS MANY THINGS"

He was a spokesman before he found exactly what he was speaking for. And he tried on many hats before he found the one that fit.

Retrospectively, Barney created a narrative to explain why his career had been delayed, his dreams thwarted. He told Hess that the business had been doing exceedingly well, and after he graduated in February 1927, Abraham offered both sons full partnerships: "stay a while, make some money, then walk out after a year or two, about $100,000 richer" able to do what they pleased. Everyone, "including the level-headed Gottlieb, urged him to accept the proposition." But "just as he was scheduled to metamorphose into a full-time painter living off a small but comfortable income, the firm was wiped out in the crash"[1] and Barney spent unexpected years with his father untangling the corroded finances. The truth is less romantic: it was not the crash that caused the business to fail, but the turmoil in the trade and mismanagement two years before. Ordinary family responsibility ensnared him, not great historical upheaval; moreover, it was convenient. Barney simply was not ready to commit to an artist's life. Nibbling around the edges, as he would for the next two decades, he finagled his qualifications and applied to become a "teacher of drawing" in New York City high schools. The Board of Examiners agreed to accept the approximately 144 hours, none of them post-graduate, "which you have successfully completed at the Art Students League as part of the 300 post graduate hours necessary to establish your eligibility for license."[2]

In the years between October 1929 and the beginning of World War II, Barney helped keep Abraham Newman & Son afloat, personally collecting money, writing advertising copy, relocating five times, defending lawsuits. But he also made his own the cause of civil servants— launching a magazine, pitching newspaper columns, mounting a relentless campaign to win a Guggenheim Fellowship for an exhaustive historical study. He "managed" a theater troupe, co-wrote its "manifesto," produced its plays, and waged publicity campaigns. Responding to civil service listings, he twice applied for federal government positions as an inspector of clothing factories and once as a teacher in an Indian Community and Boarding School. He wrote poetry, and righteous essays (mostly unpublished) on cultural events, briefly ran for mayor, taught art in public school, lobbied for a bylined "art news" column in a teachers' magazine. He offered himself for hire as a professor of art at the nascent Queens College; "discovered" fine art applications for the silkscreen process, taught it, and expected to write about it for *Popular Science*. All of these, pursued with the hyperbole, bravura, and brio that were by now becoming characteristic, were just career options he was trying out. This sort of disparate resume was not uncommon during the Depression as members of his generation chased after a living wage. What is notable about Barney is that so few of his initiatives could have realistically led to a reliable income.

He also studied ornithology and botany; contemplated becoming a rural land-owner before he decided, a few years later, that he did not want to "own anything"; wooed and wed Annalee Greenhouse; summered as a civilian in artists' enclaves in Maine and Massachusetts; and moved his domestic residence seven or eight times. He steadfastly pursued a patent violation lawsuit on behalf of his father-in-law. He regularly attended the sorts of political and social-activist meetings and rallies that were so much a part of the anxious cultural landscape in those years. He continued to look at art—a bit defiantly at Marie Harriman Gallery, at Valentine Dudensing, at Wildenstein, at Knoedler, where students were not generally welcome—and he continued to *study* painting, infrequently at the Art Students League, during the summers, and in informal evening sketch groups with Gottlieb at Milton Avery's. Occasionally—it's not clear under just what circumstances—he shared Gottlieb's studio across from the Jewish Maternity Hospital at 270 East Broadway.

What it appears he did *not* do was produce "finished" paintings. No artworks at all by Barney—if indeed any were made—from this period survive, or are recalled being seen by anyone. Only two amateur-sounding examples are documented in writing.

In today's thinking, one might project that he had some form of attention deficit disorder—if he didn't focus so *much* attention on each endeavor. But it's more illuminating to think of him in terms of the ancient Greek fragment, "The fox knows many things, but the hedgehog knows one big thing," used with elegant subtlety by Isaiah Berlin of Tolstoy: he "was by nature a fox, but believed in being a hedgehog." Barnett Newman was a "fox" so extreme—he had too many subjects, he had no *subject*—that, ultimately, embodying the hedgehog in his work was the only way for him to survive.

In January 1930, to accumulate some of the hours required for his teaching license, Barney returned to the Art Students League for the one-month, three-and-a-half-hours a day, six-day a week session of John Sloan's Life Drawing, Painting, and Composition class. The family, in financial difficulty, in April moved a few blocks east to the West Farms area in the Bronx and, although George had gotten married six months earlier in the Bronx Borough Hall without his parents' knowledge—he wore a ring on a cord underneath his shirt—all four children still lived at home.[3] For the moment, both Barney and George worked for Abraham. A year later, pushed by his brother, George went to work as a civilian draftsman at the Brooklyn Naval Yard, and Barney expected to begin teaching when schools opened on September 14, days after Abraham Newman & Son filed for bankruptcy.[4] But an outbreak of infantile paralysis—polio—claimed nearly 3500 children during the previous ten weeks and the schools did not open. It was a grim shadow over a young man's first independent initiative.

Years later, Annalee would complain that all three of Abraham and Anna's older children had to "get jobs" because Anna was a very proud woman and "had to have her fur coat and her diamond ring,"[5] but most adults took jobs during those years—if they were lucky enough to find them. Teaching was the choice of Barney's college friends: Siskind taught elementary school, a job where he "would have a little time to write,"[6] and Jesse Lowenthal taught English at Stuyvesant High School (Theodoros Stamos was at one point in his class). But Barney had failed the New York City art teacher's licensing examination at the end of the 1920s, and the existence of peer models doesn't explain why he would psychologically invest himself in a job for which he did not have the qualifications, in which the deck seemed to be stacked against him by an authority for which he had no respect, and in which he was bound to feel inadequate in his most cherished, and vulnerable, aspiration.

Art in the public schools was related to a commercial curriculum—"Make an effective design in color for a box to be used by a florist for delivering corsage bouquets," "Design and illustrate on a ten-inch figure a school costume suitable for a high school senior" were typical questions on the licensing exam—and Barney simply didn't have that training. Gottlieb had attended Parsons School of Design to prepare for teaching, passed the written exam and failed the drawing, but taking himself seriously as a painter, saw it as a joke. "I decided the hell with it, and never bothered again." He took instead "part time jobs which wouldn't be too demanding . . . summer camp, sign painting, retouched photographs, taught at various settlement houses, arts and crafts" in order to be able to pursue his vocation.[7] For Barney, who between 1937 and 1939 took the exams to become a permanent teacher of fine arts in both day secondary and junior high schools at least seven more times without acquiring credentials, it was an odd way of sabotaging himself and it fed his already ripe sense of injustice.

Nevertheless, in the first half of the decade, he was content with substitute status, which provided an income—even if teachers' salaries, in 1932, were dramatically cut—and allowed him the flexibility to fantasize. Living as an artist was too hard a slog.

"Art came in like a growth, bothering me, [not] really a choice, but kind of like fate. I had to do it." William Baziotes, who arrived in New York from Pennsylvania, in August 1933, described what a young artist had to tolerate to pursue his work. The general atmosphere "was awful. Continuous wave of poverty. Coffee lines. Riots. I doubled up with a relative who had a room on Fourteenth St. . . . I wanted to go to the Art Students League. Saw prices: $25 a month . . . . the National Academy of Design [was] free."[8] Juliana Force, of The New Deal Public Works of Art Project, which was finally funded that November, saw "the utter destitution of the artists, and how their courage is failing at the thought of facing another winter." Over 350 painters and sculptors "of first rate importance are desperately in need of jobs," she wrote.[9]

Gottlieb, while remaining a close friend and sometime studio-mate, pursued his work in the company of and within the structures of artists' society. He showed at the Opportunity Gallery (which became the Secession Gallery), and received a positive notice from the influential critic Henry McBride; along with Mark Rothko, whom he met at the Opportunity, and whom he introduced to Barney around 1931, he studied almost daily with Milton Avery. Within a few years, he would help form The Ten and find work on the Works Progress Administration (WPA).

Barney, however, chose not to engage himself in the artists' world, as even his sister Sarah had. After graduating from Hunter College in June 1933, Sarah took classes at the Art Students League—later she would describe herself as a protégée of Yasuo Kuniyoshi[10]— eventually worked for the Art Teaching Project of the WPA, and applied for the Easel Project.[11] Whether or not it was, as Barney maintained, because of family pressure, or whether it was artistic insecurities, more self-aggrandizing ambitions, or reluctance to give up a bourgeois life, this was not the path Barney followed. The project was a little too structured, or, perhaps, a little too blue-collar—there was a "degrading requirement of taking the poverty oath" and "an investigation which in most cases involved much duplicity," and indignity, according to Gottlieb—for his deeply defended personality.

With Gottlieb married in 1932, Barney spent his mental energies philosophizing and scheming with Borodulin.[12] It was a close and intensely vital relationship for the next few years; they argued over, and cracked to their satisfaction, the big issues of ethics, morality, politics, science, and culture. As Barney was considering the purchase of "5 to 10 acre plots" in upstate New York at the end of the summer of 1932 and seeking advice,[13] Borodulin nostalgically recalled a vacation four years earlier when "a storm found us in a tent together . . . . Our status quo rests easily still, then as now, and except for experience whose only signal is a grayer hair, we're where we were."[14] Borodulin was writing mathematical–philosophical treatises, poetry, and—impacted by Clifford Odets's political, cynical *Awake and Sing* for the Group Theatre —socially concerned plays. Barney was subbing at Grover Cleveland High School Annex in Ridgewood, and, as such, was now in the "civil service." Characteristically, he thought he knew better how it should be operated.

From his E. R. Tripler shoes up to his Cavanagh hat, Barney was a man of the city. If the new American metropolis was "a theatre of social action," in the words of Lewis Mumford, New York was something more, a *consciously* dramatic setting: the city "fosters art and *is* art; the city creates the theatre and *is* the theatre" where "man's more purposive activities are formulated and worked out, through conflicting and cooperating personalities, events, groups."[15] In the years of Barney's young manhood, beginning in the 1920s, the participants in the metropolitan drama were suddenly vastly more informed, sophisticated about institutional workings, and able to imagine themselves players because of the explosion of journalism and media. It was "the first age of the media, of book clubs, best-sellers and record charts, of radio and talking pictures"; by 1929 a third of Americans owned a radio and a record player and three out of four went to the movies at least once a week.[16] Barney consumed the city's offerings, participated in its life, and channeled its agita by assuming a Zelig-like spectrum of personas that ran from the wise-guy operator Damon Runyon through the professorial anthropologist Franz Boas through the worthy liberal commentator Heywood Broun through the Jewish intellectuals of the *Partisan Review*.

Is there a "radio set" in the home? The census asked this question for the first time in 1930. Yes, the Newmans responded, there was one in their new 85-dollars-per-month apartment at 1715 Vyse Avenue. By the early 1930s, radio had become so ubiquitous in New York that much of the population heard the same music, comedy, and serious drama; gossip, variety shows, and amateur hours; sporting events; pundits, personalities; news. The 1932 Hoover–Roosevelt election was the first to be covered as it happened,[17] and in March 1933, when the president began his "fireside chats," millions felt that they knew him. It was a sea change in America's relationship to celebrity.[18]

Trials became a subset of popular entertainment: that of the Lindbergh baby's murderer was broadcast live; the Hahn–Duveen case, which occupied the particular nexus of fine art, "expertise," and slander that would come to obsess Barney, was covered in over a hundred articles in the *Times* alone. Major criminal trials were transformed into "crystallizing media events" through the knowing and slangy, vivid present tense of Damon Runyon's reporting.[19]

Runyon, one of the day's most important columnists, was a dandy, "a man who regarded his suit as the first sentence of his day's story."[20] Barney—whose 1939 paean to downtown is perfumed with the same aftershave as E .B. White's classic of nine years later—was moved by the romance of New York that Runyon "practically invented."[21] So much of what later acolytes and friends found so charming about Barney—the studied dress, the night-owl life, the bottomless stockpile of New York lore and casual comfort in haunts like Stillman's Gym, Sweet's (Fulton Fish Market) restaurant, and tucked-away suppliers and boîtes—can be admired in Runyon's world as he "turned from news to delivering myths [which] became one of the few things ever to spring out of the Broadway cement and last." Mostly, though, it was that desire to mythologize in a particularly *vernacular* idiom—to make life more fun and interesting—that they shared. Runyon had *style*, and was a counterpoint to Barney's cosseted-Jewish-son intellectual self-presentation. He was a man's man, saturated with the kind of masculine urban appreciation that Barney himself loved: baseball, horse-racing, "the fights," the character-filled restaurants, the repartee with waiters and cab drivers.

Runyon made the sport of litigation metaphorical: "The trial is a sort of game," he wrote. "An enterprising radio outfit will unofficially broadcast the proceedings, play by play, so to speak."[22] Barney, a lifelong fan, adopted Runyon's voice. Anyone who attended a match with him would be treated to sports metaphors to punch up artistic heroism, and art metaphors to make more profound the athletic competition.

To a striking degree, newspapers—the central nervous system of the city—created Barney's reality. Habitually, almost obsessively, he clipped, saved, and shared clippings from a range of ephemeral printed media; his archives are filled with the crumbling evidence of once-urgent topics and personalities. Press coverage was the catalyst for Barney's *responsa*. Inspired, enraged, righteously provoked, or simply piqued, he formed at this time the lifelong reflex of citing newspaper articles as reliable source or dependable defense. And because he paid such close attention, and so consistently invoked that which he read, those occasions when reaction is glaringly absent too become part of Barney's story.

There were over a dozen daily newspapers published in New York, morning, afternoon, evening; middle-class New Yorkers typically read several each day.[23] The 1933 smash hit on Broadway, *As Thousands Cheer*, by Irving Berlin and Moss Hart, was a review "right off the front pages of the newspapers," with individual sketches based on headlines.[24] The *Times* and the *Herald Tribune* covered international as well as local news; the morning tabloids sensational events, crime scenes, and trials; the afternoon and the evening papers business, politics, and society shenanigans. No one was out of reach of the explosion of advertising for canned foods, washing machines, refrigerators, synthetic fabrics, telephones, motion pictures, automobiles, radios.[25] Clothing ads, crucially, offered a range of possibilities for coded self-presentation. It was "the golden age of myth-making journalism," with the exploits of Jack Dempsey, Babe Ruth, and Bobby Jones evoking greater interest than "hard news."[26]

Columnists defined popular culture: the two Walters—the erudite and magisterial political pundit, Lippmann, considered by many the most important journalist in America, and the self-promoting gossip-monger, Winchell, with his 50 million daily readers; the liberal Heywood Broun and the rage-filled conservative writer of scandal-creating exposés, Westbrook Pegler.[27] Writers developed identifiable, bold, personal styles to supply the many small magazines born during the Depression. When the grand *Life* magazine began publishing in 1936, it apotheosized these figures in photographs. Media, it was clear, was the path to getting your product—or yourself—noticed.

That Barney, a habitual reader of at least the *Times*, the *New York World-Telegram*, the *Sun*, the *New York Post*, and the Yiddish-language *Der Tog*, invented himself as a character to whom attention should be paid in this era is not coincidental. In a 1934 letter, he had the self-assurance to castigate the *World-Telegram*'s Broun for being pushed around by the conservative Scripps Howard management that had acquired the previously liberal Pulitzer-owned *New York World* (Broun was a holdover) and he made sure to identify himself as "an unsuccessful candidate for Mayor [see below] on the issue of Culture instead of Reform. See W.T. Nov. 4, 1933. I sent you a manifesto to join our protest but you entirely disregarded it."

In 1933, Abraham Newman & Son moved into the *New York Tribune* building at 154 Nassau Street, a "sumptuous Victorian conglomerate in glorious Ruskinian color"[28] designed by Richard Morris Hunt. Between 1935 and 1937, they were in the gold-domed Pulitzer Building, 63 Park Row, home of the *New York World*, and until the repeal of Prohibition, the location of "Doc" Perry's drug store, a hangout for reporters with a speakeasy in the rear famous for its "orange" juice and a storied history of patrons including John L. Sullivan and Mark Twain. Both buildings were in the heart of "Newspaper Row," somewhat diminished from its pre-telephone heyday when proximity to City Hall, the West Street piers, police headquarters, and the criminal courts was all-important, but still the center of New York print journalism. It was a universe of competing newspaper offices and facilities, reporters' restaurants and haunts, quick lunch "German kitchens" and oyster bars in former saloons "under the bleak shed of Brooklyn Bridge or on those cobbled streets slanting down to the East River," many open all night, and the "shoddy shops—upstairs shoe parlors, downstairs pool halls, melodramatic movies, passport photo galleries and 'reliever' cellars" of Park Row.[29] For the next six years, Newspaper Row would be Barney's base of operations. In 1939, as he was leaving the last Abraham Newman & Son office, he wrote an elegy to it.

> What is this neighborhood really like? It is built on an old American pattern around two open parks that act as commons where the people who work in the neighborhood can still sit in the sun during lunchtime. Around City Hall are the relics of New York's newspaper row, the old New York Times building facing the park, backed by the building of the old Commercial, flanked by the Tribune and the World. Diagonally opposite to the Times, the Herald and the Sun. Nearby were the Telegram, the Globe, the Evening Post. Here Greeley and William Cullen Bryant and Joseph Pulitzer and Hearst talked for the city and the country; and in between these noisy personalities were the cheese markets, the vegetable markets, the fish markets, the meat markets, and the politicians' markets that fed and ran a city.

The rhetoric of journalism, its power to publicize personalities, to articulate and argue philosophical positions, and to promote products, Barney absorbed during this period. He could be like Greeley, like Bryant and the others; he could wield these methods for his own purposes. Did a newspaper article (for instance, on car accidents) rankle him? He would put on a columnist's hat:

"Deadly Weapons"

> Do you want a picture of automobile safety? Then declare the automobile for what it is—a deadly weapon. Like revolvers make it illegal for men to own them, except for those purposes that make ownership of weapons legal—use.
>
> Make it illegal for anybody to own a car except a truck. You will rid the streets of the man to whom a car is a toy like the six-shooter of our ancestors.[30]

But against other provocations, his Walter Mitty illusions were no match. Among the small collection remaining in Barney's desk at Annalee's death was a 1936 *Fortune* magazine substantially devoted to "Jews in America," a subject that qualified as "news" during the 1930s. Forty percent of all Jews in America lived in New York—at two million, the city's largest ethnic group[31]—and for them, alongside shared economic challenges, the Depression years saw a growing American anti-Semitism: organized hate groups, Father Coughlin and his followers, the Silver Shirts, and aggressive employment discrimination.[32] The editors at the conservative Luce publishing empire felt the need to elucidate for their four hundred thousand readers just how insignificant they believed discrimination was, how much it was imagined by Jews and brought upon themselves. For Barney, the disingenuous effort must have provoked nausea.

"Misgivings and uneasiness have colored the thinking of American Jews," *Fortune* reported. The "record of Nazi barbarities," and the "proposal of Sir Herbert Samuel that they aid in the enormously costly deportation of all Jews from Germany," had shocked into fear "leading members of the Jewish community in the United States—men who had previously looked to the future with complete confidence." If, as the magazine wrote, the "apprehensiveness of American Jews has become one of the important influences in the social life of our time," it nevertheless concluded that "Shaken down to bare fact . . . American organized anti-Semitism is a poor thing indeed." Notwithstanding that an "estimated half million people may attend occasional anti-Semitic meetings, etc., there are probably no more than 15,000 loyal Jew-hating group members in the whole United States."

The true difference, *Fortune* reassured its readers, was "cultural. All other immigrant peoples accept the culture of the country into which they come. The Jews for centuries have refused to accept it . . . . even many of those who have deserted the traditions of their people and accepted in every detail the dress and speech and life of the non-Jewish majority are *still subtly but recognizably different* [emphasis added] . . . . Indeed the very fact of the existence of discriminatory quotas and barriers and the like in industry and education and the professions is proof, not only of Gentile injustice, but also of the Jewish tendency to inundate a field where other Jews have made entrance."

The magazine catalogued exactly how many Jews, in what positions, could be found in banking, on the stock exchange, in heavy industry, the automobile industry, coal, rubber, oil, textiles, meat packing, manufacturing, liquor, large retail, publishing, media, theater and movies. The most prominent were named, but there was "no basis whatever for the suggestion that Jews monopolize U.S. business and industry." Although there were numbers of Jewish lawyers and doctors in New York, *Fortune* determined that they did not necessarily hold "power." As for politics:

> The second-generation Jewish intellectual with his background of Talmudic dialectic is mentally predisposed to Marxism to a degree which he himself rarely appreciates . . . It is not the natural propensity of the Jews for revolution which produces the impression [of overwhelming identification with Communism]. It is their natural propensity for journalism and excited, persuasive speech.

Finally,

> Granted all this, it still remains true that the future of the Jew in America is puzzling . . . . The first condition of their success will be the quieting of Jewish

apprehensiveness and the consequent elimination of the aggressive and occasionally provocative Jewish defensive measures which the country has recently and anxiously observed.

Appended was a list of "Principal Anti-Semitic organizations."[33]

On Monday evening, March 27, 1933, with hundreds of police, veterans, and fife and drum bands jamming the streets, with the elevated stations and stairs "black with detrained passengers," and midtown brought to a standstill, "20,000 Jews," according to the *Times*, crowded into the old Madison Square Garden.[34] Organized by Rabbi Stephen S. Wise to denounce Hitler's treatment of Jews in Germany and increasing incidents of anti-Semitism in America, the meeting heard speeches by Senator Robert Wagner, Mayor John P. O'Brien, Governor Al Smith (who announced that pressure had been put on him not to appear), several Catholic bishops and prominent figures of all faiths. "Thirty-five thousand others at overflow meetings outside and in Columbus Circle participated in the protest. Those in Forty-eighth Street and Eighth Avenue heard the addresses in the Garden through amplifiers. The speeches were broadcast throughout the land and across the sea. Hundreds of similar meetings were held in all parts of the country. It was estimated that fully 1,000,000 Jews participated in these demonstrations."[35] The Saturday before, congregants throughout the city heard coordinated sermons in solidarity.[36]

Barney, identifying as middle class, secular, remote from the ghetto, educated, high-minded, and painstakingly turned out, was daily living in the world that provoked these publications and events. He chose to make his life here, rather than in the bohemian subculture in which artists typically moved—however much he may have fantasized about that existence—and even that subculture was not protected territory. "These ten artists who happen to be nine . . . in the Montross Gallery are worth seeing," began the estimable McBride's review of the first show of The Ten in December 1935. "Their names are Ben-Zion, Ilya Bolotowsky, Adolph Gottlieb, Louis Harris, Kufeld, Marcus Rothkowitz, Louis Schanker, Joseph Solman and Tschacbasov. Hard names for New Yorkers to circumvent, but possibly citizens of Moscow and Odessa would find them easy . . . . They attack a canvas with as much fury and excitement as they would spend in attacking a government."[37]

Many first-generation American Jews like Barney were not looking to live a particularly Jewish-centric life, but the culture did not allow that luxury. As they were identified as Jews, it became impossible to avoid seeing the world through that lens. " 'Christians only' want ads ran regularly in mainstream newspapers."[38] The city's telephone and gas companies routinely rejected Jewish applicants. Insurance agencies, banks, and law offices also regularly refused to hire Jewish workers. Prospective Jewish teachers were often "identified and excluded through an oral examination designed to detect particularities of Jewish speech."[39] In March 1939—a few weeks after tens of thousands of Nazi sympathizers gathered in New York—City

College-educated Barney failed the oral test on a New York City licensing exam for teaching English because of "unsatisfactory use of English." He appealed the ruling: "I have been teaching at the Grover Cleveland High School for almost eight years <u>continuously</u> [as a substitute art teacher]. This long stay of many years at one school, my survival of innumerable turnovers of substitute personnel, indicate unqualified, successful teaching ability. What is more important, my long stay has enabled my principal and supervisors to observe me over a long span and has, therefore, given them the opportunity to know with certainty, my characteristic and normal speech pattern. As the attached letters prove, my principal and supervisors have not only failed to discover any speech defect but they have all commended my speech pattern, both in the classroom and before the faculty at conferences, as distinguished, highly cultured and of especial merit as a model for student imitation."[40]

During the worst years of the Depression, the odds of someone in Barney's demographic finding a white-collar job were approximately one in twenty. Notwithstanding the hurdles, teaching, government jobs, and civil service presented the "best conditions for Jewish employment."[41] As he could not abide his character being questioned by DeWitt Clinton High School, he would not have his "merit as a model for student imitation" challenged. Barney until his death never betrayed his immaculate and distinguished self-presentation. Initially a matter of upbringing, eventually a matter of honor, ultimately an idiosyncratic kind of branding, its roots can be found in his characterological response to the trauma of these years.

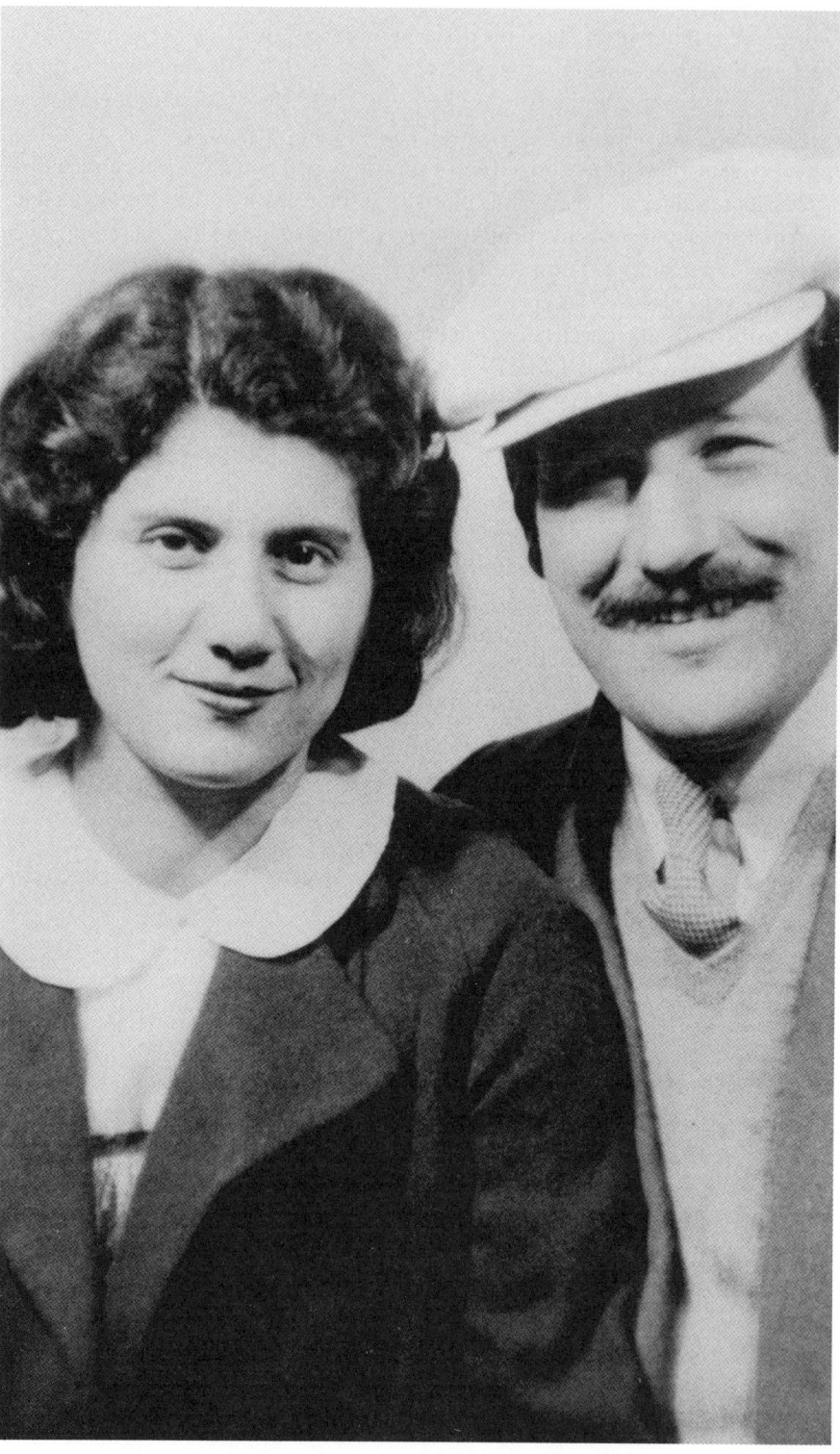

PART TWO

THE VOICE
1933–47

FIVE

THE CIVIL SERVICE MAN

"Biltwell Clothing Company, Clothiers-Tailors to The CIVIL SERVICE MAN Exclusively" read Abraham Newman's letterhead since the 1920s. Civil service was estimable, it was honorable, and it provided a dependable wage. And so, in June 1933, when he was frustrated as a substitute art teacher, Barney applied for a government position as "Supervising Inspector of Clothing Factories." Inflating his qualifications—almost an instinct, rather than simply a pattern, throughout his life—he overreached: "You do not show that you have had the required supervisory experience, including design and manufacturing processes, in a large clothing factory engaged in the manufacture of STANDARD clothing for MEN," the United States Civil Service Commission in Washington wrote, rejecting him. Now Barney's identification with civil service became an obsession.

Civil service jobs historically had been matters of political patronage, but toward the end of the 19th century there were reforms and regulations: New York State, for example, stipulated that civil service employees would be appointed and promoted based on competitive examinations to determine "merit and fitness,"[1] and even if sometimes manipulated by political parties, "merit and fitness" became popular notions. By the 1910s, the editors of *McClure's* magazine thought the result was a "Jewish Invasion of New York."

> Twenty years ago, the Irish occupied not far from ninety percent of all the positions in the city departments of New York. That was the period of the spoils system. . . . Now, however, nearly all of the 6,500 positions in the city government are awarded on the basis of competitive civil service examinations. As a result, the Jews are rapidly driving out the Irish, the Germans, and the native Americans. The East Side branches of the public libraries find themselves unable to supply the demand for books that are supposed to prepare one for civil service examinations. The Jews study hard and long, and their examination papers are so immeasurably superior to the average offered by representatives of other races that they invariably secure preferred places . . . They are the city's searchers, process-servers, and law examiners. Most of the municipal office boys are youngsters from the East Side: the stenographers and typewriters are nearly all Jewish girls.[2]

But if educated young Jews had grown comfortable assuming they owned these jobs, by 1932, when the positions were even more prized because they meant contractual security, there were new threats. That summer the newly formed Citizens' Budget Commission (CBC) put a bull's eye on the legally locked-in salaries and benefits of the civil service.[3] "A fact-finding, non-partisan, non-profit making body incorporated to study the cost of government in New York City and to urge specific economies," the CBC was made up of New York grandees to advocate a trickle-down-economics tax-cutting program, "the most comprehensive effort at budget control in the history of New York."

Barney and Borodulin decided to weaponize the words of the CBC. They developed the idea for a "new weekly newspaper" presumptuously titled *The New York Wednesday Answer*, "artistically designed and printed" for civil servants. At this conceptual stage, it was to have a rich mix of investigation, news, think pieces about the "Nature of Society," correspondence, cultural listings and reviews, "consumers' ideas," and classified ads. Barney invited Gottlieb to write, but Gottlieb was worried about producing articles. "It would not be so bad if I were required to do say one good painting a week."[4] There was a list of "Books We Recommend"—by Kropotkin, Spinoza, Plato, Voltaire, Tolstoy, Dr. Johnson; and "Books We Condemn"—by Hegel, Marx, Lenin, Bertrand Russell, and Anthony Adverse. Barney drew up a diligent writer's self-help reading list, including Edith Wharton's *The Writing of Fiction*, Coleridge's *Biographia Literaria*, Lafcadio Hearn's *Talks to Writers*, Katherine Mansfield's *Journal*, E. M. Forster's *Aspects of the Novel*, Virginia Woolf, Irving Babbitt, Henry James, Longinus, Alexander Pope, and T. S. Eliot. If one were looking for *some* thread to relate the works, it would have to be that "good" writing required a moral dimension.

Barney overly designed an awkward logo, created a layout template, had letterhead printed. They sent out advertising solicitations:

> The articles, features, editorial, and advertising policies will present an entirely new point of view that will make it indispensable to every serious thinker and man of culture throughout the country . . . What will govern our advertising policy? Two principles: First, only quality products will be accepted. Inferior, adulterated, or condemned merchandise will be barred. Second, advertisements must base their appeal on SPECIFICATION ONLY. They will be factual, informative, explanatory, and educational. Those that base their appeal on emotion, sex, or other irrelevancies will be barred.

Nothing came of this first foray: the two men were distracted by a more ambitious plan. Seven months after Stephen Wise's Madison Square Garden rally, a leaflet was distributed in New York, and a sign with the same content was carried in "the Jewish section of the city."

> American Gentiles: Do you realize that we are nothing but JEWISH SLAVES? Do you realize, the danger which confronts us by the Jews in the United States, is much greater than we all anticipate? . . . The Jewish sharks own already New York City, let us prevent them from CONQUERING our whole U.S.A. . . . their religion and business is nothing but an international racketeering blood sucking gangsterdom, exploiting the poorest of the poor to the last drop of their blood . . . Make it a principle to BOYCOTT EVERY JEWISH BUSINESS . . . The Jews are the lowest international race on earth . . . they are our biggest enemies.[5]

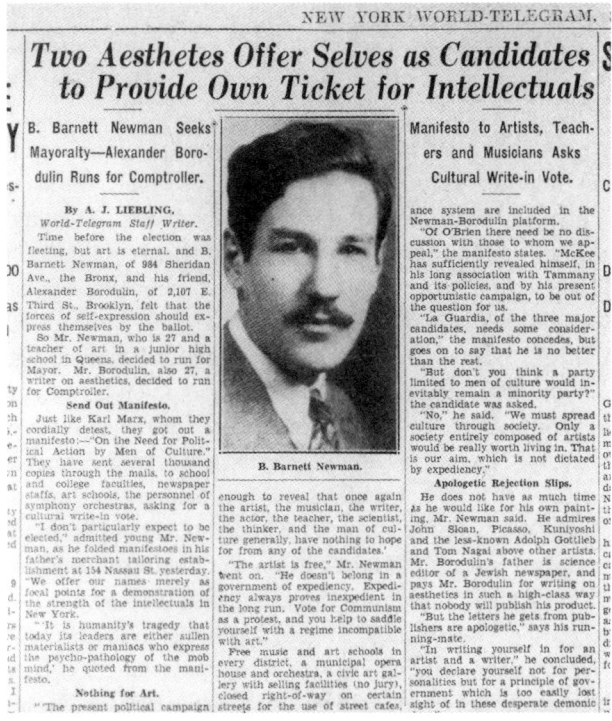

NEW YORK WORLD-TELEGRAM.

Two Aesthetes Offer Selves as Candidates to Provide Own Ticket for Intellectuals

B. Barnett Newman Seeks Mayoralty—Alexander Borodulin Runs for Comptroller.

Manifesto to Artists, Teachers and Musicians Asks Cultural Write-in Vote.

By A. J. LIEBLING,
World-Telegram Staff Writer.

Time before the election was fleeting, but art is eternal, and B. Barnett Newman, of 984 Sheridan Ave., the Bronx, and his friend, Alexander Borodulin, of 2,107 E. Third St., Brooklyn, felt that the forces of self-expression should express themselves by the ballot.

So Mr. Newman, who is 27 and a teacher of art in a junior high school in Queens, decided to run for Mayor. Mr. Borodulin, also 27, a writer on aesthetics, decided to run for Comptroller.

Send Out Manifesto.

Just like Karl Marx, whom they cordially detest, they got out a manifesto:—"On the Need for Political Action by Men of Culture." They have sent several thousand copies through the mails, to school staffs, art schools, the personnel of symphony orchestras, asking for a cultural write-in vote.

"I don't particularly expect to be elected," admitted young Mr. Newman, as he folded manifestos in his father's merchant tailoring establishment at 154 Nassau St. yesterday. "We offer our names merely as focal points for a demonstration of the strength of the intellectuals in New York.

"It is humanity's tragedy that today its leaders are either sullen materialists or maniacs who express the psycho-pathology of the mob mind," he quoted from the manifesto.

Nothing for Art.

"The present political campaign

enough to reveal that once again the artist, the musician, the writer, the actor, the teacher, the scientist, the thinker, and the man of culture generally, have nothing to hope for from any of the candidates.'

"The artist is free," Mr. Newman went on. "He doesn't belong in a government of expediency. Expediency always proves inexpedient in the long run. Vote for Communism as a protest, and you help to saddle yourself with a regime incompatible with art."

Free music and art schools in every district, a municipal opera house and orchestra, a civic art gallery with selling facilities (no jury), closed right-of-way on certain streets for the use of street cafes,

ance system are included in the Newman-Borodulin platform.

"Of O'Brien there need be no discussion with those to whom we appeal," the manifesto states. "McKee has sufficiently revealed himself, in his long association with Tammany and its policies, and by his present opportunistic campaign, to be out of the question for us.

"La Guardia, of the three major candidates, needs some consideration," the manifesto concedes, but goes on to say that he is no better than the rest.

"But don't you think a party limited to men of culture would inevitably remain a minority party?" the candidate was asked.

"No," he said. "We must spread culture through society. Only a society entirely composed of artists would be really worth living in. That is our aim, which is not dictated by expediency."

Apologetic Rejection Slips.

He does not have as much time as he would like for his own painting, Mr. Newman said. He admires John Sloan, Picasso, Kuniyoshi and the less-known Adolph Gottlieb and Tom Nagai above other artists. Mr. Borodulin's father is science editor of a Jewish newspaper, and pays Mr. Borodulin for writing on aesthetics in such a high-class way that nobody will publish his product.

"But the letters he gets from publishers are apologetic," says his running-mate.

"In writing yourself in for an artist and a writer," he concluded, "you declare yourself not for personalities but for a principle of government which is too easily lost sight of in these desperate demonic

Fig. 6 *New York World-Telegram,* November 4, 1933

On October 19, 1933, Barney attended a mass protest at Brooklyn's Savoy Mansion called by the New York Committee to Aid Victims of German Fascism in response to the leaflet and similar actions.[6]

There were, in those days, plenty of meetings, attended by plenty of people. What makes this particular meeting interesting with regard to Barney is that less than two weeks later he decided to run for mayor of New York. Using stationery for *The New York Wednesday Answer,* on October 30 Barney ordered five thousand copies of the broadside "On The Need For Political Action By Men Of Culture," and on November 4, he burst into the pages of the *New York World-Telegram:* "Two Aesthetes Offer Selves as Candidates to Provide Own Ticket for Intellectuals," read the headline over his college graduation photograph, his handsome face thin, sporting the mustache he would have for the rest of his life and a full head of dark wavy hair.

What caused Barney to mount a quixotic, if not entirely prankish, mayoral campaign, moreover one with a pie-in-the-sky cultural platform? The retrospective retelling tends to the "how typical" assessment: Barney always put himself forward, front and center—as he did in the famous 1951 *Life* magazine photograph of "The Irascibles." But in 1933 he was a 28-year-old *garmento,* working both at the diminished family business and as a substitute art teacher, and there is no evidence of any forethought for this move—other than the lesson passed on by Jewish fathers in the face of anti-Semitism: "A Jew's best weapon is his mouth."

In 1969, Barney told Hess he had become interested in municipal politics and over a late coffee at Bickford's restaurant "he attacked all three mayoral candidates" and announced 'I'll vote for myself.'" For years after, the candidacy was a "joke in the family"—it had appeared so out of the blue. Barney and Borodulin distributed their overblown statement and persuaded no less than A. J. Liebling of the *New York World-Telegram* to write a story that ran at the top of page 5, three days before the election. "Just like Karl Marx, whom they cordially detest," Liebling wrote, "they got out a manifesto . . . . They have sent several thousand copies through the mails, to school and college faculties, newspaper staffs, art schools, the personnel of symphony orchestras, asking for a cultural write-in vote."[7]

"The artist is free," Barney told Liebling. "He doesn't belong in a government of expediency . . . Vote for Communism as a protest, and you help to saddle yourself with a regime incompatible with art." Twenty-three years later, while being questioned in court during Newman vs. Reinhardt, Barney reiterated that "specifically to oppose the possibility that a lot of intellectuals were being roped into the Communist Party, I ran myself, as you might say, as a token figure for intellectuals who wanted to resist Communism and vote for me."[8] But never did he acknowledge, if he were indeed aware of it, that the Communist Party candidate for mayor in 1933 actually *was* an artist. Robert Minor was the highest paid cartoonist in the United States before he went to Paris to attend the École des Beaux Arts. Having moved away from his earlier Anarchism to a more established Socialism in the labor movement, he worked for numerous left journals and was involved in the factional wars and unifications of Communist Party sects. Minor had served prison time and run for various offices by the time Barney—artist and Anarchist—entered the 1933 mayoral election.

It was the most contested ever seen in New York. Six hundred seventy-two petitions were filed for independent nominations, containing 1,216,922 signatures. An unprecedented 407 independent candidates were nominated for 170 offices. Fourteen parties ran candidates, and since voting machines only had nine rows, on one there were four different party nominees for mayor and comptroller. Forty-seven new election districts were created because registered voters had increased by over eight hundred thousand.[9] The field was so crowded that it felt as if anyone with a single idea—there was a Five-Cent Fare Party—could run. The three major party candidates were: the incumbent Democratic–Tammany John P. O'Brien, the winner of the special election to finish the term of Jimmy Walker, who was forced out by scandal in September 1932; the Recovery Party nominee, Joseph V. McKee, who served briefly between Walker's resignation and O'Brien's election; and the Fusion Party nominee, Fiorello LaGuardia, who was frequently attacked as a radical.[10] The election was also unusual in that it attracted partisan support from a Federal official—James Farley, the U.S. Postmaster General, supported McKee—and, for the first time, no commitment from the popular ex-governor of New York, Al Smith.[11] Voter turnout was larger than for any election other than the presidential election of the previous year; the campaign was strikingly bitter and nasty; and election day, spectacularly violent: "Thugs"—read a headline—"Terrorize Voters in Wide Disorder at Polls."[12]

What were the "municipal politics" that "interested" Barney? Candidates addressed Tammany boss rule, water taxes, highway construction, Federal recovery funds, education budget and curriculum. Some shared the conservative perennial: government was too big, too wasteful, and too involved in people's lives. But considering the timing of his decision, it appears that McKee was the "issue" that got Barney's dander up. McKee, President of the Board of Aldermen under Mayor Walker, had been a teacher at De Witt Clinton High School until shortly before Barney entered. While there, he wrote an article for the *Catholic World* that relied on fear of Jews to inspire Catholic boys to stay in school. The article caused a great uproar, one that Barney would have been unlikely to know about as an entering student. But now, in a heated political campaign, this article was resurrected by LaGuardia in the last weeks of the contest, and kicked around—with prominent Jewish figures lining up on both sides. On October 17, two days before the meeting at the Savoy Mansion, the *Times* reprinted the article in full. "True education, to be worthy, must be based upon knowledge of existence of God and have for its end closer union of man with his Creator," McKee wrote, and claimed that although Catholics paid taxes to support public schools, "when we examine the enrollment of our city high schools, we find that less than 25 per cent are Christians—that more than 75 per cent are of Jewish stock. Although the Jewish people are in such a minority, their children possess an overwhelming majority in our high schools . . . . Here is a school containing about 5,000 boys . . . . Yet of these 5,000 boys hardly 10 per cent are Christians . . . Surely such a condition warrants immediate attention." (The figures were not considered to be accurate.)

McKee worried that Jewish boys would be the shapers of thought and public feeling in the future, and that "in overwhelming numbers these students are Socialists . . . whose ambition is the furtherance of Socialistic dogma." In

oral discussions on such topics as "Is Lying Justifiable?" or "Is It Wrong to Cheat?" their words consistently show that they recognize no code of morals, and are governed by no motives higher than those originating from fear of detection and consequent loss in money. Surely we cannot look for ideal results from such material. It is to such as these that our children who are without the benefits of education must bow in later years.

None of this, of course, appeared in the final platform of B. Barnett Newman, Artist–Teacher, for Mayor, and Alexander Borodulin, Writer, for Comptroller—except by implication. But, whether intentionally provocative, witty, ironic, or simply naïve, the two men's agenda was indeed rather Socialist—and utopian. It was also prescient both as a kind of performance art and as a blueprint for much that would come to exist in more forgiving economic times.

The present political campaign in New York has now run long enough to reveal that once again the artist, the musician, the writer, the actor, the teacher, the scientist, the thinker, and the man of culture generally, have nothing to hope for from any of the candidates. Once again we find repeated that barbarism of American life, the political campaign, conducted by politicians dedicated to personal ambition and sold to civic corruption. In the whole gushing flood of execrable prose and stilted oratory poured out by the contending parties, with a flotsam and jetsam of recrimination, back-biting, and lies, *not one word is given to any real issue*, not one thought is expressed with an appeal to the intelligent, and no trace whatsoever is revealed by any contender *that culture is the foundation of not only our present society, but of all our hopes for all future societies to come.* In the face of this, all men who pretend to any culture whatsoever, are confronted by the dilemma of for whom to vote . . . not with a hope for political victory, but as a show of political strength and action by all men who understand and value not the lower but the higher principles of human society . . .

We declare ourselves for the establishment, maintenance, and development of every institution and activity that will add to the cultural life of the city [emphasis added].

They had a "Program of Education":

A Free City Art School . . . A Free City University . . . A City Planetorium [sic] . . . A Complete Educational Movie House. Completely Adequate Salaries for All Teachers . . .

a "Program for the Arts":

Municipal Opera House. Municipal Orchestra. Cultural Municipal Radio Station . . . Municipal Music Festivals . . . Civic Art Gallery with selling facilities. No Jury. Civic Art Theatre and School of Dramatic Arts. A Civic Non-Commercial Art Movie Studio . . .

and a "Program for Cultural Life":

A Clean Air Department . . . Department of Local Waters to clean up the bays, beaches, and rivers . . . extensive Waterfront parks. All Parks closed to automobiles. Low Price Park Casinos . . . cafes. Public Works connected with City Planning, to clear slums and beautify city. A Local Playground and Parks System. A Large Indoor and Outdoor Public Forum Free of Police Licensing.

To subsidize this magical land? The candidates suggested:

New York City be self-supporting through the ownership and sale of public-utility services, so that it become almost tax free, with rentals accordingly reduced for all . . . a Municipal Bank with its own funds which are always at hand . . . a

Municipal Insurance Corporation to sell insurance and with the income provide a complete cultural program . . . That the city take over all subways, "L"s, trolleys, and bus lines, to own and operate for income, out of which to provide for a complete cultural program.

Borodulin's early draft was in a classic political radical's voice, Barney's was more idiosyncratic and personal, score settling. About McKee, he wrote, "Holy Joe McKee who has gone into this fight in real canine fashion is worse than O'Brien. His is the soul of a prostitute. Educated in N.Y., a member of New York's teaching staff (he taught at Clinton) . . . he wants to destroy the most fundamental, the lowest step in the ladder of culture, the high schools of N.Y. . . . . 'Send them to private schools,' he says, 'the way I do my own son.'"

Their vision, and their concerns, did not emerge in a vacuum. The intrepid gallery owner, Edith Halpert—no slouch at bold gestures and public relations—the following month proposed to Mayor-Elect LaGuardia that with his support a large-scale show of American artists should be mounted in the city. As so many Americans were benefiting from relief programs, she asked, "What about the artist? Will he fit into the new philosophy, the new life pattern? We must find a place for him. We must give him the means to continue. We cannot afford to liquidate our greatest asset—culture." Where Barney ran for mayor, Halpert enlisted the help of major league players like Nelson Rockefeller, Alfred Barr, Herbert Winlock of the Metropolitan Museum, Juliana Force of the Whitney Museum, and several other heads of institutions as a selection committee for the "First Municipal Art Exhibition"—over a thousand works of art in the main lobby of the RCA Building at the end of February, 1934.[13] That twenty thousand viewers attended the show in the first week, attracted by the art and by the enormous publicity that Halpert arranged—there were tie-in radio broadcasts every day—might have gratified Barney as fulfillment of his vision.

SIX

MISS GREENHOUSE

Barney himself struggled with the reality that all his efforts had not gotten him any-where. Attempting to explain—or excuse—his lack of success he romanticized his failure to launch in the autobiographical "Story of Communism, or 'Hope' by An Anarchist."

Winsted Archer was a real poet. Although words interested him so he sometimes spent a full day studying the dictionary, he was too sensible though to turn his art into a vest pocket edition of so called <u>beautiful</u> words. His disposition was philosophic enough despite its natural tendency to be mystic, to have solved for him long ago the problem of aesthetic technique and idea. Many sleepless nights, and prolonged worry over his art had given him a power that comes with insight so that he never had any trouble distinguishing between appearance and reality when it touched his art. In other words, he knew the difference between sound and sense.

But he had the failing of every poet's. Rather the failing that is part of youth since Winsted was still a very <u>young</u> poet, which consisted of a powerful, over-whelming feeling of hope. Not hope for himself—hope for society for mankind for the world. So strong was this feeling that it blinded him. No matter what the facts were, no matter how coarse how brutal the manifestation of human behavior in the countless examples of daily life and daily papers he still felt the world could be made better, people could be good. Human activity was based on moral law.

That year life was worse off than ever. Tutoring, translating, even odd jobs with their drudgery was [*sic*] becoming more and more difficult to obtain. With-out consciously realizing it, he was eating less, looked shabbier, walked more, seeing his friends more often when a few short years back he was able to attend concerts, the theatre and other expensive events on the small allowance his father gave him. Even the year before working his own way, his father having stopped his allowance, there was no change in his prosperity. As a matter of fact, he felt better, enjoyed things more since he was earning his own way. This last year had been very bad. Yet all around him he saw that people were happier, less worried, smugger. All the talk was of prosperity yet things were harder. His only possi-ble excuse was that people were becoming used to things and were tired not to smile. Now that it was January and the beginning of a new year, and colder, his ever hopeful, pleasant disposition was beginning to weaken and he felt himself sinking more and more into the dumps. Here it was Tuesday and he hadn't really been out of the house since Friday except to eat at the corner cafeteria. It was too cold to walk. Doing anything would mean borrowing money and although he could get some money from his mother who never said no he felt he couldn't do it. Certainly he couldn't go on. He couldn't write for thoughts of how he was going to last the winter. With these feelings, he stepped out of his room about 8:30 to go to the cafeteria where he sometimes ran up a small till for his supper. He waited this long though he could have done without the meal. For a few months now, he had been deluding himself with the trick of postponing his breakfast and lunch until as late as possible with the hope that he could save supper. But he was successful only once and it turned out to be a bad experience. So that he always tried to but always gave in to the demands of his patient intestine before he went to bed. That night he thought up a new economy at the cafeteria. He would go in for concentrated foods. He would eat more chocolate. It was cheap and it would keep him satisfied. And he would buy the big ½ bars sold at those cut rate candy and cigar stands that seemed no bigger than the bars themselves. When he came home pleased with this new adventure in diet, he found a note from De Santis, a[n] art teacher in the city schools he had met several times at Tom's house. It read "Sorry I missed you. Dropped over to tell you they need a sub in English over at Buchanan H.S. Ridgewood. Tom's friend Hal Levy is a big shot there. Go over fast and see him. Tell him you're Tom's friend. And you may get a break. Let me know how you make out—Luck."

He was too self-conscious to make art—"he knew the difference between sound and sense"—but he was also too self-indulgent. His evocation of the bohemian artist's romantic suffering during the Depression fell comically flat: "his father having stopped his allowance," "he could get some money from his mother who never said no." In a poem he wrote at the same time, "TO ARCHIE Upon The Occasion Of His Prolegomena," a wild mix of meta-phors—scripture, pugilism, Prohibition (just repealed), oeno-culture, and hab-erdashery—was itself an excellent meta-phor for his own focal extravagance and ambition.

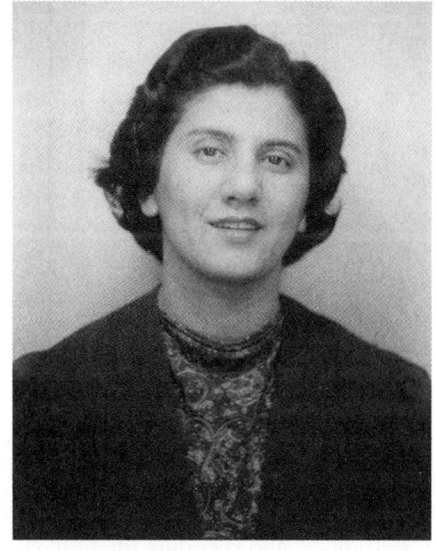

The Civil Service, the Citizens' Bud-get Commission, his hopes for *The New York Wednesday Answer*, would continue to occupy Barney's mind. But, in Feb-ruary 1934, for the first time, someone would occupy his heart. He met and fell for Annalee Greenhouse. Every success that came to him for the rest of his life was enabled by Annalee, and not simply because she was the early breadwinner in their marriage. She *believed* in him, absolutely and unconditionally. And she

Fig. 7 Annalee Greenhouse, c.1936

was resolute. The sentiments that would characterize their relationship for the next thirty-three years never wavered from what she wrote to him in 1937.

Dolly;

I want to do whatever is best for you and you never taking your eyes off the objective. You can't go along hit or miss taking the easiest way and expect to set the world on fire. You've got to remember always what you are trying to do and always insist on going in the direction. Even if you don't want to startle the world, you must remember that men with convictions or men with motives will go on imprinting their words and their thoughts on the world and since you are a man with convictions, you must make your imprint on the world . . . .

You have the clearest, the keenest mind I know. And I'm not exactly a dope myself. You see the world, life, people in their true life and without emotion. You understand their motives, their weaknesses and you set them up, look them over, and then pin them down to their little spot amongst all the cross currents of human deception. You do this philosophically, without the slightest bit of moralistic barking because you have the far-seeking vision of a clear mind that distinguished the prophets . . . .

You not only understand the world but you see it in a sharpness and penetration of a true artist. Every event records itself on your mind and vision. You operate like a fine seismograph. The needle vibrates at the slightest quake. Everything affects you. You find yourself disturbed unable to keep moving in your original direction. You find yourself hurt or upset. But you must remember that this wonderful gift of vision and penetration must be kept a gift and not allowed to become a hurt . . . .

I despise women who sit on their asses all day while their husbands rot at routine-staggering jobs so that they can have unnecessary leisure. I think that life for thinking people should add up to something constructive, some contribution before they take up their eternal space. I want my contribution to be the giving of a great mind to the world.

A Hunter College graduate, Annalee found that her degree in 1930 could get her "a job running the elevator at Altman's." To ensure her independence, she decided to learn secretarial skills and qualify as a teacher of those skills—shorthand and typing—in the public schools. In February 1934, with two years of teaching under her belt, the 25-year-old Annalee was transferred to the annex of the Grover Cleveland High School on the border of Brooklyn and Queens. Barney, who had two and a half years' experience of the Cleveland routine, was teaching six classes on four days each week (including "a course in philosophy . . . which course has no registrants"), and spending the fifth day hanging out in the school office. Although Annalee "had seen him around," she was too anxious about her work to pay much attention. A great deal of "clerical work" was expected of the teachers that she had not done before, and she was terrified. "I was so timid anyway—I was so slow, I was so afraid of everything, I didn't trust myself, I was afraid I'd make a mistake. It just terrified me." Barney "saw that I was terrified, and he tried to help me." It worked: "I wouldn't have gotten through by myself."

Annalee was on the rebound; she had had an on-again off-again boyfriend, whom she was "crazy" but naïve about. By the time she got to Grover Cleveland the relationship was over and she was unhappy. "And then I met Barney. And Barney was awfully sweet." This supportive friendship defined their relationship until six months later when at the end of the term, he escorted her to a formal dinner. They walked in Central Park, had something to eat. When Barney brought her home "all the way out to the end of Brooklyn," Samuel Greenhouse was waiting: "Well, my daughter out till three o'clock in the morning?" Annalee was "absolutely shocked," he noticed. She didn't think her father paid any attention to her doings at all, and that perception determined her emotional expectations from life. "It didn't dawn on" her that she could "ask for anything" from her parents. Then Barney appeared, and through him she found a way into her father's life that she could not have imagined.[1]

Annalee had been a precocious but dreamy girl. She loved poetry, music, French, and reading great literature—Horace, Stendhal—underlining parts that were romantic and aesthetically elevated, and those about "genius." If her high-mindedness and cultural aspirations resonated in the same key as Barney's, their personalities dovetailed. He was the golden vessel of the hopes and dreams of his family; she was groomed to be the handmaiden to "genius." Her older sister, Leah, with whom she had a fraught relationship—both adored and a lifelong rival—was treated by their parents as "the bright one." Leah was slated for a career in music, she was "lovely to look at," and the Greenhouses "made a fuss about her and didn't treat Annalee properly," something regularly reiterated that she felt "very intensely."[2] "Your mother did not send the tennis racquets," Annalee's sister-in-law wrote to the 28-year-old married woman, "because—now be calm—you are too heavy, and she would rather not have you exercise so strenuously."[3]

Samuel Greenhouse came from Belarus, and Anuta, their mother, from Ukraine, where she escaped into literature, particularly Tolstoy. After the death of their first child, they emigrated from Russia to Ottoman Jaffa, where another daughter died at eighteen months from a head injury, and Leah and Annalee were born—the former in "the Jewish place" and the latter in "the Turkish place," according to family lore. In Palestine, their life was difficult.[4] Anuta coped by imagining the future, sitting by the sea for hours with her daughters to "dream and look into the distance of life."[5]

In 1910, the family came to Akron, Ohio, where Samuel eventually had a small bottling plant for carbonated beverages, a delivery wagon pulled by a horse named Nelly, and, in 1913, a son, Nathan. After the family moved to Forest Hills, New York in 1927, Leah gave up her own fantasies of studying in Europe and worked as an usher at Carnegie Hall while getting a degree from Herzliya Hebrew Teachers' College. By 1929, she was a homemaker married to Philip Hochstein. Annalee, who had completed one year at the University of Akron before the family moved, finished her B.A. at Hunter College, and much to the family's surprise, it was she, not Leah, who went to France, to Nancy-Université in the summer of 1932—the nadir of the Depression.

The letters the sisters wrote to each other almost daily that summer were full of gossip and affection. Annalee arrived in Paris on Bastille Day and joined the "laughing, singing, dancing" crowds. She visited the Louvre, her head "swimming . . . so much splendor all at once." She complained that her French relatives were very "grabby" and just wanted money sent from America, and she shocked herself with her adventures: dancing, drinking "cocktails!" until midnight. She told Leah that while she had loved Corneille, in Nancy she became more sympathetic to Racine.[6] "Why can't you be here with me now?" Annalee wrote. "We would have the most wonderful time discovering Paris."[7]

Three years later, Annalee put aside her polite, sycophantic role and revealed her "honest" feelings of competition with her sister, her deep sense of ethnic embarrassment, and her need to justify—to herself, the recipient of this diaristic missive—her attachment to either Barney or the mystery man of her unrequited love. She had been reading George Bernard Shaw's *The Intelligent Woman's Guide to Socialism and Capitalism* and watching one of the many demonstrations common during the period:

> It all started several days ago when upon seeing the demonstrations at 14th Street, I expressed a vehement dislike for Communists. I said that I hated them—I didn't want them here—I felt th[at] if they loved Communism so much they should go back to Russia, for I feel instinctively they will cause us all a great deal of trouble some day. Leah upraided [*sic*] for being bigoted, as she called it . . . . But why is it that one sees only Jews among the Communists—why must we always be hated . . . why cannot they use their heads and work together—work with the Socialists—plan constructive movements—instead of all of this bickering—instead of waving flags and trying to arouse mob violence. And if after rationalizing their point of view—they cannot agree—let them go where they can find what they are seeking. It is not that their ancestors have lived in one place for centuries—it is not that strange environments overwhelm them and crush their ambitions. They are the wanderers of the world.
>
> The trouble that is now arising between Leah and me can be traced back to the days of our childhood when Leah was the older sister who was very bright and knew best. Through all the years of my life until she went away to school her influence was the dominating one. When I disagreed with her—when I thought her bigoted—I kept my thoughts to myself. Mama too, tried very hard to dominate me. Since I have been teaching—and been away—I have gained a little of that confidence I should have had all of these years. Who was Leah to judge me, who was she to tell me what to do, to influence me with regard [to] my behavior towards him? . . . no my dear sister—I am very practical. It is you who have romantic ideas . . . .
>
> I say these things because I am very honest.

Whether Annalee was timid and terrified at Grover Cleveland, as she described it, or strong and "vehement," defending Wagner against Barney's preference for Mozart (as he told Hess), by August Barney was truly "in the first flush of love"[8] with the serious young woman with a mass of dark hair, engaging smile, and—it must be said—distinctively pitched, whining voice. He courted her ardently, with awkward sonnets and effusive letters.

SEVEN

THE SEARCH

In the spring of 1935, Irving Stone's *Lust for Life* seemed to be on everyone's lips. The book novelized the life of Vincent van Gogh into a romantic pot-boiler, and burned into the public's imagination the very icon of the misunderstood genius—"this agonizing inferno of the human spirit."[1] For the next quarter-century no average person would ever hear the word "artist" without thinking of a tortured soul. A few months earlier, *Adam's Ancestors*, Louis Leakey's account of his stunning discovery of humanoid fossils in East Africa, presented revolutionary information about Stone Age cultures to mainstream readers.

Channeling the zeitgeist, the Museum of Modern Art worked both territories in their 1935 season: in March, 600 pieces of unfamiliar tribal art were exhibited; in November, 125 paintings and works on paper by the Dutch master. Formal aesthetics were served up in "African Negro Art" because, as the *Times*'s reviewer put it, plumbing its "deepest depths" would be too difficult.[2] Van Gogh was something else: "Day after day for six cold weeks the pedestrian queue—augmented continuously by arrivals in taxicabs, Rolls-Royces, and meaner conveyances—averaged some 3,000 persons, and at the end over 120,000 had waited in line . . . . cash customers, paying twenty-five cents apiece to view 127 pictures by an epileptic Dutchman . . . dead forty-five years." The staggering popularity could be attributed at least partially to Stone's book.[3]

The conjunction of these events—the popularization of van Gogh's agony and Leakey's research into human origins—is a key to the way Barney lived his life, both for the next decade, when he rarely made anything, and for his final, productive, twenty-five years. It provided the grain of sand in his gut, the initial irritation that twelve years later enabled him to spit out the polished pearl: his definition, his *credo*, the point of making "art."

> Man's first expression, like his first dream, was an aesthetic one . . . a poetic outcry rather than a demand for communication. Original man, shouting his consonants, did so in yells of awe and anger at his tragic state, at his own self-awareness and at his own helplessness before the void.[4]

The early years of the 20th century saw a quantity of academic work (mostly, but not entirely, Continental) on typology of tribal art. The peripatetic artist John Graham—a close friend of Gottlieb and in the late '30s or early '40s of Barney as well—was significant in bringing the vogue from France to New York art circles, advising collectors and collecting himself. Tribal art was mined as new territory for art critics, as aesthetic forms for artists, as a market for collectors, and as fodder for exhibitions. But Barney, almost uniquely, was interested in none of these aspects.

Barney was interested in the making and the *maker* rather than what was made. It was the "outcry" that identified the artist.

"Outcry" was a weighted term for Barney, one that recurred in fraught situations, and that had biblical and cultural references of which he was well aware. In vernacular Yiddish, *geshray* is translated as both "outcry" and "lament," and in Hebrew, *mah rash* is translated as a "noise"—often of biblical proportions, as when the Lord is present. Barney wielded these terms, for instance teasingly pointing out his mother-in-law's inappropriate overreactions. Barney knew when and for what reasons an "outcry"—the yell of "awe and anger"—was acceptable, and it was not to be wasted on anything less than the existential: man's tragic state, "self-awareness . . . helplessness before the void."

It took him more than a decade before he could articulate this—and act on it. In 1935 it was only an intuition, an aspiration. What he did know, categorically, was that he was *not* going to assume the role of the artist in the ordinary way, by painting pictures of things or scenes, or joining groups, like The Ten at this time or, a little later, the American Abstract Artists, or applying for jobs through the WPA.

Regarding "the project," Barney said a lot of things about why he never joined. In 1959 he told *Life* magazine that because he was a philosophical Anarchist, he didn't want to take government money, that "he would have had to go on relief to do it, and as long as he could get any job at all he would not go on relief."[5] In 1964, he said privately that the WPA was "very important for everyone" but it wasn't for him since it "emphasized subject, to the point of moralizing over [whether it was] a Negro or a Jew with a beard on a fire escape," or worse, encouraged the "neo-plastic boys" who thought they had the answer—based on a misunderstanding of Mondrian and Malevich—that abstraction was "purely visual, mere design."[6] And, in 1966, he acknowledged that: "The WPA did bring a lot of artists together. But I wasn't on the project. I was against the idea of a project for myself. So I went out and taught high school kids. I made a day's pay that way, so I didn't need the project, but I think that that was the hindrance" to his career.[7]

Nor was he willing to make work that would be acceptable to a gallery or museum but meant nothing to him. The ambition to show would come later, when he figured out how to manifest the "outcry." In the meantime, he would remain an artist–citizen. "He wanted to make New York the art center of the world. He wanted to help his fellow artists," recalled Annalee. "As a citizen, he felt a strong concern and had a strong sense of responsibility, for his fellow man. As an 'artist citizen,' he felt a strong concern and had a strong sense of responsibility for his fellow artist." In these years, "he did not feel the need to concern himself with his own place in the world. That would somehow take care of itself."[8]

The relationship with Annalee, far from causing him to narrow his focus, seems to have fueled the fire under him. While she grew in ambition, taking courses at City College and New York University in Business Law, Organization and Management to earn a Master's degree, Barney was very busy on many fronts.

Following the election, he and Borodulin sent a letter to newly elected Mayor LaGuardia recommending the establishment of a high school specifically devoted to music and art, and when The High School of Music and Art opened in upper Manhattan in 1936 they took credit for it with anyone who would listen.[9]

For the family business—now listed in directories as "clothier" and "tailor" rather than "wholesale production," he wrote ad copy in Yiddish. He "knew good tailoring," and was "very skillful, very good with his hands. He could cut, he could fit, he could sew."[10] He "learned about the nature of plasticity in the cutting room, the meaning of form, the visual and tactile nature of things," he later said, "the difference between a form and a shape . . . that women's clothes are painting and that men's clothes are sculpture."[11]

He continued as a substitute at Grover Cleveland, for 7.50 dollars a day, taking charge of "visual publicity" for General Organization membership drives and the school newspaper's circulation, the Art Club, and designing honor rolls and posters for performances.[12] At the same time, he enrolled at the City College School of Education to acquire credentials for a permanent position teaching English.

But Barney always needed a consuming initiative, and in the spring of 1935 it was "The Theatre Troupe," created to promote the plays that Borodulin continued to write.

Barney was manager and Borodulin's brother-in-law, Phillip Albaum, was director. They mounted an operation with all the intensity, publicity, and ideology of the mayoral campaign. As in that campaign, the troupe's principles defined a "new concept"—Barney always felt that only by breaking ground was something worth his while. Like that campaign, Barney's persistence resulted in media attention, and like it, as well, it was a one-shot wonder. In the space of one month, Barney wrote and sent to a diligently assembled, comprehensive list of newspaper and magazine drama editors, a press release, a letter, and a manifesto.

A new theatre organization inevitably presents itself to the world both as a new entity and as a criticism of that which already exists . . . . the various art theatres have but a pseudo-commercial character, and as such the plays they present are quite unsatisfactory . . . . It is only the repertory theatre that can maintain a truly non-commercial form . . . . Certainly, it will be no turgid question as to what we are about. We shall be all that we pretend to be, actor, director, stage designer, and playwright too! . . . From the least off-stage murmur, to the play's most esoteric implications, we shall be all of it. This is our solution and guarantee of a truly organic theatre.

On Monday evening, May 13, 1935, "Feminine Hygiene, A Realistic Drama; The Young Must Hope, A Poetic Interlude; and A Fig for Broadway, An Honest Farce," were performed at the Artef Theatre on West Forty-Eighth Street. "Artef," a Yiddish acronym for Arbeter Teater Farband (Workers' Theater Union), was considered "the most important example of the potent mixture of politics and theater in the Yiddish world."[13] Barney and Borodulin, however, had no official connection with the organization, and their production is not recorded in its history: the theater would have been dark on a Monday, rented out to make a few dollars.[14] That night, "The Theatre Troupe" took its first and final bow.

Barney was incapable of aligning himself with a position he didn't author, but his bespoke response was to the same political events that the Artef acknowledged. The spring had been filled with both anti-war and anti-fascist demonstrations, whose literature Barney collected. As he was releasing The Theatre Troupe's manifesto, college students across the country and high schoolers in New York were striking, and he was reading the Anarchist journal *Vanguard*.

> The elementary task of the Anarchist movement is to take an active, militant part in the life of the masses, to radicalize, revolutionize, nurture and encourage the revolutionary tendencies with the mass organizations . . . [not] become enmeshed in the utopian aspects of our ideal.[15]

Barney never took an "active, militant part in the life of the masses"; he had principles, but he had limits. Given his scattered commitment to The Theatre Troupe, to municipal politics, to *The New York Wednesday Answer*, or to so many other passionately promoted, one-off, endeavors, one could be forgiven for noticing that Barney's commitment was to *passionate commitment*—as a way of living vividly.

And vividly was how he continued to court Annalee—although how seductively is open to question. Writing from his briefly rented studio on West Thirteenth Street to Annalee in Schroon Lake in the Adirondacks, where she summered before their marriage, he marked her birthday:

> Today you are twenty-six years old and the thought of your birthday made me terribly lonesome . . . . I've begun to write but had to stop because of my general unenthusiasm. Today, however, I felt better in spite of my loneliness because I spent the afternoon writing your birthday sonnet. I think I'll be able to do some good work next week. How are you sweetheart! . . . Remember your letters are the only things I look forward to now . . . . Tell me what you think of the poem. I spent the day reminiscing over last year's summer [when I] gave you my first poem as a gift. Unfortunately although we are both a year older, I am in the same position and still cannot give you anything as a gift except myself which you will find attached. Still, I hope that nothing I'll ever be able to give you will have more worth or meaning than the same.

The sonnet:

> To Annalee on the Occasion of her Twenty-Sixth Birthday
> The world now lives by stealing; some find time
> To sugar the name. "Profit," they smile, "is love."

Yet who splashing through the sweetened slime
Can stand up clean? Stand white as Noah's dove?
To men lying dead in mire and tent
Wind and rain play their crazy scale of chime
While bankers and widows use their dollars for rent
And cut graveyard roses before their prime.
Let them all grow! Flowers, men, child and self
Growth is God's old word for true happiness
You fools who crush God's miracle for pelf
Think you immune from the same, cold caress?
But each year shall, my sweet, you and I bless
For, never will we each other's growth transgress.

Love-Barney

Just days earlier, the tone had been very different. Barney was concerned for Annalee's health, mental and physical. Before her trip there was an emotional crisis, even talk of suicide. Two days before her birthday, he tried to comfort her with encouragement and humor:

I know you will get over this condition. Even two weeks in the country will strengthen and relax you enough to cure you of the first trouble—overexcitement and tenseness. And someday—when you have a couple of kids— you will get over thinking about yourself . . . . You know I expect to see a brand new Annalee when you come back to add to my album of special Annalees—Saturday night Annalee, last year's vacation Annalee, Annalee of the white dress, and the brown dress with lace collar. I just remembered how you looked when you came back from last year's week in Vermont, and the time you and I bought your brown plush hat at Tardy's!

And yet, his best efforts came with a stunning insensitivity. He sent Annalee an obituary of Charlotte Gilman, the writer, lecturer, and figure in the women's suffrage, labor, and "social problem" movements, who committed suicide rather than face slow death by cancer.

"I am sending you a clipping I know will interest you because it treats of the problem of suicide as 'a personal right' which you used to talk about (except the Gilman woman treats it sensibly) and which I am certain you have driven out of your head. The clipping interested me especially because of her views on men which coincide so well with those I expressed to you and because here is one woman, at least, who understands herself and the world." The clipping read:

At first an ardent feminist who resented the attitude of superiority of man over woman . . . Mrs. Gilman later admitted, with some reluctance, that man was, after all, the "whole thing" in life. In the human world the men are the best of everything . . . . They are the best cooks, the best milliners; they build ships and the big bridges and do all the important work [underlined by Barney].

If there should come a big pestilence and all the women of the world should die, the men could get along very well indeed without the women [last sentence circled].[16]

Immediately after, Barney detailed his overreaching efforts to interest big advertisers—Wanamaker's, Eastman Kodak, Planter's Peanut Corporation, Spalding—in the forthcoming *The Answer*, as *The Wednesday Answer*, never actually published, resurfaced with an abbreviated name. "Letters are coming in," he wrote, "all with the same melody. Nice idea—no money."

And the following day's letter reported his progress:

The whole thing is beginning to annoy me. Unless I get ads for the first issue I've made up my mind not to accept commercial advertising under any condition. I'll make this part of the magazine's policy—A publication without ads.[17]

Considering Barney's state of mind, it's worth wondering who—Annalee or himself—was the actual subject of the sonnet. Who "Can stand up clean? Stand white as Noah's dove?"

"Sometimes after thinking a lot about you my feelings become too strong so that I lose desire to work," Barney told her. "I've begun, however, and I think I'll be able to do a good job. If I finish soon I'll send you a copy for appraisal." On the day he began "Deadly Weapons," his "editorial" about the dangers of cars, he noted, "These constant, petty worries and distractions are keeping me from writing, as much as I would like." He asked for a photograph of Annalee in shorts and "other sports outfits," and for "rocks for our collection" and he kept her informed about "the rising infantile paralysis epidemic" and the likelihood that schools would again have a delayed opening. He offered to send her money to finance an extra week of vacation.[18] And when Annalee *did* react to Barney's callousness, he wrote her another sonnet in apology.

Neither painting nor drawing is mentioned once during this time.

EIGHT

THE ANSWER

Bricklayer: Go to Work!

Jones, the bricklayer, is out of a job.

Smith has $25,000 to invest. He can borrow another $50,000, buy land and build a new building. If he does that, Jones gets a job.

Smith is willing to buy the land and construct the building if he can be sure of $2000 a year above all expenses.

He could be sure of that income except for one thing. His taxes would be so high that he cannot expect more than $1700 a year after paying expenses including taxes . . . to pay for City employees who are not needed . . . who get more pay for their work . . . longer vacations and shorter hours than private business can afford . . . for huge deficits in the City's subways . . . So Smith keeps his money in a bank . . . and Jones, the bricklayer is still looking for a job.[1]

For three years The Citizens' Budget Commission had distributed such leaflets at banks. In August, while Barney was soliciting support for *The Answer*, A. Newman & Son moved to the Pulitzer Building and he discovered that his *bête noir*, the CBC, had opened offices there a few months earlier. He recognized the perfect foil for the first issue. Through the fall and winter he wrote content, contacted a range of civil servants, and prepared a promotional "circular for general distribution."[2] Beneath the rhetoric of societal, political, economic and cultural polemics ran the psychological current that underlay Barney's every future step, the absolute, fundamental, *sine qua non* of human existence: the urgency of respect.

Civil Service Leaders!

Your Greatest Enemy Is The Sneer!

Bankers, real-estate owners, industrialists, politicians and newspaper owners are building up forces to destroy Civil Service rights, Civil Service tenure, Civil Service salaries. They are looking to undermine the entire Civil Service structure . . .

What psychological factor latent in the public mind do these forces intend to encourage and to exploit? What are they brandishing as a weapon?

THEY INTEND TO MAKE THE PUBLIC'S SNEER THEIR FRIEND!

THEY INTEND TO MAKE THE PUBLIC'S SNEER YOUR ENEMY!

They are fostering the sneering impression among business people, working people, doctors, lawyers, and lawmakers that Civil Service men and women are lazy, inefficient, overpaid parasites who are preventing the country's recovery . . . .

IF YOU WANT TO KILL THAT SNEER, check the enclosed post-card and mail post-free to . . .

The Answer appeared in January 1936: the magnum opus of his early life. Of approximately twenty-four thousand words, over eighteen thousand were written by Barney; he designed, laid out, produced, and mailed it to subscribers he himself solicited. He wrote the statement of policy, "Free as the Seas," under a page-wide shot of "View of the Sea from Martha's Vineyard" by his college buddy Siskind:

WE are free! Free of any and all political, financial, commercial, party, Republican, Democrat, Socialist, Communist, propaganda, department or organization influence! We are not the mouth-piece of any politician or office-seeker looking for power! We are free even of the vicious though subtle influence of ADVERTISING . . . . We are a free press, as free as the seas, owing allegiance to no one except the principles of the merit system . . . . Since we have chosen not to live by advertising, you must support us by subscription.

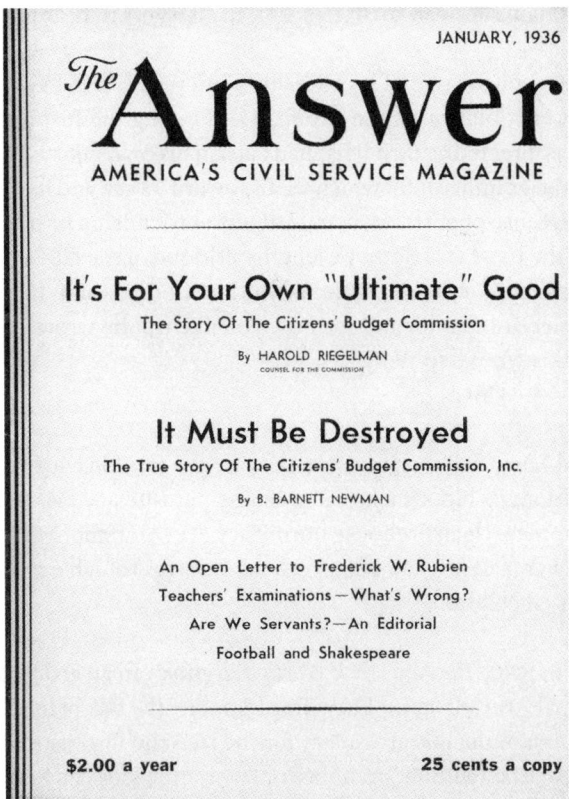

Fig. 8 First and only issue of *The Answer*, January 1936

He wrote the editorial, "Are We Servants?":

> Men steal while men sleep . . . . In Italy, one man, shouting "for the glory of Rome" has made it the excuse to seize every government office, every Civil Service function to be owned and operated by and for him alone . . . . In Germany, a group of political madmen, hysterically screaming their fantastic theory of "Racial Purity," and their new-found paganism of "Germanism uber Alle"' have created the most vicious excuse for a spoils system known. Birth has been made part of the Civil Service law . . . . In Russia, a group of "idealists" idealistic enough to use every fascist tool and weapon, invoking the name of the "working class revolution" and the "classless society" have found the holy excuse to seize every human activity and liquidate its membership for the benefit of its own party members . . . . This is the picture of the new Europe. The tragedy is that it is becoming the picture of the new America. In Louisiana . . . . In Washington . . . . But no holy need can excuse these men for setting aside the very basis of democracy, the merit system. Nothing can excuse the creation of a spoils system . . . .
>
> Shall we stay mute in the face of surrounding danger? We must wake up and give the world our answer. THE ANSWER itself wants to hear it.

And he wrote several articles of specific, local interest. But in "Teachers' Exams— What Is Wrong? A Solution of the Problem of Finding the Inspired Teacher," his opprobrium was directed against what had caused his own injury. The merit system was based on "the examination," which should award "work and its privileges to him who qualifies because of performance—not out of friendship or prejudice."

The core of the issue was Barney's lengthy critique of the CBC, "It Must Be Destroyed!: The TRUE Story of the Citizens' Budget Commission, Inc."

"Read this piece of slander and see how you like it!," he wrote, directing his audience to "Bricklayer: Go to Work!"

According to the CBC:

> You, Mr. and Miss Civil service employee, are the trouble with this country! You are its ruination, its bloodsucker, it crushing parasite . . . . Mr. Fireman, dozing there in your nice, clean firehouse dormitory . . . . You, too, Miss New York City School Teacher [salaries had been cut], who wastes valuable money pampering those ungraded children.

On January 6, 1936, *The New York World-Telegram* ran an article about the temporary Municipal Art Gallery on Fifty-Third Street—the talk of local art culture. As the "country's first municipal art gallery for the free and uncensored exhibition" of New York City artists, "without prejudice or favor,"[3] the idea had been a cornerstone of Barney's 1933 campaign manifesto. Now his name was in the same day's news, though not for anything related to art. "A revision of the examination for high school teaching licenses . . . to find the 'inspired teacher' as against the teacher with only a 'fact-absorbing brain' is urged in an article in the current issue of the monthly civil service magazine, The Answer, published and edited by B. Barnett Newman, a former teacher," reported the *Times*.[4]

Using that publicity, Barney continued for a while to solicit subscriptions but it was too heavy a lift for one man; in part he attributed its failure to "too ambitious [a] format."[5] He did walk away with a small victory: in June, the Citizens' Budget Commission was forced to add "Inc." to its name on its stationery and literature, after Barney made the New York State Department of Law aware that "provision of law" required they indicate that they were a corporation.

It is not surprising that Barney had legal procedure on his mind. A dispute over rent for 154 Nassau Street had been pending in the courts and, on May 12, judgment was rendered against the defendants, Barney and Abraham, with damages affixed at 669.05 dollars (14,814.84 dollars in 2023). Just the day before, Barney had made inquiries about a wedding reception for twenty to thirty people at the elegant Hotel Brevoort on Fifth Avenue above Washington Square. And a week earlier, he had presented Annalee with a hand-finished, double-breasted blue tweed suit. The jacket had a severely masculine cut, with very wide lapels, and the skirt was unlined, as if it had been made by someone accustomed to making high end men's suits. And so it had been: "Newman Tailors / Built Well Clothes" read the label. In the jacket's inside breast pocket was the "custom" tailor's label: "Anthony [illegible] / 53–63 Park Row, Room 911 / New York City"; with the handwritten addition, "To my sweetheart / with Love / Barney 5-8-36." It was intended to be her wedding costume, but the wedding was postponed.

In February, while Barney had been consumed with subscriptions, advertising, and the CBC, the *Times* declared "the sudden realization on the part of many different kinds of people that artistically the city has come of age," with a critical mass of distinguished collections and a new interest in contemporary art.[6] Swept along, the artists began to develop a ragged communal identity inflected by a churning mix of art and politics, according to Will Barnet.[7] Barnet was one of the organizers of a gathering that month of over five hundred artists and guests "against war and fascism" at Town Hall and the New School for Social Research, recently expanded with German refugee professors to form the University in Exile. Picasso was the expected speaker, but at the last minute he sent a telegram to "Comrades" bowing out, replaced by José Clemente Orozco. Although the event was organized by the Popular Front-influenced American Artists' Congress, which had been founded just that month—Avery, Gottlieb, and "Marcus Rothkowitz" were members—the attendees were of many different schools of thought. It was there that Meyer Schapiro delivered the lecture "The Social Bases of Art."

Few of the younger generation of New York artists remained impartial regarding the crisis in Europe; certainly Barney's friends were not, but they also were actively finding and exploiting opportunities to promote their art. Although there were very few galleries, Gottlieb, an organizer of The Ten, was able to find "a great many office buildings which had sufficient space," and owners very willing to "let us use a floor, in a very desirable location, without any charge," hoping to make the space more appealing and rentable.[8] Siskind gathered a "group of young photographers into the Feature Group to work on small features, small documents."[9] But throughout 1936, and at least through 1937, Barney's professional identification, to the extent that he associated with any group, remained with civil servants as a whole, and teachers in particular, rather than with those artists. In his correspondence he refers to practicing art not at all, apart from the unfairness of the art teachers exam, and barely mentions looking at it—although his sister Sarah's letters to him do both.

And yet, Barney was an "artist"—as *he* comprehended the calling. "The artist," he later said, "identifies himself with the painters, not the paintings of history."[10] An artist wasn't someone who made things for the sake of making things; an artist was someone who defended human dignity—"the ultimate subject matter of art." It was "inconceivable," to Barney, "that original man, that Adam, was put on earth to be a toiler." Rather, Adam, "by eating from the Tree of Knowledge, sought the creative life to be, like God, 'a creator of worlds' to use Rashi's phrase."[11] In college he knew William James's *The Varieties of Religious Experience*, which emphasized the individual rather than the institution, identified "emotionality" as the "sine qua non of moral perception," "intensity" as "the essence of practical moral vigor," and the "love of metaphysics and mysticism" as a vehicle to "carry one's interests beyond the surface of the sensible world." Art, for Barney at *all* times in his life, was his variety of religious experience. His anarchism determined his refusal to satisfy his search in organized religion, yet he was not afraid to salt his work—verbal and visual—with traditional religious references, should anyone miss what he was after: to go beyond the surface of the sensible world. Barney's relatives "always" thought of him as an artist.[12] Certainly, it was as an "artist" that he presented himself to Annalee.

NINE
MARRIAGE

Annalee watched him assume burdens for both of their families. She saw him doggedly take charge of George's application to "become an architectural draftsman." She saw her father's dependence on him "taking up too much of his life." She saw him "absolutely destroying himself for everyone," his generosity, his "terrific spirit," a sense of responsibility for others that she'd "never seen in any other person." He "did everything, he was in charge," and she wasn't about to let him spend his life this way. She "felt very strongly about the fact that Barney was giving to the whole world and everybody was very selfishly taking from him." She wanted to enable him to be an artist because she thought he was brilliant. "I believed in him and thought that he deserved it. I wanted to be the Rock of Gibraltar for him. I wanted to devote myself to him. I made up my mind that's what I wanted. He said: 'You know I have to be an artist and we cannot have a family' . . . because it would be too great a burden." He didn't talk about success, or glory, or career, just that this "was the person he was." She would have to work, there was no possibility of his being able to sell his work. "I said that that was fine."[1]

But it was "a long time" before they got to that point. For Barney, according to the way he presented the issue to Borodulin, it was not a matter of doubt or absence of love, but of principle—he wanted to be unencumbered: he "fought two years against the marriage convention," before he "bowed."[2] As for Annalee, she claimed she "never thought about marriage at all," she "wasn't one of those" types. "I was always dreamy . . . . I never asked for anything." When, in 1936, Barney was again unable to pass the teachers' exam, and his application for a Houghton Mifflin Literary Fellowship was rejected, "we finally decided that there was no point in waiting anymore, that he wasn't going to get a regular job . . . . He didn't want to go on teaching art . . . . he *had* to be an artist or he could not live." Annalee decided she would make that happen.

Either they were impulsive or just discreet; their colleagues at Grover Cleveland were completely surprised as news trickled out over the summer. No arrangements were made for a marital home, a small wedding breakfast arranged by friends wouldn't occur until September. The actual wedding, on Tuesday, June 30, more closely resembled one of the screwball comedies so popular at the time than what a girl who received love letters in Shakespearean sonnet form might have dreamed of. If the players were Cary Grant and Irene Dunne, Ray Milland and Rosalind Russell, the antics might seem less stressful, sad, or neurotic, or, possibly, ambivalent.

Because Barney simply wanted to go to City Hall, Annalee asked if her sister's husband, a well-connected newspaper editor, could engage a judge. Philip Hochstein did one better: he arranged for Mayor Fiorello LaGuardia himself to perform the ceremony. Annalee had forgotten that Barney ran against LaGuardia, and "didn't take it that seriously" anyway, but Barney's reactions should have surprised no one. "Absolutely not! LaGuardia will never marry me!" Abraham's efforts that evening, and Samuel Greenhouse's the next morning, were to no avail. The ceremony had been scheduled for 11:30 a.m., but when Barney rejected the arrangement, to save face the family told LaGuardia's office that the couple had eloped.

Barney went to his office. That afternoon, Annalee went to see him. "If you don't want to get married by LaGuardia, we can go to Rabbi Steven Wise Free Synagogue and get married by Rabbi Steven Wise or his assistant." Barney agreed, but it was already late: seven-months-pregnant Leah, Philip, and the Greenhouses had gone to dinner. Barney's parents and sisters assembled "in the shop" with Fan Cohen, Annalee's friend. Annalee kept calling her parents without success and said, " 'okay, let's just get married without them.' Barney refused. Parents 'have to be here when we get married.' " By the time she got hold of her family, and "told them to get into the car and come right in" Rabbi Wise, impatient, had left. An assistant did the honors. Annalee was wearing a dark blue silk dress, and Barney a suit and a tie. Fan Cohen and Alex Borodulin were the witnesses. Annalee said, " 'make it short and sweet.' So it was a very quick ceremony, but by the time it was all over, it must have been 10:00."

"Instead of taking us all out to have a drink or something, my father said, 'well, I guess we should all go home,' because it was so late, and because everyone was concerned about Leah. Barney said, 'okay, you go home with them.' So I went home, and Barney went home." The next morning, with Barney wearing "a beautiful white suit," they met at a pier on the Hudson River to take a "floating palace" to Providence, thence, by train, to Boston, to begin their lives together.[3]

They spent two nights at the Hotel Statler in Boston. From there, appropriately on July 4, and because Barney at that moment was interested in Thoreau, they went to Concord, spending hours at the library where Barney read about the Transcendentalists[4] and Annalee made a detailed chronology of Thoreau's life.[5] They stayed for three days at Wright's Tavern with the great-niece of one of Thoreau's friends who entertained them with stories and artifacts and drove them to Walden Pond. Unfortunately, if it were an experience similar to the 19th-century writer's that the Newmans were after, they were to be disappointed. Walden in 1936 was far from being the place to find intimacy with nature that Thoreau knew, resembling more closely the Coney Island that had so depressed Annalee the year before. Much of the forest had been cut down. There were public bathhouses offering swimming lessons; there was boating, fishing, and picnicking. Nearly half a million visitors came during the previous summer, and on a Sunday—for example, July 5, when Barney and Annalee were there—twenty-five thousand visitors was not uncommon. Notwithstanding the crowds, the stay was "*very* special," Annalee wrote to her mother that evening. Barney hoped to go on to climb Mount Monadnock in New Hampshire, the object of an inventory of natural phenomena by Thoreau and subject of a poem by Emerson, but for Annalee, terrified, "climbing a mountain was not my idea of a holiday."[6]

They went on to Ogunquit, Maine for the remainder of the season, establishing a pattern of spending at least part of every summer in New England artists' colonies

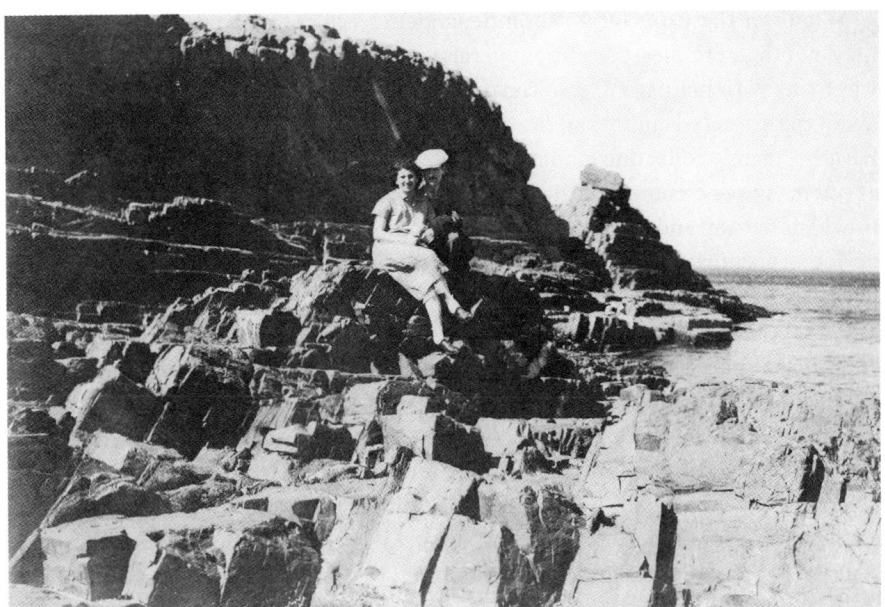

Fig. 9 Annalee and Barnett Newman on their honeymoon, Ogunquit, Maine, 1936. Photograph Aaron Siskind

that they followed for the next eleven years. Annalee was a happy honeymooner, savoring new experiences.[7] But Barney, who previously had spent only a very few nights outside New York, required some adjusting. He found their initial accommodations uncomfortable and disappointing. He developed a rash, which a doctor told him was "induced by the water or the sand—claims my skin supersensitive—which is peculiar. I've been in salt water and sand for years," and which "interfered" with swimming. He wrote home for books, and another suit, and an additional suitcase.

Finally, they found a tiny, charming, shingled cabin on Whistling Oyster Lane with a screened porch and window boxes full of flowers, named it "Newman Cottage," and printed as a postcard a photograph of Annalee beaming in front that they sent to family and friends. Barney began to revel in the "abundant variety" of landscape in Maine, "from sand to mountain within five miles," the "marvelous sand bar . . . the fishing and the boating," and the "veritable geologic museum—rocks, rocks, everywhere."[8] The couple joined a sketch class at the Art School in Perkins Cove, where Annalee learned from Barney "how to put the figure on a page,"[9] and Barney learned about photography from the local camera-shop owner.[10] For a moment, he suggested using the nest egg Samuel had given them to stay for a year. But, although he had "hoped" he "could do some work here,"—writing? drawing? he doesn't say—by late August he admitted he had "failed miserably."[11] He seemed unable to take a mental vacation; all of his commitments and preoccupations persisted in distracting him. He continued to clip newspaper articles that upset him; he fretted about the shop, *The Answer*, civil service, and the theatre troupe.

Whatever the expectations of independence the couple may have had neither they, nor their families, were about to relax any kinship bonds. Sarah Newman, who was living with her parents and Gertrude, wrote several times a week, with details about the extended family and the business responsibilities she had taken over from Barney—mainly collecting monies owed—and it's clear that Barney responded nearly as often. Annalee communicated with her family in awkward Yiddish and English to which Barney added his own fluent and idiomatic Yiddish addenda. This was a period of acclimating for Barney, and not just to the sea and sand. His old and new lives—in the persons of the two families—competed for the ready involvement and attention that they had come to take for granted.

Annalee's parents needed to be calmed: "We're OK and happy. Don't worry about us, worry better about yourselves. We have enough money . . . . Stop worrying."[12] "Don't work too hard. Take it easy and don't worry."[13] "My dear Mother-in-law and Father-in-law," Barney contributed, "I'm being written from all sides that you're worried—very worried. So I ask, as is written [in the liturgy]—*mah rash?* [what's all the noise about?] What's all the fuss about? Why the big *geshray*? [outcry]—why so upset? Why the big commotion? You think I've left my wife? God forbid. There is no running away. My hands are tied—one with fish, the other with beets! We're both well and strong."[14]

Barney's family, on the other hand, barely acknowledged the change in status. Sarah, especially—working with children at a vacation bible school during that brutally hot summer under the Teaching Project of the WPA—eagerly fed his ego, maintained their accustomed intimacy, and relied on him as a sounding board. In letters addressed to Barney alone, she praised him, encouraged him, indulged him, looked to him for approval, and, in recounting her daily life, made clear the responsibilities she shouldered so that he could be less encumbered: the roots of Sarah and Annalee's rivalry, which persisted for the remainder of their long lives. Sarah provided family news: a son was born to George and his wife less than a week after Barney's wedding; the Newmans held a party for relatives "in your honor"; a cousin for whom Barney was advocating secured the job; no need to worry, papa "isn't throwing out any of your papers"; and regular updates on Abraham's hay fever. She kept Barney abreast of current events, sent newspaper clippings about civil service and the Citizens' Budget Commission; and offered commiseration: "I'm sorry Ogunquit turned out so poorly for your purposes. I should have known artists, of the type that flock to art colonies, haven't much taste or regard for comfort."[15] And she kept up the kind of mentally stimulating conversation that she knew he thrived on: the Museum of Modern Art's exhibition of illustrations for La Fontaine, Maupassant, Flaubert and Balzac by Matisse, Rouault, Dufy, Redon, Picasso, and Maillol "gave me a big surprise. Book Illustrations can be high art . . . . What startled me was the similarity lots of these had to my sketches." "There is no geologic map for the district you are in. Maine, however, is famous for its granites and glacial deposits. You should be able to find crystals of quartz, tourmaline (black & elongated), calcite and etc. which occur in igneous, dike intrusions." Barney's vivid descriptions were a "Godsend to all of us."

One response "sounded like a gurgling brook—fresh, clear and flowing. Was it a gust of Maine air that pervaded it?" There was "nothing" she could add to his "scientific analysis of the region. However, I doubt whether there is any sedimentary rock in that region. It probably is igneous rock that has been uplifted, folded, smashed, etc." Often Barney's questions were about Sarah's artwork. She assured him that although she had done "practically no painting" since he left, "the week that mama will be away I plan to do a canvas a day. Honest!"[16] But, when, during that week, he inquired whether she had "social evenings" and whether she was painting, she replied, "I can understand now why Cézanne was not a social creature. It's physically impossible to create and dissapate [sic] at the same time. No, I haven't done much painting, I've been too busy dissapating."[17]

On the topic of art, Sarah assumed Barney's support, and righteous collusion. At an outing of the bible school the principal asked, " 'Miss Newman, are you orthodox?' When I told her that to me art was stronger than religion, she opened her eyes wide and stared at me as though to ostracize me for my infidelity . . . . God, how can people be so narrow-minded as to shut truth out of their souls and expect those souls to be elevated to heaven! It is no wonder that they are beset with prejudices and inhibitions. The core, for persecuting Jews, rests in the tough skin of religious fanaticism. In fact all prejudice grows out of fanaticism."

As engaged as Barney was with his father and mother, it was his relationship with Sarah that was both the most codependent and most satisfying one in the family. Sarah, who never married, was every bit as brainy and curious and as complicated psychologically as he was, and his benevolent mentor-disciple dynamic with her was a kind of prototype for the way he later related to women other than Annalee. To admiring women, as to admiring men, he was supportive, unfailingly charming and witty, and intellectually generous. Most unusually in the culture of artists and intellectuals in which he later moved, he did not engage in sexual innuendo or flirt, nor was he provocative in any way. Among all the artists who came to be associated with the so-called New York School, Barney was the only one, the critic Harold Rosenberg claimed, to never put a hand on a knee. But his "vibes were sexual to people who enjoyed language," as Alfred Leslie put it. "If you loved words . . . you could fall in love with Barney immediately."[18]

Sarah herself led a remarkable life. At Hunter College she majored in biology; her real interest was anthropology, but as a relatively new field, the department did not have enough credits for a major so her program was supplemented with meteorology. (She would later claim to have majored in geology.) After graduating in 1933, she followed her brother's path to the Art Students League, studying with Kuniyoshi, Zorach, Soyer, and Brooks on and off between 1933 and 1935, and maintained her membership, which entitled her to draw from the model, through 1943. But she took a different route from Barney's as regarded government assistance: beginning in 1936 under the auspices of the Federal Art Project, Sarah intermittently taught at the Henry Street Settlement and at various parochial schools, and later was an assistant and "researcher in Aerodynamics" for James Brooks's enormous mural

Flight for the Pan American Seaplane Base Building at LaGuardia Airport. For a brief period, Barney and Annalee shared an apartment with Sarah at 71 Barrow Street; neighbors recalled them as "a family of artists."[19] In 1947 she told co-workers she had assisted her brother, who was "interested in Art and Poetry," with his artwork.[20] But much more intriguing is the work that Sarah did through the 1940s and 1950s for the United States Military, the Office of Strategic Service (OSS), and the Voice of America.

Sarah told friends that because Barney, the oldest son, was unable to support his parents in their advanced age, she felt she had to.[21] She began working for the War Department, stationed at Fort Monmouth, New Jersey in late spring 1942. From there she was transferred to the Army Air Corps in Washington as a meteorologist until November 1943, when she was transferred as a research analyst to the Office of Strategic Services (OSS), writing confidential "climate," "geographical and sociological" reports for the OSS before the D-Day landings. She became a propaganda analyst in the Office of War Information and subsequently an information specialist in the Army Air Force, in New York. After the war ended she was vetted for a job by the FBI, a "top secret" position on a Columbia University Research Project "producing 50 volumes covering scientific discoveries" during the war. "This should be my cue to stop & start painting. However, after 3 ½ years of messing around the way I did I want to walk into the kind of racket that will keep me alive to paint and not occupied with meeting conditions for a government dole." Nevertheless, she continued to bounce between Washington and New Jersey, processing sensitive information for the Army.

Barney was kept up to date regarding the logistics and geographical landings of his small, chain-smoking, fishnet-stocking-wearing sister's employment peregrinations, if not—in her circumspect letters at least—of their titles or substance. A constant theme was dissatisfaction: she felt underutilized, underappreciated. Her deceptions about specific qualifications—"in the field of Geology, my major field and one in which I am highly skilled"—didn't help her land the jobs she truly wanted, and she was continually searching: "teach geology at Hunter College? . . . Be something of an electrical engineer, work in Naval Ordinance Laboratory . . . Be a writer of oceanographic reports . . . Be something or other with Office of Strategic Services . . . Be a desk geologist at Office of Economic Warfare . . . Be a Wave at Special Devices or in Meteorological Reports."[22] She harangued superiors in letters sent first to Barney for his "approval."[23] She sounded exactly, in other words, like a female Barney. (Years later, in 1950, she was cleared by the FBI for an appointment with the Voice of America, where, with interesting timing, in the middle of the decade she became the well-paid Vietnam desk editor.)

But in the summer of 1936, she and Barney, with the shared certainty that art was their "religion," were both frustrated in their ambitions. The former, a disciple for whom the value of art was sufficiently established by her idol's say-so, wanted only the serenity to paint. Barney, however, was searching for the core that would make his conviction meaningful, and his quest was existential. "I was in limbo," he said of that time. "I knew I'd be a painter. But I got terribly introspective," and was in "despair . . . . I was involved in a hunger about myself."[24]

He was not alone. The *Washington Post*'s art critic, summing up the first season of eleven shows at New York's Municipal Art Gallery, wrote, "the large public is again aware of the necessity of art in all people's lives," but he warned that, "so many alarmists predict the 'death of painting' (not through stopping to paint, but through the mediocrity of productions) that it is no use laughing off the threat. A serious effort must be made by artists and by critics both in Europe and America to raise the artistic standards of merit."[25]

There is no contemporaneous record of what Barney thought of the two landmark events for New York artists that year at the Museum of Modern Art: in March, "Cubism and Abstract Art" with Alfred Barr's deterministic diagram on its catalogue cover, and in December, "Fantastic Art, Dada, Surrealism." Were they inspiring, invigorating, or demoralizing? In later years, MoMA became something of a *bête noire* for Barney largely because of the aesthetic–historical position concretized in these seminal shows. He would talk about the "issue" for artists in the late 1930s and early 1940s: "What are we going to paint? Surrealism? Cubism?" He said to Gottlieb, "It's finished," and Gottlieb gave him pep talks, urging him "to persevere and keep going." From so much of what he said, and from everything he did, however, it would appear that the question gnawing at him in 1936 was less the meaning of *art* than the meaning of Barnett Newman's life. Which is why he stirred up activity, in some cases so frantically, on so many different fronts.[26]

Living as an artist was not a casual choice. "We were in a desperate situation, and it was a struggle just to be an artist; one had to be willing to sacrifice everything in order to just paint," recalled Gottlieb. "Economic and cultural conditions and the cultural climate" all "conspired to make it difficult to be an artist, to make it difficult to survive as an artist. And any artist of my generation whom I knew who was any good either had to try to make a little money outside of his painting by teaching or by doing some other sort of work, or his wife had to work. You were lucky if you didn't have any children . . . the economic problem was too much of a load."[27] Barney's friends, the people he chose to be with, *were* such artists. Siskind and his wife, toward the end of the summer, came to visit the Newmans in Ogunquit.[28] The Gottliebs, when Barney and Annalee returned to New York, gave a celebratory wedding breakfast for them, where Annalee met Mark Rothko and his first wife, Edith Sachar. Tom Nagai, an old friend from the Art Students League, urged Barney to "try to get" to the "First American Artists' Congress" show, "you will meet every body [*sic*]."[29] So many artists during this time, like Barney struggling to find their subjects, seemed sufficiently able to endure the deprivation and the disquiet to "persevere." But *that* struggle, more than the financial struggle, undid Barney's ability to move forward. How to be an artist with *dignity*. How to produce work that was self-evidently *confident*, how to appear not to have *doubt*.

Because doubt was not something Barney's temperament could tolerate, his creative energies, if not his self-identity, continued to go elsewhere. If he, like Sarah, could find work with the pre-war government, if he could pass himself off as qualified to be a college professor, if some newspaper would take his column on the civil service, if some newspaper would take his column on "art news," if some foundation would support his writing, if some house would publish his comprehensive history of the civil service, if he could prove that the teacher's licensing exam was fatally flawed, his life would have had meaning.

When the newlyweds returned to New York in late September they moved into a room with a small kitchen unit at the Hotel Holland on Forty-Second Street, near Ninth Avenue. It was an odd choice for a couple whose work was in lower Manhattan and Queens, whose families and friends lived in the Bronx and Brooklyn, and who complained about sub-par accommodations in summer communities. The hotel, built in 1918 as a luxury residence, was currently the site of bankruptcies, foreclosures, and labor problems, and the far west stretch of the street was grim.[1]

They left the Holland after one month and briefly shared a sublease in Greenwich Village with Sarah, while Annalee resumed teaching—part-time, at Washington Irving Evening High School—and Barney didn't. In December, they moved into their first home, one room in a nineteen-story building at 300 West Twenty-Third Street; the monthly rent, 51 dollars, was nearly a quarter of their income that year. Immediately Barney had problems. "We are being annoyed beyond all endurance," he wrote to the landlord, "by the Owners and Tenants Electric Company, who have been demanding a deposit of five dollars, or five and one half months' security for a ninety-cent bill. The five-dollar amount in itself is insignificant but the insulting attitude of a company which has never sent us a bill for services but instead had persisted in insulting us had made me determine to refuse this demand." Unless the landlord took action, they would "be forced to seek remedies." It was routine that Barney felt insulted; but from this time forward the threat of legal action became an epistolary trope, his unproductive rage expressed in self-righteous, lecturing, hectoring—albeit intellectually sound and brilliantly argued—letters and written monologues. By March, Annalee had developed the serious intestinal problems that would plague her for the rest of her life.

Financially the Newmans' situation was difficult, but no more so than that of other aspiring artists. With Annalee determined to devote her life to making Barney's work possible, with a settled home, a new bank account with 450 dollars in savings, and domestic stability—they ate most of their meals in a Consumers' Cooperative Cafeteria—there was little to prevent Barney from finally facing the terrifying loneliness and uncertainty of the studio. But face it he did not. He did not paint, he did not seem to aspire to paint, but through the remainder of the 1930s tilted at windmills old and new.

The Consumers' Cooperative Services, which ran bakeries, grocery stores, and restaurants, was in December in the midst of a strike of workers at the Twenty-Fifth Street cafeteria that the Newmans patronized. At heart was a divisive and complicated issue: was the primary loyalty of the workers to the cooperative, of which they were members, or to a union, of which they were also members? Barney took up the cause of the strikers and led a minority wing of shareholders, writing position papers supported by research into the international history of cooperative philosophy: "The labor and cooperative movements are two parallel movements for improving the living standards of the people." Characteristically, Barney took a righteously moral stand, and what jumps out, over eight decades later, is his characteristic motivation—dignity. "Our surface violation of cooperative principles tends to make us a laughing stock."

For the second time, he applied to the United States Civil Service Commission for the position of Supervising Inspector of Clothing Factories, Federal Prison Industries (4,600 dollars per year), and for the second time his application was incomplete. He hedged the formalities: regarding the December due date, he wrote in February, "I regret very much that illness made it impossible for me to answer it until now, and trust that it has not too greatly inconvenienced you." Yet no "illness" had prevented his leading the Consumers' Cooperative Services workers.

And still he had his teeth in the Civil Service. On the back of a flyer for a mid-April symposium on "Aspects and Dangers of Nazism," Barney scribbled research notes about the English Civil Service, still working on his projected magnum opus despite his failure to secure the Houghton Mifflin Literary Fellowship the previous spring.

The cause of Civil Service for Barney was not casual, nor was it simply a place-holder until he found his footing as an artist. While he was in the grip of his crusade, he endowed it with exactly the same meaning and significance that he sought in art. It found him, so to speak, at the intersection of his haberdashery clients, his own teaching, and the immediate question of WPA workers being absorbed into the Civil Service *without* formally establishing "merit." In Barney's eyes, Civil Service as a social philosophy, *if properly understood*, had the potential to save society from everything base and dishonest, and the potential to reward everything dignified and superior in human beings. Later, Barney would transfer that precise ambition to art. And he would be as categorically enraged at artists, artworks, and critics who did not rise to that challenge as he was now enraged against the Citizens' Budget Commission and the spoils system. Even accounting for the hyperbole one would expect in a fellowship application, Barney's submission seems untenably grandiose; and yet, for all its inflation of his expertise, its object is not self-aggrandizing as much as messianic—picking up the mantle of his hero, the 19th-century social philosopher Alexander Herzen. ("I have served one idea . . . war against all imposed authority . . . in the name of the absolute independence of the individual."[2])

"Next to taxes, Civil Service will become the leading political issue of our coming presidential campaign," he had written in his Houghton Mifflin proposal. "The book I intend to write . . . will be a new social philosophy written for the layman and based on the truth of the merit principle which rewards on the basis of merit."

> Chapter III: Civil Service and Honesty . . . the age-old quest of every political system—the guarantee of honesty . . . the basis of every reform movement, the stimulant for every utopia, the principle behind . . . our democratic form of government. 1. Honest will be defined in absolute terms . . . . 3. It will prove in abso-

lute terms that the only honesty possible in social organization must be based on the merit or Civil Service principle. The corrollary [sic] to this proof is that the Civil Service man or woman is per se *the only honest creature in society* . . . . Chapter VII: Civil Service and Freedom. *The elusive term freedom will, for the first time in history, be clearly defined.* It will show that the Civil Service principle is the only guarantee of complete social freedom. Chapter VIII: The American Way Out . . . I offer a sick world looking for social salvation amidst the muck of a thousand crackpot utopias, the merit system (which gives security, work and freedom on the basis of merit regardless of race, creed, or political affiliation) as the only safe, fool-proof, permanent, American way out.

I feel that *as a leader and thinker in the field of Civil Service* that I am exceptionally qualified for this work . . . .

How about the market? . . . it includes millions of people who are trying to find a way out amidst the glut of hundreds of books preaching every type of crackpot utopia from Coughlinism to Communism [emphasis added].

It had been a miserable spring, chasing down debtors. Sarah, when she covered for Barney in August, described the process:

I go to see Torney, told he's on vacation, be back Monday, came Monday, find he's been transferred. Will look him up to-morrow. Go to see Johnson, he's on vacation, go to see Dean, says he made agreement with you for 1st of every month, not 15th. Go to see Irving, his afternoon off. Go to see Joseph—left 10 min ago + etc. Finally got $2 from Hunt. If that's what you call business, it'll be no business of mine . . . . 7th Ave, 8th Ave, Queens, Bklyn subway tracks, which lead here, there + yet wind up no where. [sic]. . . . todays developments. Got $3 from Weston, after acting bloodhound. Got $2 from Hunt $15 . . . $5 . . . $3 . . . $1 . . . Is it true Dean pays on 1st only? Moore said he'd come to office Sat + maybe pay whole bill. Shall I trust him? Have to get Ziegler Tues. He left early to-day, so did Irving. Will go to see about Fitzgerald myself to-morrow. Telephone call doesn't work out because there are thousands of Fitz's there + nobody seems to know.[3]

In April, Biltwell Garment, Inc., the firm for which A. Newman & Son manufactured clothing, declared bankruptcy.[4] In May, A. Newman & Son relocated within 63 Park Row, was paying off debts, and in August it moved again, downsizing to a small office at 12 John Street. This is where, for the next year at least, frequently under his father's letterhead, Barney tried to find his footing. Shortly before he decamped for Chilmark in August to share a cottage with the Siskinds, he had moved the elder Newmans from their Bronx apartment to a two-story attached house on Clyde Street in Forest Hills, near the Greenhouses. Socializing with Cora and Benjamin Ginsburg (of the antiques firm), Leo and Alice Yamin and the Lipkinds, the unpressured days in Chilmark were "the first in months that I have had a chance to relax," he wrote Borodulin.[5]

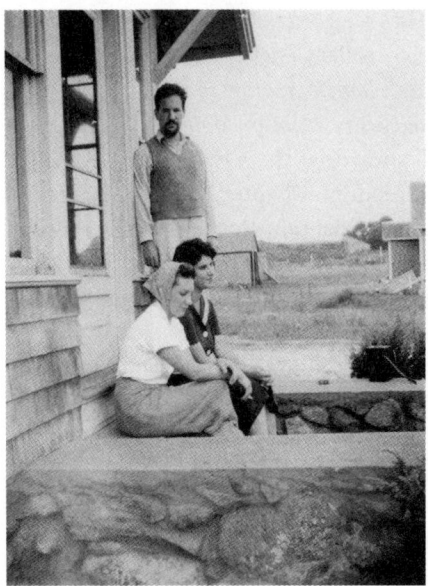

Fig. 10 Barnett and Annalee Newman with Sonia Siskind, Chilmark, Massachusetts, 1937. Photograph Aaron Siskind

Hess repeats Barney's story that Abraham suffered a heart attack sometime in 1937, at which point Barney was "free to liquidate" the business—the implication being that Barney was then also "free" to become an artist,[6] but this narrative was surely finessed: the economic downturn made liquidation inevitable, the business had failed in the spring, the heart attack didn't occur until late October or early November, and it would be years before Barney would paint.

"My father's condition making it necessary for me to carry the load of two families," he told Lipkind, reminding him of 72 dollars owed for an overcoat, a suit, and a topcoat, "this amount is very important to me now." As Annalee increased her hours as a substitute at East New York Vocational High School and at Washington Irving Evening High School, Barney's activities suggest he was panicked.

A new City University college was about to open in Queens, and by mid-October he jumped on it. It was an opportunity to expound his philosophy, customize the imagined position, and vent his resentments. "Dear Dr. Klapper," he wrote to the newly appointed president,

> I understand that you have not as yet organized the art department of Queens College. May I, therefore, offer you my name as a possible candidate?
>
> I am interested in the opportunities Queens College represents for live, creative art education. I am writing to you directly, I am writing to you at all, because I know that you, as one of American's great educators, intend to build your college on the principle of merit rather than on privilege. For the first time, higher education offers a hope of—higher education.
>
> Before I present my list of qualifications, should we not define the specifications they intend to meet? Should we not, in the manner of Socrates, ask what is this merit?

"What shall be the criterion of art education at Queens College?" he asked.

> Is it to be another outcrop of that sham that poses as art throughout the length and breadth of America's University Schools of fine Arts—<u>design</u>? Is it to be a continuation of the study of the trick formulas Pratt Institute specializes in for the

better selling of liverwurst? Or is Queens College to become another haven for some dingy portrait painter who cannot lick his way into the National Academy, to smother the creative spark that may fly into its halls?

And the criterion for the professor?

Is not a professor of art one who can inspire creation? Is not a professor of art one who can inspire love of the plastic expression of the human mind? Is he not one who knows paintings and painters, not as names in a catalogue or history text to be remembered at examinations for higher licenses and to be avoided in daily life, but as his living intimates, as his constant interest and inspiration?

"Merit in this case," should take for granted "that the candidate have the ability to give to art education in this country the dignity that it had gained . . . in England from Prof. Herbert Read."

After an exaggerated history of his training, and an accurate one of his teaching, Barney continued:

I am, however, much more interested in the creative art process and in the philosophy of art . . . . Four years ago, appalled at the petty political squabbles between O'Brien, McKee, and LaGuardia, I offered my name as an opportunity for intellectuals to express their determination for a higher cultural communal life . . . . The fact that a great part of the cultural program I offered at that time has been carried out by Mayor LaGuardia testifies to the inherent worth and substantial merit of my action and to the fact that I had no little part in its fulfillment, especially since I have the Mayor's letter informing me that he, "would give your (my) suggestions serious consideration." . . .

I am sending you a copy of THE ANSWER, a Civil Service magazine I conceived, wrote and published in an attempt to dignify, with serious thinking, the merit system, a philosophy of life I am convinced is very important . . . . This magazine met with unusual success and interest not only in the field of Civil Service but in the fields of education and educational philosophy . . . .

Finally I am enclosing a copy of a letter from Houghton, Mifflin, and Company informing me that although I did not succeed in winning their literary fellowship, [my] "project was one of the small group selected by the judges for special consideration."

He closed by giving as his home address the Queens residence of his parents.[7]

Then he sat for the two-day, fourteen-hour first part of the art teachers exam. And then, immediately after, his quest to get his Civil Service study funded—as opposed to written—began to approach a mania.

The proposal Barney submitted to the Guggenheim Foundation on October 28 was past the deadline and much of the data was fudged. He claimed to have taken graduate courses at "CCNY? Hunter."[8] He listed his current occupation as "Publisher of THE ANSWER" and "member of the N.Y. City High School System." The spaces for the "learned, scientific or artistic societies" to which he belonged, and the "scholarships or fellowships" that he had held, were left blank. He claimed accurate degrees of fluency in French and Hebrew, and exorbitant ones in German, Spanish, Italian, and Latin. Among his references were Leah's husband, George's wife's cousin the journalist Norman Cousins, and the jury of the Houghton Mifflin Fellowship, which had rejected but praised his project. He estimated that his comprehensive study would be completed in one year. It is painful to see how baldly, and ingenuously, he exposed himself—as he had done two weeks earlier writing to Queens College.

"A Study and Analysis of the Civil Service in America," was to include "a complete history of Civil Service in America, its present position as an institution and social force, the nature and the meaning of the merit principle, its implications and promises for the future, its significance as a way of life. In other words, it is to be a complete and definitive work on the merit system in this country." From the day he mailed his proposal to the end of February 1938—sixteen weeks—Barney wrote at least fourteen letters to Henry Allen Moe, the secretary general of the Guggenheim Foundation, most prompted by daily newspaper clippings that Barney felt supported his application. The letters grew in length, substance, and urgency, taking on a life of their own—increasingly presumptuous about the impact his study would have, increasingly omnivorous in identifying examples of his subject, increasingly righteous, repetitive, and sloppy. It was an adult version of an extended temper tantrum, a desperate and self-defeating attempt to enforce his "dignity," provoked as much by stresses in his life as by insistence that his *rightness* be acknowledged. "The question had never been studied"; "news from Europe . . . France . . . general strike . . . Rumania . . . the rejection of all Jews from government service . . . prejudice in the establishment of 'merit'"; he was sending "*actual clippings . . . from our most important newspapers* as tangible proof of this need." State examiners for high school teachers "admit they would refuse a license to Arturo Toscanini." He was "forced to write by the pressure of events," he told Moe, how could he "resist"? How could he "refrain"? He was "compelled." These were the very words, in the last decades of his life, with which he answered questions about why he made the art that he did.

He seemed to be genuinely innocent of what constituted qualifications—that original research and reporting were required, that scholarly authority didn't reside in newspaper reports of events. There is a striking disconnect for someone so deeply invested in the "merit system."

The high school art teachers exam that Barney took on November 11 and 12, 1937—the one that seemed to be the last straw (although not his last attempt), that provoked him to write letters of protest and to solicit letters of support, and which led, a year later, to his organizing a *salon des refusés* and publicity campaign—was widely agreed to be meaninglessly vague, confusing, and incompetently administered. The

New York Teacher, magazine of the Teachers Union, confirmed Barney's rage. The same position was taken by art department chairmen and the director of art for the New York City High Schools, Forest Grant, who called it "the worst managed, most incompetent examination in my experience." The uselessness of the exam as a test of "merit," the insult to teachers' "dignity," undoubtedly contributed to Barney's assault on Moe. Certainly ego was involved in these battles, but there was also economic urgency: the Newmans' combined income of 2887 dollars—over 61,707 dollars in 2023—was sufficient for a middle-class life in New York, but not the style to which they and the senior Newmans were accustomed.

A "Fine Arts Substitute Association" was created in June, the "business" address officially registered as 12 John Street; the new letterhead read simply "B. Barnett Newman." Its purpose was the organization of "all substitutes who have been failed in the second performance test of June 1938," who were encouraged to file appeals, apply for the next exam—while reserving "all rights in connection with the previous exam"—and attend a meeting at the Consumers' Cooperative Cafeteria. Barney was the association's "chairman" and compiler of the "List of Demands" resulting from the meeting. Within a month there were power struggles and resignations.

The previous August, Barney had met Thomas Hart Benton in Martha's Vineyard. Venting his frustration at the test—specifically the section on mural design—to the famous muralist and teacher when they returned in 1938, Barney interviewed Benton about his process and drew from him an expression of support: "If I had tried it, I would have failed." Written up as a piece of feature journalism, Barney "released" it to the *Times*.[9] Thus prodded, the newspaper ran a small item in September, "occasioned by the announcement of the Board of Examiners last week of a list of thirty eligibles out of 207 candidates," but did not mention Barney.[10]

He petitioned the *New York Teacher*, where he had contributed to an "Arts" column, to engage him to write a recurring feature. Instead, the editors informed him they would "dispense with [his] services" entirely. Having his voice, and indignation, thus silenced, Barney at the end of November staged an exhibition at A.C.A. Gallery on West Eighth Street, "Can We Draw? The Board of Examiners Says—No!," of work by substitute teachers including Sarah Newman, who had also taken and failed the exam. Barney wrote to "Honorable Fiorello LaGuardia" asking for his support, and issued a six-page press release/manifesto, and a brochure:

> To teach art in the city high schools, a candidate must pass half a dozen examinations . . . . the Board of Examiners has been using this "test" as an eliminating device [but] the board does not hesitate to license these "incompetents" to work in the schools as substitute teachers . . . without tenure, sick leave, or vacation pay, ineligible for social security and unemployment insurance, without rights, [many] for from six to ten years . . . . They are regular teachers, every day except payday.

The exhibition included a coup—the inclusion of a work by Max Weber, who failed the test in 1909. Weber, who had by this time a significant reputation, was nevertheless every bit as indignant as Barney: "It does my heart good to see this whole mess placed before the public. I wish you had done it sooner. My own experience with these inferiors is even sadder. I wasn't even given a chance to substitute. Keep up the good fight. I'll go the limit with you . . . . This dirty deal I got at the hands of this little band of pigmies . . . has been lurking and simmering in my heart all these years. It does me good to give vent to this pent up feeling . . . . I honestly believe that they do not want progressive teachers with ideas and higher aims, they fear them. Manifestations of genuine contributive educative aptitudes in applicants are to them what signs or symbols of culture are to the Nazis. Mediocrity and servility in applicants seem to be desirable."[11]

The handout included a unique testimonial to "MISS SARAH NEWMAN." The *New York Post* critic was "particularly struck by the distinctive charm of frankly naïve paintings by Sarah Newman"; the *Art Digest* reproduced one, and quoted Barney as saying of a second that while yes, the wheels of a tricycle were not round, "the painter did that on purpose to give the impression of freedom." *Newsweek*—a *national* magazine—focused entirely on Weber; there were other articles and even an editorial noting that the question at stake was economic, rather than skill.[12] The Board of Examiners ruling was not reversed, and Barney did not get his sinecure in the civil service.

But the show marked a debut: *Studio in the Country*, a watercolor by "B. Barnett Newman" is listed but not illustrated in the brochure. How Barney persuaded A.C.A. to host the show, what this work looked like and what became of it remain a mystery.[13]

ELEVEN

DIGNITY

If his ambitions were grand, if he were grasping for an anchor, in 1938 his quotidian life went on in a quotidian manner. His combative energies were focused on his campaign for a teaching license, writing agitated letters, accumulating references, petitioning the Board of Examiners for reconsideration. He was encouraged by Borodulin, who had self-published a modest literary magazine, to "restart the ANSWER on a mimeograph basis."[1] When, in the early part of the summer, Annalee spent a bored week with her mother in upstate New York, Barney enjoyed his bachelor life, celebrating his "sudden freedom [staying] out until 3:30 A.M." wandering the city, going to late-late movies, but also doing domestic chores like having Annalee's dresses cleaned. He composed "not the [literary] writing" Annalee expected, "but letters and briefs." One evening, he went to a "mass meeting commemorating the 2nd anniversary of the war in Spain" at Madison Square Garden, where twenty thousand in the audience approved a resolution calling for the American government to end the Spanish embargo. "Last night's meeting was quite spectacular . . . The Irish priest was excellent—his remarks are quite important," he wrote to Annalee and sent her a clipping of the *Times* story with those words circled: "*I say to every Bishop of the church that if you accept your politics from the Pope you are not worthy of citizenship in any country of the world except Vatican City. And I say to the Pope, 'You are not infallible about anything except religious matters.'*"[2]

It is impossible to overemphasize the impact of the cultural nutrient in which Barney's crusades were waged. If his acute perception of disrespect, if his tactics to provoke affirmation, if his annoyingly *thin skin* appear in today's world as excessively sensitive or symptomatic of a rampant narcissism, in the 1930s they were more like a healthy refusal to be, on the one hand made a scapegoat, and, on the other invisible. The thinking and exhortations of Jews who had achieved distinguished and respected positions—like the journalist James Waterman Wise, whose "Open Letter to My Fellow-Jews" Barney read in August 1938—demanded that enlightened Jews not "degenerate into [the] hysteria . . . of certain sections of our people in the present crisis" of anti-Semitism, not listen to those who demanded that "some Jews should abandon or soft-pedal their political convictions so as not to endanger the political rights of other Jews." When Wise, who covered the Spanish Civil War for the *New York Post*, wrote disparagingly of Jewish collaborators who "demand that Jews do not support the democratic struggle of the Spanish people—lest the Catholic *hierarchy* react against us," he repudiated the commonly held fear that Barney had acknowledged in his letter to Annalee. Wise warned that, "When we surrender the right as free and equal citizens of our country to maintain any political opinion, or to participate in social and economic movements which are [progressive] we tacitly invite further demands by our enemies for self-obliteration and auto-enslavement." Jews *should* align themselves with the CIO (Congress of Industrial Organizations), the American League for Peace and Democracy, the North American Committee to Aid Spanish Democracy, because "the whole meaning of Jewish history is to be found in our age-long struggle against those brutal and oppressive forces which have sought . . . to enslave the spirit and body of man." Acquiescent, less noisy Jews, according to Wise, say, "Better . . . that a Jew be a Mr. Zero than an Einstein, a non-entity than a Sigmund Freud, an ignoramus than a Brandeis!"[3]

There was no way that Barney was going to be a Mr. Zero.

"We're enjoying like the goyim—eating, sleeping, [breathing the] air—a people without worry," Barney wrote to his in-laws from Chilmark in August. But the chatter in the community was not so idle. That summer in *Partisan Review* Leon Trotsky had both thrown down the gauntlet to artists and verbalized what so many were struggling with: they had to make a choice about whom or what their art served. "Art can become a strong ally of revolution only in so far as it remains faithful to itself." This was followed, in the fall issue, with "Manifesto: Towards a Free Revolutionary Art," bylined Andre Breton and Diego Rivera but generally believed to have been drafted by Trotsky.

Trotsky sounded several of the chords that had already been resonating within Barney, that he already had sung in a different context, and which were responsible for his aesthetic paralysis—or rather, the atypical manifestation of his aesthetic faculty—during these years.

> Generally speaking, art is an expression of man's need for an harmonious and complete life . . . . That is why a protest against reality, either conscious or unconscious, active or passive, optimistic or pessimistic, always forms part of a really creative piece of work . . . .
>
> The decline of bourgeois society means an intolerable exacerbation of social contradictions, which are transformed inevitably into personal contradictions, calling forth an ever more burning need for a liberating art . . . . Art, which is the most complex part of culture, the most sensitive and at the same time the least protected, suffers most from the decline and decay of bourgeois society . . . .
>
> Art can neither escape the crisis nor partition itself off . . . . It will rot away inevitably . . . unless present-day society is able to rebuild itself. This task is revolutionary in character. For these reasons the function of art in our epoch is determined by its relation to the revolution.[4]

Barney would not have allied himself with the *Partisan Review*'s politics. But it would be wrong to completely divorce his ambition from Trotsky's fundamental charge: that art had a crucial, progressive role in shaping the world. How else to explain Barney's boldface pronouncement ten years later, that if his work were properly understood it would be the end of state capitalism and totalitarianism?

The couple returned just before the historic "Great Hurricane of 1938"—the "Great New England Hurricane," the "Long Island Express"—on September 20 destroyed most of Chilmark's quaint 17th-century fishing harbor, with 25-foot-high waves and tides 8 feet higher than any recorded in Chilmark's 244-year history.[5] But there was no escaping the next "hurricane" at the end of the month: the Munich Agreement, annexing the Sudetenland to Nazi Germany. The front page of the *Times* on September 28 carried the six-column, all-capital-letter headline "Roosevelt Appeals Again To Hitler As Hope Wanes; Reich Sets Attack For Saturday, Denies New Deadline; Britain Mobilizes Navy; Chamberlain Makes Final Plea." Two days later the headline was "Chamberlain Hero of Munich Crowds: People Stand Outside Hotel for Hours to Get Glimpse of Him and Cheer Him"; there were four-column-wide photographs of Hitler and Mussolini and Chamberlain. Barney, who became a truffle pig when searching for newspaper coverage with any relevance to civil service issues, left no indication—no clippings, no letters to editors—that the week's news provoked any particular rage or action on his part. But he wasn't immune. Whenever there was historic agitation or turmoil, in the city, country, or world, Barney didn't simply "go on" with his life but instead created his own tornado in which he could make certain that he remained the center. It was his reflexive way of metabolizing anxiety, a way to displace feelings of powerlessness into an arena in which he could have an impact. In October 1938, he began to organize the press blitz for "Can We Draw?"

The country was preparing for war that fall, but art and artists made good stories, a distraction from the economic news and reports of European appeasement. Anticipating the hoopla around the Museum of Modern Art's tenth anniversary and opening of its new building, *Fortune* magazine in December devoted over 7500 words to the phenomenon that was the museum, granting "its share of the credit for the gradual increase in the popularity and appreciation of modern art on this side of the Atlantic."[6] The Museum of Non-Objective Painting (later the Guggenheim) was shortly to open in rented quarters on East Fifty-Fourth Street. Even stylistically radical artists received mainstream coverage. The Ten had been showing together for four years, but in November, when WNYC radio aired "What's Wrong with American Art" to highlight "The Ten: Whitney Dissenters"—an exhibition at the Mercury Galleries coinciding with the Whitney Annual—it was "perhaps the ultimate" attention they had received. (Their dissent, according to the catalogue, was to enlighten "a public which has had 'contemporary American art' dogmatically defined for it by museums as a representational art preoccupied with local color . . . aggravated by a curiously restricted chauvinism which condemns the occasional influence of the cubist and abstractionist innovators while accepting or ignoring the obvious imitations of Titian, Degas, Breughel and Chardin."[7]) Rothko, teaching part time at the

Brooklyn Jewish Center School since 1929, and Gottlieb were in The Ten, and as members as well of the left American Artists' Congress, they were able to identify both as advanced artists and political men. Other artists of Barney's generation were attending Hans Hofmann's lectures in Greenwich Village that winter, where formal issues were paramount, and just as many (often the same ones) were exploring paths of spiritual expression opened up by John Graham's surrealist take on primitivism. Many, struggling to live on the WPA salary, led a rough, bohemian life; in Baziotes's words, "lots of drinking, lots of sex, lots of dancing," 25-cent-a-beer parties with "architects, photographers, businessmen, college students, wealthy women, Antoine de Saint-Exupéry, the surrealists, Paul Robeson, Auden, MacNeice, John Garfield, art dealers," and a "whole lot" of talking about art.[8]

In contrast, for Barney and Annalee life had become more middle class when they moved in November to the top floor of newly completed 315 West Twenty-First Street. In two-and-a-half large, well-lit rooms they had a host of "modern conveniences": "Venetian Mirrors . . . Concealed Radiation . . . Spacious Closets . . . Radio Outlets . . . Interviewers [intercoms] . . . and Electric Refrigeration." They installed the luxury of their own telephone. Annalee continued to work toward a master's degree taking business law and management courses at New York University, and returned to teaching stenography and typing as a full-time "substitute" at East New York Vocational High School; Barney returned to teach art at Grover Cleveland.

As they settled in, the front page of the *Times* was dominated from Friday, November 11, to Wednesday, November 16, by three- and four-column headlines and twenty-four articles about *Kristallnacht* and the escalating persecution of European Jews. They made a 35-dollar donation to a Jewish charity refugee organization, but it wasn't a sufficient response. Barney needed his own war to channel the complex variety of his pain and in which he hoped to dominate. He embarked upon what would be the last, and greatest, of his civic—as opposed to aesthetic—campaigns for justice and respect: the Greenhouse patent lawsuit.

For ten years, Annalee's father had been bedeviled by what he considered infringement upon the patent of his beverage-carbonating invention. Either he found in Barney just the general to mount the battle he wanted waged (according to Barney and Annalee, and Samuel's own letters), or Barney, hoping to redress the family's years of disrespect toward Annalee by surrounding her with his reflected glory when he "prevailed," took advantage of Samuel's vulnerability and persuaded him to fight (according to Leah's family lore).

Joe Hochstein, Leah's son, remembered stories about his grandfather's "little bottling plant" in Akron, Nellie the horse, and how "the kids helped" in the plant. It was a big deal, after only twelve years in America, when Samuel invented and applied for a patent for "A Method of Bottling Carbonated Beverages." The "Greenhouse CO_2 Gas-Saving, De-Aerating and Purifying" device involved an "automatic constant escape valve for the gases, which assure[d] a continuous and constant escape of air and lighter gases from the beverage filling station, regardless of minor fluctuations in water level and pressure." A patent was granted in September 1928, about a year after the family moved to New York. But by that time, Crown Cork & Seal, who had been unsuccessfully negotiating with Greenhouse to purchase or license the device, began manufacturing its own version and selling it to bottlers throughout the United States.

Samuel was racked by suspicions that his work had been stolen, but was unable to confirm the construction of his competitor's process.[9] It was after the 1938 bottlers' convention, where a distraught Samuel abased himself by shouting at, and chasing after, the "terribly embarrassed" offender that Barney stepped in. It was unbearable to witness how profoundly the elegant Samuel, revered by his family, experienced the piracy and absence of acknowledgment as an assault on his dignity. After strategizing with his son-in-law, in January 1939 Samuel began a heartbreaking pursuit of justice. As evidenced in the hundreds of

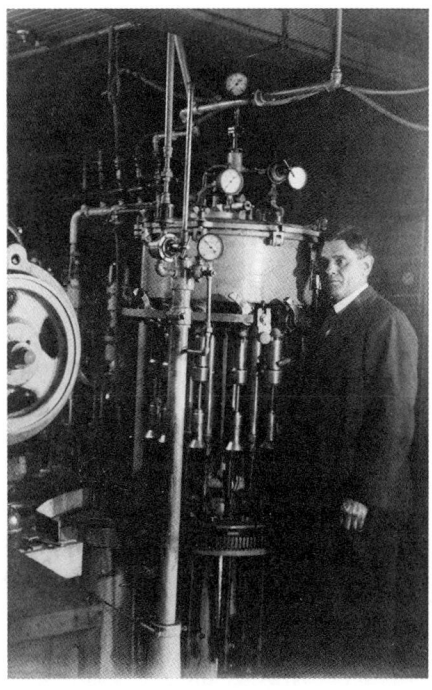

Fig. 11 Samuel Greenhouse with his "Gas-Saving, De-Aerating and Purifying Device," 1920s

pages of correspondence—letters to lawyers and co-defendants drafted by Barney and sent out over Samuel's signature, letters between Barney and Samuel in the colorful Yiddish that so exquisitely expresses hurt—and legal documents, the two proud but financially strapped men, their lawyer (with whom Barney continuously argued about fees), and their single expert witness were the David to the Goliath of Crown, with its "four sets of lawyers and about twenty-five experts against us."[10] This was a fight of a different sort than Barney had picked before, and this arena was a different place. The legal system was not benignly interested in his narrative the way the newspapers earlier had been. This time there was money, not simply principles, at stake, and companies in business to make money were not amused when challenged.

Barney was in it heart and soul. He collected advertising literature and radio scripts, service manuals and drawings, "searching diligently for proof."[11] Apart from the case against their actual adversary, Samuel's erstwhile partners in Akron and the lawyer they all agreed upon required constant corralling. Barney's commitment and custodianship did not waver, and the multi-front battle tormented both Barney and Samuel through the entire period of the War in Europe.

The seven-year experience left Barney deeply scarred and shaken. He was still churning about the injustice twenty-five years later. Friends heard the story of "the great tragedy of pin point carbonation . . . many, many times. More times than you can imagine," to the point where they "tuned the story out."[12] Before, he really did seem to believe that a man of principles could make his case, logically and rationally, and receive appropriate consideration, if not prevail. After, he would say that he had been naïve. The lawsuit was a life-changing experience; he realized, he said, for the first time that what actually happened didn't matter. The operative criterion was how you spun it, how you made it look.

The struggle confirmed his enormous empathy for the *pater familias*, confirmed the father as the "tragic figure."

The two fathers with whom he was involved—his own and Annalee's—had both, even as first-generation immigrants originally without English, managed to achieve some degree of financial success and social standing, only to end their lives frustrated and humiliated by their business failures and weakened by illness. Did Barney see a loving Abraham forced to be distant and formal in a world that moved beyond him? Perhaps that's all there is to it. On the other hand, we have Barney's amplification, twenty-one years later, to his friend B. H. Friedman: "Everything good in the world had come from a patriarchy and everything bad from a matriarchy. The matriarchy . . . is involved with generation fucking; the patriarchy, with love."[13]

The pronouncement had come in a long—philosophical, not specific—disquisition to Lee Krasner and Friedman, "a series of Talmudic paradoxes. In brief he said, I worship women and therefore thank God I am a man." Barney spent eighteen years following his father's death in 1947 taking care of his mother, invariably performing as the good son. If he found Anna overbearing, if he resented her ambition and blamed her for the toll on Abraham, he left no indication. Obliquely, with a laugh, he would refer to her "favorite phrase" in acknowledgment or envy of the fortunate on whom American prosperity rained: "They should be walking around the streets yelling, 'America I love you!' "[14] The black painting *Abraham* (1949), made, if not titled, less than two years after his father's death, is a magnificently complex and tragic painting. But *Anna's Light*, 1968, made after his mother's death, is unambiguously glorious: an enormous, enveloping, penetrating red radiance. "My mother was an extraordinary woman—a remarkable person whose loss to me is immense," he told Robert Motherwell after she died.[15]

With whom did the son identify? Never having become a father, did he nevertheless include himself in that formulation, man = father = *mensch*? Once he overcame the distractions and doubts, and determinedly became a painter in the late 1940s, Barney played the role of fantasy father figure—benevolent and encouraging—to numbers of appealing young men in whom he recognized potential. He charmed and advised, educated in Barneyalia and entertained in one way or another, architects Tony Louvis, Hans Noë, and Richard Meier; artists Robert Murray, Harold Cohen, Alfred Leslie, Cleve Gray, Malcolm Morley, Donald Judd, and Dan Flavin among others; and various assistants, writers, dealers, collectors—including Lawrence Alloway, John Kasmin, Alan Power, Brooke Alexander, Bill Ehrlich, S. I. Newhouse; and the enigmatic Tom Crawford, his last studio assistant. During one lunch when a young Larry Poons enlisted him in an "attempt [at] a reconciliation of some sort" with his father, Barney delivered a disquisition on the ur-patriarchal story of Abraham and Isaac.[16] The associations could be as brief as a couple of evenings, or friendships that lasted years. But he left these young men feeling they had been touched by something very special, that they had the parental approval, formal but wise and loving, that everyone craves and feels affirmed to receive.

And yet his own father, "incapable of displaying his emotions and feeling toward one he likes," as Sarah once wrote to comfort Barney, was restrained and formal in apportioning just those qualities.[17] "I was very pleased to read in your letter that at least you became a good boy following the old good habit of 'early to bed and early to rise,'" Abraham wrote to the 35-year-old Barney, while he was attending the Audubon Nature Camp in Maine in August 1940.

> I hope you will continue same through coming years . . . . Keep on your good work and when you will get through the intensive course in nature study you'll come to the conclusion that: all we know about nature can be written on one page, but all we don't know millions of pages would not be sufficient. I am also to remind you that your vacation time is very short before you look around will be over and another year of hard work is waiting for you try to make your vacation more restfull and cherfull [*sic*] hoping to extend you a hearty welcome when you return home in good health I remain your father Abraham.[18]

The only fathers Barney knew were Jewish men of a certain generation, those who came to America without the language, without credentials for work here, whose deracinated families were to an extreme degree dependent upon them. As marginal people in Europe, they had little importable structure they desired to duplicate. They did not have the kind of support the Catholic Church provided so many other immigrants; and they were subjected to prejudice on every front once they did get situated. There was ambition, there was defensiveness, and there was, grievously, shame; and the children of this generation internalized that heritage. "My fear . . . is, when I think I'm speaking for man, I only speak for the Jews, more precisely, the Jews most like myself," Clement Greenberg—for much of the 1950s a constant social presence in Barney's life, and his earliest critical supporter—wrote around this time.[19]

Greenberg came from a family similar to Barney's and, he too, worked with his father—in a dry goods business—during the Depression. His diaries are filled with tortured references to his father—his weaknesses, his judgments—and the specifically "Jewish" shadow he cast over the critic's life. Greenberg never wrote "the father is the tragic figure" but he, like Barney, wrestled with the same legacy that history had sculpted, and his self-analysis provides an insight into Barney's own bombast. "Pa is one of the 36 just men on whom the world rests." "My tendency to start everything with a flourish, by going off the handle: to start out of control, on a high note—like the capital letters in my writing, especially at the beginning of a sentence. Exhibitionism; also designed to get Pa's attention for what follows—and just to get his attention."[20]

At the very end of 1938, for the first time, there is a record that Barney purchased art supplies—ink, pad, two brushes, a tube of "Brush White," a pen, a set of forty-eight sticks of NuPastel, and pastel fixatif. He did not deduct them on his tax returns, where he continued to identify himself as a teacher, but the date is a milestone in his evolution.

All through the following spring, as he was notified of his failures in teaching exams for both fine arts and English, he wrote letters protesting the grades, compiled dossiers of others' letters in support and finally, in May, took his complaints higher—to the New York State Commissioner of Education.[21] The endless, defensive re-presentations of his credentials, answered with arbitrary and detached rejections, deeply wounded him. He felt he was not being taken *seriously*.

He applied for a teaching position in an "Indian Community or Boarding School"—apparently never questioning its mission. These had recently been in the news because the application rules for teachers had changed. After his New England summer experiences, he may have considered himself something of an outdoorsman, reveling in his nature walks and geological specimens. Gottlieb had recently returned from the desert near Tucson. Rothko and his first wife spent summer vacations camping in upstate New York or the Far West. William Lipkind had been in Nebraska studying the Winnebago language, and since 1937 was in Brazil doing field work on the Carajaacute. If these vicarious adventures weren't in Barney's mind when he considered the schools—"mostly in isolated localities of the Far North and West, where bad roads, inclement weather, a meager population and other elements present problems to which the teacher cannot find answers in textbooks"—what was? On the other hand, the challenge to "plan original programs, adjust to changing conditions . . . respect primitive cultures, build programs on needs and customs of a special locality, discuss intelligently social and economic problems of low-income groups and the natural resources of the region, and willingness to lead in community enterprises" would have appealed to every impulse that fed into his public rhetoric.[22] But did he really mean to so drastically relocate when he applied in June 1939 to the Civil Service Commission? He never had to make that decision, fortunately: his application was "disapproved because [he] failed to submit special form sent."[23] It was just as well: "young married men [were sent] to the most inaccessible of all, the one-teacher schools," the *Times* reported. "Their wives get appointments as 'special assistants' and are expected to do community work, handle home economics problems and cook noon-day lunches in stormy weather."[24] It's hard to imagine that Annalee, with her high cultural tastes and chronic stomach problems, was an enthusiastic supporter. And anyway she had in February gotten a placement as a regular full-time teacher, a position that Barney later noted was "the highest standard" among all civil service groups.

Instead of a romantic (and inevitably disillusioning) fantasy, Barney indulged in the "needs and customs" of the "special locality" of New York. He went to lectures— Jan Masaryk on "After Munich—What?"; Franz Boas on "Democracy and Intellectual Freedom"; and those of Cooper Union's "Forum Series": "Adventures in Ideas" (Max Lerner, Reinhold Niebuhr, Karen Horney, Ernest Nagel, Sidney Hook); "The Power of Criticism"; "Art for Virtue's Sake"; "Art for Art's Sake"; "Contemporary Art Quarrels"; and "The World's Fair as an Expression of Contemporary Art." He sought out the opening at Carnegie Hall of the Third American Writers Congress of the League of American Writers in June, where Langston Hughes spoke on "Democracy and Me" to "thunderous applause," and Thomas Mann delivered the keynote.[25] The most memorable session, held at the New School and closed to the public but generously covered in newspapers[26] was Kenneth Burke's presentation of his essay, "The Rhetoric of Hitler's 'Battle,'" which examined "the role of the critic and the function of criticism in a democratic society." *Mein Kampf* had only in February 1939 become available to Americans in two unexpurgated editions; it was on bestseller lists and had been treated in a deluge of reviews. Burke reacted to the critics who condemned the book for its content while missing the rhetorical prowess: "book reviewers provided the public with what they wanted to hear about Mein Kampf rather than what they needed to hear."[27]

The lesson in the power of extreme rhetoric was not lost on Barney when the opportunity arose to take "revenge at all the teacher organizations that have been flopping around and refuse to see the right direction."[28] New York State planned to cut 10 million dollars from the allotment for education, including the salaries of teachers—a cut urged by Barney's nemesis, the Citizens' Budget Commission. An opposing coalition of the city Board of Education, teachers, and parents called for public hearings in Albany and organized a mass demonstration. "We refuse to stand idly by while those looking for this year's dollars sacrifice the citizens of tomorrow," Barney wrote to Annalee.[29] This battle, continuing into the summer, led to a new fixation, and draft after draft of "Problems of the Teachers."

Previously, he decided that this was the moment he would make the leap. "How do you like your freedom? Are you working hard? Have you adjusted yourself to the life of an artist?" Annalee asked him in August from the Jersey Shore. But if they expected paintings to emerge that summer, they were to be disappointed.[30] Barney was indeed "working hard," but the only creations he produced were partisan and verbal excuses not to paint.

"I'm sure you will be happy to know that . . . I am on page 3 of my stuff," he wrote to Annalee, with the Writers Congress fresh in his mind. "It isn't bad though by no means good. But if I plug along—now that I am free—I think I'll be able to finish by the end of the week."[31] "Things haven't been too good with me, I've discarded both my beginnings and I am starting a third—The first two needed _fire_."[32]

The city's teaching organizations had been:

> the strongest civil service pressure group in the State. They have been the envy of all other Civil Service pressure groups who have these last 20 years stood by to watch the "teachers lobby" get almost anything they wished for until the teachers of NY have achieved the finest living standards and working conditions obtainable in the globe . . . . Legislators have always seemed anxious to appease the teachers lobby not out of any love for teachers or education, but out of fear . . .

Barney wrote, illuminating just why he fought so long and so hard to gain his full-time license. But now the teachers were "inexcusably caught asleep [and] disillusioned all civil service groups by their utter helplessness." Relying on "old time methods of buttonhole and back-room lobbying" and dumping record loads of telegrams on the legislature in Albany, the teachers missed "the true enemy": they themselves were "definitely to blame for their inflexibility to fight back" against "official sounding groups like the Citizens' Budget Commission Inc," which used "the shrewdest of propaganda methods yet devised for reactionary propaganda in any democracy to date."

If, in this latest attack, Barney was aiming for a style with "_fire_ . . . Plenty of pepper,"[33] he dexterously adjusted his rhetoric in a strange tale written for his little nephew, where he channeled Kipling. And he pivoted again, striking a deeply tender and loving—if still righteous—chord in a paean to his cherished downtown Manhattan. This unfinished draft, so vividly previewing the Virgil of New York he became, guiding scores of good friends and casual acquaintances around the city, was provoked by a controversial rehabilitation of City Hall Park by Parks Commissioner Robert Moses, who insisted that the "handling of telephone wires, subway kiosks, conduits, telegraph lines and the like involved more problems than the landscaping of a 'New England village green.'" Opposition in the city government hadn't only focused on the excess of asphalt and dearth of trees and shrubbery; the concrete, they worried, would provide an "immediate gathering place for Communists."[34] Barney's objections were—in a voice rarely heard in his writing—much more elegiac and sentimental: Moses

> desecrated . . . City Hall Park . . . a perfect example of an old American common. On its west side, right behind the Nathan Hale statue, is a large plot where stood two of the oldest elms in New York with a large patch of green meadow between them, a beautiful silky lawn, a vignette of landscape beauty. The trees are gone— they couldn't stand the hurricane of '38—but they most likely wished it so, for the hand of Robert Moses planned to destroy them.

Although he had seen only bits of New England in America, and none of Europe, Barney did not hesitate to claim that

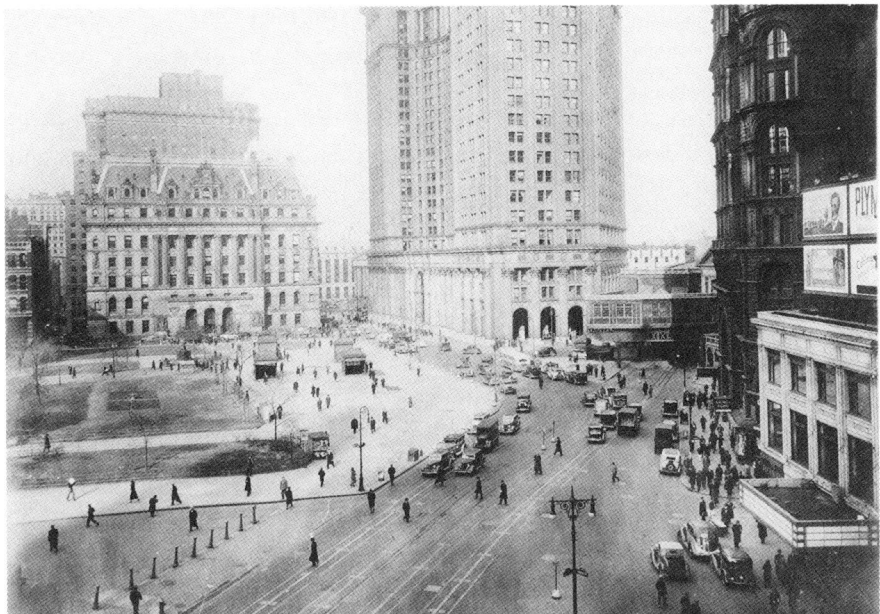

Fig. 12 City Hall Park, 1936. New York City Department of Finance

The artists and the writers who have gone to Europe to come back yelling "America" have proven their dislike of America by their insistence on linking New York with Europe. To them, America is the fields of Kansas and the dirty waters of the Mississippi. Have they forgotten that New York was America long before Kansas was even seen by a white man?[35]

"New York" is so suffused with affection, it's easy to overlook its overstatements and naïveté.

The world knows New York by its new landmarks . . . . Yet there is a part of New York where one gets . . . the sense of history, the charm of age and tradition. This is the district around City Hall . . . . The tip of the island of Manhattan forms a compact heterogeneous cosmopolis where one can still have the charming feeling of living in two centuries, where one can still catch the friendliness of the small town, where one can still savor the distinctive American flavor. Hemmed in by two rivers on its sides, where a short walk can take you from one to the other, and by two old-fashioned commons on the north and south, Bowling Green and City Hall Park, one feels a sense of the whole city and its past. The huge wall that lined the narrow lanes of a colonial village, the skyscrapers and the two-story Revolutionary houses, the marketplace and the central office directing the Transcontinental corporation, the tiny churchyard and the huge railroad terminals, the old landing piers and the gigantic bridges, the tiny shops and the huge department stores, the old bookshop and the immense newspaper plant—all are jammed close together as can [happen] only in New York . . . .

Thomas Street, one of the few private thoroughfares left, is the center of the cotton textile industry. Here one can catch the flavor of New England, not only because of the concentration of dry goods but because it is the most perfect remaining stand of nineteenth-century architecture . . . . The Hall of Records, the most perfect example of neo-Renaissance architecture in the whole city . . . one might think one is in the Paris Opera House, with its grand staircase, its many-colored yet sober marble walls, its old-style metal trim . . . . Washington Market, small brick buildings . . . where one gets a deeper realization of the nature of vegetables than on a farm . . . . one is overcome by the vastness, the variety and the concentration of objects; the smells of cheese, of raw beef, of fish tantalize the appetite; and the place is full of restaurants where the gourmet can eat Maine lobster and Ipswich clams and exotic fruit . . . . Les Halles of Paris is not more picturesque. Walking out of the market . . . out of the brick canyons into the free, open air where you can still see sky and water and boat masts and huge liners and freighters with their romantic overtones . . . Cortlandt Street . . . stores jammed full of radios, wire, tubes, aerials, radio chassis . . . . Here also you can get the best glass of beer in town in a wide open saloon without any walls, where the men who drink beer are not barflies.

"The sense of focus, of people and things and time, is immense, and one feels one's self at the steering wheel of enterprise," Barney all but sang his great love. "We can forgive the pride New Yorkers feel that from here the country and the world are being run."

TWELVE

THE STANCE

"One quickly gets used to living well and having nothing to do," Annalee wrote from Ogunquit in August. Just before they left New York the newspapers were filled with headlines announcing the non-aggression pact between Germany and the Soviet Union and the mortal threat to the country Barney's parents had left forty years earlier. Within a few days, the German Army invaded Poland; the Federation of Polish Jews in America announced that it would "be ready to give not only financial and moral support, but also their very lives";[1] and Barney had, within his family circle at least, stolen the limelight. "We flew to Boston in an airplane and liked it a lot."[2]

"The clouds can't get over your aerial visit yet. But then, you people always do things with a bang, when you get around to them," Sarah wrote before getting to the real news. "Hitler, like most maniacs is raving stark mad with the sun invisible. So, do come back by boat or train, to clear up matters."[3] Leah, glued to the radio, wrote "Polish cities had been attacked by planes . . . the whole day has had a nightmarish quality."[4] Speaking for Anuta Greenhouse, who was "too upset" to respond herself, Nathan's wife wrote, "And then you come along with a 'bombshell.' Your airplane trip, of course. It's a good thing you are so far away, or would you 'get it.' "[5]

By mid-month "the town of Lomza was captured after particularly heavy fighting."[6] Lengthy, vivid descriptions of stampeding refugees and "panic-stricken civilians afoot, on bicycles and in peasant carts drawn by emaciated horses" choking the roads appeared on page one of the *Times*.[7] No correspondence exists concerning Newman relatives who remained in Poland but Annalee was in touch with her uncles, Anuta's brothers, and her cousins in France, whom she had met during her student sojourn, and their letters were alarming.

America was not yet at war; but the non-aggression pact—along with the Soviet Union's invasion of Finland in December—would impact Barney in a way entirely unforeseen. They were the significant cause, some months hence, of the breakup of the group known as the American Artists' Congress, which had been formed in 1936 under the influence of the Popular Front of the Communist Party.[8] In April 1940, seventeen artists including Avery, Gottlieb, "M[ark] Rothkowitz," and art historian Meyer Schapiro resigned.

The American Artists Congress, which was founded to oppose war and fascism and to advance the professional interests of artists, at its last membership meeting on April 4, endorsed the Russian invasion of Finland and implicitly defended Hitler's position by assigning the responsibility for the war to England and France . . . . It has failed to react to the Moscow meeting of Soviet and Nazi art officials and official artists, which inaugurated the new esthetic policy of cementing totalitarian relations through exchange exhibitions. Moreover, congress officials have informed members that participation in a projected fascist show at Venice is a matter of individual taste. The congress no longer deserves the support of free artists. We, therefore, declare our secession from the congress and call on fellow-artists within and outside it to join us in considering ways and means of furthering mutual interests which the congress can only damage.[9]

Gottlieb and Rothko—he changed his name that year—were among those who founded the Federation of Modern Painters and Sculptors "to promote the welfare of free, progressive artists working in America."[10] The artists, who experienced "the repercussions [of German aggression] as strongly as though they were only yards away," affirmed their "social obligation to keep and protect freedom" by standing for the "kind of artistic independence the world struggle symbolized."[11] It was through this group, in 1943, that Barney, not a member and not yet painting, would officially enter the most vital segment of the New York art community.

At the same time that Barney's future cohort—already entering middle age—were feeling internal pressure to clarify their place in the world philosophically, the very experience of the world was changing optically. And that, too, they were forced to confront.

At the World's Fair, which opened in April 1939 and ran through October 1940, the public saw for the first time a multitude of wonders: television, color photography, and the marvel of fluorescent lights. This was a vision entirely new: "linear stick[s] of brightness" occurred nowhere in nature.[12] Although the science for fluorescent lamps had been understood for over seventy-five years, it had languished, unexploited and unseen; a practical use had only been devised in 1938, and even then it wasn't clear whether they would simply replace incandescent lamps as a more efficient light source—as incandescent lamps had replaced flames—or if industrial designers and architects would elaborate their unique characteristics. The designers working on the World's Fair, realizing the potential, arranged to channel the lights into the fair as a "proving ground," and the very first installations appeared there. Dazzlingly, streets and walkways were lined with fluorescent light; magically, the fair's numerous "zones" were distinguished by different colors. At the Glass Center, "patterns of lamps reflected in ceilings and windows, produced an effect never seen before"; the Netherlands pavilion incorporated columns of light into the building structure. Of all the unimaginable information, sensations of motion and speed, unexpected flavors, and unfamiliar eroticism that would enchant giddy fairgoers, the transformative qualities and playfulness of the light caused—literally—the profoundest experience of enlightenment.

The fair was a stunning undertaking. Its scale and ambition—cultural and geographic—were intended as a kind of vitamin B12 therapy for a society still scratching its way out of the crater of the Depression. It was promoted with unprecedented coordination by the public relations genius Edward Bernays: the federal government, New York sports teams, Albert Einstein, Howard Hughes were just a few of the recruited boosters.

The visual art component was enormous. Older art was prominently featured in various pavilions: Vermeer's *The Milkmaid*, in the Netherlands hall; "Five Centuries of French History Mirrored in Five Centuries of French Art" in the French. In a "Masterpieces of Art" building, in 1939, 13th- to 18th-century works, and in 1940, 18th- to mid-20th-century works, were loaned from mostly American collections. These were insured for 30 million dollars (over 664 million dollars in 2023) each year—the price tag itself a source of wonder. In its thirty-five galleries there hung works by Leonardo and Michelangelo, Rembrandt, Hals, Caravaggio, and Bellini.

But the fair was specifically charged with imagining the *future*. "Dawn of a New Day" was its slogan, and a view of "the world of tomorrow" its promise. "The eyes of the Fair are on the future—not in the sense of peering toward the unknown nor attempting to foretell the events of tomorrow and the shape of things to come, but in the sense of presenting a new and clearer view of today in preparation for tomorrow . . . . To its visitors the Fair will say: 'Here are the materials, ideas, and forces at work in our world. These are the tools with which the World of Tomorrow must be made.'"[13]

At least *some* fairgoers wanted to see what the artists would have to say about the world of tomorrow. The major fair-sponsored exhibition "Contemporary Art Today" was conceived late in the planning, in April 1938, following protests from the art world at the absence of art programming.[14] In what was either an emphatic display of democracy or abdication of professional responsibility, artists were selected by votes of nationwide sub-committees, and visitors voted to have works purchased and given to museums.[15] "Every school and every phase of opinion in the American art world" was represented on the selection committees, assured Holger Cahill, director of the exhibition.[16] The 40,000-square-foot Contemporary Arts Building—later called the "American Art Today Pavilion"—displayed eight thousand works in twenty-three galleries.[17] Not surprisingly, the approach made for "a dull, vapid promise on mediocrity," even the conservative critic Peyton Boswell had to admit.[18] It certainly confirmed in Barney a lifelong, virulent opposition to juried shows, and to participating in any. Although Cahill was concurrently the national director of the WPA's Federal Art Project, the 1939 exhibition did not have a WPA connection. In 1940 that changed: as the new organizer, the WPA abandoned the juried approach and mounted a curated show

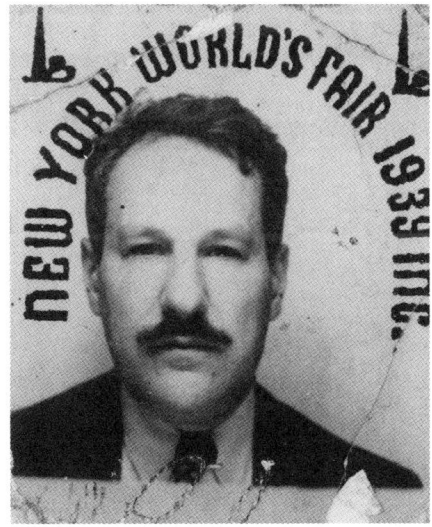

Fig. 13 Barnett Newman's 1939 World's Fair press credentials

of progressive works by American artists. This time the result, wrote Boswell, possessed "a higher aesthetic level and more frequent peak of individual achievement than last year's lamented consensus."[19] Sixteen New York art societies, including the American Abstract Artists and American Artists Professional League, participated in 1940, and the Federation of Modern Painters and Sculptors installed a separate show in the rotunda of the pavilion.[20]

Officially, 105 murals and 102 sculptures were commissioned for the fairgrounds.[21] As "contemporary" as the work was, under the influence of Cubism, Futurism, and Fauvism—all of which had been known in New York since the 1913 Armory Show—the visual impact of the startlingly new lighting, and the transfiguration of the futuristic grounds could only have made depictive painting seem inadequate to Barney and his peers. Especially, as the war began, they despaired of painting's usual content.

"The general feeling, I suppose, was that it didn't matter what you painted, as long as you made the painting plastic, that you got a living quality into the color, that you expressed yourself in terms of mood. So that the accents were on self-expression," Barney told an interviewer in 1963 about pre-war painting. "We thought, perhaps, that it was a moral commitment, but we began to question . . . how much of a moral commitment one was making when one painted a cello player in a distorted way, or took the figure and distorted it to represent our own feelings. Somehow the subject matter . . . became highly questionable. And, also, the nature of the subject matter was then *random*. As a result of the WPA, as a result of all that subject matter" with its overtones of "folklore, one began to ask oneself the question, what is painting? Like, What *IS* it?"[22] Others were feeling similarly disheartened. "A crisis," said Baziotes of this moment. "Got depressed. Couldn't paint . . . I didn't care for the spirit about New York City."[23] It had become "difficult to assume anything," wrote Greenberg, theorizing about the avant garde more broadly, but, significantly, writing in New York. "All the verities . . . are thrown into question," the artist is "no longer able to estimate the response of his audience to the symbols and references with which he works."[24]

Barney in the following months studied works by Cézanne, van Gogh, Toulouse-Lautrec, Redon, Gauguin, Rouault, Picasso, Derain, Modigliani, Degas, Maillol, Despiau, Gilbert Stuart, and Chardin at the exhibition and sale of "The Entire Collection of Mrs. Cornelius J. Sullivan" (a founder of the Museum of Modern Art). He went to see "Italian Masters" at the Museum of Modern Art—Titian's *Pope Paul III*, Botticelli's *Birth of Venus*, Raphael's *Madonna of the Chair*, Masaccio's *Crucifixion*, and Bernini's *Costanza Buonarelli*, among twenty-eight art-historical landmarks—and "Courbet: Tenth Anniversary Exhibition" at Marie Harriman Gallery.[25] He was trying to find a way for himself. Many years later, he spoke about what gripped him about the experience of original works: "In those years . . . anything that I knew or studied about 'art history' came from my encounter with the original works. It was not through photographs, reproductions or from slides . . . . What was important for me was something that went beyond the work, that had to do with the men who had done them. Here was a world of miracles made not by magicians or by an apocalyptic muse but by men, creative men . . . . who said clearly that art is a human activity . . . . The thought that others had done it and lived it only whetted my desire to create, that I could do it—not what had been done but that which hadn't *yet* been done."[26]

It was always, for Barney, about the men. In 1947, to answer a question about "attitudes of . . . artists on their art and contemporaneousness," Barney came up with one of his famously clever—and carefully self-confirming—aphorisms: "An artist paints so that he will have something to look at; at times he must write so that he will also have something to read."[27] But he was much more explicit about the agency driving him in private correspondence: "In discussing . . . the crisis that exists in painting in America today, it occurs to me in rethinking our conversation that we were . . . really discussing the crisis of artists as men, as human beings not the crisis in the art, for *the crisis of artists as men is no different from the crisis of other men*, but I fail to see any crisis in the art [emphasis added]." Minimizing the formal or aesthetic influence of the European "refugee painter" in America, he located their impact elsewhere: they "gave the American artists a sense of dignity, a sense of self respect for he saw them as fellow artists struggling to delve into their inner recesses."[28]

He was "very depressed"; he was "drifting away" from the idea of painting and was "casting about."[29]

All over New York people were meeting to listen to and discuss the crucial issues of the day. Some congregated informally, some riotously; Barney was attracted to the dignified presentation. He continued to follow the new season of the Cooper Union Forum: Saturday evenings addressed developments in and philosophies of astronomy, psychology, sociology, education, law, the sciences, and religion; Tuesday evenings were devoted to "This Critical Year"—political and social questions; and Friday evenings, "Bread and Roses": "The Artist's Place in the World at War," "Diaghileff: Or How a Personality Became a Synonym for an Art." The seeds of the 1948 Friday night speaker sessions of "The Subjects of The Artist School" were planted at this time.

Also incubating, and not just within Barney, was the justification for *teaching* art: what exactly was the point? Mark Rothko, whose lost "theoretical treatise on painting" dates from this time, produced the fragmentary *Scribble Book*, an outgrowth of his years teaching children and his credo that there is a "difference between sheer skill and skill that is linked to spirit, expressiveness and personality." These were exactly the sorts of issues that drove Barney crazy in the bureaucracy-fraught teaching exams. Rothko's *Scribble Book* referenced Plato, Kant, and Nietzsche, and relied heavily on the philosophy and psychology of art-education developed by Franz Cizek. Although he was equally well read, Barney's ideas were more firmly based *in* the empirical experience of teaching in schools, his frustration, and his memory of how a great teacher could be a transformative experience.

During this time of Barney's fixation on the *profession* of and qualifications for teaching "art appreciation"—aspects that, at this moment, would blur in Barney's mind with the idea of actually *being* an artist—he clipped Edward Alden Jewell's review of *Gist of Art* by John Sloan.

> Loved for his sympathetic attitude toward people and their individual or collective problems; respected for his consistently liberal views, his uncompromising independence, John Sloan has long occupied a very particular niche in the realm of contemporary American art. He is the artist's guide, philosopher and friend. He is himself the artist through and through. And he brings to the profession of teaching a fervor so intense that it might almost be described as mystical. There are, to be sure, many liberal and independent minds. There are many artists, many teachers. There is only one John Sloan.[30]

In March 1939, Barney had asked Sloan to examine the drawings that were failed by the Board of Examiners "in spite of my nine years of teaching experience . . . and my many years of study at the Art Students League in your class and with others. At that visit," Barney wrote to Sloan one year later seeking his help, "you were very favorably impressed with my work done for this test and you promised to give me a letter to that effect . . . . At the present time, circumstances are such that I can really fight the Board's decision and I would very much appreciate the letter concerning your reaction to my test papers."[31]

The new "circumstances" were that Barney would now get his "case" heard at the state level. Somehow he had managed to testify at a public hearing of the Commission on Quasi-Judicial Action of Administrative Agencies in June and to have his self-edited testimony entered into the record. "The leaders of the Federal Art Project . . . succeeded in achieving educational values that were comparable with the best teaching of the progressive movement," Barney read and underlined in a catalogue for an exhibition of children's art; they had "effectively undertaken the salvation of the creative spirit of youth in the largest and most complex city in the world."[32]

The *salvation* of the creative spirit. That is what Barney in his testimony warned was at stake if the contribution of the substitute teacher were not recognized.

> One of the most interesting phases of American art history in the last decade has been entirely overlooked. Occupied with the ever changing complexion of American art no time has been found to examine the changes that have taken place in our art audiences. No longer is it confined to the sugar magnates and the expatriate aesthetes. The depression with its New Deal have [*sic*] created an entirely new audience—the taxpayer. Either as a direct buyer of art or facsimile reproductions, or as the indirect purchaser of WPA Post Office murals, or as the purchaser of bargain newspaper reproductions of Van Gogh the artist knows he must depend for recognition and livelihood not on dealers and connoisseurs, but on the high school graduate.

Without a "conscious audience" art could not "thrive"; without "high school courses in art appreciation" there could be no conscious audience. "The art teachers are the builders of America's art audience."

> Today 22,000 are studying art in the New York high school to 2,700 ten years ago. The improvement in tastes both concerning the fine arts and industrial design is visible everyplace . . . . From fountain pens to a locomotive, from a circular to a mural every object must meet the approval of sensibilities. The WPA art project is reframed by youths who only a few years ago were in our high schools.[33]

In his testimony, Barney spoke about the need to educate to "honestly appraise, enjoy and recognize beauty everywhere." Later, he would discard "beauty" as a worthwhile value: it was weighted with a "pseudophilosophic attitude . . . that saw it as the moral expression of society" and obscured true art's true nature, and he completely denied "that art has any concern with the problem of beauty and where to find it."[34] Here, in 1940, Barney rejoiced that art education created the improvement in industrial design that is "visible everyplace." Later, the conflation of art with design—specifically in the Bauhaus-inflected art department of Brooklyn College and in exhibitions at the Museum of Modern Art like "Useful Household Objects Under $5" and "Bauhaus 1919–1928"—became a particular *bête noire*. He was "repelled" by commercial art, "with its useful objects, superficial designs and ideology of the commonplace."[35]

That Barney was inconsistent or equivocated in his principles only reveals the consistency of his nature. He was as invested in his pre-painting activities of the 1930s and early '40s as he was in the conviction that he was an artist. Unlike other artists, who took jobs with the knowledge that they were the means to support their "real" work, Barney was one hundred percent committed to *everything* he did, and he bled and suffered one hundred percent on every commitment's behalf. It was a characteristic that marked his entire life, regardless of the ups and downs of his career. He felt most alive when he was taking a stand. *End of Silence, Be, Vir Heroicus Sublimis, The Way, Right Here, Not There—Here, Here, Here, Here*, he would title paintings and sculptures. Friends and compatriots individually came to terms with the endearing and admirable, and irritating and exasperating, quality. He loved a good contentious fight. He loved to make a point. "He loved to make a point so much that he would sometimes make it over the wrong issue."

Ben Heller was one of those friends. "You [had] to understand the Stance. With a capital S. He had to take stances on certain issues. Then if he had the stance . . . he got the theoretical construct afterwards."[36] Every one of Barney's vocations was selected, a conscious, intellectual choice by the sentient man, and the man was an artist. The true purpose of art was "the expression of intellectual content." Its true *origin*, though, was not its utility as a "social" act, but the "ecstatic outburst" of power: man's "artistic nature."[37]

THIRTEEN
OBJECTOR

He was 35 years old; more than half his life was over. He was beginning to thicken around the middle and jaw-line but still had a thick and bushy thatch on his head, even as he sought advice from diet books and weight-loss programs and *Save Your Hair!* He had bedrock principles, he had many talents, he had intelligence, perseverance, and taste. His wit and charm were acknowledged. He had identified his short-term goals and his ultimate ambition. But he was not ratified—neither in public nor in his gut—as a teacher *or* as an artist. As the former, at least, he had the confidence to passionately engage the battle, he never cringed from the campaign, nor was he deterred by pride: perversely, he was willing to humiliate himself in the crusade for his dignity. As an artist, however, his fortitude failed him. The risk was too great, the exposure too extreme.

Ensconced in yet another new apartment, "Our Cooperative House," at 433 West Twenty-First Street across from the Theological Seminary, he appreciated the amenities suited to one chronically irritated in his surroundings: "quiet neighbors . . . a little [Consumers' Cooperative Services] cafeteria on the ground floor where you can slip in for an inexpensive meal . . . or, if you are tired, have a meal sent upstairs to your apartment . . . . The independent Subway, the Ninth Avenue 'L', the new 23rd Street Cross Town buses, and ferries to New Jersey" close at hand. Again, it was an aspirational step up: they could have had one room and kitchen for 60 dollars per month, or two rooms and kitchenette for 65 dollars, but they splurged on a three-room, plus kitchen, apartment on the fifth floor at a rent of 75.85 dollars. They acquired the grand piano that would be with them for the rest of Barney's life.

In the sun-filled rooms, with "cool fresh air from the river and a view of the Hudson"[1] he was suffering from a colossal case of procrastination. He was all over a map that did not have a painting studio on it. In a manic burst of initiative, between the end of March and the beginning of June, while he was preparing his testimony, he sent out letters. He wrote to Sloan. He wrote to Marian Anderson—weeks after the "publishing sensation of the year," Richard Wright's shattering portrayal of Black experience in America, *Native Son*, was released—requesting an interview:

> My dear Miss Anderson: I am writing an article on "The Metropolitan and the Negro Singer" which will be a study of the relations between American Opera houses and Negro talent . . . There is a feeling growing that the stir in Washington over your appearance there is by no means the real issue. Far more serious is it that the Negro is being barred from the great music institutions of the country. Only by gaining entrance there, can the Negro artist hope to break down permanently the doors of the D.A.R. Halls throughout the country. [She was not available.][2]

He wrote to George Backer, publisher of the *New York Post*, offering himself as a columnist for a proposed "civil service page":

> as Councilman, you are very much aware of the important role civil service is playing and will play in the public and political life of our community, and as New York's most progressive publisher, you should not overlook this valuable field of readers . . . . I assure you that I shall be able to make the New York Post the most important voice for leadership among civil service people and a source of enlightenment to the general public.[3]

He wrote to the director of WQXR radio station to propose a series on "the classical and popular music of the Pan-American republics":

> The whole idea, it seems to me, has unusual merit from an artistic and educational point of view and the added value of timeliness since the World's Fair this year is accenting the Pan-American theme.[4]

He wrote to Ralph Ingersoll, publisher of *PM*, "A new kind of Newspaper," before the first issue had even appeared:

> do you realize that you are overlooking the very important field of civil service? . . . This valuable news field must be covered in PM by means of a civil service page or column . . . . May I offer my services to you as the logical writer of such a feature . . . I am confident that should you permit me, I can establish PM as a model in the field of civil service journalism.[5]

Again he was needed to move his mother and seriously ill father, and Gertrude and Sarah, this time from their ground-floor apartment in Forest Hills into an apartment on the Upper West Side adjacent to the Columbia University campus. And he continued to strategize and write endless letters in the patent fight. By the time Alex Borodulin contacted him in the middle of June with an oddly ambitious proposal—in the spirit of Barney's own compulsiveness—Barney was verging on exhaustion.

"The war, of course, has completely gone to my head," wrote Borodulin in June 1940, a few days after Paris fell to German troops.

> The abject stupidity of the ruling castes of the Allies has brought us to a point where it is not only going to cost us money and liberty, but also life. As far as I can see there is no other alternative than military preparation.
>
> I saw a picture of the newly designed uniform for the coming army. From the waist up . . . it consisted of at least six buttons—with as many buttonholes. The whole idea was at least a full generation away from the kind of war that Hitler induces. I have in mind the photographs of men . . . returning from Flanders, many

without their pants, some without their jackets. In short, the modern uniform is perfect for the last war, but needs complete redesigning for this one.

I have in mind to design a practical efficient uniform, one that can be cut out of one sheet of cloth (woven, if necessary, to specifications) which would open and close in one operation by means of a zipper . . . I should like to work with you on this, both because of your experience with clothes, and your letter-head. If we can accomplish something intelligent then I would be prepared to go to Washington with it.

All my activities have been suspended while I hang in front of the radio and pull my quickly graying hair at the stupidity that emanates . . . Petain's fatuous speech . . . . Mussolini from the Piazza . . . . our rulers, the ones who submerge millions of people into slaughter's hot river.[6]

Barney's response was more focused on covering his own buttocks:

These last few days have been hectic—I've appeared before the State Commission on Quasi-Judicial Action of Administrative Agencies—there's a name for you—in private and public hearing to make long speeches. I've had to worry about full-day hearings before lawyers and with a piano to buy amidst everything I couldn't answer your letter—

I do not know whether I could help you in the undertaking because I would have to decide whether the design of a military uniform would not involve a betrayal of my pacifist position. I would need decide it as a moral question first.

But I would like to hear your plan and help you as much as I can if it is possible for me to do so.[7]

Both men relished self-righteous intellectual combat, and the opportunity for disputation; Borodulin could not let that phrase—"involve a betrayal of my pacifist position . . . moral question first"—pass. As his old partner in secular *pilpul*,[8] Borodulin was the one who could knock Barney off his pedestal.

I think it is characteristic of pacifism that it can no more adjudicate a particular instance than any other generalization. . . . The principle which is higher than pacifism, since it rules among rules themselves, is what Buddha calls the Cardinal Sin—Stupidity. My reaction was to military stupidity, not to any issue of war or peace. If a human being is going to be put into uniform, then my principle says that for good or evil the uniform itself should not be a hindrance to the man, at least no handicap . . . . Morality is not a force, but an ideal. And only forces can be manipulated.[9]

"Whilst all pacifists need not be anarchists," Herbert Read wrote in *The Modern Monthly*, "all anarchists must be pacifists" since "if pacifism is not possible, then anarchism is not possible." If there were a requirement for Barney to justify logically his position, to establish what Ben Heller called the theoretical construct for his prepositioned "Stance," it would be this. But philosophy was not the only thing on his mind: the first peacetime draft in United States history would go into effect on September 16, requiring all men 18 to 65 to register; those up to 45 years old were eligible for immediate induction. As early as April, he was collecting literature from the War Resisters League,[10] and in July contacted The Community Church of New York: "I am very anxious to know whether it is true that you are conducting a registry for conscious objectors. If so, will you kindly send me the necessary forms or applications and information concerning this very important haven?"[11]

"Conscientious Objector" status was granted to those who could demonstrate "sincerity of belief in religious teachings combined with a profound moral aversion to war" (the War Resisters League information included "Special Problem of Some Conscientious Objectors of Jewish Birth") and there were practical repercussions: the law explicitly required "work of national importance under civilian direction"— designing a military uniform would not have compromised his application—and conscientious objectors often performed long hours of hazardous work in Civilian Public Service Camps. Of the seventy-two thousand men who registered, fifty-two thousand received the status. How or whether Barney validated his case, he did not receive the classification nor perform alternative service. In 1941 he had a physical and was classified 4F, unfit for service, for an unrecorded reason. Ordered to report for another physical some months later, he protested, writing that he was instructed "to disregard notice to appear . . . since you already classified me as 4F. I fail to understand, however, why you have not at the same time classified me as a conscientious objector as it seems to me that such classification supersedes any other?" The Selective Service System did not agree. *They* prioritized 4F. "Should there be any change in the rules of Selective, you will be notified. We trust that this answers your question."[12]

It was an answer, but it didn't satisfy Barney's point. It wasn't simply that he preferred not to go to war; he had his "Stance." And, in this case, he later told Hess, he took "a radical anarchist stand—that he did believe in killing, and would kill Nazis, but didn't want anybody to tell him who to kill. 'Joining the army would deprive me of my right to kill.' "[13]

The schizophrenia of daily existence in 1940 was regularly on display in the magazine *Life*. Did Barney buy the May 27 issue—with its tightly cropped cover photo of a German soldier's profile and weapon and the single word, "INVADER"—because of its coverage of the "lightning war," which brought Hitler's army to the English Channel and cut off Allied troops, or because of the generously illustrated "Cranbrook-Life Exhibition: Great Detroit Art Center Holds a Democratic Show of 60 Paintings by Living Americans"?

The lead story called the *Blitzkrieg* "like the Apocalypse, like the end of the world." Maps traced the "German Wave Sweeping Westward," a wave into which Barney's

Polish relatives had disappeared and behind which Annalee's French aunts, uncles, and cousins were trapped.

Dovetailing with the "Nine days that shook the world," the Cranbrook layout was meant to swell the patriotic breasts of readers with paintings that were symbolic "of America's increasing responsibility as a democratic world art center." Edward Hopper, John Curry, Zoltan Sepeshy, Ernest Fiene, Fletcher Martin, with a host of forgettable others, were represented by their most jejune work, Peter Blume by one of his "happy pictures."

They were just the type of paintings that brought Barney and his crowd to despair. In the summer issue of *Partisan Review* Greenberg declared the "present superiority" of abstract art in his coming-of-age essay, "Towards a Newer Laocoon." Barney was, as much as Greenberg, uninspired by "realistic illusion in the service of [the] sentimental and declamatory." But he was not convinced by the art of avant-garde, abstract "purists"—"isolated, concentrated and defined" by the medium. And so Barney decided "it was more interesting to study nature than to paint it,"[14] and escaped to a naturalist camp in Medomak, Maine. The Newmans had been attending courses at the Brooklyn Botanical Gardens, learning about flowers and trees. Barney had been intrigued by the camp run by the National Association of Audubon Societies since it began in 1935, and at least once before had come close to enrolling. Something in their lives at this point felt settled—or *un*settled—enough for them to go now.

The camp promised "to provide teachers, youth leaders, and other interested adults with field experience and practical program suggestions for developing genuine interest in birds, mammals, insects, plants, marine and other wildlife." For 102 dollars (partially funded by the Greenhouses) Barney and Annalee spent the two-week session "out-of-doors by the sea, participating in informal field classes," and picnics, games, songs, swimming, and nap time. "Lights out" and "absolute quiet" would prevail at 10:00 p.m. It must have been quite an adjustment for the smoking, drinking night-owl Barney. He and Annalee diligently noted physical descriptions and attributes, habitats and behavior, in their notebooks, providing inspiration for at least one poem, a bizarrely dark vision for Leah's son: "To Joseph on the Occasion of His Seventh Birthday."

> Do you know, that now, the snowy egret
> Would, to you, be a vanished secret
> That men with knives cut out their lives
> For pennies, so other men's jennies and wives
> Ugly and smugly, foolish as cats
> Could strut new impudence with feathers in their hats?
> But Audubon, busy with brush in hand
> Such a blush of shame painted o'er the land
> Now men spend their lives to give life to the egret
> Now it thrills with its flight, its plight brings no regret.

(The frustrated irritability so present in Barney's letters, and his racking doubt, became something more tortured in his occasional poetry. Earlier in the year, he wrote the extraordinarily revealing "To a young poet age 4" addressed to Joseph's sister: "I hear, little Judy, you want to be a poet / A poet? What it means, do you know it? / A poet to most men is a man idiotic / A fool, an idler, of course a neurotic / A man who talks in accents periodic / . . . Who needs such a one in a world so chaotic / Unwanted the poet with accents emphatic / . . . He contemplates the true *nature*.)"

As the story goes, upon returning to the city Annalee said "I want a divorce." "Why?" Barney asked. "Because I married a painter I didn't marry a teacher."[15] And so to free his days Barney began seven years, four nights a week at the Washington Irving Evening High School teaching "Block-Printing, Batik, Silk-Screen and Other Textile Processes." Yet *still* he avoided committing to his own painting, *again* he retreated to his comfort zone of writing, *again* he presented himself as an expert in an area others (he claimed) had not recognized. Silk-screen "is a new printing process which has been adapted to the textile industry only within the last few years and it is expected that it will help capture for America the leadership in the field of luxury textiles," he wrote to the editor of *Popular Science Monthly*. "I have found the demand and need for information . . . to be so unusually great that I am convinced that an article describing it would be of interest to your many readers who are looking for a hobby, scientifically fascinating, artistically stimulating and commercially profitable. Would you . . . consider such an article."[16]

For the fifteen months following his return from Audubon Camp, until the attack on Pearl Harbor—a day further dramatized by the funeral of Abraham's bachelor brother, the small and dear Elie—there was notably little production of any kind on Barney's part. "We were very hard up, but I insisted that Barney stay in his studio," Annalee recalled about those days. She was paid once a month, the checks arriving close to three o'clock, which made it almost impossible to get them into the bank before the next day. "Barney and I worked out his schedule so that he would come to the school, to the side door, and wait for me. I would bring him my check and then he would rush off to deposit it before three," when banks closed for the day.

They were living close to the edge, but agreed that appearances must be maintained. One day, a clerk from the school office came to Annalee's classroom to tell her that the bank had called. "The president of the local branch got on the phone, and said: 'Mrs. Newman, you have made a check out for a loan. We didn't think a nice person like you would have a loan. Is it true?'"[17]

"Nice" people like the Newmans attended the Metropolitan Opera—Ezio Pinza in *Le Nozze di Figaro* and *Don Giovanni*; Rose Bampton as *Alcesti*; *The Bartered Bride*; *Fidelio*—and programs at Carnegie Hall and other venues. The tickets were likely appreciation from Annalee's music-loving family, for Barney had been constant regarding the anguish and tribulation, the "passion" of Samuel Greenhouse—and Samuel, as it turned out, was vulnerably, not to say manipulatively, reliant upon him.

Samuel's gnawing feelings of injustice resonated with his empathetic son-in-law. He raged at the lawyers, he raged at his partners, he raged at the accused, and, intermittently he raged at Barney: the lawyer was "not the man for it. And yet every time Shannon came to work you took him out for a good time!" Then he would turn around, recount the goings on in excruciating detail, and plead for Barney's help: "I'm tearing up this letter because I don't want to cause you any trouble. If you could type it in English I'll sign it." Or: "It's hard for me to write. When you type my letter include not just yourselves but our whole family. I think there will be fireworks." Or: "this time I will not let them off the hook. We can't let this moment pass us by. It is an opportunity for us . . . . Write me your reply right away."

The letters continued through the summer of 1941, reaching Barney and Annalee at Cornell University, where they pursued their studies in ornithology and added "Trees and Shrubs (Botany)." Barney wrote draft after draft of letters for Samuel to send to the various parties, lawyers, co-plaintiffs, expert witnesses, while both he and Annalee filled course workbooks and personal notebooks with written assignments, field work, and notational sketches. These new studies—like almost every experience in Barney's life—ignited almost random fires of inspiration, creativity, and somewhat arrogant showboating.

Not satisfied with playing the student, he devised a system to categorize birds along a scale from most primitive to most advanced according to the complexity of their song. Most primitive was the loon with no pattern or variation to its single cry. Finches, wild sparrows, and canaries had patterned songs of many notes with many variations and each offspring had a different song from its parents. His theory was received skeptically. Although Barney did respectably in the undergraduate-level course, he told a friend twenty-two years later that the teacher, the distinguished Dr. A. A. Allen—famous for his work recording bird calls—was "always making him a fool."[18] Nevertheless, Barney would forever after enlist this six-week session as evidence that he was scientifically trained, and that "I know what I'm talking about."[19] More significantly, the notebooks from that summer provided the raw visual material for a group of wax- and oil-crayon, and pastel drawings that Barney would make three years later—the earliest of his works that survive.

Shortly before they went to Ithaca they moved again. It didn't start out well.

Day after day has been spent shivering and my wife and I have been sick as a result. For the first time in my life I developed a chest cold . . . . ever since we moved in to this apartment we have never had a temperature of 70° . . . If 64° is the best you can do with a new furnace, boiler, steam units and all the coal you claim you use then this is hopeless. As you know I have been put to terrible inconvenience + hardship . . . I have invested $200 <u>our complete savings</u> in improving an apartment because we were anxious to be happy here . . . . I ask that you release me from my lease. I will leave you all of my improvements and go my way and you will get a new tenant who will perhaps better appreciate your "services." . . . I am not the right tenant for you + you are not the proper agent for me . . . I have had to . . . write you letters to fill a whole file. I have done it until now but I refuse to continue to spend the rest of the year degrading myself.

He threatened to remove the steam vents and pay "a cold water flat rent" or, in language remarkably akin to that he used to the landlord of their first apartment in 1936, "be forced to go to court to invalidate the lease on the grounds of 'destructive eviction.' "[20]

But they stayed in the floor-through apartment in a remodeled brownstone at 343 East Nineteenth Street for sixteen battle-scarred years. The run-down area had been known since the late 19th century as the Gas House district in acknowledgment of the number of large storage tanks just to the east. When Barney and Annalee arrived, all but four had been felled for the construction of the East River Drive on landfill from bombed British cities, and almost immediately the area began to change drastically, with planning for the massive development of Stuyvesant Town. By the time the first occupants arrived in 1947, 600 buildings containing 3,100 families, 500 stores and small factories, three churches, three schools, and two theaters had been razed in "the greatest and most significant mass movement of families in New York's history."[21] As had happened on the Lower East Side and in the Bronx, Barney was once again smack in the middle of enormous physical and demographic change and growth, and it was reflected in his own domestic life. Stressing his seriousness about painting a few years after the move, Barney asked Tony Smith for advice. "The first thing you have to do is get rid of all this bourgeois Jewish furniture," Smith told him.[22] The apartment's furnishings shifted from overstuffed to simple sturdy and functional office pieces, and Barney began to acquire the classic solid oak "Bank of England" chairs that, over his life, became as identified with him as his monocle and mustache. But the Steinway grand piano remained, creatively positioned in the living room by Smith, and several prized possessions—antique Chinese and Persian rugs, a 17th-century English table,

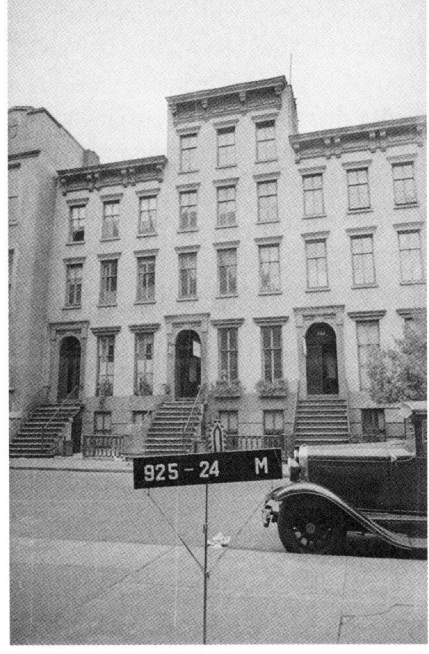

Fig. 14 343 East Nineteenth Street (center), 1940. New York City Department of Finance

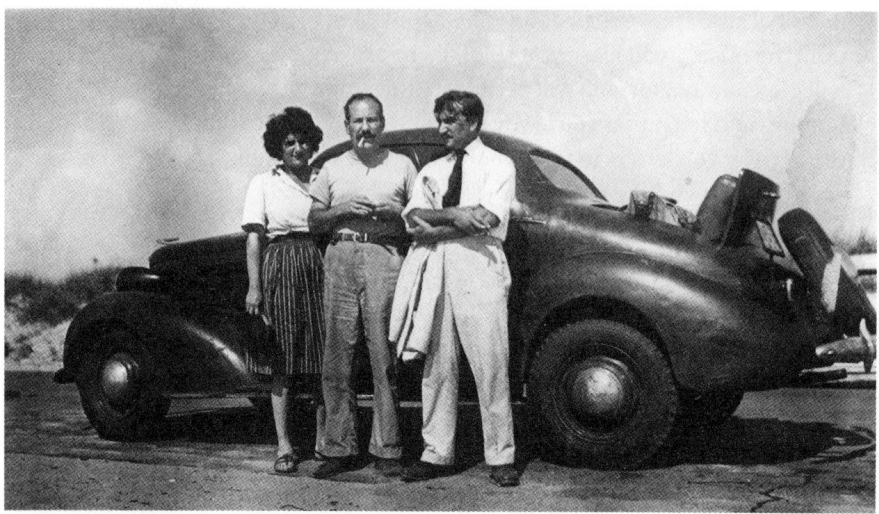

Fig. 15 Annalee Newman, Barnett Newman, and Theodoros Stamos with the Chevrolet Master Deluxe Sport Coupe in Provincetown, Massachusetts, 1946

an "imported" Chinese wicker chair, a French Provincial table, some "Louis XVI antique needlework"—were eventually incorporated, along with what he claimed were "1000" books.[23]

Notably for someone in Barney's situation where it was in no way a necessity— and even friends who routinely left the city relied on trains—he acquired his first car: a 1937 Chevrolet Master Deluxe Sport Coupe. Cars had been among the most aggressively promoted, and most glamorously seductive, visions of the future at the World's Fair and advertisements in eye-popping color filled popular magazines. Barney's dignity-defending missives were intended to present a refined persona but made him sound like a crotchety old grandfather; and his sense of *comme il faut* self-presentation pretty much stalled at the fashion of this period. But inside him there also lived an adventurer like the popular character Bulldog Drummond. Just as he had intrepidly boarded an airplane when civilian flights were exceedingly rare and terrible accidents were common, Barney saw himself sweeping into his brilliantly imagined future in the appropriate vehicle.

And there was another change: all the passion, impersonal *com*passion, intelligent discrimination, and rhetorical skill that were lavished on the various campaigns of the previous years would shortly be marshaled in the service of what he always believed had called him: the unique power of art. As he conceived it. He never doubted that was his bedrock, but *how* to manifest it?—that had paralyzed and deflected him. With the war, with humanity threatened, he became a zealot for a route to the meaning of life. Or, at least, his own life.

FOURTEEN

POLEMICS

"Physical custody or the temporary importation of European artists and works of art . . . [is] only a small part of our task," *Art News* under Alfred Frankfurter put its readers on notice at the end of 1940.

> The most remarkable fact about art in 1940 . . . is that there was art at all. Art, that is, worth writing about: art as a living thing created, seen, felt, as a world force. All this there was in America in the year of the Blitzkrieg and the fall of Denmark, of Norway, of Holland, of Belgium, of France; in the year of the Battle of Britain and the Battles of Greece and Egypt . . . . If that is an occasion for thanksgiving, it is also a warning against complacency. It is a clear indication of *the duty that lies before America, of the cultural mandate we must take up on behalf of the now darkened continent from which our own civilization derives* . . .
>
> No matter whether America goes to war or not, one thing is clear. We are today and in the near future the guardians of those arts that demand, for their creation and continuance and safekeeping, at least the outer tranquility and security insured by our geographic position. . . .
>
> We must build our own culture, and build it strongly, securely, purely on American terms, because when peace comes our culture will be offered the dominant place in the world . . . [emphasis added].[1]

Within less than a decade a cadre of ambitious New York artists and their supporters—unlikely to be led by the stodgy *Art News* but living in the larger cultural petri dish it reflected—would receive unimaginable recognition, even, many would say, had staked "the dominant place in the world." But during the pre-war anxiety-filled year of 1941—the year Henry Luce would declare the "American Century"[2]—there remained a gnawing insecurity and professional dissatisfaction among Barney's friends. It was the European artists—escaping the war and arriving in New York in numbers significant enough to capture public attention—with whom the Americans had to come to terms. In New York, particularly the Surrealists' work and their lives had an odor of privileged decadence that was quickly seen by many to be out of sync with the time and place, but their presence was a provocation, and one that catapulted a generation of previously provincial artists to maturity.

Even as Alfred Barr at MoMA didacticized abstract European art with "Cubism and Abstract Art" in 1936, he found the spirit running out of steam. Months later he declared that it was Surrealism that was "growing . . . . now active in a dozen countries of Europe, in North and South America, in Japan" and having the broadest influence "outside the movement."[3] Meyer Schapiro, responding to Barr's codification of abstract art based on formal motivation, agreed that "the older claims of abstract art have lost the original force of insurgent convictions." Nevertheless, Schapiro averred that "the ideas underlying abstract art have penetrated deeply into all artistic theory, even [that] of their original opponents," the Surrealists.

Looking back, what jumps out of Schapiro's essay is how urgently polarized artists' discourse had become: " 'Objective' painters strive for 'pure objectivity,' for the object given in its 'essence' and completeness, without respect to a viewpoint, and the Surrealists derive their images from pure thought, freed from the perversions of reason and everyday experience. Very little is written today—sympathetic to modern art—which does not employ this language of absolutes."[4] Although the Surrealist camp was the flavor of the week and artists' language was charged and oppositional, for a time there was intermingling and overlapping. Like neutrons during atomic fission, under the controlled circumstances of seminars and exhibitions and temporary alliances, artists crashed together and spun apart. Within a few years the energy exploded.

Schapiro's lectures at the New School for Social Research were wildly popular. Hegelian in philosophy, they emphasized style and form and historical context over matters concerning conscious and unconscious sources of inspiration; Picasso, Braque, and Miró were the artists he commended to his students, who included Fairfield Porter, Joan Mitchell, Thomas Hess—and Sarah Newman. At the same time, in 1941, among his colleagues at the New School were the Surrealists Stanley Hayter and Gordon Onslow Ford, a British-born member of the Surrealist Group. The flier for *that* program commended the Surrealists' adventure "in tapping the unconscious psychic world. The aim of these lectures is to follow their work as a psychological barometer registering the desire and impulses of the community." For many New York artists who were searching for a new vision, among them Baziotes, Jimmy Ernst, Robert Motherwell (who landed in New York after sojourns on the West Coast, at Harvard, Columbia University, and in Mexico), and possibly Gorky, Pollock, and Rothko (anecdotal evidence leans both ways)—the lectures and the accompanying small exhibitions were revelatory, challenging them to pursue personal experiment in order to bring about a revolution in consciousness through painting.

At the Riverside Museum the conversation was mostly about Americans. Hans Hofmann—almost a de facto American because of his total embrace by, and encouragement of, a generation of native artists—in February 1941 presided at a symposium on abstract art in conjunction with the fifth exhibition of the zealous American Abstract Artists group. "Every creative artist works continually to penetrate the mysteries of creation," Hofmann acknowledged, but the "correlation between color and form is the plastic basis of painting." Never "was an epoch great through the presentation of a particular subject but rather in this: how such a subject matter was aesthetically presented . . . . A painting that does not fulfill this aesthetic necessity is rather everything else but painting."[5]

Hofmann, Bavarian-born, studied and showed in Germany and Paris in the early 20th century with many of the pillars of modernism. His teaching in America after

1932 emphasized pictorial structure, spatial tension, and color relationship. At the Riverside Museum, his presentation was Hofmann 101:

> a plastic work has always . . . a decorative quality, but not every decorative work has a plastic quality . . . positive [decorative quality] is not only the effect of the resulting tensions in the correlation between form and color but the result of the relationship under the created tensions. It provides the work with the technical quality of translucence and furthermore with the technical quality of expansion and contraction. This is painting in the highest sense of the word and only a few artists ever have reached this high.[6]

Barney sought his own path through these tangled woods. He was uninterested in Cubism or geometric abstraction, which he felt was simply design, "building parts," and he had little sympathy with what was perceived as the Museum of Modern Art's line. MoMA, as far as he was concerned, was a "Cézanne museum" and what he was looking for was the "reaction against Cézanne." The "three-dimensional tactility" didn't interest him, and he "objected to the *cannon-balls* in Cézanne." In Roger Fry, Barney read about "the apple that is more than an apple," and he "didn't get this kind of mysticism," thought it was a vulgarization. Picasso, in Barney's eyes, was a "straight expressionist." Cézanne was a "counter-revolutionary" to what interested Barney. *That* was "the Impressionist idea of even surface [with] no edges." It was the overlooked Pissarro, and Monet, who "did something tremendous . . . changed the painting world."

There were also problems with Surrealism. While he respected the Surreal*ists* Barney "disagreed with the Marxist–Freudian content"[7] and saw it as a "continuous performance."[8] His initial antipathy was concretized a few years later, after the influential Greenberg pronounced that in spite of being largely "literary and antiquarian" Surrealist painting was not entirely without merit since "the reliance upon the unconscious and the accidental" lifted inhibitions and allowed the artist to surrender to his medium. "Surrealism, under this aspect and only under this, culminates the process which has in the last seventy years restored painting to itself and enabled the modern artist to rival the achievements of the past."[9]

One hundred eighty degrees from Greenberg's position, Barney would insist that "the great contribution of surrealism was in its *revival* of subject matter, which had been deliberately avoided by the strong antirealist program of modern art [emphasis added]." He wrote this as visual evidence of the concentration camps was emerging, and could not bring himself to take a hermetic, aesthetic, stance: "the subject matter of surrealism was the most important of our time and definitely linked to our time." The work was

> in the nature of prophecy. For the horror they created and the shock they built up were not merely the dreams of crazy men; they were prophetic tableaux of what the world was to see as reality.[10]

Whether flirting with Surrealist "play" led to better formalist painting or a reinvigoration of meaningful subject, one thing was certain: most American artists felt obligated to reevaluate what they were doing, who they were. And for many, this led to dark places.

"In the 1940s, when artists got together of an evening . . . . playing surrealist games . . . . everyone in the room had to say what it was that destroyed him," Barney wrote in the late 1960s. "I said that I felt destroyed by established institutions. I was surprised to hear one of the artists present say that what destroyed him were people. He was perhaps wiser than I, for I had to go through that Darwinian lesson . . . . I think we were both right, because only those people practice destruction and betrayal who hunger to accept completely the values of the establishment in which they seek a place. It's the establishment that makes people predatory."[11]

In 1941, no matter where on the spectrum of political or aesthetic opinion, the cultural community was galvanized by what they seemed to agree was America's responsibility to Western culture. In February, two months after Frankfurter's announcement that America had a "duty" because "when peace comes our culture will be offered the dominant place in the world," Henry Luce agreed with Herbert Hoover that America was fast becoming the sanctuary of the ideals of civilization. But he also agreed with Frankfurter—envisioning a broader, if less sophisticated, canvas than did the editor of an art magazine: "for the moment it may be enough to be the sanctuary of these ideals . . . [but] not for long. It now becomes our time to be the powerhouse from which the ideals spread though the world and do their mysterious work of lifting the life of mankind from the level of the beasts to what the Psalmist called a little lower than the angels."[12]

The clarion to which the *artists* paid attention occurred in August, while Barney and Annalee were basking in nature at Cornell, the "Garden of Eden . . . where one can forget all worries."[13] Sam Kootz dropped what became notorious as his "bombshell"—a challenge to American artists in the *Times*.

Kootz, the future gallery owner, had written a decade earlier in his book, *Modern American Painters*, that except among his chosen few artists, he did not "find any healthy signs of original impulses."[14] A collector and sometime curator of small shows, Kootz was also a lawyer who worked for years as an advertising executive, and that experience was useful when he took to the print media at the end of 1931 to attract attention to himself and to castigate chauvinism in the art community.[15] Now, in the summer of 1941, Kootz wrote to the *Times*'s powerful art critic Edward Alden Jewell a letter he wanted made public:

Under present circumstances the probability is that the future of painting lies in America. The pitiful fact is, however, that we offer little better than a geographic title to the position of world's headquarters for art. . . .

Consider what our present record is. The recent national roundup at the World's Fair was a representative cross-section, no matter how depressing it seemed. For all our big shots were shown, and a diligent search unearthed the best men in each region. The inference was appalling.

In spite of a decade of gallery-going, Kootz had "not discovered *one* bright, white hope . . . not seen one painter veer from his established course . . . not seen one attempt to experiment, to realize a new method of painting." He was dispirited by both the "pleasant, harmless" subject matter, and the "class-struggle" painting of a few years earlier, which had its potential "killed . . . by no effort to invent new techniques." Not in years has an established painter "wondered *why* he paints that way." Isn't there a *new* way, he asked, "to reveal your ideas, American painters?"

Jewell printed the letter in his column. "Mr. Kootz . . . puts the whole thing right up to the artist himself . . . . If we are seriously interested in art we should be willing to consider . . . any challenge issued by any one, anywhere, at any time." It was "a truly shattering bomb," the critic declared, assuring that the issue would be joined.[16]

Artists answering in the letters column, and in the bars and on the street, agreed with Kootz—the interesting art was not on view. But it did exist, they maintained, in studios. To them, Jewell offered a "concrete proposal":

those artists who have invented a "new way," a "new method,"—let them come out of their studios and organize. Let them form an exhibiting organization and, in some readily accessible place, prove to Mr. Kootz that the picture he drew of American art today is too black . . . . It is up to the artists somehow to come out of their studios into the open . . . . A sort of experimental *Salon des Réfusés* [*sic*] operating . . . on an annual, a permanent, basis.[17]

FIFTEEN

WHAT ABOUT ISOLATIONIST ART?

Barney sat with Gottlieb in Union Square "right after Pearl Harbor." He thought painting was finished, but Gottlieb was more optimistic. Here was Barney's dilemma: everything he saw around him "bored [him] stiff,"[1] and yet he continued to be exquisitely attuned to "vision, the power of vision," and it gnawed at him. "When somebody sees a stroke on a canvas, it does something to them that doesn't happen when they see a movie or read literature. They get either *very* hostile, they get very excited, or they get very passionate. They have to own it."[2] *What* was this thing, "painting" that had such an effect on him?

Gottlieb's state of mind was buoyed by his work; he felt he was finding a different direction, one that eventually would allow Barney to find his own. "Mythic painting started then—around Pearl Harbor," was how Barney connected the events.[3]

Barney had enough insight—or interpretative inclination—to see that there was more than an intellectual interest drawing Gottlieb to the Oedipal myth, that he was refracting the situation with his own mother through Freud. But when Barney contrasted his own "interest" (such a flaccid word for something so powerful) in "terror"—he liked the "*wildness*" of the birds he had studied, he said by example—he didn't, at least publicly, plumb his own psychology,[4] how the omnipresent perturbation sparking between the poles of terror and dignity accounted for his expressive paralysis.

Although Barney had not yet found any *actual* subject, he would forever after identify this moment as pivotal. The artists with whom he identified had accepted that "subject matter didn't matter so much . . . . it didn't matter what you painted, as long as you made the painting plastic, that you got a living quality into the color, that you expressed yourself in terms of mood." The "accents were on self-expression." But suddenly any subject matter that had supported that expression "became highly questionable . . . *random*." As he struggled to identify what he wanted to paint, he was "totally unsatisfied" with "all painting. It didn't say, really, what was crucial."[5] There was yet no physical evidence of any painting by Barney, but there was a lot of *thinking*, and a great deal of discussion certainly with Gottlieb, and Gottlieb was having "many many" similar, searching, discussions with Rothko. They, too, "shared [the] feeling of wanting to find something, and they began using "mythical images verbally"—as titles, not literal images—because the titles "evoked what they were feeling."[6]

The presence of the European Surrealists, Barney later wrote, had enabled the Americans to separate themselves from the literal subject matter that the WPA encouraged, on the one hand, and on the other, theory-driven abstraction—as in the theories and work of Piet Mondrian, then showing at Valentine (Dudensing). But what exactly was emerging? No one was sure.

Gottlieb worried whether the "pictographs" he began making then were "something that could be considered art or not? That is the question [that] came up at that time." Even though he had been exhibiting for many years, at his new work "people seemed to be rather aghast . . . . they didn't consider it painting at all . . . . [it was a] rejection of almost everything . . . that existed as a standard of what good painting is."[7]

"Not only did the artists [Gottlieb and Rothko] have difficulty in deciding whether they were Surrealists or not, but people like Sidney Janis," who placed Gottlieb's *Pictograph #4* and Rothko's *The Omen of the Eagle* under the surrealist label in his 1944 book, *Abstract and Surreal Art in America,* "couldn't decide" either.[8]

Barney's jeremiads, previously about everything else, now became lectures in correct thinking about *art*. More significantly, a new identification emerged. In helping Gottlieb and other members of the Federation of Modern Painters and Sculptors write the screeds and issue the press releases to wage their battles, Barney easily began to use "we."

"We feel it is our duty to protest the change of policy that is implied in the current exhibition at the Museum of Modern Art called Americans 1942," he drafted when the museum in January mounted the first of what would be six sharply focused and selected "Americans" shows. Subtitled "18 Artists from 9 States" and chosen by Dorothy Miller, who had only just risen to associate curator of painting and sculpture at the museum, it included Darrel Austin, Hyman Bloom, Raymond Breinin, Samuel Cashman, Francis Chapin, Emma Lu Davis, Morris Graves, Joseph Hirsch, Donal Hord, Charles Howard, Rico Lebrun, Jack Levine, Helen Lundeberg, Fletcher Martin, Octavio Medellin, Knud Merrild, Mitchel Siporin, and Everett Spruce.

> This exhibition is not only misleading . . . it marks the abdication by the Museum of its lofty position as the citadel of the modern art spirit.
>
> From the Museum's inception it has consistently maintained a policy of excellence that has made it a veritable shrine where all, artists and public . . . have flocked to participate in the companionship of the most advanced, progressive and vital thought in the world of art. Those of us who have seen the official art of Europe as presented at the various European pavilions at the World's fair realize how well the Museum has displayed a definite and consistent sense of selection that avoided the banality of an art whose only merit was that it existed in the region.
>
> It is therefore a profound shock that in the Museum's attitude towards American art it has not similar courage and conviction and has abandoned its standards and point of view to cater to mediocrity on the specious grounds that this exhibit represents American painters from the four corners of the country . . . . the public that has learned to rely on the Museum's taste in matters of European art can only be misled to believe that this American art had similar excellence. This is tantamount to a betrayal of confidence . . . .
>
> But this is more than just a betrayal of the Museum's past standards . . . The Museum is not a private hobby or business. Its position is now a public trust.

That is why we feel compelled to speak out against this exhibit because it marks a betrayal of a public trust.

These are serious charges. But these are serious times.[9]

It wasn't only failures of quality that had Barney's back up in the arena that he now fully identified as his own. In "What About Isolationist Art?," written about four months after the strike on Pearl Harbor, he began to lay a polemical framework for the manner of art that he decided the times demanded, and an almost legalistic case against what he saw as a nefarious and dangerous support system for American Scene painting. As written by the 37-year-old with almost two decades of hyperbolic diatribes under his belt, it was a familiar reflection of his righteously engaged personality and disputational bent, but his new panoramic focus on art was almost a byproduct. This polished but unpublished essay in which the personal bubbles below the objective, shows Barney wrestling with his own rationale for his dubious pacifism—now becoming harder to justify in principle. The essay is haunted by Hitler.

Years later, he recalled this time: "The real thing that happened, to me personally, and for those artists, painters that I knew personally, was the crisis created in our lives by the war . . . . I suppose only men of my age remember how it *felt* at that point, to live in New York with the U.S. being at war and . . . Hitler moving through Europe. And it became very obvious to me in a strong emotional sense—that is, it wasn't obvious to me *intellectually*—but in terms of the whole being, that it was no longer possible . . . just to be sensitive. That the sensitivity had to move towards a *real* consideration of what a painter is really involved in . . . . You couldn't be complacent, when people were being killed by the hundreds."[10] [!]

Even before Pearl Harbor, the war was closing in on Barney's home. "The incredibility, the preparations, the regimentation and the utter loss of individuality are to me distasteful—but I am for the present a soldier and I must obey," wrote his cousin, "Burrie" Siegel, a doctor in the Medical Corps. Their cousin Nathan Libby—the boy Barney had once balanced on his bicycle handlebars—was in the Navy, and another cousin, Harry Pollack, was an Army medic in Europe. George was working at the Brooklyn Naval Yard. Annalee, following the tragic story of her French cousins, as it emerged bit by discreet bit in letters, took the Red Cross first aid course as so many women did.

By early 1942, the "mobilization of American industry [was] at a blistering pace"; civilian industries were "wiped out with a speed that . . . stunned business men"; and consumer rationing had begun.[11] Sarah, previously attending New School lectures, was now at City College under the Government War Training Program, studying Map Preparation. As early as April, she was a meteorologist with the Army Signal Laboratory in Eatontown, New Jersey, within a year was at the Pentagon, and by late 1943 was a research analyst with the OSS.[12]

In February, nearly half a million new registrants in New York City were called under the third Selective Service registration, in which men 20 to 44 were eligible, marriage was no longer an automatic excusal, and eye and teeth health requirements were relaxed. Varieties of alternative service were promoted for those who failed the physical. In April, the "Old Man's Draft" collected information on the skills of men born between April 1877 and February 1897 for a complete inventory of manpower resources available for national service.

The year before, the jingoist Luce had written of the "moral and practical bankruptcy of isolationism."

> Once we cease to distract ourselves with lifeless arguments about isolationism, we shall be amazed to discover that there is already an immense American internationalism. American jazz, Hollywood movies, American slang, American machines and patented products, are in fact the only things that every community in the world . . . . recognizes in common . . . . America as the dynamic center of ever-widening spheres of enterprise, America as the training center of the skillful servants of mankind . . . and America as the powerhouse of the ideals of Freedom and Justice.[13]

But not everyone understood the "bankruptcy of isolationism" in the same way. In the very same issue of *Life* in which Luce declared "The American Century," there ran an article on the sculptor Mahonri Young—"one of Brigham Young's 300-odd grandchildren," who "disassociated himself from his ancestral religion," lived in New York, and taught at the Art Students League. Young made just the sort of sentimental, academic, America-firster sculpture—a cowboy *Rolling His Own*, *This Is the Place* (Brigham Young gazing over the Great Salt Lake), a galloping *Pony Express*—that would cause Barney to gag in his own response.

"Is isolationism dead?" Barney asked in his unpublished essay.

> No one can tell what Pearl Harbor will bring us, but we can feel certain that no matter what, isolationism as a factor in the political life of America has seen its best days. But does that mean that it is dead? . . . To get rid of these enemies of world progress, we must drive them from every field they have penetrated. And make no mistake, unless we do, isolationism will again rise to poison and corrupt American life.

Barney saw isolationism as a powerful intellectual movement that dominated "the cultural life of America with a hand of iron" and found its "most blatant penetration" in the peace movement, where leaders, whose standards "must be . . . incorruptible," found strange bedfellows.

> The [Edward Joseph] Flynns, the Norman Thomases, the Libbys, even some of the Quakers who were yelling no compromise with war, showed by their alliance with the Lindberghs, the [Burton Kendall] Wheelers, the [Gerald Prentice] Nyes, the [Reverend Charles] Coughlins, and the [Hamilton] Fishes that they were willing to accept Hitler's peace.

At least the shock of Pearl Harbor "put an end to the tolerance of these corrupt peace leaders, who could not tell the difference between peace and surrender."

What a contrast we find when we examine another field of American culture where isolationism is rampant. In the field of the arts the grip of isolationism is absolutely [unbroken]. Art in America is an isolationist monopoly. Publishers and critics, art dealers and museum directors willingly or unwillingly are completely dominated by an isolationist aesthetic that permits no deviation . . . . The whole art and literary world, is, to use Hitler's phrase, theirs.

Yet they have had their Pearl Harbor. The death of Grant Wood and Gertrude Whitney, archisolationist art men [*sic*] (can they be called artists?) so recent and so close to the events of Pearl Harbor that it seems an ominous coincidence, could have been a symbol of the end of an era, a symbol as forceful as Pearl Harbor itself. Yet these isolationists leaders died in a blaze of eulogy . . . .

Like so many other cultural movements, this one found its battleground in the field of painting . . . . Isolationist painting, which [is] named the American Renaissance, is founded on the bad politics of chauvinism and on an even worse aesthetic . . . . inhibiting the production of any true art in this country . . . . Isolationism, we have learned by now, is Hitlerism. Both are expressions of the same intense, vicious nationalism . . .

To those who think that the identity between isolationism and Hitlerism is an exaggeration, an examination of the methods used by the isolationists in the field of painting, where their leader, [critic] Thomas Craven, was on time, will prove enlightening. Craven's methods and the methods of his friends were the methods of Hitler . . . . the "great lie," the intensified nationalism, the false patriotism, the appeal to race, the calling of names, the reemphasis of the home and homey sentiment. The art of the world as focused in the "Ecole de Paris," these men ranted,

and here, Barney channeled Craven's voice:

is degenerate art, fine for Frenchmen but not for us Americans . . . . And who are their American fellow travelers? A bunch of New York Ellis Islanders who aren't even fifty percent Americans, most of them communists and internationally minded, etc. What we need is a good old one-hundred-percent American art based on the good old things we know and recognize.

Barney quoted Grant Wood: "I started to analyze what I really knew. I found out. It's Iowa. I'd found the answer when I joined a school of painters in Paris after [the first World War] . . . They believed an artist had to wait for inspiration, very quietly, and they did most of their waiting . . . with brandy. It was then that I realized that all the really good ideas I'd ever had came to me while I was milking a cow . . . . I had in mind something which I hope to convey to a fairly wide audience in America . . . . the picture of a country rich in the arts of peace, a homely, loveable nation, infinitely worth any sacrifice necessary to its preservation."

This attitude made Barney's blood boil. Although he wasn't able to articulate it then, he would have said, he told an interviewer in 1963, "painting is ridiculous . . . people are dying, my relatives are being killed, innocents . . . the problem of the war." With hindsight, he could recognize what was happening to him. The important issue was, and continued to be, "how you should live a human life."[14]

> The isolationist aesthetic has become known as the American Scene. It is based on two fallacies so flagrant one wonders how they could have succeeded with any group [of artists] that was not intellectually corrupt.

The fallacies were, one, that an American art meant painting "AMERICA."

> What was this America that artists were to paint? Was it a certain national character one was to express, a point of view, a taste, a cultural nuance? Not at all . . . . America was the geographic life around them. The crassest philistinism.

And, two, that the isolationists

> didn't mind a bit if the artist stole European painting styles and techniques, so long as they were confined to the American scene . . . . Benton painting cowboys with a palette stolen from the Venetians; Wood painting the farm with a Flemish primitive contour; Curry, Marsh, Cadmus, and Fletcher Martin, with colors and distortions stolen from the postimpressionists . . . .

"Leftist" social painting, Barney stated, was "still American Scene," essentially

> a struggle by leftist artists, who had been ostracized as Ellis Islanders by the original regional tinge of the American scene movement, to join the philistines . . . . All they wanted was to be able to include the worker, the Pittsburgh smelter alongside the Kansas farmer. The whole mess a cheap, successful, new commercial art.
>
> Every nation has its commercial artists, but no nation, not even the fascist nations, claim that they have made art history with them . . . except America. Here our commercial official art is called an American Renaissance by our critics, dealers, and museum directors. They fill the American wings of our museums; they dominate our art schools, our art galleries. They have their own museum. They have penetrated the Museum of *Modern* Art!

To blame for the situation, Barney moved from Gertrude Whitney's money and old family society to Yale and Harvard's "museum-director graduates," dealers, publishers, and "prize committees."

It is time for artists to wake up and reexamine their aesthetic foundations . . . . It is time they understood the political foundation of the art . . . refused isolationist money, repudiated the art dealers, the favor of museum directors . . . . the deaths of Grant Wood and Gertrude Whitney were as strong a symbol as Pearl Harbor for the end of an isolationist era.

"What About Isolationist Art?" was provoked by Miller's Americans show, by what Barney and Gottlieb, speaking for the Federation, had seen as "placidly accept[ing] the false standards so thoroughly exploited by the flag-waving isolationists," and their hope for "higher standards from the Museum of Modern Art than from *Life* magazine, Thomas (America First) Craven, Holger Cahill, or from those 'museums' who follow the market."[15] But it was also prompted by genuine despair, and Barney's characteristic confidence that the disaffected grousing of rap sessions could become the stuff to provoke meaningful manifestos. "We always—at least I always—thought . . . that the function of [art] was to be part of the intellectual and cultural life of an elite group," Gottlieb said, and Barney would have agreed.[16] He had always been an advocate; it was his talent, his skill, and, it's obvious, his joy—how else could he keep it up with such energy? Now he finally made the decision about the professional team on which he was going to play. His ardent—and unselfconscious—offense could be put to use advocating first for Gottlieb, and ultimately for himself.

At the McMillen Gallery, the painter John Graham, in a bold maneuver, juxtaposed Picasso, Braque, Rouault, Modigliani, Bonnard, Derain, and de Chirico with established Americans Stuart Davis, Walt Kuhn, and Graham himself, newcomers Jackson Pollock, Lenore (Lee) Krasner, and a few others, to promote those he considered heirs to the avant-garde Europeans. Two months later, on behalf of Gottlieb, Barney began a correspondence with Paul Rosenberg, whose galleries in Paris, London, and New York[17] showed Cézanne, van Gogh, Picasso, Braque, and Léger, among other modern masters. "The establishment of your gallery in New York had created the first real hope for modern art in America. All the other galleries pay false homage to modern art only to promote mediocrities . . . to satisfy vulgar taste. I know that your gallery, which has a young spirit, will elevate taste . . . . [its] important, not to say heroic, role . . . requires that you show American artists . . . it would be impossible to do otherwise . . . unless you want to become a second Durand-Ruel—a tomb for old art. I am sure you hope to become an important force in the culture of our time," he wrote in a long letter of excellent French, aided by Annalee, fluent in the language as well as in typing. "What is this culture?" Barney asked, before recapitulating the "tragic combination" of America-first patriotism and *faux-artistes* that "destroyed art in America," described in his essay on isolationism. As support, he used the classic Newman rhetorical trope, citing the *New York Times,* in this case their extravagant coverage of a new portrait of Sara Roosevelt and a show of academic painters as opposed to the "paltry lines given to your show of [Max] Weber in the same article."

This remarkable letter—written by a nobody to a star—was the first explicit articulation of what Barney demanded contemporary art *should be*, what made art worthwhile, rather than how so much of it failed. And he formulated exactly in what way that art should be displayed: with no mediation.

> Don't despair . . . I have seen the new work of one of the rare intellectual American artists . . . one of the only who has fought vulgar influences for twenty years . . . the new works are masterpieces . . . . a series he calls "pictographes" on the subject of Oedipus Rex . . . . remarkable for their originality, the artistic power and their absolute insistence on plastic elements. And there is the issue. How can one emphasize the plastic without losing the subject? The artist has resolved this admirably. He has chosen a subject that is classical and at the same time psychological. He surpassed the subject's limits without falling into the errors of abstract or surrealist painters . . . . Viewers of the paintings know the subject before and can thus concentrate on the plastic elements.

Imagine how powerful a show "could be made!" Barney told Rosenberg. No catalogue. No reference to each work. No list. Upon entering the gallery, one got a program with notes explaining the history of the legend. "Each visitor must look only for plastic elements or be lost."

As someone who had "devoted his life entirely to art, first as a student, then as an artist and finally as a teacher of art in New York high schools," Barney declared these works "true masterpieces" by the "best intellectual artist in New York." If Rosenberg would like to discover "an artist who is the equal of Picasso, Matisse, Miro [*sic*] and the other avant-garde spirits who advanced art," Barney would arrange it. "Gottlieb is not unknown," he reassured the art dealer. He was the vice president of the Federation of Modern Painters and Sculptors, he showed his work at The Artists Gallery, he was appreciated by a circle of admirers, recognized as "the most important artist in our country."[18]

Rosenberg responded: members of his staff had seen Gottlieb's work, but he would be happy to view them himself. A visit was arranged through Barney and, unfortunately, Rosenberg was not sufficiently impressed. But Barney was not satisfied by simply getting the gallerist's attention; he had taken a stand, and needed to feel "vindication." A year later, after a burst of public attention for Gottlieb and Rothko that Barney was instrumental in instigating—a rash of newspaper coverage, and letters, eventually an appearance on radio—he abandoned the calculated nicety of using French and wrote again to Rosenberg, in English:

> More than a year ago . . . before you began showing any Americans [conveniently forgetting the Weber show], I called your attention to the work of Adolph Gottlieb, the innovator of a real art movement . . . The art page in today's TIMES vindicates my judgment and sincere advice to you. For Mr. Jewell considers the work of Adolph Gottlieb and M. Rothko (who is allied with him) of sufficient

importance to name it a new art movement—the first in two decades. There can be no doubt that this work is the first during this time in America that is at all challenging; that offers hope for a new art.

You may feel that Mr. Jewell's opinion and taste do not carry sufficient weight for my vindication. Precisely the point! Mr. Jewell admits he does not <u>like</u> the work. He only recognizes its import . . . .

You will, therefore, I hope, pardon me if I chide you now for not having had the perspicacity then when you had the opportunity.[19]

SIXTEEN

WHAT DID YOU DO DURING THE WAR?

Barney's 4F was safe through another "Old Man's Draft" in June. He never received conscientious objector status, but that didn't stop him from later claiming it: "I was a conscientious objector," he said in 1963, "not because [I claimed] religious grounds, because I could kill, that's what I told them; but I don't want to die as a soldier."[1] Nor did others of his cohort.

Fritz Bultman (b. 1919), like "everybody, was worried that [he'd] have to go." Bultman went to his physical, "and he was turned down," his wife recalled. "And Tony Smith laughed and laughed at that. And then *he* went and he was turned down . . . . They didn't want artists [and the artists] didn't want to go anyway."[2]

Robert Motherwell (b. 1915) was called when he was 27. He had a history of asthma, but to be safe his family "sent [him] to see some psychologist." When she saw that he'd gone to prep school, she asked how many "homosexual relationships" he had had, and refused to believe him when he answered "none." "I assure you," he told her, "I live in an art world. Nobody could care less what my sex life is." "You don't really want to go, do you?" he was asked. " Do you? " he answered. He received his 4F. He didn't "want to name names," he later recalled, "but a lot of the artists I knew, one very famous one, learned to simulate some psychotic state, like always staring at the floor and never looking anybody in the face. And also fortunately my draft board was Greenwich Village, and I imagine that draft board more than other one would have assumed that painters and poets and those types of people very likely weren't very good soldier material."[3]

David Hare (b. 1917) "didn't want to be drafted . . . . First because you're scared to death and who wants to be shot, and secondly, who wants to shoot somebody else? . . . Obviously, Hitler was wrong and we ought to [have done] something about it . . . [but] my reaction was that it's too far away. I didn't want to have anything to do with it."[4]

Jackson Pollock (b. 1912) didn't want anything to do with it either. In 1944, he wrote to his brother, Charles, "I have really had amazing success for my first year of showing . . . If it weren't for this god-damned war I'd head west for a while."[5] When he was first called in 1941, he persuaded his analyst to petition the draft board for a 4F on psychological grounds. She requested a psychiatric examination at Beth Israel Hospital, and he received the classification.[6]

Mark Rothko (b. 1903) received a 4F as well, probably because of his bad eyesight.[7] "The Rothkos," Mark told his first wife, "are not heroes."[8]

Philip Guston (b. 1913) spent 1941 to 1945 as an artist-in-residence at the University of Iowa. His "contributions to the war effort," according to his daughter, "took the form of commissioned murals on celestial navigation and illustrations for naval air training, published in *Fortune* magazine."[9]

Willem de Kooning (b. 1904, Holland) as an immigrant had the option to enlist, but "never talked about whether or not he tried." One story, attributed to his wife Elaine, that he "was deferred as an alien" and became ineligible at the age of 38, is suspect since men as old as 44 were being taken. Another story blamed a bum knee. "In any case, he hardly yearned to become a soldier."[10]

Many of the artists who one way or another avoided the Army found ways to do service stateside. Gottlieb (b. 1903) was one, going to work at the Brooklyn Navy Yard. Barney was cognizant enough of public opinion regarding who served and who didn't that, in a December 1943 press release for Gottieb's show at The Artists Gallery, he wrote: "Although the artist has now put aside his brushes to devote his skill to doing special work of a high order of craftsmanship in an aeroplane and glider plant, he has not neglected his art. His paintings are now being shown . . . . thereby serving his country in a double capacity for while helping to fashion the instruments of war, he is at the same time contributing to home front morale."

Jack Tworkov (b. 1900, Poland) became a citizen in 1933 and worked in an "engineering house" mostly "on government contracts, war contracts." He was enthusiastic: one, "it was the most marvelous way to get off the Project, at last I had a WAY of getting off the Project; two, because I wanted, really wanted to work partly in the war effort, was happy to do it; and thirdly, it was a marvelous thing for me to find out that I COULD work and could get something else if I had to."[11]

David Smith (b. 1906) lived in Schenectady from 1942 to 1944, assembling M7 tanks and locomotives during the 11:30 to 7:30 a.m. shift for the American Locomotive Company.[12]

Clyfford Still (b. 1904) said that from fall of 1941 until summer of 1943 he "worked in the war industries—shipbuilding in Oakland, California, as steel checker for the Navy in the making of submarine tenders [and] later in San Francisco as Materials Release Engineer for Hammond Aircraft which made assemblies for the Douglas A-20 planes."[13]

Franz Kline (b. 1910) briefly did some sort of work for the Army on Governors Island, and in the summer of 1943 was a second lieutenant in the Citizens Military Training Camp at Fort Monroe, Virginia—a program of basic military training that entailed no obligation to active duty.

There are no enlistment records for William Baziotes (b. 1912).

Clement Greenberg (b. 1909) was drafted in early 1943 when he was 32. He went through basic training, had a psychological collapse, and was discharged that fall.[14]

Philip Pavia (b. 1911), who didn't serve, acknowledged the impact felt by draft-age men: "The war kept us together—it was terrible. You never knew what was going on. The radio was on 24 hours a day everyday. You couldn't sleep too well at night. In a way it made us become strong individuals. You didn't take life for granted, though."[15]

And Alfonso Ossorio (b. 1916) recognized just how few of the artists were directly involved. "It's extraordinary to think that of all the abstract expressionists I can think of none who were in the Army."[16] Ossorio himself was one of the few who was—from 1943 through 1946.[17]

He wasn't entirely alone. Conrad Marca-Relli (b. 1913), drafted before the war, was out before Pearl Harbor; by the time he was recalled he was working as a draftsman for the Bureau of Ships. Ad Reinhardt (b. 1913) was in the Navy and James Brooks (b. 1906) the Army. Harry Jackson (Harry Aaron Shapiro, b. 1924) won a Purple Heart as a Marine. Milton Resnick participated in the second-wave assault on the beach in Normandy and became the head of a reconnaissance group—relying on the sort of maps that Sarah Newman was producing.

But, by and large, the men who each in his own style would later contribute to the extraordinary pissing match that characterized the so-called "New York School"—the various associated groupings, "clubs," "schools," and the splintering of tenuous and unstable alliances—abstained from the bigger historical battle. Many expected through their work to write—or control the writing of—the history of their time. Precedence, who came first, was never so important—to the actors in this drama—as it became in the early 1950s. Friedel Dzubas compared it to politicking for votes, with surrogates—wives, girlfriends, poets, other "partisans"—working the "populace" and the "elect." For as long as there have been records of their activities, artists have been known to be egocentric and competitive. But these men—the women among their numbers until years later were nearly silenced in the male onslaught—took their antagonism to new levels. They would create their own war, mount their own campaigns, fight for nothing less than *moral* high ground—something to which Barney was particularly well suited. These men were the inverse of what has come to be known as the "Greatest Generation"—the veterans who returned from the Far East and Europe and built postwar America. Confronted by those heroes, the artists, instead of being satisfied with channeling their bravura and insecurities into their artwork, at the beginning of the 1950s would carry on as if it were not their talent, or genius, or historical consequence, but their very *manhood* that was at stake.

At the Reed Studios in Gloucester, Massachusetts, a school of "Modern Art" had been run by the painter Ernest Thurn since 1929. Thurn had studied alongside Vaclav Vytlacil at the Bavarian Academy of Art and with Hans Hofmann in Munich. Hofmann himself taught in Thurn's school shortly after his arrival on the East Coast. Not only artists, but "former GI's, retired business men, executives and even lady lawyers, with 'hayseed in their hair' [spent] many happy relaxed weeks each summer in the Reed Studio building."[18] For a period during the war the school was closed, but the studios remained open and it was there that in August 1942 Barney and Annalee spent their vacation, swimming, eating lobsters, and sailing on Gottlieb's funky boat.

At Washington Irving High School Barney was geographically in the midst of artists' studios, artists' bars, and the cafeterias they frequented. He had become a sort of Cyrano de Bergerac, writing but not signing official artists' statements. At Reed he had the perfect opportunity to externalize the identity he carried inside, to put what was in his mind not into *words* but into *pigment*. But again he dodged the moment: no works, if they were made, survive.

In the early summer of 1942 a small news item in the *Times* reported an "announcement of the Polish Government in London" that

> 700,000 Jews were slain by the Nazis in Poland. The report was broadcast by the British Broadcasting Corporation and was recorded by the Columbia Broadcasting System in New York yesterday. "To accomplish this, probably the greatest mass slaughter in history, every death-dealing method was employed—machine-gun bullets, hand grenades, gas chambers, concentration camps, whipping, torture instruments and starvation."[19]

Later that fall, incontrovertible, unavoidable, and personal evidence of the violent destruction of the Jewish communities in Europe, from which the New York Newmans and Greenhouses were less than one generation removed, crashed into their lives.

Abraham regularly shared with Barney communications from Stephen S. Wise, chairman of the World Jewish Congress. In one of these, in late November, Wise confirmed that half the estimated four million Jews in Nazi-occupied Europe had been slain in an "extermination campaign." Annalee's cousin Emile wrote from France: he was able to "safely come back from the war," and found his wife and daughter in Marseille, but his father and brother, who had been in a "camp" near Paris since the previous year, had been deported to unknown whereabouts. His and Annalee's uncle, Felix, his wife, Simone, and their son had been deported as well, leaving their 17-year-old daughter Renee, whom Emile found living in Paris with his own mother, required to wear a yellow star and forbidden to use major streets and boulevards. Acknowledging "all you have done for us during the war," he now implored Annalee to help his wife, Lisette, who "was born in Paris and whose father was killed in the war of 1914–18," to come to America.[20] (All but Renee were ultimately murdered.)

Annalee and Barney hadn't left their families across the ocean or across the country, with only occasional visits or annoying letters, as was the case for so many other "New York" artists. Their engagement in their families' lives was relentless. Samuel's lawsuit, Anuta's train tickets, Abraham's business and health, Sarah's job applications, daily, lengthy, phone conversations with Anna;[21] money passing back and forth. Barney made a point of telling Hess that he "never had a generation gap with" his father or mother;[22] indeed, far from a "gap," there often seemed to be no distance at all. Which makes Barney's ability to compartmentalize seem especially prodigious.

Yet, compartmentalization was true of the great proportion of American Jews, those from Eastern Europe—the *Ostjuden*—who carried the trauma of historical abuse and aspired to assimilate and seize new American opportunities, as well as their "Our Crowd" co-religionists, the haute-bourgeois German Jews who arrived in the mid-19th century,[23] concerned to protect their privileged status and avoid shame by association with the newer immigrants. For these reasons, psychological and social, the decimation of Jewish culture in Europe was not talked about except by a few prominent leaders: it was considered a *shanda*, an embarrassment in front of non-Jews, an affliction that brought unwanted attention. Particular fears and vulnerabilities were provoked by world events that were also significantly personal events, and this aspect of culture was something Barney thought a good deal about. In later years he would talk about cultural ritual "as if it were philosophy," about immigrants' lingering loyalties to countries of origin, about first-generation individuals and multi-generational families, and their attitudes toward America. How culture was constructed by these attitudes—this, rather than a particular belief system, was the way he presented his Judaism.[24] Others with the same background might metabolize their history in attenuated intellectualizing; Barney developed a conspicuous compound of thin skin, inarticulate terror, and articulate fixation on dignity. And this was a combination that mightily thwarted, if not entirely defeated, the very thing an artist must do, which is to suffer exposure, to audaciously take risks.

When he meditated about the impact of the war years on his work, his thoughts were about *not* painting. He had "never considered that what a man is is the result of his environment . . . a man finds what he has to say in spite of the environment." And yet, "there is no question that time plays a role in a man's life," and, as he thought back, "Pearl Harbor had a very serious effect on my work as well as on my life." Before, "the war and Hitler were far away"; but after the attack he was "to question the subject matter of painting. Getting into the war meant that we were no longer on the side lines and although I had always felt from my earliest youth that I was committed to what I was doing, I had really to examine the nature of the commitment. I found self-expression in relation to the physical world around me was not enough. Distorted cello players, half-nude figures seemed inadequate to the depth of the despair I felt at that time."[25]

The shows in the fall of 1942 provided no guideposts for his search. In mid-October, the notorious "First Papers of Surrealism" exhibition at the Whitelaw Reid Mansion on Fiftieth Street consisted mainly of works by Surrealists in exile—"first papers" referred to their residency filings—with a few American artists of similar persuasion like Baziotes, Hare, and Motherwell, the last of whom had only begun to identify as an artist a year or two earlier. The European work was confident and cynical, playful and, in Barney's eyes, precious. The installation, significantly obscured by Marcel Duchamp's sixteen miles of criss-crossed string, did not manifest the high moral purpose Barney sought. The inaugural exhibition of Peggy Guggenheim's Art of This Century Gallery was equally entertaining: her "entire collection of paintings, objects and sculpture representative of the various movements that, during the last three decades or so, have gone to compose modernism"[26] was showcased in an installation designed by Frederick Kiesler, at that time the director of the laboratory of the School of Architecture at Columbia University. The serpentine wall of the room of Cubist and abstract work was covered in dark blue canvas, and Surrealist work was shown in a room with concave wood walls; most pieces were unframed and suspended in air—the traditional frame, Kiesler explained, was a "symbol and agent of an artificial duality of 'vision' and 'reality,' or 'image' and 'environment' "[27] that separated the world of the viewer from the world of the work—and some rotated. There were World's Fair-worthy devices that showed Paul Klee paintings one by one for ten seconds each, and a hand-turned wooden wheel that revealed through a peephole reproductions from Duchamp's *Box-in-a-Suitcase*. The media had a field day with the gallery, the artists, the installation, Guggenheim, and Kiesler. A *Times Sunday Magazine* made it all look particularly glamorous and wacky.

The presence of the Surrealists was a "stimulus," but had no "direct influence" on Barney. While they had been "chased" out of their "security . . . it had not really affected their work because they were doing the same painting they had been doing before the rise of Hitler. But I had no immunity to the crisis of the time so I had to dig into the real problem of what to paint, otherwise painting could not have stood up to the seriousness of the events."

This was a *stunning* formulation: it elevated Barney's personal trauma—that of the conscious witness—over that of the victims, the war refugees themselves. It was also a tacit acknowledgment that he *hadn't* been seriously painting, for if he had had a body of work it would have provided some sort of "immunity." The Surrealists and the "Neo-plastic refugees and their American followers" were "totally inadequate to the intensity of my life at that time. I had to break through into a new way of saying what was really me to make the painting express the totality of my being instead of just the finger tips of sensibility."[28]

Later, he would regularly reiterate that the war was the source of his block. "You couldn't be complacent, when people were being killed by the hundreds [*sic*] . . . . In my own case, I began to write some poems in the early '40s, because painting seemed inadequate."[29] "I didn't paint for a couple of years, I wrote."[30] And certainly, on his tax returns for 1942 and '43, he identified himself as "writer—freelance" forgoing the previous "teacher." "We all were writing then," he said, noting that "Mark had written a book." Tworkov, too, had begun a book—about the social and historical context for art—but never completed it.[31]

Poetry came toward the end of the war. Around this time Barney wrote random sketches which couched what was on his mind in passes at disinterested scholarship, like the possibly satiric "The Future of the A B C Crap"—a polemic urging the adoption of the Roman alphabet: *The time will come when every language on earth will be printed in the A B C design . . . . When that day comes and the alphabet barriers are removed, it will mark another victory for international friendship*[32]—or stylish "fiction," like "Artists Prefer Schoolteachers."

The person to whom Barney spoke most about his aesthetic/functional impasse was Gottlieb, "because he was also involved in this crisis."[33] But their conversations, often at the Gottliebs' Brooklyn Heights home, were not exclusively concerned with existential meaning. Money was a topic. And marriage. And, sometimes, how the two intertwined. It was good if an artist's wife worked, Barney and Gottlieb agreed. Esther

Gottlieb, who taught tailoring at the High School of Needle Trades until she retired in the mid-1960s, said at one point during the Depression she was supporting several artists: she gave her paycheck to Adolph, he lent money to David Smith, who lent to someone else.[34] When Baziotes had no money coming in, Barney told him, "You have a wife. Send her out to work."[35] Later, Barney liked to joke, "well, fellas we're going to have to gird up our loins and send our wives out to work"[36] and de Kooning, "Vat we need is a wife."[37] They agreed that "you were lucky if you didn't have any children."[38] For both Annalee and Esther, that turned out to be a very painful decision.[39]

As in his courting poems to Annalee, drafts of "Artists Prefer Schoolteachers" indulge Barney's awkward romanticizing of his preferred feminine qualities—and by implication what he found in his wife. As in "Story of Communism, or 'Hope,'" the drafts are suffused with imaginative projection.

> I began to realize for the first time that visits made regularly twice a week [to D's house] were not made entirely to discuss my newest problem in painting or to see D's newest work. I [was] to great extent drawn out of curiosity, envy that always ended up in self-pity at the happy solution D had found to his life's problems. For D had married a school teacher. <u>Do you realize what that meant to an artist?</u>

Later, Barney replaced artist "D" with "Adolf."

> From the very beginning when I first saw her at A[dolf's] studio I felt she was no ordinary beauty. All girls have beautiful eyes, or hair, or skin, or figure and after painting the figure for 10 years I could pick them out with ease. A was no ordinary combination of eyes, skin and membrane. She had that vivid living aesthetic quality you cannot see only comprehend. Many the night I and Adolf had spent arguing to exhaustion over the same problem in painting. What makes a great painter—What means good color, great line.— All men use the same colors and all lines are alike, black scrawls, I used to shout. I'm sick of hearing all these objective critics who keep extoling these trite idiocies [like] significant form and are blind to the real "life" in a painting. And rummaging through the catalogue of women I had seen and studied they were all breasts, eyes, hair, skin of every degree of beauty and delicacy but all flesh. Here suddenly like the appearance of a new genus (artist) A came into my life and to me I saw a work of art Her expression . . . . I have never been able to decide whether it was her body or her manner or her character . . . . It therefore gave me a good deal of satisfaction to be able to adapt an aesthetic theory that I had used in my arguments with A to include my A.

Another draft is Barney at his most exposed, a revealing fantasy, and justification, of his life so far:

> The very first time my wife and I met, of course she wasn't my wife then, we took to each other like soap and water. It was at Keats Sheldon's studio, he wasn't as

famous then as he is today. Then he was only a promising artist, just as I was. He and I had been college mates at Ohio State and had shared our room and clothes, our troubles and fun, our hopes and ambitions like true fraternity ΔΠΦ brothers. That ambition was to become America's greatest art team. We had dominated the art life of Ohio State, ran the Merc—cartoons, gags, and front covers (we alternated one a month between us) to the point where some of the radicals accused us of a conspiracy to maintain a monopoly!

I had convinced Keats to come to New York. He was a boy from Ohio, I was a native New Yorker. Though we were different we were united by our strong common interest and ambition and because we each thought the other a hell of a nice guy. So we both banged into the Art Students League and took away all honors and the best looking girls in the place. But somehow instead of me taking the leadership in my own home town, Keats was leader. He found entrée into the exclusive salons, the exclusive night spots, he knew the best lookers in all Greenwich Village and he was beginning to meet the art directors. He knew which magazine needed this kind of a cartoon, that is I knew them too but he was getting them. And before I knew I was doing a half dozen things that had no connection with art at all. Here I was selling automobiles, doing a bit part in a play, a job as bill collector, public relations man for Carmelita Peponina but Keats was painting. I've never understood the mystery. The other night at the Jumble Shop I was discussing this very point with my friend John Underfield, who is a fellow in psychology at NYU. He claims it's the psychology of it. He says I'm a native New Yorker and see New York as a home. I can participate in its life. To me, he claims, it is perfectly natural to be relations man for Carmelita and watch the phony game of nightclub entertainment. I enjoy being part of the city. But not Keats. To him New York is a foreign city full of strangers. He is an outsider and he fights to maintain his identity. To him New York is to be used, for its fun, for its luxurious living, for its opportunities to get ahead. Participate in its life, join its toiling masses. Why he can do that back at <u>Oneida</u>. He didn't have to come to New York to be the lawyer or small merchant or work in the bank or be public relations man for the entire joint in Elmer's "Oneida News." "Are you any different" [the] professor of psychology says to me, "when you go to Gloucester" for the summer. "Do you feel part of the place. Don't you live a life richer than any native even the best. Do you think they eat the dinners you do at the Blacksmith Shop, and the Old Mill. Do you think the natives go swimming, sailing, sunning and spooning the way you do. You use the place for everything it's got from subject matter to paint, to their best Essex clams. You wouldn't want to stay and live the life of a fisherman would you, no matter what Kipling and Spencer Tracy have done to glamorize Gloucester fisherman: New York is Keats Gloucester." There was nothing I could say. Maybe there is something to this psychology stuff. Maybe this is the answer to the mystery. "You" my professor continued, "should have gone to Paris."

But I have forgotten about my wife and she's the main point of this story let alone my life.

And here the manuscript ends.

Barney's efforts now became more concerned with the "aesthetic theory that I had used in my arguments with A," and Gottlieb's career was the convenient hook on which to hang it. Gottlieb, along with Rothko, were "not any more overlooked than anybody else was," according to Esther Gottlieb. "They were less overlooked than many of the other artists." But they had a strong *feeling* of isolation, not from their own artist friends, but from the larger society, absorbed by the war and with only the most embryonic infrastructure for contemporary art. "They both felt that they were outcasts and the public was not interested in them." [40] Attracting attention in public was something Barney knew about.

A few months earlier he was enlisted to call to task the Museum of Modern Art for its failures in "Americans 1942"; in December Barney was again acting as public relations man, not for "Carmelita Peponina" but on behalf of his cohort. Again the action grew out of a protest. At the Metropolitan Museum, "Artists for Victory"—a loose cooperative including the Federation of Modern Painters and Sculptors and the American Abstract Artists—choreographed a titanic juried show of what they called "contemporary" art, with jurors and artists that Barney's pals did not recognize as modern. (Unlike MoMA's approach, large juried shows enabled the responsibility—and blame—to be spread.) The "mammoth nation-wide exhibition," sweetened with 52,000 dollars of purchase awards, included over 1400 paintings, sculptures, prints, and "miniatures," chosen from 11,000 works submitted. Inevitably, artists were left out. Jewell found the show mixed and confusing, with works good, boring, overly familiar, and "some of the most horrible pieces of right-wing academism ever exhibited in New York." [41] There was of course a response: a new group, a separate show, and a mission framed by Barney. In a brief, unsigned catalogue essay for the "first annual exhibition" of the "American Modern Artists" at the Riverside Museum, Barney rehearsed the arguments of "What About Isolationist Art?" He put the public on notice: what was being shown at the museums were "false artists and their movements." America had the opportunity to become the cultural center of the world, and "this exhibition is a first step, to free the artist from the stifling control of an outmoded politics"—isolationist art, Regionalism. "For art in America still is the plaything of politicians."

In the earlier essay his thoughts were elaborated; here they were so condensed they disappeared into slogans. Jewell in his initial review wrote that the statement covered "vehemently, though not too explicitly, the genesis of this latest group effort"; he called it an "explosive manfesto" [*sic*] that boiled down to "something of this sort: We are the only 'right' artists." In his later Sunday column, he continued: little seemed "path-blazing," and "the new group's barrage, printed in the catalogue [was] rather puzzling." It needed clarifying, he concluded. "It is one thing to cry havoc and another to make the bogy more plausible than the Don of Quixote's windmill."[42]

Reducing his thoughtful essay to a rallying cry had in this case done Barney no service. He clipped and saved a column by the *New York Post*'s editorial page editor that confirmed the instinct he would remember to obey: "To impose your own conception above that of the enemy, to follow it out in detail with remorseless logic, is 'style.' "[43]

Still, it was a gratifying step into the professional art arena for Barney, even if only his friends knew. Before the exhibition he added his name as a painter to a list of American Modern Artists members and persuaded Vincent Spagna, the organizer, to include four of Sarah's paintings—although none of his own. His goal was to kick up dust, but it was the beginning of a sirocco. Writing from the U.S. Signal Corps Laboratories in the War Department, Sarah was bursting on Barney's behalf. "It's amazing what a thrill I got reading the art page this Sunday in this quiet, dull town of Bethlehem . . . so far removed from the small revolution that was happening in Jewel's [*sic*] column that it made the incident so much more remarkable . . . . The truth is the catalog really won a real victory by forcing Jewel [*sic*] to give the show so much publicity (no ads were printed) and link the show with his 2 pets the Whitney & Met & Penn [Corcoran] Annual."

"It's too bad Barney," she concluded, "your [*sic*] wasting your talents on a bunch of artists that are jellyfish & not using your ability freely in your own fight."[44]

It had been a season of large group shows of living American artists, but as far as Barney and Gottlieb were concerned, not of significant, living American art. *Their* coup would come in early June, in events around the show at Wildenstein Gallery put on by the Federation.

In February 1943, Jewell had been merely unimpressed by Gottlieb and Rothko's works in "New York Artists Painters."[45] Now, reviewing the Federation of Modern Painters and Sculptors, he wrote a single sentence: "You will have to make of Marcus Rothko's *The Syrian Bull* what you can; nor is this department prepared to shed the slightest enlightenment when it comes to Adolph Gottlieb's *Rape of Persephone*."[46]

It was a backhanded slap at the two for their persistence—abetted by Barney—in demanding recognition for a "new," "modern" art. Four days later, to repair his cavalier dismissal, Jewell in his Sunday column quoted at length the show's unsigned leaflet: "Today America is faced with the responsibility either to salvage and develop or to frustrate Western creative capacity."

This country has been greatly enriched, both by the influx of many great European artists . . . and growing vitality of our native talent. In years to come the world will ask how this nation met its opportunity. Did it nourish or starve this concentration of talent? . . . In the last analysis the quality of a civilization is largely judged and understood through its art. It follows that to understand one's own time one must experience the art of one's own time. Since no one can remain untouched by the present world upheaval, it is inevitable that values in every field of human endeavor will be affected. As a nation we are now being forced to outgrow our narrow political isolationism . . . . it is time for us to accept cultural values on a truly global plane.

He allowed the artists their say, but withheld his approval: "Strive" as he would, Jewell concluded that he "couldn't seem, in the true sense of the term, to 'experience' some of the art."[47]

Gottlieb promised an additional statement. A week later that clarification, "calculated to disperse befuddlement (which I had freely confessed) over certain paintings" appeared in Jewell's column, and *Trijugated Tragedy* by Theodore E. Schewe, *The Syrian Bull,* and *Rape of Persephone* were reproduced. Schewe provided his own explanation, but it was the letter signed by Rothko and Gottlieb, written by them and Barney, that became the focus.[48] Except for one sentence, it was quoted in its entirety, and because of the prominence given it, and its protracted engagement by Jewell, it has come to be considered the verbal opening salvo of "Abstract Expressionism."[49] If their explanations of the paintings were a bit foggy, the large point was crystal clear: the locus of serious art was in the serious human being who was "compelled" to make it.

"To us art is an adventure into an unknown world, which can be explored only by those willing to take the risks," Gottlieb et al wrote. "This world of the imagination is fancy-free and violently opposed to common sense . . . . It is our function as artists to make the spectator see the world our way—not his way." And, most famously, in repudiation of formalism: "There is no such thing as good painting about nothing. We assert that the subject is crucial and only that subject-matter is valid which is tragic and timeless. That is why we profess spiritual kinship with primitive and archaic art."[50]

Not surprisingly, Jewell received many letters—most, but not all, flummoxed by the "mess of private symbols." At the end of the month, he wrapped up the controversy by declaring that the "Globalists"—the name he insisted on giving the Federation artists—had "accomplished precisely nothing that is intelligible." He suggested they "band together and put on a comprehensive exhibition of their own that may disprove this unintelligibility."[51] It may have been this slap and this challenge that would provoke Barney's most ambitious foray—the unpublished, multi-draft, "The Plasmic Image" in which he verbalized the philosophic position of the band of artist brothers whose group success he had taken upon himself to support. But for the moment, it was the published letter that articulated, and publicized, their ambition.

Rothko initially drafted his own reply to Jewell's criticisms, points of which were incorporated by Gottlieb into a joint version. Barney was then consulted for input and editing. The two artists whose work was at issue had written "polite" and slightly rambling explanations. Barney established a more militant, "antagonistic" tone, reflecting his experience leading campaigns and writing press releases.[52] He reformulated the ideas of his friends and created a "Stance." It made the names of Gottlieb and Rothko emerge from the pack. And in recognition and gratitude, Rothko gave him *The Syrian Bull* and Gottlieb *The Rape of Persephone*.[53]

There were five days between the appearance of Jewell's first article about the Federation's show on June 2 and Gottlieb's delivery of the letter on June 7, 1943. While Gottlieb, Rothko, and Newman struggled over the most effective tone and declaration of principle (and while Barney's maternal relatives were still in Poland) the newspaper they were obsessed with published other reports of historical consequence and other calls to arms. "The massacre of Jews by mean of gas chambers has been speeded up in Poland through the enlargement of the lethal plants . . . Polish radio [claims] that Germany has killed off 90 per cent of the Jews of Poland, leaving only 300,000 out of the pre-war population of 3,000,000 . . . [Treblinka camp] gas chambers can handle as many as 7,000 executions daily."[54] "The most widely known military secret in the world today is that the combined American–British–French armies that ran the Axis out of Africa are about to move against the continent of Europe." "In Hot Springs, Va., last week there came to a formal end the first full-scale international conference in the history of the United Nations."

On Sunday, June 6, at Rothko's home on Fifty-First Street, Barney tried to convince him to sign the latest version of the letter and Annalee sat outside on the stoop watching Rothko's wife, Edith, make silver jewelry. A couple of blocks away at one of several rallies in the city called to enlist five hundred thousand volunteers for civilian defense, James M. Landis, director of the Office of Civilian Defense, told tens of thousands in Rockefeller Plaza, "Volunteer workers had become the front line of home defense against possible attack by the enemy." On the day Gottlieb brought the letter to Times Square, twenty thousand were at another rally at Madison Square Garden on Fiftieth Street.

On June 11, after a month of unprecedented, relentless bombardment, the island of Pantelleria was invaded by the Allies in advance of the push into Europe; this event was reported in hundreds of news articles, many front page. But in the art pages, where on June 13 the question of whether "to be valid, subject-matter must be 'tragic'" was being debated, Pantelleria was only a distant echo of the bomb dropped by Gottlieb, Rothko, and Newman.

That the artists *felt* they were engaged in the world conflict was obvious from the leaflet for the Wildenstein show: "*No one can remain untouched by the present world upheaval* [emphasis added]." That they saw their campaign as some sort of commensurate response was either visionary or deluded. But it was, in their minds, the option that was open to them. The "world upheaval" demanded action in a similarly urgent register.

Barney was more worried about "isolationist art" than isolationist artists; certainly, at this moment, he had isolated himself from ordinary means of engagement. He locked out every quotidian, practical way that he might address the unbearable pressure of events. If Gottlieb was "agitated" by the need for a new subject, Barney's quest was ontological: in what *form* could he, without a natural gift, realize what he considered the only important role—the *job*—of art, which was to make visual the "outcry" of the artist. Most specifically, the outcry—against the war, against the destruction of his people, against his father's failures of business and health, against injustice done to his father-in-law, against the unfairness of "the system," against landlords, against daily humiliations, against regular assaults on his own *dignity*—of Barnett Newman.

There was no respite found in Gloucester that summer of 1943. Reed Studios was closed and barren; the Coast Guard was much in evidence, demanding identification at the piers. The cost of accommodations rose suddenly, without warning, without recognition of existing agreement. Sarah's career questions, Abraham's debts and receivables, and Samuel's case required Barney's immediate attention.

"Unless this very considerable weight of evidence is convincingly rebutted . . . it is almost certain the Federal Courts will decide the suit against you," warned the Greenhouse's single expert witness. "Now it is no easy undertaking to establish that 15 or more sworn witnesses were all untruthful or had all forgotten how those Fillers were operated in 1920 . . . To do this effectually . . . I suggest you have Mr. Newman help you to prepare these statements."[55]

By November, it had become clear that Samuel was not going to prevail. But neither was he backing down. The question of whether it was Barney or Samuel who persisted in pressing the case became a matter of disagreement in the family. Samuel and Barney had developed a genuine affection, and in many ways were alike. Her father, Annalee said, "cared more about being known for his great achievement than for any monetary gain." He had long tried unsuccessfully to bring the partners in Akron and New York together to get the action started against the company that, he believed, was infringing on his patents. Then, "Barney got everybody together, he got the case going, he was in charge. Barney made it all happen."[56] Still, Samuel himself was consumed by the fight. The suit proceeded through 1944, at a financial cost that was staggering for people in their position in those years, and an emotional cost that ultimately proved fatal to Samuel, who was ordered by his doctors "not only not to testify but was forbidden even to be present at the trial" the following April. The lawyers "and of course, myself have worked night and day on this matter," Barney wrote to the Akron principals as they awaited a judgment at the end of June.[57] They had "put up a magnificent fight" and the witness thought that the "Defendant's tricky and deceitful brief" would result in a favorable ruling. But it did not. They were overwhelmed by four law firms and over twenty witnesses.[58]

In the fall of 1944, after the judgment against them had come in, Barney wrote under Samuel's name to one Akron party that he would "have to appeal. There are very good grounds and I intend to proceed in this matter." The cost would be 5000 dollars, and Samuel/Barney asked "all interested parties who do not wish to finance this case to contribute half of their shares." In the event, there was no appeal, but Samuel/Barney did seek a higher adjudication. They wrote the U.S. Department of Justice requesting an investigation into whether perjury was committed at the trial by the Crown Cork & Seal witnesses. On January 2, 1946, the Justice Department wrote to Greenhouse that no action would be taken.

Samuel died of a cerebral hemorrhage on January 5, the day after he received the notification from the Justice Department. Family lore has it that Samuel was found with the letter in his hand. The Greenhouse relatives agreed that Barney was "very manipulative," but they also recognized his absolute conviction, that he was not "playing tricks on people," not pressuring them against "their own self interests," and that the verdict knocked the wind out of him.

In a frame of mind conditioned by the war news, by the Greenhouse setbacks, and with the Gottlieb–Rothko–Jewell–Federation of Modern Painters and Sculptors–Museum of Modern Art skirmishes under his belt, Barney heard about the demotion, in October 1943, of Alfred Barr, the founding director of the museum, to "Advisory Director," a post without administrative or curatorial responsibilities.[59] The news provoked a bile-filled article, "The Museum of Modern Art—A Failure," which, at the same time, was movingly desperate in its search for a meaningful anchor, for *something* in which Barney could believe—even if he had to invent it.

> The real danger the Museum holds for the American artists lies in its high-pressure attempts to inflict its shrewdly worked out aesthetique on the public and on un-suspecting artists. This aesthetique of bad taste had been dressed up in evocative labels, "Magic Realism," "American Romanticism." Under these magic titles the Museum hopes to confound a confusion that will lead to a chaos of taste. It is founded on the bad logic that since art is universal, everything therefore is art. It can only result in rendering the meaning of art meaningless. Its victory will be the sabotage of modern art in America.[60]

SEVENTEEN

BETTY PARSONS

Barney met Betty Parsons at Gottlieb's home in the winter of 1943, shortly after he had written promotional material, a press release, and polemical statements for Gottlieb and Rothko's WNYC radio appearance in connection with "The Portrait and the Modern Artist," at the 460 Park Avenue Gallery.

Parsons was a fey and fascinating spirit, the offspring of generations of wealthy and distinguished American families, one Northern, one Southern, unhappily united by her parents. Born in 1900, by the time she was in Gottlieb's living room she had already lived a picaresque epic as a rebellious socialite with an unfortunate failed marriage, a series of relationships with both men and women—including, she implied, Greta Garbo—bohemian residencies in urban and rural Europe and America, and years as an eccentric artist during which she acquired a spectrum of friends and connections, famous, artistic, and wealthy. She had a sympathetic bent for the mystical and spiritual side of life and a conviction about the revelatory nature of art; her come-to-religion moment occurred at the 1913 Armory Show. When Barney met her she was settled back in New York and, since 1936, had been selling art to her coterie initially at the Midtown Galleries (where, recommended by Robert Benchley, she showed her own watercolors), then at the gallery of Mrs. Cornelius J. Sullivan, and, ultimately, at the gallery in The Wakefield Bookshop, on East Fifty-Fifth Street. At the Wakefield, finally in charge of the gallery operation, Betty was newly confident in her "eye" and ability.[1]

Barney and Betty—they "took to each other like soap and water," Barney might have said—were one of the great combinations. Barney became Betty's advisor and provided her with intellectual gravitas, and Betty's endorsement and the platform she gave him legitimatized Barney's presence in the New York art community. She nicknamed him the "Great Statesman," instantly recognizing and appreciating his sophistication. For his part, he was drawn to her spunk, her breeding, her social charm, her informed worldliness (in Paris she was friendly with Brancusi and Giacometti), and, not incidentally, to her as someone who recognized and appreciated his sophistication. "All the others were country, the far west," she told an interviewer. "But Newman was really a definition of the urban man . . . . *Everything* about him."[2] The opportunity to work with Parsons was flush with potential, exactly what Barney had been waiting for.

When Gottlieb was offered a drawing show at Wakefield, Barney was the obvious choice to pen the brief, ardent catalogue essay Betty needed.

In the art of the Western world, he wrote,

the artist never dared to contemplate the human figure in terms of body and soul. That he left to the poets and philosophers. It is a pleasure, then, to see Adolph

Gottlieb repudiate . . . this attitude, to face the age-old philosophic problem of mind and matter, the flesh and the spirit, on equal ground with the philosophers. And he sets it forth with simplicity and dignity . . . . In these burning heads that are the soul, there glows that inner splendor, the "dry light" of man's eternal quest for salvation.

He closed by quoting Heraclitus: "The perfect soul is a dry light / which flies out of the body as / lightning breaks from a cloud."[3]

This language, this articulation, was a revelation for Parsons, who also believed in a creative "elite." She saw in Gottlieb's work, and in that of 21-year-old Theodoros Stamos, which she showed in late 1943, "secret forces of nature, mysterious knowledge" that she could not yet herself define, describe, or convey. But she intuited that there was "a miracle . . . in the making, [that] artists of the 20th Century, through the mystical powers of art, were in the process of recoding human sensibilities, of opening the human mind and spirit." As time went on, Parsons found that the words that Barney crafted "exactly reflected" what she was feeling and enabled her to form her feelings into thought. " 'Barney' became a touchstone in [her] life, a friend with whom she discussed virtually every aspect of the gallery and of her own progress as an artist; above all, Barney was both the theorist and artist by whom Betty measured all others."[4]

The harmony in their vision of art was not the only chord that resonated. In a passive and hidebound art market unrecognizable today, Parsons began to understand the importance of *championing* that vision if she were to succeed as a dealer: her artists deserved notice even if she had difficulty making sales. Already embedded in her life was Rosalind Constable, whom Parsons met in 1939 shortly before Constable became the "culture scout" for Time-Life Publications. The synergy between culture and the press that was Constable's arena, and to which she introduced Parsons, was something for which Barney brought a finely developed instinct.

And so, when Gottlieb's show received negative reviews from critics—the *Times*'s Howard Devree mocked not just the drawings, but the quoting of Heraclitus; Jewell didn't think "the idea clicks at all"; and the *New York Sun*'s Henry McBride gave sixty words to the "extremely puzzling pictures"—Barney was quick to respond.[5] He shot back a four-hundred-word challenge to McBride about his double standard: "it is all right for Europeans and South Americans to function as modern artists . . . to consider painting a medium for the expression of thought, no matter how involved, but woe to the American artist who dares to consider himself their equal."[6]

At last, Barney had the creative outlet for which he had spent years in training. It coincided with the most agitated period of the Greenhouse suit and Barney was energized, cycling high. He had lived his life up to this point as a *Luftmensch*; now he began to think of himself as "The Breton of American painting."[7]

In the middle of May, "Pre-Columbian Stone Sculpture" opened in the gallery at the Wakefield Bookshop. Three months earlier, the newly renovated Mexican and

Central American Hall in the American Museum of Natural History had reopened with great fanfare and drama: vibrantly colored walls, massive sculpture, dramatic spot lighting. Attending a performance of *Norma* at the Metropolitan Opera, Barney missed the celebrations but read the review—"one of the richest collections in the United States of works of art created in Middle America long before the Spanish conquest . . . the rarest creations of original American art [from] those fabulous civilizations that flourished south of the Rio Grande . . . for 2,500 years"[8]—and soon was writing to Dr. Harry Shapiro, chairman of the Department of Anthropology at the museum, to propose a "mutual show" at the Wakefield.[9]

Many artists, collectors, and writers had been involved with so called "primitive" art for at least three decades; now, in his brief catalogue, Barney's would have *his* turn.

While we transcend time and place to participate in the spiritual life of a forgotten people, their art by the same magic illuminates the work of our time. The sense of dignity, the high seriousness of purpose ["the sublime plane of 'moral state' " was added in a later version] evident in this sculpture makes clearer to us why our modern sculptors were compelled to discard the mock heroic, the voluptuous, the superficial realism ["the exercise of virtuosity" was added] that inhibited the medium for so many European centuries. So great is the reciprocal power of this art that while giving us a greater understanding of the people who produced it, it gives meaning to the strivings of our own artists.[10]

Parsons was persuaded to do the show because Barney, "a great authority on the primitive," in her opinion, told her that "the primitive world was a free world and this world that I was now in was a free world. It was no longer under the pressure of the academic world or the rules and regulations that I was brought up by."[11] Barney's own interest was more focused. He found in these "primitive" works a sanction for contemporary art other than the values of the Renaissance; they provided the "only way [he] could get out of the history of art as [he] knew it"—an ambition crystallizing in his mind at this time.[12] But he was not unaware of an extra-art "hook." Latin America was a hot topic. It was the focus of governmental attention as an important sphere of influence in postwar geopolitics, and culture was a useful evangelizing tool. American films, radio "sets" (to receive U.S. pro-graming), and cultural exhibitions were seeding several countries; regional wines were featured at Macy's Latin-American Fair.[13] Students were being exchanged, American universities adding programs, and star violinist Yehudi Menuhin went on an eleven-week Pan-American concert tour. Newspapers at this time did their part by reporting that since 1938 the Axis powers had greatly expanded their propaganda and espionage presence in Latin America. Barney was not a national propagandist, but he knew how to pitch a story.

In the summer of 1940 the Museum of Modern Art had presented "Twenty Centuries of Mexican Art," a monumental exhibition that filled the entire museum and sculpture garden. During the war years, MoMA organized nineteen exhibitions of contemporary American painting to be circulated throughout Latin America. In 1943 the museum showed "The Latin-American Collection of the Museum of Modern Art."

Around the time of "Twenty Centuries," MoMA's president, Nelson Rockefeller, was appointed to the newly created post of Coordinator of the Office of Inter-American Affairs, responsible for a "friendship crusade."[14] In that capacity, he met Rene d'Harnoncourt, an Austrian artistocrat who lived in Mexico in the 1920s and had become a well-connected diplomatic expert in Mexican art and antiquities, advising collectors and creating exhibitions, and shortly after Alfred Barr was fired as museum director Rockefeller, now Assistant Secretary of State for Latin American Affairs, had the talented, intelligent, and elegant d'Harnoncourt placed on staff at the museum, intending that he, with his Latin American expertise, would succeed Barr.[15]

Barney didn't know much about the museum staff's complicated Latin American associations, although he did have an opinion about its involvement generally: in "The Museum of Modern Art—A Failure," he wrote "that they had no pioneer leadership can be seen from the way they have exercised their position in another foreign realm—South America. There Barr and his backers have waddled in the official art with as much pleasure as they fawned on Cézanne."[16] But what Barney did know was that Latin America was *news*, and that was the context in which his show was mounted and publicized. He was not above pandering: "The growing aesthetic appreciation of pre-Columbian art is one of the satisfying results of our inter-American consciousness . . . . the excitement of the aesthetic experience will achieve the very aims of statesmen and scientists who feel that our common hemispheric heritage is a vital link in inter-American understanding, since it is by comprehending the spiritual aspirations of human beings that permanent bonds can best be built."[17]

And so when Luis J. Navascués, the editor of *La Revista Belga*—an official Belgian government, Spanish-language, New York-based, wartime magazine aimed at Latin America—asked Barney to expand the essay into an article on the show, he was alert enough to begin: "A friendship between peoples that is founded only on a common danger must be ephemeral. When the war is over . . . shall we then look for a new friendship based on business?"—before he got to his aesthetic agenda.

> If friendship between the Americas is to be permanent, we must build on a moral principle . . . . Permanent friendship resembles, as Aristotle explains, a moral state . . . . In art, the tangible expression of man's innermost, intangible, spiritual aspirations, we have a great school for interhuman learning. Through art, we comprehend the deep stirrings of man's soul . . . .
>
> It is a hopeful sign for our cultural rapprochement to watch the growing aesthetic appreciation of pre-Columbian art. For here we have ready-made, so to speak, a large body of art which should unite all the Americas since it is the common heritage of both hemispheres . . . . the moral base for that intercultural community.

The Wakefield show was a family affair. Of the fifty objects exhibited, ten came from the collections of friends of Barney, from John Graham or the journalist Frank Crowninshield, whom Graham advised; two from Parsons's friend the artist Henry Schnakenberg; and two very small Guerrero diorite figures were the property of "B.B. Newman"—the name under which Barney signed the essay—which he had purchased from Graham. Twenty objects were borrowed from the Museum of Natural History, which also consigned publications for sale. Parsons persuaded the Metropolitan Museum to loan display pedestals and a case; Siskind photographed pieces for the catalogue.[18]

Barney was feeling his oats—or his *chutzpah*. In late April, while plans for the show were "progressing satisfactorily," he wrote again to Shapiro at the Museum of Natural History: it "occurred to me tonight that important as it may be to bring the art of the ethnology museums to the attention of the art public, it is equally as important to bring to the scientific public an appreciation of the aesthetique involved in this art. I should like very much to do it. What do you think of a possible article for Natural History [the museum's magazine] on the subject matter of our exhibition—i.e. 'Sculpture in America before Columbus,' or 'The Modern Artist and Pre-Columbian Art.'" He promised it would be a "serious discussion," neither too technical nor popular "in the cheap sense," and it would help to focus attention "on our mutual show at the Wakefield and the Museum's extensive collection in its Mexican Hall."[19] The idea was a "good one," Shapiro responded; Barney should write it and "decide upon its disposition later."[20] But a month later, enclosing reviews, Barney wrote that he had been so "busy with the show that he had no time to work on the article."[21] Shapiro called the show a "highly successful experiment."[22]

Barney assembled a dazzling list of names to receive notice of the show and invitations to the preview, including Countess Gulda Toptani, Princess Fharaddin, Prince Osman, Mrs. Cornelius V. Whitney, Walter Chrysler, Ralph Pulitzer, Jr., Mrs. Theodore Roosevelt, Jr., Granville Winthrop, Duncan Phillips, Billy Rose; every member of the press who ever touched on art or culture; and museum professionals inside and outside of New York. He wrote to Lester Markel, Sunday Editor, proposing an article with Siskind's photographs for the *Times Sunday Magazine*; "it will have to be handled by Mr. Jewell on the art page," Markel responded.[23]

He got his name to appear—for the first time in relation to an *art* show—in the *Herald Tribune* section "Art of the Week" and a small ad in the *Times*: "The Macmillan Company, publishers of Medieval American Art by Pal Keleman, congratulates the WAKEFIELD GALLERY and Mr. B.B. Newman for the fine exhibition of PRE-CO-LUMBIAN STONE SCULPTURE now on display at the gallery." Always thinking synergistically, he produced a proposal for "a book that will present the sculpture of Pre-Columbian Mexico from its earliest archaic period to the coming of Cortez," characteristically attentive to multiple interests, commercial, as well as intellectual, citing the "growing appreciation in this country of this great artistic expression. This interest has been enlarged since the war as a result of our inter-American, Good Neighbor policy. (Witness the best seller-sales of 'Medieval America' by Keleman, at the high price of $22.50)." And he tried, unsuccessfully, to organize a symposium with an art critic, the "Mexican Consul General Sr. [Ricardo] Hill and Dr. Harry Shapiro" to open the show.[24]

He had achieved a certain standing from which he could pontificate on two platforms, the gallery and *La Revista Belga*, that carried more authority than brief catalogue forewords and cranky letters to art critics. The reality that his audience was nevertheless still quite limited did not seem to undermine his resolve.

He had "been mulling over" ideas, he wrote Shapiro. His motivation in organizing the Wakefield show "was the fact that the art public was not sufficiently aware of the Museum's art treasures." It now occurred to him that "the Museum could do . . . the converse of the Pre-Columbian exhibition by putting on exhibits of outstanding examples of modern art . . . with exhibitions of its own art objects removed from their ethnological background in true art-gallery style," and "put itself on the itinerary of all those who go to art shows," as did the Metropolitan Museum's concerts and the Brooklyn Museum's modern design shows.

> I have plans for several shows of outstanding modern sculpture and painting which I should be happy to share with you . . .
>
> Frankly, if you like the plan and if you have no one qualified, I would like to work it out. I wish to make clear to you that I am not looking for or trying to create a job for myself. I would be willing to offer you my services if there is some way of doing it without becoming involved in a formal job . . . .
>
> I hope you will forgive my exuberance, but I feel strongly about the need for a wider appreciation of primitive art and would like to do something about it.

Shapiro did not dismiss Barney's idea; in fact, he said it had "already occurred to some of us." And, although it was financially and administratively "unfeasible," he offered to talk it over with Barney "sometime." Barney immediately came back with a concrete proposal: an exhibition of the "Art of the Fighting Fronts of the Pacific." "Starting with Alaska, it would include the art of the Eskimo, North-west coast and Oceanic Islands . . . . Such an exhibition could be popularized on the slogan—'Know the art of the peoples your son is freeing from Japanese aggression.'" Shapiro responded, "the prospects are not by any means closed."[25]

Waiting for Shapiro's replies in Gloucester, he immersed himself in Jules La Forgue's "Physiological Origin of Impressionism." New York intellectuals had recently taken up the French Symbolist poet,[26] an early devotee of Impressionism, Schopenhauer, and ironic existential angst. During stretches of 100-degree days in August, Barney, with Annalee's help, embarked on his own translation of La Forgue—something notoriously difficult to do (T. S Eliot declared the poetry "impossible")—and a congenial interpretation. La Forgue dismissed as a dead academic language the "prejudice for drawing" through contour, perspective theory, and perceivable color, and he rejected as "school-engendered chimeras" (in Barney's translation) "the beauty of Greece, the color of the Venetians." These enunciations helped Barney clarify his objections to the narrative told by the Museum of Modern Art, and provided sustenance as he began to formulate a series of position papers and articles: "The Problem of Subject Matter" (unpublished); "The Anglo-Saxon Tradition in Art Criticism" (unpublished); "The Plasmic Image" (unpublished); and "On Modern Art: Inquiry and Confirmation," his review of MoMA's "Art in Progress," which *was* published—in *La Revista Belga*.

A story about an esteemed art historian—that he taught himself how to ride a horse by researching the subject at the library—comes to mind in relation to Barney's education around this time. Although he certainly *looked* at paintings constantly, his overwhelming identification with the maker, his ardor for the artist, could get in the way of developing his "eye." And so, when he found himself, finally, with a soapbox, he relied perhaps too much on his immersive reading. How else to understand, in "The Problem of Subject Matter," his claim that "were all knowledge, written and oral, of the dates of production of those great works that make up the art treasury of Western Europe to be lost (let us hope the work is not), all of them, from Veronese to Delacroix would become a dateless jumble. No man could trace its chronological progress with accuracy, so unified is its general appearance." To support a claim that "for good or bad, impressionism [gave] art an unmistakably different look" he felt it necessary to blur the evidence of every work in every society in Europe between Veronese and Delacroix, declaring all of it "blanketed by the velvet standards of the school of Venice."[27]

He wanted to both sound like and take on the historians and critics he was reading.[28] Critics from "Clive Bell to Herbert Read," Barney wrote, "have made careers for themselves as 'friends of modern art' by broadcasting the sophism that the values of modern art were a continuation of the great traditions of European painting begun in the Renaissance," and thereby concealed "its revolutionary character." The "shrewd popularization of the big lie that modern art isn't modern succeeded in establishing the position of respectability modern art now enjoys with museum directors and professional art lovers, but it wreaked havoc with the creative forces struggling for a footing, wherever this false thesis took root."[29] In other writings Barney wanted to establish the new painting as *sui generis*, and he was temperamentally and ideologically opposed to deterministic systems. But here he built one to support an insight awkwardly achieved but genuinely relevant to his peers: that historical justification for their work, and affirmation for themselves, could be found in the radical, tradition-defying way the Impressionists constructed their paintings, used color, and treated the flat surface of the canvas. This justification and affirmation he found to be outside the agenda of the overweening, canon-establishing Museum of Modern Art, which owned not a single Monet.

If we could describe the art of this, the first half of the twentieth century, in a phrase, it would read as "the search for something to paint"; just as were we to do the same for modern art as a whole, it must read as "the critical preoccupation of artists with solving the technical problems of the painting medium."

Here is the dividing line in the history of art! Whereas every serious artist throughout history has had to solve the problems of his medium, it had always been personal, a problem of talent. It was not until the impressionists that a group of artists set themselves a communal task: the exploration of a technical problem together. With them, talent became axiomatic. What to do with it? That has become the earmark of modern art movements. This critical reevaluation of the artist's role, this refusal to continue blindly the ritual of what art professors like to call tradition, had become a dividing line in art that is sharp indeed.[30]

The "artist's role": Barney could not separate the two words. It was not enough to *be* an artist as it was traditionally understood. The *role* the artist filled needed to be Olympian.

By the time the historic "Great Atlantic Hurricane" began traveling up the East coast in the middle of September, Barney and Annalee were back in New York, driving out to Long Island in his Chevy Sport Coupe. The car had a rumble seat, and in it, "frozen to death," were Siskind and his girlfriend Ethel, the roommate of Mary Alice ("Mell") Beistle—the future second Mrs. Rothko. With the hurricane approaching, they arrived along with Rothko at Motherwell's house, where "all the guys sat down in a circle," talking about painting and life, while "the girls"—Motherwell was married to Maria Emilia Ferreira y Moyers, whom he had met in Mexico in 1941—stood around, waiting for the dancing and fun to start. Motherwell, mimicking Breton, suggested that the men say what they thought they were "really about, why they were painting, why they were doing what they were doing."

Rothko had lost all faith that social agencies, like the Artists Union, could help people; "you had to do what needed to be done yourself"; *that*, he told the men, was his theme, "that was what his painting was all about." He—and, he added, Gottlieb—were "fed up with the political people [who] they felt . . . had a motive that had nothing to do with the integrity of painting." Siskind said his motivation was a "need for order . . . . my whole being was disturbed and disorganized." Disappointed by his past activism, he also had little faith in "politicians and social agencies"; the way he could feel a "sense of order was to make a picture, and that is why I thought that the picture had to be an absolute and unique thing."[31]

Motherwell had recently given a lecture at Mount Holyoke College, "The Place of the Spiritual in a World of Property," and he was preparing it for publication as "The Modern Painter's World" for the November number of *DYN*, the short-lived magazine edited by Wolfgang Paalen, an Austrian-born, Mexico-based Surrealist painter and theorist. "The function of the artist is to express reality as *felt*," Motherwell wrote. "The function of the *modern* artist is by definition the felt expression of modern reality." Not all values were eternal. Some values were historical—or social. The modern artist's "social history is that of a spiritual being in a property-loving world," and "the function of the artist is to make actual the spiritual, so that [it is] there to be possessed." Without "any vital connection to society"

> modern artists have had, from the broadest point, to replace other social values with the strictly aesthetic . . . . This formalism has led to an intolerable weakening of the artist's ego; but so long as modern society is dominated by the love of property . . . the artist has no alternative to formalism.[32]

Within this unfavorable reality, the artist was required to progress and create something new; if he failed to do so, history could not move forward. This challenge was fresh in Motherwell's mind with his first one-man show about to open at Art of This Century, but it was also on the minds of all of the painters who were neither pure abstractionists nor Surrealists. "When the intellectual habits of his culture become radically changed, the artist must concern himself with 'theories' whether he wants to or not," wrote Paalen in the first issue of *DYN* in spring 1942.[33]

Barney got to know Paalen later, at his Nierendorf Gallery opening in 1945, but he already was familiar with the entire run of *DYN*, especially what has become the most famous of the six issues, the "Amerindian" of December 1943. Articles by Paalen, Miguel Covarrubias, and Alfonso Caso, and reproductions of Paalen's collection, were "instrumental in the reception of ethnographic art and culture in the Americas and abroad."[34] Barney was captivated by Paalen's collection of Northwest Coast art, and talked to him about it at parties, but Paalen's theories of "primitive art" were too allied with Surrealist philosophy, and the man himself too "introverted," to become a friend.[35]

It was a confused moment. For artists who did not know how to categorize their work, as Gottlieb didn't when he worried whether his pictographs could be considered "art"; for artists who felt their identities and purposes were being taken out of their hands, as several did by Sidney Janis's book, *Abstract and Surrealist Art*, and its companion show at Mortimer Brandt's gallery, 1944 was filled with the sort of reflection and self-evaluation that Motherwell demanded of his guests.[36]

There's no record of how Barney answered Motherwell that evening, but he had already written about the "why." It was the "what" he hadn't yet formulated. Although he later claimed that his earliest surviving drawings were already begun in that summer of 1944, there is little evidence: no mention or indication in any of his writing, nor in Sarah's letters to him of what would have been an enormous breakthrough in Barney's life. Indeed, far from making art in the fall, he was frantic trying to raise the money to mount the Greenhouse appeal; he was resentfully teaching evenings at Washington Irving High School, and he was again channeling his pent-up rage about provincialism. On the back of a letter from the principal—"You have six late stampings on your card. Please explain"—Barney scribbled:

> Why is regionalism in art, in literature, in publishing an evil: Because it must live on hate, hate for the city, for the cosmopolitan, for Europe, for the foreigner, for the immigrant, for anyone or anything that is not of the region—for the outsider.

How else can it live than by fostering this hate of the competitor & the destroyer of regions. Whereas the city if not based on love is at the worst neutral—it is tolerant, tolerant of the country, of folk—its vision being broader it has not petty loyalties. As a matter of fact there is a tendency of city folks to idolize & idealize the country the regional cultures—because the city is a cultural idea—and as such fosters a respect for any culture & all cultures. In essence then regionalism must become anti-cultural anti intellectual.

He was also writing what he later called his "monologues," elaborating a grand philosophical–aesthetic stance. He grappled with the Museum of Modern Art's "canonical" genealogy; he formulated objections to "Anglo-Saxon" art criticism; he digested the mash-up of late 19th-century French art history presented in *Impressionists and Their Contemporaries*,[37] the new book by his bane Jewell. And in La Forgue's 1883 essay he found a way to harness his train of thought to the new agenda on which he was embarking with Parsons.

There is an immediate message in this article by La Forgue for the present day American artists, inherent in its revolutionary postulates. The last few years have seen a tug of war between artists, artists' organizations and the Museum of Modern Art. We have also had high hopes for a great American art renaissance by the use of government subsidy. The WPA, the cry for a permanent Secretary of Fine Arts, a national theater, etc., have been put forth as the possible key for a resurgence of art in America, the all-over catalyst for creative production, for an American culture. La Forgue's manifesto should wash all that from our minds.

The fact is that the Museum of Modern Art—that no museum—can act as a revolutionary force. It must in its very nature be the citadel for some academy . . . the Museum of Modern Art cannot be looked to for leadership by avant garde artists. To date, the Museum has never "made" an artist nor has any true artist needed the Museum . . . .

The artist must realize once and for all his revolutionary responsibilities. *Hope for help can lie only with sympathetic dealers.* Only when the artist learns to stand on his own feet instead of clamoring at the gates of the Museum is there any hope for an art renaissance in America. He should enlist the support of young and energetic new dealers who believe in his art and have the character to defend him. *The responsibility of the dealer is great indeed* [emphasis added].[38]

EIGHTEEN

THE BRETON OF AMERICAN PAINTING

At the end of 1944, Mortimer Brandt offered Parsons the opportunity to run a venue for contemporary work in a section of his Old Master gallery at 15 East Fifty-Seventh Street. Artists she had shown at Wakefield—Stamos, Hedda Sterne, Joseph Cornell, Gottlieb—encouraged Parsons to make the move. Wakefield was planning to close the gallery, anyway, and many followed her. Gottlieb urged Barney, whom—in spite of his philosophical participation—they had no reason to believe was a *painter*, to formalize his position, too. "Why don't you go in with her?" Gottlieb asked. "You're enjoying this activity here and you're writing." But Barney was firm. "I don't want to be a dealer. I want to be the Breton of American painting."[1]

Betty was happy to have Barney at her side in whatever capacity he chose. He "really knew everything there was to know about art. Nothing surprised Barney but good things made him smile." Over the next few years they would together regularly visit artists' studios, the Metropolitan Museum, the American Museum of Natural History. They would speak for hours and hours about the "timelessness of art, the eternal qualities of art, the *truthfulness* of art to the human spirit—regardless of the time or place that defined the *art history* of the piece." This was the "essential fiber in the total fabric of their conversation and friendship." In Parsons's estimation, Barney was "the most intelligent of all of the artists." What he impressed upon her, she said, was that it was "most important to struggle to dignify the work."[2] On the back of an envelope he wrote, "The responsibility of the dealer is to judge the buyer not to allow the buyer to judge the picture."[3]

That first season the "Modern Division" of the Mortimer Brandt Gallery had shows of Stanley William Hayter, Louis Schanker, Maurice Sievan, Graham, Stamos, Sterne, Boris Margo, Alfonso Ossorio, and John Stephan; several would become important in Barney's life. Other friends also had shows at the beginning of 1945, Gottlieb at the 67 Gallery, Rothko at Art of This Century (Jewell took another slap at *The Syrian Bull*), and Avery a well-received two-venue exhibition at Rosenberg and Durand-Ruel.

Affiliations and bonds formed during the Depression and WPA were left behind. A new, reshuffled art community was coalescing that retained for a while the old collaborative instinct, and Barney was well connected. He continued to look for ways to promote the work of his expanding circle of friends, who were thrilled to have him do so, and, especially, to *re-orient* to his satisfaction the way living art was thought about. Over and over in this period he describes others' interpretations with words like "faulty logic," "mistake," "complete misunderstanding," "contrary to prevalent opinion," "confusion," "misses the point," "full of confusions and errors."

But he also was willing to satisfy a commission—especially, at this time, one from Navascués, the person who had given him a secure, regular outlet for his written opinions. With a nod to his Mexican audience and his Belgian employers, Barney began "The Painting of Tamayo and Gottlieb" by announcing that although the "individuality" of their art was "very strong" there was good reason to look at the two together: an analysis of "working aesthetics should give us a clue to the attitude that ought to motivate our American artists . . . concerned with the establishment of an 'American' tradition." And with a nod to the Newman Doctrine, Barney elaborated the comparison:

> Tamayo and Gottlieb are alike in that, working in the free atmosphere of the art tradition of the school of Paris, they have their roots deep in the great art traditions of our American aborigines . . . . Only by this kind of contribution is there any hope for the possible development of a truly American art, whereas the attempts of our nationalist politics and artists, in both South and North America, have failed and must continue to do so.

Given the "great struggle of the Mexican revolution" it was difficult for a young artist to reject the call for a nationalist art by "the archnationalists Rivera and Orozco," but to not reject it indicated a "lack of understanding of what art is about—of its nature. Art is a realm of pure thought," and much greater would the contributions of artists be if they "had been given the status and *respect* [given] our scientists" (emphasis added).

In Tamayo's engagement with the "basic terror, the brutality of life," he looked to pre-Columbian art and the "present-day life of the Mexican Indian." In Gottlieb's attempt to "capture a sense of the tragedy of life," he looked to the abstract symbolism of the "healthy, primitive, well-integrated societies of the Northwest Coast."

"Man is a tragic being," Barney declared,

> and the heart of this tragedy is the metaphysical problem of part and whole. This dichotomy of our nature, from which we can never escape and which because of its nature impels us helplessly to try to resolve it, motivates our struggle for perfection and seals our inevitable doom. For man is one, he is single, he is alone; and yet he belongs, he is part of another. This conflict is the greatest of our tragedies.

"The Painting of Tamayo and Gottlieb" is noteworthy because Barney explicitly enunciates his excruciating consciousness of life; but it is far more significant for the marginalia on its handwritten drafts. Riffs on his earliest extant drawings, they constitute a dramatic break from any doodles he previously made—most of them typographical variations on the letter "B"—and establish a date, early 1945, for the birth of the artist we know.[4]

Barney's sixteen earliest wax- and oil-crayon drawings—some with pastel—and the slightly later brush-and-ink drawings, often described as evoking forms of biological germination and genesis, are rooted in the botanical and ornithological visual jottings that filled his notebooks from his summer sessions at Cornell and the Audubon

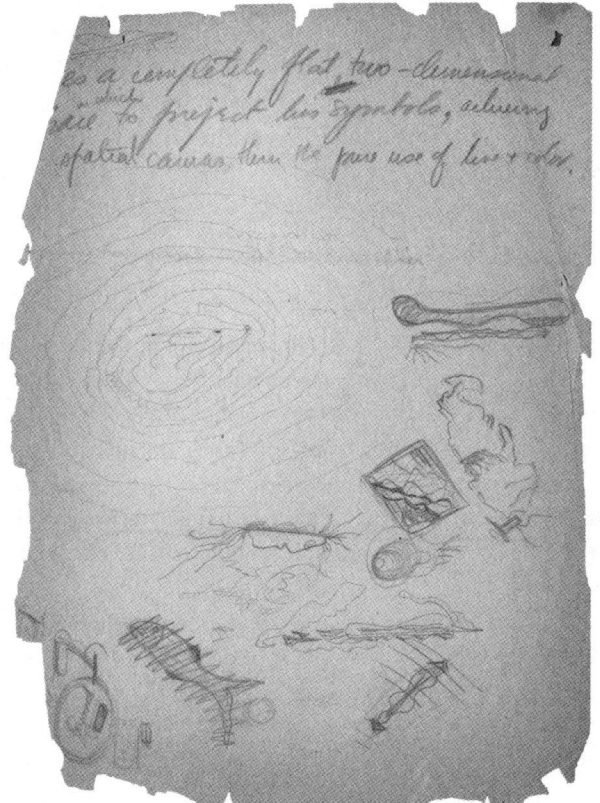

Fig. 16 Barnett Newman's doodles on a draft of "The Painting of Tamayo and Gottlieb," 1945. Pen, 11 × 8 ⅛ in. (28 × 20.7 cm), irregular

Camp. Sketches of the internal organs and systems of birds—skeleton, bladder, intestine, "duodenum," "proventriculus"—and topological schema of flora—shrub, "vaccinum," lobed, segmented and veined leaves, "hypogynous" and "epigynous" plant ovaries, "strobili" and "sporangia"—are precisely indicated and identified in Barney's notebooks.[5] These classroom and field notebook drawings were made years earlier; what encouraged him to mine them now? The scholar Brenda Richardson notes the confluence in March of memorial exhibitions of Wassily Kandinsky at the Museum of Non-Objective Painting and Piet Mondrian at the Museum of Modern Art. "Here were the two artists whose work, more than that of any others, both symbolized and manifested the two extremes of modern abstraction—the expressionist and the geometric—while yet sharing very specific kinds of spiritual foundations for abstract form." From around this time through 1946 Barney produced forty-nine drawings in a "tremendous burst of exploratory energy."[6]

We don't know the exact dates of these works, but Barney did not consider them ready for prime time. No one mentions seeing them—indeed, only one was shown before 1960 and many were unknown until after his death—and he seems to have told none of his friends about them before 1969, although Betty Parsons in 1978 said she was familiar with Barney's "early insect drawings."[7] But as he continued to write with a new focus, and as he continued to assist Parsons with enormous zeal—because "the responsibility of the dealer is great indeed"—Barney was an altered man. He wrote and curated with a different sort of confidence from his earlier, defensive bravura. He had made the first concrete move toward claiming his destined portion among those he considered his peers.

However the others viewed him—as co-conspirator or ally or equal—he had an expanding crowd who were finding, as the Newman family and the Greenhouses and Gottlieb had already found, that he was extraordinarily entertaining and generous with his assistance in whatever was needed. When a residency issue complicated Rothko's remarriage, Barney came to the rescue, enlisting Leah's well-connected husband, Philip Hochstein, as a fixer.[8] If Parsons needed him to, he himself manned the desk at the Brandt Gallery. He made lists for mailings. He wrote catalogue essays. He helped hang shows.

The Newmans became part of a social scene; especially they saw "a lot of Adolph and Mark, and Baziotes, [and] Jackson later." Pollock saw one of the shows at the Riverside Museum and told Peggy Guggenheim she had to see Gottlieb and Rothko;[9] Barney's essay put the former on Guggenheim's radar. He and Annalee became frequent guests at her home, and on occasion, she came to their apartment. On Saturdays after gallery visits people congregated at Betty's. Clyfford Still had relocated from the West Coast, where he met Rothko in 1944, and in the late spring of 1945 was briefly in New York.

The artist Buffie Johnson, a friend of Gottlieb's, made an introduction to Howard Putzel. Putzel, as Guggenheim's advisor, had brought many of the Americans—Pollock, Baziotes, Motherwell, Reinhardt, Hare, Rothko and through Rothko, Still—into Art of This Century. The previous winter, Putzel left Guggenheim and opened the 67 Gallery where his first show, "Forty American Moderns," included works by Avery, Baziotes, Stuart Davis, Gottlieb, Morris Graves, Hofmann, Roberto Matta, Motherwell, Pollock, Richard Pousette-Dart, Rothko, and Mark Tobey.[10] It was where Gottlieb had his January exhibition. "Barney wasn't painting" yet, "he was philosophizing," but Johnson remembered he made "a circle with sort of spatters coming off it" (likely *Pagan Void*, not exhibited until 1958), because he "wanted to be in the exhibition" Putzel was planning.[11] Putzel was less messianic than Barney, but the two men were after the same thing: to encourage, promote, and enlighten the public about artists whose works "indicate genuine talent, enthusiasm, and originality," as Putzel put it. "I believe," he wrote, "we see real American painting beginning now."[12]

"There has been a new spurt of activity in the Fifty-seventh Street galleries . . . that indicates that the art public is becoming aware of a new movement. Spontaneous, unorganized, emerging from several points, its force is being felt not by artists alone, but also by critics and dealers," Barney wrote, tipping his hat to his—and Parsons's—confrere. "Mr. Howard Putzel has gone to the trouble of organizing an exhibition of this trend as 'A Problem for Critics' in an attempt to give the movement a crystallized appearance—a name."[13] Putzel invited Barney to curate a show of Eskimo art the following October.[14]

"Milton Avery is an example of an advance-guard painter who has achieved the highest success without having his work properly understood," Barney wrote hyperbolically.

> The leading artist of the most distinguished dealer in America, Paul Rosenberg, Picasso's dealer, he stands at the peak of success in art circles, his work selling on equal grounds with the most distinguished Europeans. Yet his success is based on a complete misunderstanding of his work and of his statement as a painter.

Barney responded point by point to Jewell's *Times* review, denying Avery was simply a tasteful, charming, lesser "fauvist," an American disciple of Matisse. Avery himself disdained the "angle of whimsy [which] has been welcomed by his dealers, who use it to talk away his distortions and unconventionalities so that they can capitalize on his sensuous appeal" and turn him into a "decorative painter of sweetness and charm." In fact, he was "a leader in the fight that the American painter has had to undergo to free himself from the realism, the chauvinist isolationism, and the provincialism of American art. He has raised American painting to a level of equality with the work of Europeans."[15] Influenced by an ignorant and specious "journalistic attitude," dealers had shown the least risky work; in his best, Avery "has learned to get rid of personal sentiment, personal feeling, to arrive at a level of statement where his achievement is more universal."

And it was here that Barney introduced a concept not heard from him earlier. Surprisingly, for a man whose correctness of presentation from intellect to appearance was so precisely engineered, Barney praised in Avery's work

> an abandon, a nihilist explosiveness, a Dionysian orgy of freedom that is overwhelming . . . . It is no longer a question of reaction; it is a question of participating in *the* moment of communion.

Language reflecting this primal desire to find release from one's self began to appear around this time: the "ecstasy of true understanding" in "The Plasmic Image"; the "ecstasy man feels whenever face to face with deep insight" in "The Painting of Tamayo and Gottlieb"; "the original ecstasy of scientific quest" in "The First Man Was an Artist."

"Milton Avery" was written in January 1945. Overseas, in the background of Americans' lives, the Battle of the Bulge, the United States's most costly of the war, raged on. Eyewitness accounts of Nazi death camps began appearing the previous fall, with pictures later that spring. Brutally explicit photographs of dead "slave laborers" and "prisoners"—the word "Jew" was entirely avoided—were published in *Life* in May. Banner headlines and relentless war coverage reported the slaughter of American war prisoners, the total destruction of Warsaw, civilian panic in Germany, unimaginable atrocities, and, of specific interest to Abraham Newman, urgent debate surrounding the rescue and immigration of Jewish war refugees to Palestine. This was also the moment that Barney and Annalee finally tracked down Renee Rabinovitch, Annalee's 19-year-old French cousin, through Abe Rappaport, an American Greenhouse cousin stationed in France, and established contact with Renee herself in a stream of heartrending letters. They were sending money and clothing and shepherding the cumbersome process of arranging for Renee, who never recovered from the trauma of witnessing her parents' and brother's deportation, to come to America. (She had no further information and assumed they perished in a camp.) World events were reaching a crescendo of horrors: the destruction of Dresden; the extended battles of Iwo Jima and Corregidor; "Operation Meetinghouse," which unleashed upon Tokyo the most destructive bombing raid in history. First-hand reports came via Rappaport, who by May was in a "little town just across the Rhine" near where Mannheim had been before it was "wiped off the map by air bombardment."[16] The Newmans' phone bill, never small, was more than twice its usual size that June, the equivalent of 332.73 dollars in 2023.

In "Surrealism and the War," written that spring "now that World War II is coming to an end," Barney addressed these crises, making of them intellectual fodder to support his position regarding art. "Surrealism is dead," the dealers have acknowledged it. Nevertheless,

we must not overlook that the great contribution of surrealism was in its revival of subject matter . . . . They showed us the horror of war; and if men had not laughed at the surrealists, if they had understood them the war might never have been.

No [better] painting exists than the photographs of German atrocities. The heaps of skulls are the reality of Tchelitchew's vision. The mass of bone piles are the reality of Picasso's bone compositions . . . . The monstrous corpses are Ernst's demons . . . . The sadism in those pictures, the horror and the pathos are around us. Had men not laughed at them, they might not have needed to cry at them, to be them, to live in them![17]

He longed to find meaning through some sort of hyper-experiential channel. This was understandable and common in the cataclysmic climate: in the domain of literature, there was an upsurge in intellectuals' interest in writers like Danish theologian Søren Kirkegaard, Roman Catholic Jacques Maritain, and Arthur Koestler, who saw a movement toward spirit and away from science and reason. But as an ur-credo—"the ecstasy of my preoccupation"[18]—it continued through the rest of Barney's life, through, some twenty years later, his definition of man's birthright as "his urge to be exalted"[19] and his infatuation with the Dionysiac rock musical *Hair*—

he saw it at least four times—and the youth culture of the late 1960s. "Go down to the Electric Circus at the Dome on a Saturday night to see hundreds of young people sitting and standing in the greatest spectacle of piety that I've ever seen."[20] He would tell "rhapsodic" stories of the Hasidic temperament, about the state of ecstatic joy Hasidim achieved through dancing. Tony Smith, especially, immersed himself in this aspect of Barney's entertaining oratory; so "totally and completely" under Barney's spell, "he became Super-Jew," according to the painter Al Leslie, "he would quote Barney over and over" and "grew his own Hasidic beard."[21]

Barney turned again to poetry, the outlet in which he gave vent most fully to the existential crisis. The multiple drafts of the few poems that survive expose his turmoil and vehemence and despair, his struggle to integrate the parts of his life and to justify his ambition. They are quite literally a *geshray*, an unfiltered outcry.

"RHYMES FOR A BOMBED OUT NURSERY" (originally "Rhymes for an Anar-
    chist Nursery")

"LULLABY" (June 1945)

Alone a child is crying, glad
The world is coming to its end
His mother lies 'cross iron rails
Her head is full of iron nails [originally Her head tattooed with iron nails].[22]
Airplanes fly home for their beers
Amid cheers from a million hands
There women lie limp, their teeth in leers
And naked men are making their peers.

When will the wind stand still?

The men are marching through the trees
Eating salt and sugar
All ears, all eyes, all shivers
Their priest lies torn to slivers.
Birds of paradise stand on his knees,
Eating his wafers, corpus Christi,
Great leaves fall, the men all sneeze
The birds in Paradise are singing sweetly.
When will the wind stand still?

The rain falls slowly to burn the town
Fire eats up its river
The marble streets melt, the church turns brown,
The generals are eating liver.

Never never never never
The people chant as they drown
Peace peace peace peace
The rain keeps falling down.

When will the wind stand still?

Poetry "permitted the artist to approach that abstract handling of the language usual in music . . . to react . . . in a purely abstract way, or, in other words, to react to the words themselves."

This was an aside in Barney's impassioned reaction to "Spatial Form in Modern Literature," the essay in the July *Sewanee Review* that established the reputation of the young critic Joseph Frank as a literary theoretician. The idea that comparison with modern painting could help explicate Eliot, Proust, and Joyce was "perhaps one of the most valuable analyses of modern literature to appear in recent times," Barney granted. But Frank "misse[d] the point . . . of the modern concept of space," and this misunderstanding catalyzed Barney to define it for himself. Modern painting was a return to its "primitive function . . . as a vehicle of human expression." It was not something that could be explained by "following a Hegelian dialectical line" or what Barney called the "false philosophy of art" of German scholar Wilhelm Worringer; none of them "knows what art is about." Frank's essay got Barney into such a lather that he titled this last section of the unfinished, unpublished essay "Frankenstein":

the important truth underlying the creation of any art form and determining any art style concerns man's relation, not with the universe, but with himself. It is man's attitude toward himself that determines the form of his artistic expression . . . . It is the man who is terrorized by his sense of personal weakness who becomes concerned with divinity . . . .

The artist among primitive peoples was anything but a commentator. He was a maker of gods that had animate life, that had intrinsic meaning. As soon as we realize this, so soon will we understand his product, so soon will we understand the artist's function and return, perhaps, to the artist's original role.[23]

Surrounded by U.S. Navy vessels, Provincetown, Massachusetts was not entirely divorced from the war, but it did provide respite; in the years before air conditioning, escaping New York's stifling summer heat and pollution and concrete was an egalitarian imperative. The city itself, schools, restaurants, theaters, felt largely shut down.

Many artists among Barney's friends new and old summered in Provincetown—some like Buffie Johnson, Bill and Ethel Baziotes, Fritz Bultman, Nick Carone drawn by the presence of Hans Hofmann—and in the summer of 1945 so did Barney and Annalee, forsaking Gloucester. They escaped in early July for two months, an atypical stretch for them but not for the artists who were now their community. Their cabin, a studio right on the water, was "very cute . . . the nicest house we have ever had," Annalee wrote to her mother.[24] If internally Barney was churning, venting in poetry and theoretical/rabbinical *responsa*, he was also very happy to feel he was finally where he belonged. Mark and Mell Rothko came to visit, and found the "proficiency and charm" of their hosts, and the "native charm of the place itself" combined to make it "quite the best vacation in our memory."[25] The Gottliebs, sailing over from Gloucester the following month, felt the same: we "look back upon our Province-town stay as one of the most enjoyable trips we've ever had."[26]

The beach, with its socializing and fraternizing, was "the theater of activity . . . the tail wagging the dog" according to Ethel Baziotes: if you made it in the social life, your career was in good shape. Barney was not yet painting, and the community—who didn't know he thought of *himself* as an artist—still considered him as first a "public school teacher" and then an "art theorist." But Ethel fondly recalled he had "plenty of *saykhel*"—smarts—"he was a smarty-pants." He knew the "new center of the [art] world was going to be A or B," and he wanted to influence which form it would take.[27] Carone, on an Army furlough studying with Hofmann, ran into Barney on the beach with an elderly European couple, Hofmann students, talking about the philosopher George Gurdjieff. Barney did not present himself as an artist, he was not "compet-itive" as the artists were, he did not talk about his "own" painting at all. "He would be on the beach like he was an intellectual living amongst artists . . . . He would talk to you, and you would listen like you would listen to a professor."[28]

The Hofmann school was not so much a place where you learned, "as where you were exposed to other people and their ways of thinking," recalled Jeanne Bultman, a tall, elegant beauty married to Fritz. And one of the things Hofmann's wife, Miz, contributed was the advice to artists not to procreate. "Artists don't have children. They can't afford them. It gets in the way of the work." Not everyone took this to heart, including the Bultmans, who had two,[29] but those, like Barney and Annalee, who had come to their own similar determination, enjoyed the reinforcement. "I want both of us to have the most beautiful wives in captivity," the recently remarried (and temporarily childless) Rothko gushed about Annalee's new hairstyle. "Both of us seeming to have an untenable romantic attitude about this shady business."

More seriously, the friends considered how to amplify Barney's "possible function in the picture," something made more urgent by Putzel's ill health. After returning to the city, Rothko wrote to Barney that he was working toward "further concretizing my symbols," and hoped Barney was "jealous" of his focus, and would "be spurred to greater labors. Remember your promise of two chapters [of exactly what is not stated] one of which I expect by mail in a week or two."[30]

The most enduring event of that far from placid summer for Barney was meeting Tony Smith, who was building a studio in Provincetown for Bultman. One day, Barney saw a man sitting astride a house, banging in shingles. "Who is that crazy character sitting on a roof?" Barney said to himself. "Who is that dopey Englishman?" said Smith to himself, spotting Barney with his mustache and un-beach-worthy clothes.[31] Buffie Johnson introduced them.[32] Smith, not yet prominent as the architect and sculptor he would become, had studied art at the Art Students League, architecture at the short-lived "New Bauhaus" in Chicago, and apprenticed with Frank Lloyd Wright. He was also a scion of the A. P. Smith Manufacturing Company in New Jersey—the company whose name is on fire hydrants far and wide—whose economically comfortable childhood was marked by tuberculosis, a period of isolation, and a few years of rigorous Jesuit education. During the thirties, having grown a beard and become something of a clotheshorse, he "began to demonstrate the gifts of conversation and social charm for which he would thereafter be well known."[33] Smith's wit and disciplined intellect, as likely to be cast upon the ordinary as the profound, were what Barney had missed in a friendship since he grew apart from Borodulin. He immediately recognized Smith as a "man of terrific mind," he could discuss Mozart with his wife, opera singer Jane Lawrence, and the two men would eventually become soulmates. Smith, Barney told Irving Sandler, *understood* what the Parsons-plus-Gottlieb group was after; he became "passionately" involved in their work, he was "inside our private discussions. We had no inhibitions with him. He was part of the situation of our family."[34]

On August 6, Rothko telegraphed Barney the shocking news: "Howard Putzel died." The obituary ran in the *Times* a day later, the same day as the front-page banner headline, "First Atomic Bomb Dropped on Japan."

Emotions ricocheted wildly. "We are very happy at the good news that the war is over," Annalee wrote to her parents. "We had quite a celebration. I didn't know they could make so much noise here." All the fishing boats and navy boats were blowing their whistles. Everybody ran out to the main street shouting and singing. Stores were closed. Everyone was drunk.[35]

Even as the joy and relief, and the serial concussions of the war, of the camps, of the bombs began to sink in, the artists who had become so optimistic about their futures because of the initiatives of Putzel struggled with bereavement. Barney, the "artist–citizen," instinctively conflated the events, and again wrote to Jewell:

> Now that martyrdom—devotion to a cause even at the cost of one's life—has become an everyday role for millions of people, martyrdom for the sake of art is still a unique phenomenon, full of wonder. Howard Putzel lost his life in the service of art. That he was a dealer rather than an artist from whom society expects such sacrifices, makes it that much more remarkable . . . .
>
> He believed in the new art around him and that this art, the first authentic art movement to come out of America, deserved a home and a champion . . . . He let the world know that in New York, separated from the leadership of Paris, artists were expressing a mature statement completely their own . . .
>
> What is the nature of this statement? Essentially it is a religious art, a modern mythology concerned with numinal [*sic*] ideas and feelings . . . . The present

movement transcends nature. It is concerned with metaphysical implications, with the divine mysteries.

Barney rehearsed his conclusion from his July essay, "Frankenstein." These new painters "have brought the artist back to his original, primitive role—the maker of gods."[36]

Then he revised with increased bitterness the poem, "RHYMES FOR A BOMBED OUT NURSERY," "PRAYER (September 1945)."

Save me from the selfless life
Of love
With its blissful state of sleepy being . . .
The man who loves a woman
To be with his woman

The man who loves money
To be with money
The man who loves nature
To be in Nature
The man who loves ART
To be with his love feelings
The man who loves his country
To be with his countrymen
And the man who loves power
To be the power.

Save me from the fate of lovers . . .
The women-lovers
Who practice slavery
The money-lovers
Who never give
The mankind-lovers
Who march meek to the gas chamber
The my country-lovers
Who die in uniform
The ART-lovers
Who never create
The success-lovers
The power-lovers
Who die without principle.
For there is no silence
Like the love in blind eyes! . . .

The man who hates women
Will free them
He who hates men
Must save them
The man who hates money
Will abolish it
He who hates Nature
Must conquer it
The man who hates ART
Will create art
He who hates his country
Must live in the world
And the man who hates power
Will destroy it . . .

The Church says that God says:
Men are evil, so I shall destroy them!
And yes, it is true
Men are evil.
So why not destroy all men?
But I, Oh mercy,
I am a man
And I hate myself
Shall I destroy myself?
But I, mercy, mercy,
I am a man
And I love my self
Shall I destroy myself? . . .

Oh, if only all men were blind
With hate . . .
And hated themselves
And everyone else
And everything on earth and in Heaven
That they might act
To destroy the world
To build a Heaven for each
And every solitary Son of
A man.

Each himself
By himself

For himself
Forever and ever.

Amen

Barney reacted to the end of the war with affect strikingly different from his disposition during its prosecution. In the early forties he was righteously confident, externally energetically engaged in everything *but* the world conflict. The conclusion, however, provoked profound self-reflection. Years later, recalling the circumstances around the genesis of the poem "Rhymes for a Bombed Out Nursery," originally called "Self," he told an interviewer that after the war, he "became very aware of *myself.*" In the poem, he "felt that the real issue is the self . . . the whole notion of existence . . . the notion of being." At the time of the interview, 1963, he said he was misunderstood as "being involved in the denial of self"; it seemed "so strange that it isn't clear: that I am *asserting* the self above all extraneous matters." For Barney, as always, it was a *moral* issue: the insight may have been brought on by the war, but he rejected the idea that "the question of war or non-war is the necessary imperative for a consideration of moral issues." To take one's life "seriously" did not mean taking one's "career or . . . place in the world seriously." It meant to "take the *meaning* of one's life seriously."[37]

For those who had been at it a long time, making art in the new, post–Depression, postwar world seemed a less foolhardy choice than before. Looking for a new gallery in New York at the beginning of September, Gottlieb did not "feel pessimistic . . . Howard [Putzel] did enough for me in the past year, to carry me along this year on momentum alone."[38] Rothko wrote that he was working on his "symbols"; it made his head hurt, but it was "exhilarating." Even Sarah was relaxed about losing her job—the Army Air Force Information office where she was a specialist had been broken up. "This should be my cue to stop + start painting."

Barney's quotidian struggle was no less financial than Sarah's, if self-inflicted: exorbitant telephone bills, summer rentals, car insurance, restaurant tabs—in the interest of *bella figura*, Barney could be irresponsibly generous. There were luxuries like fine suit fabrics and an obscenely expensive ultraviolet sun lamp that helped "defense workers and service men keep physically fit." He was bouncing checks, had at least two bank loans, and was borrowing from family members. But he had just begun making drawings he considered worthwhile and the only obstacle he recognized was how to make them meaningful—"moral." For that, he had to take himself seriously, and he began scouting a proper artist's studio.[39] An independent studio was not required for an artist to be considered serious; many didn't have one. "You used part of an apartment, selecting the largest room with the best light, and that became a studio," recalled Esther Gottlieb.[40] But Barney craved the symbol.

The groundwork, his aesthetic foundation, had been laid on his own terms. "I have to say what I think because if I don't say what I think somebody else will say what I think and it won't be what I think."[41] He assumed the world was prepared for him. "Barnett Newman was a mystic in art," was the way Ethel Baziotes interpreted Barney's trajectory. He "had the need to go from verbalism to the paintbrush . . . he wanted the art world to know what was in, was *within*, Barney Newman's soul and psyche," before he jumped with both feet.[42]

NINETEEN

THE PLASMIC IMAGE

John Graham's *System and Dialectics of Art* provided precisely the reinforcement that Barney needed to formulate his aesthetic position. The 1937 book had among artists "cult status," establishing a "lexicon for speaking and writing about art." The two men met at the Art Students League in 1923 when Graham was the monitor in John Sloan's class,[1] but Barney's copy, with its undated, affectionate, multilingual inscription, likely dates from the early 1940s, when their friendship was at its closest: "*To my dear friend Barney / Friend and poet in token of appreciation* IOANNUS MAGUS SERVUS DEI / *Ex ungue leonem / Qui bene castigat bene amat / L'art est comme le suplice du pol* [sic] *ça commence bien mais ça finit mal.*"[2]

The Newmans very rarely acquired works by other artists, but at some point they came into possession of *Portrait of Elinor Graham*, 1943, purchased or—like *Syrian Bull* and *Rape of Persephone*—a gift. The older artist's contribution to the Federation show was dismissed by Jewell as unceremoniously as was Rothko's and Gottlieb's—"John Graham continues his bizarre experimentation with paint, giving us this time a device called just 'Painting,' which might perhaps derive in some queer sort of way from Lautrec, though it also might perhaps not. One can hardly say." Graham was not a co-signer of the notorious letter to Jewell, but he felt the same gratitude to Barney, found him a sympatico ear and loyal friend during the '40s.

Barney and Graham's personae were in sync: both were flamboyantly cultured, with little formal training in art but holding deeply developed theories and opinions, and Graham was well known for embodying art as "a way of life as well as a way of seeing."[3] They both had a kind of *noblesse oblige* that inclined them to be—Graham at this time, Barney, later—extraordinarily generous mentors to younger generations. Junior by eighteen years, Barney saw in Graham an acknowledged, recognized artist occupying a robust alternative to the kind of deprived artist's life that Barney already had rejected as something foreign to himself, impossible to imagine. It must have been soothing to Barney that "Graham could go for extended periods not making art at all [abstaining] when his vast energies were tapped by" a variety of pursuits and experiments, "or dire finances sidetracked him to supply life's necessities."[4]

System and Dialectics of Art was structured as a kind of primer, or instruction manual—it was called at the time of publication, a "catechism of art"—a format that concurred with Barney's own pedagogical, lecturing bent. The text invoked the unconscious—"Abstraction as a figure of speech opens the unconscious mind and allows the truth to emerge"—which nodded to Surrealism, an ethos with which Barney was not comfortable. But its self-regard was very particular, even narcissistic, and that ran parallel to Barney's philosophical and psychological disposition.

"What part does art play in human civilization?" Graham asked. "It urges humanity to make efforts for no use."[5] Or, as Barney would say, "the necessity for dream is stronger than any utilitarian need."[6]

"What is Talent?" Graham asked. "Talent is just an animal ability. There is no merit in talent itself . . . Until mind and intuition build it up into a source of organized expression talent has no value."[7] Or, as Barney would say, "men of skill and taste . . . play with color, line, and shape . . . instead of creating an expression that is abstract in the sense that it makes articulate an abstruse concept that can be expressed in no other way—that is, the abstract thought of the creator."[8]

"Genius," Graham wrote, is "talent brought to consciousness," a man "capable of projecting his personality into the future . . . an explosive mixture of boundless self-indulgence, vision, capacity for making stupendous efforts, sorrow-worship, self-sacrifice and destiny." Genius, being a gigantic engine, "devours ideas, space, time, paint, canvas, paper, women, wine . . . scorches everything in his vicinity: wife, children, friends, animals, objects. [He] is modest when appreciated and arrogantly confident when defied. At all times genius is cognizant of his value." Virtuosos, by contrast, are "facile, witty, and sociable . . . . acclaimed, admired, successful . . . . They wear long hair, flowing neckties . . . they look the image of the artist. A real artist, on the other hand, never looks the part. Picasso looks like a tailor."[9] Barney, who dressed like a banker, and advised other artists to wear a coat and tie when photographed or out in polite society,[10] had contempt for the tasteful "manipulation" of the elements of painting that led to "virtuoso art." He would rage at the "credo of a virtuoso, of the salon painter, of the social and public man." A man's work and the man who makes the work, he wrote, "form an equation. The same virtuosity that begs in the work for public approval has been the means whereby moral issues against the philistine world could be juggled."[11]

Every artist in Graham's orbit could find in *System and Dialectics* the justification for their own work and their own lives. Barney wasn't unique in hearing the book speak to him; rather he found what he required as he was contriving his own aesthetic theories: not a directive, but a confirmation that the vocation was noble. And, not insignificantly, confirmation that it is the *artist* who is exalted, for only a genuine artist could produce genuine art. "What is the ultimate, logical destination of a work of art? . . . The reduction of the same to its minimum elements," Graham said. "Painting starts with a virgin, unified canvas and if painted upon ad infinitum it reverts again to a plain, unified surface (dark in its color) enriched by *experience lived through* [emphasis added]."[12]

"What is painting?" posed Graham. "Painting is a creative exploitation of the potential value of a plain surface. Painting is the Space articulating . . . . What is art? Art . . . is a systematic confession of personality . . . . A work of art is a creative, significant and unique expression of one's point of view."[13]

In a sense it was Graham who provided permission in February 1944 for Barney to quote Heraclitus in reference to "the stirring that takes place in [Gottlieb's] pictures": "The perfect soul is a dry light / which flies out of the body as / lightning breaks from a cloud."[14] And when, a little over a year later, Barney produced his most ambitious enunciation of the ideas upon which he had been ruminating, Graham's opus provided a shadow model.

As Graham did in *System and Dialectics*, Barney organized "The Plasmic Image" pedagogically. His explanations, less systematic and more long-winded, are equally prescriptive. Like Graham he is concerned not only with identifying what was genuine but, significantly, what was specious in art as it was practiced. And Barney was not afraid to go further. Graham might be satisfied that art was a "systematic confession of personality," but for Barney, that solipsistic source was insufficient, meager: "the truth is not a matter of personal indulgence, a display of emotional experience. The truth is a search for the hidden meaning of life." Barney posited a more vainglorious fountainhead: "In his will to set down the ordered truth that is the expression of his attitude toward the mystery of life and death . . . the artist like a true creator is delving into chaos. It is precisely this that makes him an artist, for *the Creator in creating the world began with the same material* [emphasis added]." The artist's role was to "wrest truth from the void." For Graham, the source of creation was sorrow: "An ability to suffer is a gift, a gift possessed by few," talents "deprived of the gift of sorrow, produce only near-values," and "capacity of perception depends greatly on capacity to suffer. Suffering is the measure of one's genius. Suffering extends the limits of consciousness." But "sorrow" was too New Testament for Barney. *His* wellspring was the more Old Testament "terror."

Like Graham's, Barney's system could only have been developed by someone bucking tradition. Barney spent years thinking about art, analyzing, searching for "this mythic, fundamental thing which somehow one felt was important,"[15] but he had had very little traditional training, and very little experience of actually making something he was willing to recognize as the genuine article, so impossibly elevated were his standards. Unlike the other artists with whom he exchanged ideas, he was not developing a mode, a new approach, an *evolution* of his style. He had to live as "the new painter": "concerned not with his own feelings or with the mystery of his own personality but with the penetration into the world-mystery . . . . attempting to dig into metaphysical secrets . . . his art is concerned with the sublime. It is a religious art which through symbols will catch the basic truth of life, which is its sense of tragedy."[16] Artists throughout history have had analogous intentions, have thought of themselves as performing as mystical, spiritual, religious—in Barney's sense—a ritual. But in Barney's case the "Stance" came first, and the stance enabled him to make the art. He was giving birth to more than a style; it was a different genre, one in which he could excel, and that would acknowledge, even lionize, what he had to contribute, something newly capable of satisfying "the intensity generated by man's"—or at least Barney's—"spiritual need." To do that he had to achieve nothing less than the delegitimation of the values of "Western European art." The Stance was a matter of *will*, and it arose from the heroically undeluded recognition of the human condition. It was "an address to the unknowable."[17]

In this embryonic stage his conception depended upon an aesthetic–spiritual notion that he called "mental plasma." He used the description only once, but it constituted the very basis of the "plasmic," Barney's neologistic response to the formal—"plastic"—qualities that Anglo-Saxon critics insisted serious art should have. He had to vanquish "the propaganda for plastic form" which was "so disarmingly powerful that it has become the most difficult and entrenched enemy of the new painter." "Plasmic" was an ultimately ineffable quality that rose from the *will* of the artist. And Barney found it in what was then called "primitive" art. It was the first iteration of Barney's assault on the received ideas of "Western European aesthetics."

It was common at this time to find in primitive art "plastic values" as they were currently understood—qualities of color, line, shape. But Barney proposed an entirely different understanding.

> If we are to understand primitive art . . . we need to get rid of, to slough off, the skin of "beauty" in which we have grown up, which has become the cover that we use to include the art works of our world. We do not enter into the world of primitive art by reading into it the concepts of plastic form we know or by attempting to correlate these primitive works with our own expression. We must educate ourselves to look at them through the eyes of their creators . . . . *the only way of describing these works is outside the terminology we have developed for the works of our culture* [emphasis added].

A new set of terms was needed to describe the power to "link the beholder with essences."

"Plastic," implied "heightening" or "glorifying" forms already known, or "sugar-coating" a thought "so that its impact will be made by stealth, by intriguing our senses," whereas Barney's "plasmic" denoted "forms that carry or express abstract thought, a presentation in tangible symbols of some inner idea or concept."

> Essentially, comprehending the work of the primitive artist involves a denial of Western European art. Essentially, the new painter who is emulating the primitive artist by his preoccupation with plasmic instead of plastic form is also denying Western European art.
>
> It is about time that we reconciled ourselves to this denial. The history of the revolution in art known as the modern-art movement is an attempt at this denial. The cubists, the fauvists, and their followers . . . have been afraid to make a clean break . . . [The new painter] is declaring that the art of Western Europe is a voluptuous art first, an intellectual art only by accident. He is reversing the situation by declaring that art is an expression of the mind first and that whatever sensuous elements are involved are incidental to that expression. The new painter is therefore the true revolutionary, the real leader who is placing the artist's function on its rightful plane, the plane of the philosopher and the pure scientist who explore the world of idea, not the world of the senses . . . [in the pursuit of] *the ecstasy of true understanding* [emphasis added].

Barney's ruminations were provoked by the spring 1945 Museum of Modern Art retrospective of Piet Mondrian, who had died in New York the year before. "There has been a great to-do lately over Mondrian's genius. His point of view, his fanatic purism, is the matrix of the abstract aesthetic. His concept, however, is founded on bad philosophy and on faulty logic." Abstract, "purist" art, Barney derided as empty, "mere arabesque." To be valid, to be meaningful, the plastic elements must be "converted into mental plasma" which would enable "sympathetic participation on the part of the beholder in the artist's vision." Only then will the work have "the living elements within it that will carry the living thought."

> To the new painter . . . art is a realm of thought . . . to express an idea, a concept that will agitate the mind of the reader . . . color, line, shape, space are the tools whereby his thought is made articulate. They are not pleasure elements that the artist should dote over . . . it is not the plastic element that is important; [not] the voluptuous quality in the tools that is his goal, but what they do. It is . . . the subjective element in them that will in turn stir a subjective reaction in the reader of the language that is important. *Here is the real difference between the traditional abstract painter and the new painter. Whereas the abstract painter is concerned with his language, the new painter is concerned with his subject matter, with his thought* [emphasis added].

Art must become "a metaphysical exercise" because the new painter is in the same position as the primitive artist, "always face-to-face with the mystery of life . . . always more concerned with presenting his wonder, his terror before it" than with "plastic qualities."

"The subject matter of creation is chaos."

Who read this treatise? With whom did Barney share it? What did he hope to *do* with it? He was not someone who would "rush into things," Annalee would tell interviewers after he died, he was "the kind of guy who had to think through things very carefully, think out his ideas."[18] In Parts One through Six he elaborated a reasoned statement of philosophy, moving from the general to the specific; in multiple drafts he struggled to work out principles, to *logically* support an ultimately supralogical "metaphysical exercise": how to penetrate the "world-mystery" and achieve the "ecstasy of true understanding."

A coherent ontology established, he could move beyond paralysis in the face of his own ambition. In Part Seven, he targeted the "highly articulate school of art criticism"—the formalism promoted by Clive Bell, Roger Fry, and advocated by the Museum of Modern Art. It was motivated by "the American urge for popular education," and it was "the greatest handicap to any artist who wishes to advance art and to find individual expression."

Barney elaborated these objections and pulled them out as a separate essay, "The Anglo-Saxon Tradition in Art Criticism." Since making the cause of Gottlieb and

Rothko his own, Barney was familiarizing himself with a growing body of literature. "The book on modern art has become a new genre, and the writer on art a new profession . . . . Already it has a tradition," which Barney identified as beginning not with Ruskin, whose approach developed from literature, but with Fry whose "attitude was conditioned by the scientific interest of his time."

Fry's purpose was:

> determined by the educational impulse that makes up so much of rationalism: to make everything in the world crystal clear even to the average mind. His scientific aims were framed by the desire to give the average man the "know-how," the key to the world of art, just as English industrialism was giving people the pragmatic keys to science. His books were for laymen, not for artists.

Since Barney's lifelong quest was to establish his superiority, to distinguish himself from "the average man," he was not sympathetic to the idea that "if one understood Bell's 'significant form' one could understand *art*." It could be argued, Barney granted, that this impulse was required in "Anglo-Saxon countries where beauty and art are ignored, where no natural taste exists [and an] effort needed to be made to separate aesthetic values from all others so that English-speaking peoples would show tolerance to abstract aesthetic properties." But, he noted, philistinism is a "universal . . . an international fault," and, notwithstanding that, the story of French criticism was very different:

> written for the artists or for the writers, or, if you will, for the intellectual classes. Instead of the objective approach so characteristic of art criticism in our language, French criticisms were projections into literature of the painters' affirmations. Instead of coldly analytic exegeses, theirs were poetic effusions, obscure, lyric, personal, completely subjective.

La Forgue, Apollinaire, Breton, "the voices of modern art . . . developed a creative tradition of art criticism alongside the very creations of the painters and sculptors themselves"; instead of writing about "form and shape" they "produced a type of criticism that is mystical, metaphysical, poetic.

"French criticism has attacked the problem from the point of view of the creator, of the artist, while our criticism has always been written from the point of view of the layman . . . [and] although this layman's point of view has produced some fine and intelligent writing, it cannot motivate the production of art."[19]

Although Annalee filed twelve "sections" together as "The Plasmic Image," Barney's original intentions are unknown and Parts Eight through Twelve are written in an entirely different, more journalistic, voice than the earlier seven. Repetitious and overlapping, they are less theoretical, more promotional, and appear to be drafts for an article or catalogue introduction. The war is not yet over, but its "international character . . . had the effect of muting, if it did not completely silence, the professional Americanists who [have] spent the last two decades trying to foster a cheap popular art under the guise of an isolationist political slogan." He described the "new spurt of activity in the Fifty-seventh Street galleries," and it is clear that Barney had moved beyond the issues raised with Jewell nearly two years earlier, even as he couldn't resist noting that Jewell "tried to belittle and label this 'new' movement as 'Globalism.' It is significant that Gottlieb and Rothko are now at the forefront of this present trend."

The span of time spent writing "The Plasmic Image" marked a sea change. If the later parts assumed "unmistakably a movement in the direction of 'subjective abstraction,' " and could marshal evidence of critical recognition, in the early parts it was obvious that Barney still felt the need to construct a meaningful theoretical basis for the importance of his friends' radical new work. But just as clear is that Barney was creating the space to enter himself.

TWENTY

THE TERROR

"The defense of human dignity is the ultimate subject matter of art," Barney wrote a few months after Samuel Greenhouse's humiliating loss and tragic death. "And it is only in its defense that any of us will ever find strength."

The context was a catalogue foreword he was asked to write by the Polish expatriate constructivist Teresa Zarnower for her show at Art of This Century. In her new work, Zarnower felt that "purist constructions in a world that she has seen collapse around her into shambles and personal tragedy" were not enough. "*Art must say something* [emphasis added]." Barney was depressed, so disillusioned by losing the fight against the cruel "system" that, when Peggy Guggenheim herself asked him to review her autobiography, he managed only three limping sentences: "Peggy G is like a character out of Henry James. P.G. in this story of her life gives us a picture of an America, Americans want to forget. The America that having just come out of its role as a frontier country to become the frontier millionaire producing country."

But if in the writing he vented his bile at the injustice rampant in America, on the same page something more interesting happened: doodles that riffed on the drawings he was now producing covered the lined paper. There are swooping, wrist-driven curves, implied hollow sacs, and worm-like cursive meanders formed into "compositions." One sketch has a proportionally large hollow with a radiant aura that found further elaboration in an oil and crayon drawing and in the oil painting *Pagan Void*, where they are layered with amoeba shapes from the same distracted little sketches (plate 3). Another vignette has the sprouting verticals, disk, and sloped shaded area that were reconfigured in the very early oil on canvas *Genesis—The Break* (plate 2).[1] Barney was closing in on a way to superimpose his conceptual ideas with their physical manifestation, to make his "vehicle" and his "abstract-thought complex" congruent.[2]

Fortuitously, *Ambos Mundos*, a new magazine started by the publisher of *La Revista Belga*, invited him to review "Art of the South Seas" at MoMA, which the curators linked to surrealism. He was diligent, collecting maps, scholarship, and other research materials, but he knew what he wanted to say, whether the science supported it or not: in an early draft, he duplicated language from the museum's catalogue regarding Melanesia's climate, only to dispense with it in the final version because the scientific evidence conflicted with his intended interpretation.[3]

"All life is full of terror," he wrote, and "we, living in times of the greatest terror the world has known, are in a position to appreciate the acute sensibility primitive man had for it." He had a theory: that the source of terror varied among civilizations, and impacted the art they produced. "The distinguishing character of Negro African Art is . . . terror before nature as the idea of nature made itself manifest to them in terms of the jungle." Mexican art contained "a terror of power." In contrast to those traditions, the distinguishing character of Oceanic art was "its sense of magic,"

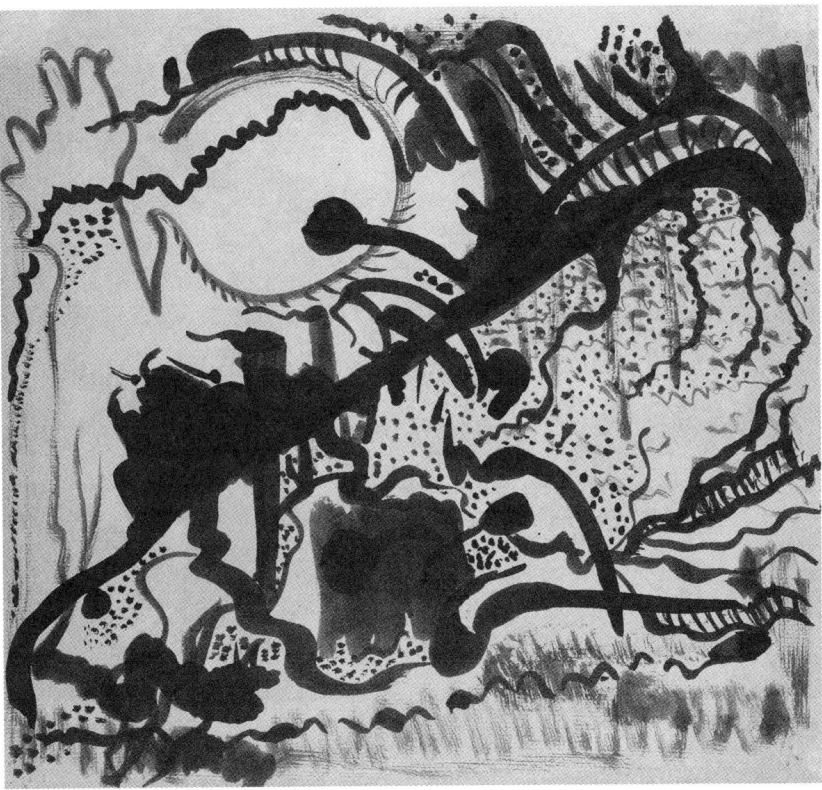

Fig. 17 Barnett Newman, *Untitled*, 1945. Brush and ink on paper, 14 ⅞ × 16 ⅜ in. (37.8 × 41.6 cm). National Gallery of Art, Washington, D.C.

which, while also based on terror, was defined by Barney—with what one scholar called "unembarrassed arbitrariness"[4]—as "unlike the African terror before nature [because] this is a terror before nature's meaning, the terror involved in a search for answers to nature's mysterious forces."

> In Oceania, terror is indefinable flux . . . the sea and the wind, unlike the static forest and the jungle, approach metaphysical acts. Whether benign or catastrophic, they arise out of the mystery of space.[5]

It all led to an epiphany of sorts: the congruence Barney sought could be found in "the mystery of space." That is what, as an artist, he would need to translate onto canvas. And later, when he did, he understood that "the terror of that blank area is the whole issue."[6]

In May, when Mortimer Brandt decided to return to England, Parsons had to choose to suspend her business or to take over his lease for 15 West Fifty-Seventh

Street and open under her own name. She put together 5500 dollars from her savings and loans from artist–friends Hedda Sterne, Saul Steinberg, Hans Hofmann, and Henry Schnakenberg, and socialite friends Dorothy Haydel "Dumpy" Oelrichs and Hope Williams, and rented the space. She stripped it bare, painted it white, emptied it of furniture, and installed bright lighting. "A gallery isn't a place to rest. It's a place to look at art. You don't come to my gallery to be comfortable," she said, claiming that hers was the first gallery with the "pure, large, bright open space" that the new breed of artist—*Barney*'s breed of artist—required. She would open in September.[7]

"What do you need to make a place the center of the art world?" Annalee reconstructed Barney's reasoning: "Well, you need some good artists, you need a sympathetic museum—and he thought the Museum of Modern Art *could* be sympathetic, although Barr really liked European art more—and you need a dealer. And who is a dealer? A person who cares about art and who is willing to sit with art a whole day and not be bored. [In] a room with an open door where painting could be hung. And Barney felt that Betty, because she was an artist herself . . . was the person."[8] He went to work to make sure Parsons had that roster of artists, the exact formula he thought would most brilliantly establish the Betty Parsons Gallery. He made lists and fantasy schedules for the gallery, plotting not just a stable of artists—Avery, Rothko, Siskind, David Smith, Calder, Tamayo, Matta, Lam—but also ambitious shows that would respond to the zeitgeist, including "modern" artists from South and Central America, "music of John Cage," "Impressionists (a reevaluation)," "aesthetics of Industrial Design," "Monet and Kandinsky," and "Gothic form."

Barney was alert to a newly ecumenical sense of possibility in the city. Delegates to the new headquarters of the nascent United Nations flooded into temporary quarters in Queens where the World's Fair had been seven years earlier; "Miss America" was not only from New York, but was also, for the first time, a Jewish girl (Bess Myerson). Manhattan's old-fashioned trolleys were being replaced by modern buses. Barney's old destination, the City Hall IRT station, had to close because it could not accommodate new, longer subway cars. And culture was a growth industry. *Oklahoma!*, the first musical theater to fully integrate songs and classical dance into its dramatic plot, was a huge hit on Broadway, joined by *Annie Get Your Gun* and *Born Yesterday* (called a "Marxist farce" by some reviewers) and the dark, bitterly disillusioned *The Iceman Cometh*.

The new publishing house Farrar, Straus & Co. was formed to focus on young writers, especially war veterans. People were reading Christopher Isherwood's *The Berlin Stories*, George Orwell's *Animal Farm*, Evelyn Waugh's *Brideshead Revisited*, Frederic Wakeman's acerbic novel of the burgeoning advertising profession, *The Hucksters*, Robert Penn Warren's *All the King's Men* (inspired by the life of the Southern demagogue Huey Long), dark comedies by veterans Thomas Heggen

(*Mr. Roberts*) and Max Shulman (*The Zebra Derby*), and the early monument of "New Journalism," John Hersey's *Hiroshima*.

The Best Years of Our Lives swept the Academy Awards, but Hitchcock's *Notorious* and the noir classics *Gilda*, *The Postman Always Rings Twice*, *The Big Sleep*, *The Stranger*, and the feel-good *It's a Wonderful Life* were audience favorites. Bing Crosby, Danny Kaye, Bob Hope, George Burns and Gracie Allen hosted "variety" radio shows; and Perry Como, Frank Sinatra, Jo Stafford, and Nat King Cole had the top songs.

The contemporary "art scene" in postwar New York was less socially stratified than it had been previously, and more naturally heterogenous. Especially for those artists who were part of a settled couple, socializing most often took place at home. The Newmans had small dinners with Buffie Johnson, Tony Smith, Bill and Ethel Baziotes, the Gottliebs, occasionally Peggy Guggenheim, sometimes Navascués and his wife; "Boy, how I miss one of [Annalee's] gorgeous meals," Navascués wrote in one of his numerous and dense letters.[9] Their friendships described a wide circle, the young Guggenheim–Putzel discovery, Charles Seliger, for instance, with whom Barney had a memorable night that included the senior West Coast mystical painter Mark Tobey.[10] On another occasion, when Ruffino Tamayo was a guest, Barney's old college friend Jesse Lowenthal and his Cuban wife the artist Carmen Herrera were invited so that there would be someone with whom Tamayo could converse in Spanish.[11] Frequent meetings on the street with Jack Tworkov, whose studio was down the block from Barney's apartment, would segue into visits; Barney was also friendly with the painter Janice Biala, Tworkov's sister.[12] On the occasions they did go out it would almost always be to a Chinese restaurant.[13] Barney's group didn't spend much time at the Waldorf Cafeteria with the less domesticated Gorky, de Kooning, Kline, James Brooks, Ibram Lassaw, Reuben Nakian crowd, although Baziotes was able to straddle both worlds. Nineteen forty-six, according to Philip Pavia, was the moment when "the avant garde spirit started on 8th street," and "Baziotes was top . . . . We always thought that everything ran around him."[14] "Barney was not then a painter; he was the sort of philosopher for the trio"— Gottlieb, Rothko, and Newman—recalled Buffie Johnson.[15]

There was fluidity in the galleries, unlike the later committed relationships. John Graham's "Three Musketeers" of the 1930s—Stuart Davis, Gorky, and de Kooning— were then showing in three different galleries, Edith Halpert's Downtown Gallery, Julien Levy, and Charles Egan respectively. Sam Kootz exhibited Baziotes, Carl Holty, Léger, and Motherwell in a group and mounted one-man shows of Motherwell and Baziotes. Parsons, at Mortimer Brandt, showed Rothko watercolors.[16] Gottlieb, after Putzel died, showed at Nierendorf, but Kootz recruited him in April as more congenial with Kootz's stable,[17] which at that early moment included Byron Brown, Baziotes, and Motherwell. Art of This Century also had shown Rothko, Motherwell and Baziotes, and Pollock. Recommended by Rothko, Still had a solo exhibition there in February. Barney first met Still at the opening, but they were already known to each other. On an advance copy of the little "catalogue" listing fourteen paintings with a few paragraphs written by Rothko, Still scribbled a note: "Dear Newman: I'll be looking for you. And wish me luck."

Thus began an extraordinarily intense ten-year friendship that would leave, at least on Barney, long-lasting scars. As sympathetic, warm, and supportive as was Barney's relationship with Tony Smith, that with Still was rocky, buffeting, and, on Still's part, false and manipulative. Barney later fell out with one-time friends over ordinary professional competitiveness that he cast as moral corrosion; but, regarding Still, the scales never fell from his eyes. Given Barney's core identity as an overly defended, first-generation Jewish boy from the streets, Still—tall, handsome, disdainfully *American*—was the symbol of the unattainable, baggage-free, paragon; he was the ultimate "*shiksa* goddess."

With Motherwell's help, the Rothkos set up in Springs, Long Island, in the summer of 1946, and they urged the Newmans to visit. Instead, Barney and Annalee drove directly to Provincetown, in his sports car, with clear plans, as he told everyone, to make good on an excess of commitments. "Do you like living away from the crowd? Can you manage to get some work done?" Sarah asked.[18] Rothko, interpreting Barney's description as "an ideal set up for work and play"—beach antics and frolicking *au naturel* with old friends Ben and Cora Ginsburg, and new ones like Theodoros Stamos—wrote, "I hope that you are doing considerable of each."[19] The truth was that people on all sides wanted things from him, and he developed the painful back trouble that would surface at similarly stressful times throughout the rest of his life.

Even as he understood his dilemma—that to realize his ambition to paint he had to come to grips with the "self"—his *own* self—it was the isolation of the self that terrified him. Later, after the panic had been somewhat conquered, he was able to acknowledge the dread. "What is the most difficult thing about painting? The most difficult thing is sitting in that room by yourself. That's it. That's really terrible. You have to sit there by yourself. It's not like sitting at a place with a desk and other people are talking to you and the phones are ringing. You are there all alone with that empty space."[20] Barney feared the "mystery of space," both literal and metaphoric, the "terror of that blank area." And so he lived in many parallel worlds, and that was a matter of choice. It was the choice that had always been his default.

A letter Barney received from his father that summer was a multi-layered communication that the two intimate and sympatico men understood as almost a private dialect. The overblown, exceedingly formal, literary style of modern Hebrew was a hallmark of a dedicated Hebraist, a diasporic Zionist whose Hebrew would be used in certain controlled circumstances (as opposed to daily spoken Hebrew, which was less formal) and of a well-educated Jew, who could invoke biblical cadences and poetic imagery to support emotional content. (When he wrote Abraham's obituary—for the *Times*—Barney made certain the brief notice included that he was a "founder and trustee of . . . an institution dedicated to the revival of Hebrew as a living language."[21]) Abraham was confident that Barney would appreciate the linguistic, philosophic, and contextual complexity—and wit.

Sunday, the 21st of Av, 5706
August 18, 1946

To my dear son, Master Baruch, Shalom!

In truth, I must justify my prolonged silence. How else would you know that I am burdened these days with a dual labor. The domestic work of helping my dear wife, your mother, long may she live, with the housework. I must do something to lighten the heavy burden she shoulders as the house-wife. To return each item to its place, in a disciplined, orderly manner and pleasantly, as is her soul's desire, which strives continuously to anticipate our household needs in a timely manner in order to satisfy not just each and every household member's necessities but also the needs of those strangers who are residing with us. This requires an alert eye and industrious hands and my assistance is needed. Additionally, due to my new position, I am also slightly burdened with public service, zionist work, which is very beloved to me, for how could a Hebrew heart be silent at such a time when the surviv-ing remnants, those embers that were on the brink of extinction and saved from the fire, are in need? The fate of our entire nation is about to be tried—it will either come to a halt or see mercy; slavery or freedom; imprison-ment or redemption. Is there a man possessing a beating human heart who witnesses this and doubts its significance? I am content to assist, even if only a bit with my minimal energies . . . .

From all that is written above you will comprehend my unending tears and I beg your pardon; however, you too have not bothered to explain your absence. We only received one letter from you the entire summer and my soul yearned to know if throughout this time you had managed to find yourself in a place of Torah, as you did last year. And are you among learned intelligent people who are "conversant with the revelations of the wise," among whom it is pleasant to be?

In the hopes of receiving your letter informing us in detail, I remain your father who inquires after your well being all the days of your life.

Avraham[22]

Annalee's cousin Renee, led to believe she'd have a visa by mid-summer, need-ed affidavits and other administrative assistance to emigrate, but discovered that "only GI's fiancees" were receiving them.[23] A facilitator had to be arranged, and the requested chocolate, shoes, and clothing, probably fated for the black market, sent. Anuta, in mourning for Samuel, and overwrought with anxiety about Renee, required reassurance.

There was Navascués, whose professional relationship with Barney had evolved into a rich, affectionate, intellectually omnivorous, and demanding one. As the Spaniard was taking a faculty position at Franklin and Marshall in Pennsylvania and trying to negotiate a future for the failed *Ambos Mundos*, his American friend was needed as an errand-doer and sounding-board for business dealings and scholarly mash-ups. Their energetic correspondence addressed ancient Greek, American, English, and Continental literature, from Aeschylus to Shakespeare to Eliot to Camus; criticism, anthropology, theater, and occasionally art.

And, most consumingly, there was Betty Parsons, whose gallery would open in September. Barney was the middleman between Parsons and Rothko, Still and Ad Reinhardt; questions and concerns were floated through him. Parsons tasked him with arranging for insurance. She expected an article for *Art News*. "I know Rosamund Frost, A.M. Frankfurter . . . Robert Hale, Thomas Hess," she wrote, listing the editorial staff, "so if you send along the letter I will send it to them—with a suggestion that your article gets into the October number . . . please <u>hurry</u>." She pressed him for the public announcement "<u>now</u>." Peregrinating through the summer resorts of New England, to Barney in Provincetown she wrote, "I hope you and Annally [*sic*] are not working too hard."[24]

TWENTY-ONE

ONLY THE PURE IDEA

Betty Parsons believed—and believed that Barney corroborated for her—"that chosen human beings, abiding by the laws of the cosmos, could find the wellsprings of art, could draw forth the deepest meaning and most profound spiritual truths as they formed their art." In turn, the works the "chosen" produced would provoke in the receptive viewer a measure of spiritual experience. And so she was delighted to inaugurate the Betty Parsons Gallery with the show of Northwest Coast Indian art that Barney proposed; it would both "bless the new space and bow to the mysteries and aesthetic forces that in her judgment lay behind all art."[1]

Native American traditional art, like pre-Columbian art, had already a following widespread enough among artists that it generated various "camps"—although the motivation, "to go beyond Europeans," was the universal impulse. The 1940s saw only the latest twist in a fraught history.[2] From the end of the 19th through the early 20th century, Native American works were blithely absorbed into European–American design culture via the same eyes and intentions as were Arts and Crafts movement pieces: "as symbols of a solidity, purity, spirituality, and integrity increasingly missing from everyday life." They were sold at Wanamaker's department store and displayed in dedicated areas—"Indian corners"—of middle-class homes. Arthur Wesley Dow's influential 1899 textbook, *Composition*, suggested the work as a "tool with which [non-tribal] students might get in touch with their inner, 'natural' self." Many of the Indian Boarding Schools, where Barney had hoped to teach in the '30s, used a curriculum specifically developed both to feed the fashion and to promote traditional arts drained of meaningful context and content.[3] In 1941, 1500 years of "Indian Art of the United States," organized by the Indian Arts and Crafts Board of the U.S. Department of the Interior, was shown at the Museum of Modern Art.

This overdetermined history was repressed by those "modern" artists who, in the 1930s and '40s, wound up on the East Coast. For them, the story generally began in New York's museums. "Rather than frequent the Metropolitan, as we had all done when we were younger," Peter Busa, Motherwell, Steve Wheeler, and Pollock "used to spend a great deal of time at the Museum of Natural History" and the Brooklyn Museum.[4] Often the objects were covered in dust and one had to ask to have them removed from bins and vitrines. But in them Busa saw a way to "work in a concept that was *completely* removed from my earlier training of Cubism." The "Indian Space" painters—Busa, Will Barnet, Wheeler—found thrilling the "total idea; that you couldn't tell the difference between the object and the so-called 'space' around it. It all seemed to have equal emphasis."[5]

"We wanted to go beyond the Europeans, beyond Paris, beyond Picasso, beyond Matisse, beyond Kandinsky, beyond all these people," recalled Barnet. "From my point of view there was a culture among the Indians of how to handle space that was

not European but American for the first time . . . . And that's what interested me."
For the Indian Space painters it was not the symbols that they found interesting, but
"how they put the symbols together . . . . The formal ideas of how space works."[6]

Northwest Coast art held a specific fascination for other artists who, prompted by
Surrealism, found inspiration in its content. The December 1943 "Amerindian Number" of Wolfgang Paalen's *DYN* was instrumental in that respect, but Pollock, with
Reuben Kadish, had already been visiting the Natural History Museum's collection
of "large carvings in the Northwest Coast Indian room" as early as 1936 and, a little
later, under the influence of Jungian theory, he found there vital creative sources.
Busa remembered Pollock telling Paul Wingert in the museum, "This is art," to which
Wingert, a scholar of American–Indian art, replied, "Nobody else seems to think so."[7]

For Barney, however, the emphasis once again was not on new formal potential,
nor on archetypes that would resonate in the collective unconscious. It was, instead,
on the *ritual*—the specifically male ritual—of making, and the use of "abstract symbols . . . without regard to the contours of appearance," to express the "metaphysical
pattern of life" in two-dimensional *paintings*.[8] He made a distinction between the
"mythology and the mythic thing." He "didn't really care about the Thunderbird,"
he explained. He was "interested in the *fact* that those people were interested in the
Thunderbird."[9]

As Paalen had when he traveled to the Northwest Coast in 1939, the art historian
and curator Katherine Kuh in 1946 focused on totems. Kuh was working in Sitka,
Alaska, sent by the Office of Indian Affairs of the Federal Department of the Interior
on a 'special mission . . . to make a detailed report on Indian totemic carvings.'[10] That
project was typical of the times: both advanced, in directing attention to the works,
but also retrograde in focus and approach. It was that cultural bias that Barney was
addressing when he wrote: "The art of the Northwest Coast Indian, if known at all,
is invariably understood in terms of the totem pole . . . . I have been eager to shift the
focus to this little known work"—in other words, to *painting*—"whether on house
walls, ceremonial shaman frocks and aprons, or as ceremonial blankets." He insisted
that "it would be a mistake to consider these paintings as mere decorative devices,"
that they constituted a kind of heightened design. "Design was a separate function
carried on by the women and took the form of geometric, non-objective pattern."[11]

"Barney had a very male point of view on things, to put it politely, and one of the
things that fascinated him about Northwest coast native art was that the men painted
the designs for these Chilkat wonderful heraldic-shield-like blankets with long white
goat hair tassels," recalled his close friend Robert Murray. Men painted the design
on shaped cedar boards, which the women wove, making a symmetrical, mirror
replica. "Barney just thought that that was amazing because in those days there was
no sense that what native or indigenous people made was art. Not only did they not
have a word for it, or a concept for it, but the anthropologists never treated it that
way. It was part of anthropology. It wasn't part of the art world. Well, Barney had
this notion, this vision, this sense."[12]

That the landmark show opened at Parsons on September 30, 1946, is almost a miracle. Not until September 15 did Barney phone the Museum of Natural History to arrange their participation; Parsons followed up with a letter without specific requests, confusing Harry Shapiro. Only after did Barney visit the museum to make choices, and on September 20 the museum completed the loan agreement, providing brief descriptions of the functions for which the objects were made. Then on September 23, Shapiro received a classic Barney letter: "I am very unhappy and disappointed over the fragmentary nature of the exhibition . . . Mrs. Parsons is spending close to $2,000 and I all of my energies, without hope of any return for either of us except some possible prestige for our educational effort. That prestige is in question because of the fragmentary nature of our exhibition material but no more so than the prestige of the Museum's collection if we fail to make our point." Barney had a radical idea, and that idea, to be persuasively advanced—to "click" with the work of his contemporaries—needed a large-scale wall painting. The museum owned only two of these, both house fronts; they were very rare, very fragile, and the museum prized them "very highly." But Barney's puffed-up indignation persuaded Shapiro, "contrary to my judgment," to lend him one. It arrived on September 27, too big, it turned out, to fit in the elevator that served the gallery—it was hoisted on the top of the elevator, which infuriated Shapiro when he found out[13]—and too late to be in the catalogue.

The installation of leather skins, woven blankets, drum heads, and pattern boards was challenging; Tony Smith stepped up with a novel idea—pin them to drapier's racks and hang the racks on the wall[14]—and it was during the installation of the show that Smith and Barney bonded.[15] Parsons's opening exhibition was "quite the most novel show of the week" noted the *Times*. "In an introduction to the catalogue, B.B. Newman points out that the dominant esthetic tradition in the little-known art of the peoples of this region was abstract . . . . The exhibition has been admirably installed."[16]

Not until a month after the show closed did Motherwell, in the middle of November, weigh in. "On rereading [your preface] . . . it seems to me even better . . . . But if you had the space, I would have liked to see you mention the other important thing, how we <u>differ</u> now from the primitives; nothing could be more different than our concrete individualisms and anarchism: it is in this regard that modern art for me tends to be, on the part of the artist, a tragic enterprise." Motherwell's point, finally, was to invite Barney to contribute to "our new magazine."[17]

Navascués, too, wanted Barney's writings to appear more widely. With Barney's consent he wrote to a British publisher to ask him to print an expanded, English version of "The Art of the South Seas."[18] And John Stephan, a transplanted Chicago painter who would shortly join Parsons's gallery, made it clear that he would be counting on Barney's contribution to his forthcoming magazine, *The Tiger's Eye*.

That is why, one evening at the apartment when there were a few people at dinner and Barney was improvising at the baby grand piano, and Tworkov had "the impression that he was trying to tell us that he was really interested in composing music," he turned to Barney "and just asked him simply . . . 'Forgive me, but really what do you consider your work?' " It was early 1947, and Tworkov recalled his answer: "He said, 'Well, essentially I'm a writer.' "[19]

And yet.

Even as he became recognized and appreciated and depended upon for his literate advocacy, he had other plans. The previous December, he had signed a lease on his first painting studio, the entire fourth floor of 114 Fourth Avenue, near Grace Church. That winter was so cold Barney would rush in, light the kerosene stove, and run out to a cafeteria to wait for the place to warm up. Often, he would have coffee with de Kooning, who had taken a studio across the street.[20] Tworkov would soon be in the building with de Kooning; Franz Kline, Conrad Marca-Relli, and Milton Resnick were nearby.

Now, a studio became not simply a matter of wishful thinking or magical projection. Barney had a painting in the Parsons Christmas Show, which ran a "gamut from the ultra-realism of Walter Murch's textural still-life to the bitter surrealism of Alfonso Ossorio . . . and the sheer nonobjective compositions by Reinhart [*sic*], Slobodkina," and the "newcomer—Pennington West."[21] If the identity of the landmark piece is lost to history, the debut was a thoughtfully considered action, combining the *saykhel* of Barney and canniness of Betty. The nationally syndicated columnist Elsa Maxwell, an intimate of Dumpy Oelrichs, one of Betty's oldest friends and a gallery backer, devoted her entire December 20th column to breathlessly reporting on Parsons's show. "I heaved myself into the elevator and arrived on the fifth floor . . . . 'Betty,' I said, 'let me see your Christmas show.'" Hofmann, Pietro Lazzari, Boris Margo, Murch, Ossorio, Hedda Sterne, and "Rathko," were mentioned, and also that "Betty has a Newman." Maxwell demurred about her art critical skills, but advised, "anyone who wants to spend $100 or $150 for a picture by one of the younger American abstractionists may eventually own a masterpiece. Who can tell? . . . So don't turn down our own artists, no matter how silly or funny you think them. Their dreams are real and their aspirations pure . . . . Some dissenters scream, 'Hang the abstractionists.' I echo: 'Certainly, but why not on your walls.' "[22]

Maxwell's flippant "hang the abstractionists" was no joke. It was a paraphrase of what President Truman said that season about the "ham and eggs school of art," the "vaporings of half-baked lazy people," which was provoked by "Advancing American Art," a U.S. State Department-organized show meant to tour Europe and Latin America. Including work by many contemporary artists—some identified as leftists, some abstractionists—the exhibition was forced to cancel by a coalition of conservative congressmen and Hearst newspapers. About Kuniyoshi's *Circus Girl Resting*, Truman famously said: "If that's art, I'm a Hottentot."[23]

Betty was no fool. She had spent time in Hollywood, and knew the power of the press. " 'I read it in the newspaper,' was, she knew, a popularly acceptable citation of authority." Toward the end of her life, she recalled the Maxwell column: "It was exciting. It was wonderful! I knew I was on the bean! I knew I had an eye! I knew, dammit, that *my* artists saw into the future. And that's what interested me. I never looked back."[24]

As Howard Devree noted, Parsons's stable "ran the gamut"; and they wouldn't be corralled by the ideology expressed in Barney's writings and implied by the two "primitive" shows. And so, to annoint the spear carriers, he organized in January 1947 the exhibition "The Ideographic Picture." His catalogue introduction was as brilliantly engineered as Maxwell's appearance at the gallery. It began with reinforcing definitions of "ideograph/ic":

> A character, symbol or figure which suggests the idea of an object without expressing its name. Representing ideas directly and not through the medium of their names. . . . (Century Dictionary). A symbol or character painted, written or inscribed, representing ideas (Encyclopaedia Britannica).

Then Barney projected what was in the Kwakiutl maker's mind: "To him a shape was a living thing, a vehicle for an abstract thought-complex, a carrier of the awesome feelings he felt before the terror of the unknowable." And, finally, he presented the "epistemological paradox that is the artist's problem."

> The basis of an aesthetic act is the pure idea. But the pure idea is, of necessity, an aesthetic act. . . . Not space cutting nor space building, not construction nor fauvist destruction; not the pure line, straight and narrow, not the tortured line, distorted and humiliating; not the accurate eye, all fingers, nor the wild eye of dream, winking; but the idea-complex that makes contact with mystery—of life, of men, of nature, of the hard, black chaos that is death, or the grayer, softer chaos that is tragedy. *For it is only the pure idea that has meaning. Everything else has everything else* [emphasis added].[25]

Voila! He had *tailored* the definition of what art is to something that would fit him. "As early as 1942," he wrote, "Mr. Edward Alden Jewell was the first publicly to report" a new force in American painting. "Since then, various critics and dealers have tried to label it, to describe it. It is now time for the artist himself, by showing the dictionary, to make clear the community of intention that motivates him and his colleagues." Suddenly, with this announcement, Barney, known as a writer, as an advocate, morphed into "the artist himself."

Barney became serious, shopping like a professional for pigments, stretcher strips, a "studio easel." The white cotton duck from John Boyle and Company on Duane Street in lower Manhattan had the kind of patina that appealed to his inner historian: since the mid-19th century Boyle had made clipper ship sails, Civil War tents, tarpaulins and mailbags, Conestoga wagons covers, and circus tents.[26] The reality of the raw, cold studio may have been more authentically bohemian than he bargained for and he had not renewed the lease. But in March 1947 he had over 15 yards of canvas delivered to his home.

"It was purely for my own education," Barney told Irving Sandler, a decade later, about "The Ideographic Picture." He was trying to make the distinction between abstract design and abstract painting, but the name "didn't click."

Two works were hung by each artist: Hofmann, Lazzari, Margo, Reinhardt (whose first solo show at Parsons had appeared the past fall), Stamos, Rothko, and Still—who had moved from Art of This Century.[27] Barney had one painting and one oil-crayon drawing.

To strengthen the argument, he had wanted to include Gottlieb and Motherwell, but by then they had joined Kootz Gallery, and Kootz (who had a policy of paying his artists a 200-dollar monthly stipend in lieu of commissions) would not allow it. This was stunning to Barney: Kootz allowed his artists to participate in shows at the Museum of Modern Art, he said. "Why is this any different?"[28] If the show couldn't make the most comprehensive, most persuasive statement for his ideas, the only alternative, he decided, would be to restrict it to Parsons artists alone, thereby also eliminating Pollock, who that very month had shown his first "all-over" drip paintings at Art of This Century. One astute critic noted that Gottlieb's new paintings could be seen across the hall at Kootz during the run of "The Ideographic Picture."

But even with the artists absent, Barney's presence loomed. He could not write the catalogue preface for Gottlieb's show, but Victor Wolfson's essay used Barney's words and ideas from "The Painting of Tamayo and Gottlieb" and other recent pieces. Wolfson—gratuitously in the context of writing about art at that time—brought up the term "Kabbalistic," a subject upon which Barney, uniquely, would discourse. And in *The Nation*—during the run of "The Ideographic Picture"—Clement Greenberg also invoked Barney's terminology: "Jackson Pollock's fourth one-man show . . . is his best since his first one and signals what may be a major step in his development— which I regard as the most important so far of the younger generation of American painters . . . Pollock has gone beyond the stage where he needs to make his poetry explicit in ideographs."

Jewell's review of "The Ideographic Picture" quoted a significant portion of Barney's preface, and acknowledged its ambition: "drawing a deep breath, the spectator may then suppose himself prepared to begin his journey about the walls." But he concluded that while "many of the designs [ouch!] are handsome and striking, considered just as abstract expression . . . to apprehend the special meanings intended by the artists may prove considerably more difficult." Mentioning Barney several times as the impresario, Jewell wrote about his painting only that it was in the show. The critic Maude Kemper Riley, more generously, allowed what Barney was up to, with a wink; among the gallery artists, she wrote, "is a writer who has assumed the role of interpreter, B.B. Newman . . . Newman's *Gea* is made of maternal forms and his *Abyss* is certainly black." The exhibition was not "overwhelming in its content" but "may make history if the name . . . catches on."[29]

Gea (plate 1) was an example of what Barney later described as his first principles: "Those first things that I did in the middle forties . . . always included a kind of a void . . . always had sort of an empty circle from which emanated aspects of creative life that I projected purely out of nothing."[30] "I was involved with the void [but] I disliked it. I was hopeful and I depicted the 'abyss' as the point to start anew. But I created a fantastic landscape."[31] He had been working with circles, with a "void" of black or white inside, and "life" outside, he told the art historian Barbara Reise in 1964, beginning the story of his development not with the work that Annalee dated as his earliest oil, *Untitled*, 1945, but with what is now known as *Pagan Void*, 1946 (plate 3), a composition nearly unique in his oeuvre but whose elements are found doodled on the notes for his review of Peggy Guggenheim's autobiography. A "little later" in 1947, he told Reise, he painted what is now known as *Genetic Moment*, which contained the same ovarian form, but in a much less ectoplasmic iteration. The various tendrils, membranes, bird, and plant innards of his earliest drawings (including *Gea*) were now gone, as was the suggestion of viscous nutrient in which they swam. In its place was a carefully irregular scaffolding—*not* to be confused with that of Mondrian or other "purists"—and Barney's "void" was set in a roughly defined box between stalwart verticals that ran from the top to the bottom edges. One had a thorny-tipped hooked branch and the other, more gracefully swaying, bifurcated in its lower third like a mangrove trunk or ginseng root.[32]

The background, more uniformly scumbled than in the earlier drawings and marked with small, completely non-referential forms, projected a surer intention and touch. But *Genetic Moment*, which was documented and named before 1948, was not the work he hung in "The Ideographic Picture." Along with *Gea*, he chose to show a work far removed from any lingering hesitancy—except for its size. Only 28 by 22 inches, *Euclidian Abyss* (fig. 18) was indeed, as the critic said, "black," and no longer were there any figures on a "field." The ginseng root retained a bend—more a sway, having lost its legs—and was still yellow, but a much flatter, more vibrant yellow. Its "male" counterpart had been moved all the way to the right, where its curved branch was squared off, and co-terminus with part of the bottom edge. Everything else on the textured paperboard was a rough black. It was an aggressively unexpected work, not partaking of any known "art" rules. Its trangressiveness must have been thrilling for Barney, and he later would say it was the "first painting where I got to the edge and didn't fall off." But would anyone consider it art? That question was by his friends politely—and by others rudely—ignored.

Professional validation "was limited to recognition of and by each other as artists and a few critics or patrons . . . and whoever had a space in which to show the works," Herbert Ferber said of this period. "It was pretty much an enterprise that was self-supporting." They were friendly with each other because "altogether there

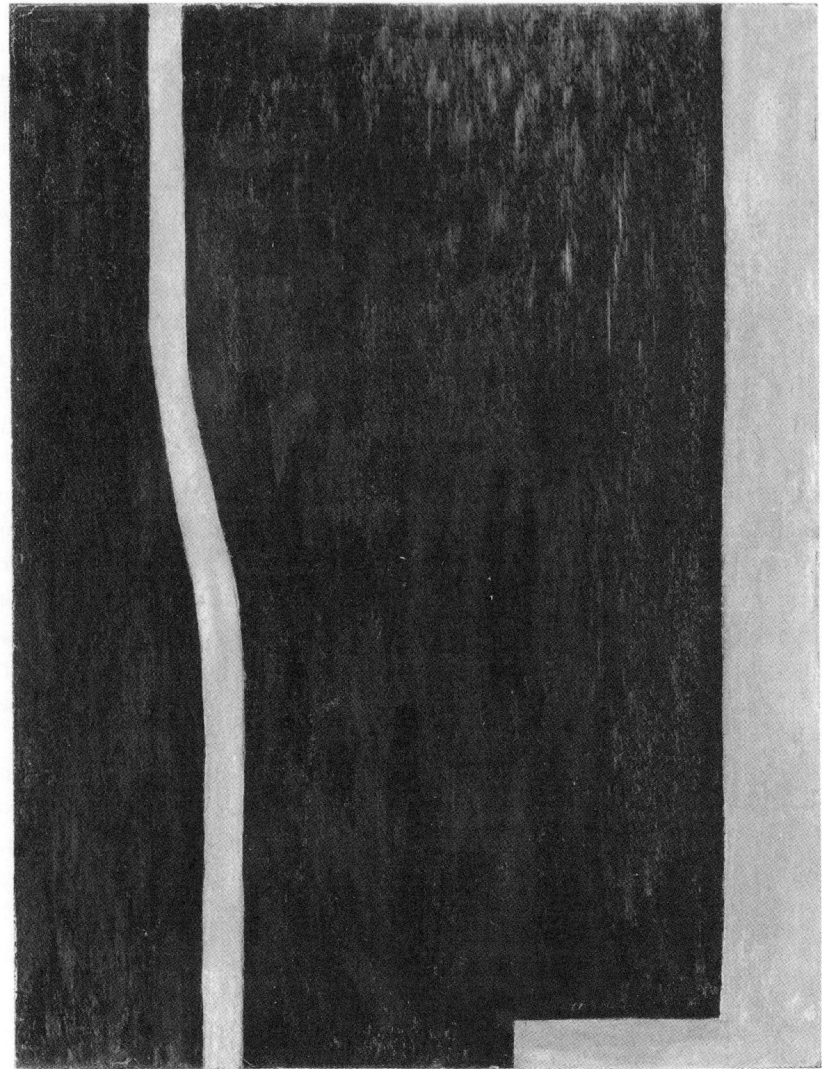

Fig. 18 Barnett Newman, *Euclidian Abyss*, 1946–47. Oil, oil crayon, and wax crayon on textured paperboard, 27 ¾ × 21 ¾ in. (70.5 × 55.3 cm). Private collection, Atherton, California

were only maybe a dozen or 15 of us. The sculptors hardly counted . . . David Smith was showing. I was showing. Lipton began to show a little later at Betty Parsons. Lassaw was showing . . . . There was a constant communication between us about the problems of what later became known as the New York School. What it meant to be an artist who was doing non-figurative painting or sculpture, or painting or sculpture which had other motivations than representation." In this community, the monkey wrench thrown by Kootz was understandably surprising. Tony Smith saw a difference in intent between the dealers: Kootz started out on a "promotional basis" with theme shows, rich-looking carpets and frames; Parsons had "none of that." Kootz painters did more "sophisticated, sensuous" work, while Parsons "went in for more visionary painters."[33] But "the lack of obvious jealousy or competitiveness amongst the artists," was "beautifully sentimental in those days," according to Ferber. "Except for a very few cases there were no enmities, and although we were in different galleries we never thought of . . . any one of them being more important than another. They were all simply a stage where our works could be displayed, a showcase. And we cut across gallery lines."[34]

Barney wrote a catalogue essay for Stamos's February show and one for Hofmann's March show (rejected). He brought Tony Smith to help him hang Hofmann's work and devised an installation principle—one that honored *each* work—that he would carry forward as an ethical doctrine. "I wanted to make latest work visible," Smith recalled. But "Barney wanted to make each picture concrete in itself and not to indicate development or growth." Smith "always respected Barney for this," and resented [Alfred] Barr "because he didn't consider a thing as itself but as a stage."[35] Barney installed, deinstalled, and stored, Still's April show, while Still was in California.[36] And his support made the crucial difference in Siskind's career. The photographic community was not interested in Siskind's "abstract, non-social photographs," so he would show them to Barney, who appreciated what he was doing; Barney pushed him to show them to the dealer Charlie Egan. The exhibition that Egan made in April 1947, Siskind always maintained, formed a crucial connection with the artists: "The guys came up to see. Pollock was very impressed . . . . And that was the beginning."[37]

Most importantly, Barney educated, reinforcing the *stature* of the men. "In the '40s, it was Barney Newman who was the big articulate one who talked and talked and talked and talked and talked." Future art dealer John Bernard Myers remembered Barney standing in the gallery, enlightening visitors about the work. "He was very good at explicating what these people were doing. And since explication seemed to be the order of the day he certainly was very articulate about it [and] Barney played an important role."[38] Tony Smith, newly teaching at New York University, never forgot what Barney told him when they ran into each other on the Fourth Street subway platform: "The students want to love you. What you must insist upon is respect."[39]

There were some—in later years they grew in number as Barney grew in renown—who claimed to agree with Motherwell that "we didn't take him seriously in the '40s. He was more a kind of wonderful uncle friend. If you had a baby he would have a celebration . . . things like that. Might invite you for a turkey on Thanksgiving. Was benign and friendly and so on."[40] But that evaluation is not borne out by the reality. They relied upon him, they were anxious to use him for what needed doing—including Motherwell himself, who solicited Barney to discuss and contribute to "our new magazine"—and often they only knew what needed doing because he identified it for them.

In Ferber's memory, those were "very beautiful years when we were all friends and all felt able to discuss all kinds of problems openly and without very much rancor." They "were constantly in each other's homes." Nobody could afford to prepare dinner for large groups, "but we were always able to manage drinks after dinner." They would meet at 8:30 or 9:00 and sit around until the early morning "talking, talking, talking" about "each other's work, about European art, about ideas, about books, about everything," except "where you were showing or what you were selling, or what commissions [you'd] gotten." The "milieu" was "electric." It was "always about the ideas involved in the breaking away from or developing toward a new form or a new idea. And these were very, very exciting and very stimulating and very sparse days for all of us. Nobody was making any money." But they "all learned from each other."[41]

Ferber was a practicing dentist, and his home on Riverside Drive was a focal point. "Perhaps we had a little more money and it was a little more stable matrimonial situation at that time" than some others. The apartment became known as "a meeting place" and people would ask him "about their medical problems." Including Barney, who relied on "Dr. Silvers"—his full name was Herbert Ferber Silvers—for his and Annalee's dental care during the late 1940s. In return, for his December show at Parsons, Ferber would have a catalogue essay by Barney that struck a now familiar chord: "By insisting on the heroic gesture, and on the gesture only, the artist has made the heroic style the property of each one of us, transforming, in the process, this style from an art that is public to one that is personal. *For each man is, or should be, his own hero* [emphasis added]."

Pollock was around less, having moved to Springs on eastern Long Island. And he was shy. The Newmans invited Pollock and his wife Lee Krasner over for dinner. "Mrs. P. said 'Let's make it a quiet evening, just invite de Kooning or someone we already know,'" but the Pollocks arrived with a posse of three of Jackson's brothers. Pollock, who was not drinking, said very little, but after this "meet the family" event, the fraternal attachment of unlikely mates was cemented. They always celebrated their birthdays—Pollock on January 28, Barney on January 29—together.[42]

Parsons was uncertain about Pollock, and so Barney took her to Springs to see the work. (Atypically, Annalee passed, worried that the overnight excursion would cost a day of teaching.) For Barney it was a memorably horrible night: very cold, and upstairs where he was staying had no heat. Even with all the covers he could find, even fully dressed, he was freezing, but too shy to come downstairs where the Pollocks slept and there was a stove. He reported to Annalee that he just "toughed it out through the night in this freezing room" with all his clothes on. "Betty, what did you do?" he asked the next morning; "Me? What did I do? I just opened up the window, and let the air in. It got warmer!"[43] Gallerist and artist would close the deal.

Still and Rothko formed a particularly, effusively supportive camaraderie. In the fall of 1946, after they had seen each other a few times in New York and on the West Coast, they became a mutual admiration society, albeit with hints of future discord. Still gushed about Rothko's show that August at the San Francisco Museum of Art: to Parsons, it was "without question the best show I have ever seen in the gallery for years and it commanded the highest respect from those out here who know good work when they see it."[44] To Rothko: "You have some real fans out here, they await further work almost with reverence, and all are hoping that you get the luck you have so long deserved. Certainly they will do everything in their power to bring it about . . . . All the other bastards will of course follow when the noise becomes sufficiently loud. And it will."[45] In June 1947, when the Rothkos were again in San Francisco, "Clyff" was "constantly with us."[46] Rothko told Parsons that Still's show at the California Palace of the Legion of Honor "has left us breathless both my students and everyone else I have met."[47]

TWENTY-TWO

THE FIRST MAN WAS AN ARTIST

"How is the painting?"[1]

For the first time, Rothko acknowledged Barney's pursuit. The term "ideographic" may not have clicked but Barney's direction, on canvas and in life, finally had.

Those he thought of as his peers were teaching in college art departments—Still, at the California School of Fine Arts in San Francisco, Rothko there for the summer, Reinhardt at the Brooklyn College Department of Design. No longer at Washington Irving Evening High School, Barney unsuccessfully applied to Brooklyn College for a summer teaching position. The Newmans needed the money. Multiple rents; car registration, insurance, parking, repairs, gas; loan repayments to banks and friends and family; the culture that Barney could not deny himself—theater tickets, art (a coveted Black Sun Press portfolio, four small totem poles, 25 dollars a month to Avery for *Pink Umbrella*[2])—they lived beyond what should have been Annalee's adequate income.

Abraham was ill, and failing. He was emaciated, he had "congestive failure, difficulty breathing, high blood pressure, liver pathology," and his ankles were disturbingly swollen. It all took an enormous toll on the family. Barney was in constant consultation with the doctors but because of Abraham's overall deterioration they recommended only palliative care. At the end of June 1947, Abraham died.

It was a blow that the normally communicative Barney could not easily acknowledge. No one had thought to notify his oldest, closest friend, Gottlieb, who was in Provincetown and "shocked to learn that he passed away June 30 and we did not know it all summer."[3] Ferber and Parsons, who were on the spot in New York, gave the news to Rothko on the West Coast.

Barney and Annalee did not leave the city that summer until late August, when they joined the Ferbers in Orleans, Vermont. They delayed their departure until after the wedding of Barney's sister Gertrude to Philip Master had taken place in the West 121st Street apartment that she had been sharing with Anna and Abraham and Sarah, who was temporarily back in New York. Things at home were "a bit confusing," Sarah reported shortly after Barney and Annalee arrived in Vermont. Anna was depressed, and spent her time "cooking for the newlyweds," who continued to live in the family apartment. The building had been bought by the Jewish Theological Seminary and the rent was raised.

Like Samuel, who had died without reclaiming his dignity, Abraham died less than one year before he would have seen *his* life's goal—the State of Israel reclaiming the dignity of the Jewish people—come to pass.[4] The two deaths within eighteen months of men he admired and adored, to whom he had made unconditional commitments of every resource he had, jolted Barney to his core. Esther Gottlieb suggested the Newmans join them in Provincetown for a "long weekend over the Jewish holidays."[5]

They didn't, but returning from Vermont, Barney prepared to observe in the middle of September the occasions of Rosh Hashanah—when the Torah portion that is read, from Genesis, is the story of the birth and binding of Abraham's son—and Yom Kippur in reflection upon the meaning of a man's life, on how close to or far from fulfilling his potential he came. "Hashem, what is man that you recognize him?": this is precisely the agenda of the "High Holy Days."[6] As generally non-observant as he was, Barney was always cognizant of, frequently referenced, and occasionally privately enacted, rituals of the faith. Out of respect for his father he was obligated to be in synagogue for the *Yizkor* (Remember) prayer on Yom Kippur, to evaluate his own life, and commit to worthy actions. This Barney did in September 1947.[7]

And it was in this state of mind that he wrote for the first issue of *Tiger's Eye* in October "The First Man Was an Artist," with its "ecstatic outburst" of power, its reference to Genesis, and its tossed-off invocation of "Rashi," the medieval colossus of Jewish Biblical commentary.

Recent articles about two paleontological discoveries being studied at the Museum of Natural History caught his interest. Barney mashed up the news, objected to the journalists' leap from description of what was found to a speculative narrative, substituted a personal teleological standard, and made the news the essay's hook.[8]

A scientist has just caught the tail of another metaphor. Out of the Chinese dragon's teeth, piled high in harvest on the shelves of Shanghai's drugstores and deep in the Java mud, a half million years old, he has constructed Meganthropus palaeojavanicus, "man the great," the giant, who, the paleontologists now tell us, was our human ancestor . . . .

Paleontology, like the other nonmaterial sciences, has entered a realm where the only questions worth discussing are the questions that cannot be proved. We cannot excuse the abdication of its primal scientific responsibility because paleontology substituted the sentimental question *who* for the scientific *what*. Who cares who he was? What was the first man, was he a hunter, a toolmaker, a farmer, a worker, a priest, or a politician? Undoubtedly the first man was an artist.

Of all the manifestos that he wrote, of all the petulant letters and indignant *responsa* to come, "The First Man Was an Artist" is the most revealing statement of who Barnett Newman was.

A science of paleontology that sets forth this proposition can be written if it builds on the postulate that *the aesthetic act always precedes the social one* [emphasis added]. The totemic act of wonder in front of the tiger–ancestor came before the act of murder . . . . the necessity for dream is stronger than any utilitarian need. In the language of science, the necessity for understanding the unknowable comes before any desire to discover the unknown.

Man's first expression, like his first dream, was an aesthetic one. Speech was a poetic outcry rather than a demand for communication. Original man, shouting his consonants, did so in yells of awe and anger at his tragic state, at his own self-awareness and at his own helplessness before the void . . . .

The human in language is literature, not communication. Man's first cry was a song. Man's first address to a neighbor was a cry of power and solemn weakness, not a request for a drink of water . . . . The purpose of man's first speech was an address to the unknowable. His behavior had its origin in his artistic nature.

Just as man's first speech was poetic before it became utilitarian, so man first built an idol of mud before he fashioned an ax. Man's hand traced the stick through the mud to make a line before he learned to throw the stick as a javelin . . . . The God image, not pottery, was the first manual act. It is the materialistic corruption of present-day anthropology that has tried to make men believe that original man fashioned pottery before he made sculpture. Pottery is the product of civilization. The artistic act is man's personal birthright.

The earliest written history of human desires proves that the meaning of the world cannot be found in the social act. An examination of the first chapter of Genesis offers a better key to the human dream. It was inconceivable to the archaic writer that original man, that Adam, was put on earth to be a toiler, to be a social animal. The writer's creative impulses told him that man's origin was that of an artist, and he set him up in a Garden of Eden close to the Tree of Knowledge, of right and wrong, in the highest sense of divine revelation. The fall of man was understood by the writer and his audience not as a fall from Utopia to struggle, as the sociologicians would have it, nor as the religionists would have us believe, as a fall from Grace to Sin, but rather that *Adam, by eating from the Tree of Knowledge, sought the creative life to be, like God, "a creator of worlds," to use Rashi's phrase, and was reduced to the life of toil only as a result of a jealous punishment* . . . . [9]

It is the poet and the artist who are concerned with the function of original man and who are trying to arrive at his creative state. What is the raison d'être, what is the explanation of *the seemingly insane drive of man to be painter and poet* if it is not an act of defiance against man's fall and an assertion that he return to the Adam of the Garden of Eden? For the artists are the first men [emphasis added].[10]

"Seemingly insane drive" echoes his advice to Annalee's young niece, *I hear, little Judy, you want to be a poet / . . . . A poet to most men is a man idiotic / A fool, an idler of course a neurotic . . . . / Who needs such a one in a world so chaotic*; the phrase laid bare the self-imposed, parentally imposed, or societally imposed barrier he felt in his life so far.

Barney would write a few more pieces to announce his intentions, or to satisfy promises to friends and help them out, but he was done dancing around the main event. He no longer had to justify himself to the patriarch who demanded to know if he were spending his time "among learned intelligent people who are 'conversant with the revelations of the wise.'" He would not die unfulfilled, un*dignified*, a "tragic figure" like his two fathers.

He realized that in all of his theorizing he was "substituting an imaginary set of apparatus for a known set of apparatus." His "crisis" had nothing, any longer, "to do with world conditions, because the war [was] over. It ha[d] to do with my own life," he said in 1963. He had been writing in various ways "about the 'bric-à-brac of history'"; but what he really meant was the "superstructure used to tell an old story. And eliminating the superstructure you get back to the fundamentals of what it is to be [a] human being and to say something that expresses one's humanity." What an artist feels had to do with a "dialogue with one's contemporaries, but also with one's history." He had been substituting "one set of monsters for another" and the "mythic" that he had been writing about had lost its interest.[11] One could not think of one's self as an "Artist with a capital 'A'," as a lawyer thought of himself as a "Lawyer." The problem of painting, he told an audience at the Guggenheim Museum in 1966, "has to relate to me as a person, as a man, rather than as an artist"; otherwise, "you begin to knock out work that relates to your self-image rather than to your sense of self."[12] A man's painting was a matter of "birthright." All he needed was "Barney" himself.

"A seismograph to the complex cultural moment" is how *The Tiger's Eye* has been characterized.[13] The "little magazine" of art and literature put out by John Stephan and his wife, Ruth, a poet and Walgreen's heir, had only nine issues between October 1947 and October 1949, but its readership counted. Barney was involved from the beginning; the "joy of participating at the birth" was an experience that, he told the Stephans, he and Annalee "shall not forget,"[14] and he assumed a portion of the credit for its success. Barney encouraged the reproduction of Rothko, de Kooning, Pousette-Dart, Gottlieb, Avery, Stamos, Still, Motherwell, and Tomlin—the last three "violently" opposed by the Stephans—and it was because of his "knowledge and advice" at a time when "the only American painters [the Stephans] knew were Gorky and a guy named Barney Newman," that *Tiger's Eye* had a reputation "as an avant-garde magazine in the plastic arts."[15]

Despite the friendship that developed between Barney and the Stephans, and their reliance upon him—he was on the masthead as an associate editor in the second and third issues and the fourth ran an "appreciation for the special assistance of Barnett B. Newman"—the magazine was by no means a personal mouthpiece for Barney. He claimed never to have asked to have a work of his reproduced, although three—*Death of Euclid, Two Edges,* and *Genesis* (as *The Break*)—were, the last two upside down. *Tiger's Eye* published reproductions by an ecumenical range of artists along with self-consciously described features—"Stories of Intuition," "American Poets in Ironic and Heavenly-minded Moods," "5 Diverse Opinions" on something or other (Sartre's *Age of Reason* or Blackmur's *The Good European*)—and all manner of fiction, poetry, criticism, book excerpts, and "opinions" by illustrious writers past and present: Henry James, Joseph Campbell, Georges Bataille, Paul Goodman, Van

Wyck Brooks, Jean Genet, Thomas Merton, Allan Block, Marianne Moore, Kenneth Rexroth, Lionel Abel, Stephen Spender, Jorge Luis Borges.

Most of the visual artists would not have been Barney's choices. However, the "convictions" that guided those decisions, announced in the first issue, jibed with his own.

> That a work of art, being a phenomenon of vision, is primarily within itself evident and complete; That the study of art remains an afterthought to the spontaneous experience of viewing a work of art; That too close an association between art and the profession of art criticism creates a marriage of hypocrisy for neither the artist nor the critic are motivated by altruism towards each other.

The intention was to "keep separate art[ist] and the critic as two individuals who, by coincidence, are interested in the same thing, and any text on art will be handled as literature."

Barney around this time—in other words, when certain critics began extolling certain artists of his peer group—started to make the analogy between critics and lawyers: "all these guys come with their lawyers." He didn't understand why "articulate" artists—which is what *he* was—needed critics to speak on their behalf, and in *Tiger's Eye* he encouraged the separation to avoid the unholy marriage. Within a number of months, the credo that "the artist should talk for himself" became briefly enshrined in the Subjects of the Artist "school."[16] And yet his exceptionalism allowed the author's note for "The First Man Was an Artist," which flew in the face of the announced "conviction" to separate artists from their "lawyers": "Barnett B. Newman, a painter and a spokesman for contemporary painting, who also has arranged exhibits of primitive art. He has been singled out by traditionalists as a man to watch (or to watch out for) because of his cognizance of the changing forms in art."

When he chaperoned the *Tiger's Eye* survey, "The Ides of Art: The Attitudes of 10 Artists On Their Work And Contemporaneousness," he began to have second thoughts. He wrote to Stephan, "In discussing with you the 'Ides of Art,' the crisis that exists in painting in America today, it occurs to me in rethinking our conversation that we were talking about crisis out of habit; that we were really discussing the crisis of artists as men, as human beings not the crisis in the art, for the crisis of artists as men is no different from the crisis of other men, but I fail to see any crisis in the art." Picasso, he added, speaking from Barneyworld, "never had any influence on the American artist really. He was the play boy of the collectors and the museum people."[17]

For his contribution, Barney first drafted:

> We are beginning to wonder whether the new crop of weeping, professional friends of the American artist, is any improvement over our former friends, who disillusioned with the world, insisted that the American painter contemplate the American fields. For where these old friends saw only storms, our new friends, weeping before the heroes of history, now see a vast, bare desert. Perhaps we can

comfort them by explaining to them that we do not, require, as they seem to, the plush of hanging gardens, that if it is a desert we are in, many of us are painting so that each of us can have something to look at. And I for one find that I must write too, so that on this desert isle I shall also have something to read.

What he ultimately submitted, however, was

An artist paints so that he will have something to look at; at times he must write so that he will also have something to read.

Barney felt on solid enough footing to include himself among artists with greater track records in the "Ides." *Euclidian Abyss*, retitled *Black with Yellow*, was chosen by Katherine Kuh for inclusion in the Chicago Art Institute's 58th Annual Exhibition of American Paintings and Sculpture—a wildly ranging show of abstract and surrealist art, that included a number of Europeans in spite of its name. Although there were 251 other artists in the show, this was no small honor—though an unusually large number, thirteen, were represented by Parsons. The catalogue noted that Kuh traveled over fifteen thousand miles in the United States, visiting studios, galleries, art schools, and museums and concluded that "the number of professionals has probably doubled in the last ten or fifteen years." Barney was among the eighty-five who had never been exhibited in a major national exhibition, and his brief biography read: "Has organized exhibitions and written articles on primitive and modern art." (Maud Morgan was identified as a "housewife raising two young children" and "A.D.F. Reinhardt" as an "original and witty cartoonist.") It was an enormous leap: exhibited in the Art Institute of Chicago, one of the country's preeminent museums, and included in a substantial book of a catalogue. *Black with Yellow* was purchased from the show, by Emily Hall (Mrs. Burton G.) Tremaine, an intrepid pioneer collector of postwar art, for 200 dollars. His first sale.[18]

The Chicago annual was a large pond seen by a small audience. More consequential was Clement Greenberg's notice: "Gottlieb is perhaps the leading exponent of a new indigenous school of symbolism which includes among others Mark Rothko, Clyfford Still, and Barnett Benedict Newman," he wrote, reviewing Gottlieb in *The Nation* that December.[19] Motherwell might claim, long after Barney was no longer alive, that "we didn't take him seriously in the '40s," but clearly Greenberg did.

Barney, being Barney, could not say "yes." He was compelled to challenge Greenberg—the first to critically acknowledge him as a painter—to get it right. It was no longer about identifying a new movement; Barney felt required to substantiate his *own* art, and to do this it became *especially* important to separate not only from learned European conventions, but from a European *conception* of art. He had been developing his argument for some years but it appeared it hadn't sunk in.

Greenberg had doubts about the "importance this school attributes to the symbolical or 'metaphysical' content of its art . . . . As long as this symbolism serves to stimulate ambitious and serious painting, differences of ideology may be left aside for the time being. The test is in the art, not in the program." Barney insisted there never was any "program."

> When a number of American painters are found using the abstract idiom in a fashion that is unique, that is unfamiliar anyplace else, I am convinced that it indicates a singular fact in American painting of historic importance. The only reason for a literature is that this work cannot be described within the present framework of established notions of plasticity. Any formulation that I have attempted I have done to help meet this need; I have never tried to speak à la Breton as a program maker.

By necessity, to clarify the point, he had "on occasion entered the critic's realm."

The American painters, he wrote to Greenberg, "start with the chaos of pure fantasy and feeling, with nothing that has any known physical, visual, or mathematical counterpart, and they bring out of this chaos of emotion images that give these intangibles reality . . . . the struggle is to bring out from the non-real, from the chaos of ecstasy something that evokes a memory of the emotion of an experienced moment of total reality.

"To put it philosophically, the European is concerned with the transcendence of objects while the American is concerned with the reality of the transcendental experience."[20]

Before Greek civilization, "a work of art was concerned with the problem of meaning and was a visible symbol of hieratic thought." But then the Greeks "succeeded in secularizing their divinities to make them things to admire rather than objects of worship." Barney continued his exegesis of the history of art in "The New Sense of Fate," in early 1948. Here, Barney chose an interesting word to disdain Greek civilization, to cast doubt on its value—at least in *his* mind. Commenting on the manner in which the Greeks transformed Egyptian "totemic fanaticism," he wrote, "their will to achieve the monumentality of the barbarian's symbols was always frustrated by the awareness of their own *effeteness*" [emphasis added]. We now know, Barney insisted, that "beauty—that is, the love of ideal sensations—creates in us today sheer physical embarrassment." One wonders whom he meant when he wrote "us."

At the Waldorf Cafeteria on Eighth Street and Sixth Avenue, members of the so-called "downtown" arm of the "New York School"—Landes Lewitin, de Kooning, Kline, Pavia, Giorgio Cavallon, Reuben Nakian, James Rosati among them—had spent the war years sharing the tables with the virile "ammunition loaders." Under the influence of the charismatic Aristodimos Kaldis, who "walled out everyday reality with his Greek idealism," their discussions of the "long-standing problem of symbol and abstraction" tended to glorify the Greek sensibility over the Egyptian: artists "love to talk and talk about the golden ages of art when it was full of beautiful secrets" was how Pavia characterized the conversation.[21] Many of the same crowd, a little later, could be found acting out their own virility, overdrinking, passing around and casually engaging with various women at the Cedar Bar or in after parties at The Club. Barney, in contrast, was embarrassed; he maintained his dignity.

Rejecting Greek ideals of beauty was not sufficient; prevailing concepts of "classic" and "tragedy" had to be overturned as well. Once again, Barney felt these to be based on a fundamental misunderstanding: the very idea of "classic" was itself *romantic*. A reexamination of Greek art must dispel the "generally accepted" notion that as Egyptian art moved through Crete to Greece, it "miraculously moved away from [the] Egyptian dream to become an absolute style of classic value . . . For despite their distortion of it and despite their inability to understand it properly, the entire Greek tradition was deeply involved and overwhelmingly dominated by the romantic quest to achieve the sublime content of the Egyptian symbol."

> There has never been a classic style in history . . . the possibility of classicism is not only in itself an expression of the highest [romantic] mysticism . . . but a dangerous and misleading hope. Those who believe that classicism is possible are the same who feel that art is the flower of society rather than its root.

In contrast, because Greek *writers* were not seduced by foreign *forms* "they could concern themselves with the raw problem." Greek literature, with its "unequivocal preoccupation with tragedy" continued to be "the fountainhead of art."

> Contrary to the prevailing psychological interpretations—that it was concerned with individual frustration, with the problem of human failure and success—Greek tragedy constantly revolves around the sense of hopelessness: that no matter how heroically one may act, no matter how innocent or moral that action may seem, it inevitably leads to tragic failure because of our inability to understand or control the social result; that the individual act is a gesture in chaos, so that we are consequently the helpless victims of an insoluble fate.

Primitive societies existed alongside terror, but

> terror can exist only if the forces of tragedy are unknown. We now know the terror to expect [and we know it can be without limits, an early draft included]. Hiroshima showed it to us. We are no longer, then, in the face of a mystery. After all, wasn't it an American boy who did it? The terror has indeed become as real as life. What we have now is a tragic rather than a terrifying situation.

Barney was wise enough to place Hiroshima at the crescendo of what is, underneath its decorum, a gut-wrenched essay. Those two sentences—"We now know the terror to expect. Hiroshima showed it to us"—are the ones that are regularly quoted. In the coda, however, are the words that expose the personal scaffolding, the—as he called it—"dialogue with one's [own] history": Barney's impotence, in spite of his best efforts, in the face of the decimation of European Jewish civilization, to save Samuel and Abraham.

> Our tragedy is again a tragedy of action in the chaos that is society (it is interesting that this Greek idea is also a Hebraic concept); and no matter how heroic, or innocent, or moral our individual lives may be, this new fate hangs over us. We are living, then, through a Greek drama; and each of us now stands like Oedipus and can by his acts or lack of action, in innocence, kill his father and desecrate his mother.[22]

"The New Sense of Fate" wasn't written simply to unspool Barney's theoretical formulations, or to promote the new American painting, or to memorialize what many of the artists were thinking and saying—all of which it did not neglect to do. If we are to believe his own genesis text, as he was composing the article, which was meant for, though too long to publish in, the third issue of *Tiger's Eye*, Barney's own eye was struggling with an object he had just made. He had prepared a canvas, and covered it with a warm, very opaque, mineral tone. He tested a second color against it, running from top to bottom. And then he stopped.

It was the first painting that "contained" nothing concrete, that was two parts of a single field united by what, many years later, some would call a "zip." No image, no figure, no ground, no atmosphere, no metaphor; "not space cutting nor space building, not construction nor fauvist destruction; not the pure line, straight and narrow, not the tortured line, distorted and humiliating; not the accurate eye, all fingers, nor the wild eye of dream, winking,"—the "epistemological paradox that is the artist's problem" described in "The Ideographic Picture." Yet it announced itself as complete, as an assertion, as "the idea-complex that makes contact with mystery,"[23] as "something that evokes a memory of the emotion of an experienced moment of total reality."[24] And to understand, and legitimize, this extraordinary, *sui generis*, creation he needed to sound the final death knell to any remaining attachment to the inherited ideals of the Greek notion of beauty.

Ever since the letter to Jewell written with Gottlieb and Rothko, Barney had been incubating the *logical* argument, the "Stance" regarding contemporary art—just as he had nurtured his stances regarding civil service and carbonation. In his private drafts, in his catalogue prefaces, his articles for *La Revista Belga* and *The Tiger's Eye*, and in personal letters, he closed in on the definition, characteristics, and, most importantly, *specious* qualities, the strategies used by weak or inadequate pretenders to mask or distract. Through the first two thirds of his adult existence he produced writing in that Talmudic, or Jesuitical, framework, reason above all, and for the remainder of his life, even after he identified as a painter, he continued to speak, and argue, and privately fume, in the same way. But his identification as a painter was not based or reliant on that overworked talent of Barney's. It was, in fact, a matter of *revelation*. The drama of the moment, for Barney, was that in looking at the work that became known as *Onement I* he found himself, very possibly for the first time in his life, in an oasis where he heard no static. No newspapers, no logical arguments, no historical or philosophical recitations, no angry or scholarly *responsa*; no trotting out of credentials or *comme il faut* clothes. Whenever it actually happened, on January 29, 1948—his 43rd birthday—or sometime later that year, and regardless of any post-creation narrative he developed, *Onement I* (plate 4) was very likely the first unmediated moment in Barney's oppressively mediated life.

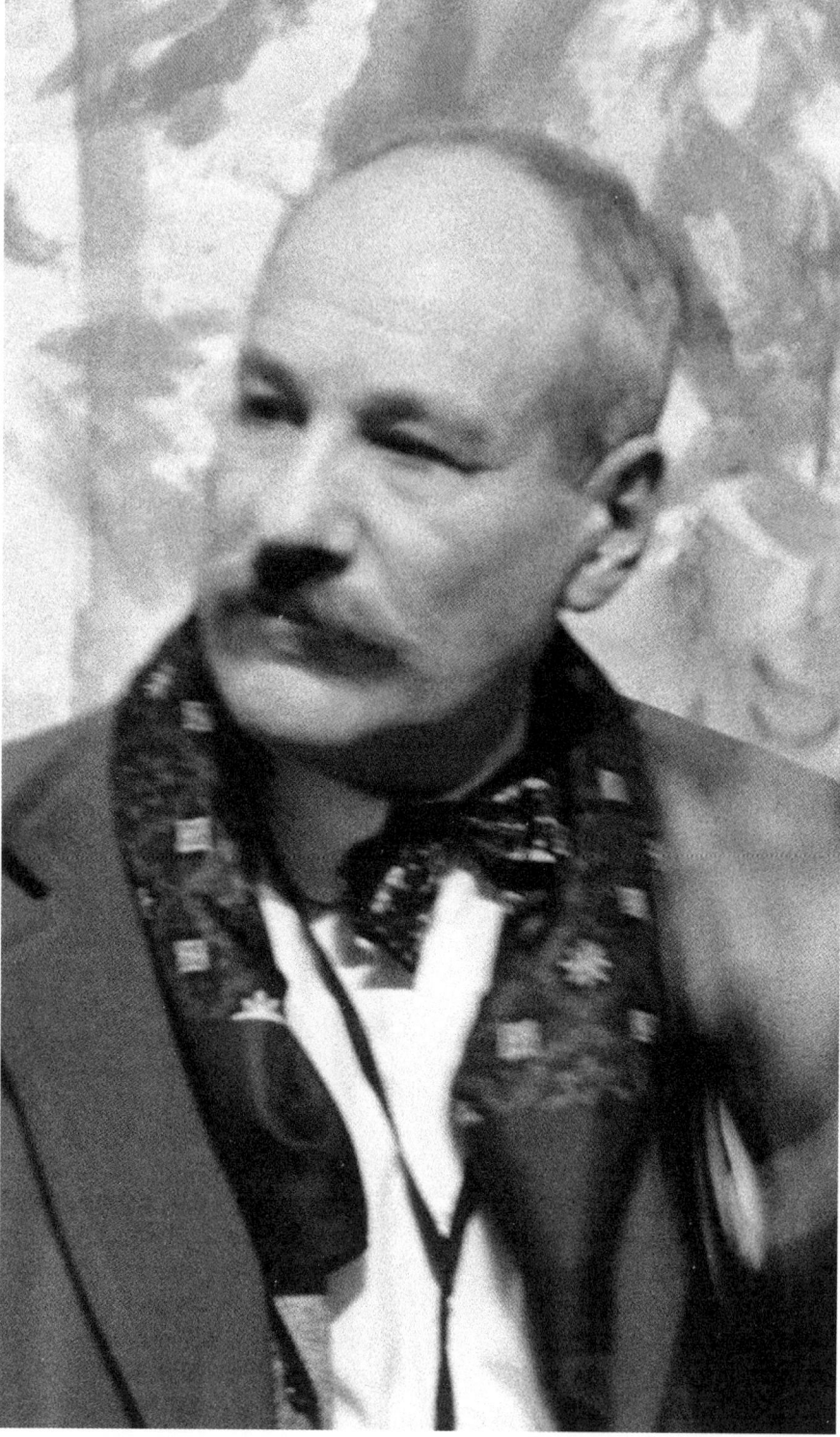

PART THREE

OUTCRY
1948–58

At the end of the decade one of the best-known origin tales belonged to Ernest Hemingway.

Hemingway was the "most famous writer" in the world, at least according to the *New Yorker* in 1950, and one of the stories he liked to tell about himself is that he began his first book, *The Sun Also Rises,* on his birthday in 1926, wrote it in two months, put it aside, then thought about and revised it for many months more. Is it true? Or did it simply tickle "Papa" to establish a dramatic creation myth for himself and what many consider his first mature work?

Barney's own origin story—that he painted what came to be called *Onement I* on his birthday in 1948, looked at it for eight or nine months (the period of human gestation; auspiciously, Yom Kippur, the Day of Atonement, fell in 1948 precisely nine months after January 29) wondering what he had done, and was ultimately struck by its satisfying inevitability—began to be told many years after the fact, sometime in the mid-1960s. With this story—"the beginning of my present life"[1]—Barney memorialized the moment when he finally realized that the single stroke on that canvas "made the thing come to life for me."[2] Previously, he had been "filling" a canvas with atmosphere in order to make it "viable"; this particular painting was immediately full. And when he saw in late January the Giacometti exhibition at Pierre Matisse Gallery, it provided close to an epiphany, confirmation of his gut: the sculptures looked "as if they were made of spit—new thing, no form, no texture, but somehow filled," he told Tom Hess.[3]

The catalogue for that show, designed by Herbert Matter, has become something of a convenient conspirator in Newman studies: it featured a cover with a narrow die-cut vertical slot, through which the 1947 *Grande Figure* was made to look like "the same column of fire and smoke as Newman's 'zip' of *Onement*," according to the Swiss scholar Franz Meyer.[4] That graphic presentation hardly gave birth to *Onement I*; Barney had earlier played with a dominant vertical. But what certainly happened is that he saw *those* Giacometti sculptures in *that* installation and isolated on *that* catalogue cover, and the experience reinforced his belief that his own vertical could contain an analogous assertive humanity.

It might have pleased Barney to fancy himself a lusty, virile figure along the lines of Hemingway. He enjoyed establishing himself as a man's man, as when he told an interviewer that his post–1952 coffee-district studio was in "a very masculine world," where he never "bumps into anyone walking poodles or trips over fur coats."[5] Hemingway's highly developed romanticizing of pugilism, horse racing, baseball, and his pleasure in mining them for analogies to the creative life; his stout-hearted way with alcohol, male companionship, and dedicated handmaidens; his constant, and favorable, measuring of himself against a historical canon (Turgenev, de Maupassant, Stendhal); even his Abercrombie & Fitch plaid wool clothes were all distinguishing features that Barney assumed as well, especially into the 1950s as he edged his persona from writer to artist.[6]

It made a good story, but it matters not whether *Onement I* was actually done on January 29, 1948, his 43rd birthday, or whether that singular painting was, in fact, the first painting Barney was content with. *Onement I* is not documented—verbally or physically—until 1952, when it was reproduced in Motherwell and Reinhardt's vividly contemporaneous document, *Modern Artists in America, First Series*. If we credit Barney's discussions with Barbara Reise in 1964, there is reason to suspect that *End of Silence* was the first, the one he "lived with . . . for a year trying to understand it." If we credit Hess's discussions with Barney at the end of the 1960s, the work he looked at for months was the one now known as *Onement II*, which was exhibited publicly (without that name) in October 1949.[7]

Only after the fact—about four years for the artists, up to decades for those Barney called the "book-makers"—did it become a matter of supreme urgency to establish whether it was Newman or Clyfford Still, or somebody else, who deserves the credit for a singular "breakthrough" in so-called field painting. What is intriguing is that Barney adopted the same *strategy* as Hemingway to announce his artistic maturity. There was something "chosen" about that narrative, something necessary for one who always believed he would be an important painter but had not yet made the medium cooperate with that conviction. "All these guys were dribbling paint, and schmearing paint, and doing fancy tricks with the paint," he told his friend painter Harold Cohen around 1960. "I wanted to do it with nothing."[8] The birthday anecdote had a whiff of the uncanny, it suggested that Barney had been touched by an angel. From then on his path was clear: he had, he understood, "to give up any relation to nature, as seen," including abstracting from nature and "atmosphere" from his earlier, tentative forays. In *Onement I* he was confronted with "the thing that I did." It was a painting that, for the first time, "had a life of its own."[9] As in Hemingway's telling, this self-realization was heroic.[10]

The work that putatively provoked these flights was 27 ¼ by 16 ¼ inches of canvas covered with cadmium red dark vaguely mottled top to bottom with black; it was the least inflected surface at which Barney had yet halted. Perhaps he was thinking about subtly modulating this "background"—as he had in *Moment, The Word I*, and *Two Edges*—or placing some sort of "figure" against it—as he had in *Death of Euclid* and *Genetic Moment*. To test a second color, he ran down the center a strip of the one-inch masking tape he had been using to create sharp edges and covered it with the more orange cadmium red light paint. What struck him, what he was moved to think about—whether it was for months or weeks or days—was that he had made not a picture but a painting. Not a scene, or a composition, or a design; "not an arrangement of objects, not an arrangement of spaces, not an arrangement of graphic elements," but a *declaration*.[11] He decided not to remove the tape.

"*Onement I* does not 'mean,' it confronts," wrote Harold Rosenberg years later. "It must be grasped as a whole, must be felt as a presence. It has the intrusive arbitrariness of an act or an event . . . *Onement* was something he had done, not conceived.

No wonder the artist himself was baffled in contemplating it . . . . Instead of invoking symbolic references, the painting calls for blank recognition of itself."[12] Like meeting a new person, Barney felt.

Later, Barney would say that the "fully held image" was characteristic of all of the "good guys" in his generation. This type of painting could not be explained or parsed, because it "deeply involves the whole being." They "were trying to make painting more visible." But, "also," Barney significantly added, he aimed to make "*myself* more visible."[13]

He gave the painting to Annalee in December. It was a gesture of profound gratitude.[14]

For thirty years he had managed his insecurities and demons by conceptualizing his experiences grandiosely even as he engaged with life on his own terms. He turned the disappointments of his family's decline in fortune and frustrations, the grim and compulsory demands of every day during the Depression, into ideas for reformation, into quixotic actions, overreaching pantomimes, and romantically impractical gestures. His writings, as reactive to immediate events and grounded in specific arguments as they were, relied too heavily on his own brand of utopian or "anarchist" abstractions. And then, sometime in 1948, all of his intellectualizing and circumvention narrowed to a focus in one slightly bigger-than-a-bread-box pronouncement.

"I had done this painting," he said in one variation of the story repeated often enough for it to take on a quality of liturgy, "and stopped in order to find out what I had done."[15]

The conundrum then—as it continues to be for those who confront his paintings today—was how to ensure that the fact and the significance of that content would be *visually* available to viewers who were unacquainted and unconcerned with how he arrived there.

Barney labored over "The New Sense of Fate," but his habitual intellectual acrobatics were derailed by his psychological turmoil. It was too long, too cumbersome; *Tiger's Eye* rejected it. And so, as he would reduce the content of his painting to a single outcry, he reduced the nearly two thousand words to just over a hundred to satisfy John Stephan's needs:

> Greece named both form and content: the ideal form—beauty, the ideal content— tragedy . . . . This tortured emotion . . . is always refined. Everything is so highly civilized.
>
> The artist in America is, by comparison, like a barbarian. He does not have the superfine sensibility toward the object that dominated European feeling. He does not even have the objects.
>
> This is, then, our opportunity, free of the ancient paraphernalia, to come closer to the sources of the tragic emotion. Shall we not, as artists, search out the new objects for its image?[16]

Among the portfolio of twenty-one reproductions included under the rubric "Ivy on the Doric Column"—"The quotation is from Fredrich [*sic*] Nietzsche's essay *The Birth of Tragedy*" wrote *Tiger's Eye*—Barney, in one of his final acts as associate editor, included not the (putatively) still perplexing *Onement I*, but, tellingly, the work from the previous year that he entitled *Death of Euclid*—a title appropriate to, but challenging, the issue's very loose classical theme. As in his original written submission, which concluded "each of us now stands like Oedipus and can by his acts or lack of action, in innocence, kill his father and desecrate his mother," Barney had murder on his mind.

He did not contribute to the next two issues. When he filled out his 1948 tax returns, he was no longer a "writer/artist" but an "artist/writer." His mental and emotional energies were directed toward the visual.

It was a very different "art world"—if that term can even be invoked. Works were not immediately photographed and indexed. Artists did not yet think of careers in terms of stylistic developments aligning with gallery shows at regular intervals or installations at international fairs. There were no price databases that logged relative monetary values nor PhD theses that assigned genealogical/aesthetic values. Artists worked, tried some things, rejected some things, combined some things, experimented and consolidated and trimmed. Then they started fresh.

In Barney's case the difficulty in ascribing a chronology to the thirteen known paintings and fifty or fifty-three drawings preceding the presumed creation date of *Onement I* is evidence of just this. If we accept the received order, the botanical and visceral residue and the voids that were abandoned early in the painting chronology continue to reappear and disappear in the drawings, even after, in the kind of baseball metaphor he would have loved, Barney found his "cutter."[17]

After 1948, every subsequent work had a composition structured around, or derived from, the edge-to-edge contrasting band that, in his words, "activates and gives life" to the painting's expanse. Yet they cannot, accurately, be described as "field" and "gesture," "background" and "foreground," "figure" and "ground": there was too great a variety.[18] Barney played with degrees of modulation and mottling; facture with a brush or a palette knife; shafts of light or simply stripes of paint; edges falling in the middle or the far boundaries of the canvas. Occasional subtle atmospheric conditions occur in both elements of the composition. There was color companionability, or color aggression, or an extreme color subtlety. At times, there was barely any color at all. There was no formula.

Of course, some accounting is unavoidable, if only to puzzle over why Barney—or Annalee—fudged a few sequences. Of the five paintings currently dated to 1948, only *Two Edges*, first reproduced in December 1948 and *Onement II*, exhibited publicly in October 1949, are documented. Between those confirmed dates, *Onement I*, *Untitled 1, 1948*, *Untitled 2, 1948* (plate 5), all ascribed to 1948, and *End of Silence* and *Onement III*, 1949, are conceptually and chromatically related, regardless of where *Onement I* fits into the group. Several—but not all—drawings dated 1946–48 use the simplified composition of the later works and are executed with the same level of assurance in both structure and facture. Barney's assurance was so great, in fact, that after 1949 he seems to have abandoned drawing entirely for ten years.

Fittingly, the painting *Genesis—The Break* is at the frustrating center of efforts to describe the story of Barney's own genesis and break with his earlier production. All agitated, indecisive marks anchored by a serene orb, the painting was purchased by John and Ruth Stephan from Parsons, and first reproduced in the October 1949 *Tiger's Eye* with the title *The Break*. According to Barney it was upside down. It was also unsigned, and, in the caption, dated 1948. There is no sontemporary record of any protest at the time, nor did any perceived offense prevent Barney from participating in several additional issues of the magazine—until, in fact, it ceased publication. But in 1959, after *Genesis—The Break* was shown in Barney's landmark exhibition at French & Company, he inscribed in the upper left corner his name, the title, and "1946" to emphatically "correct" the record. If there remains any question that 1946 is too early for that painting, there can be little doubt that 1948 is too late. *Euclidian Abyss*, which was exhibited and documented in 1947, marked a division in Barney's output. No painting documented after had any of the pictorial elements or treatment of materials seen in *Genesis—The Break*.

In 1959, the controversy around the painting focused on the circumstances of its acquisition and reproduction, and Barney's desire to buy it back. It was, he wrote, his "clear feeling" that the couple had "no real pleasure in this painting . . . you hung it upside down in your house . . . misnamed it and misdated it in Tiger's Eye . . . . You bought the painting without my permission and I have always felt that you . . . were involved in buying it as an act of bounty to me for services you felt you owed." Barney denied Stephan's claim that he had a photograph in which Barney agreed to the orientation,[19] and recounted the events of 1949:

> At the time you were publishing Tiger's Eye, No. 9, my painting was hanging on your walls at 40 Fifth Avenue upside down, which I protested. At that time, you wanted it reproduced in the Night issue but you did not like the Biblical name, Genesis. [The issue's theme was "A Selection on Night—A Darkness of the Mind Or Of Nature."] You called me by phone and asked if I would allow a change of name so that you could reproduce "your" painting in your own magazine that you yourselves controlled. I told you (if you could read the first chapter of Genesis you would know it yourself) that the first act of Genesis was the separation of "The Break" between night and day. You were happy and asked that the word, "The Break" be given you so that you could include it in your Night issue even though you befouled it by reproducing it upside down. As far as the title was concerned, I knew that "The Break" was the same as Genesis.

After the career-making French & Company show, the Stephans were not about to part with the painting, and became suspicious when the gallery delayed returning it to them. Barney explained that he had asked for time to sign and photograph the work. It was during the course of the progressively vituperative correspondence that the Stephans promulgated that Barney *requested* the painting be reproduced in *Tiger's Eye.* Barney responded with his own recollections.

> That I solicited the reproduction of this painting . . . is an outrageous, slanderous vilification of my good name, an outright malicious lie. The only soliciting was the soliciting that you did when you asked me to advise you and to help you concerning art in America. It was I who "asked" you to reproduce Clyfford Still, Mark Rothko, Bob Motherwell, De Kooning, Pousette D'Art [*sic*], Gottlieb, Tomlin, Milton Avery, Stamos—never myself . . .
>
> You now come and insist that I join you in the vilification of my own name, by allowing you to continue to defame my work physically. How ludicrous can you get that you expect me to forfeit my reputation . . . .

"What is involved here is not a painting but my reputation—my life."[20]

TWENTY-FOUR

EMBATTLED

If you were looking at newly made art in New York or collecting or critiquing it, 1948 was all about labels. Not only labels that identified "schools" or styles, or preferences, but labels that called into question and sparked debate about whether something was actually "art" at all—the alternative was not "bad" art, but subversive propaganda—and whether it was legitimate for anyone to support it publicly. Virtually no art event was free from attenuated political shadows.

An exhibition at the National Gallery in Washington, D.C. of "the most remarkable collection of early Italian, German, Flemish, Dutch and French paintings ever brought together on this side of the Atlantic" both broke attendance records *and* gave rise to "as bitter dissension and criticism as anything in the whole art history of our country," because the original international agreement offered the consideration that the works would be returned to Germany in "as good, or better, condition than when they were received."[1] When, after public agitation, the 150 works were allowed to travel, "Pictures from the Berlin Museums" became the Metropolitan Museum's most popular show that season—not solely because the European masterpieces were *real* art in the public's mind, but also because they were victor's spoils, treasures liberated by triumphant America and presented in cooperation with the Department of the Army, their official custodian. The museum's guards were enhanced by military police.

In March, the Whitney Museum, still located on Eighth Street, expiated some amount of collective guilt by presenting its first one-man show of a living American artist: Yasuo Kuniyoshi. A revered teacher, Kuniyoshi, was not only one of the artists singled out by President Truman to represent what he considered the base quality of some current American art. He was a Japan-born American painter who had been an outspoken propagandist against the Japanese government during the war, but nevertheless was classified as an "enemy alien." Earlier in the year, Oscar Niemeyer, the Brazilian architect and planner of the United Nations headquarters, was invited as a visiting scholar to Yale, but denied entry into the United States because he was a member of the Communist party of Brazil.

These episodes were in the wake of early anti-communist hysteria in America. Loyalty oaths were demanded, government and private enterprises were anxiously hunting what they called subversive elements, the Attorney General Tom Clark developed a list of "totalitarian, Fascist, Communist, or subversive" organizations that included schools, labor groups, the American Christian Committee for Refugees, the Jewish People's Fraternal Order, and the American Artists' Congress. In November 1947 the grandees of the motion picture industry voted unanimously to refuse employment to Communists and "to discharge or suspend without compensation" ten movie industry figures cited for contempt of Congress for refusing to answer questions about their political beliefs before the House Un-American Activities Committee. Industry executives reassured the public that "nothing subversive or un-American has appeared on the screen."[2]

In this suffocating atmosphere, the Museum of Modern Art, the Metropolitan Museum, and the Whitney Museum began negotiations about how best to define and fulfill their roles regarding contemporary art. When did a "modern" painting become a "classic"? Under what conditions should it be hung? In what context or company should it be seen? Battle lines were drawn between "those who claim contemporary art will never be any good and those who championed modern art twenty or thirty years ago and are reluctant to admit part of it has already become traditional."[3] Works were exchanged among the institutions in a chimerically optimistic solution to divvy up historical periods and draw lines of territory. But what was really at issue was something much larger.

To convey in the 21st century just how controversial abstract painting was in the mid-20th requires as great a leap as explaining a "party line" telephone to a person born in 2000. And yet, party line phones were an accepted fact of life in 1948, and so was a heightened paranoia about the new painting. This was something other than a matter of mass versus elite taste; no advanced artist expected the man on the street to be his champion. The shock was that great subversive motives were attributed to "modern" art by *cultural* figures and institutions. This art was not simply to be dismissed, it had to be fought against: it represented a "cult of bewilderment," an "attractive playground for double-talk, opportunism and chicanery," according to James S. Plaut, the director of the Boston Institute of Contemporary Art, in a widely publicized announcement explaining why he changed the name from the Institute of Modern Art.[4] Plaut "enjoined" artists to "come forward with a strong, clear affirmation of truth for humanity." If it was not surprising that Plaut's letter was enthusiastically supported by the conservative *American Artist* magazine and more mildly by *Art Digest*, it was a shock that many presumed friendly to advanced art did not object.

Plaut insisted that his proclamation was not "an invitation to reaction," but as Boston artist Karl Zerbe responded, "The harm is done. The reactionaries have not only accepted the invitation; they have adopted the statement."[5] Even John Graham, the author of the influential manifesto of abstraction of merely twelve years earlier, wrote to Barney from his new base in Florence: "No doubt you read the condemnation of the abstract and surrealist trend in art in works of Prokofiev and Shostakovitch in Russia. I think they are right because all this abstract art is only a game of a perverted mind, is analytical and destructive." Critics in America and England weighed in. The message was that modern art was a mystification, and a potentially dangerous one—an attribution of potency that was not disagreeable to Barney, who around this time first said, to a question variously attributed to Harold Rosenberg or Motherwell about the meaning of one of his works, "That picture will destroy the whole capitalistic system."[6]

Perhaps not coincidently, one of the earliest successes on the nascent medium of television—a hundred thousand homes had the large boxes with tiny screens—was a popular weekly show called "You Are an Artist." Originally ten minutes, it was expanded in 1948 to fifteen, during which the low-key, plaid-shirted Jon Gnagy drained art of all profundity and passion, and supplied a "plan and method of putting on paper what the beholder sees in such simple basic forms as ball, cone, cube and cylinder," from which his amateur audience could progress to landscapes, still-lifes, and figures.

None of the feeble dithering, arrogantly negative pronouncements, or popular emasculating of art was missed by the vanguard artists who, shaken by the vituperative cancellation of the government-sponsored show "Advancing American Art" and rising official anti-Communist paranoia, understood Plaut's announcement in the broader cultural context. "It is most likely that you yourself have noticed recently a journalistic and pseudo intellectual wave of animosity directed against the spirit and name of Modern Art," wrote Bradley Tomlin, Paul Burlin, and Carl Holty in a letter to select artists asking for a strategy meeting. "We invite you to meet with us because we consider it undignified to suffer the insults and insidious attacks leveled at us and to remain silent."[7] Hundreds attended the general meeting at the Museum of Modern Art in May; among others, Gottlieb and the former curator of the museum James Johnson Sweeney spoke, and George L. K. Morris castigated writers of popular criticism—naming those at the *Times*, the *World-Telegram*, the *Art Digest*, the *New Yorker,* and "those twin enemies of culture, *Time* and *Life*, Inc."—who concocted "'tip-sheets' for the public, brewed from snap judgments, unsubstantiated appraisals and highly questionable pronouncements of taste." Understanding art, like understanding every other professional arena, proclaimed Stuart Davis, required aptitude, education and experience: "Art galleries, museums, and writers on art have the power to bring art to the people, or separate it from them by misrepresenting its character"; but they were *not* responsible for directing its course. Enjoining the artist "is not the function" of a museum, wrote Juliana Force, the director of the Whitney, in a letter of support; it was a dangerous step toward suppression of artistic freedom.[8]

Rubbing salt in the wound, 117 works—including pieces by Gottlieb, Avery, and Baziotes—from the canceled "Advancing American Art" tour were offered for sale by the State Department, who responded to "pressure from those interested in modern art" by declaring the paintings "war surplus." The sealed bid auction was thought to be a diplomatic solution: it allowed the works to "be disposed of in the least ignominious way."[9]

"The violence of human living is at its highest daily pitch" in American society, Barney declared in July. The artist was "reminded every minute of his state of futility."[10]

Those artists who were becoming known as some sort of group—if not, as Barney had suggested, the "Ideographic" painters; nor, as Sam Kootz would hope in September 1949, as the "Intrasubjectives"; nor, as Motherwell would tag them in a

1949 lecture, the "School of New York"—were undeflected from their work by any of this chatter. But they acknowledged the impact on their state of mind: their own paranoia, their own defensiveness, their own competitiveness were heightened by feeling embattled within the culture.

In the toxic atmosphere every affront was experienced as a mortal wound. "Men like us . . . fester with indignation," wrote Rothko to Bay Area painter Clay Spohn, when a personal slight escalated into high dudgeon; he could not stomach the "stinking mess" on Fifty-Seventh Street.[11]

On the West Coast, Still reacted to maneuverings in New York with characteristically immoderate rhetoric, telling Rothko, "To hell with the whole lot of picture-sucking pimps. Men of art, farts without number, buggers of buggers, pricks without balls. May their foreskins drag the ground, & their bowels replace their faces that men can <u>see</u> them stink. We will yet make a path over them—tramp them into the slime from which they presumptuously rear their heads. We <u>will</u> have the last word."[12]

Clement Greenberg, focused on only the artists he deemed "serious," described "The Situation at the Moment" in *Partisan Review*.

> Given the obstacles American art continues to face since the Civil War, the situation still opposes itself to the individual artist with an unfriendliness that makes art life in Paris or even London idyllic by comparison . . . The American artist has to embrace and content himself, almost, with isolation, if he is to give the most of honesty, seriousness, and ambition to his work. Isolation is, so to speak, the natural condition of high art in America . . . .
>
> Isolation, alienation, naked and revealed unto itself, is the condition under which the true reality of our age is experienced. And the experience of this true reality is indispensable to any ambitious art.

The immediate reality, Greenberg said, was "the shabby studio on the fifth floor of a cold-water, walk-up tenement on Hudson Street; the frantic scrabbling for money; the two or three fellow-painters who admire your work; the neurosis of alienation that makes you such a difficult person to get along with."[13]

Arshile Gorky, who had a burnished reputation among the artists and shows and sales, was not living in a fifth-floor walk-up. He had recently moved into an early 19th-century farm house near Sherman, Connecticut, that had been renovated with startling glass walls. In February 1948 *Life* magazine ran a photo spread: "The house shown here is an outstanding example of how an old-fashioned dwelling can be transformed into a striking modern home" that "comfortably houses tenant Arshile Gorky, an artist, and his family in its eight rooms." Photo captions identified where the "Gorkys entertain guests" and "lie in bed mornings and watch the sun come up." There was a distant view of the woodshed that was "remodeled into a studio for Painter Gorky." But there was no art to be seen, and no words about Gorky's work, career, history, or reputation. A few days after the article appeared, Gorky came upon Barney and Baziotes at a party. "I was glad to see you as the first American artist to be featured in *LIFE* magazine," Barney recalled saying. "I'm very happy," he added, thinking, "this was an achievement because we were all underground." "Yes, but didn't I look sad? Didn't I look unhappy?" Gorky responded. "To hell with *LIFE* magazine. The important thing is life."[14]

Five months later, Gorky, fatally sick with cancer, recovering from a broken neck, reeling from a fire in his studio, cuckolded and in despair, hanged himself in the barn on that Connecticut property. Barney later said that he heard the news while he was at de Kooning's studio, and perhaps he was. But de Kooning, at Black Mountain College, was not. It was June 21, the day after Barney formally ended his year of mourning with the unveiling of Abraham's headstone, emotional enough in itself and dramatically freighted by the realization one month earlier, of Abraham's personal quest: the birth of the state of Israel. Barney, along with Jews the world over, closely followed the end of the British Mandate and its repercussions—the immediate invasion of the new state by five surrounding armies. He purchased a subscription to the Yiddish-language newspaper *Der Tog*, and preserved the May 15, 1948 issue with its banner headline. Barney did not know Gorky well at all, but likely recommended by de Kooning, he wrote a bizarre tribute to the older painter. "Arshile Gorky: Poet and Immolator" was, like "To a young poet age 4," Barney *Agonistes*.

Arshile Gorky had the supreme poetic sensibility to make every moment of his life an act of high ceremony, so that from the very beginning, painting was for him a fulcrum that he hoped would lift up his life to make it a personal pageant of glorious poetry. Gorky's final gesture, therefore, was not a simple act of violent escape from a desperate personal despair. Wandering through the scattered maze of hanging ropes, he knew he was making the poet's grand gesture of immolation.

Every human act is an act of violence. In its refusal to confront this truth lies the failure of social morality . . . .

Moral systems cannot be sound if they avoid or ignore the violent nature of human actions . . . . *The only moral act is the useless one, and the only useless act is the aesthetic one. The artist is the only man who performs an act for no useful purpose; he is, indeed, opposed to its usefulness. His behavior is completely, unalterably, and profoundly futile* [emphasis added].

No man was more fanatically and passionately devoted to the futile life of the artist than Arshile Gorky . . . . One might say that his art and his life were a search for the perfect act of futile heroism.

While the futility of an artist's act gives him his strength, at the same time it intensifies the tragedy of his life above the normal tragedy of other men, who suffering equally with the artists, cannot, in their suffering, permit themselves the despair of self-awareness, this sense of futility. Gorky's life would have been tragic in any country and in any society. Here in America, where the violence of human living is at its highest daily pitch, where there is never, as in Europe, any respite or "good living" between holocausts, Gorky's tragedy was more conspicuous. For the artist in America has the special privilege of being told and reminded every minute of his state of futility. The world here makes no bargain of expediency with him in the name of culture.

To Gorky, however, the futility of his life inside and outside the studio was not sufficiently intense. Every artist understands the feeling of its inadequacy. Sometimes, so deep is his despair, the artist feels he must make the *absolute* futile gesture. It was Gorky who chose to do it for us. When he walked into his barn to perform his private Passion, he made clear to each of us the nature of our own act and our destiny: that no matter how violent the artist's will may be against the world, his real target is the artist-man himself—that the moral act is an act of self-destruction. In showing us the morality of the moral act, Gorky saved us from the drastic violence he himself assumed.[15]

What could Barney have been *thinking* to write, a mere three years after the horrors overseas, "Here in America . . . there is never, as in Europe, any respite or 'good living' between holocausts"? Lionel Abel, the scholar and critic, and editor of the little magazine *Instead*, for which he had invited Barney to write the obituary, declined to publish it. Certainly, Americans in creative professions were under attack; certainly the foundational creed of America was under attack. Barney was overwrought, as millions were, by the House Un-American Activities Committee hearings, the blacklisting of hundreds of creative artists in the film industry, by the riveting coverage of the testimony of Meyer Schapiro's Columbia College friend Whittaker Chambers, a former Soviet spy and current editor at *Time*, against the accused spy Alger Hiss. Barney's response was a mixture of displaced rage and slashing oblique jabs by an agonized soul caught in a trap: an artist was a "fool, an idler, of course a neurotic" he told his little niece. "Who needs such a one in a world so chaotic." And yet he saw no other identity for himself.

The Parsons–Kootz–Egan painters felt out on a limb. They were not members of a formal academy or even a recognized group—such as Alfred Stieglitz's vintage avant-gardists—with a social or didactic support system. There was no meaningful market for their work, and that, combined with the lack of wide sympathy for their mission—"that speculative spirit without which a living Art is impossible of achievement," as Tomlin, Burlin, and Holty put it in their call for a meeting—created an atmosphere of beleaguered but stubborn resistance to compromise. It was as much a mutually enabled psychological reflex as a reflection of an objective reality. The idea of making adaptations that would enable their vocations, such as teaching or commercial work equaled, in their minds—and spitefully, competitively, in the minds of peers—a corruption in their art. Most could not or would not believe that a diminution of their misery wouldn't corrupt the authenticity of their work. And they could not or would not comfortably accept acceptance, the modicum of attention, audience, and sales that within a couple of years would shatter any fellow feeling with bitter accusations of plagiarism, falsification of history, and—through a 21st-century lens, quaintly—"selling out." But for the moment, their insecurities, anxieties and ambitions made them a community. Even Baziotes, one of the more successful, did not evade the psychological trough; with every sign of success he would experience a degree of psychological and physical collapse.[16] "The art world boys are in a crisis—the painters that is. Plenty of frustrated ambitions," he wrote to his brother.[17]

In months of reviews that read as pontifications, Clement Greenberg proclaimed a "crisis" of the easel picture; declared Willem de Kooning "one of the four or five most important painters in the country"; discovered the Palestinian painter Mordecai Ardon-Bronstein to be "one of the strongest painters of his generation"; predicted that Pollock would "in time be able to compete for recognition as the greatest American painter of the twentieth century"; and parsed Motherwell's efforts into yeses and no-nos. Barney expressed his irritation to Still, who leapt on it. "I recall a remark you made this summer at your house in which you quoted a local magazine hack by the name of C. Greenberg to the effect that he, in reviewing the works of his betters in the galleries, considered himself one who gave marks to the pictures he saw (in the manner of an Iowa art school teacher)." Still was so delighted that he asked Barney to repeat it precisely so that Still could arrange to have it appear in a "national magazine," so that the "bore" would be placed in his proper relation to his "obligations, and intended victims."[18]

The artists were "*very* disappointed in the late 1940s," remembered Fritz Bultman.[19]

"No one was selling any work," according to Grace Hartigan. One day Kline came to hang out at her studio and told her that he didn't have his rent but he had a collector who was going to meet him at a bank. "Franz didn't have any money for the subway. So I cashed in some soda bottles" for the fare, so he could "meet the collector to get the money to pay his rent. It was that rough."[20]

Pollock was also broke. At Guggenheim's gallery he had received a monthly stipend and his shows recognition and attention. At Parsons for his first show in January 1948 of drip paintings there was neither—other than Greenberg's praise in *The Nation*. Two paintings sold, but his old contract with Guggenheim stipulated that the proceeds went to her.[21] He looked for teaching jobs at the Art Students League and at Cooper Union; he thought he might design textiles. Escaping the cold of Springs where he couldn't buy the wood to heat his house, Pollock turned up at the Newmans' apartment; Barney took him "around the corner to the New Star Market [to] cash a ten dollar check," which bounced.[22] There were more of the feared episodes of extreme drunkenness and violent behavior.

At Egan, de Kooning's first one-man show in April was an artistic triumph. The ten black-and-white paintings, all of them less than a year old, had an outsized impact on the community, especially the so-called downtown artists, many of whom were seeing his work—not just hearing about it—for the first time. The popular press barely noticed it, but in *Art News*, which because of Hess's presence was fast becoming the journal artists paid attention to, a young critic was effusive, and Greenberg in *The Nation* called the show "magnificent" and de Kooning "one of the four or five most important painters in the country."[23] But because nothing sold during its scheduled month-long run, nor through June as Egan desperately extended it, it was a public embarrassment to the artist equal to Still's when, for the same reason, Parsons closed his 1947 show early;[24] and de Kooning, too, was broke. That fall he could not sufficiently heat his Fourth Avenue studio, where he lived whenever he was separated from his wife, the artist and critic Elaine. The evening drop in temperature brought the choice "to go to bed or to go out."[25] If there was cash available, artists would go to the Jefferson Diner, where Aristodimos Kaldis showed friends how to pilfer food. Conrad Marca-Relli, Ibram Lassaw, and de Kooning figured out ways to disable gas meters to avoid utility payments.[26] Fritz Bultman discovered that going to cheap double features, often with Léger, was more economical than paying for heat.[27]

Kootz, who represented Baziotes—perhaps the most successful of his peers—was unable to pay him money owed from recent sales at his gallery. Despite a contract with Kootz that ran another year, Baziotes also placed work with Parsons. "I haven't sold anything at Betty Parsons," he wrote to his brother in Reading, Pennsylvania, from whom he was borrowing money for "household finance." "Business in the art world is worst since depression."[28]

Barney himself was juggling more loans—from banks, from loan societies, from Parsons, from family members. But never would you hear these sorts of stories about him, nor see any indication of the wrenching, if obscurely motivated, sense of futility he described in his tribute to Gorky: he believed it was "bad manners to actually say one is feeling bad."[29] Unlike his witty and clever friend Reinhardt, who seemed to coolly manage by teaching and producing sharp and satirical magazine drawings, Barney maintained his *bella figura*, as always, through the total and devoted support of Annalee. She was teaching both day and evening sessions at Bryant High School, and it was obvious to everyone how tired she constantly was, how she "had to struggle," how she neglected herself for the benefit of Barney. The painter Yvonne Thomas noticed a button missing on Annalee's winter coat; the following year the same button was still missing. But friends also recognized it was a grand love, "a love to end all loves: the way she loved him, the way he loved her."[30] Of course Annalee had to be appropriately turned out for work, but the regular monthly outlays to an ecumenical assortment of department stores, Abercrombie & Fitch to S. Klein's, also subsidized goods and services for Barney. He kept up his car and his liquor cabinet, while Annalee did not drink anything harder than the antacid Gelusil.

Friends saw a man energetic and enthusiastic, even exuberant, a very well-dressed, very well-maintained character who liked to perform. He convincingly manifested an almost excessively upbeat attitude, mirroring what was being sold in other cultural arenas, like popular magazines' spreads of baseball players, bathing beauties, ballerinas, and babies; films like *Mr. Blandings Builds His Dreamhouse* (in which a family of four, with household help, managed nicely on 15,000 dollars a year), or the breathlessly promoted exhibits at New York's Golden Anniversary Exposition at Grand Central Palace: "actual uranium. . . . silver dimes transmuted to cadmium, working models of atomic power plants, mines and other [secret] processes."[31]

"To Barney Newman/The Grandest Grandee in the whole kingdom," wrote Pierre Garai, a young Frenchman at City College whom Barney and Annalee had taken under their wing, in a handmade book of peculiarly informal photographs of the "grandee," who allowed himself to be seen—and recorded—smoking in pajamas in a rumpled bed. Garai's text consisted of riffs on "Barneyisms": "Yes, I have thought about it a good deal—But don't you see that if, as you claim, the earth is <u>flat</u>, and it is the eyeball which is curved, that makes truth and consanguinity elliptical?" / "Do you realize what that would mean in terms of Pre-Columbian Jewish Prophets?" / "(Mrs. Newman rushes off to escape his Newmanship's dire answer to his own question.)" / . . . . "And, after all, what the hell does it matter as long as my wife remains delightful, my painting absorbing and my friends neither for Trotsky nor for that other fellow, Joseph something or other."[32]

There were big bawdy parties at Cora and Ben Ginsburg's in Tarrytown with Barney's old City College crowd—Leo and Alice Yamin, Bill and Maria Lipkind, Max Margulis, Aaron and Sidonie Siskind. There were modest upstate picnics with Mark and Mell Rothko and Richard and Evelyn Pousette-Dart. At Richard's parents' home in Valhalla, New York, Barney positioned himself imposingly against the sweep of a grand piano as it was being played and told jokes like a Catskill *tummler*. The first time Bill and Ethel Baziotes visited the apartment on Nineteenth Street Barney stood in the middle of the living room with one hand on his hip and the other holding what he said was a copy of the Kabbalah, raised above his head. Barney declaimed passages while they drank vodka.[33]

Declaiming from the "Kabbalah," like telling jokes, or singing arias from *The Magic Flute*, or reciting from memory passages of Corneille, was the kind of thing Barney would do. But the Kabbalah has attracted special attention in Newman studies, given both too much and too little weight.[34] For Barney, familiarity with Kabbalah—actually the *idea* of the Kabbalah—was one of many hallmarks that he appropriated to define his historical person—he regularly referred to it in conversation, along with the Torah and other Mishnaic texts—but it did not define his religious beliefs. The scholar Gershom Scholem's *Zohar: The Book of Splendor* was published in English in 1949, and indeed Barney had a copy, as he had many books on Jewish "folklore," ethnography, rabbinic literature, and personal stories of varities of Jewish religious experience. (Scholem himself was a Zionist; his writings were intellectual not pious, focused on the historical–philological aspects, not the accrued interpretations that were the object of spiritual Kabbalah study.) Barney also had texts on Buddhism, Gnostic Christianity, the Bhagavad Gita, and Rudolf Otto's *The Idea of the Holy: An Inquiry into the Non-Rational Factor in the Idea of the Divine and Its Relation to the Rational,* alongside Martin Buber's 1948 *Hasidism*. Barney loved books, and filled the

Nineteenth Street apartment with them. Sometimes he bought them new, but mostly they were secondhand; he browsed in the books the way he browsed in the stalls where he picked them up along Fourth Avenue's "Book Row," and browsed in Job Lot—the legendary emporium of random bargains on Vesey Street—and the other lower Manhattan treasuries of the unexpected that he had written about in 1939.

The Kabbalah was largely unknown to American Jews in the mid-20th century. Only adherents to ultra-orthodox movements, after years of preparation, were entitled to study it as a *religious* text, one that had been passed orally from the Abrahamic era until it was transcribed in the Middle Ages as the *Zohar*—the source for Scholem's studies. Barney was saturated with Jewish culture, learning, and tradition—he had family stories of revered Hasidic relatives in Poland as well as secular Zionist ones—but if he was psychologically attracted to all things mystical his Jewish practice was secular, like that of his *Menorah Journal*-reading father.[35] Being an informal Kabbalist is as impossible as being a little bit pregnant. It was certainly Scholem's book—not the "Kabbalah"—that Baziotes saw him holding aloft. The *Zohar* itself is all but impenetrable to anyone whose life is not primarily devoted to its study.

Nevertheless, if his art were not Jewish, in the sense of promoting or illustrating or practicing the creed, the person who created it *was*, and he would not let anyone forget it. "Pious" he wasn't, but identified he was, with a thumb-in-the-eye attitude about it, dropping both recondite and intimately tribal references provocatively in letters, essays, statements, and conversation. Being Jewish wasn't something relevant to his art, he would maintain, if he were forced to state a position, but his contrarian personality relished opportunities to evoke it, wear it, use it, then deny any significance for his work. Still, a deeper, resonant, meaning was there: it was the sum total of a life of a Jew during a certain span of modern history. It was his sign of an intellectual culture, a badge won in combat, a chip on his shoulder. It created the man who made the art. Over the years he would bring up the story of being overwhelmed at the Passover seder when the first night fell on a Friday. As the Sabbath was the more exalted observance, a prayer in the order of the seder was altered, and his brother-in-law gave him "the honor" of reciting it: "Blessed be Thou, oh Lord, who distinguishes between what is holy and what is *holy*" (or "the holy and the still holy"). "The holy and the HOLY," Barney would repeat. The concept "shook" him. "That's my aesthetic. I thought, 'those Jews were *some smart* Jews!'"

The story perfectly illustrates how Barney deployed his traditional/individual, educated but selectively absorbed Judaism. He knew something—enough to sound learned—and he counted upon his audience knowing less, on there being no one who could call him out. He may have been referring to 1948, when the first night of the holiday fell on a Friday. That seder, the first since Abraham had died, would have been spent with his own mother and family: Annalee traditionally celebrated the holiday with the Newmans, and Barney himself would have been the presiding male. Or, he may have been thinking of 1950, when the first night fell on Saturday, and a prayer marking the end of the Sabbath and the beginning of the holiday was recited—"Blessed is God who separates between one holiness and another." As his

Greenhouse nephew and nieces did not recall Barney and Annalee at their seders, the gesture of respect by his brother-in-law is dubious, but the story did make for a brilliant addition to the Barney canon of epiphanies, and he repeated it regularly.

Bringing up the Kabbalah at once both identified him with the rigorous scholarship of the tradition and jibed with the generally mystical philosophies to which he was intellectually attracted. Thus he managed to walk a tightrope across the agitated and fraught landscape of *how* to be a Jew—after pogroms, exile, and Holocaust—in 20th-century America. It was a singular moment: the realization of the Zionist dream of a safe Jewish state, liberal revulsion at the consequences of ideological nationalism—the "herd" mentality, Greenberg called it—and a prevailing Existentialist zeitgeist. Many voices energetically held the position that "defense against assimilation" was "more urgent than defense against [antisemitic] discrimination."[36]

Questions of "Jewish loyalty, security, commitment, and survival"; "fundamental disagreements about what could be said by and about Jews in public"; and "whether nonconforming individuals had a right to speak 'as Jews'" were much deliberated at the end of the 1940s,[37] taken up by Jean-Paul Sartre, Hannah Arendt, Nathan Glazer, Max Horkheimer, Theodor Adorno, Bruno Bettelheim, Morris Raphael Cohen—to name only a few. Two were daily voices in Barney's life: Harold Rosenberg and Clement Greenberg. "As is usual with metaphysical problems, this issue of what we are and what we shall choose to be presents itself among Jews in an immediately practical, not to say painful, form," wrote Rosenberg in June.[38]

Psychology had only recently emerged in America as a significant field of study, and the concept of "Jewish self-hatred"—eventually as acknowledged a prominent trope in literature as the Oedipal Complex—fostered and abetted by émigré intellectuals, was put under a microscope, endowed with social scientific authority. A contemporaneous "Jewish Cold War" developed, "a contentious public debate revolving around the question of Jewish group loyalty, Jewish group 'survival,' and Jewish nationalism" in which the "escalating polemics of self-hatred forced the universalists to define and defend their Jewishness in the face of charges of disloyalty to the Jewish collectivity."[39] The urgency was such that Rosenberg and Greenberg chose to enter the fray in *Commentary*. "What have I in common with Jews?" asked Rosenberg. "I have hardly anything in common with myself."[40] "What loyalties do I possess?" asked Tworkov, as the effects rained down on those who were not ideological participants in the secular iteration of disputation. "Except for self-defense what do Jews want to group themselves for?"[41]

Greenberg, for one—perhaps *the* one as far as the artists were concerned, since his arguments were consistently engaged by them—addressed the issue full-frontally in an ugly and self-mortifying article: "One looks into oneself and discovers there what is also in others. A realization of the Jewish self-hatred in myself, of its subtlety and the devious ways in which it conceals itself, from me as well as from the world outside, explains many things that used to puzzle me in the behavior of my fellow Jews . . . I have become persuaded that self-hatred in one form or another is almost universal among Jews."[42]

The preoccupation with Jewish self-hatred in the aftermath of the Holocaust cannot be discounted when considering Barney's righteous defensiveness—or Rothko's or Gottlieb's or Resnick's or Tworkov's. Their guts were made up of entirely different matter than de Kooning's, Still's, Pollock's, Reinhardt's, or Motherwell's. Resnick recalled that after his 1949 show, Rothko asked de Kooning what he thought. "You're yourself now, Rothko," was the Dutchman's reply with, what Resnick, who was present, called "his sincere young Christian soul." Before the war, Resnick explained, they "all wanted to be new; after they wanted to be themselves." But "as ethnics we [the Jews] didn't want to be ourselves; we wanted to be new."[43]

Barney was not a partisan or even a participant in these debates; most assuredly, he wanted *both* to be new *and* himself. But with his family background, his father's burdensome legacy, his own political Zionism, his vanished Newman patrimony, his shattered, refugee cousin, and, most importantly his intellectual engagement with many of the players, he was caught in the complicated and complex web. It was a cultural climate in which Greenberg could write:

> Is not a "Jewishness" defined almost entirely in terms of group loyalty and group conformity, and whose only context is its function as differentiation, being elevated as the supreme criterion by which everything and every Jew is to be judged?

Regarding the " 'positive' Jew," who asserts that he has no self-hatred to express, Greenberg had serious doubts that he meant it "all the way down."

> The pressure of the larger society within which we live, according to whose traditions the Jews as a whole do not cut an attractive figure . . . is far too strong to enable one to escape self-hatred simply by feeling oneself 100 per cent Jewish. On the contrary, such a feeling may even increase self-hatred. The pressure of the opinions of the larger society reaches everywhere . . . and one may well resent oneself all the more for sensing oneself undilutedly Jewish.[44]

This did not describe Barney. *Barney* hated what the world did to Jews, but he did not hate himself. Annalee maintained, and everything in his life and actions supports, that Barney was "always comfortable" in his Judaism,[45] and he did not overtly wrestle with it as Greenberg and others did. He made his statement by smuggling—sometime provocatively, sometimes playfully—his comfort into otherwise unconnected conversations, statements, letters, and activities. In social situations he discoursed, in his manner, upon the Kabbalah. In interviews he invoked the Passover prayer story. He unnecessarily but deliberately introduced the observant Jew's tractate of ethics, the *Pirkei Avot*, to forestall criticism of his startling interpretation of *The Stations of the Cross*.[46] In a contemptuous—commissioned but unpublished—review of Hess's 1951 book, *Abstract Painting*, Barney randomly marshalled Hebrew philology: the idea that sensation is physical experience + that by calling one a sensation painter that he automatically has no content but eye pleasure [is] a new kind of Philistinism under the guise of intellectualism. The scholastic thinkers understood this better. Kabalistic thinking is fundamentally built on the mystery of vision and although too complex to explain in a review *anyone who understands the kabalistic explanation* of the Hebrew letter ע which means eye must know that sensation involves the total being, neither the aesthetic reaction alone and certainly not the intellectualism [emphasis added].

Hess *must understand*?[47]

When the Jewish Museum in New York invited Barney to participate in a discussion, he wrote to interim director Hans van Weeren-Griek to "express my disgust at [your] sponsorship of the Am Haoretz [Barney's terminology, not the museum's] debate 'What About Jewish Art?' . . . I cannot emphasize enough the repulsion I feel for there is something here that is more serious than just a Am Haoretz performance. What the Jewish Museum has done is to compromise me as an artist because I am Jewish."[48] It was 1965, when his reputation was secure, when established and respected younger Jewish critics (who hadn't his history) were to appear on the program without fear of ghettoization. Even his good friend and committed supporter Ben Heller, collector and sometime curator at the Jewish Museum, could not "quite understand the depth of feeling to which it seems to have driven you." Barney reacted out of principle. At the same time, however, he wanted to make very sure the director knew who *was* and who *wasn't* Jewish and van Weeren-Griek was not. One could not get more tribally dismissive than *Am Haoretz*—literally "from the land," but idiomatically vulgar, boorish, uneducated, bumpkin, ignoramus. Doubly ignoramus, since van Weeren-Griek, and in fact most younger Jews themselves in 1965, would have no familiarity with the term Am Haoretz at all.

Barney was a master of submerged verbal symbolism. His identity as a Jew was neatly folded into his identity as an artist. Just like the Jew in Egypt—he couldn't resist making the comparison to an interviewer—the artist was a person in exile. "I believe in exile, a self-imposed exile . . . . As I, as [an] artist, am separate from the world, so a picture is separate from the world of things."[49]

TWENTY-FIVE

THE SUBLIME

Barney had not had an "artist's" studio since December, but in mid-May Jeanne Reynal, the mosaic artist, helped him rent a storefront under a frame shop at 304 East Nineteenth Street, a few yards from his apartment. The new studio had running water and heat but was so small Barney would be able to maneuver around canvases only by creating a bridge from wood planks laid across milk crates. He had it plastered and painted and mopped, then he was knocked back by Gorky's death and hesitated: "The futility of an artist's act gives him his strength . . . the despair of self-awareness." But by the middle of the summer he began to paint with a focus and commitment he had never experienced. Between August 1948 and December 1949 Barney made twenty paintings, some of them his most memorable. Never again would he sustain so concentrated an explosion of work.

How to get to the place of sublimity where he needed go—while doing it "with nothing"? *Onement I* and most of the other works during this period used traditional oil on canvas, but he was searching for alternative materials. He experimented with masking tape, orientation of the canvas,[1] and oil and wax crayon. He played with various recipes for varnish, and irregular applications. In January 1949, he bought a Paasche spray gun. He tried unusual mixtures of oil and casein on canvas for the profound blackness of *Onement IV*, oil and Magna—a non-water-solvent acrylic paint newly formulated by the legendary artisan Leonard Bocour—for the even profounder blackness of *Abraham* (plate 6), and, most unusually and effectively, egg tempera and oil for the ethereal, infinitesimally modulated, hear-the-angels-sing white-on-white transcendence of *The Voice* (plate 7).[2] Barney wasn't alone in his quest to push painting into a different register. Pollock was having his most productive, inventive period as well, which Barney witnessed firsthand during summer visits to Springs.[3] Still's and Rothko's paintings invested "the physical dimensions of painting with the values of a human realm that had been inaccessible to western art" according to the catalogue for the annual exhibition at San Francisco's Palace of the Legion of Honor.[4] When in December the Stephans devoted *Tiger's Eye* to "The Sublime" it was likely that Barney encouraged the idea of an encompassing label.

"How can we be creating a sublime art?" That was the question Barney posed in "The Sublime Is Now."

"If we are living in a time without a legend or mythos that can be called sublime, if we refuse to admit any exaltation in pure relations, if we refuse to live in the abstract, how can we be creating a sublime art?"

In rehearsing the arguments he had made in "The New Sense of Fate," Barney was engaging with many others in the debates over what constituted "art" in the contemporary world. He was responding to both the rhetoric of the enjoiners and that of the prescribers; to both the genuine and the self-styled intellectuals who were filling the air around upper Madison Avenue and Times and Herald Squares with skepticism and know-nothing contempt, and the air around Eighth, Tenth, and Fifty-Seventh Streets with elevated theoretical justification.[5]

For centuries in Western culture the "easel picture" cut the "illusion of a boxlike cavity into the wall behind it" and organized within that cavity "the illusion of form, light, and space." Now, in April 1948, Clement Greenberg had declared it to be in "crisis." A different approach, a "relatively undifferentiated surface" that was "tightly covered, evenly and heavily textured"—Greenberg located its origin in Monet and Pissarro, as Barney had in his unpublished 1944 "The Problem of Subject Matter"[6]— was not an "eccentric phenomenon," but an "important new phase in the history of painting." The uniformity, the "dissolution of the picture into sheer texture, sheer sensation, into the accumulation of similar units of sensation" Greenberg said responded to "something deep-seated in contemporary sensibility."[7]

Greenberg continued his offensive in a review of de Kooning's first show later that month: the "canon of the profiled, circumscribed shape—as established by Matisse, Picasso, Mondrian, and Miró seems less and less able to incorporate contemporary feeling." Upon the rejection of that canon depended "the possibility of originality and greatness for the generation of artists now under fifty."[8]

A few months later, in "The Herd of Independent Minds: Has the Avant-Garde Its Own Mass Culture?" Harold Rosenberg had very different ideas about what was "deep-seated in contemporary sensibility," its sources, and satisfactions. In a contradictory frame of mind, he argued that *any* broad cultural statements—whether mass or "small group" (intellectual)—were suspect as "constantly *in the process of making themselves true* by causing people to experience their common lives in those terms." The "authentic" artist "by way of his own humanity" moves "spontaneously towards the humanity of others"; but only "the individual can communicate experience, and only another individual can receive such a communication."[9] Barney read both *Partisan Review*, where Greenberg's article appeared, and *Commentary*, where Rosenberg wrote. These issues were the social currency in their set. They were all buzzing in the same hive, a community that was drenched in discourse—what they considered *urgent* discourse—and cross-pollination was endemic.

What was art meant to do? In his hope of being definitive, of brooking no argument, Barney in "The Sublime is Now" grandly hit those high moments of Western culture with which he was familiar, nodded to the names people were talking about (Kant, Mondrian), and ignored acres and acres of more subtle discussion. His leap-frogging sprint through centuries of philosophy and art, assigning his own version of motives and goals, ends in the failure of all—except, notably, Michelangelo, whom Barney insistently identified with and frequently invoked as the standard-setter for "his Newmanship's" definition of sublimity (although "only in his sculpture"). "I want to say something Michelangelo didn't say," he told an interviewer in 1963. "The reason I raise the issue of Michelangelo [is that] maybe I know him better than

the guys who write about him. There is something there that I think I understand."
The books "just tell stories. The [historians] don't identify. The artist identifies himself with the painters, not the paintings." To a certain extent, he maintained, "I belong
to the context of the dialogue in which, let's say, Michelangelo and I participate."[10]

"It was no idle quip that moved Michelangelo to call himself a sculptor rather than
a painter," Barney wrote in "The Sublime Is Now," as if the "divine one" himself hung
out at the coffee shop with him and the guys. "The failure of European art to achieve
the sublime is due to [the] blind desire to exist inside the reality of sensation" and
"the Greek ideal of beauty," whether romantic (active) or classic (stable).

> Modern art [Impressionism, Cubism, Purism] caught without a sublime content,
> was incapable of creating a new sublime image and, unable to move away from the
> Renaissance imagery of figures and objects except by distortion or by denying it
> completely for an empty world of geometric formalisms . . . . became enmeshed
> in a struggle over the nature of beauty: whether beauty was in nature or could be
> found without nature.
>
> I believe that here in America, some of us, free from the weight of European
> culture, are finding the answer, by completely denying that art has any concern
> with the problem of beauty and where to find it . . . . We are freeing ourselves of
> the impediments of memory, association, nostalgia, legend, myth, or what have
> you, that have been the devices of Western European painting. Instead of making
> *cathedrals* out of Christ, man, or "life," we are making [them] out of ourselves, out
> of our own feelings. The image we produce is the self-evident one of revelation,
> real and concrete, that can be understood by anyone who will look at it without
> the nostalgic glasses of history.

But he didn't need the selective history, or weak and specious reasoning. The crux
of the matter was very fundamental, very basic, and very simple: "We are reasserting
man's natural desire for the exalted."

And that, in December 1948, was—with one important exception—pretty much
the last public statement Barney made on behalf of "we."

By the end of the year "modern art" had been called a formula of "deformation" by
the lapsed advocate of the Museum of Modern Art, Lincoln Kirstein, in *Harper's*—
even as he was the champion and prime mover of George Balanchine's revolutionary
New York City Ballet, which had its first season in 1948.[11] The contemporary artist
was called a "flat-chested pelican, strutting upon the intellectual wastelands and
beaches, content to take whatever nourishment he can from his own too meager
breast," by Metropolitan Museum director Francis Henry Taylor in *The Atlantic
Monthly*; the "innocent layman visiting the national exhibitions may be forgiven for
suspecting that the chief purpose of American art is to illustrate the Kinsey Report."
Mainstream America, which had not paid much attention to the little community of

advanced artists on the east and west coasts, picked up the gauntlet. *Life* magazine reported that the layman's discomfort with the art was supported by "the fire of distinguished thinkers" like Arnold Toynbee and Aldous Huxley; was a "situation" that, "from the point of view of our civilization as a whole . . . certainly has its dangers"; and raised the question, "How can a great civilization like ours continue to flourish without the humanizing influence of a living art that is understood and enjoyed by a large public?" Within less than a year the U.S. Congress was informed that modern artists were "human termites . . . boring industriously to destroy the high standards and priceless traditions of academic art."[12] The presumed defenders of contemporary art—the Museum of Modern Art in New York and the Institute of Contemporary Art in Boston—were locked in a 24-month tense negotiation about how best to exercise damage control while subduing the unintended consequences of Plaut's original statement.

But cracks in the wall of resistance began to appear. If, in October 1947, avant-garde artists in America had "no reputations" beyond "a small circle of fanatics, art-fixated misfits who are isolated in the United States as if they were living in Paleolithic Europe,"[13] a year later mainstream institutions were paying attention—some of it positive, some not entirely negative. When Peggy Guggenheim's collection was shown that summer at the Venice Biennale, it included six works by Pollock. In October MoMA bought a work by de Kooning, and a painting of his was included in the Whitney Annual. In 1945 Henry Luce's *Life* had covered the Museum of Modern Art's Mondrian show by noting—with cavalier disregard for accuracy—that Mondrian "was probably the only artist in history who never drew a curved line," opined that "most gallerygoers are alternately bored and exasperated," and mockingly described the artist as dancing by himself to boogie-woogie music while sucking on an orange. In October 1948, in a postwar society of booming media, advertising, and hunger for the new—the cover of the issue had a glamour photo of a "Television Discovery"—it was obliged to acknowledge "the strange art of today" along with its favored living documentarians and amateur artists in "A *Life* Round Table on Modern Art."[14]

"Round table" discussions were a popular device; they signaled engagement with a subject while avoiding a particular position. *Partisan Review* held one in August on "The State of American Writing, 1948" and the *Magazine of Art* would, in March 1949, ask a range of minds to describe "The State of American Art."[15] In April 1949, a three-day "Western Round Table on Modern Art" at the San Francisco Museum of Art involved a range of disciplines, with George Boas, Gregory Bateson, Kenneth Burke, Marcel Duchamp, Alfred Frankenstein, Robert Goldwater, Darius Milhaud, Andrew C. Ritchie, Arnold Schoenberg, Mark Tobey, and Frank Lloyd Wright addressing explicitly defined spheres: The Cultural Setting, Art and Artist, The Critic, The Collector, The Museum.

"A *Life* Round Table on Modern Art" was held at the Museum of Modern Art with fifteen "distinguished critics and connoisseurs" who were posed the questions "Is modern art, considered as a whole, a good or a bad development? That is to say, is it something that responsible people can support, or may they neglect it as a minor and impermanent phase of culture?" The participants represented a spectrum of taste, but *Life* had to report that at least they were "unanimous" that not all art characterized by "unrecognizability and strangeness" was bad, and that, on the other hand, even "the 'radicals' . . . gave at least partial approval" to some "'conservative' pictures." To be fair, the printed *precis* of the discussion was lengthy and balanced, with Meyer Schapiro having the most prominent role; but the take away—given the introduction and the loaded terms in which the magazine described modern art—was that the "young" Americans whose work appeared on the pages were "Extremists" (an intentionally *political* word), as the headline put it, and the critics "leave us in confusion" about the "values of modern art."[16]

Despite their confusion, the editors reproduced five works: de Kooning's *Painting, 1948*; Baziotes's *The Dwarf*; Stamos's *Sounds in the Rock*; Gottlieb's *Vigil*; and Pollock's *Cathedral*. And the discussion had been joined in a genuinely popular venue with the participation of a number of genuine thinkers. But it was a conversation about contemporary art conducted in the voices of museum men, professors, professional intellectuals, and writers. Where, artists could not help but wonder, were *their* voices? The artists of Barney's circle took steps to bring *their* discussions—up to this point held in coffeeshops and bars, in living rooms and tearooms, in the pages of miniscule-circulation short-lived journals—into a different arena. To call this arena an "institution" would be laughable. It was a concept—the casual fantasies of Still and Rothko and Motherwell—that coalesced in a small loft space at 35 East Eighth Street, in close proximity to the Waldorf Cafeteria, the NYU school of art education where Tony Smith, Robert Iglehard, and Hale Woodruff were teaching, and in the neighborhood where so many artists had their studios.

That summer, while visiting New York, Still had a conversation with Rothko that he reconstructed years later: "Talk shifted to the 'school.' The idea of creating a center of free activity for imaginative effort . . . . A group of painters, each visiting the center one afternoon a week, each an entity different from the others, each free to teach in whatever way he chose or free to stay away, every student free to work or remain away, attend every teacher's meetings or none. Workers would, of course, be selected with emphasis on intelligence and 'drive.' "[17]

By mid-September Still had returned to California "in order to take over a job in San Francisco that will pay my living expenses this winter," telling Parsons he was too concerned "with the problem of basic survival to know what the future plans will include."[18] But Baziotes, Motherwell, and the sculptor David Hare were moving ahead with the "school." In the rented loft they opened a ten-week session in October with a distracted and depressed Rothko, whose mother had died earlier in the month and whose funeral in Portland, after much agonized consultation with Barney and Annalee, he did not attend. For comfort and advice regarding a variety of conflicts with Motherwell, Rothko also relied on Barney for a sympathetic ear. Everyone knew that Barney was an insomniac and a night owl who slept late into the day—Annalee attributed his odd sleeping habits to his "bohemianism." But Rothko rose early, and after painting for a few hours, "full of angst" he needed to talk—to "kvetch" and complain, according to Annalee. He got into the habit of waking Barney up at 11:00 or 12:00 for therapeutic telephone venting, after which Rothko would go to lunch, and Barney, exhausted, would fall back asleep. As the school took form, the conflicts became one of their topics; Rothko wanted Barney involved as a buffer between Motherwell and himself.[19] (There was also dissention between Motherwell and Hare.[20]) It was a moment when to outsiders it appeared that Barney and Rothko were most in agreement "on the one subject: their careers in the art world."[21]

Initially, Barney was not particularly interested in the school, and dealing with Motherwell gave him bouts of sciatica.[22] Moreover, he was enormously productive, finally finding the satisfaction that had been elusive in his work.[23] His conversations with Pollock were his touchstone; they would talk about painting "with a capital P," as not a way toward leading "an 'artistic, bohemian life,' but [as] *life* itself."[24] Barney's temperament, and habit, however, were no less inclined to the verbal or expository than they had always been, and his conviction that the artist was of value to society for more than the value of his products was no less absolute: he could not keep himself from getting caught up in the new venture. The artists should speak for themselves, he insisted; no one else should be speaking for them. That was something he personally could not abide: if Annalee, who heard him say something over and over again, would volunteer a version, Barney would look at her and say, "you know, I'm very articulate. I can speak for myself."[25] On the other hand, so identified with Gottlieb, Rothko, Still, Pollock, and a few others was he that he gave *himself* a pass. These were the artists who—he said years later—woke up in 1940 to find that "painting did not really exist," and they had to start from scratch, "as if painting never existed before"[26]—so any historical preparation or justification for it was moot. Starting from scratch suited Barney just fine; it provided the same liberation that his alliance to Anarchism had: if you functioned by the rules of an institution you were accepting the authority of that institution—and that would not do. At the new school there were to be no models, no objects. And, he hoped, no compromised History. Conveniently, it also made insignificant—in his mind at least—the absent record of his own history as an artist.

"All of these guys come with their lawyers," he would say. The artist should take matters into his own hands, say his own piece, say what he had to say about his work and himself, without having someone speak for him. If the artist were not sufficiently "articulate," he could take his painting, put it up on an easel, and stand with it: "this is what I do and this is who I am."[27] The curriculum was the artist himself. Which is why Barney suggested "Subjects of the Artist" be added to the original name "A New Art School."

And then he went on to contribute to "The Sublime Issue" of *Tiger's Eye* a text that said "the image we produce is the self-evident one of revelation, real and concrete, that can be understood by anyone who will look at it without the nostalgic glasses of history" and a full-page reproduction of *The Two Edges*—later called simply *Two*

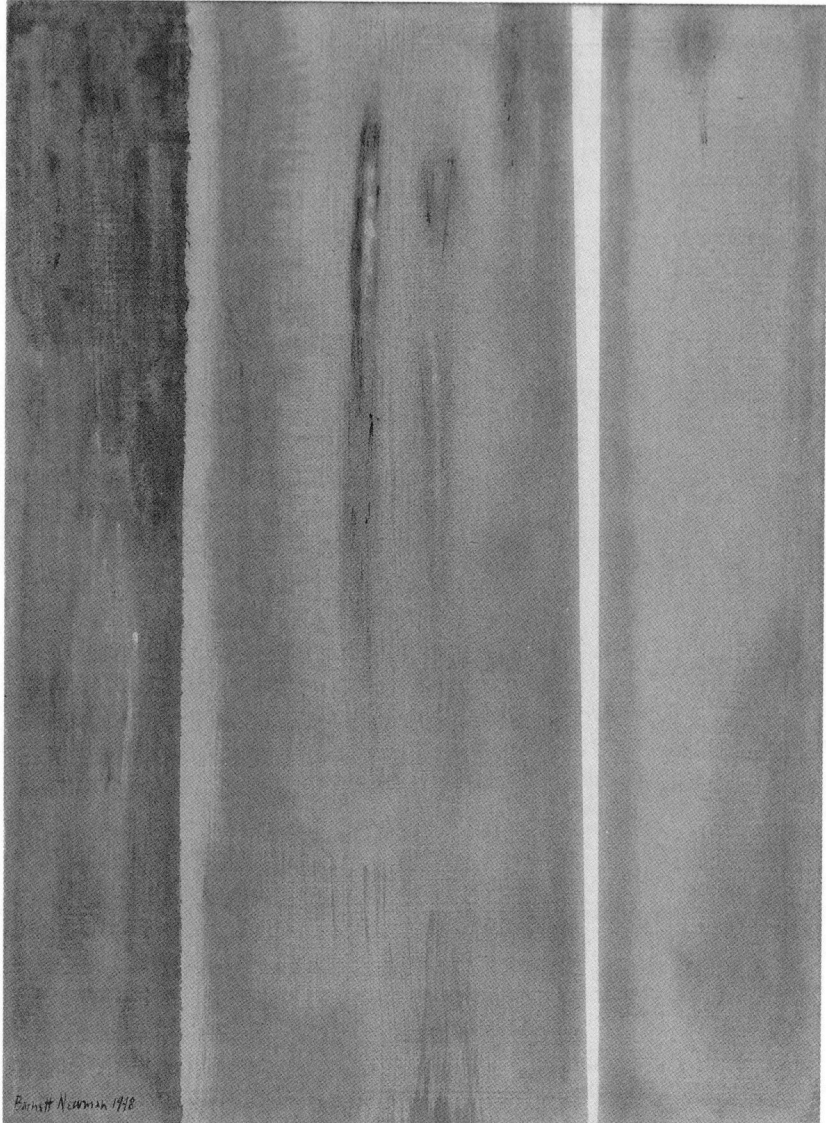

Fig. 19 Barnett Newman, *Two Edges*, 1948. Oil and egg tempera on canvas, 48 × 36 in. (121.9 × 91.4 cm). The Museum of Modern Art, New York. Gift of Annalee Newman

Edges—a mid-sized painting in shades of mottled ochre with a lighter ochre vertical and a tapering shaft of starker white, not unlike a shaft of sunlight on knotty pine paneling.

Whether chosen by Barney or Stephan, *The Two Edges* was an interesting choice at that moment.[28] Of the five paintings and two drawings now dated 1948, none were exhibited or illustrated before 1949 except this one. Both Rosenberg in 1963, and

Barney himself in 1970, identified *Two Edges* as the final pre-*Onement* painting; it retains the pronounced "atmosphere" that was quickly evaporating from his work, and two tentative versions of the verticals that, following his breakthrough, were invariably stalwart.[29] Barney ever after said it took nine months to absorb the powerful direction to which the breakthrough *Onement* pointed. If we take his narrative at face value, by the December 1948 *Tiger's Eye* he would have arrived at his mature style; he told Hess that he "began to paint again" that October.[30] It's strange, then, that he would have allowed a less secure work to represent him—and again upside down—in the permanent record of a printed magazine.[31] One explanation may be that *The Two Edges* was the only 1948 work that had enough articulation to "read" in a black-and-white illustration, although the 1952 publication *Modern Artists in America, First Series* would reproduce *Onement I*—in black and white, with no title—to powerful effect.

A different explanation might be that *Onement I* had not yet been painted. And that years later, given the often-repeated story of the Subjects of the Artist School and his imminent participation in it, Barney's appreciation of grand performance dictated a bespoke artist's narrative to secure his position among his peers. Thus—a seed was planted on his birthday; it gestated for nine (!) months; and, with a characteristic private–public nod to his ethnicity around the Jewish New Year and Day of At*onement*, a fully matured signature was born. By the time this story had achieved currency it was no longer—if it ever were—needed. The fact that anyone was listening to him tell it was proof enough that his reputation had been earned. But Barney was never interested in being known only for the artifact. "The pictures were painted by a painter conceived by" Barney Newman, said William Rubin.[32] And it was around this time that *that* particular "onement" was realized.[33]

TWENTY-SIX

SUBJECTS OF THE ARTIST

"Our school is coming along O.K. + the lectures given here every Friday nite are sure getting known around N.Y. as a very lively bunch of people," Baziotes reported in February, 1949.

They called their students "collaborators."[1] There were about a dozen, most female; Gandy Brodie, who would become a favorite of Meyer Schapiro, was the rare male. No one formally directed the school during the first semester the previous fall, with Motherwell the public face. One of the artists came each day and one each evening to discuss the students' work, but the principals would get into heated arguments with each other and the students were left hanging. By the beginning of the second and final semester in January Barney agreed to join the dysfunctional "faculty," with the stipulation that he would only be there occasionally. Nevertheless, his magnetic personality changed everything.[2]

Barney inaugurated the series of Friday night artist's talks. The idea was to broaden the students' experience, but, with the school "going under," the founders were very happy to publicize themselves to a larger audience in the charged cultural atmosphere in which *Life* suggested the new art was "a silly and secretive fadism."[3] They "had to get to the public," Barney said, to show "that we weren't screwballs," that the distinction between "personal expression and realism" had become too attenuated, "both were human and neither was insane."[4] Those "who were interesting and doing something on their own terms" were who they were after; they wanted a dialogue, they did not want to "promote a movement—like Surrealism." Three "ground rules" were agreed upon: only those who were creative artists in their field could speak; no faculty could speak; and the entire proceeds from the admission fee, minus the chair rental and the speaker's pre-event dinner, went to the speaker.[5]

At the first session, in January, Joseph Cornell showed rare pioneering films from his collection: "Méliès Magic," Pathé's 1905 "A Detective's Tours of the World," and Chaplin's "The Count." The following week, John Cage spoke about "Indian Sand Painting, or the picture that is valid for one day." Richard Huelsenbeck, the 58-year-old legendary Cabaret Voltaire habitué and provocateur spoke about "Dada Days"; and Jean Arp, with Frederick Kiesler interpreting, attracted the biggest audience in February.

"I am surprised to be here this evening reading my piece, for I do not think I am up to it," began de Kooning's comments the next week, and, in fact, at the last minute he didn't read it, so self-conscious was he about his Dutch accent. Motherwell, generally master of ceremonies, filled in, "talking in [a] very patronizing way about" how good it was, "sort of patting Bill on the back." "Barney Newman decided it really," de Kooning's text continued, "and he even gave the evening a name, 'The Desperate View.'" Barney was more emphatic: he "bulldozed" him when, at the

Newmans' apartment, de Kooning, his wife, the artist and critic Elaine, and Barney jointly drafted what he would say.[6]

> My interest in desperation lies only in that sometimes I find myself having become desperate. Very seldom I start out that way. I can see, of course, that in the abstract, thinking and all activity is rather desperate. When an idea is given, one is stuck with it . . . .
>
> The subject matter in the abstract is space. [The artist] fills it with an attitude. The attitude never comes from himself alone. One is with a group or movement because you cannot help it.

Fritz Glarner, the émigré European, showed his De Stijl- and Bauhaus-influenced "Relational" paintings; Cornell returned to screen additional rare movies; Julien Levy, on Barney's instance, recounted the history of his involvement with Surrealism and how he became a dealer; Gottlieb spoke about the "Abstract Image"; Reinhardt about "Abstraction"; Harry Holtzman on "Every man his own hero." Pollock, Tomlin, and Tony Smith were invited, but passed, and the series of twelve wrapped up in early April with Cornell and more early films. So ambitious were the founders thought to be, that someone created a satirical card in the school's format: "Prof. Albert EINSTEIN, the violinist" would speak on "The Atomic Bum & Academic Painting,—'a disparate view.'"

The evenings were a fantastic success. Tiny ads were placed on the *Times*'s art page, and announcement cards were mailed, but promotion was mainly through word of mouth, and the little loft felt mobbed with 85 to 115 artists, hungry for just this sort of intramural exchange. Gottlieb and Cornell drew big crowds, Cage, de Kooning, and Glarner smaller ones. Barney had the ceiling plastered and took care of the printing. Annalee—the only "regular" wife, in her words—kept the accounts, secured and returned chairs from a nearby restaurant, and collected the entrance fees. On one occasion, the room was so crowded that, not recognizing him, she turned away the Museum of Modern Art's Alfred Barr. Barney took the guests to dinner before they spoke—he felt that a good meal would ensure a good performance—and, ignoring Annalee's assurance that "he'll *never* get tired," waited for Motherwell to weary of being master of ceremonies so he could step in.[7] Inevitably, the discussion spilled over into the Cedar Bar a block away and lasted half the night.[8]

Nineteen forty-nine was "the year when the idea of a group crystallized." The genealogy, from Tworkov's perspective, was thus: "Egan came into being in 1946. I had a show in 1947, de Kooning in 1948, Kline in 1949. In the meanwhile Pollock was having shows at Parsons. By 1949 you began to see that there was something going on . . . . There was suddenly hope after the war. People suddenly were working hard."[9] At midnight on January 1, the New Year's Eve celebration in Times Square was broadcast to televisions across America for the first time, and in the biting cold and bitter winds, the communal ebullience and optimism could have been meta-phor for the fresh start in Barney's own life: he was where he always wanted to be, in a community of artists as—in his mind at least—a *peer*. There was a noticeable joyfulness as he "found himself"[10] and allowed his natural buoyant charm to eclipse the armor of paranoia and rage at injustice of his earlier days.

At the school, he was a big hit especially with the women, among them Yvonne Thomas, Mary Abbot, Florence Weinstein, and Rosemary Beck, who would come down from Woodstock on Fridays to hear the speakers. Abbot, a former debutante descended from Henry Adams, came to the school through a friendship with Hare. That she was extremely pretty made her popular with the "teachers"; that she was extremely serious about her art made Barney take her under his wing. He "changed everything" for her, "opened up all kinds of things," a way to understand abstraction. "It was marvelous" for her. "I had come from an Art-Students-League, Washing-ton-museums-schools kind of background. Barney showed me you didn't have to paint objects. You painted what you thought, what you felt." He spent time talking to her, about matters of the mind and spirit, and very much about matters on the canvas. Abbot "*got* it and Barney got me *doing* it."[11] Thomas, whose Newport, Rhode Island society friend, Patricia Matisse (later Matta), gave her a letter of introduction to Motherwell, was another of the enthusiastic students who caught Barney's eye. "Being French," Thomas was particularly taken with the way he had "invented him-self as some kind of a personage, *American*," always well-dressed, thumbs hooked in the armholes of his waistcoat, supremely articulate, "with a jolliness, an affirmation of good humor." The advice he gave unstintingly was always about painting[12]—that impressed her—whereas with Rothko, Thomas discussed many things peripheral to art but *not* her painting.[13] Barney never condescended to the women. "He treated you like a person," remembered Abbot, whose other experiences were often derailed by her loveliness. "You and he talked. Not like some of the others. He didn't throw you to the ground." Thomas was struck that "he thought it very natural that I was there . . . . He felt so genuine, and he would be the first to denounce someone who wasn't."[14]

What he passed on to them was the same insight that he would pass on to many younger painters over the next twenty years. "To create a work of art" meant, to Bar-ney, "to express something that is so deep in one. It's not acting out one's neurosis, it's not [an] expression of one's sensations. It is an attempt to put down what you really believe and what you really are concerned with, what really moves you and interests you, in terms of *being*."[15] This was what he had learned from the Passover prayer: to separate the "holy and the HOLY." Work could only proceed from a moral base. "If you had to sum up his message in one sentence," summed up Robert Murray, it was just that: "the importance of being an artist in society was that it was, in many respects, maybe one of the last moral professions, one of the last professions with *any* degree of morality."[16] And what made it so compelling for a younger generation was Barney's model, that he lived his life in that way.

Barney was elated. The attention he had so longed for fed his best angel and al-lowed his good humor to flourish, making him popular beyond his core *compañeros*.

His circle expanded and his social life had more gaiety and gusto, drinking and danc-ing—at both of which he shone. Alfred Leslie, then only 21 years old, met Barney when Elaine de Kooning brought him to "a little show" that Leslie, Robert Good-nough, and a few others had put up. Suddenly, Leslie began to notice Barney and Annalee at glamorous cocktail parties at the Central Park South studio of the fashion illustrator René Bouché.[17] At one of the famously festive dinners at the West Village townhouse that Jeanne Reynal shared with a large population of caged birds and her future husband Thomas Sills—an African–American eleven years her junior whom she met at the liquor store where he worked as a delivery man and who recently had begun to paint—Reynal's neighbor Meyer Schapiro and Barney conducted an erudite discourse upon Mozart while Hess eavesdropped.[18] At the parties at Thomas's Park Avenue apartment, Barney captivated her mother-in-law, Blanche Marie Louise Oelrichs, the Newport socialite, author, and poet (under the pen name Michael Strange). During her first marriage, Oelrichs had been involved with Bloomsbury; her second husband was John Barrymore; she was accustomed to being entertained, and Barney did not fail her.[19]

By May, the Subjects of the Artist School, as originally conceived by Motherwell, Hare, Baziotes, and Rothko, was over. "The Club," was taking shape two doors away at 39 East Eighth Street, spurred by a different group of artists, the fellows who had been making the Waldorf Cafeteria their clubhouse but were now feeling unwel-come by a new clientele of toughs that didn't particularly care for the artists and by pressure from the *patron* to buy more than a cup of coffee. Those from around Ninth and Tenth Streets who were hanging out together most nights—Conrad Marca-Relli, Franz Kline, John Ferren, Herman Cherry among them—began to talk about renting a space.

It explicitly began as a social club, and did not exclude the "uptown group"—the "rabbis," as Cherry called Barney, Still, Motherwell, Gottlieb, and Reinhardt, "a closed group of intellectuals" as opposed to the "bummy artists."[20] There was a "real feeling of fraternity," according to Marca-Relli, "unquestionably . . . one of the most vital and exciting periods in the history of art for us." Others agreed that although The Club's lectures and panels were frequently "boring," the "vital thing was that they stimulated conversation later."[21]

Barney noticed that the most active members were "those who had no wives," and when the group "swung for a large audience, there were too many camp fol-lowers. Bill [de Kooning] and Kline fell into this situation and Reinhardt became a foil for a debate on Abstract Expressionism as if it were an issue." Barney wasn't interested; he and Rothko avoided it, they felt the discussions "had nothing to do with" them.[22] Reinhardt felt The Club was "another academic institution where artists talked all the time, and young artists learned how to act . . . they all learned their *chutzpa*, you know, from their masters talking all the time."[23] He called it a "weekly Kaffeeklatch."[24]

"Do they wear gardenias and striped pants," wondered Tomlin in response to Barney's mocking description, encouraged that at least "there is a place to go besides that ghastly Cedar Bar."[25]

In retrospect, these non-political and non-activist groupings were a doomed-to-fail attempt to sustain the camaraderie of purpose that arose during the Depression and war years. There was something else in the air—barely noticeable, easy to brush off for now—about prominence and preeminence and, inevitably, jealousy. Some artists were emerging from the pack in spite of the general climate of perplexity. Some dealers were emerging as more successful in helping their artists emerge.

"The art world is still in a peculiar state . . . . Too many guys are a bit bitter," wrote Baziotes to his brother. Kootz was "dumb enough to think he was so powerful he could give up the gallery and still be a big shot in the art world. Well, I know he is not being considered at all—that is, no one cares—not many invitations to openings—no one calls him up to ask him to speak etc. And so he starts to feel bitter . . . in a mood for taking cracks at different people. . . . scared shitty that Betty Parsons will prove that what he said was impossible for him as a dealer . . . . So underneath I know he wishes her the worst."

"That's the art world."[26]

Perhaps Baziotes's "peculiar state" had to do with individual, rather than collective, adaptive resistance to a cultural situation increasingly frightening. Because their work was solitary, fewer artists than writers and actors were blacklisted, but no one was untouched by the mission of Attorney General Tom Clark and the House Un-American Activities Committee: that was enough to chill souls and undermine any sense of business as usual. Representative George A. Dondero of Michigan spent the first half of 1949 repeatedly impugning the motives of artists from the floor of the House of Representatives; in "Modern Art Shackled to Communism" in August, he called out by name Barney's fellow "faculty" Motherwell, Baziotes, and Hare, as well as his buddy Pollock, for "stabbing our glorious American art in the back with murderous intent." Modern artists were:

> human termites . . . boring industriously to destroy the high standards and price-
> less traditions of academic art . . . . from deep Red Stalinist to pale pink publi-
> cist . . . [art] is a weapon in the hands of a soldier in the revolution against our form
> of government, and against any government or system other than communism.

A main artery ran "from the black heart of the isms of the Russian Revolution to the very heart of art in America." It was no use to bring up the dull and programmatic official art of Russia as a counter-argument. "The Communist art that has infiltrated our cultural front is not the Communist art in Russia today . . . [the] art of the isms, the weapon of the Russian Revolution is the art which has been transplanted to America . . . . So-called modern or contemporary art in our own beloved country contains all the isms of depravity, decadence, and destruction." Dondero called the "roll of infamy":

dadaism, futurism, constructionism, suprematism, cubism, expressionism, surrealism, and abstractionism. All these isms are of foreign origin, and truly should have no place in American art.

Herbert Read and Peggy Guggenheim, whose autobiography, *Out of This Century*, was "vile," were enemies. Dondero was horrified that the "Hallmark Christmas Card Co." selected Kurt Seligmann, "a leader in surrealism," and Kuniyoshi, "presumably a Buddhist but unquestionably a Red Fronter," to the panel of judges to choose *Christmas* card art. Jews were a subtext, and Thomas Craven was admiringly quoted for disparaging the "effeminate elect" trained at the Fogg Museum—"the rendezvous of an effeminate and provincial tribe"—to be museum directors who jammed "art trash down the throats of the public."

Add to this group of subversives the following American satellites, and the number swells to a rabble: Motherwell, Pollock, Baziotes, David Hare, and Marc Chagall. The last named is lauded by Communist publications and is a sponsor of the School of Jewish Studies, cited by Attorney General Tom Clark "as an adjunct in New York City of the Communist Party" . . . .

The question is, what have we, the plain American people, done to deserve this sore affliction that has been visited upon us so direly; who has brought down this curse upon us; who has let into our homeland this horde of germ-carrying art vermin?

Communist art, aided and abetted by misguided Americans, is stabbing our glorious American art in the back with murderous intent.[27]

Dondero was not a lone, erratic voice in the wilderness and his fulminations were effective. Congressional threats forced the Library of Congress, which did not want to be in the position of compromising intellectual and aesthetic standards, to cancel its prizes in literature, music, and art. "We are back at the criteria of excellence voiced today with such alarming frequency: intelligibility and style to suit the lowest common denominator of taste," wrote Aline Louchheim that September, "despite the fact that a work of art is not a common but a peculiarly uncommon thing." It was "The temper of our times," she wrote, that made acceptable the "twisted conclusions" of Dondero's "campaign against modern art, using with ugly finesse every unpleasant technique."[28]

The art community's social medium in 1949 was highly evolved and almost exclusively face to face. Any show that appeared in New York would get an immediate reaction the day after at The Club. "You would see all your friends there, they would talk about it, they would say, 'did you see the show?' 'What do you think of the Giacometti show? How did you like that?'" recalled Marca-Relli. "And if something was, we'll say, a lousy show, we all knew it, we all shared opinions. It affected museum directors, because they were there. And the critics began to take part with the artists."[29]

"Every damn article that came out," was discussed, especially those by Greenberg, according to the young dealer John Bernard Myers (who didn't particularly agree with the critic).[30] Certainly, when *Life* magazine ran the feature story "Jackson Pollock: Is he the greatest living painter in the United States?" in early August, it was noticed.

Life magazine was not an organ in which whatever constituted the art world in those days expected to find meaningful discourse. But because of its circulation and visibility it had an outsize role in suggesting to average Americans what they should think. The self-identified intellectual highbrow Greenberg took notice of what *Life* wrote as much as did the avid popular-culture-consuming Barney.[31] When, earlier in the year, it covered provocatively the "Revolt in Boston: Shootin' Resumes in the Art World"—which hit the stands as Barney titled de Kooning's talk "The Desperate View"—it was not simply a news story, but a piece of cultural propaganda. If "modern" art were so bereft of significance, why respond so aggressively? It was a story of interest to the larger, middlebrow audience of *Life*'s readership because *Life* made it that story: abstraction was a "totalitarian" formula and the people who thought that it was "art" undermined America.

"The U.S. art world is full of temperamental people who have been wrangling for years over whether modern American paintings . . . are works of art or unintelligible nonsense," wrote *Life*. "The lid blew off the wranglings last year when Boston's Institute of Modern Art decided it could stomach the word 'modern' no longer" and "assembled an exhibition to show the main trends in U.S. art of this century," which, *Life* interpolated, "are chiefly rooted in native traditions that are romantic or realistic."[32] Four pages of large color reproductions of representational paintings followed.[33]

Life's demeaning take on Pollock—"Pollock drools enamel paint on canvas," read one caption—was given a special tweak. In the same issue a fashion feature extolled "dime-store" accessorizing; one photograph of a model prominently holding a Museum of Modern Art brochure of International-style design purity was captioned "Cheap White Touches set off an expensive dress."[34] The Pollock article could have served as Exhibit A in Congressman Dondero's "Modern Art Shackled to Communism" speech a few days after.

On the other hand, as Milton Resnick noted with twelve years' perspective, *Life*'s pictures of Pollock and his paintings represented one of the "most important revolutions in this country" because "the first thing that occurred to millions of people is that he looked like everyone they know. He didn't look like a foreign type, a strange man, a Jew; he really looked all right. He looked like Saturday night."[35]

There were so many opportunities to get noticed and to calculate one's standing.

A different form of competition took place that summer among the artists making the caravan to Provincetown. "French Art vs. U.S. Art Today," a symposium, was organized on August 11 by Gottlieb for those who hoped to measure themselves against the Europeans.[36] On newsstands the previous week, along with *Life*'s Pollock article, was the twenty-fifth anniversary issue of the *Saturday Review of Literature*: "Does Our Art Impress Europe?" The question made the artists sit up and listen. James Thrall Soby, vice-chairman of MoMA's Committee on the Museum Collections and the magazine's critic, briefed the 20th-century history of American artists vis-à-vis Europe, trends within American art, and the effects of postwar economics on art's reception.[37] It all set the stage for his conclusion, a call for Federal involvement—not, he made explicit, State Department involvement, citing the debacle of the dismantled collection, but something along the lines of a "Federal Department of Fine Arts." The best possible effect of such an entity, Soby said, would not "regiment artists in a nationalist cause [because that] would be to destroy the character of the cause itself," but rather to engender the "dignity and standing for the arts and for artists" that was *assumed* in Europe. In France, "no one questions the absolute importance of art; it is only the relative quality of various kinds of art that is the point of dispute. The same cannot yet be said of this country, despite the protestations of those who claim to detest only one species ('modern'), when in reality they are suspicious of all."[38]

Dignity. That was what resonated with Barney. The factions in Provincetown—those indebted to Paris and those proclaiming independence—had a different agenda. They were interested in the "species" of art, and in asserting themselves as representatives. Surely there were disagreements with Motherwell, who had come to Provincetown that year with de Kooning, when he spoke about finding an identity as a painter and attempted to universalize the calling: "One might say that we artists of the School of New York are a collection of co-existing separate pasts. So are the individuals who constitute the School of Paris. These two handfuls of individuals are closer to each other in their essential acts than either is to the herd of individuals who constitute his national culture, French or American."[39] But disagreements notwithstanding, Motherwell's coinage turned out to be the most enduring result of that particular summer episode. "New York School"—whether the artists liked it or not—stuck, probably because it easily piggy-backed on the commonly used "School of Paris." It was certainly more graceful linguistically, and less limited aesthetically, than "Intrasubjectives"—the name that Sam Kootz essayed in the show he mounted in September.

TWENTY-SEVEN

MAN IS PRESENT

Throughout 1949 Barney was busy.

He was corralling speakers for the Subjects of the Artist School, anticipating and arranging details—announcements, logistics, projectors—editing texts, providing dinners and encouragement. At the gallery, Parsons depended upon his intellect, his discernment, and his advice. He negotiated exhibition schedules, refereeing agitated arguments among the artists at the Horn & Hardart automat over who would have the next show.[1] He came in the Sunday before an exhibition to install "indefatigably" and brilliantly, the artists confident in his "great eye."[2] He was a vivid presence in the art life in the city, a "first-rate intellectual [who] knew a great deal about what was happening"; he went to other galleries and expostulated, "exciting for the artists listening to him."[3] And he hoped soon to have a show of his own.

Over many months, as he made list after list for the coming season at Parsons, he scheduled his solo debut during the winter of 1950 in between Rothko and Pollock, then between Tomlin and Pollock, then Pollock and Rothko. Maybe a placement between Sonia Sekula and Pollock would show him to better advantage. Or should it be between Rothko and Baziotes in the fall? His show should open on his birthday, January 29, he decided, between Stamos and Reinhardt; or between Stamos and Still; or Reinhardt and Walter Murch. (It finally opened January 23 between Rothko and Hedda Sterne.) He wrote his last article for *Tiger's Eye*. And he decided to apply to teach at New York University.[4] Previously when he was energized by satisfying work he became a little manic, hungry for more, and 1949 was no different.

The *real* work—his painting—was going well. A year earlier, Greenberg announced that important painting needed space: painting "seems to become trivial when confined within anything measuring less than two feet by two."[5] At the Waldorf Cafeteria Barney complained about how tired he was from painting. "My wrist hurts," he would say.[6]

He produced eighteen or nineteen paintings in that year of 1949 to January 1950. They ranged from the brushy and restrained *End of Silence* and the brushy and lyrical *Concord* to the rigorously deliberate *By Twos*; from the bold, declarative *Onement IV* to the profound and wrenching *Abraham*. Their colors ran the gamut from the earthy sienna brown, pale buttercup, and black of *Covenant*, to the discordant burnt sienna, chrome yellow, and cobalt of *Untitled I, 1949*, to the dignified formality of the black, off-white, and gray of *The Promise*; from the blistering lemon of *Yellow Painting* (plate 8), to the proto-pop vermilion and gray wash of *The Name I* (subliminally evocative of a *Life* magazine cover of the period), to the tropical sensuality of turquoise, canary, and coral of *Dionysius* (plate 9), to the staggering confrontational red of *Be I*. The formats were those of traditional easel paintings, or the extreme vertical limit of easel paintings, or door-sized panels, or racing horizontals. They had a single screeching filament of a "zip" (a term that is useful for description, but one that would not be employed by Barney until the mid-1960s) or four of various widths and strengths, or two in different colors, or one or two speeding along horizontally. They were oil on canvas, or oil and casein, or oil and Magna. The variety in the mediums, degree of solution of pigment, and method of application led to almost literally living surfaces, responsive to every slight variation in light and viewing angle. Several were *tours de force* of paint apparently exhaled onto the surface, a correlative of the ideal exalted state in which they were made. A few—like *Concord, Abraham*, and the tragically damaged *Be I*—eventually would be considered masterpieces.

Still, in San Francisco, saw "reproductions"; "good work," he told Barney.[7]

Tworkov, whose studio was across the street from Barney's storefront, would "occasionally . . . peek in to see what was going on." All he could see was "canvases being stretched. And for a long time the only thing I saw were more and more canvases. Then I went away . . . . when I came back there was this Newman show at the Betty Parsons Gallery."[8]

But both Barney and Annalee were suffering. Much of August—the month of the French-American faceoff and musing over whether Jackson Pollock was the greatest living American painter—was for them occupied with attending to their health. To Ferber, Barney complained of how little "time we had away from doctors." Annalee's gastrointestinal problems—she regularly took the benign, over-the-counter Gelusil, but was often on a regimen of belladonna and phenobarbital traditionally prescribed for colitis or hiatus hernia—required a battery of medical tests. Barney had a node on a vocal cord that was in danger of rupturing. He was told to radically limit his speech. Only by leaving New York could he avoid socializing, entertaining, daily hours-long phone calls to his mother and sister. He could not go to Provincetown, though he had been invited by Weldon Kees to lecture. Instead, he would go someplace where he could, atypically, keep his mouth closed.

He and Annalee decided to make a trip to Ohio, where she had spent her youth. "He had gone to meet Annalee's family," was the often repeated story transmitted through Hess, suggesting a certain benevolent, if inopportune, flexibility that doesn't bear scrutiny.[9] Annalee had very little, if any, family remaining in the state, and the timing was strange and infelicitous: Parsons had decided to exhibit his work and work needed to be produced. On the other hand, the journey led to an extraordinarily felicitous encounter.

It was an ambitious road trip. Barney and Annalee drew up a long list of plantation houses, churches, courthouses, and other notable architecture to visit throughout Ohio. Nine years earlier, with "stupendous" amounts of money, material, and publicity, the Pennsylvania Turnpike "super-highway" had been rushed into construction for national defense purposes.[10] In the last week of August it allowed the Newmans to efficiently cut through the mountain wall between Harrisburg and Pittsburgh and by the second night reach Akron, which Annalee found so changed that she "practically couldn't recognize it."[11] They took two rooms for three nights, but, closely watching their budget, downgraded to one for the next two. Over seven days they circled through Ohio: in historic Marietta, they toured the first permanent non-native set-tlement of the Northwest Territory; in Cincinnati, they hit the Terrace Plaza Hotel "Gourmet Restaurant," famous for its Joan Miró mural.[12] In an unsent postcard to Robert Motherwell, Barney referred to the tours they made of the ancient Indian Octagon, Mound Builders, and Wright earthworks of Newark, Ohio and the 750-year-old Fort Ancient site as, simply, "an experience." But to Tony Smith he was more can-did: "Talk about art for the wild and in the wild—It is overwhelming."[13] A *revelation*.

In the wilderness, the earthworks had for centuries been undisturbed. When Barney and Annalee arrived, it was not yet the wildly popularized destination that Walden had been in 1936, but a century and a half of farming, lumbering, canal excavation, mills, and the Central Ohio Railroad—which ran right through it—left their mark, as had sixty years of scholarly and touristic visits. The original earthworks had been eroded, partially restored under Depression-era relief programs, and in some areas park-ified—even country-club-ified.[14] None of that fazed Barney's fertile conceptual processing. He decided that "picnics and golf were really ceremonies" akin to the ancient ceremonies on the sites.[15]

Ignoring the transformation, the Newmans saw a complex system of geometrical earth embankments that enclosed the remains of what was postulated to have been dedicated social, religious, and funerary spaces used by the Hopewell tradition. Some of the mounds, the so-called "effigy" type—for example, a 6-foot-high, 240-by-210-foot mass in the shape of an eagle in flight—had been found through excavation to contain sacrificial altars. Other, simpler, mounds were for burials. The remark-able quarter-mile-long Serpent (effigy) Mound was particularly well preserved and awe-inspiring. Ornamental and ceremonial artifacts found in conjunction with the earthworks were displayed in a museum. Typically, Barney educated himself thor-oughly about everything he saw, collecting tourist brochures, but also scholarly articles from specialized journals he located in libraries. But the mountain of facts and information that he accumulated—what was known about the civilization and about the mounds that grew over burial sites—turned out to be entirely beside the point. The point, for Barney—exactly as he had written to Motherwell before he even understood it well enough himself—was the *experience*.

Standing before the Miamisburg mound, or walking inside the Fort Ancient and Newark earthworks, surrounded by these simple walls made of mud—absolute—one is confounded by a multiplicity of sensations, that here are the greatest works of art on the American continent—before which the Mexican and North West Coast totem poles are hysterical, over-emphasized monsters—that here in the seductive Ohio Valley are perhaps the greatest art monuments in the world; for somehow the Egyptian pyramid by comparison is nothing but an ornament—what difference if the shape is on a table, pedestal or lies immense on a des-ert . . . . Here is the *self-evident nature of the artistic act, its utter simplicity* [em-phasis added]. There are no subjects—nothing that can be shown in a museum or even photographed—a work of art that cannot even be seen so it is something that must be experienced there on the spot, the feeling that here is the space, that these simple low mud walls make the space . . . . Suddenly one realizes that the sensation is not one of space or an object in space. It has nothing to do with space and its manipulations; that the sensation is the sensation of time—and all other multiple feelings vanish like the outside landscape.

What is all the clamor over space? The Renaissance deep space . . . the Impressionist flat space, cubist space, shallow space, positive and negative space, trompe l'oeil enigmatic space, the pure space—the space of "infinity"—Mondrian's universe. There is so much talk over space that one might think it is the subject matter of art . . . .

Only time can be felt in private. Space is common property. Only time is personal, a private experience . . . . Each person must feel it for himself.[16]

Critics, he wrote, insist on space as if all modern art were an "exercise and ritual of it," because "it includes them, it makes the artist 'concrete' and real because he represents or invokes sensations in the material objects that exist in space and can be *understood*." Barney was suddenly not concerned with being understood.

"The concern with space bores me," he realized. "I insist on my experiences of sensations in time. Not the <u>sense</u> of time but the physical <u>sensation</u> of time."[17]

Recounting the epiphany to Hess years later, he referred to neither space nor time precisely. What stunned him, he said, was "a sense of *place*, a holy place. Looking at the site you feel, Here I am, *here*." Out beyond there was chaos; "but here you get a sense of your own presence." He became involved, he said, "with the idea of making the viewer present: the idea that 'Man Is Present.' " It was less an *insight* than a *feeling* that gripped him.[18]

He saw the Ohio earthworks less than four months before he was to have his first one-man show, when he had already painted a number of the works that would appear in it. But what would be the Stance for this debut? How could a minimally trained artist, a man defensive of every move and statement he ever made, a Jew in 1949, an anarchist–rejector of his society's rules and strictures, become a lodestone? His paintings were, above all, the expression of the "Imperial Self," as literary scholar Quentin Anderson termed those writers for whom, "to accept the conditions of action in the society or the community, to pin [themselves] to a particular role," to capitulate, would be insupportable and result in an "impulse to a total self-abnegation."[19] Standing within the dramatic landscape, quiet and unchallenged, without any need for guile or defense, Barney found just what he required. He succumbed to the overwhelming significance of himself. In the circumstances, he endowed the earthworks with cosmic meaning as much as the primitive earthworks endowed legitimacy to the radically reduced pronouncement of his art.[20]

In this temperament he continued to edit his last submission to *Tiger's Eye*.[21] The subject was Trigant Burrow's *The Neuroses of Man*, and Barney, interested in Burrow because of Herbert Read's praise, was one of six invited to review it. Burrow was a pioneer psychoanalyst whose reputation was based on his early identification of a person's psychological state as a social construct. For Burrow, there was a complicated back-and-forth interplay between individual neurosis and an enabling society, which could only be countered through treating the individual as a part of society, acknowledging the tether as a given of human life. Burrow's thesis, according to Barney, was that when man behaved as part of society he was "in a state of integration . . . but as an individual entity he is full of prejudice, ambitions, aggressive desires"—in a word, "neurotic." This Barney felt as a frontal attack on the purity, the revelatory nature of his recent experience, which the preceding year of small successes and mild reinforcement after a lifetime of resentments and minor rebellions had left him poised to receive. In Ohio he had seen the light and was born anew.

Barney could respond to Burrow only with sputtering rage. "The proper manner to review this book . . . is to dismiss it." Either the "I" needed to be paramount (Barney), or the unrestrained "I" set up barriers to the health of society (Burrow). The "Imperial Self" or Burrow's "I-Persona"? Barney knew where he stood: unequivocally, individually, uniquely, *Here.*

The Betty Parsons Gallery mounted a group show in October. Helen Carlson, art critic at the *New York Sun*, was the only writer to review it. In staccato phrases she noted Sonia Sekula's "labyrinthine maze of line and color"; Stamos's "delicately gradated violets"; and Pollock's skill as a "master weaver" of "ribbons of color." Measured in column inches—Carlson devoted a full one and a half to the piece now known as *Onement II*—Barney should have been overjoyed; but in his case she wasn't dismissive, she was livid: "Barnett Newman's mural size canvas painted an unrelieved tomato red with a perfectly straight narrow band of deeper red cleaving the canvas neatly in two is something else again. It's as pointless as a yard rule, which at least has the advantage of being functional. Is Newman trying to write finis to the art of abstraction?"[22]

Parsons's show followed Kootz's ambitious "The Intrasubjectives" at his revived gallery in September: Baziotes, de Kooning, Gorky, Gottlieb, Hofmann, Motherwell, Pollock, Reinhardt, Rothko, Tomlin, and the West Coast artists Mark Tobey and Morris Graves, who were represented by Marian Willard. A brief, peculiar essay by Rosenberg would have persuaded no one except an initiate of the art's value—in fact, as Kootz himself noted in his essay, the artists abandoned "the curious custom of painting within the current knowledge of the spectator" in order to "enlarge the spectator's horizon" through the artists' "self-experience."

"The modern painter is not inspired by anything visible," wrote Rosenberg, "but only by something he hasn't seen yet . . . . In short, he begins with nothingness [and] the nothing the painter begins with is known as Space . . . the canvas before it has been painted." The space "speaks to him, quivers, turns green or yellow with bile, gives him a sense of sport, of sign language, of the absolute."[23] It was to this description of his new peer group that Barney, not included in the show and thus both literally—because of the node in his throat—and figuratively voiceless, felt compelled to respond in "Ohio,

1949": "The concern with space bores me. I insist on my experiences of sensations in time . . . the physical <u>sensation</u> of time." Man is present; "Here I am, *here*."

Perhaps it was fortunate for those around him that Barney was under strict doctor's orders: "<u>Absolute Voice Rest</u> that means NO TALKING, but being a 'hoomin' being', and being you, one might as well sentence you to jail," wrote the consulting doctor, Barney's cousin Borie, who was also very careful to respond to Barney's injunction. "As far as telling my mother [who would have told Barney's mother] about your status, remember I too have 'ethics,' and moreover am aware of the utter impracticality of such a procedure!" Barney would have to find another excuse to disrupt the phone conversations with Anna. If he wanted to avoid surgery, "DO NOT USE THE VOICE," closed Borie's note. "Here's a chance to soliloquize [on paper] on what it is to be speechless for a while."[24]

TWENTY-EIGHT

"A SHOW AT THE BETTY PARSONS GALLERY"

He was still ailing when in mid-November 1949 his show was locked in for January 23[1] and created new, unaccustomed burdens. Familiar was the financial juggling that enabled their middle-class lives, including monthly charge account invoices from at least seven department stores. Less typical were mounting bills for lumber and tape, 4- and 5-inch brushes, a spray gun and the compressor and hose to make it work, paints and cotton duck—nearly 18 yards purchased on January 11. In the weeks before the show cash outlays more than doubled. They took another bank loan. With his old tailoring skills, creating patterns to maximize the yield, Barney was able to be thrifty with the fabric. But he would not scrimp on the costly dry pigments he mixed himself. They were "colors"—what he thought of as an "inert material." His "job," as he saw it, was to turn that material into "COLOR"—like a baker would use "wheat to make bread." *Color* was what he worked with, and on which he depended "entirely."[2]

Only days before the installation it appears he completed two of the most chromatically daring paintings: *Yellow Painting*, the 5½-foot-high, zinc yellow presence with two white "color areas" (as he liked to call them at that time)[3] toward the edges and one slightly lighter yellow area in the center; and the dazzling "reditude"-inous *Be I*, 48 square feet of cadmium red dark with a single, central, quarter-inch-wide line of white.[4] Next to them, even the all-black *Abraham* might have seemed more perplexing but less transgressive. The nearly 6-foot-wide horizontal, cadmium orange *Argos* was likely also completed days before the show; it was not exhibited, but Barney did include another horizontal work, *Horizon Light*, 6 feet of alizarin crimson with a single monastral green horizontal, probably to confound any smug expectations created by his dominant format.

If—as the story has come down to us—there were surprise, or confusion, or grumbling, or competitive feelings on the part of his crowd at his sudden metamorphosis from spokesman into art *maker*, none show up *prior* to the show. Parsons described him as a "very original and provocative painter" to the artist Amy Lee, whom she planned to show in a smaller gallery at the same time as Barney.[5] Motherwell wrote he was glad that Barney was painting.[6] Tomlin empathized, one painter to another, with the anxious "state of mind you are in if my own is anything to go by . . . . I heard reports of your astonishing canvas in the group show. Atta boy Barney up and at 'em . . . I hope the painting goes along beautifully Barney. I am so happy that you are showing. As to your madness you are of course mad. We are all mad."[7] Still wished him luck.[8]

January was unpleasantly wet and warm, with stretches of 60- and 70-degree days. Rothko's show of twenty-two paintings had closed on Saturday, and Sunday and Monday were frantic days of installation. The established tradition at the gallery was for artists to install each other's shows, and Rothko was there for Barney. A sizeable crowd came out on the rainy Monday evening of January 23.[9]

The gallery had sent out a thousand announcements and took ads in *Art Digest, Art News*, the *New York Times, World-Telegram*, and *Partisan Review*—charged back to Barney, as were all expenses.[10] Siskind photographed him in the installation. Barney cut an impressive figure in his beautifully tailored dark suit, his tightly knotted silk tie, his shined shoes—his shoes were *always* shined as far as anyone remembers—his dark wavy hair neatly trimmed and only slightly receded. He was still slim, unmonocled, and unjowled. From the looks of him he might have been a Reuters editor or a mid-level diplomat. At a time when "all the guys wore jackets and ties," the fine dark fabrics of Barney's clothes distinguished his from their typical tweeds.[11] Observers might have thought, as Degas told Whistler, that he dressed as if he had no talent—his decorum was as extreme as Whistler's flamboyance.[12] Although Barney posed himself contemplating the large red painting in a way to project confidence and control, it was obvious to Siskind that Barney was very anxious about how the show would be received.[13] He personally invited old friends and acquaintances from his previous life, like the principal of Grover Cleveland High School where he had been the obstreperous substitute teacher. The inclusive guest list turned out to be fortunate: the one painting that sold, *No. 24* (later *End of Silence*) for 350 dollars (4515 dollars in 2023) was bought by Annalee's old chum Fan Cohen. After the gallery's commission and expenses Barney would earn 84.14 dollars.[14] But so what? A wildly record-breaking exhibition of works by van Gogh—the patron saint of no-sales, misunderstood-in-their-time artists—had just closed at the Metropolitan Museum, with the city buzzing about him and buying tens of thousands of catalogues in his honor.

Siskind's installation photographs recorded only three of the four walls, hung with nine works now known as *Onement III, Covenant, The Promise, Be I, Yellow Painting, End of Silence, Concord, Tundra*, and *Horizon Light*, which was hung incorrectly—its "zip" ran vertically—at Rothko's insistence, according to later complaints by both Barney and Annalee.[15] But Barney showed eleven paintings,[16] and since at the time all were identified by numbers instead of titles, the two works not visible have been a matter of speculation ever since. That additional works may have hung in the "backroom" of the gallery instead of the public area complicates a reconstruction.

Why care? Because it later became *very* important to Barney. Beginning sometime in the 1960s, he would say that *Abraham* was in the show, but it's hard to believe that not a single reviewer mentioned the *shock* of the "first" (according to the poet, critic, and curator Frank O'Hara) virtually all-black painting, especially one nearly 7 feet tall—as Stuart Preston did when *Abraham* was shown in Parsons's June group show, writing "At one extreme is Barnett Newman's black on a blackish ground"[17]—though every one of them described what they saw.[18]

"Take a canvas about five feet wide and eight tall. Cover it with flat paint in a rich, beautiful shade of unbroken red so it looks like the side of a red barn. Bisect it with a white strip of paint about a quarter of an inch wide," wrote one;[19] "Each of the pictures is simply a colored surface cut vertically by one or more lines,"[20] another; and

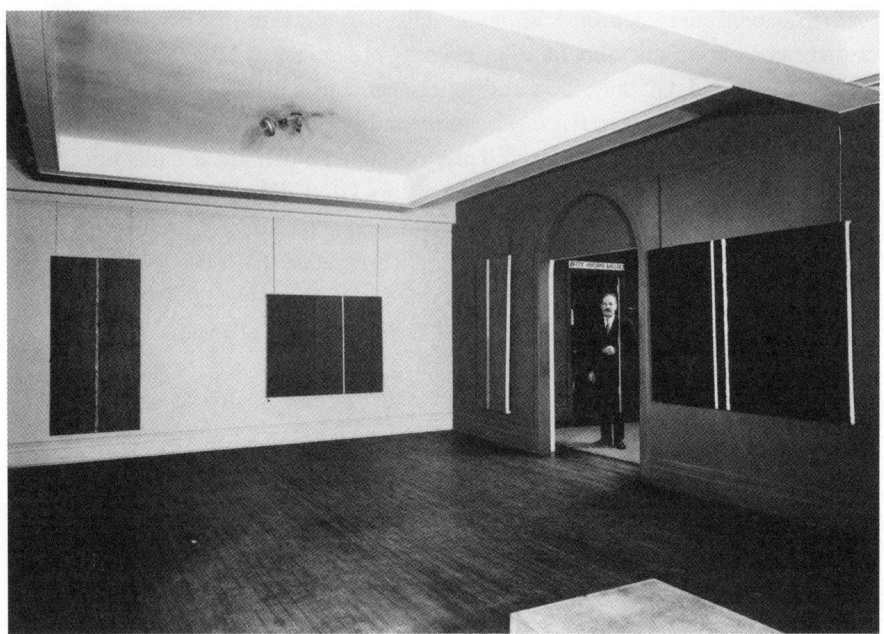

Fig. 20 Barnett Newman's first show at Betty Parsons Gallery, January 1950. From left: *Onement III*, *Covenant*, *Horizon Light* (displayed vertically), *The Promise*. Photograph Aaron Siskind

"The majority of his large rectangular canvases are covered with a single flat color and divided into two or more areas by one or more lines in one or two colors . . . [a] kind of *reductio ad absurdum*," a third.[21] Even *Time* magazine's inaccurate *reductio ad absurdum* "Barnett Newman, 45, was a man of few lines—one, or at the most, two, to a picture. The lines ran straight up & down, bisecting huge canvases that were painted one bright color apiece,"[22] did not seize the opportunity to ridicule the all black *Abraham*—if it *were* there. Hess—the critic most up-to-date, most intimate with and respected by the artists, who had become the executive editor of *Art News* in 1949—described "large canvases painted in one even layer of color (scarlet, yellow, blue, etc.) and on which runs a vertical line (or lines) of white or a contrasting hue."[23] The poet Nicolas Calas, at Studio 35 in February, talked about "those reds and those browns," the "fulness [*sic*] of a red's red" and the "redness of the Now"; he said the poet who faced chaos was "forced to adopt a hermetic attitude," but mentioned *nothing* about the mute profundity of a black-on-black work. (Ten years later, Calas reconstructed the talk in an article for the journal *It Is*. Barney read—and corrected—the draft to read, "we can <u>now</u> say that Malevitch [*sic*] is famous for not having painted black on black."[24])

In 1969, trying to reconstruct the show for the critic Lawrence Alloway, Annalee drew up three lists postulating the tenth and eleventh paintings. On one, in Barney's handwriting, *Abraham* was inserted, and Barney sketched a floorplan which included *Abraham*.[25] Annalee included *No. 20 Two Edges* and *Dionysius*, but no reviewer mentioned the unique horizontal bands in the latter work—assuming it were hung as it has been seen ever since. In the 1960s, Barney loved to tell the story of Buckminster Fuller's visit to the gallery: knowing that Fuller was "full of speculative ideas" and trying to make conversation, Barney offered that in 1949 he did a number of paintings with horizontal "color areas," but he inevitably returned to his favored verticals. Fuller responded, Barney said, in his most oratorical fashion, that "the earth being round, if one moves in a horizontal, in relation to the earth, it [ultimately] comes back," whereas if you move vertically you are "aiming at a *star*."[26]

If we believe the Fuller story, which implies no horizontal was on view, Barney had no objections to the installation at the time of the show. But in 1955, in a private tirade to score a point in his obsession with precedence, Barney wrote that *two* pictures "which were painted horizontally" were hung vertically in that first show against his will,[27] suggesting *Dionysius* was the tenth—unphotographed—painting exhibited. Regarding the paintings' intended orientation, we are left with the choice to credit Barney's words of 1955 or those of the mid-1960s. But we are no closer to knowing for certain the identity of painting 11.

"Everybody" came to the show because Barney was so popular—if only as a writer.[28] But the *reaction* to the show among artists had shifted from their earlier encouragement, and it was personally devasting. Barney couldn't fathom why they didn't see what he was doing, why the response was so stunningly different from the plaudits and laurels and sales that greeted Pollock's show two months earlier. Or the collegial acceptance of the stylistic breakthroughs of so many other artists around this time—Rothko, Kline, de Kooning. With very few exceptions, his fellow painters were "shocked," the "downtown" artists especially vocal.[29] Will Barnet could not remember what was in the show or even whether he actually saw it, but he *did* remember the atmosphere: "negative."[30] Tworkov remembered the show was a "surprise to everybody. Everybody was astonished." Although he had seen drawings that Barney had made, he "took them as I took his piano improvisation. It didn't have any meaning for me."[31] The extravagantly fur-clad, flamboyant dealer of European Surrealism, Alexander Iolas, arriving at Parsons with Nick Carone and a titled European collector, mocked the paintings brutally.[32] Dore Ashton, a 21-year-old future critic, had the impression that "not one" of the guys she hung out with—among them Guston, Kline, Tworkov, James Brooks—had "thought of Barney as an artist or a painter."[33]

Retrospective responses to the show were increasingly dismissive as Barney's stature grew and that of many others did not, and the accounts of the early dismissals have become inflated in direct proportion to the respect Barney subsequently earned. Tales from the Cedar Bar, later enshrined by Hess, were repeated so often that they became a kind of unsourced oral tradition:

> The artists played a bar game. If every painting was a self-portrait, where would Barney Newman be found? The winning answer: "Barney's walking into an

elevator, and just a split second before the doors close, he turns around and looks at you."[34]

Franz Kline was sitting in the Cedar when a member of the community came in, enraged, after seeing Barney's show.

"How simple can an artist be and get away with it?" he sputtered. "There was absolutely nothing there."

"Nothing?" responded Kline. "How many canvases were in the show?"

"Oh, maybe ten or 12—all exactly the same. Just one stripe down the center."

"All the same size?"

"Well no. They were different sizes."

"Same colors?"

"No Different colors. Each canvas painted one flat color—you know, like a housepainter would do it. Then this stripe down the center."

"All the stripes the same color?"

"No."

"Were they the same width?"

The man squinted. "Let's see. No. I guess not. Some were maybe three inches wide, some a little more."

"Was the stripe painted on top of the background color or was the background color painted around the stripe?"

The man became uneasy. "I'm not sure. It could have been done either way."

"Well, I don't know," said Kline. "It all sounds damn complicated to me."[35]

It was "complex, innovative work," thought Ileanna Sonnabend, at that time a young collector and nascent gallerist, a "magnificent exhibit." But the Club artists, all of whom came to see it, felt "threatened," in her evaluation, "by the purity of his work and treated him very shabbily . . . . De Kooning was put off by Newman's rigorousness," and, she said, turned others against Barney.[36]

"Well, now we don't have to think about *that* anymore," Guston said to de Kooning after they left the opening in total silence.[37] Charlie Egan, the dealer who represented de Kooning, Tworkov, and Kline, and showed Siskind's photographs at Barney's suggestion, told Barney at a gathering at Siskind's apartment, "I can't go to your show . . . because if I do, they will kill me." Annalee was quite certain that Egan meant the paintings, but it's not impossible "they" referred to the coterie around de Kooning.[38] Barney later claimed that one unnamed (painter) friend, "got terribly upset and had tears in his eyes and began to abuse me." Barney asked what was the trouble. "You made me aware of myself."[39]

"Artists can sometimes be quite cruel and envious," Sonnabend said.[40]

Pavia remembered that "the Club gave him a great homage . . . . Table tops, chairs, et al, were festooned with tape, alluding to Newman's zips. The Club loved him."[41] But others recalled it very differently. De Kooning "put up a card table which had a split in the center of the table on the wall" and Barney was "rather offended."[42] Or, "Elaine [de Kooning] found some feathers in the street. It was just a coincidence that some of Barney's paintings were the same size and proportion as a card table. She took a card table, folded the legs under, nailed it to the wall, and stapled these feathers on it for the stripe. That's all. When he saw that he stood there and cried. Because it was a joke."[43]

During the run of the show, one of the paintings—according to Barney—was vandalized, smeared with paint.[44]

A birthday party was thrown for Barney on Sunday night, January 29. Both Motherwell and Tomlin sent their excuses the following day. Motherwell claimed he had the "grippe"; he "greatly admire[d] the intelligence and jauntiness" of the exhibition, "the rationalization, less so," although he tipped his hat to Barney "with real respect"—underscored as he addressed the letter to "BARNETT NEWMAN PINX" (Barnett Newman has painted).[45] Tomlin told Barney that he liked the show "immensely" but not the unidentified party giver: "I really do <u>not</u> get on with your friend and I can practically never bring myself to the point of going to the houses of people to whom I am strongly unsympathetic."[46] There is no record of Gottlieb's opinion; his eleventh solo show, appearing nearly concurrently at Kootz's new space at Fifty-Seventh Street, was praised in the *Times* for moving away from paintings that had become "monotonous."

"Mark speaks of your latest work in superlatives," wrote Still, who was relying on Barney to manage and install his April show while he remained in San Francisco, "I am very anxious to see it. From his description I catch an excitement that indicates you have landed on a very profound work . . . . With interest I note that Time magazine spoke of your work with fewer than usual of the snide flipancies with which they customarily entertain the ineffectual at the expense of the able." He was "delighted again," he responded to a letter from Barney a few weeks later, "that most worthy response to your pictures came forth. This is good. I share your hope and excitement. Odd, isn't it that I seem to have no competitive feelings whatever where your work and Marks, Rhineharts [*sic*], Tomlins, and Baziotes is concerned. Yet out in this place . . . I become furious with frustration at what has happened to the idea which generated these new forms." He wanted to have one of Barney's paintings, he said, and hoped they could arrange a trade.[47]

As for "Mark," Annalee's recollection was that Rothko, after hanging the exhibition, became depressed by it, feeling that somehow Barney had gotten out ahead of him. But Barney told Hess that Rothko was "appalled" by the show and had a "near nervous breakdown"; Rothko looked upon him as "a guy who would write notes for his catalogue."[48] Certainly, he was depressed, but whether the cause was Barney's emergence with the unexpectedly blunt paintings from such a fussily verbose man, or the mixed reviews *he* had received for his show the previous month,[49] the death of his mother eighteen months earlier, or the new competitive situation in the art community, Rothko decided he needed to leave the scene for a while. Within a few weeks, holding a compact Welta camera that Barney bought for him at a Third

Avenue pawn shop, and with Barney on board to see him off, Rothko and his second wife Mell were on the *Queen Elizabeth* headed for Europe.

In the reviews of Barney's show (at least he *did* get reviews) he was judged as both too extreme—"They may not be art, but they certainly are the image of a void"; "Newman is out to shock, but he is not out to shock the bourgeoisie, that has been done. He likes to shock other artists"; *and* too tame—it may have seemed transgressive "back in the days when no advertising layout man had heard of Mondrian. Today . . . it is rather shocking for another reason: that a presumably serious and well-trained painter should find absorbing material in so sterile and played-out a game."[50] Only Louchheim wrote favorably. She was "hypnotized" by him and the paintings, Barney told Hess in 1968, "it was like being raped," he bizarrely added. Her review was "pretty much" what he told her,[51] and it is as good an indication of how Barney wanted the show to be received as we have.

> There are many who will sneer mercilessly when confronted by the canvases in this debut . . . . But I wonder if they will remain unmoved. These pictures have, for me at least, an undeniable attraction—vibrancy, mood, impact, wholly direct and visually induced. Newman believes that line, intensely concentrated upon, can become a pure means of conveying emotion.
>
> This work has nothing in common with Mondrian, no reasoned probing of structure, no logical investigation of relationships in space. Space as such is not defined; it is as if the colored surface were simply part of a continuum in which the sharp or wavering line exists as an emotive element, without frame of reference, without objective meaning. I cannot tell after one viewing whether these pictures will quickly wear themselves out. But this is serious work which does evoke genuine response.[52]

Four days after the opening, Barney was defensive at Studio 35—the new identity of the Subjects of the Artist School, which disbanded in May 1949.[53] There, where he had been the major domo but never the star, Barney talked about what he felt at the Indian mounds in Ohio and how the experience helped him understand his paintings. According to Milton Resnick, when Barney "climbed the mound and stood there looking out on the horizon he said, 'Bad art.' When he climbed down and turned to face the side of the mound he said, 'Great art.' "[54] While there was "nothing to look at" the experience nevertheless created "a sense of presence" of what was real, even "ominous."[55] Resnick interpreted it thus: "He took the horizon and turned it on its vertical. Instead of looking at where it contracted, you saw where it expanded. He solved his problem and that's what he painted . . . . All he had left to do was ennoble the color, emphasize it with many coats 'til he felt good about it."[56] In other words, turn "colors" into *color*. Resnick meant to be belittling, but Barney knew exactly what he was doing.

It was an "art experience where you couldn't see anything." He spoke about *intent*—"you had to feel it, you couldn't do it with your mind," as Spinoza recognized, "if you got the feeling, all else was unimportant." And he spoke about the idea of the "holy."[57] His sketchy notes recorded the session: "I have been involved in an act and I hope a vision that now seems to me to stand visible on the walls . . . . I am in the position of being asked, almost tested to prove that my pictures are really real. The best I hope to [trails off] . . . . call it God—the transcendental experience, the miracle, the unique experience God—anything you like"; he was "the creator of an embodiment of experience of reality—what is reality—It is a felt experience no space, no time, no image—the wrestling with this experience is the meaning of tragedy."[58]

Hess in *Art News* called Barney "one of Greenwich Village's best known home-spun aestheticians," obliquely acknowledging the art community's surprise that he was now painting. It did not escape notice in that community that Hess found it hard to "even say that Barney painted paintings," calling them instead "products" and "canvases."[59]

Whatever they were called, they were a stark assertion. Since he had collaborated on the statement with Gottlieb and Rothko in mid-1943 Barney had been refining the prescription for "the painter of the new movement." The works that *he* now recognized as art emerged during a nervous state that he likened to "terror": "Where do I get the *nerve*? What's going to happen?" It was a "physical and psychological and psychic state of high intensity," a moment of "intuition on the highest level." Not, he was careful to say, "blind intuition," not "feminine in that sense," but Spinozian, knowledge "being a very intellectual intuition." Normally, Barney acknowledged, that would be "a contradiction in terms" but "only in the point of contradiction" could he describe the state: "One suddenly has a vision."[60]

When he later decided to title his visions, however, he couldn't resist the pedagogical urge to drive his point home, to make sure he was understood *precisely* the way he wanted to be understood. *Tundra* was named sometime after it was exhibited in the January 1950 show, and he would tell a story that nicely amplified the epiphany at the Ohio mounds. The artists would play hooky by going to the movies; one day, he said, he and Pollock went to a theater near Times Square to see *Valley of the Eagles*, a British-made black-and-white thriller whose climax in Swedish Lapland is a terrifying reindeer stampede in whiteout conditions. The "stark landscape, and its burnished pale copper color, of the midnight sun"—the words are Hess's, the faulty memory Barney's—reminded him of the painting.[61] It is a wonderful story, full of the specific, resonant detail fondly identified as characteristically "Barney."[62] The association was an effort to make explicit what Barney had in mind, and what many viewers in 1950 were too hidebound, too rigid, too defensive, or too blind to allow themselves to see. Was it an unfortunate consequence, or an impish intentional strategy, that the retroactively assigned titles of the early works might lead to intellectual overdetermination and precisely belie an unmediated "vision"? This is the conundrum that is in the soul of Barney the man and at the heart of his paintings.

If it is unlikely that the radically self-possessed work titled *Abraham* appeared in Barney's first show, it was certainly in process at that time. On January 11 Barney wrote an unusually large check to Leonard Bocour, who developed Magna; only he and his designated agent, Goldsmith Brothers, sold the "revolutionary," "permanent plastic" paint, with pigments "*locked* in the molecular structure of the vehicle."[63] Of the many square inches of canvas covered with black exhibited or reproduced between early 1949 and April 1951, the date of Barney's second show, only *Abraham*, documented in June 1950, used Magna. As is the case with *Onement I*, it makes little difference in the 21st century which end of a very productive six months' span saw the making of a single painting; it occurred within this time and did not alter the direction Barney's art was taking. But in the immediately ensuing years, the precise date of this "first" all-black work would matter a great deal to Barney, Still, admirers of Reinhardt (although not Reinhardt himself),[64] and legions of art historians. And so Barney would place its appearance in his first show. Over the years, in letters sent and unsent, in interviews and in talks, engagements with artists and critics, with museum directors and received accountings of avant-garde history, he (and after his death, Annalee) waged a campaign to have the dating of his heroic move acknowledged.[65]

Barney's motivation in making the work—as it was for all of his works, he repeatedly said—was above all an expression of his state of mind. And although it was not exhibited with the title *Abraham* until 1957, there's no question that it is an eloquent enunciation of mourning made within two years of his father's death. But Barney meant the content to encompass "more" than his father. He was after the "tragic," and in his mind the "*most* tragic figure is the father." He was "doing," he said, what "Abraham" *meant* to him. He wanted to push it as far as he could, he wanted it to be "more than black on black."[66]

"Abraham" is a brilliant name for the work. Not only Barney's own father, but the Jewish and Christian and Muslim patriarch and *all* of his accumulated resonance over nearly six thousand years—theological, historical, anthropological, aesthetic, psychological, up to and including the Kierkegaard text so discussed among Barney's peers in the early 1950s—could be brought to bear on Barney's mute, ultimate expression of dignity. It was not enough, in 1950, to have had his debut as an artist; for Barney it had to establish him as not simply a presence among his peers, but as *sui generis*, a pioneer, a general in the avant garde.

TWENTY-NINE

"THE BIGGEST SCANDAL IN N.Y. ART WORLD"

In February, while Barney's work remained on view, *Vogue* magazine stylishly digested the subject that had been given so sharp an edge the previous year in *Life*. Six sculptures and forty-seven paintings "out of the great store of living work, ranging from conservative to non-objective, by artists with such melting-pot names [!] as Noguchi, Benton, De Kooning; ranging from seventy-nine-year-old John Marin to twenty-seven-year-old Theodoros Stamos" were mashed up and reassembled by "school of New York" intimate Herbert Matter to mimic the indubitably artistic 17th-century depiction of the collection of the indubitably aristocratic Archduke Leopold Wilhelm by David Teniers.[1]

Under the creative direction of Alexander Liberman, *Vogue*'s upper-crust and worldly inability to be shocked did not represent the greater culture. The 20th century was exactly half over when Barney—whose life closely coincided with those fifty years—had his show. If, reading about the reaction and looking at the work from a 21st-century vantage point, we can imagine that it seemed radical, it's almost impossible to reconstruct just how radical it truly was without pausing to recapitulate what had happened in New York. For "anyone who has lived his lifetime here" reminisced *Cue* magazine in December 1949, "it is no trick at all to recall the jokes about the Flatiron Building and the wind which [would] blow the girls' skirts, revealing a forbidden bit of ankle encased in a high button shoe" and "an era when the Empire State Building was of the same dream stuff as Jules Verne's submarine"—all now replaced by overcrowded subways and traffic jams.

Cue quaintly catalogued changes for its privileged readership: "brownstone life, as pursued by the majority of the middle class" until 1925 had vanished; "you telephone where once you left cards"; and women may "venture into the street sans hat." Radio "predigests news" where families previously might have read "three morning and four afternoon papers." Evening society had become unrecognizable from the time when "nightclubs were known as cabarets, and thought to be a little 'fast' [and] there was no such thing as the cocktail hour"; the theater became a "battleground" exemplified by plays like *Death of a Salesman* instead of a "suite of coy boudoirs or Ziegfeld shower baths." Movies, radio, and "more lately, television" contributed to the "demise of the [stage] gallery god," supplanted by the "Hollywood visitor whose exploits are recounted on the air [or] in the press," and painting moved from "John Sloan to William Baziotes." New York no longer belonged "to its natives," but was "the mecca of everyone with a purpose in mind"; the city contained the "concentrate of all the changes that have marked the first fifty years of the century anywhere and everywhere in the world."

"Everything that has happened, two world wars, prohibition, the atom bomb, psychiatry, woman's suffrage, radio, airplanes and electronics have left their imprint."

Not to mention—as *Cue* did not—the Depression, the Holocaust, the G.I. Bill, two-piece bathing suits, and frozen foods, Norman Mailer and Charlie "Yardbird" Parker. And the unprecedented international prominence of the United States.[2] And the double-sided paranoia brought on by conservative-stoked fears that card-carrying Communists had infiltrated the State Department and the imminent Senate Foreign Relations subcommittee hearings that proposed to root out disloyal Americans.

The old life that was recalled so nostalgically may not have resembled Barney's or Gottlieb's or Rothko's, as much as that of Parsons, establishment critics, and the expanded audience for art in 1950. But the trajectory from the Lower East Side or the Bronx or Dvinsk was, if anything, steeper and more disorienting.

This was the forward-looking but agitated and somewhat shellshocked world that would be contemplating *Be I, Yellow Painting,* and *The Promise* at the beginning of 1950. The reviews be damned. Barney had gotten what in 1933 was only a pipe dream: a major gallery show that demanded to be acknowledged and reckoned with. And on his own terms.

If there were polite tolerance or incomprehension, beefs or sour grapes, on the part of his peers—even his most supportive buddy, Tony Smith, had doubts—some less entrenched and younger artists now fell under his avuncular spell. By that cohort Barney began to be thought of with Rothko and Pollock as on a level by themselves, different from many other artists who had been showing longer, like Stamos and Baziotes.

Smith was pivotal in this development. He and Barney were appealingly alike in their prodigious and infectious enthusiasms, but with very different styles. Smith was the "Trevi fountain . . . . Things were always bursting forth. The moment you saw him it started to come out," and the flow of psychic energy only stopped "when he passed out—and even then it probably continued with his eyes closed." Whereas Barney, recalled Hans Noë, a young architecture student whom Smith took under his wing at Cooper Union, was "a really unusual, unusual person: friendly and sweet and nice, but he was like a mountain in the distance, and never, never was close to you, you were never close to him. He was like this wonderful guy encased in ice." Although Smith loved Barney "there was an element of formality between them that was always there."[3]

Barney inherited many of the coterie of devoted, if not to say adoring, colleagues, mates, and novitiates that Smith had assembled. He developed his own relationships with them and began the routine that he would follow with younger friends for the next twenty years. He took them to humble but surprising Chinese dinners, on "educational" field visits to his favorite New York City architecture, regaled them with wide-ranging stories and philosophic insights and intellectualized if superficial references to Kabbalistic mysticism and random facts and political positions that he wove into unexpected connections. If they were artists he provided inspiring—but diligent enough not to appear fulsome—critiques.[4] They would appreciate him. And sometimes stretch a canvas or move a painting for him.

Tony Louvis was a Smith student who became involved with Studio 35, along with the artist Robert Goodnough—at that time a G. I. Bill-supported graduate student—setting up the room and collecting the 50-cent admission fee. A future architect, Louvis was happy to assist Smith and Barney with hanging shows at Parsons or installing mirrors in the bedroom closet at the apartment on Nineteenth Street, where he spent many evenings.[5] When Barney learned that Louvis was studying operatic voice, he was invited to perform with Barney's piano accompaniment. When Frank Lloyd Wright discussed "Cities: Medieval or Modern" with developer William Zeckendorf, Louvis was invited to the gathering to watch on Barney's small, grainy, black-and-white television.[6] And when Louvis became a conscientious objector during the Korean War, Barney offered his educated assistance in writing the required position statement—"a very long drawn out affair, going through various levels of meaning."[7] Ritualizing ordinary activities was a hallmark of Barney's theater, and one of the many qualities that some people cherished and drove others mad.[8]

Noë, a recent immigrant, a Holocaust survivor, who grew up in an upper-middle-class Jewish family, "didn't know what the hell was happening" to him when he landed in the company of Smith, Newman, Pollock, Rothko. It was "like thunder and lightning," a world he didn't recognize and didn't know existed. Hired by Smith as the draftsman for houses the architect was designing in Connecticut, Noë began working in Smith's skylit studio at his apartment building on Sixteenth Street, flummoxed by the "shocking" and "inexplicable" Rothko and Pollock paintings on the walls.

When more space was needed, Smith rented a storefront on Nineteenth Street between First and Second Avenues, the block where Barney lived and had his storefront studio. They would retire to a luncheonette at the corner, often remaining through the evenings until they were in danger of being thrown out. Noë, who didn't speak much English at that time and had a hard time understanding what they were saying, watched as Tony and Barney talked and Annalee "would sit there, exhausted . . . . Every 45 seconds she would say, 'Um-hm,' no matter what it was. It didn't matter who spoke. It was like a metronome. She made this sound of establishing her being there."

Barney took Noë, "sometimes Tony, sometimes other young kids" who worked for Smith, always Annalee, down to Wah Kee in Chinatown. Ordinary customers ate in front, but Barney would walk through the kitchen into a little prep room with a couple of tables in the back. "They knew him . . . . All the artists used to go there"—de Kooning made a print, *Wah Kee Spare Ribs*, because in that room they would place in front of you a teacup and saucer, "both filled with rice wine . . . . Everybody was slightly drunk the whole time."[9]

The schmoozing generally took place during the afternoon or at night. Early evenings Barney and Annalee could be found watching the news on television, after which Anna Newman would phone, beginning a long conversation. A second call followed, with Barney telling Sarah everything he and Annalee had done that day. He felt guilty, Annalee said: Sarah was taking care of his mother, and "he wanted to share his life with her, he wanted her to have a vicarious experience."[10] Only after would they go out. Barney had trouble sleeping; he'd be up until two or three[11] but back at his gallery duties in the morning.

His show had hardly come down when Betty was off for vacation in Florida with Barney left in charge of the daily business and the following season's calendar.[12] Barney would "gladly" do "chores" for both himself and Rothko, Still confidently assured the latter—without first checking with Barney.[13] While Still remained in San Francisco, Barney and Annalee hung his April show, arranged to store the works afterward, per Still's request, then shipped them back to the West Coast for a hastily organized show there.[14] He was the show-runner and promoter for Still's show but it was, in Barney's view, a washout. "Barr, Greenberg, Preston etc saw nothing. I had quite a row with Greenberg over it," he told Rothko. "I've written Clyff as much as I could without upsetting him. Living through it, however, left me at a new low. With Clyff away, the experience of his show became like a sharp mirror of our lives that was unbearable."[15]

"I hope the show was not a disappointment to Betty," Still wrote to Barney, "but if it was it is the price she must pay for knowing one as single in his will as I. To sell these canvases involves a change of reference quite total in regard to the cultural whole. Such shifts are not easily made if made at all by very few people."[16]

"My work, as yours," Still added in a letter that followed, "is made to establish an idea, an hypothesis offered, rather than for cash. And no compromise, even of size, is permitted. Even the seemingly empty spaces are important."[17] Rebounding from his own show's reception, Barney's ego found succor in Still's words, and he took on the mission of defending Still as he wanted to be defended himself.[18] And for a moment, Barney was richly rewarded for his loyal feelings of fellowship. From the person whose own self-grandeur, ambitious vision, and disdain for compromise made it the most highly valued, he got the sort of explicit affirmation he had only dreamed of. About "those lines in your last show,"

As I see them in their vivid blaze they were no "Portrait of a Line" but in their magnitude and intensity they were the outpouring, the gesture of a man who had seen the totality of his culture and those behind it, and found them wanting. And you stood before those big canvases and made a blaze come down and turn its way through man's guts and up again. With the totality of your being you laid a stroke through men's eyes whereby for a moment at least they could see as you saw, and feel as you felt. For you had found something big and a way to make vivid this new thing, that for the moment you were. Something more than all that which had preceded you in all their creation. You saw, and felt, and put it down, and by God they will never forget it![19]

"The despair of self-awareness," Barney had written about Gorky. Of course he succumbed to Still's grandiose charisma. Barney could not have said it better himself.

Still's show coincided with both the first official foray of the "second genera-tion"—"New Talent 1950," an invitational show curated by Greenberg and Meyer

Schapiro at Kootz—and an event that has come to be seen as the Seneca Falls Convention of Abstract Expressionism. As the Studio 35 evenings were about to end, Goodnough encouraged the artists who had been involved as speakers and audience to memorialize their experiences by sharing thoughts about the future. Three afternoons were set—4 to 7 o'clock on Friday, Saturday, and Sunday, April 21, 22, and 23—to hold a freewheeling discussion that was closed to the public and recorded by a stenographer. "Dozens" were invited; twenty-five men and women participated in one or more of the sessions.[20] In jackets, ties, and, on Hedda Sterne, a chic hat, they sat around an enormous table in a small room with pretzels, chips, lots of beer, and plenty of ashtrays. Richard Lippold moderated on the first day and Motherwell on the third. Alfred Barr, whose current title Director of Museum Collections at the Museum of Modern Art did not adequately define his influence and impact, and who participated on the condition that there would be no discussion of MoMA and no allusion to his title or position there, was the only participant who was not an artist; he was invited to attend only the Saturday session, which he moderated without knowledge of what had happened the previous day, and the end of the Sunday session.[21]

By announcement there was to be no "criticisms of museums . . . involved in the talks."[22] There was no agenda, no one knew exactly what they should be discussing. "We don't just want to hear everybody talking about his own point of view," began Hare. Ferber thought they should "attempt to identify our relationship to the public." Since the public asked "What does this work mean," Ferber thought they should "adopt" an attitude—"either discarding the question or trying to answer it." Gottlieb said that despite their differences, there was a "basis for getting together on mutual respect and the feeling that painters here are not academic." Lippold didn't care about the public; he was concerned with problems of "creativity."

Barney's concern, not surprisingly, was something different, and notwithstanding his public cheek, poignantly reflected insecurity about his recent history. He reformulated Gottlieb's proposition: "Do we artists really have a community? If so, what makes it a community?"

Hare thought that the "group activity [the] gathering together" was a "symptom of fear"; but Reinhardt thought it was pertinent. He thought it would be productive to "find out what our community is and what our differences are, and what each artist thinks of them." If one were to diagram it, the discussion would resemble a map of the New York subway system, with tracks only occasionally intersecting. The relationship of the "artist" to museums and tradition and Europe came up, as did "titles," "subjects," "external agony," "purity," "quality," and whether or not signatures were appropriate.

Even though the record of Barney's track was in its brevity most like the Forty-Second Street shuttle, there's no disputing that he had spent a *lot* of time thinking about art. For a few moments, everyone was in the same station discussing the definition of "finished." While most of the artists' answers involved facture, Barney was particularly, and distinctively, exacting: he thought "the idea of a 'finished' picture

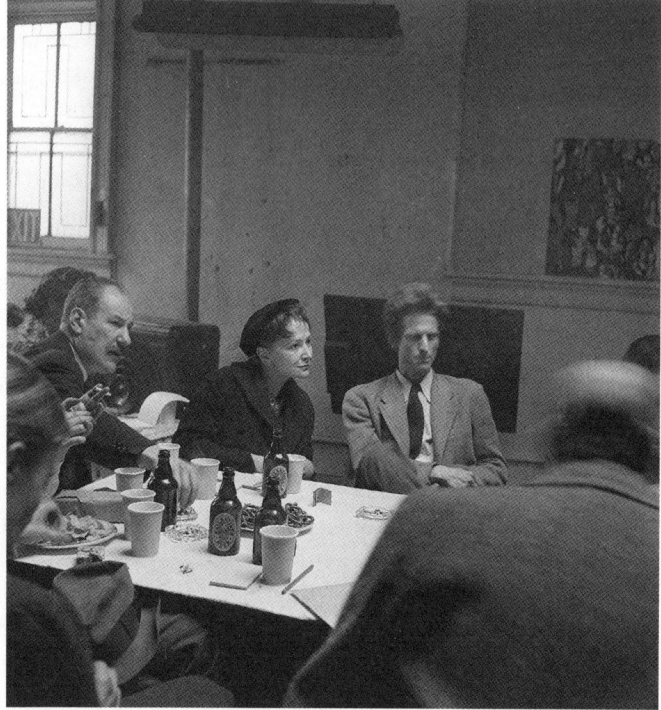

Fig. 21 Artists' Sessions at Studio 35, April 1950. From left: Barnett Newman, Hedda Sterne, David Hare. Photograph Aaron Siskind

is a fiction. I think a man spends his whole life-time painting one picture or working on one piece of sculpture. The question of stopping is really a decision of moral considerations. To what extent are you intoxicated by the actual act, so that you are beguiled by it? To what extent are you charmed by its inner life? And to what extent do you then really approach the intention or desire that is really outside of it. The decision is always made when the piece has something in it that you wanted."

"Do you regard painting as a profession?" asked Motherwell on Sunday. By this time the group, generally tired and even a little more cranky than usual, irritably brought up unions, licenses, and hours devoted to the job.

"The thing that binds us together is that we consider painting to be a profession in an 'ideal society.' We assume the right of insisting that we are creating our own paradise. We should be able to act in a professional way on our own terms. We go out into normal society and insist on acting on our own terms," was Barney's contribution.

"You mean that we are not acting in relation to the goals that most people in our society accept?" asked Motherwell.

"Yes," Barney answered. " 'Professional' for me means 'serious.' "

Toward the end of the third day, the group addressed a question that Barr had posed: "What is the most acceptable name for your direction or movement? It has been called abstract-expressionist, abstract-symbolist, intra-subjectivist, etc."

"I would offer 'self-evident' because the image is concrete," offered Barney, having *almost* the last word.

"It is disastrous to name ourselves," inserted de Kooning, the final statement in Goodnough's edited transcript (if not in fact)—a passive assertion of his actual preeminence in the art world at that moment.[23]

They couldn't simply walk away from this consuming and contentious but extraordinary experience, Barney felt, without something concrete emerging. He wrote Rothko that in toto it was "so much blarney," but he used it "to get everybody to agree to a letter of protest to the Times for giving Clyff the brushoff."[24]

Barney's draft, prickly, verbose, and combative, accused daily journalistic art criticism of a multitude of sins: it was "notorious for its lack of quality . . . . lack of taste . . . inept scholarship." The signatories could not "tolerate and wish to condemn the lack of responsibility" and protested "the alliances they make with reactionary groups among dealers and museums," the promotion of "mediocrity and reaction." The critics attacks were "personal rather than objective, vindictive rather than sincere." And the treatment of Still's show by Emily Genauer and Stuart Preston were the "most flagrant recent examples."

One more example of "the deliberate attempt to promote mediocrity and reaction" was tacked on last. In terms of posterity, however, it turned out to be the art community's equivalent of Archduke Ferdinand's assassination, the first shot that led directly to the way the artists would be inscribed in "history."

The present exhibition of young American artists organized by *Life* magazine and the Metropolitan Museum of Art which we charge was deliberately done to confuse the public concerning the true picture of the state of art among the young painters of the country. It is a well known fact that the great majority of the youth of our country is painting in the abstract style and is at a much more advanced aesthetic level than *Life* Magazine indicates . . . .

We wish to condemn these deliberate attempts to ignore, malign, and to distort the state of art in America in this headstrong drive to promote reaction in art here and to confuse the public [and] to prevent the public from knowing the truth.[25]

As the artists in the loft were ruminating about what they were doing and whether they had a community, the Met was presenting contemporary art selected by—of all authorities—the editors of *Life* magazine.[26] Ironically, it would be the reaction to that show, "19 Young Americans," that cemented the idea of a New York artist's community in the public's mind.

At the beginning of the year, the Met had announced two initiatives focused on living art. In recent years the grand institution demurred regarding contemporary American art according to its agreement with the Whitney. But circumstances changed when toward the end of 1948 the Whitney abrogated the agreement;

about to move physically closer to the Museum of Modern art—from Eighth Street to Fifty-Fourth Street—they were also moving closer aesthetically, with an aim to cooperative ventures. Perhaps feeling betrayed, the Met determined its own next moves. The *Life* show was one. The other was a biannual competition promoted by Artists Equity Association.[27] The first was for oil painting, and would result in a show in December, with four prizes to be awarded. Five regional juries, each with a representative from the Met, one from a local museum, and three area artists made the initial selections. The final judging was to be by a seven-member jury in New York—five members from the regional groups and two selected by the Metropolitan. Entry forms would be mailed by May 1 and due back July 1. This perceived insult loomed as the twenty-five artists and Alfred Barr sat around the table drinking beer at the final Studio 35 sessions.

The Met's approach—its *abdication*—was what made it hard for the pretzels to go down. The Whitney annuals were, at least, rigorously curated; the Museum of Modern Art's 1946 "Fourteen Americans," as an up-to-the-moment group survey, was even more selective, highlighting a particular taste. Instead of "'giving the artists what they want,'" as Louchheim referred to those represented by Artists Equity, "the Metropolitan might have filled a different need by bringing its own selective point of view and standards into the arena."[28]

This is what simmered beneath the letter supporting Still. Although he was equally offended, Reinhardt radically tempered Barney's draft, and it was this version that was shown to the other artists.

> We, the undersigned, protest the summary dismissal by your critic, Mr. Stuart Preston, of the exhibition of paintings by Clyfford Still . . .
>
> Clyfford Still is a mature and advanced artist and belongs to a group of artists who are working at the periphery of known art experiences and therefore presents a new challenge to the art public. These paintings consequently require a greater imaginative effort on the part of the serious critic.

"Everybody agreed until it came to the signing when Herbert killed it with his 'right of the critics to ignore, praise etc etc.,'" Barney wrote.[29] It turned out that one artist's negative reception was not an "issue." But in the Metropolitan Museum's December show they found one.

For once Barney was laconic in a draft of his report to Rothko in Europe: "At the conference Adolph brought up the Metropolitan show,—and a letter was written (mostly by Bob) using less people than those who attended. I wrote the releases and it hit the first page of the *Times*."

In fact, it took nearly a month of coordinated negotiation to formulate something on which a large enough group—a critical mass—could agree. Ultimately, twenty-one of the Studio 35 sessions artists plus Pollock, who had been in Springs,[30] Rothko, in Europe, Still, and four others signed mimeographed copies.

On Saturday, May 20, Barney walked the consensus statement, "Open Letter to Roland Redmond, President of the Metropolitan Museum of Art," up to Fifth Avenue and Eighty-Second Street. By the standards of manifestos of the '40s it was pretty moderate—until the part about "consequential contribution to civilization":

> The undersigned painters reject the monster national exhibition to be held at the Metropolitan Museum of Art next December, and will not submit work to its jury.
>
> The organization of the exhibition and the choice of jurors by Francis Henry Taylor and Robert Beverly Hale, the Metropolitan's Director and the Associate Curator of American Art, does not warrant any hope that a just proportion of advanced art will be included.
>
> We draw to the attention of those gentlemen the historical fact that, for roughly a hundred years, only advanced art has made any consequential contribution to civilization.
>
> Mr. Taylor on more than one occasion has publicly declared his contempt for modern painting; Mr. Hale, in accepting a jury notoriously hostile to advanced art, takes his place beside Mr. Taylor.
>
> We believe that all the advanced artists of America will join us in our stand.[31]

The next, miserably hot, day, Reinhardt and Barney, "looking more like a businessman or politician than an artist" in his dark suit and tie and shined shoes, managed to get a meeting with the weekend editor on the *Times* city desk.[32] (Ironically, that day's Sunday magazine section featured "Rebel With a Paintbrush: At 79, artist John Sloan's revolutionary American scenes win him recognition as an Academy 'immortal.' "[33]) On Monday, at the bottom of the front page ran the headline, "18 Painters Boycott Metropolitan; Charge 'Hostility to Advanced Art' "; most of the letter was printed and all of the signatories listed. "Mr. Newman, one of the artists" (the last words on the front page before the jump) "explained that he and his colleagues were critical of the membership of all five regional juries . . . but were specifically opposed to the New York group, the 'national jury of selection' and the 'jury of awards.' "[34]

"The biggest scandal in N.Y. art world, ever," wrote Baziotes to his brother that day, "it was terrific. The same thing hit the N.Y. Tribune, World-Telegram, & N.Y. Post.

"Everyone thinks it's fantastic."[35]

Not exactly everyone: "The Irascible Eighteen" was the unsympathetic editorial's headline in the *Herald Tribune.* The writer (some supposed it to be Genauer) accused the group of a kind of prior restraint, and pointed out that eleven of the signers had works exhibited or owned by the Metropolitan, four were included in the *Life* magazine show, and three were to be included in a June show of American art in the permanent collection. Loftily, the editorial chided the artists: "surely misrepresentation—actual or implied—such as is incorporated in their highly publicized protest to the museum, can only harm their cause. In time, museum directors are apt to become so irritated with unjustified criticism they will develop a protective armor thick enough to render them immune not only to constant sniping but also to new ideas."[36]

Barney angrily scribbled a volatile anarchist's response, accusing the Metropolitan *and* the Museum of Modern Art *and* the Whitney *and* university art museums around the country of failure to take a position of responsibility toward American art—"its stature, its genius, its merit or lack thereof." He called on them to "desist from meddling with painting in America," to give up their "token activity." But there were cooler heads—Gottlieb's and Reinhardt's—and a proper corrective was written: "Our concern is not that any specific advanced artists would be excluded from the show, but that, because of its choice of jurors any representation of advanced art will be on the basis of masking the real politics of the Museum."[37]

In spite of a favorably partisan article by Weldon Kees in *The Nation*, the group was on the defensive. *Time* magazine, in contrast to the small intellectual journal, reached a wide national readership with predictably mocking coverage. The story was still news on July 4 when an omnium gatherum of seventy-five painters, including former allies of the renegades Milton Avery and Will Barnet, issued a statement defending the integrity of the juries and Hale in more column inches in the *Times*.[38] How ironic, then, was the effect of the *Herald Tribune*'s scolding. With "The Irascible Eighteen," echoing the "Hollywood Ten," the unnamed writer did more than all of Motherwell's and Gottlieb's and Reinhardt's fine rhetoric, more than twenty-eight artists' petulance (ten sculptors supported the painters' "stand"), more than Barney's honed public relations savvy, to etch the group into the public's mind.

When Preston reviewed the end-of-season Parsons group show, he couldn't resist an acknowledgment—and a dig: the gallery's stable, he wrote, "are as much in the front line of today's avant garde as they are highly conscious of being there. Their admirers make almost as much noise as their scoffers. Just what is all the shouting about?"[39]

It could easily appear decades later—as it did to Preston at the time—that the artists' position was navel-gazing and narcissistic. But something much more serious was at stake, the "real politics of the museum," as Gottlieb and Reinhardt wrote. If, for much of the group it was more deeply metabolized than intellectual or conscious, Barney had already described the problem in 1942 in his unpublished "What About Isolationist Art?" In 1950, Meyer Schapiro felt it was urgent to be explicit.

"It is instructive for the student of social life as well as of art," wrote Schapiro about the 1913 Armory Show, "to observe how a single event in a long series may acquire a crucial importance because it dramatizes or brings into the open before a greater public what is ordinarily the affair of a small group." Schapiro's was a not-so-coded message about the Luce publications, Congressmen McCarthy and Dondero, the publication of the scurrilous, destructive, *Red Channels: The Report of Communist Influence in Radio and Television*, and Francis Henry Taylor. His lengthy, considered, erudite discussion of the historical motivations for radical-seeming art concluded:

> Today, almost forty years after the Armory Show, modern art is still a recurring problem for the public, although so many more painters and sculptors practice

this art. The hostile criticisms made in 1913 have been renewed with great viru-
lence. We hear them now from officials of culture, from Congress and the president. The director of the Metropolitan Museum of Art has recently condemned
modern art as "meaningless" and "pornographic," and as a sign of the decay of
civilization in our time. These criticisms are sometimes linked in an unscrupulous
way with attacks on Communism, foreign culture, and religious doubt . . . . Those
who demand a traditional and consoling art, or an art useful to the state, have
nothing to hold on to in contemporary painting and sculpture, unless it be some
survivals of the academicism of the last century, or hybrid imitations of the modern art of fifty years ago by mediocre conforming painters.[40]

Kootz tried to "cash in." He had been "against the original enterprise" but "while
Betty was on vacation [he] tried to maneuver through Bob [Motherwell] to get us
into a show with him," Barney reported to Rothko.[41] "None of us at Betty's wanted
Kootz's show (with the exception of a couple of innocents)."

Kootz's show was stillborn, the dealer blaming Barney, Pollock, and Parsons "for
killing it." But the episode brought Barney even closer to Jane and Tony Smith, who
had "some terrific ideas" for his own presentation of the artists that Barney thought
would "change the whole picture for all of us . . . . I love them both," he told Rothko,
and he meant it. "Ad also has been wonderful. He fought for Clyff like a bulldog and
has helped make life bearable for me. I have also gotten to know Pollock better. He
is a changed man and has developed a sense of solidarity with the men in Betty['s]
gallery that is genuine." But Barney was "really finished with Bob . . . I just can't
stand [his] Jesuitical mind any more," and Tomlin felt the same.[42]

"The art world has been unusually active," Parsons told Still, "not in sales but
in controversy." She "never approved the whole idea," of Kootz's show and Barney
"not only got into a fight with Kootz but a terrible fight with Bob, who accused me
of betraying him forgetting that he had betrayed all the 'irascibles.' "[43] The agitation
took a toll on Barney's emotional and physical health. He was depressed and in
"constant pain" suffering from "sciatica rheumatism that practically kept me in bed"
for eight weeks.[44]

Rothko was sympathetic, but even more, he was in agreement. In hindsight the
months between May 1950 and January 1951 appear to create a historical narrative
of a group coalescing. But for a number of the artists themselves—as much as they
appreciated the attention and even notoriety—it was quite different. "We must find a
way of living and working without the involvements that seem to have been destroying us one after another," Rothko wrote to Barney in August. "I doubt whether any
of us can bear much more of that kind of strain. I think that this must be a problem
of our delayed maturity that we must solve immediately without fail. Perhaps my
ranting against the 'club' was no more than a cry of despairing self protection against
this very danger." While he was still safely in Europe, Rothko had received Kootz's
invitation; his first instinct was to run it by Parsons, then he decided not to "involve"

her, and ultimately did not respond at all. But the competition between the dealers had insinuated into his mind his next move.[45]

In Venice, Pollock, de Kooning, and Gorky, chosen by Barr, represented the United States at the biennial;[46] at Black Mountain College, "de Kooning's influence is everywhere," Stamos told Barney; and in Provincetown, "Post-Abstract Painting 1950: France, America" had, during its preparation, caused "a complicated series of maneuvers by [French art dealer Louis] Carré and others that was unbelievable," Barney told Rothko. "They were all resolved and I had no small hand in outwitting them." Meanwhile, he held the fort at the Parsons Gallery, which was showing the work of 9-year-old students from the Dalton School.

The isolation was just what he needed. Neither the disagreements, drafting, organizing, maneuvering, and other "intrigues,"[47] nor the judgment by Preston in his review of Parsons's group show that *Abraham* contributed "nothing," seem to have distracted Barney from his work. He bought Belgian canvas from New York Central Supply—more refined than the commercial duck remnants from John Boyle—and he allowed to expire his substitute teacher license, renewed as recently as September 1948.

The best news—the thing that gave him "a sense of hope"—was a new studio.

"Where do you think it is?" he asked Rothko. "On Wall St. of course. Think of it I'm now Barney the wolf of Wall St. Me and the House of Morgan. I can't stay in my place and I could not get anything near me, so Monday we went down to my old haunts and there on Wall St I found a beautiful place with a view of the river just like in Provincetown.[48] Unfortunately they are going to build an East Side Express Highway on South St that will kill the view. It's simply impossible to achieve a sense of rest here but at least I have a big place and I feel great about it."[49]

On the first floor was a restaurant; the second a barber shop, and the third—just the thing to delight Barney with his old identification as a naturalist—a "mineralogist." It "tickled him pink to think that he had a studio on Wall Street. He couldn't get over it."[1] But once he got there he faced the "problem." Before anything could happen he had to "get rid of the physical restrictions," make "the environmental space" disappear so he could create his own "sense of place by feeling myself where I was."[2] He cleaned and plastered and painted the walls. He invited people, including Dorothy Miller, the curator at the Museum of Modern Art.

A "man's studio is his sanctuary," he insisted. One would "never walk into another's studio unless invited, never look at his work unless asked." Barney loved the ritual, the "politeness of our relationships" before the galleries became central to their lives. "The ceremony was that you called on your friend or your friend would invite you. You would sit in your living room and you would be drinking coffee or prohibition whiskey or something. You knew that a certain moment he would say, 'would you like to come into the studio?'" The artists would wait for "the right psychological moment to say 'come in' [because] he doesn't want to be seen on a disinterested basis. 'We've had our coffee, you're feeling good. Would you like to see my work? . . . Then he introduces you to his work. It is like 'would you like to meet my wife?'" It didn't matter whether he was working, or not working, if someone dropped in it was a "terrible intrusion." When the ceremony disappeared and people dropped in unexpectedly, he couldn't continue. He felt "paralyzed."[3]

He also loved the ceremony of the "physical work" required before painting: examining the fabric for irregular "nubbins," constructing the stretcher, stretching the canvas, shrinking the canvas, sizing the canvas with glue: it "warmed" him up and destroyed what he called "the romance" of the fabric. As he demanded of the studio space before he could work, of the color before he could use it, he required the canvas as well to be "inert." If he wanted the silence broken, he would turn on the radio and listen to news, or a ballgame, or popular music, but never Mozart. He couldn't have Mozart because it was too powerful, because he would have felt it necessary to "start talking to him."[4] Sometimes it was the natural light he needed to shut out.[5]

Painting provided exactly the antidote to the relentless cerebrating. He was looking for a feeling that was "natural," like "walking or talking or reading," but definitely not a loosening of inhibitions. He set deliberate barriers for himself, so that he wouldn't be seduced by the easy or comfortable—colors or textures or formats with which he might be "in love." When it worked, the act of painting allowed him to tap into a "heightened feeling," something "extremely true to my way of thinking," a sense of "vividness": what could be called his soul.[6] And because of who Barney was—not libidinous like de Kooning, not unbridled like Pollock, not delusionally

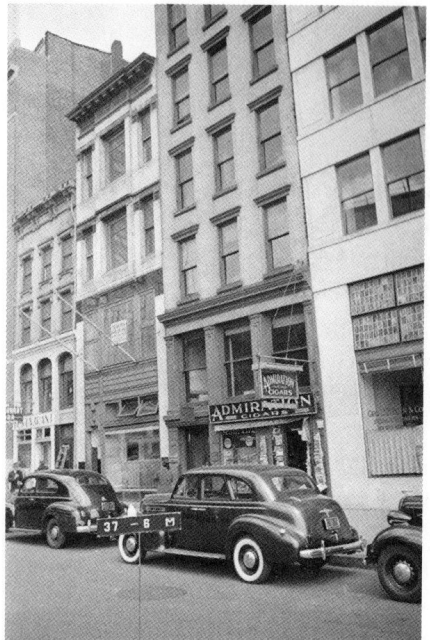

Fig. 22 110 Wall Street in 1941, Barnett Newman's studio from August 1950 through August 1952. New York City Department of Finance

potent like Still or chronically unhappy like Rothko,[7] or artistically confident like Gottlieb—his work inevitably was pressured by his punishing reluctance to violate decorum.

He didn't want to "use painting as an instrument," as he felt many others did, to "interpret their feelings . . . interpret their emotions, their experiences . . . act out their psyche." He was not at all interested in it as a "form of psychiatry, therapy, a form of uplift." For Barney painting was something else, "the opposite of interpretation": it was a "total involvement, involving your whole being as a man whereby, you might say, an objective fact is created." In that sense, he felt, painting was "a tool." It emphatically was not a performance "interpreting life."[8]

But once he was "in it" all kinds of emotions began "to develop." It's easy to scoff at his description of the experience as a kind of "metaphysical terror"—the paintings seem so simple—but that belies the colossal effort to suppress the public persona and live for a few moments in the naked state which that personality had been erected to armor. Of course a man so publicly buttoned up, so guarded, so self-edited, experienced "every stroke" as "violent. Because once you make it, it's there and you've got to handle it," to own it. A man accustomed through his adult life to control whatever circumstances might be controlled, to immaculately tailor his life and self-presentation, who produced countless drafts of everything he put to paper, was faced, in his own words, with a "fantastic series of choices" that involved "the most intense expression of one's experience." It's bad enough, he analogized, when one is making a choice in a horse race. "You pick the horse and you put down your money—which might be a week's pay—on it." But the money was not the issue, he said. It was the choice: "Out of six horses, you choose number three, and the damn horse didn't come in." Most people would curse bad luck, or fault the jockey or the mount. Not Barney. A man would figure, he tellingly concluded the story, "something was wrong with me, not the horse. Well, in painting the choices are more crucial and they are more manifold."[9]

"There is something about being alone the whole day in the studio which is pretty tough . . . . Nobody can help you. You are there alone. It is a desolate, miserable life." And it left him completely spent and physically exhausted.[10] After, he would "relieve it" with whiskey. "How can a painter be a painter without alcohol?" he asked. "Apparently, we need turpentine. But we also have to have alcohol."

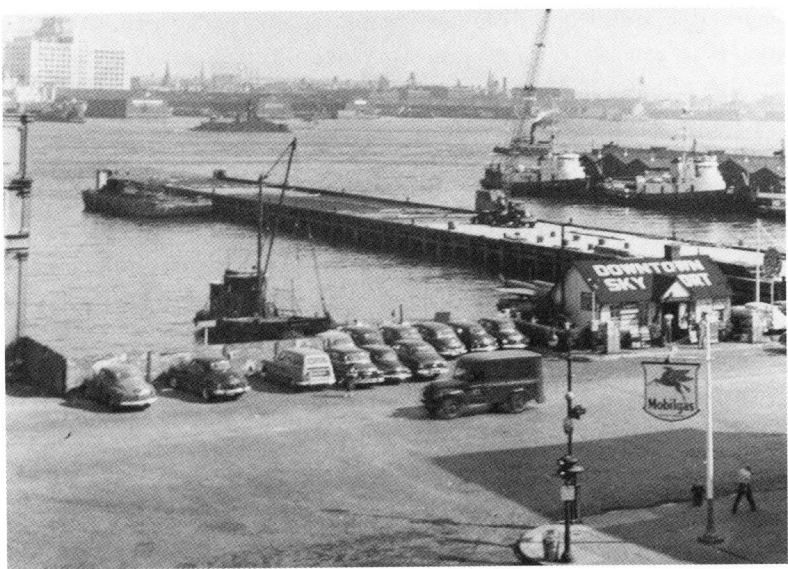

Fig. 23 The view from his studio was "just like in Provincetown," Newman told Mark Rothko

"When one is working," he explained the process many years later, "one is at his greatest intensity." In this heightened state, in these first years of his career, in his romanticizing mind, Barney's model and soul-mate was Pollock. "When I used to meet Pollock when he also had been working at his greatest intensity . . . there would be a rapport which was special . . . We [both] knew the important concern: what is painting about?" They would "stimulate each other to go back to the studio to really use the highest level of our ability."[11] Later on, to somewhat distance himself from the awesome responsibility of having made a choice, he would use the word "compelled": he was "compelled" to make this painting, "compelled" to make this sculpture.

For many in the *Herald Tribune*'s "Irascible" group the fall season was suddenly lively. Gottlieb, Motherwell, Pollock, Reinhardt, Stamos—but not Still, Rothko, or Barney—were among the twenty-two painters in "America Paints—2nd Exhibition" at the Argent Galleries. De Kooning, Pollock, Reinhardt, Rothko, Tomlin, and Sterne were paired with French artists in Janis's "Young Painters in the U.S. and in France." In October, Kline, who had not been at the Studio 35 sessions but was a fellow traveler from The Club, showed at Egan; in November the Whitney Annual included Baziotes, Gottlieb, de Kooning, Motherwell, Pollock, Reinhardt, Rothko, and Tomlin; Motherwell opened at Kootz and Pollock at Parsons. In December, following up on the previous season's Greenberg- and Schapiro-curated "new talent" exhibition, Kootz invited the gallery artists Baziotes, Gottlieb, Hare, Hofmann, and Motherwell—now apparently the older generation—to make the selection.

When Ferber, Gottlieb, and Motherwell were approached to make work for Congregation B'nai Israel in New Jersey, the very idea of a commission forced an ethical debate. They felt they had "been rejected by the largest part of the public, [including] the museums and the collectors," remembered Ferber, "we felt considerable antagonism to the outside world as we looked at it. So that when an architect such as [Percival] Goodman, who was really the first architect in America to face up to the problem of using abstract art on his buildings . . . came along everybody began to discuss it as if it were a questionable thing to do." Reinhardt was opposed to the artists doing anything as "commonplace and public as a sculpture for an architect"; he dismissed that sort of work as "Chagallerie." But Barney encouraged Ferber. Ferber vividly recalled a cafeteria lunch with himself, Tomlin, Reinhardt, Barney, Rothko, and "perhaps Motherwell . . . . Ad said, 'You just can't do that kind of thing.' And Barney Newman said, 'the only way to do it is to get your art out . . . in the public eye.' "[12]

As for Barney himself, he optimistically invested in yards and yards of canvas, and regularly attended performances at the Metropolitan Opera and Carnegie Hall.

In other words, by late November, when what has become the singular, iconic image of the so-called New York School was created, one would have had a hard time making the case that—*apart* from Barney—these protesting artists were under-acknowledged. Three years later, when Barney looked back at 1950, he described the year as "crucial in the transformation of a situation that until then was fluid. What seemed . . . to be a crisis" at that time had, by 1953 revealed itself to be "rather a surrender on the part of the artist, intellectuals critics art historians, museum directors, to the same desire + what appeared like a struggle turned out to be a[n] amalgam of the forces that desire a painters + sculptors Hollywood."[13]

Shortly after *Time* ran its condescending story in June, its sister Luce publication *Life* began to plan a story to coincide with the Metropolitan's December juried show. Although it would reproduce only exhibited works—and therefore not any made by the "Irascibles"—*Life* wanted for its own dubious purposes a photograph of the eighteen posed on the steps of the Museum. The artists, however, "refused to agree to their cute ideas" to be photographed "with paintings under our arms."[14] They didn't mind having a picture taken, Gottlieb told art editor Dorothy Seiberling after conferring with Newman and Tomlin, "but we're not going to be photographed that way, under those circumstances, because that would look as if we were trying to get into the Metropolitan and we were being turned down on the steps."

"They asked us what we want[ed]," remembered Barney of a meeting with Seiberling, Tomlin, Motherwell, and himself. "We wanted nothing; we weren't a group." The artists agreed to be photographed only in "neutral territory"—a rented studio— and "in an honest way—like doctors, not like clowns, and not an organized group."

"We called a meeting to deliver a message to artists. Pousette-Dart went into a tirade against museums and the Establishment. Rothko opposed [the] idea, [he was] against mass culture. I didn't give a damn either way, because [a] photo was clean. As the committee, we couldn't say we wanted it because it would have appeared we made a deal with *Life*. Still agreed because [the] photo was to be honest. Mark made a turn around and was for it. The vote was among a dozen or so who were there." The choice of who was included, according to Barney, was accidental. "Friends brought friends, or rather guys we respected." Fifteen artists showed up on November 24.[15]

Fellow feeling was in short supply. Several artists were out of town and didn't want to be inconvenienced. Pollock was again drinking heavily, partially provoked by just this sort of "celebrity"; since September he had endured the escalating ambitions of photographer Hans Namuth who, possibly inspired by filmmaker Robert Flaherty's recent successes, was filming Pollock working.[16] The evening before, the Newmans shared Thanksgiving dinner at the Rothkos' home with a temporarily relocated Still, and deep competitive rifts were already appearing. Adhering to studio etiquette, Barney did not follow when Rothko called Still out of the living room to show Still his new work. When Still returned he told Barney that New York was a "nest of incest," and he, Still, had to leave—which he did in April.[17]

No one, except perhaps Barney, who insisted that they should present themselves with the same dignity as bankers, recognized that the photograph could become historic. Resentments stewed for decades—in Krasner's case, for a lifetime—in no small measure due to Barney's maneuvering himself into the pivot of the image, although he insisted, and Sterne confirmed, that Nina Leen, the photographer, "arranged us—the way she wanted."[18] Barney wore his best, Italian-tailored suit and a brand new pair of gleaming shoes that Annalee, not working because of the Thanksgiving holiday, had run out to buy that morning.[19] It was a good thing, too, because, whether it was cause or effect, those shoes were, with the rest of Barney, right in the center.[20]

Barney might have had in mind as a model the stylish Irving Penn photograph of eighteen *New Yorker* cartoonists elegantly arrayed around a studio scaffolding that had appeared in *Vogue* three years earlier—most of the men in dark suits and ties, the (two) women in dark dresses and hats. These artists did not consider themselves a group unified in any position or goal, but Penn had made a handsome and respectful photographic composition of individuals. At least two were Barney's friends: Sterne's husband, Saul Steinberg—centrally placed and wearing an unusual light jacket that stood out—and Otto Soglow, the fourth musketeer, with Gottlieb, Borodulin, and Barney, of the college and Art Students League salad days. But in the Leen photograph, Penn's wry, comfortable, and unclouded subjects are transmuted into a tangled knot of anxious discontent.

Everyone in *Vogue* was facing front, artfully knit into a group; in *Life*, Sterne, standing on a stool, rises like an ascendant Madonna while the male subjects are jammed together, their body language asserting their independence. Rothko, close to the foreground, face turned and eyes side-glancing, appears shifty and uncomfortable, Gottlieb in the back is focusing to his left, Motherwell looks bored, and de Kooning, his hair plastered to his head, has hunched shoulders and a beetled brow. Reinhardt is erect and broad-shouldered, facing forward, but his expression is impatient. Everyone's face is smudged by awkward shadows, Still's deep-set eyes nearly obscured entirely. Ruggedly handsome with his bald head catching the light, Pollock, placed directly behind Barney's own bald egg-shaped light-reflecting head, echoes

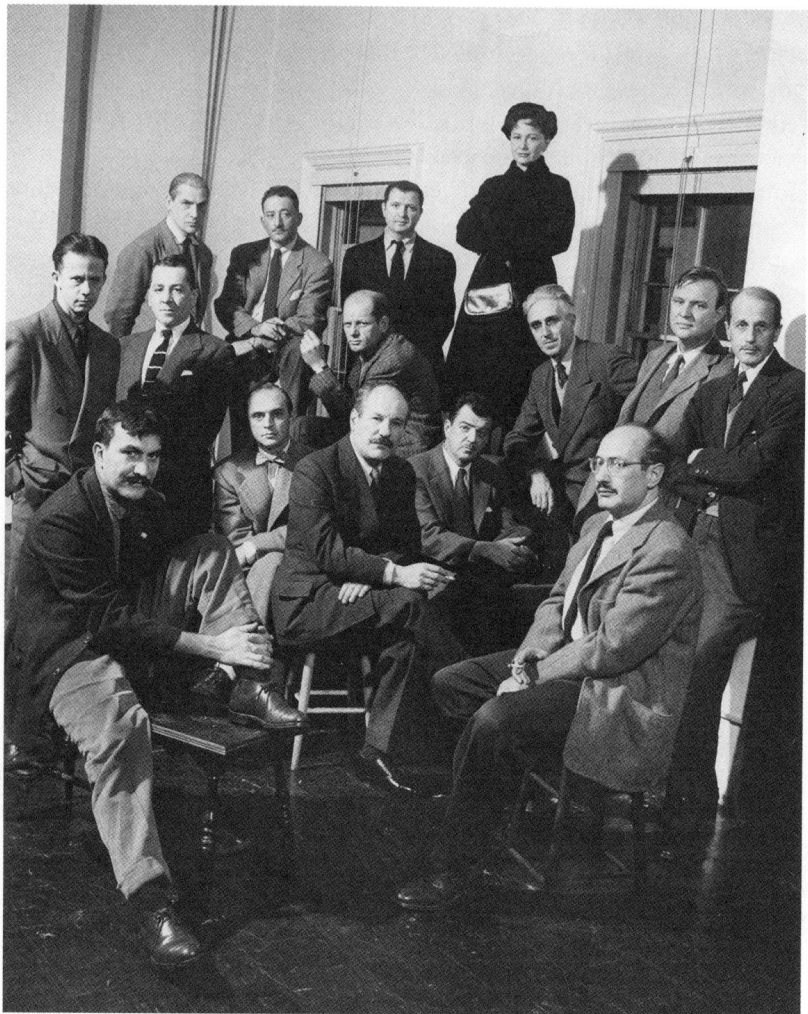

Fig. 24 "The Irascibles," 1951. Top row, from left: Willem de Kooning, Adolph Gottlieb, Ad Reinhardt, Hedda Sterne; middle row, from left: Richard Pousette-Dart, William Baziotes, Jackson Pollock, Clyfford Still, Robert Motherwell, Bradley Walker Tomlin; bottom row, from left: Theodoros Stamos, Jimmy Ernst, Barnett Newman, James Brooks, Mark Rothko. Photograph Nina Leen

Barney's mass. Only Barney seems unaffected by the stress of the photo shoot. He is completely poised, relaxed yet imposing, his face perfectly bisected by shadow, his beautiful hand, as always holding a cigarette, artfully lit and in dramatic relief against his dark suit. (Eighteen months later in a portrait she painted of him, Sterne would make that hand her central subject.) He is not simply at the center of the photograph; he is the physical and psychological weight in an intentionally dissonant ensemble.[21]

The photograph appeared in the January 15, 1951, issue of *Life*. "The solemn people above, along with three others, made up the group of 'irascible' artists who raised the biggest fuss about the Metropolitan's competition," stated the text. "All representatives of advanced art, they paint in styles which vary from the dribblings of Pollock . . . to the Cyclopean phantoms of Baziotes, and all have distrusted the museum." Their opinion about the Met aside, the artists were quite right to mistrust *Life*'s motives. "The effect of the revolt of the 'irascibles' remains to be seen, but it did appear to have needled the Metropolitan's juries into turning more than half the show into a free-for-all of modern art."[22]

In fact, the article in spite of itself assured the "effect of the revolt." Across the double page spread the artists faced the work of others in the Met's show, and through the text—their "outbursts unleashed blasts and counterblasts across the country, echoing in museum corridors, art galleries and newspaper columns"—they faced their new very public identities.

"It was the first time that there was a breakthrough to the public," said Reinhardt years later. "It wasn't one crazy person like Pollock whose career was built out of adverse publicity. The protest against the Met brought things out into the open." It was "key."[23]

Barney was happy with the way the photograph had turned out, especially since its prominence countered his exclusion from "The School of New York" at Frank Perls's West Coast gallery, which opened a few days earlier.[24] "Without prejudice, it is one of the best photographs 'Life' has ever published: the arrangement, the naturalness of it, the really human qualities of it," Luis J. Navascués responded to Barney's ask. "Also you as the 'putative' father of the group, right in the center, and not only a physical one."[25] Yet his appearance as a respondent in a Club evening, "Art in Anti-artistic Times (on the third volume of Malraux's book)," while the "Irascibles" issue was on newsstands deliberately ambiguated his status: was it as the central artist, or Hess's "genial theoretician" that he sat between Clement Greenberg and Meyer Schapiro—all three "one hundred percent against Malraux"?

By this time, for most of them, the Metropolitan Museum was almost irrelevant; the fortunate had already received the seal of approval from the Museum of Modern Art. "Abstract Painting and Sculpture in America" opened on January 23, 1951, the museum's first survey of what it finally decided was "one of the most controversial movements in modern American art." Of the fifteen painters in the "Irascible" photograph a week earlier, only Gottlieb, Sterne, Still, and Barney were not in the show.[26]

Did Leen accurately capture the essence of each artist as he (or she) was, or did the artists become their *Life* avatars? When Michel Seuphor, a sympathetic French critic and editor, arrived in New York for the MoMA exhibition and the activities around it, he confirmed what all could see on the page. "Shall I sketch a few portraits?" he asked. "Pollock is sullen. What loads does this man carry on his shoulders? What is the remorse that gnaws at him so? . . . Motherwell looks very gentle. Is he really as gentle as all that? Civilized. Too much so? A bit of decadence could not harm an art as subtle as his . . . De Kooning, quicksilver, frank, enthusiastic, every day torn with some new anguish, which every day's act of painting relieves . . . . Reinhardt observes the world and speaks not, while a very slight smile floats on this round face. There is a hidden humor behind the willfully indifferent glance . . . . Stamos swarms in all directions in feverish search of—what?" And yet Seuphor, like David Sylvester before him, became completely ingenuous in this crowd: "Everything is open in this city, everything is easy to know and get into . . . . In the artistic circles, the groups do not fight and do not consider themselves exclusive, do not wave doctrinaire banners. There are no airtight partitions; all the artists know each other and see each other. This does not mean that there is no competition, but it is not ferocious." It was so unlike Paris, Seuphor said, where the literary and artistic life is "rotting with intrigues, trickery, wire pulling, sordid calculation, murderous gossip," where "jealousy and bitterness reign over all."[27]

Seuphor was as off-base as those who saw a group identity in the "Irascibles." The media noticed some artists, curators anointed others, and still others were beginning to think about "reputation." As inconceivable as it was a few years earlier, there were those preparing for their place in "history."

One of the earliest to think along these lines, and to calculate the management of his reputation, was Still. At the end of 1948, he asked Parsons to withdraw all of his canvases from view because, he felt, the damage caused by showing work no longer representative of his evolving style would cause him "the greatest of injury" leading to "blood on the floor."[28] Frequently his positioning was at Barney's expense. In early 1950 he had "no competitive feelings," and happily put his paintings and show into Barney's hands,[29] yet later he would tar the Barney of that time as a "little man with the flipping fist" and a "conspicuously morbid (even sinister)" clown, who engineered the "unauthorized" reproduction of Still's painting in the December 1948 *Tiger's Eye*, and "manipulated" the name and date, who was guilty of "amoral hypocrisy" and the "totalitarian technique of verbalizing the sublime while performing painting and acts which [were] its total antithesis."[30]

In July 1950, Barney "and Mark, and probably others" were the hope to keep the "love and energy alive" in New York, "to protect this heat from the ghouls and dogs";[31] in November, New York was a "nest of incest."

In April 1951, Still told Barney the previous winter was a very "valuable" period that sharpened his judgment of the "personalities and principles involved"; he was "measuring the field," saw its "pathetic limitations," and counted on Barney to be at his side when he returned to New York, and together they would "smash them open and correct the blur so obvious that it blinds."[32] Days later, he confided to Rothko, "Certainly all of us are getting famous. On several occasions I have had to slap people down for speaking of Betty and her gallery and artists in contemptible terms. Young smart-alecs from here [San Francisco] and elsewhere are now peddling the most libelous tales of conduct and attitudes. Jealousy rampant all over the place."[33] But only a couple of weeks later, the loyalty vanished: although "Barney's relation to me has often been full of kindness and truly generous in spirit," Still had to "speak ruthlessly . . . because I will continue to separate friendship and its compromises from the almost absolute issues of our work . . . . Barney is a very lonesome man. He is a childless father whose need is so great that he has almost become his own child. To compensate he would be all things. He is intelligent above most to know that the arts are the road to the only real power . . . . I see Barney, for all his energy a man of almost pathetic impotence. With a good mind he is incapable of transcending ambition . . . . I am always on guard with Barney now."[34]

Nevertheless, in June 1953 Still would invite Barney to drive across the country with him, offering an introduction to Grace Morley, the founder and director of the San Francisco Museum of Modern Art. They had gotten as far as Ohio in the best of spirits, they had what Barney called a "glorious" day, but twenty-four hours later the trip was suddenly aborted because of "car trouble."[35] Two months later Still would slander Barney to Dorothy Miller, who was perceived to hold an artist's reputation in her hands, calling him "a ruthless, crafty, dedicated gangster, a little Molotov who is sharp enough to see that art is important as a political weapon and as a personal entrée," and was "interesting chiefly as a relentless, willful, vengeful + often a horrifying scoundrel,—as an animal is often horrifying"; he wanted to disassociate himself from Barney in "every position of act + mind + motive + feeling"; "certainly no one but a completely impotent man, one who must live by envy alone, could have such need to destroy, or trample the virtue he parodies, whether in words or paint."[36]

A few months after, Still compared "Newman and Reinhardt" to "whimpering frightened little boys hiding behind their women's skirts when I put the pressure on,"[37] but nine months later he wrote affectionately to Barney about Rothko's "technics [*sic*] of assault + capture," hoping Barney's "resentment is not as deep as mine, for it is not a good thing to feel + know." Rothko was a "very bitter masochist and welcomes anything that will give him the chance to cry 'persecution,' even if he has to roll in a spiritual gutter to achieve it"; he was a "very bright + very mean 'operator'. (In lighter moments I have wondered if he were not a 'woman' in search of a husband—he often talked + acted like it.)"[38]

Still regularly undermined his artist "friends" to each other and to non-artist third parties, while maintaining a sometimes gushing united front with the target. However much the artists shared stories that would allow them to see the pattern, it could not have been enough, but Still's Iago-like behavior was not solely responsible for the bad faith that was brewing. This was a group of men who had chosen a profession that left them uniquely exposed. Most not war veterans, they were especially vulnerable in a culture blooming with postwar confidence and public glorification of a particular mid-century American fantasy of manly virtues in which they had small participation. How were they to define themselves as men, when the popular culture around them was shining a klieg light on veterans and heroes in best-sellers like Norman Mailer's *The Naked and the Dead*, Irwin Shaw's *The Young Lions*, James Jones's *From Here to Eternity*, Herman Wouk's *The Caine Mutiny*, John Hersey's *The Wall*; or wise and stabilizing family anchors in movies like *Cheaper by the Dozen* and *Father of the Bride*. But, if they might have found affirmation in fellow feeling, Still, at least, worked diligently against that.

None of these men bothered with a foolish consistency. Still could write about Barney, "I can have deep feeling for Barney and yet say that his pictures that I saw were in their ambivalence, a death act against the human spirit . . . . The passion that deplores the evidence of the free human hand and the groping of the spirit is but the passion of the knife . . . an aesthetic of the wound," and at the same time, a few paragraphs later, about himself: "When I hang a painting I would have it say 'Here am I; this is my fist, my feeling, myself. Here I stand implacable, proud, alive, naked, unafraid. If one does not like it he should turn away because I am looking at him . . . ' Certainly I will not be the subject of any man's judgement."[39] To be fair, Barney's boast that he "killed painting" while pursuing it might rankle even a less volatile personality than Still's, especially as Barney, after events in 1952, dedicated himself to having his contribution acknowledged by the very institutions for which he had such anarchist disdain. Nevertheless, Still's language of unremitting contempt regarding Barney, written to other artists and representatives of institutions, even as he cozied up to Barney with fulsome praise in his parallel campaigns against others—Rothko, Reinhardt, Janis—was cruelly dishonest. While Barney continued to admire Still and bask in his Americanness until the mid-1960s—the Bronx native sharing his beloved Yankees and his stature at Stillman's Gym with the west-coaster, eventually even purchasing Still's trophy Jaguar—Still two-facedly sustained a "friendship" that included the road trip, gallery visits, empty gestures of support, and—especially—goading Barney's worst angels. And he conducted a similar dynamic with others. He was a quadruple agent in the service of Clyfford Still.

"Still was a sort of force for disintegrating friendships of people," was Dorothy Miller's evaluation after experiencing years of his antics. "It was a very sad thing but it was just the way he [was]."[40]

"The thing that binds us together is that we consider painting to be a profession in an 'ideal society.' We assume the right of insisting that we are creating our own paradise," Barney had said near the conclusion of the Studio 35 sessions in April 1950. "We should be able to act in a professional way on our own terms. We go out into normal society and insist on acting on our own terms."[41]

A year after Barney's declaration, a group of artists who hung around The Club would do just that. In a rented storefront on East Ninth Street, Conrad Marca-Relli and the fresh art entrepreneur Leo Castelli became impresarios for a new breed of salon, inviting artists by word of mouth to show one work each. Over fifty came, some with emerging reputations, some hardly known, along with the de facto lion of the downtown artists, de Kooning, and the now international star Pollock. Kootz did not want the artists in his stable to mix with the Club boys, but Motherwell was always happy to take advantage of exposure.

It turned out to be a "historical phenomenon" that, along with other events of the spring, solidified perception about what was going on in New York art. "People talked. And, in art, money often follows talk." Sidney Janis and Castelli were alert enough to be the beneficiaries of the rising tide.[42]

To almost everyone's surprise except perhaps Castelli's—after all, it was only four months since the "Irascibles" presented themselves as embattled—the show "became a fashionable event." Joop Sander told Mark Stevens and Annalynn Swan that the opening was like "old newsreel pictures from a movie opening in Grauman's Chinese Theatre in Hollywood [with] people getting out in evening clothes." Alfred Barr was "stunned by the number of unfamiliar artists who were included. It confirmed for him and many others that what was happening in New York represented 'a movement' and 'a scene.'"[43]

Barney did not receive a letter of invitation, nor, initially, did he pay much attention. To the "downtown" artists like Nick Carone, Barney wasn't one of them, he "was an outsider, a friend of artists . . . . a 'professor,' a wonderful mind"—even though his second show at Parsons, a major exhibition at a major gallery, had been hanging until the week before. That Motherwell published more, lectured more, and organized more was not held against him. But Barney "didn't live in East Hampton," according to Carone, and this was "the time when everybody went to East Hampton."[44]

For one version of an artist's standing in the still very insular New York art community, a good place to go is Ad Reinhardt's elaborate, sharp, and witty cartoons and genealogical "trees," useful shorthand for an unofficial view of the situation at any given moment. They could be caustic with their inside-joke categories but Reinhardt could hardly be accused of being partisan: he was more widely inclusive than any other compendium of the time and an equal-opportunity cynic. His capsule edits of artist's and critic's verbalizations and staked territories were sometimes savagely satiric but not mocking, and the attention lavished on these charts was proof enough that Reinhardt indeed thought of them as "family trees" and that he was embedded in the eccentric family. His 1946–47 cartoons for *PM* mentioned very few living artists by name, but by early 1950 that had changed. The one that appeared in *Art d'aujourd'hui* while the Ninth Street Show was up, "Imaginary Museum 1951: Modern Art in America," included Barney in the "leaves" among all of the great artists and movements in world history and the better part of contemporary American artists. "Social Realists & Surrealists at work" were marginalized with a "Detour . . . Not the main Road" sign.

"Certainly all of us are getting famous," as Still noted.

One of the first paintings he made after he occupied his Wall Street studio in July 1950 was *The Voice*, a nearly square, 8-by-9-foot work in either egg tempera and oil or an unusual combination of egg tempera and enamel that created a nearly imperceptible contrast (plate 7).[1] It was entirely white.

"My search is for a picture that is simple and self-evident," he said at the time of his first show, "what is there is there."[2] He wanted "a pure means of conveying emotion"[3] and *The Voice* distilled that aspiration with a grand, not to say grandiose, flourish. It might have been a petulant response to Preston's June dismissal of *Abraham*, it might have been a joyful, optimistic response to the clean slate of the new studio— like his first home, a block from the East River. Whatever emotion he was turning into objective fact, the work itself provides an almost holy experience: a physical manifestation that rises above earthly problems to celestial realms, a different kind of outcry, an incandescent whisper of exultation. In a lifetime's oeuvre of undeniable subtlety, it is a singularly subtle but gripping work. Twelve years later, the most passionate collectors would be competing to possess it.

The Name II, virtually the same size but rotated 90 degrees, was made just after *The Voice*. Also white, it was made with oil and the acrylic Magna.

Even this early in his career, working toward what was only his second solo show, Barney was anxious "not to take a formal position." *That* would reduce his work to a "certain kind of product" and he didn't believe that painting was a product. "What happens in painting is to a certain extent a kind of miraculous event"; if he copied himself the work would be dead.[4] Neither did he struggle to be formally innovative. Rather, as a somewhat unnatural artist without an innate facility, he challenged himself to push the canvas as the vessel of his presence in the universe, to remain true to, to distill even further, his conviction that the "artistic act" is, plain and simple, "man's personal birthright."

In the winter of 1950–51 he made a number of paintings that improbably managed to be an outcry even more transgressive than any with which he had surprised his friends or shocked his doubters in his first show. In six works, the vertical dimension echoed his previous work—36, 48, 56, 74, 77 inches—but the horizontal dimension was radically out of proportion. As he worked through the idea, the width shrank progressively from 6 inches, to 5, to 3, until he made the astonishing 95 ⅜-by-1 ⅝-inch piece that he eventually named *The Wild* (plate 10). He wanted to prove that the narrow colors in his earlier works were not "lines" but "areas"—in this case, red wrapped on either side by blue. He was nervous, he was "terrified," but he was emboldened. His self-satisfied pleasure radiates in a photograph from the installation in which Barney, arms tucked confidently behind his back to present his chest ("ornithologists explain the cock's crow as an ecstatic outburst of his power"[5]), trousers high and necktie short in the fashionable way of the time, and Betty Parsons, head thrown back and pencil gripped in her right hand like a maestro about to strike the downbeat, flank *The Wild*.

The Wild was not what a painting was expected to be, but neither was it "sculpture." Barney's first genuinely three-dimensional work, *Here I*, was created in a different context. Other painters—Barney's friend, Pollock, for example—had been experimenting with, and even exhibiting, three-dimensional work. "Sculpture by Painters" at the Museum of Modern Art in 1949 had fifteen from Eakins through Pollock, and his chicken wire and Japanese paper piece was in the March 1951 "Sculpture by Painters" at the Peridot Gallery.[6] But Barney likely found the audacity to pursue his cheeky vision once again in Giacometti, whose second American show opened at Pierre Matisse Gallery four months earlier. There Barney saw *La place*, *La foret*, and *La clairiere*—each work containing multiple attenuated figures of different heights on a platform rather than a pedestal. And once again, Barney saw how the European did it with "spit." Giacometti's radical vision gave Barney the courage to abandon "the principle of composition for [the] immediacy of the total work."[7]

With a show of his *painting* only a few weeks away, abruptly all of the agonizing choices available to him narrowed down to a single focus, and one path suddenly became overwhelmingly urgent.

"I was compelled" he would say ever after, to make *Here I*. Two slim white-skinned elements—the surface of the wider one roughly clotted plaster, and that of the narrower smoothly applied paint—jut 8 feet vertically from hardened mounds of plaster set on a wooden milk crate. It was so stunningly unexpected that when, a few years later, B. H. Friedman first saw it in Barney's studio, he remembered it as "a bucket of cement that [Barney] stuck a piece of wood in," and concluded that Barney "was a Dadaist."[8]

"It came to me as a desire . . . . It came to me in such a way it dominated my whole [life] for days," Barney explained, in some way deflecting his responsibility for it. He had "to stop painting"; he ordered plaster (or was it already handy, previously ordered for repairs in the new studio?); he "couldn't pick up a brush until I had worked with the plaster."[9]

Over ten hectic days, as Annalee remembered it, they "didn't eat or sleep." "I had this vision or desire [and] I had to do it with my hands." Now, instead of Michelangelo, Barney compared himself to his favorite composer: he had "a sense of Mozart's totality," because he "saw not

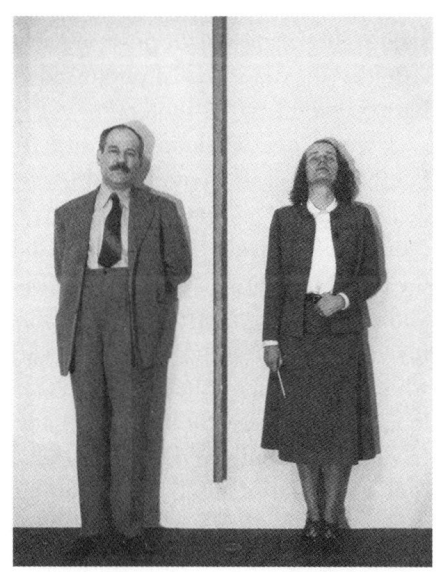

Fig. 25 Barnett Newman and Betty Parsons with *The Wild*, 1951. Photograph Hans Namuth

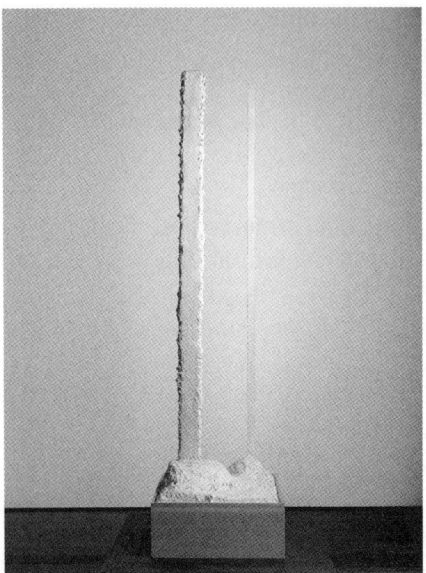

Fig. 26 Barnett Newman, *Here I*, 1950. Reinforced plaster, wood, and a wood-and-wire crate, 96 × 28 ¼ × 26 ½ in. (243.8 × 71.8 × 67.3 cm) excluding base. The Menil Collection, Houston. Gift of Annalee Newman

this particular sculpture," but "a piece of sculpture." The execution was, like Mozart's composing, simply "making an 'exaggeration.' "

Betty "was extremely nervous . . . she thought I would never get ready for the show because I had a few paintings that were, you might say, three-quarters finished. They were there but also I needed more. I was supposed to work, I was under the pressure of a show. But I am very bad about pressure. I don't care, I refuse to submit to pressure." He made a detour to make *Here I*.[10] "I thought I was doing the sculpture only for myself, but the pressure of friends and colleagues that I showed the piece was so great that I allowed myself" to have it in the exhibition.[11] Pollock, especially, "urged him to show it," he often said. That choice, too, then, was out of his hands.

Between making the all-white paintings and the narrow paintings, before he made an idiosyncratic sculpture that seemed to come out of nowhere, Barney took another bold leap. He made what art historian Eugene Goossen identified as, after Pollock's 16-foot *Number 1* (1949), the second earliest "big" canvas of the postwar period.[12] Alex Liberman remembered the "macho attitude," the way it was "pronounced as a powerful outward sign of strength," when Barney would say "18-footer."[13]

It was 18 overwhelming feet of red—or, rather, potentially overwhelming.[14] A numbing effect, the complete drowning of the viewer, was avoided through the deliberate intervention of very thin vertical areas that firmly establish what Barney thought of as "scale"—an inarticulate but insistent felt presence—as opposed to the crude measure of "size."[15] He finished the painting, he said, in December 1950 (although the receipts for large purchases of cadmium red paint date from February 1951) with five proto-zips: two red variants, black, white, and translucent ochrewhite. "But then, in the spring of '51" (it was April 11), "one band was a little soft to me . . . . And so I took it and I changed the color, very, very slightly. And then I turned on the radio and that was the moment that Truman fired MacArthur." He "got a kick out of that," he said, and it prompted the title, *Vir Heroicus Sublimis* (plate 11). Why that name—Man Heroic and Sublime? "The "emotional complex" that the incident provoked in Barney was that "man can be, or is, sublime in his relation to his sense of being aware."[16]

Truly, Barney was exquisitely aware of himself. He was creating some of the boldest art works yet made *and*, during the frantic month of excitement and stress, anxiety, and pressure preceding his show, proposing to Washington Irving High School that he would again teach a course, and encouraging Still, teaching at Brooklyn College on Rothko's recommendation, to find a position there for Barney. (Nothing came of either.) His risk, he would say a few years later, was as great as MacArthur's—no, in fact, greater. He recalled "how terrible the terror it took for me" to make the line; it was "a true act" not "a piece of rhetoric."[17] And the extravagant title was provoked by an "emotional complex" even more complex than he later acknowledged.

A few days earlier, when Barney picked up his newspaper, four headlines across the top of the front page caught his eye. Because Sarah Newman had just begun working for the USIA/Voice of America, he was interested in "Ocean-Going Radio Station To Send 'Voice' to the Reds" for use in its "campaign of truth" against the Communist world. Because of his Zionism, he was interested in "Israel's Aircraft Bomb Syrian Area in Reprisal Move." Because he was an American Jew, and because the photographs of Julius and Ethel Rosenberg looked so familiar—they could have been Barney, or Rothko, and Annalee—he found shocking "Atom Spy Couple Sentenced to Die; Penalities for Rosenbergs Are First Under '17 Law."[18] And because he was feeling intrepid and transgressive, "M'Arthur Wants Chiang Army Used on China Mainland; In Sharp Digression From U.S. Policy, He Views 2d Front Diversion as Logical."[19]

Barney chronically personalized, and overidentified with, public events; they focused his insecurities and rage and provided useful metaphors and referents in his writings. On the eve of his second show, having made what could easily be considered outrageously schismatic works of art, he badly needed to feel heroic.

It wasn't only Barney who seized upon MacArthur in the spring of 1951.[20] In the days after the brilliant and revered World War I veteran, commander of World War II's Pacific theater, and hero of Inchon, had been relieved of his position as Commander-in-Chief of United Nations forces in Korea, MacArthur was actually compared to a god. "Well, I guess I have to relieve God!" President Truman said. A televised speech that the general gave before Congress on April 19 was "a masterpiece of restrained emotion delivered with all the skill and oratorical power of an Anthony burying Caesar." The *Times* reported that national sentiment was such that "apparently television viewers all over the country wept buckets of tears," provoked by the man's presence itself: "To the public he seems completely to fit the phrase of Shakespeare: 'This was the noblest Roman of them all.'" The day Barney's show opened, April 23, "MacArthur the man cast a long shadow across the country . . . as the nation recovered from its biggest emotional binge in many years."[21]

Only the title *Vir Heroicus Sublimis* would be appropriate for 18 feet of defiant Red.

In 1951, the critics did not see the terrible terror or the heroic effort to overcome it. They saw the "extreme detachment of this artist's emotions." They saw not risk, but intellectual "arguments that have more to do with philosophy than with art criticism";[22] not a "kind of miraculous event" but "arid optical hypnotics . . . which seems to have little to do with the special art of painting" (this from the previously overwhelmed Louchheim).[23] The "end results are occasionally striking, stark, and intellectually provocative, but elements of sterility, preciousness, and above all pretentiousness mark all but his modestly scaled canvases."[24]

"This genial theoretician," punned Hess in *Art News*, "again wins his race with the avant-garde, literally breaking the tape."

"A Cecil B. de Mille-size number in Indian-red with five verticals" was one of "the better ideas presented," Hess continued, unable to call the works "paintings" and cruelly misspelling the artist's name, as if he had not registered in the critic—and magazine's editor's—mind.[25] Robert Scull, soon to form an important collection of American art, read Hess's review aghast: "Seven lines in which he ripped Barnett Newman to pieces." Scull kept it as a kind of talisman.[26]

Self-satisfied "educated" viewers, the critics saw what they were looking for—for instance, a variation of Malevich's *White on White*, which at least "was small"—rather than submitting to Barney's specific works. "I want to know with what standards one measures works like these," wailed Genauer. Barney's lecturing tone in his 1950 statement that "These paintings are not 'abstractions,' nor do they depict some 'pure' idea. They are specific and separate embodiments of feeling, to be experienced, each picture for itself. They contain no depictive allusions. Full of restrained passion, their poignancy is revealed in each concentrated image,"[27] and his 1951 instruction, posted on the gallery wall, "There is a tendency to look at large pictures from a distance. The large pictures in this exhibition are intended to be seen from a short distance"—did not help, and added fuel to the mockery. As did the show's announcement, which he designed: a white card, with his name, Genauer wrote, "almost indecipherably printed in white. One gets the feeling that in this whole concept of reducing the specific to the point of near non-existence, the mere thought of a blunt, specific signature was distasteful." Genauer, "willing to go along," did not mention the name "Barnett Newman" in her review.[28]

As had been the case so often with his writing, Barney's apodictic distillation of his meaning did him no service. What he meant was that regarded from a distance the painting became a "picture," a discrete illustration—something that was not his intention at all. Too close, and it became atmosphere, a mood. "A short distance"—that was, as the art historian David Rosand would say, the correct way to view a painted work: the length of an arm plus the length of a brush. That was where one could find the maker. "The subject that motivates me," Barney said, that helped him move on from painting to painting, was "the nature of self. And naturally I can only do it in relation to understanding myself."[29]

Barney, Pollock, Krasner, and Smith—with Noë, Louvis and Dick Schust providing the muscle—hung the show on Parsons's pale gray walls in the windowless room. *Vir Heroicus Sublimis* barely made it into the approximately 10-foot-high, 20-by-30-

foot gallery;[30] two 11-foot works, later titled *Day One* and *Day Before One*, did not. *Vir Heroicus Sublimis* filled an entire wall—the same that, four months earlier, had Pollock's slightly smaller *Autumn Rhythm*. Although photographs show only those paintings subsequently titled *Vir Heroicus Sublimis*, *The Voice, Eve, Adam, Joshua, The Wild,* and the so-called "study" for *Vir Heroicus Sublimis* (Barney always denied that he made studies), and the sculpture *Here I,* a total of fifteen paintings, including five of the extreme narrow works, were included on the contemporaneous price list. In the "back" room, two of the narrow paintings hung behind the desk: *Untitled 4, 1950* and *Untitled 3, 1950* (installed 180 degrees from the way it was later shown). Genauer reported there were "eight canvases and a single sculpture."

Astonishingly, no critic, no contemporary account, addresses or even describes the narrow paintings. Nor does the sculpture *Here I,* installed in front of *The Wild,* get more than a mention. Perhaps aesthetic faculties and intellectual curiosity were exhausted in the confrontation with the "Cecil B. de Mille-size number," the "elephantine panels" that were pushed "to the point where either they or the gallery walls will have to give"; and the shock of "white on white," "Huck Finn's invisible ink." None of Genauer's rote "standards" applied, and she was frustrated and enraged. Neither the artists nor the critics seem to have *seen* these works, seem to have been able to cognitively grasp them; they had used so many brain cells to be snarky and clever.

The critics were particularly ungenerous to Barney. The month before, Preston tempered his review of Rothko's show—"Rothko is a subtle and sensitive colorist . . . But works of art have other obligations"—with "No artistic judgments can, or should be final."[31] Immediately following Barney's exhibition, a very young and green Robert Rauschenberg showed insouciantly monochromatic pieces, some with splatches on unconventional, "unprofessional," supports, and Preston, perhaps relieved not to engage with an artist's verbal rhetoric, indulgently noted the "most successful" were "semigeometrically planned oils, in black, white and yellow areas."[32] But regarding Barney's show, Preston was categorical. "Art has finally been emptied of content."[33] This unusual treatment did not go unnoticed. Belatedly, Greenberg, in the *Partisan Review,* acknowledged Barney had "met rejection from a quarter where one had the most right to expect a puzzled judgment to be a suspended one."[34]

These evaluations were hardly more negative than they had been for Barney's 1950 show. And, to be sure, Genauer described a "crowd of excitedly chattering, worshipful youngsters," and the show as "by a contemporary New York artist who will, within a few months, I warrant, be the new darling of the avant-garde."[35] What stung Barney was the reaction of many of his peers. In his mind they were still a confraternity.

Siskind, the only photographer included in the Ninth Street Show—exhibiting the kind of abstract work that Barney had been so instrumental in encouraging—saw the paintings in Barney's Wall Street studio. "The thing that shocked me," he recalled, "was the fact that the color was so solid and insensitive . . . . There was an idea there, the stripe, the zip and all the crap. And I just didn't say anything . . . . All of his old friends from college didn't care much for it."[36] Annalee's memory reflected the Newmans' experience. "The reception of the second show was even worse" than that of the first, where "at least the artists came [although they] rejected it"; to the second "they didn't come."[37]

Although Buffie Johnson was "electrified" by the show—"just so exciting I was overwhelmed, one beautiful shock after another"[38]—and Pollock, Krasner, Greenberg, and his brand-new girlfriend, Helen Frankenthaler, had a jovial dinner with the Newmans to celebrate "Pollock paints a picture" just out in the current *Art News*, Parsons understood the fragile bonds among the fragile egos in her stable. The show was a "hot one!" Parsons told Still.[39]

Still had not seen the show, but he was anxious to distance himself from Barney and his perceived failure. "Your reactions to Barney's show were of course interesting points to me," he wrote to Rothko. "Although you did not state them I feel the issues involved keenly, and you indeed have my sympathy."[40] Hess's review had not yet come out, but gossip had spread through the artists' community. Still unleashed his analysis of Barney's work—"a death act against the human spirit"—and his "almost pathetic impotence." In Still's view, his own emotional sources were authentic, Barney's contrived; while Still needed no external verification, Barney was using art to satisfy his ambitions for power.[41] Faced with the negative reception of Still's show in April 1950, Barney had tried to rally the other artists in support. But now, with Barney on the ropes, Still conspiratorially preened and flattered. Praise and criticism, Still preached to Rothko, were both dangerous, and must be measured by the man who gives them. "I will feed any man, give him a bed or my shirt. But let him touch my work, my spirit, and his blood will be on his own hands."[42]

Rothko, whose show at Parsons immediately preceding Barney's had gotten unfavorable enough reviews—"Is there some kind of affrontery to common intelligence here? It would seem so"; "they look like sections of a rainbow arranged by a creative response to the extreme line taken by certain twentieth century painters"[43]—was not unhappy to hear Still's opinions of Barney. Rothko was "afraid of other artists," in Tworkov's estimation. All artists wanted "appreciation from others, other artists, critics, the entire art world . . . . [But Rothko] wanted it more than anybody," said Tworkov, "and he wanted it at the highest level, he always wanted to be numero uno."[44]

Later on, in 1965, when Barney's stature had soared, Still continued to discredit the early years of Barney's career: "When I took up residency in New York in 1950, I slowly discovered the range and depth of [Newman's] schemes. And during 1951 I began my repudiation of him and what I had to call the Parsons gang. However, much damage was done by that time and the violation continues to this day in spite of my efforts to separate the free and creative from the parasitical and authoritarian."[45]

Barney didn't "go into a decline"; that was the way some were wont to recount what followed. He was not happy, but he didn't doubt himself. The problem was with the others, who didn't understand or appreciate what he was doing, or—as is possible from the extremity of their reactions—felt threatened by it.

"Barney's show continues to baffle and bewilder but it has also been enormously admired," Parsons told Still, certainly unwelcome news in the ragingly competitive environment.[46]

Editors from *Look* magazine were coming to the gallery for a fashion shoot. The previous spring, Rothko was featured in *Vogue*'s interior-decorating feature, "Make up your Mind: One-Picture Wall or Many-Picture Wall"; a month earlier, also for *Vogue*, Cecil Beaton photographed models in the newest fashions against Pollock's paintings at Parsons. Now Barney decided to require the agent for *Look* to sign a waiver: "It is agreed that under no circumstances is LOOK magazine to use any photographs of models against the large red 18' painting with five stripes by BARNETT NEWMAN or any part thereof. It is agreed that only the smaller pictures are to be used."[47]

"Anita Colby's recipe for Well-dressed Beauty: Everyone can learn the art of making the most of herself," photographed "at the showing of Barnett Newman paintings in the Betty Parsons Gallery" appeared in September. " 'When in doubt, underdress.' Simplicity is the best taste any woman can have," the text read. "Line . . . proportion . . . color [can] create the illusion of the ideal."[48] Barney recalled the episode to make a point about popular capitulation when he had an audience of young acolytes in 1958. It was too novel an experience, he told his students, for him to think ahead, but he did demand that the whole, uncropped painting be included in any shot. When the issue hit the stands long after the show was down, Barney's embarrassment was such that he had his "lawyers" contact the publisher of Colby's forthcoming book, to make certain that the photographs of his paintings as model background would not be used.[49]

It's not surprising that he took that position. What he didn't appear to mention—ever—was that the red "painting" behind Colby was not from the show, nor was it his. Nor, probably, was it even a work of art. And it could have been for this reason that Barney would tell of an otherwise inexplicable "settlement": Annalee got a dress.[50] Whether the *Look* editors decided Barney was too difficult to deal with, or more likely, that the paintings they were given permission to use—those later known as *Adam* and *Eve*—did not flatteringly compliment the red of Colby's "Castillo design for Nanty," they substituted a flat red painted surface for Barney's work. It was an extraordinarily brazen act of philistine contempt for his art. Executed without overt acknowledgment—unlike *New Yorker* cartoons of the period referring to Rothko or Pollock—it was an unforgiveable assault on his dignity. "A man and his work are one," was his creed.[51]

He continued to be bothered by *Adam* after the show closed; it needed something more to become "the real statement [he] wanted to make." He added an additional vertical, then dated the painting "1951, 1952" not "1951–1952." He had done the same with *Vir Heroicus Sublimis*—"1950, 1951"—because he did not want to suggest, or imply, that he had worked on it over a period of time. The point—the stance that he had to make clear vis-à-vis the work—was that "I didn't study the painting, I did it in 1950 and it had something. But it bothered me. Well, at one moment in 1951, I made an absolutely impulsive change which worked, so I date it 1950 plus 1951 just historically to make it correct."[1]

This story entered the gospel, and it had everything to do with pressure engendered by Still and Rothko—at least equally entrenched in their own signature formats—and their coalescing supporters. The precise dating of paintings, the detection of traces of submerged influence, had become almost more urgent than the impact of works themselves. "The American myth of sacrosanct originality . . . has made the possibility of derivation more unmentionable than that of venereal disease," wrote Hess that spring.[2]

The atmosphere was that sour. By the summer, Reinhardt claimed he couldn't "even remember the other nine [?] of the Irascible Eighteen."[3] Still wrote to Parsons, "Regards to all those who are still on speaking terms with me."[4]

So aggressively did Still seek primacy that even the New York territory with which Barney had become identified—Stillman's Gym, Yankee Stadium—Still now proclaimed as his.[5] His relentless bad-faith maneuvering behind a friendly front was a virus that corrupted Barney's life and career, even as Barney, somewhat naïvely, was a willing host. He loved Still and believed that Still loved him. And the next few years of odd, even self-destructive, behavior by Barney cannot be understood apart from this dynamic.

"Newman said a few nights ago that since I got here it seems to him that he has been on a spree, and now doesn't intend to leave this fall. Whether it is the heat, my crazy energy, or just a combination of a lot of things I don't know. But things have certainly been rolling," reported Still.[6] Since there is no other indication that Barney was thinking of "leaving" in the fall—unless one counts his habitual delinquency regarding electric bills—it may have been Still's invention. Reinhardt, a few months later, confirmed Barney's high spirits: "Mark and Mell say they see only people with kids these days," he wrote to Rita Salomon, the woman who would become his wife. "How many couples make their own world in order to cope with their lives!—As a contrast, Barney & Analee [*sic*], because of Barney are in quite a social whirl."[7]

Not Barney, but the mercurial Still left—a month after he wrote "New York continues to be 'it.' " Parsons "is not having an opening group show here this fall so no opportunity is lost to exhibit the work in that quarter."[8] He had stayed around long enough, however, to be lauded with the rest in Aline Louchheim's article for the October *Vogue*, "Betty Parsons: Her Gallery, Her Influence." "Twelve Abstract artists, all constant and provocative exhibitors," each photographed with his or her work, surrounded a head shot of Parsons: Stamos, Reinhardt, Ferber, Rothko, Tomlin, Day Schnabel, Walter Murch, Lipton, Pousette-Dart, Pollock, Still, and Barney. Barney was singled out as "the artist who occupies a special position in the group . . . . [Parsons] seems to have special respect for Newman's opinions." There was no protest—indeed, Still remarked that it was "a pleasant surprise."[9]

"Barnett Newman has very small, sad, closely-set eyes under a high, balding forehead, a slow, rambling manner of speech, larded with mystical phrases," wrote Louchheim, so taken with those words eighteen months earlier. "Newman is incontrovertibly one of the Parsons Gallery's most controversial painters"; when he first exhibited paintings there, Parsons was "nervous as a mother hen."[10]

On WNYC radio Parsons answered charges that she had made a place where her artists lived in an ivory tower. Without condescending to the audience, nor mystifying in support of her group, she praised their seriousness. They "created a world truly related to life, rather than follow the historical trends of art, notions of tradition, and conventional ways of living . . . . Only the mature can make a real history of the living," whereas "the adolescent is involved in imitation of style, modes, fashions of modern art, which produce pictures that may have great style but are devoid of content."[11] Listeners might agree that she made an excellent representative; not so the thorny bunch that made up much of her stable. *They* wanted sales, and some thought Parsons made "a point of not selling." She would "go into her back room if a rich buyer entered," said Alexander Liberman, "you had to sort of rape Betty, violate her" to buy a painting.[12]

Those patrons and collectors in 1951 came from a segment of the population more likely to be reading *Vogue* than *Art News* or, even, *Life* or *Time*; they were the people about whom Louchheim wrote "almost every Parsons' show . . . furnishes fuel for dinner-party conversation."[13] Here, precisely, was the schizophrenic nature of an artist's life reflected back at him. Three months later this deep discomfort led the four artists she most admired—Still, Rothko, Pollock, and Barney—the ones she thought of as "the Four Horsemen of the Apocalypse,"[14] "The Giants,"[15] to call a meeting in her Fortieth Street apartment and confront Parsons with an ultimatum: she had to stop showing most of the other artists in the gallery.[16] From the beginning, Parsons had shown both talents in whom she believed and friends—including some investors—who believed in her. Now, the four would demand a change. If she focused on them, they would "make [her] the most famous dealer in the world," they grandiosely promised.[17]

Whatever the precise number, or nature, of the meetings that followed—testimonies vary—and whatever the individual reasons, and in spite of participating in commemorative group and anniversary shows, neither Still, nor Rothko, nor Pollock, nor Newman would have a one-man show at the Parsons Gallery again.

"De Hooch to de Kooning by de Hess," Barney called *Abstract Painting: Background and American Phase*. Hess's primer began with an elementary walk through a formal analysis of four 17th-century paintings by Pieter de Hooch and continued into 1951, but did not include Barney. It was the unkindest cut of all that season of Barney's second show. The crack delighted Dorothy Miller ("Barney loved to do things like that"), his wit barely concealing his irritation but entertaining everyone around. It wasn't that Barney had a late start and was missing some *bona fides* that kept Hess from including him. Hess gave space to, in his own words, the "self-taught" Balcomb Greene, and "almost entirely self-taught" Gorky, and "mainly self-taught" Tworkov; and to Motherwell, "trained in philosophy, art history, and a gifted writer, [who] only began painting seriously in the summer of 1941," and to Franz Kline, who "did not have his first one man show until 1950—the year of his fortieth birthday." And it wasn't only "downtown" artists clustered around Hess's favorite, de Kooning, who received attention: Reinhardt, Gottlieb, and Rothko of the "uptown" artists were there. It seemed to Barney purposeful and mean that Hess respectfully quoted Rothko and Gottlieb's 1943 letter to the *Times* without acknowledging Barney's contribution.

Hess genuinely did not "get" Barney's paintings. His own limitations hobbled his writing about the new art: beautifully crafted, erudite, and often poetic words required a relatively rigid construct to support them. In *Abstract Painting*, it was the generative connection between Expressionism and abstraction—which displeased many of the artists while cloaking them in a terminology not of their choice. "Painting is both eye and hand and when words attempt to intercept their vision and motion they must either digress or approximate," the text acknowledged.

> We can wander into the fields of chronology or biography or speculate about contemporaneous sensibility . . . . We can try to communicate a similar response with different materials and, like a Lewis Carroll character, break into little poems of our own. Then, usually we feel that the picture under discussion is standing by contemptuously, untouched, untroubled, and vastly unenlightened.

Yet Hess was loathe to jettison the crutch, to attempt to have and convey a fresh, unprocessed response; he liked to be able to chart an evolution. About Barney's work, there was nothing Hess could say. Eighteen years later, after he had come to appreciate passionately the painting, he fell into the same trap of requiring a system. And so he was dependent to the point of embarrassment on "secret symmetries" and popish interpretations of Kabbalah.[18]

Although it was aggressively promoted as "the book you have been waiting for on abstract art," Hess's volume pleased almost no one. Even downtown, The Club held panels on the "Hess Problem." Invited by *Partisan Review*—some thought at the suggestion of Greenberg—to review it along with *Revolution and Tradition: Modern American Art* by John Baur, the head of the Brooklyn Museum's Department of Painting and Sculpture, Barney was defensive after the reception of his show.[19] To soothe his ego he returned to a familiar device, the excessively rhetorical, intellectually contemptuous essay. Still encouragingly fanned the flames. "I hope that you are deep in your reply to the travesty on painting by Hess of recent note. My wishes go strongly with your effort, that you will find it pleasant, potent, and effective fun . . . . This is a war, not a lollipop exchange."[20]

In agitated handwriting, in rage-filled draft after draft, Barney bristled at the very idea that American artists needed to explain themselves. But quickly he got to what was really eating him: Hess himself, who had been so mockingly dismissive of his show. Hess was

a bureaucrat [at an] art trade paper, hates his role, and given to believe by some of his artist friends that maybe he is an intellectual if he only would give himself a chance. The chance came and here is a book to prove that he is not a hack, that he really can think better than the intellectuals and artists who have [made] him so faithfully their servant. The result is a vicious, ugly book that can serve the avant garde no useful purpose + can only harm Hess himself for the book cannot die a quick death. Its danger lies that it may impress the bureaucratic institutions and the high fashion magazines may now fill their pages with his stuff.

Barney compared his support for de Kooning to what Craven did for Benton, but "more complicated and pretentious more highly dissembled but consequently less effective." The overdetermined theory was "disastrous for De Kooning because he has to stand on Hess's brain— + it is just a bit soggy for any kind of solid pedestal." De Kooning "is the master virtuoso" of all "the child prodigies now in New York," and most other "American 'avant gardists'" are involved in sensation, in eye titillation . . . empty, hypnotic, subjective, private."

Calling one a sensation painter [meaning] that he automatically has no content but eye pleasure [is] a new kind of Philistinism under the guise of intellectualism. The scholastic thinkers understood this better. Kabalistic thinking is fundamentally built on the mystery of vision . . . sensation involves the total being, neither the aesthetic reaction alone and certainly not the intellectualism.

Nor could it have pleased Barney to read Hess's dismissal of his heroes Monet and Pissarro. Monet, Hess wrote, "became involved with paintings which he must have known could not work. The Haystacks and Rouen Cathedral series are among the first sacrifices of art to avant-garde."[21]

Barney could not simply disagree with Hess, or mock his weaknesses, as Hess did when he reviewed Barney. The book, Barney argued, was "dangerous," not only "bad but sinister."

I see the implications in it of a case theory for a slave art . . . . This is the perfect art for state capitalism, for the dominance by institutions, and art of mumbo-jumbo, for clarity may lead to freedom so why not feed the ambiguous man with ambiguous art? [The reference to the "ambiguous man," Barney said, derived from Sartre.]

Moreover, Hess excluded "Matta, Clyfford Still, Barnett Newman, Stamos who have all played an important part" in American painting, but included "such moot figures as Hyman Bloom, Lee Gatch, Balcomb Greene who are all involved in depictive paintings."

This intemperate version was not the one that Barney submitted to the editors of *Partisan Review*; that essay's rhetoric was significantly toned down, prudently missing his final remarks about "a police state."

"There are a good many artists who already stand like unemployed policemen. Now comes Mr. Hess and with his stalinic thinking makes a bid to serve"—and here, once again, in a passionate rage Barney lost all sense of proportion—"as once did Abetz," the German ambassador to Vichy France. Hess was a Jew who didn't understand "the Kabalistic explanation of the Hebrew letter ע which means eye," he was "stalinic" and a Nazi. Barney was angry enough that the manuscript that *Partisan Review* did see included the statement,

art books are notorious for not being read; it is the reproductions that count; publicity is publicity, etc. etc. . . . But when by some misfortune, the book is read, what then? I believe that a bad book is a bad book even though some of my colleagues, or should I say some of my best friends, appear in it . . . Mr. Hess's book is a bad one because it misses the point of what is taking place in American painting. Mr. Hess thinks that it lies in that endless talking-war going on at Eighth Street . . . . instead of a sincere critical examination, he uses the artists he discussed to build for himself a fantastic tower of Babel from which, in his stalinic dream, he imagines he can dominate the American artist.

"Loads of people thought Pollock was a terrific figure and to be respected; but when it came to an entourage they camped with Bill" de Kooning.[22] It struck John Bernard Myers, who had just co-established the Tibor de Nagy Gallery to represent a younger generation, that it was "extraordinary" that people had to choose between de Kooning (representing "tradition") or Pollock—representing a "totally modern concept."[23]

As happened with Barney's obituary for Gorky, those who commissioned it did not publish the essay. Barney always insisted that Hess "brought so much pressure"[24] that it was killed, but a careful review of Hess's own relationship with *Partisan Review* at this time suggests that was unlikely.[25] That didn't stop it from festering with both men—Hess had gotten wind of the substance—and in 1955, when Barney's emotional condition was especially attenuated, this episode was dramatically revisited.

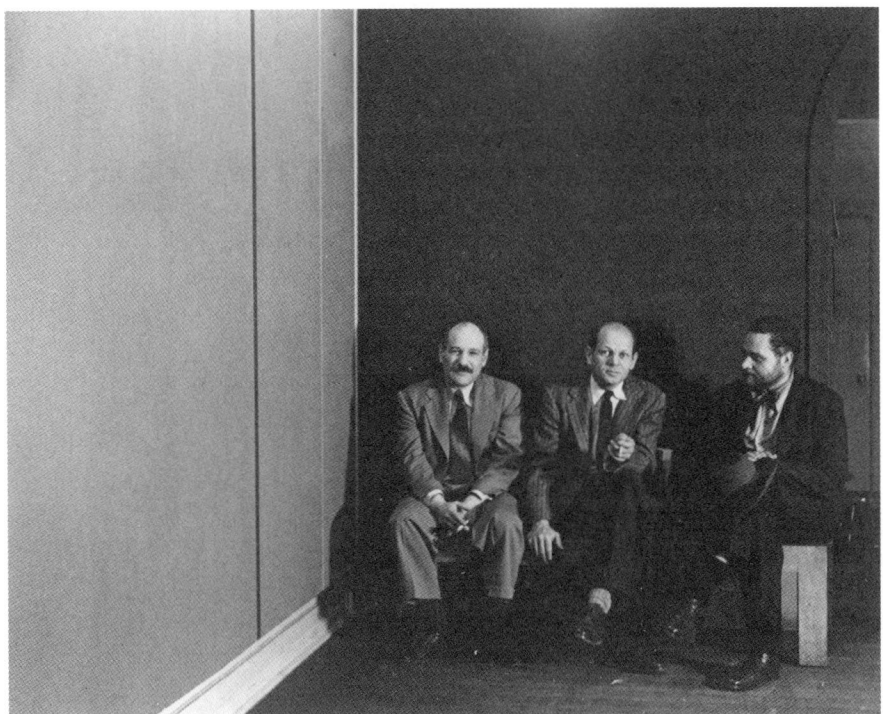

Fig. 27 Barnett Newman with Jackson Pollock and Tony Smith at Betty Parsons Gallery for Newman's 1951 show. At left is *Vir Heroicus Sublimis*. Photograph Hans Namuth

Barney, Pollock and Tony Smith fill a bench in the corner of Parsons's gallery perpendicular to *Vir Heroicus Sublimis*, the three men companionably sharing a smoke and a moment of relief (fig. 27). Several frames from a roll taken by Hans Namuth on the warm spring evening opening of Barney's second show are among the most reproduced photographs of Abstract Expressionist painters ever taken. Earlier, in a whirl of motion and emotion and anxiety they had installed the show together, but now they were satisfied. Pollock's eyes are a little glazed, but there is no other indication that this was a rare sober interlude in a binge that had been going on for several months, during which Smith and Pollock had become almost co-dependent as Pollock had fallen off the wagon and Jane Smith had gone to Europe to study and perform. Barney and Annalee, at their finest when permitted to indulge their profound *Menschlichkeit* instinct, had been anchoring influences for the two men.

Both Newmans loved Pollock. "You wouldn't find many people around of whom that was true," recalled a friend who "gave Pollock a very wide berth." He could be "extremely aggressive and difficult; if I saw him at a party, I would sit on the other side of the room. It was that bad. Many people who had a huge respect for him as a painter didn't want to get too involved," but he never showed that side of himself to Barney and Annalee. There was never any judgment, "they always spoke of him with real love and reverence,"[26] and the time they spent together was "mostly . . . unspectacular, like any friends." They walked around, talked about cars, went to plays and movies—especially fight movies but not the fights themselves, because procuring tickets was "too complicated." They kidded about "getting away from it all."[27] They celebrated their birthdays together—Pollock's was January 28 and Barney's January 29. When Pollock, capriciously, viciously humiliated Lee, Barney and Annalee's presence and support for Lee forced a small measure of contrition. When Pollock went on a bender in Manhattan, Barney and a Springs neighbor of the Pollocks, Dr. Joel Gribitz, searched through the city, tracked him down, and got him back to Long Island. Gribitz recognized Barney as "one of Pollock's real friends," not, as was becoming common, a member of Pollock's entourage.[28]

On a visit to the East End, Pollock and Ossorio came to meet Smith and the Newmans at the station. "He was obviously intoxicated. Barney and I got in the car, and Jackson started to drive. It made me very nervous," Annalee recalled. " 'Jackson,' I said, 'I have to get out.' " She told them she would ride in Ossorio's car. Barney was rarely provoked by his wife, but now he was "very angry . . . . He said that my getting out of the car made it worse, because Jackson insisted on driving. If I had stayed in the car Jackson would have driven a little, and then he would have fallen asleep. Barney would have pushed him over, and he would have driven. But since I got out of the car, Jackson had to prove that he could drive, and he was driving from one side of the road to the other."[29]

When Smith was apart from his wife, depressed and in debt, Barney and Annalee wrapped him in emotional support and encouragement.[30] When Jane wrote from Germany, it was not unusual for her to write a single letter to "Annalee, Barney, Lee & Jackson"—so sure was she that Barney and Pollock were in constant communication. And Smith reciprocated; he had faith in Barney, he didn't just love him personally. "Don't criticize Barney, he knows what he's doing," he told doubters.[31] Sympathizing with Barney's frustration about the language critics used, Smith tried to enlist his old childhood friend, Elizabeth "Sitty" McFadden, to do "some pieces in terms of straight reporting instead of the jargon."[32] Barney made multiple visits to Guilford, Connecticut to encourage the progress of the compound overlooking the Long Island Sound that Smith designed for the Fred Olsens, characterizing one wall as "light, soft, yet intense as the finger of God," and another as having the "quality of the resurrection." This was the kind of language they used with each other.[33]

With Reinhardt, too, the Newmans had a deeply affectionate relationship, their time together considered "family" time. "Fix up your car, see you in a few weeks, let's hit the Connecticut hills," Reinhardt, teaching a summer session in Laramie, Wyoming, wrote to "Squaw Annalee, Chief Barney."[34]

As intimate as Barney and Reinhardt were as friends, as mutually supportive privately and publicly, the latter never dropped his cynical assessment of the endeavor in which they were all involved. It was not confidentially parceled out in Still's manner, each fulminating rant tailored to the individual listener's vanity; Reinhardt flaunted his intellectual and witty cynicism democratically. All of the Studio 35 session artists' pronouncements and condemnations and competitiveness of the previous few months were burlesqued in Reinhardt's "Museum Racing Form: The latest Racing Dope, pigeonhole the ponies, a page of COMICS," published in the tiny journal *trans/ formation* that Harry Holtzman edited. Twelve dense text-and-image panels strained the horse-racing conceit, but those in the know could imagine the sources of "Out of the Horses' Mouth" paraphrases: "An artist should never speak, but"; "I'm a primitive . . . I don't know what I'm doing . . . please buy my masterpieces anyway"; "I'm more advanced than the advanced"; "I look through outer reality to see the inner reality"; "My painting paints me." Just about everyone was comprehensively and unjudgmentally skewered. The "18 scratches" in "the Bandwagon" panel was not an arbitrarily chosen number. Nor did Reinhardt spare the superstructure of museums; nor critics and their "tip sheets"; nor kingmakers—"Leading Jockeys" Craven, Soby, and Frankfurter rode Benton, Shahn and Lebrun (respectively) and Genauer, Greenberg, Barr, McBride, and Hess rode Rattner, Pollock, Lippold, Tchelitchew, and de Kooning. Reinhardt's pun-filled art comics provide as good a barometer as we have to the chatter around the scene.

Divorced from his first wife, Reinhardt was in love with the beautiful young artist Rita Salomon, a Jewish refugee from Germany who had gotten to know several of the New York artists when she was studying with the painter Norman Lewis. The summer of 1951 when Reinhardt was teaching in Wyoming, and struggling with insecurities about his career, the maneuverings in the art community, the decision of whether to get married again, it was Barney with whom he'd ruminate. "There's no relation between love and marriage," Barney often told him, Reinhardt wrote to Salomon. Did what followed—"Marriage is a relationship between two people, practical, social, sober, of the real world, ordinary, every-day reality, real life, and love is like art, fantastic, special, wild, subjective, transcendent, illogical, non-sensical, irrational"[35]—come from discussions with Barney as well? It's fascinating to imagine Barney as an authority in such tender matters. His early romantic poetry written to Annalee notwithstanding, he had extraordinarily limited experience with "the babes," as he liked to call them. But he did know marriage. It must have been tremendously affirming for Barney that a worldly man such as Reinhardt looked to him for life advice. "Barney tells me that there's an article on wives in the current issue of Life 'The Wife Problem—wives of business executives.' "[36]

Over the next couple of years, the two couples—Salomon and Reinhardt, and Annalee and Barney—formed the closest thing Salomon had to a family. "Rita was a little Polish [*sic*] girl living with an English family during the war," was the way Annalee remembered the younger woman from this time; reminded of the suffering of her own French cousin, Annalee felt maternal and protective toward Salomon. Shortly after coming to New York and a brief first marriage, Salomon "met Ad [who] was on his own; his wife had just left him . . . . going out with a different girl every night. But [Rita] fell madly in love with him." Ad was fond of Annalee because she "once told him what I thought of him after two martinis," leaving out the mystery of what that was, as well as what circumstance made the normally abstemious Annalee drink two martinis.[37] From Europe in mid-1952, Reinhardt sent multitudes his now famous postcards, but those to Barney and Annalee were especially warm.

Until the "pious absurdit[y]"[38] of Barney's lawsuit in mid-1954, they were extraordinarily close. They talked about everything, including what Reinhardt was writing. Salomon felt like Barney and Annalee were surrogate in-laws. If the Newmans spent an evening at the Reinhardts and it was approaching Annalee's bedtime, both Barney and Reinhardt would escort her home, and then continue walking and talking, sometimes for hours.

To a significant extent, the substitute family of Newman, Reinhardt, Smith, and Pollock psychologically sustained each in the dark and challenging years of 1952, 1953, and most of 1954.

Nineteen fifty-one did not end well for Pollock. In November he showed recent so-called "black and white" works—actually thinned black Duco enamel on raw canvas—that included figurative references. The reviews were intrigued: the "new work seems . . . to have gained immeasurably" wrote Devree in the *Times*;[39] Pollock had "materially increased the formal impact . . . there is more to conjure with and to evoke poetic meaning and feeling" noted Carlyle Burrows in the *Herald Tribune*.[40] But the work was not well received by his peers and there were very few sales. The artist spent most of the holiday season drunk.

It was not a good time for Barney, either. Between the end of September and the end of November he bounced twelve checks. He was in arrears with all of his bills.

For Still, too, things had gotten "a bit out of hand," again he found New York inhospitable and he returned to San Francisco earlier than intended.[41] To Barney, he wrote that it was "imperative that I continue in the way we spoke of many times this fall and winter. The gallery situation has now become even more sinster [*sic*] and socially debauching than the Universities, if that is possible. I am convinced that we must clear ourselves of the implications of the entire exploitive idiocy before we are lost in the bog of its careerism, its neuroses, and its intellectual corruption. We have already been to a great extent sold out, our meanings obscured [*sic*] by ignorance and good intentions and our very survival jeopardized by those so anxious to show what they have found. And all for love, you know, always for love———. I am definitely through with the Gallery on 57th street as now constituted. I cannot afford from any point of view to pay the price they exact of the man and his work. I doubt that either you or Mark will continue with it much longer. Pollocks [*sic*] world is another matter. I am not nor ever was any part of it."[42]

Back in San Francisco Still immediately regretted his decision and made plans to return to New York in mid-January.[43] He was committed to "denying" the "[Andrew] Ritchies . . . Barrs, Parsons[es], every one" who was "a block to, or perverter of, my meanings."[44] But he was also very happily cultivating a sycophantic relationship with Dorothy Miller, who was at that moment selecting the artists for the April installment of her next "Americans" exhibition.

THIRTY-THREE

"FIFTEEN AMERICANS"

"Give us billboards!" demanded Barney—or Rothko. Condé Nast art director Alex Liberman had invited them to a luxurious luncheon in October 1951 after the article he commissioned on Parsons and her artists appeared.[1] The celebration at the exclusive restaurant Chambord may have been the first and last occasion when Parsons, Pollock, Rothko, Still, Reinhardt, and Barney were all together in high spirits. Big was the direction they agreed should be followed . . . and then, almost immediately it became one more territory to contest.

Six months after he completed *Vir Heroicus Sublimis*, Barney was working on the equally enormous blue ocean of *Cathedra*—unfinished at the time of the luncheon, and unfinished when Still saw it in Barney's studio, "just before" Still "did his own large black painting"—as Barney later claimed.[2]

The careerist calculations, the dissembling and shifting alliances, infected them all. "I'm making a special effort to finish my 12 foot canvas this year," Reinhardt reported to Salomon at Christmas, "Though Mark and Barney don't want me to show it because they say its [*sic*] different from the rest of the work—this is my biggest problem these days."[3] Deferring to what he assumed were best intentions, Reinhardt allowed Barney and Rothko to hang the show in early January. "I'm more pleased with this show than any I've had and both rooms look exactly like I would have wished them to look."[4]

Barney had reason, in the beginning of 1952, to feel his career was secure, even if opinions of his work were not. His name was now recognized enough that Preston in the *Times*, reviewing a show of early 20th-century abstraction, could casually drop the observation, "who knows, there may be, this very moment, a Pollock behind the Iron Curtain, a Barnett Newman in some Shangri-la."[5]

And, finally, he had Greenberg's considerable intellectual weight behind him. At the same time that *Partisan Review*'s editors were dunning Barney for his review of *Abstract Painting*, the critic wrote that Barney's two shows:

> exhibited both nerve and truth . . . . Newman is a very important and original artist. And he has little to do with Mondrian . . . . People have been bewildered by this art, but there is no question of shock value; Newman simply aimed at and attained the maximum of his truth within the tacit and evolving limits of our Western tradition of painting. Some of his paintings come off, some don't; one can tell the difference. They may not be easel pictures, or murals in any accepted sense, but what do difficulties of category matter? These paintings have an effect that makes one know immediately that he is in the presence of art.

Mentioning no specific work, Greenberg had a wider agenda:

Newman took a chance and has suffered for it in terms of recognition. Those who so vehemently resent him should be given pause, however, by the very fact that they do. A work of art can make you angry only if it threatens your habits of taste; but if it tries only to take you in, and you recognize that, you react with contempt, not with anger. That a majority of the New York "avant-garde" gave Newman's first show the reception it did throws suspicion on them—and says nothing about the intrinsic value of his art.[6]

In the same column, Greenberg wrote about Pollock that his new pictures hinted "at the innumerable unplayed cards in the artist's hand. And also, perhaps, at the large future still left to easel painting . . . he has a lot to say."[7]

It was in this atmosphere—each man wrestling with his own demons and illusions of solidarity, and with Parsons having in her hand a request from Dorothy Miller for loans of Pollock, Rothko, and Tomlin works for the upcoming "Americans" show[7]—that she had to face the ultimatum by her favorite artists at the end of January.[8]

Virginia Wright, hailing from a Pacific Northwest timber family and in 1952 fresh out of Barnard, found Parsons somewhat too casual an agent when she attempted to buy a Rothko painting. "Oh, well, you know, this is not an important sale for Rothko, so you'll have to talk to him about it," Wright recalled Parsons saying. "I can see why they left her . . . . there was this sort of mental set then that art was not a commodity."[9] Rothko finally agreed to sell Wright his painting, on two conditions: one, she must agree to hang it at that moment. And two, she must not lend it to any museum for at least a year. "Well, you know, that was a no brainer because nobody was asking. That was the way they carried on in those days. The art was so important and you had to do right by the art."[10]

In the early 20th century there was very little of anything that could be called publicity or media attention concerning contemporary art, and what existed was very limited: the number of those intellectually or economically invested was miniscule. Interest increased through the '20s, '30s and '40s, and because of the political history of those years, the buying, showing, and selling of art was—in the artists' minds—burdened by a fuzzy ethical responsibility. The new ascendency of Janis Gallery, which had opened across the hall from Parsons in late 1948, combined with the looming "Americans" show at MoMA to provide something of a catalyst and a focus to a significantly altered American "art world"—more precisely, the beginning of the "art world" as we have come to know it. Was it necessary to obey strict lines of jurisdiction? What was wrong with a little mutual back-scratching? Janis seemed so much more on the ball in the postwar media–cultural–economic dynamism. He could show both acknowledged European modern masters like Léger and Rousseau, *and* avant-garde Americans.

Janis mounted the "American Vanguard Art for Paris Exhibition" at the end of December 1951; after, it would travel to introduce the "Parisian art-going public" to advanced painting of the U.S.[11] Parsons men and women Rothko, Pollock, Reinhardt, Sterne, and Tomlin were installed alongside Baziotes, Gottlieb, Guston,

Kline, Motherwell, Tworkov, and others with the assistance of a young Leo Castelli in what Janis hoped were resonant pairs. It was not lost on the restless painters that Janis represented the estate of Gorky. De Kooning, who had begun to consider Egan's representation "amateurish,"[12] had already formed an understanding with Janis by the spring of the previous year. Kline and Baziotes followed.

As soon as an artist defected to Janis, the dealer would raise prices. Collectors "seemed to rather spend a little bit more for art than a little bit less," noticed the future collector Wright, who worked in Janis's gallery after she graduated from college.[13]

The jockeying for stardom became more sophisticated. To the 21st-century spectator it can appear like a reality show—"The Real Artists of New York City"—filled with posturing, vicious backbiting, undermining, shameless fawning, and engineered "together" time. But to the artists at the center, it felt like a matter of life and death. The "downtown" painter Friedel Dzubas saw "going out for votes" by consorts. Elaine de Kooning "pulled in Tom Hess and directed the campaign . . . . She played politics with the populace . . . and the young poets, like [Frank] O'Hara." Lee Krasner (Pollock) "played with the elect—Rothko, Still, Ossorio, Clem." De Kooning's "partisans pushed Still aside as they pushed Newman aside. They did the same to Rothko."[14] The "uptown" artists, who had less active mates, fended for themselves with the critics, curators, and dealers.[15]

Still was at Pollock's studio when Greenberg was working "with Jack and Barney" on the *Partisan Review* essay; the three were interested in coming to his studio as well so that he "too could get a plug," Still told the painter Edward Dugmore, his former student and close friend. "When I refused to play ball with the sordid nonsense my name was not mentioned" in the article. Then he crowed that he was forced to consent to be shown in Miller's exhibition in order to make clear that his "departure from 57th street does not mean absolute suicide or censorship,"[16] and carried on with his regular, fawning correspondence with Miller and her husband Holger Cahill—forgetting that two years earlier he told Barney that "To recognize or be recognized by these public punk balls [San Francisco art appreciators] is to strike into oblivion damn near equal to that generated by the Museum of Modern Art."[17]

Rothko, who since 1946 lived and worked out of a studio on Sixth Avenue a couple of blocks from MoMA, frequented the small Italian restaurant on Fifty-Second Street where Miller and Barr ate. After a while, he began joining them, to "sit and talk," Miller noted. Soon, he would see Miller more regularly, when in 1952 he took a studio at 106 West Fifty-Third Street and he sought, and was given, a special pass to wheel his baby daughter's carriage around the sculpture garden.[18]

Barney, too occupied with waging war in his head against Hess to properly court Miller himself, relied on Greenberg's endorsement. Pollock, who had Greenberg's blessing and Krasner's shrewdness in his camp, was trying to cement a relationship with a dealer other than Parsons—someone who had the proper stature for an artist as major as he, plus business acumen. "Caught up in the idea of getting art out of the 'arty' circles," Barney told an interviewer, Pollock began to consider as an agent Grant Mark—a Dr. Feelgood psychologist he had been seeing and who had grandiose marketing ambitions. But when, at Pollock's urging, Barney met Mark, Barney put the kibosh on the plan. "I used to be in business with my father," Barney said, and he recognized an operator when he saw one.[19]

There was synergistic publicity around MoMA's show. Wildenstein Gallery asked the regular critics from seven publications to select their "favorite" 20th-century American paintings. *Art News*'s editors invited Reinhardt to submit "A Nosegay for the Art-Schmeckers," a two-page spread filled with the artist's brazen and disdaining puns, including, close to home, "peeping-tom hessbackwards." And *Life* ran a feature on the dealer Edith Halpert and her stable at The Downtown Gallery, "New Crop of Painting Proteges: Dealer with an Eye for Talent Tries to Pick Tomorrow's Stars." An "Irascible"-type photograph of her "oldtimers" including Stuart Davis, Jacob Lawrence, Shahn, and Kuniyoshi reinforced Halpert's prominence. But the work of her "discoveries" was derivative and had no urgency—which is why *Life* had nary a discouraging or snarky word. One of the artists—Irving Kriesberg, a middling painter later called a "figurative expressionist"—had been chosen for inclusion in "Fifteen Americans."

"Fifteen Americans." That was the biggest prize in the immediate universe, and the grail that eluded Barney—and Reinhardt. Artists were doing more than jostling for inclusion: they wanted to—and felt newly empowered to—wrest control.

Miller wanted to show Ferber's just-completed commission for the Congregation B'nai Israel synagogue, and Ferber went up against those who had commissioned it to make clear that was also what he wanted, even before it "leaves New York" and even though, not insignificantly, as Miller wrote to the rabbi, "this would mean postponement of the dedication date for the works of art in Millburn."[20]

Still, who generally did not allow studio visits, had a list of conditions before he agreed to let Miller in. Once there, she selected "more paintings than there would be room to hang" because she wanted to have "a range of works" from which "to make the final choice." They had agreed upon a "tentative arrangement . . . when Still was inspired to make that [13-foot] black painting"[21]—the one Barney (referring to himself in the third person for the historical record) claimed was a "take off on Newman's black on black and big ones"[22]—which replaced two "normal sized paintings" in the previously approved installation.[23] Still only agreed to appear at the opening if Miller promised to escort him herself.[24]

She selected "15 or 20" paintings at Rothko's studio. When the truck arrived at the museum, however, it was clear Rothko had made drastic changes, adding a number of pictures for which there would be no room. He would not allow Miller to arrange his gallery, he would not accept the museum's lighting. He wanted his paintings hanging edge to edge around all four walls, with twice the museum's illumination in each fixture in addition to the overhead lights. Miller thought it was a fear that he would "literally be outshined by Still," even though Rothko magnanimously had originally suggested him. (Miller already intended to include Still.[25]) Barr and Rene d'Harnoncourt eventually wore Rothko down,[26] but to his further irritation, Still's painting could be seen through a doorway. Miller strategically placed potted plants.

De Kooning agreed to participate, then withdrew, and Pollock, of course, was selected.

At least one contemporary critic noted Barney's absence. A. L. Chanin, in the liberal newspaper *The Compass*, judged that "Still will probably emerge as the sensation of the show—and the season—at least by virtue of novelty, and his ruthless disregard for even the slightest conventions of tradition . . . . While Still seems the last word and the most extreme example in discarding traditional values, and giving us so-called 'pure' painting, there is another painter, Barnett Newman (not represented) who is hot on his trail, with even 'purer' art, and closer to either fragmentary statement or almost nothingness."[27]

Still told Barney that Rothko had lobbied against Barney's inclusion, a story Rothko obliquely confirmed years later. (This was probably the first step in the dramatic decline of the relationship between the two men, with earlier insults invoked retrospectively.[28]) In 1981 Miller told historian Avis Berman that the first time she had gone to Still's studio at Cooper Square, "I asked him if he would be in this show of mine, and I was sure he would say no. And he said, 'Well, who else is going to be in it?' He had to know that. So I said, 'Newman and Rothko.'" She added, and "'a group of . . . more realistic painters.' And he said, 'Well, I'll think it over and tell you tomorrow morning.'"[29] Miller never finished the story and it's not clear if she was talking about "Fifteen Americans." In the early 1990s, asked why Barney was not in "Fifteen Americans," Miller told Lynn Zelevansky that in her opinion, "He just wasn't good enough." But Still and Rothko, Miller elaborated, acted as if being with "other people would contaminate them" and perhaps that influenced her opinion. Provocatively, in his statement in the show's catalogue, Still said, "The anxious men find comfort in the confusion of those artists who would walk beside them." Whatever that meant. He signed a copy of the catalogue "to my friend Barnett Newman who, also, should have been represented in this exhibition. Clyfford Still."

Barney *thought* Still and Rothko and Ferber were his friends. Pollock certainly was. And Baziotes and Tomlin. But Barney was not celebrating with them at the festivities on a Wednesday night in early April. The opening conflicted with the first night of Passover—an added insult, especially to the rabbi of the Millburn synagogue who had graciously delayed the dedication of his enlightened commission and had to decline—but Barney did not, as was his habit, participate in the Newman family's seder. Instead of Fifty-Third Street and Sixth Avenue he was at Thirty-Ninth and Broadway, where he heard the Jewish star baritone Robert Merrill sing Rodrigo in *Don Carlos* at the Metropolitan Opera. To emphasize the purposefulness of this, Annalee filed the ticket stub with the "Fifteen Americans" catalogue and reviews.

And then, after the weekend's Easter holiday, he and Annalee went to Cape May and Atlantic City, where they stayed at the formerly grand but now declined Hotel Traymore. The year had taken a toll on Barney, who was physically changed—older-looking, softer, with the beginning of the jutting belly that would come to seem so characteristic of him—but still wearing a suit and tie and fedora on vacation at the shore. He took photographs that mimicked his now signature motif—a trope that became popular among his friends who regularly sent him their own versions. He was not a natural photographer; his pictures were never well focused nor composed nor uncomposed enough to be interesting. But now over and over and over in Cape May he shot the tall, thin columns of the historic Congress Hall hotel loggia in myriad configurations. And when he returned, to most observers he had recovered his equilibrium. A show of Maud Morgan's work needed to be installed and Parsons asked the artist to hang her own show, as there was no janitor to be found. Morgan found herself up on the ladder when the elevator door opened and "a pleasant-looking, heavy-set man walked in and looked around. 'This show looks terrible,' he said." Removing his jacket, Barney told Morgan, " 'Let's take it all down and start over.' "[30]

Before "Fifteen Americans" had closed at MoMA, Pollock had joined Janis's stable; by November he had a show at the gallery, and a "Retrospective" at Bennington College organized by Greenberg.[31] Within a few months of the ineffective confrontation with Parsons, Still had withdrawn all works from the gallery but kept her as his agent into the next year. In December 1953 he joined Janis, although he never exhibited there;[32] Virginia Wright recalled many "persuasive" letters from Janis, and many angry replies from Still.[33] Rothko followed in early 1954.[34] Barney made no official announcement about his future. Nor did he investigate what any other dealer might offer him.

THIRTY-FOUR

AESTHETICS AND ORNITHOLOGY

The harbinger of a dark period was often a real-estate imbroglio. The substance might be a simple annoyance, a run-of-the-mill hiccup, but it would conveniently appear when Barney needed to focus rage and provided a useful nexus for all of his injustice collecting. It allowed him to be righteous, a way to vent about situations in which he was powerless. Four days before it became clear that Miller would not include him in "Fifteen Americans," and just as he was fulminating over being ignored by Hess, and, with his fellow "Four Horsemen," bullying Parsons over the inadequacy of her representation, Barney was informed that he was going to lose his "sanctuary."

He loved the Wall Street studio, he assumed he would keep it "at the same rental and under the same conditions"—60 dollars per month—after the lease expired at the end of July. But in January, tired of dunning for the chronically late rent and utility bills, the landlord claimed it had already been rented to a new tenant. In fact the building was for sale, and was more attractive without encumbrances. The lie was exactly the sort of underhanded manipulation that pushed every one of Barney's buttons, the sort of thing he simply could not abide.

He was also warring with the landlord of his apartment, and this only escalated over the following three years. There were repairs not made, heat not supplied, and contrary to earlier practice and Barney's expectations, the floors were not "shellacked." This last provided the impetus for voluminous correspondence, multiple drafts of angry, self-righteous letters, rent-withholding, lawyers contacted, Housing Commission applications filed, affidavits sworn to and answered. Barney didn't really want the floors done, the landlord maintained, because it kept rent low; Barney refused to answer his calls, was "hiding" in the apartment when the workman rang the bell, and shellacked the floors himself. At one point, he claimed significant damage to all of their belongings on Nineteenth Street. An antique Chinese rug and antique Persian rug, a Steinway grand piano and its bench, "antique" and "imported" furniture, cushions, four men's suits, a thousand books, Venetian blinds. He was out 400 to 1100 dollars depending upon whether the Steinway needed a factory refinish—"which it should have." Ten oil paintings and a "plaster sculpture" were also itemized.[1]

Once he depleted his rage and frustration, he was freed to paint. The work he produced through this otherwise anguished period must have thrilled him: three paintings named for Greek heroes, *Ulysses*, *Prometheus Bound*, and *Achilles*. In none of these works did Barney follow a formula, as undiscerning critics had described his approach. There were areas of color bound together on the surface of the canvas, but the bands were skinny, or wide, horizontal or vertical, at the sides, in the middle, on the top or bottom. In *Achilles*—named for the hero whose shield, its artist–maker the god Hephaestus promised, would "the cruel stroke repel, / As I shall forge most envied arms, the gaze / Of wondering ages, and the world's amaze!"—the "zip" was wide, two thirds of the canvas, and never reached its expected destination, being torn ragged in blood red.

Asked by Hess about the title, Barney said "red and fiery"; Hess added that it was "the shield form."[2] Can we say that Barney, the classics student, "surely" knew (as Barney would later say of Jesus) the glorious description in the *Iliad*, in which the shield itself encompassed virtually the whole world? "The image of the master-mind; / There earth, there heaven, there ocean . . . / The unwearied sun, the moon completely round; / The starry lights . . . / The pleiads, Hyads." Homer's 130-line description was famously one of the earliest examples of "ekphrasis"—a literary description of a work of art. Achilles's shield could not have been more pertinent to Barney, whose 1951 reviews most boorishly criticized his work as contentless: its appearance in the *Iliad* is a prelude to a stupefying letting of blood and vengeance.

By the third week of April, with "Fifteen Americans" on view and the impending loss of the studio—which he would claim interrupted work on the oceanic *Cathedra*—Barney was torn. He considered taking "the faith to a calmer land."[3]

"One of the greatest injuries that I've ever suffered," he recalled years later, "was when I was put out of my studio on Wall Street by the landlord in July" of 1952. He had "been working all spring," was "involved in a big painting and it was unfinished." He did "everything" he could to keep the landlord "out"; he "changed the locks on the door"; he "went to court." Barney fought for that painting "because . . . it was a large painting—18 feet long—[and] you have to roll that, and [to] go into a new studio would have been a blow. Well, I finished. I held onto that. And I fought the landlord, I was under a great strain."[4]

The reference to the "big painting" is confusing: no 18-footer is dated 1952. Barney himself dated *Cathedra* (plate 12) 1951, and in a letter to *Art News* years later, he wrote that Still had seen it—unfinished—in his studio in the fall of that year.[5] In November, after visiting the blockbuster "Henri Matisse" at MoMA, Barney may have been inspired to continue adding layers: works like *The Dance I*, *Bather*, *Nasturtiums with "Dance" (II)*, *Goldfish and Sculpture*, *Flowers and Ceramic Plate*, and *Portrait of Mme Matisse* had more startlingly uninterrupted acreage of barely modulated blueness than had been seen in painting since Renaissance frescoes. Because there is physical evidence that *Cathedra* was worked on over an extended period of time,[6] it's quite possible that Barney revised it through the summer of 1952, so both stories—how the painting was a crucial influence on Still *and* was victimized by the landlord—could be true. Especially, if as he did with *Adam*, Barney used a date when he first "had" the painting. In 1952, the later date was useful in a fight against the landlord; in 1965, the earlier date was useful in a fight against Still.

Toward the end of June, as it became inevitable that he would very shortly be out of that studio, Barney did something odd: he had delivered to 110 Wall Street a 23-foot length of cotton duck and unusually large amounts of both pure blue pigment and ground oil paints—Cerulean Blue, Ultramarine Blue, and "Bocour" (phthalocyanine) Blue. Whether to adjust *Cathedra*, or embark upon the six radiant blue paintings it inspired over the next two and a half years, it was a last-ditch strategy to save the studio, since the interruption, as the eviction notice came, would feed his victimhood. On a late afternoon in early July, Greenberg and Ossorio visited the studio and saw work in progress, but left no description.[7] "I hope you've had a chance to finish the work you were in the midst of & that you had some good news about yr. present or future studio," wrote Ossorio toward the end of the month.[8]

Then the Metropolitan Museum of Art did it again. While Barney was in his most outraged temper at the end of June, the museum called for entrants to the 1952 juried exhibition, "American Water Colors, Drawings, and Prints." This time there were *two* juries in each geographical region—one "modern" and the other "conservative"[9]—and entering artists could "specify" to which of the two "they wish to submit." Once again an open letter was written to Roland Redmond, the president of the museum. Once again objections were raised to the jury system and its declarations of "impartiality," the "leveling prize system"—all "attempts to conceal this lack of real commitment, this lack of respect the museum entertains towards the artist and his work." Once again the story hit the newspapers and Barney was quoted in the *Times* and the *Post*.

But things had changed in art institutions' attitudes to the "Irascibles." After "Fifteen Americans" no one could make a serious claim that an abdication of responsibility "to make any commitment towards any American artist; his stature, his genius, his merit or lack of any thereof" was "common practice among the directors of the museums of this country." And yet six of the artists signed this letter under "Barnett Newman"—Still, Rothko, and Ferber, who had been included in Miller's show, and Gottlieb, Motherwell, and Reinhardt, who had not. They agreed with Barney that Francis Henry Taylor's assertion that "we must be dispassionate" obligated a reply; at several meetings of the seven they encouraged him to be their useful mouthpiece. And then some ran away. "Barney saw another chance of getting his name in the paper so insisted on playing spokesman and damn near cancelling out the merit of the reply," Still told Miller. "I can never have another such association with him. His lust for power is beyond anything I ever saw."[10]

It was the summer, most of the artists left New York shortly after the Metropolitan fiasco; Still was in San Francisco, Reinhardt in Europe; others were in New England and Long Island. Betty had "a wonderful rest in the south of France, [and was] again spending a few days in Paris" on her way to Brittany, confident that Barney would negotiate a new lease for the gallery on her behalf.[11] Half a year after the demand to Parsons had been issued, there had been no satisfactory resolution for those who remained. "Betty seems to realize (too late?) that her 'authoritative position' depends only on the few men she can talk about & is obviously bothered by her friends & social activity around the gallery & certainly doesn't know what to do & looks to you Barney for some secours in this here circonstance critique," Reinhardt wrote in his version of Franglish after running into Parsons in France.[12]

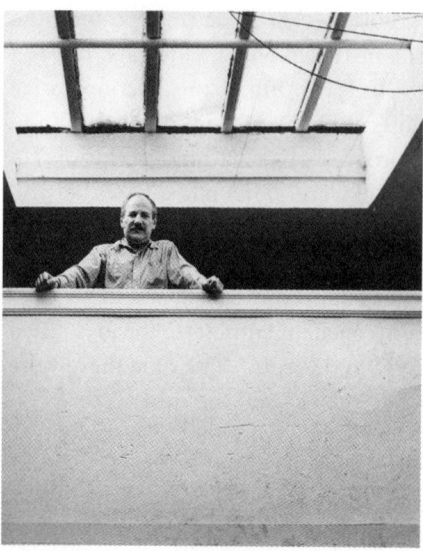

Fig. 28 Barnett Newman in his Front Street studio, c.1952. Photograph Hans Namuth

Regarding his own studio, "my attorney" was invoked,[13] the situation was resolved, Barney would vacate by the end of July. But he refused, emotionally, to accept that he hadn't prevailed. He "didn't work for quite a long time" after he moved, he said, "because it took me a long time to overcome the being pushed out. I felt like a refugee. I didn't like the idea of being pushed. I didn't. I went into a better studio, but the fact that I was pushed had a deep psychological effect on me, and I couldn't work for a while."[14]

One Hundred Front Street was in the district of coffee roasters and blenders. Barney loved being near the East River—which loomed in his earliest memories—and particularly liked the "very masculine" feel of the area.[15] The smell of coffee was constant and permeating. "It beats Soutine," Robert Murray later reassured him when Barney worried that his paintings would absorb the aroma. "His paintings smelled of rotting meat."[16]

It was a beautiful studio—the whole fourth floor, front and rear—with a dramatic interior balcony and a leaky skylight. When Smith saw it, he was filled with excitement: the sloping roof, he felt, freed the pictures "from that trapped look of being held by floor and ceiling."[17] The building's shape reminded Barney of a boat, and he had to "conquer" the architecture to make it a "place" where he could feel "I was Barney Newman."[18] To create a space appropriate for the pursuit of art as serious, dignified, moral, he developed rituals—always leaving his brushes immaculately clean, always vacuuming the floor before he left. Watching him years later, Murray thought of a hockey foreword as Barney "stickhandled around the studio and under the sparse furniture with serious determination, every movement economic and efficient."[19] He would occupy this studio for the next sixteen years, until its landlord, too, took action against Barney when he stopped paying rent in protest. But by that time, as a precautionary measure, Barney was prepared with an already-baptized back-up.

Barney did not stop painting after the blow of "Fifteen Americans" or the blow of losing his studio. But he did take a step back, and in that he was not unique. "Art" was becoming a mainstream business, and artists, almost before they could see or understand what was happening, intuited that they had to take a position, to acquiesce, or to rebel. *Day One* and *Day Before One*, two works from 1951, were typical of big paintings of the "first Abstract Expressionist period," Hess later understood:

"not only unsalable, but unexhibitable." There was "no chance at all that they could be sold or even seen by anybody but the artist and the friends he invited to his studio."[20] In less than ten years that intimacy would be gone, replaced by a full-fledged carnival: 1952 was a "turning point in the intellectuals' shift from alienation to accommodation," *Partisan Review* confirmed. In four issues the landmark symposium, "Our Country and Our Culture," examined "the apparent fact that American intellectuals now regard America and its institutions in a new way" no longer "hostile to art and culture."[21]

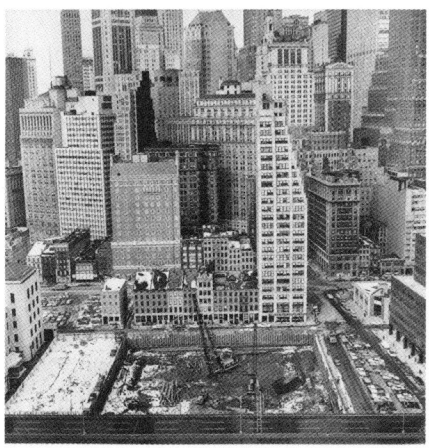

Fig. 29 View toward Barnett Newman's Front Street studio in 1967, when the early 19th-century Greek Revival buildings he treasured were replaced by "fumes" and the racket of excavations "going day and night." Photograph Carl Gossett © *The New York Times*

This was not a trend easily accepted by many of the artists who self-identified as outsiders. Many needed time and space to adjust—or to cave. "Fifteen Americans" had been open just over a week when Still, who had gotten the most audience buzz, whose work Miller hung to be the "climax of the show,"[22] refused to allow his seven paintings to be part of the exhibition when it traveled. He told her he felt "stripped," "quite naked." In irresponsible hands the work could become "a dangerous force." He felt compromised, and he did not publicly show again for seven and a half years.[23] Rothko was motivated by the same shock—the dramatic juxtaposition of a satisfyingly in-depth hanging of his work in the midst of work by others that "contaminated" it—and refused to show in the Whitney Annual that year: "Since I have a deep sense of responsibility for the life my pictures will lead out in the world, I will with gratitude accept any form of their exposition in which their life and meaning can be maintained, and avoid all occasions where I think that this cannot be done."[24] Gottlieb didn't show new work between 1953 and 1957. De Kooning battled with *Woman I*, enacting in painting the conflicts and agita. Pollock, needing to produce work for his first one-man show at Janis in November, procrastinated, complained, drank, and otherwise acted out, agonizing over the canvas that would become *Blue Poles*.

Neither was Barney alone in avoiding those he no longer trusted in the dubious dynamics. As recently as a few months earlier they all spoke continually about their work, their ideas, and all the insignificant details that made a life. Now, many former colleagues, if not friends, were no longer speaking. There were new people with whom to socialize and chew over philosophy.

"Barney has remained invisible," Rothko wrote to Ferber from New York. But Barney was not invisible to Greenberg, and his paramour Frankenthaler, with whom Barney and Annalee would share summer nightcaps and a growing camaraderie.

Or to Buffie Johnson, Ossorio, and Pollock. Or to Hedda Sterne, at whose weekly dinner parties the Newmans were often guests,[25] and who painted pendant portraits of the couple. Sterne's work ranged from abstraction to surrealism to representation, from landscapes to lettuce to agricultural machines. When she thought a person was "fully developed" and she was "stimulated extremely" she would paint a "face." For the Newmans she chose a rare format, large and in oil, in scroll-like dimensions. Barney's, 89 by 27 inches, was a witty reference to the thin paintings or *Here I* from his show of the previous year. His bulky torso occupied the lower third of an otherwise empty canvas, a sly modern transliteration of a Kamakura ancestor portrait,[26] hardly more than a grisaille sketch except for his prominent, pigmented hand, the same hand so prominent in the "Irascibles" photograph. In the other, Annalee, standing in a slip and skirt, is a Spartan goddess crossed with Stella Kowalski crossed with a

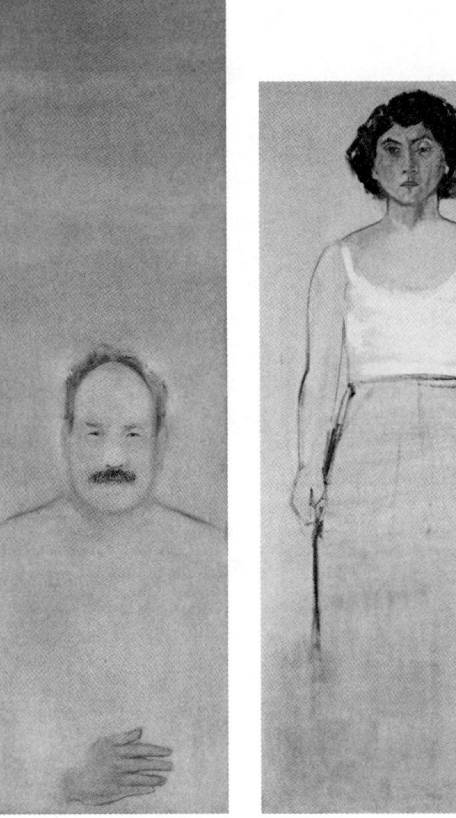

Fig. 30 (left) Hedda Sterne, *Portrait of Barnett Newman*, 1953. Oil on canvas, 89 × 27 in. (226 × 68.6 cm). Collection of the Francis Lehman Loeb Art Center, Vassar College. Gift of the artist

Fig. 31 (right) Hedda Sterne, *Portrait of Annalee Newman*, 1953. Oil on canvas, 79 × 35 in. (200.6 × 88.9 cm). Collection of the Francis Lehman Loeb Art Center, Vassar College. Bequest of Priscilla Miner Morgan, class of 1941

contemporary schoolteacher version of Sargent's *Madame X*. She fills entirely the tall, skinny panel and stares straight ahead, her black hair a halo and her thumbs tucked into her clenched fists. Sterne kept this painting on view in her house, and later in her studio, for years.[27]

And Barney was not "invisible" to a large audience at the end of August in Woodstock. Days after the disorienting and wrenching move to Front Street, Barney and Annalee went to the old artist's colony in rural New York to participate along with George L. K. Morris, David Smith, Harry Holtzman, and Ben Shahn (among others) in an annual event sponsored by the Woodstock Artists Association. The 1952 topic was "Aesthetics and the Artist," and as an invited "guest of the panel," Barney was treated with the deference he craved by Rollin Crampton, an art administrator and painter, and member of the Artists Association board.[28] Motherwell, too, had been invited. Rothko, bathing in the "after-glow" of "Fifteen Americans," and getting itchy in the city, visited him in Long Island and the two went off together for the weekend to Woodstock, where Rothko found that "the perfect weather plus copious drinks and food did much to drown" what he called "the banal words which were even more copious."[29]

"There seems to be no news or gossip important enough to justify the continuance of this wrestling match with the typewriter," Rothko concluded a letter to Ferber after the conference,[30] avoiding entirely what he had heard in Woodstock, including the decidedly not "invisible" Barney's words—among them those that turned out to be the single best-known expression to emerge from Barney and enter "art history."

George Boas, the Johns Hopkins philosophy professor, was keynote speaker. As the "Society for Aesthetics" was the co-sponsor, and the *Journal of Aesthetics* expected to publish the proceedings, it was suggested that the panelists prepare a "statement of perhaps five hundred words . . . [on] any topic you feel will contribute to a clearer understanding between the artist and the aesthetician."[31] Given Barney's frame of mind, and his decades-long antipathy to approaching art through any sort of scientific method, "five hundred words" was not going to be forthcoming.

He had prepared remarks: the conference would have value—as an "anthology"—only if each speaker presented a point of view. He was not interested in a debate which would be a "spectacle," a form of "entertainment, where one can watch the better arguer exhibit his brilliance." He wanted only to express his own point of view. He was not there "to defend a group, a movement, an ideology or a style of painting." Here was a radical turnabout: Barney's announcement that he was flying solo, the days of mutual support were over. That month's studio relocation had made him feel like a "refugee"; now, as he made notes while listening to the other speakers, he scribbled the word "exile."[32]

Art was miraculous and each manifestation could only happen once, like "Michelangelo's Sistine Chapel [or] Rembrandt's" *Night Watch*. "Unless some clarity is brought into the distinction between a fact of art and artifact, the whole thing becomes a simple device for propaganda whereby, by invoking the holy name of science and scientific method a new priesthood arises that gives itself the authority of acting as an intervenor between the artist and the public. I see no difference between the aesthetician's invocation of science in the matter of art than the middle ages' invocation of divine authority in the intervention between man and his soul."

And here, logically for his written argument, Barney planned to propose the analogy of ornithology. "I have never come across a single ornithologist who dreams that his science is intended for the birds or that he can in the end contribute to bird life." Ornithologists had saved some rare species of birds from extinction, "but they have not done so by getting the birds to study their science. They have saved the birds by leaving them strictly alone. They have saved them by getting people to stop shooting them. They have gotten people to let the birds keep their feeding grounds . . . . In this regard, the best the aestheticians can do, I suppose, is to leave the artists alone, to stop shooting him, to give him his feeding grounds. Art under these circumstances, I am positive, would flourish.

"It is the aesthetician . . . who is involved in art. The artist is involved in life . . . [in] creation."

Barney intended to use the opportunity to dismiss his former pals and settle scores. "The tragic thing to me is to see the rise of a specific kind of aesthetician, the artist as aesthetician . . . . There are many men who claim they are artists whose main preoccupation it seems is the Kunstwissenschaftig activity of telling us where beauty can be found. The social realists, the neo-plastics, the surrealists, the expressionists, and more recently the abstract expressionists." Motherwell, Hess, and "those involved in Buicks, Matisse, Sartre, Whitehead, in Life magazine, Kenyon Review" and "the Philistines where anything is art, the shape of a screw driver, the look of a chair, the design of a layout, the look of photography"—he meant the Museum of Modern Art—are "creating a new form of society I can best describe as Democratic Fascism."

Barney wanted to close by claiming for painting "status as the flower of a society that can create roots for new societies" and by quoting the Ben Jonson poem "The Noble Nature."[33]

But Barney didn't follow his notes. Instead, he extemporized, responding to Boas's presentation, which maddened him in its impartiality and disinterestedness ("the aesthetician must not try to appraise but merely to find out why certain things are happening"), and to Susanne Langer's "claims" to have created a science and a philosophy of art. He got a big laugh when he said he had no prepared statement, as he shuffled a sheaf of paper. He announced that he was not there as a painter, "even though I have been so invited," but as a citizen—an identification he brought up repeatedly. His misrepresentation of Boas's words brought a chorus of "nos" and rumbles of discomfort and Barney was ruffled.

In a style of delivery recognizable to everyone in 1952 as radio and television columnist Walter Winchell's—pugnacious, nasal, New York-inflected, punched staccato phrases that ended with drawn out syllables and significant pauses—Barney surged on, including, in his fashion, a couple of jokes and puns, but delivered with no mirth or participation in the audience's polite laughter. Langer and other aestheticians, he said, made the "false identification of reality with nature." What is art and what does the artist do? "As a citizen," Barney proposed,

> what I think the artist does is to create reality, and that what seems to be reality is really an imitation of art, of what the artist has made. By "reality," I mean human reality. The artist does not make the hills and the rivers, but whatever reality we have as human beings has been created by the artists and only by the artist. It seems to me that by identifying art or reality with nature, the artist had been reduced so that he's really just a performer.

It was "Dr. Boas's attitude of 'no commitment'" that gave credence to the Dada artists, Duchamp, and museums that showed

> screwdrivers and automobiles and paintings. [Laughter] And have accepted this aesthetic position that there's no way of knowing what is what. Well, if there is no way, I feel that it's time for the Museum of Modern Art, for example, to put on an exhibition of machine guns. After all, they're beautifully functional, they're wonderful forms, they're full of content, and they actually make noise. [Laughter]

And because his dander was up, and because he felt himself flayed by recent events,

> Will the modern aesthetician who takes this position, if he's confronted with the parchment lamps that were made from the skins of the Jews that were killed by the Nazis, just criticize [them] on the grounds that it's pretty good work? [total silence]

"Painting is a fine art," he said. "The word 'fine' means 'end,' and I feel that painting is an art which is the end in itself," not something that could be "reduced to a fact in order to find some greater truth." His was not an art-for-art's-sake position; what he was saying was that "the world is created by the artist. Reality is what the artist makes . . . . Life is an imitation of the reality set up by the painter. [Great laughter]" Aestheticians have nothing to do with the artist; but they are "very anxious to capture the public."

By this time, almost twenty minutes in, Barney was urged to wrap up; there was irritation all around, and he became flustered as he skipped ahead to a condensed version of the story he had prepared:

> I have insisted on coming here as a citizen because I feel that even if aesthetics is established as a science, it doesn't affect me as an artist. I've done quite a bit of work in ornithology. I have never met an ornithologist who ever thought that ornithology was for the birds.

The audience erupted in laughter and applause. Barney had them in his palm.

After Barney's comments, Langer, wounded, challenged his characterization of her work. It was clear that Barney misunderstood or misrepresented her position; they were talking at cross-purposes, they were using different meanings for "nature," "reality," "concrete," "art." But Langer's actual position didn't matter to Barney: he required a foil to make his point about his work. It was a brilliant performance—notwithstanding his rejection of the artist as performer. And as time passed, very few remembered what Langer had said, but everyone quoted Barney. Actually, later writers would quote not what was said at Woodstock, but the quip derived from it, one that Barney himself would repeat: "<u>Aesthetics</u> is for the artist as <u>ornithology</u> is for the birds." Although Barney was always happy to remind people of his studies in ornithology (or botany, or geology), the art world's most famous amateur ornithologist at the time was Alfred Barr, the founding director and the conceptual designer of the Museum of Modern Art—the palace of well-designed screwdrivers called out in Barney's talk—and he might assume that reference would not have been lost on many in the audience.

When Reinhardt returned from Italy, Switzerland, France, Germany, Holland, Belgium, and England, and was living on Nineteenth Street a block away, Barney and Annalee saw him and Rita regularly. In October, on Halloween, the two men, along with Parsons, went on WNYC radio as part of an "Art Festival," in which, to the organizers' surprise, the disaffection from August spilled over.

Parsons took the opportunity to settle scores. To pointed questions about whether she showed "intrinsically incomprehensible and unintelligible" work, she gave very firm and clear answers. Some people, she said—the world of privilege, money, and the status quo—wanted to escape, to be reminded of the past. Facing the present "means one is facing oneself," changing one's attitude. There was nothing wrong with her painters; she supported them with her whole being, with complete trust. "I do not take on painters because of their past financial success or popularity," she told the popular radio audience, her ungrateful renegades, and Sidney Janis. "In fact some of the painters that I have introduced I have lost because they became successful enough for someone else to capitalize on."[34]

Reinhardt bemoaned the "big business," the "fat commodity," the "hucksters" he saw in the art-interested community, who made a "fantastic combination of 'art authorities' and 'art susceptibles.'"

"Looking over the topics and items of this program," Reinhardt concluded, "I would say, right here—this WNYC 'art festival' is a questionable activity, is a quandary, and a funny business if I ever saw one!"

What, Freud might have asked, do artists want?

One autumn weekend Barney and Annalee and Tony Smith went to Springs to visit Pollock during a particularly blocked period. Pollock had his Janis show coming up and an eight-painting "retrospective," organized by Greenberg, at Bennington; he had a 16-foot canvas on the floor of his studio and felt paralyzed. After hours of alcohol consumption, the three men went into the studio to look at the canvas Pollock had started months before on a freezing, drunken night with Smith. According to the story Smith told the art critic and novelist Tom Robbins, Pollock and he were going through bottles of Old Gran-Dad when Smith told him he had to get back to color. "Color forces you to make some decisions." Whereupon the two of them embarked on a spree of orange and blue that ended, Smith said, with "ruined good canvas," and Pollock passing out in the studio. Now, in the fall of '52, Barney asked to see the canvas, he wanted to get it going again. Barney, Smith told Robbins, "put the poles in . . . [and] Pollock worked on it some more." That was *Blue Poles*. And that was the story—originating with Smith—that was told many times over.[35] But Annalee, who was there at the time, categorically maintained that it was untrue: Smith and Barney did go into the studio with Pollock, and they did each squeeze "one tube of paint."[36] That was all. But their moral support helped Pollock get the canvas ready for his show.

"The painter no longer approached his easel with an image in his mind; he went up to it with material in his hand to do something to that other piece of material in front of him. The image would be the result of this encounter." When "The American Action Painters," Harold Rosenberg's coded dismissal of Pollock and valorization of de Kooning, appeared in the December number of *Art News*, its impact was enough to almost reunite the estranged "uptown" artists.[37] "At a certain moment the canvas began to appear to one American painter after another as an arena in which to act—rather than as a space in which to reproduce, re-design, analyze, or 'express' an object, actual or imagined. What was to go on the canvas was not a picture but an event." This statement is now a cliché, a tenet in the Artist's Bill of Rights. But in December 1952 it was a thunderbolt.

Rosenberg's essay was cryptic, written for a certain narrow audience that he knew would catch his meaning, and all but indecipherable to any of the uninitiated. It called for a radically new definition of criticism, of the way to approach the new art.

Criticism must begin by recognizing in the painting the assumptions inherent in its mode of creation . . . the spectator has to think in a vocabulary of action: its inception, duration, direction—psychic state, concentration and relaxation of the will, passivity, alert waiting. He must become a connoisseur of the gradations between the automatic, the spontaneous, the evoked.

With a few important exceptions, most of the artists of the vanguard found their way to their present work by being cut in two. Their type is not a young painter but a re-born one. The man may be over forty, the painter around seven. The diagonal of a grand crisis separates him from his personal and artistic past. . . .

The test of any of the new paintings is its seriousness—and the test of its seriousness is the degree to which the act on the canvas is an extension of the artist's total effort to make over his experience. . . .

By its very nature, action painting is painting in the medium of difficulties.

And here Rosenberg threw down the gauntlet:

> Weak mysticism, the "Christian Science" side of the new movement, tends in the opposite direction, toward *easy* painting—never so many unearned masterpieces! Works of this sort lack the dialectical tension of a genuine act, associated with risk and will.

Without naming names—it was, after all, the era of Senate Internal Security Sub-committee hearings, but the writer was being coy, not careful—Rosenberg dismissed the work of Pollock as "apocalyptic wallpaper," and Rothko, Still, and Newman as purveyors of "the cosmic 'I' that turns up to paint pictures . . . a megalomania which is the opposite of revolutionary": a unique signature that only seemed "the equivalent of a new plastic language."

Barney could only have read what followed as directed precisely at him (Rosenberg was a notorious punner): "In a single stroke the painter exists as a Somebody—at least on a wall. That this Somebody is not he seems beside the point."

The unnamed Pollock was "the painter himself changed into a ghost inhabiting The Art World," of whom the statement " 'I have bought an O.' (rather than a painting by O.) becomes literally true. The man who started to remake himself has made himself into a commodity with a trademark," the subject of articles in "big-circulation magazines." Authenticity, the "genuine act," was the only art that had any value. The rest, whose motivation Rosenberg somehow knew was inauthentic, were like "canned meats in a chain store," "all standard brands."

Those who actually created the art, however, could not abide this. Still wrote to Rosenberg—and sent a copy to Pollock—to say he was "downright ashamed" of him for the obvious motives and crudeness of his "hatchet job"; Rosenberg, he said, was an "intellectual lout." To Pollock, Still wrote that the attacks were on the two of them, and offered solidarity.[38] "The Abstract Expressionist movement may turn out to have been around de Kooning," Reinhardt said years later, "but we didn't see it that way."[39]

THIRTY-FIVE

L'ERRANCE (THE WANDERING)

The more Barney, Rothko, Reinhardt, and Still—and Parsons—tried to explain, ver-
balize, or defend their position, the more hermetic or charlatan-ish they seemed.
Their work was caught in a catch-22 of which they were more than subliminally
aware. Robert Wolff, the chairman of the Brooklyn College art department where
Rothko, Still, and Reinhardt taught, called it a "trap that awaits every manifestation that dares leave the protective anonymity of privacy" for public exhibition.
Artworks became victims of "the swift infectiousness" of official pronouncements,
contaminated by "congealed meanings." To exist as art in the society, they had to go
through "the machinery of authentication (one-man shows, museum exhibitions and
purchases, prizes and awards)," becoming pieces of "artistic merchandise"—Rosenberg's "canned meats in a chain store." Thus they assumed the "image of a meaning"
which they were created "to destroy": not merely "accepted aesthetic concepts" but
the "whole meaning structure of mid-Century materialism."[1] In other words, what
Barney had meant—and been ridiculed for—when he said his painting, if properly
understood, would "mean the end of state capitalism."

The men could capitulate; they could sputter and rage, and take barely com-
prehensible moral positions; they could develop a bespoke armor; or they could
withdraw from the fray to preserve their "honor." Still went back and forth, affili-
ating himself with Janis in November, never showing there, and debating "whether
to withdraw totally, or go in and spend another chunk of life slugging it out with
Newman, Reinhardt, and Rothko."[2] Pollock went to East Hampton, "able to live
off his work. He didn't make a big *geshray* about exhibiting," collector Ben Heller
recalled of this time. "He painted it. He put it up. No arguments." Heller was struck
seeing him standing against a wall at Janis's, "in his brown and beige tweed suit with a
vest . . . dying on his feet and suffering and taking it. The others flinched. Everybody
else flinched from that kind of attitude. Even Bill, with all the support that Bill had,
Bill flinched. Barney went through a mechanism of rationalizations for why he wasn't
accepted, to get accepted solely on his own terms . . . . He went through idiocies,
crazies, *mishugas*."[3] Barney would not show again with Betty, he would not submit
a piece to the "Stable Gallery Annual"—formerly the Ninth Street Show—although
in 1953 he was invited.

With the Parsons Gallery no longer central command of a unified front, Barney
was no longer so needed by Rothko, Ferber, and Still. He was moving away from
them and the Egan group and Motherwell's coterie; he was happier with Pollock
and Smith and Reinhardt. As Greenberg was involved with Frankenthaler, Barney
was drawn into a different circle, often centered around Frankenthaler's apartment
uptown, sometimes just the four of them, or with the Pollocks when they were in

Manhattan, or with a crowd that at times included Friedel Dzubas, *Partisan Review* editor Philip Rahv, and artist and Bennington professor Paul Feeley and his wife.

Alexander Liberman was a new friend. The brilliant Condé Nast art director had been making paintings. Priscilla Peck, a witty innovator he hired as layout designer for *Vogue*, introduced him to her chum Parsons and arranged for the dealer, Greenberg, and Barney to visit Liberman's studio. A decade later, Barney would open art-world doors for Liberman; at this moment it was Liberman—graceful and debonair, socially connected, an intimate of the famous European artists he photographed—who would dramatically expand Barney's world, as Liberman and his wife, the aristocratic (by marriage) and outrageous (by design) milliner Tatiana du Plessix included the Newmans with *Vogue* bold-face names in their salon. Liberman, born to a wealthy Jewish family in Ukraine, had a mother who lived the extravagant cultural richness that Barney's mother dreamt about, but by the time he arrived in America he was a refugee from occupied France. The two men recognized each other as soul-mates. For all his outward ease, Liberman found life "a torment" and "navigating through life . . . very difficult"; he was painfully "sensitive to all form of criticism," because in his heart he found "all criticism somehow probably true." Like Barney, he believed that at its best, art could bring one close to a higher spiritual realm—without any "structure of institution" or "intermediaries" like religion,[4] and he empathized with Barney's struggle to reach the sublime. Barney was the "essence of the American artist that I was trying to become," he said. Quickly they became addicted to long, almost daily telephone conversations and became indispensable to each other's equilibrium.[5]

Far from shriveling up and retreating to a corner as many reported, Barney continued to work. But he mostly socialized, conducting the New York excursions that over the next sixteen years reliably showcased his most charming, appealing, and entertaining self. Instead of the irritable and irritating provocations of his Mr. Hyde-side, the Dr. Jekyll pronouncements at these times were intellectual, visual, unverifiable but impishly "Barney." The way the light hit the canvas-floored ring at Stillman's Gym would lead to a captivating discourse on Vermeer. A baseball game was narrated in ritualistic, religious terms: "Now here comes the high priest on to the mound."[6] Mies van der Rohe was a great architect, but his greatest buildings were not the ones standing up like the Seagram building but the ones lying on their sides, like Newark's Colonnade apartment building, which joined the tour in 1960.[7] You could digest the overwhelming meal he ordered at Sweet's as long as you ate a grapefruit after. And just get him started on movies: "In English movies, there's a knock on the door, the woman opens it up, the guy says [assuming a British accent], 'I'm from Scotland Yard.' And she says, 'Won't you come in and sit down?' A French movie [is] always about eating. A loaf of bread, a woman is breaking beans, a man eating chocolate. In an American movie, the guy's not polite, [he] says 'I'm from Scotland Yard' and pulls out his gun! You'll never see an American movie, *never*, with anybody eating. You'll see them drinking but [never] a guy putting anything in his mouth and chewing . . . . A guy will take a girl to a restaurant and you'll see two glasses, cocktails, but you'll never see a guy cracking lobster or eating beans . . . . You can always tell an Italian movie because in five minutes the guy got the girl, he grabs her by the dress and goes 'zingo!' and she's naked. I say, what kind of cotton do they use?"[8]

He knew the last remaining dive on lower Second Avenue that had a music-playing puppet-limb orchestrion, and the oldest fish restaurant in Brooklyn, Gage & Tollner—the one from 1892 that still had walls of arched, cherry-framed mirrors, gaslight fixtures, and Lillian Russell's perfume. He'd take out-of-towners to be advised by his special contact at Sam Goody's, the Smithsonian Institution of vinyl record emporia. He was welcomed by the chefs of obscure but authentic Chinese restaurants. He knew that when everything else was closed for the night Ratner's, the Lower East Side dairy restaurant, would still be going strong, and he would escort Pollock there when he showed up falling down drunk on the doorstep of Front Street, where Barney would be in his studio hours after midnight.[9] He was *the* arch-appreciator of Damon Runyon, and now *Guys and Dolls* was *the* hit on Broadway. (Was it a taunt, a strange tip of the hat, or a perverse reminder of the autographed "Fifteen Americans" catalogue when Still presented Barney with a program from the performance he attended autographed by . . . Still![10])

He and Annalee kept up their shopping habits for clothes and books and records; they attended classical music and opera performances, and well-publicized culturati events, like a revue of the Gamelan Orchestra and Dancers of Bali, the Azuma Kabuki Dancers and Musicians, the National Theatre of Greece's mounting of *Electra*. He went to jazz clubs in Harlem. In other words, whatever their debts, they pursued the self-consciously cosmopolitan but bohemian-inflected middle-class life for which they had been bred.

In February 1953, the Newmans convinced Reinhardt to marry Rita Salomon. The four regularly spent time together and, regularly, the subject of marriage came up. The Newmans were encouraging: Salomon was a "nice Jewish girl," they wanted the best for both of them. "Finally," Annalee recalled, "he said he would marry her, but he never would set the date. She implored me to help her. One day, when we were all together, I said to Ad, 'When are you and Rita getting married?' Ad said, 'We'll get married, but you and Barney would have to be the witnesses at City Hall.'"

After the wedding, Barney announced that they had to have a celebration and took them to Andre's, a classic newspaper row eatery, at the corner of Nassau and Frankfort Streets where Abraham Newman & Son had been located in the mid-1930s. It was a bit "fancy": "Un repas sans vins est une journee sans soleil" the restaurant advised, "Le Vin Dissipe La Tristesse et Rejouit Le Coeur." While the others had a drink, Barney ran out to borrow money to pay the bill from "Yudel, who used to do some work for his father."[11] Ad and Rita, Barney and Annalee, and Rita's friend Helen Triesel signed and exuberantly decorated the menu as a souvenir. "*Mazel Tov*" Barney and Annalee each wrote in Yiddish. Exultant, Reinhardt broke his rule—not trading or giving works to other artists—and made an exception, presenting a work to Annalee. Greenberg invited them all for drinks at the Ritz Towers. Parsons threw a party.

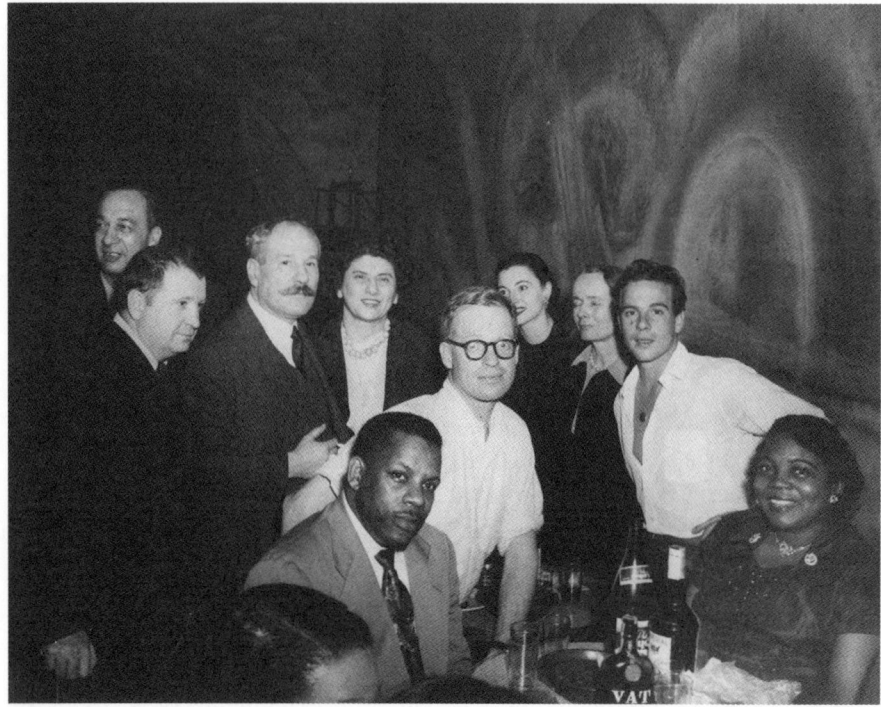

Fig. 32 At a nightclub in Harlem, 1953. Standing, from left: unidentified, Ad Reinhardt, Barnett Newman, Annalee Newman, William Congdon, Rita Reinhardt, Betty Parsons, Gianni Silvestri; seated, from left: Thomas Sills, unidentified

When Lucille Ball's pregnancy was incorporated into the plot of the country's most popular television show, *I Love Lucy*, three-quarters of all sets tuned in to follow the story that reflected what the rest of postwar aspirational America was doing. A few years earlier it was shocking for self-regarding "avant-garde" artists to have children, as "Miz" Hofmann told the Bultmans in 1945. When Evelyn Pousette-Dart became pregnant in the late 1940s, "everyone was horrified!"[12] and Still's two daughters were out of sight on the West Coast. Now, in the Newmans' circle, there was a change. Kate Rothko had been born in 1950 to the 47-year-old artist. Both Tony and Jane Smith's first daughter, and Ad and Rita Reinhardt's daughter were born at the beginning of 1954. Annalee loved children, and confidentially told friends that she would have liked to have a family and told her sister she was "desperate" to—but it was impossible because Barney was struggling.[13] He called children "little mortgages."[14]

During 1953 Barney made only two paintings, but they are two of the most sensuously beautiful he ever made, profound blue universes: *L'Errance* (plate 13), moodily atmospheric with blood red slicing through the far far left, and *Onement VI*, with a single narrow central greenish-white area. This latter painting—not radically small, not radically large, no longer radically colored nor radically composed—became, when it was exhibited in New York at the Guggenheim Museum in 1961, the work that converted the non-believers.

In spite of the absence of exhibitions, in spite of there being no grand statements, or gestures for some time, Barney could no longer be ignored. In a blithe compendium of contemporary culture—ballet, cinema, legitimate theater, musical theater, fiction, poetry, philosophy, and art—published for the international passengers on the new luxury steamships "United States" and "America," Hess himself felt obliged to include eleven words about "Barnet" Newman: "straight lines down color; and [sic] extreme of painting which sacrifices painting." Rothko, Still, Reinhardt, and Motherwell fared only slightly better in Hess's descriptions.[15]

Intrigue persisted. By the time Barney saw the magazine, he was discreetly planning his cross-country trip with Still in search of a job. "Darling: We arrived in Salem Ohio, 6:15 P.M. today + I have just finished my dinner of blue pike," he meticulously reported to Annalee. The adventure had been kept on the down low, and he warned her to deflect Pollock's questions. "It will interest you that [Clyff] sent Jackson a telegram saying goodbye so that Jack knew Clyff was going," Barney told her. "He wasn't fishing to find whether Clyff had gone—I think he wanted to know <u>who</u> was the passenger."[16] Then the trip ended abruptly the next day, with Still claiming that the car was not working properly. Two large and arrogant personalities crammed into a small Jaguar taking each other's temperature, provoking each other's demons: it was inevitable that impulsive action would ensue.

Almost immediately, Barney contacted Ossorio, who owned the little 36-by-6-inch work from the 1951 show: he had borrowed money and wanted to repay the 200 dollars Ossorio loaned him to move his studio, even though that had been understood as a "payment on a future painting."[17] The real objective became clear a few days later.

After a great deal of thought and upon long contemplation of my feelings, I have decided to withdraw all of my "small" canvases at this time, from public view.

This does not mean that I am denying them. On the contrary, it is because I feel so strongly that they are authentic and personal expressions, that they have the authority of my being, that I must act so.

The conditions do not yet exist for me, either physically or in the realm of idea, that can make possible a direct, innocent attitude towards an isolated piece of my work, particularly one of my "small" ones. Without the proper context, the larger issues in my work are lost, or what is worse, become distorted to be just tour de force—from the tiny to the immense. I have, of course, done both sizes but I have never been involved in tour de force—in size for its own sake—and although I do not care what may be said about my work (I am not interested in whether or not it is liked), I do care intensely that it be seen for what it is and not for what it is not . . . .

I may perhaps have to do the same with my large ones—but that must wait for more thought.[18]

Barney returned what Ossorio had paid for the canvas, and, in a postscript, wrote that although he had "no objection that my decision be known," nevertheless, "Since it is personal, let us keep it confidential."[19]

Still's car, meanwhile, quickly got "fixed," and he had a "terrific trip across the great plains."

Still had been working at Ossorio's Long Island home before he left because dealing with the art crowd was "too much like handling shit with the bare hands,"[20] but he remained in contact with Ossorio, who reported Barney's decision—so much for confidentiality. Still was predictably contemptuous. Barney "is the most completely political man I know, and I say it most objectively. And I use the word 'political' in the way it pertains to achievement of 'social' power by psychological and technical means, and the compulsion to achieve these ends so urgent that any means can be used without ruth or qualification." They had had "furious arguments"; they always ended "friendly persons" but total enemies regarding "the individual versus the virtue of power."[21] That summer, behind his back, Still called Barney "a ruthless, crafty, dedicated gangster, a little Molotov"[22] and a "a relentless, willful, vengeful + often a horrifying scoundrel";[23] but that autumn, and for another couple of years, at least, the two men managed to remain friendly enough to go together to ballgames, "push" into Janis's back room together to look at Pollock paintings, and to collaborate in a vicious letter campaign against Rothko.

Whatever happened on the brief road trip, Barney returned in a state of agitation not sufficiently quieted by his decision about his work. He was, in a way, looking for trouble, and within another few days found a hook in reliable sources of provocation. Buried in the *Times*'s coverage of the wide-ranging, wildly diverse summer installation at MoMA was the half sentence "Paintings recently acquired include Monet's 'Poplars at Giverny,' one of the impressionist's solider achievements."[24]

Barney was off.

OPEN LETTER TO WILLIAM A.M. BURDEN, PRESIDENT, MUSEUM OF MODERN ART

The Museum of Modern Art has just acquired and is now quietly exhibiting, as part of its yearly show of new acquisitions . . . "Poplars at Giverny," painted in 1888 by Claude Monet, the Impressionist painter.

This cannot be considered as just another addition to the Museum's collection. The acquisition of this picture involves a basic issue of Museum policy of far-reaching importance to the American public, which the Museum, it seems, would like not to be noticed. No one, nowhere in the exhibition or in the public announcement, has indicated that this picture is not only the first Monet acquired by the Museum of Modern Art but also that it is the first important picture by an Impressionist painter <u>ever</u> acquired by the Museum in its almost 25 years of existence. Until now the Museum has owned neither a Monet, nor an important Pissarro, nor a Sisley.

Why the silence? Is the institution that has dedicated itself for a quarter of a century to the false art history that modern art began with Cézanne afraid now to admit that it is changing its position?

Is the Museum that has, by dedicating itself to the myth of Post-Impressionism invented by the English critic, Roger Fry, promulgated the theory that the Impressionists were failures—mere experimenters—now renouncing this policy? . . .

Is the Museum ready to abdicate the authority that has established Cézanne as the father of modern art, Marcel Duchamp as his self-appointed heir, and the Bauhaus screw-driver designers who have proclaimed the millennium . . . to fight for a new concept of art? . . . As an artist-citizen, I feel the responsibility and the right to demand to know.[25]

Once more, Barney issued his missive as a press release, but the letter was covered only in a single New York tabloid. "It being holiday weekend," the *Daily Mirror* noted, there was no one at the museum yesterday to answer the artist's many questions."[26]

Miller understood the action to be retaliation against her and the museum for excluding Barney from "Fifteen Americans"; Still saw it as a prime example of Barney's "political" maneuverings and "power" grab: the timing over July Fourth was savvy, with many hard news reporters on holiday. No doubt, his "stances" were becoming fatiguing for many of his peers. Nevertheless, Barney's point, and the importance of making the point publicly, was not wrong, and even enlightened. What "power" did Still think Barney was grabbing? Certainly it was not about getting his art seen in the short run, certainly it would make him no friends in high places; even Barney could not have imagined that it would have had that effect. There was no strategy when he responded to Burden's disingenuous and dismissive reply by quoting definitions in the museum's "official publication" to strengthen his argument. He was simply "compelled."[27]

Like all of the artists, Barney was anxious that his art not become a commodity, not be used for what they considered corrupt or base ends. But Barney alone among them always aspired to have consequence through his role as a "citizen," and so he reached farther than those whose lobbying was aimed only at the insular art community. He had a meta-understanding of the forces at play, and it was something about which he was forthright. If he was "obsessed," as Reinhardt later said, with the concepts of popular "success," and "publicity," it was because he admired most the artists who "had or made an impact on the public" as opposed to an impact on the gate guardians: museum curators, critics, collectors.

Reinhardt said Barney told him he would have liked to have been a "TV master of ceremonies or disc jockey," but that diminishes his ambition.[28] The ubiquitous gossip-political-social commentator/friend of presidents Walter Winchell was as much a source of identification for Barney, as the journalist, author, and wise guy Damon Runyon had been in his earlier life. The correspondence with Burden was no Machiavellian calculation to promote his own paintings: Barney saw something dishonest, disinformation that would, he thought, undermine ART. Because everything for him was part of the big picture of cultural forces.

Reinhardt was one of the invited speakers to the Woodstock conference later that summer, on a weekend in mid-August. During their previous evenings together, and during their four-block walks back and forth between their apartments, he and Barney talked about his presentation. Naturally, it would take the kind of sardonic tone that Reinhardt's drawings and his postcards took: his "humor, jests and cartoon-poetry [had] always," he assumed, "been obvious and self-explanatory." It would be, like his magazine work, a caricatured description of the vanguard artists' own attempts to define what each uniquely did and to separate themselves from the pack while at the same time being anxious to find sustenance from identifying with the pack. "The Artist in Search of an Academy," he called it. He grouped fifty-two of his artist contemporaries into four categories, each category representing a "general" idea of art and a "stereo-type" artist—"a lampooning of how contemporary art history is written today by art historians and critics with their arbitrary and accidental choices of artists and their label-thinking."[29] In other words, it addressed exactly what had been on everyone's minds and tongues for the last eighteen months.

Barney was put in the category of "the artist-professor and traveling-design-salesman, the Art-Digest-philosopher-poet and Bauhaus-exerciser, the avant-garde-huckster-handicraftsman and educational-shop-keeper, the holy-roller-explainer-entertainer-in-residence (Albers, Bolotowsky, Chermayef, Diller, Ferren, Greene, Holtzman, Holty, Morris, Motherwell, Newman, Wolff, Vytlacil, etc.)." It was galling to him, considering how aggressively he always separated himself from any Bauhaus aesthetic and any "design" connection.[30] But if his choice was that or "the café-and-club primitive and neo-Zen-bohemian, the Vogue-magazine-cold-water-flat-fauve and Harpers-Bazaar-bum, the Eighth-street-existentialist and Easthampton-aesthete, the Modern-Museum-pauper and international-set-sufferer, the abstract-'Hesspressionist' and Kootzenjammer-Kid-Jungian, the Romantic-ham-'action'-actor" where de Kooning, Gottlieb, Pollock, Rothko, Still were placed—well, it was a hard choice. Reinhardt would later give himself great credit for including Barney at all—despite his short "career"—although by this time even Hess could not honestly omit him from accounts and Greenberg, too, would include him in describing the most interesting of "the new American abstract painting" in *Art Digest* in September.[31] Not to mention that at the very same venue, the previous year, Barney himself was something of a star. But if Barney objected to his company or Reinhardt's description of that camp, he had many opportunities, Reinhardt later told lawyers, to tell him personally before the talk was given, and again before it was published a year later.

As Barney and Annalee had the previous year, the Reinhardts were planning to stay with Rollin Crampton, and because Ad wanted Barney there, he asked the Cramptons if they'd have room for the Newmans. As it turned out, Barney and Annalee did not go to Woodstock—instead, they had the pregnant Rita over for dinner while Ad went alone—and so didn't hear the reactions to the satirical pigeonholes and their occupants. The fact that many were thinner-skinned, or had less of a sense of humor, than Reinhardt expected did not alter his own: the following week, from the airport in Florida, he wisecracked to his wife that he took out travel insurance with which she would be able to "take care of all my families and all my friends even the artists I'm currently slandering."[32]

Hess, at least, took no offense: he wrote a praise-filled and thoughtful article—the first magazine feature on the artist—in the December issue of *Art News*. In the opening paragraph of "Reinhardt: the Position and Perils of Purity," Hess noted that Reinhardt had exhibited with "such men as Rothko and Newman"—an independent acknowledgment of Barney's status as an artist. A couple of months later in his review of the Stable Gallery "salon"—the third incarnation of the Ninth Street Show—Hess specifically noted that among the 150 artists he included "Rothko, Still and Newman" were "absent from the list because absent from the exhibition."[33] James Fitzsimmons did the same in *Art Digest*: "The best known abstract impressionist, Rothko, is missing (as are Still and Newman)."[34] These mentions, ironically, provided the three men with greater prominence than they would have had if they elected to exhibit with the enormous group.

Barney found no gratification. He was a master at inflating so many less meaningful references to himself (as he did his "credentials"), and reading between lines to find offenses—fulminating and castigating—yet he seemed to miss legitimate confirmation when it was offered. He vigilantly kept his eye on the ball, but it was a different ball from the one he claimed. If he were looking for recognition as an artist he would have seen it arriving. What he truly hungered for, the hollow in the pit of his soul that would never be sufficiently satisfied, was public avowal that his work reflected back upon himself the dignity that he had determined was the "ultimate subject matter of art."

In November, Barney—one of those artists Reinhardt was "slandering"—remained unoffended enough to join Reinhardt and Parsons to propose that *Life* magazine—the enemy *Life*—do a story on the gallery and its remaining artists.[35] Approached for his cooperation, the even thinner-skinned Still, simmering with anger at the Woodstock presentation, finally told Parsons he joined Janis.

Still's description of these happenings to Miller are the preamble to the shocking events of the next eighteen months. "Adolph Reinhardt," he wrote, "had just inaugurated his effort to haul me into the arena of the public brawl via an assault in print. He learns fast from his colleague Newman, that the way to notoriety is to climb on a better man's back." And now that the ice was broken with Janis, he promised Miller, "you will see an interesting act or effort. Newman and the others will move toward Janis, the thing already started with Barney's espousal of Jack . . . . In fact, I heard Newman say that he would try soon to bring Betty and Sidney together and organize them, for some kind of grandios [*sic*] propaganda machine for the display of his concept of himself as Jaweh, (the latter words are mine)."[36]

Still warned Miller that "Newman and Reinhardt . . . seem to be nice guys when one talks to them, at first. Then the frustrations reveal themselves in the calculated deceits and the unguarded gestures. I have always insisted that these men can never take what they dish out, and I have had the pleasure of seeing them both collapse to whimpering frightened little boys hiding behind their women's skirts when I put the pressure on." Their frustration was so great, Still believed, that "they must kill what they feed on or they would die themselves."[37]

THIRTY-SIX

INDIGNATION

Who can say *what* set Barney off, or when precisely it happened? As always, it took a critical mass, rather than a unique instance, of perceived injustices to provoke the extravagant, disproportionate, *geshray*.

Over the months of 1954—and through the next three years—as Barney's injustice collecting escalated so did his capricious, eventually reckless, behavior, at odds with his squire's presentation but not his resentful sense of entitlement. Burdened by debt, he didn't unload the car, or cut back on shopping. Stuyvesant Liquors became a regular stop—to cash checks for his increasing demands and satisfy his increasing thirst.

At the end of 1953 Hess, reviewing Reinhardt's Parsons show, was serious and laudatory.[1] It was bad enough that Hess, whose book Barney had done battle with for months, had praised in Reinhardt exactly what he hadn't in Barney: that any evidence to the contrary, the work did *not* derive from Mondrian or the Bauhaus; that its heart was non-verbal, that it was best described by what it was "not"; that despite the "impersonal distance" in paint application, the pictures betrayed "an individual (if cool) involvement" with material; that the difficulty in talking about the work derived from the uselessness of "aesthetic qualities whose labels [were] bankrupted by generations of sloppy thinking." Hess didn't mind that Reinhardt was combative and that "declarations of his art's independence [were] often needlings of some one else's position," nor that he was "generous with needles," nor that there were "many difficulties in Reinhardt's [theoretical] position." Reinhardt was "cool," "funny," and satiric. Likable, from Hess's point of view, not irritating like Barney—and so his more restrained personality allowed Hess to *see* the art, rather than just swallow it.

Barney may have been the farthest thing from Hess's mind when he wrote about Reinhardt's work, but it didn't seem that way to Barney, as Hess parsed the meaning of "fine" in "fine arts" just as Barney had the previous year at Woodstock.

There were genuine victims in the American cultural community. In the prevailing climate of hysterical red baiting and virulent homophobia, actors, writers, directors, choreographers—artists of many sorts—lived in oppressive fear or were compelled to compromise their ethics by naming names or to destroy themselves by refusing. In Barney's needy and self-aggrandizing reactive manner, he elevated his own perceived plight, at least in his mind, to mirror those he followed in the news. Scratch-pad venting and furiously compulsive doodles preserve Barney's agitation: the first half of 1954 was filled with tantrums. Barney wanted a fight, but no one seemed to be listening.

Art Digest asked a heterogeneous selection of eight artists about their "Creative Process." Rollin Crampton, the New York supervisor of the WPA mural project—and Woodstock host of Barney and Annalee in August 1952 and of Reinhardt in 1953—answered that "Modern painters whose beliefs are similar to my philosophical

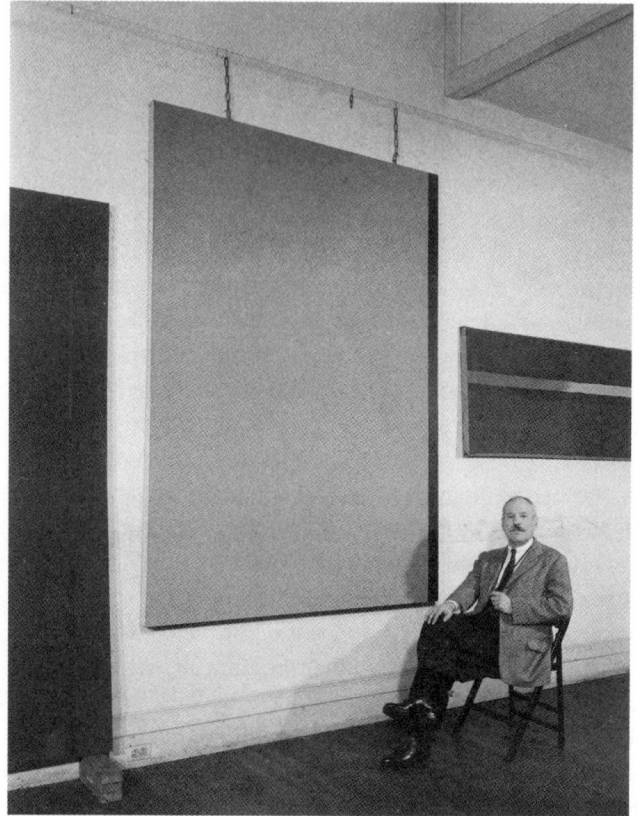

Fig. 33 *La bella figura*: Barnett Newman in his Front Street studio with *Adam, Eve,* and *Horizon Light,* early 1950s. Photograph William Vandivert

searching, such as Ad Reinhardt, Barney Newman and Mark Rothko, I find vital." Undoubtedly, Crampton wanted to associate himself with one pole of what by now were generally accepted as the most progressive artists and it was a minor note in a long article. But it was not minor to Barney, who embarked on one of his campaigns of righteous indignation—huffy drafts and revisions of a "Letter to the Editor," accompanied by letters to the editor, Hub Crehan, negotiating about its publication.

"Kindly advise your readers that Mr. Rollin Crampton and I know each other so little and for such a short time that Mr. Crampton has no basis by which he can make the claim that <u>my</u> 'belief' [*sic*] is similar to his "philosophic searchings." The crucial point, though, had not to do with Crampton, but others. "His statement is even more serious when it insinuates that I maintain a body of belief and that such doctrine is held in common with Ad Reinhardt and Mark Rothko. This is unjust to everyone concerned." Barney invoked his "work and published writings" to make "precisely" the point that he was "against dogmatic belief,"[2] conveniently overlooking the fact that some of those writings—for example, in *Tiger's Eye* five years earlier—supported Crampton's assumption: "I believe that here in America, *some of us,* free from the weight of European culture, are finding the answer . . . . *We* are reasserting man's natural desire for the exalted . . . . *We* do not need the obsolete props of an outmoded and antiquated legend . . . . *We* are freeing ourselves of the impediments of memory, association, nostalgia, legend, myth . . . . The image *we* produce is the self-evident one of revelation [emphasis added]."[3]

This, rather than any "dogmatic belief" was what was implied by Crampton. But by the end of January 1954 Barney had made up his mind to be associated aesthetically with no other artist. And this, "precisely," would drive the rest of his life. He was *sui generis*.

It was a leitmotif in his ongoing conversation with Reinhardt. "The only piece of wisdom now (a variation or version of your wisdom?) and the only weltanshauung [*sic*] to take [is Sam Goldwyn's] when he said 'include me out!'" read a May postcard to Barney from Paris.[4] Before he took off for six weeks overseas, Reinhardt had readied his Woodstock talk of the previous summer for publication in the forthcoming *College Art Journal*. His handwritten notes were transcribed on one of Annalee's typewriters by either Annalee or Rita, and the article ended with a story that Barney characteristically picked up from a news report and told Reinhardt: "A friend of mine," Reinhardt wrote,

> heard Roosevelt tell a story at a Jackson-Day-dinner as he introduced a Republican, about a teacher who asked her class one day who wanted to go to heaven. When Johnny was the only student who didn't raise his hand, the teacher asked, "What's the matter, Johnny, don't you want to go to heaven?" "Sure" he answered, "but not with them guys."[5]

Reinhardt also left behind, in the April *Art News*, "Founding Fathers Follyday" ("Avantgardekunstvereinabstractexpressionistnewyorkschoolfoundlingfathersapril fielddaysportsguide"), an especially complicated program of the art world, with genealogical trees, institutional advertisements, and bowling-, wrestling-, and boxing-match cards. Heavyweights, welters, middleweights down through bantams: artists were matched against each other in pun-entitled venues. Barney alone did not face off against an artist (Motherwell fought Motherwell in an "all out knock down grudge fight"). The heavyweight match in "Limbogymnasium" was "Newmanvs-Beelzebub (supermanvssdemigod)." By this time, at least, Reinhardt was sensitive enough to Barney's stance not to have set up a spurious association. But Beelzebub? Limbo? Barney was not in a joking mood.

He was especially agitated that month, prickly with friends and strangers alike. A lawsuit and countersuit—over property damages and personal injury suffered and non-payment of rent—between Barney and his landlord had been ongoing since 1952, with a retrial date set for May 20, 1954. He began a festering resentment with Herbert Ferber (Silvers) over money owed for dental visits by both Newmans; the argument, largely in his own head (where its submerged source was Ferber's continuing friendship with Rothko),[6] would not be settled for ten years—when Barney decided to make a case that he, Barney, was owed 167 dollars for the catalogue foreword he had written for Ferber's 1947 show at Parsons, and Ferber wondered why it took seventeen years to "apprise me of your fee for a work on which I have always felt a high enough value could not be set."[7]

Everything provoked him. Reading about MoMA's acquisition of the American Pavilion in Venice and the Guggenheim's acquisition of *The Clock Maker (The Man with Folded Arms)* by Cézanne, Barney revived his dispute with MoMA in the very place Reinhardt had him duking it out with the devil: *Art News*. He appealed to Alfred Frankfurter and Hess, respectively editor and executive editor of the magazine, to publish the correspondence in order to "act as a starting point to reexamine the policies of museums."[8]

By May, his indignity intensified. He had been to the Guggenheim to view the Cézanne that he had previously only seen reproduced in the *Times*[9] and noticed that it was displayed without a frame. "As one of the first artists in America to eliminate frames from his own work, as one who has consistently opposed the use of frames for himself," this was too much. The Impressionists might have been against the gilt frames of the Salons, but "they liked and did use their own frames." Showing Cézanne without a frame was "edited art history."[10]

He drafted a letter to James Johnson Sweeney, director of the Guggenheim, to inquire about the "full meaning" of the museum's new Cézanne—"a nineteenth-century picture." Did it mean that the Guggenheim intended to become "a general museum"? Did the Guggenheim "intend to repeat or to follow the pattern of slanted art history" of MoMA? To establish "yourself as an authority that will trace the development of art" from Cézanne through Duchamp to the "Bauhaus screwdriver designers?" Answers were demanded: "As an artist-citizen, I call upon you to [respond] to eliminate the uneasiness the American artist and the American public feel at the possibility of an additional fake art history being promulgated."[11]

Of course, indignation was not solely Barney's province; much of the country's population was feeling morally bludgeoned. The Army–McCarthy hearings[12] easily trumped personal peeves. Immediately before the proceedings began to be broadcast in April 1954 Barney bought a new television. Although for the most part visual artists were not a focus of Senator Joseph McCarthy and lawyer Roy Cohn—Rockwell Kent and Ben Shahn were notable exceptions—for everyone from nail-chewing suburban housewives to Tony Smith in Germany (glued to American radio broadcasts) and Reinhardt in England (complaining about the ten cents for the *Paris Herald Tribune* "in order to find out how the hearings are going"),[13] they shadowed everyday life.

There was certainly a penumbra touching the Newman family. The previous year the Senate committee had investigated employees at the Voice of America, where Sarah Newman was working, and now it was searching for spies and Communists within Fort Monmouth in New Jersey, where she had been stationed on and off since the war. Undoubtedly a minor character, she was investigated by the House

Committee on Un-American Activities at least once, at the end of 1950, and, having held a position with the Office of Strategic Services (precursor to the CIA), was on their radar.[14] But Barney found an even more personal stake. As he invoked Holocaust horrors in his tribute to Gorky, as he would invoke MacArthur in a 1956 exchange with Rosenberg, Barney very soon found a way for the national trauma of McCarthyism to amplify his own private torment.

"Have you no sense of decency?"

Spoken live on television while hundreds of thousands watched, these words, if not a thunderbolt in the maelstrom of the Army–McCarthy hearings, nevertheless were a startlingly dramatic wakeup call on June 9. What had people been thinking? How had they let this travesty go on so long?

If one were a righteous narcissist, someone feeling sorely used, unappreciated, *unacknowledged*, this might have been an inspiration to expose the "frustrated leeches," to thwart and expose "frauds." In late June, Still debated, in a letter, whether it was worth his energy. But when the time was right, he assured Barney, "I will <u>act</u>, as always—with considerable directness + vigor."[15] In a community where chronological priority was the prize, it was almost a dare.

While he was in Glasgow, or Paris, or Madrid, or Munich, or Greece, Reinhardt's text version of his Woodstock talk had appeared in the summer issue of *College Art Journal*, the College Art Association's peer-evaluated quarterly. Across the country, Still was steaming.[16] The mention of Reinhardt's name induced in him a "nausea identical with" the one he experienced on his "first visit to a slaughter house" in Spokane—and that was one of the nicer things Still had to say.[17] While he never ceased biting Barney's back,[18] from the side Still continued to whisper like Iago in his ear, and, ever vigilant in the face of imaginary oppressors, he encouraged an alliance between them. And yet as recently as March, Still had been complaining to others about what he viewed as the opposed alliance and "antics" of Barney and Reinhardt;[19] "the cartoonists in the art-rags are at least contributing to their own demise . . . not an utterly unhappy thought," he told Miller.[20]

Reinhardt, for his part, did feel an alliance with Barney, but of a friendlier, more supportive sort than Still's imagined power-plays. Before he left the U.S. in May, Reinhardt had voted against recommending Rothko for tenure at Brooklyn, and "kept writing" notes to Robert Wolff, the head of the art department, to recommend Barney as the "best possible replacement for Rothko."[21] But as his travels wore on he grew increasingly disaffected. "I'm preparing some more aggressive post cards for artist-friends, I don't know why I'm mad at all of them, even slightly at Barney."[22]

There's no question Barney needed a job; he had also, unsuccessfully, applied for—even assumed he had been promised—a position at the University of California for which Still had paved the way.[23] In his own injured and resentful state of mind, Barney concluded that his categorization in Reinhardt's text was responsible for him not getting it[24]—notwithstanding that many of the others with whom he was grouped *did* have secure teaching positions, that he was in no way singled out; in *his* mind, as always, being singular, he *was* singled out. He began to collect newspaper clippings about libel suits, a practice he continued for the next couple of years. On June 29, he read that historically large damages—175,001 dollars—were awarded to Quentin Reynolds in his action against Westbrook Pegler and two Hearst corporations.[25] Within a month Barney contacted a lawyer to press his own libel suit, very specifically urging that the complaint should include not only that the name-calling ("i.e. 'artist-professor'") was defamatory, but also that the association with "men who willingly represent the Bauhaus and Neo-Plasticism makes me a disciple and a follower of an aesthetic line and of a political line that is damaging to me—and is deliberate slander."[26]

A talk, delivered in person with intonation and pauses for laugh-lines was one thing. But the *College Art Journal* was a "very important magazine, a very serious magazine," where, in Barney's mind, "all the important things about art" were memorialized in print.[27] Perhaps he could handle the joking when he was feeling stronger, his dignity intact. But what he could not bear was looking like a *shmo*.[28]

On a pad with uncharacteristically agitated doodles, spattered with copious drips of what might have been coffee, or whiskey, but also might have been blood from his vocal nodes or chronic stomach inflammations—he occasionally coughed up blood—along with sketches for a synagogue that anticipate the one he elaborated nine years later, and notes analyzing the science of the race track and various betting "systems," there are drafts of an inflammatory, and not entirely rational, "press release."

> Barnett Newman considered by some [changed from "many"] art critics, the most extreme [changed from "advanced"] artist in America, (see N.Y. Times Jan 29, 1950, Apr 29, 1951, Vogue Oct 1, 1951) today filed suit for libel in the amount of $150,000 against Ad Reinhardt, ex-cartoonist for PM and the Art News and the College Art Association publishers of the College Art Journal for publishing an article in their current issue by Reinhardt. The subject of the article is the same as an address made by him at the Woodstock Art Conference. In doing so he is protecting himself and the good name of all practicing artists.
>
> Mr. Newman accuses Reinhardt and the College Art Association of damaging his professional reputation by deliberately false, untrue and malicious statements concerning his activities as an artist, of holding his work up to ridicule by linking it with the work of a group of painters selected for the purpose. In the article, Mr. Newman charges "Reinhardt has tried to make himself the only 'fine' artist by defaming not only me but every important artist in America. Over forty names are linked and unlinked and their work and characters maligned."
>
> In this article Reinhardt called Newman an artist-professor, a newspaper philosopher-poet, a Bauhaus exerciser, a traveling design salesman, the avant-garde huckster handicraftsman and educational-shop-keeper . . . and linked him with Albers, Bolotowsky, Chermayeff, Diller, Holtzman, Morris, Motherwell, Wolff etc.
>
> Every name mentioned by Reinhardt is or has been a university professor including himself. Reinhardt is Assistant Professor of Design at Brooklyn College.

"All except me. I have never and do not now teach in any college or university. It is no disgrace that the others do but it is a complete falsehood concerning me. So are the other defamations."

Mr. Newman continued "there is all the hullabaloo about what McCarthy called his fellow senators. *Nothing that McCarthy called them approaches the shameless libel Reinhardt has committed against me and over forty of my fellow artists,* by means of the most nasty abuse and through name linking. It disqualifies him together with his work from being called an artist [emphasis added]."

It was another instance when Barney's narcissistic and self-righteous hyperbole (not to say disingenuity, since he was at the time chasing a teaching position) obscured an issue worth considering. Reinhardt's motive was not in doubt: he was fed up with the maneuvering that characterized the scene and infected institutions. But Barney thought the College Art Association, "an organization of university art professors," had something else at stake.

"The college boys were glad to use Reinhardt to discredit his colleagues so that they could put a stop to the practice now current in the colleges of employing practicing artists rather than art professors. Why did they make sure to eliminate the names of several professional professors? Why did they protect their own against Reinhardt and let him loose on the practicing artists?"

And even here, in an action that was certain to bring nothing good—a "grotesquely quixotic public gesture"[29]—Barney could not resist asserting his priority.

This is perhaps the first time an American artist is suing an artist for libel. It is the first time an artist has dared to sue an organization of art educators.

As he wrote his lawyer, "time is important. A delay may bring complications should others seeing this material decide to use it for their own purposes."[30]

Still had been canoodling with Barney, empathizing with the latter's "effort . . . to keep 'free from the mess' "; he teasingly implied that Barney was the friend "one is extra fortunate" to have to "talk to freely." But the message was mixed: "Following the initial nausea and feeling of outrage" as he left New York earlier that year, came the recognition that the whole tumult "should have bored me." Meanwhile, his own work and vision would, *on his own terms* "continue to be of highest importance in all decisions I chose to make. The corruption of utility and the obscenities of logic will be relegated to their proper and low position in the heirarchy [*sic*] of values."[31]

Having egged Barney on, Still now was coy.

All the while, Reinhardt remained confident that he and Barney, at least, were on the same side, addressing Barney from Europe as a comrade in arms. In July, after he returned, the Newmans spent a sociable evening at his and Rita's apartment viewing slides from the trip. After, when he couldn't reach him, he wrote postcards to Barney from down the street—"Have you gone away? For a long time? Long distance?"—filled with familial quotidian minutia and digs at those Reinhardt assumed were irritations in common—"Motherwell's mad at me. Cliff [*sic*] sent me via Pat [Garske] a poison pen note and I sent him via Pat a four worded nasty card." Feeling detached from so many but secure in this friendship, he reported the "news of the month as if I had led a social time and knew those people above very well still."[32] Not yet aware of the depth of *Barney*'s sense of betrayal, Reinhardt was not innocent about others' feelings. Motherwell was "still mad at me for an article which I wrote calling him an educational-shop-keeper, a traveling-design-salesman, an art-digest-philosopher-poet, and a professorial-button holer, can you imagine anybody getting sore just for that?," he joked to Smith in August.[33] Rothko, too, was unhappy.[34]

Through August, when he wrote to Smith (in Germlish), "Die Newmans oder BB's, answering nicht der telephone so mussen sie vieleicht away gegangen haven etwas ein bischen vacation zu enjoyin also analee must soon zurick zu arbeit gehen nach laborday, so wir expecting zu horen von sem soon" (The Newmans or BB's are not answering their phone so they may have gone away a little in order to enjoy a short vacation also Annalee must soon go back to work after Labor Day so we are expecting to hear from them soon),[35] through Rosh Hashanah—he sent a fanciful, scroll-filled "Happy New Year" drawing at the end of September—Reinhardt seemed not to suspect that anything was amiss.

But Barney had already acted. On August 18, a court summons was issued, and Barney and Annalee made arrangements to return to Cape May, to an Audubon Center, for a brief birdwatching vacation in the middle of September. They were back in time to see the riveting, heavily promoted and covered, television production of the jury room drama, "Twelve Angry Men." The story of one honorable man standing up for what was right in the face of overwhelming pressure could not have been more timely.

The complaint was filed at the very end of September. "It's easy for me to understand the thing, but for pulling it into the legal world, making it a vulgar act that's not easy to forgive, and a fantastic fluke," Reinhardt wrote to Parsons. "I can explain to you perhaps why I listed names," in four groups for "four general ideas," four decades, thirteen artists in each group "all of them my friends and colleagues, all of them distinguished."

"But how explain the listing of BN's name as a way of 'including' him as a way of 'not excluding' him in any consideration of influential artists?—How explain my 'tongue-in-cheek' writing as a kind of self-questioning? Which BN knows? And knew??"[36] Having sent these words to Parsons, Reinhardt knew they would find their way to Barney. Which they did, with no effect. The painting which Reinhardt had given to Annalee during more halcyon days was now found on his Nineteenth Street doorstep with no explanation.[37]

Estranged from Reinhardt, with Smith in Europe, and with Pollock himself alternating between rage and despair, Barney was by turns susceptible to Still's goading or left on his own. He had declined to show again with Parsons; he was not included in the summer's "Younger American Painters" at the Guggenheim; he was not to be included in the four hundred works by forty-five artists—as were de Kooning, Still, Tworkov, Grace Hartigan, and the recent *Art News* annointed Lee Gatch—in the Museum of Modern Art's 25th anniversary show; not hung in the new quarters of the Whitney Museum. He kept careful track.

He was feeling, as always, very pinched financially, spending more and more on alcohol. Fortunately, here his *amour propre* served him very well. Unlike so many of his peers, whose increased drinking made them mean, violent, aggressive, embarrassed them or worse, Barney never *appeared* inebriated: his imbibing seemed to help him function, help him to turn down, to control the external static stirred up by his agita. He finally sold his car. He lost face with the rest of the Newman family by appearing at his cousin's wedding without Annalee and without a gift—not even, his relatives always pointed out, a "little painting." He began to consider playing the stock market. He did more than consider playing the horses.

Barney had begun a serious study of horse-racing in the middle of 1953. As he had done with botany and ornithology and geology and tribal art and Indian mound building—and weightlifting, harmonica playing, and floor shellacking—he diligently developed his own curriculum, now systematically studying the layouts of the tracks around New York. He read turf reports and *The Blood-Horse*—which analyzed such specifics as sires and earnings—and signed up for the Hugh Matheson lectures that he read about in *Time* magazine that September, conscientiously filling notebooks with tenets of this new "science."

"No good horse player ever counts on luck," was Matheson's credo. His course promised to teach how to decipher the fine type in the form charts, so that a good handicapper could judge "a thoroughbred's breeding, consistency and condition, its ability to carry the assigned weight, the skill of the jockey and the ability of the trainer" and confirm his judgment in the paddock. Done wisely, Matheson promised, a man could earn a living.[38]

He began to avoid phone calls, even in the middle of the night, when Pollock would often try Barney at 3.00 a.m., waking Annalee. Barney, she would tell him, was at the studio.[39] He discoursed "rhapsodically about the Hasidim, and the culture of fidelity. The culture of devotion to ideas." The ecstasy, the joy through dancing, the "Hasidic temperament."[40] (The ecstatic and moral were often conflated in Barney's ethos.) To Pollock, who was putting together a group of artists to visit the Barnes Foundation, he telegraphed: "My dislike of Barnes Foundation and what Barnes stood for is so intense I could not accept any invitation. This should not influence your desire to visit the place my revulsion is my own, it goes back to my teens when it enormously affected my life and thinking."

His "revulsion was his own," as well, when the "brand" of avant-garde art reached its most prominent public position and inspired the most high-falutin rhetoric in October, around the celebration of the twenty-fifth anniversary of the Museum of Modern Art. D'Harnoncourt and Barr, speaking on prime-time television about the "relation of modern art to everyday living"—anathema to Barney—and carefully placed magazine articles built anticipation. On October 19, in an opening ceremony extravaganza, a recorded speech by President Eisenhower that cited the artist's freedom to create as "one of the pillars of liberty" was heard by an assembly of 2500 people in the sculpture garden and broadcast on radio and television: "For our Republic to stay free those among us with the rare gift of artistry must be able freely to use their talent . . . . As long as artists are at liberty to feel with high personal intensity, as long as our artists are free to create with sincerity and conviction, there will be healthy controversy and progress in art." UN Secretary-General Dag Hammarskjöld said that modern international politics must be approached in the same spirit as modern art. And several others, including Mayor Robert Wagner, and the chief editorial writer for the *Herald Tribune*, August Heckscher, generally echoed one theme: that modern art, and especially MoMA, contributed to "the central struggle of the age," as Heckscher put it, "the struggle of freedom against tyranny."

A week later, the new home of the Whitney Museum, previously on Eighth Street, opened adjacent to MoMA. In neither building, in neither celebration, did Barney figure.

And so, when Barney received an invitation from the Sidney Janis Gallery to an October opening, he could only continue to comfort himself by condescendingly reveling in his outsider status, his absolute purity, "the dedication, integrity and sincerity that the artist has in the creation of his work" that was the primary test of a fine artist.[41] He would *not* go to heaven with "them guys." "Dear Sidney," he wrote:

> It seems strange to me that after six years, you have decided to invite me to the openings held at your gallery.
>
> As you know, I have attended all of your shows during these years, as an artist member of the general public. The only openings I have come to were those given by Jackson Pollock because I was specifically invited to them by him.
>
> I should prefer it if we let things continue as they are. I realize that you may feel this to be severe; that it is better late than never. To me, however, there is also that which is—too late, and I do not wish to become involved in the pathos of mistakes and oversights.
>
> I have, therefore, refused to accept your recent invitation.[42]

Psychologically wounded, Barney focused and clarified and amplified his grievance against Reinhardt. "The Artist in Search of An Academy" became the vessel in which to pour all the doubts and wounds and rejections and secretly felt inadequacies of a lifetime of semi-successful repression behind beautiful suits and elegant intellect. Excruciatingly he flayed himself, as, to his lawyer, he expanded on his official legal complaint.

Because the "primary test of a fine artist involves the dedication, integrity and sincerity that the artist has in the creation of his work," the meaning of the article, he wrote, was:

> That the plaintiff is not a fine artist or an artist at all but is instead masquerading as an artist or a fine artist and is a charlatan and a fake; that the plaintiff is incompetent as an artist and incapable of being one; that the plaintiff is a laughable and ludicrous individual; that the plaintiff is egotistically exploiting the fact that he is "a public art image" and makes himself ridiculous; that the plaintiff is a presumptuous "artistic character" and a freak and is engaged in clownish activities; that the plaintiff is dishonest, a man without the integrity of a dedicated artist and without the sincerity and seriousness of a fine artist engaged in the true practice of his profession; that the plaintiff is involved in a public hoax and is exploiting art for commercial and social purposes; that the plaintiff is not devoted to the creation of his work but that he is involved in an absurd activity for the sake of getting public attention; that the plaintiff is constantly debasing himself instead of maintaining the ideals of a fine artist.[43]

Laughable, ludicrous, a freak, and a clown. A month before he would turn 50, is this what his life had amounted to? Whatever the source of the drops on the writing pad, Barney was bleeding.

By November, as the lawsuit was moving forward—stunning, or embarrassing those in the community who knew Barney and Reinhardt—Still, on the East Coast since September, was enmeshed in maneuvers with MoMA over a painting, or a "replica" of a painting, and avoided the put-upon Barney. "I wish you would call me," Barney wrote, "we have so much to say to each other."[44] Ducking Barney's calls Still may have been, but he used Barney in his own campaign to have Reinhardt fired. The *Art Journal* article was "widely read" in libraries and colleges "throughout the land," and had made Brooklyn College, "as well as the artists named, the butt for contemptuous obscenities and vulgar derogations," Still wrote to the dean. To strengthen his case, he told Dean Gaede that Reinhardt and the *College Art Journal* had been sued for libel by one of the artists, and assured him that "there is every reason to believe that the plaintiff will be wholly successful."[45] Just before he returned west, Still did meet Barney in the middle of December and described him to Ossorio as full of friendly feeling toward all except Rothko and Reinhardt.[46]

Back in San Francisco, even as he continued to lobby Brooklyn College against Reinhardt, Still assumed the mantle of a statesman. He wrote to Barney that, "from this view [of] the 'scene' . . . what were once dilemmas calling for most absolute decisions have a way of being seen years later as mere mistakes or errors of judgement obscured by pity, hopes, or outrage"—cruelly detouring to the high road and leaving Barney stranded on the low. Nevertheless, he enlisted Barney to collect information that would enable Still to pursue (or to make Barney believe he was pursuing) his quest to convince the "highest board" members at Brooklyn College of the difference between "freedom of thought + freedom to libel."[47] A week later, he coyly reported that although he had "prepared for further action," he had moved on from Reinhardt, and hoped to involve Barney in eviscerating Rothko, whose recent solo show—his first since 1951—at the Art Institute of Chicago was a sharp thorn in their sensitive hides.[48]

To Ossorio, Still now declared that he had "with finality" turned his back on the "scene," and the "farce" that over the past few years had "taken place in the Parsons Gallery," and which had now come to its "sordid and inevitable conclusion." And yet he would be back in March 1955, conspiring in "long and probing discussions" with Barney over an entirely new "gambit."[49]

THIRTY-SEVEN

THE BLACKEST PERIOD

On January 29, he turned 50. Armies of men mark the occasion by buying a new car and so did Barney. Amazingly, it was Still's 1946 convertible that he chose—a broken-down car of constant sorrows, which continued to run only because Still himself was able to maintain it. He tried to write an "important" play with his old friend Luis Navascués.[1] He tried to learn to play golf from a book. But these classic compensations were not sufficient. At the beginning of his *annus horribilis* he needed to scream.

It was the "blackest" period of his life, he later told Hess. He hadn't shown in four years, there were no sales. He was embarrassed that Annalee was still supporting him, that he had to borrow from his family. He pawned his watch and binoculars, even while he was spending more than ever. He tried to make money buying and selling IOUs in the garment district, kiting checks and covering them at the last minute with loans. He wrote to a tailor offering to become a fitter and dreamed of "chalking up"—fitting—Jock Whitney.[2] When Parsons asked someone how she could get hold of Barney, she was informed "his studio is among the trees at Belmont" racetrack on Long Island.

As if by evil design, his little apartment building had been sold. As bad as his relations had been with "Discreet Realty Corporation," those with the new owners would be much worse. The East End Temple, located on Fourteenth Street, was not in the real estate business and was not acquiring the building as a residential property; they were interested in occupying it themselves. In January, tenants were asked to give "immediate and serious consideration to securing other quarters."[3]

In order to defend his own dignity, and the dignity, the intense seriousness that he demanded of "fine" art, he screamed and screamed and screamed in the most undignified way possible. Thus began months of unrestrained correspondence with East End Temple, with Janis about Rothko, and with Whitehorn & Cowin, the law firm pressing his suit against Reinhardt. He picked fights with Greenberg over his inclusion in a highbrowed essay; with Hess for only including him in a footnote in a review of a show he was *not* in; with *Time* magazine, and with the Jockey Club of America. Barney's rage and sense of injustice were so all-consuming and widespread, it is sometime difficult to parse the insults and nerve-endings torched.

His reliable and mutually supportive relationship with Parsons—consulting, advising, installing—was frayed. Of course he avoided Reinhardt's show at the end of January. Required by his lawyers to respond to Barney's amended complaint, Reinhardt begged them to "never mention the name Newman again."[4] The papers submitted to the court by the white-shoe law firm Rosenman Goldmark Colin & Kaye, which was retained by the College Art Association, were based on extensive correspondence with Reinhardt and explicitly humiliating to a degree far beyond the original satire.

The plaintiff has been and has sought positions as an art instructor, is a frequent writer of letters and comments published in art magazines and journals, has instigated and injected himself into numerous controversies and disputes in the art world and elsewhere, and is considered by those artists who know him as one who constantly talks about, writes about, expounds and seeks to explain and popularize art and his theories of art, rather than as a true "fine artist" . . . .

Plaintiff, by his actions and by reason of such reputation as he has succeeded in creating for himself, is in truth a member of the category of artists described in the twelfth paragraph of the article . . . .

The professional reputation of the plaintiff in the art world among persons familiar with his activities, works and philosophies is bad in that plaintiff is thought to be an over-aggressive, unimaginative, insignificant and incompetent artist.

And yet, they insisted, the article had been "without malice."[5] But if that were the case in June 1954, the assertions in the court documents could only support Barney's conviction that malice indeed existed. In print, in the public record, these words viciously abraded his deepest insecurities.

On a particularly bad day, he drafted a letter to Parsons to explain:

I know that it is being said for example that I did not come to Reinhardt's show because I am angry at him and I am suing him for libel. It is also being said in regard to others that I have removed myself from the art world, that I seek privacy, that I am bitter, that I have quit. And that is why I am not showing. Nothing could be farther from the truth. . . .

I wish to make public now that I did not go to see Reinhardt, not because of anger in that I am suing him for libel, but out of apprehension that should I have gone I would need to institute another law suit for plagiarism. For it was Reinhardt himself who said to me at the time he came to ask me for advice on how to receive Hess who was to do an article on him . . . that even though he knows that people will say his work stems and looks like mine he did not think it really did. I agreed it was a parody and told him to speak only for and about himself . . . .

It was Reinhardt who said . . . that he felt his role as painter was pure and should not be contaminated. He painted and as for the rest it wasn't his responsibility. What happened to the pictures or to himself was Betty Parsons' impure needs in an impure world. The evils were her guilt. In these sophistries he hid his ambition to reduce you to become the doer of his dirty work. For him to be the saint he needed you for his devil.[6]

In early March, he boiled over. *Time* magazine was amused to report that the French artist Mathieu, currently showing at Kootz, "by adroitly publicizing himself," had become "the reigning darling of advance-guard art" and referred to the "laudatory essay" in *Art News* that described a balletic performance in which he made abstract works titled after episodes from early French history.[7] "To paint an abstraction of the 13th-century Battle of Bouvines . . . he dressed up in black silk pants and jacket, a white helmet, and greaves fastened to his shins with white cross-straps."[8] The association with "abstract expressionism" could not go unchecked. Barney pounced.

To the Editor, Time Magazine:

> Are there any readers of TIME who wish to join me in sending a pair of sterling silver roller skates, suitably engraved, to George Mathieu so that he may re-do his I WAS THERE dance routine of the Battle of Bouvines into a big Blitzkrieg production?
>
> Too bad he and his Tapié friends could not find a more recent fighter-ancestor, so that they could have done the choreography for, let us say, the breakthrough at Sedan, but I suppose they had no relatives who were fighting in 1940 . . . . [9]
>
> TIME may be laughing at Mathieu's press-agent antics but when its Art Editor says that his works, "surpass the average of their kind precisely because they fail to be quite meaningless," it is obvious that he cannot tell the imitation from the originals "of the rock'em, sock'em school of abstract art."[10]

Days later, Still admonished Kootz, against the "witless propagandist Mathieu" and his "vicious and sterile tart's gambit."[11]

Barney, upping Still's ante, continued the attack on multiple fronts. To Kootz:

> Last month . . . I saw the Art News. My outrage at the deliberate insult to my intelligence and to my values . . . compelled me to write the Art News, that very day.
>
> It is only fair, then, that I now, send you a copy of my letter, since your name is mentioned in it and you are the responsible representative of this "artist".
>
> P.S. I am sending copies of my letter enclosed to all those mentioned in it.[12]

To Joan E. Gibson, at *Time*:

> This is to confirm our telephone conversation. I must refuse to allow the use of any photographs of my work in connection with my letter on the Mathieu article.
>
> The letter either deserves to be printed or it does not. I wrote it not to enter the Mathieu game of publicity and I do not think that I should be asked to do so under any specious claim of "fairness," "hear all sides," etc.

I am protesting the travesty this Mathieu trickster has made of serious American artists and the imitation he has impudently fashioned of their serious work.[13]

The April issue of *Art News* brought Hess's gushing review of Rothko's first show at Janis: "one of the most enjoyable shows in several years, and once again emphasized the international importance of Rothko as a leader of postwar modern art. His leadership (like Clyfford Still's) is in the direction of simplification." Bramante, Piero della Francesca, Bonnard were invoked.

As long as there have been artists there has been competition: Who will have the honor of creating this tomb, this temple, this basilica? Who will be granted membership in the guild? Who will be awarded the commission for the doors of the Florence Baptistery, the hall of the Palazzo Vecchio? Who will enter the king's court, be voted into the Academy, be exhibited at the Salon? Brunelleschi or Ghiberti? Leonardo or Michelangelo? Ingres or Delacroix, Turner or Constable? There were always concrete rewards along with glory. In mid-20th century America, a topsy-turvy biome where commissions were sniffed at and juries abjured, where the most critically acknowledged artist could barely make a living, a vestigial, if no less fierce, rivalry remained, but it was without concrete reward. Now the pure ambition was to be unequivocally recognized as top dog.

April 9

Dear Mr. Janis: . . .

I have just received two invitation [*sic*] from both the painter and from you, to attend Rothko's show. I have, after much thought, decided not to. I feel, therefore, that I owe you an explanation.

I am not going to Rothko's show for the same reasons that I did not attend those of Mathieu and Reinhardt. I am frankly bored with the uninspired, or to put it more accurately, I am bored with the too-easily inspired. It was Rothko who said to me that it does not matter that an artist "looks" at other painters. It is not what he "sees" but what he "does" with what he "sees" that counts. This is the credo of a virtuouso [*sic*], of the salon painter, of the social and public man, and whether it be Mathieu, Reinhardt, or Rothko, this easy ability to be inspired . . . is so at variance with my own point of view that I can only reject everything it involves.

Anybody can make a painting, and there are some who can do it with dash and brilliance. However, it is a different matter to <u>create</u> a work. I am not interested in cadenzas, no matter how ecstatic they may seem and no matter how seductively a painter may improvise them. The time has come to speak out against them . . . .

Why should I look at [Rothko's] death image? I am involved in life, in the joy of the spirit . . . .

A man's work and the man who makes the work form an equation. The same virtuousity [*sic*] that begs in the work for public approval has been the means whereby moral issues against the philistine world could be juggled. It is true that Rothko talks the fighter, He fights however, to submit to the philistine world. My struggle against bourgeois society has involved the total rejection of it . . . .

I must unequivocally separate myself from Rothko because he has publicly identified himself with me . . . .

I insist that a man and his work must not only say what he means, but they also must mean what he says. And it is on this proposition that I stake my life.[14]

This was *personal*, a wailing *cri de coeur* from a man possessed by his vision and standard of morality, over which he was willing to self-immolate.

And yet, a few days earlier, Janis had received from Still his own letter, four times the length of Barney's, and even more filled with grievance, vulgarity, and accusations.

Dear Sidney:

A few weeks ago when I visited your gallery you extended to me an invitation to attend your exhibition of work by Mark Rothko. Insomuch as it is very doubtful that I will accept your request I consider it an appropriate time to explain my decision. For Rothko's presence is one of the significant reasons why I was unwilling to have an exhibition in your gallery at this time.

Ten years ago I came to New York with hope, and disciplines of thought and a vision which have since most literally cut through the shoddy fabric of centuries of self-deception in art and aesthetics, and with almost naked hands, created new and individual "forms" to extend man's comprehension and revelation . . . . I naively desired to share my "conception" and purpose . . .

Insomuch as the "form" of this painting and the man who makes it are as one, Rothko requires that his paintings be read as an exercise in Authoritarian imagery. When they are hung in tight phalanx, as he would have them hung, and flooded with the light he demands that they receive, the tyranny of his ambition to suffocate or crush all who stand in his way becomes fully manifest . . . . Not I, but himself, has made it clear that his work is of frustration, resentment and aggression. And that it is the brightness of death that veils their bloodless febrility and clinical evacuations.[15]

The overlapping language, and consistency of attack, leaves no doubt that the two men plotted together—as Still told Ossorio and Betty Freeman.[16] They incited each other's anger and sense of betrayed purpose, and whipped each other into action.

But by the end of the month, when he sent to Ossorio a copy of his rant against Rothko, Still included a letter expanding upon it.[17] "I speak of Rothko as a man who had committed treason, for he has lent his hand to the enemies of life. Also, with few changes, except for his lesser ability and probably therefore greater effectiveness and need, I would have to include Barnett Newman."[18]

What provoked the latest turn against Barney? Greenberg's " 'American-Type' Painting," his treatise on what he considered the most advanced ambitious painting in America, which appeared in the spring issue of *Partisan Review*. ("American-Type Painting" is what the work was called in London.) On the same day that he condemned Barney to Ossorio, Still wrote to Pollock that he had "been apprised of an article by C. Greenberg in the most recent Partisan Review. My name was used in relation to several points, some good, some foolish. For the interest and favorable attitude I wish to give you and your spouse major credit. Therefore, thanks.

"May I add that I wish he had never seen my work or heard of it?"[19]

For Barney, it could not have come at a worse time. Without doubt, his psychological makeup made him unusually vulnerable to feeling unappreciated; but, also without doubt, he was playing with the mean boys. Following soon after what he considered the insult, the vaudeville show, of Mathieu's antics (more directed against his friend Pollock, and his "friend" Still), following *immediately* upon Barney and Still's plotting and their united attack on Rothko, Greenberg's essay cruelly included both the most thoughtful treatment of Barney's own work, *and* further humiliation.

The article began well. De Kooning, according to Greenberg, remained a "late Cubist" but was able to continue Cubism without repeating it. In certain of his works, "The brilliance of the success achieved demonstrates what resources that tradition has left when used by an artist of genius."

About Motherwell, Greenberg wrote that he stood out among the other painters known as "abstract expressionists" by reason of his "lack of real facility," and by having painted "some of the feeblest pictures done by a leading abstract expressionist." Gottlieb was "uneven," capable of a greater range of "controlled effects" than the others, but hampered by "some lack of nerve or necessary presumptuousness"; his 1954 paintings, however, in which there was a display of virtuosity, "were liked better by the public than anything he had shown before," and he seemed to Greenberg "one of the least tired of all the abstract expressionists."

Pollock, having achieved a major breakthrough with "four or five huge canvases of monumental perfection," in 1951, had "pulled back." His 1954 show, "the first to contain pictures that were forced, pumped, dressed up," nevertheless had been a popular success. On the relative value of Cézanne, Cubism, Malevich, and Mondrian on one hand, and Monet and Pissarro on the other, Greenberg and Barney were in agreement, mutually reinforcing.

Greenberg anointed Still "one of the most important and original painters of our time—perhaps the most original of all painters under fifty-five, if not the best." His paintings, Greenberg continued, were the "first abstract pictures I ever saw that contained almost no allusion to Cubism." Still's art "has a special importance at this time because it shows abstract painting a way out of its own academicism." And it was then Greenberg committed the unforgiveable sin: "An indirect sign of this importance is the fact that he is almost the only abstract expressionist to 'make' a school; by this I mean that a few of the many artists he has stimulated or influenced have not been condemned by that to imitate him, but have been able to establish strong and independent styles of their own.

"Barnett Newman, who is one of these artists . . . ."

Greenberg *knew* the reaction this would get from his friend. It was the moral equivalent of Reinhardt's parodic grouping, a frontal assault on the holy grail of precedence, priority, and *sui generis* uniqueness. That Greenberg ostensibly meant it as praise of Barney's *craft* as a painter carried no weight. Barney didn't give a fig about being praised for craft. He cared about onement, the covenant, the voice, and the name; about "be," about man heroic and sublime. He was not part of *anyone*'s "school." At his most vulnerable moment, into his most tender spot, Greenberg thrust a lance.

In the same way that Rosenberg would gratuitously use Barney's name to make a point that didn't need it, Greenberg now flippantly named Barney to say something about Still: Still's was the first "Whitmanesque" painting, infused with and transcending "that stale, prosaic kind of painting to which Barnett Newman has given the name of 'buckeye.'"

Greenberg didn't need to name Barney, since he immediately devoted over four hundred words to the history and application of what was meant by "buckeye"—"probably the most widely practiced and homogeneous kind of painting seen in the Western world today"; it could be seen in the Barbizon School, in Greenwich Village restaurants, in Washington Square outdoor shows. "Buckeye" was a common enough term, and its meaning (banal, shallow) was known among the artists. It appeared in the published letter Gottlieb and Rothko sent to Jewell in 1943; it appeared in several of Reinhardt's cartoons. Greenberg himself was part of a 1953 *Art Digest* panel at which Tworkov used the term. There could be no innocent explanation. Greenberg was publicly needling Barney, knowing Still would assume the critic and Barney had dissected his work privately, that Barney would take the bait, that the two artists would come to verbal blows.

It hardly mattered to Barney that what followed in Greenberg's essay was the most positive, most serious, highest praise that he had yet received—and that it came a full four years since a work had been seen in public.

Barnett Newman, who is one of these artists [in Still's "school"], has replaced Pollock as the *enfant terrible* of abstract expressionism. He rules vertical bands of dimly contrasting color or value on warm flat backgrounds—and that's all. But he is not in the least related to Mondrian or anyone else in the geometrical school. Though Still led the way in opening the picture down the middle and in bringing large, uninterrupted areas of uniform color into subtle and yet spectacular opposition, Newman studied late Impressionism for himself, and has drawn its consequences more radically. The powers of color he employs to make a picture are conceived with an ultimate strictness: color is to function as hue and nothing else, and contrasts are to be sought with the least possible help of differences in value, saturation, or warmth.

The easel picture will hardly survive such an approach, and Newman's huge, calmly and evenly burning canvases amount to the most direct attack upon it so far. And it is all the more effective an attack because the art behind it is deep and honest, and carries a feeling for color without its like in recent painting.

More so, Greenberg implied, than Rothko's—although he calls them both, again, "the Still school," before demurring that the "abstract expressionists" had diverse aims, and "did not feel, and still do not feel, that they constitute a school or movement."[20] None of them could let this pass.

Still:

April 12

Dear Greenberg:

Your article in the latest Partisan Review makes it necessary for me to write you a rather unusual letter . . . . After taking the venom of Barnett Newman's jealousy for over two hours yesterday afternoon, it required some considerable control to see your last effort in an objective relationship.

I am not going to discuss your article here except to say that I think you are a completely honest man (a very rare person in these times), that you said many right and pertinent things about my work, eg. . . . . the character of my influence and ideas on the art world today. Unfortunately, also, you set me up as a target a few times, eg. "buckeye," in a way that will make life pretty nasty socially for some time . . . .

It seems to be a consistent paradox of human frailty that those who owe the most to another in the realm of the fine arts are those who will most deeply resent and deny the debt . . . . What guilt or impotence rises to choke these men or boys, sometimes with an intensity that touches on madness, I can only guess . . . .

Thus I arrived with you, at a point where I have to warn you, however unethical it may be, in order to try to protect my work, my meanings, and even self respect, from some of those same men . . . .

Would it be asking too much to request that before you take farther into your confidence, in regard to me, any of the men who have presumed to educate you or speak for me or my work, you check their evidence, definitions, analyses, or terminology, especially where equivocal idioms are used, with me?—in person. For I know about these things; but especially do I know about the motives and ambitions which lie in the guts of these frustrated ones . . . . I would appreciate it if you will use more than a little caution before you accept weapons in the guise of metaphors or bouquets which may be poisoned to kill us both. . . . spit has already been thrown in my face,— inevitably it marked only a preliminary gesture in the serious business of assault and defamation to follow.[21]

Greenberg:

18 April

Dear Clyfford Still,

I'm glad you didn't find my piece in PR too far wrong about your painting, but if Barney's upset about it I'll be upset too. I know he's been difficult lately, but he's one person I make allowances for (which have nothing to do with his art but with him personally) and I'll have to try to straighten it out with him. If he's said hard things about me behind my back, that's too bad, but it won't make much difference in the way I feel about him. I just can't help liking him no matter how impatient he might make me.

But let me tell you meanwhile that, before I finished the article, neither he nor any one else tried to "educate" me about your art beyond the point of saying that they liked it or didn't like it. The Pollocks did say that you had influenced Rothko and Barney, but I knew that anyhow. Barney, like the Pollocks, Rothko, and Ossorio, has in expressing his admiration for your painting never attempted to characterize it or explain it in my hearing. Nor has any one ever told me anything that you yourself have said about your own work or your attitude to painting in general . . . .

Barney was the first one I heard name a certain kind of painting as buckeye, but he did not apply the term to yours . . . . In any case Barney has always praised you and stood up for you, and done it more steadfastly than most people do for artists they admire. Nothing he has ever said to me about you could be construed as indicating the slightest jealousy. I wish I myself had a defender like him.

"I never saw anything really good come along in art that didn't require the artist concerned to sweat it out before getting recognition," Greenberg added. "(I assume we all want recognition; I know I do.)" "A lot of Barney's present bitterness comes, I feel, from his unwillingness to sweat it out with his art."[22]

Chastized, Still rejiggered his swipe at Barney, this time tarring Greenberg with the same brush:

Having made the unfortunate blunder of permitting my work to enter the public domain some twenty years ago, I found it a moral responsibility to try to be articulate in the defense of the issues concerning its implications. That I have not been able to achieve more clarity up to the present moment is due almost totally, not to my enemies, but to my "defenders,"

he wrote, before he terminated the "rather morbid exchange."[23]

And between labeling Barney jealous, impotent, and mad to Greenberg, and treasonous to Ossorio, Still alerted Barney to a teaching job in a small college in Springvale, Maine, for which he had withdrawn his own application—because the dean there offended him.[24]

Barney did not react to Greenberg's article immediately. It was a challenge to weigh the two poles of the critic's essay—the praise for Barney's work on the one hand, and the errors of fact and misleading implications (including the idea of "school of Still" and placing Still's 1946 first show at Peggy Guggenheim's in 1944) on the other. And, with so many urgent affronts that demanded timely address, he stewed in his dilemma for a few months. Certainly, being labeled the "*enfant terrible* of abstract expressionism," and (favorably) the artist who made the "most direct attack" upon traditional easel pictures, made him proud—and, he understood, it could be usefully trumpeted.

The tirades weren't solely the competitive posturings, the one-upsmanship, typically occurring among peers. Barney would take a stand on any issue—art or otherwise— that he was convinced *insulted* him.

To Pollock—who would about once a week come to Manhattan and drop into the Cedar Bar where he had become "a kind of talisman," where many of the next generation, as well as his peers, pressed in, slapped his back, bought him drinks, playfully punched his arms, admired and teased and taunted him, and (according to at least one sympathetic observer) turned him into an "object"[25]—Barney wrote during the Greenberg–Still imbroglio.

You kept asking me last night, why I did not go to Mark Rothko's show? I could not explain it to you over the phone . . .

To go to a man's show is to honor him. What shall I honor Rothko for—our friendship? It is true that I have been his friend as everyone knows. But has he been mine? I am convinced that throughout these years Rothko has been not only not my friend but my active enemy . . . . shall I honor him for his work? . . . shall I honor him because we are involved in a common struggle for moral issues . . . ? *For my own self-respect* I must declare myself separate from him. [emphasis added].[26]

The following day, after receiving a saucy—a *disrespectful*—note from *Time* explaining that his letter about Mathieu would not be published, Barney, his funk deepened, wrote to New York Governor Averell Harriman to protest the "debasement and vandalism" about to be visited on Hempstead, Long Island's racetrack, Belmont. And, *again*, there was a "Press Release."

New York State's four main "flat" race tracks had long been operated by local racing associations. They had fallen into varying states of disrepair and seen dropping attendance, when the aristocratic Jockey Club, fifty-six racehorse owners and de facto supervisors of the sport, pressed to buy all the shares of the local associations and form a non-profit Greater New York Racing Association to operate and massively rehabilitate the Saratoga, Aqueduct and Jamaica tracks, and raze Belmont to build a new "Dream Track." The plan needed state government approval.[27]

It was yet another outrage as far as Barney was concerned, in a season of outrages. He had flayed himself to pursue the suit against Reinhardt, every nerve ending was exposed and had been harshly abraded by the Rothko–Janis–Still–Greenberg drama. Now, it was not simply his newborn fascination, nor his old New York connoisseurship and nostalgia, that prompted his tantrum. In the very center of this story he found his devil.

April 26, 1955
Governor Averill [*sic*] Harriman

Honorable Sir:

I as an artist and native New Yorker, who loves and respects the art treasures of New York respectfully call upon you to veto the Jockey Club Bill . . . . a selfish tax-saving device . . . . But above all . . . to destroy Beautiful Belmont is sheer vandalism . . .

It is highly significant that the leader in this attempt at vandalism, this cynical desire to destroy a work of art for the sake of escalators and restrooms in modern décor, is none other than Mr. John Hay Whitney, who is also chairman of the Board of Trustees of the Museum of Modern Art. There he has helped to develop the same dangerous policy, the same kind of tax-free private government that initiated this set of values, in this case, towards the plastic arts, so that painting and sculpture have become the hand-maidens of our plumbing and kitchengadgets.

John Hay Whitney—the very man who Barney dreamed of "chalking up" if he found a new career as a "fitter."

The record of the Museum of Modern Art as a debaser of artistic standards already stands. Let not your hand join his to spread this debasement and vandalism. Save Belmont.[28]

"In a letter to Gov. Averill Harriman, the artist Barnett Newman considered by critics to be the most advanced painter in America (see current issue, Spring 1955, Partisan Review for article on 'American-Type Painting' where he is discussed by critic Clement Greenberg) called upon him to veto the Jockey Club Bill to save the

Belmont Park race track from <u>vandalism</u>." So began Barney's press release, another opportunity to vent accusations against MoMA, but also another mechanism to publicize Greenberg's praise.[29]

In isolation, or at almost any other time in his life, Barney's puffed up posturing and grandiosity would prompt smiles or headshakes. Surely, in earlier, similar announcements, manifestos, applications, he knew what he was doing, cannily aping the rhetorical theater of Damon Runyon and Walter Winchell. At this moment, in the second half of 1955, however, Barney's behavior was *his* version of Gorky's "grand gesture of immolation."

On June 27, the New York Supreme Court denied Rosenman Goldmark Colin & Kaye's motion to dismiss on behalf of the College Art Association and Reinhardt. The trial would go forward.

By this time, the East End Temple had begun emptying 341 and 343 East Nineteenth of the nine tenants. Two apartments—including that of the Newmans—had leases that were renewed three months before the building's transfer and would not expire until the end of August 1956. Counterintuitively, counter-productively, self-defeatingly, health-damagingly, Barney and Annalee made it their Alamo. In some perverse way, Barney was going to take his stand on Nineteenth Street and it would answer for his helplessness while the ugly suit against Reinhardt was in the lawyers' hands, with reams of correspondence on both sides, one pursuing dismissal, one insisting on a trial. Fighting eviction would answer for not being included in "Modern Art from USA," a selection from the Museum of Modern Art appearing at the Kunsthaus in Zurich, for not being included in the Whitney Museum's "The New Decade: 35 American Painters and Sculptors," for praise-filled reviews of Rothko's show. For the next year, exactly coincident with the lawsuit, Barney and Annalee held out against their own Santa Anna, the East End Temple, who fought back with every harassing tactic available, until, eventually, they were the only remaining people in the buildings, until they had to acknowledge total defeat.

With real estate values about to soar as the Third Avenue El was torn down, with the neighborhood about to change, evictions would begin by mid-September, and remaining tenants were being harassed.[30]

July 20

Miss Constance F. Burr, Tenant Relocation Bureau, Inc.:

> The time has come to speak out concerning the "efforts" being made by you and your mentors, The East End Temple, to find us an apartment.
> My wife and I have visited the places you have recommended . . . obvious run-down slum tenements. . . . We can only assume that passable apartments are offered us as pure fiction . . .

Do you really think that we can live in these apartments? You have seen how we live.[31]

The vocal cord node that had been giving Barney trouble since 1949 was removed at around this time.[32] "Absolute Voice Rest . . . NO TALKING" he was told at the time the problem first emerged. "DO NOT USE THE VOICE write all things out on paper," and so Barney did now, even more compulsively than was usual. He would never have been harsh in speaking, anyway—it simply wasn't his style. But he had to "defend" himself, he refused to lose by "default," according to Annalee, and when the rage built up, he was compelled to "sit down and write with a very sharply pointed pen."[33]

Within days, the Whitney Museum was caught up in the rage: "I have just seen the catalogue of your recent show the New Decade and I am shocked to find that my name has been incorporated into the show as part of Motherwell's biography."

Barney had no works at the Whitney. But in text about Motherwell appeared the sentence, "With Baziotes, Hare and Rothko, later joined by Barnett Newman, [Motherwell] started an art school on 8th Street in 1947." It might have seemed a minor matter. But because he had such a small resume it was not minor to Barney.

Are you in the habit of using names without getting permission?
The use of my name here was unnecessary since a flat, simple statement saying that Motherwell was one of the original founders of the school would have been adequate.

The museum "willfully" tried to "tell the story of painting in America these last ten years" but only succeeded "in telling the story of the Whitney's history these last years." His work was "not part of the exhibition," he had "never been part of any Whitney function," his "position in regards to these popularizations" was that they were "useful attempts to confuse the public" and "so many included in the show itself have dipped their brushes into my work to make adaptations and burlesques of some of my pictures." His appearance in Motherwell's biography was "not only unnecessary it was completely unwarranted." The "exhibition is traveling the country. It does not have my work . . . it in fact has only my rejection and a good many of my imitators."

He insisted that the catalogue be withdrawn.[34] But even that would not have calmed the waters. He vented in a draft to Motherwell:

When the lending of any name, yours and mine means giving power to an institution, and in this particular situation, an institution which knowing my position has not only never invited me to any of its shows, whose officers, Mr. More and Mr. Baur have not even seen a single one of my pictures, who have willfully boycotted me as they know I did them; on every other occasion that you have had to discuss the scene, when you wrote your letter to Barr, when you organized the NY School show in Los Angeles, when you write for the Art Digest, you did me the honor to leave me out . . . . to have included me here . . . was I must say thoughtless and unfeeling.

And then it took several drafts to fully vent his simmering rage toward Hess:

Having just come from the Whitney version of the New Decade, I found your review of it in the summer Art News of interest.

By pointing out that the Whitney has "committed graver errors of omission and commission," you make clear that this show is the history of the Whitney these last ten years rather than an accurate exposition of the last ten years of painting in America.

You are also to be commended for pointing out that the "absence of these four (Gorky, Hofmann, Rothko, Still) seriously damages any survey of recent American painting."

However, I too must point out "some graver errors of omission" that you yourself made in your review. In correcting the Whitney's "omissions," you, by making your own "omission" of Newman, when you knew that the Whitney had included in its show those who had dipped their brushes into my work, damaged your own position. Your article, by this failure, becomes identical with the Whitney exhibition.

I cannot make myself believe that you were personal in this "omission" even though you have given me, goodness knows sufficient reason to do so.[35] I cannot overlook the fact that on several occasions (The Stable show, U.S. Lines) you did discuss my contribution to painting in America. I can only assume, therefore, that your criticism of the Whitney is only a mild chiding and that you are fundamentally in accord with their evaluation of painting in this country. This accord is made specific by the fact that I am "included" in the Whitney show—that is, my name exists in their catalogue as a footnote to Motherwell's biography.

May I remind you that in your own previous attempt to describe and evaluate the same ten-year period, in your book, "Abstract Painting" you likewise included me as a footnote to Gauguin's biography? . . .

Well, you know what Euclid said—things equal to the same thing are equal to each other. The Whitney show and your book thus become one and the same even unto and of course by means of the footnotes.[36]

And, finally, on the following day, Barney decided he could no longer *not* reply to Greenberg. He saw personal mockery, ill-will, ill-use, and implications of "clownishness" accumulating around him.

August 9

Greenberg [the most moderate of the versions on the spattered and stained pad, and the one sent]:

I have now reread your article and I find that the errors of fact that you made in discussing me are even more serious than when I first saw them. I feel they must be corrected.

First: " . . . so Still's painting is infused with that stale, prosaic kind of painting to which Barnett Newman has given the name of 'buckeye.' "

No reading or rereading of this phrase can avoid the implication that I invented the term, "buckeye," and that I applied it to Still. You do not specifically say that I did these things, but you do not say clearly enough that I did not . . . .

You know that I did not invent the term—that I did not "give" it. I only used it, as I am certain (since the word goes back for several centuries) other painters from Hogarth to Eakins have used it.

You know that at no time in my discussion did I mention Still's work or any other artist's work, and that you in no way indicated to me that you were involved in an operation of your mind that went beyond the pictures on the wall [of the White Horse Tavern] . . . .

Second: " . . . like Newman, he (Rothko) soaks his pigment into the canvas, getting a dyer's effect . . . "

To a reader, the words, "soaked, dyed," imply that the surface is as if stained by dye-like color. This may be a description of Rothko's surface but it is in error and entirely misleading as a description of my work. You know that my paint quality is heavy, solid, direct, the opposite of a stain . . . . You should have made the distinction between something that is "dyed" and something that is whole as if cut or stamped by "dies." I think that this play on your vocabulary gives a clearer picture of my paint quality than the erroneous link you made.

Third: " . . . an indirect sign of his (Still's) importance is the fact that he (Still) is almost the only abstract expressionist to 'make' a school; by this I mean that a few of the many artists he has stimulated or influenced have not been condemned by that to imitate him but have been able to establish strong and independent styles of their own. Barnett Newman is one of them . . . "

Here you have made the most serious error of all. For here you are not examining my work. Here you have assumed the authority arbitrarily to tell its history. And the only interpretation possible from your phrases is that I am derived from Still. The facts are otherwise. . . .

By 1946 I had already done a series of pictures which culminated in the picture I called "Death of Euclid"[37] . . . .

I first became acquainted with Still and his work during the winter of 1946 at the time of his first show at Peggy's. (In your article you incorrectly place Still's first show at Peggy's in 1944. The correct date is [February] 1946).[38]

For all of Barney's history of fudging or arrogating exaggerated qualifications or acclaim, bad faith is still bad faith; he was correct about that. Barney may have been of little concern to the powers at the Whitney, but he made himself so puffed up and so almost irresistibly teasable that some took a cruel pleasure in hitting the target.

The letter to Hess was, unbeknownst to Barney, particularly bad timing. Hess was at that exact moment developing material for both the 1955–56 *Art News Annual* —"U.S. Painting: Some Recent Directions"—and a new book, partially based on that article, *American Painting, a Modern History.* Aiming to include eighteen to twenty-six artists, Hess had to make choices.[39] It smarted that Barney questioned his motives. "My opinion of your pictures . . . has nothing whatsoever to do with my personal feelings about you. The fact that you have had an important influence on other painters is clear . . . . An article in the forthcoming Annual, my first on younger American painters, does take into account, briefly, your historical position," Hess wrote back.

But he also took the opportunity to suggest that Barney's letter was "motivated, I suppose you would say, personally," asserting that Barney's review of *Abstract Painting*, after being rejected by *Partisan Review*, was shopped around "without success. I can only conclude that you made a number of 'personal' attacks which the editors felt were beyond the scope of criticism or fair comment. You could allay these rough suspicions by sending me a copy of your review so that I could assure myself that our relationship is pure."[40]

The copy was not forthcoming. For a period, people noticed Barney wasn't around. "I've been invisible," he told a friend who, sometime later, asked about his absence.[41]

As his lawyers received Reinhardt's responses to the complaint, and orally silenced by his vocal-cord problems, Barney got away from it all—if only for a couple of weeks. He and Annalee took a road trip north in Still's old car, stopping first, like *Guys and Dolls'* Nathan Detroit, at Saratoga a few days after Governor Harriman, himself a horse owner and former member of the Jockey Association, dedicated a new National Museum of Racing there. (Detroit's song, "Call a lawyer and sue me, sue me," might have been playing in his head, as Barney pressed not only the suit against Reinhardt, and the suit against the East End Temple, but also a suit against the landlord of his beloved studio. This last, at least, was settled in Barney's favor in October.[42]) The couple continued up through New York to Niagara Falls, and, hugging the south edge of Lake Erie, within two days had made it all the way to Chicago, where Barney had drawn up a list of significant architecture to see.

They returned in a couple of days of marathon driving through Detroit and lower Ontario, back in Manhattan by September 8—Annalee had to work—where they awaited the State Rent Administration's decision on whether the East End Temple would be allowed to proceed. By the beginning of October, it was certain and tenants began to be dispossessed. A court-ordered three-month stay gave them until the middle of January; there was an additional three months' extension "if they could not find new apartments within the allotted time." In late October, when all but four apartments were empty, the Newmans informed the lawyer they required three or five rooms in Manhattan at about 100 dollars per month.[43] He made plans to "institute proceedings in the [New York] Supreme Court"; he had an existing lease through September 1956.[44]

It was no longer simply the Alamo. Now, figuratively cut off from most of the city's destinations and public transportation by hundreds of men armed with "sharp-tongued torches" and "the grinding, throbbing cranes" odiferously and brutally dismantling the 77-year-old Third Avenue El colossus a block away, isolated within his own building, Barney was a Zealot on Masada: it was almost a holy mission. He was relying on his god—the Rule of Law, *Justice*. But this god had let him down in his father's bankruptcy and in his father-in-law's patent suit, would let him down again in his righteous quest to hold onto his home, and would not protect him from being portrayed as a "clown" by Reinhardt. Time and again, it was this god he would return to for recourse, and, eventually, dramatically, it was this god—Justice—he was forced to acknowledge had "forsaken" him.

Maybe Hess was a little chagrined by Barney's letter, maybe he felt bullied. Maybe he thought Barney had a point. When Hess's review of that fall's Carnegie International appeared in the November issue of *Art News* it included this sentence: "The inevitable absence of Rothko, Still and Newman from all such exhibitions is once more to be regretted." But the recognition only served to reopen this particular wound in the hemorrhaging body. No version of a reply was actually sent to Hess, but Barney wrote one—many times—and it exists as a private diary of his overwrought, not to say litigation-crazed, state of mind.

November 26

Mr. Thomas H. Hess [the incorrect middle initial in this final draft a response to the times Hess misspelled Barney's name]:

Since my return from a trip to Canada [on September 8] to find your reply to my letter of August 8, I have not had a relaxed moment in which to respond until now.

I am of course very pleased that you agree with me that, as I pointed out in my letter, it was not a personal matter towards me that you failed to discuss my work when you castigated the Whitney "New Decade" show for "graver errors of omission and commission" . . . .

I am, however, astonished at the rest of your letter in which, after asserting your lack of personal feeling and in the name of what you call "the pure," you heap a collection of charges against me based on irresponsible "assumptions" which you make in an attempt to excuse your article. You . . . charge me with attacking you personally in a review of your book that I wrote for

Partisan Review. "I can only conclude that you made a number of personal attacks which the editors felt were beyond the scope of criticism or fair comment." May I make clear to you that nothing remotely constituting a personal attack was expressed in the review of your book by me. If your "conclusion" is based on things that anyone has told you, the person involved is a contemptible liar and I should very much like to know who it is so that I can deal with him. In my review, I discussed your book seriously, cogently and respectfully and it would have been, had it been published, on the basis of what I have seen, the best review you received.

Could Barney have really forgotten that he submitted a review in which he wrote of Hess's "stalinic dream" from which "he imagines he can dominate the American artist"? That, accusing Hess of glorifying ambiguity, he wrote that "ambiguity as a deliberate act . . . can lead only to some form of slavery"? Both comments were deleted in the magazine's edit, before it declined to publish the review, and it was likely those comments that Hess was "told" about.

I wish you to know the facts. In the first place, my review was not rejected. It was <u>outvoted</u>. There were those on the editorial board who wanted it. There were, however, others who, involved in the immediate publicity values your book may have had for their artist friends you feature . . . preferred that it exist as a publicity manual for the small careers sought by their artist friends. This is why my review was not published. If this treatment of your book as an exercise in public relations does you honor, you are welcome to it. Your charge however, that I solicited other magazines for it is so ridiculous, I can only take it to be malicious![45] . . .

The review of your book was contracted for by Partisan Review months in advance of the appearance of your book when I had not the faintest idea whether I was to be in it or out of it. There was no motive except to have a painter's point of view concerning an art book . . . . If I were in the habit of making charges and conclusions and assumptions as easily as you seem to be, it would be very easy for me now to say that you left me out of your book because you knew that I was to review it and to call for your original notes to prove to me that your personal relationship to me is "pure." However, I do not play such games nor am I in the habit of putting men on trial . . . .

But you wish to put me on trial. All I can say to you is that I would very much like you to read my review. I regret that the review never appeared. No matter what its position, it was fair, unbiased and written with dignity and grace, seriously examining the aesthetic, and philosophic content and the practical application of your position as critic. Unfortunately I do not have a copy readily at hand, for the copy I submitted to Partisan Review was never returned to me.[46]

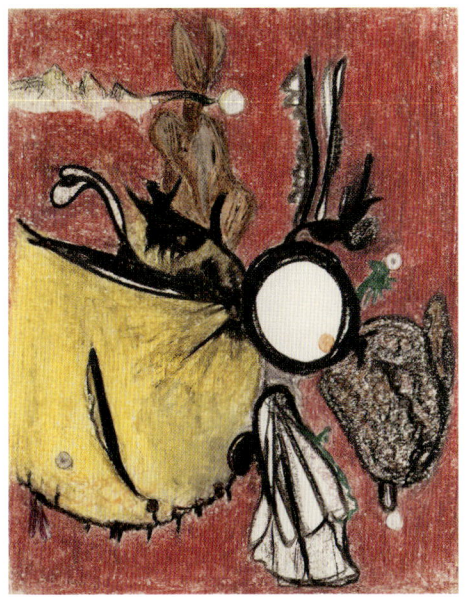

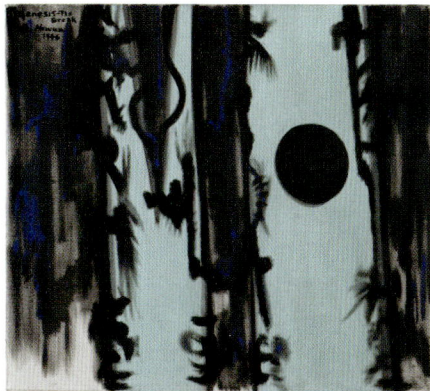

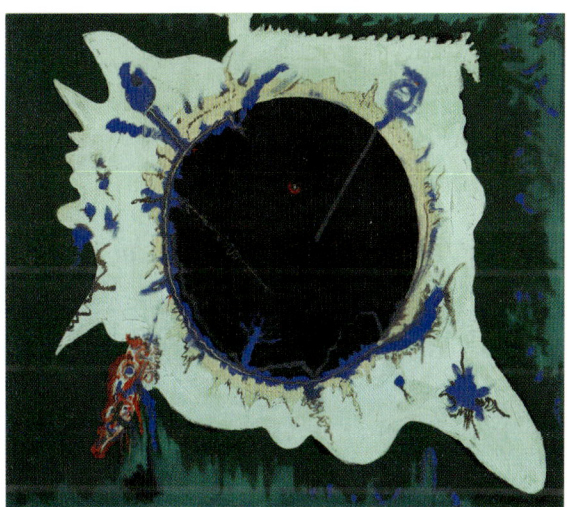

Plate 1 (top left) Barnett Newman, *Gea*, 1945. Oil and crayon on cardboard, 28 × 22 in. (71.1 × 55.9 cm). The Art Institute of Chicago. Through prior gift of The Charles H. and Mary F. S. Worcester Collection

Plate 2 (top right) Barnett Newman, *Genesis—The Break*, 1946. Oil on canvas, 24 × 27 ⅛ in. (61 × 68.9 cm)

Plate 3 (above) Barnett Newman, *Pagan Void*, 1946. Oil on canvas, 33 × 38 in. (83.8 × 96.5 cm). National Gallery of Art, Washington, D.C. Gift of Annalee Newman

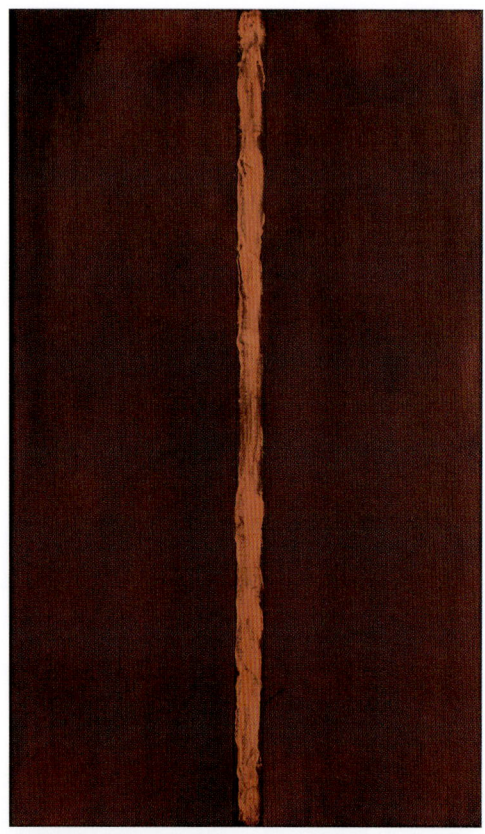

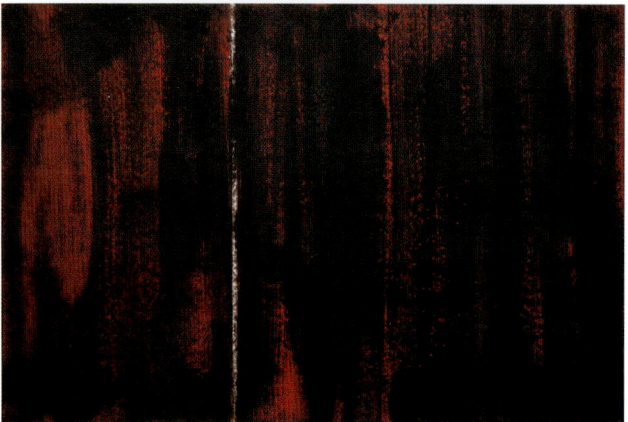

Plate 4 (top) Barnett Newman, *Onement I*, 1948. Oil on canvas and oil on masking tape, 27 ¼ × 16 ¼ in. (69.2 × 41.3 cm). The Museum of Modern Art, New York. Gift of Annalee Newman

Plate 5 (above) Barnett Newman, *Untitled 2, 1948*, 1948. Mixed media on paper, 24 × 36 in. (61 × 91.4 cm). Location undisclosed

Plate 6 (opposite) Barnett Newman, *Abraham*, 1949. Oil and Magna on canvas, 82 ¾ × 34 ½ in. (210.2 × 87.7 cm). The Museum of Modern Art, New York. Philip Johnson Fund

Plate 7 Barnett Newman, *The Voice*, 1950. Egg tempera and oil on canvas, 96 ⅛ × 105 ½ in. (244.2 × 268 cm). The Museum of Modern Art, New York. The Sidney and Harriet Janis Collection

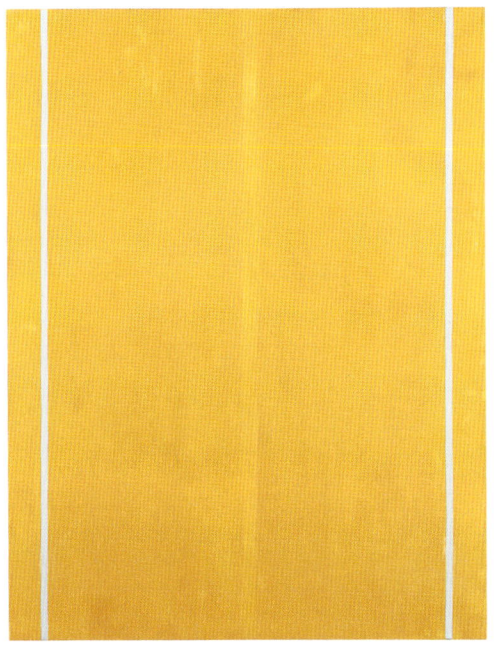

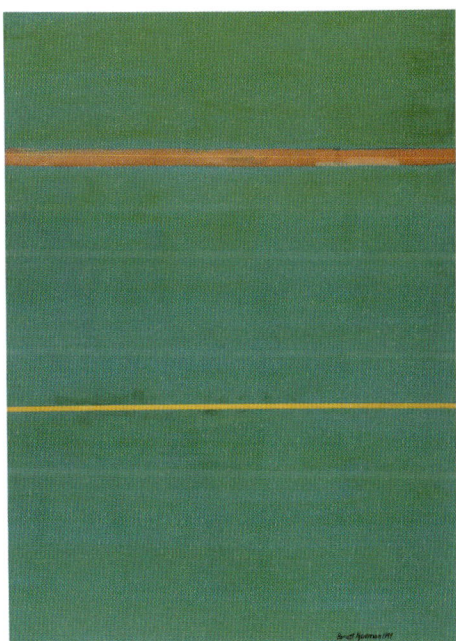

Plate 8 (top) Barnett Newman, *Yellow Painting*, 1949. Oil on canvas, 67 ½ × 52 ⅜ in. (171.5 × 133 cm).
National Gallery of Art, Washington, D.C. Gift of Annalee Newman

Plate 9 (above) Barnett Newman, *Dionysius*, 1949. Oil on canvas, 67 × 49 in. (170.2 × 124.5 cm).
National Gallery of Art, Washington, D.C. Gift of Annalee Newman

Plate 10 (left) Barnett Newman, *The Wild*, 1950. Oil on canvas, 95 ⅜ × 1 ⅝ in. (242.3 × 4.1 cm). The Museum of Modern Art, New York. Gift of the Kulicke Family

Plate 11 (right) Barnett Newman, *Vir Heroicus Sublimis*, 1950, 1951. Oil on canvas, 95 ⅜ × 213 ¼ in. (242.3 × 541.7 cm). The Museum of Modern Art, New York. Gift of Mr. and Mrs. Ben Heller

Plate 12 Barnett Newman, *Cathedra*, 1951. Oil and Magna on canvas, 96 × 214 in. (243.8 × 544 cm).
Stedelijk Museum Amsterdam

Plate 13 Barnett Newman, *L'Errance*, 1953. Oil on canvas, 86 × 77 ½ in. (218.4 × 196.9 cm). Collection Denise and Andrew Saul, New York

Plate 14 Barnett Newman, *Uriel*, 1955. Oil on canvas, 96 × 216 in. (243.8 × 548.6 cm). Private collection

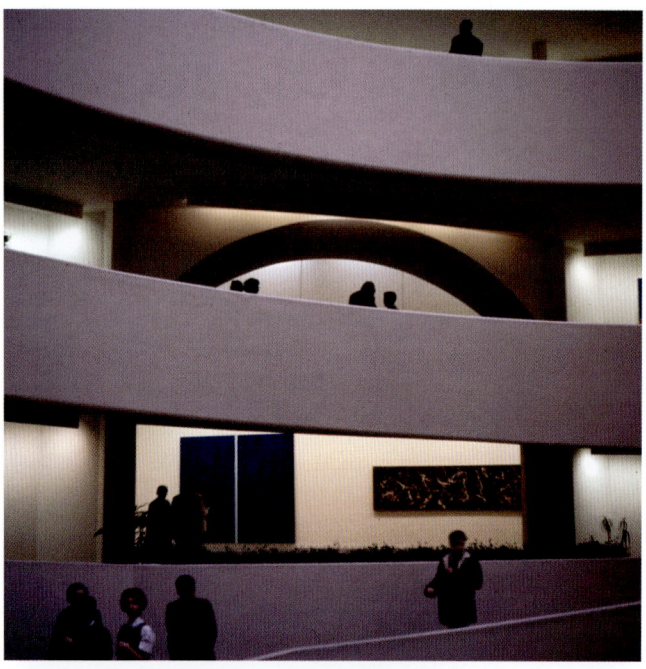

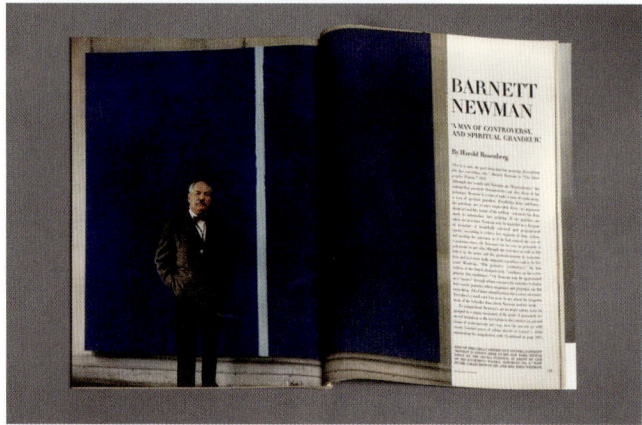

Plate 15 (top) "American Abstract Expressionists and Imagists" at the Guggenheim Museum, 1961. Barnett Newman's *Onement VI* next to Jackson Pollock's *Number 2, 1949* in the High Gallery

Plate 16 (above) Barnett Newman and *Onement VI* photographed by Alexander Liberman for a *Vogue* feature article, published February 15, 1963. Photograph Bruce White

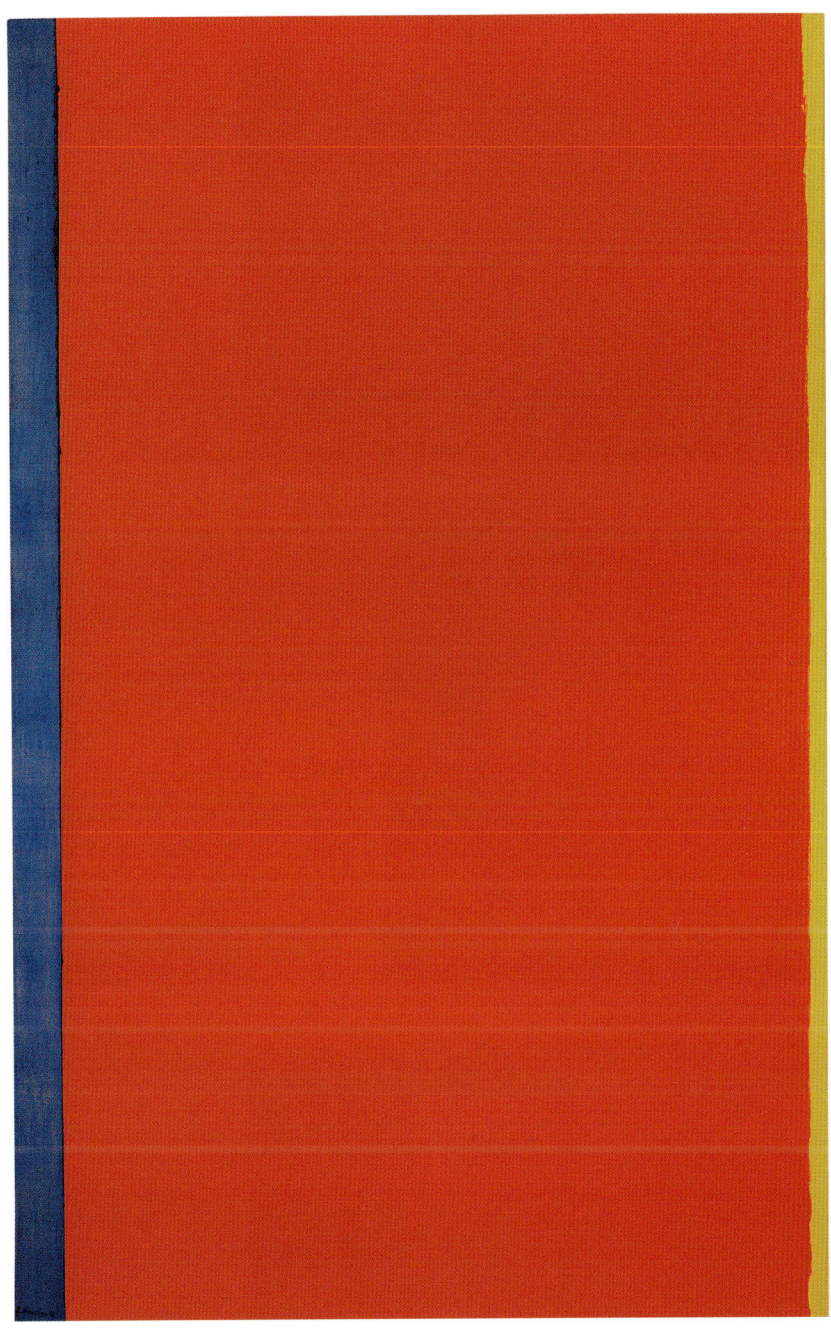

Plate 17 Barnett Newman, *Who's Afraid of Red, Yellow and Blue I*, 1966. Oil on canvas, 75 × 48 in. (190.5 × 121.9 cm). Private collection

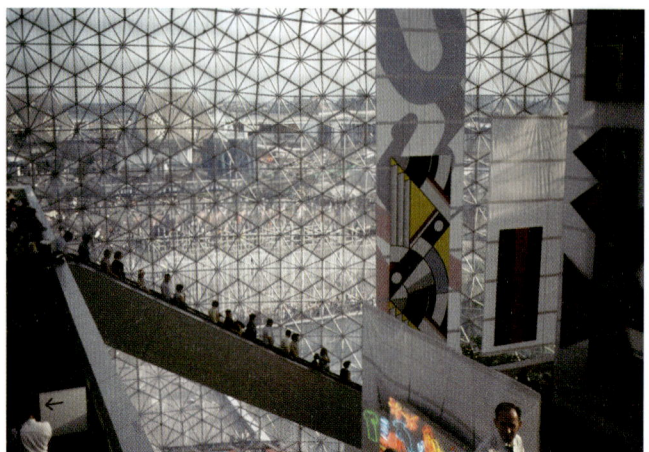

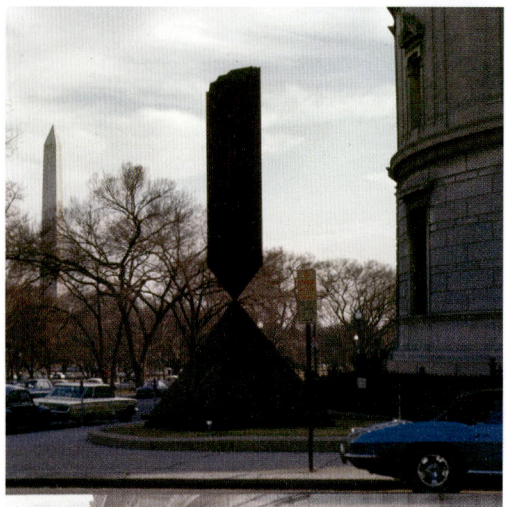

Plate 18 (top) Buckminster Fuller's "geodesic skybreak bubble" at Expo '67 in Montreal, with Roy Lichtenstein's 30-foot *Big Modern Painting* and Newman's 18-foot *Voice of Fire*. Photograph Robert Murray

Plate 19 (left) *Broken Obelisk* in Washington, D.C., 1969

Plate 20 (below) Barnett Newman and *Who's Afraid of Red, Yellow and Blue III* (incorrectly titled and dated in text), photographed by Alexander Liberman for a *Vogue* feature article, published March 15, 1969. Photograph Bruce White

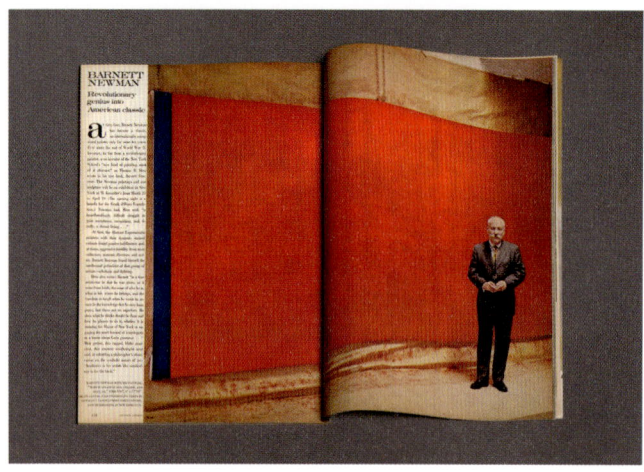

"NEWMAN INTERESTS US MUCH MORE"

"Whether or not the public acknowledges it, the status of American art vis-à-vis that of the rest of the world has radically changed in the last ten years," wrote Greenberg in a catalogue note. "This is a triumph." And, "one of the notable scenes of that triumph" was "the Betty Parsons Gallery."[1]

The Art Students League *News* and *The Nation* seconded Greenberg's praise. "Miss Parsons . . . has done more for modern art in America than anybody now living . . . . [her] role has been unequalled."[2] It was a gallery where the *artists* came to look, because "the art shown, good or bad, is almost always courageous, adventurous and explorative."[3]

It must have been hard for many of the artists to believe, hard for some to remember, but the Betty Parsons Gallery was ten years old. In December, Parsons mounted an anniversary show that, because she had personally purchased pieces or had sold them to friendly collectors, could include works by all of "her" artists—even those who left her. With the exception of Maud Morgan's, none of the pieces was dated later than 1952: Pollock's *Night Dance* was from 1944, and Rothko's *No. 26* from 1947. In a sirocco of agitated brushstrokes by Calvert Coggeshall, William Congdon, Hofmann, Boris Margo, Ossorio, Pousette-Dart, Pollock, and some of the others, *No. 7*, 1949, Barney's first publicly exhibited painting in almost five years, was a powerful oasis of intention. As Parsons's indispensable advisor, he was also at least partially responsible for the accolades. But he had moved beyond that. The work later titled *Horizon Light* would finally be displayed without Rothko's interference, in its intended horizontal orientation, and as a record-correcting rebuke to others' assertions of influence or priority.

December 1

Dear Betty:

I am sending this note with the picture so that you will have, in writing, a statement of my responsibility, should anything come up concerning this picture.

No one is to see this picture before the show officially opens, except the reviewers. No one means artists and their "lovers," officials, collectors, etc. No one.

No explanation of the picture is necessary except to tell the facts. I am not showing it to confound the wise. I have never tried to do that. It is the wise guys themselves who have confounded each other. It is they, be they critics or artists, art officials and art "intellectuals" who have misled themselves by constantly trying to label me a "straight-line painter," who have tried to type-cast me for their own purposes, as if the art world were just another Hollywood.

Maybe it is but I am not one of its performers. It simply is not true that I paint a particular kind of picture. In those years and now I have done many pictures with verticals, horizontals, and every which way kind of line. Here is a picture that was done and seen by artists and others in 1949. If the question arises that other painters are now doing this kind of a picture, the answer is still the same. I did this one in 1949, long before theirs and it has been part of the same pictorial concept as my others. I am not involved in stylistic gimmicks or aesthetic kicks of either color or line. I am a painter of pictures—not of a particular kind of "line"—formal or otherwise and I wish by showing this picture at this time to show a picture I love and to assert my freedom from labels and type-casting. I am a painter of pictures with content and here is one done in 1949.[4]

The "painter of pictures" got his recognition. Pollock's piece seemed "almost tame" at this date, said *The Nation*, "but there are extremists like Clyfford Still and Barnett Newman to arouse ire or interest."[5] The *Times* took for granted his stature: "this gallery has promoted adventurous talent which later received wider recognition. Hans Hofmann, Barnett Newman, Jackson Pollock, Ad Reinhardt, Mark Rothko and the late Bradley Tomlin."[6]

When, in January, the 1955–56 *Art News Annual* appeared, Hess's imperial "U.S. Painting: Some Recent Directions" tied the previous twenty-five years of New York artists' activities up in a neat—if questionably packed—box. Barney's name was mentioned twice—in text, not the dreaded footnote—but left out where one would have expected to see it, in reference to "very large scale" paintings, for instance. In fact, left out was the whole generation of his peers. Rather, the essay featured twenty-one artists, abstract and representational, who, "following (and in many cases influenced by) the painters who came into prominence in the previous five years" reacted "individually from the forces already at work in the international art world." These had "to follow on the stage of public scrutiny the applause and catcalls which have greeted Abstract-Expressionism since 1940"; they were a new generation with, in Hess's opinion, diminished ambition, the result of what he termed "G.I.ism," and characterized by the "admonition 'Never volunteer.'" G.I.ism was "the perfect expression of American culture in 1955. It is as safe and sound as the currency that floods the nation; and it will fight for its integrity only at the point of 'you can't push me around'—as do all self-respecting capitalists."[7]

The 20th-century avant-garde "dream" of painting that could communicate "glowing universalities" was gone. "Today almost all painters are content to communicate with their own small but expanding universe," Hess concluded.

The artists were "inveterate museum and gallery visitors . . . strict about the moderns but [with] a connoisseur's affection for all the past." They most frequently cited

Rembrandt, the Italian "primitives, and the second half of the French 19th century"—with the exclusion of Gauguin and Monet (surprising to Hess)—and "the older New York School painters were given equal status with" Matisse and Picasso. "Willem de Kooning, Pollock and Gorky were most frequently named; after them, Kline, Hofmann, Motherwell, Rothko, Still and Newman (the last three being rejected by most of the non-avant-garde painters)."

One evening, Parsons brought Barney to a party at Ellsworth Kelly's. Kelly was one of those veterans who had had the extraordinary opportunity of studying under the G. I. Bill, several in Paris. He had come to New York in 1954 and in 1955 landed in a space at Coenties Slip, a stone's throw from Barney's studio, and invited a few people over to baptize it. He had been discussing representation with Parsons, but was surprised when she showed up. He didn't know who her "very impressive" companion was, although it was obvious she relied on him. Very little of Kelly's work was visible, and Barney and Parsons left quickly. When he later learned from the dealer David Herbert, who first introduced Kelly to Parsons, who "the gentleman was," Kelly knew enough of Barney's stature to be deeply "chagrined" at the missed opportunity.

A few months later, B. H. Friedman, a young enthusiast, was talking about Pollock to the equally young Robert Rauschenberg and Jasper Johns.[8] Friedman was "astounded" when the artists—especially Johns, who had been very reticent and quiet the whole evening—"spoke almost in chorus. 'Newman interests us much more.'"

"That's bizarre," was Friedman's reaction. "How can anybody compare Newman with Pollock?"[9]

"The Great International Art Market," *Fortune* magazine's two-part series, appeared in December 1955 and January 1956. Appropriately for a (Luce) business magazine the articles, focused mainly on blue-chip historical art, were entirely in the language of economics—commodity, investment, appreciation, hedge, immoveable assets, self-regulating currency; the "cold socialization" of the drift of great art from private to public hands, stimulated by income taxes and death duties; the different arrangements French and American galleries had with living artists. Except for a very small de Kooning painting reproduced to represent "American Younger Contemporaries" on a chart of price levels, the articles had virtually nothing to do with art. And yet there was an impact: for the New York artists, at least, no matter how deeply they buried the worm, it would never again be possible to avoid the issue of the marketplace.

In a postwar heartbeat, the end of 1955 had brought a "triumph," a torch-passing, and a business economy.

Suddenly, Barney had become an unavoidable *eminence* after barely having had a career. None of Barney's rich and powerful cerulean blue, and black and red paintings of the last five years had been seen outside of his studio—not because no one would show them, but because he decreed it be thus. Still and Rothko and Pollock had left Parsons, but Reinhardt (among others) had stayed, and Barney could have exhibited there at any time if he wished. The bind in which this put him—his pride required him to be as brashly impetuous as the most brashly impetuous—did not diminish his resentment of Reinhardt. Nevertheless, he insisted on his credits, his "props," and it put critics and writers and other artists, too, in an impossible position. Now, with the next generation of artists pressing for attention, it became a solution to simply include Barney's name as a member of a group—and that was *precisely* what inflamed his choler. Barney's greatest success up to this point was shooting himself in the foot.

And yet it's clear that it was only through this process—this pressure—that the work could be made. Where some might have seen a line or three on a field, Barney saw everything. The "first man," the "terror" of existence, the "defense of human dignity"; Hitler, pin point carbonation, landlords, Reinhardt, Rothko, Still, Hess, Rosenberg, John Hay Whitney, MoMA, the Whitney. *Everything.*

"I don't show because my paintings wouldn't be seen," Barney announced to the group that had assembled at B. H. Friedman's home a month earlier, on November 28, to celebrate the opening of Pollock's new show at Janis. "I don't want to become invisible." He sat in the middle of the living room with, as always when he orated, a group around him.[10]

"What's the difference between Barnes and Rockefeller?" he posed, rehashing his gripes. "One's totalitarian; the other's charitable. It's better to lock some people out than to let everybody in. At least Barnes was interested in art. The Modern is only interested in history [and] in objects. Paintings don't have meaning when they become objects. It's just like they're spoons and egg-beaters and chairs. If they're going to show us good design why don't they show us what America's really making. We're not involved with chairs. They should show us the real thing. Like machine guns. They're beautiful, functional, they make music. And jet planes . . . when they really want to show us, they'll put The Bomb on exhibit—out in their garden."[11]

Plenty of artists had heard this before from Barney, but that night there were at least two people in the room who hadn't: one was intrigued enough to record Barney's words in his diary, and the other to take up the challenge when Barney declared that there was no audience, no collectors, no interest for work like his.

"Okay. Here you are. Here I am. Here's Bob Friedman," said Ben Heller. "Where's the work?"[12]

Heller, a 29-year-old businessman, had already begun to collect some of the New York painters' works; he was shortly to buy *Blue Poles* from Fred Olsen, and it was Pollock himself who told him, "you ought to see [Barney's] work." *Horizon Light* would be sent to the Parsons Gallery two days later, but, perhaps with Heller and Friedman (among others) in mind, Barney had forbidden Parsons to show the painting before the opening on December 19. Thus began a pattern Barney would follow for the rest of his life. A collector, or a critic, or a museum director or curator, who had heard about Barney and who was interested in seeing the work, was first required to get to know Barney the man. At times—especially if the person were tall, good-looking, and athletic, as both Heller and Friedman were—this dance could become an elaborate quadrille: visits to Barney's favorite restaurants, tours of

New York sites and neighborhoods, long post-meal conversations over drinks about subjects as unexpected or remote as baseball arcana, Kabbalistic concepts, the finer points of woven textiles, birds and film and food. Only then, after the interested party had been seduced and Barney felt comfortable that his own finer points were appreciated, could the work be unveiled.

That's how it would evolve; now, at the beginning of 1956 it was more rudimentary, but not without a certain romance. A date was made for Heller and his wife Judy, Friedman and his wife Abby, Pollock, and Krasner to accompany Annalee and Barney on a visit to the studio. The Friedmans were already good friends and collectors of Pollock's, and it was through Pollock that Friedman, like Heller, recently had met Barney, quickly realizing they had "things in common." First among them being "the drinking."[13]

The group approached through the coffee district on Front Street surrounded by the "marvelous" aroma of roasting coffee beans—which, in those days, before Starbucks appeared on every corner, was a rare exotic perfume. They climbed the three flights of stairs and entered the double-height studio, which was bisected by an elevated walkway, approached by more stairs, from which one could look down. The red *Vir Heroicus Sublimis* was there, and the black *Abraham*—Heller heard them referred to by their names, not numbers or descriptive titles. The four newcomers "wandered around and wandered around and wandered around."

And it was "a non-experience," remembered Heller.[14] (The blue *Cathedra* was nowhere visible; when Heller first saw it in December 1958, it was the polar opposite of a non-experience.)

Friedman already "felt very affectionate toward Barney," but for a long time he did not take him seriously. He was "slow on Barney." He thought of him "as a Dadaist."

"He said many things that I found extremely witty, and we had fun together." Although Friedman had no interest in boxing, he was charmed when taken to Stillman's Gym, where "all the boxers loved" Barney,[15] and the way, seemingly off the top of his head, he came up with the "strangest analogies." But at the studio that day, Friedman saw "a bucket of cement that [Barney] stuck a piece of wood in"—*Here I*—and was convinced by that that Barney was a "Dadaist."[16] Neither was Heller impressed. He "didn't like them"; he "didn't see anything there." But it "bothered" him, he said, because he felt "the man was serious."

Heller "got out of there as quickly as I could," and he told his wife it was the emperor's new clothes; but he continued to be "bothered." What it was exactly that bothered him, he couldn't identify. "Jackson said I should look at it, [but] what does it mean I should look at that? There's nothing there. What's going on?" He decided to go back. And then back for a third visit, at which point he understood that Barney was a "great painter."

"When I'm in front of something that is, quote, 'marvelous,' I get it in my stomach and the hair on the back of my head. That's where I know what I'm thinking. Because . . . you can talk yourself in and out of anything, you can rationalize anything. But you cannot rationalize or dispute true feeling. If you're open to that true inner voice, that's what you have to go by . . . . And my feelings about Newman were the same I got in front of the 'great' paintings."[17]

Heller got those feelings in front of the painting Barney called *Adam* and the one called *Queen of the Night*—"one of the most outright shocking paintings around," Heller told *Gentlemen's Quarterly* in 1958. Within a year of his eureka moment he had acquired both,[18] but already, on that third visit, Heller was formulating ambitious plans to get the work seen. He and Pollock and Krasner and Barney talked about reviving Tony Smith's idea of an installation of big works by Barney, Rothko, Still, and Pollock. It was decided that Barney would call Still, and Pollock would call Rothko. But "by then the world had split" and Rothko refused.[19]

When, eighteen months after the first meeting, Heller made a commitment to purchase the two large works, it was, in his opinion, "a big shake in Barney's world."[20]

That world was already trembling. On a frigid Friday in late January 1956, Barney received the "final notice of eviction" from a marshal of the Municipal Court of New York—although it turned out, as he persisted, that it was not quite the final one. He was expected, the next day, in Springs, to "celebrate" his and the equally depressed Pollock's birthdays with the Smiths, but Barney did not want to go, and tried to resist Pollock's urging, telling him it was too cold to get the repairs needed for the car, the evening too "icy" to drive in its condition. But the weather on Saturday suddenly turned balmy, and the Newmans went, bearing a new recording of *The Magic Flute* that they listened to into the night.[21] The following week, he read in the Sunday *Times* that at the annual convention of the College Art Association—Reinhardt's co-defendant in the libel suit—the young Princeton professor, William Seitz, who had spent much of the previous months in artists' studios, delivered a paper on "Monet and Abstract Painting." Barney, whose noisy position was that he was the first, and for a long time the only one, to make the connection received no visit from Seitz nor any acknowledgment.[22]

And then, on February 14, 15, and 16, Barney and Annalee—who had tried and failed to dissuade him from pressing the suit[23]—appeared as the only plaintiff's witnesses at Barnett Newman v. Ad Reinhardt and College Art Association in the New York State Supreme Court.

Barney had been talking to Greenberg about the trial; he may have assumed, expected—or hoped—that Greenberg would also testify; after all, "I wish I myself had a defender like him," the critic told Still. Coincidently, the week before, Greenberg was on jury duty in the Supreme Courthouse, where Barney and his lawyer met him for lunch and strategizing. But Greenberg did not testify.

Barney also expected support from Still. He continued to expect it until the last day of the trial, when Still dispatched Pat Garske (whom he married in 1957), to carry a letter. "I got reckless with the bursitic knee last evening, made too many trips up the stairs, and am pinned down again for my effort. Hence this note, with sincere regrets that I cannot meet your attorney this morning as planned."

It was probably for the best, Still continued, since he was convinced that "the ambiguities of the situation" would make the "absoluteness" of his commitment a "hazard" to the case. Still's letters to universities, his "conclusive" separation of himself and his work from the public arena in "total contempt," made him "most probably the least useful voice you could find for your purposes." It was a fact not of Still's "choice or desire or making," he wrote. "I sought a moral position; I found a mass of writhing, frightened vermin, from top to bottom of the 'art world.' A representative assortment are to be found defending one of their number in your courtroom." Barney would have to settle for Still's "moral judgment."[24]

It was a depressing performance in the courtroom. Questioned about the July 1954 slide-show evening, Barney said he asked Reinhardt:

What happened. Did that article ever get published? . . . I thought it had been rejected.

"Yes," Reinhardt replied, "but I brought pressure on [*Art Journal* editor Henry R.] Hope on the grounds that they didn't have the courage to print something controversial and I also agreed to eliminate the names of [Robert] Goldwater and his wife, Louise Bourgeois, who are active in the College Art Association. So I took their names out and they printed it."

Barney said he asked to see a copy; Reinhardt didn't have one; Annalee went to the College Art Association office and bought it. That was the first time, Barney said, he saw the article or "knew any of its contents."

Some of Barney's testimony rings true: on one of their walks before the Woodstock talk, Reinhardt, according to Barney, said "I am going to talk about the whole scene. I am going to talk about everybody and I am going to talk about you, Barney. I am not going to leave you out," and Barney said he answered, "Why do you have to talk about me or anybody; since you are invited to talk about art, why don't you talk about art and about yourself and your work." Some of the testimony may or may not have been true: Barney denied ever having seen the speech or the text, while Reinhardt told his lawyers he had. And some of the testimony is agonizingly, disingenuously, manipulated: Barney dissembled about the authorship of a quote describing him as a "former philosophy student, painter, art teacher of long standing and authority on primitive arts" until he had to acknowledge that although it had not come from a "catalogue" it *was* from the "typewritten piece" Barney had "tacked on the entrance arch" of his second show; when asked whether he had done "no other work other than . . . as an artist and as a teacher," he foolishly neglected to mention *The Answer* or his "run" for mayor (both of which he personally had publicized in the press) and was exposed. Most shamefully, he equivocated about his and Reinhardt's friendship.

He was very badly prepared by his own lawyer, and tactically bullied by the lawyer for the defense. But not as badly as was Annalee.[25]

At the close of the case for the plaintiff that first day, Judge S. Samuel DiFalco dismissed the suit, and ordered Barney to pay a judgment of 152.85 dollars, the defendants' "costs." Immediately he discussed with his lawyer an appeal and memorialized their conversation: "I willingly assume all the financial risks involved in making an appeal to the Appellate Court." His lawyer pleaded with him: "The only way in which you can be reimbursed for the expenses of the appeal is obtain a reversal and to then obtain a judgment in the second trial of $4,000.00 or more." But it was to no avail. "I would like very much that you institute proceedings in the matter as soon as possible. I do not wish to yield to what I know is a miscarriage of justice because it may prove expensive to resist."

Although he was willing to "take a retraction as final settlement" he wanted every attempt to be made to "compel" them to pay his incurred legal expenses. [26]

Now began the negotiating about a "settlement." In April, Barney proposed a retraction:

> Editor's Note: In our Summer 1954 issue, we published an article, "The Artist in Search of an Academy," by Ad Reinhardt which contained certain statements concerning Barnett Newman. We find that they are in error and we, therefore, are publishing a corrected statement by the writer of the article. [signed] Henry R. Hope, Editor
>
> I wish to make clear to the readers of the College Art Journal that the statements made by me in my article . . . were made in error. I, therefore, wish to correct this mistake and to point out that Mr. Newman is not an "artist-professor", that he is not a "traveling-design-salesman" . . . an "Art-Digest-philosopher-poet" . . . a "Bauhaus-exerciser" . . . an "avant-garde-Huckster-handicraftsman" . . . an "educational-shop-keeper," a "holy-roller-explainer-entertainer-in-residence" . . .
>
> Neither . . . a "Professional jobber", nor a "Pepsi-cola-humanist" . . . a "Professional-buttonholer."
>
> Neither did I intend to associate or group his name with the other names mentioned.
>
> In no way did I intend to question his dedication to his work or to question his integrity as a fine artist.
>
> (Signed) Ad Reinhardt

It was "of course, understood that the retraction is to receive the same prominence of display given the original article in the main body of the magazine and is not to be buried in the back pages."

And then, he couldn't control himself: "Inasmuch as the magazine, if it accepts this retraction, is getting off easily, I do not consider it out of order for you to make a request that they pay something of my expenses for the sake of fair play and even though I have agreed to accept only a retraction. I think it is deserving of a try."[27]

The lawyer for Reinhardt and the CAA was amused: "tell Mr. Newman to proceed with his appeal. Certainly this statement would make your editors look as silly as Mr. Newman looks," Doskow wrote to one of the editors.[28]

Reinhardt agreed that it was a "silly thing." But he did counter that he would be willing to say that he was sorry that Barney's "feelings were hurt by his misconstruing anything I had written or said," and that "there were many occasions" he could have told Reinhardt how he felt. Barney "was not a particular issue":

> I did intend to associate with and group him with the most distinguished and prominent artists of America. This is no error.
>
> I did intend to question the integrity (?) or character? or professional nature? of the fine artists in America, all of them representative or not of anyone else. And I did intend to make fun of the arbitrary historical methods, divisions in time, terminology, etc. of American contemporary art historians.[29]

And in the next month's issue of *Art News*, Reinhardt grandly did just that. "A Portend of the Artist as a Yhung Mandala," was a bitterly satiric take-down of the entire art scene that, in an elaborate, karmic interpretation, recycled the mocking categories of "The Artist in Search of a New Academy" but included not a single proper name.

Two days after the cocky, not to say arrogant, suggested "retraction" was written, as the last remaining tenants in the building, the Newmans received the last of the "final" notices of eviction. In the wee hours Barney read "Jackson Pollock: The Maze and the Minotaur," an article in the 1956 *New World Writing*. At 3:00 a.m.—too late for a phone call, too urgent for a letter—he sent Sam Hunter a 350-word telegram in praise. Hunter, a future Princeton professor who by 1956 had been a critic for the *Times*, editor at the new art-book publisher Harry N. Abrams and *Arts* magazine, and professor at UCLA, sought out Barney and the two had been meeting at the Howard Johnson's on First Avenue and Third Street to talk about current artists.[30] "Congratulations," he wrote, "I have just finished your article on Pollock, and late at night as it is, I wish to thank you for the pleasure of this good reading. I think you deserve that I do not wait."

> At a time when art in America is being presented by the "experts" in mass image terms, as a herd creation, without regard even to the facts of their creation, it is refreshing to see you present an artist so that the man and his work emerge; to see the facts of his life properly respected so that the painter stands as a separate self without being isolated, so that he can be seen for what he is and not submerged under the jargon of fake movements, schools and styles. . . .

Although there are a number of ideas in your article that I cannot agree with . . . It is serious, thoughtful, respectful of the real facts of the man.

If the rest of Hunter's book were as "full in the presentation of each man," Barney enthused, it would be "a true achievement." He could only hope that "the same could be achieved for my work." And he offered Hunter "access to any material and facts" he might desire.[31]

Hunter responded immediately, appreciative of the praise, and engaged Barney's doubts in a measured, conversational, and friendly way. Barney saw a brush-off.

Impulsively, Barney again saw "misunderstanding," the necessity to clear up impressions, and prickliness all around—and an opportunity to assert priority. At least temporarily, Barney had learned a lesson: he wrote his response after just a few days, but he didn't send it off until over a month later, explaining the delay in mailing as caused by "the pressure of trying to find a place to live."[32]

Hoping that the same treatment could be given to him was "the highest compliment I could pay you and your article. It was an expression only of spontaneous feeling, an expression of optimism," that Hunter would write the story of art in America instead of "the <u>art world of America</u> which is what the official institutions are now doing." (Barney's original draft read "which is what the Barr's and the Hess's have already done.")

His invitation was "not a calculated piece of flattery to get equal space or publicity with Pollock" and was based on their original conversation in Howard Johnson's. Hunter had concluded his reply with "I hope our paths will be crossing again soon," and Barney was clearly shaken by it, since their meeting, he said, was anything but casual. Hunter had sought him out and it involved "mutual responsibility."

"But perhaps I take all these things, painting, writing, too seriously."[33]

THIRTY-NINE

LOSSES

On a brutally hot Friday in mid-June, an Auer's moving van transported the earthly belongings of Barney and Annalee out of Manhattan over the bridge three blocks into Brooklyn. The previous day a wild-cat transit strike paralyzed the city with an infusion of private vehicles and thousands of pedestrians crossing bridges—nearly all overheating in a chaotic inferno. It could not have appeared propitious.

Built not long after Barney was born, 62 Pierrepont Street, the "Woodhull," was a rare, beaux-arts luxury building in a neighborhood of 19th-century houses—"Manhattan's Bedroom"—with a spectacular view. In 1910 it was touted for being "in the centre of the choice Columbia Heights section, overlooking New York Harbor, three blocks to Subway entrance" and "within 10 minutes of Wall St." For a few months it was the tallest building in the world. But by the 1940s, having fallen into decline, the area was considered a "slum" and Barney's once and future nemesis Robert Moses targeted the major neighborhood artery, Hicks Street, for the "Brooklyn–Queens Expressway," cutting off the historic access from the bluff to the water.

Enter Barney and Annalee. By 1956 Moses's original proposal was dead and an advance-guard infusion of professional and artistic blood, among them Norman Mailer and Truman Capote, joined a population the *Brooklyn Heights Press* deemed "undesireable"—"Puerto Ricans" and "exhibitionist homosexuals." In the reimagined 1954 plan a highway ran along the waterfront, a magnificent landscaped public "Esplanade" was cantilevered over the two-tiered road, and a vital community campaign had begun to preserve the "unique charm" of the area. Capote's yellow-brick Victorian, down a block from the Woodhull, was memorialized in *A House on the Heights*. This was something right in Barney's wheelhouse: he was a passionate warrior against the corruption or destruction of New York's cultural heritage.

The East River was also comfortably familiar: if not quite as close as it had been to the Cherry Street tenement, it was an everyday presence, as it was at the Wall Street and Front Street studios. But Barney was not to be comforted. Forced again to adjust to the trauma of dislocation, he was embarrassed by having "Brooklyn" on his biography, traumatized by having to capitulate to the East End Temple, and boiling over the dismissal of the Reinhardt/CAA lawsuit. He wallowed in his grievances, and papered his files with support for his moral position. Someone—probably Bill Lipkind's brother, Norman, a special deputy clerk in the court—had sent him a copy of a recent *Record of the Association of the Bar of the City of New York*, directing him in a note to the transcript of an address in which Judge Harold Medina decried the remarkable inefficiency, disarray, and old-boy, partisan political attachments in the court system of New York State. "New York procedure is a horrible example of confusion and complexity, seemingly almost designed for technical gymnastics, dilatory tactics and excessive paper work rather than inexpensive, speedy justice," wrote Medina. The article did not alleviate Barney's sense that he had been treated unfairly.[1]

It was also abrading that critics were so happily moving on into the future. Dorothy Seckler identified Pollock, de Kooning, and their peers as a "fire-breathing *middle* generation" (emphasis added) in *Art in America*—by no account the most up-to-date journal.[2] Hess, in his review of MoMA's current "Twelve Americans," took a bizarrely unwarranted—from the artists' point of view—almost elegiac tone about the fire-breathers: "the inclusion of Pollock, Rothko and Tomlin in the [1952 "Fifteen Americans"] exhibition was belated recognition—of greater importance to collectors than to the artists themselves"![3]

Barney drank, painted the apartment, settled in. He kept up his dutiful visits to his mother on the Upper West Side and Annalee's mother in Queens. He and Annalee took a distraught but determined Krasner to the West Side pier to see her off—as they had Rothko years earlier—to Europe on the Queen Elizabeth.

When the unimaginably horrible news came, on a Sunday morning a month later, of Pollock's death, Barney immediately had the car serviced, and he and Annalee rushed out to Springs. Krasner, who had flown back from Paris, wanted Greenberg to speak at Wednesday's funeral, but he refused. Greenberg suggested, and Krasner rejected, Barney as a replacement. In the end, no one but the hired preacher spoke. The Newmans remained on Long Island for a few days among the shell-shocked, spending time with Greenberg and Frankenthaler. (There, they were tracked down by the East End Temple. Unwittingly or wittingly, Barney had neglected to return the key to 341 East Nineteenth Street.[4])

Pollock had been the one person Barney could most reliably count on for what he experienced as *peer* recognition and encouragement—as incomprehensible as it would have been to the other artists, or to critics, or museum people, or the mass media that they were "peers." It was *the* great, inconceivable, loss after the loss of his home and his pride.

"For the first time in history, no one is sure who the art audience is. Today, the question, For Whom Do You Paint . . . can only be the beginning of a speculation, if not of an angry controversy."

Harold Rosenberg's screed in the November *Art News* took to task the popular idea that the problem with advanced art was that it failed to communicate with the average man, since such a population was an illusion.

> Today everybody is already a member of some audience . . . self-conscious in their tastes . . . Science-fiction pulp, tabloid sports columns, rock 'n' roll gossip, the New Criticism [all] assume various levels of terminology on the part of their readers . . . even an afternoon broadcast designed for the suburban housewife addresses itself to an expertise . . . [which] differs from that of a Museum of

Modern Art first-night less in intellectual capacity . . . than in the form of its interests and their social expression.

"A practice establishes itself as a profession . . . through self-consciousness . . . . The essential mark of a profession is its evolution of a unique language . . . . The more incomprehensible this lingo is to outsiders, the more thoroughly it . . . elevates it out of the reach of mere amateurs." But if specialized language was accepted by the culture in disciplines like physics, plumbing, social anthropology—and, he might have mentioned, economics, such as the language of *Fortune*'s "The Great International Art Market"—it was not likewise accepted in regard to art. A critic who wrote in comparable "lingo" about painting "would be treated as a genocide by audience builders. In their turn, artists, responding to the surrounding professionalization, become convinced that the secret of art, as well as its honor as a calling, resides in the jargon of the studios."

Along the convoluted way, to illustrate the segregation of professions, or professional philosophies, Rosenberg seemed to randomly invoke two public figures: Ezra Pound (Pound's "broadcasts for the Italian Fascists showed no trace of the language master. But without poetry what was Pound? . . . a professional echoing the jargon of another profession which he only partly understands"); and Douglas MacArthur ("a general to whom the proper way to fight meant carrying out Pentagon directives could never understand MacArthur)." In the "ritualization" of professions, Rosenberg wrote, "each metier is moved to detach itself from the social will and to ignore every other form of thought except as it can absorb it into its own technical procedures."

Rosenberg bemoaned that all of this had led to the powerful influence of "intercessors" who, by delivering "modern painting to the public" achieve only "work totally taken away from its creator and totally falsified." Without naming names, he was opposing his own aesthetic ideology—in references the initiated readers of *Art News* would understand—to that of Greenberg. It was the same stealthy technique he used in "The American Action Painters." But then, out of the blue, *uniquely* in the essay, a *single* artist's name appeared.

> Manifestations of such dissociation may seem absurd or vicious to members of other professions, but a Barnet [*sic*] Newman dropping his line down the middle of a canvas is in no different position than the Supreme Commander in the Pacific trying to solve the problem of Chinese Communism by "hot pursuit" across the Yalu.[5]

Ezra Pound, Douglas MacArthur . . . and Barney!

Earlier in the year *Life* magazine ran in five installments excerpts from President Truman's memoirs. In the same February issue that featured those concerned with the Korean War, there was an editorial about Ezra Pound that provoked a responding editorial in *Art News* ("Life and the Crazy Artist") and a second editorial, "Artists at Liberty," that provoked a letter to the *Life* editor from one Harold Rosenberg.[6] Between the issues of *Life* with the Pound editorial and the one with Rosenberg's letter was the memoir installment describing MacArthur's "hot pursuit."[7] These three magazines were sitting on Rosenberg's desk, and it was this conjunction that inspired his choice of examples—Barney having brought the association with MacArthur upon himself with his by-this-time titled *Vir Heroicus Sublimis*. And it was with a similar conjunction of Truman's memoirs and the *Times* coverage of "Old Bolshevik" Vyacheslav Molotov's ascension to primary responsibility for Soviet culture, *and* other world events that November, that Barney now unleashed a tsunami upon reams of abused draft paper.[8]

Barney read paragraphs of implication between every line, and with some justification—since he *was* the only artist mentioned—interpreted "Everyman a Professional" as particularly poking him. Rosenberg's:

> Comparison of my work to MacArthurs "hot pursuit" is not only an example of R's inability to read work but unwarranted. My work is an act, unplanned, immediate concept and thing . . . whereas Mac was involved in a plan for "action" a rhetorical gesture.

And from there Barney segued directly into his old, narcissistic pattern: the insult of Rosenberg's flick became inseparable from his agony over Pollock, over Reinhardt, over current events. Typically, he found echoes of his personal misery in political conflicts, and news reports were useful—if an inchoate stretch—to confirm the righteousness of his indignation:

> it was unfortunate that political considerations forced Truman not to agree with Mac for it is obvious that it would have been better for all of us if Mac had engaged in hot pursuit and the bombs had fallen over the Yalu. Perhaps they would not be falling now over the Nile and the Danube.

In July 1956 Egypt had nationalized the Suez Canal, and in late October Britain, France, and the State of Israel—Abraham Newman's bedrock, the territory where Annalee was born—were allied in a war. Barney as always experienced it personally. "How can I tell you how moved I was to read your letter except to tell you how also moved my sisters and Annalee were by your deep feelings and heartfelt concern. At a time like this," he wrote to the Libermans, "your friendship and Tatiana's friendship sustain one as nothing else can."[9] In the same week Soviet tanks moved into the streets of Hungary.

Barney collapsed it all into his drafted reaction to Rosenberg:

> seriously why this incessant desire by you and your artist friends to restore art to the people. Do you all feel that Molotov will fail

H.R. calls it "professional" Molotov calls the same art for art's sake "bureaucratic" H.R. in discussing my work calls it "manifestations of such dissociation" . . . Molotov calls it "deviations from orthodoxy."

"What is shocking," Barney wrote, was Rosenberg's confessed "inability to make the distinction between pure and applied art. Somehow he makes the same mistake made by his painter friends who have been debating this same straw man question now for six years."

> Today the argument of the pure and impure goes on and try as they may they cannot get me into it. Rosenbergs friends, the De Kooning and Reinhardt, Rothko and Motherwell debating this false "issue" . . . created and carried on by shrewd theoreticians . . . but in reality the impure dick and din school of painters could fight the pure ones . . . the Bauhaus art professors from our city colleges conducting club forums and saloon seminars, [and] the soirees of the official art world.

The polarity between "those fathered by Surrealism and those fathered by the Bauhaus [was] a struggle over who has 'The Truth.'" The "real"—and "dangerous"—thing that was taking place, according to Barney, was the "amalgam between the Surrealist and Bauhaus Ideas," which accepted everything but Barney's art, which they called "art for art's sake."

As the drafts piled up, as the language became more convoluted and the logic more tangled and the writing more visibly agitated, it is easy to see Barney, still in the "appeal" stage of his lawsuit against humiliation, and with works by the victorious Reinhardt praised in the current *Art News* ("They represent only the glow, the ultimate thing—the artist—after artistry has been . . . eliminated"[10])—feeling more and more abused, uniquely singled out and mocked.

> Mr. Rs distinction is not a pure one [but] psychological warfare.
>
> As to the comparison with MacArthur it is again no true distinction and a psychological trick . . . . For Mac was involved in a plan while my picture is a totally useless statement not of truth but of my truth as an individual . . . .
>
> Ten years ago at a dinner party attacking the intrasubjective content [of] abstract painting for its lack of social content & political "meaning" HR turned to a picture of mine on the wall & challenged me to give him "the reality" of it. I explained to him that if he could read pictures he would see that the intensity of its content properly understood its political implications would destroy state capitalism & state socialism . . . .
>
> But why the article? Why [make it] around my name & mine only? . . . .
>
> I didn't see the need for the parallel analogy R made bet my work—Gen MacArthur. But if had to make an analogy why him . . . there is an important difference. *My line is a true act—R will never know how terrible the terror it*

took for me to do it whereas MacArthurs was an "action" and like all "actions"
political, social, artistic, judicial performed as contemplated, no act at all but
only a piece of rhetoric [emphases added].[11]

Turmoil, and big ideas, and powerful sentiment was what Barney was made of.
Sometimes he was able to wrangle the mixture into an "act"—and art was the result.
At other times, it eluded his control and a cyclone blew in. At least he existed in an
arena in which both were possible. Hess liked to quote Stuart Davis: "It's great to
be Picasso in Paris, but what would it be like in some hick town where every one
thought you were nuts?"[12]

It was in this frame of mind that he attended the memorial at The Club on a Friday
night at the end of the wracked month of November. The death of Pollock had brutally eliminated one pole of the de Kooning–Pollock axis, but de Kooning "remained
obsessed" with the other artist, "who in some respects was a more formidable rival
dead than alive."[13] At the memorial he infuriated Barney—and many others—by
suggesting that Pollock was, in a way, a John the Baptist who had "broken the ice"
for him. Afterwards, Barney reacted in drafts of a letter. This time, though, his wit,
albeit bitter, remained intact:

> Shame on you, Willem! I still cannot forget that on Friday <u>we</u> came to praise
> Jackson but you, like a cheap 14 Street Mark Anthony, you came to bury
> him . . .
>   You, who condemn the museums [that] "put us in pigeon-holes. Who the
> hell ever told them we were pigeons." you did not hesitate to put Jackson
> into a pigeon hole—on a pedestal of cracked ice!
>   Shame on you, Willem! . . . First, the defunct Duchamp cracked the ice
> of "freedom" for you . . . then Gorky cracked ice for you and now you would
> like to make it that Pollock served you too. Tell me, with all this ice-cracking
> to give you room, when are you going to learn to swim?

More was at issue for Barney than de Kooning's behavior at the memorial. He saw
powerful factions aligned against him.

> P.S. I have owed you a letter that would properly express my contempt for
> a long time now . . . . You used a sacred occasion not only to show your
> cynical intentions but you told me that <u>nothing</u> would stop you from the
> vilification you have practised against me for years now. I therefore wish
> to serve notice on you to desist . . . . I therefore would like to recommend
> that you ask HR[osenberg] whom you seem to respect to explain to you that
> words unlike paint cannot be slung around with impunity.[14]

That day, he wrote to Parsons, continuing their conversation at the memorial: they should see each other, she had told Barney, she would like to buy some of his work, she wanted to show his work. "The things seem intertwined for you," he responded. "For me they are completely separated." Of course they would see each other, they had been close friends for fifteen years, and he hoped for at least fifteen more. But he had questions about her interest in his "pictures":

"You say you have money now. You had money before when I helped you organize the funds to buy Mark & Clyff's work. To have bought me then would have helped me out not only financially but at a time when reputations were being made. Now it is all done and everyone has his place or doesn't have it."

He challenged Parsons's motivation: "even now you tell me you want my stuff not for itself but because Clyff isn't selling." He also challenged her basic sympathy for his work, since she was showing Reinhardt and Ellsworth Kelly, both of them making "things," in Barney's estimation, while his work was a "matter of the spirit."[15] But "the most important thing of all" was that she could imagine that he would show in the same gallery as his "defamers and libel sayers"; it made him doubt that she understood him at all. "You claim you must be neutral. Yes all of my friends have taken the same position. I have wondered whether the issue was one of neutrality or just plain indifference."[16]

Barney staked his life on his independence and self-sufficiency, yet he could sound like the kid afraid of eating alone in the cafeteria. In his righteous letters, he chronically invoked friendship—as if only he stood on principled positions, and others' loyalties were based on with whom they drank, danced (at The Club), slept, or played baseball (in East Hampton). Mathieu and "his Tapié friends"; Hess and his "artist friends"; *Partisan Review* editors and their "artist friends"; Rosenberg and his "painter friends." He wasn't being dismissive; it was a way of telegraphing how profoundly he felt left out: the word and the idea was freighted with meaning for him. He could not honor Rothko for their past friendship because Rothko was not his true friend but "active enemy," and to Barney "friendship is man's most sacred trust."

And now all of those he thought were his friends were indifferent to his pain. But in the midst of his perceived rejection, the friendship of *Vogue*'s Alex Liberman and his wife Tatiana "sustain[ed] one as nothing else can."

As the Liberman's guests, Barney and Annalee attended a charity ball at the Plaza Hotel. Annalee looked "quite attractive" in a black dress. At the time it was the fashion to begin a hot Charleston in the middle of a slow blues number. Liberman had always thought of Annalee as a "rather calm, and noble and sedate person." Suddenly, to his astonishment, he "saw Annalee *twist* and *wiggle*, with a *fantastic* shimmy and energy," and he "understood the vitality and the energy, attractiveness that Annalee must have had when she first met Barney. It was still [there] in her." It was a "moment of revelation. Because she was so *noble, serene* and *wise*. And [here] was this extraordinary physical energy Barney knew and must have loved and appreciated."[17]

He would begin a new chapter with new friends, new bank loans, and his constant, stalwart, partner.

FORTY

TURNING POINT

The privileged audience members who were invited "Under the Auspices of The Museum of Modern Art" to view the collection of Ben Heller at his home in May 1957 were treated to an exhibition of recent New York art that they could see nowhere else. Immediately upon entering the foyer at 280 Riverside Drive they were overwhelmed: oils by Still, Pollock, Guston, Rothko, punctuated by a Joseph Cornell box, a gouache by Miró, and a 3000-year-old Mycenaean figure. Advancing into the living room, there were major pieces by Kline, Rothko, Esteban Vicente, Pollock, and numbers of African, Eastern, ancient Greek and Mexican sculptures. Progressing through the apartment, Pollock, Rothko, Tomlin, Kline—and two paintings by Barnett Newman.

There was nothing that could have been better for Barney in 1957 than to be in this company, on these walls, with the imprimatur of Heller, a true believer and patron. A dealer's commitment, tainted by finance, could always be suspected and doubted; critics existed to criticize. It's not to say that Heller was not interested in "investments," or, a little later, in making financially beneficial sales. He wasn't a saint, but he put his money where his mouth was. He had these works where he lived. And he was extraordinarily supportive to those artists in whom he believed.

With a little help from his new friends—Heller and Liberman among them— Barney's world would finally turn right side up.

If the year began with more letter-writing, the tone was entirely different. To William Burden, he was full of praise for the Sam Hunter-curated Pollock exhibition at MoMA. The show was "not only poetic" but made apparent "the stature of the painter." He *congratulated* the museum for an exhibition that was a "living experience and unforgettable." He also congratulated the museum on its recent acquisition and prominent display of Monet's 1916–26 *Water Lilies*, recalling their 1953 exchange of letters: "I did not then nor do I now wish to supplant Cézanne with Monet or with anyone else in the promulgation of any theory of art or in a struggle over art influences. I have been concerned that a healthier, fuller picture should emerge concerning French 19th Century painting." He had *complimentary* things to say about Alfred Barr as well, and, so unlike his wounded and aggressive earlier style, very diplomatically suggested that Barr, who did so well with the Cézanne and van Gogh exhibitions in the early days at the Heckscher Building, might bring the same expertise, drama, and excitement to a show of Monet and Pissarro.[1]

Ten days later, after reading that a number of Monet shows were planned in museums across the country, he wrote to Barr himself: "I should be disappointed if, because of this, an exhibition of Monet directed by you, is not held at the Museum." But should that be the case, there was an "even greater opportunity [to] fulfill a public need" by presenting a comprehensive show of Pissarro, whose work was "virtually unknown to artists and public alike in this country." His interest, he assured Barr, was "not one of affiliation" but only "an act of respect—in the name of Painting."[2]

"Thank you for your thoughtful letter . . . . It was very considerate of you to write expressing your approval of recent Monet acquisitions by the Museum," Barr responded, genially, genteelly, reflecting his allergy to Barney the man, a sensitivity that he would very soon have to overcome for the greater glory of Art.[3]

If the positive attitude, the gracious, measured prose might have belonged to an entirely different person, Barney's thin-skinned and prickly self could still be provoked. At the opening of Frankenthaler's show at Tibor de Nagy, looking trim and handsome, silk scarf perfectly coordinated with soft silk bowtie, Barney was having a good time holding forth in his most charmingly jovial manner when he was introduced to journalist Clay Felker and Magnum photographer Burt Glinn. "Dear Miss Frankenthaler," he drafted a few days later, "I presumed that I was among friends and that your friends were doing a souvenir of the show." When he discovered that they were working on "Upper and Lower Bohemia" for *Esquire* magazine, Barney blew his top, "shocked" by her "trickery," feeling used. "As the daughter of a judge and coming from a family of judges you must have known that my privacy was being invaded and that I was being taken advantage of."

"My attorneys have already written to the men involved" to demand that they not use photos of him or anything he "may have said that evening." In the letter he actually posted, Barney left the "attorneys" in, but was less angry, if much more condescending: To "Dear Helen: Art is cunning, so say the dictionaries, but it is time that you learned that cunning is not yet art, even when the hand that moves under the faded brushwork so limply in its attempt to make art is so deft at the artful."[4]

His "attorneys." In his own confusion, or ambivalence, about his identity—bohemian artist? radical anarchist? proper "banker" avatar?—Barney again shifted mode to a man who had on retainer attorneys. And at that moment he was indeed keeping them busy, preparing, in "accordance" with his request, the brief in the self-destructive pursuance of the Newman v. Reinhardt et al appeal.

The "Bohemia" article wouldn't appear until July, but the world it described— telegraphed by Hess's summation in "U.S. Painting: Some Recent Directions"—if unnatural for Barney, was not so for Frankenthaler's generation. Unlike Rosenberg's sour and judgmental description of "everyman" locked into his own specialized jargon and world-view, *Esquire*'s take was based on Russell Lynes's essay, "A Surfeit of Honey." Upper Bohemians, "whether lawyer, editor, or architect—or even a businessman who is patron of the arts after office hours" were the "cultural purveyors" of the era, the top tastemakers of the day, flitting from one specialty to the others. They functioned as a "bridge between the creative artist and the public." Pages of photographs showed parties and jazz clubs, openings and rehearsals—David Smith, Larry Rivers, Grace Hartigan, Arnold Newman, Frank O'Hara, Allen Ginsberg, Merce Cunningham. Laid out next to photographs of her fashionable opening, shots of

Frankenthaler in a skirt and rolled up sleeves hovering over a canvas on the floor were a Bizarro World echo of the *Life* magazine photographs of Pollock that had been so disturbing to the public eight years earlier.

Barney had anticipated Reinhardt redux: let down his guard with a "friend" and it could turn out to be fodder for mockery. But by the time the article appeared, he would not have been able to deny that he was indeed entering this world. And, ultimately, he entered and navigated it with more success and finesse than any of his former cohort.

A new world for contemporary art really was about to take shape, and oddly enough, notwithstanding all the pompous rejection of old-world models, the impetus would come from abroad.

Counterintuitively, the fresh air began to drain from the *work* of Barney's generation any conceptual, mystical, or philosophical radicality—in the minds of all but the artists concerned—while at the same time making the *men* themselves more heroic. And it would turn out to be especially beneficial for Barney.

From London, a young curator and critic named Lawrence Alloway unwittingly but perfectly identified the evolving order—and coincidently, several aspects that would, within a few years, particularly impact Barney—when he wrote to Tom Hess to ask for "four things": would Hess put his friend, the sculptor William Turnbull, in touch with New York artists, "including the newer ones"; would Hess organize statements from de Kooning, Rothko, and Rosenberg for the BBC "egghead" affiliate's feature on "Action Painting"; would Hess help E. J. Power, "England's only important collector of what-do-you-call-it post-war painting," to find the works he was looking for; and would *Art News* be interested in a piece about "the aesthetics of popular art (meaning, need I say, the mass media—Hollywood, Science Fiction, Fashion, Ads). The subject seems to me to get more and more important and in some ways it puts the fine arts on the spot. When pop art gets very good in quality can it be described in traditional aesthetic terms? *Or, when modern art goes into the area of expendability does it become popular*" (emphasis added). There was now a fine-art / popular-art continuum, Alloway noted, but it was ignored by the critics: "How much longer must pop art be left" where Greenberg put it in the "outdated" essay "Avant-garde and Kitsch"?[5]

From Switzerland came Arnold Rüdlinger, the director of the Kunsthalle in Basel, who arrived in New York in March with the intention of organizing a major exhibition of Abstract Expressionist painting for his museum. Previously the director of the Bern Kunsthalle, where he mounted three adventurous shows of international contemporary art, this charismatic and energetic modern-art partisan met in the early 1950s a number of American artists who lived in Paris. One of them, Sam Francis, a "second generation" abstract expressionist championed by Michel Tapié, became an especially involved friend, and persuaded Rüdlinger that he needed to come to America.

Having been impressed in Zurich with the 1955 Museum of Modern Art International Council show, "Modern Art from USA," Rüdlinger hoped to mount a show of Francis, Kline, Motherwell, Rothko, and Still. It's hard to imagine what harm a well-selected show at a prestigious European museum might have done them,[6] but the last two, ever on the alert for any nefarious "trick"—using "one artist's name to force the hand of another," as Still reported to Ossorio[7]—scuttled the idea by refusing to participate. Now, after his studio visits, Rüdlinger was considering de Kooning, Reinhardt, and Barney. That show, too, never happened because the Basel Kunsthalle could not get it financed,[8] but Rüdlinger's enthusiastic presence alone was galvanic. All of the players in New York, whatever they felt about each other, whatever animosities festered, were interested in him, and he was interested in them. Greenberg, through Francis, was a voice Rüdlinger heard. Heller, involved with the Museum of Modern Art, was another voice Rüdlinger heard. And both men believed in Barney, even if MoMA itself did not. Rüdlinger "was the very first museologist to get to Newman."[9]

European recognition came also from Paris: Barney was invited to contribute to a show organized by Michel Seuphor and Galerie Raymond Creuze. (He did not.)[10]

In the U.S., Stanton Catlin, the curator of American art at the Minneapolis Institute of Arts, was interested. The beneficiary of significant public and local corporate support, the museum had been conservatively focused on building a collection until the appointment of Richard Davis as director eighteen months earlier, when it embarked on an ambitious program around modern art. Now it announced what would be one of the first comprehensive surveys of postwar American painting, directed by Catlin. Ten years younger than Barney, Catlin had already had a career in South America (at times with United States Military Intelligence, at times affiliated with the Museum of Modern Art); in Europe during the war (at times with United Nations Relief and Rehabilitation Administration, at times with the United States Fine Arts, Monuments and Archives Division); and in the early 1950s was writing reviews for *Art News* while a graduate student at New York University's Institute of Fine Arts. Catlin was no provincial suitor.

Catlin traveled "coast-to-coast," looking at art, and when he got to New York, Greenberg, who had been spending endless hours listening to Barney's "issues" in his "relentless, droning voice, nasal, wheedling . . . as Annalee hummed" in the background,[11] told Catlin: "You must see Barnett Newman. He is really the wave of the future."[12] Barney's work seemed to Catlin to "bear no relation to what was going on in the abstract expressionist idiom at this point," but Greenberg was adamant; it was the only suggestion he made to the curator, and so it was taken seriously. Especially since Catlin had heard that "Newman had refused to show for ten years in New York"; *that* really intrigued him.

Barney could always be counted on to give good studio and when Catlin approached him in April he was treated to the full seduction.[13] Barney "received" him, Catlin recalled years later, in his Front Street studio. "He liked me, I guess, from what I said, and we got into a discussion." Then they walked through the district, and Barney led him through the "great, coffered porticos of Wall Street [the Municipal

Building at the end of Chambers Street] and he said, 'See that? That's strength. That is masculine. They may be bastards down here, but they are real men. They are not shopping, shopping, shopping, shoppers, as they are uptown.'"[14] Catlin said he wanted to borrow work.

Greenberg and Hess "couldn't believe" that Barney agreed. When Hess asked Catlin why, Catlin told him that the "main reason" was that Barney "did not want to be identified with the reasons given by other artists who have refused to participate in group shows, such as Rothko and Still." It was an answer that Hess respected: "That's a good reason," he said. (To Heller, Barney was more explicit: "The issue is not why I have not shown publicly or privately to friends, etc. etc. The question that has to be answered by those who ask it is—why have they shown? What was it that they thought they had that made them show mechanically year after year?)"[15]

The inclusion was, Catlin felt, crucial for the show: "The real turning point was Barnett Newman."

"I had Los Angeles painters, I had San Francisco painters." But Barney's work "was the keystone," so far as "the importance of the show." Later, Catlin summed up what he saw in the work, a crystalline response to the anxieties of the mid-20th century: the "vertical shafts cut through aeons of time and space"; they brought the macro- and micro-cosmic into "proximity with man's sensibility." Paralleling "science's farthermost methodological explorations—quantum mechanics, partical [sic] physics, and the biology of the origin of life—Newman blaz[ed] a path for the human spirit to accompany the mind."[16]

"We got along," Catlin said, "we became friends."

One might have expected Barney to be overjoyed at the recognition. But whether genuinely anxious about *how* he would be shown or residually cognizant of Still and Rothko's petulant decisions not to be shown with *any*one else, Barney was coy. He found showing "very painful."[17] He played both hard to get—setting conditions, testing his suitor, insisting upon seeing the entire checklist of 146 works by 55 artists before he would commit—*and* literally hard to reach, refusing to take phone calls. This was often the case with Barney; it made ultimate contact feel so much more special and rewarding. Finally, Barney was persuaded to participate, and at the beginning of June, titled as they have since been known, *Abraham, Onement* (the numeral "III" was not included), and *Vir Heroicus Sublimis*—Barney's trump card—were sent to the Midwest, insured for 14,300 dollars (over 155,000 dollars in 2023). Barney wanted to hang the works himself. When he was told that was not possible, he never came to Minneapolis at all. And so, when he saw photographs of the installation, which were taken through a doorway because *Vir Heroicus Sublimis* was so large, they seemed to confirm his worst fears: paintings by Reinhardt, hanging on the outside of the portal appeared to abut Barney's canvas, "made Newman think that he was being placed alongside of Ad Reinhardt," and "he blew his stack," Greenberg told Catlin.

He needn't have fretted. The buzz that month was around the *Art News* parody of Reinhardt, more cutting than any Reinhardt had written about other artists. "Adolf M. Pure" demanded that his paintings must have no color, wrote Hess's special friend,

Elaine de Kooning, in "Pure Paints a Picture," a satirical version of the magazine's series and a riff on Hess's own 1953 article, "Reinhardt: the Position and Perils of Purity." "Therefore his shelves are lined with tubes of color that he never touches." He slept sixteen hours in twenty-four, to ensure that no ideas might creep into his work; " 'ideas are harder to get rid of than roaches once they get a foothold.' " Any viewer's projection of subject matter was "erroneous. 'Art can be corrected but, alas,' Pure sighs, 'the public cannot.' "

" 'If any paint remains on the picture-surface at the end of a day's work, I have failed,' " the imaginary Pure was "quoted" as saying, and to fail " 'should be the highest aspiration of the fine-artist.' "[18]

June also brought Heller's check for *Queen of the Night*—already hanging in Heller's dining room for the MoMA tour—and the "brown" one—*Adam*. Barney wanted 3000 and 1000 dollars respectively, the prices at the time of his Parsons show, but Heller recently acquired a Still painting for 2000 dollars and a Rothko for 2250 dollars, and didn't feel he should pay more for Barney's. With no dealer's commission involved, the two agreed on 3000 dollars (32,530 dollars in 2023) for the two.[19] It was an extraordinary sum to fall into Barney's hands, and a psychological gift. In an unbearable insult, the Appellate Division that week "unanimously affirmed, with costs" the judgment against him. Five days after Heller's check arrived, in Maspeth, Queens, Barney laid down 630 dollars of it to purchase a beautiful black Jaguar Mark V sedan (Still's was a Mark IV), and arranged to garage it at considerable expense. Its elegance was so unexpected that Annalee's nephew, on leave from Fort Meade and taken for a spin, forever imagined the dazzling wood dashboard when he heard the name "Barney."

The previous summer, he had begun wearing a monocle—an accessory that, in those days, was mainly associated with the ventriloquist's dummy Charlie McCarthy or the spokes-legume Mr. Peanut. However much it solved a real problem—the need for reading glasses after a certain age, the regular misplacement of those glasses by anyone who has ever used them—a monocle, suspended from a black silk cord around the neck of a portly, extravagantly mustached, middle-class New Yorker in 1957 was not simply a practical instrument. Inevitably it called attention to its twinkling self, inevitably its use provided opportunities for the idiosyncratic gestures that distinguished one who wielded it for flourishes and punctuation. It was, as Cyrano de Bergerac would have called it, Barney's *panache* (Dan Flavin, who loved him, called it "preposterous"[20]), and the monocle became what everyone mentioned when speaking of the man. Now the man, the mustache, and the monocle would tool around in an appropriate vehicle.

If Barney's paintings were the turning point of the Minneapolis show, his inclusion was the turning point in his life.

Not only had he required special urging to show, his work required the most explicit and special treatment. He sent two single-spaced pages of instructions for preparing the canvases to be returned: the kind and size of cardboard facing;

the kind and method for fastening wrapping paper for *Abraham* and *Onement*. *Vir Heroicus Sublimis* needed to be unstretched, laid flat on new canvas, all loosened staples needed to be accounted for, kitchen freezer paper handled by at least two men needed to cover the back in a particular way, the painting needed to be rolled around a cardboard drum by at least three men who had re-washed their hands and put on clean gloves. Barney supplied the gloves. Et cetera. His anxiety was palpable and warranted. He asked that these instructions be followed "not out of fussy nervousness, but because I know from experience that they are necessary." Even now, *after* their public exhibition and reception, Barney felt it critical to emphasize his uniqueness. "The surfaces of my pictures are such that even a scratch can destroy the picture effect, whereas those pictures with many forms and colors, a scratch only affects the specific area around it. I must also point out, that contrary to the general impression, it is more difficult technically to paint a single color over a large area than it is to paint a complex of many colors."[21]

And this, precisely, may have been Barney's most brilliant artistic initiative—his own "breaking of the ice." He had truly made his paintings in such a way that they required more than professional handling. By their nature, Barney's paintings *demanded* the tender, devoted, worshipful treatment that the man himself longed for. Wherever they went, for their entire existence in this world, this demand might be ignored but it could never be forgotten. Without that treatment they would absolutely lose their—and Barney's—presence.

"The surface lies exposed and naked before you, offering no shelter, and the slightest flaw in composition or technique is blatantly apparent," wrote a particularly sensitive critic after the first large-scale showing of work. "The sureness which this approach requires is extreme, and it is typical of Newman to challenge himself in this way."[22]

He had "added a new range of meaning to painting," remarked one of the younger generation of artists upon whom he had a profound influence, "the symbolism of what one does, as opposed to the symbols involved in the images one makes."[23]

"Your pictures make one of the most important contributions to the show," Catlin recognized. "'Vir Heroicus Sublimis' has no peer in purity, in the high tenor of its conviction, and through these in power of ablution."[24] For the remaining twelve years of his life, Barney suffered the torments of hell brought on by inadvertent scratches, intentional vandalism, and accidents, and the sometimes flawed responses of restorers, conservators, and insurance adjusters. He thought it was "wrong for an artist to have his work, once it's bought, the victim of the buyer. As if it were an automobile," Barney said years later. Depending upon the "sense of kindness" of a purchaser felt like "blackmail" to him.[25]

It could have been anticipated that crisis would ensue. Despite the packing instructions, *Abraham* was returned "marked up with at least six spots of green paint." The same were discovered on *Vir Heroicus Sublimis*. And it could have been anticipated, as well, that no satisfactory remedy could be taken.

"I am afraid that things have turned out as my husband predicted," Annalee wrote a few months later to insurers when *Abraham* was under consideration to be included in a Museum of Modern Art show. "His fears, that the restoration of the two paintings which were mutilated in Minneapolis require much more delicate and complex skills and involved a much greater danger to their proper restoration than was previously contemplated, are true."[26]

While the local Minneapolis reviewers were respectful, a scathing review in the *New Republic* was contemptuous about the whole endeavor: it was "the kind of show the Walker [the more *au courant* Minneapolis institution] might have mounted two years ago . . . . More and more, month by month, abstract expressionism reveals itself as more fraud than Freud." Brutally mocked were Hofmann, Pollock, Brooks, Guston, Joan Mitchell, Albers, and Reinhardt. But "the most asinine thing on board is Barnett Newman's 'Vir Heroicus Sublimis,'" the reviewer, Frank Getlein, wrote; it was hung in what he called "the Design Division" of the show. "Eight feet high, 'Vir' is damn near 18 feet across . . . . At the opening somebody told Catlin the Institute could have saved a good chunk by getting the plan and having the thing run off by the janitors with rollers."[27] (Barney immediately wrote to Catlin to confirm whether the remark was truly made to him. Catlin assured him it was not.[28])

Vacations did not seem to relax Barney, or diffuse his indignation; instead, they provided time to stew, and he often returned with his sword sharpened. Barney waited until after the summer's road trip—Saratoga, of course, Fort Ticonderoga and Ausable Chasm, and up to Montreal—to react. As was his well-honed technique, he ignored the context and company, and found an immediately at hand issue of political importance as a strained "hook" for his rejoinder.

> The same issue of the New Republic . . . that had as its feature article, the excellent report by Robert Guillain on the methods of thought-control used by the Chinese Communists to coerce their writers and artists (The Chinese Intellectuals) also included a report on American Paintings in Minneapolis by Frank Getlein, who uses these same Chinese methods to attack my work.
>
> In his ill-tempered, "cussing" article, Mr. Getlein throws at me the label of "Design Division" with its implied charges of formalism, subjectivity, separation of practice and theory and parallels, thereby, the Communist charge of "ideal-ism" which Mr. Guillain reports is the device used by the Chinese against their artists . . . .
>
> Mr. Getlein's methods can have no effect whatever on me. However, I must protest his use of them and his attempt to brain-wash your readers who, not able to see my work, cannot judge for themselves.
>
> 1. It was unnecessary for Mr. Getlein to swear at the "damn" size of my picture when a glance at the exhibition catalogue would have given him the exact size.

2. . . . my picture . . . has no elements of "design." . . . . To the knowing my work stands as the strongest threat to the "Design" Painters because of its complete opposition to their principles and practices . . . .

3. Anyone who knows anything about art techniques knows that to paint the large areas I do in free space in terms of a whole image requires the greatest skill and artistry.

When these pictures were first shown years ago, the shock they created then was understandable, and I am not surprised that they still shock Mr. Getlein since they embody a vision and a way of looking that never existed before. However, there is a great difference between the critical eye blinded by shock and the prejudiced eye practicing psychological warfare. Is Mr. Getlein critic or Chinese commissar?

To which, Getlein, obviously giddy with his own condescending and racist "wit," replied with a single word: "Clitic."[29]

Barney prolonged his reactions to the *New Republic*'s review and insurance claims for the injuries suffered by his paintings—insurance claims began to be a leitmotif that replaced to a large extent lawsuits—throughout the fall and early winter, but, in a good humor, could acknowledge that Getlein was, " of course, of small consequence." He shared his ripostes with the friends by whom he felt securely supported—Catlin, Greenberg, the Hellers: "Here is the epilogue to the Minnesota show which I hope you will find amusing." He even sent it to Hess, with whom, since Hess's trip to see the show, his relationship was now entering calmer waters.[30] "I'm glad . . . that the incident brought us together for a drink," Hess wrote to Barney. "Perhaps you will consider writing something for Art News?"[31]

And in the same easier frame of mind, he reminded Ethel Schwabacher, concerning the (one-sentence) history of black paintings in America that she had in her Gorky monograph, that he "recall[ed] mentioning" to her that Pollock had a "complete one-man show" of such work at Parsons, and she also forgot "the work of a guy named Barnett Newman . . . . The historical fact is that the first all-black painting that included no white and no other color besides black was done in 1949 by me." This appears to be the first instance of Barney trying to memorialize that date for *Abraham*.[32]

FORTY-ONE

"MENSCH. TIMES TEN"

What exactly did Catlin see when he was invited to the ritual of a showing, the recitations, the ceremonial laying out of brown paper backdrop, at the Front Street studio the previous spring? What convinced him and brought him around to Greenberg's position? What might he have seen had he returned later in the year? The issue of the paintings' dates is always in the background of Barney's story.

Hess, recording what Barney told him, wrote that *Uriel* (plate 14) was the only work he painted in 1955, and that no pictures were made in 1956 or 1957, and that is the way these years have been written about and understood ever since.[1] Yet there is something puzzling about including 1957 in that narrative; even Hess, as he recorded the official version, equivocated about Barney's rationale. "Things seemed to be improving," he wrote, noting the sales to Heller. Hess concluded that "the blackest years" were unbearable to Newman not only because of "outside hostility and rejection, but also because he had come to a serious problem in his painting." Constructing a complicated theory that mixed mathematical proportion and his own projected Kabbalistic logic to interpret the oeuvre's development, Hess decided that what was missing from the story was something *formal*, an artistic endgame. *Uriel* was a "culminating" picture that foreclosed further challenge: "His impetus toward a breakthrough had stopped."[2]

But Barney's approach to his work, disciplined and professional, was anything but "formal"—in the Bauhaus sense—anything but literal, and absolutely anything but programmatic or predetermined. He would find himself "compelled" to make paintings while in the studio not by an act of will, but through a complex of "intellectual intuition." And in 1957, the churning agitation and static noise that blocked that "spiritual . . . [and] psychic state of high intensity" had settled down.[3]

There is no evidence of, or possible reason for, depression or despair as in previous years; on the contrary all signs support something entirely different. Beginning with the rational tone of his letters and his first significant sales to an important collector, through a social calendar packed with new acquaintances—who were less competitive, less judgmental about his person (if not his work), who sought him out and who reveled in his company and his stimulating, eccentric philosophizing—his life had improved immeasurably. There was intellectual play with Greenberg and Liberman; museum people in his studio; his own (not Still's) Jaguar. Instead of gut-churning, irritable, or conspiratorial correspondence with friends of dubious allegiance, there was clever and affectionate repartee on a range of high and low culture with a host of supportive new partners.

Barney had purchased virtually no painting supplies in 1954 and 1955 and 1956, the years in which he waged so many angry battles. But strikingly, in 1957, instead of avoiding Dykes Lumber, John Boyle canvas, Bocour and Goldsmith Brothers and New York Central Supply colors, he was buying more than ever. And this mirrored his actual state of mind. So the fact that no works are dated 1957 is more than intriguing.

What seems likely is that the uniquely serene three large paintings, *The Gate*, *The Word II*, *Primordial Light*; the smaller *White Fire I* and *Right Here*; and the "culminating" colossus *Uriel*—all featuring the viridian and "Bocour" greens that were bought in quantity in 1957— were made not in 1954 through the beginning of 1955, the period of extreme agitation, rage, lawsuit-pressing, angry-letter-and-press-release writing, as they have previously been dated, but at this time. The variety of airy aquas produced when the greens were mixed with white turned out to be surprisingly cheeky, but in a seductive and polite way. Reminiscent of a suburban pool, the color was assertive, would not play second fiddle. Most of all, it had inner illumination, a visual and conceptual clarity: these paintings had a calm and a confidence not seen in Barney's work before. This is true in *The Gate,* where the color occupies nearly a third of the canvas in spatial balance with other hues, and true in *The Word II*, where it is saucy and fearless in the central quarter, uncowed by the obdurate black of the left half of the canvas or the deeper blue of the remaining quarter to the right. And it is true in *Primordial Light*, where an area bigger than and blacker than *Abraham* is held in check by a thin turquoise band on each vertical side. The surprising "light, greenish turquoise," as he called it, was felt to be compelling by Barney. It took over the canvas in *White Fire I*, meekly interrupted by a vertical of ochre-beige and a thinner one of bleeding blue-black, as well as in *Right Here*, where just a few inches of the cerulean favored in 1953 escaped its taped border at the left edge. Finally, a version of the color ran rampant across 13 of the 18 feet of *Uriel*, before thin stripes of black, light blue, burnt sienna, and white introduced a large burnt sienna area. These were not paintings Barney would have been "compelled" to bring forth in anger or depression. These paintings have a lighter heart, an ease, even, one might say, hope.

But he *was* compelled to establish 1954 as the date for all but *Uriel*. In brief form letters Barney made gifts of all except *White Fire I* to Annalee; the transfers are dated 1954–61, the works 1954. (Before December 1956, he put dates on only two of his fifteen gifts.) They do not appear on tax returns. No exhibition accounts, and no documents other than his letters of transfer, no photographs, anecdotes, or reports confirm the dates. What possible reason might Barney have had to date these works earlier? Not one of them was needed in the olympics among Still, Rothko, Motherwell, Reinhardt, and Barney; a 1954 date, even by that year, no longer relevant for that competition. But later, establishing 1957 as a nadir *would* be important.

During the latter part of his life—when he was receiving the amount of attention that one is tempted to say was beyond his wildest dreams, except that in Barney's case it was exactly what he always assumed he *should* get—he would maintain that he was unable to paint in 1957. Barney understood the power of an engaging narrative. The nine-month gestation/origin story endowed *Onement I* with its seminal status. Likewise, it was crucial for 1957 to have been a bone-dry period to ensure that what followed would have the appropriate drama. As Barney told it, he began to paint seriously in the early 1940s; he began to show in the late 1940s; he painted for a few more years—1952, 1953, 1954—but was so unappreciated that he stalled, lost, wandering in the desert. Then a genuine crisis occurred: Barney had a massive heart attack, forcing a recalibration—"instant psychiatry," he would say—and he emerged *resurrected*. "Resurrected"—he rejected that word as a title when it was suggested by at least two parties after being struck down. "Forsaken." *That* was the title for him.

It was with uncomfortable equivocation that Annalee, after his death, when his legacy and, finally, his myth, were left in her hands, semi-supported that story. "Barney said he didn't work in '56 and '57," she told an interviewer in 1991. "Well, actually I suppose he did a little work, but maybe he didn't like what he was doing so he destroyed it." But would she "have worked day and night, driven myself crazy working" while "Barney was doing nothing? . . . Barney was a sensitive man." He liked to tell his story the way he wanted the story to be told. He "rolled those away" to force those paying attention in 1957 to see exactly how important he was in 1952—the time of "Fifteen Americans."[4]

And then, with a shockingly unanticipated turn of events, the hidden chronology of those rolled-up works could be used to tell an entirely different tale.

If Reinhardt's work, so adamantly principled, lent itself to satire, the richly limned protean persona that Barney had nourished for so long invited capture in fiction— both affectionate and cynical. His young friend Pierre Garai, now an advertising copywriter whose information about the art world came mostly from Barney's own lips, in 1958 reacted to the heart attack with a mock news feature: "Bullet balled 'BB' Newman trapped in Love Nest."

Behind the arrest of the man who once boasted that the brush was mightier than the airgun lay a story stranger than pigment, Assistant DA Dutch Picasso revealed in an interview at his Whitney Headquarters. Even as he spoke, vicesquad detectives were bringing in the scum of Tempera Alley, including the notorious "Mushy Finger" Rothko whom Newman once nearly rubbed out for fucking around with paint. In a surprise raid last night, detectives seized Newman in a sparsely furnished love nest beneath the Brooklyn Bridge . . . .

Fluent in Chinese from the days of his childhood, "BB" had first made his mark as an importer of chinese cookies at the turn of the century. With the advent of Graham Crackers, he folded, reappearing soon afterwards in the role which made him famous, boss of the oilfront . . . . His syndicate was world-wide, his word law wherever cubes were split, splattered, dots dimpled, blots blotched, drips dried.

Twice elected mayor of New York, he twice declined to serve . . . . An enigma to those who worked with him, a legend to his many fans, he was above all an inspiration to struggling lads with talent. When the supply ran low, he grumbled. When it ran dry, he left the hiring hall he had called home for half a century, stretched his own canvas, took up his work again.[5]

A few years later Hess created a character somewhat based on Barney to illustrate his own discomfort with the evolution of the "art world." A broad parody of Balzac ("The Unknown Masterpiece"), "Mensch-the-artist and Mr. Big," was a Jekyll and Hyde fable about a cagey and manipulating "pioneer New York modern painter" who had a dutiful wife who kept his "ship-shape apartment . . . as snug and cozy as a Norwegian poorhouse," and who himself kept a "complicated verbal record of the publicity which [his] colleagues have received in the daily press, in magazines, on radio and television."

"You know, a funny thing happens when I paint . . . I change. I really change. 'I' go out of my body; the body is transformed. Something else and somebody else paints the pictures." Barney's abdication of self when he was "compelled" to make work is, in Hess's tale, not metaphorical.[6]

Barney's persona was becoming beloved among many new entrants into the New York art community—professionals from beyond the city foreign and American, enthusiastic consumers, and a new generation of artists. The attention was like a steroid shot to Barney's natural charm. In his fifty-two years of changing the hats that covered a brain of febrile intelligence he had accumulated an astonishing archive of factoids, and he was particularly skillful at tailoring his charismatic tutorials to his audience. With Greenberg it was art, of course; but also semantics and "the spelling of goulash on a menu."[7] With Heller, the subject could be Jewish texts and traditions, the textile business, Samuel Beckett, ancient and non-Western art. With Liberman, it was the scars left by anti-Semitism, as well as the fine points of cotton duck and where to find it, recommendations regarding technique—like "the means of dulling" black paint or how to avoid changes in paint color in canisters over time—career strategy, and the "sanctifying power" of work.[8] With Friedman, he carried on about old New York real estate, architecture, and trivia; boxing, television shows, and popular journalism; theater and baseball and how to publicize Uris, Friedman's family property business—everything *but* art. Sheridan and Francile Lord, aspiring artists with a foot in the East End of Long Island, were recruited for serious birdwatching in Central Park. Others were treated to discourses on rocks, carbonation, Indian mounds. He would develop "shticks."

Friedman, who had only become close to Barney about a year earlier, never saw the truly angry man; instead, he saw him "explode" when he was "really amused." When Friedman wrote a letter to *Architectural Forum* defending the aesthetic of the new Uris building at 2 Broadway against another firm's buildings, Barney advised him on the fine points of libel. "You're like a guy who's got a good shot but picks the wrong target." Friedman protested that he was not attacking other buildings but protecting his. "Mass bombing is always attacking," Barney told him. "Bombing specific targets is protective, defensive. I'm involved with specific targets." This was "the way Barney's mind worked"; Friedman thought it was "really very funny." Rather than attributing bad faith to Barney, Friedman appreciated his playfulness—even if it was not always kind. An announcement photograph of Stamos showed only one eye; Barney wanted to send a telegram, "Cyclops=½ Oedipus." It was "castrating,"

Friedman thought, but Barney disagreed. "Well let me put it this way," Friedman told him, "if you think sending him the telegram will make him happy, send it." Although it was "obvious" that Barney wasn't entirely serious, Friedman recognized he was capable of being taunting and provocative. Also "capable of changing positions entirely—within a sentence sometimes." What was "marvelous about Barney is that both possibilities existed."[9]

Heller, too, understood that "Barney was happy even as he was complaining."[10] The younger man had been very close to Pollock, very close to Rothko, to the painter Paul Brach. He associated with many of the artists and knew the range of their complicated artist-temperaments. But for him, Barney was unique, a "mensch. Times ten."

The few genuine friends of the previous decade—Smith, Pollock—were credulous, and therefore put a burden of consistency on Barney. These new men, friends who "got" him, who were not competitive with or threatened by him, who could see past the contradictions to the complicated stew of DNA that was their source and *enjoy* his performances with open eyes, were an entirely different experience.

As one late-life friend would say, Barney flourished in an atmosphere of complete approval.

"Let all of us, in accordance with our hallowed custom, foregather in our respective places of worship or in our homes and offer up prayers of thanks for our manifold blessings. Let the happiness which stems from family reunions on Thanksgiving Day be tempered with compassion and inspired by an active concern for those less fortunate."

As President Dwight Eisenhower in his official proclamation on November 28, 1957, urged, Barney and Annalee foregathered in a family reunion of a sort at the Pollock homestead in Springs, Long Island, with Sheridan and Francile Lord, Bob and Abby Friedman, and Lee Krasner. On a balmy but wet day, the two young couples were casually and lightly dressed, Krasner had a coat thrown over her shoulders, and the Newmans were elegantly buttoned up and hatted—her topper very Miss Marple, his Irish flat cap perched at a jaunty angle. Barney looked robust and happy in suit, necktie, monocle, overcoat, dandyish walking stick, and ever-present cigarette as, giggling and hugging, they posed for pictures. The Friedmans were interested in purchasing a 1947 drawing of Barney's; Krasner made a turkey dinner.

Despite his manifest pleasure, a dark gray cloud hung over Barney. In the current issue of *Time*, where there was a 180-degree course change regarding mid-century abstraction, Still mocked his fellow painters as "the Bob Hopes of 57th Street." Only he "fought my own way out of this ocean."

The subject of the article, archived by Barney, was the "venturesome" collecting policy of Buffalo's Albright Art Gallery (now the AKG Art Museum), but the focus was on Still. He was "the most original painter alive" (quoting Greenberg) and one of the "top four U.S. abstractionists" (quoting MoMA). It said the museum considered its

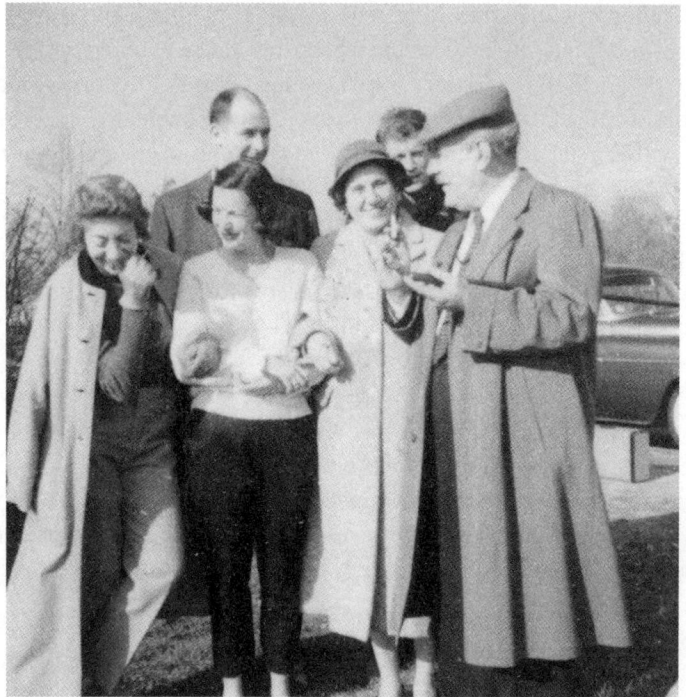

Fig. 34 Thanksgiving 1957 at Lee Krasner's home in Springs, Long Island, fifteen months after Jackson Pollock's death and days before Newman's heart attack. From left: Krasner, Abby Friedman, Annalee Newman, Barnett Newman. Behind them, B. H. Friedman, Sheridan Lord. Photo Francile Lord

"prime acquisition to date" the stunning 1954 *Red and Black*, which was reproduced in color. "Merely to own a Still is a rarity. [He] is so cantankerous that he flatly refuses to sell his work to any collector or museum not of his own choosing, and then is likely to offer only one painting at a take-it-or-leave-price."[11]

Barney didn't have a chance to compose the inevitable riposte. On Friday, at the foggy, humid Bridgehampton nursery where he and Annalee had gone to purchase bushes for Pollock's grave,[12] he began to feel ill, and so they returned to Brooklyn. He felt no better on Saturday morning, but, not wanting to miss the last day of Elaine de Kooning's show at Tibor de Nagy he went to Sixty-Seventh Street and returned home even worse. Nevertheless, he was determined to attend a dinner party that evening at Jeanne Reynal's house on West Eleventh Street. It would be the type of soiree that Reynal and her husband Thomas Sills—they married in 1953—held nearly every month. About thirty people. Jeanne Bultman would tease Barney about his work, "oh, Barney why are you doing those? I don't like them at all," and he would good naturedly tease her back, drawling, "Oh, *Jeanne*." Often, after dinner, they rolled up the rug and there would be dancing. Barney and Annalee did a mean Charleston. But on this night, during dinner he excused himself, went to the bathroom, and was found a little while later, stretched out on the floor, by Sills.

The doctor who was called diagnosed indigestion. Barney insisted it was a heart attack, and "insisted on having an ambulance take him to the hospital."[13] There is no longer anyone alive who was at that party, and so no one can explain how, under what must have been frantic pressure, the decision was made to bypass St. Vincent's, Beth Israel, New York University, Lenox Hill, and New York-Cornell Medical Center—all good hospitals that were closer—and take Barney from the West Village up to East 100th Street to Mt. Sinai Hospital. To Heller, it made perfect sense: Mt. Sinai was "Jewish," and it had "the big reputation"; any other option was inconceivable.

It took about a week for him to be well enough for Annalee to issue the news. Letters came from friends old and new, who were stunned: "You're one of the last people we know of to strike us as being liable to illness," wrote Greenberg.[14] Even Still sent a note: "Have heard from several sources that the heart has been acting up."[15]

When Heller visited, he brought the little "study" for *Vir Heroicus Sublimis* that Barney had given him. Heller removed the hospital art on the wall facing Barney's bed and replaced it with the painting. "You see that?" Barney asked a nurse. "That's what I do. That's by me." The nurses "flocked to him, gave him extra care." As long as he "wasn't angry and being stupidly crazy, *mishugena*—which he could be [when] riled up on a theoretical point," people "couldn't not love the man."[16]

One could almost imagine Mt. Sinai's Klingenstein Pavilion as a giant incubator. During the six weeks that Barney convalesced in the hospital his presence and position in the outside world altered profoundly. While Barney the man grew stronger and stronger, Barney the problematic duckling was about to emerge a swan.

With Barney sick, Annalee soldiered on; barely a beat was missed in what had suddenly become the Barney business. She quickly arranged to have the Jaguar put on blocks in Washington Heights and canceled the insurance. She wrote the pile of monthly charge-account, rent, utility, and loan-payment checks that Barney always took care of. And she handled what was a refreshingly new kind of correspondence.

"Dear Mr. Newman: I have admired your work on several occasions, and I would like very much to see what you have done recently," wrote Gordon Washburn, director of the Department of Fine Arts at the Carnegie Institute, who was scouting for artists to include in the 1958 Pittsburgh—"Carnegie"—International.[17] The Carnegie was unusual—it was the only regular exhibition in the United States to include international works, and unlike the Venice and São Paulo Biennales, for which committees consulted, Washburn was making the selection himself. It was his third time, and the first, he said, that he was forced "into a relationship with the moment" and had the "courage to come up to my time."[18]

Preparations had begun, as well, for what would become a landmark exhibition—praised, adored, reviled, and condemned in critical discourse over the next sixty years—being organized by the Museum of Modern Art. Encouraged by Rüdlinger's enthusiasm for the American artists he saw,[19] curators and administrators at the museum began shaping a show to tour Europe and forming tentative lists of participants. It would be called "American Art of the Past Decade" or "Americans 1947–1957," or "Abstract Expressionism in America." As of mid-December, it would include "approximately five works each by approximately twenty painters and sculptors," Porter McCray, director of the International Program, told Heller, who was depended upon for loans.[20]

Now Heller began negotiating. In December, he told MoMA that he "hoped" Gottlieb, whose show was still up at the Jewish Museum—Heller was chairman of the museum's exhibition committee—would be included. By the beginning of February, Motherwell was added at Heller's suggestion and the name became "The New American Painting" to accommodate Barr's doubts about who was or was not an "abstract expressionist." And by February 20, only three weeks before paintings were loaded onto the Holland–America Line and sailed off, Barney was in.[21] This would be the occasion when Europeans would get the full impact of what had been taking place in American art. The show was "really about leading trump," Heller told Barr, "and Barney Newman is trump."[22]

"Leading trump" would be important that spring. "Expo 58," the Brussels World's Fair—three years in preparation and highly anticipated—was turning out to be a face-off between the Soviet Union and the United States.[23] Art planned for the official American pavilion was grouped in four areas: contemporary sculpture, folk art, Native American art, and contemporary painting. This last, "Seventeen Contemporary Painters" (all "under 45") included Baziotes, Richard Diebenkorn, Hartigan, Kelly, Marca-Relli—among others—and Motherwell and Reinhardt.[24] Other works, specifically requested by an international committee of "art experts," were to be shown in other, curated, international exhibitions. By general agreement, the show was a mess, "a curiously dispirited and undistinguished array . . . that is far from being fully representative of our painting and sculpture today," as the *New Yorker* put it.[25] This time it was not the ailing Barney who fired off a round, it was Hess, who wrote in *Art News* that the show that the U.S. was sending was a "scandal": "American culture will appear at Brussels in a propaganda as well as in its own cultural context. And our propagandists . . . adopted the advertising method of telling the clients what they want to hear. The European visitor . . . will find all his stereotypes about America confirmed, his prejudices reinforced," a cultureless America, "land of soft-headed high-living, of thoughtless epicures . . . chromium and carbonated drinks, cowboys and Indians, and paintings the way grandmother used to make them." Where are those American artists, he asked, who have "exerted an international influence, from Japan to Rome?"[26]

The occasion forced a gut check for every cultural institution—from the Metropolitan Opera to the future Lincoln Center, Hollywood, the fashion industry, and broadcast television; the need to act in an international arena became the impetus for American culture to enter the modern world with more energized intention. In mid-April—just as "The New American Painting" was appearing in Basel—the fair opened. By the beginning of June, even popular media was paying attention to what was at stake; President Eisenhower sent a personal emissary to check it out.[27] "The American Pavilion at the Brussels World's Fair is under fire. The most outspoken critics of our exhibit are American citizens. Most Europeans are more polite." It was assembled by "scattergun techniques. Some shots have hit the mark, others are as wild as a left-handed rookie pitcher who can't find the plate. Good and bad are commingled as if there had been no consistent discrimination of choice." The art pavilion failed to give "the thing it cries out for—a coherent and concentrated point of view," which was a "reasonable reflection of the uncertainties and divided counsels that bedevil so many of our attempts to show and explain our way of life and ideals." Those responsible "probably have to keep looking back over their shoulders worrying about the comments of backseat drivers," whereas the Russians behave as if they have a clear and definite idea of what they wish to achieve . . . confident and optimistic, fresh from . . . the launching of the sputniks." Their means were crude but effective.[28]

That "Expo 58" was a misrepresentation and a missed opportunity was obvious. At the same time, while Washburn was traveling in search of works to include in the Pittsburgh International, he discovered a "greatly increased prestige of American painting in Europe," with collectors adding American works to their collections, and galleries "eager" to have American exhibitions.[29] In London, "The Impact of American Art in Europe" was dissected at the Institute of Contemporary Art. Several members of the panel—among them artist Richard Smith, Whitechapel curator Bryan Robertson, and the chair, critic David Sylvester—would soon form a solid and passionate bloc of support in England for Barney, although, since "The New American Painting" did not reach the Tate until February 1959, none had yet seen his work in the flesh.

But there was another story that summer of 1958, as the MoMA show reached Madrid. At the Venice Biennale, Mark Tobey, whom Barney considered a weak artist, won the International Grand prize for painting—the first American since 1895, when it was awarded to James Whistler—and two artists Barney resented, Rothko and the sculptor Seymour Lipton, were in the American Pavilion.[30] More troubling to one only beginning to be recognized, the curated international show, "Fifty Years of Modern Art," leap-frogged right over Barney and included the very young radical Jasper Johns.

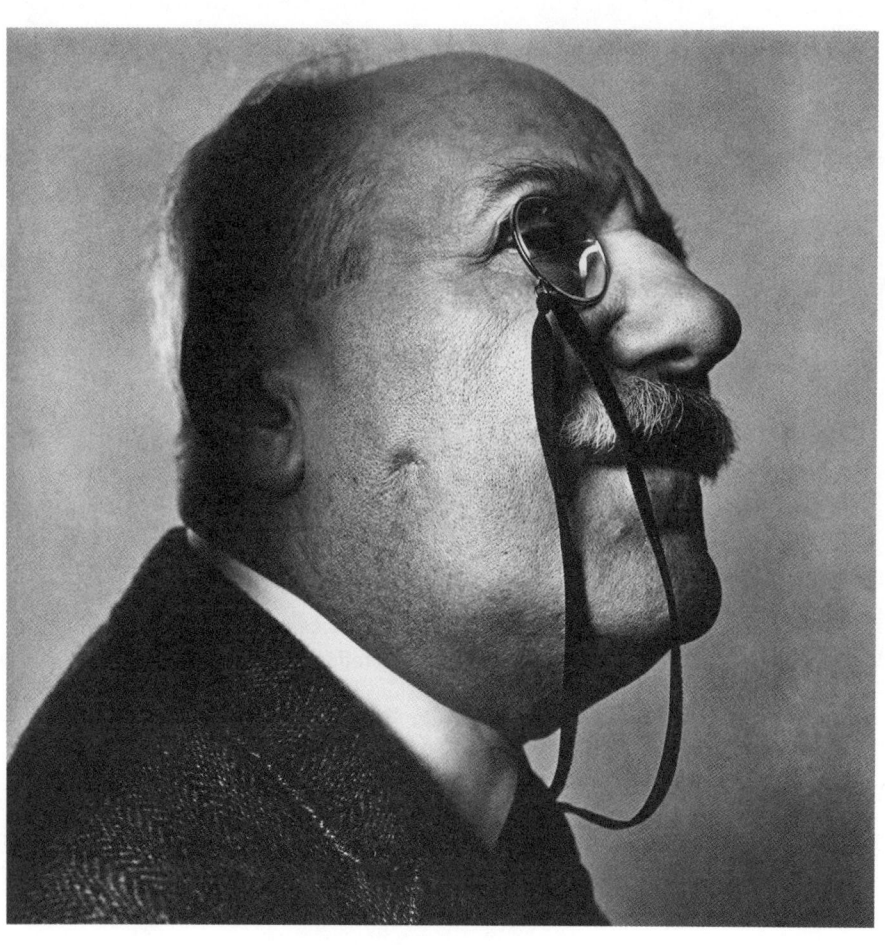

PART FOUR

VIR HEROICUS SUBLIMIS 1958–70

FORTY-TWO

"THE NEW AMERICAN PAINTING"

The week before Barney was tapped for "The New American Painting," Annalee held a gathering at the Front Street studio where Heller had "installed" Barney's paintings. There was a party atmosphere, with enough alcohol to ensure good spirits. Greenberg was there, and Krasner, but the important guests were Barr and Dorothy Miller; the scuttlebutt among younger artists was that Barney had one leg out of this world, and the MoMA royalty did not want to miss their opportunity.[1] Because many of Pollock's works were committed to a touring solo exhibition, and Rothko and Still refused to loan, they could not ignore Heller, the owner of important pieces, and Heller was passionate about Barney. Irritated by Barney's attacks on the museum and himself, Barr was not so favorably disposed, and neither was Miller.[2] But this evening with Barney himself, his enormous personality, his monocle, and his attitude absent, they were persuaded by what they saw.

Ultimately, they borrowed from Heller, *Adam*; from Barney, *Abraham*; from Parsons, *Concord*; and from Reynal, *Horizon Light*.[3]

Now, instead of Bulldog Drummond, the image that comes to mind for the convalescent Barney is Charles Laughton's post-heart-attack Sir Wilfrid in that year's *Witness for the Prosecution*: short-tempered with his caretaker, stubbornly committed to his smoking and drinking, vainly concerned about his appearance, strategically deploying his monocle, and crankily resistant to relinquishing any control. On a frustrating 1500-calorie daily diet prescribed by his cardiologist, Barney hesitantly began to walk again, slowly strolling along the Esplanade propped up by Annalee. But he was still Barney, and there were to-be-expected hiccups relating to his participation. While he directed, Annalee, Sarah, and the otherwise disenfranchised Parsons executed.

Abraham, *Horizon Light*, and *Concord* were discovered by the museum's conservation staff to have serious condition issues. The priming of *Concord* was cracked, and the others, on poorly constructed stretchers, were warped; because *Abraham* was "off-square," restretching it would require losing at least a quarter inch of painted surface.[4] This was infuriating and embarrassing, especially because he had personally spent over 1000 dollars on restoration that April, and Barney set about reconceptualizing how a stretcher should be made. He "invented" a universal joint—"a joint no matter what its structure or nature that has sufficient extension so that it can be attached to any kind of length of material as a board of wood, or strip of metal, glass, or synthetic material or manufactured material that will give that length of substance a joinable end"—and being Barney, wanted legal protection and applied for a patent.[5]

Instead of a comprehensive essay, Miller opted to include statements from each of the artists. Barney's went through multiple iterations; the first submission was not simply to be replaced, but needed to be "destroyed," and the final version sur-prisingly—given recent history—was aggressive, feisty, and, for its European public, oblique if not impenetrable. In suffocatingly compact prose, it took both high and low roads—reiterating the bedrock "freedom" at the core of Barney's ethos (now, freedom from World War I-engendered deterministic styles, instead of, as ten years earlier, freedom from Greek concepts of beauty and "the velvet standards of the school of Venice"), *and* hitting the critics who got under his skin and their "artist friends." In other words, de Kooning, who, during the 1958 season, was enjoying his moment as the undisputed king of the New York art community.[6]

It is precisely this death image, the grip of geometry that has to be confronted.

In a world of geometry, geometry itself has become our moral crisis. And it will not be resolved by jazzed-up kicks but only by the answer of no-geometry of any kind. Unless we face up to it and discover a new image based on new principles, there is no hope for freedom.

Can anyone, therefore, take seriously the mock aesthetic war that the art jour-nalists and their artist friends have been waging against the new Pyramid—while they sit in it under a canopy of triangulation—with their feeble frenzy-weapons of the hootchy-cootchy dancer?

I realize that my paintings have no link with, nor any basis in, the art of World War I with its principles of geometry—that tie it into the nineteenth century. To reject Cubism or Purism, whether it is Picasso's or Mondrian's, only to end up with the collage scheme of free associated forms, whether it is Miró's or Male-vich's, is to be caught in the same geometric trap. Only an art free from any kind of the geometry principles of World War I, only an art of no-geometry can be a new beginning.

Nor can I find it by building a wall of lights; nor in the dead infinity of silence; nor in the painting performance, as if it were an instrument of pure energy full of a hollow biologic rhetoric.

Painting, like passion, is a living voice, which, when I hear it, I must let speak, unfettered.[7]

What must the Swiss and the Italian, Spanish, German, Dutch, and other audi-ences have made of the "feeble frenzy-weapons of the hootchy-cootchy dancer" as "The New American Painting," which opened at the Basel Kunsthalle on April 5, traveled to Milan, Madrid, Berlin, Amsterdam, Brussels, Paris, and London over the next twelve months? As they saw for the first time *Adam* and *Abraham, Horizon Light* and *Concord*, what would they have understood about the maker from a paragraph that began with "death" and continued as pure rejection until its last sentence? And why would Barney believe that this was the way to "lead trump" to the centers of Western civilization?

Whatever was understood of the translations of Barney's—or any other art-ist's—statement, the paintings were what mattered. Rüdlinger called the works an "autochthonic American event,"[8] and "The New American Painting" succeeded in enshrining the participants as the heroic generation of American art in the minds of tens of thousands. And, over the year, Barnett Newman became enshrined as a particular hero to a new generation of artists. After 1958, it would be very hard to exclude Barney—except by his own choice—again.

On the cover of the January 1958 *Art News* appeared *Target with Four Faces*—a 1955 painting and sculpture combination by Jasper Johns. Hess was a smart enough editor to feature the extraordinary object by an almost unknown artist, but his personal opinion of the work was equivocal: "A target will always be an attractive magazine cover," he wrote a little over a year later, but Johns "does not paint very well."[9] If it caused discomfit to those still engaged in the world of the previous generation—the flags, targets, and alphabets were "all very puzzling" to Preston at the *Times*[10]—it wasn't shocking to younger artists, or new collectors and dealers and writers with their ears closer to the ground. The old internecine feuds, and competitions, and arguments about sources and who did what first, and who did it with the purist purity, were becoming moot. At Castelli's young gallery it wasn't one thing or the other. Johns's first solo show, in mid-January, was an earthquake—the Museum of Modern Art bought three paintings and lined up trustee Philip Johnson to buy a fourth, committing in a way they never had for an Abstract Expressionist.[11] But the gallerist didn't make a seismic break with his early professional life; his following show was of Friedel Dzubas, a "second generation" abstract expressionist painter and member of The Club. Then the March exhibition of Rauschenberg's work—"old rotogravure photographs, bits of comic strip, daubs of paint, a thin slab of metal and even a hat with bepainted crown"[12] and the now iconic *Bed*, *Odalisk*, and *Rebus* signaled to the gate guardians that they weren't in Kansas anymore.

Heller noticed that the atmosphere had even changed at *Art News*. "Some of it, I flatter myself, is due to a point I made one evening at The Club." Hess, Barr, and Rosenberg were discussing the "perennial question, 'has the situation changed?'" and continually referred only to de Kooning. When Heller rose to point it out, and to point out that the same occurred in *Art News*, he was met with a burst of applause. In articles and editorials there began to be new names.[13]

The newly extended art family continued conducting itself and its business in much the way it had been doing: first generation, second generation, and a now-emerging unrelated generation (metaphorically) working side by side. Claes Oldenburg. Jim Dine. Red Grooms. One of Allan Kaprow's earliest "happenings" took place at the young sculptor George Segal's chicken farm in New Jersey, followed by others in the fall. Some of the established critics comfortably moved on, for example Greenberg to the so-called Color Field painters. But some, specifically Rosenberg and Hess, had to have seen Johns and Rauschenberg—flippantly undermining the autographic brushstroke, coolly engaged with mass culture, unconcerned with heroic origins—as a threat to everything they had staked their lives on. They needed to protect their territory, they circled the wagons. Barney was no longer what had to be feared; "shocking" as he was, he was nevertheless one of them.[14]

And now began the conversion of Hess and Rosenberg from Newman doubters to believers. And with that, although by no means entirely because of it, came the eventual apotheosis of Barney.

In the March 1958 *Gentlemen's Quarterly* article on Heller's collection, Hess might have heard a curious, inverted echo of the dismissive 1950 reviews. But now virtually the same words were used in praise instead of mockery: " 'I buy from many painters who are unknown,' " Heller was quoted as saying. " 'Take this painting here,' he said pointing to a seven-foot-high canvas in his office that was a solid blue except for a thin white stroke running along the left edge of the painting. 'This is one of the most outright shocking paintings around. It's by a man named Barney Newman.' " The work was a "series of lines on a canvas with practically nothing else going on except the slightest quivers" but it made Heller respond in the same way he responded to the best paintings—old masters included—he had ever seen. Because of this, Heller told the interviewer, "I know him to be good, that he's terrific, because he has created a new dimension to the definition of painting."

If a heart attack was "like instant psychiatry," as Barney told Hess years later, a retrospective, for a painter, could bring karmic rebirth.[15] Already in the works by the time Heller's praise appeared, such an event was being prepared by Eugene Goossen, recently arrived at Bennington College in Vermont, where he became a professor of art and exhibition director of the New Gallery. Earlier shows of Hofmann, Gottlieb, and Pollock had been organized at the college by Greenberg; now a former carriage house became a dedicated exhibition space. Tony Smith and Paul Feeley, both teaching at Bennington, persuaded Goossen that this was the moment for Barney. Goossen requested eight to ten works; Barney sent eighteen.

And not just any eighteen. He had been left out of New York museums' survey shows and most of the critical literature in the 1950s, missing from Venice, from "Expo 58," and "The New American Painting" had not yet arrived in Europe. A "stream of events established the strong sense that a history was being written, a history that would not be unwritten soon, and one in which Newman was wholly absent."[16] Barney saw Bennington as the opportunity to correct the record. Or, at least, that was Annalee's interpretation of why he chose only paintings that already existed at the time of Miller's "Fifteen Americans" show in 1952. In other words, works that *could* have been included had Miller not been prejudiced or benighted.[17] And it was equally crucial that Greenberg began his catalogue statement, "Barnett Newman is part of the splendor of American painting in the *past decade and a half*," (emphasis added) and addressed, in forty-two compact lines, virtually every single criticism and charge thrown at Barney over the same period.

During two weeks in April, as Greenberg delivered the prestigious and influential Christian Gauss lectures in criticism at Princeton, the two men discussed this text, what Greenberg called the "blurb."[18] They met at Greenberg's home and Barney's studio, and their conversations were not without conflict. Barney "was quite upset"; he had not been consulted about the title—"Barnett Newman, First Retrospective Exhibition." "How many retrospectives can a man have in his lifetime?"[19] Then, atypically, he relented. "Let's forget the nonsense" he telegrammed the critic.[20] At the final version, they celebrated, Greenberg acknowledging the moment as the "beginning of the Vita Nuova."[21]

The paragraphs redefined an art experience by telling viewers not to be led astray by what they *thought* they were seeing. Did the works seem detached from intellectual substance? Did they seem to be easily made?

His art is all statement, all content; and fullness of content can be attained only through an execution that calls the least possible attention to itself. We are not offered the dexerity [*sic*] of a hand or the ingenuity of any eye. Skill and ingenuity cannot convey directly enough what has to be said. Newman is not concerned to demonstrate how well he can draw, shade, or tint; he knows (and so do several of us) how well he can. The truth of art lies for him, as for any genuinely ambitious artist, somewhere beyond what he knows he can do.

"There is no program, no polemic . . . they do not intend to make a point, let alone shock or startle." Barney was not "interested in straight lines, right angles, or empty spaces as such, or in bareness or purity. He pursues his vision," Greenberg emphasized.

The vertical stripes enter as a result, not as part of a layout. The color comes first and does the controlling. The stained surface spreads, ascends and descends, and in certain places it pauses. The line that marks the pause does not demarcate or limit; it simply inflects a continuity, and all it needs in order to do this is to proceed as directly as possible from one point to another. This has to do with economy, not geometry.

This kind of painting has far more to do with Impressionism than with anything like Cubism or Mondrian.

That was an error made by those who were "color-deaf."

With repeated viewings, Greenberg himself had become aware of the complexity of the tensions between "different light values of the same color and between different colors of the same light value." Thus was introduced "an almost entirely new area of interest for our tradition of painting, and it is part of Newman's originality that he should lead our sensibility toward it." Barney enlarged the "capacities of the art of painting in general," and that is why Greenberg deemed "this first retrospective exhibition of his art an historic occasion."[22]

It was all a more graceful way of taking care of the business Barney had wanted to transact in "The New American Painting" catalogue, a more gracious way of saying exactly what he decided—or was persuaded—to cut from that original, a point-by-point rebuttal of what "the American press has already said . . . about me":

> My work, they charge, is empty of content, when what they mean is that it is empty of familiar forms and shapes.
>
> My work, they say, is antiart, when what they really mean is that is antidogma, that it is anti-the kind of stereotyped picture they expect.
>
> My work, they claim, is antipainting, when what they mean is that it is antitechnique, antibrushwork, and that the large open areas I use require, as the restorers of my work are beginning to realize, the highest artistry.
>
> My work, they say, is involved in line, when it is obvious that there are no lines.
>
> My work, they charge, is so many optical color tricks, when what they mean is that I have no colors, that I am involved in color.
>
> My work, they claim, is based on nonvalue painting, when what they mean is that I depend specifically on the most subtle set of values and that value to me is of the utmost importance.
>
> My work, they shout, is involved in geometry, when what they mean is that they miss the geometric pattern of colors, shapes, and line diagrams they are familiar with.
>
> My work, they say, is more advanced than Malevich's, when what they really mean is that I have reduced Malevich to yet another color scheme, so that his white-on-white is just another syntactical device no more significant than black-on-white.
>
> My work, they say, is more advanced than Mondrian's, when what they mean is that I have broken the barrier of his dogmas.
>
> They say that I have advanced abstract painting to its extreme, when it is obvious to me that I have made only a new beginning. In short, they find me too abstract for the abstract expressionists and too expressionist for the abstract purists.

The twenty-day retrospective opened in Vermont on May 4. There was a luncheon, a cocktail party, a preview, and an "opening." It was quite a coming-out party for an invalid, who was still restricted in his movements. While Parsons and the other VIP guests stayed at the Elm Tree Inn, Barney and Annalee made do at the "less attractive" New Englander Inn where there would be no steps to climb.

The previous January, not six weeks after the heart attack, with no prospects on the horizon, Annalee had decided that Yaddo, the bucolic scholars and artists retreat in Saratoga Springs, would best suit them the coming summer. They had come to love Saratoga and were encouraged in this plan by Meyer Schapiro, whose two-month residency was confirmed at the same time that Parsons made an initial approach on behalf of Barney and Annalee. No question that he needed a vacation; but, as for everyone, there was an application *process*, and work needed to be submitted to be judged. As so often in the past—when he was applying for fellowships, or overreaching for various staff positions and teaching jobs, or, even, "running"

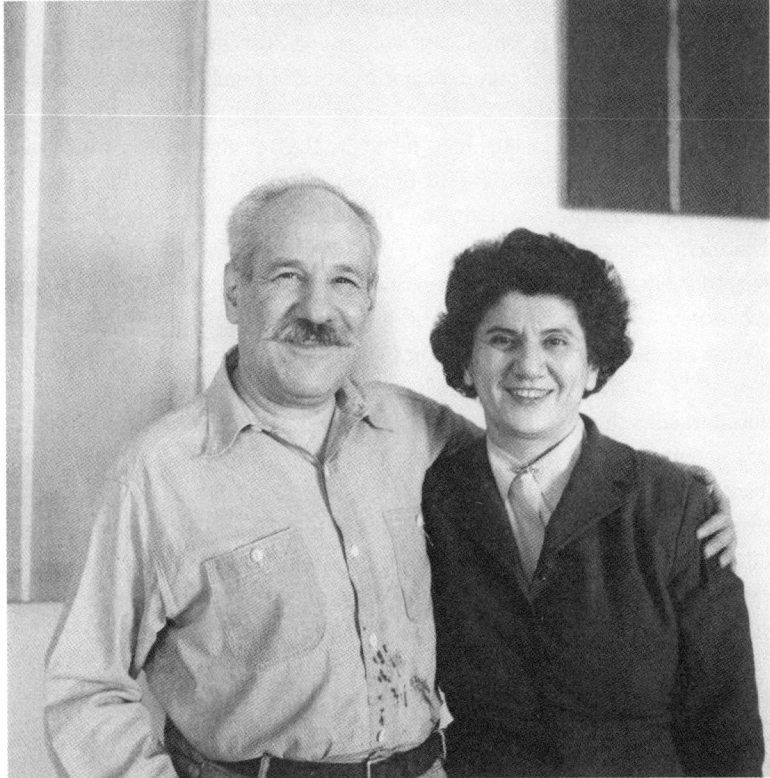

Fig. 35 Barnett and Annalee Newman, 1958, in an outtake from a formal portrait session. Photograph William Vandivert

for mayor—Barney faced the stunning reality that he was not above or immune to or excused from the rules. Plus, there was a "rather long" flight of stairs involved.

Now in the spring, with a suddenness unimaginable four months earlier, pursuing Yaddo did not seem so urgent. Barney was publicized and feted, making arrangements for the MoMA, Bennington, and Carnegie International shows. He was photographed by the esteemed photojournalist and Magnum co-founder William Vandivert, looking significantly aged since the November photographs at Springs, and wearing a shirt with a too-neat paint-spatter (cropped out in the college's catalogue) although he had done virtually no painting recently.[23] Most importantly, over one third of all the paintings Barney had ever made were on public view, eighteen of them in Vermont.

"That weekend I spent at Bennington, while your show was going up, and meeting you in New York, was one of the highpoints of my US visit," wrote Lawrence Alloway to Barney the following year. The 31-year-old had recently left the London ICA, and had a Foreign Leader grant from the U.S. State Department to educate himself about American art. His friend Greenberg insisted that Alloway see the show and Parsons drove Alloway to Vermont. Dumbstruck by the "violent economy of means"[24] he could barely wait to take the subway to Brooklyn Heights. "I count it as one of the most fortunate encounters of my life," he wrote Barney after he returned home, and it turned out to be most fortunate for Barney as well.[25] When, back in England, he reviewed "The New American Painting" during its appearance at the Tate, Alloway could confirm, "Newman's pictures with their stretching fields of colour, some wide, some narrow" survive "a changing relation to [their] witnesses: his art is a massive defeat of noise. This, combined with the spirit of gravity and momentousness which is Newman's reason for working justifies such ambitious titles as 'Concord', 'Abraham', 'Adam' . . . . His art is like a rock."[26]

Friedman sent the Bennington announcement to his social acquaintance, the important British collector E. J. Power, advising him that Barney was "beginning to release some of his paintings more widely to collectors and institutions, and inevitably . . . the prices will go up."[27] Months before "The New American Painting" arrived in London, before Alloway's review, before he had ever seen a painting by Barney in the flesh, Power's agent from the Arthur Tooth Gallery contacted Parsons to inquire which in the show might be for sale.[28] Of the four, only *Concord* was Parsons's to sell.

Heller arranged a private plane for himself, his wife, and the Friedmans—Barr and Miller declined his offer—to make the round trip to Vermont for the closing. It was an extraordinary, thrilling adventure in 1958: landing on the hockey field, the four were met by Feeley and Goossen. Barney once told Friedman that he wanted "to rid my work of *atmosphere*," and it was at this moment that Friedman, emerging literally out of the atmosphere, knew "what he meant."[29]

The poet and writer (and brother of Diane Arbus) Howard Nemerov, who taught literature at Bennington, wrote an appreciation. Barney treasured having inspired it: "you so beautifully create an image that throws insight into the nature of the miraculous." He read it "to all my friends."[30] He encouraged Nemerov, a future Pulitzer Prize-winner who had already published a number of collections, to send it to the *New Yorker*—"Nobody hates the New Yorker more than I do. (I cannot stand a magazine without a table of contents). [But] If we are going to deal with a middle-class journal, let us deal with the real middle-class journals."[31] It belonged in "the best literary journal," or the *Evergreen Review*. He sent it to Gordon Washburn, to Dorothy Miller and Barr (whose somewhat backhanded comment Barney took for praise and quoted to Nemerov); and filed it in the thin archive of encomia that he would trot out to prove his *bona fides*. Ultimately, it was published, in *The Nation*.

On Certain Wits

> Who amused themselves over the
> simplicity of Barnett Newman's

paintings shown at Bennington
College in May of 1958

When Moses in Horeb struck the rock,
And water came forth out of the rock,
Some of the people were annoyed with Moses
And said he should have used a fancier stick.

And when Elijah on Mount Carmel brought the rain,
Where the prophets of Baal could not bring rain,
Some of the people said that the rituals of the prophets of Baal
Were aesthetically significant, while Elijah's were very plain.

When Barney showed Hess the poem he "decided against using it,"[32] but *Art News* did publish "the first article ever devoted to Newman in any magazine"[33]—Goossen's "The Philosophic Line of B. Newman"—in the issue that was in people's hands by June.[34]

Goossen addressed Barney's work without defensiveness or derisiveness; he confronted the paintings themselves, rather than Barney's words, and was a bit awestruck. He was serious without jargon or what Rosenberg would have termed "professional lingo," and by the time he wrote that *Vir Heroicus Sublimis* seemed to him "one of the truly moving pictures of recent times" that struck "into a territory of effectiveness on a level with the large pictures of Picasso, Matisse and the late Monet," and that Barney had "produced a number of pictures complete in themselves which can stand with the best of modern art as examples of the infrequent heroism of our awkward times," it did not read as fulsome promotion.

Even people who did not see the show at Bennington, including, and especially, a generation who had not seen the shows at Parsons, were persuaded by Goossen's article. It was hard to question that Barney was an artist whose work had to be reckoned with and not a footnote, not the last name in a list. But this was not simply the first article about the work. It was also the first iteration of the personal myth, and that, too, took hold.

"Just seven years ago Barnett Newman closed shop. That is, he brought his pictures home" from Parsons's gallery. The Parsons shows, Goossen wrote, "faded into the past. Meanwhile Newman remained sufficiently in evidence himself . . . making frequent sorties into vanguard art society where his wit, aggressive concern with principle, and his poetically enigmatic pronouncements seemed to be headed toward placing him permanently as a personality rather than as the fine artist he is. The artist, however, has now been reconfirmed" by the Bennington show.

The article ignored the earlier notice by Greenberg in " 'American-Type' Painting." It ignored the growing respect among Europeans and a younger generation of Americans. It ignored that Barney's "aggressive concern with principle" was often simply aggression, and that his pronouncements were far from "poetically enigmatic," but were, in the term Norman Mailer would coin the following year, "advertisements for myself." But *because* Goossen summarized the history of Barney so casually and briefly it became the accepted, repeated, shorthand—not incorrect, exactly, but so less than complete.

Also (tactfully) missing was the guilt and remorse that were the reaction to Barney's unmentioned heart attack. In its grim usefulness as punctuation it too played a grisly role in the myth.

FORTY-THREE

THE LEMA SABACHTHANI AND THE GLORY

Very quietly, very tentatively, alone in the Brooklyn Heights apartment while Annalee was at work and before his sister or his mother arrived in the afternoon, Barney began to paint on unprimed, manageably small canvases. He produced a *geshray*, and called it *Outcry*, 82 by 6 inches of ultimately vertical shriek that could only have been painted horizontally, given Barney's condition and the physical limitations in the apartment.

Now Barney began to emerge for a rare social occasion—dinner with Reynal, Schwabacher and Greenberg, Stanley Kunitz and Elise Asher's wedding. He took the Jaguar out of dead storage. And, when Heller decided to leave his Riverside Drive apartment in the early summer, Barney saw it as an opportunity to move back into Manhattan: the luxury building would allow him to "be a good patient" and "follow his doctor's orders" not to climb stairs. (In Brooklyn he had an elevator, but not the appropriate status.)[1] Unfortunately, Heller had gotten ahead of himself in suggesting Barney take his own about-to-be vacated apartment: Barney's finances did not meet the landlord's requirements, and Heller, trying to let him down easy, only stirred up his *amour propre*. Barney struck back at Heller, calling him unmanly, accusing him of throwing a "line of shit," of insulting both Annalee and himself, and, as the "son-president" of his father's business, not such a hot shot either—oblivious to how dedicatedly the collector was working on Barney's behalf.

Heller felt "much too affectionately" toward Barney to respond in an analogous key.[2] Barney quipped to Friedman, himself comfortably from a real-estate family, and equally trying to help, "I've seen democracy in action along the promenade at Newport: the People looking into the homes of the aristocrats and the aristocrats looking out at the people."

His "ideal apartment house" would have "one self-service elevator for my informal needs and one with an operator for when I'm with Annalee"; the "ideal kitchen" would have "two stoves, one for the husband and one for the wife."[3] An apartment found on West 103rd street would have been "perfect"—a "nice place to play house"—except for the location. "It's a little frightening when we go out at night. The trouble is thugs never ask what you do, or I'd tell them I too live by my wits. They see a guy who's dressed well and they assume he's rich. They don't recognize style, as such. If they rob you or hurt you or kill you, it's always a case of mistaken identity." He considered buying a brownstone that he couldn't afford because the ground floor was formerly a store. "I hate to live above the store," he told Friedman, "but if I have to, I prefer it to *be* a store."[4]

He finally found the place, a fifteenth-floor, six-and-a-half-room apartment on Ninety-Third Street and West End Avenue, a boulevard of solid, early 20th-century buildings with a rich *mitteleuropean*–Jewish culture, and unreliably safe side-streets with brownstones occupied by a demographically varied population. The sixteen-story 1923 building was known for the musicians—violinist Jaime Laredo, the pianist Rudolf Serkin—and judges among its tenants. It didn't hurt that the other residents initially thought Barney was a banker and came from a very wealthy family.[5] A block to the east was Broadway with every type of local shop and trade and restaurant, movie theaters (four between Ninety-Sixth and Eighty-Eighth Streets), buses running the length of Manhattan island and an express subway station within a short walk for Annalee. A block to the west were mansions and apartment buildings on Riverside Drive, the Olmsted-conceived Riverside Park, and the Hudson River. The apartment had spectacularly gracious proportions, a 14-by-20-foot dining room, a 17-by-21-foot living room, a wide, 20-foot hallway, and they filled it with Barney's paintings—*Vir Heroicus Sublimis, Primordial Light, The Word II, Pagan Void, The Way I*—and little else. It was a dramatic shift from a bit of bohemia to the belly of the bourgeoisie, but he hadn't entirely left the art community behind: the Gottliebs, Leonard Bocour, artists Paul Brach and Mimi Schapiro, Will Barnet, and several others all lived within a very short distance. The Newmans moved in October, and Barney was diligent about informing Miller so that she could change his residence to "Manhattan" in the press material for the final stops of "The New American Painting."

Returning to his downtown studio was a bigger problem. He had had to "accept" the idea of working at home while in Brooklyn, but not happily.[6] In the colorful anecdote described by Hess, Annalee "arranged for the basketball team from the high school where she was teaching to carry Newman up the three flights of stairs to his Front Street studio. It was a dramatic sight, and not without an air of high triumph— the hero's return—as well as of low comedy, which Newman enjoyed enormously."[7] The story enacts the resurrection beautifully, but if it indeed happened—no interviewed members of the team recall it, or even that "Mrs. Newman's" husband was an artist—it was likely at the end of April, when packing materials were delivered to Front Street and works were being readied for Bennington rather than to paint. More seriously, if less heroically, Bob Friedman took up the long-term challenge. As a "'welcome home present,'" Friedman had an architect design a "cat-walk" between the roof of 100 Front Street and the roof of an adjoining, elevator-equipped, building to provide access. But it required the landlord's approval and—even though Barney engineered his cardiologist's visit to the studio to confirm this was a medical necessity—he never had much luck with landlords.

On Pierrepont Street, Barney had begun painting on 78-by-60-inch canvases. To conserve his strength they were unprimed, and he initially used only black paint, now Magna, now oil. Where *Outcry* has small bits of blue leaking through its wide, craggy black band, the next two each had one solid band of paint cleanly occupying the left edge, and one narrow "negative" band created when thinned paint was brushed neatly or randomly over a length of tape which was then removed; the remaining canvas was completely naked, raw. (When Barbara Reise looked at these at the beginning of 1964, she called the white line a "screech," so pleasing Barney he spontaneously enveloped her in a hug.[8]) Later, when these two became the first of fourteen paintings of the same size and with the same foundation intentionally embodying a "particular subject"—the cry "Why has thou foresaken me?"—Barney would say in "hindsight" that he was "compelled"—meaning psychologically, emotionally, spiritually—"to do [them] in black and white on raw canvas." In mid-1958, however, they were the first steps in getting back to work within the physical limitations his doctor had imposed. Heller saw the two in the Brooklyn Heights apartment, and Barney's "excitement about being able to do *something.*"

"I had a doctor make me do this," Heller recalled the gist of their conversations. "I had to come up with [this]; . . . . put this amount of black . . . this amount of white . . . if I put this on top of this."[9] *If* he could "make an area of canvas come to life with the one line," as he had previously, he would be "satisfied with it."[10]

"Barney thrived on not acceding to life," said Heller. "Did he have to accede to the doctor when he had a heart attack? You're goddamned right he did. [But] could he figure out a way to make a triumph over it? And if he could, both exult *and* exalt? Yes!"

"Minimal work. For maximal value. What a triumph. Excuse me, what a *goddamn fucking triumph.*"[11]

He did the first two. Then over the following years he did two more, and then two more. When he did a sixth in mid-1963 that was "similar in structure," he felt he was, without planning it, "doing something unique," that he was "involved in a series."[12] But before that he already saw in them *lema sabachthani* ("why has thou forsaken me?").[13]

"Even tho I know that I died many times," he wrote Tony Smith in 1962, he didn't experience his recovery as a resurrection. "All I could experience and remember was the agony and not my salvation. Now that I finally have come out of it," he said, explaining the subtitle, *Lema Sabachthani*, he attached later, in 1966, to the fourteen *Stations of the Cross*, "I understand it better, i.e. not only the Lama Sabachtani [*sic*] but the glory."[14]

The students who had been in the class on "New York School" painters that Meyer Schapiro was permitted to teach only after challenging hidebound faculty at Columbia—the university did not yet acknowledge postwar art—were told by Schapiro the following spring that they must see "*the most* important show"[15] at French & Company Gallery. On the basis of Bennington buzz and their personal friendship, Barney—whose work was not addressed in the curriculum—had been among the artists Schapiro invited to speak during the fall 1958 term. For late 20th-century "art history" this was a defining moment, since around Schapiro's seminar table sat William Rubin (future professor and director of the Painting and Sculpture Department at the Museum of Modern Art); Max Kozloff (future influential critic and editor of *Artforum*); Maurice Tuchman (art historian and future founder of the Modern Art Department at the Los Angeles County Museum of Art); Carroll Janis (art historian and scion of the Janis Gallery); Jack Spector (university professor); Carl Baldwin (university professor); Lucas Samaras (brilliantly eccentric artist); and Barbara Rose (art historian, prolific author and curator) who, as a Barnard student, was auditing. Also enrolled was Donald Judd (seminal critic and foundational artist of minimalism), but he was absent on the day Barney spoke.

"Toward the end of the session, Schapiro drew four rectangles on the blackboard, outlined an object in one, filled the second with dots, the third with interlocking forms, and the fourth with disassociated elements. Newman understood it to be a 'typology of modern art history,' each rectangle standing, in turn, for Realism, Impressionism, Cubism, and Surrealism. Schapiro asked him where he fitted in; Newman walked to the blackboard and erased the dots; then he drew his 'zip' vertically down one edge of the rectangle. 'I had to think fast,'" Newman explained to Hess when he related the episode. "'I had to think fast, so I wiped out Impressionism.'"[16]

"Barney didn't have the star luster about him. It wasn't like we were meeting Pollock or de Kooning or even Rothko; he was a guy who we thought was maybe in the second rank," recalled Tuchman. But after his visit, all the minds (with the exception of Samaras) were changed.[17]

With the help of another exceptional young man introduced by Smith, a playwright and member of Tennessee Williams's circle, George Franklin, Barney stretched and hung the nearly 18-foot blue leviathan *Throne* (later known as *Cathedra*) in the studio for viewings by Gordon Washburn, Heller, and, he hoped, Barr.

"One of the pictures of our time," raved Heller, and that is what he told Dorothy Miller, who now began to address Barney in much more friendly terms.[18] When Arnold Rüdlinger returned to America in November with a budget to purchase the "new" American painting, he naturally went to Heller's apartment, because Heller's apartment had the single highest concentration of such works on view. He was "knocked out" by *Adam*. Barney, relaxing in his new apartment far uptown, was immediately summoned to open the studio for Heller and "Noldy," as Rüdlinger was affectionately known. What Noldy saw left him "smashed."

"If you want to buy a great Newman, you should see the one [already sent to the] Carnegie" (which opened on December 5), Heller told him, and offered to buy the plane ticket.

That painting could be found not in the "spacious and airy" first-floor galleries, nor in the second-floor central gallery with works by Gottlieb, Rothko, Kline, de Kooning, and Reinhardt and sixty-eight other artists, but at the very end of the installation, with thirty-five others in Gallery Q—of A through Q—which, unfortunately for Barney, at least one critic called the "gallery of 'Purism.'"[19] As it turned out, Washburn had chosen not *Throne/Cathedra* for the International, but the 11-foot-high contemporaneous *Day Before One*—similarly hued, yet as profoundly different in appearance and effect from *Throne* as a cabochon sapphire is from one of the highest clarity. If the installation irritated the artist, he left no record of it. Probably because Rüdlinger committed to purchase *Day Before One* immediately.

Barney was not simply being at long last recognized; he was being recognized as relevant. At The Club—the epicenter of the very critics and "their friends" that

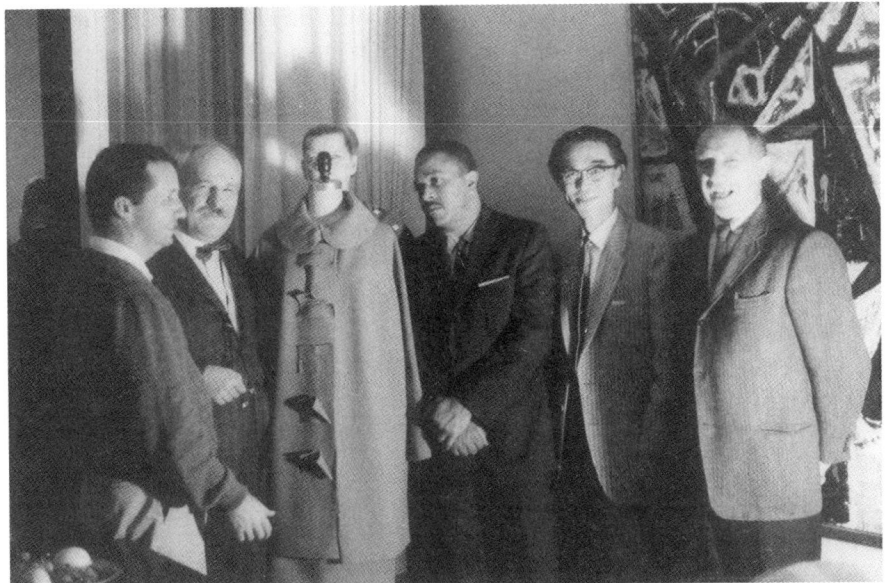

Fig. 36 Party at the Bultmans, 1958. From left: Fritz Bultman, Barnett Newman, Jeanne Reynal in a Dada disguise, Thomas Sills, Kenzo Okada, Jack Tworkov

Barney regularly railed about—Nicolas Calas, the poet and philosopher, spoke in his defense. On the street in New York, the young, irreverent upcoming artist Ray Johnson enthusiastically talked and "TALKED," with Barney, repairing to a bar to continue.[20] Schapiro's students recognized that he was the one with whom they would remain in touch. By the time "The New American Painting" arrived in London in February 1959, Barney was the one English artists—Richard Smith, Robyn Denny, Peter Blake, John Hoyland, William Turnbull, to name a few—would be buzzing about. "Your work . . . stole the show as far as many of the younger painters were concerned," wrote Alloway. "Your name had become known here, among the experimental artists, as a result of Clem Greenberg's references . . . and as a result of talk by William Turnbull . . . and myself. Your work, now that it has been seen, caused a big impact."[21]

In *Pageant* magazine (he saw an advance copy) Barney was the only artist of "Ten Americans to Watch in 1959: A . . . forecast about people you should know." The sculptor David Smith, who as 1958's anointed named his successor, called him "a painter whom few except artists know and who to my mind has broken a barrier in visual realization."[22] Barney sent tear sheets to friends and foes alike.

But despite—or possibly because of—the new respect, the promising future, the upscale apartment, his improved health, Barney felt more vulnerable than ever. Now he had an actual position, a standing, which required renewed vigilance against indignity. He had once again slipped into a dark funk, irritated, angered, overreacting to actual slights and seeing others where none was intended, writing letters that he knew—or Annalee told him—not to send.

"The Lama Sabachtani" *and* "the glory." It was the brutal co-existence that was so destabilizing.

Anarchist, secularist, newly successful, an American "to watch," Barney nevertheless was in pain. This was not some "schtick," as Friedman would say, performed for his own, or others' amusement. He was unable to let go of any slight, unable to acknowledge his own role or responsibility as provocateur. He did not feel empowered. He felt *personally* forsaken.

It was the old crowd that opened old wounds.

"I want to mention a marvelous book: Kierkegaard's *Fear and Trembling*, which deals with the sacrifice of Isaac by Abraham." While speaking at Pratt Institute in Brooklyn, Rothko—who in 1949 was, for a moment in Barney's eyes, a prelapsarian Jacob to Barney's Esau—invoked the 19th-century work that had in the 1950s become a sacred text of Existentialism. Fresh from having ten paintings shown in Venice and a couple of months into a commission for the Four Seasons restaurant murals, Rothko was battling his own demons, his own "*mishigas*," he told Heller. Underlying his remarks was a degree of self-loathing that stemmed from success in the face of his generation's obsession with the idea of "selling out." But when Barney read critic Dore Ashton's account in the *Times* a couple of days later, he saw only that it was directed at him.

Rothko "firmly dissociated himself from any movement and, above all, from the 'abstract expressionist' movement," Ashton wrote. There were "many noted artists in the 'new American painting' movement (as it is now called in Europe), whose hackles rise at the mention of expressionism and whose philosophies deliberately exclude expressionist tendencies toward unchecked impulse and athletic gesture," she continued, obliquely referring to the painters in the Museum of Modern Art's traveling show. "Foremost among them is Rothko."[23] Since it was the case that at one point in its planning the show was titled "Abstract Expressionism in America," that Rothko allowed himself to be included at that point, and that the title was in large measure changed to accommodate Barney's work, Barney went ballistic.

He saw in Rothko's words "one of the most immoral statements I have ever read." In a blistering unsent letter to Ashton he diminished Rothko's work and demanded that "since he has paraphrased some of my statements the story of the exhibition should be told to the public and the statement I made published."[24]

In an unsent letter to Heller he sputtered, "This week you became witness to how psychological warfare is transformed into history. This is what I meant by the true story . . . of what went on in Mid-Century, 1949–50 . . . I know that your buying my work is what forced [him] to strike out against you . . . . It seems to me Ben that since you are taking an active interest in the history of our time that you now have an opportunity almost an obligation to tell the true story of the show and to get my statement published."[25]

It was not the first nor the last time that Barney refused to consider that another artist with a similar history working in a similar environment could independently arrive at a similar thought. On the other hand, as Barney well knew, there was a basis to assume that Rothko *was* needling him, since Barney had explicitly needled Rothko. In his statement for "The New American Painting" catalogue, Barney declared that he could not find a living art by "building a wall of lights"—knowing well that "Rothko's Wall of Light" was the title of Hub Crehan's discussion of the artist's 1954 show at the Chicago Art Institute, and the description had achieved currency.[26]

A freewheeling interview in *Evergreen Review* with Franz Kline catapulted Barney back into Reinhardt-reaction mode. "Barney Newman . . . knows what a painting should be," Kline said, suggesting (in Barney's mind) the idea preceded the creation. "He paints as he thinks *painting* should be, which is pretty heroic." The "so-called conversation" was "not only a self-serving political attack on me but is also slanderous," Barney wrote to the editors, Barney Rosset and Donald Allen, and he expected "equal space."[27] (It may not have been incidental to his fury that Rosset had been married to painter Joan Mitchell and "friends" with the "downtown" artists.)

And so, when W. McNeil Lowry of the Ford Foundation informed Barney that he, along with several hundred other artists, had been nominated for one of ten 10,000-dollar awards and a possible retrospective—which entailed delivering works to a "regional center" for judging, and, if chosen, donating a painting—there was a full resurgence of the righteous, self-important, and (understandable) churning wrath of the man who had not passed the misguided and defective teacher's licensing exam.

"I fulfill the requirements," he wrote directly to Lowry, "yet the program of the Ford Foundation is inadequate for me to be properly considered . . . . There is no question in my mind that my work merits the award, and . . . I am at a stage in my career where, due to illness, outside assistance would be of considerable help . . . . How can I send paintings that are 18 feet long . . . who will unroll them? Who will stretch them? Who will crate them? . . . each of my paintings . . . is more expensive than the actual reward. And I cannot guarantee that the painting I will paint under the grant will be cheaper . . . you have been badly advised as to the nature of painting in America . . . based on the notion that painting in this country is still on an easel-painting level and that it can be bought cheaply . . . moral issues concerning the submission to juries . . . humiliation suffered . . . in the very act of achieving some temporary economic freedom, you force the painter to paralyze his creative spirit."

"The Ford Foundation has created a complicated system of 'buying' a painting when it could very simply pay the price of an artist's work . . . and thereby build a collection."[28]

Into this dark storm in Barney's soul, landed Rüdlinger's own project—how to purchase paintings to form the collection that he wanted for Basel with the generous, but not generous enough, funds that he was given.[29]

In 1959, the Swiss National Insurance Company would celebrate its seventy-fifth jubilee; the director of the company, Dr. Hans Theler, was also the president of the

Basel Kunstverein (Art Society) which ran the Kunsthalle, where Rüdlinger was director. As a gift to the city, Theler gave Rüdlinger 100,000 Swiss francs (246,000 dollars in 2023) to cover his travel and to purchase American paintings for the Basel Kunstmuseum, and it was with this sum that he now, in early November, arrived in New York, hoping to acquire five or six.

But he found that prices had risen with the attention received by the traveling show; he broke his arm in an accident and was delayed; and by the time he got to Barney's studio with Heller he had only 3000 dollars left. (Thus Heller's offer to provide the ticket to Pittsburgh.) Knowing what was paid for Rothko's picture, Barney expected the same. The choice was a smaller work or a price reduction. Again, Heller stepped in and offered to make up the difference (even if he had to raise it from others).

Despite the fact that this was an enormous plum, his first painting to enter a museum, one of only four artists represented in the first European museum collection of postwar American art, and despite having allowed Rüdlinger to return to Switzerland thinking the deal was done, Barney dug in his heels: if none of the other artists' fees were supplemented privately, he would not allow his to be either. But that wasn't the point he made to Rüdlinger. "What really matters is that there is an ethical question here which I feel certain you will understand . . . . I cannot <u>accept</u> any money in the purchase of my painting that does not come from Swiss sources. It is not only unethical for <u>me</u> to take American money, but for you to do so would defeat the integrity and the nobility of this Swiss gesture . . . . and it certainly would hurt me since it involves my painting . . . this gesture can be meaningful only if the <u>entire</u> gesture is done with funds from Swiss sources." Barney set the following conditions: The price of the painting was 5,000 dollars. He would accept the 3000 dollars that was available on account, and was "willing to wait for the balance of $2000 if you think that it is possible to raise this money from . . . Swiss sources only."[30] As letters crossed over the Atlantic, Barney prematurely received the 3000-dollar check "as downpayment" from Theler: "Please convey our sincerest thanks to your American friends which have contributed the remaining $2000." Barney responded as he had to Rüdlinger: he insisted that "the purchase of my painting will be on the same basis as the purchase of the other American paintings."[31]

Rüdlinger proposed they split the difference. Barney refused. "You know how very much I admire your work and I ask myself whether you could not meet my wishes half way if you really think you could not accept American money. I find it strange that you connect ethical reasons with facts as relative as the prices of pictures . . . if you are determined to refuse any American help there are only two possibilities left: you accept a price reduction in view of the whole collection and let us have the painting for $3000 or we must renounce your participation."

Although he spent a lifetime asserting his exceptionalism, he would *not* be treated in an exceptional way. There was a bit of the horseplayer left in him and the gamble paid off. Before Rüdlinger had even posted the letter, he showed it to Theler, who in the "last moment" caved: "he would like to offer you a supplement of $1000 hoping you may agree to make a similar gesture."[32] Theler's proposal amounted, Barney noted, to a "20% institutional discount instead of the regular 10%" and, as his "contribution" he was "pleased to give it."[33]

But it did not end there. After the negotiation had concluded, Barney "accepted the invitation to exhibit six years" of paintings "(the same show as at Bennington College) at the new galleries of French & Company," he wrote to Rüdlinger, as if this were the most ordinary thing in the world, and not the single most prominent showing of his work in his career so far. "Mr. Clement Greenberg, art consultant for French & Company, and French & Company," he repeated as if he himself could not believe it, "would very much like to include 'Day Before One' in the show inasmuch as with my show, French & Company will be dedicating their new galleries.

"I, of course, would like to have it in the show because it has never been publicly exhibited in New York City . . . . This would mean that it would be shipped at the end of March."[34] But the Swiss players in the drama surrounding *Day Before One* were adamant that it was required for a brief showing at the St. Gall Kunstverein of "all paintings bought in the United States." The American ambassador was to open the show. Somehow, with a new opportunity on the horizon, Barney quickly forgot the international significance of what Rüdlinger and Theler had accomplished. "New York's loss is Basle's [*sic*] gain," he casually wrote it off.[35]

It was the beginning of a new gallery relationship, *without* history, without, as well, the comfort and understanding and sensitive indulgence that Parsons allowed him, and *with* all the agitation that a person as controlling as Barney could experience. He agreed to the show—and demanded that French agree—only on the condition that he have "total personal and artistic freedom." That meant the gallery would not have "exclusive dealership rights" (Barney could sell to "anyone who comes to me"); the gallery would not be allowed to make any frames or stretchers, to include his work in group shows without his written consent, or to sell any other than the works he would indicate ("total release of my work is [not] in my interest at this time"); and Barney had the "right to reject any prospective buyer."[36]

In the midst of the Swiss sale negotiations and the French show anxiety, Barney's cab, driving down the West Side Highway, was in a fender-bender. A police squad car arrived, and he asked the officers to call a cab to take him home, but, in Barney's words, the police were "unwilling" (likely, not permitted) to call for anything other than an ambulance. He found a taxi, took it directly to the 16th Precinct station house on Forty-Sixth Street near Ninth Avenue, a burdened precinct responsible for seedy Times Square, West 52nd Street jazz joints, the theater district, and the docks on the Hudson—"the gaudiest, the most violent, the lonesomest mile in the world," notorious enough to be the tagline of a popular radio police drama *Broadway Is My Beat*—and "raised the issue" of his rights as a private citizen to ride home in a cab. He sent the Police Commissioner Stephen Kennedy an 8-dollar telegram narrating his position and complaint, and called his lawyer, who told him he didn't have a case.[37] "Do you see the issue between a taxi and an ambulance?" he asked Bob Friedman a few nights later. "Do you recognize the invasion of privacy?"[38]

From his own point of view, he was "always proceeding from a moral base"; that was what everyone understood about him.[39] This "Talmudic" stance was tempered with extraordinary benevolence—the word "moral," constantly used when friends talk about him, is matched by the word "generous"—when it didn't affect his self-regard, or the regard he felt was owed him. One friend compared his complicated rigor to Cromwell. It was not beyond question "that Barney's positions always *were* moral," but there could be no doubt that "he always assumed" that they were correct.

So it seems natural to justify Barney's irritability, or crankiness, through the immoderate standards of morality that friends were impressed by or acquiesced to. Especially easy, because, as Heller accurately summed it up, he was a "mensch. Times ten." But every once in a while an eruption makes unavoidable the conclusion that, rather than an intellectually arrived at, *philosophical* stance, the source was emotional and psychological. And the story of the West Side Highway incident shifts the ground just that measure.

"The true story . . . of what went on in Mid-Century" would finally be told. In March at "the city's most extravagant showcase for contemporary art"[1] Barney happily sacrificed exhibiting twelve or thirteen confident and mature paintings to show, as he had at the sleepy Bennington, only works made through April 1952. And in the enormous space, he would strengthen his case for the early years.

He had a "strong desire" that in the catalogue the 1946–47 *Euclidian Abyss* be one of four color reproductions—the first time his work was published in color anywhere. He chose one of his earliest drawings, one of the first appearances of a characteristic "zip" from 1945, for illustration, but not exhibition. He wanted a "special effort" made to include the painting that John and Ruth Stephan had purchased. Like the conditions placed on the show itself, this last transaction enabled him to settle another old but festering score.[2] And with a particularly vindictive, but presumably satisfying, flourish Barney wrote letters to both "Mr. & Mrs. Mark Rothko" and "Mr. & Mrs. Clyfford Still": "This is to make certain that you know that you are both not welcome to my show."[3] Rabbi Julius G. Neumann from Congregation Zichron Moshe, the temple on East Twentieth Street where Barney occasionally had helped to make up the daily *Minyan*, on the other hand, *was* welcome, to make known that he was not just any "shmo."[4]

French was the distinguished, century-old purveyor of the sort of decorative arts that American robber barons demanded. A year earlier the firm had moved from Fifty-Seventh Street to 978 Madison Avenue and, with Greenberg consulting, added contemporary art to their business. Now, the fifth-floor showrooms were being designed by Tony Smith—who had reconfigured the physical space for Barney's previous shows at Parsons and Bennington—and public-relations hot shots were engaged. And yet, toward the end of February, so overcome by nerves and doubts, Barney notified French that he was "postponing my show until such time as the gallery is physically a gallery instead of a collection of rooms with shops"—French's antiques inventory—"in between." Furthermore, he wanted it to be crystal clear that the postponement was caused by the gallery, and not the painter. If this were inconvenient for French, "perhaps the best thing is for me to withdraw entirely."[5]

It was not necessary. "Plush quarters" achieved, the twenty-nine paintings, two of them 18 feet long and three others over 10 feet high, were moved from his studio and his apartment to be shown "under the most advantageous of circumstances, both in regard to the physical setting and the interest and excitement generated."[6] Nemerov's poem, Greenberg's Bennington comments, five images, and the same grave photograph of Barney by Vandivert—one of very few in the session that made him look neither diminished by illness nor excessively jolly—made a catalogue appropriate to the occasion.

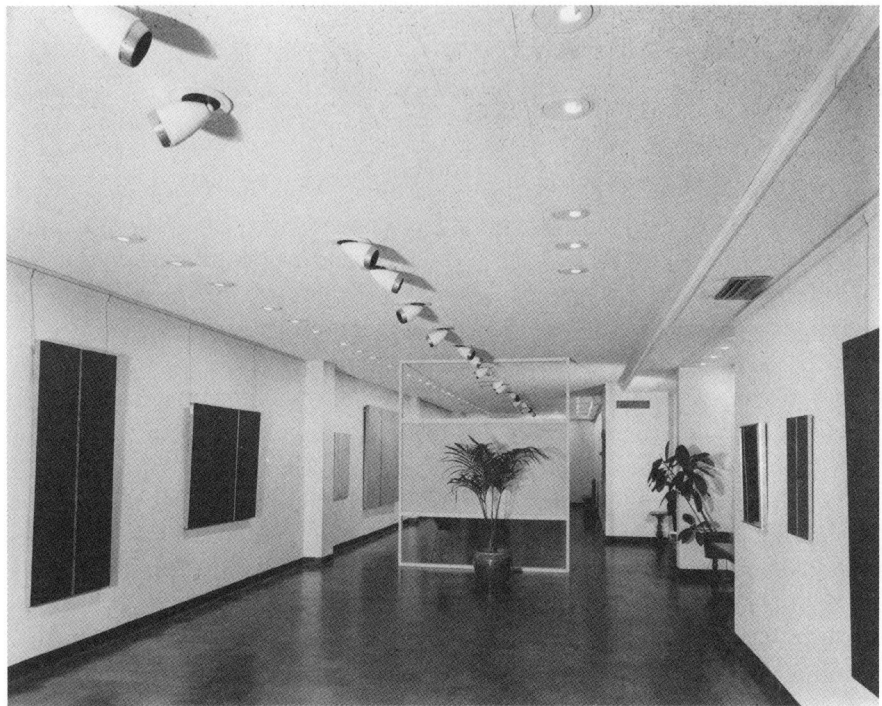

Fig. 37 French & Company show, 1959. From left: *Onement III, Covenant, The Beginning, Tundra, Euclidian Abyss, Onement I, Onement II* (partial view)

Notwithstanding the absence of *Onement VI, L'Errance, The Gate, Primordial Light,* and *Uriel*—all completed after "Fifteen Americans"—and *Be,* an exhibition that had *Vir Heroicus Sublimis* and *Cathedra* and *The Voice* and *Day One* and *Achilles* had to have been staggering. It certainly was to the Museum of Modern Art, which was organizing the United States representation for Documenta II in Kassel over the summer. They quickly requested *Cathedra* and *Tundra. Abraham,* already in Europe, wasn't at French, but the equally tragic, 11-foot-tall *Prometheus Bound,* obdurate, black with a thin white brushy-edged bottom, was. Heartbreaking, if not tragic, was the saga of *Be.* Under Barney's watchful eye, Annalee and George Franklin removed the 8-by-over-6-foot canvas from its stretcher, and, carrying it "like a hammock," began to descend the studio stairs. As they made the turn on the landing, the painting bent, cracked, and a thumb-sized area of paint broke off. It was withdrawn from the exhibition (although consigned for sale[7]) and Barney would never allow it to be shown again.[8] ("Good gracious!" was Smith's reaction, not believing that Barney kept it out of the show. "He should have put some lipstick on it!"[9]) Greenberg corroborated *how* the painting was damaged, but said it happened while being moved for the Bennington show, and that Barney hoped Bennington's insurers would compensate him.[10] When that failed, he blamed a French & Company chair. "This painting in some way fell against some heavy Renaissance furniture with large protrusions which cracked large sections of the paint film down through the sizing to the bare canvas" was the way Barney described the accident.[11] Unable to recover anything from French, Barney deducted 7000 dollars—"two thirds of its value"—on his tax statement, which, with all of his other deductions for depreciation of "desks, tables, typewriters, easels, books, fans, furniture, entertainment," et cetera, led to a negative taxable income of almost 6000 dollars and provoked one of his many audits.[12] The deduction for *Be* (later designated *Be I*) was disallowed "since loss is limited to cost and as the cost has been recovered through deduction in prior years for supplies, paint, canvas, etc."

Yet again, the critics were confused, unaware of the strategic reasons behind the 1952 end date. "The artist, I'm told, was ill for a while, but that was some time back. The last work he felt ready for showing was done seven years ago."[13] They were snidely unpersuaded, but no longer able to ignore or smugly dismiss the artist.[14] Ashton devoted twelve *Times* inches to make her point that the show was "like the old proposition about how many angels can stand on a pin. For those who believe angels exist, it is a possible speculation. For those who do not, it is an absurd proposition."[15] That she expanded her remarks at significant length in the May *Arts & Architecture*—invoking Malevich, Mondrian, and Vasarely—and wound up in the same place, belied her contention that the paintings were "reticent," "docile," and "not at all irksome." They clearly irked her. And irked her again in the bilingual review, *Cimaise*.[16]

In a particularly noxious review Crehan reacted as much to Barney's running his mouth to the press as to his art. "I don't want to show anything hot off the griddle" Barney had been quoted in *Newsweek*, and described his studio in the coffee district, around the corner from Wall Street, and across the street from "where the government smelts its gold" as a "very masculine atmosphere. There isn't anybody walking dogs, and you don't trip over fur coats." Crehan not only dismissed the work, but took *ad hominem* swipes at what he decided was Barney's "proud and inflexible archaic, male sensibility . . . lifted from the Old Testament." He translated *Vir Heroicus Sublimus* as *Heroic Man Erect* and mocked Barney for arriving at the opening on a freezing, snowy March evening wearing a "hunter's cap and looking like a modern Madison Avenue Nimrod . . . possessed by the myth of the patriarch."

"But we live in another world, really, one certainly that is in need of the phallic charge, although the *new man* . . . will be aware that we should have more music with the dancing. It takes two to tango [emphasis added]."[17]

"You've got to be able to tell the men from the boys," Barney had told *Newsweek*.[18] Appearing in the April *Art News*, Crehan's tweaking was once again under the aegis of Hess. Somehow Barney managed to hold his tongue and pen—maybe Hess's praise in his January Carnegie review and his gratuitous, if ambiguous, mention in the March issue implied Hess was coming around to Barney's work.[19] But clearly infatuated with his own wit, Hess could not resist rubbing salt. In the May issue, under the pseudonym "H. Rumbold" (the barber who would be hangman in "Barney" Kiernan's pub in Joyce's *Ulysses*), Hess wrote a letter with a deluge of literary references. "I was reminded of the words of T.S. Eliot commenting on the book by John Middleton

Murray in which he makes an analysis of D.H. Lawrence. Eliot wrote that never had the sacrificial victim been more beautifully arranged for the obsidian knife."[20]

In 1959, this was an ugly subtext, and a defense was compulsory; barely meta-phoric language became the steps in the dance and Hess got what he was looking for. "I could not keep my promise to myself to ignore it," Barney wrote a friend.[21] His response ("only the complete letter may be used for publication") ran in the summer *Art News*.

I want to assure Mr. H. Rumbold . . . and anyone else concerned that Mr. Hubert Crehan, in his attempt to slaughter me, only killed himself. The sacrifice that Mr. Rumbold describes did not take place. What did take place was Mr. Crehan's suicide. Let there be no doubt that the intended victim is very much alive. For vilification is an old substitute for art criticism. The force in my work must be very alive to have compelled Mr. Crehan to commit so drastic an act that in his self-fury he could only strike at my person, to lose himself completely in an orgy of self-hate at his own impotence.

I have seen a parade of magazine criticism in my time that has demanded of its practitioners that they be deaf, dumb, and blind but this is the first time (ART NEWS has made it possible) that one of them insists that his main criterion, his main qualification is castration.

Mr. Crehan's assault on my person, my manhood, my clothes, my appear-ance, his twist of the biblical metaphors of Mr. Nemerov's poem are, of course, beneath contempt. What is to be pitied is his love of impotence, his stupid fear of the creative man—man spelled masculine. What is not to be pitied in him is the unpardonable crime of blindness. I did not come to my opening wearing a brand new hunting cap. It was an old cap that I had been wearing all winter and which is worn by skiers to keep out the cold. Neither do I sport a mythical, patriarchal white beard. It is only a white moustache. These are important differences for one who claims he can see . . . . It is smear tactics.

Mr. Crehan attacks my steadfastness, my "masculine" strength by saying it takes two to tango. To him this is the essence of real painting. Is the painting-dance <u>that</u> easy? I have a feeling that Mr. Crehan's two dancers are eunuchs. Some day Mr. Crehan may learn that no matter how many it takes to tango, it takes only <u>one real man</u> to create a work of art.

As for the editors of ART NEWS who permitted this smear to appear, how is your tango?[22]

Disgruntled media critics—perhaps looking for more obvious sensationalism in the season of *Lady Chatterley's Lover* and Lenny Bruce—could keep sputtering; the artists disagreed. In their eyes, and in those of the opinion-makers in museums, the recent shows were revelatory, and Barney was a star. Ashton might see an archi-tectural "bourgeois . . . backdrop," Genauer, "shenanigans"; Jerrold Lanes saw the artist as clairvoyant, far ahead of his contemporaries, "masterful, but better than virtuoso . . . content to make his statement without asking you to admire how it is made," and the work as "at opposite poles from an applied, and perhaps even an applicable, art."[23] Even Rothko wanted a part in his new esteem: "I taught Barney Newman how to paint," he told a friendly painter.[24]

Alloway hoped to mount a one-man show in London.[25] A young Henry Geldzahler, teaching at Harvard, was so moved by the show that he gave impromptu talks to his students on the importance of Barney.[26] The flood gates had opened. "Newman's work will never have a more sympathetic audience than it has right now," announced *Arts*.[27]

During parts of the spring and summer of 1959, almost thirty works were hanging in New York, four works in London, and *Day Before One* in St. Gall, Switzerland. *Onement V*—a mid-size cobalt painting that, with a central stalwart army-green band, has an almost military presence—was shown in the Kimura Gallery in Japan.[28] Three paintings remained at French for the summer group show; *Dionysius* was shown in Rome; and *Tundra* and *Cathedra* were in Documenta II in Kassel.[29] At the end of May, "The New American Painting" returned to the U.S. to be shown at MoMA. And still, not one work publicly exhibited was made after 1952.

And, in what should have been the ultimate confirmation that the ancient wrong had been righted, *Abraham*—traveling around Europe through 1958 and 1959—entered the collection of the Museum of Modern Art. Barr was drawn to the painting from the time he first saw it in the studio with Heller, but, like Rüdlinger, had financial- and trustee-commitment issues. In this case, as he often would, Philip Johnson came to Barr's "rescue": Johnson had established a "Purchase Fund" in 1956 to circumvent the acquisitions committee by acquiring works himself with the "definite intention" of giving them to the museum.[30]

The blows and the praise, the excitement and the stress, the unfamiliar demands and solicitations—over the next several months galleries in Columbus, Los Angeles, Paris, and Milan wanted loans for the following season; he was invited to be in the Whitney Annual for the *first* time; he was invited to be on a College Art Association panel; he was "trending" enough to be asked for a recipe for an artists cookbook—the radical ups and downs were handled with a punching bag hung in his hallway (for rehabilitative exercise on his doctor's advice) and a great abundance of alcohol. But now, since the heart attack, his drink was not whiskey but clear vodka—which made it very difficult, despite her best efforts, for Annalee to monitor. Many noticed Barney's "water glass" being constantly refilled, but no one could say with exactly what.[31] And so perhaps the vodka can be blamed for how Barney ricocheted between the poles of irresistible charm and righteous, petty hostility. He "went to practically every opening of a young artist," noticed Liberman, where he "was a very touching and benevolent-looking figure." But, "he was not in reality. He had a harder side."[32]

Alan Power, the son of the British collector E. J. Power, who had been trying to purchase a work, came to the U.S. on business. "Oh, by the way," his father told him before he left England, "if you're in New York, try and look up four or five of these abstract expressionists." The younger Power worried that he was "as green as a cucumber, and didn't know anything about these guys or how to talk to them." Fresh from a traumatizing lunch with Still, who barely spoke at all, and would not show him any paintings, he called Barney. "He was wonderful. He said, 'Oh yes!' delighted to meet anybody who was interested in paintings, particularly from Europe." The French show had closed, but Barney arranged a visit to the Hahn Warehouse on West 107th Street, which he had recently begun to use, and had them "strip off the neat paper wrapping."

Power didn't know how to respond, and that was Barney's forte. He took him to the apartment, poured drinks, talked and talked. He took him to a Yankee game, and narrated it in awe-filled language—"the high priest" on the mound—and explained the field and action with metaphors that "amazed" the young man. With Tony Smith they went on an "architecture tour" and, with flair and drama, educated the Englishman about Louis Sullivan; he "could not have wished for a better guide to show me New York's great and controversial buildings."[33] But Barney also felt that Power was not ready to buy a "Newman," that he did not really appreciate what was going on.[34] "I agree with you Barney," Power wrote after speaking to Parsons about acquiring work from the French show and returning to England, the "issue is quite separate from the fact that we had a great time together in New York."[35] What might have seemed to some a manipulative tease, was for Power a clear indication of Barney's "moral stature."[36] And a magnificent representation of his generous and gregarious nature. "Nevertheless," Power added, "E. J. and I would very much like to hang those pictures."[37]

Yet over exactly these same few days of jovial and avuncular handholding, Barney's dark angel continued unabated in other interactions. He didn't initiate the ugliness with Crehan and Hess, but he did with John and Ruth Stephan, in protracted and nasty correspondence because, Barney told them, "my doctor sets strict limits on conversations on the telephone."[38] Righteous and snide, he sought to redress his wounds from 1948, his "clear feeling" that the couple had "no real pleasure in" the painting *Genesis*.[39] But there was also a new urgency to curate his output. The only satisfactory solution was for him to buy back *Genesis* and he sent the Stephans a check, which they returned.[40] From condescension, Barney's letters escalated to accusations of "persistent" attempts by the Stephans to "ruin my reputation, to slander and libel me" and "maliciously injure me," among "artists, dealers, critics and whomever you come into contact with." He demanded that they "desist from this attempt to ruin my reputation professionally"—using his lawyering-up language. "What is involved here is not a painting but my reputation—my life."[41] French was caught in the middle: they had mistakenly returned the painting to Barney rather than the Stephans. And, yes, "attorneys" became involved.[42] He lost the short game, as he probably knew he would, but Barney certainly won the long: during the delay he signed the face of the canvas "Genesis—The Break" in the upper left corner (to show its correct orientation) and dated it clearly: 1946.

He promised *The Promise* to Greenberg. It, like *Be*, had been marred during the show, and was sent to Barney's favored restorer S. J. Fishburne. Fishburne was not available, which led to glitches, which led to contretemps, with questions of responsibility turned into moral offenses. "Here is Fishburne's letter dated April 23, 1959," Barney wrote to Greenberg, "which is my answer to your uncalled-for insults and your public attempt to humiliate me this afternoon." (Greenberg had told people he had to "fight with Barney" for the offered "wedding gift."[43]) This, only two months after Greenberg wrote from Kassel, Germany, that *Cathedra* was "positively the best thing in Documenta painting section,"[44] and two weeks after Barney giddily responded: "Do you realize that it is the first time you ever used 'best' in connection with my work?"[45] No wonder Greenberg responded to the accusation of public humiliation, "I can't believe you're serious."[46] Even his best friends had trouble navigating through Barney's barometric pressure shifts.[47]

But it was a new, more pressing, worry that was on his mind. In French & Company's summer show, his work was hanging with those by a new generation of artists favored by Greenberg—Morris Louis and Kenneth Noland. He solicited the critic's "objective opinion": how did *Prometheus Bound* stand up in New York? "That interests me more than Germany."[48]

It was all so much static. His chronic, intermittent, back pain was now constant.[49]

FORTY-FIVE

"A MAN AND HIS WORK"

They sat gazing out across a narrow lake in a remote spot in central Canada, a band of western light squeezed by thick clouds and the treeline on the opposite shore. Far away physically and psychologically from the tornado that was New York, Barney and a young artist talked about the extraordinary "compression of light" and how as painters they might "deal with that phenomena in nature." The young man had never seen *Horizon Light*, and Barney didn't mention it, but when, a few months later in New York it was the first painting of Barney's that Robert Murray saw, he understood it instantly. It was not a transcription of something in nature, but an analog, an objective correlative of the compression.

The workshop at Emma Lake was a four-year-old summer program of the art school of the College of Regina, which itself was a satellite of the University Art Department in Saskatoon. Ken Lochhead, the director of the Regina College School of Art, had recently decided to keep the Emma Lake summer art school open for an additional two weeks in late August. Practicing Canadian artists from the three prairie provinces were invited as "students" and, with the goal of alleviating the artists' feelings of isolation, a more "cosmopolitan" guest was invited to lead the "seminar." In 1959 the guest was Barney.

The invitation on Will Barnet's recommendation came in February from Arthur McKay, workshop coordinator, just as Barney was organizing the French & Company show: "The purpose of the program is to provide opportunity for painters and sculptors to work and exchange ideas over the two-week period under the leadership of an artist of established and contemporary reputation . . . . The form and content of the program is decided by whoever leads the workshop . . . . There is no structure . . . . and any program desired by the artist is entirely possible."[1] To which Barney replied that yes, he was very interested. He had "been so busy getting things ready for an exhibition of my work in New York these coming months that I have not had an opportunity to make any plans for the summer," he wrote coyly, "and I, therefore, will be available."[2] The honorarium was appealing, as was its funding by the Arts Board of Saskatchewan's Co-operative Commonwealth Federation—the first Socialist government in the Americas, voted in during 1944 and widely covered in the U.S.

Barney could not have realized at that time in February how much, by August, he would need the quiet and relative isolation, the freedom from judgments and insults, demands and extraneous responsibilities—the escape from what he called the "drivel of New York art world" in order to regain his equilibrium.[3]

A previous workshop in 1957 had been led by Barnet. Barnet's name is not one that generally comes up in Barney's history, and yet their friendship led directly to one of its benchmarks. The men had met each other at various openings and Barnet never forgot their earliest "real" conversation. He was standing in front of the old

St. Moritz Hotel on Central Park South when he ran into Barney, who "grabbed" him: "'I'm very angry,' he said. 'Something in the *Art News* bothered me. I'm very angry about it.' And he grabbed my arm and said, 'I'm going to do something about it.' I said, 'Really Barney? Why do you get so excited?'"[4] After Barney moved to West End Avenue they spent long evenings together, beginning with dinners at the Barnets' or the Chinese restaurant on Broadway that became a favorite of Barney's, where philosophy and religion and art were on the table, and continuing "way into the wee hours because Barney liked to talk a lot." He would "always pontificate; he was mainly the speaker of the evening: he had these ideas and he felt deeply about them." Eventually, Barnet would begin to check the clock because he had to teach the next morning, aware that "Barney was *not* teaching and could sleep as late as he wanted to." But Barnet indulged him because Barney had a "certain quality" that he found very appealing. He "stood up straight. He had a sense of expansion, of feeling. Of really being someone important with important ideas." It was in his gestures, in the way he behaved. "If you met him, you'd realize the man is important."[5]

A revered fixture at the Art Students League, Barnet would, "from time to time" when he was traveling, invite Barney to substitute for him in his classes. Barney was already "quite famous" in their eyes, he impressed the students by being "positive," "upbeat," interested in and supportive of them, unlike other substitute teachers, who were "sour."[6] Barnet decided Barney was the right person for Emma Lake.

Barney and Annalee's last wilderness excursion, their 1936 honeymoon, was guided by Henry David Thoreau, but even then they paid little heed to his admonishment, "I say, beware of all enterprises that require new clothes, and not rather a new wearer of clothes. If there is not a new man how can the new clothes be made to fit?" Now it was out the window entirely. They rushed around—Harry Rothman, Gimbels, Bloomingdale's, Lord and Taylor, and Barney's "dream shop,"[7] the old Abercrombie & Fitch. For the outback, he equipped himself with casual collared polo shirts and slacks, and Annalee—most unusually—with an awkward pants suit, slacks, pastel sweaters, and cardigan. They bought sleeping bags and air mattresses, and a secondhand camera from the painter Kenzo Okada.

The Newmans arrived smartly outfitted for traveling to find a scene resembling Boy Scout camp. Fourteen artists—all male in 1959—lived in rustic cabins with no electricity or plumbing, in the woods "where the Canadian prairies meet the parklands of the North Country";[8] meals took place in a bigger "dining" cabin. The cabin that Barney was offered was promoted as the "largest and most comfortable . . . two bedrooms, a kitchen and a large living room," but in fact was quite small and mean. The common studio itself was a timber building with a truss roof and a great many windows that would have allowed for the northern light to pour in if it hadn't rained nearly every day. Keeping warm was "a constant and major effort." Post-heart attack, Annalee fussed over Barney continually; he, on the other hand, especially concerned to appear to be a "tough camper," not an "effete Easterner," was verbally brutal to her.[9]

In spite of the harsh conditions, he reveled in the landscape: "going out meant going to the prairie or deeper into the brush so that each experience was a true

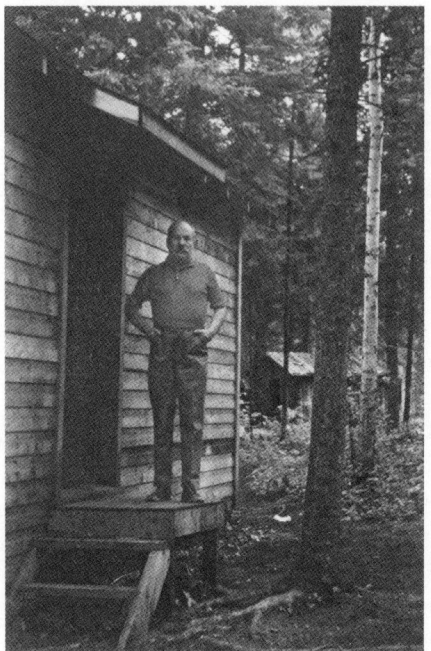

Fig. 38 Barnett Newman at Emma Lake for the summer art school, 1959. Photograph Annalee Newman

adventure." He was in a "constant state of excitement." They had "every possible weather—sun hot and yellow—white, blue clouds, rainstorms, hail as big as walnuts, rainbows, a dome of sky constantly changing, the greatest to me of all dramas—with the most fantastic sunsets, some massive, some like Turners—others thin as if painted with dry brush—just so many hairs." In Winnipeg they were "surrounded by four horizons, a circle of 360°, and a dome of 180°—but on *land*—not at sea—the difference is tremendous."[10] Bear, deer, elk, and "countless water birds, ducks, grebes, loons, & partridge, grouse, rabbits, muskrats" were part of an experience for which he was, in a sense, preparing his whole life.

Barney did no painting himself, nor did he "critique" the others' work in the typical art-school way. What he did do, in long and intense sessions, was impart the spirit of what it meant to be an artist and to take that role *seriously*. Painting was a *moral* activity. He "threw down the gauntlet" and left up to the fellows whether they would pick it up or not.

The students had never seen a work by Barney. But they had read Goossen in *Art News* and Jerrold Lanes in *Arts*—"Newman is an exemplary painter . . . in the mastery and economy of his means and in the purity of his purpose [and] in the clarity of understanding with which he grasps both . . . . He is an intellectual painter"—and seen the reproductions in that magazine in May. It seemed to them that Barney was as *au courant* as anyone could be. Murray, who had been at previous workshops but was at this moment busy with his first sculpture commission, was urged to return. McKay, who *had* seen the French show, wrote to Murray in Mexico: "Come back early, and come to the workshop. I've invited this guy Barnett Newman."

Barney wandered around the studio in a Yankees cap and the Cowichan sweater that he had just bought in Saskatoon; if an artist was so disposed, Barney would talk to him about his work. But in the morning, and then in the afternoon, and often very late into the night, they would have "unbelievable" discussions. Facts were one thing; but where Barney took them was "his own personal amalgamation" of philosophy, history, anthropology, and a variety of other disciplines.

"The most memorable occasions spent with Barney," recalled one participant, "were always outside the context of the workshop, the painting that we were doing. Whenever we got together over a bottle of vodka . . . he would spin for us that mythology and all of its legendary heroes and non-heroes and un-heroes and their women there, various and valourous women."[11]

Here, in the forest, with a captive audience of flannel-shirted younger men far removed from New York, Barney could write history the way he wanted it written. His tales brought to life a merry-*ish* band of men, and the evident respect he had for their work led some of the Canadians to consider themselves as having "group status and some sort of family resemblance to Newman, Pollock, de Kooning and company in New York" in the 1940s.[12] "Galvanized by Barney," four of the participants, joined by Lochhead, would become the "Regina Five" and exhibit together at the National Gallery of Ottawa.

They were awed by the seriousness he exuded. When a group of visitors drove up the long road into the woods and began wandering around the site (as people did during the regular summer session), Barney summarily threw them out: the studio was a place of "sanctity" and reflected the sanctity of one's work.[13] He specifically told them under no circumstances to allow fashion models to pose in front of their paintings.

Most importantly, he opened their eyes, made them aware of how an artist might function in modern society with a degree of focus for which one was *entitled* to receive respect. And that there was "no need to apologize for being an artist because you weren't doing useful work." He gave them "the guts to be alone in the world and not be overwhelmed by the lack of interest that the world might have in what we were doing."[14] He instilled in them the importance to society of those who were artists: it was perhaps the last profession with any degree of morality.[15] And the regard was reciprocal: *finally* Barney received, from these men, the unquestioning respect for which he always longed.

"This is really what I tried to do here," Barney wrote under the influence of the magical, and adoring, climate, "to explain that geography means nothing. *Place* means everything and place is created—and created by men with vision."[16]

Unlike the other students, Murray, who had been housesitting a log cabin on a nearby island, was able to have some time with the Newmans away from the group. He took them in a canoe to see a waterfowl nesting area at the north end of Emma Lake. They talked about how, as painters, to engage with phenomena in nature, about Corot and Pissarro and Monet, and developed a deep and resonant relationship. And so, at the end of the session, it was natural that Murray was delegated to drive Barney and Annalee to the airport in Saskatoon—a five-hour drive. But when they saw the castle-like Bessborough overlooking the Saskatchewan River—a vintage railroad hotel of the era when such establishments meant the luxury of heavy silver and fine china and elegant linens—Barney insisted on staying. Like a classic "Barney" dinner, the journey went on and on and on. Barney experienced things he never had before through Murray's enthusiastic efforts; Murray saw things as he never had before through Barney's unique eyes. Annalee, on sabbatical to watch over Barney's health and outfitted like Dame May Whitty in *The Lady Vanishes*, kept a vigilant eye on the vodka and hummed.

Very shortly thereafter, the Hollywood-handsome Murray moved to New York, and he became the colleague, sidekick, son *manqué*, and completely loyal friend that Barney had always wanted.

"Man against the mob"—one of Barney's favorite phrases—that was what Murray had taken with him from Emma Lake. "The real danger was the unthinking mob, mob psychology." Murray recognized it as one of the demons Barney struggled with.[17] "Just being a practicing painter does not free one from the herd," Barney wrote to Power when he returned, summarizing what he thought he had imparted to the Canadians. "No matter how one rants against institutions, museums, etc. It is not enough to bitch—it is action—one's work and one's <u>actions</u> towards the herd instinct in <u>oneself</u> that count. Since a man and his work are one it reveals itself best on the canvas."[18]

Reinforced, reinvigorated, ready for the future, Barney had returned from Arcadia to Manhattan. But the exhilaration didn't last long. The "art world" was still quite a small world, but at the beginning of October a "man and his work" revealed a vision far removed from "the canvas." In a new type of event, a "happening," Allan Kaprow actually courted a "herd."

For some—Norman Mailer, for example, in *Advertisements for Myself*, published that month—there were "the hints, the clues, the whispers of a new time coming . . . a universal rebellion in the air." If Mailer's form of aggressive and aggrandizing New Journalism didn't impress Barney that fall, Ornette Coleman's strangely unstructured music, his transgressive white plastic alto saxophone, his "free jazz" that debuted at The Five Spot Café on November 17—with Barney, Mailer, and a cadre of celebrities and less famous in attendance—did hit its mark.

It wasn't a casual occurrence that Barney was there. He was a deliberate and selective aficionado. He would bring guests to every night of a particular singer's run at the Village Gate—a compliment she repaid by fawning over him—then not return for months.[19] He did the same for the brilliantly innovative tenor saxophonist Sonny Rollins, at The Five Spot, a club created in a Bowery bar after the Third Avenue El was torn down, which quickly became a popular hangout for the downtown artists and beat writers who lived in the area. The Five Spot was the venue to which one "graduated" to hear the most significant, newest, jazz, where people "lined up three and four deep to get in."[20] He educated himself about jazz exactly as he had about his other enthusiasms, with regular consultations at Sam Goody's and discerning purchases of jazz 45s and newly-released LPs—Lionel Hampton, Thelonious Monk, Bill Evans, Charlie Parker, Stan Getz, and (a specialized taste in those years) Jimmy Giuffre. Many he would send to his British friends as gifts.

Before the French show, Barney would write "press releases" about his activities and his breakthroughs and his significance, and he personally delivered them to news desks. Then, he would bristle at those like Mathieu who successfully engineered their own "buzz." Now there was hardly a distinction: medium-stretching serious artists like Coleman and ego-driven publicity hounds alike cluttered the cultural radar.

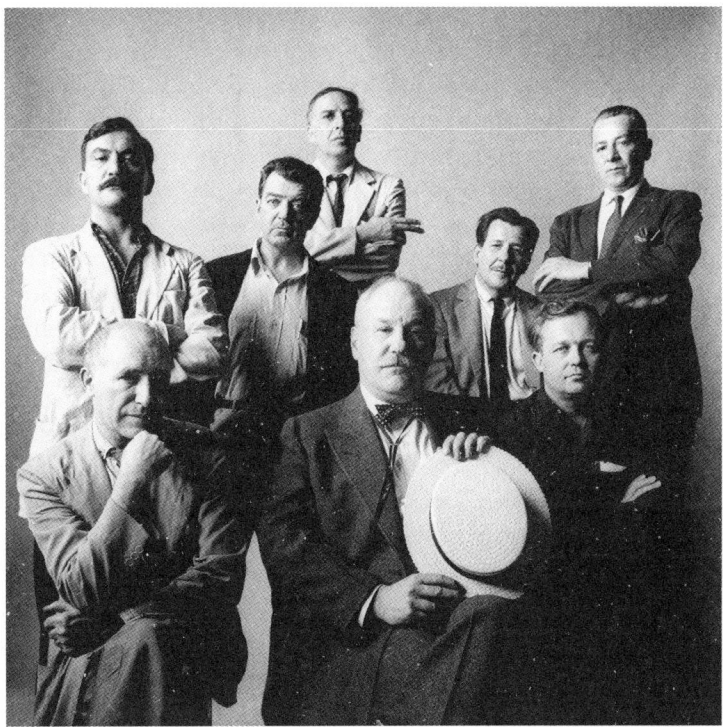

Fig. 39 "8 New York Painters," *Vogue*, October 15, 1959. Back, from left: Theodoros Stamos, James Brooks, Philip Guston, Franz Kline, William Baziotes. Front, from left: Jack Tworkov, Barnett Newman, Sam Francis. Photograph Irving Penn

The international exposure of "New York School" artists during the previous season had forced the hands of mainstream American institutions. In *Vogue*, under Liberman's art direction, the notice met with Barney's approval: "Few American painters have more international effect than these men, part of a larger group of New York Abstract Expressionists, all with influence; each of them begat imitators in other countries." Irving Penn's regal and polished photograph (unlike Nina Leen's tense and shadowy one of eight and a half years earlier) flattered Tworkov, Francis, Stamos, Brooks, Kline, Guston, Baziotes—and once again smack in the middle—Barney, "a sharp, genial, witty man, who wears a monocle, pin-striped suits, and in summer a straw boater." All the men were unusually, almost unnaturally, well-groomed, but only Barney's accoutrements were noted in the text, the straw boater held vertically in Barney's lap like a great white moon bathed in his reflected light.[21]

But in *Life*, which declared abstract expressionism "the most influential style of art in the world today," from Barney's perspective the coverage could not have been worse. "Its creators are a handful of Americans who have become the most talked-about painters on the globe. But in spite of the established reputations of the artists and the impressive prices their paintings command, the work . . . is a source of bafflement and irritation to the public at large."

The first installment of the glitzy two-part article was entirely about Pollock: twelve pages of text, photographs, "source" images by earlier artists meant to prove a reputable heritage, and impasto-accentuating details. Art editor Dorothy Seiberling's researchers had interviewed everyone, including Barney, so the article was no surprise. Part two, however—devoted to Still, Rothko, de Kooning, and Kline—was a genuine shock. Several color reproductions were so enlarged that the pages could only accommodate small sections of paintings. The opening spread showed actual, not metaphoric, flames of yellow and orange against a black background on the left facing a tight, full-page black, white, and yellow detail of a version of Still's *1956-J No.2 (PH 1074)*. Astonishingly for an artist so notoriously opposed to promotional flimflam, a black shadow of his American Gothic profile was silhouetted against the white area to echo the jagged form of black paint.[22] The three others were treated similarly. A photograph of muscular construction scaffolding against a blue sky was next to a Kline painting, while hard-edged shadows raked across the artist's portrait. A telescoped view into a forest floor was meant to help viewers comprehend a tiny detail of a work by de Kooning, while he himself, groomed to look so much like an Ivy League professor as to be nearly unrecognizable to those who knew him, leaned against a leafless tree whose analogue was roughly implied in the painting propped in the high grass behind. Rothko fared no better. He sat in deep shadow, his face ruddily lit with orange light, its attenuated shadow cast onto a detail of a painting, while immediately below was a second photograph of an uncannily mimicking sunset. No titles were given. It was cringe-worthy, it was almost a *New Yorker* cartoon. Barney should have thanked his stars that he wasn't treated in this manner. Except. A fourth full page devoted to Still had his now clearly visible face, once again in profile, against so tight, and so *un*characteristic, a detail that it evoked no Still painting at all but did read, to anyone who had seen the French & Company show, or had been to Documenta, or Barney's studio, as the magnificent *Cathedra* by Barnett Newman.[23]

Still, ostentatiously self-isolated from the "scene"—the story was that he had "turned down the offer of a one-man show" at the Venice Biennale, afraid that it would be "misinterpreted as catering to 'the praise of Vanity Fair'"[24]—at just that moment had manipulated his own publicity coup. After seven years of not participating in any display of his work, he negotiated an arrangement with the Albright Art Gallery. He would show seventy-two paintings, *if he* hung them, and *if* no other contemporary work was shown in the museum, and *if* the catalogue made explicit that although "the paradox manifest by the appearance of this work in an institution whose meaning and function must point in a direction opposite to that implied in the paintings—and my own life," he "accepted" that paradox.[25]

Also confronting that paradox was Rothko, as the Four Seasons awaited his murals.[26] Since they were not yet in the restaurant (nor, as it happened, would they ever be) Friedman could not comment on them in his witty but scathing dissection of "The Most Expensive Restaurant Ever Built" for *Evergreen Review*. But he did not have high hopes. Rothko's "recent and regimented paintings can hardly exist, except as historical objects," Friedman wrote. "It will be a surprise if he . . . transcends décor."[27]

Barney "raised an issue" when Friedman asked him for editorial advice: did Heller and the Museum of Modern Art (who lent works to the dining room) sanction "the restaurant and its vulgarity"? Heller, who lent Pollock's *Blue Poles*, "was in the clear," Barney decided. The "issue is whether what is lent is or is not art. In Bens [*sic*] case it is. In the museums [*sic*] it is questionable," Barney telegraphed to Friedman.[28]

But he was far less rational about *Life* magazine. Of the "Four Horsemen" of Betty Parsons's early days, only Barney was missing. "There are lots of spoilers around," he told *Newsweek* at the time of the French show. "You know what a spoiler is?" he said pointing to the punching bag. "It's a boxing term for a fighter who never gets to be champion, but he makes the champ look like a bad fighter."[29] It was all fine and good to be hailed now. But nobody appeared to understand that his shows were about *historical* 1952. All the attention of the previous season, and all of the new audience for his work, did not make up for having been left out of "Fifteen Americans." This realization struck at his dark place as much as it ever had.

"Everybody had their own way of being difficult in those days," recalled the English art dealer John Kasmin. "Being difficult was what you were supposed to be." Furthermore, "half these people are Jewish, and for all Jews the *record* is pretty important. Whatever gets written down gets carved in stone. So getting the record straight, even if it meant nudging it around a bit your way, was pretty important because it was going to last."[30]

At the end of 1959, there was a new urgency. Miller's 1956 show, "Twelve Americans," was filled with solid and interesting and talented artists, but it had not left the kind of mark that the 1952 show had. "Sixteen Americans," about to open in December 1959, announced something completely different, a *cooler* future, characterized by the hard-edge abstraction of Ellsworth Kelly, the so-called "neo-Dada" of Jasper Johns and Robert Rauschenberg, the unclassifiable art of Jay DeFeo, and work that appeared shockingly new by the 23-year-old prodigy from Princeton who had just been taken on by Castelli: Frank Stella. "It was *staggeringly* important" that Barney get the record "carved the right way"[31]—even if the only recipient of the corrections were his own files.

November 23, 1959

Dear Editor:

Life should be commended for its attempt to bring modern art to the attention of the people. But there are two ways of doing it. One is the good way of discussing a man and his work as it is which is what your first article on Jackson Pollock exemplified. The other is to assume the role of high priest . . . who tells the story of its history which can only be good if it is accurate and can be bad if involved in partial truth and propaganda . . . . Were these men really the pioneers? How is it you did not identify the paintings by dates? By what authority are some of these men included and others left out? Doesn't the photograph of Still in front of his painting look as if he is standing in front of a Newman. Is not Rothko's painting a horizontal version of another Newman?[32]

Dear Mr. Barr:

In visiting the museum's show for a New Museum I was impressed . . . [but how] do you account for showing the Rothko and the Monet? The acquisition of the Monet corrects the historical situation but what is the story about the Rothko? Should it not be made clear that the color schemes used there, the browns and the reds were never used by him until Mr. Heller acquired Adam by Newman who from my knowledge of modern painting was the first to combine these colors and the first to use the open space concept.[33]

Dore Ashton:

Congratulations on an excellent general analysis of Still's exhibition and work . . . I have always been suspicious of his attempts to equate innate character of a work of art with the vanity of self-exploitation in order to become a personality.
Your remarks that he reaches "the height of his present style" . . . are very true but how is it you are unable to give credit to the man who made it possible for him to open up his painting?
Don't you recognize that your own description of his work is an accurate description of Newman's painting?
Don't you realize that the legend of his reputation begins in 1952 and that in the "Fifteen American [sic] Show" the bulk of his work is the soft painting that antidates [sic] the big black painting which is a take off on Newman's black on black and big ones?[34]

Dear Miss Seiberling:

I find your article on the pioneers very misleading. I have seen Clyfford Still's work and reproductions of it ever since he first showed at the Peggy Guggenheim gallery. He never showed a picture that looked like the one on Page 77.
In 1951, Aline Saarinen described his work as follows: "paints canvases where murky dark pigment is sparked by bold flicks of color."
In the same article Aline Saarinen describes the work of Barnett Newman, as follows: "paintings where a single line of colour plunged down a canvas

flatly covered with a different colour." It doesn't take a great deal of research
to see the truth . . . .
What is worse, in the case of Clyfford Still you even used a cropped
picture . . . .
If you study this cropped photograph carefully you will find that it is not
at all the pioneer work of Clyfford Still but that of the pioneer Barnett
Newman.[35]

Later he would tell an interviewer "I have given no attention [to] where I am
going to lie in the cemetery of history."[36] But after 1959 his attention never wavered
from just that.

At the beginning of the season, before *Vogue*, before *Life*, the *Times*'s new art editor
introduced himself with a startling agenda: "The New Year in these parts has so
little to do with the first day of January and so much to do with the first Monday
in September that Labor Day's Eve . . . would be a good time to ring the bells and
blow the whistles while everyone wishes everyone else the best of everything for
the next twelve months—including a lot less pother about abstract expressionism,"
read the first sentence of John Canaday's first paragraph. "With any luck, 1959–60
might even go down in history as the year abstract art in general accepted the responsibilities of middle age." The abstract expressionists should "feel embarrassed
in their protracted adolescence."

The best abstract expressionists were "as good as ever they were," Canaday allowed, but they were surrounded by "freaks," "charlatans," and the "misled." Anyone
"can paint in a kind of abstract expressionist idiom," he wrote, invoking "the highly
personal work of Betsy the Ape, conspicuous not long ago in the newspapers"; it
was, "of course, not art," but "it was certainly abstract and, in its own way, quite
expressive."

"Professors, museum men and critics," had "tried to atone to a current generation
of pretenders to martyrdom" for previous eras' blind spots. Canaday left no doubt
that he would be happy to martyr himself to correct the situation.[37]

This was not going to be a discussion of different values, a parsing of approaches,
or an argument over which beakers of ice deserved laurels; this was a declaration of
war, of carpet-bombing, scorched earth. Canaday's lengthy responses to objecting
letters from Daniel Catton Rich, former director of the Art Institute of Chicago and
current director of the Worcester Art Museum, and collector (and banker and diplomat) Donald Blinken, made manifest that this was his precise intention. "On the
tenth day of May, 1944, on the drill field of the Marine Corps Base at Quantico, Va., as
the only dissenting member of a company of recruits that had received the command
'column left,' this writer executed a brisk right turn."[38] Canaday was the paragon of
virility who would clean the field of the "starry eyed" adolescents, "the freaks, the
charlatans and the misled," the ape apers.[39]

His focus was relentless: whether reviewing the chatter-generating show of the season—"New Images of Man" at the Museum of Modern Art[40]—or a small photography show at the Metropolitan, Canaday used every opportunity to denigrate abstract art. "Sixteen Americans" was so dangerous, he attacked it in *four* columns for its "intellectual stunts," and "examples of painting that seemed to me utterly stale and pointless . . . displayed as a spectacle."[41]

An outraged group began to coalesce, monitoring the critic's campaign; eventually they formed themselves into a more organized outraged group. And where there was outrage there was a place for Barney. He always preferred to vent his spleen highly polished; here was an occasion professionally sanctioned, like his Rothko-Gottlieb-Jewell crusade, and unlike his Still-Seiberling-Life eruption. Throughout the 1960 season, as Canaday spewed his contempt and harumphed at those reigning from other platforms, like Hess at *Art News* and Barr at MoMA, while blithely exempting his own pontifications as the "art critic in chief of the most powerful and respected newspaper in the United States with about 1,400,000 copies sold every Sunday"[42] (as Barr noted), Barney clipped and saved the articles. And throughout the same period the "organizing committee"—Barney; collectors Blinken and Heller; artists James Brooks, de Kooning, John Ferren, Gottlieb, Hare, Raymond Parker, Pavia; and critics Hess, Rosenberg, and Irving Sandler—met in Ferren's or Sandler's apartments to discuss action. They composed a letter and solicited others to sign it, or, should the *Times* refuse to publish it, to fund an advertisement in the paper. Eventually, in February 1961, a letter, signed by forty-nine artists, art historians, professors, collectors, architects, poets, and writers, was finalized and published and reacted to. "Reading Mr. John Canaday's columns on contemporary art, we regard as offensive his consistent practice of going beyond discussion of exhibitions in order to impute to living artists en masse, as well as to critics, collectors and scholars of present-day American art, dishonorable motives, those of cheats, greedy lackeys or senseless dupes." He waged a "polemical campaign under the guise of topical reporting." His "terminology of insults" included "built on fraud"; "hobby"; "freaks, charlatans and the misled"; "exceptional tolerance for incompetence and deception"; "critics and educators . . . sold down the river. We have been had"; "brainwashing . . . in universities and museums." The letter left out Betsy the Ape and the occasion when Canaday mockingly "critiqued" a blob of ink.

If Canaday "has a political or social or esthetic 'position' or philosophy, let him state what it is and openly promote his aims," read language familiar from Barney's writing from the late forties. Every period in art had "imitative or uninteresting artists." But Canaday's relentless focus on the worst "to impugn the whole, instead of attempting to deal seriously with the work of the movement, is the activity not of a critic but of an agitator."[43]

The brouhaha went beyond the *Times*; it was national news in *Newsweek* and *Time*. Two weeks before the joint letter appeared, a small item in the newspaper reported that Canaday had been censured by the American Section of the International Association of Art Critics for "having treated a fellow critic"—Dore Ashton, a "part-time" art news reporter—"in a manner unbecoming the profession of criticism . . . infringing basic principles of freedom of criticism by his accusation, demands and threats, aimed at forcing compliance with his own views and methods in matters of judgment."[44] All of it had virtually no effect on Canaday, but the impact for Barney was enormous. Through sixteen months from September 1959 to February 1961 a broad coalition of art world establishment figures was united in war, and Barney, with Hess and Rosenberg, his earlier tormentors, was among the generals on the "organizing committee."

Thus began his marathon phone conversations with Rosenberg. Murray, who had recently arrived in New York, recalled occasions when Rosenberg would phone the apartment while he and Barney were in the midst of some task. The calls went on for so long—for "hours"—that Murray simply got his coat and left. "They would go over things left, right and center, up, down, sideways." Somehow, extraordinarily, the days of the "Yalu River" had been put behind them.

And it was this episode that resulted in Hess's profound change of heart as well. When, in mid-1962, Canaday published his collected writings, *Embattled Critic: Views on Modern Art*, Barney was "challenged" by Hess to review the book.[45] Other reviewers found the book so weak in supporting its positions, and so filled with contradictions, that it was easy for them to dismiss with polite dispassion. Barney's review was more personal: the "now famous letter of censure," he wrote, was the "*raison-d'être* of this book." But, as published, the review showed a great deal more restraint than had characterized his previous *responsa*.[46] For here he knew he was not alone, he had the organizing committee and thirty-six others behind him. They were on the same side.

By 1962, Schapiro, Rosenberg, and Hess had become not only genuine friends, *mishbucha*, as Heller, or Barney, might have put it. They were, crucially, Barney's most ardent supporters.[47]

FORTY-SIX

"NEWMAN STANDARD TIME"

He was too distracted to make paintings in 1959 or early 1960.

Dionysius had come back from Italy with scratch marks. Was it injured in Rome or during shipping? One insurance company's coverage, for air freight, had ended on November 30; the painting was incorrectly shipped by steamer on December 16. Who was responsible? Rome? New York? The maritime company? Restoration costs totaled 600 dollars. Barney felt mugged. Parsons would spend nearly four years fighting this particular battle on his behalf.[1]

Cathedra—a presence so transgressive, so radiantly revolutionary that it could have borne the title "Who's Afraid" before the artist assigned it to other works—came back from Documenta heartbreakingly damaged: the metal cables from which it had been hung snapped.[2] The work was to some degree a victim of its own sensitivity, the unvarnished, thin, matte paint—partly applied with a spray gun—was crisscrossed by structural cracks that were barely noticeable from the front, but obvious in raking light. It felt to Barney almost like a penalty, or a punishment for success, for having so many works out and on view: every single time every single work left his care there was mortal danger. Like Barney's, its skin was too thin, its spark too fragile, its soul too exposed and too easily hurt. "The paint layer is utterly tender . . . it is comparable to velvet," wrote one of the most accomplished and esteemed conservators in New York, Caroline Keck, about *Cathedra*. Its tenderness was "inherent in its nature. It has nothing to do with the accident. The painting is an item which I do not know how to preserve . . . this is beyond me."[3] She might as well have been speaking of the artist himself.

"One of the pictures of our time," in Heller's opinion, *Cathedra* had become in Barney's eyes a "total loss." And in his distress, he felt he "must ask for complete restitution," 35,000 dollars, the "sales price" of the painting.[4] The negotiations with the German underwriters "over the settlement of claims," Porter McCray wrote in November 1960, "have been bitterly contested and prolonged for a period of time beyond any reasonable patience on your part." On behalf of the International Program of the Museum of Modern Art, which organized the American representation in Kassel, he commended Barney's "generous patience throughout [the] excruciating delays" and reported he was now optimistic. But not until February 1963—when prices for his paintings had risen significantly—and not until the predictable volume of letters, did Barney finally receive a check for 10,000 dollars.[5]

"Aside from all the personal aggravation" restoration and insurance battles caused him, he wrote to an underwriter, "I wonder whether you are aware of the additional damage I have suffered. It seems that I am being boycotted by some of the out-of-town institutions because my paintings, they say 'get damaged.' This is an obvious attempt to make me, who is the victim, the blame for their negligence."[6]

If so relentlessly facing the repeated traumas of injured paintings developed into a kind of phobia, made him fearful of undertaking major new works, at least he would draw. After producing—or at any rate saving—only four drawings in the previous ten years (all dated 1959), in 1960 Barney made twenty-two. In fact, he made *all* of the drawings, with one exception, that he would make during the remainder of his life. All twenty-two were small—between 14 by 10 and 12 by 9 inches—and made with brush and black ink. Profoundly beautiful and absolutely assured, they feel both spontaneous and deliberate, composed according to the ambition he began to pursue shortly after his illness: how to make the white of the ground sing like a color would. Together they constitute a symphony—perhaps the symphony that was always in him,

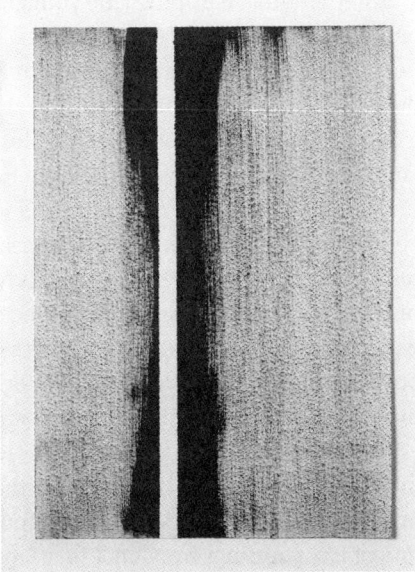

Fig. 40 Barnett Newman, *Untitled*, 1960. Brush and ink on paper, 14 × 10 in. (35.6 × 25.4 cm). Private collection, Connecticut

that he hadn't finished decades earlier. The drawings are not studies for the paintings that would follow over the next six years, but, as the scholar Brenda Richardson called them, a "kind of incubation for the Stations," to confirm his "visual instincts, to achieve a sense of conviction . . . about the direction he found the work taking."[7] They were intimate, they were not exhibited, they could be kept safe from harm.

And, not incidentally, there was emerging great interest in drawings by Barney. As the contemporary adventure of French & Company was ending, the last man who had been hired to try to keep it going, Everett Ellin, headed back to Los Angeles to open his own gallery with a show of drawings. Unpacking the crate of those he had gathered in New York, he saved Barney's—six dated 1945 to 1949—for last, delaying the gratification he anticipated after the seductive immersion of his Newman studio visit. It was "an experience I shall long remember," he told the artist. "Barney, you knocked them dead! I just can't take my eyes off of those drawings of yours and they take on new significance for me each day . . . no-one else comes close. The West Coast is in for a real treat."[8] Prices were set at 600 to 1200 dollars.

In New York, the painter and innovative frame-maker Robert Kulicke would buy one. On the West Coast, the collectors Fred and Marcia Weisman—whom Barney had met at a cocktail party at Heller's—bought one and hung it prominently; the Los Angeles artist Ed Moses wanted another "desperately," possibly the one reproduced in the magazine *Frontier*.[9] It's not impossible that the twenty-two drawings that are dated 1960 were as provoked by financial considerations as by sudden artistic inspiration.

After months of griping (the younger painters "make it all so simple: they think being creative is the way to be happy"),[10] after socializing and side projects (he hung Liberman's first painting show at Parsons), after an immersion in avant-garde dance, and existential and absurd theater, after the existential and absurd honor of a *Saturday Review* cartoon mocking his work,[11] after a jaunt to Boston to catch the landmark Courbet show and see the five Henry Hobson Richardson buildings in Easton, and fortified by quantities of vodka ("I drink, but I don't get drunk" he said about whether he drank when he worked. "I just drink enough to get closer to the metaphysical terror"), Barney was ready to paint again. Now he would buy only the best quality canvas, obsessively inspecting each bolt for nubs or irregularities that would interfere with his surface, and the best quality stretchers. But he still loved to buy his beautiful English house painter's brushes, his Chinese bristle brushes, and his tools at Job Lot, thrilled to get a bargain.[12]

In May or June, he again made a black-and-white painting on unprimed canvas in the same dimension and format as the previous two. A couple of months earlier, luxuriating in the works at the MoMA opening of another groundbreaking show, this one of late paintings by Monet focused on the *Haystacks, Poplars, Cathedrals,* and *Water Lilies,* Barney was struck by the concept of "series." But he quickly "forgot about it," he said, as he made a fourth 78-by-60-inch painting on unprimed canvas with black; he simply "wanted a few paintings that [were] similar." After all, he was "not doing the haystacks." But by the middle of 1963, after he had done two more, he recalled the Monet show, and realized, yes, he was "involved like in a series."[13]

There were eventually fourteen paintings and in many ways they crystallize everything about Barney's character: learned, extreme, provocative, magnificent, and marvelous. Like Barney, uncategorizable. They *seemed* to be a series, but were not exactly a series, rather "*like* in a series." They would be titled *Stations of the Cross,* but they had nothing to do with the canonical narrative. The events therein recounted, the Passion of Christ, were uniquely the domain of Christendom, but these fourteen were painted by a Jew who unapologetically refused to relinquish the name. In fact, he righteously *changed* the meaning of the name and righteously defended his act. If, historically, the Stations of the Cross referred to episodes in the Passion, these particular stations would be the Passion compressed: "*Lema Sabachthani* . . . Why did you forsake me?"—as he tellingly translated.

They might have *appeared* empty, but they were burstingly full. One might be able to dismiss them with a verbal description; one could not dismiss the overwhelming *effect* of the experience.

Would he be able to carry it all off? "Who's afraid?" Barney might have asked defiantly.

Later, when they were shown at the Guggenheim Museum in 1966, a tempest swirled around Barney, with Canaday its Prospero, and Barney and others devoted many many *many* words to explanations. In 1960, however, none of this was an issue, even for those, like Murray, who were intimately present during their creation. (Of course, not *in* the studio; nobody was ever actually in the studio when Barney was painting.) It was in early 1961, between, as Barney said, the fourth and fifth canvases, that he began to think of them as the *Stations of the Cross*. Specifically, the *Lema*. The very same cry wailed that season by the devout and pure victim of the corrupt charismatic preacher at the hellfire climax of Oscar-winning *Elmer Gantry*. "My God, why hast thou forsaken me?"[14]

That was the pattern: there were highs—this show, that notice, a potential sale—but they were always accompanied by dark lows. If a piece in a group show converted a doubting critic into partisan, he might nevertheless be excoriated for having the wrong reason; if a pristine canvas left viewers awestruck overseas, it was carelessly installed and so disfigured by the "hair dressings" and "prolonged fondling of the surface by sweaty hands" that "under no circumstances [could] it be considered a work of" his.[15]

If he and Annalee—who had earlier in the year taken driving lessons—arranged a road trip for their first visit to Washington to see Sarah Newman, the museums, and the striking petroglyphs from Bald Friar, Maryland, there would be multiple car breakdowns, unscheduled overnights in random towns with unscheduled costs for food and phone calls, and accusations of false advertising by the garage (Barney preserved proof of the advertised "special"). The drama of insurance companies, stopped checks, collection agencies, and threatened lawsuits would go on for months.[16]

Barney's indignation and irritability are easy to recount because he left so much evidence. Much more elusive are the charm, the wit, the joy, the warmth, and generosity and kindness that made people adore him so devotedly, made them want to be in his company and listen to his monologues, experience things through his eyes, and forgive him for the furious outbursts. He left no drafts of the improvised sermons he delivered on excursions to restaurants, New York walking tours, art viewing or shopping outings; or at Passover seders at the Hellers, or Christmases with Hess's sister, or election night and New Year's Eve parties at Hess's townhouse, or at boldface-name-filled luncheons at the Liberman's; or of his extemporized colloquies with cab drivers or waiters. Or of how genuinely interested he was in many of the younger artists, how much focus he brought to their interactions. Or of how much *fun* he was to be with.

It is precisely the same with Barney the man as with Barney's paintings: they require, they insist upon, first-hand, *personal* attention. Neither can be grasped in reproduction.

With a characteristic smile and chuckle, "he liked being difficult or making simple things seem difficult. He would have a look, and you could tell that he knew that he was making things slightly more complex than necessary, but he quite liked adding weight to simple things." He sought profundity in simple things. "It was, generally speaking, solemnizing things, but with a sense of humor. He had a sort of a twinkle, and you knew that deep down he really wanted this all to be as though it was all being noticed and written about."[17]

Whatever magic dust he sprinkled over such random proceedings has long since been dispersed into an impossible-to-capture hazy aura. What might have been in other company quotidian occurrences were recounted, even half a century later, with excited delight. Certainly, the sophisticated consumption of alcohol is a leitmotif—"Barney and I used to knock off a bottle of vodka trying to figure out what bar to go to," laughed Murray—but that alone cannot account for the glow.[18] Think Pollock. Think de Kooning. Stories about New York School artists' drinking rarely involve intellectually singular, or beguiling experiences.

At the Five Spot with Alan Power, Coleman Hawkins himself came over to the table to chat. At a new Chinese restaurant "discovered" by Jonathan Holstein, the master chef emerged from the kitchen to greet old friends from previous obscure restaurants, Barney and Annalee.[19] On Barney-arranged excursions to New Jersey it was "very, very important to go to see" Mies van der Rohe's glass-skinned Pavilion and Colonnade Apartments in Newark.[20] Then to Tony Smith's place for copious drink and Smith's multi-voiced performance of *Finnegan's Wake*.

At the Barney Greengrass "appetizing" store and café, the aristocratic Swiss art dealer Ernst Beyeler and the Stedelijk Museum men, Wim Beeren and Edy de Wilde, were introduced to New York lox and bagels. When the Swiss museum director Carlo Huber and his wife came to visit, they were sent on the flight home with a box of smoked fish sandwiches on ice.[21]

John Kasmin dropped that he loved buying records. So Barney took him to Sam Goody's near Times Square, where he "had a particularly good relationship with

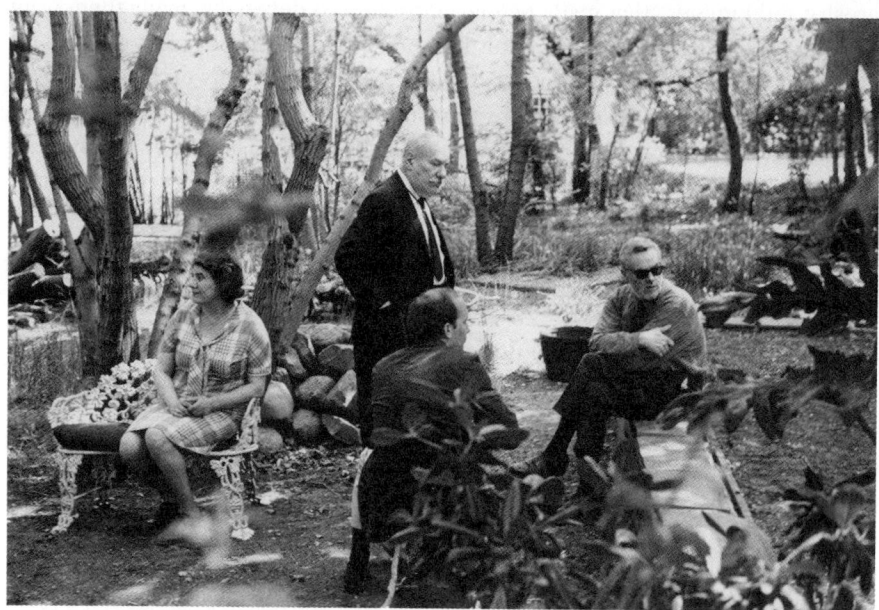

Fig. 41 From left: Annalee Newman, Barnett Newman, Richard Smith (back to camera) and Tony Smith at his home in New Jersey. Photograph John Kasmin

one of the guys. He'd chat with him forever . . . big discussions about whether Otis Redding was better than James Brown," and insisted Kasmin buy the brand-new—now standard-setting landmark—jazz album *Undercurrent*, by pianist Bill Evans and guitarist Jim Hall.

During Christmas season, he knew the premier place to hear carols was the historic Romanesque Revival St. George's Episcopal Church on Stuyvesant Square—during his life it was known as J. P. Morgan's Church—where the brilliant African–American composer and singer Henry Thacker Burleigh had left a unique and indelible musical legacy.[22]

When, on one extraordinarily hot summer night of no available cabs, he was forced to take a subway, violating Annalee's post-heart attack prohibition, Barney overwhelmed Donald Gratz, the metal fabricator, with the complete history of the New York City underground system; he explained that he chose to take the Independent line because it was deeper than the IRT, and so "cooler." Typically, Barney's arrival home was delayed by a detour for drink and continued conversation at Gratz's stop.[23]

When Friedman wrote "Whisper," a riff on Allen Ginsberg's "Howl," Barney gave a performance in his living room to an audience that included Krasner, Parsons, and the dealer David Herbert, "declaiming" the poem in the same tones he had used years earlier when reciting Racine on the train from Long Island.[24]

When the British-born artist and critic Andrew Hudson sat down to interview him for the *Washington Post*, they both became "very inebriated"—or Hudson did, as, in his eyes, Barney "showed no sign." It became "very jolly, very intimate and very exuberant," with Barney revealing "all sorts of juicy and gossipy and extravagant" things. Unfortunately for the readers of the *Post*, and for posterity, at the conclusion Barney "grabbed whatever the machine we were using and said 'Annalee will transcribe the tape.'"[25]

These episodes became as much the substance of the Newman legend as the work itself, because, exactly as was the case for the work, Barney's best self was in evidence when he had a live audience. And in the last ten years of his life the feeling was abundantly returned. "So many of us who knew Barney thought of Barney as our audience, of all the people you would want to see and comment on your work [it] would be Barney."[26] Sol LeWitt had Barney's obituary taped up on his studio wall. Saul Steinberg continued to "monologue with Barney" after his death.[27]

Liberman relied on Barney to help choose and hang the work for every show: he had a counterintuitive, but "very subtle feeling that the strongest painting should not be immediately visible" but should be happened upon "unexpectedly." Liberman tried "to learn from" from Barney, he "always subliminally hoped" he could "capture some of his magic . . . the wisdom, the mind, the depth of the mind, the sort of silent contained power . . . . [and] tremendous psychic energy." The two had long phone calls—"the longest conversations of my life with anybody"— virtually every night, about critics, openings, art. And, endlessly, technical matters. Barney would always end these by saying, "Alex, we've had a good visit." After Barney's death, Liberman continued his "wonderful conversations with Barney," but he didn't "get

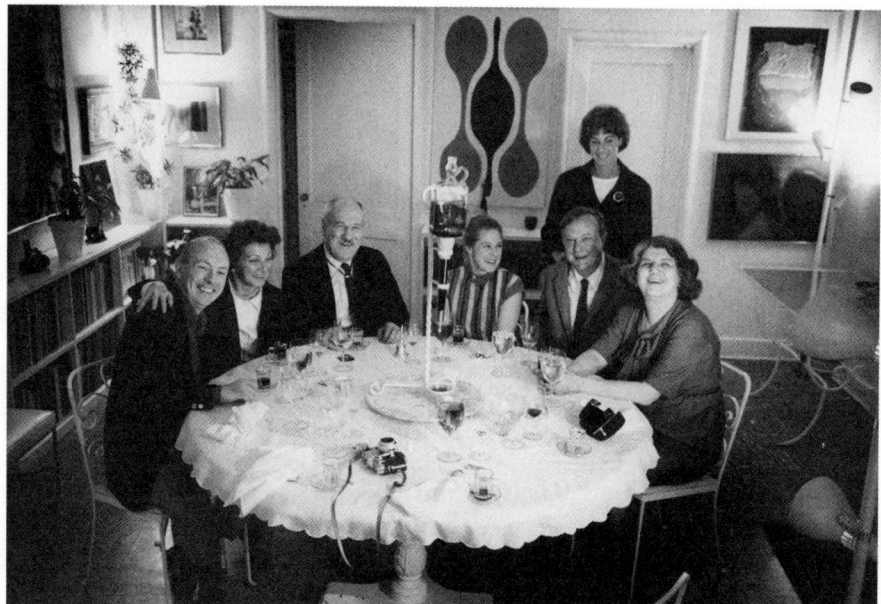

Fig. 42 Lunch at the Libermans. From left: Lawrence Alloway, Beatrice Leval, Barnett Newman, Sylvia Sleigh, Helen Frankenthaler (standing), Robert Motherwell, Annalee Newman. Photograph Alexander Liberman

his wonderful responses anymore." He considered Barney his "best friend" but he discovered that he was only "one of Barney's friends." That was how people felt with Barney, he gave them so much.[28]

The person with whom he did have a unique relationship in the last ten years of his life was Robert Murray. Murray and his wife moved to New York in September 1960, immediately after Barney and Annalee's ill-fated road trip. From Murray's respectful perspective, as someone who had met Barney at Emma Lake, a generationally structured situation, he couldn't call Barney the minute he got into town; he felt that the appropriate thing to do would be to "find an apartment and get settled, and then invite him over." But from Barney's affectionate perspective, knowing when Murray was supposed to arrive, he was immediately as concerned as any major domo—or parent—would be: he called the police "to see if there had been any accidents." When, shortly after, temporarily settled in the Madison Square Hotel, Murray finally phoned, the adventure that led to ten years of epic friendship began immediately.

"Where have you been? Why didn't you call? When did you get here?" And, "Look, we're going out to Jeanne Reynal and Tommy Sills place tonight. It's too late to have you invited to dinner, but I'm going to call Jeanne, and maybe you can have coffee and dessert. And then we can go out afterwards and have a drink." They had dessert surrounded by "de Kooning's *Pink Angel* . . . a whole bloody roomful of Gorkys, and on one wall an early Rothko and Barney's *Horizon Light*." Murray knew immediately that it was the painting they'd talked about in their conversation at Emma Lake.

After they left Reynal's, they went to a nearby bar. Finally, the Newmans dropped them off at the hotel. Within minutes the phone rang. "You remember that cab driver?" Barney asked. "You remember I asked him where he cabbed? Because he didn't seem to know Manhattan . . . . So I gave the guy your name," Barney continued, excited. "He's just been up to Saskatchewan to settle his brother's estate. A place called Wakaw. Now, didn't we drive past?"

"What do you mean you gave him my name?" Murray interrupted. "Well maybe you can recommend a lawyer." There ensued a long story: the brother lost a hotel he owned in a poker game. Murray recognized the tale, the man who won it was the father of someone he had introduced Barney to at a "very special Chinese restaurant" in Saskatoon. Barney "absolutely flipped." He called Murray back four times until dawn was breaking to have the story repeated, to get more details.[29]

That was only the beginning. Every time they would go somewhere, it seemed to Murray, there would be some similar experience. "Barney began to count on it"; or maybe, being Barney, he somehow *found* it.

For the next five years—until his wife gave birth to twins—Murray saw Barney nearly every day. And if he didn't see him they spoke on the phone. If something came up in the conversation that wanted clarification—the proper height of a stair riser, for example—a field trip, with tape measure, was arranged for the following day. Barney took him to openings, to restaurants; to the Woolworth Building, the Central Park Obelisk, and the Brooklyn Bridge; to baseball and hockey games, and Stillman's Gym. He gave Murray his own tickets to museum openings and debriefed him afterward over drinks. He introduced him to everyone he knew. When they visited artists' studios, as they so often did, Barney was always curious about their materials, how they prepared their canvases. It felt "like a couple of art students" jawing. Barney "never pulled rank."[30] And although Murray, in his late twenties and conscious of Barney's physical vulnerability, offered to help stretch and size canvases in the studio and, for example, with the installation of an 18-foot painting in a collector's home, Barney never once called him his assistant. He always introduced Murray as a sculptor. "It takes a sculptor to figure this out," he would say, acknowledging Murray's skill.[31]

During Murray's first winter in New York, Barney took him and his wife and George Franklin and his wife—a very attractive French model—to dinner at Sweet's. As often happened with Barney, they closed the place down. It was a bitter night. Saskatchewan blizzards with temperatures of 40 degrees below had not prepared Murray; he had never felt so cold in his life. But Barney insisted on a tour of the Fulton Fish Market's 1869 "Tin Building." They went out onto the off-limits pier where the trawlers came in. "Where are you out of?" Barney asked a fellow having a smoke beside the boat. "Gloucester," came the answer.

" 'No kidding,' Barney said, 'I used to have a friend who owned a sailboat up there.' " He fished through his wallet and found a Second World War pass to Gloucester Harbor. " 'Come on, you have to see the inside of one of these things,' " he said to the two young women, who went down the hatch, where there were four or five drunken sailors watching the sudden appearance of two attractive women in short skirts "descending the gangway into their abode." The men "thought the welcome wagon had arrived." In the semi-darkness, the French girl let out a blood-curdling scream, and up they shot "like two corks out of a bottle."

Barney had seen none of it. "He *chose* to see none of it"—not his freezing, shaking, terrified guests, not the drunken sailors. And, amazingly, magically, Murray recalled the whole episode not with anger or irritation, but with affection. "Dinner with Barney was always an adventure."[32]

If Barney was enjoying himself, he never wanted the night to end, he had no sense of time. What he had was a sense of ceremony. If the Murrays, who lived near Gramercy Park in the East Twenties, and the Newmans were going out together, Barney would insist that they come to West End Avenue and Ninety-Third Street first, have a drink, and then they would all travel back across the same territory to the final destination. He liked to begin an evening out by having everybody gather in his living room. It made them in a way his guests.

"Barney operates on Newman Standard Time," Murray once told Alloway, who, with his wife Sylvia Sleigh, knew well the experience of Barney talking and talking, taking no notice while waiters put the chairs on the table and donned their hats and coats. Alloway thought it was hilarious, and repeated it to Barney. "I'm always punctual!" Barney yelled at Murray when he phoned at one o'clock in the morning to ream him out.[33] Liberman was less flippant, but equally victimized by Barney's "different tempo," his "extraordinary slowness and sort of methodical approach." On the occasions when the Newmans were invited to one of the Liberman's dinners, it could take forty-five minutes to say goodbye to Barney after his "five, six, seven vodkas."

"He would stand on the landing, then he would start a conversation on the steps. Then he would talk in front of the front door."[34] It drove Tatiana mad. It drove her daughter, Francine du Plessix Gray, who "adored" Barney, mad. The Newmans would spend weekends in Connecticut with Francine and her husband, the painter Cleve Gray. "A uniquely brilliant and fascinating talker who was very fond of his vodka," Barney kept them up "way past midnight, engaging in soliloquies that ranged from Virgil to the development of American labor unions to Tintoretto's compositions, as Annalee hung on to her husband's words, saying 'Aha, Aha.'" When Gray, thinking of the early wake-up times of their two children, tried to end the night, Barney continued speaking "as he climbed up the stairs to the guest room, blowing kisses to us and saying 'more tomorrow! More tomorrow!'"[35]

It could be very difficult to arrange a lunch date with him, it could feel "like organizing an expedition to the North Pole." It was complicated, he had "things he had to resolve, and things that he had to figure out" before he knew whether it was going to be possible.[36] But once he would go to that lunch with a visitor it was like no other lunch, and by the time they left the restaurant would be setting up for dinner. Barney once explained to Murray that you only had your very best friends to your apartment, and you didn't have them to your studio if you were working, unless you had just finished a painting. And you didn't go casually to somebody else's studio. So bars and restaurants were the solution; and while they might have their own schedules, those were ignored if Barney were entertaining.[37]

Especially after his heart attack, he did not think about taxicabs as a luxury but as a basic convenience; he often treated them as he would a personal limousine. He would take a cab from West End Avenue, stop on East Twenty-Second Street to pick up Murray, go back West to Job Lot on Vesey Street to buy discount hardware or tools, and tell the cab driver, "just wait." He would justify this by telling people—like the Australian sculptor Clement Meadmore, who violently protested—"Well, it's hard to get a cab down here, you know?"[38]

Driving down Fifth Avenue in 1966 to see the *Stations of the Cross* at the Guggenheim, their cab driver, eavesdropping, pointed to a building and told Barney and Murray, "my boss took us in there to see a big painting."

"Is your boss [taxi fleet owner] Robert Scull?" Barney asked.

"Yeah."

"Who was the painter?"

"Oh, Rosencrantz and Guildenstern—something like that."

Barney and Murray understood that he was referring to James Rosenquist, whose *F-111* Scull had loaned to the Jewish Museum some months earlier. When they arrived at the Guggenheim, Barney said, like he always did, "Just leave the meter running. Come in and see *my* work."

This was typical: as long as it was not written by a critic, as long as it was not in print, he believed he could discover things about his paintings through someone else's observations. He craved people's reactions to his work. "Never assume you know who your audience is," he would say to Murray.[39]

For the 1961 World Series between the New York "Yanks" and the Cincinnati "Reds" (a Cold War-era dream)—the end of the magical season in which Mickey Mantle and Roger Maris had chased Babe Ruth's home-run crown—Barney got a television set, set it up on a card table in his living room, and ordered a case of Trommers beer from Brooklyn. Although he never drank anything but vodka after the heart attack, he told his guests, "you gotta drink a bottle of beer when you're watching a ballgame."[40]

He liked the companionship, but equally, he liked "giving his version of events to people that were in town as newcomers"—particularly English newcomers. "He liked to be a sort of guiding light. He had his own view of the way things were, and he liked being able to get impressionable people. He was always ready for a drink and a chat." And the young people and visitors liked "his manner and his mannerisms; they were what they thought of as 'old fashioned America.' He made them feel as though they were in touch with H.L. Mencken's American."[41]

"How do you get to Carnegie Hall?" asked the out-of-towner. "Practice, practice," answered the New York native.

From his days working at Abraham Newman & Son, when he wrote his ode to lower Manhattan, New York was his great love and project. When he moved his home or his studio, when he read about a site being threatened with destruction or alteration—City Hall Park, Belmont racetrack, the Produce Exchange building, the East River waterfront, and later the cast-iron buildings of SoHo for the planned lower Manhattan Expressway—he collected brochures, historical documents, news reports. He wrote letters. Since he was, it often happened, one step ahead of the wrecking ball descending on his neighborhood, preservation became for him another *personal* cause, like civil service had been, like irresponsible critics had been, like museums' distortion of history had been, like non-geometric abstract art was.

In 1960, one catastrophically poised wrecking ball was stopped, and Barney found a way to share in the victory.

Three years earlier it was announced that historic Carnegie Hall would be demolished by its new owner in spring 1959, with construction of its replacement slated for late 1960. The design for the mixed-use office building was shocking as depicted in *Life*: a 44-story bright-red porcelain-paneled monolith. The drawing showed the narrow Fifty-Sixth Street side in shadow—a full-length, darker red, "zip," a coincidental, monstrous caricature of Barney's 1950 *Eve*.[42]

Carnegie Hall was considered by most New Yorkers to be a "consecrated house," filled with memories of great artists and great performances in the minds of three generations—including, vividly, Barney and Annalee's. Not only did it have a concert auditorium with what was widely acknowledged to have among the best acoustics in the world, a recital hall, and a basement theater; it was also home to 193 artists' and eccentrics' living and working studios, among them those with ghosts of Isadora Duncan, Charles Dana Gibson, Jan Paderewski, Enrico Caruso, and the more recent fingerprints of Marlon Brando and Marilyn Monroe. But by the beginning of 1960, even as public opposition to the demolition ballooned, eviction proceedings had begun. The saga was an epic New York City battle that was closely covered by the press that Barney—now subscribing to the *New York Mirror* as well as his *Times* and *Tribune*—combed through daily.

Most of the tenants lost their leases, but the building not only escaped demolition, it was brilliantly restored. On September 26, Mayor Robert Wagner cut through a blue-and-gold ribbon and invited the public in at the ceremony marking the rededication of Carnegie Hall. The following night Leonard Bernstein led the New York Philharmonic with Isaac Stern, who led the preservation effort, as violin soloist. And four days later, on September 30, in the midst of the Canaday confabulations with his new coterie, Barney made a two-month security deposit for a three-year lease on studio 910 in the Carnegie Hall Studios.

Twenty-four years earlier, Barney had dadaistically challenged Fiorello LaGuardia for the mayoralty of New York City. Now, *Fiorello!*, a musical comedy based on the Little Flower's life was a hit on Broadway, and Barney was in Carnegie Hall with his own mythology. How satisfying it must have been. For the first time he was making real money—more than Annalee. This was a colossal change in their lives: in 1960 his income from sales of art was 16,000 dollars while Annalee earned 6300 dollars from two teaching jobs. If he felt "forsaken," he could also feel vindicated. He had a place in what was then the most glamorous cultural address, across the street from the Art Students League where it had all begun for him, next door to the Russian Tea Room where the city's elite culturati lunched and where Barney now opened a house account. He had an elevator and could nap on his cot before the evening activities of Fifty-Seventh Street gallery openings or opera or theater.

Like his timeless Cavanagh hats, like his solid Jaguar sedan, like the steadfast Annalee, there was in Carnegie Hall something abiding. It suited him. It was, in a word, his style. In his life choices he risked nothing, so that he felt able, in his art, to risk everything.

What exactly was there to be risked?

Abstract Expressionism was "currently by far the most favored style of contemporary American painting." It was confirmed by the hip but suavely aloof *New Yorker* in a profile of the dealer Sidney Janis, who represented a "veritable pantheon of contemporary Americana," several of them "Abstract Expressionists" whose exponential price increases the article tracked: Baziotes, de Kooning, Gorky, Gottlieb, Guston, Kline, Motherwell, Pollock, and Rothko.[1]

Accurate or not, the November 1960 magazine described a situation in which "clients whip out their checkbooks." Janis's "American painters are so popular with collectors that most of them cannot, or will not, produce fast enough to meet the demand." Some had "become so well-to-do that their output is governed not only by their inner necessity but by a far more mundane force, the income tax." Even the U.S government, "through its tax laws"—which allowed the donor of a painting to a tax-exempt institution to deduct its full value, pay no capital-gains tax, and retain lifetime rights while the value rose—was "one of the current art boom's staunchest supporters." Indeed, the author surmised, "there may be some collectors of Abstract Expressionist paintings whose chief concern is not artistic merit at all." He made much of Janis's May 1959 show of de Kooning's paintings, which sold out, "the lot bringing well over a hundred thousand."[2]

Milton Resnick dreamt he was "in a police lineup." Speaking at The Club on New Year's Day 1961, he continued, "I am innocent but everyone I see is in uniform. They have hard faces. Here are the questions they ask me. Am I real? Am I committed? Involved? Passionate? Do I have experiences? By this time I have a guilty look . . . . Where do I go summers? In what gallery do I show? Am I a new artist? There are more questions but I give up."

The session was entitled "Attack," in response to "Why Fight It?"—the Janis profile—and also to Rosenberg's "Literary Form and Social Hallucination," a Brandeis lecture published the previous fall in *Partisan Review*.[3] The "downtown" artists were furious about what they found to be inaccuracies and innuendos in current press coverage. What had the descriptions to do with their lives? "Ten years ago," Resnick said, the only thing he "felt illegal about was that I lived in a loft." His long-range plan had been to paint pictures that "had something to do with the future"—open, "free." Now he was confronted by the question posed in *Partisan Review*: "How can art be true if it is used by the state and by *Time* and by *Life*?" And he was forced to "feel so bad" by a "system worked out in another magazine by which they can grade or tell which came first and who did whatever it is they did."

"They don't say what anyone ever really did," Resnick complained; he "never found out what someone was supposed to have done. But they have a list" that determined who were the imitators, because those imitators were despised for "cashing in." Resnick had been called an "imitator."

Reinhardt, picking up the ball, pointed to the artists' share of responsibility. It was easy to complain that professional painting had "become a racket like every other racket, a business like every other business." But the "worst thing" he could imagine was "the artist as company man."

The evening dissolved into an ugly shouting match. Resnick, Reinhardt, Hess, de Kooning, and several others argued about the relationship among institutions and critics and artists, about the artists who permitted *Life* to treat their work "as pictures of flames, girders, grasses and sunsets," about those who "practically made a career out of 'Me 'n' Pollock,'" about selling, about the meanings a work of art accrues after it leaves the artist's hand, about *corruption*.[4]

Many in the audience came from a new generation of "downtown" artists, a group that was "very small from one point of view, but enormous underneath the few who rose to the top." There were "loads" of these artists who occupied the old real estate but with a new sense of community. They shared visits with their kids, were involved with different institutions (like nursery schools), and clustered around the Tenth Street cooperative galleries scene—Tanager, Hansa, Camino, Nonagon. They thought Barney's monocle off-putting; they didn't see the point of his feud with Reinhardt, which appeared unnecessary and sad.[5] But if Resnick and Reinhardt's complaints seemed poignant and nostalgic, to some, like Greenberg, the younger downtowners seemed provincial. "If Eighth Street in the late thirties and early forties meant catching up with Paris, Tenth Street in the fifties has seen New York falling behind itself."[6]

On at least one issue, however, the painters could find common cause.

At this moment, the concern with—the *fixation* on—corruption was urgently felt to be *the* pressing problem.[7] A panel at the Camino, "Corruption in the Arts," devised by gallery director David Rosenberg (Harold's brother) and moderated by Regina Bogat, Reinhardt, and Carl Holty, was mobbed. The subject was "on everybody's minds because money was starting to pour into the gallery system. Artists were selling, and everybody was very uncomfortable or jealous or both" about the ethical implications. That evening, voicing a theory that had become prevalent in the art community, Holty specifically blamed women: they "did not want to be so poor, and urged their husbands to paint in a way that would make the paintings sell."[8]

Away from both the angry and the earnest downtown scenes, while the battle was taking place on New Year's Day at The Club, Barney was uptown, enjoying champagne and nougat. As much as the agony of having been misunderstood in the period between 1948 and 1952 persisted, he operated in a second, parallel world; the risk with which *he* was concerned was the same one he had faced in 1946 and in 1956: to "bravely abandon" the "securities of familiar pictorial geometries" in favor "of untested pictorial intuitions," as one scholar wrote that February.[9] A suggestion that he might be influenced by Still inspired simple rage; a suspicion that Barney himself was an "imitator" of a Newman "style" was soul-searing, *unbearable*.

The doubt defiantly manifested itself as he confronted the 81 linear feet of 10-foot-high cotton duck that had been delivered to his Carnegie Hall studio at the end of October.[10] The terrifying prospect was to paint in a "total state of beginning again," not to "do something which I've [already] done." What had to be avoided at all costs was repeating himself, "making myself into a cliché."

"I don't believe that painting is a product . . . and I don't think I'm a product," he told an interviewer in 1963, when he had achieved the dubious honor of being as "marketable" as the artists included in the Janis profile, "although some people are beginning to move towards me as if I *am* a product." *That* had become one of his "troubles."[11]

A cynical observer could be forgiven for thinking this was disingenuous, that, of course, Barney "repeated himself." But, unlike Hess's satirical "Mr. Mensch," who *became* a different person in order to make work, Barney had to *find* himself, psychologically, in a different place for each painting. At times he actually had to *be* in a different place to find the different emotional place; this was one of the reasons he accumulated studios.[12] If he felt a painting was a copy of a "Newman" it was "dead" for him; what made a successful painting was, "to a certain extent a kind of miraculous event." Not religious, precisely, more like the extreme emotion, the extreme self-awareness that could result from some forms of meditation, during which "one is in the presence of a kind of presence [of] oneself," the "heightened feeling that I [have] said or done something that is extremely true to my way of thinking, so that I have a sense of being, a sense of vividness."[13]

Sometimes a canvas would reflect back to him the emotion in so intense a form that it was almost unendurable. Such an instance occurred toward the end of his life, when, in a section of the spare bedroom on West End Avenue, behind a purple curtain that he had hung for privacy, he worked on the painting known as *Yellow Edge*—93 ¾ by 79 inches of black acrylic with a vulnerably thin strip of yellow at the far right. It was as if the darkest night had almost swallowed completely life-giving sunlight, the last moment before a total eclipse. While Barney was alive no one else, not even Annalee, set eyes on it, so potent was its effect on Barney.

In the final months of 1960 Barney's social and professional calendar was bursting: Canaday protest organizing meetings with de Kooning, Sandler, Hess, and Rosenberg; lunches and dinners with Murray, Smith, Heller, Ellin, Kulicke, and Robert and Ethel Scull—young collectors who were on the scene buying Kline, de Kooning, and Rothko; late night pow-wows with gallerist Lawrence Rubin at Reuben's Deli on Fifty-Eighth Street; Monday-night fights with Krasner and her sometime companion British dealer David Gibbs at the St. Nicholas Arena on West Sixty-Sixth Street; country weekends with the Sculls on Long Island or with the Grays in Connecticut.

If Barney's boldness was habitual, the more comfortable reception it now received in more estimable quarters was new. "It is so necessary to correct the half-cocked conclusions, even of the great" he wrote to Schapiro, regarding the latter's 1956 "Leonardo and Freud: An Art-Historical Study," which Schapiro had recently sent to Barney.[14] "I have always considered Picasso an autobiographical painter. But your analysis of him as an occasional painter, the 'painter-laureate' makes the point so much sharper. Nowhere have I seen so beautiful a statement of the trivia of his subject matter. When he is personal, he is banal. When his subject is 'important,' he is making journalistic comments on the political issues of our time," he opined to Alloway.[15] He was invited by the *Second Coming*, a small but highly regarded journal, to write his "reminiscences and opinions about the New York School in its early days."

James Elliot, the assistant chief curator at the nascent Los Angeles County Museum of Art, who had been overwhelmed on his Ellin-engineered visit to Barney's studio, strategized about mounting a Newman show for the museum's new home.[16] "I told him that his Museum would have a real scoop by staging your first major museum show," Ellin wrote to Barney, "and that I thought that you might be receptive to the idea if properly approached."[17] And, "everybody" in London wanted a show "so badly." Alloway, urging Barney to come to England to capitalize on his popularity, began planning itineraries and a lecture schedule.[18]

Commercial interest in Europe, too, was heating up—and with it, precisely the momentum and competition that fed many of the artists' fears about their work morphing into mere "product." The dealer Lawrence Rubin, brother of William Rubin (who had purchased *Prometheus Bound*), had been negotiating with Barney the previous January, establishing himself as an agent on behalf of clients in Germany and France, and galleries in Italy and England and Switzerland.[19] Dipping his toe into the Newman waters, he bought and resold *By Twos*—the 1949 work that was reproduced upside down in *Art International*—to E. J. Power. He cultivated European clients for Barney's paintings, and began arrangements for a show (never realized) at the Morsbroich Museum near Cologne.[20] Now, in his new Galerie Lawrence in Paris he expected to show Barney's work "as an opener," expected all of Barney's pictures to be for sale "during the entire round of the european [*sic*] capitals," and made the unfounded assumption—given Barney's known antipathy to such ceding of power—that he was the artist's "exclusive dealer in Europe for the next two years at least."[21]

Reeling from the sudden death of his own brother, George, Barney was "shocked at the presumption." Based on intercessionary conversations with Bill Rubin, during which he felt "bull[ied]," he deduced that the "exclusive" was Bill's idea and did not serve Barney's interests but was a bullet to be dodged. Venting his anger in multiple—unsent—letters, Barney fulminated: he saw Larry's loyalty divided between his painter and his brother ("your art counselor") and Bill's divided among the many parts of himself: "collector, art historian, big brother, and dealer." It was an "emotional triangle" that was "bound to fail."[22] He canceled the exhibition and connection with the gallery.

Barney himself had sold two works to the London dealer Gibbs—who had recently left Arthur Tooth for Marlborough—in an arrangement that did not include Rubin, for 9,000 dollars each, one and a half times their prices when shown at French & Company.[23] This was the price level Barney *thought* Larry Rubin had agreed to, but found to be otherwise. Now, Rubin's sale of *Tundra* to the major Belgian collector Philippe Dotremont (twenty works from his collection were shown at the Guggenheim Museum in 1959) was at risk of becoming a sacrificial victim of the standoff. Ultimately, the billing was finessed to accommodate the purchaser, Rubin, and Barney's new price level.[24]

He was flush with money. On January 22, 1961, the *Los Angeles Times* reported in its "Art News" column that "An 18-ft. canvas by New York abstractionist Barnett Newman has been sold to collector Ben Heller for $35,000" ($356,675 in 2023)—nearly as much as Yankee Roger Maris's new, Most-Valuable-Player contract. "This is the highest price ever paid for a painting by a living contemporary American painter, according to the artist's West Coast representative, Everett Ellin. Williem [*sic*] De Kooning previously held the record with $18,000 for one of his abstractions."

Although neither involved with the sale nor Barney's exclusive representative, Ellin, an engineer and lawyer who had previous stints at Columbia Pictures and the William Morris Agency, happened to be in New York the week of the announcement, where Barney saw him several times. Whether by coincidence or calculation, this public relations coup could not have come at a better moment. Four days earlier, a 54-work retrospective of Mark Rothko's oeuvre—culminating, according to the press release, in eleven never-exhibited "dark red" murals from the Four Seasons restaurant commission—opened at MoMA. As Barney and the group censuring the biased Canaday continued to refine and polish the letter that would be published a month later, the very critic who was their target, on the very day of the *Vir Heroicus Sublimis* sale announcement, wrote about Rothko that "The phenomenon of giantism in contemporary painting may sometimes be only a bid for attention . . . but Rothko is one of those painters to whose art large size is intrinsic . . . . During the last two years he has increasingly . . . reduced the contrasts in his paintings toward the point of lowest visibility."[25]

Although the sale was not completed until early 1963, *Vir Heroicus Sublimis* was already hanging in Heller's new Central Park West apartment in January 1961. The installation, immediately before a large party, was a production worthy of Barney's bent for "solemnizing" events. The painting had been removed from its stretcher and rolled on an 18-inch by 12-foot tube from a builders' hardware company in Queens; the windows of Heller's living room were removed and the painting-wrapped tube hoisted up by a winch on the roof. Once inside, the canvas was restretched on the floor by Barney in vest and loosened tie, Murray and Franklin, with Annalee, frantic about his health, fluttering and yelling. Later, at the reception, the champagne was red. It felt to Barney like Heller was "crowning it with laurel."[26]

In a room already hung with Pollock's *One* and *Blue Poles*, and Barney's *Adam*, Heller's first reaction was "expansive": the work "enlarged everything, the space, the world around it." He reported to Barney that all of the guests, and all of the people working at the party, were "quite involved" with it, and did not question whether or not it was "art." To which the painter, in his newfound security, responded, "I have always had intelligent and passionate response on the part of people. It has always been the art experts who think they should know the subject and what is good for the public who have always given me a hard time."

FORTY-EIGHT

"MR. NEWMAN, WHY DO YOU PAINT?"

The torch had been passed to a new generation. The televised Nixon–Kennedy presidential campaign debates thrust into the foreground charm, charisma, and personality, and the election of a 43-year-old with a young family, an excitingly fresh postwar style, an interest in high culture, and an atmosphere of optimism and promise reinforced the new direction taken by events in Barney's life. To his youthful posse of Murray, Holstein, and their families, he added the young painter Cleve Gray and his wife, Francine du Plessix, the stepdaughter of Liberman. They met Barney at a dinner given by Betty Parsons's nephew, William Raynor, and now were included in ritualized whiskey sour-, scallops- and monologue-dinners at Sweet's.[1] The Grays' home in Connecticut became the site of ritualized birdwatching.

Again Tony Smith, teaching at Bennington—which encouraged instructors to take a personal interest in students—stepped up, sending to Barney a short-term studio assistant. Barbara Marcus, as Smith described her, was "an odd type who intended to work in the circus as a clown," during her non-resident term, but needed to fill a gap in her schedule before that job became available. She was also interested in painting and architecture, and she told Smith, as he wrote to Barney, that she wanted "to make a building that could be perceived at once as a whole and in all its aspects 'like a painting by Barnett Newman.'" Smith thought Barney would "like this girl," because she was, in addition to being energetic, pure, warm, good-humored, and dependable, "screwy . . . a kind of angel." He thought she would "take the heat off a little." Barney was smitten. Both he and Annalee loved Marcus, and formed an intense familial bond with the first unattached young woman to enter their orbit.[2]

Whatever else Marcus did in the studio it is clear that *listening* to him, as had the painters at Emma Lake, was her most important contribution. They talked about life, about the regard of others, about the self-congratulatory exclusivity of "circles."[3] As he had with Alan Power, he continued the lectures in correspondence. "In discussing the 'circle' what I tried to bring out was the fact that in all walks of life there are the 'bright talkers' who aren't much at doing."

"I did not mean for you to avoid [circles]—rather the opposite—to enter into them for what they are worth and to talk with the self-confidence of your own abilities. The issue is not to find a place there, that would be submitting to the herd, but to hold your own so that you will be respected for what you are. That you do not find favor is not important. Do not confuse love with respect." He sent her a copy of Turgenev's *The Life of a Sportsman*, the "moral" of which "is not to [be] bullied by the clever tongues."[4] When she returned to Bennington, where Barney was "admired greatly," Marcus reported that she found her status among other students raised "about 100%."[5]

Over the next year "Mr. Newman" wrote to her of his triumphs and disappointments, relying on this extremely young woman's praise and commiseration. He developed a worthy disciple: reading his early Northwest Coast Indian Painting catalogue, she could hear his voice. "In one swift motion you do away with painters like de Kooning, in fact you do away with all these people ('toymakers' and 'women') who call themselves painters, but are instead the imitators and parasites, the wolves in sheep's clothing who depend on and live from the men who possess and create '. . . the awesome feelings felt before the terror of the unknowable.'"[6] He so counted on her naïve regard that, at the thought of her working elsewhere for her next non-resident term, he called to offer to pay her to work for him.[7]

With Marcus's help (and probably Murray's), he stretched the biggest canvas—114 by 174 inches[8]—he had yet challenged at the Front Street studio. Then he waited for the physical encounter to inspire him.

On Wednesday, February 1, the thirteenth day of blizzards and brutally frigid weather, a day that Ham the chimpanzee rocketed into space, and Black demonstrators in the South were arrested *en masse* for marking the first anniversary of lunch counter sit-ins, and the impending trial in Jerusalem of Adolf Eichmann for crimes against humanity filled the newspapers, and the appointment of Thomas Messer as director of the Guggenheim Museum occupied the minds of art worlders, 54-year-old George Newman collapsed while getting into his car in Manhattan Beach, Brooklyn, and died of a heart attack. Only three days earlier, while Barney was strategizing

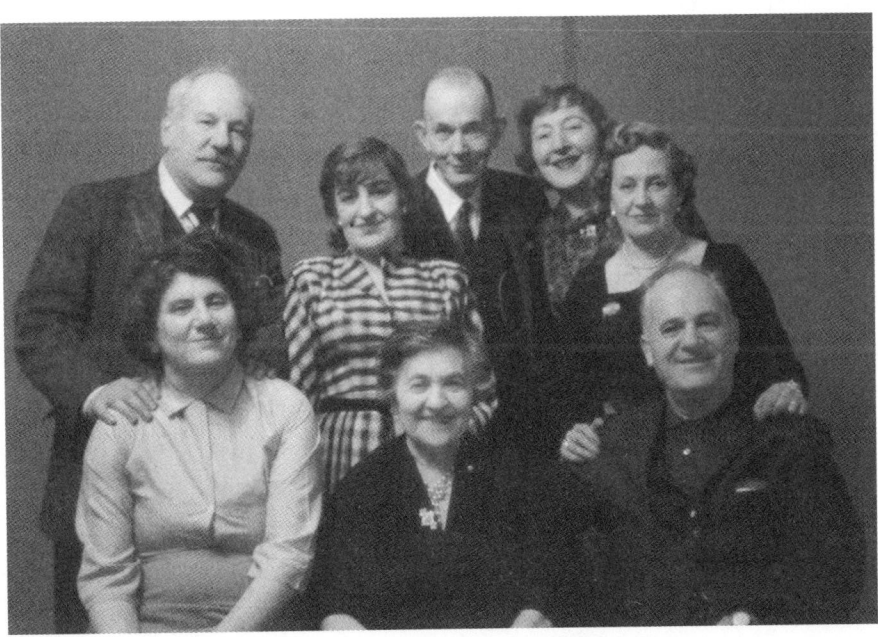

Fig. 43 The Newman family, 1960. Back, from left: Barney, Sarah, Philip Master (Gertrude's husband), Gertrude ("Goldie"), Ethel (George's wife). Front, from left: Annalee, Anna, George

with Ellin on West End Avenue, George had phoned to wish his brother a happy 56th birthday. But on Thursday, with the temperature dipping below zero and under pressure to beat the imminent strike of workers in Jewish cemeteries, George's funeral took place in Coney Island.

The rug had been pulled out from under Barney. Behind all of his socializing and public performance, he was a family man, sustaining and sustained by his relationships, especially with Sarah and his mother, but also the connections with George and Goldie. Now, after his own heart attack, and the death from the same of Abraham, he was compelled to face his own mortality. Barney placed an obituary—not simply a death notice—in Thursday's *Times*.

In mourning and depressed, Barney went shakily on. In mid-February, in a cab with Annalee and Murray on the way to fulfill a commitment to lecture at Pratt, he was in another fender-bender. Ashen-faced, he sat at the front of the room and lowered his head onto his hands, visibly distressed. Finally, a young man broke the silence and asked, "Mr. Newman, Why do you paint?"

"Well, I once composed a symphony because I wanted something to listen to," Barney responded. "And I paint for pretty much the same reason."[9]

An unanticipated but not unfortunate consequence came to pass from the chronological proximity of George's death and the lecture at Pratt, where Cleve Gray was beginning to experiment with lithography[10] under the guidance of master printer Arnold Singer. By late February, Barney was able to conduct his affairs, but completely stalled in his painting. Since his own recovery, four of the future *Stations of the Cross* paintings had been completed, as well as two other black-oil-on-exposed-canvas works, the larger *White Fire II* and the small *Treble*: the first a symmetrical declaration of strength and grandeur, the second a delicate, intimate whispered question. Now it seemed impossible to get back to the work.[11] Regularly checking in with Barney to take his emotional temperature, Gray hit upon the idea of inviting him to the Pratt studio. After non-committal visits to the workshop, Barney had lithographic stones sent to his apartment.[12] In the spring, after a battle between his will and the new medium's non-negotiable characteristics—the obdurate stone, the oily crayon, the "inevitable white margins,"[13] Barney created the first three prints—other than the despised batiks from 1940—in his career. On three different sizes of paper he continued his exploration in the endless cosmos of blackness on white, and struggled to discover, with greasy ink, crayon, and stone, a new universe, a way his demarcated areas—he had not yet begun to call them "zips"—could function within a galaxy limited by a *border*. Over the next nine years he would make two more particularly productive excursions into the territory of printmaking.

"I felt as if approaching the very residence of the Deity; the tears started into my eyes; and I remained, for moments after . . . in that delicious absorption which pious enthusiasm alone can produce.

"I pity the man who can coldly sit down to write a description of these ineffable wonders."[14]

Robert Rosenblum, writing about Abstract Expressionism, invoked the words of an early 19th-century Irish Romantic poet who gazed upon Niagara Falls. It was one of the earliest instances of 1958's "New American Painting" being treated almost retrospectively, *historically*, as other approaches to painting filled most of the growing number of galleries, and fascination with market forces was ascendant.

Rosenblum had been spending long evenings of "good food, good drink, & good conversation" with Barney since he wrote about him for a French audience in 1958.[15] In his landmark essay in the February issue of *Art News*, the young associate professor of art history at Princeton rehabilitated the "esthetic category" of the Sublime—Longinus, Burke's "obscurity," Kant's "boundlessness"—as it "suddenly acquire[d] fresh relevance in the face of the most astonishing summits of pictorial heresy attained in America in the last fifteen years." The nature of this heresy he called "The Abstract Sublime," and Barney was its "fourth master," along with Still, Rothko, and Pollock.

As in certain paintings of the earlier period—like those of Turner—enormity alone did not suffice; the effect also required "bewildering structure . . . outside the intelligible boundaries of esthetic law." Barney explored a "realm of sublimity so perilous that it defies comparison with even the most adventurous Romantic explorations into sublime nature." *Vir Heroicus Sublimis* "puts us before a void as terrifying, if exhilarating, as the arctic emptiness of the tundra," the terrain he had a "strong desire to visit," to be surrounded by four horizons in a "total surrender to spatial infinity." Likewise, in its "passionate reduction of pictorial means," *Vir Heroicus Sublimis* achieved "a simplicity as heroic and sublime as the protagonist of its title."[16]

Inspired by Barney's disquisitions, appearing within days of his brother's death, the analysis only reinforced Barney's "terrifying" void. But within a few months, the impact of the praise enabled Barney to rise to the "exhilarating" heroism. Notwithstanding his recent depression, he met the battle when the prodigiously learned, eminent art historian of Netherlandish and Italian Renaissance art, Erwin Panofsky—a man with his own god-like stature in scholarly circles— noticed a caption error in Rosenblum's article: "*Sublimus*" instead of "*Sublimis*." The contretemps, which continued over five months, has become one of the most enduring anecdotes about Barney.

An eminent faculty member of the Institute of Advanced Study in Princeton, Panofsky was not a close follower of contemporary art. His primary area of study was iconology, the interpretation of symbols and historical meaning in works of art, with a focus on the Northern and Italian Renaissance. He was sent a copy of the February *Art News* because in it the art historian and philosopher George Kubler reviewed Panofsky's *Renaissance and Renascences in Western Art*, something that made Panofsky "a little uneasy," he wrote in a letter that appeared in April, because "his kind words seem to encourage contemporary artists to read my book [whereas] it is really directed only to what a less well-meaning colleague has called 'the pedants.'"

Panofsky continued: "Conversely, I find it increasingly hard to keep up with contemporary art, particularly with the titles affixed to some of the objects." Like Hess ten years earlier, he wouldn't call them paintings. "A signal example has appeared . . . where Mr. Barnett Newman's composition is entitled *Vir Heroicus Sublimus*." He found himself "confronted with three different interpretations of the curious form 'Sublimus': does Mr. Newman imply that he, as Aelfric says of God, is 'above grammar'; or is it a misprint; or is it plain illiteracy?" He signed the letter "In the optimistic assumption that the first of these possible interpretations is true."

Barney would answer virtually anyone about almost anything, but this was particularly irresistible: Professor Panofsky suggesting Barney considered himself, like God, above the rules. It mattered not that the typo in the caption had absolutely nothing to do with Barney. The opportunity to shine in such venerated—such *sublime*—company, at a moment when Barney could be witty and highhanded instead of embarrassingly bitter, was too delicious to pass up. And it did not hurt that the magazine's executive editor, Hess (unlike during the exchange with Crehan), and Schapiro (with a long history of indulging Panofsky's delicate one-upmanship in the most arcane scholarly personal correspondence) were now in Barney's camp, egging him on.[17] They were in the thick of the Canaday caper and Panofsky was Canaday's friend and ally. It all came together symphonically, with Schapiro conducting.[18]

Readers might have been forgiven for seeing in the letter that Barney wrote yet another instance of his thin skin. Lacking a familiarity with typical exchanges between Panofsky and Schapiro, they would have missed entirely the droll satiric performance, the opportunity for Schapiro to have a little fun at the master's expense. For example, in 1946:

Dear Meyer,

Many thanks for your note! I'm afraid, however, that your quotations do not quite fill the bill. What interests me is the application of the adjective Gothic to the representational arts within the context of such writings as apply the adjective to the specific period of mediaeval architecture which we thus designate . . . . (In spite of the reference to Jean de Bruge, who, likewise serves only as an exemplum of an antiquated, pre-Renaissance style), and in the dissertation by Paillot de Montabert the term is probably used for a style antedating even the Middle Ages in the narrower sense of the term, that is to say to the "Barbarian", pre-Carolingian phase . . . . in keeping with Mabillon's and Felibien's usage who designate the self-portrait of Airardus on the bronze doors of St. Denis . . . .

But many thanks and cordial wishes! Pan[19]

And, in 1961, at the very moment Schapiro was sending Barney "sublimus" ammunition:[20]

Dear Meyer,

You are really an amazing man! Only you could have fished out that reference to Galileo from Bernardin de St. Pierre . . . . The agreement between Rousseau's thought and Galileo's is indeed remarkable, all the more so since we can safely discard the possibility of Rousseau's having known the Galileo letter which, so far as I know, remained unpublished until it appeared in the Edizione Nazionale.[21]

And so Barney would write a letter to the editor—Hess—of *Art News*: "I feel compelled to initiate a clinic in remedial reading." Professor Panofsky's difficulty in reading "requires more than a reprimand. He needs repudiation and disciplining." (This last sentence was cut when the letter was published.)

Had Panofsky read the article, it would have been obvious to him that it is a misprint . . . . Only in the caption is it "Sublimus."

Were I to follow the Panofskian dialectic, I could charge that he is above reading the text, or that he did not read, or that he cannot read. I shall not, however, stoop to the Panofskian techniques in order to hope that the third of these is true. I shall be generous enough to believe that he attacked me without reading the text.

"However," Barney was not done.

What I wish to do here is to defend Art News' use of the word, "sublimus." It is important to make clear that Art News printed a misprint but that the magazine did not commit an error.

Ernout and A. Meillet, the authorities on Latin etymology, in their famous dictionary on the subject, give "sublimus" as a collateral form (Doublet archaique). This fact can be verified in other dictionaries. Of particular importance is the fact that "sublimus" was used by the Roman poet Accius (170–86 B.C.) who is quoted using this construction, by Cicero.

It is not for me to argue over Panofsky's Latin. It is enough to point out that he does not know quite as much as he thinks he does. He should, therefore, be flunked not only for bad research but also for poor scholarship.

What is left is the mark he can get for effort. It is sad to find that Panofsky, who claims to be a scholar engaged in the discovery of truth, hopes instead to find arrogance and evil. [This irresponsible hope for an obscene delight instead of truth] This violation of the ethic of science, must, it seems to me, make his scholarly findings suspect.

As for the matter of Aelfric, the tenth century monk had a greater sensitivity for the meaning of the act of creation than does Panofsky. One would think that by now Prof. Panofsky would know the basic fact about a work of art, that for a work of art to be a work of art, it must rise above grammar and syntax—*pro Gloria Dei.*[22]

No one treated the 69-year-old Panofsky in that way. "Mr. Barnett Newman's letter . . . referring to a personal communication which was printed without my knowledge or consent—assaults not only me (which I don't mind) but also the Latin language; and this I do mind," he answered in the letters column.

"Sublimus," was indeed a correct, but *archaic* form, he agreed, but it could be used only literally, not metaphorically, and "it habitually precedes, rather than follows, the governing noun." Panofsky listed several such examples. If he were shown a "classical author" using the form as the typo had it (and as Barney argued it could be used) he should "be glad to think of Mr. Newman as a PICTOR SUBLIMUS."[23]

"At the time of the publication of my [first] letter, I was aware (and so were the Editors of *Art News*) of the complete list of allusions that Dr. Panofsky has suddenly found in Kuhner's Latin grammar," Barney shot back of Panofsky's "attempt to impress with his erudition."

He was enjoying himself, as correspondence among himself, Hess, and Schapiro makes clear. Now, he would refute what he said was Panofsky's "fabricated . . . Darwinian theory of linguistic evolution" by applying it to English.

If someone were to use the work "shoppe" instead of "shop," as for example in a shopkeeper's sign as . . . "Haberdasher Shoppe," Dr. Panofsky would argue that the word "shoppe" is not correct grammatical English. If one proved to him that the spelling was classic because both "shoppe" and "haberdassher" occur in Chaucer's Canterbury Tales, he would insist that Chaucer never used them *together* and challenge you to prove that he did. And his original issue of grammar would suddenly become an issue of style. I am certain that if it could be proved that they *were* used together, Dr. Panofsky would then argue that "haberdassher" in Chaucer's time was spelled with two s's so that the question of rhetoric and style would suddenly, in order for him to win the argument, again become a problem of spelling. And yet according to Dr. Panofsky's theory, phrases like "coffee shoppe" and "gifte shoppe" would not only be grammatically correct but high style.

The whole argument was beneath both men; Barney mocking just the sort of intellectualism that he himself aspired to and revered.[24] But he did have a point that he wanted to make, and finally, after his college-quad-bully performance, he made it. What was at stake was Panofsky's "attempt to deny the artist's right to create poetic language, the right of '*potestas audendi.*' "[25]

How different is the attitude of the great Otto Jespersen, who says: "This is one of the reasons that impel poets to use *archaic* words; they are 'new' just on account of their being old." . . . .

The issue is simple. My use of the Latin "*sublimis*" is correct. The *Art News* use of "*sublimus*" is also correct. Dr. Panofsky's attack was unwarranted and unbecoming. Nothing that he writes now changes matters. Yet I hope that he is not convinced for to be called "*Pictor sublimis*" *or* "*sublimus*" by one who has consistently shown himself to be unfeeling towards any work of art since Dürer is too much. If Dr. Panofsky had really read Prof. Rosenblum's article, he would have found that I have already been so named.[26]

FORTY-NINE

PROMETHEUS BOUND

In the months following George's death, instead of painting Barney managed his growing career. Heller had possession of *Vir Heroicus Sublimis* but the formal contract was not signed until May, and the final payments were not made until two years later. The Sculls wanted *L'Errance*, a large, exceptionally sensual blue and red painting; the cost was 7,000 dollars ("less discount 50%"), and he agreed that he would receive eight monthly installments, according to the protocol that had been established by a few collectors who, in Heller's mode, bought quickly and paid slowly.

Barney could be maddeningly obstructionist or reluctant to part with a work when something didn't click with a collector, no matter how otherwise qualified by wealth or position. There could be a frustrating stretch between desire and consummation, because he wanted to make sure that it went to someone worthy.[1] But with those who pleased him he would transfer the work and wait—sometimes for years—for the cost to be paid off.[2] At the same time that they acquired *L'Errance*, the Sculls had their eyes on *White Fire II*, and although they had it in their possession by June, it was not invoiced until the following year at Barney's "new rate," and payment was not completed until March 1963 in an oblique arrangement that involved the Scull's usual dealer, Leo Castelli. In a similar installment plan (the contract vetted by Barney's lawyers and filed with the New York County City Register), Bill Rubin had, early in the year, purchased *Prometheus Bound* for himself.

Swiss dealer Ernst Beyeler, anxious to corner the European market for Barney's work, came to New York expecting to negotiate an agreement. Barney put him through his paces: Gage & Tollner in Brooklyn, Barney Greengrass on the Upper West Side, the Russian Tea Room, Madison Square Garden for the highly publicized Archie Moore–Giulio Rinaldi fight. He impressed Beyeler by having his program signed by the aging great Jack Dempsey. For Beyeler's benefit he lectured on American food, comparing it to the development of American painting. "There's not so much American cooking," he told Beyeler, "many of the best things come from Europe and we absorb them." Likewise, there was European influence on American artists—at least that's the way Beyeler *recalled* the conversation—but then the new American art developed "on its own."[3] And Barney conducted Beyeler, along with Beyeler's guest, a Reverend Hassler, and Barney's guest, Charles Delloye, a French art critic based in Montreal who had recently become a Newman acolyte (if not sycophant), on the Long Island Railroad to see the Scull's new and newly "hot" collection.[4]

Over the past year, the Sculls' house in Great Neck was a trendy destination. (Shortly after, the Sculls would move to the Upper East Side in Manhattan and a house on Georgica Pond in East Hampton.) The couple had begun by acquiring

Abstract Expressionists, concentrating on de Kooning, but also Rothko, Kline, Stamos, and many less prominent painters, in the late '50s. Now met with "hostility" by those artists, but "actually encouraged" by Barney—who thought the choice was "daft" but genuine—they had become interested in newer art, in John Chamberlain, Mark di Suvero, Larry Poons, James Rosenquist, and in "Pop" art. And Pop "came with [an] entire Pop scene in which everything was Pop." It was "truly an expression of its moment," Scull said, "the clothes, people, vinyl, movies, fads . . . it was so new that it took our breath away." The "high luster of it" also described the way the Sculls "were living, the parties we were giving, the good times," the scene.[5] People came to see the collection and people came for the parties; and Barney thoroughly enjoyed his place in it. On occasion, he even performed on the piano. Two weeks before Beyeler's visit, on Memorial Day, the Newmans were there along with de Kooning, Larry Rivers, Jasper Johns, and Rosenquist, who had met Barney when he first came to Coenties Slip and noticed, a couple of blocks away, a skylight covered with what appeared to be decorative awnings. Intrigued, Rosenquist walked into the open door in spite of the "Private, Do Not Enter" sign announcing, "Hi. I'm a painter. I live in your neighborhood," settling in for a chat with the welcoming Barney. Now, at the Sculls, standing together with drinks in hand and looking out the window, Barney pointed to a single stick emerging from the pond. "That's it," he said, "That's what it is, that's what *it* is," as he regaled—talked "at"— Rosenquist with the story and meaning of *Onement*.[6] Rosenquist understood it as an obligation to challenge one's self-consciousness when looking.

When Beyeler returned to Basel on June 14, he was confident that the negotiations between him and Barney had resulted in a much more positive multilateral agreement. But Barney delayed making any commitment, likely because Beyeler had written upon his return that he was also talking with Kline and de Kooning, and the words "This would naturally also help your works very much when they are connected with these more known names over here." Neither did it contribute to the seduction that Beyeler's arrangement with Janis about those artists also involved Rothko.[7] It was the same as it had been with Rubin, the same as the "joke" he told Reinhardt years earlier: Barney would be happy to be in heaven, but not with "them guys."

Two months later, still waiting for a commitment and anxious to show work "to some good European collectors," Beyeler was "very astonished" that he had "no answers to my letters."[8] Not until another month had passed did Barney respond, easily excusing himself. He

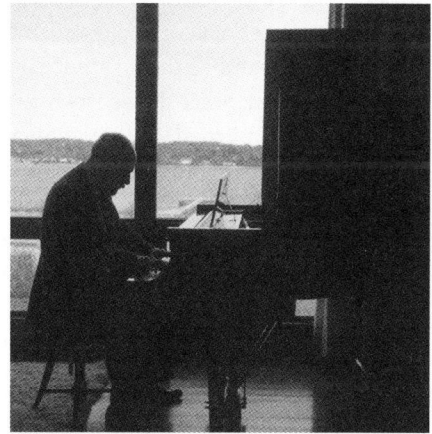

Fig. 44 Barnett Newman playing the piano at Robert and Ethel Scull's home on Georgica Pond, East Hampton, c.1961

"really had nothing to report . . . . I thought you understood how complex and complicated my situation was."

Robert Scull thought Barney was "wonderful," "extraordinary," "such a brain," and their friendship flowered. Scull owned a fleet of yellow cabs that he took over from his father-in-law, a taxi-insurance company, and garages. Barney always saw a trophy car as certifying success. Even as he became more ensconced in Manhattan real estate, and even as his weekend trips were usually made by train, he coveted a Lincoln Continental—at the discounted price that Scull could arrange. Along with the standard Lincoln power brakes, steering, and windows, and white wall tires, Scull proposed the luxury options: air conditioning, power seats, leather interior, tinted glass. Then Barney seems to have turned his attention to a new Thunderbird—also at Scull's professional discount. He wanted a convertible, but in 1961 only hardtops were made. Then he dropped the idea and held onto his Jaguar.

The benefits for Scull were more profound and more enduring. Scull was famous for having a lot to learn about conducting himself in the polite company of the art world and Barney seemed to be the rare person who helped, rather than disdained, him. Barney taught Scull about "a whole world of things," taught "a great deal about the word 'respect'"; taught him how to "deal with museums . . . about loans and how to handle them, and who would handle paintings." He taught him when asked for a loan to learn "what other painters were going to be in the show, what kind of catalogue would [be done], would the painting be handled with any respect, would the carrier be people that would come with white gloves. He taught me to respect the actual canvas; that nobody should lay their hands on it unless they were trained to do so. He taught me that when canvases are stretched the wood should be waxed." Scull knew nothing concerning "the actual painting itself . . . how delicate paintings are and that they must be taken care of."[9]

Barney taught Scull to "make sure that there were enough guards in the museum"; to ask "who is handling the insurance because some insurance companies are not as reliable as others"; that the artists one collected should be "handled with respect. Sometimes," he warned, "you would get a letter from a museum saying 'we think you have the greatest so-and-so in the world,' and then when it came time for the painting to be reproduced in a catalogue no one could find it."[10] In other words, Barney passed to the young enthusiastic but naïve collector not only the wisdom acquired from operating in harsh reality, but also the moral seriousness about the practice that was in his DNA and for which he'd been fighting since the crusade against the art teachers' exam in the 1930s, since he wrote "the defense of human dignity is the ultimate subject matter of art," in the 1940s, since he wore well-shined shoes to represent the "Artist" in the 1950s.

Scull became such a passionate acolyte of Barney's, that, like Heller, he used whatever force of personality and leverage he had to support him. At one point, he began a letter to Barney with a complete transcription of Hess's 1951 review of

Barney's second Parsons show, and continued: "Well, only eleven years have passed since the above review appeared in *Art News*, and believe me Mr. T.B.H. has learned a great deal since he printed these immortal lines, which proved a great testament to his state of blindness."

"I had the pleasure of meeting Mr. T.B.H. at Larry Rivers' studio only a couple of weeks ago, and in that meeting he learned a little more about you. However, this time he was a good natured pupil. When Ruv [Rabbi] Scull preaches the Gospel according to St. Barnett, I am told it is a real revelation."[11]

When it became clear that no work by Barney would appear in the 1961 Carnegie International, Scull, a self-declared "relative newcomer to the Monde d'Art" (also, newly in possession of *White Fire II*), dashed off a huffy letter in language resembling that of the artist himself to Barney's erstwhile supporter Gordon Washburn. It was an edited version of a draft written on the Newmans' typewriter.

> For some time now I have heard most disturbing rumors concerning some allegations that the winner of the forthcoming Pittsburgh International has already been chosen . . . . that the winner is a foregone conclusion . . . .
>
> My next problem is related to the foregoing in that it concerns the exclusion of Barnett Newman from the International this year . . . .
>
> Last month I was fortunate enough to obtain an eight foot high masterpiece of Mr. Newman's, created in 1960. It is quite indescribable, but . . . it does not take an art historian to recognize at once the influences he exerted over such artists as Still [Still was not in the show] and Rothko. Without Barnett Newman's experiments a host of painters today, many of whom were chosen for the International this year, could not have been able to attain their current success.[12]

"The real issue," Scull continued in a follow-up, was that "One could hardly consider any judging of a 1961 Biennale in the least bit definitive or even the least bit serious without the inclusion of a work by this acknowledged master." Scull sent copies of the entire correspondence to Barney, conspiratorially (jokingly) scribbling on the bottom of one page, "I am now dedicated to bring this man to his knees! He will beg for mercy—I will hound him until he publicly admits his chicanery! I will not cease—like a pestilence—until he cleanses himself with a one man retrospective of the work of Barnett Newman—a great artist—and my friend! We must prevail—because we are right."[13]

Scull was channeling Barney's perturbation—expressed to friends, including the 21-year-old Bennington student, Marcus, who hailed from Pittsburgh.[14] Barney himself went over—or tried to go over—Washburn's head. To John C. Warner, the "President of the Carnegie Institute" Barney wrote that it had come to his "attention that several painters whose work I respect . . . have not been invited to this year's Pittsburgh International . . . . This means that by a process of elimination the director creates a clear field for certain painters to receive awards," circumscribing "the aesthetic judgment of the members of the jury." It "occurred" to Barney that in order to free the jury from pre-selection, "there should be an award for artists not invited by Mr. Washburn." He enclosed a "check for $500 to be used as an award for any artist the jury would like to honor regardless of any restrictions. The award is to be known as "'The Barnett Newman Award for an Artist Not Invited to the Pittsburgh International,'" and he offered to create a trust to make the award permanent.[15]

It was a brilliant and witty move by the old anarchist, a way of inserting himself where he had not been invited and, not incidentally, to very publicly announce that he had newly expendable income. But it wound up something of an embarrassment—if Barney were capable of embarrassment: Warner was the President of the Carnegie Institute of Technology and had no idea what was at issue; the letter was routed to James M. Bovard, the President of the Carnegie Institute, who brought it to the Fine Arts Committee of the Board, who unanimously rejected it. The check was returned.[16] There was no press release issued on this occasion, just crowing letters to friends. And thus this episode, too, became part of the Newman catechism.

In spite of all the sales, in spite of being included in 1961 museum shows in Darmstadt, Chicago, and New York, and already chosen for the Fine Arts Pavilion at the 1962 Seattle World's Fair, Barney had not gotten past 1952. Nor had others, for other reasons. The early, radical nature of his work, for Barney and his supporters, established his *bona fides* as a seminal figure for the art of the '50s and the nascent '60s. But there were still those who were as "blind" as Hess in 1951. When a women's committee from the Art Gallery of Toronto approached Heller to assist in forming a collection with the limited amount of money available to them, he recommended they purchase the vibrant orange *Day One* that had been too tall to hang in Parsons's gallery in 1951. It was part of an ambitious season for the Women's Committee: they also offered to donate a Canadian work from their respected annual exhibition to New York's Museum of Modern Art, chosen by a representative of MoMA. Alfred Barr himself was enthusiastic.[17]

The sale of *Day One* was completed and the painting sent to Canada. Then Heller got a phone call: "the ladies" wanted to visit him. "There was a furor." Audience was offended, trustees were offended. Some newspaper articles condemned Toronto for being retrograde, others condemned the painting as "awful and [said] they shouldn't have it." They were "very upset, they wanted to return the painting." Heller was "horrified. Because you just don't do that."[18] He told his visitors "the only way that I would even speak to Barney is if you would allow me to put on an exhibition of painting of the period, and then I could speak to both the committee and to the board of the museum." Persuaded by Heller, Barney agreed to take it back on those terms.[19]

Heller arranged "a phenomenal exhibition" including Pollock, Rothko, de Kooning, Hofmann, Kline, Motherwell, Gottlieb, Guston. "The upshot was that we lost the battle and won the war."[20] It was an "occasion which should have taken place in Toronto five years ago," wrote the critic in the *Toronto Daily Star*. "None of the paintings in the room . . . lets us look 'into' a part of the world; none bears any relationship to a window; none refers to any objects, even distorted objects, outside the painting; none makes any concession to traditional structure. Each is a painting," and this was the "essence of the revolution which the American painters have made."

But the "enormous surprise," in the critic's judgment, was *Day One*: "so simple . . . that to describe it makes it seem ridiculous—yet on the wall it had a magnificent authority which no reproduction of a Newman has ever conveyed to me."[21]

Barney had a cot installed in the Carnegie Hall studio so that, as a "natural insomniac," he could nap during the day,[1] and—with hired help—began to rid it "of the physical restrictions," erase "the environmental space," and create his own "sense of place by feeling myself where I was." On the day in late July that he wrote to Bob Friedman praising the maturity of boxer Archie Moore, his "brains + skill" and "show of style" that impressed him in the championship fight against Giulio Rinaldi, Barney summoned his own brains, skill, and show of style, on the way to return to painting. He bought new "workclothes" and "supplies."[2] Within weeks, having had a psychologically satisfying lunch with "somebody from the art world," he returned to his Front Street studio, looked at the 114-by-174-inch canvas that the young Bennington intern had helped him stretch more than seven months earlier, and, feeling "brave," in one session painted *Shining Forth (To George)*.[3] He did not have his glasses, only his monocle. "I had such a strong feeling . . . that I did it with this one glass," he told an interviewer. "I just felt that I had to do it, and I could do it now. And if I didn't do it now, I never would be able to paint that painting." He didn't go home, he didn't stop to eat; he had a "full belly of food," and there was no reason to leave.

It was "the biggest painting I did in relation" to the direction he was exploring, in the as-yet unnamed *Stations*—black paint on unprimed canvas. It had "very little on it." But it was "exactly what I wanted." It looked like a *tallis* for a Jewish titan.[4]

Barney didn't "remember the kind of day it was." He didn't "remember whether it was a sunny day or not." He supposed the man he had been lunching with "had something to do with it." He "enjoyed talking with him." Maybe he "had some anxiety in meeting him. And maybe it was gone when we talked. Maybe I was depressed before I met him."[5]

Very possibly that person was H. H. Arnason. Arnason had come to the Guggenheim Museum as vice president for art administration from the Walker Art Center in Minneapolis the previous December, to ease the transition after James Johnson Sweeney's departure while Thomas Messer was getting his footing.[6] His new position did not specifically have a curatorial function, but a year earlier in Minnesota Arnason had mounted "Sixty Painters for 1960" and in the Guggenheim interregnum he was putting together "Vanguard American Painting," for the USIA, *and* a less "rapidly" gathered, more thoughtful "Abstract Expressionists and Imagists" exhibition, he told Barney. Barney had not been in the Walker show, criticized it as "supposedly depicting American Abstract Expressionism," irritably unloaded his vexation on Arnason, and was not inclined to trust him.[7] For his part, Arnason now *did* want Barney's participation, but was concerned—exuding tact, good feeling, and empathy after he extracted Barney's stinger—about the "many stories to the effect that you would not exhibit in group shows."[8]

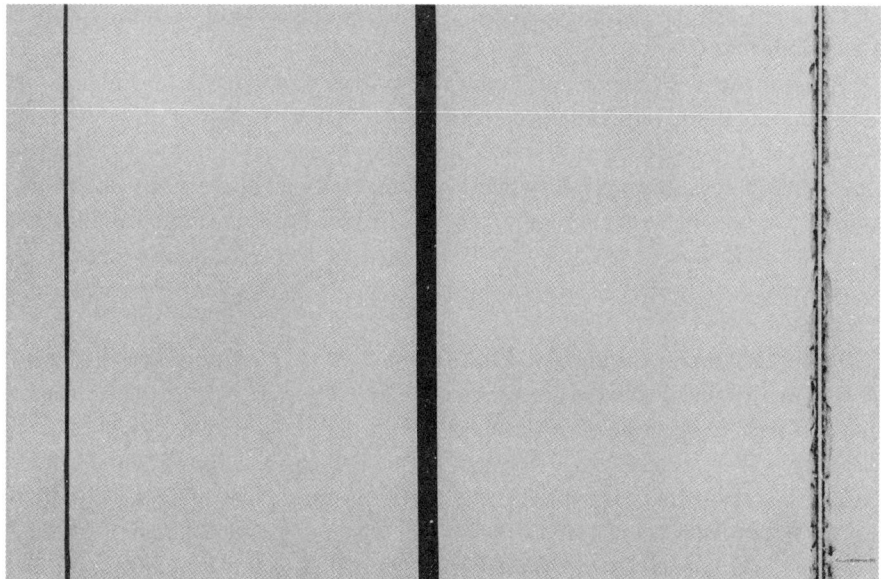

Fig. 45 Barnett Newman, *Shining Forth (To George)*, 1961. Oil on exposed canvas, 114 × 174 in. (289.6 × 442 cm). Musée National d'Art Moderne, Centre Georges Pompidou, Paris

"My whole position in regard to group shows seems to be completely misunderstood," Barney drafted in a reply preempted by Arnason's studio visit. He had issue only with "certain group shows," and wished to "separate myself from the dislikes of some of my colleagues who hypocritically reject certain shows at the very moment that they are participating in others." He disliked "didactic and cross-section group shows," but not presentations "of the existing painting milieu in which I have a place, it seems to me, by right." He wasn't so sure about the proposed Guggenheim show. "Will this show be brave enough to show the influence that I had on the men of my own generation?"

Was this how Barney had come to feel "brave enough" to begin to paint again? Was it Arnason who "had something to do with it," whom Barney "enjoyed talking with," whom he "had some anxiety in meeting"—anxiety which "was gone when we talked"?

"Maybe" he "was depressed before" he met the unidentified man, Barney later narrated. There would have been ample reason. He was still in mourning for his brother. It was the "summer of crisis" about Berlin, the Vienna summit, Soviet ultimatum, troop buildups, escalating fears about nuclear war, local talk of "fallout shelters." For four months horrific revelations from the trial of Adolf Eichmann were detailed daily in the press, with "highlights" broadcast on U.S. television. "The volume of evil unfolding in the trial . . . has grown so huge in three weeks that it seems no longer manageable, at least not within the bounds of normal, rational thinking" the *Times* reported at the end of April, even *before* two months of survivors' testimony, and American, British, and Russian films of the camps at liberation were shown.[9]

Arnason met with Barney on August 17, two days after the trial concluded, four days after the Berlin border had been dramatically closed by Soviet divisions. Business as usual "seemed terribly trivial," David Sylvester wrote to Meyer Schapiro. "I did little but sit around feeling futile and angry; I expect everyone else did the same."[10] Or, maybe, it was simply difficult for Barney to digest the thought of MoMA's show of Rothko traveling to six European countries. But what Arnason proposed was very promising: he wanted to show at the Guggenheim the competition-crushing *Cathedra*.[11]

Barney celebrated his improved state of mind by attending the smartest, trendiest, activities that a New Yorker had available that September. He was in Yankee Stadium to see Roger Maris hit his fifty-fifth home run on a Thursday night, and, on Saturday—"Whitey Ford Day" in honor of the pitcher—his fifty-sixth and Mickey Mantle his fifty-second. He was at City Center for the much-touted Greek Piraikon Theatron's ritualistic performances of Sophocles's *Electra* and Aeschylus's *The Choephori* and *The Eumenides*. He heard his friend Ornette Coleman's sessions at the Five Spot, and on the very hot, soupy night the Alloways disembarked from the ocean liner Rotterdam for a year's residency at Bennington, he insisted on bringing them to Coleman at Birdland.[12] For the first time in months, he bought yards of cotton duck from John Boyle.

In mid-October, "American Abstract Expressionists and Imagists" opened at the Guggenheim Museum in New York and Heller's eight-day show opened in Toronto.

One "might ask what it added up to," wrote *Time*. One might ask, as well, why *Time* was covering a local story from Toronto, and who placed it. The comments on both the artist and the painting were mocking—"Day In, Day Out" was the headline—but the Vandivert photograph that accompanied it was clearly supplied by Barney.[13] Barney had a plan, worked out with Ellin. Having been rejected by "the ladies," the Canadian city, and the Luce voice of *Time*, *Day One* became especially desirable. On the West Coast, Ellin, who had been trying to sell *Cathedra* to the collectors Fred and Marcia Weisman, now was anxious to have the notorious *Day One* as a cat's paw for other sales.[14] If *Day One* were placed in the Los Angeles County Museum of Art "we will have achieved a major victory with respect to the future."[15]

"The more I think about it, the more I am convinced that the plan we discussed concerning the presentation of your image in California is the only way to win this fight," Ellin wrote to Barney.[16] If the Weismans did not want *Day One*, Ellin would show that painting, *Achilles*, and *Onement VI* "as a special event" in his gallery in January.

Earlier in the year, three paintings by Still hung together in a single room, on extended loan from three different collectors to the existing Los Angeles County Museum's shared building in Exposition Park. This fact, and the dates Still had assigned to the works—1950, 1956, and "1951–52" (to a work purportedly in Miller's 1952 show)[17]—gave Barney the kind of indigestion Ellin knew well. His proposed "special event" would "underscore our victory over Toronto and Still," he assured Barney.[18]

That Still remained a thorn in Barney's side, even though their paths hardly crossed and Still did not show in galleries and had moved to rural Maryland in July, might seem unusually obsessive even for Barney. But the competition was entirely mutual. On at least one recent occasion, Still did not miss the opportunity to lash out at Barney—and in a way that Barney would be certain to notice. When *Art and Culture*, the edited collection of Greenberg's writings, appeared in the spring, it contained the essay "'American-Type' Painting"—originally from 1955, revised in 1958—which credited Barney for the most dramatic break with the easel picture. Still's "point," Greenberg had written, was "easier to grasp." For whatever that was worth, it proclaimed Barney's "priority"—and this, almost more than their continued development, was paramount to both men.

Still was so incensed by the re-publication that he could not write to Greenberg himself (or so it was said). Pat Still's signature (in Clyfford's handwriting) appeared at the bottom of the typed letter: "Believe me, there is something rotten in you impotent souls that makes it so necessary to defile the work and purposes of your betters."[19]

As it happened, the Weismans had already committed to the purchase of *Onement VI* (invoiced in March 1963); Fred and Marcia had each seen it in the studio independently, six months apart, and both of them knew it was "the" one. "If ever I knew a painting belonged to anybody, I knew this belonged to you two," Barney told Fred.[20] It was *this* painting—not *Cathedra*—that was chosen for Arnason's show, and it was *that* presentation of *Onement VI* that would go farther than any strategizing by Ellin to "win this fight," to establish once and for all Barney's historical position.[21]

"I never saw anyone so excited about a painting as is Fred," Betty Freeman, the California writer, patron, and collector, told Barney. "Everybody (like Irving Blum & Everett) who saw it at the show say that its radiance shines over everything."[22]

"The sight of your blue painting . . . towered over everything else in the show, and made a lot of it seem prissy, futile and superfluous," another art-world insider told him.[23] The remark turned out to be not as fulsome as it might have originally appeared. *Onement VI* at the Guggenheim (plate 15) was the turning point for entrenched holdouts.

Eight and a half by ten feet, the cobalt/phthalo blue *Onement VI* could be seen as a "compression" of the more cobalt/ultramarine *Cathedra*, equally commanding and sensual without the breadth. The central placement of its single, stark light mint band insists on an immediate confrontation instead of the more gentle, generous invitation posed by *Cathedra*'s muted white and exquisitely subtle phthalo green asymmetrical ones. Barney, still fixated—obsessed is not too strong a word—on the ten-year-old iniquity, was thrilled with the hanging. The "big room as it 'works' with the rest of the show will make clear the real story of the painting of these many important years. It will be a landmark in the struggle for clarity," he told Arnason.[24]

The exhibition included a single, 1959–1961 work by 64 artists ranging from 81-year-old Hofmann to 25-year-old Stella. Most lived in or near New York City. There were seven exceptions to the bracketing dates: Paris-based Matta had a 1942 painting; the deceased Gorky, Tomlin, and Pollock, works from 1943–48, 1952–53 and 1949, respectively. Works from the Scull collection represented Rothko (1957) and Still (1951). According to the catalogue, Barney lent *Onement VI* (1953) himself—although it was already committed to the Weismans. Arnason told Barney that he intended to point out "how many of the younger artists, not only the free abstractionists but also the newer precise or hard edge group, stem from the experiments which you and a few others started over ten years ago."[25]

Critics were skeptical. Generally, it was felt that the conceit, and the limitation to the previous couple of years, did a service to no generation: many of the older artists' works were uncharacteristic and made them look more exhausted than they were, the younger artists appeared less challenging. Nor was it a service to the public to exclude any work with a representational element. "A false polemical position," one critic called it, invoking Picasso's dictum, "there is no such thing as abstract art."[26]

But whether through Arnason's design or Barney's manipulation or Ellin's strategy, or simply luck, the choice of the 1953 *Onement VI*—made in the prime years of discovery and urgent experimentation—turned out to be golden. In the company, and by its placement, it dominated the great bowl of the Guggenheim.

Most of the works were distributed two, three, or four per bay across twenty-seven bays spiraling around four ramps. In the museum's airy "High Gallery," opening from the middle of the lowest ramp, Tomlin's *Number 10* and Gorky's *Untitled* hung on perpendicular walls visible only upon entering the gallery. On the long wall, visible through an arch from almost every vantage in the museum, were Pollock's *Number 2, 1949* and *Onement VI*. One critic described Barney as "probably the most 'modern' of all the mentors" and his aesthetic position as "occupied magisterially," and that was exactly what the hanging reinforced: "the cleansing logic" was heroic. "This painting has a presence and speaks a language like no other in the show."[27]

It was what Barney had been waiting for. He crowed to Weisman that he would have enjoyed "seeing 'Onement' in the place given it by Arnason and the way its impact moves through the entire Museum," the way it was used "to establish, on the wall, what many are beginning to realize is the real dialogue."[28]

Newman's "paintings have borne many children," his influence was "considerable," Allan Kaprow wrote in a surprisingly loving, philosophical meditation that he began to formulate from a most unexpected corner of the younger generation at this time.[29]

Forty years later, Sandler, who had not previously been persuaded by Barney's art even as he enjoyed the man, remembered the sight: "The single picture of his . . . the unforgettable *Onement #6*, opened my eyes wide—and those of many of my contemporaries. It literally riveted our attention, and also that of younger generations." He "castigated" the 1961 Carnegie International for omitting Barney's work, and denounced "their rejection as 'inexcusable' and 'scandalous.'" Barney's prize proposal delighted him.[30] "Downtown" painter Paul Brach and his good friend Heller always argued about Barney. Heller, in the hospital when Arnason's show was on, got a visit from Brach. "He said, 'I *finally* get it.' The Newman hit him on the head."[31] Speaking at a Club panel arranged by Sandler on "New Image Painting," Brach said that the school of de Kooning was no longer interesting; Barney's paintings were. Challenged that he had changed his mind, he replied that yes, he didn't know how good Barney was.[32] Years later, Lucy Lippard still recalled it as providing "one of the most memorable and intense color experiences" she had ever had.[33]

It was yet another "group show," but it had extraordinary prominence, and Barney found a way to accommodate his participation policy and play nicely with its curator.

In the mid-1950s, planning for the sort of ambitious, optimistic, and frenzy-generating world's fair that is now hard to imagine was undertaken by the city of Seattle. "The Century 21 Exposition," scheduled to open in April 1962, would showcase "modern science," "space exploration," and the "progressive future," and, not incidentally, encourage business, population growth, and all the other catalysts required to boost Seattle into the world-city league. The U.S. government was enthusiastic, NASA was involved, and so were several of the country's biggest corporations, and numbers of foreign countries. The fantastical Space Needle, with a rotating restaurant 605 feet above the ground, and the futuristic Monorail became the fair's visionary icons. World-famous musicians, dance companies, and Elvis Presley were attractive draws. And organizers were smart enough to attend to visual art. Unlike the mystifying American selection made for Brussels four years earlier, the execution was masterful.

The revered director of the Stedelijk Museum in Amsterdam, Willem Sandberg, was invited to organize a "cutting-edge" show, "Art Since 1950," and Sam Hunter, since 1960 the director of the Poses Institute of Fine Arts and founding director of the Rose Art Museum, both at Brandeis University, was charged with the American portion. "In Sandberg's sort of spontaneous and somewhat idiosyncratic way, and Hunter's more historic and dogmatic way, each of these two exhibitions—being separate entities but back-to-back in the exhibition hall—told a very interesting story about what was happening in the world [and] made a lot of converts for contemporary art," recalled Jan van der Marck, the art historian, future curator, and director of museums, who assisted Sandberg. Not least of the enthusiasts were collectors Bagley and Virginia Wright.[34]

If Hunter felt manipulated by Barney in 1956, all was now forgiven: a December dinner with the Newmans was "delightful" and all Barney's "good-humored, sagacious talk" gave Hunter "quite a lift."[35] By the time the show opened in April 1962 the works they agreed upon—the Weismans' *Onement VI*, the Sculls' *White Fire II*—had major collectors' names attached, burnishing Barney's newly achieved luster.

The shows were covered in *both* the third and fourth issues of *Artforum* magazine, the new kid on the block, created to cover art activity on the West Coast, but quickly becoming the journal of the most interesting, most intellectually relevant, most current art and aesthetic dialogue. Very little postwar art had been seen in that part of the country and the exhibition was revelatory. The Washington-born painter Chuck Close remembered the excitement of seeing de Kooning "not in *Life* magazine but in the flesh."[36]

Where Arnason's show extravagantly inserted Barney into the old history, Seattle would be an opportunity for a fresh history to be written. Underscoring Barney's place in that history, *Onement VI* was one of only two American works reproduced in color in the catalogue (the other was Hofmann's *In the Wake of the Hurricane*). Through Hunter's negotiation, the 114 works by 87 artists would travel intact to the Rose Museum outside of Boston.

Samuel Wagstaff, the paintings curator at the Wadsworth Atheneum, over several meetings won Barney's participation in "Continuity and Change: 45 American Abstract Painters and Sculptors," an exhibition that, by including early, middle, and late work by each artist, would be "*of* contemporary painting and sculpture as well as . . . *about* it."[37] Desired or not, Wagstaff also won Barney's "time + kindness + suggestions." "All I can say is that you + Lee [Krasner] changed it + I hope for the better."[38]

For this occasion, in which a few of Barney's generation went back decades for their early piece, and almost all to the previous year, 1961, for their late work, Barney chose only from his earliest four years: the 1945 *Gea*; the 1947 *Death of Euclid*; the 1949 ink wash *Sketch of Rothko*—entirely eccentric in the context of his career and his emotional complex—(the last two owned by Parsons); and the 1949 *Horizon Light* (owned by Reynal and Sills). Almost spitefully renouncing the opportunity to include a prime recent painting, he again, as was his habit, refought the old battles, reiterating his earliest work when in the company of his peers, as if to prove that a) he was not a maker of "a certain kind of *product*";[39] b) Rothko had wronged him in 1950 by hanging *Horizon Light* vertically and in 1952 (in Barney's mind, at least) by lobbying against his inclusion in "Fifteen Americans"; and c) he knew how to "draw." By including the fluid and charmingly referential portrait sketch, Barney was certainly anticipating the kind of reaction to the show that *Time* magazine did, in fact, have in a five-page feature with large color reproductions: "The Atheneum exhibition should do away with one outworn illusion: that abstract artists are abstract because they cannot paint images."[40]

By any measure he had achieved the recognition whose absence had caused him a lifetime of emotional agony. The critics that he respected respected him (and satisfyingly, the ones who were benighted, didn't); curators sought him out; younger artists sat at his feet; important collectors courted him. He would never acknowledge that the financial rewards that now came his way had anything to do with his definition of success—or, more importantly, were any sort of index of his "dignity"; but he was astutely managerial about his prices (and investments) and sometimes cringe-provokingly small about what he felt was his due. "On leaving the Kootz Gallery, 555 Madison Ave., at about 7:30 p.m.," he wrote to his insurance company as the Seattle fair was about to open, "I noticed smoke coming out of my wife's pocketbook.

I opened the pocketbook and found it totally ablaze. Some friends, spectators and myself ripped out the suede lining of the bag which was ablaze and stamped out the fire." The pocketbook itself, "an English bag, made of leather and lined with suede, bought at Abercrombie & Fitch 4 months" earlier, a pair of eyeglasses, and a leather wallet were "badly damaged and beyond repair." He wanted to make an insurance claim for the total of 60 dollars.[41]

"When I was 19 years old," he told Dorothy Seckler, he decided "I don't care what posterity thinks of me. I already have my opinion of posterity." He began conversations with the critic at the beginning of 1962 for an article that would run in the summer issue of *Art in America*. For the magazine, it was an obvious journalistic decision—Barney was now established. From Barney's perspective, his "career," and his evolving old master stature was less on his agenda. Whenever he had an opportunity he used it for the same purpose: to make understood what exactly he was doing and what exactly he was *not* doing, to foreclose the misinterpretation that he felt was the by-product of renown and exposure and that would turn his work into a "cliché" and to separate himself from *everyone* else.

He did not pre-ordain what his paintings would look like when finished, he did not work from sketches. He did not make copies or tweaked versions of works that were passed off as the earlier ones—as he, and others, accused Still of doing. When he found the quiet and psychological peace to paint, he had no plan other than to paint. Every time he worked he tried "to begin as if I had never painted before"; and that was possible because the impulse came from feeling, and *that*, at least for Barney, could not be pre-facto sketched or post-facto duplicated.[42] His paintings said something personal, but if they turned out to also say something universal, so much the better: he was "enacting his dream" but he hoped that his dream was "more real than reality."[43]

His relationship to painting was fundamentally different from that of other artists. He compared the dynamic to *The Perils of Pauline*. Most "action paintings" were, in Barney's opinion, "episodic," an event that implied the next event, with a whole series of sequels: "The excitement always ends at the brink and leaves the subject" hanging off the cliff. "The next painting repeats the excitement, in a kind of ritual. What he was interested in, by contrast, was "saving the girl."[44]

He had said most of these things before to smaller—usually much smaller—audiences. But now, in January 1962, with the twenty-two drawings of 1960, the three prints of 1961 and eight black-paint-on-unprimed-canvas recent works on his mind, he discoursed on a new idea, one that "no writer on art has ever confronted."

"Drawing is central to my whole concept," he announced to Seckler.

I don't mean making *drawings*, although I have always done a lot of them. I mean the drawing that exists in my painting . . . . I am always referred to in relation to my color. Yet I know that if I have made a contribution, it is primarily in my drawing. The impressionists changed the way of seeing the world through their kind of drawing; the cubists saw the world anew in their drawing; and I hope that I have contributed a new way of seeing through drawing. Instead of using outlines, instead of making shapes or setting off spaces, my drawing declares the space. Instead of working with the remnants of space, I work with the whole space.[45]

A canvas full of rhetorical strokes may be full, but the fullness may be just hollow energy, just as a scintillating wall of colors may be full of colors but have no color. My canvases are full not because they are full of colors but because color makes the fullness.

"The *fullness thereof* is what I am involved in," Barney announced, quoting (but not citing) Psalm 24.[46] "The land and the fullness thereof are the Lord's; the world and those who dwell therein." That is what Barney, the creator, was "involved in."

After a New York lunch in 1960, after Fred Weisman and Jim Elliot had peeled off, Barney asked Marcia Weisman, "Would you care to come to my studio and see my sculpture?"

"What could you sculpt?" she asked in sheer amazement. "Well, you'll see," he responded provocatively.

In the dark corner of the studio, where it had been for years, was the white *Here I*, two 8-foot elements jutting up from lumpy plaster.[1] She was "astounded," she could "not believe that such a thing could have been done. But on the other hand, it was so obvious it was what Barnett Newman would have to do in sculpture." She asked when he made it. Nineteen-fifty was the answer. She asked when he was going to cast it. "I'm thinking about it." She told him he had been thinking long enough, and began to bug him, sweetening the relationship by arranging for hard-to-get tickets to the World Series. It turned out to be the final game at Yankee Stadium managed by Casey Stengel, who had been fired for turning 70—an occasion tailor-made for Barney.[2]

It wasn't until the early part of 1962 that he dove into the casting of *Here I*, now subtitled *To Marcia*. "The Art of Assemblage" had been the Museum of Modern Art's fall 1961 blockbuster show. Of 250 wildly diverse works by 130 artists chosen by William Seitz, *Here* was not one, although it nicely fell into the museum's description—"varieties of art assembled from . . . unorthodox materials"—or, as Robert Coates of the *New Yorker* wrote, "anything not fashioned by casting or by the chisel."[3] It is intriguing to think that the casting was Barney's riposte.

Typically, Barney made the endeavor into an adventure. The Modern Art Foundry was in Astoria, Queens, in a neighborhood with a large Greek population, and a particular restaurant that Barney came to love. He and Murray would lunch there on supervising visits to the foundry, and on a couple of nights they "took the babes"—their wives—to watch belly dancers perform.

The original plaster and wood sculpture that he was "compelled" to make in 1950 while he was preparing for his second show at Parsons, had, as its base, an ordinary milk crate with casters, added after the show, underneath. Murray made a sort of cradle for the whole piece, and rode in the truck as it was transported, steadying it on two pieces of thick foam. "You're not going to do the milk crate, right?" Bob Spring, the proprietor, asked Barney when he began to make the molds. "We should end it right here?"

"Well, I don't know," Barney replied. He had not thought about it before. Back and forth, Barney and Murray teased out the concept. The mesh in the milk crate supported the verticals, but with the casting, that became unnecessary; was it a part of the sculpture or was it a temporary base? They decided to forgo the crate. After it was done, Murray and Holstein placed it in front of Astoria's fanciful 19th-century Steinway Mansion, "lugging it up the hill like Sisyphus," to be photographed.[4]

There was a protocol that foundries followed when a sculpture was cast in bronze. The original was used for making wax molds, and if it survived intact it might be returned to the artist; but the molds remained with the foundry. The technique for *Here I* was slightly different—molds of the dismantled sculpture's parts were made from Tuffy, a synthetic rubber—but the custom was the same: it was "unheard of for the artist to get the molds."[5] Barney, as usual, insisted on tailoring the protocol. He told the foundry that he wanted the whole business back, and, with his newly elevated stature, he prevailed.[6]

Everett Ellin and James Elliot, the Weismans, and Betty Freeman were so enthusiastic, so encouraging, such a fresh source of galvanizing support, that the Newmans did something that was, for them, extraordinary. In a burst of spontaneity while Annalee was on a sabbatical they went farther west—past Ohio, past Saskatchewan—than they'd ever gone before, to mingle with their new friends. With an astonishing 23,000 dollars (232,060 dollars in 2023) deposited into various accounts during January and February 1962, and 18,500 dollars (186,655) more expected before the year was half over, Barney was in high spirits. Days after they helped "inaugurate" the studio Smith designed, at Barney's suggestion, for Gray in Connecticut, they were greeted with flowers from the Weismans and the Freemans at the new Beverly Crest Hotel, in Beverly Hills.[7]

There were parties in their honor. At one, Barney saw in the Weismans' living room the work by Still that would later become the focus of another vicious skirmish. Barney had already embarked on the project that Marcia Weisman had coaxed him into, a bronze cast of his inspired, wonderfully messy, casually plastered sculpture of 1950, *Here I*, and they were excited to review its progress.[8] Dinner at Chasen's, the watering hole of Hollywood elite, and an outing to the winter season at Santa Anita Park in Arcadia, famous as one of the most scenic racetracks in the world with the finest horses, were the authentic Los Angeles experiences that Barney could not miss.[9] In Santa Monica, in one of the apartments in the fantastical Moorish–Byzantine–Spanish–colonial Hippodrome that still existed above the carousel, Elliot was the host, introducing Barney to the young southern California artists who only knew his work from magazine reproductions. He spent quality time with the new generation, visiting Venice studios in a beautiful dark blue suit, a necktie, and his monocle, which, among the youthful, laid-back, paint-smeared-khaki-and-beach-shirt-attired Californians left a much less negative impression than it had among the "downtown" artists of New York. The image remained engagingly vivid half a century later.[10]

A "cross-section of painting and sculpture by the so-called 'School of New York' " had been the star attractions in a number of Los Angeles galleries during the previous eighteen months: drawings at Ellin, Jasper Johns at Ferus, and Kline, de Kooning, Pollock, Guston, Goodnough, Hartigan, Ray Parker, and Larry Rivers at Dwan.[11]

While Barney was there, a Motherwell retrospective was on view at the Pasadena Art Museum.

The exposure to the West Coast artists may have been responsible for the introduction, in three paintings of 1962, of an assertive, sunny yellow and saturated orange, the likes of which he had not used since *Yellow Painting* in 1949 and *Day One* in 1951. It was the first time he had used *any* color since his heart attack, except for the cautious appearance of a ragged and brushy blue emerging behind the black in *Outcry* and, possibly, the thin cadmium red strip on the left edge of *Be II*. This last, a unique combination during this period of acrylic, oil, pigmented polymer emulsion, and Magna, is dated "1961, 1964," but is first recorded when it was reproduced in a catalogue—although not exhibited—at the end of 1962 as *Resurrection*. From 1958 through the end of 1961, Barney made ten paintings; all but *Be I* were black on raw canvas.

Now, in Los Angeles Barney looked at the clear-eyed, fresh, untroubled surfaces of work by Larry Bell, Craig Kauffman, Billy Al Bengston, John McLaughlin, Robert Irwin, Joe Goode, Charles Arnoldi. By this time, New York had seen early minimal, hard-edged, and Pop works, but there the atmosphere, for an older-generation artist identified as an abstract expressionist, had become fraught: "Like giving a Jewish kid a hot pork sandwich on the day of his bar mitzvah" was the way Guston squeamishly characterized to Barney the transgressiveness of Andy Warhol.[12] In the sensual, effulgent southern California light, with friendly, admiring, adoring faces surrounding him, Barney was light-hearted and happy: it was "like Brooklyn and East Hampton pushed together, with no Manhattan in between."[13] And so, a few months after he returned, he put some of that light on canvas. *Not There—Here* and *The Moment I* featured egg-yolk-in-a-sunny-kitchen yellow on white casein and on exposed canvas, respectively, and *The Third* was 101 ¼ by 120 ⅛ inches of mostly Sunkist orange, with thin "stops"—as Kaprow named them before Barney came up with "zip"—of yellow and an area of orange-brushed exposed canvas.[14] When *Not There—Here* was shown in November, Cleve Gray found it "enormously interesting . . . to see + feel the tremendous difference in emotion created by the new color range; it was wonderful for the spectacle of it and also because it made me realize that you are still discovering and expressing new emotions in your own world." Gray was happy to see "that the output is now flowing strongly."[15]

It took some time for the output to flow, a delay before "the immediate exercise of total commitment" that he required to make what felt, to him, authentic, a total experience, rather than an "episode."[16] As soon as he returned from California, he was on the train to Philadelphia, where he had agreed to be visiting critic for the spring semester at the University of Pennsylvania. He arrived with Annalee and a brown paper bag holding a bottle of vodka, from which she periodically filled a small paper cup. One of the students, who was Armenian, was prompted to draw an analogy: "the priest was sitting at the head of the table . . . incredibly impressive."

"He began talking about his work and the significance of the single line, how critical that decision was to him: it was everything." In inspiring, poetic terms, he made clear that the stakes were "life and death." These young artists, like the artists at Emma Lake before, or the young Californians, saw nothing of the demons that still surfaced in Barney's drafts of letters, or interactions with those who disappointed him. What they saw was a master of extraordinary, encouraging "generosity." They had "never met another artist who was like him. He didn't have anything to prove," whereas the other established artists who had come to speak to the seminar "were very angry about European art being valued so highly," and how they had earlier been "ignored."[17]

Barney's "really top-rate job" in the seminars "was more than we had any right to expect," wrote James Van Dyk of the School of Fine Arts, and "the general consensus [was] that you are a superlative teacher and human being, and this is not to overlook the contribution that Mrs. Newman made by her presence."[18]

This last was particularly welcome when, a few days later, Bryan Robertson reviewed *American Art of the Twentieth Century* by the Whitney's director and associate director, Lloyd Goodrich and John I. H. Baur, for *The Listener*, the British Broadcasting Corporation's popular and respected literary weekly. Barney was not in the book, because he was not in the Whitney collection, and the authors limited their discussion to artists who were. Nevertheless, Robertson, who mused that the American moment might be over, ended the review with what he considered an amusing anecdote. The situation in New York had "its occasional humours."

That arch exponent of monumental simplicity and puritanism, Barnett Newman, walked recently into a small downtown gallery in New York and bleakly surveyed the daubs on about eight vast canvases by a very young artist. They were very slight daubs, the brush marks were a bit dirty and there was a lot of bare canvas. "These kids . . . " mumbled Newman from the depths of his single-colour majesty, in rolling W.C. Fields-like tones of stern disapproval: " . . . these kids, they think it's *easy!*" Mrs. Newman's motherly heart was similarly unmoved. "Why," she said, "when Barney goes into his studio we just *never know* what's going to come out."[19]

It was a singularly stupid, lazy, and wrong piece of writing. Barney *never* mumbled. He *never* appeared inebriated—as the comparison to Fields suggested. He, almost alone of his generation, was famously supportive of young artists. And what purpose could be served by lampooning Annalee, who was so staunch and reserved that she was virtually unlampoonable? In his misguided way, Robertson, "a man with a heart of gold," but who could also be "catty,"[20] clearly thought that even though Goodrich and Baur had left out Barney, he, Robertson, would appear embarrassingly uninformed in the middle of 1962 if he did the same.

Barney wrote an outraged letter, Robertson wrote a response, but in the interests of minimizing the spilling of "bad blood," *The Listener* condensed the long letters into one paragraph. Barney: "No such incident occurred, no such exhibition existed, no such conversation took place, no such remarks were made either by me or by my wife." Robertson said he was told the story in New York: "It seemed . . . quite a funny, rather nice, story and it ended my review of the book on American painting as a device meant only for amusement—friendly amusement . . . . I have great respect for Mr. Newman's work . . . . I apologize unreservedly if it has caused him or his wife any irritation."[21] But that did not satisfy Barney; instead of identifying the original story as a "flagrant falsehood," the paragraph called it "inaccurate," and there was no "moral regret."[22] He called on Roberston to name his sources. He enlisted the well-connected Murphy Radio magnate E. J. Power, father of Alan Power—whom he had not yet met—to persuade the BBC to properly address the "outrageous smear": a lot of things "have happened to me in my life but nothing quite this raw." He enlisted the cultural affairs officer at the American Embassy (whom he *had* met) for the same: he wanted his full letter printed, only *that* would "clear my name and my wife's name." He wrote to the director-general of the BBC.[23] It continued to simmer for six of the otherwise best months Barney may have ever had. He tracked down the "source" of the story as Rosenberg, who, now that he had abandoned his antagonism, detailed to Barney a version of a game of "telephone" in which Robertson elaborated the affectionate retelling of a long-ago conversation between Barney and de Kooning—to "show he was an insider."[24] Barney took weeks to settle before he grudgingly accepted Rosenberg's account.[25]

And so, when he was asked, along with numbers of others, to contribute a few words to the sixtieth anniversary issue of *Art News* in December, he still had the tar on his hands. "Having just had an amazing experience with a 'culture' magazine in England," he began his tribute, "published by a branch of the Establishment, and having found out how an artist is treated there, I understand more than ever how thankful all of us here should be for the '*Art News*' [and] for the vigor with which it has fought for what it believes in and for making an area of freedom where all . . . have an opportunity freely to express themselves."[26]

The biggest impact of being included in "The Century 21 Exposition" in Seattle was the friendly reconnection with Hunter. At the Poses Institute he was responsible for programs that, in the early 1960s, captured the attention of multiple generations of artists, and an emerging generation of art critics. Some had been under the tutelage of Greenberg, some came from other quarters: academics, artists, and poets, who were finding new outlets, wider exposure, and, propelled by 1960s economics and demographics, an *au courant* and informed audience interested in cultural exchange. The nascent energetic and provocative *Artforum* magazine had a catalytic effect on the existing outlets as well: *Art News, Art in America, Art International*, even the mass media, began to up their games. On more than one occasion all eyes were on the Poses Institute's events, as well as on the reinvented Jewish Museum, whose newly appointed director, Alan Solomon, initiated a focus on advanced art in New York.

In the busy spring of 1962, Barney was invited to be a "discussant" at the first conference at the Poses in Boston, "Modern Art and Mass Culture." With Motherwell, Guston, Seitz, and Hess, Barney was asked to consider the "effect of commercial and popular pressures in the present period of material prosperity; the possible conflict between maintaining high standards of excellence and a broadened public appreciation of art; [and] the role of critics, collectors and public institutions in guiding taste."[27] In other words, all of the very issues that had him churning for fifteen years. But, at this moment—with his works in important exhibitions in Hartford and Seattle and owned by prominent collectors on both coasts, with his ethos being digested in Philadelphia and appearing in *Art in America*, respected enough to throw around his weight, with a *financial* advisor—it would require a new lens in his monocle to accommodate an altered perspective.

When Hunter refined the question a few weeks later—what was the "effect of 'mass' culture, of affluence and an intensified promotion and prosperity around the avant-garde on its old positions of protest . . . . Is acceptance, in fact, a reality?" and, secondly, "how does the environment 'mass' and 'pop' culture affect expressive forms. Who is avant-garde anyway, Jasper Johns or your generation of pioneers?"[28]— Barney begged to withdraw. It was an "entirely different matter," he wrote, the day after attending a memorial for Franz Kline, who had died suddenly in mid-May, from a "discussion of modern art and the problem of mass culture."

"I am certain all the things you mention, which you would like to have the panel discuss, are of interest to you and to others. They do not interest me . . . . What started out as a conference over ideas [is] developing into a debate over other painters, in the style of the Club."[29] The tremendous disjunction between his principles and the "reality" of what had occurred in his career was impossible to accept. He didn't have, or desire, the new lens.

And yet, in spite of developing a toothache and debilitating leg cramps—a lifelong pattern of stress-related ailments invoked as excuses—he would rise to the occasion. The weekend was fun; the conference was "revealing" and "made clear that the struggle is constant. The opposition never ceases."[30] He was "the star" of the panel (in the opinion of Hunter's Harvard graduate students) jovially tossing around Yiddishisms to modulate what might have appeared to be whining.[31] As if in confirmation of Barney's philosophical discomfort, on the day of the second session, the "feuds and personalities" of the art world were acknowledged as fodder for mass entertainment. In an unprecedented move, NBC television broadcast over 118 affiliate stations a debate—compared to a wrestling match—between Hess and Canaday in the garden of the Museum of Modern Art.[32] A couple of months later, in August, a tape of Barney and Guston's performance at the Poses aired on WRVR-FM radio, competing for attention with a presidential news conference.

Guston's retrospective had opened at the Guggenheim shortly before the Poses panel. He seemed to his daughter "almost as disturbed" as he was honored. He had canceled the show once; he had had a "collapse about it," worried that it would destroy "certain hopes and myths about myself that I needed." The day before the

Guggenheim opening he told his family, "I'm a goner." His daughter had the distinct impression that his "growing sense of personal crisis . . . [was] clearly connected with what was happening in the art world."[33]

For Barney's generation "of pioneers" the "struggle" was indeed constant. It was a massively enlarged heart since childhood and the years of heavy drinking and smoking, not the pressure to metabolize their new reality, that caused Kline's fatal heart attack just days before his 52nd birthday.[34] But the shadow of the well-liked Kline's death contributed to an aggrieved tone on the Poses panel. It was, as de Kooning's biographers put it, "a powerful symbol of the changing of the guard."[35]

"Bill deK is building and so is the Museum of Modern Art. Similar scales"—Hess relayed the local news to Schapiro, in California.[36]

The other artists coped with the impact of success in their own ways—"Clyfford Still has moved to Maryland . . . Ad Reinhardt has definitively flipped," in Hess's opinion; Rothko, depressed, was medicated for a variety of ailments in a vicious cycle of cause and effect.[37] Like de Kooning, Barney found reassurance in real estate.

In August he expanded to the entire third floor at Front Street—he already had half plus the fourth floor—and in early September he and Annalee looked to buy a large apartment in the once regal future landmark Osborne, a building festooned with glazed terracotta, Tiffany glass, mosaics and marble, works by John La Farge and Augustus Saint-Gaudens on West Fifty-Seventh Street, catercorner across Seventh Avenue from Carnegie Hall and the Russian Tea Room.[38] It was a long way from East Nineteenth Street—or the downtown living quarters of many of his peers—and just the right, slightly stodgy but culturally resonant, civilized, and substantial, announcement of the couple's new standing. The 14-foot-high ceilings in the grand apartment would be the perfect setting for Barney's decidedly unstodgy art.

The newly successful painters had begun thinking about "financial planning for artists"; Weisman, who was advising Barney, now urged him to become serious about arrangements for deferred compensation.[39] That is how the idea to invest in real estate was likely initiated. When the deal at the Osborne fell through, Barney and Annalee pursued a number of other possibilities, mostly off Park Avenue but including the baronial Dakota on West Seventy-Second Street—all of them significantly upscale from the pre-war classic on Ninety-Third Street.[40] In the end, they did not move.

FIFTY-TWO

"THE REPUTATION OF BARNETT NEWMAN"

"I had a 4-hour, 24-vodka, Arab lunch with Barney Newman," Hess wrote to Schapiro at the end of August. "He is about to have a 2-man show to open Allan Stone's new gallery, with (of all people) Bill dek. Barney says, 'It's like Babe Ruth and Lou Gehrig.' I resisted saying, 'Watch out, it might be like Joe Louis and Max Baer.'"[1]

In the last week of 1962, John Kennedy faced down Nikita Khrushchev in Cuba; "New Realism," soon simply known as "Pop" art, faced down Abstract Expressionism in a temporary outpost of the Janis Gallery in a storefront on West Fifty-Seventh Street; and one of the original giants of Abstract Expressionism, de Kooning, faced off against the ascending star of his peer, Barnett Newman, at the opening show of the Allan Stone Gallery in a second floor loft at 48 East Eighty-Sixth Street.

As were so many other young men, Stone, a lawyer who had been painting for over a decade, was swept up by Barney's charisma. It was one of the "glorious things about Barney"—how he genuinely involved himself in the lives of so many of the next generation.[2] Stone found it "uplifting" to be around him. "He knew so much, [he was] like a Talmudic scholar . . . . Architecture, music . . . cheap, obscure" places to eat. Barney took Stone around to view work, advising him whom he should be showing, trying to make Stone into a "dealer's dealer," and encouraging him to "get the original group together again." Don't bother with "the pie guy," he advised Stone about Wayne Thiebaud, whose *Pies* merited an enormous color reproduction in *Life*.[3] Even so, Barney took Thiebaud and his wife along when he arranged a visit to West Orange, New Jersey to see "something that's gonna blow your mind," Barney told Stone of Smith's "six-foot-square" sculpture. "Isn't that magnificent? Don't you get it?" The men drank, and Smith recited *Finnegan's Wake*.

Stone was already buying de Kooning's work, and he was interested in mounting shows that would create a dialogue. He seemed to think that Barney and de Kooning were not on speaking terms, but only the previous year they were friendly collaborators in the small group delegated to fashion the letter protesting Canaday's bias. Barney basked while de Kooning, in his Dutch accent, told him he always loved him.[4] In Sandler's apartment, with the critic acting as a "kind of secretary," the letter could not get written because the two artists "began reminiscing about the old days."[5] When Stone arranged a meeting at Barney's apartment, "Barney pulled out a huge bottle of vodka" and "drank most of it himself," without showing the smallest sign of intoxication. They agreed to the show.

De Kooning wanted intimate spaces for the work, Barney wanted the opposite, and suggested, once again, that Smith design the exhibition, which he did brilliantly, in everyone's opinion, satisfying them both. De Kooning had no interest in the installation; Barney wanted to supervise; Stone agreed he could be present. Barney wanted to write the catalogue, Stone told him firmly, "no words," then proceeded to write a one-page note himself. And Stone gave his own names to some of the works: an untitled drawing became *The Void*; *Be II*, which Barney may not have considered finished, was not exhibited but appeared in the catalogue as *Resurrection*. The work later called by Barney *The Third*—the enormous Sunkist-hued, post–Los Angeles work that had been completed only months earlier, and which Stone was hoping to buy—was emphatically named *Orange Colossus*. Barney was furious.[6]

It was the broadest selection of Barney's work ever to be exhibited together. The eighteen pieces included very early drawings, and paintings from 1947 through 1962—those with horizontal and those with vertical bands.[7] The 95 ⅜-by-1 ⅝ work untitled in the 1951 Parsons show and named *End of Silence #1* at Bennington was now titled *The Wild*, and would have been one end of another spectrum if the 18-footer *Uriel*, illustrated in the catalogue, had been included as intended; but its old stretcher was warped, and a new stretcher Barney commissioned was not ready. Its absence caused him "great damage," and Barney telegraphed the vendor asking for the 275-dollar payment to be refunded, once again using language that set the stage for litigation.[8] When Stone asked him why go to such lengths, "it's a matter of principle," was Barney's reply,[9] and he engaged a new law firm to pursue the suit.[10] It was an entirely different story with the tall and narrow canvas: Barney brought it to Robert Kulicke, challenging him to create a frame for a *painting*, not an *object*. The solution so pleased Barney that—Barbara Kulicke claimed—he not only named the work *The Wild* after a particularly enjoyable weekend at the Kulickes in New Paltz,[11] but gave Robert the option to buy it.[12]

The fifteen less deliberately selected works by de Kooning described an analogous chronological and stylistic arc.

In enthusiastically embracing the idea of the show—"like Babe Ruth and Lou Gehrig"—Barney may have considered how vulnerable de Kooning was. His reputation had taken a hit in Arnason's show, especially in a lecture that Greenberg gave at the Guggenheim, "After Abstract Expressionism." About de Kooning's work the critic used the most damning term possible—"mannerism"—to condemn what he called the "homeless representation" that had crept into de Kooning's recent art. His March show at Janis had been thin and disappointing, and even his most committed supporters could not deny it. His personal life was chaotic and alcoholic benders were not infrequent. He had moved from the city to Long Island and had not been painting; he felt he was "not in the public eye . . . he was sort of being forgotten," and had gone into debt to build his grandiose, fantasy studio in Springs.[13] At this moment, with Barney rising and de Kooning—temporarily—declining, Stone's ambition to put Barney and de Kooning "on the same plane"[14] cut two ways.

"Barnett Newman and William [*sic*] de Kooning are founding fathers . . . . This exhibit is not a competition. The purpose is not to pick a winner, but to raise issues," Stone began his paragraphs. Both men, he wrote, "loom as artistic and intellectual giants."[15]

And that was how the critics treated them, as two great powers. In *Art International*, ignoring Stone's "disclaimers," Michael Fried called it an "agon."[16]

Almost metaphorically, the show opened the evening after President Kennedy addressed the nation on television about the "Soviet military build-up on the island of Cuba" whose purpose could be "none other than to provide a nuclear strike capability against the Western Hemisphere." That morning the *Times*'s headline ran across eight columns: "U.S. Imposes Arms Blockade on Cuba on Finding Offensive-Missile Sites; Kennedy Ready For Soviet Showdown." On Madison Avenue, there was a line around the block, waiting to get into the gallery, "everyone [on it] wondering if there was about to be a war," recalled Stone.[17]

"Two of the most remarkable artists alive today," wrote Hess—considerably more respectful since he had published Barney's review of Canaday's book in September. "De Kooning and Newman do not confront each other as rivals, and although it would be hard to find more unlike colleagues, their work seems to share a certain quality of light and of place, perhaps because, as Barnett Newman once remarked, 'it's the artists who made New York,' and the city, in turn has impressed its sense of urgency and beauty on their images." As Scull pointed out to Hess a few months before, it was less the chicken who was blind in 1950 than the critic.

Hess praised equally both men's work and "continuing and profound" influences on younger artists. And he finally "got it" as Barney might have said. If Barney's assertion of the "contemplative spine appears simplistic, consider some of its consequences." "Rational means and ends both are transformed into mysteries . . . . He makes a multitude of radiant negations. His aim is simply to produce the greatest masterpieces in the world."

"Newman focuses on the Universal Man he has discovered inside himself. In each Newman painting, there are years of other Newmans, each inflecting the other, quietly, remorselessly."

Hess called for "large, thoughtful" museum exhibitions of both.[18]

"Newman's canvases look unequivocal, but their meanings are complex. They are vertically aspiring and static, contained and expansive, at the same time," Sandler wrote in the *Post*. "Newman's paintings are intransigent and difficult, but they refuse to be ignored. They have been and continue to be a challenge, and this is their strength."[19] To be fair, there were critics who were not impressed; Fried, and Sidney Tillim (in *Arts Magazine*), for instance, could only place the work in grander contexts of deterministic art history and, in attributing motivations that Barney never had, found it wanting. Those critics were interested in a different generation, in different purposes for art. No one, however, thought to dispute Barney's *right* to be shown with de Kooning.

The "war"—if there was to be one—would not be between Barney and de Kooning, but between abstract art and the Pop artists showcased at Janis one week later in "International Exhibition of the New Realists," where a "modernist" felt "like a follower of Ingres looking at the first Monets," and the New Realists eyed the "old abstractionists like Khrushchev used to eye Disneyland—'We will bury you.'"[20]

Hess's review of Janis's exhibition was placed immediately below his review of Stone's. "A great deal has been written about these artists, and they are eminently writable-about": art magazines, gallery shows on both coasts, upcoming exhibitions, and symposia at museums addressed the "ideas about art beyond Art . . . commercial displays, advertising mediums, industrial design—all of it shoved forward at the spectator with undisguised delight." He contrasted this work to the "Abstract-Expressionists, whose masterpieces convince you at non-verbal levels (i.e., esthetically) and whose masters are shy of press-conferences."[21] But the particular "point of the Janis show," Hess bristled, "was an implicit proclamation that the New had arrived and it was time for all the old fogies to pack. What *Life* (the magazine) calls the 'Red-Hot Take-Over Generation'" was in.[22] Certainly that was the way the artists who, just a few years earlier, Janis had seduced away from Parsons, saw it. Now Janis literally evicted Parsons from her space and, symbolically, the older artists from his.[23] Motherwell, Rothko, Guston, and Gottlieb—who had joined Janis in 1960—left the gallery in protest. Guston may have found the "pork sandwich" indigestible, but Barney had an adventurous appetite. Janis recalled that alone of his generation, Barney came to see the show and kept in touch with the younger generation.[24]

And Hess acknowledged why it was reciprocated. "Given the stripe, you can assume Jasper Johns's American Flag. More important, once given Newman's assumption of the possibility of enormous psychic energy behind the most obvious-looking 'composition'—the symmetrical disposition of two planes interrupted by an obviously sensitized stripe—you can extrapolate the idea of the banal image itself, taken from the most banal sources—advertising, comic strips, etc."

Hess was the original partisan of Abstract Expressionism. Nevertheless, having participated in the outcry over Canaday's sclerosis, and recognizing his responsibility as a critic and an editor, he dutifully added, "just because something is bound to happen does not make it easy to do." There was indeed a group of "brilliant young artists" at Janis.

"The 60s were a very bad time for all the Abstract Expressionists," recalled Grace Hartigan.[25] "I don't know why they have to knock one thing for the other," de Kooning would say. "In Europe . . . masters were allowed to rest on their laurels. Here in America they were forced to prove themselves again and again and again." At one point he humiliatingly traded physical blows with Greenberg, who had thrown his authority behind the "color field" painters Morris Louis, Kenneth Noland, and Jules Olitski.[26] Rothko publicly shunned the Pop artists when he encountered them.[27] Not only did Barney's generation feel that they were being replaced, many felt they were not *respected* by the young.

But Barney, for whom respect was the central ethos of his entire life, did not, at least publicly, succumb to this darkness, nor did he compromise the standard to which he held himself and his art—whatever *internal* accommodations he had to make. Finally, it was his enthusiasm, his curiosity, and his warmth that prevailed. He *was* respected by the newcomers.

The hook for Seckler's article,[28] published in June, was the "surprisingly swift emergence of what the Guggenheim has called the 'abstract-imagist wing' of abstract expressionism," and Barney's placement "among the leading 'imagist' precursors" in the installation. But she also had in mind the "flurry of critical activity," mainly Greenberg's lecture, "After Abstract Expressionism," published in October in *Art International*. "Of the artists that 'king-making' critic, Clement Greenberg, has successfully sponsored," Seckler wrote, "Barnett Newman is the last to enter the Pantheon of the museums. But perhaps the very severity that has made his work too forbidding to many, has given it greater prestige and influence among those of his contemporaries who conceive of progress as a race toward ultimates."[29]

Greenberg had provided a sort of tip sheet, naming those artists who he said were in decline because they had succumbed to "homeless representation" and "painterliness"; he praised "three New York painters who stand somewhat apart from Abstract Expressionism"—Newman, Rothko, and Still—"who have renounced painterliness . . . for the sake, precisely, of a vision keyed to the primacy of color." This, of course, set the stage for Greenberg's newly favored, "color field" artists.

But Barney was *onement*, he renounced nothing for the sake of a style, and would not set the stage for anyone. He certainly would not allow Greenberg to submit his *sui generis* uniqueness to a formal dissection, or to use him for his own purpose. "He always puts Still and Rothko in the same bed with me, now he's putting Noland and Louis in the same bed. With the five of us, it's kind of crowded."[30] Nor would he allow Seckler to breezily accept Greenberg's determinism. "My quarry," Seckler wrote in her introduction, "was skillfully skirting all traps baited with 'style' or influence.'" She found him to have an "extraordinary capacity for attention to the particular," to "discrimination of qualities" in her "tape recorder, Latin suffixes, the predicaments of young artists, and the complex pattern of sounds in a bird's song," and, to her frustration, not least in the person and art of himself.

Since Greenberg in his lecture said that Barney (and Rothko) had subordinated "drawing" because it got "in the way of color-space," Barney made sure to tell Seckler that "drawing is central to my whole concept . . . yet no writer on art has ever confronted that issue. I am always referred to in relation to my color." Where Greenberg said "Newman's pictures look easy to copy . . . but they are far from easy to conceive, and their quality and meaning lie almost entirely in their conception," Barney tied himself into knots, while speaking to Seckler, to distance himself from "those involved in the notion of the dogmatic and who have some idea of how a painting should be made . . . painting with a capital P." Greenberg used the word "conception"; Barney called himself a "direct painter," which was something very different. He did not pre-conceive, he "never worked from sketches, never planned a painting, never 'thought out' a painting." If the final appearance seemed "organized," that was "somebody else's problem."[31]

Now, in November 1962, after Greenberg's lecture appeared in print, Barney was very specific. At a lecture at Hunter College ("my alma mater-in-law" he began, winningly and wittily; Annalee and Sarah Newman had both graduated from Hunter) he used the platform for the activity that defined him *as a person*: to *react* when issues were raised. Thus, for the benefit of the students, he reacted to several "things that [he'd] been reading" recently—by Ada Louise Huxtable, by Harold Rosenberg, by Allan Stone in the catalogue of his own show—building up to his reaction to Greenberg. He went through this exercise in order to unequivocally declare that *as a painter* he, Barney, did *not* react. He created: each day's painting created a new place, the "place"—not geographical—"where I am" that moment.[32]

With his generation, "for the first time in history, painting moved from the picture" of something—even an abstract something—to "painting," and painting, "certainly" in his own work, was "a complete thing" in itself.

> Painting can no longer depend on a given set of facts, it has to depend on what you really have to say yourself. And at the same time, since it has content, and people are beginning to understand that it *does* have content, that the *content has to be determined at the very moment that it's being made* [emphasis added].

And, in a direct blow to Greenberg, he expressed hope that "the time will come very soon that there will be some attempt made to read the work . . . not in terms of its *paint,* not in terms of its structure, but in terms of its result!"[33]

As he told Seckler, "the meaning must come from the seeing, not from the talking." The counter—and the more accurately sympathetic than Greenberg's formalist—description of Barney's paintings came from Alloway, in a BBC broadcast that month, when he described his experience at Bennington in 1958.

> This was certainly <u>not</u> geometric art. The bands, I discovered, when I moved closer, were often fluttery and rough at the edges; the great planes of colour were painted firmly, but without fanaticism, giving a factual but relaxed surface, quite unlike the finish of geometric painting. The colour had an intensity and grandeur which was a new experience . . . the expansion of one colour in a field. Newman's paintings resist analysis into separate parts. They exist, commandingly, as indivisible units . . . a sense of existing as a whole, primal and irreducible, majestic yet compact, which is uniquely Newman's gift.[34]

Alloway described the feeling of exaltation that "comes from one's sudden domination by the work of another man," and doubt that "stems from not knowing what it is that has been done." Understanding and admiration follow, and the "the acceptance that precedes a verbal grasp of the work is a unique moment."

Alloway's broadcast demonstrated more than an innate, sensitive understanding of the art; it was one of the first instances of a critic's compassionate understanding of the man. Alloway, who suffered from epilepsy, was recognized as independent, rigorous, and astute, but not known as an especially amiable personality. But for the few months that he had been at the Guggenheim, most days would begin with a friendly call from Barney. They spoke on the phone until lunchtime, when they would meet to dine together and continue talking until three.[35] Now, instead of pained letters from the artist himself, a critic would pick up the baton and point out Barney's grievances from the sublime to the ridiculous: that with his absence from Hess's *Abstract Painting* (1951) and Ritchie's *Abstract Painting and Sculpture in America* (1951) and Miller's "Fifteen Americans" (1952), "Topical art history [was] being written without the presence of a key figure"; and that Barney's 1947 words about "the revived use of brown" in America pre-figured "the use of such colours by Rothko" and was "missing from the art history of American Art." His goal, Alloway announced, was to "re-introduce Newman"—by quoting Barney's early writings "that can be verified and looked at in context"—"into New York art history."[36]

As soon as the Stone show had been planned, Alloway proposed to James Fitzsimmons, the editor of *Art International,* a two-part article: part one would be essentially what became the BBC broadcast and part two would be a selection of Barney's writings, "accompanied by a full 'scholarly apparatus' of bibliographical notes, etc."[37]

Alloway's broadcast was tellingly entitled "The Reputation of Barnett Newman." Barney could stop carrying the weight alone. The hagiography had begun.[38]

A "burlesque of art history," Barney's surprising new champion Rosenberg took on Greenberg in *Art News* in December. "Artists vanish, and paintings spring from one another with no more need for substance than the critic's theories." On the other hand, the "current revival of illusionism in art through techniques of physical incorporation of street debris and the wooden-faced mimicry of senseless items of mass communication"—Pop—was an art of "impenetrable farce," the "new slapstick art." The superiority of Abstract Expressionism—in Rosenberg's parlance, "Action Painting"—required defending from attack on all sides.

> To forget the crisis, individual, social, esthetic, that brought Action Painting into being, or to bury it out of sight . . . is to distort fantastically the reality of postwar American art. This distortion is being practised daily by all who have an interest in "normalizing" vanguard art, so that they may enjoy its fruits in comfort: these include dealers, collectors, educators, directors of government cultural programs, art historians, museum officials, critics, artists—in sum, the "art world."

In sum, every force that would render impotent the *power* of Barney, now that he was being feted.

Sure, Rosenberg acknowledged, the "rich Action Painter stoically enduring the crisis of society in his imported sports car" was easy to parody. But that was the opinion of "materialistic cynics for whom high sales prices decide everything."

"The net effect of deleting from art the artist's situation, his conclusions about it and his enactment of it in his work is to substitute for the crisis-dynamics of contemporary painting and sculpture an arid professionalism that is a caricature of the estheticism of half a century ago."[39]

At Hunter College in November, like a yeshiva rebel, Barney transgressively challenged the received interpretation of Genesis. The "apple was not the issue," he told the audience. Man *willfully* "rejected Paradise." A "choice of how one will die consequently left [one] free to live."[40]

FIFTY-THREE

BLACK AND WHITE

"Barney Newman is about to 'take over,'" Hess reported to Baziotes, at the end of January, even as Jasper Johns filled Castelli Gallery, and Rauschenberg's retrospective loomed at the Jewish Museum.[1]

To Schapiro, he joked, "Harold Rosenberg is becoming an art critic (we are all aghast)."[2] Hess had been publishing Rosenberg for years in *Art News*; what Hess really meant was that Rosenberg's feature, "Barnett Newman, 'A Man of Controversy, and Spiritual Grandeur,'" was about to appear in *Vogue*.

At Rauschenberg's opening at the end of March, *Glamour* magazine corralled twenty-nine artists for a group photo: once again in the center was Barney (next to the man of the hour). Select quarters of the younger generation—artists and critics and collectors—were suddenly discovering, and being thrilled by, Barney's work. "Newman begins with the trial of a premise of a perfect vision in a calm, unruffled world, and ends with a cataclysm," wrote Kaprow in *Art News*. "The flood of utter chaos, of sheer color inundating us, of lines crashing into splinters and vanishing into the vibrating deluge, is the 'terror' Barnett Newman refers to when he speaks of his work."

"This terror and passion is as close to our marrow, as unsettling to us emotionally, as anything of Pollock's."[3]

The Allan Stone show was the "best" of the season, of "such importance that . . . it should have embarrassed most of the museums in the vicinity," wrote Frank O'Hara. Barney hovered as one of "the best artists" in Janis's "New Realists" show—self-evident in his influence on Johns and Rauschenberg.[4]

The 1950 *Joshua*, sold in January for 9000 dollars (89,600 dollars in 2023), was featured in a Museum of Modern Art tour of the serious and fashionable collection of the Leon Mnuchins; *L'Errance* (1953) and *White Fire* (1960) in a museum tour of the Sculls' apartment. A few months later, *L'Errance* appeared on the opening page of a glamour piece devoted to the Sculls in what Alfred Barr called the "exceedingly elegant" French magazine *L'Oeil*.

In *Vogue*, Liberman's photograph of *Onement VI*'s deeply saturated cobalt spread across a page and a half, with Barney before it, looking unusually trim with bow tie and monocle, hands casually in his pockets à la J.F.K. (plate 16).[5] Three years earlier, readers of *Life* saw Clyfford Still's enormous profile, god-like, in front of a tiny detail of a painting, cobalt with white ribbon—an entirely uncharacteristic color and brushstroke—enlarged to a full page in a disingenuous masquerade. Now *Vogue* settled that score: "One of the great American painters, Barnett Newman is shown here in his New York studio down by the docks, standing in front of one of his enormous works, 'Onement No. 6,' now in the collection of Mr. and Mrs. Fred Weisman," read the caption, confirming his regency and crucially his authorship.

"You stand before the canvas as if you were lecturing to America on How to Look at a Newman; your relation to the painting is like Kennedy standing in front of the American flag," wrote Schapiro.[6]

A couple of months later, for an hour-long special on CBS television, Barney was one of fifteen New York artists ranging from Stuart Davis and Hofmann to Warhol and Oldenburg who were featured speaking in their studios. He agonized over every word in the final script, revising endlessly to distinguish himself from the crowd, identify himself as singular personally as well as artistically. And he was successful. When the show was later screened to Yale art graduate students who were thinking about how you "physically make the image, what to do and how," Barney talking about stretching the canvas, restretching it, wetting it down, etcetera" in a "Platonic" way, made the big impact.[7]

It was not unconsidered that Rosenberg began the *Vogue* encomium by proclaiming that Barney's "outstanding personal characteristics are also those of his paintings." Barney's "taste," courting of "controversy," and "spiritual grandeur" were the same qualities that inhered in the paintings: "impeccable décor," an "argument about art and life," and the "sublime." The total identification of man and work was not simply recognized, but touted in a mass medium for the consumption and benefit of the fashionable audience.

Rosenberg worked hard—and faithfully to Barney, warts and all—to deflect any doubt. The paintings, he wrote, balanced "the intellect on pivotal issues of contemporary art (e.g., how far can one go with evenly brushed areas of colour devoid of forms?), while summoning the imagination . . . to a ritual stripped of myth." Rosenberg conceded that the work's reception had been a slow process; it was not psychologically easy to hold several "active" responses at once. Understanding had to overcome "piecemeal" analysis, assault and apology, dialectical warfare, and specious resemblances to the work of others. The last, Rosenberg wrote, engaged "Newman in a protracted campaign of distinctions and clarifications not unlike that conducted by his celebrated ecclesiastical namesake."

Barney was endowed with "a rare strain of ideological persistence" and "a highly developed skill in disputation" that led him "at times to the border of hairsplitting, though one who resists losing patience will usually discover that the particular hair was in need of bisection. This tendency of Newman to draw lines of division is, of course, an aspect of his painting, though in it the lines have also other reasons for being."

The "heroic," the "cosmic," the "mythic," the "primitive"—with Barney "these are all one sentiment, experienced in his paintings as the sentiment of one-ness . . . . In the last analysis, singularity is their subject, a singularity beyond human reach." Barney's paintings were no less than a "short cut to the unattainable."[8]

The article was a short cut to apoplexy for at least one of Barney's peers. Clyfford Still, who had been for some time working closely with Betty Freeman on a book that he hoped would become the first major iteration of his own mythos for posterity, seized on the article to advance his pawn. "Amoral hypocrisy," "totalitarian technique," courting "public attention and public success at any cost to manhood," were some of the things of which Still accused Barney, calling him one of the "conspicuously morbid (even sinister) clowns."[9] When a skeptical Freeman asked Still for any early evidence, Still responded that the "papers you requested" were in deep storage.[10] When Freeman sent him an essay by Alloway in which the critic, continuing the mission assumed in his earlier radio broadcast, assigned intellectual precedence to Barney for articulating the postwar "sublime" in his writings, Still responded that it represented the "degree and extent to which a colossal hoax has been effected" and revealed the "utter shameless and moral depravity of Newman."[11]

In "The American Sublime"—the offending article—Alloway praised the work of Newman, Rothko, and Still as "a moral model for human action," "the product of an intense moral act," and the artists themselves as connected to "the prophet, the sage and the seer" through whom "the sublime is reached."[12] Moral competition was such that, in the company of the others, any of the three might have felt the victim of a "colossal hoax."

It was 1963, nineteen years after a loose group of artists responding to the tragedy of World War II expressed an urgent longing for a way to approach the sublime, and at least six years after a younger generation had responded to that (too-excoriating) longing in a world more comfortable and cynical than traumatized with a variety of emotionally distanced work. Barney, as emotionally invested as ever, understood he had to tailor his rhetoric to the times and his earned stature. But there was no adjustment in Still's bombast, no change in the kind of hysterical language that Still continued to employ behind Barney's back to an array of curators, critics and collectors, now—happily for Barney—with less and less effectiveness. By November, Still felt "compelled personally to enter this murderous arena" (the art community) and to "drop the matter" of a book written by anyone but himself.[13]

Rosenberg told Barney that he had written the *Vogue* piece "with deep affection for you and with that noble image of you in the photo propped up before me. The affection kept" him from "being overcome by the image." The critic recounted in *Vogue* the story of "colored feathers found on the street [that] were pasted in vertical bands on sheets of cardboard and segments of the wall" at The Club after the Parsons's 1950 opening—implying it was to honor Barney for developing an "insignia" and not owning the mocking gesture originally intended. Now, Rosenberg ended his letter, "Perhaps I shall make myself another feather 'Newman' as a souvenir of this gratifying event"—the hagiographic essay.[14]

No wonder Barney was almost giddy at Rosenberg's birthday party a week—it might as well have been a lifetime—later. The two men were swimming in *yiddishkeit* fellowship and "deep affection" for each other, and Barney and Rosenberg—one of the participants in The Club caper—were able to joke about it. For Rosenberg's annual celebration, to which artists were accustomed to bring gifts of their work, Barney's was a drawing of a sort of heraldic circle in which a sword and a feather were crossed. "To Harold or should I call you Chacham [Hebrew for "Wise one"]. In honor of your birthday, here is the souvenir feather you asked for—what is more fitting for one who lives by the 'feder' [Yiddish for pen] and can turn it into a feather or into a sword. And what is more fitting than that I who thirteen years ago was asked to read his signature in feathers should now have his feathers joined by your feder—thirteen years later—a regular bar mitzvah or is it a federation. Birds of a feder flock together."[15]

The interview with CBS producer Lane Slate thoroughly illustrated the kind of "hair-splitting" that long amused and had so recently begun to impress Rosenberg. The challenge for Barney, he again articulated, was to overcome the material—the canvas, the paint; and the danger was that the result might become an "object." He didn't "crop" like some artists; he didn't make "objects" as others did; although he had written about the Sublime, he now found that "ridiculous." He was not interested in talent or beauty, but in "genius"—and here he told the story of the prayer recited at the Passover seder when it fell on the Sabbath, thanking God "who distinguishes not only between the holy and the unholy but between the holy and the HOLY."

"Those who think that the world is made up of objects must inevitably think of man as an object," he began. "I am not interested in adding to the objects that exist in the world. I want my painting to separate itself from all and every object that exists in the world. It not only has to be unique but the uniqueness has to be meaningful for living men."[16]

As the final script took shape he revised his language. "I'm against aesthetics. I'm against any kind of aesthetic way of making a painting . . . . But I do insist on painting**S**." He did "insist on the power of that work [to change] people's lives. There's a difference in making an aesthetic object and a work of art. To create a work of art means, to me, to express something that is so deep in one. It's not acting out one's neurosis, it's not expressing one's sensations, but it is an attempt to put down what you really believe and what you really are concerned with or what really moves you and interests you, in terms of being." This was the final language on which he settled after at least seven revisions.

But many revealing remarks were edited out by Barney, or left on the cutting room floor, perhaps deemed too indiscreet for the program's purpose of exposing a wider public to the newly fashionable contemporary art.

"How do you feel about your success?" Slate asked, perhaps not realizing how recently earned that success was. "The thing that does give me some satisfaction is that whatever has happened to me has happened to me outside, without, and in spite of, the system," Barney answered. "I have had no real career. I have never had a dealer." ("I have no museum. I am not fondled by the Buffalo Albright Knox Art Museum," he penciled in on one edit of the script, in a disgruntled dig at Still, who had negotiated the 1959 condition-laden exhibition.[17]) "It has happened without the help of *Time* and *Life* and I have never been the white-haired boy of curators. I hope that my success has been the power of my work. It found support in the courage of young collectors here and in England."

Actually, he corrected Slate, he was not a popular success. "My work is still very controversial and inaccessible. Even now, the public can only see one example of my work in one institution on this continent. My work is extremely controversial and not many have enough courage to take it."[18]

The more opportunities that came Barney's way, the more opportunities he created, the more hyperactive he became. He was able to do nothing halfway—which meant that not only was he exquisitely demanding of himself as a craftsman, but also that he had to perform fully as "Himself"—orating, charming, seducing each new potential conscript he encountered to the crusade. As always during his manic periods, he was incapable of marshalling his energy and physical and mental resources to protect himself.

Thus, at the beginning of 1963 he committed himself to the grand ambition for the growing group of black-and-white paintings—that they would be his defiant take on the Passion cycle: "as for Barney's Stations of the Cross, he says he'll write about the issues and ideas himself," thus Hess declined Schapiro's offer to *Art News* in January.[19] And he had—*possibly*—begun calculations for what would be *Broken Obelisk*, arguably the first fabricated monumental abstract sculpture.[20] Before the summer he enlisted in the exciting revival of fine art lithography, and made a Barney-esque incursion into architecture. He installed Liberman's third show at the old Parsons, and after "an amazing and painful lunch" during which Barney and Alloway "forced her not to" show her own work as she planned,[21] he conceived and wrote paragraphs for a surprising show that would inaugurate Parsons's new gallery space in September: "Amlash Sculpture." Before the fall, he had presented in a Princeton symposium on world affairs, and sat for long, thoughtful sessions with two interviewers that allowed him to shape and control and polish his ambition for posterity, but that, unfortunately, never produced published works.[22] He acted as his own agent, negotiating terms of sales with Weisman, Heller, Leon Mnuchin, William Rubin, and Kasmin, and negotiating business arrangements with Ellin, who hoped to return to New York and open a gallery. Schapiro encouraged him to write his memoirs.[23]

That fall, *Primordial Light* and *Shining Forth* were loaned to a group show at Janis; *The Way* (1951) was in a Poses-organized show that proposed Abstract-Expressionist roots of current painting; and Alloway requested *The Third*—a.k.a. *Orange Colossus*, "insurance value" 40,000 dollars—for the Guggenheim International Award Exhibition to be held the following January.[24] Wagstaff wanted work for a January show at the Wadsworth Atheneum; the Whitney, *Noon-Light*; Stockholm's Moderna Museet *Right Here*; and two other paintings, including the 9-by-14-foot *Shining Forth* were on their way to the Jewish Museum for the Heller-organized "Black and White." Barney always found showing very painful, according to Annalee,[25] and every single one of these loans entailed all the usual apprehension, prolonged anxiety, and multiple-party correspondence about packing and shipping arrangements, condition, restoration, and insurance—and the self-imposed obligation on Barney's part to, whenever possible, intervene and influence the exhibition's agenda. "You gave me some fruitful (fertile?) food for thought in relation to the catalogue, and I am anxious to get at the essay," wrote Sam Hunter from the Poses Institute, in words that echoed Sam Wagstaff's earlier ones.[26] Visitors from England and the U.S. arrived, expecting the legendary treatment.

"Barnet [*sic*] Newman (or 'Himself') is in fine shape," Hess reported to Schapiro that spring. "He has recovered from several attacks of the sniffles this winter, mainly through the heroic ministration of Annalee, and has put to the Torture of the Telephone Harold Rosenberg (see Vogue article), C.B.S. (their program on art), myself . . . and the usual group of small museum officials. On a Sunday evening, he located the chief script writer of the C.B.S. program in a Third Avenue bar where even he (the script writer) didn't know he was."[27]

But it had been a "bad winter," Barney told Weisman,[28] as he looked back from July, "very tough," Hess confirmed to Schapiro. Baziotes, broke, was found to have terminal lung cancer after Janis "fired" him; Gottlieb was still recovering from a heart attack. "Kay Sage killed herself . . . Otto Gerson dropped dead . . . Lee Pollock's brain operation was very long and difficult."[29] Throughout Barney's life a range of physical symptoms both undermined him and readily provided excuses when the terror neared unendurable. He may have hoped the cigarettes and vodka—and the rituals associated with cigarettes and vodka—would dull the agita; of course, they only made it worse.

Barney's ailment wasn't just "several attacks of the sniffles," but noteworthy enough to be noticed and worried over by many friends. During the same period, he was having problems with his gums and his eyes, and was sufficiently agitated to be given by a St. Louis doctor, whom he had only met socially, Librium for the tension and nitroglycerin for chest pain, with prescriptions for their continued use.[30] "Whip lash [from] an old automobile accident"[31] had acted up, and he was, for a while, in "traction" for a hip injury that he pursued in small claims court. He was unable to work because of his "sacroiliac." Annalee felt her own anxiety about his health, hovering over him. Since his heart attack in 1958 she had worried constantly about—in fact, "couldn't stand"—him being in the studio alone. She took all the "sick days" the Board of Education allowed to stay with him. She taught herself not to talk, to sit quietly, "absolutely observant" and anticipate his needs. She would run errands, buy supplies like big jugs of distilled water, paint, and a great many tweezers to remove any stray brush hairs from a painting.[32] Half jokingly, Alfred Leslie recalled her walking five feet behind Barney carrying his foul-weather galoshes.[33]

But Barney soldiered on. Whether they were genuine, hypochondriacal, psychosomatic, or conveniently deployed excuses, no ailment—not even the "traction"—kept him from anything he chose to do, including traveling. His correspondence records a litany of problems, his checkbook a regular log of doctors' fees. Socially, however, he aimed to appear "laid back"; the only giveaway was a "terrible sort of twitch in his jaw muscles."[34]

Convoluted negotiations among Ellin, attorney Bernard Reis, David Smith, Rothko, Guston, Motherwell, de Kooning, and Barney, and then Frank Lloyd of the international powerhouse, Marlborough Gallery, stirred the pot and set off alarms. It all came to nothing for Barney—except a new diplomatic role with Janis, *Shining Forth* shown in his gallery, the twitch and the chest pain.[35]

Harold Diamond, a private art dealer whom Reynal had introduced to Barney, owned a dashing black Buick with tail fins and a white leather interior.[36] Everyone knew that de Kooning, even though he didn't drive, had so loved the Diamonds' previous car, a white Pontiac with red leather upholstery, that he swapped a number of paintings for it, and now Barney got it into his head to do the same, despite the reality that trading work for something else was, for Barney—as Hester Diamond recognized—"totally improper and totally contrary to his idea of the respect that he owed to his own work." Since Barney had been painting the black-and-white pictures, Harold said to him, "well, the car is black and white, and it's 17 feet long. So I think you should trade me a black and white picture, 17 feet long." That summer, there were weeks of test drives. The Diamonds would pick up Barney and Annalee at Ninety-Third Street and West End, go up the West Side Highway, and take the newly completed, surprisingly empty Cross Bronx Expressway to City Island to eat lobsters. His hunger satisfied, Barney decided he did not want the Buick, but it was enormous fun, the Diamonds became fast friends, and Barney had a new audience for the ritual telling and retelling of the "great tragedy of pin point carbonation"—the heroic lawsuit against the Crown Bottling Company on behalf of Annalee's father, his revolutionary insights about the evolution of complex birdsong, and lessons about the perfidy of dealers.[37] But Barney's high spirits had already begun to wane.

When he sat for the lengthy, probing, uncharacteristically revealing interview by Karlis Osis, Michelangelo was on his mind.[38] An English translation of the divine master's poems and selected letters had just been published and was being reviewed in the publications Barney regularly read. It struck a chord when the *Times*'s critic wrote that Michelangelo notoriously "saw enemies, or—if they were artists—rivals at every turn."[39] The day before he sat down with Osis, *Born Under Saturn*, Rudolf and Margot Wittkower's seminal study of the particular temperament of great artists, was discussed in Barney's morning paper.[40] Michelangelo didn't "see in the world that which I feel is my meaning," he remarked to Osis right off the bat. He wanted to "say something that Michelangelo didn't say. At the same time, I do think that what I'm saying will also interest Michelangelo . . . [because] to a certain extent, I belong to the context of the dialogue in which, let's say, Michelangelo and I participate."

Barney told the parapsychologist that even though he—Barney—was "supposed to be a father to a lot of people," what was involved was merely "interpretation," and that fact was sometimes so threatening to him that he felt a "sense of total despair"—because it indicated to him that his work was entirely misunderstood. "What the hell am I doing?" he asked.[41]

Every new professional occasion offered a fresh crop of passionate and driven specialists, large personalities, with whom to collaborate. And likewise every new occasion reproduced the kind of dynamic—learning, teaching, entertaining, feeling appreciated and adored—that he had always craved, but, now, like an addict with a boundless source, could feed without moderation.

William Lieberman, the curator of drawings and prints at the Museum of Modern Art, had not been a notable fan of Barney's work. Barney had not been a notable fan of lithography. But it was Lieberman who suggested to Tatyana Grosman that she invite Barney to make work at Universal Limited Art Editions (ULAE), the lithography workshop she had started seven years earlier in West Islip, Long Island. By 1963, Motherwell, Frankenthaler, Johns, Rauschenberg, and Rivers were among the artists who had made prints in the bucolic, communal, camp-like atmosphere of the workshop. And not simply individual lithographs. ULAE was giving new life to portfolio editions, as contemporary prints were now as likely to be bought by collectors—appreciated like manuscripts or autographs—as they had been previously by decorators to hang on a wall.[1]

Grosman, a Russian Jew, and her husband, a Polish Jewish painter, fled invading armies during the war. The couple had climbed through the Pyrenees, Tatyana's feet frostbitten, to Barcelona and found their way to New York. Of course, Barney had "a great deal of empathy and sympathy for somebody like that" recalled Bill Goldston, who, groomed by Grosman, became ULAE's director after her death.[2]

On several trips in early 1963, Grosman and her young master printer, Zigmunds Priede, brought four or five stones, each weighing 30 to 40 pounds, and a box of lithographic crayons to the apartment on West End Avenue. Barney approached the stones as he would a canvas, thickly layering crayon. Priede would then collect the stones, "process" them to stabilize the image—which inevitably washed out all but the first layer of crayon—and pull a proof. Then Barney "with a kind of formality about his presence" would arrive to view the result, like a "little business person coming out to the country." He wanted very little, if any, adjustment to the images, but when he saw the proofs hanging on the wall, he bent and tore and folded the proofing paper, so maddened was he by the unwilled, offending margins. Originally he intended to make a few individual prints, but, over the course of a year and a half, he wrestled the margins to a draw—they were still there, but he was satisfied—and produced eighteen, spending as long as seven hours testing proofs on various paper.

Priede lived in Manhattan, and at the end of a working day he and Barney would be dropped off at the Babylon station. "It was usually about 10 or 15 minutes before the train came but that was a long time for Barney, he had to get a few shots before," and they "ended up at the bar" across the street. "By the time the train came it was so close that we had to actually rush up the steps, step into the train, and the door would be closing right behind us."[3] During the Long Island Rail Road rides and the group lunches Barney would never stop talking. One of his subjects—Priede had never heard about it before—was Jewish mysticism and the Kabbalah. Later, some related that to his decision to make eighteen images and an edition of eighteen, but it was not his original intention. Although Barney's fondness for eighteen is real—the Hebrew letter *chai*, "alive," has a numerical value of eighteen, which in turn signifies luck—it's another instance of a Jewish cultural tradition, or habitual superstition, not requiring *mystical* investment or piety.

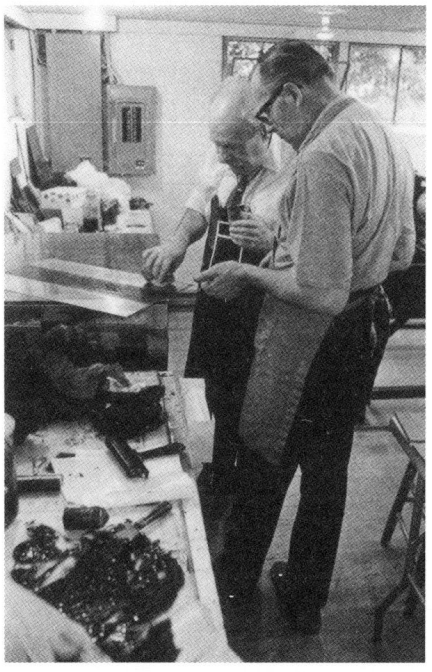

Fig. 46 Working on the *Cantos* with Zigmunds Priede at Universal Limited Art Editions, 1963. Photograph Harry Shunk

Any such meaning assigned to eighteen in this case was a poetic post-facto rational for Barney's reluctance to stop "grappling with the instrument," as he put it, and the indulgence of his collaborators.[4] It was late in the process that he decided to call them "Cantos."[5]

In his three black-and-white lithographic experiments two years earlier at Pratt, his "areas" floated on the paper, solidly inked, textured or scumbled. In two attempts at a narrow band, Barney could not overcome a graphic, drawn quality, as he had in the paintings. But a third version, in which the band was implied between two not-quite abutting areas, was more successful, and it was this to which he returned—with the felicitous addition of color—in twelve of the eighteen on Grosman's stones. Rather than mix his pigments, he "accepted the already premixed colors that came in the cans," which he layered and overlapped, requiring large numbers of proofs with all possible permutations, before Barney made his very simple, but very difficult, choice. The beauty of it, as far as Priede was concerned, was that they used "simply what was in a can, straight, pure pigment." But printing only one or two colors, and staying consistent through the edition, demanded extraordinary attention. There was no room for any variation; either it was "right on or it was not good."

It was the old battle between his stated desire for the work to be seen as "self-evident" as the Ohio earth mounds were, and his fear of being misinterpreted. The viewer needed to recognize his struggle, the decisions that were made; otherwise his effort might go unacknowledged. He was obliged to write a Preface. "I should say," he began,

> that it was the margins made in printing a lithographic stone that magnetized the challenge that lithography has had for me from the very beginning . . . I would create a totality only to find it change after it was printed—into another totality . . . . To crop the extruding paper or to cover it with a mat or to eliminate all margins by "bleeding" (printing on papers smaller than the drawing on the stone) is an evasion of this fact. It is like cropping to make a painting. It is success by mutilation.

In the eternal Newmanian Paradox, Barney was entirely in control, and yet irresistibly compelled.

Each of the eighteen, printed in a unique size on one of four precious papers, had "its own personal margins."

"Each print and its paper had to be decided by me." When a print existed in two iterations—the margins different—it was because each imprint meant "something different to me," Barney tautologically explained. As in other formal "statements"—notably in "The New American Painting" catalogue—he was insistent in memorializing what he was *not* doing.

> I had no plans to make a portfolio of "prints." I am not a printmaker. Nor did I intend to make a "set" by introducing superficial variety. These cantos arose from a compelling necessity—the result of grappling with the instrument,

in other words, the stone. And the viewer could not be trusted with them until instructed.

> Here are the cantos, eighteen of them, each one different in form, mood, color, beat, scale and key. There are no cadenzas. Each is separate. Each can stand by itself. But its fullest meaning, it seems to me, is when it is seen together with the others.

This insight, which emerged from the process, led, ultimately, to Barney's plan for the portfolio's exhibition, unusually precious for the time. Rather than framed and hung, the eighteen were to be viewed flat, the leaves turned, and experienced, as an archival book, or—as they were shown in Los Angeles in 1965—supine in specially constructed vitrines. After Nicholas Wilder in Los Angeles and Gertrude Kasle in Detroit—two gallery owners with whom Barney maintained very friendly relationships—purchased portfolios only to sell the prints individually, Barney bought back from Grosman the eleven remaining portfolios.

As in his show with Stone, where he received the sales proceeds and personally paid Stone his commission, as with the Modern Art Foundry, where he retained the ownership of the molds for *Here I*'s casting, Barney's financial arrangement with Grosman departed from the industry norm.

One May evening, at the Jewish Museum's opening of "Toward a New Abstraction," Barney ran into Richard Meier, a young architect who recently left the office of Marcel Breuer to work on his own; Barney had seen Meier's own paintings in Stella's studio. While a student at Cornell, Meier had taken the course in 20th-century art taught by Alan Solomon, and the two men developed a friendship that continued after they both moved to New York, and Solomon became director of the Jewish Museum, where his advanced program—the first museum shows of Rauschenberg and Johns, the ground-breaking show of minimal sculpture, "Primary Structures" (curated with Kynaston McShine)—created an enviable buzz and drew a large new audience.

At first, the museum's board was swept up in the excitement, but by early 1963 they began to question what it all had to do with the mission of the institution. On the beach on Fire Island, Solomon would talk to Meier about the situation, and Meier conceived of a solution: he would curate a show of recent American synagogue architecture. He knew Louis Kahn was struggling to have his design for Mikveh Israel built in Philadelphia, and, while at Breuer's office, Meier had worked on a large synagogue in New Jersey, so he felt he had "something to contribute." It was a "eureka" moment: if he could show Kahn's design in a museum it might help that specific building to be realized, and raise the level of synagogue architecture in general.[6]

Architecture was never far from Barney's mind: special guests had always been treated to his New York tours and visits to Mies van der Rohe's New Jersey apartment buildings. With friends old and new—Smith, Friedman, Murray, and now I. M. Pei—he enjoyed discoursing on proportion and scale and the mysterious achievement of ineffable qualities of "presence."[7] So he was more than intrigued when Meier told him what he was working on.

"Oh, *I've* designed a synagogue," Barney told Meier.

"Great," was the reply, "I'll put you in the show. Where is it?"

"Well," Barney answered, "I'll have to find it. You know, it's sort of on the back of a napkin somewhere."

And, then the full-blown agitation exploded. Despite visits to a range of doctors in New York, he turned to Dr. Edward Massie of Missouri for help with anxiety and stress. He wrote to the Carnegie Hall manager, who inquired whether he wished to renew his lease, that he hadn't been able to use his studio for three years because of the "incessant and obsessional Hi-Fi playing machine" that his neighbor ran "day and night," the distress he suffered was inexpressible, and he wanted assurances that the "overbearing clatter of mechanical machines" would cease before he would renew.

Juggling lithographic stones and crayons with one hand, Barney and his reliably helpful and enthusiastic comrade Murray began, with the other, to make somehow concrete the general ideas Barney had talked about with Smith in 1950 and developed at the time Gottlieb, Ferber, and Motherwell had contracted to work with Percival Goodman on Congregation B'nai Israel in New Jersey. "The outside is a box. The inside is the essence of an open, living space, the true theatre in the round, where everyone feels himself in it," as he noted of the Touro Synagogue.[8]

It did not result in the most important work in Barney's oeuvre, and the pressure was deleterious to his health. But the episode turned out to be one of the most happily intense stretches in his life. It had all the right components: a problem to be solved, a new creative challenge, virgin territory on which to plant his stake, and the always welcome excuse to spend concentrated hours, days, and long nights, talking, working, eating, and drinking vodka in the company of a partisan young cohort: Meier, Murray, Holstein, sometimes Solomon, sometimes Meier's brother, Jim. Whichever English visitor was in town. If Meier had other plans, Barney was insistent that they be canceled: "You gotta come over." If Murray were in the messy midst of constructing a model of a concept and it was dinner time, Barney made him wash, button his shirt, and put on a jacket. "I don't want these guys thinking you're the hired help." There were *de rigueur* dinners at the Old Peking on Broadway, where the group would close down the restaurant long after midnight. Sometimes they met on West End Avenue, sometimes in the Front Street studio where the final model was built, sometimes in Murray's apartment on East Twenty-Second Street,

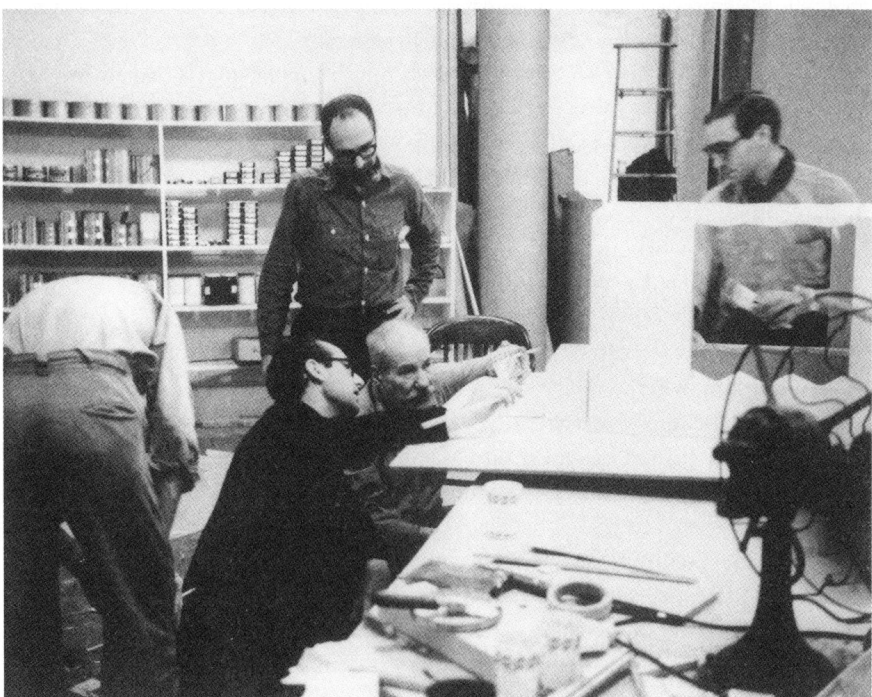

Fig. 47 From left: Robert Murray (bending), Richard Meier, Barnett Newman, Alan Solomon (standing), and Jonathan Holstein building the synagogue model, 1963. Photograph Annalee Newman

where Murray worked on drawings and a small trial plaster and plexiglas model. It was ritualized, and it was fun.

On a draft of the statement for the Jewish Museum's catalogue he inscribed, then crossed out, "1951," implying it had been fully thought out by the earlier date. But something to exhibit—a three-dimensional model—had to be built. All the details needed discussion, parsing, opinions knocked around, trial runs—and, naturally, amplification through all of the wide-ranging influences, sources, and implications that Barney could unearth. Meier may have thought Barney's participation was something of a lark, capricious, resulting in a "folly." But as much as he was enjoying himself, Barney was not at all casual about the project. Philip Johnson's design for a synagogue in Port Chester, New York was to be in the exhibition; Barney wanted to show Johnson that he was a better architect, he told Meier.

Alongside the diligent notes Barney took in English and Hebrew while listening to the British writer, biblical scholar, and "mythologist" Robert Graves and the Israeli anthropologist, biblical scholar, and "folklorist" Raphael Patai discuss "Hebrew Myths" and the parallels with Greek mythology at the 92nd Street Y, he made rudimentary sketches.[9] He mashed up physical details like the zigzagging way groined vaults were depicted on a schematic floor plan, the zigzagging peaked roofs of the surrounding town and building exterior of Prague's "Pinkas Synagogue" as depicted in a 1955 book that he bought secondhand,[10] and the spiritual aspiration from a history of Congregation Shearith Israel, New York's landmark Spanish and Portuguese synagogue. "The synagogue is a place of holiness where we come for inspiration and spiritual stimulation, a 'makom kadosh,' where we stand in God's presence. 'Know before Whom thou standest,' are the words inscribed atop the Ark containing the Torah scrolls," read the brochure produced by the temple's sisterhood,[11] which Barney adapted in his printed statement: "'Know before whom you stand,' reads the command . . . . The synagogue is more than just a House of Prayer. It is a place, 'Makom,' where each man can be called up to stand before the Torah." He visited old synagogues in New York, and initially enlisted Smith's, and Noë's, help with the design and drawings. A book on Polish wooden synagogues was being passed around among some artists, and he acquired that as well. Field trips were arranged to tiny lower Manhattan *shuls* to confirm the required elements, and to grand public buildings to experience firsthand impressive interior spaces or to measure the height of a stair riser—which had "nothing to do with the synagogue" but everything to do with Barney's love of the open-ended discussion it inspired. A "short course in Judaism"—why, in orthodox houses of worship, men and women were separated, the meaning of the eternal light that hung over the ark—was given to Murray.[12] One preliminary drawing made by Barney—not by Murray or Noë as some were—of a perspective view makes the windows resemble draped pleated fabric; Barney scribbled in Hebrew "and the skirts of his robe filled the Temple." The phrase is from Isaiah, specifically from the portion that the 13-year-old Barney was required to learn and read on the day he became a bar mitzvah:

In the year that King Uzziah died, I beheld my Lord seated on a high and lofty throne; and the skirts of His robe filled the Temple. Seraphs stood in attendance on Him . . . . And one would call to the other, "Holy, holy, holy! The Lord of Hosts! His presence fills all the earth!" . . . Then I heard the voice of my Lord saying, "Whom shall I send? Who will go for us?" And I said, "Here am I; send me."[13]

The other projects in the show—by Frank Lloyd Wright, Kahn, Breuer, Goodman, Eric Mendelsohn, Johnson, and nine other individuals and firms—were represented by drawings, photographs, and models. Barney wanted his representation to be different. Once the momentum began, he not only wanted to be in the show, he wanted to have the biggest model—even as he told Murray that he didn't want it to have any sense of materiality at all, that he wanted it to be an idea, an idea that, in his opinion, everyone else missed.[14] "In the synagogue, the architect has the perfect subject because it gives him total freedom for a personal work of art . . . . Nothing happens that is objective. In [the synagogue] there is only the subjective experience in which one feels exalted." Unfortunately, architects were concerned "not with the emotion of exaltation and personal identity called for by the command but with the number of seats and clean décor."[15]

He wanted to somehow reify a creation myth, the squeezing of the elements, the "Zim-Zum"—in the Kabbalah, "God's self-contraction to allow room for Creation"—that would enable one to experience "a total sense of his own personality before the Torah and His Name." Light was critical. Initially, Smith suggested a way to configure the windows and the building. But that plan was too tangible, no longer an idea. Barney took over. Thinking like a painter, not an architect, he specified light pouring in from two sides without regard as to how to make it happen. The vehicle for the effect, Murray told him, had to be structurally supported: a pane of glass would not just float. Murray folded a piece of paper like a fan; it supported a two by four piece of wood. Barney liked the resonance, he was reminded of walls Smith had built for the Parsons Gallery. The zigzagging glass walls that became so identified with Barney's synagogue were now in the plan.

He wanted to tie the building to the American experience as well as the Jewish experience, and in his intention to have a central *bimah*—the platform where the Torah is read—as in Touro, as in Shearith Israel, as in the 17th-century Portuguese Synagogue in Amsterdam and other Sephardic synagogues generally, he found witty, attention-grabbing, inspiration. He was not at all interested in the outside of the building, but the inside would derive a layer of meaning from being analogized to a baseball field.

"The men are seated in dugouts secluded—private . . . ready to be called up to the mound—not the stage—to take his [*sic*] turn before the sacred book. The women instead of hidden" behind a curtain as they were in Amsterdam, "sit up front in the clear light . . . to see what is taking place not as wives, or in some abstract way but as persons. They need not mount the mound to do so anymore than they need walk out onto the baseball field to take part in the baseball play."[16]

The architects in the show were interested in issues like how many people could fit in the building. Barney's issues were of another order. Should the rabbi be on the mound or at home plate? That discussion occupied hours. There would be "bleachers" where the women would sit; what was the perfect proportion? That's when Murray took him to the Twenty-Sixth Street Armory to look at stairs that he thought looked very "Egyptian." The men would sit in the "dugout" and its overhang would provide a structural opportunity to support the window glass.

Originally, the model was to be photographed, and the photograph would appear in the show. But the first maquette was too small, impossible to photograph successfully. Murray built a large version in homasote that was lying around in the Front Street studio, about 2 feet by 2 feet with a larger base. Too large, it turned out—when Barney somehow got Solomon and Meier to agree to put it in the exhibition—to pass through his studio door.[17] The night before the opening, having cut the model down in a way that could be reassembled, Allan Stone, who had a van, was conscripted to drive it to the museum. It was 2:00 a.m. on October 1, an unusual hour for activity at the museum, and police were called. Barney was in heaven; it had turned into a caper. They returned a few hours later for the opening.

For years, he and Lee Krasner argued about the position of the female in Judaism: Krasner rejected the tradition, Barney insisted on its benevolence. His point of view was that she misunderstood it; hers was that she "understood it too clearly."

"Lee, have you seen my synagogue?" he approached her at a large party while the show was on view. "It will resolve that argument we've been having all these years."

"In what sense?" she asked.

"You will approve of where I placed the women in the synagogue. It will end the argument."

"Where did you place the women, Barney?"

"On the altar."

"You sit up on the altar," she told him. "I just want the next empty seat in the next pew that's vacant."[18]

It's a story often cited to indicate Krasner's antagonism toward Barney. In fact, they could have this sort of argument only because of their almost familial closeness. "When I think of Barney," she said after his death, "St. Thomas More's quote, 'Finally it is not a matter of reason; finally it is a matter of love,' expresses my feeling best."[19]

Almost non-stop, almost every day and every night of the months preceding the organized chaos of his participation in the synagogue show, and continuing into the fall, there were hours-long phone conversations with Liberman, or Alloway, or Rosenberg; lunches and dinners with Bill Rubin, Liberman, Reynal, Tony Smith, Parsons (Barney was advising on her September move from 15 East Fifty-Seventh Street to 24 West Fifty-Seventh Street, and Smith's redesign for the space), Elliot, Ellin, Heller, Krasner, Gibbs, Motherwell, Rosenberg, Hess, Gray, Grosman, Stone, Larry Poons, and Larry Rivers; Metropolitan Museum curator Geldzahler and Walker Art Center curator Jan van der Marck, and the private dealer, Harold Diamond; a cadre of British artists who made a bit of a pilgrimage to see him (William

Turnbull, Harold Cohen, Victor Pasmore, Edward Paolozzi); the Chicago collector Muriel Kallis Steinberg Newman, the dealer Kasmin and his business partner, Lord Dufferin, and his sister, the novelist Lady Caroline Blackwood and her husband, composer Israel Sitkowitz; and the Swiss museum men Arnold Rüdlinger and Harald Szeemann. And of course there were the "working" meals with Murray and Holstein, Terry Syverson, Hans Noë, and their wives and dates, at the Russian Tea Room, Billy's, Gloucester House, the Sherry Netherland, Lindy's, Ratner's, Schrafft's, Paris Brest, El Faro, Reuben's, Wah Kee, and assorted other Chinese restaurants. With Alloway and Sleigh, with Motherwell and Frankenthaler—they were married in 1958—there were luncheons at the Libermans and dancing at Tavern on the Green.[20]

A lot of people had similarly active social lives and could manage to get work done. But an important distinction was that a meal with Barney was a ritual that could easily—and would typically—last four or six hours. The conversation with one interviewer involved a preliminary brunch at Barney Greengrass, a preliminary lunch at the Russian Tea Room, and a session at West End Avenue that lasted at least six hours and one or two bottles of vodka.[21]

On November 22, 1963, Barney and Murray were on their way to Treitel-Gratz, the fabricators who would make two of Barney's next sculptures,[22] when they stopped at a Third Avenue bar and grill for lunch. That's where they heard that President Kennedy had been assassinated. Barney was "white as a sheet" as they watched the coverage on the bar's television. As it did for virtually every American, his normal life came to a dramatic halt. It's an index of the staggering impact that Barney did not even try to connect the trauma with his personal agon. He did not respond to the Still painting on the cover of *Art News*, the lengthy text inside, or the comments by Still in *Time* that were fuel and fodder for their decade-long competition.[23] Only a short time before, to an interviewer, Barney dismissed Still as "a Johnny-come-lately."[24]

He told Muriel Newman, who was pursuing *The Voice* (1950), that he had been confined to bed since Thanksgiving with "serious trouble with my sacroiliac" as he equivocated about selling her the exquisitely virginal white painting. The confinement may simply have been an exaggeration, or it may have been a metaphor for the pain the entire country was experiencing, but his activities resumed in early December with the opening of "Black and White" at the Jewish Museum where *Shining Forth (To George)* moved after its public debut at Janis the previous month, along with *Onement IV*. At least one critic recognized that in the monumental canvas Barney was "measuring the universe,"[25] consolation after *Time* described Still's work as "a machete in the jungle."

In the ensuing years, Barney's arguments with Still, with Rothko, and with Motherwell, and theirs with him, were framed in outbursts as an inventory of "firsts." But that was a crude catchall for what genuinely irked Barney. His battle was against "contrived" spontaneity[26]—and it was because of that specifically that priority mattered. He lived the all-black painting; Still, a few months later, merely adapted it.

Barney and Annalee were crossing the pond.

The decision to go to London seems to have been made with some suddenness. Meyer Schapiro immediately rued the missed opportunity to connect Barney with the philosophers Richard Wollheim and "Freddy" Ayer.[1] Even Alloway, the well-connected Englishman with whom Barney was in near-constant communication, socializing and strategizing, had not known about the trip until they were gone.[2] Only a few weeks earlier the Newmans, Alloways, and Motherwells had danced in the unfinished New York State Pavilion in Flushing Meadow Park, having gone to the World's Fair construction site to watch the installation of their friend Liberman's work.[3]

But the worldly and well-traveled Alex and Tatiana du Plessix Liberman were informed, and they shepherded the anxious Newmans through their jitters on a Thursday evening in May as they departed from New York, earning Barney's eternal gratitude by escorting him and Annalee via limousine to the newly renamed John F. Kennedy International Airport and lingering to see them safely off.[4] In his pocket, Barney carried an introduction to Evangeline Bruce, the cosmopolitan and cultured wife of the American ambassador David Bruce.

At Heathrow, E. J. (Ted) Power was waiting to whisk them to the Grosvenor House hotel facing Hyde Park, around the corner from E. J.'s home and where the managing director was a friend[5] and then immediately after checking in, to Westminster Abbey. Astonishingly, it was Barney's first visit to a cathedral building.[6] The following day he went to the races at historic Kempton Park in Surrey. On Monday, Alan Power, fulfilling Barney's "childhood" dream, took him to see the 12th-century fantastical (but heavily restored) Ely Cathedral in Cambridgeshire. At the Lord's Ground to see a Middlesex v. Sussex cricket match, Power assumed Barney, like most Americans, would be bored in three minutes; he patiently explained that the batsman didn't necessarily "slog" the ball, that he also had to defend his wicket. "Alan! This is amazing!" Barney cried, raising his hand to his brow. "This guy's defending his wicket? This is a game of grace."[7]

The Newmans saw "Black Africa—Ballet Africains" the national ensemble of Guinea, the exotic interest of the season with its bare-breasted dancers and fantastic bead and feather costumes,[8] and boxing at The National Sporting Club. And they saw *White Fire I*, which E. J. had earlier purchased from Gibbs, and *White Fire III*, which he bought from Barney only months before, installed with a Brancusi sculpture in the Powers' pristine, 1950s-modern flat.[9] A show of Frankenthaler's paintings opened at Kasmin's gallery and there was a glamorous party with the art and society friends and aristocratic relatives of Kasmin's partner, Sheridan 5th Marquess of Dufferin and his fiancée, Guinness Brewery-heiress Serena Belinda (Lindy) Rosemary Guinness (a descendant of the dukes of Rutland).[10]

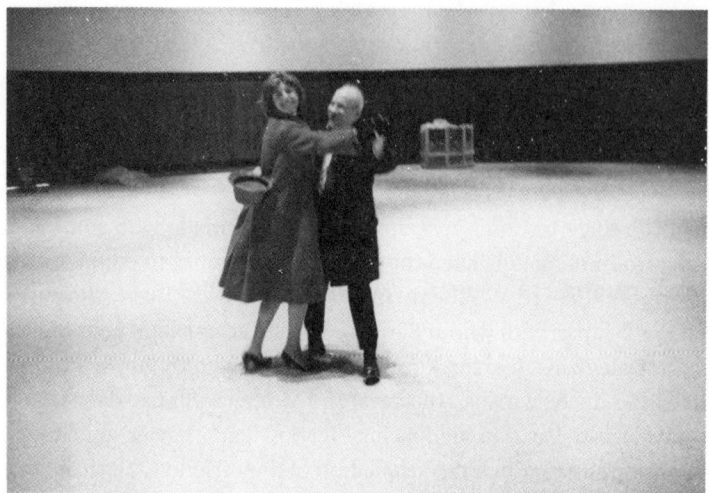

Fig. 48 Dancing with Helen Frankenthaler at the site (under construction) of the 1964 World's Fair in Flushing, Queens. Photograph Alexander Liberman

It was as if they had walked into a fantasy.

Many British artists still carried a charge from the lightning bolt of "The New American Painting" at the Tate in 1959. Barney's work "changed our idea about how to [make] a picture," William Turnbull said after seeing the show. "You had to say is it silly or meaningful . . . . We had to rethink what painting is."[11] A few codified that experience in "Situation," an exhibition of works "not less than thirty square feet," organized in 1960, with Alloway advising.[12] They were thrilled to meet Barney or renew an acquaintance begun in New York. The brothers Harold and Bernard Cohen, Robyn Denny, John Hoyland, Richard Smith, Peter Stroud, and Turnbull were among these so-called "Situationists." "New London Situation," chosen by Alloway and Gibbs, both enthusiastic partisans of Barney's work, followed in 1961. With that group the two-week visit at times felt like a festive Barney-con. But Barney saw others as well: lunch with Edward Paolozzi and the expatriate R. B. Kitaj, dinners with Victor Pasmore and Richard Hamilton, an evening with Henry Moore.

He was the "gayest and most indefatigably energetic companion," according to Whitechapel curator Bryan Robertson—who only a year earlier had so offended Barney's "single-colour majesty"—"with huge zest for life and an unequalled flair for turning all occasions into talking marathons, loaded with hilarious reminiscences, that reduced everyone to helpless laughter." Barney regaled an appreciative audience with his plan to defeat the arch-conservative Arizona senator, Barry Goldwater, whose campaign for president had been announced in January and was gaining traction. Barney's plan was to have some of the most striking members of the New York art, music, and dance avant garde (this was the sixties) on an enormous float, with a banner declaring "Artists for Goldwater," driving up and down Fifth Avenue to "confuse the issue." It "was typical of Barney's exuberant sense of the ridiculous," thought

Robertson.[13] Kasmin remembered the whole of Barney's visit, choreographed by the younger Power, as a grand "performance."[14]

Barney and Annalee made the trip for two reasons. In late 1963, Barney was invited to participate in "54–64 Painting and Sculpture of a Decade," supported by the Calouste Gulbenkian Foundation at the Tate: over three hundred works made during the previous decade by a range of artists from Matisse and Picasso, Léger and Lipchitz, to the 29-year-old Jim Dine. Rauschenberg's *Monogram* (with stuffed goat and automobile tire) and Johns's *Large Target Construction* (encaustic target with sculpted body parts) were included. The organizers, Courtauld Institute art historian and future Tate Gallery director Alan Bowness and artist, curator, and educator Lawrence Gowing, visiting New York, had chosen from Barney's studio *The Three*, 1962 (40 square feet of mostly black oil and exposed canvas with a thin white band) and the 18-foot, aqua, black and brown *Uriel*, 1955—just the sort of work that so enthralled the Situation artists. But Barney believed *Uriel* was too fragile to unstretch, roll, ship, and restretch. The alternative—Barney's idea—was for Kasmin to loan his recently purchased 1954 *Primordial Light*, the shipping costs from New York worked out between the Tate and the dealer.[15] The 1961 stark black-and-white *Noon-Light*—which had been in the recently concluded Whitney Annual—was added.

After negotiations between Bowness–Gowing and Kasmin had been concluded in January 1964, Alan Power showed up in New York in March, overlapping a lengthy, Barney-event-filled visit by his parents. Barney took Power *fils* to his Front Street studio—the sanctorum for which he had been judged not ready in 1959—and there, looking past the recently returned model for the synagogue, he saw *Uriel*. Power was "absolutely flummoxed and knocked out," all seven of his chakras "vibrating."

"How much do you want for that painting?" he asked Barney.

"Well, I don't know, it's big. I suppose 50,000 dollars" (491,455 dollars in 2023).

Normally, Power would have negotiated; he didn't have that kind of money to throw around. But now he couldn't be bothered. His only thought was, "I don't care if this is the last painting I ever buy. I have to have this."[16] Barney took him to Sweet's to seal the deal.[17]

Because he did not have a place to hang the painting, when he returned to the tony district of Richmond where he was living, Power decided to acquire a London flat exclusively for his art. He made significant alterations, removed a vintage fireplace, and got his long white wall. It was a sort of private gallery—Power never lived in the space—where *Uriel* could hang with the other American pieces he had acquired: a 16-part *Jackie Kennedy* by Warhol, *Jasper's Dilemma* by Stella, works by Kenneth Noland.

And so with great trepidation, but happy with the financial bonanza, Barney acquiesced; *Uriel* indeed wound up being sent to London rolled on a barrel. (Power's late attempt to loan it for the Tate show was not successful.) Embarking on his own trip, Barney was both excited to see his work in the "biggest exhibition of modern art ever staged in Britain"[18] and looking forward to the ceremonial ritual of having *Uriel* restretched under his personal supervision.

The location of Power's flat in Ennismore Gardens in Knightsbridge—a block from Hyde Park, a brief walk from the Royal Albert Hall, the Natural History and the Victoria and Albert museums, and Harrods—was the real-estate equivalent of a bespoke suit, a brigadier's mustache, a monocle, and watch fob; it was undoubtedly the sort of site Barney would have chosen himself, if he had known the city at all. He loved the busy barges on the Thames, the noises, hustle and bustle, and the "quiet dignity and sense of pride that even the little children" had.[19] The stretching went well, a "fast and perfect" execution by the Cohen brothers assuming the roles previously played by Murray and Franklin, with Barney hovering over them, directing, "in his braces."[20] But the Tate show, in Barney's eyes, was a shock.

Even before he left New York, he became aware that the paintings' traveling frames—conscientiously built and attached to prevent finger marks and other damage—were mistakenly left on for the formal hanging.[21] When he saw the installation two days after he arrived, the frames were gone, but the situation was far worse. "The Tate show . . . is a mess. Badly hung and badly selected. My things are miserably presented and already seriously damaged," he wrote to Liberman;[22] to Alloway, it was the "messiest presentation of art works ever organized . . . my things are [so] damaged that I believe they are beyond recall."[23]

They were hung on a panel in a narrow passageway. *Noon-Light*, 9 feet tall, rested on the floor, the top 12 inches extending beyond the support's top edge. Barney had "never seen a painting so presented. Ordinary common sense would have placed the painting a foot above the floor so that the passerby, his heels and toes would not be kicking the painting and the hair of the men and women passing by, their umbrellas, bags, etc. would not be hitting the canvas." When he protested, he was told that the paintings "could always be restored." He asked that *Noon-Light* be removed from the exhibition and the others rehung in a "safe place" or removed. Back at his hotel, in agitated handwriting, Barney drafted a letter to Kasmin to relieve him of his obligation to purchase *Primordial Light* since it had "always been [his] policy to deliver guaranteed perfect work."

It was less than ideal, it was disrespectful, it was an insult. It turned out his fear for the safety of the works was justified. *The Three* was badly dented and scratched. Orrin Riley, the preeminent painting restorer, was able to "disguise" the damage sufficiently that Barney did not disown the painting, but *Noon-Light* was another—"tragic"—story. The damage was "not only permanent" but had "completely disfigured the painting so that under no circumstance can it be considered a work of mine," in Barney's estimation.[24] Indeed, it was never sold or exhibited again during his lifetime.

It was not simply egoism, then, that drove Barney to send extravagantly explicit instructions for handling when he loaned *Black Fire*, *Achilles*, and *Ulysses*, as requested by Rüdlinger, to "International Painting since 1950" at the Basel Kunsthalle that summer.[25]

Leaving London for ten days, Barney and Annalee made the essential aesthetic and cultural pilgrimage to view Matthias Grünewald's staggering *Isenheim Altarpiece* in Colmar, Alsace—an ambition of Barney's at least since Reinhardt, when he was still on excellent terms with the Newmans, had shared his experience of it in late 1952. On the way, they travelled through Zurich and stopped for a brief visit with Rüdlinger—and to *Day Before One*—in Basel. Rüdlinger was an excellent cook (and drinker), and he and his wife Pia threw a party in Barney's honor at their old and magnificently sited home. Georg Schmidt, the former director of the Basel Kunstmuseum, was there, and Franz Meyer, Schmidt's successor (and eventually Rüdlinger's as Pia's next husband), and Carlo Huber—Meyer's assistant, who would follow both men at the Kunstmuseum—and his wife Helga. Barney spent much of the evening buttonholing Schmidt in an intense, intimate conversation, the first speaking only English (with perhaps a bit of Yiddish), the second only German; but there was no doubt in any observer's mind that they understood each other.[26] And then—since jazz was the rage in Germany—records were played and Barney suddenly had the guests standing in rows while he and Annalee expertly taught them to dance the Charleston.[27]

Barney thought the complicated nine-painted-panel masterwork in the Unterlinden Museum, in which expressive crudeness and vulgarity coexisted with extraordinary grace and spiritual elevation, was the most moving and beautiful work he had ever seen in his life. And the idea that it required a dedicated journey added to the allure and enhanced its maker's power. Thereafter, an introduction became a "great gift" that he conferred on people: "You've never seen the Isenheim Altarpiece? That's crazy. You must go. *Immediately*."[28] Armed with an early American Express credit card, the Newmans also enjoyed nearly as much staying in a river-view room at the luxurious Trois Rois Hotel in Basel and, following that, at the Bristol in Paris for a few days. The many photographs Barney, or Annalee, took from their room in Basel of the bridge over the Rhine are, in the canon of Newman photographs, almost uniquely in focus, well composed, and properly exposed; from most evidence, Barney seems to have been almost incapable of taking a "good" photograph. At the Bristol one of them waggishly recorded every part—the "European" bidet and the twin sinks in the beautiful grisaille mosaic bathroom, the black satin bedspreads and burled-wood headboards of the twin beds, the ecru and chestnut-colored brocade overstuffed furniture and marble mantel. They did not photograph—or even visit—the Louvre, but immediately on arrival hired a car to take them to Chartres. It was not the famous facades or the stained-glass windows that Barney wanted to see, but the interior. He had told people that as a schoolboy he drew a floorplan of the cathedral; now he couldn't wait to experience the thrill of being in its overwhelming, awesome space. Although he had only visited any cathedral for the first time ten days earlier, he would later say that he was struck by the subtlety of Chartres, how, because there was "no narthex," one simply passed over the threshold and was immediately confronted with the rows of columns and side wall light, "gripped by the tremendous experience of this dynamism."[29]

He continued his buoyant revelry in Paris, and had "passionate" discussions with local intellectuals.[30] But he had been gored. Once again, he launched a crusade to collect from insurance companies, this time for *Noon-Light*; in 1967, he would even threaten Norman Reid—who had by then become director of the Tate but was deputy director at the time the damage occurred—that he would go "to court." As was the case with most of his insurance battles, one can believe that it was less about the money involved than it was an outcry: the artist himself had been severely wounded, and nothing less than an official acknowledgment, in legally recognized papers, could stanch the bleeding.

In the weeks before he left for England, the New York media was filled with descriptions and images of Michelangelo's *Pietà* as it arrived in the city *appropriately* packed in a "watertight case inside of a case inside of another case,"[31] and was exhibited *appropriately* in its own niche in the Vatican Pavilion at the just opened World's Fair in Queens. This was how an artist and his work deserved to be treated. Now, in the torment that he saw depicted at Colmar, in the weeping plague sores, in the gushing wound of Longinus, in the stigmata of Grünewald's crucified Christ, Barney could recognize the brutal blows to his work, the irreverence that it—and he—had suffered.

It was "precisely the moment when Europe was ready to turn with enthusiasm and sympathy to American art, and to accept it as a major international cultural force,"[32] wrote Alan Solomon in his report.

Although the word among his friends in New York was that Barney's English visit had been "triumphal,"[33] the excited buzz in the city's art hive concerned that summer's Biennale in Venice. The federal government, through the USIA, had taken over the official sponsorship of the American representation, the aesthetically audacious Solomon had been appointed commissioner for a newly ambitious participation, and there had been high hopes and expectations. "Everybody recognizes that the world center for art has moved from Paris to New York," Solomon boldly stated, antagonizing especially the French, and leading to an allegation in *Arts* magazine that the Americans had conspired with the Communists against the French.

"How can you be an art critic in Paris when there are no more painters in France," *Newsweek* quoted one French art critic a few months later, in a cover story that echoed Solomon. Art had "become globalized, with London, Düsseldorf, Warsaw, Rome, Madrid, Tokyo, and Osaka as the new city-states." But New York was the "capital."[34]

As if to drive home the point, Leo Castelli touted that for the "first time" in the Biennale's sixty-year history an American—Rauschenberg—was awarded the grand prize, ignoring that Mark Tobey won in 1958. Rauschenberg was also, symbolically, one of the youngest artists to win it—although, through extraordinary incompetence and confusion on the part of the Italian authorities, his works appeared not in the Biennale proper, but in the temporary annex Solomon negotiated because of the small size of the American Pavilion. The award was not uncontroversial—many suspected it was a conclusion pre-ordained by Castelli's politicking, and there were .
sour grapes in the mouths of some Europeans and other American artists' camps.

Lawrence Rubin and fellow Greenbergians favored painters Noland and Louis, for example—the only two artists actually installed in the small, "official" American building in the Giardini.[35] One Italian critic stated what seemed to be a consensus opinion: "The most important painter of the whole Biennale is another American, Morris Louis," who had died in 1962. (Biennale rules prohibited posthumous awards.)[36]

What was uncontested, was that the award signaled that young American art—represented by Rauschenberg's *Bed, Tracer,* and *Canyon,* Johns's *Three Flags, Painting with Two Balls,* and *Gray Numbers,* Oldenburg's *Soft Typewriter* and *Ghost Toaster,* and Dine's literal *Green Shower*—was sexy. The unavoidable corollary was that Barney's generation—secure in history, "venerable patriarch[s] like Cézanne" as they were called in an Italian newspaper[37]—was not.

"The survivors of the band who made [the] revolution—de Kooning, Robert Motherwell, Barnett Newman, Mark Rothko, tread the new scene warily, shaking their heads over the Vanity Fair that has sprung up on the old battlefield, bedeviled by their own myth, like guerrilla fighters finding it hard to adjust to the city conquered by their revolution," was the conveniently glib packaging by *Newsweek.*[38]

The venerable Marlborough Gallery had been positioning itself as the place for those "survivors." They signed with Krasner to represent the Pollock estate and a major show of Pollock's work was at the gallery when Lloyd came courting. The discussions among Barney, Lloyd, and Ellin went well; by the end of February 1964, Lloyd was set to "do everything in my power, supported by our entire organization all over the world, to make your work better known to the wide public," he had told Barney. "An artist of your importance deserves a much wider public . . . both in America and in Europe."[39]

The previous November Marlborough's highly anticipated New York space had opened with a benefit show in tribute to the dealer Curt Valentin (1902–1954), showcasing over three hundred works by mostly European "master" artists he had introduced. It was packed, there was "chaos" and drama. The "head of Rene d'Harnoncourt, the towering director of the Museum of Modern Art, could be seen above the crush. Shorter people, like the publisher Samuel I. Newhouse and his wife, were completely engulfed." Larry Rivers was served with a subpoena on behalf of Tibor de Nagy, who still had the artist under contract.[40] With two thousand people inside, some in evening dress, the Fire Department denied entry to enormous numbers waiting to get in.

Yet, in the end, Barney did not sign with Marlborough. His resistance to monogamous representation was philosophical and principled: if a collector desired a work by Picasso, Barney explained, he had the option of six different dealers and could choose the one he trusted most. Even a dealer who did not have a Picasso in his possession knew how to find one for a client. Why was it not the same for American artists? Why did these artists, like himself, have to be "handled"—he said it with contempt—by one dealer? It was "so elementary," he said, it was "almost unAmerican."[41]

A couple of evenings before he got on the plane to London in May, Barney attended an auction of "Abstract Expressionist and other Modern Paintings, Drawings and Sculptures" at Parke-Bernet Galleries. In the catalogue he recorded the estimates—7500–8000 dollars for a 1953 Kline, 1000–1200 dollars for a small Pollock, 12–15,000 for a mid-to-large 1955 Rothko—that would establish the market and guide his placement in it.

But even earlier, Barney had begun to up his business game. When Kasmin agreed to purchase *Primordial Light* at the end of 1963, he was given a 40 percent discount off the price Barney had set; two months later he found himself explaining to Kasmin that since his "inventory" of works ten years old was dwindling, he would be reducing the discount rate.[42] And although Barney immediately calculated how far Kasmin's 12,000-dollar check would go toward shares in American Motors and AT&T, his goal was more career management than simply economic, and in that he could step on his own feet.[43] He kept stringing along Muriel Kallis Steinberg Newman in her escalating quest to own *The Voice*, and later in the year, a discreet approach by Virginia Wright was "totally rejected" when Annalee made it very clear that one didn't just say "I want a Newman." Wright was made to understand that it was "sort of vulgar to bring up the idea of buying a work of art"; one had to "really commit to it and get to know it and it must be part of your life."[44] That both suitors were rejected in spite of their obvious and genuine passion and the extraordinary collections they had amassed would be regrettable. Muriel Newman had been frequenting The Club since its beginning, and acquired a stunning collection of works by Gorky, Guston, Kline, de Kooning, Pollock, Rothko, and David Smith before the mid-1950s; in 1964 she purchased a painting by Still. Wright's collection in 1964 was about to be shown at the Portland Art Museum; a painting by Barney would have taken its place among those by Gorky, de Kooning, Guston, Pollock, Rothko, Kline, Stamos, Rauschenberg, Johns, Noland, Kelly, Lichtenstein, Oldenburg, as well as selected West Coast artists. Or, it's possible the company was exactly what had to be avoided.

This was the way Barney and Annalee felt most comfortable, happiest, controlling his career. It is impossible to imagine that he ever considered the arrangement stipulated by Lloyd where he would agree, for a period of five years, not to make any direct sales, not to directly negotiate with—or, more importantly, appraise—a potential owner, not to have approval over reproductions and catalogues. It's a wonder that Barney ever seriously entertained the idea, and more than likely that he only allowed the appearance of doing so to be able to refuse. In that way he would certainly distinguish himself from Rothko and Motherwell, Gottlieb and "them guys."

In the same way, he took himself out of contention for the 10,000-dollar main prize—which Harry Guggenheim imagined as the Nobel Prize of art when he established it in 1956—and the five 2500-dollar prizes at the Fourth Guggenheim International Award Exhibition that January. Alloway had spent two years making the selection of eighty-two artists from twenty-four countries; a jury of Hans Hofmann, German art historian Werner Haftmann, and Arnold Rüdlinger would select the winners. Barney had grandly declared himself opposed to this sort of beauty pageant when he was left out of the 1961 Carnegie International, and now he stood on his principles. He was at last genuinely in a position to disdain the money, and it was a brilliant gambit to remove himself from the often meaningless—sometimes invidious—comparisons that reviewers would inevitably make.

He and he alone would manage his career. It was the way he wanted it, the control was comforting, the role empowering. But the frequent downside was that, as was famously said of Henry James, he chewed more than he bit off.

He and Alloway were speaking "in detail" about a proposed exhibition in two parts at the Guggenheim Museum; in fact, by July it was "the main project" occupying the curator's mind. After Alloway had taken Messer to Barney's studio two years earlier, there followed a series of lunches, Barney and Alloway, Barney and Messer, with Barney "circling around" the idea of a show. He set a "wonderfully absurdist" condition: build a square tower with level floors in the atrium, with little bridges from the floors to the ramps: in Walter Hopps's eyes the vertical would have turned the whole museum into a "Newman."[45] Finally, the museum men decided they had to "face Barney together and make a very clear proposition, and either he will take it or leave it" but they could not continue with the "monkey business." Cornering him at the Century Club, where Messer was a member, they "got his clear agreement,"[46] which Alloway memorialized in July 1964. "Spring 1965 for the Stations," and fall 1965 for "the retrospective selection of your works." It was "pretty much the timing" Barney "had in mind for the revelation of the new work as a group" in the context of the entire oeuvre.[47] The Guggenheim geared up but Barney dilly-dallied.

While those latest discussions were taking place, and with the excuse of the "suffocating" heat, Barney, unwilling or unable to end the eighteen-month relationship with ULAE, was dodging Tatyana Grosman. When the Newmans quietly escaped to the East End of Long Island for a long weekend, Grosman got wind of it, and drove over to physically dragoon him into committing to the final prints for the *Cantos* portfolio. It took them seven hours of "back-breaking" work, but the project was, once and for all, finished.[48]

When the weather broke in August, after a month of city-wide racial tension, subway attacks, and five days of violent riots thirty blocks from the Newman's Ninety-Third Street apartment, Barney was either able to knuckle down to work in the studio—according to Annalee—or he was not, because of "a lot of interference"—according to Barney. But somehow during 1964 he made six paintings including those he identified as the seventh, eighth, and ninth *Stations*—the last white paint, instead of black, on exposed canvas. A few months before he left for England he had begun a focused study of the origin and textual meaning of the Stations of the Cross.[49] Now, having committed himself to the canonical number—albeit with a unique interpretation—Barney was at least five paintings short when he and Alloway planned to show them the coming spring.

"A near-vegetarian diet was served at Meany Hall last night for the first art symposium to be held in Seattle with an all-star cast as chefs."[1]

It was a far cry from the red meat of Barney's first star turn at Woodstock in 1952.

Hunter, Hess, Rosenberg, sculptor Gabriel Kohn—who had replaced a "petrified of symposiums" Ellsworth Kelly[2]—and Barney were, in the opinion of a local critic, somewhat too "ingratiating" and "well-mannered." They seemed "constantly on the verge of speaking more significantly about 'Problems and Issues in Art Today,'" but never quite got there, although what was absolutely clear was that none of the men were happy with current developments in art. The new mass audience had "an aggressive indifference to art," according to Hess; Kohn called Pop art "castor oil." Barney "furnished some of the most nourishing morsels," among them that the artist himself was of greater value to society than the value of his products.[3]

"I didn't think I was traveling 3,000 miles to spend an evening talking about Pop Art," said Barney to an unexpected capacity audience of two thousand, when it became clear that Pop was the goat to be sacrificed. What he objected to at the Poses panel in 1962—that "what started out as a conference over ideas [is] developing into a debate over other painters"—equally bothered him now. It seemed to him that it wasn't fair, that it was "self-serving" for them to either "attack or defend" without a Pop artist present. What Barney had on his mind, what he characterized as "an illness in this country," was the larger situation crystallized by the tumult at the ongoing Venice Biennale and the subtext of Greenberg's "Post-Painterly Abstraction" show at the Los Angeles County Museum of Art: the inclination to think of "art as moving in terms of some kind of rhythm of ten-year cycles." In the "thirties it was Benton and the American scene, in the forties it's us guys—that is the late forties and fifties— and now it's like we were all dead." He didn't "understand it, really it's an American phenomenon." He'd never heard "anybody defend Dubuffet by announcing Picasso is dead [or] defend Mathieu by announcing that Dubuffet is dead."

What particularly irritated Barney was that the "younger generation" wouldn't fight, wouldn't put up their dukes, were silent. Hunter said they were "cool" and the others agreed.

"Historically, my generation did not have that audience [that Pop now has] . . . no critics talking for us . . . no dealers talking for us . . . no museum men talking for us. And so we had to talk ourselves. Everyone of my generation did talk or write or in some way make clear what interested him." The new artists, Barney continued—metaphorically, in a merging of so many of his complaints—had "lawyers."

"I'm not going to talk about painting or sculpture with another painter and have his lawyer answer me." The rest agreed it was an "excellent," a "very important" point.

And without blinking, Barney inconsistently but unabashedly insisted that he was not "involved in commentaries," he was "involved in texts."

"If I am strong enough to make the painting I'm also strong enough to invite those who don't make paintings to talk about paintings, because I can't even talk about them. And since I can't talk about paintings, and paintings can't be talked about, then the only thing to do is to try to talk about them. And I suppose I'm here to find out what I want to say." He was not "entering the society of the writers and critics," he was "inviting them to enter" his world.[4]

"At first these good men tried to communicate with their audience," a local observer reported. "Then they tried communicating with each other. Failing that, they communicated with themselves."[5]

If the formal proceedings were tame, the participants, at least, had a rollicking good time. A "water" pitcher of vodka was passed around the symposium table, in secret defiance of the university's ban on alcohol. The artist Morris Graves made a great show of stomping out. Coming off Barney's grand treatment in Europe—fawned over and entertained by aristocrats in stately surroundings—the arrangements in Seattle felt appropriately doting. The timber heiress Virginia Bloedel Wright—the Janis Gallery assistant of the early '50s—was a founder of the new Contemporary Art Council of the Seattle Art Museum, which, as its inaugural program, organized the symposium with the University of Washington School of Art.[6] The travel arrangements were made with an eye sensitive to the Newmans' maximum convenience and comfort; they were met at the airport and housed, with Rosenberg and Hess, in the beautiful and historic Beaux Arts home on Capitol Hill that Wright's grandfather built with architect Charles Platt. The breakfasts at the house—with Wright and the museum's director John Denman joining to witness the gossipy fun—were far more lively, entertaining, and nourishing than the "vegetarian" symposium had been.

Annalee officially retired from teaching a few days before in order to accompany Barney on this trip, and she was in high spirits. Rosenberg had extolled the old Pike Place Market when he was writing state guide books for the WPA, and now Barney went there looking for the giant crabs that Rosenberg promised,

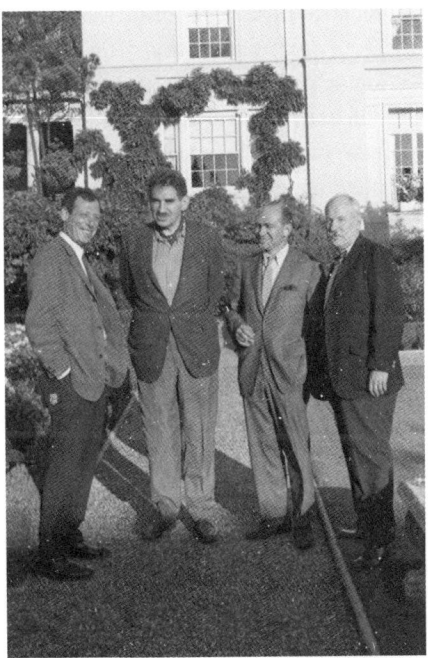

Fig 49 Seattle, 1964. From left: Thomas Hess, Harold Rosenberg, Sam Hunter, Barnett Newman

the fifteen different kinds of salmon, and the giant fruit—"a tomato as big as a football"—grown by Japanese farmers who had reclaimed lands devastated by logging. Of course, they were to be disappointed: the market was a tenth of what Rosenberg had seen and the Japanese, their property confiscated since the war, were gone.[7] With Rosenberg and Wright, Barney and Annalee took a ferryboat to Bainbridge Island in Puget Sound. Delighting in the majestic views of Mt. Rainier, they climbed up and down the hills, wandered through the markets and the waterfront and Yessler Way—the original "Skid Row," Annalee excitedly noted—and explored the unfamiliar flora of a distant, off-shore island. And then there was the elegant and elite soiree at the Wright's own house and a grand reception after the symposium.[8] Several painters whom he knew from Emma Lake journeyed to see Barney.

The Guggenheim agreement "in principle" had already been pushed; the survey was rescheduled for fall 1965 and the *Stations of the Cross*—"for the first time . . . as a group"—for spring 1966. But even with the reprieve, Barney's stress was too great to continue as planned "to celebrate Annalee's retirement" by travelling to British Columbia.[9] Ever since the heart attack Annalee never relaxed her vigilance: Barney felt ill, and they returned to New York.[10]

If the final composition of the *Cantos* portfolio was strung out, if the tens of multiple-personnel-assisted iterations of the synagogue were elaborated into a cultish ritual, the monumental indenture of the looming Guggenheim shows was the largest challenge to Barney's commitment-phobia yet. But a museum's exhibition schedule was not something to toy with, and Thomas Messer, the museum's director, was becoming concerned. As it turned out, there would be only one show and it didn't happen until April 1966. When, in the fall of 1964, Barney agreed to be interviewed by Frank O'Hara for a half-hour filmed television segment, it was still with the memory of his triumphal march through London and Basel and in anticipation of the two lionizing shows.

Arrangements for the interview appeared to be finalized. Just as Barney got to Channel 13's studio on the West Side of Manhattan, however, the producer decided a painting should be in the background. Always worried that any time a painting was moved it could be damaged, Barney was vociferously against the idea. But the producer prevailed, and *Cathedra* was transported from the Hahn warehouse. With Barney and Annalee supervising, *Cathedra* was uncrated not by art handlers but by television stagehands who were "knocking it around," when Murray stepped in to take charge. Barney was getting increasingly upset, Annalee was attempting to calm him down, and Murray was trying to get the unpacking done correctly, when he called a halt. Barney had turned chalk white and Murray was certain it was another heart attack. Annalee escorted Barney to an anteroom where he could lie down; his shirt was removed, a glass of orange juice was produced. When Murray finally got the enormous work uncrated and hung, O'Hara walked in and asked, "where's Barney?" Murray didn't know. "He was sick and lying down."

Everyone was frantic, when "suddenly Barney walked in, dressed perfectly" and the interview commenced. At first, the atmosphere was toxic and Murray thought "they were going to kill each other." But when it was over "they were all hugging and kissing" and the Newmans and Murray, O'Hara and his friend Bob Cohn, Motherwell, Bryan Robertson, and the poet and art critic Bill Berkson went to Paris Brest to celebrate.[11]

On a Tuesday evening in early December, immediately following a "Conversation with Eric Hoffer," the Bronx-born blue-collar philosopher, and in competition with the comedy–variety "Red Skelton Hour," the lighthearted spy show "The Man from Uncle," and the oddly lighthearted military show "McHale's Navy," television viewers could turn to the public station to see "Barnett Newman (American painter)" on "Art New York."

For the most part, Barney recapitulated the points he had become accustomed to making in interviews over the previous twenty-four months. But it was the first time a *mass* audience would hear about the despair among artists after the war, the search for a new art, or Barney's early preoccupation with the "void"; how Buckminster Fuller at the 1950 Parsons show talked about the horizontal versus the vertical; how he didn't work out of habit or to keep himself busy, but asked himself every day, "why am I painting?"; how he did not want to paint "Newmans" and reduce himself to a "cliché." Prodded, Barney was also very specific about his work—"I will only answer questions if I get the right questioner," he told O'Hara. "Color is really what I work with. I depend entirely on it, as I don't use line," he said provocatively. What an observer might think was a line, Barney considered "color areas." But colors themselves—what anybody could buy and squeeze out of a tube—were "inert." It was his "job" to transform that obstinate material "into COLOR."

And—not revealing that he was working on a cycle he called *Stations of the Cross* and planned to exhibit it as such—he said, "Titles for me are metaphors ["metapherrs" in his New York-ese] for emotional content," given after the work was completed. His example was *Abraham*: "In my mind the tragic figure in life, the most tragic figure," he emphasized, "is the father." With his "more than black on black painting" he was painting what Abraham (the Patriarch as well as his own father) meant to him—the tragic—and only *after* "decided to call it *Abraham*."

"In regard to my own work [there is the] physical reality at the same time I hope that there is some moral and ethical and meaningful content." When O'Hara attempted to somehow reduce, or simplify, or explain Barney's meaning as "religious," Barney objected: " 'Religious' is a rough word to use today—because religion implies 'church' etcetera. Life is more complicated."[12]

Complicated enough for Barney to feel able to separate the words "stations of the cross" from their historical use and endow them with what he considered their ultimate meaning.[13]

The Abstract Expressionists were "artists of intense response," wrote *Newsweek* at the beginning of 1965 in an extensive cover story on the changing of the art guard, "men who painted with their own nerve endings."[14]

"If only," Barney may have thought. His nerve endings were so inflamed they often made the act of painting impossible. Parsons's description of him in the article as the "great statesman of up and down" was more revealing than she probably realized. It was the thumb up or thumb down of an emperor: Barney sat in judgment.

As far back as he could remember—in public school in the Bronx, in Latin class at City College, in requirements for teaching licenses, civil service regulations and representatives, mayoral candidates, private art collections and public museums, in critics, landlords, police and insurance companies, and art handlers—Barney found not simply what he considered incompetence, but rather non-comprehension. Misinterpretation. And he believed it was his obligation to set the offenders straight. When Alloway wrote, "What looks like geometric abstract art is not," in *Artforum* that spring, he was channeling Barney. "What may seem to be, from the title, a religious painting is not an idol, but a presence."[15] Nobody else understood the implications. Believe "nothing till you hear from me," in the words of Duke Ellington.

Thus it would be, most publicly, regarding the *Stations of the Cross* when he exhibited them in 1966. The true meaning of Christ's last day and course on the Via Dolorosa was *lema sabachthani*, "why did you forsake me?," a single cry, not fourteen "sentimental illustrations." That he needed fourteen canvases to "make clear the wholeness of the single event" was the result of eight years and a number of "spontaneous, inevitable" urges, not any prescribed, programmatic structure.

And thus it would be with many in the growing population of those who *thought* they were supporting him. Even *they* required correction.

When the (non-Jewish) acting director of the Jewish Museum, Hans van Weeren-Griek, invited Barney to participate in a panel discussion, "What About Jewish Art?" he was operating under the naïve but not craven idea that an artist who was a Jew would not object to being identified as a Jewish artist—after all, the cultural climate in the American diaspora had shifted from a shocked and ashamed silence in the postwar years to a new (if modulated) public pride. Instead, the topic unleashed a torrent of derision. "I cannot emphasize enough the repulsion I feel for there is something here that is more serious than just a Am Haoretz performance. What the Jewish Museum has done is to compromise me as an artist because I am Jewish." Barney put van Weeren-Griek on notice that it was now "impossible" for him to show in the museum in the future.[16]

How embattled did Barney continue to feel? On how many fronts could he be vigilant and mount defenses in the name of his person and work? The threats only increased as Barney's renown, and demands for morsels of him, increased. The unfortunate corollary of fame is fame's very vulnerability to missteps and misjudgments. In the mid-1960s, the artist's representative—a dealer—carried much of that burden. But Barney trusted no one to be conscientious enough; he was compelled to be his own representative. "It must be understood that my situation is somewhat unusual, in that I am involved not only in the role of an artist, but also in the role of a dealer. Many of the expenses itemized below would not have to be borne by an artist who used a conventional art dealer and who did not also have the responsibility of selling his own works," he responded when his 1965 taxes were audited.

> I show my paintings on a seven-day-week basis . . . maintained a studio at 100 Front Street, a studio on West 57th Street, and a studio as part of my apartment . . . paintings and sculptures were located in each . . . as a result of the wide dispersion of my works, I have consistently had high transportation expenses . . . [in] an average week, I have shown my work to approximately five persons . . . necessary for me to take my visitors from studio to studio by taxi . . . as well as expenses in taxiing to and from art supply stores at all hours of the night . . . .
>
> I have been required to spend substantial cash sums for tips and gratuities in connection with showing and moving my work . . . warehouse employees . . . janitors, superintendents, elevator men and doormen . . . seven days a week . . . . [17]
>
> On a daily basis, I make approximately eight to ten telephone calls from booths to persons with whom I have appointments or to keep track on incoming telephone messages . . .
>
> Because I do not adhere to a regular schedule, I frequently paint at odd hours of the night . . . I will often need additional colors, brushes, hardware or other supplies, which I can obtain only at one of the few art supply stores open at those unusual hours. [18]

Whether or not his justification of the "approximately $5,000.00" ($49,150 in 2023) in undocumented expenses was accurate, the affidavit provides a vivid description of how he understood his life. It was an ingenious, if subconscious, adaptation to the new (art) world order. He could never have the "cool" of the younger artists—the absence of "worry about the sins of society," of "moral attitude," of "sensitivity" that *Newsweek* noted about the new generation. [19] But he could, unlike de Kooning—whom Rauschenberg notoriously "erased"—or Rothko or Still, span the generational divide, be the "man of the world" that Kaprow called for the previous fall. [20] That generation had its "lawyers," as Barney said in Seattle. If a lawyer were needed, Barney would fill that role himself.

He refused to grouse about the new art, even if he telegraphed his preference for his own. He would manage every opportunity that came his way—and he would make himself available for those opportunities—to be certain they were about himself and his work no matter how he might be baited.

The adjustment was not easy; the constant vigilance took an emotional and psychological toll. But it was worth it: he became the most *au courant* of the older generation.

In 1957 Barney's work was "the real turning point" of Stanton Catlin's exhibition in Minneapolis; in 1961 it was the fulcrum around which Arnason built the Guggenheim show. In 1964, Greenberg—as much as he had moved on in his affections—accorded

Barney's work important relevance to a new generation. In early 1965, Sam Green, the 25-year-old director at the University of Pennsylvania's ICA, identified Barney as one of the seven painters who made 1943 to 1953 "The Decisive Years."[21] Now, Walter Hopps, the director of the Pasadena Art Museum and curator for the Eighth São Paulo Bienal, recognized Barney as a "locomotive" for a "kind of train, full of the work of young men of high purpose, who, not being too well known," needed one.[22]

With Barney, Hopps planned to show the New York artists Frank Stella, Donald Judd, and Larry Poons, and the Californians Larry Bell, Billy Al Bengston, and Robert Irwin in the prestigious show in Brazil in September 1965. But regarding Barney, the pot was at full boil by May.

A 1964 military coup against the elected leftist government in Brazil was instantly recognized, if not engineered, by the United States; United States involvement in Vietnam had dramatically escalated and so had mass anti-war protests and suspicion of all things officially U.S. government. But at issue for the former anarchist, who claimed he hadn't been on the WPA because he refused to take government money, was not that the American participation was sponsored by the United States Information Agency—objective: propaganda—but that there might be the impression that Barney was a "practitioner of a formal art."[23]

Dear Walter:

It certainly was a blow to me to see your announcement of the São Paulo Biennial [*sic*] in this morning's New York Times . . . . It is clear to me now . . . that you intended something other than what I had been given to understand. It was my impression that you were honoring me for my work and that you were including six younger people because you were also committed to their work. I had no idea, and somehow you never expressed it in conversation, that you had chosen me and the others because you felt that we were practitioners, whether major or minor is irrelevant, of a stylistic idea. Or, that this show was going to be used by you as spokesman for these six painters with me as the "senior colleague" to represent an "art movement."

The press represented the American selection as "formalist." As far as Barney was concerned, that was "very much in the style of prevailing polemical journalism," and it involved

a kind of advocacy against which I have fought my whole life. What is more serious, it indicates a misunderstanding of my work. . . . All I wish to say is that you have made it impossible for me to participate in the Biennial [*sic*].

"Formalism" was more than an "old-hat style"; it was an "international dirty word in every field of thought." He was never "involved in formalist art."[24]

The impact that I have made on the young and for that matter, on the old too, is precisely the other way, that they feel that I am the most radical anti-formal painter.

If Hopps were under the impression that he was using the term as the opposite of "informal" painting Barney could only answer that he was "the victim of the fallacy of linguistic cognates"; formalism was very specific and did not apply to him.

This does not mean that I have not made some very important formal contributions, inventions and revolutions but that does not make me a formalist painter.

There was no question that Rembrandt "invented chiaroscuro, but he was not a chiaroscuro painter." After all the texts—from *Tiger's Eye*, from his show statements and interviews—that Barney had given Hopps to read, how could he have been so wrong? [25] As wrong as Hess had been in 1951. As wrong as Rosenberg was in 1956.

At issue was a brief news item by Grace Glueck in the *Times* previewing the show. Glueck, with severely restricted space, quoted only individual words or short phrases: the show had no theme, but was "keyed to what Mr. Hopps has called the new American 'formal' painting, as opposed to 'symbolic' and 'narrative' art . . . Head man in Mr. Hopps' line-up is 'a major practioner' of the new painting, 60-year-old New Yorker Barnett Newman."[26] Hopps—who was notoriously exasperating in his own way—naturally claimed he had been misrepresented. Barney found his excuse insufficient, telegraphing, "I believe I warned you about the kind of pressure she would give and I thought we agreed that the only thing to offer her was your name and serial number . . . . I cannot willingly become a partner to any ambiguity concerning this matter."[27]

A month earlier, interviewed by David Sylvester for a radio broadcast scheduled to air in November, Barney made explicit the distinction between his art and that of Mondrian, to which it continued to be compared. Mondrian "was definitely related to the theory of nature; that is, his horizontals and his verticals moved in relation to, you might say, Platonic essences about the nature of the world . . . a Utopian idea about the nature of life." Mondrian's ambition, Barney said, was to "purify all attitudes into the perfect painting, into the notion of the perfect painting." It was a "non-tragic art." But his own work "should give a man a sense of place, that he knows that he's there, so he's aware of himself." And, aware of *Barney* as well, because "I was there," something he did not neglect to point out.

His ambition was to give "someone, as it did me, the feeling of his own totality, of his own separateness, of his own individuality. And, at the same time, of his connection to others, who are also separate." Formalism's "disdain for the self" was something he didn't "quite understand."[28]

When he received the telegram at his office in Pasadena, Hopps grabbed all the petty cash, asked his secretary to make a reservation on the next plane, and high-tailed it to the airport. Upon landing in New York, he went directly to West End Avenue, where Barney got out the vodka bottle, dismissed Annalee, and they talked.[29] Although Barney had clearly stated that his withdrawal from the Bienal was "irrevocable," he wisely decided to let Hopps off the hook; he was now back in, but his wrath not spent, it landed on Glueck. The matter dragged on for more than two months. Barney wrote to the publisher and president of the *Times*, Arthur Ochs Sulzberger, asking for a retraction; managing editor Clifton Daniel conveyed Glueck's "regrets for the misunderstanding" and invited Hopps to write a letter for "possible publication." Barney demanded a correction in Glueck's column. "Nothing else will satisfy me." Then the real lawyers got involved. Barney had, in the meantime, been collecting examples of corrections recently published in the paper. Now, Leon Mnuchin, the prominent attorney (and owner of *Joshua*), wrote to Sulzberger that Barney felt "seriously aggrieved at the manner in which he has been presented to your reading public, and is most insistent that this be appropriately corrected" only by having a second article with a mea culpa. "If this is done, Mr. Newman will seek no monetary damages. His interest is in an *appropriate retraction of the libel* [emphasis added] on him and his work."[30]

It was not until a column in mid-October—six weeks after the Bienal had opened— that Glueck, repeating verbatim the offensive lines, wrote that Barney notified her that "Mr. Hopps has advised me that he never used these words," printed a convoluted definition of "formal" that Hopps had supplied to her, and quoted Hopps: "Barnett Newman, beyond question, in any sense is not a 'formal painter.' "[31]

In 1965 this was not a minor matter. If "formalism"—as in Bauhaus, as in Mondrian—was always in the background, always shadowing Barney, now it had emerged as a battle cry. A new generation of rigorously educated thinkers was taking up art critical writing in the medium-centered, self-reflexive mode promulgated by Greenberg. In a recent article that listed Barney as among the best artists in America the young, philosophy-trained critic Michael Fried made the case that "formal criticism, such as that practiced by Roger Fry or Mr. Greenberg, is better able to throw light upon the new art than any other approach."[32] That spring, Fried had curated an attention-grabbing show at Harvard's Fogg Art Museum, "Three American Painters: Kenneth Noland, Jules Olitski, Frank Stella," which grounded their work in the abstract expressionists, while grounding the strength of the abstract expressionists' work not in "any fashionable metaphysics of despair" but rather in "formal intelligence."

If some found that position disingenuous, to Barney it was heresy: Fry had particularly gotten under his skin since at least the mid-forties.[33] It was the *opposite* of what he believed in. Hopps, Glueck, Sulzberger, even Mnuchin might have rolled their eyes at what they recognized as Barney's characteristically immoderate response to Glueck's minor mistake; but Barney himself knew he was a bulwark against a rising tide.

Nothing went by Barney. "Everything was parsed," according to Holstein, who was summoned late one night to contribute an interpretation of the meaning of an irritating article. How many years and how often did Barney have to rail against others speaking for him? At Emma Lake, and at every other occasion when he spoke to the next generation, what he wanted them to take away was not how to be an "artist" but how to be a "human being." Boiling over Glueck's characterization, he pointedly told an interviewer that his generation's works "have never been successfully pigeonholed." They had been labeled "abstract expressionism, abstract impressionism, action painting, informal, tachisme, field paintings, color painting . . . . None can stick the way 'pop' and 'op' have, because the meaningful work [of the older artists] is so powerfully personal that stylistic slogans at best can only apply to individuals."[34]

Because of his generosity toward younger artists, his sincere belief in the human impulse at the root of their work and ambition, he accepted each one individually. It mattered not to Barney if Greenberg or anybody else put them into a box. But if *he* wound up in the box—even if he were placed there with misguided reverence—that was something entirely different.

The generational relationship was much more complex than simply Oedipal: both older and younger artists bore responsibility for tensions and fissures. Hopps, "a surrealist at heart,"[35] was far from an ideologue of formalism and had precisely this in mind. "Of all the New York School artists," Barney was his "philosophical and spiritual guide."[36] Philip Leider, the young editor of *Artforum*, recognized that securing Barney's participation allowed Hopps "to break, for the first time, the solid front of hostility which the Abstract Expressionist artists had presented to the new generation for over half a decade. Newman's courage in being the first of his generation to openly acknowledge the validity of the younger group cannot be underestimated; it will go a long way in clearing up the confusion which narrow self-interest and critic-fed misunderstanding had created."[37]

Barney more than "openly" acknowledged the younger men. Always the *pater familias manqué*, he could not have been happier to have another opportunity to preside and bask. The other artists did not travel to the Bienal, but Barney already knew several of the men, and, to some degree—whether greater or smaller is a matter of unreliable anecdotal evidence—had a hand in choosing them.[38] On the basis of a "fan letter" Poons wrote at the time of the French & Company show, he was invited to a party at the Newmans where he was thrilled by the presence in the apartment of both *Vir Heroicus Sublimis* and *Cathedra*. (Poons later said that his "first color 'experience' " was standing before *Vir Heroicus Sublimis*.[39]) As the party wound down, Barney asked him to hang out a while and the two of them drank and talked about poetry and painting and fooled around on the piano. For Stella, as well, the French show was "stunning. Huge," and Barney's presence, especially on panels, was "magisterial."[40]

Barney first met Bell in Los Angeles in 1962; then, at a New York party in 1964 Annalee befriended Bell's mother, engendering a lifelong affection. Judd, a student in Schapiro's Abstract Expressionism seminar (the one who was absent when Barney spoke), had been a fan of Barney's since he saw the "great" *Shining Forth* in the Jewish Museum's "Black and White" show at the end of 1963; he made it the focus of his *Arts Magazine* review[41] and planned an extended consideration for the German magazine *Das Kunstwerk*. Judd had an insight into the work that, at that time, was rare. Unfortunately, the article was not published until February 1970, in *Studio International*; but, as so often happened, it was the unlikely soul-recognition between the two men—the 36-year-old large, handsome, confident Judd and the 60-year-old short, soft, amiably righteous Barney—that was most consequential.

Before Barney left for São Paulo, Barbara Rose, the art historian and critic who was at that time married to Stella, threw a party to celebrate the participants. "Everybody was sitting around in a circle" in the living room in the unglamorous apartment on Seventy-Third Street and Madison Avenue. "Barney was sitting in a swivel chair so that he could address everybody, and he swiveled from right to left to right to left, and he talked for an hour and a half straight, and he absolutely did not take a breath," remembered Rose. Bell recalled him "holding court," gesturing with the ever-present cigarette between his index and second finger, in "a very spirited discussion about fine nuances of baseball."[42] John Cage walked in and Jasper Johns, who brought sushi chefs from a Japanese restaurant. "Barney was going on, 'and this and this, and this' for another hour. Finally, Barney took a breath, and John [Cage] said, 'And then what did you say Barney?' And Barney started again." When the Stellas' 3-year-old daughter Rebecca toddled out, she said, 'That's enough Barney. Now it's my turn.' "[43]

If Barney saw the Brazil show as about a certain approach to art, one which he adamantly did not share but to which he was willing to supply heft, others saw it at least in part as a validation of work being done on the southern West Coast. At the time, months after the grand opening of the new, Wilshire Boulevard building of the Los Angeles County Museum of Art "amid a numbing succession of banquets, receptions and other rituals of civic self-congratulation,"[44] Hopps's choice of three local artists along with three from New York plus Barney was pointed. The appointment of Hopps himself—a California native, champion of California art, and Los Angeles gallery partner before his appointment at the Pasadena Art Museum—was made with that expectation, and it provoked commentary on whether there were different indigenous characteristics.[45] Alan Solomon, visiting California, found that the artists "were the only people in L.A. who did not refer constantly to New York . . . . unlike the collectors, the museum personnel and the dealers, who practically commute to New York."[46] This was in particularly high relief immediately before the Bienal opened when "New York School: The First Generation, Paintings of the 1940s and 1950s" was on view at LACMA. Well over a third of the 122 pieces in the show came from California collections, a bias that an energetic local art community hoped to correct.

Art was a boom business. Critics and commentators and art consumers were sated with the packaging of the past, their appetites for something fresh whetted by a burgeoning art industry. But for Barney the two shows of the summer of 1965 were a one-two punch as he struggled mightily to retain control of the posterity that he claimed he "didn't care about." The unfolding of each impacted Barney's reactions to the other, in increasingly anxious attempts at choreography.

Maurice Tuchman was another who had been in the seminar room at Columbia the day Barney came to speak, and he was another young man who thereafter developed a genuine friendship, getting Barney's "eyes on things" while lunching at Barney Greengrass.[47] Tuchman had recently left a position at the Guggenheim to become the first curator of 20th-century art at LACMA. As his inaugural exhibition, he excitedly told Schapiro, he would mount a show of "only ten or eleven of the first generation artists, the choice to be almost identical with the eleven artists we studied in your seminar on Abstract Expressionism, with perhaps the only change being Tomlin omitted and Barney Newman added."

But this approbation, too, demanded Barney's tailoring. For the catalogue, Tuchman proposed two large sections of documentation: a selected anthology of artists' published statements of the 1940s and early '50s, and a "very select and small anthology of the best contemporaneous critical writings on the movement."[48] And therein lay Barney's "issue." An accurate reconstruction of history was *exactly* what he always wanted, but the record of the time did not accurately represent events from his point of view. From his point of view, he was the most radical and advanced in his thinking and in his painting. The "contemporaneous" critics were tardy. And, of course, some of the artists had in the years since fooled around with dates.

After preliminary discussions the previous fall, Barney agreed to be included. In January, however, with the catalogue already gone to press, Barney told Tuchman "as things stand now, I must decline your invitation to participate." A show that was a clear reconstruction of the period "would be of great importance." But here was the concern: "Mine are <u>known</u> works. What makes me wonder about the show, however, is how about the works of others? For example, Still? Do you intend to show his known works for the years mentioned above or do you intend to use his newly discovered 'unknown works,' to use the language of scholars? . . . (As an example, Clement Greenberg's discovery in 1955 of an 'unknown work' by Still claimed for 1948)." Unless this standard were assured, that there was an exhibition or reproduction history that confirmed the works existed in the years for which they were claimed, "I must be excused. I do not intend to stand as a witness to questionable historical facts."[49]

Tuchman had been promised loans of eight paintings by Barney from the artist and collectors, one from each of '46, '47, '49, '50, '53, and '58, and two from '54. Only one, *Outcry*, 1958, had never been shown before; for the others Barney provided precise, incontrovertible exhibition citations—proof that they were made in the year claimed. He expected the same evidence for all of the other artists.[50] "I do not intend to go into a game where the master of the house lets some of the players use loaded dice."[51]

Tuchman didn't budge but Barney did not withdraw. He simply continued to gripe about the title, and about excerpts from his early writings being used without notifying him.[52] Instead, he began to plan his counterpunch. On the phone, after the show opened, Barney told Tuchman, "What I take issue with is that all eight paintings that you showed by Still as being from 1943 through the late '50s were all painted in the last couple of months. And he painted them all in the last couple of months in order to show that he—his size—was bigger than mine and the other artists."[53]

In the summer of 1965 Barney pulled off a hat-trick. *Artforum*'s cover blazed with *The Third*, *Art in America* featured the *Cantos* portfolio, and *Art News* ran a six-page interview. Yet Barney ping-ponged between crises.

As news of the Watts riots was gripping the nation, the printed São Paulo catalogue arrived on Barney's desk from Los Angeles. He "could not believe [his] eyes."[1] A typo had crept in, and it was not simply a misspelling or a dropped article. It was as if all his adversaries and detractors, real and imagined, over the previous seventeen years, all of those who were scheduled to be finally vanquished by his elevation in São Paulo, had slipped into the printers in darkest night to sabotage him. In *Art in America*, Hopps had written that Barney held a "special significance"; it was "the meaning and stature of his art that establishe[d] the essential nature" of the exhibition.[2] But in the catalogue, the sentence that was meant to read, "There were few artists of Newman's own generation *who remained untouched* by issues raised in his art dating from the late 1940's," had become, on that printed page, "There were few artists of Newman's own generation *touched* by issues raised in his art dating from the late 1940's" (emphases added). Thousands of corrected pages in English and Portuguese needed to be permanently pasted over the false one. "I take this matter very seriously since, as you know, I do not need that this statement be made for my sake," but it was an injury "to all the young artists."

"In discussing my influence on the young, I felt it would protect them and clarify my position if you would also discuss my influence on the older artists. . . . This new version leaves the old out and puts my hand only on the new. This is re-writing history."[3]

This—the recording of history—was particularly attenuated at just this moment. If no action were taken, the game might be lost for good.

To rectify the "re-writing" of history at the Los Angeles County Museum, Barney persuaded Hess to arrange an interview for the September issue of *Art News* in which Barney would argue his case. If it wasn't a set-up, it certainly read like one:

NEWMAN: Tell me, what is the purpose of this interview?

[NEIL] LEVINE: It is not so much to review the show . . . . [that wouldn't] tackle the real problem—namely, the issue of history, the attempt to reveal sources . . .

NEWMAN: As I understand it, you want us not only to discuss the show as an exhibition of important paintings but also to talk about its subject and the big, ambitious catalogue that records that theme.

It was "odd," Levine pointed out, that Barney "and the others represented in the show were not asked to tell what you know of the story. Historians are always bemoaning the passage of time, their inability to find out the facts once a man is dead. Yet maybe that is the way they really want it." Barney agreed.

It took Barney only four sentences to get to his central point: "it is particularly strange that the paintings included in the exhibition by Mr. Still are paintings that were never shown in New York, either during the time he exhibited here or since. With the exception of [Still's] work, I know every painting in this exhibition."

He had "advocated" for this type of show for years, to show the early paintings as "historical events"; but "a great opportunity was lost." An "accurate presentation" would have maintained a strict chronology, "so that everyone would know what was visible when and where." He was unhappy that the show ended in 1959, which itself undermined historical objectivity, "as if there is nothing in the sixties." Barney would have preferred a concentration on "1949–50 or 1948–51. Then the world could see what the artists themselves saw at one specific, particular moment." And, it should have included works that were in the artists' studios, as well as galleries, those done in "utmost solitude." Who were "the artists who were most personal, most original, most effective, and when?" he asked, feeling his own opportunity to correct history slipping away.

The artists were a "collection of individual voices . . . . The only common ground we all had is in the creation of a new, free, plastic language. Some of the voices in this language are strong, some hollow, some thin." And then he tipped his hand: "Before this can be truly discussed, the event has to be accurately recreated so that everyone will know what everyone else is talking about," and that included exposing the Stills in the show as including later versions.[4]

The very name was objectionable; "New York School," he claimed, "exists only in California"; the first time the name was used was in Motherwell's preface for the 1951 Frank Perls gallery show. Since birthdates, but not places, appeared in the catalogue, Barney wondered if the organizers were "trying to hide" the fact that none except he and Gottlieb were born in New York. Nevertheless, New York "institutions" did "not do that much" for Barney. On the contrary: "I helped make New York a place, as did Pollock, de Kooning, and the others."

The catalogue was indeed inadequate in its attempt to objectively encapsulate a story: the critical excerpts and bibliography were incomplete and sloppily presented—reprint dates, for example, were confused with dates of original publication. It was all indicative of a kind of abdication. Barney concluded by bemoaning "the new art historian" who was not searching for "truth" but performing a "new professionalism—the running of the new immense culture establishment." Clarity, if it would ever come, "will have to come not from the new art historians but from a real historian."[5]

A few weeks later, after dinner with his mother and Sarah, Gertrude, her husband, and Anna Greenhouse, he and Annalee got on the plane to São Paulo.

But the storm in Los Angeles did not end there.

To show his contempt for the publication of Barney's take-down, Still's response was again sent "to the editor" over the name of Pat Still. Calling Barney a "frequent visitor and *student*" (emphasis added) of her husband's, "she" wrote that Barney's claims about altered dates for works that, she said, had been visible in "New York City and Easthampton [*sic*]" would "be dealt with by Mr. Still at a time of his choosing. It was in the hope of forestalling this typical political maneuver that he felt constrained to permit his pictures to be shown in this exhibition in spite of what he considered a debatable title."[6]

"It is an unpleasant task to have to silence another man's wife in public, but if that is how the man wants it, chivalry will have to wait," began Barney's answer when both letters were published in *Art News* in November. He pointed out discrepancies in size between the paintings shown in Los Angeles and those that had been exhibited at MoMA in 1952 and in Still's studio in New York in the late 1940s. "A 9-foot painting in 1947 by anyone in New York would have been very conspicuous," Barney wrote, and indeed Pat Still had acknowledged in her letter that "the second version . . . barely distinguishable" from one shown at Parsons in 1951, was the one included in the Los Angeles show.[7] (At the same time, Still, under his own name, wrote to the art historian Katherine Kuh that he would have had more respect for Barney if he "would apply himself to the lessons of the Talmud rather than those of Paul Joseph Goebbels."[8])

Barney arrived in São Paulo late on a Thursday at the end of August with a 38-day American Specialists grant from the USIA. As Abercrombie & Fitch had outfitted him for Emma Lake, now it was the equally *comme il faut* F. R. Tripler & Co., est. 1886 ("Ours is a distinctive, high quality business that appeals to gentlemen of quiet good taste") where he found appropriate garb for Brazil.[9] Expenses guaranteed, itinerary planned, phrases at hand courtesy of three LP records—*Listen and Learn Portuguese*—he and Annalee could anticipate a remarkable tour of the country to "lecture and meet with Brazilian artists."[10] But before they could embark on another triumphal march, to Rio, Brasilia, Salvador, and Belo Horizonte, they faced an unanticipated cloudy horizon.

His seven paintings and two sculptures—the first bronze cast of *Here I (To Marcia)* and the recently conceived and fabricated Cor-Ten steel *Here II*—plus thirty-seven works by the other Americans arrived in Brazil on Friday night, less than one week before the opening and only one day before the judging would begin. An East Coast shipping strike had delayed the scheduled transport, and because it was the weekend, Hopps—who was constitutionally, famously, unable to cope with these sorts of details and problems, who notoriously would disappear when confronted with such "machinations"[11]—was forced to run to the homes of seven Brazilian officials to get the signatures necessary to unload the art at the port of Santos, just as Barney was sitting for a press conference and an interview for Brazilian radio.

Word had gotten around that an "elderly, big deal American" who does "very mysterious art" was coming, and the whole press corps lined up. Annalee was terribly nervous, but Barney, looking very distinguished, was perfectly at peace. "What is the

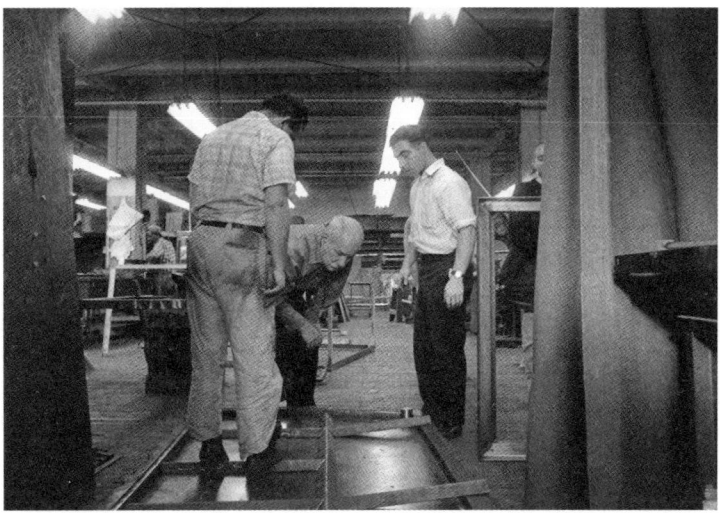

Fig. 50 Donald Gratz (right) and Barnett Newman with an unidentified worker consulting on *Here II* at Treitel-Gratz fabricators, 1965. Photograph Ugo Mulas

essential meaning of your art?" he was asked. The day that all nationalist divisions in the world fall to ruin, he said in response, "the meaning of my art will be perfectly clear." Was it Communist? Did it address the agitation in Brazilian streets? Was it some obscurantist intellectual wisdom? Nobody knew what it was that he said, but they were mesmerized.[12]

Here II was three rolled steel verticals, each emerging from its own trapezoidal base, all sitting on one thin plate. At Treitel-Gratz's new, pin-up-festooned location in Astoria, Queens the incongruously attired Barney had supervised the fabrication with the kind of obsessional concentration that he had given to the synagogue model, to the *Cantos*, to everything he touched. Donald Gratz, with whom he developed a "kind of father-son relationship," so "adored" the older man that he jumped through hoops to please him,[13] providing wood mock-ups, and good-naturedly indulging Barney as he endlessly adjusted the placement of the verticals. The plate at the base had been a particular challenge, cut with an oxyacetylene torch to achieve uneven edges that could be experienced as analogous to the painted edges of his "areas." One corner had a "bite" removed like the title page of the *Cantos,* which may have been printed on a chipped lithographic stone. But now that *Here II* was in Brazil, there was a problem: Barney did not like the surface, it was "shiny." The steel had not patinated as much as he expected it would. Hopps's assistant, Dagny Corcoran—the same young woman who, dragooning her friend, had rubber-cemented the errata pages into the catalogue—was instructed to "do something" and found herself on a ladder in the exposition hall pouring lemon juice and Coca-Cola over it. The solution worked like a charm. Lost to history is who came up with that formula, but very shortly afterwards Barney began to tell the story of how, at the port of Santos, he had cured the sculpture with orange juice—since "there were so many oranges around."[14]

On Sunday, as Barney was picked up by a U.S. embassy driver and whisked off to see the Brazilian national hero Pelé play a soccer game, the São Paulo state police provided a motorcycle escort for four trucks from the port to the museum; the crate protecting *Vir Heroicus Sublimis* alone was 24 feet long, 12 feet high, and weighed more than a ton. At the Oscar Niemeyer-designed pavilion, where five miles of walls were already packed with nearly five thousand international artworks, Hopps, consulate staff, and museum employees hustled frantically to install the American exhibition.[15] The next day, as Barney challenged the installation of his canvases that Hopps had worked out on paper in Pasadena, Corcoran and others, with gloved hands, shifted the seven paintings under Barney's watchful eye for hours, finally returning to Hopps's original. Poons thought that Barney simply liked "situations where he could be mayor"—be fully committed and enjoy the "foxiness" of the proceedings at the same time.[16]

Irwin remembered the show being described as "six tugs pulling a major liner into port"—a very different image from Barney's locomotive for a "kind of train, full of the work of young men of high purpose" who were not "too well known." All six, each differently and to a different degree, blurred the distinction between painting and sculpture. For these and other artists working in this "Third Stream," as it was called by the critic Lucy Lippard, it was precisely Barney's "uncompromising attitudes and articulate statements" that made him "a kind of hero"—as well as his "thin" paintings that blurred the distinction as early as 1951.[17]

Within his rigorously limited selection, Hopps's agenda was manifold: not only to complicate categories and generational and geographical "divides," but also to open possibilities of practice. The choice of Judd and Bell, one critic noted, "may be the first clear recognition of the fact that sculpture, in the hands at this moment of [only] the most tenuous few artists, may, in the course of this decade, achieve the flowering which, for one reason or another, it had never, with one or two exceptions, been able to achieve during the Abstract Expressionist period."[18] And so, yes, Barney was there with the perfectly named *Here I* and the barely finished *Here II*.

Hopps, Solomon told friends, had shown " 'almost suicidal' courageousness in selecting not a single 'easy' artist."[19] This time it was not Barney's, but Irwin's paintings that were cruelly, intentionally, damaged—cut with knives, punctured with ballpoint pens, scribbled over. People hated the work, he was told. He had already raised hackles by refusing to allow photographs of his work to appear in the catalogue. It maddened Barney, who felt it was an affront to the others: it implied that photographs could be taken of their work "that approach the experience [but] not of his."[20] His rigor was even more confusing to the public than Barney's had been, and therefore more threatening.[21]

If the regal image of the ocean liner, or the "locomotive," seemed in some way inevitable, or inspired, initially it was anything but. Characteristically, Barney had been scrupulous about engineering the presentation of both his work and himself.

The USIA public affairs officer in Brazil, at the end of 1964, strongly recommended that the coming exhibition of American painters show "the tendency away from

the abstract toward the semi-represen-
tational." He suggested a "gamut from
Jackson Pollock to Andrew Wyeth,"
with some sculpture "preferably all by
one outstanding artist." Examples of
"pop art were not desired."[22] Unsurprisingly, that advice was not followed.

Also unsurprisingly, before the dust
had settled from the *Times* and the catalogue skirmishes, Barney began his expert alterations. Hopps had chosen four
pieces. By the beginning of June Barney
had charmed Lois Bingham, the chief of
the exhibits division of the fine arts section of the USIA. Well into the planning,
she let Hopps know that in her opinion
the four pieces constituted "an incomplete statement" of Barney's "exceptionally cogent concept of purpose [and] his
multifaceted way."

"The Newman statement will remain
incomplete," she told Hopps, "until we
add, first, one of his great, long, spacious
canvases with its magnificent sense of
pace and interlude and color"—either
Cathedra or *Vir Heroicus Sublimis*—and
secondly, a piece of sculpture as evidence that both his painting and sculpture stem from the same fountainhead

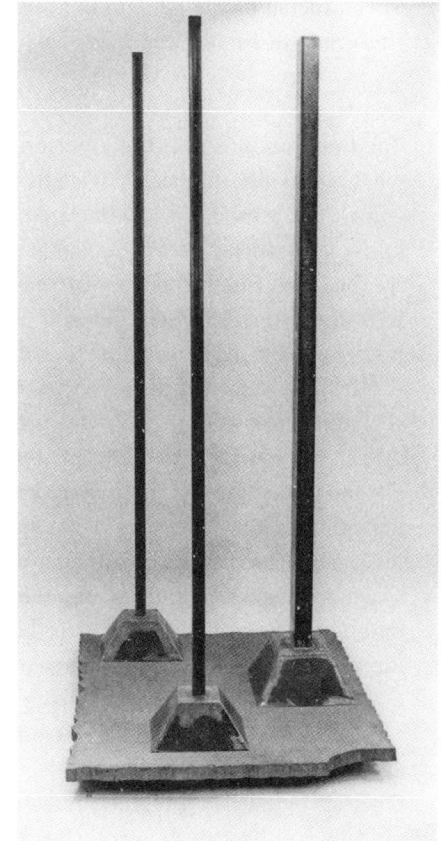

Fig. 51 Barnett Newman, *Here II*, 1965. Cor-Ten
steel, exemplar "B/2," 113 ⅞ × 78 ¾ × 51 ¼ in.
(289.2 × 200 × 130.2 cm). National Gallery of
Canada, Ottawa. Photograph Jonathan Holstein

of reason and inspiration." Although she understood that it would be awkward for
Barney to have twice as many works as any of the others, "to present fewer of his
works, especially when they do not fully reveal the scope of his art, is counter to the
purpose of the show."[23]

That accomplished, Barney got to work on another front.

"I regret that the terms you suggest in your letter . . . make it impossible for me to
accept the invitation so kindly extended by the Embassy in Brazil," he wrote to the
representative of the State Department's Division for Americans Abroad—collapsing
his hunger for deference with an instinctive need to *handel*.[24] He claimed the grant
was far less than his "usual honorarium"—the greatly exaggerated 500 dollars plus
first-class travel and expenses for both him and Annalee—and that he had a competing offer for his time.[25] The State Department made a counter offer, 1500 dollars
per month, pro-rated for thirty-eight days, "the highest compensation authorized by
the Department"; they regretted being unable to provide first-class transportation.[26]

It proved such a happy bargain that, upon his return, Barney requested a "second grant to visit the same area."[27]

> The freedom of space, the emotion of human scale, the sanctity of place, are what is moving—not size (I wish to overcome size), not colors (I wish to create color), not area (I wish to declare space), not absolutes (I wish to feel and to know at all risk).
>
> The fetish and the ornament, blind and mute, impress only those who cannot look at the terror of Self. The self, terrible and constant, is for me the subject matter of painting and sculpture.
>
> The play of formal devices, their manipulation, the framing of space, the association—free or not—of areas, colors, lines for whatever their sake, abstract or otherwise, must lead to the denial of the self through fetishes with—threats of fire and brimstone and through ornaments with—voodoo ecstasies. Instead of the falling in love, what comes through is the falling in love with oneself, the self-love of the sha-man. Like the man-made image of an artist instead of the artist as a man, inspired and inspiring, the fetish and the ornament demand only one emotion—the worship of the artist himself by himself and by those whom he can intimidate. Instead of an eloquence that means what it says, that gives life to mud, one is left, no matter what the magic and the techniques, with so much mud.
>
> Life, as is a true work of art, is, after all always positive.

Once again, Barney produced a statement for an exhibition catalogue that was so cryptically condensed, so perplexing, that one wonders what the audience in São Paulo—whose political freedom, at that very moment, was under siege—might have made of it (not to mention how it must have read in the Portuguese translation). The critical interpretations that he was battling, the scabs ripped off old sores by what he considered the hypocritical behavior of Rothko and Still (a 250,000-dollar contract for murals at a Houston Chapel by the first; a 31-painting, heavily encumbered donation to the Albright Knox Museum by the second), "re-written" history in Los Angeles—all of that, not simply his own work, invisibly shaped a statement of koanic density.

And yet the statement was so unlike the man!

The Brazilian press adored him. He was "so extravagant and so marvelous." People would ask him what he thought of Brazil, and he would say things like, "Oh, the earth is red and red is the color of love and I love Brazil";[28] "the red soil of São Paulo" was "good coffee country" and the paintings of his that were shown there, "were for the most part painted in the Coffee Exchange district" where his studio was located. He spoke about coffee for so long that the interviewer finally had to interrupt him: "Now we know that you like coffee and know something about it, but can we hear something about your work as an artist?" Characteristically, Barney then described all that he was "not involved" with, before discoursing on football (soccer), and taking his "hat off to [the] great *artist*"—Pelé.[29]

The show was heavily promoted by the Brazilian government, which provided funds for press junkets, even as hundreds of leftists were rounded up to prevent disruption of the September 7 Independence Day celebrations. Elizabeth (Betsy) Baker was a young editor at *Art News* when Hess chose her to go.[30] "Look up the Newmans when you get down there. It will be interesting." As it happened, their itineraries overlapped. Barney was "not in terrifically good shape," Baker remembers, but he nevertheless worked very hard, giving a press conference in every city, and visiting multitudes of studios with a "heroic degree of stamina" and a "little pint bottle of vodka" in a paper bag. He would be "white as a sheet," clearly making a great effort during the day; but by the evening he would gather momentum, and by dinner time he was going strong. By two or three in the morning, Annalee would be dozing off and Barney would be having a ball at the late-night bars and restaurants.

On every adventure, whether it was an elegant lunch at a collector's home, a visit to a favela, the racetrack, or a bar, or literary parties in Bahia and Salvador, or (without Baker) a bullfight, or tennis match—Barney was in a suit, with a tie and his monocle.[31] Even at the swimming pool at their hotel, with Annalee in swimsuit, Barney wore a long-sleeved, buttoned-up, collared shirt over his trunks.

And near Ouro Preto, famous for its multitude of elaborate Baroque churches, they visited Congonhas do Campo, where, climbing up a hillside to the Sanctuary of Bom Jesus do Congonhas, were seven chapels containing sixty-four polychrome cedarwood statues depicting the stations of the cross.

At every stop they went to see dealers in stones and they returned with their bags stuffed with amethyst and topaz and other semi-precious crystals and geodes to add to their collection. Airlines charged high supplements for excess baggage, and so when Baker, who was continuing on to Peru, saw them off she had their rocks in two Pan Am flight bags and hid behind a post as they checked in and had their baggage weighed. In those days, before airport security was barely thought about, Baker was able to walk Barney, Annalee, and the rock-filled bags up the stairs, right into the plane.

In the end, the State Department remained unhappy that the American participation was aimed at "a far-out restricted group of artists and critics" instead of the "upper middle class from which most visitors come." But the final report had to acknowledge that Barney was a stunning success.

The authoritative and affable presence of Barnett Newman during the opening rush of the Bienal proved to be an asset to the post in recouping, somewhat, former U.S. prestige and presence at other Bienals. Mr. Newman charmed reporters with his frank admiration for architect Oscar Niemeyer and world-famous soccer star Pelé, and—more importantly—impressed São Paulo artists with his encyclopedic knowledge of the history of art, intellectual authority, and brilliant apologia of his own work . . . . Mr. Newman was unfailingly cordial and communicative with artists and laymen alike. The press conference the day after his arrival resulted in very favorable and fairly extensive coverage . . . . At an informal three-hour discussion meeting with about twenty local artists, Mr. Newman delighted the participants by demonstrating his interest in the works of young artists and explaining his own ideas on trends in modern art and the meaning of art itself.

"In a word," the State Department public affairs officer drew his own conclusion, "the São Paulo public found Mr. Newman far more fascinating than his paintings."[32]

Two weeks after Barney returned from the long ambassadorial tour of Brazil, while his professorial interview in *Art News* was still being argued over by his former cohort, his stature as a master and, possibly, his acumen as an agent were confirmed when, shockingly, Robert and Ethel Scull sold thirteen of their abstract expressionist works at Parke-Bernet to support "younger artists without dealers."[33] In full public light, in the first auction sale to offer "only abstract expressionist paintings" (according to the *Times*, although some of the artists included—Rauschenberg, or Rivers, for instance—might have differed), an event notable enough to be covered in the major newspapers, and in *Time* and *Newsweek*, Barney watched from the audience as *Tundra*, a work the Sculls had purchased less than three years before, achieved the very dignified price of 26,000 dollars (251,500 dollars in 2023).

On the ninth of November, at the age of 84, Barney's mother Anna died suddenly of a heart attack. In a poignant coincidence that would not have been lost on Barney, early that evening the entire city of New York and much of the Northeast was plunged into total darkness and virtually paralyzed by the biggest power failure yet in history. When, in 1968, Barney made in her honor the largest painting in his oeuvre, he gave it the name *Anna's Light*.

"She must have been an extraordinary woman," Motherwell wrote to Barney, "because of your own attitude toward women, which I think is largely formed in sons by their mothers."[34] She was "an extraordinary woman—a remarkable person whose loss to me is immense," Barney, who spoke to her at least once most days, agreed.[35]

How to characterize his "attitude"? Women could be relied upon—up to a point ("If there should come a big pestilence and all the women of the world should die, the men could get along very well indeed without the women," he quoted to the young Annalee pre-marriage); encouraged—up to a point; respected—*up to a point* (they were the "basket weavers" rather than the artists); and their valor lauded, as he explained to the young men around the campfire in Canada. And, up to a point, they could be idealized: "I worship women and therefore thank God I am a man," he once explained to Krasner, echoing Talmud. In all of this, Barney was completely typical of his demographic and time. Perhaps a bit less typical was his discomfort with women physically, and when discussing women throughout his life—in text or in the memories of friends—the terms were aesthetic and conceptual, witty but definitely not sensual. His painting *Eve* was "one of my most poignant and one of my most firm—like a girl should be";[36] a "girl" seen at an opening had a "beautiful front but a bad back" because she had "a flat ass, and didn't understand Pollock's work."[37] The idea that child-bearing was linked to age was foreign to him. But what he *did* understand was that the women in his life provided him with what he needed from them.

Had Anna lived three months longer, she would have had the satisfaction of reading on her son's 61st birthday, in the very newspaper that had defined his struggles over a lifetime, of his "immense prestige and acclaim," which commanded "respect, even awe, among artists of similar persuasion the world over."[38] Five months longer, and she would have seen a temple dedicated to his tenacious will.

FIFTY-EIGHT

STATIONS OF THE CROSS

Give a man enough rope, they say, and he'll hang himself. The adage received double proof this week at the Guggenheim Museum. That body hanging from the rafters belongs to the painter Barnett Newman, and the companion object swinging alongside is Lawrence Alloway, the museum's curator . . .

A third casualty is the museum itself. The Guggenheim can no longer be taken quite seriously as a first-rate institution . . . . Since cigarette manufacturers are required to state on their packages that smoking may be hazardous to your health, it is unfair that the Guggenheim should be allowed to operate without posting a notice.[1]

Thus John Canaday, nursing a chronic contempt for contemporary abstract art and a particular grudge against Barney—who repeatedly, publicly, challenged his weak and specious analyses—began his *Times* review of the *Stations of the Cross* finally installed at the Guggenheim in late April.

Here, it was the word "counterfeit" that he flourished. But Canaday had a much bigger agenda than simple disregard for a particular type of art; this was very personal. Without the title, the work would have been "harmless," but now the verticals resembled "unraveled phylacteries."[2] The message in the review was clear to his readers: How dare a Jew take on this subject?[3]

One could not say that Barney didn't enjoy the *scandale.* So charged was the atmosphere, that at a public "Conversation" between Barney and Hess at the museum on May 1, Barney immediately—and wittily—addressed the elephant in the room: "Some people have read the notice [for the event] sort of fast and instead of conversation they think perhaps it is going to be a conversion."

Defending himself on both flanks—from those who objected to the specific, identified, content as well as those who objected to the idea (for which he had been fighting since the mid-'40s) that "abstract" art had any content at all—seemed to make his juices flow.

Hess: The idea of subject matter and picking a subject matter almost always appears to be an affront, and certainly a number of our journalist/critics in New York have taken the affront and been howling about it . . . .

Barney: Well, I think, Tom, that the critics would have taken affront if I had any kind of paintings without any titles . . . . Everybody knows what you are referring to, and . . . no matter what I would have had on the walls, because I was involved in opposing the situation there [at the *Times*], that the use of my work for a personal vendetta would have occurred anyway . . .

I think the other issue [is] of whether I am involved in just making paintings as things [or] paintings that have something to say. I have always felt that a painting says something.

Messer, the museum's director, had a particular flair for display—"It was what I do best," he claimed—and was a fan of the Guggenheim building that many found inhospitable to art; he was itching to direct the hanging. Nevertheless, because of the longstanding relationship between curator and artist, Alloway was put in charge. As it turned out, both museum men had to cede. Barney had something in mind. He personally directed the installation of the fourteen *Stations* and ever after, they would always be shown together in the specific order he established—although not necessarily proceeding in the same direction—with the additional single canvas *Be II* as final punctuation.

Three months earlier, in January, Barney was back and forth between New York and Washington, where the American section of the São Paulo show was shown at the National Collection of Fine Arts.[4] The galleries were in the natural history museum, just past the rotunda displaying an enormous elephant, and had only recently been occupied by the art museum. Barney was mainly concerned about the lighting—he kept asking for it to be lowered—and the lovingly coaxed patina of *Here II*. The labor crew was a "pretty rough bunch," but Barney spoke to them with politeness and respect, informed them how the work was made, about Cor-Ten steel, and how delicate, and easily marred, the surface was. At the end of the lecture, when one of the men immediately, clumsily stepped on the base, Barney did not anger, he just turned away, shaking his head.[5] But it was different with Hopps, forced into a confrontation with Barney's "preconceived notion of how the space should be." Ornate architectural detailing high up on the wall where his paintings hung "bothered" him.[6] Still, nothing was done until Irwin arrived a few days into the installation and discovered that the spot allotted to him had an "ornate marble dado," which made his painting look "like a pig skewered on a spit." His solution—to make the rail disappear by repainting the wall in degrees of gray that functioned as a "reverse trompe l'oeil"—inspired Barney to reconsider. Since no one could duplicate the subtlety of Irwin's magic in the more complicated physical situation, a Potemkin fix was demanded.[7] Hopps built "a false wall about ten meters high, at great expense and difficulty."[8] Not surprisingly, Barney was absolutely correct: it was the most prominent showing of his works in a public institution, and the room was pristinely beautiful—as could be seen in a television film shown the following summer.[9]

Frank Lloyd Wright's architecture for the Guggenheim Museum was a breed of another sort, known for a continuous span of shallowly recessed, curved-wall galleries spiraling up a ramp while describing a widening circle around an open atrium. But it also contains the eccentric "High Gallery"—what would be a roughly 38-by-48-foot room jutting off the spiral, had not the enormous arc of the ramp sliced through its area. On each end, a short straight wall met a short curved wall; between them

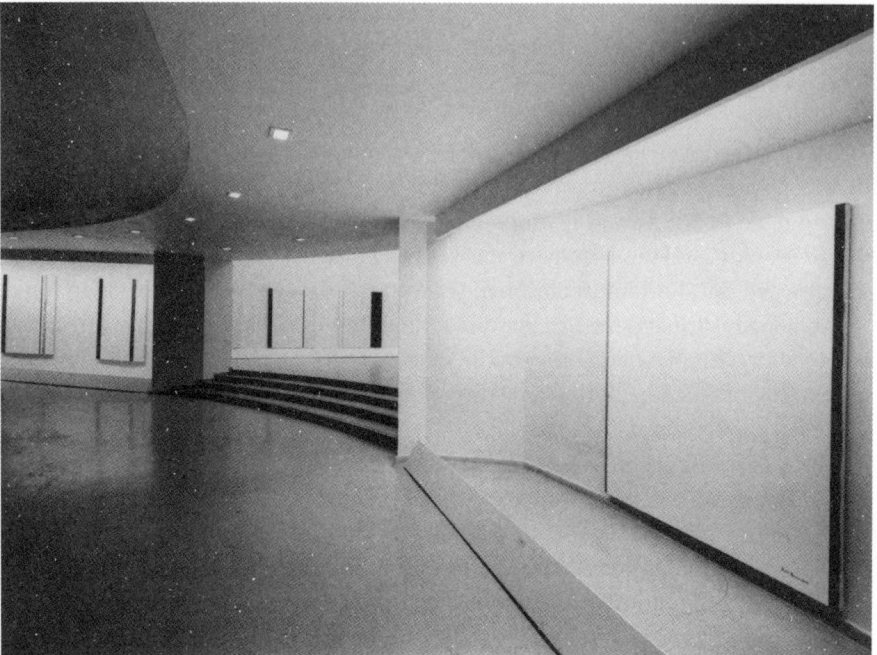

Fig. 52 Guggenheim Museum, 1966 installation of *The Stations of the Cross: Lema Sabachthani*, looking into the High Gallery from the ramp. Photograph Robert E. Mates

was a 23-foot curved open span. To enter the raised High Gallery, one mounts four 23-foot-wide steps off the first arc of the museum's lowest ramp. Twenty-three feet is also the height of the room. It was in this sanctuary-like space that Barney created his "Sistine Chapel."[10] The first four *Stations* did indeed begin a linear progression along the ramp just above the High Gallery. At that point, the viewer turned left into the room to be enveloped by the remaining ten. Returning to the ramp, she would see *Be II* to her immediate left. In this way, a viewer might experience the cumulative effect of the individually conceived but identically sized black-on-white or white-on-white vertical paintings not as variations on a theme, or a narrative, but rather as something akin to being surrounded by singing prayer bowls, each with its own resonant frequency, in a Tibetan monastery. *Be II*—the painting called *Resurrection* over Barney's objections in the 1962 Allan Stone catalogue—somewhat larger and with a cadmium red zip on the far-left edge of an otherwise white-and-black canvas, was the final gong, "in a sense the resolution of the event," in Barney's words.[11]

In the two years since he made *White Fire III*, the 1964 white-on-exposed-canvas work that E. J. Power purchased from his studio, Barney painted what are now known as the ninth, tenth, eleventh, and fourteenth stations in various white paints on exposed canvas, and what are now known as the twelfth and the thirteenth stations in black on white. Three weeks before the show opened, while the catalogue was being printed in Holland, Barney decided that "the painting labeled 14th Station is now to be 13th and the 13th becomes 14th."[12] The Stedelijk van Abbemuseum in Eindhoven was negotiating with him to purchase *Resurrection* after it had been exhibited at the Guggenheim. That was "a name given by others," Barney corrected the director, declined the offer, and decided to keep "*Be, #2*" with the *Stations* and "take it off the market as a separate painting."[13]

Less than a year earlier at the Castelli Gallery, where it wrapped around the 22-by-24-foot walls, and then at the Jewish Museum, the installation of James Rosenquist's spectacular *F-111* knocked the socks off New Yorkers. It was *F-111*'s subject matter that was thematically and visually explosive, but Barney responded to something else. He and Rosenquist would have conversations about the viewer's *orientation* to a work of art, about Barney's "theory of the effect of peripheral vision" that everything that is "fed into the side of one's eyes is what lays claim to reality."[14] Rosenquist's masterwork may have been the first independent—not commissioned—contemporary artwork that was publicly installed as a surrounding environment and the enveloping, and sheer *amount*, of real estate allocated to a single monumental statement could only remind Barney of the old master pantheon in which he always assumed he had a place.

Certainly, both that tradition *and* the popularity of Pop were on his mind as he spoke to Hess. "I always thought that you were a staunch atheist, a pragmatist," the critic began.

I don't think that I have to be a believer in that sense to say something about a subject that has meant something to me all these years. I wasn't commissioned to do this by a church and I felt free to express something that I had feelings about. *I think when the Pope asked Michelangelo to do the ceiling, he didn't give him an examination to see if he knew the creed* [emphasis added].[15]

But particularly noteworthy, for future Newman studies, was that during the conversation, amid several references to "stripes," for the first time *publicly* Barney said, "Zips. I prefer zips."

BARNEY: I have as many paintings without stripes at all as I have with stripes, so to speak. If that's what you want to call it.
HESS: Zips.
BARNEY: Zips. I prefer zips.

Much scholarly ink has been spilled upon why, at this moment, Barney featured the name. As spoken, it had the energetic urgency of the comic-book sounds depicted in Roy Lichtenstein's paintings, and the punch of the vocabulary used to describe Pop art. Just before the *Stations* opened at the Guggenheim, "Word and Image," curated by Alloway, was seen at the museum—a show, according to the critic Hilton Kramer, that promoted Alloway's positing of an "aesthetic community of interest between abstract expressionism and pop art."[16] But there's a danger of overburdening the inspiration for—and Barney's commitment to—the adoption of the word.

Consider the immediately preceding circumstances: between January and the April 20 opening, Barney's schedule of travel, interviews, discussions, and general public relations was particularly, almost alarmingly, packed. Consider Barney's mindset: he was preparing, in a typically focused way, to defend and amplify the *content* of *The Stations* against the inevitable backlash, reading theology, meeting multiple times with Theodore Gastor, translator of the Dead Sea Scrolls and possessor of an elite Zionist pedigree (Gastor was named for his father's friend Theodor Herzl), and Lionel Abel, a rabbi's son, New York intellectual, and friend of artists. Consider how casual and uninsistent this first mention of "zips" was: in interviews during the spring Barney was still using "stripe," "line," "band," "color areas"—but never "zip."[17] It is unlikely that there was premeditation to introducing the term; in fact, he had privately used it at least since 1963, and, other than in the interview with Hess, the only time he is recorded as using it publicly is in the 1970 interview for the film *Painters Painting*, where he distanced himself from it: "my so-called 'zip.'"[18]

What seems likely is that in the collegial and verbally playful discourse with Alloway and Hess, Solomon, or Rosenberg—Barney's frequent punning-partner, who was a last-minute cancellation as interlocutor at the Guggenheim that evening—it had surfaced. As a musical-comedy fan, he may even have had a giggle over Lorenz Hart's song "Zip" in *Pal Joey*, enjoying the riff, like the internal dialogue of an exotic dancer, who, as she practiced her own art with "intelligence," thought about Walter Lippmann, William Saroyan, Schopenhauer, Allah, Whistler, the Schubert brothers, and the Kabbalah. (A popular Broadway revival with Bob Fosse opened in 1963, the same year Hopps heard Barney use the term.)

The workings of a mind, especially an intelligently ravenous one, are never entirely knowable—even to the mind's owner. So it should not be ignored that Rita *Zipr*kowski was the maiden name of the wife—genuinely loved by both Newmans—of Barney's nemesis, Reinhardt. And, since Barney was so inclined to witty word-play himself, the son of the menswear manufacturer likely appreciated its particular aptness, as Frank Stella noted: zippers join pieces together into one inseparable whole.

Barney never diverged from his insistence that he was not a brand, that if he ever thought he was painting "Newmans" he would give up. But others—critics and writers—who, recognizing in the name a way to distinguish his "stripe" from the increasingly prevalent stripes in others' works, seized upon it as a kind of trademark. Exactly what he abjured.

Already in his 20s, Barney placed the artist above dogma. "Without its special literary qualities, the Tanach would hardly have had so profound an effect," he wrote in "The Literature of the Jewish People." "One cannot comprehend the Tanach, even as a religious book, if one is not able to appreciate the extraordinary literary art of the Biblical poets and thinkers." In "The First Man Was an Artist" he recast Genesis.

This attitude of mind enabled him—gave him the cheek—to creatively, *ingenuously*, take on the Passion of Christ for its cry. "Lema Sabachthani—why? Why did you forsake me? Why forsake me? To what purpose? Why?" Barney wrote in his catalogue statement.

This is the Passion. This outcry of Jesus. Not the terrible walk up the Via Dolorosa, but the question that has no answer.

"I suppose maybe this is blasphemous," he said to an interviewer, comparing the pain of the Romans' nails with what was "going on in Vietnam, or the sort of things that happened in Hiroshima, or the kind of thing that happens when somebody sticks his bayonet into you." It seemed to him that the main issue, "the agony," in the Passion was the *human cry*, not the "torture."[19]

"I have felt that in terms of that kind of physical suffering, it's gotten almost universal," he told Hess. "I was trying to call attention to that part of the Passion which I have always felt was ignored and which has always affected me: the cry of the *Lema Sabachthani*. Which I don't think is a complaint." He was always struck by the paradox: about those "who actually persecuted him and crucified him," Jesus "says to God, 'Forgive them for they know not what they do.' But to God . . . he says, 'What's the idea?'"

"What's the idea?"—a classic Newmanism, disarmingly colloquial. A way to charm his audience, momentarily revealing his inner Damon Runyon. "What did I ever do to anybody?" asks the horseplayer in Runyon's "No Justice." "Why can't I win?"[20]

In the writings of Gastor, the esteemed comparative religion scholar, and in their conversations at Steinberg's, the Upper West Side dairy restaurant, Barney found an intellectual, secular confirmation for collapsing two religious traditions. So that to Hess, in front of the Guggenheim audience, he could feel secure in stating that he "could have called [the paintings] the Twenty-second Psalm" because "the psalmist does say, 'God, why hast thou foresaken me?'" But that, he said, would not have made his point. "Other elements" in the psalm ("Oh my God, I cry in the daytime, but Thou hearest not and in the night season, and I am not silent") would have resulted in a painting "illustrating, you might say, a poetic expression." He felt "that it was more appropriate for me to be concerned with the *Sabachthani* ["forsaken" in the Gospel of Matthew] instead of the *Azavthani* ["abandoned" in the psalm]."

For Barney what was compelling was not a king's appeal for the faith to lead a people, but a single man's *geshray*.

The ones who are born are to die
Against thy will art thou formed
Against thy will art thou born
Against thy will dost thou live
Against thy will die.

"Jesus surely heard these words from the 'Pirke Abot,' 'The Wisdom of the Fathers,'" Barney wrote with stunning *chutzpah*—"surely"?—and evidently without checking with Gastor, since the *Pirkei Avot* did not exist before the third century, when oral traditions were compiled into the written *Mishnah*.[21]

It was a "declaration" of "the human condition," he clarified for a mass audience, in an interview recorded at the time and broadcast in July after the show closed. It meant "*more*" than the anecdotal walk on Calvary. That was its "*power*."[22]

No detail had been overlooked. Herbert Matter, who designed the small catalogue, was told by Alloway that it would be "absolutely inappropriate to use any kind of graphics"; "no verticals"; a "somber, but not too symbolic looking" color might possibly be used for the cover but it "should definitely not be too ecclesiastical a purple." And, "without slighting the title would you give the artist's name somewhat more emphasis."[23]

There was the matter of timing: Parke-Bernet auctioneers announced that eight sales of the property of the recently deceased Helena Rubinstein would be held between April 20 and May 4, and Barney was worried that the buzz surrounding them would steal his thunder. He asked to reschedule the show. Not possible, Alloway said, and reassured him that the daily newspapers had writers "assigned specifically to sale rooms, which are treated separately from museum and art gallery reviewing."[24]

Then there was the matter of the opening: Barney and Alloway were concerned that "though the show is a small one, the celebration should not be too minor in view of his major reputation."[25] Fortunately, another friend of Barney was on the job. To build an audience, Messer had recently hired the very well-connected Everett Ellin as one of the first public affairs officers at any museum. Ellin became, as he said, the Guggenheim's "Perle Mesta"—the great society hostess of the 1950s.[26]

As luck would have it, the *Stations* opening coincided with the trustees' dance at the Whitney—its "final social gala" before it moved into its new building—*and* the celebrity-packed first night of the Bolshoi Ballet at the old Metropolitan Opera House, which would be demolished after the Bolshoi's performances. It coincided, in fact, with what one society page claimed was "widely held to be the most hopelessly overscheduled evening" in years, with "nearly everybody who is anybody socially" out on the town attending at least six "major events"—and didn't even mention the one at the Guggenheim.[27] But it made no difference: a large, beautifully dressed and spirited crowd showed up nevertheless.

It was a "very special occasion" for Barney, "everyone came"—peers, younger artists, critics, curators, "celebrities, beautiful women." It was, according to the WNET feature program filmed at the event, a "happy opening, perhaps the nicest of the season." In any case, it was memorialized as such when the television show was broadcast in July.

Time and *Newsweek*, genuflecting to Barney's "pioneer[ing]," "second to none" influence, had abandoned even the whiff of their earlier mockery: there was a "spiritual as well as a visual atmosphere, a call to contemplation." And in that rarefied air hung Barney's "own existential question as an artist . . . Why paint?"[28]

For Canaday, and for Genauer at the *Herald Tribune*, who found the works in the show as empty (and "pretentious") as she had always found Barney's work, the years, and the shows, and the critical commentary, and the legion of admiring and influenced artists since 1950 might never have existed. But in the *New York Post* it was 1966. Reviewing what would turn out to be a landmark show, "Primary Structures"—three floors of radically new sculpture appearing at the Jewish Museum at the same time—the *Post*'s critic judged that it honored "as its source Barnett Newman's paintings and concepts." Barney in the *Stations*

> Synthesized space and its emotional freight. He has used the mysteries of space, its intervals, its volumes, its expansions, its constrictions to evoke direct emotive responses.[29]

There seemed to be no end of points of controversy.

Many expected supporters were disappointed: the "insistence" of the story; the synthetic paints used on nine of the fourteen was too easy a medium and didn't require the effort that oil had; black and white avoided the struggle with color; the title was considered the "ultimate chutzpah," the "grandiosity" was "over the top."[30] Do you want visitors "to walk up the ramp carrying a two by four on their shoulders?," Gottlieb joked to Barney at the opening.

Messer would later repeat that he and Alloway did not know the title of the works until immediately before the catalogue went to press, and that, in fact, Alloway's essay in the catalogue was written largely when "there were no *Stations of the Cross* on the horizon."[31] That is contradicted by correspondence between Barney and Alloway as early as July 1964 and Barney and Messer by December 1965.[32] Understandably, Messer was concerned about the impact of inevitable controversy on Harry Guggenheim, the ultimate power at the museum; Guggenheim was among many, Messer said, who "considered it a debacle." Canaday's review "was more or less what [Guggenheim] would have thought himself, not only about Barney, but about abstract art in general." Messer was forced "to conclude that this is not something that I can do every two weeks."[33]

The exhibition supplied fresh fuel to the split with Rothko, who was "particularly disgusted" and angry, he told Katharine Kuh, because he considered his own work "religious at its core," and felt that Barney had invaded that private territory,[34] that he had co-opted Rothko's own identification of his 1964 Harvard multiple-mural commission with the Passion and Resurrection of Christ.

It provoked, in *The Nation*, the dubious, if high-minded and respectful, thoughts of Max Kozloff, another member of Schapiro's seminar at the time of Barney's visit. Kozloff was unimpressed since his earliest criticism: "underneath the cold exterior of a Newman painting beats a heart of stone" he wrote in 1963,[35] as Barney reminded readers in the *pilpul*-like letter responding to Kozloff's negative review of the *Stations*. Carey McWilliams, *The Nation*'s editor, was less indulgent than Hess had been; Barney's letter was not published "word for word" as he insisted, thus avoiding Panofsky redux.[36] Barney's campaigns against critics, in which the charges always alleged bad faith rather than bad taste, had become known as "Barney Newmanism" among artists, and some—like Flavin—considered it complimentary.[37] But now, even Schapiro, reliably supportive when Barney needed it, in private notes expressed his exasperated fatigue with Barney's "insistence to fight all critics so persistently."[38]

But it was Canaday's hatchet job and thinly veiled anti-Semitism that provoked the most extended and concentrated linguistic and logical exegesis. The critic's "contradictions" and "unintelligibility" were "flagrant," Barney wrote to Arthur Ochs Sulzberger, who had experience deflecting Barney.

At first, a coalition was formed to write to Sulzberger: Elizabeth Bliss Parkinson (collector and MoMA trustee), Messer, John Baur (associate director of the Whitney at that time), Robert Sarnoff (president of RCA), Schapiro, and Vera List (philanthropist, collector, and Jewish Museum trustee), with Barney and Heller leading. The planned communication would address Canaday's "accusations of bad faith on the part of a museum when it exhibits work he does not like" and the paper's complicity in a "personal vendetta" against certain artists.[39] Ultimately, that proposal was shelved; it's possible that, with a *Times* eleven-page feature on Leo Castelli ("Sort of the Svengali of Pop") and his artists on the newsstand, some of the art-world grandees thought twice about the appearance of sour grapes.[40] Barney, however, wrote his own letter, which went somewhat farther.

Since Canaday's "reckless doubletalk brings his good faith into question, there can be only one conclusion—that [he] had other motives in writing his piece. Although he does not know what he is saying, there can be no doubt that he knows what he is doing," and what he was doing was payback for Barney's review of *The Embattled Critic*, and "the fact that I signed a letter, together with 48 others, protesting this type of abuse." He noted Canaday's unprofessional retaliation against some of the others, including David Smith, Motherwell, and Frankenthaler.

Finally, Barney addressed the slur: "What do you make of his remarks that turn the ritual phylacteries into an epithet?" he asked Sulzberger. "Is he attacking Jesus because he was a Jew and had to wear them or is he attacking me because he knows that I am also a Jew?"

"It is not inappropriate at this time to mention again the religious slur that was able to transform the crosses of Calvary into the gallows for us. I am writing to assure you that none of us intend to mount them."[41]

Before the correspondence ceased, the WNET show "USA Artists: Barnett Newman" aired. Producer Lane Slate, with Solomon consulting, gave Barney the most respectful, thoughtful, accessible—and sychophancy-free—presentation he had yet received. But despite having been crowned on television, and despite further, increasingly petulant and aggrieved arguments from Barney, the *Times*, like *The Nation*, would not publish his letter "word for word."

Of all the many controversies Barney provoked or joined, the one surrounding the *Stations of the Cross* had the most legs. It was "amazing" to him that it seemed "to penetrate [critics'] most intimate beliefs," he told Schapiro,[42] at the same time fomenting just that sort of perturbation and ostentatiously courting some broad acknowledgment of his grand theological insight. He invited theologians to the opening at the Guggenheim: Father Charles Whelan of Fordham University Law School, Dr. R. Shaull of Princeton Divinity School, Dr. Marc Tanenbaum of the American Jewish Committee, Benjamin Payton of the Council of Churches, Gabriel Vcharian of Syracuse University. Venturing into new territory, he began to be a spokesman of a sort about contemporary art and religion while carefully avoiding the trap of "Chagallerie"—illustration. He was invited to ecclesiastical conferences to be held the following spring.

With the Museum of Modern Art he pursued an elaborate plan, requiring the construction of specially built, fabric-covered false walls, to install the *Stations* in the Founders Room for a reception for one of those conferences, the National Council of Churches' International Congress on Religion, Architecture and the Visual Arts, at which Barney would be speaking; the intention was that they would remain on view for a month. The paintings were moved to the site, the museum agreed to cover half the 5000-dollar cost, and Barney lobbied to raise the remainder from "the religious groups" the museum would be hosting. Enthusiastic support, but no funds, came from Barney's contacts, and the exhibition did not happen.[43] He fantasized about a sale to the Vatican,[44] and implied to Evan Turner, the director of the Philadelphia Museum who hoped to exhibit them, that a mysterious potential sale was in the works.[45]

Not a few people felt that whatever spirituality Barney claimed for the experience was ruined by the appearance on the front surface of the otherwise pristinely absolute canvases of his signature.[46] It announced adamantly his conscious construction of the experience, something many decided was at odds with the intention, leading some, like Bob Friedman, to go so far as to consider the fourteen pieces a "dada gesture"—as he had labeled *Here I* when he first saw it. Others, however, like Heiner Friedrich, the collector and dealer of minimal and conceptual art, recognized it as absolute integrity: Barney *owned* his work. He had never deviated from the foundational principle of his art: every work had content, and the content was "The Subject of the Artist."

The dissonance of the signature on the canvas, the self-consciousness imposed on the primal, was Barney's acknowledgment that:

> This overwhelming question that does not complain, makes today's talk of alienation, as if alienation were a modern invention, an embarrassment. This question that has no answer has been with us so long—since Jesus—since Abraham—since Adam—the original question . . . .
>
> No one gets anybody's permission to be born. No one asks to live. Who can say he has *more* permission than anybody else?[47]

Of course he had anticipated the art world's reaction, *of course* it must have been satisfying to the aggrieved old anarchist in him on so many levels. But it was no counterfeit art, or dada-type gesture. "The agony and the glory were one," he told an interviewer.[48] For Barney the culmination of the Passion was "why? Why . . . Why . . . . Why?"[49]

As he articulated years earlier in "The First Man Was an Artist," that outcry before the terror of existence was the essence of being human, the single strongest determinant of his life, the driver of his career, and the framer of his art—the aesthetic act that preceded the social act. And although he developed his magnificent social persona, his loquacious, avuncular personality, his notorious talent for discoursing on subjects from paleontology to L'il Abner, ornithology to the Fulton Fish Market, geology to Grünewald's altarpiece, when he went to bed—rarely to sleep—it was with the cry before the terror.

And when he woke in the morning he faced the fear that he would "make another Newman that I made yesterday" and become—like the "tragic figure," his father—nothing better than a "manufacturer."[50]

The *Washington Post* called Barney "one of the giants of postwar American painting" when the São Paulo show was at the National Collection of Fine Arts (now the Smithsonian American Art Museum), and he determinedly assumed that role. He collapsed the opening festivities, during which all seven artists were finally together with the exhibition, with his birthday two days later; for some celebrating with him, watching his attenuated elegance, his happy entitlement to "life's pleasures"—like heavy cream in his coffee—was pure joy.[1] The first two months of 1966 were filled with partying in both Washington and New York. The *Village Voice* reported that the 61-year-old artist had been spotted frugging with Poons, Alloway, Castelli, Dennis Hopper, and Warhol at the early February performance of Rauschenberg's "Statue of Liberty" Happening.[2]

On lunchtime visits to galleries or his studio, Liberman had been praising Barney to *Vogue*'s publisher at Condé Nast: "Barney's visits to the studio for me were the most important thing in my life," their conversations were his "lifeline to another existence."[3] In the magazine's April 15 issue, "People Are Talking About . . . : Barnett Newman," a stunning portrait by Irving Penn, tightly-cropped, all monocle, silk cord, mustache, and cigarette, loomed. Finally, Si Newhouse decided to see for himself. On a Friday in May, they met at West End Avenue, where Newhouse saw *Outcry*—the first "Newman" he had ever seen.[4] They had the obligatory lunch at Barney Greengrass, where Barney told Newhouse about his run for mayor, and about the fun of jousting with Panofsky, and they then crossed Central Park to see the *Stations*. At the museum, a visibly concerned Barney peered through his glass at a spot he noticed on one of the canvases. As he got closer, a fly flew off, but the memory of that, his "preciseness," made a profound impression on Newhouse: it was a window into understanding the painter. Newhouse arranged to buy *The Word II* that very day; it was "a very great work of art," he told Barney, "and an important personal experience for me," later adding, "nothing that I will ever own will give me the intense gratification I'm receiving from your great painting."[5]

Newhouse was "so passionate about my painting, I can't refuse him anything," Barney wrote to Liberman, "He is pure spirit—total passion." For his part, Newhouse credited Barney with introducing him to the "culture of painting."[6] Barney immediately began to see Newhouse regularly, educating him—about art, about why he didn't like Cézanne or Mondrian, why he "resented" Greenberg and the way he wrote—and socializing in a new register. Over the next years, the Newmans would be Newhouse's guests at the glamorous haute French restaurant La Grenouille, at fashionable dinners and parties, and at special events sponsored by Condé Nast or *Vogue*. There were intimate meals with Newhouse and his companion, Nadine Bertin, an editor at *Vogue*, at Michael's Pub, not infrequently joined by the publisher's

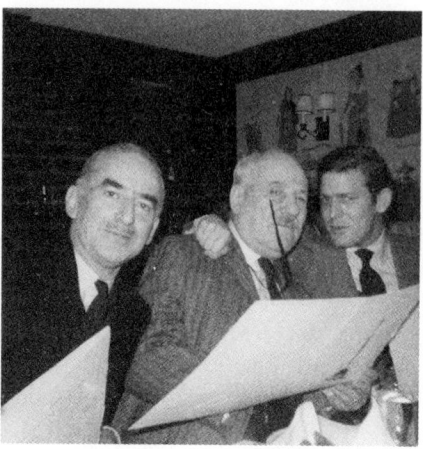

Fig. 53 Barnett Newman with Alexander Liberman (left) and Bill Berkson (right) at La Crémaillère restaurant in Bedford, New York

good friend, Roy Cohn. Somehow Barney, who went to war with Hub Crehan, with John Canaday, Clyfford Still, and Ad Reinhardt, did not have "an issue" with Cohn and his miserable history. Cohn "knew nothing about art" and had nothing at all in common with Barney, was even nervous about having dinner with "a famous artist." But the two recognized each other as "jokers" and liked each other. Their companions thought them very funny. They laughed a lot. They were "both very charming when they wanted to be." There was a brief moment when the purchase of a painting was discussed, though nothing came of it.[7]

Barney, of course, was "always immaculately dressed" when they went out together, "believing an artist should be first class in the way he looked, the restaurants he went to";[8] Newhouse was the definition of eccentric casualness. On one occasion, when Barney and Annalee were his guests at the Plaza's Oak Room, the publisher was denied admission for wearing a turtleneck. In Newhouse's written reply to the Plaza's apology the sound of Barney's chuckling can be detected: if he didn't coach Newhouse, he at least relished the exchange enough to keep both letters: "In an era when Mass is said in the vernacular and the Queen of England receives her uncle, it is an effort to work up much sympathy for your attitudes towards men's neckwear. Nevertheless, I continue to think kindly of the Plaza—as I did of my great grandmother, before her recent demise."[9]

Barney was not done with his experience in São Paulo. He was "pleased . . . to be the initiator of [a] hopeful new attitude," and extolled the exhilarating impact his work had among Brazilians, even if "this response was not shared by our American officials abroad," he told the *Washington Post*. The official report was "full of untruths," in order "to appease an ambassador."[10] It led his interviewer to pose the question, "Who should decide what gets sent abroad to represent American art at the international art exhibitions—government officials or art experts?"[11] It was a question that started to come up more frequently.

By the time the *Stations of the Cross* was installed in April 1966 much of the kumbaya illusion created by Messer, Alloway, and Ellin was dissipating. It was leaked that Alloway and Messer had been since February in conflict over the selection of artists for the U.S. Pavilion in Venice the coming summer. The government sponsors had invited the Guggenheim to curate with the idea that Alloway would present Pop art;

instead he chose Pollock, Cornell, Trova, and a work by the recently deceased David Smith, to be shown with Lichtenstein. Messer dropped Lichtenstein and Pollock, and substituted Larry Rivers and Isamu Noguchi. In New York and Los Angeles there were complaints that the show was too conservative and presented no compelling reason for Europeans to visit the American exhibit.[12] Even before the *Stations* closed in mid-June, Alloway was no longer at the museum.

But if he had lost his position at the Guggenheim, he had not lost his influence. In mid-October, the Alloway-organized "Systemic Painting" opened there: twenty-eight artists, each represented by one "geometrical . . . , hard-edge . . . , shaped . . . , color-field . . . [or] optical" painting.[13] As the fountainhead of *permission* for the genus of art included in the show—by Kelly, Leon Polk Smith, Liberman, and Noland, but also, to the immense gratification of that fountainhead, even by the mature Reinhardt—Alloway firmly centered Barney. "On the one hand he has created his own audience and influenced younger artists; on the other hand, his art was waited for."

"The essentializing moves made by Newman"—as early as 1951, Alloway carefully pointed out the date—"to reduce the formal complexity of the elements in painting to large areas of a single color, have an extraordinary importance. The paintings are a saddle-point between art predicated on expression and art as an object." Barney had spent a professional lifetime separating himself from early 20th-century constructivists and Bauhaus artists; in his catalogue, Alloway grabbed the baton. "Whereas Mondrian and Malewitch, in the formative period of their ideas, believed in absolute formal standards, of the kind a definition of Classicism requires," *now* "the systematic and the patient could be regarded as no less idiosyncratic and human than the gestural and cathartic."[14] Anyone paying attention could no longer legitimately misunderstand Barney's relation to the earlier artists' work.

Alan Solomon, too, was at work placing Barney; alone of his generation he was featured in the stylish photography book *Ugo Mulas in New York: The New Art Scene*, for which Solomon wrote the text. At the same time, the loyally admiring Solomon was, since January in New York and Washington, at work interviewing and filming Barney for a summer television program. For much of this period, the first half of 1966, Barney had been working on sculpture—the second and third exemplars of *Here III*—a single stainless steel vertical member in a Cor-Ten steel base.[15] But in the summer, with the deinstallation of the *Stations* behind him, it made perfect sense that he would return to the work of painting. Especially since Solomon was in the midst of elaborate negotiations with the USIA about American representation at "Expo 67"—the Canadian World Exhibition in Montreal the following spring. Solomon had conceived a radically transgressive installation of *very* large-scale paintings, in which they would appear to be floating in the air above platforms and moving staircases. Any work included would bear an Olympian burden to speak in a context that almost defied such speech. The number of artists was limited by the installation's ambition—only eighteen to twenty-five were at first considered—and several of the works, among them Barney's, were executed specifically for this show to conform to the size proposed.

During the "lazy summer eves" that still had "good light," Barney had the forth-coming challenge on his mind, and the "large painting" he began took a very different direction from his work of the preceding few years.[16] One might say that having once again been designated as conqueror of a territory by Alloway, Barney needed to se-cure it. But with the fear of repeating himself, of "just knocking out Newmans" weigh-ing heavily on him, he now felt that he was "competing" with himself, and he faced a new crisis he told an interviewer: to avoid "self-indulgence in self-expression."[17]

He began the new work using familiar oil paints, but in colors that appeared almost straight from the tube, not characterized by the subtle, unnamable hues of the past. And, although no title could rise to the *chutzpah* of *Stations of the Cross*, this new work pugilistically demanded Who's Afraid of Red, Yellow and Blue? Of the genesis of this first of four so-titled paintings, Barney echoed the thesis underpinning "System Painting": "Just as I had confronted other dogmatic positions of the purists, neoplas-ticists, and other formalists, I was now in confrontation with their dogma, which had reduced red, yellow and blue into an idea-didact . . . . Why give in to these purists and formalists who have put a mortgage on red, yellow and blue, transforming these colors into an idea that destroys them as colors?" he asked. In response, he had the "double incentive of using these colors to express what I wanted to do—of making these colors expressive rather than didactic and of freeing them from the mortgage."[18]

"USA Artists: Barnett Newman" was broadcast in early July. Interviewed in his studio with Annalee quietly reading in the background, Barney wore a collared shirt and his monocle, and chain-smoked filtered Kent cigarettes. He saw no benefit at all to films or photographs of an artist at work, he said. As always, his default example was Michelangelo: what would we learn from a picture of the divine master with a chisel in his hand? He was "not much of a performer," but he conceded there might be some interest in showing the room in which he "spent 14 years." Then, compro-mising, he allowed himself to be filmed mixing and applying gesso to a very large canvas—possibly the 11-foot canvas he mentioned during his Guggenheim conversa-tion with Hess. He donned a worker's jacket over his shirt and work gloves—the very flexible kind of glove that workers use when they paint bridges with lead paint, he told Solomon—and climbed a ladder, carefully brushing, smoking, and talking the whole while. In the Front Street studio, it was not his habit to work on such a large canvas vertically, and although he insisted to Solomon that he was not a performer, the ladder may have been mobilized for the camera's benefit—as he had been filmed in sport coat, tie, suspended monocle, helmet, and welder's mask directing the fab-rication of *Here III* at Treitel-Gratz.[19]

There was a script and narration, but Barney himself led the national audience through a virtual retrospective. And himself led them through the correct critical interpretation: his work "declared" space, and when properly experienced, enabled the "true feeling of what it is to be alive" because "at one instant [one] gets the whole painting and there's nothing to examine." And himself led them to his proper place in history: he was an influence *"precisely"* because he didn't insist on a "dogmatic situation." And yet, throughout the high-handed narrative, Barney managed nevertheless to project an appealing and seductive sort of modesty. He didn't paint to make himself into a "so-called ARTIST." He didn't think of himself that way (as he repeated nearly verbatim at the Guggenheim shortly after he was filmed). He thought of himself as a "man in the world," as an "artist-citizen."[20] He read from his statement in the *Stations* catalogue, concluding with "This overwhelming question that does not complain, makes today's talk of alienation, as if alienation were a modern invention, an embarrassment."

The 75-by-48-inch oil *Who's Afraid of Red, Yellow and Blue* (plate 17) made that summer may have been intended as the Expo submission and rejected by Barney as too small, or it may have been only a dry run. Over the next seven months, he worked on different formats. A 96-by-214-inch oil horizontal, was begun, but not completed; a 120-by-102-inch acrylic vertical was painted before Barney returned to the enormous horizontal. (The vertical became *Who's Afraid of Red, Yellow and Blue II*, the horizontal, *III.*)[21] But none, ultimately, was the work exhibited in Montreal. The large, vertical canvas Barney was filmed gessoing in "USA Artists" may have been *Profile of Light* or *Now II* or *Queen of the Night II*—all of them dated 1967, all made with acrylic paint—but certainly not the almost "18-footer" (pronounced with a "macho . . . powerful outward sign of strength"[22]) Magna on canvas that would be sent to Canada. And yet, "altogether it has been a terrible year for us," Barney told Schapiro in September.

Another unusually hot summer was especially brutal for the overweight, chain-smoking Barney, unbalanced by the deaths of his mother, Annalee's brother, and "many friends"—among them David Smith just over a year earlier, Hans Hofmann in February, Paul Feeley in June. In late July came the terrible news that Frank O'Hara had been killed by a car on the beach on Fire Island. Only days before Barney received a letter from him about his "awe" in front of the *Stations*: "so Moving, so eloquent, so right" that "the best way to express one's feelings is simply to burst into tears."[23] There was a story around that after Pollock's death Barney had vowed he would never return to the East End of Long Island, but for O'Hara, who had begun organizing a Newman retrospective at MoMA, he broke his pledge. He and Annalee dramatically arrived at the cemetery in Springs in a Harvey limousine.[24]

But Barney was also, as he catalogued in the same letter to Schapiro, stewing over the ongoing battles with the *Times,* with *The Nation*, with Kozloff and Ashton— whose review of the *Stations* show was "a piece of slander that makes Canaday seem a gentleman."[25] ("The Newman legend is symptomatic of a sickish turn of intellectualism . . . . If Newman's rather arcane rhetoric is sufficient to pass for the highest of esthetic thought, and if by virtue of its wide currency it succeeds in placing him in the forefront as a leading artist, there is something askew somewhere."[26])

And, in spite of his own privileged position in Alloway's history, Barney was unable to stop stewing about Reinhardt.

It was "no coincidence that the more the public is eager to consume art as a commodity, the more difficult and unavailable for consumption Reinhardt makes his art," Barbara Rose wrote in her first article for *Vogue* in November, timed to co-incide with a retrospective at the Jewish Museum.[27] Rose's insistence on Reinhardt's refusal "to adapt himself to the exigencies of the cultural boom"—she even invoked Elaine de Kooning's satirical "Mr. Pure"—just as Barney's brand of defiance was being embraced, reopened his festering wounds. The private explosion of venomous contempt—directed at Rose, at de Kooning, and particularly at Reinhardt—may have been therapeutic, but it is nevertheless shocking to find in someone so roundly cele-brated. That she chose to write on Reinhardt was her affair, Barney wrote in a letter to Rose ultimately unsent, "but to have discussed [him] in a whole article without mentioning my black painting, 'Abraham,' the first and still the only black painting in history" raised "deep questions" of her "responsibility as an art historian. He never would have painted the black paintings if he had not seen my black painting."

"Nothing pays off in the art world like plagiarism especially if it is accompanied by post cards," he concluded.[28]

The "plagiarism" charge Barney had already made two weeks earlier, when he ran into Sam Hunter, newly named director of the Jewish Museum, at the opening of "Systemic Painting."[29] The Reinhardt retrospective was billed as "directed" by Hunter with the "participation" of the artist and Lucy Lippard, and Barney had preemp-tively prepared his objections. He advised Hunter that "the use by you or Miss Lucy Lippard of any of Ad Reinhardt's material that were plagiaristic of his work would be considered by [Newman] as acts of violence against him," as his lawyer phrased it a few months later when Barney took action.[30]

The irritable letter writing is a reliable reminder of the deep disjunction between Barney's avuncular public persona and his private experience of pain. Three weeks after Anna's death he was at the racetrack; days after Nathan Greenhouse's death he unleashed his full charm offensive on Newhouse. Even as he complained to Schapiro he squired the young art historian Barbara Reise around New York and encouraged her to act (informally) as his agent during her imminent residency in London.[31] Between September and the end of December, Barney the artist achieved a wondrous break-through with *Who's Afraid of Red, Yellow and Blue I*—exhibited in a museum-quality group show at Janis. But for Barney the man, the internal churning ground on.

No matter how desperately he tried to control what people said, what people thought, how his work was treated, how it was installed, who bought it, and even who saw it, it was only in the presence of his work that he could overcome the feeling that "out there"—*everywhere*—was "chaos."[32]

Reinhardt's show presented a new opportunity on which to concentrate his agony.

"Just recovering from a back injury but will start work soon" was the reason he gave Solomon in December for not having a suitable work ready for Expo.[33] For three weeks in late November and early December virtually all of his frenetic activity had halted; he saw an orthopedist—likely for the sciatic pain that chronically accompanied his psychic pain—cardiologist, internist, dentist, and an elite ophthalmological pathologist and surgeon. By December 31, however, he was sufficiently well that he and Annalee went to a Sunday brunch of scrambled eggs and signature bagels with cream cheese and anchovies at William Rubin's apartment, along with Rubin's wife Phyllis Hattis, Stella, Rose and their children, Poons and Lucinda Childs.[34] It was such an informal, "family" affair, that Barney was shocked, *shocked*, to find a photographer present, and had to leave the room. It was a question of a "way of life," Barney told Rubin when he asked for a "sensible explanation" of Barney's position. "My way of life has been such as never to use you. However, you not only claim a moral right to use me as you see fit but you also claim a legal right to trick me into it." It was "obvious" to Barney that Rubin had cleared his position with his lawyers. "This means that the only way I had to protect myself against your way of life was to come to breakfast with you in your home with <u>my</u> lawyer standing behind me."[35]

In February, Barney was shown the proofs for an article and eight pages of photographs of Rubin's art-filled loft scheduled for mid-March in *Vogue*; it included one very small picture of the company at brunch. The question of whether Rubin invited him "properly or not" was no longer at stake: "that part of it is all forgotten."[36] The issue now was Reinhardt, whose show had recently closed, and the Reinhardt painting that Rubin owned, mentioned but not reproduced in *Vogue*. It stung that the issue of *Life* on the newsstands, with a historic cover of the three astronauts who had tragically died at the start of their mission, featured eight luxuriously illustrated pages on "Art's Master of the Minimal." Reinhardt was a "moralist," who, "concerned with the 'pollution' of the art establishment," its commercialism, and the "self-promotion of the abstract expressionists," categorized them in "scathing cartoons," David Bourdon wrote. "One abstract expressionist, whom Reinhardt called a 'holy-roller-explainer-entertainer-in-residence,' sued for $100,000. But his case was thrown out of court." Barney was not happy to be singled out and have the offending description resurface after thirteen years.[37]

It was all "part of the Reinhardt putsh" [*sic*] he told Rubin—the *Vogue* article by Annette Michelson, another by her in *Harper's Bazaar*, and Rose's earlier piece in *Vogue*—in which no mention was made of Barney's "role in the matter," his "red on red paintings," his "blue on blue paintings," and his "black on black 'Abraham,'" which, Barney now claimed, Reinhardt "hung" at Betty Parsons in 1950. The version of history Barney saw proffered by the articles was misleading, "therefore, to be photographed sitting in your house, under the umbrella of camaraderie, in which two critics have taken the position they have, when your collection also represents Reinhardt, puts me in the position of giving consent to this point of view about me," he wrote to Rubin, "the politics practiced by them has put me and you in a position where ordinary human relations become suspect." He felt "compromised" by the photograph. He "asked Alex [Liberman] to take me out" of the brunch scene.[38]

Historical priority. No other accolade could satisfy the hunger for *that* recognition. He could go on as much as he liked about his self-definition as an artist–citizen, how he had no agenda other than to embody an ideal of himself that (selectively) conformed to a civilized Aristotelian model. But that he did something *before* any of the others of the particular peer group—before Still (painted an incident-free field), before Rothko (used brown and red), before Reinhardt (made the monochrome)—well, there attention must be paid. In her 1966 adulatory essay on the *Stations*, Lucy Lippard acknowledged Barney's priority: "Since the late '50s Barnett Newman has been the name most invoked as precedent for the newest abstraction; Still and Rothko, grouped with him at first, somehow dropped out of critical vocabularies after a while, and Reinhardt, whose prototypal position is still clearer, was never as influential."[39] And so Barney was hesitant to include her—even though she had written the essay for Reinhardt's Jewish Museum show—in the Reinhardt putsch.[40] Instead, he engaged council to assert that Reinhardt's 1962 statement, "The one thing to say about art is that it is one thing. Art is art-as-art and everything else is everything else," with which Lippard opened her catalogue essay, was "definitely lifted" from Barney's own 1947 "For it is only the pure idea that has meaning. Everything else has everything else," which appeared in the catalogue for "The Ideographic Picture," a show "in which Reinhardt participated."

To anyone who had been around long enough it seemed likely that Barney was being baited—if not consciously by Lippard or even Hunter—by Reinhardt when he first wrote the words in 1962.[41] And because the museum's, and exhibition's, director, Hunter, in his preface praised Lippard's essay, Hunter "consciously and deliberately joined with Reinhardt in committing acts of violence against" Barney, according to Barney's lawyer's claim.[42]

But now Reinhardt was in the hospital with what Hunter termed "angina." "Both artists are old, established figures in world art, each occupying a distinct and independent position," Hunter responded in a long, measured answer that acknowledged the "long history of partisan dispute" between these "two fine artists on priorities and prerogatives . . . who said or did what first." While it was "arguable that in the context of the ideologies and painting styles of the forties Newman was first to reinstate the idea of 'purity' in art as a conscious program," Hunter doubted that "Reinhardt 'stole' Newman's ideas or plagiarized them, although, like so many other American artists in the forties, he may have benefitted from Newman's presence on the scene." But he also doubted that Barney had a "legal leg to stand on . . . . The fuss and feathers would waste everyone's time." The only "amends" would be "those of posterity."[43]

The lawyers agreed with Barney about the "historical distortion," but they also agreed with Hunter that there was no legal remedy.[44] Barney demanded a footnote somehow to be added to the existing catalogue; it was not. The letters continued for months. Reinhardt died of a heart attack on August 30, 1967. Barney saved his obituaries. Hunter, citing pressure by the museum's board of governors to increase the emphasis on Judaica, resigned from the Jewish Museum in late October.

Barney was a sleuth of the subtext. Because he took such intellectual and moral satisfaction in identifying—or *projecting*—masked meanings, Barney loved loading layers into his own statements, leaving breadcrumbs for his future biographer, even if unnoticed to contemporaries. Thus, at least twice in public presentations in mid-1967, he brought up the twenty-year-old published catalogue introduction to "The Ideographic Picture," the very essay in which, *verifiably*, he wrote "Everything else has everything else." In January, when *Arts Magazine* had asked "what are the ideal museum conditions for the presentation of [your] work?" he couldn't resist taking a swipe at Still. That month's *Art News*, "Special Issue: Albright-Knox Gallery, Buffalo," featured a painting by Still on the cover.

"It is the shrine and the showroom that I wish avoided since I am not moved by demands for worship. Nor am I impressed by the fake drama of display. *Nox Buffalonis caveatur pintoribus*," he closed in Latin that was tortured to make the pun. (Roughly, "Let painters beware of Knox of Buffalo.")[45]

SIXTY

"THE URGE TO BE EXALTED"

The art installation in Montreal was one element in a U.S. exhibition that was itself a three-level scaffolding-like structure with traffic flowing automatically on escalators. The whole erector set, adorned with exhibits of technology, lunar exploration, American heritage, *and* painting (Oldenburg's *Giant Soft Fan* was the only sculpture), was enclosed within and visible through a massive, transparent "three-quarter geodesic skybreak bubble" over 19 stories high and 250 feet in diameter, designed by Buckminster Fuller. Filled with natural light by day and glowing at night, the bubble also contained a multi-screen film projection depicting "creative Americans in action" and an open theater featuring "continuous live American entertainment."[1]

Colossal paintings by Johns, Stella, Poons, Rosenquist, Rauschenberg, Motherwell, and Frankenthaler, among others, were hung against enormous panels of sailcloth seemingly suspended in mid-air. Visitors to the pavilion floated by at a set rate, or paused on exposed platforms. Solomon himself was stunned by the "property of scalelessness"—"What do you do when you are asked to select an exhibition of paintings for a space like this?"[2] Viewed between Johns's 186-by-396-inch *Map*, and Lichtenstein's 360-by-120-inch cityscape *Big Modern Painting*, and surrounded by the Brobdingnagian barnacle pattern of the dome, Barney's portentously titled *Voice of Fire* seemed less the utterance of the old testament god than a semaphoric flag (plate 18).

It was not a success. Many observers thought the American Pavilion did not compare favorably to the Russian one—there was not enough military hardware on display—and most of the coverage of Expo focused on that, an intentional decision by the USIA, which hoped to deflect attention from the war in Vietnam and protests in America. Eventually, it led to Congressional hearings about federal support of international exhibitions. Nearly all of the works suffered damages—even as they were subsequently shown in the Horticultural Hall in Boston under the auspices of the Boston Institute of Contemporary Art.

It's easy to understand why Solomon insisted on only selecting very very large paintings for the pavilion in Montreal. It's much harder to understand why *Barney*, previously so nervous about showing that it was "painful" for him,[3] who could not tolerate an ornate cornice a year earlier, agreed to be part of this carnival. A few days before he went to Montreal himself, he acknowledged his chronic trepidation to an audience in Washington. The way society was going to use his art—his "act"—was "a very repulsive thing," a "problem" for which he didn't have a solution. All he had, he told the church leaders he was addressing, was the "hope that some place, some man will be moved, will have an experience, a reaction."[4]

The timing of the two art and religion conferences in which Barney participated that summer of 1967 was serendipitous; his talks allowed him to counter the pop-ish, promotional sonority of Montreal and reconfirm the *content* of his work.

In Washington, soon after early reviews of "Expo 67" appeared, he addressed the possibility of "bringing art into the church or art into society" by turning the issue 90 degrees. What Barney found missing in the conversation at the Washington Cathedral for a conference on "Contemporary Art and the Church: The Point of Intersection" was that the true position of the artist was outside of society. He told the audience that John Canaday had wanted him *hanged*. He wanted Alloway hanged. He wanted the Guggenheim closed. The "studio is a sanctuary, and the problem of what is sacred and what is secular is," he said, "very ambiguous." Instead of "looking at art as art," one should look at "the individual, the people involved . . . at specific artists," and try "to understand what he is doing." Only in that way did there seem "to be any hope."[5]

In New York in August, he said that he had "always had to answer [the same] question" that Father Thomas F. Mathews posed: whether there was an "inherent religious sensibility in what the modern artist is doing by his own choice." As early as 1947, he reminded listeners, he had written "about man's birthright, his urge to be exalted." Recently, "words like 'the self,' 'experience,' 'revelation,' 'moral crisis,' . . . not to mention 'God,'" were "repudiated by young artists as well as the hippies today." But the urge to be exalted was not, he said, quoting from "The Ideographic Picture."

It was a surprisingly apt perception. Barney understood that there was a "fantastic hunger. All you need to do is go down to the Electric Circus at the Dome on a Saturday night to see hundreds of young people . . . in the greatest spectacle of piety" that he'd ever witnessed; people congregating "as if they were in a church."[6] The idea was to be together. Instead of the organ, rock and roll played; instead of the ritual of sacrament, there were flashing images on a screen. Similarly, for artists, it made little difference what style or method they worked in: "what matters to a true artist is that he distinguish between a place and no place at all; and the greater the work of art, the greater will be this feeling."

He repeated on both occasions that what he was after was the fundamental spiritual dimension—his "life-long aesthetic"—that he found in the Passover prayer when the holiday fell on the Sabbath: the injunction to distinguish between what is holy and what is HOLY.[7]

Passover. And "the Jewish medieval notion of Makom . . . where God is." He was not reluctant to invoke such connections when speaking to the Christian groups, perhaps to dispel any lingering concerns about a Jew taking on the Stations of the Cross. But when invited at the suggestion of Marcia Weisman to consider a work "spiritual in scope" for Sinai Temple in Los Angeles, Barney appears not to have responded.[8] Through the second half of 1967 his Jewish identity would take a form more political than religious.

Barney's focus on Reinhardt only petered out shortly before the latter's death at the end of August, which was also around the time that Barney became consumed by a superseding offense by Motherwell. And he was not simply grandstanding: his constant venting to Newhouse, who was flummoxed by these episodes, attested to his very real sense of violation.[9]

"Concerning the Beginnings of the New York School: 1939–1943," an interview with Motherwell conducted as "Expo 67" commissions were being made, appeared in the summer issue of *Art International*. This being Motherwell's interview, he was at the center of the story, which went roughly thus: the surrealist Kurt Seligmann begat Roberto Matta who begat Motherwell who begat (the mature) Pollock. About 6000 words into a 6400-word history—one that by definition ended at 1943—Motherwell was quoted as saying that he thought one of the major American contributions to modern art was "sheer size. There are lots of arguments as to whether it should be credited to Pollock, Still or Rothko, even Newman. It's hard to say, probably Pollock, possibly Still."

He continued: Still's 1945 show at Peggy Guggenheim's was "the most original. A bolt out of the blue"; the work was "in a way like a present-day Newman if it were much more free-handed . . . if the line were jagged, like lightening [*sic*]." Rothko was impressed with Still, Motherwell went on, and, he implied, Newman was influenced by Rothko.

Whatever Motherwell had in mind, through intentional provocation or faulty memory, the actual paintings of those years in the late 1940s belie his account. This Barney went to great lengths to show. Motherwell seemed to find it necessary, he wrote in a "Letter to the Editor," to "take my work away from me" in "the strategy of constructing his own epitaph." Motherwell's description of Still's late-1940s work was based on that "good old logical proposition . . . if Grandma had had a different set of genes, she would have been Grandpa."[10] Barney's reaction, buttressed by photographs, was first drafted in July. After he dropped the images and replaced much of the bile with wit, a further response was printed "entire" in the September issue of *Art International* by James Fitzsimmons, the editor, who at the same moment was expecting an article on Barney's works by Gene Baro and a second on his writings by Alloway, and who, in any case, was inclined to indulge Barney throughout the ensuing theatrics.[11]

Fitzsimmons thought the letter was hilarious. Motherwell did not. Naïvely or disingenuously, considering how well he knew Barney, his own "Letter to the Editor" in October expressed his extreme dismay: Barney's response hurt "our long relationship, which I esteemed," and it was "unnecessary," because the point, "perhaps poorly expressed," was simply that in the early '40s exhibitions at Peggy Guggenheim's, Still seemed the "least figurative."[12]

"The obvious truth is that Still was the first to paint Stills, and Newman the first to paint Newmans, and neither could be mistaken for the other." The "'real' subject of Barney's response," Motherwell said, was Barney's "relentless hatred for Mark Rothko and Clyfford Still."[13]

"How coy can Motherwell get?" Barney reacted in November, although "How coy could Newman get?" Motherwell might have asked as Barney claimed he had been "urbane, responsible and spread no malice" in his letter. But this was not a minor matter for Barney, the floodgates opened and nearly 1500 offended words, roiling for years, poured forth. Fitzsimmons printed them all.

Motherwell "deliberately" smeared him personally, Barney objected. He enumerated a list of instances where he claimed Motherwell had done the same to other—now deceased—artists who were "esteemed" friends: Tomlin, Baziotes, Pollock, Gorky, Kline. His own "relationship with Still and Rothko has always been on the highest professional level," he wrote. "Whatever our differences may have been over our paintings, or concepts, our relationship has always been honorable." There had never been any quarrel. That was *technically* true, although not true at all was that no one had ever heard him "utter one single word of calumny against" Rothko, as at least Sidney Janis could attest.[14]

But it didn't end there. In his beautiful obituary tribute to Reinhardt in the October issue of *Art News*, Hess addressed "the issue of Ad's originality as an artist": because of the closeness of the New York artists, "who did what first is often lost in a tangle of later claims." But it seemed "certain that he got the ideas of blackness and symmetry from Barnett Newman." Barney thanked Hess for "straightening out the facts in connection with my black painting," although, he added, "it is unfortunate it had to be in Reinhardt's obituary."

"It will interest you," he pointed out, "that in connection with my black painting, your mention of it *has been noticed by friends of my work* [emphasis added]."[15] Now, in early December, after a particularly validating trip to Europe, with that historical priority memorialized in the art press, and finding encouragement in *Art International*, Barney continued what he called "this ugly farce." To further beat down Motherwell, Barney invoked the friendship that Motherwell denied existed: "In talking to Rothko recently," the two identified in the "Knox-Albright Museum" [*sic*] Still monograph the painting "which is the basis of this ridiculous affair"—the painting Motherwell originally described as "like a present-day Newman" if it were painted differently. Barney straightened out the rest of history by quoting what Still wrote to him in 1950: that Rothko spoke of his work "in superlatives," Barney's "vivid blaze" was no "portrait of a line" but something "big . . . vivid . . . *new*."

Motherwell, attacked on two fronts, rolled over. "I very much regret my exchange with Barnett Newman, and especially that my original interview . . . could have been interpreted by Newman as an invidious comparison, which was not my intent. In my opinion, Newman is a major and original artist, and on that premise I would conclude."[16]

Reading these exchanges, one could be forgiven for wondering how—or, more to the point, why—Barney spent mental energy on this. His calendar over the same period is a breathtaking record of furious enterprise. Back and forth to Washington, Baltimore, New Haven, Montreal, New Canaan. Not to mention the receptions, lunches, dinners, drinks with museum men Solomon, Leering (director of the Stedelijk van Abbemuseum in Eindhoven), Barr, Rüdlinger, Rene d'Harnoncourt, James Harithas (curator at the Corcoran Gallery); writers Hess, Sylvester, the television producer Merrill Brockway; theologians—stacked up two and three a day, nearly every single day. "He'd go to an opening, or he'd have dinner with friends, or he'd go to the ballet, or to the opera," and *then* he'd go work. "I'm going to schmear a little," he would tell the company.[17] On many occasions when he returned home he would call Murray at two in the morning to read the draft of a letter or conduct a post-mortem on the day's activities.

There were frequent trips to fabricators. And even more frequent meetings with his lawyers and accountants: the review and justification of claims, the writing, swearing to, and filing of affidavits for his IRS audit.[18] The dealer Xavier Fourcade from Knoedler Gallery was courting him. And, in November, there was Dublin, London, Amsterdam, Zurich, Basel, Paris. All of this, even as he insisted "the artist" was alone in the studio.

"There is no scene. The scene is the artist working in his studio; everything else depends on this," he was quoted in *Vogue*'s "The *New* New York Art Scene: Who Makes It?" that August. He may have demurred, but Solomon, the author of the boosterish article, thought otherwise: Barney's "vitality and youthful openness really makes him a key member of the new scene, even if he is a few years older than most of the others."[19]

"Nobody was as needy as Barney." Hess's sister, Betty Wolff, noticed that among her brother's many friends, Barney was unique in this way.[20] It was the beginning of the most variously active, not to say *frenzied*, period of his life.

There was endless correspondence: with the Stedelijk in Amsterdam concerning the purchase of *The Gate* and their pursuit of a retrospective; with MoMA about showing the *Stations* and dangling the Stedelijk's offer as bait to move MoMA toward a preemptive retrospective;[21] and with Jan van der Marck from the Museum of Contemporary Art, Chicago, who worked for months to have a show of Barney's work alongside a show of Flavin's. This last would have been stunning, but because too many paintings were already committed to other shows, it never happened. (Generously, Barney suggested that van der Marck devote the entire gallery space to Flavin.[22])

Over the summer, Barney was at Front Street most evenings after the brutal sun passed his skylights and the studio cooled down.[23] And, as was his habit, it was during such evenings, after the days filled with frenetic and worldly activity, that Barney painted, completing three of the six enormous paintings of 1967—*Who's Afraid of Red, Yellow and Blue II*; the 132-by-50-inch *Now II*; and the 108-by-48-inch *Queen of the Night II*. They were in acrylic paint, bought in quantity from Bocour, in spite of the particular challenge acrylic presented: because it was water-based, the color in acrylic paint could too easily become " 'lovely' color—sweet and lovely," something he continually fought against. "Thank God you and I get some intensity into these acrylics," he told Liberman.[24]

There was a certain amount of pressure to make these paintings. He had been invited to send three recent works to "Rosc—the poetry of vision," an ambitious experiment under the patronage of the Irish government to present a "comprehensive, up-to-date report on modern painting." ("The poetry of vision" was the sweet and lovely translation given to the old Gaelic word, whose original meaning was "visual perception at its brightest and most excited pitch.")[25] Fifty artists of "world importance" were selected to be shown together with ancient Celtic and early-Christian Irish stone sculpture, while other masterworks from the same period, including the Books of Kells and Durrow, the Ardagh Chalice, and the Tara Brooch, were exhibited in a separate venue.

"Who is the leading painter in the world today?" the press release asked. Visitors to the exhibition would "have a rare opportunity to decide." In a field that included the 86-year-old Picasso and the 32-year-old Jim Dine, Barney felt pressure, "to send . . . my best work," and raced against the organizers' deadline.

He delivered the address at the International Congress on Religion, Architecture, and the Visual Arts and negotiated the storage limbo for the *Stations*. He arranged loans and conditions for more than ten different shows; five recently completed paintings were shown in the final months of the year. He made eleven profound and beautiful trial drawings on acetate—his first (extant) drawings since 1960—one of which was selected for a photolithograph to be included in *Frank O'Hara / In Memory of My Feelings*, the memorial exhibition and illustrated book of poetry that MoMA produced. He wrote a 2500-word statement on criticism that would be delivered in public, in Paris, in front of an impressive congregation of international authorities.

All of this would have demanded an explosion of extraordinary energy by *anyone*—with no agent, with no staff, using mid-20th-century technology and communication—let alone by a portly, tobacco- and vodka-addicted 62-year-old who had already had a massive heart attack. As spurts of similar agitation were in the past, the agitation in the Motherwell letters was a side-effect of that dizzying effort. And a new attack by the evil demons of real estate inflamed his irritability.

Barney's familiar New York was undergoing the most radical transformation he had yet seen. The two towers of the World Trade Center had already broken ground, replacing the hundreds of small businesses about which he had written so affectionately in 1939. Now five of Robert Moses's new "superblocks" were marching east across lower Manhattan and in virtually a clean sweep most of the span from the Custom House on the Battery to Coenties Slip was in a state of demolition and construction. "The southern tip of Manhattan, the city's most famous face, looks like a disaster area," wrote Ada Louise Huxtable. The physical change from past to present was "unparalleled." Multitudes, hundreds, of the four- and five-story brick buildings—"that still have the smell of whale oil in them, the silence of dead sea captains' voices, the dust of ship chandlers' offices," the charm of "any *rue* by Utrillo," Barney had written of these relics—were demolished for fifty- and sixty-story towers. Barney had spent fourteen years with one of the city's best-preserved rows of early 19th-century Greek Revival buildings outside his window; many of the buildings— like the one that Barney's coffee-perfumed studio was in—had been in "continuous commercial use for over a century and a quarter."[26] Now they disappeared and in their place a 24-story, two-block-square glass-walled behemoth was rising.

Downtown, on Front Street, Barney was filled with "despair," he told Liberman, because the Uris brothers' corporation—"Bob Friedman's uncles"—was building a "superblock" that would cast his studio into darkness;[27] its excavation machinery was "going day and night, making a terrible racket," and gave off fumes that polluted his studio, making it extremely difficult to work ("I am a cardiac") and, he said, affected his paintings, causing a "large" one to "darken and go black."[28] Midtown, at Carnegie Hall, he could not work because of noise and vibrations from another tenant's "super-large air conditioning machine."[29]

Barney must have felt that the time spent handling so many of the things a loyal dealer could have taken care of—"having constantly to contend [with] those businessmen, people in the world that are constantly making trouble," he complained in June at the Washington Cathedral—was worth the independence and control he retained. But oh! the distraction, his disproportionate sensitivity to what he described to Liberman as the "harassment and the continuous sniping," the embarrassing public self-importance![30]

And yet, almost superhumanly, precisely while he was negotiating transactions, and conducting the petulant back and forth in *Art International*, something so much more significant for Barney's legacy than what Motherwell said, or in what group show he was included, was also on his agenda. The remarkable, gravity-defying, over-25-foot sculpture *Broken Obelisk* was fully conceived, fabricated, and exhibited in Manhattan and Washington, D.C.

"To get a piece of sculpture that gets off the floor, which means to do a vertical, is very very difficult," Barney told the television audience that spring, while he was working on *Here II* at Gratz. He brushed off any question about the legitimacy of a painter making three-dimensional work with his default reference: "These questions were never raised in relation to Michelangelo, I don't know why they should be raised in relation to me."[1]

During this time, Barney began to say that he had been thinking about a "25-foot sculpture" since 1963,[2] and that although he had an extraordinarily sympathetic working and personal relationship with Donald Gratz, Treitel-Gratz was not equipped for the scale of his ambition. In fact, there was no fabricator who worked with artists who had the facility to execute such a work. Artists who aspired to monumental scale had only the options of working with a shipbuilder or an auto body shop, where they would find little tolerance for experimentation or enthusiasm for collaboration.

But in 1966, partly as a response to the establishment of the National Endowment for the Arts a year earlier, and percent for art programs as spurs for urban renewal, Donald Lippincott and Roxanne Everett opened Lippincott Incorporated with the sole intention of working closely with artists to fabricate large-scale works. Among the first artists Lippincott wanted to work with was Murray; Murray took Barney to Connecticut to see one of the early pieces he built there, Barney and Lippincott hit it off, and Barney doodled an early iteration of the as yet unnamed 25-footer.[3]

Two events that 1967 summer encouraged Barney to make what must have seemed an inconveniently timed, significant detour. Mayor John Lindsay—who was responsible for the designation of New York as "Fun City"—named the first week in October "Cultural Showcase Week" and by June the Parks Department, acting on the idea that "contemporary sculpture can lend itself to the enhancement of our city," announced "Sculpture in Environment," an unprecedented installation of outdoor sculpture in parks and plazas throughout the five boroughs for six weeks in the fall.[4] Twenty-nine living artists were invited, plus the estate of David Smith, with the twenty-five who agreed to participate—including Barney—selecting sites for themselves.[5]

At the same time, the Corcoran Gallery of Art in Washington invited Barney, Tony Smith, and Ronald Bladen to create one massive work each especially for "Scale as Content," also opening in October. Making the invitation especially enticing, the Corcoran offered practical and financial assistance.[6] Barney, however, seems to have refused any such help: he later said he was "three-quarters finished" at the time of the invitation.[7] If, by that, he meant the physical piece as distinct from the concept, no existing records support his claim.

The blueprints that Lippincott produced, after many meetings and a formal agreement reached on July 13, show a not-too-attenuated development from the flat platform, truncated pyramid (ziggurat) base, and obdurate vertical of *Here III*. For the monumental piece, however, the pyramid culminated in a traditional angle and the vertical rose from its own inverted pyramid, which appeared improbably—*counterintuitively*—balanced point-to-point: a contact almost like God and Adam's on the Sistine ceiling, Murray thought. In Barney's early doodle the vertical column was defined at its apex by a flat, horizontal surface, as in his previous sculptures. But the working blueprint showed something different: a jagged, steeply sloping edge.

That fall, *Time* magazine featured Tony Smith on its cover, anointing him "Master of the Monumentalists"—"the most dynamic, versatile and talented new sculptor in the U.S. art world, the darling of critics," whose work was at the time being shown in seven cities. Smith was part of what *Time* called a "fast-cresting wave of enthusiasm [for] the huge, wild, pure (and impure) shapes of contemporary art" and for "a growing race of creators who have discarded modeling clay in favor of blueprints, the chisel in favor of the welding torch, and Vulcan's forge for a sheet-metal fabrication shop."[8]

At the same moment that the popular press was breathless about an epidemic of new sculpture shows and installations, old notions of monumentality itself were under siege among the younger art intelligentsia. In June, *Artforum* published "Special Issue: American Sculpture" with Sol LeWitt's "Paragraphs on Conceptual Art," Michael Fried's "Art and Objecthood," Robert Morris's "Notes on Sculpture, Part 3," and a seminal essay by Robert Smithson. The issue marked a dramatic relocation of goalposts and would retrospectively be recognized as capturing the essence of the moment. In "Towards the Development of an Air Terminal Site," Smithson described a radical way of thinking about sculpture that had nothing at all to do with an object occupying a distinct space. He postulated the unorthodox idea that something like Alexander Graham Bell's work in aerodynamics, aeronautics, engineering, and surveying could drive the making of "art"; a photograph of Bell sitting in an "outdoor observation station" of his own devising—a pyramid-shaped structure with a truncated pyramid-shaped opening cut out on one side—was reproduced. One day, Smithson wrote, we would see "aircraft that will be more crystalline in shape . . . . Already certain passenger aircraft resemble pyramidal slabs, and flying obelisks."

This provocation was published exactly during the period when Barney was frequenting the art world's latest hot spot, Max's Kansas City, where he and the 29-year-old Smithson would entertain each other. They had in common sweeping, heterodox intellects, and a metaphysical bent; they both honored the primal force felt in the presence of ancient earth mounds or disorienting landscapes, how those experiences affected a person's intuition of aliveness in the world. Barney spoke of the feeling of "compression" of light squeezed between shore and tree line, of extreme self-awareness produced by whiteouts; Smithson of "that area of terror between man and land." Barney spoke of distinguishing between "a place and no place at all," Smithson of "sites" and "non-sites." Did they talk about their current projects? It's easy to imagine the two, sitting in the noisy bar, shooting the breeze. A single sheet of doodles, in an unknown hand but preserved in Barney's papers, includes both images of figures inside peaked structures—very like the photograph of Bell in his observation station—and a crude sketch of what would become *Broken Obelisk*.

Barney would never be a follower of aesthetic theories or fashions, but neither would he succumb to some sort of mandated irrelevancy. Always the punner, for whom three or four layers of meaning were preferable to two or three—more interesting and covering more ground, and presenting a more *complex* self to the world—Barney was not going to be in the rear guard. So it would not be wrong to say that *Broken Obelisk* was, in its way, "Who's Afraid of Monumentality"; and it would not be without basis to say, as many have, that the primary forms drew on personal memories of the ancient "Cleopatra's Needle" in New York's Central Park that had infatuated Barney since high school, and drawings in his well-thumbed copy of I.E.S. Edwards's *The Pyramids of Egypt*, or even, perhaps, an eccentric typographical layout in the Babylonian Talmud.⁹ But in June 1967, "Egypt" had an entirely more pressing connotation, and the immediate inspiration for corralling those aesthetic and historical refrains appears to be something less concerned with art-world politics, something less infused with romantically perfumed resonance.

In early June 1967, shortly before *Broken Obelisk* was created, Newman, with much of the rest of the world, was watching the mounting tensions in the Middle East. The existential threat to Israel, the build-up of forces and attacks by several Arab states, the call by Egyptian President Gamal Abdel Nasser to "eliminate the shadow of Zionism from Palestine and to restore its Arabism," the daily reports of border incursions and bombings, the abrupt removal of UN peacekeeping forces from Gaza, the closure and mining of the Gulf of Aqaba, the airlifting of foreign nationals, the blame cast and warships sent by an aggressive Soviet Union—all of this was covered in front page headlines, in great numbers of daily news stories, on television newscasts. Barney was not deflected: during these same days, he sat for the final interview and filming and editing sessions with the CBS crew. He dined with Jan and Ingeborg van der Marck and Dan and Sonia Flavin to discuss the proposal for Chicago. He refined the stainless finish of the second exemplar of the 400-pound *Here III*; sold *Here II* to Philip Johnson and installed it on the grounds of Johnson's iconic Glass House in Connecticut. On Sunday, May 28, as Barney left his apartment to have lunch at the Gloucester House restaurant with Jean Leering, he would have had to navigate through a crowd of 45,000 supporters of Israel on their way to Riverside Drive around the corner, and his taxi would have run into an opposing demonstration two blocks east. If he had returned home between that meeting and his dinner at Max's Kansas City, he would have found the streets blocked by the spillover from the Israel parade's culmination a few blocks north, where a rally of 125,000 gathered, including the Israeli writer and recent Nobel Laureate S. Y. Agnon in the reviewing stand.¹⁰ Barney had told Solomon that the moral concern of an artist should be "about how he himself is and how he lives," that "worrying about how other people are, what the nature of society is" was not his concern, he was involved in his "own education."¹¹ But the distance between Barneyworld and the "world" that he told Solomon that he was a citizen of had narrowed more significantly and with greater consequence than these chance proximities would suggest.

A second-generation Zionist, Barney, along with Schapiro and Gottlieb, signed "Leading Americans Speak Out Against Arab Threat To Destroy Israel," placed in the *Times* on June 7 by the nonsectarian "Conference on The Status of Soviet Jews," whose sponsors included such prominent names as Justice William O. Douglas, Dr. Martin Luther King, Jr., Norman Thomas, and Robert Penn Warren.[12] Then he quickly suggested to the group another public statement that would go further, that would raise the issue of "whether the Russian policy in the Middle East is an extension of the policy they practice toward Soviet Jews or should the attitude toward the Soviet Jews be explained as an extension of the Russian alliance with the Arabs."[13]

And when, in mid-August, the group at a press conference released a report on Soviet Jewry,[14] Barney prepared his own statement: "It must sadden all the people of Soviet Russia to find that on his 100 anniversary the embalmed hero in Red Square is not Lenin but Pharaoh."[15] In the warm and frazzled summer months of 1967, Egypt and its glorious imagery was viewed by Barney with emotions very far from admiration or nostalgia. Even for a lifelong Zionist it was stunningly improbable that Israel would prevail; yet that is what happened, and Egypt was diminished.[16] Barney cut "carefully out of paper" and "worked out each angle for the technicians," the obelisk's jagged edge.[17] And it may simply be a coincidence that one side—the most articulated face, the one he spent endless hours working on getting right—bears a striking resemblance to the northern boundary of Israel with Lebanon and the seized Syrian Golan Heights, as it was drawn on the maps printed in the daily papers.

It is in the light of events of 1967 that the image and the name of *Broken Obelisk* must be seen. That he had thought of this work earlier is something Barney only began to say in that year and should be taken with a grain of Dead Sea salt: there is no extant reference to or evidence of the sculpture from earlier than 1967.

That's not to say that the resulting work was a political statement, or an aesthetic–political statement, or some kind of strategic move in an artists' game of priority—although Barney was invested in all of those concerns, and particularly, heavily invested at the very moment *Broken Obelisk* was made. He was an "artist–*citizen*," he always emphasized. *Everything* that made up Barney was allowed to filter through his process, he couldn't help it, he was "*compelled*"—and that is why his work is so compressed, so dense with content: the Subject of the Artist. "It's personal," Newman told the *Times*, shortly before the New York installation on Park Avenue. "Some people may think it's geometrical, but it's gone beyond that."[18] *Broken Obelisk* contained his old friend Smith and his new friend Smithson; it contained regret and rage, nostalgia and disappointment, arrogance and fallibility, a wail of anguish and a declaration of obdurate presence. It distinguished "between a place and no place at all"—as, he told his audience at the First Congress on Religion, Architecture, and the Visual Arts that September, "true" art must.

It was always part of Lippincott's plan that in building its projects it would consider how they would travel; and so the sculptures were engineered to be separate elements that could be assembled on site. Having just purchased *Here II*, which he placed on his home grounds, Philip Johnson was naturally enlisted to advocate when Barney chose the plaza in front of the Seagram Building for *Broken Obelisk*'s site—"the best place in New York to show my work," he wrote to Johnson. Other of the sculptures may have been in dramatic surroundings—Central Park, Grand Central Station, Lincoln Center—but in midtown Manhattan on Park Avenue, the act of installation of the two-story high "bright orange-rust" plinth (as the color was described in a contemporaneous article[19]), to all eyes precariously balanced, was certain to receive maximal attention. It was not only art, it was *theater*. Parks Commissioner August Heckscher was among the crowd, as were Flavin, Murray, Lippincott, and over fifty others. Newspapers could not resist running the image of the ten-and-a-half-foot pyramid or the vertical member being lowered by an enormous—by 1967 standards—crane. Barney wanted the hole used for the crane hook blocked to prevent rain entering. The perfect fix was a champagne cork, and Lippincott climbed up to insert it. In what may have been a random juxtaposition, the *New York Post's* two-column photograph of Barney crouching in front of the pyramid descending into place—the ground level perspective emphasized its mass and unquestionably evoked Giza—was run next to a similarly sized news story headlined "20 Young Israelis Start The Resettling," and a smaller headline, "Suez Artillery Duels Finally Halted by UN."

"It's like a reminder of the human and tragic . . . . Its scale put the surrounding space in perspective, prevented it from making you feel like a dwarf as you used to in that vast plaza, and instead made you more aware of your own body and gave it some sense of power," Waldo Rasmussen of the Museum of Modern Art wrote to Barney. "It also brought to mind in some curious way Viet Nam, and I thought of the sculpture, right where it stands now, as a monument about it. I wish it could always stay in that Plaza."[20]

"Your Seagram Bldg obelisk is magnificent," wrote Lippard in *The Hudson Review*, the "only example of a first-rate work in a first-rate site."[21]

"A joy to behold," wrote Hess—the second time in two months Hess went out of his way to praise Barney in an editorial.[22] Evan Turner, the director of the Philadelphia Museum who only a year earlier had hoped to buy the *Stations* paintings, was gobsmacked by the startling development in Barney's oeuvre; he couldn't understand "how such an incredibly handsome and monumental piece of sculpture . . . could have been created without my knowing who the artist was."[23]

At the Corcoran in D.C., as well, Barney achieved a placement *coup* for the second of the two exemplars Lippincott made in 1967. (A third would be made in 1969.) Unlike Bladen's and Smith's pieces, which were inside the building and, in some opinions, were aesthetically constrained by having been created *in situ*, *Broken Obelisk* was outside on the corner of New York Avenue and Seventeeth Street, visually resonating with a corner of the Corcoran building and, wittily, with the unbroken, colossal obelisk of the Washington Monument over the trees in the distance (plate 19). It was another Newman pun.

SIXTY-TWO

"FOR IMPASSIONED CRITICISM"

"The content and the form are inseparable. That's scale."

He might have been talking about *Broken Obelisk*, as he gazed from a high window of the Ritz Hotel at the Place Vendôme, which seemed to him in urgent need of his sculpture.[1] But it was in front of Uccello's *Battle of San Romano* that Barney uttered the appreciative judgment.[2]

He ended the feverish year with an equally feverish, twenty-day trip to Europe. He and Annalee landed in Dublin for Rosc, but the trip only "became worthwhile" when he discovered that the sea at "Joyce's Tower is snot-green as Joyce says." In London, Zurich, and Basel—tragically Rüdlinger had died a week earlier—he saw old friends and museums. In Holland he saw *The Gate* and *Right Here* in Leering's "remarkable" exhibition in Eindhoven ("Paintings After 1945 in New York"); Rembrandt's house and the Rijksmuseum; and the magnificent wooden, late 17th-century Portuguese Synagogue, "one of the great buildings of the world [which] makes clear why even years before it was built Spinoza didn't stand a chance." And in Paris there was "Six Peintres Americains" with *Profile of Light* at Knoedler.[3]

He made his first visit to the Louvre, escorted by the French art critic Pierre Schneider, who found him remarkably energetic and fresh—in spite of the previous two weeks' punishing schedule, the morning at the Jeu de Paume, and afternoon at the Louvre and Petit Palais—and with his irreverent singularity fully unleashed. The pure pleasure, the *fun* of spending time with Barney, a "noble savage" in the protective disguise of "old World *Kulturmensch*" comes most vividly alive in Schneider's text—the "portliness, the jovial majesty . . . the Hapsburg mustache and the monocle dancing on the chest."[4]

Mantegna's *St. Sebastian* was like Magritte: "The way he coolly takes all those arrows . . . . As soon as I got through the Hamlet image to the surrealism, I became interested." Cimabue's *Virgin* was no virgin, but "an epic statement about the mother of God"; the artist had "the same boldness that made Grünewald give his Christ the syph." Veronese's ambitious *Wedding Feast at Cana* was too symmetrical and "fussy"; it was, in Barney's eyes, "really a small painting. That's the trouble." Delacroix's *The Death of Sardanapalus* had an interesting scheme: "the cut-out forms, the jumble. *Guernica*, even Rauschenberg, is related to this. It is what in journalism we used to call circus layout . . . a three-ring circus . . . . And yet there's more to it than just the ingredients. The eggs, the salt, the butter are all needed, but the omelet is something else." What was "interesting" to him, what was "successful" was "the spiral perspective, as against processional or vertical perspective"; the picture, he judged, "really swings."

The scale of Géricault's *Raft of the Medusa* was "fantastic! . . . marvelous. You feel the immensity of the event rather than the size of the canvas." It had the kind of "modern space you wouldn't expect with that kind of rhetoric." And it diminished

Barney's old irritants Roger Fry and his favorite painter: the raft tilted "long before Cézanne."

In front of the *Mona Lisa*, he saw "the long arm."

"Notice the way the arm and the shoulder swing. The neck back, the shoulder forward, hence the lengthening of the arm. It is from her that Courbet and Cézanne learned the trick of leading with the shoulder."

But as involved with the work as he was, as always for Barney it was about the maker. Cimabue was "someone with a brain, not just a hand"; Ingres's sensuousness was "weird. Maybe he used to pride himself on how long he could hold back an orgasm . . . . He had a very false idea of his own talent."

Barney told Schneider that he "felt related" to what they had seen and to the Dutch painters he saw the previous week in Amsterdam—"to the past." Once again, he repeated what he told nearly every interviewer, that "if I am talking to anyone, I am talking to Michelangelo."

"Those who put the mustache on Mona Lisa are not attacking it, or art, but Leonardo Da Vinci the man. What irritates them is that this man with half a dozen pictures has this great name in history, whereas they, with their huge oeuvre, aren't sure."

"The great guys are concerned with the same problems. Saying something about life and about man and about himself. That's what a painter is about."[5]

In spite of the trauma of the damaged *Cathedra* in 1959, Barney again was persuaded to lend to the Documenta exhibition in Kassel, Germany. In January 1968, the organizers—among whom was Leering—proposed a room with both paintings and sculpture, and it was implied that Barney's writings would be included in the catalogue.

But Barney was traveling and was distracted. The studio on Front Street was scheduled to be demolished: he was ordered to vacate, his work on a painting he said was intended for Documenta was interrupted, he was negotiating for new studio space.[6] He was negotiating with Knoedler about representation. He was negotiating with the IRS. He was reviewing his entire life with Hess as preparation for a monograph the critic would write. Because of a teamsters' strike he could not access paintings in the warehouse. He had terrible misgivings because of his previous experience, with *Cathedra*. His viewing-lunch-meeting-drinks-opening-dinner-drinks schedule was, if possible, busier—and more glamorous—than ever. La Côte Basque, Christ Cella, the Russian Tea Room, the King Cole Bar at the St. Regis Hotel. Producer David Merrick, the Hesses, Libermans, and S. I. Newhouse and his companion, Nadine Bertin, at the studio. Dinner with governor and art collector Nelson Rockefeller in Pocantico Hills. At La Grenouille with the Libermans they were spotted by the society columnist Doris Lilly: "Mrs. Newman usually wears a house dress but rising to the occasion looked svelte and chic in simple black," Lilly wrote in the *Post*, to which Bertin, who worked for Condé Nast, took up the cudgel: "What, in your estimation, connotes a 'house-dress'? Some little flower-printed sloppy cotton in which one vacuums the rug? Have you ever seen Mrs. Newman in such garb? . . . In my opinion, and fashion happens to be my business, Mrs. Annalee Newman is always dressed in the best of conservative taste. Fortunately for her, she has matters of a broader scope than just fashion to occupy her thoughts."[7] Ever the truant, Barney delayed and delayed responding to Documenta.

But by June all was settled—there would be three recent paintings, *Profile of Light* (shown the previous fall at Knoedler in Paris), *Who's Afraid of Red, Yellow and Blue II* (shown the previous fall in Dublin), and *Voice of Fire*, the 18-foot vertical made for "Expo 67"; no sculpture, no writings. Barney was as proactively specific about the works' handling as anyone could possibly be. To meet the shipping deadline, *Voice of Fire* was in a "temporary" crate built by the reliable Hahn Brothers, preemptively screwed to the wood so that it could not move. But, he emphasized, extreme care was necessary in opening the crate and it was "not to be used for the return trip." A new crate and traveling frame were already being made. Barney made it explicit to all parties involved that only Leering was to handle his work.[8]

The massive exhibition opened on June 27. But the bad news, Barney's bad news— America was already convulsing with assassinations, protests, mass student and worker strikes—arrived days before, *the* day before, in fact, Barney physically moved his studio from Front Street to 35 White Street: in the crate were exposed nails and *Voice of Fire* was ripped. The resolution of the claims and restoration of *Cathedra*, damaged at Documenta II, took four years. The same for *Voice of Fire*—which involved, in addition to officials of, and the insurance company for, Documenta, the mayor of Kassel, the law firm of Weil, Gotshal & Manges, and a longshoremen's strike in New York—remained incomplete at Barney's death.

Earlier in 1968, during what in retrospect was a relatively peaceful time, Barney was back in Paris, only weeks after returning to New York at the beginning of December. The same Pierre Schneider who had such fun with Barney in the Louvre had invited him to address the "merits of passionate criticism as instanced by Baudelaire" at a "Baudelaire pow-wow" in January.[9]

Barney's participation—with an international group that included Theodor Adorno, André Masson, and Stephen Spender as well as his more familiar discussants Hess and Rosenberg—ushered in a markedly new phase of his life. The civic engagement of his early years—of the Gary system protests, of the civil service manifestos, of the "Need For Political Action By Men Of Culture," of the Committee against Isolationist Art—had for two and a half decades been muffled by the overstuffed pillow of art-world politics and maneuvers. He had lived through and been alert through other periods of ugliness, polarization, and upheaval; he had enough examined life under his expanding belt to know that ugliness and upheaval—like "alienation"—was not a "modern invention." But with success, security, age, wisdom—and perhaps a desire for continued relevancy in a changing world—there was no longer any reason to suppress his one side for the other. "There is no such thing as an apolitical man, especially a Jew," announced Bok, in Bernard Malamud's *The Fixer*. The content of Barney's art was Barney, and his acutely felt reactions and responses to the world were what made Barney. It was "personal," as he said of *Broken Obelisk*. His lifelong internal identification as the "artist–citizen" could fully blossom. He could stop simply telling interviewers that that was who he was. He would live it.

Baudelaire believed that artists must live *in* their historical time, and urged that criticism should "seek to penetrate deep into the temperament and activating motives of each artist." Barney wrote the text of his presentation just as he sent *Broken Obelisk* into the world.

"Baudelaire has said that criticism should be partial, passionate, political." To that Barney compared the "neutral, dispassionate, scientific" criticism of "today"—embodied, one could infer, in the unnamed Greenberg—which Barney judged to be political only among art critics themselves. The "constant hiding behind the façade of scientific method, while paying obeisance to its insufficiency, produces not art criticism but art hypocriticism." (He could never resist a play on words.) Even a biologist's scientific method "strives to maintain, at all costs, the in-vivo situation of" a specimen; the "scientific" art critic practices the "cult of art-sacrifice, carving up whatever he sees in the name of this higher truth."[10]

By comparison, passionate criticism brings sensitivity and intensity—not to be confused with zealotry—and therefore, "new poetic insights into the living quality of a work of art." It reveals the critic's living sensibility as it reveals *the artist who is its subject*" (emphasis added). It is an act of love, "a point of view that opens up the widest horizons," Barney quoted Baudelaire, honoring both "the external world and the artist himself."

They were not there to celebrate Baudelaire's ideas, according to Barney, which were not original at any rate, but had sources in Delacroix, Stendhal, even Abbé Du Bos. Nor to celebrate his taste—he had terrible blind spots, he neglected Courbet, was hostile to Manet—and loved too much the pot-boilers.[11] What they were celebrating was Baudelaire's "enormous courage to be passionate about everything that interested him . . . his own passionate nature." It was because of that nature that he understood that the "most fundamental of all the problems of a painter, the problem that every painter has, no matter what his style [was] what to paint."

Barney closed his presentation—and the entire conference—by acknowledging this was at odds with what he had said previously, that "aesthetics is for me like the study of ornithology must be for the birds," and that he had no use for aesthetics. "But I am now asking for passionate criticism because anything else fills me with a sense of humiliation."

And then, as if it had been scripted by the poet himself, Barney collapsed in bed with a fever for days, before he and Annalee continued on to Barcelona and Madrid.

True passion, by its very nature, by its sheer existence, is a political threat against the philistine and the bourgeois.[12]

Against the chaos of 1968, Barney positioned the artist's passionate commitment, renewing and reinvigorating his rhetoric of the 1940s, when he told Rosenberg that if his work was properly understood it would change the world. Three weeks after Martin Luther King, Jr. was assassinated, Barney told an audience at the University of Bridgeport, where he was a visiting professor of drawing for the spring semester, that the artist is "someone who sits all day in a room all by himself in confrontation with himself. In front of him is his empty canvas, or empty paper, or the empty piece of metal. Nobody can help him. Only he can make the decisions . . . that make possible a statement not only of what he himself believes, but if it is valid, moves the statement into a dialogue of history. And if it is creative enough, it can change the world by its revelations." But first, it had to change the artist. "If it has no effect on him, how can it have any effect on anybody else?"

Never mind that the "all day" was a description far removed from his own life. It was precisely what he believed. The burden of that confrontation with himself, the moral *responsibility* that he placed on it, was what was so terrifying. The agitation of his accustomed activity during the day exhausted Barney enough, turned down the static enough, that he could encounter the confrontation of the studio at night.

As early as 1963, Harold Rosenberg's friend Ben Raeburn, the legendary owner and publisher of Horizon Press (whose list included Irving Howe, Alfred Kazin, Frank Lloyd Wright) had decided that what Barney had to say—and his unique locution—deserved a bigger, more permanent outlet. "You may be as good a writer as a painter . . . . shall we talk about publishing a book by you?" he asked after first meeting "you and your wife." (It was always, "you and your wife." Every occasion to which Barney was invited to speak involved the non-negotiable requirement that Annalee's expenses were covered; every informal meeting, every studio visit that anyone memorialized in letters or recalled in narratives, never failed to acknowledge Annalee. Barney needed her there; ultimately, his sustenance came from what Rubin called her "glorious idealism."[13])

Raeburn "got" the written Barney. The things Barney sent him to read, especially "The First Man Was an Artist," "swing in a kind of timeless orbit of imagination . . . . This history without dates is the most accurate there is. And the research is in the living the life of the artists . . . . the sort of joy of quickening you get in reading Blake and yet the only connection is that beautiful flying sense of timelessness." What a book, in his opinion, could Barney write![14]

The right project arrived in the madness of 1968. What "the wave of student protest in the advanced countries" had as its underlying philosophy, wrote the social critic Paul Goodman in a *Times* magazine article furiously scribbled over by Barney, was Anarchism. And Anarchism—"decentralist, anti-police, anti-party, anti-bureaucratic, organized by voluntary association, and putting a premium on grassroots spontaneity"—was a political position on which Barney liked to hang his hat.

Sometime during that spring of student rebellions Raeburn decided to republish the original 1899 American edition of Prince Peter Kropotkin's *Memoirs of a Revolutionist* and invited Goodman and Barney to pen introductions. Both

Goodman's "Preface" and Barney's "Introduction" were explicitly informed by—and referenced—immediate events; both evidenced (and to different degrees indulged) a tolerance for current amnesia about historical forerunners and admonished that disruption itself was not enough without content. As Goodman put it, "Kropotkin's generation had a more interesting notion of freedom"; as Barney put it, "revolution is more than a nihilist Happening." Both praised Kropotkin's aristocratic optimism and generous nature. But where Goodman noticed in Kropotkin a "certain amount of repression," an "extraordinary" sexual reticence ("far beyond the Victorian" public standard), Barney sympathetically praised the absence of the confessional and "erotic intimacies." Kropotkin's "innate puritanism that is characteristic of the high-minded . . . was essentially his scrupulous sensitivity regarding any tyranny over the individual that made it impossible for him to distinguish between his idea of the individual and the idea of the individual's body." And in sentences that may represent the only time—at least only time recorded or recalled—that Barney discussed matters sexual, he continued:

It was only natural for him to have a special sensitivity in regard to the predatory nature of lust. This comes through when one reads how proud he was that as a student in the School of Pages he led a successful revolt against the homosexual abuses (he calls them "oriental games") inflicted by the older boys upon their younger classmates. For him these "games" were not to practice pleasure but excuses to practice force and domination. Kropotkin was a witness to the buying and selling of "souls" [serfs] as so much flesh by his father and his father's friends. He witnessed the flogging of serfs. He saw landowners practice a vicarious and perverse *droit du seigneur*. . . . It was only natural that Kropotkin would develop an extraordinary sensitivity to anything that smacked of tyranny over someone else's body. The body, therefore, was something ultraprivate to the person.

Barney's identification with Kropotkin—whom he discovered in the late '20s when the "*Memoirs* existed as one lived: in isolation," where it "broke one's loneliness inside [the] solitary confinement" of someone rejecting the popular Leftist dogmas—was ingenuously un-selfconscious, and he welcomed the reissue as an antidote to the dogmas of the New Left. Kropotkin was noble. He was both "against the man who is neutral on moral issues" and "scrupulous to the point of fanaticism in his defense of the untrammeled person." If Barney himself couldn't entirely perform that balancing act much as he tried, it was his espousal of that standard that so endeared him to younger artists. And there was something more: "Kropotkin is the only revolutionary hero untainted by anti-Semitism." (In his introduction, Barney made note of several occasions that Jews enter the *Memoirs*.)

Finally, Kropotkin provided the ballast for Barney's ethos. In the 1940s, Barney wrote, "when artists got together of an evening, there was always someone who insisted on playing surrealist games." During one, in which everyone had to say "what it was that destroyed him," Barney answered, "established institutions" while another, "perhaps wiser than I," said, "people." Looking back, Barney decided they were both right: "It's the establishment that makes people predatory."

Only those are free who are free from the values of the establishment. And that's what anarchism is all about.

The art critic Thomas B. Hess makes the point that the reason that political scientists and social planners have difficulty understanding the modern artist is that they cannot understand how anybody is able to make *anything*, particularly a work of art, spontaneously or directly—*a primo*. The idea that someone can make anything without planning, without making sketches upon sketches from which one renders a finished product, is incomprehensible to them.

Anarchism was what gave Barney hope: just as social planners and political scientists were operating in a "mirage [because] there is no such thing as political 'science,'" art critics, theoreticians, historians—all the "dogmatists"—were also operating in a mirage. There was "no such thing as art 'history.'"[15]

It was perhaps his best writing since the 1940s and it resurrected that more global, partisan voice that his early cohorts had noted and exploited for their own purposes. Raeburn had recognized the vividness achieved, the passion in a writer unfettered, when he wrote to Barney that "history without dates is the most accurate there is. And the research is in the living the life of the artist." Primed by his recent immersion in Baudelaire—his symposium remarks were printed in *Art News* in June—Barney wrote a love letter to a man in whom he saw the best of himself, the person he aspired to be.

But it was also very much a response to the urgency of specific current events; as much as he lumped all of the competing voices—"Anarchists, the writers of the Republican party platform, the Students for a Democratic Society, the southern racists, Governor Wallace, or the black militants"—together in a blanket condemnation of the clichés of doctrinal rhetoric, there was a big difference. There were "moral issues" bigger than those that beleaguered him alone—and he would act on them.

Watching the sickening violence at the Democratic Convention on television at the end of August, fifty artists decided that the actions of the police, "directed and supported by Mayor Daley and not repudiated by the people of Chicago" had made the city "unfit for membership in a civilized society." They announced a two-year boycott of the city's museums and galleries—enough time to change the political leadership. Barney asked the Art Institute to withdraw *Gea* from the Museum of Modern Art's "Dada, Surrealism, and Their Heritage" show when it traveled to Chicago in mid-October.

Very quickly, the Chicago dealer Richard Feigen, whose exhibition of Claes Oldenburg's works was withdrawn by the artist after he was thrown to the ground, beaten, kicked, choked, and called a Communist by "six swearing troopers" outside the convention hall, offered an alternative to the "ineffectual" boycott.[16] Feigen proposed to mount a show of work made in protest. "An Art Protest Turns into a Chicago Bonus: 'Richard J. Daley' [the show's title] Looks Like One of the Season's Liveliest Shows," declared a Chicago newspaper headline, and, certainly, it generated far more attention than the boycott would have received—including in the *Wall Street Journal, Time,* and *Newsweek.*[17]

Although Oldenburg, Rosenquist, and many other others made work especially for the purpose, about half, including Motherwell—the only other artist of Barney's generation—sent older work to show support. But there was one work that *everybody* noticed, one work that succeeded in being at once a protest and much more than a gesture. Barney's *Lace Curtain for Mayor Daley,* positioned in the center of the gallery, was undeniably, richly, powerful, and was mentioned in all of the accounts of the show. Although Barney's three *Here* sculptures, done over sixteen years, were not a secret, they had to date extremely limited exposure in exhibition or reproduction. But within only months of the creation and prominent display of *Broken Obelisk* Barney was sufficiently identified as a sculptor that the art historian Barbara Reise pitched a "tri-partite" article to *Artforum* with equal emphasis given

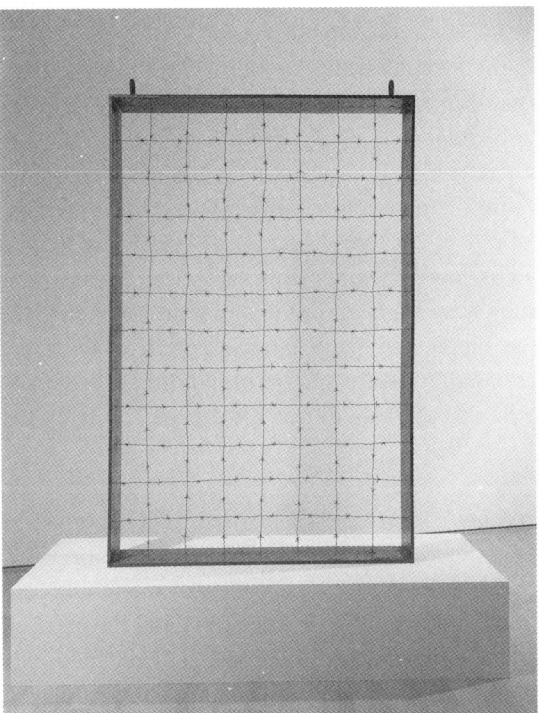

Fig. 54 Barnett Newman, *Lace Curtain for Mayor Daley,* 1968. Cor-Ten steel, galvanized barbed wire, and enamel paint, 70 × 48 × 10 in. (177.8 × 121.9 × 25.4 cm). The Art Institute of Chicago. Photograph Bruce White

to writings, paintings, and sculpture,[18] and it was as a sculptor—and a "patriarch" in the eyes of the younger artists—that he protested Mayor Daley.[19]

Surprisingly, considering both how fanatical he was about the most minute aspects of surface and condition before he allowed a work to be exhibited and how anxiously present he insisted on being during a sculpture's fabrication, in this case he phoned it in—literally, ordering it from Lippincott. His defense of this approach was that even the phone call required particular skill: "Did you ever telephone an order of sandwiches to a delicatessen and have them get it right?" he asked Hess.[20]

Lace Curtain was an almost 6-by-4-foot steel frame with red-paint-splattered barbed wire stretched within it. It existed on almost as many levels as *Broken Obelisk*. Verbally, the title—widely understood as the crude socio-economic "middle" category of Irish immigrants ("shanty," "lace curtain," "castle")—feminized the bully Daley and suggested he was in need of its civilizing decorum. Physically, the barbed wire was widely understood to refer to the police barricades in the streets around the Conrad Hilton Hotel convention venue in August, and the red paint to the bloody violence. But, as with *Broken Obelisk*, it was also "personal." No Jew who saw or read about the convention would ever forget the spectacle of Daley himself, from the audience, screaming at Connecticut Senator Abraham Ribicoff, who denounced the police tactics from the podium. What watchers agreed Daley said was either "Kike, you Jew son of a bitch" or "Fuck you Jew son of a bitch."

"Well, if that's the level he wants to fight at, I'll fight dirty too," Barney said. "There're other words besides 'kike.' "[21] The fences of Nazi concentration camps were also in *Lace Curtain*.

When a Christmas Art Sale for Peace to benefit the Student Mobilization Committee to End the War in Vietnam was organized by a group of critics, Barney donated half of any sale of one of his 1961 lithographs specifically to be used for medical expenses incurred by young members injured by the Chicago police.[22] No less than anyone else, Barney was caught up in the moment. Newhouse took the Newmans to see the anti-war, hippie and Baudelairian-passionate *Hair: The American Tribal Love-Rock Musical*; Barney, infatuated, returned three more times. That he was, in fact, born under the sign of, if not during the Age of, Aquarius, tickled him.[23]

Barney had only recently gotten settled in his new studio. The move provoked all of the emotional and psychological turmoil that accompanied his previous dislocations—at least that is how he described it to those with whom ongoing correspondence was disrupted. But bridging the move to White Street and the creation of *Lace Curtain* Barney was absorbed in discovering the potential of yet another medium: etching. And, this being 1968, that experiment, too, initially was provoked by a convulsion.

After the assassination of Martin Luther King, Jr., Vera List asked selected artists to contribute to a portfolio of prints in his honor. A few years earlier, when the Lincoln Center campus opened, List and her husband led the acquisition of major works of art for the site and theaters. Around the same time, she began a program that commissioned artists—with sensitivity to their instinctive anti-commercial positions—to create posters for events; eventually fine, limited editions of these commissions were also made to raise funds for Lincoln Center programs. It was a golden age of American contemporary printmaking and List recognized the potential the medium presented: announcing cultural messages to a wide audience, raising funds for those messages, and supporting artists. Sales of her King portfolio she intended to support the Martin Luther King, Jr. Scholarship Fund at the New School for Social Research. At the time of the assassination, the *Cantos* were on exhibition in "Suites: Recent Prints" at the Jewish Museum where List was a life trustee; she asked Barney to participate.

At ULAE, Tatyana Grosman had recently established an etching workshop—*1st Etchings*, Jasper Johns's contribution to "Suites," was made there—and the idea of the untried technique appealed to Barney. To allow him to experiment and develop a personal touch, Grosman arranged to have very small copper plates, prepared with ground, brought to the apartment in June and July.[24] Just over 3 by 6 inches, they were about the size—and the purpose—of a pocket notebook, and Barney did sometimes carry one around in his pocket.[25] When, posthumously, a suite of prints were pulled from the plates, they were titled *Notes*.

Donn Steward, Grosman's intaglio printer, who brought the plates to West End Avenue, brought as well a stylus and scrapers, and explanations. Almost immediately, the Newmans went downtown to Job Lot to look for the "best and handsomest burins and scrapers"[26] to be found, and, grounded by the fine tools, Barney went to work—or, more accurately, play: many of the marks he tried were analogous only to his doodles, more free-handed, more frisky than any that he allowed to exist in a finished work since the mid-1940s. They have what Hess called "qualities of intimacy" that enabled Barney to evoke the same in the 20-foot painting he was working on concurrently in his new studio. All were generally formatted like the paintings; seven of the proofs were left with scribbles, hatches, swoops, and dashes, and in a couple his hand reverted to the identifiable chicken scratches of Yiddish script. In October, when they were all proofed out on Long Island, he created second and third states of a few by adding aquatint to etching to achieve the density he couldn't get with the scraper alone, or by forgoing etching entirely for a field of aquatint. Twelve plates, multiple states: once again, there were eighteen individual images.

With that accomplished, he moved on to a larger size, and produced the etching and aquatint for List by early November.

"I do not recall when I have been so deeply moved nor have I ever thought a print so exquisite," List wrote of her response to the larger etching Barney made after his experiments—the image that for that one moment was titled "Requiem." It may have been the only time Barney had fulfilled an obligation before the deadline. Unfortunately, for this project the other artists didn't. Only two produced acceptable work, a "designer painter" and Romare Bearden. Feeling blindsided, Barney suggested including at least one or two others. List was inclined to go with the three. Barney withdrew and List understood.[27]

But there emerged other opportunities to honor King. One of them was an invitational exhibition held at the Museum of Modern Art, organized by Carroll Janis and advised by museum men including Rubin and Geldzahler, with sales to benefit the Southern Christian Leadership Conference. In a situation where the echo of Calvary in the three ten-foot verticals may have been unavoidable, Barney sent one of the two exemplars of *Here II*.

Somehow fittingly, the capacious *Broken Obelisk*, already densely packed, would have the civil rights martyr included in its weight. One resonance Barney did *not* have in mind when he made the piece was King, who was still alive. But later, when the occasion arose to have it dedicated, he did not object, and hoped that it would go "beyond only memorial implications."

"It is concerned with life and I hope that I have transformed its tragic content into a glimpse of the sublime."[28]

When it was newly made, John de Menil, the Houston oil executive and art collector, began to think about buying *Broken Obelisk*, but "couldn't face Barnett's price with my two eyes open."[29] (The Newmans had been socializing with one of the de Menil's daughters, Christophe, in New York for years, introduced by Philip Johnson, who designed the family home in Houston in 1950.) Then one day, in 1969, the phone rang and Annalee answered.

JOHN de Menil: Is the *Broken Obelisk* for sale?
ANNALEE to Barney: Is the *Broken Obelisk* for sale?
B: It depends who is calling.
A: Who wants to buy?
J de M: John de Menil.
A to B: It's John de Menil.
B: If it is John de Menil, say yes.
A: If it is John de Menil, it's yes.[30]

John and Dominique—the daughter of the founder of Schlumberger Ltd., the oil services company—offered to match a National Endowment for the Arts grant to Houston to acquire an important sculpture. By May, they had already exerted their customary *droit* by going around the agency's established process for choosing public work, and managed to have all parties agree to *Broken Obelisk*. The Houston Municipal Art Commission wanted the site to be the Civic Center, the patrons thought the neighborhood insufficiently diverse and lobbied for the Old Market Square. City Hall Plaza was the agreed upon compromise. The de Menils, with King's assassination on their minds, wanted an inscribed dedication, *forgive them for they know not what they do*, but the local councilmen took that personally; a simple plaque dedicating it to King was suggested. Those negotiations, too, became excessively complicated, and in August, signaling they were done with the de Menils, with the *Obelisk*, and with

Martin Luther King, the city council decided to use the NEA grant to commission an *Iwo Jima*-style monument to the Houston-based astronauts who had walked on the moon a month earlier.[31]

Kept abreast of the controversies by de Menil, Barney wondered whether the "attack" was not so much "against the Biblical quotes or the Martin Luther King dedication" but "perhaps a cover for their hostility towards the sculpture itself."[32]

With their original plan thwarted, the de Menils came up with the full purchase price—90,000 dollars—and at the end of August donated the first exemplar of the sculpture, now dedicated to King, to the ecumenical Institute of Religion in the Texas Medical Center. Barney penned a few talking points: "This great work of art—one of the most significant pieces of art of these years in America is appropriate to be dedicated to the memory of Martin Luther King whose life is a life of dedication as the artist's life is . . . . He is the general in the background and I'm the soldier. After all I did this piece when MLK was alive so that it is a celebration of his life—not his death!"[33]

In Detroit, while the negotiations between Houston and the de Menils were continuing, Barney installed the second exemplar of *Broken Obelisk* downtown on a pentagonal patch of grass surrounded by neo-classical-aspirational and mid-century-grim buildings of dramatically different heights, and stores with comfortingly 1940s commercial signage.

Two years earlier, in the summer of 1967, Detroit was the location of the worst of the riots (or rebellion, or war, depending upon who's remembering), arson, and looting rocking the country. The Michigan National Guard was deployed, and five thousand United States Army troops were sent to the city. Thousands of buildings were destroyed, many adjacent to the five acres known as the "Kern Block," which since 1966, when the Kern's department store was razed, was an unused, desolate greenspace designated an urban renewal site. Six weeks before *Broken Obelisk*'s erection, thousands of Detroit jobs were lost in reaction to a United Auto Workers strike. "Just keeping the doors open is the problem, just keeping enough police on the streets, just keeping the hospitals open," the incumbent mayor said shortly before he decided not to seek reelection.[34] In June of 1969, less than a month before Barney's visit, a white former police officer was acquitted by an all-white jury of the 1967 murder of a black teenager in the horrific siege of the Algiers Motel annex; racial tensions in the city—where 40 percent of the population was Black—were on a hair-trigger, and there was fear that the summer would bring an explosion.

"Sculpture Downtown," the outdoor show of eleven public sculptures—five fabricated by Lippincott—that was organized by the Michigan State Council for the Arts, was a boosterish effort in self-esteem and image rehabilitation. In Grand Rapids, a few days before "Sculpture Downtown" was fully installed in Detroit, Alexander Calder's 50-ton *La Grande Vitesse* was dedicated, the first example of the National Endowment for the Arts-supported urban renewal art project. If Barney were aware of the social or political implications, he didn't leave any record of it. He supervised

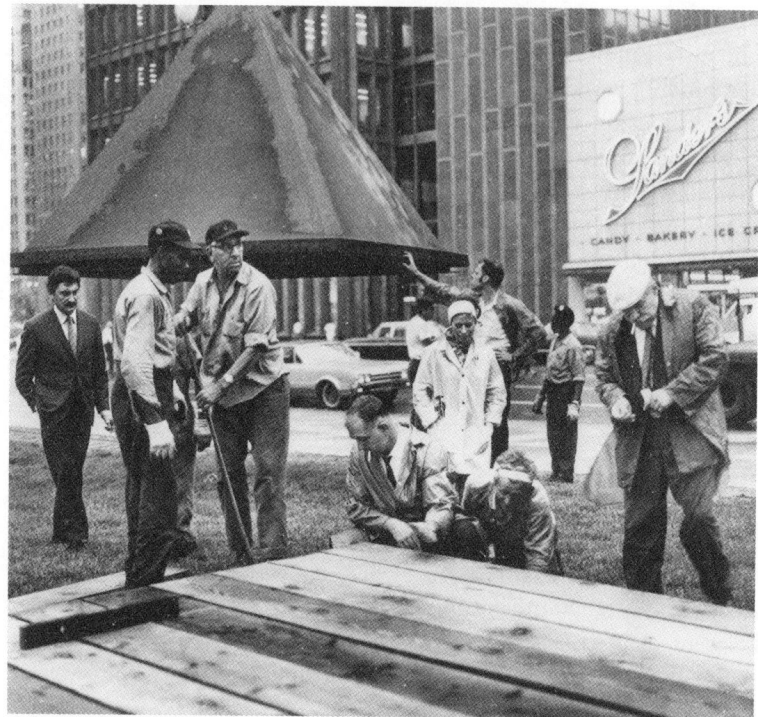

Fig. 55 Donald Lippincott (hand stretched toward dangling base), Newman, and crew installing *Broken Obelisk* in Detroit, 1969. Photograph Roxanne Everett

the installation in the most prominent spot available, near the river, with his unique flair. It had begun to rain; Annalee dashed across the street to buy cheap gray malodorous oilcloth raincoats for Barney and Murray—who showed *Megan's Red* nearby. Murray did the champagne-cork honors. It was the "one good moment" of his summer, Barney told Liberman. He was "delightful with passers-by," the Detroit dealer (and friend) Gertrude Kasle was told. "Everyone was enchanted."[35]

For all of the personal content he himself had injected into the sculpture, he seemed not to object to its accrual of other, unforeseen meanings in the time of social turmoil; moreover, whatever happened to *Broken Obelisk* happened to Barnett Newman: work and man were fused.

When "Scale as Content" closed at the Corcoran in January 1968, *Broken Obelisk* continued to stand where it had originally been placed. On that site, it became a resolute focal point for a fond audience: it both symbolized the museum's exciting new commitment to contemporary art, and seemed—to the growing dissident population in Washington, and those who converged on the city for mass protests and who thought America was itself broken—to perform a sort of counterculture balancing act with the Washington Monument behind it.

When the National Collection of Fine Arts was about to relocate to a new home in a renovated Greek Revival landmark, the special consultant Adelyn Breeskin asked Barney if *Broken Obelisk* could be moved temporarily to mark the spot and the occasion. Barney did not respond for months, then dove deeply into issues not simply of the sculpture's placement but the construction by Lippincott of a new pedestal and gravel bed based on Philip Johnson's design for the Seagram Building installation. But by late April the entire plan was aborted: "Since we are situated in a crowded section of the city, on the edge of where the worst disturbances occurred a few weeks ago we feel that the less attention we direct to the outside of the building the better until after the Poverty March has taken place," Breeskin informed Barney.[36]

And so, *Broken Obelisk* remained in its place outside the Corcoran, presiding as an honored guest for nearly two years, where it seemed to "symbolize the gallery's lively new interest in the contemporary,"[37] until, forced by circumstances, it assumed yet another burden.

The turmoil that overtook the Corcoran in July 1969 and rocked the Washington art community had nothing to do with *Broken Obelisk*, and it had nothing to do with Barney. Yet, coming right in the middle of the negotiations in Houston—not yet covered nationally, but looming in Barney's mind—and exactly as it was starring in Detroit, it must have seemed to Barney that *Broken Obelisk* was the most famous sculpture in America, and its enlistment in the moral "issue raised" was "compelled."

At the end of June director James Harithas abruptly resigned after only nine months on the job. A few years earlier Harithas, who came from the Phoenix Art Museum to the Corcoran as a curator, had called on Barney for career advice: he had interviews at New York's MoMA and at the Corcoran. It was 1965. What should he do? Barney told him, "Forget about MOMA, they'll bury you. On the other hand, there is nothing in Washington, but you could do something there."[38]

Harithas was designated the Corcoran's director in September 1968, and as Barney predicted, he was widely praised for his vision, his imagination, his flair, his innovation, and energy, and for creating a living art scene in the city, bringing local artists to national prominence. He amplified the Corcoran's role—unaffiliated with the umbrella of the Smithsonian—as a *Washington*, as opposed to national, institution. But he had done his job too well, and his success, and his impulsive personality, created problems in the organizational structure of the Corcoran, to a degree, Harithas said, that was unworkable for him.

Although the local art community reacted, initially, with outrage, ultimately all parties agreed that Walter Hopps, appointed "acting director," would be able to sustain the Corcoran's new promise. (Hopps was the director of the Washington Gallery of Modern Art when it merged with the Corcoran the previous year and had stayed on in a curatorial role.)[39] Harithas had had nothing to do with bringing *Broken Obelisk* to the Corcoran, but Barney respected him; he was a kind of anarchist in his approach, exactly the sort of independent thinker that Barney valued. What's more, Harithas was planning a major show of Barney's buddy Liberman, and that was caught in limbo. Barney took action in moral support.

In early July of 1969, Barney arrived at New York Avenue and Seventeeth Street in a white straw hat and sandals, with "his wife, two flight bags, a navy-and-white dotted bow tie, a Swedish Hasselblad camera and a monocle," according to a *Washington Post* reporter who also happened to be there with a photographer to supervise *Broken Obelisk*'s removal by Lippincott. "He seemed serene, even impish," the newspaper reported.[40] Several girls—students at the Corcoran school—carried flowers that they laid at the base. Presented with a rose by one, Annalee, too, placed it as an offering. "Had Harithas stayed, the piece would still be there," Barney told the *Times*. "Since he's not there, I see no reason for the piece to be."[41] It was "one of the most moving experiences" of his life, he told Liberman. "All the art students and older artists were on the grass mourning its removal—Girls came and decorated the base with flowers—It was a tremendous tribute to the piece."[42]

SIXTY-THREE

KNOEDLER

The Auer's van had been called once again. Barney's eviction from his 19th-century sanctuary at 100 Front Street was accompanied by all of the threatening letters, the punitive rent increase, court documents, and the mulish, self-righteous resistance of his previous real-estate traumas. More collegially, during the same few months in mid-1968, Barney finally came to an agreement with the Internal Revenue Service. The settlement checks he wrote for over 24,000 dollars (210,139 dollars in 2023) were around the sum he received from the Stedelijk for *The Gate* and stung less than they would have a few years before. A price tag of 100,000 dollars (875,580 dollars in 2023) was attached to *Broken Obelisk* when the Seattle-First National Bank, at the recommendation of Virginia Wright and the Contemporary Art Council of the museum, considered purchasing the second exemplar for their new Fourth Avenue Building plaza.[1]

Still, old habits die hard. Investments were one thing, haggling another, and with the new studio on the corner of Church and White Streets came a "nefarious" real-estate broker with whom to do battle. Jack Klein liked to work with artists because he liked to forgo his commission in exchange for artwork. But although Klein was aggressive about pressing Barney in front of witnesses to "paint me my painting," Barney never "got around to it."[2]

Barney took two floors, and then, at the last minute, he decided to take a third to be used for storage, because he did not want anybody to be above him. The floor where he would work on the big paintings was about 22 by 70 feet and had 16-foot ceilings; French windows were installed between the cast-iron façade's corinthian-capitaled pilasters to allow paintings to be removed without rolling them up. One 12-by-28-foot expanse of wall on the second floor was covered with linoleum in checks of gray and white whose dimensions—nine-inch squares—made a confounding impression on de Kooning.[3] It was an enormous, light-filled space, a few blocks north of a relocated Job Lot, and Barney seemed to be happy there, eventually painting the largest expanse—81 square feet—of the most brilliant yellow he had ever used.

In the years since Murray first came to New York, he had had twin girls, had built a career, had gotten a little older and a lot busier. His relationship with Barney had evolved into something more like colleagues. But when Barney needed to move something, stretch canvases, or install, Murray always tried to be available, and there were a few other younger men loyal to Barney who could be called upon; several were now. Murray and Holstein, their friend, filmmaker Jim Stanley, and Terry Syverson kicked in to pack for the relocation to White Street, and contrive operations—like that involved in the aborted conveyance and hoisting of a slippery roll of linoleum by timber hitch—that resembled at times those of the Keystone Cops.

Barney moved on a perfect early summer day at the end of June 1968, two weeks after the shooting of Andy Warhol and the assassination of Robert Kennedy. It is possible, as Hess wrote after the artist's death, that he was already working on his largest painting, *Anna's Light*, when he was given the copper plates for his smallest works from ULAE six days earlier, although it seems unlikely he would have embarked on the 20-footer when he had known for over a year he would have to vacate.[4] He was in the process of writing about Kropotkin. Most importantly, he had reached a tentative understanding with Xavier Fourcade and Knoedler Gallery to represent him exclusively—or so Knoedler thought. At least one thing was certain: there would be a solo show, Barney's first survey since 1959, of work since 1960 in Knoedler's New York gallery in February 1969.

By the fall the letters had gone out to collectors—the Sculls, Newhouse, Dolly Bright, John Powers—requesting loans.[5] In November Knoedler sent out a press release that announced the forthcoming show, a monograph by Hess to be published at the same time, and that "we have become the official representative for BARNETT NEWMAN." As it happened, the gun was jumped. The contract remained unsigned as Barney pondered and his lawyer, Hess's brother-in-law, Jesse Wolff, reviewed the papers and responded to Barney's exhaustive questions over many months.[6] The show was moved to late March.

Whether or not Barney had begun *Anna's Light* before June 1968 at Front Street, by the end of September at White Street it was finished. When Elizabeth Baker visited, she was able to feel, as she wrote in *Art News* before the Knoedler show, the "terrific physical impact" of its "stunningly huge" expanse of cadmium red light acrylic paint.[7] Barney knew he had to respond to a world radically different from the one in which his French & Company exhibition had taken place and Baker recognized that he was in a "dialogue with the present." Over the next six months in his new studio he would make the surprising, unpredictable, final monuments through which he assured yet another dimension of his legacy.

In mid-January, when what may have been his newest work, *White Fire IV*, was sent to "New York 13," at the Art Gallery of Vancouver, eleven of the artists were more than twenty years younger than Barney; the twelfth, Ellsworth Kelly, was eighteen years younger. The organizers hoped to exhibit three or four new pieces by each artist. As it turned out, very few of the others were "brand new," but at least one critic, who called Barney's sole contribution "without doubt the most breath-taking moment in the show," was under the impression that it was Barney's "first in two years" and coincided "with rising juices in the 64-year-old master."[8] *White Fire IV* was most certainly not made after a dry period, but one could speculate whether the artist had an ulterior motive for choosing this particular piece to go to Canada. Unequivocally countering the vulgarity of the Montreal Expo's display, it was a spectral presence, the exquisitely spiritual ghost of the heraldic *Voice of Fire*—similarly proportioned and similarly composed at about half size—that was now sent to the opposite end of the country, and eventually, as the show travelled, to Montreal itself.

Although much of what the next months would bring was unanticipated at the lively party on Beekman Place that Hess threw for Peggy Guggenheim, perhaps the date—January 29, Barney's sixty-fourth birthday—was a sign. Nineteen sixty-nine turned out to be Barney's *annus mirabilis*.

In early February, he was invited to show a monumental sculpture to inaugurate a new museum in Japan. By mid-February the Centre National d'Art Contemporain in Paris proposed a solo show, and an acquisition. By the third week in February, the Museum of Modern Art in New York committed to a "long overdue" retrospective.[9] By the beginning of March, the Tate in London wanted their own retrospective, overlapping an offer from the Stedelijk in Amsterdam.[10] And Knoedler released the announcement of Barney's "first one-man show since 1960" with "18 paintings and one sculpture."

In the middle of that month, spread over most of two pages, the gloriously red 18-foot *Who's Afraid of Red, Yellow and Blue III* jolted the eyes of readers of *Vogue* (plate 20). In the Liberman photograph an unsmiling, monocle-bedecked, immaculately dressed Barney stood before the painting in a nearly precise echo of the 1963 spread of Barney standing before the cosmic blue of *Onement VI* for Rosenberg's "A Man of Spiritual Grandeur." This time the text was brief: it no longer needed to make a case for Barney as "one of the great American painters," but could categorically declare him, quoting Hess, as "secure in the knowledge that he may have peers, but there are no superiors."

On the last Tuesday evening in March the Knoedler show opened with a Gala Champagne Preview benefit for the Frank O'Hara Foundation—effectively attaching Barney's persona and the beloved poet and curator's for symbiotic attention and attendance and heft.[11] The publicity benefits of the marriage did not go unnoticed in the art community.[12]

In April, the cover of *Art News* featured one of Barney's most radical and surprising new paintings, *Chartres*, on view at Knoedler; Barney's explanation about why he made the leap was inside. A few days after, he received an invitation to participate in the first of the Metropolitan Museum of Art's centennial celebration shows, "New York Painting and Sculpture: 1940–1970." And a freshly made, five-foot-high brush and ink drawing—his largest drawing ever and only second since 1960—was featured in "The BIG Drawing" at the James Graham and Sons gallery.

In June, a monumental sculpture, *Zim Zum*, that he had somehow managed to create the previous month, was shipped to Hakone, Japan. MoMA's show "The New American Painting and Sculpture: The First Generation," the largest ever exhibition of the so-called "New York School," opened with a prominent role for Barney. *Art News* again featured him, this time in the 1968 text "Through the Louvre with Barnett Newman," by Pierre Schneider.[13] *And* the shockingly stark, white-with-blue 1968

Shimmer Bright was first shown at Knoedler in "Arshile Gorky, Willem de Kooning, Barnett Newman," joining four other recent paintings.

Also in June, Barney's presence at the installation of *Broken Obelisk* in Detroit was a Michigan news event. In July, his presence at the *removal* of (the other exemplar of) *Broken Obelisk* from its Washington site after nearly two years was more widely covered as a sort of "happening."

Over the first seven months of the year, Barney's name appeared in the *Times* on fifteen occasions for a wide range of reasons, and sometimes for no compelling reason at all: "Howard Kanovitz . . . looks like a youngish Barnett Newman"; small bronze sculptures by Mahonri M. Young (1877–1957) were in his Knoedler exhibition "(in the upstairs galleries—that's Barnett Newman on the first floor)"; the newly appointed director of the Houston Museum of Fine Arts, Philippe de Montebello, was "interested in shows of all eras, from early Egyptian to, say, Barnett Newman."

"Speaking of Barnett Newman (weren't we?)," Grace Glueck felt obliged to write in the *Times* "Art Notes" column on July 20, the day all American eyes were on the astronauts about to land on the moon.

In October, "New York Painting and Sculpture 1940–1970" opened at the Met. It was, in a way, Barney's apotheosis—or, at any rate, the most prominent corrective to "Fifteen Americans" of 1952 one could ever hope for. In December, *White Fire IV*, completed a year earlier and back from Canada, was in the Whitney Annual. It was Barney's seventh Whitney Annual, since the great violation of 1955, his absence from "The New Decade: 35 American Painters and Sculptors."

In Barney's eyes, the single most important event of the many months of coronation may have been the May publication of Hess's slim volume, Barney's first monograph. Two or three generations of artists would see the Knoedler show and process for themselves in nearly endless ways the richness of his moves; two or three generations of collectors and observers would see the show and leave emotionally (and, eventually, financially) enriched. But Hess's book engraved in stone, for posterity, the account of Barney Newman that Barney Newman blessed.

It was an elided and compressed story, heavy on foreshadowing; it erased the injuries to dignity and the not always rational anger to create a history of charm and amusing anecdotes. Who could blame the writer and his muse? After all, it was not an entirely untrue picture: Barney was as much defined by the version presented as by the version expurgated.

The book made every thwarted ambition and pragmatic choice, every struggle and setback, a matter of elevated principle. Mainly it lovingly captured what Heller identified as "the most unforgettable character"—the thrilling roller-coaster ride of being with Barney—and it went a long way to memorializing the towering personality as well as a career mythology for younger and future generations. By clearing away, disregarding, the chaff of a packed life spent largely not producing artwork, Hess convincingly made Barney's work seem improbably *ordained*—through the mechanism that Kirk Varnedoe would later identify as "a fine disregard" for the rules.

Perhaps most importantly, Hess, who played so significant a role in the early ostracism, and whom Barney had once compared to Stalin, issued a *mea culpa*, "ashamed" of his role in "an amazing example of collective blindness."[14]

The pressure was extraordinary and the agony severe. The Knoedler show was to open on March 25, and throughout a wintry February, when Barney was still working on at least two major works, there was no heat in the new studio.[15]

Ten years earlier, French & Company engaged Greenberg to plant its flag in the contemporary art arena. Now, Knoedler, in business since 1846 selling masterworks from the 14th through the early 20th centuries to Vanderbilts, Astors, Mellon and Frick, was doing the same by bringing in Xavier Fourcade. He had already signed de Kooning, who had had no official representation for three years and was more naïve than Barney was in his relationship with the independent dealer Harold Diamond. Fourcade was reserved, with an "upper-class air . . . not the sort of man whom de Kooning ordinarily liked," according to de Kooning's biographers, but his respectful formality was exactly what de Kooning needed at the time. Barney, on the other hand, had *always* believed that artists should be treated with the same dignity as bankers, and that is how Fourcade conducted business.[16]

Fittingly, in concert with the elegiac poetry of old New York that was his ballast as he intrepidly pressed into the future, Barney's show was one of the last to be held in the six-story 41 East Fifty-Seventh Street building that had been the gallery's home since 1925, with its 18th-century English oak panels, and famous chocolate-brown French plush wall-coverings that didn't show nail holes.[17] Barney *liked* the darkness and soft texture and intimacy of the rooms.[18] But it was exactly those qualities that caused so many of Barney's friends to be shocked by the association; it seemed the antithesis of where Barney would want to be shown. Holstein was "astounded"; he could only think of how Barney would say "that's the enemy," as they walked down Madison Avenue looking at Tiffany vases.[19]

But de Kooning had filled Knoedler's spaces the month before. And a retrospective of his career was at the moment filling three floors of MoMA—guest curated by Hess. (The post-opening dinner was held at Hess's house.) Barney and de Kooning had always been on friendly terms, at times close friendly terms, and the ups and downs of de Kooning's career had been a congenial foil against which Barney could measure his own position. In the nadir of 1952, when Barney was not in "Fifteen Americans," neither was de Kooning, struggling with *Woman I*. In 1962, together at Allan Stone's gallery, Barney's own light shone more powerfully. In 1968, while Rothko, Motherwell, and the estate of Pollock had opted to be represented by Marlborough, Barney negotiated with Fourcade as de Kooning had before him. And—as MoMA announced in the fall that de Kooning's Stedelijk show would come to New York in an arrangement advanced by Knoedler—Barney, Fourcade, and Hess sat down to a meal to discuss the future.

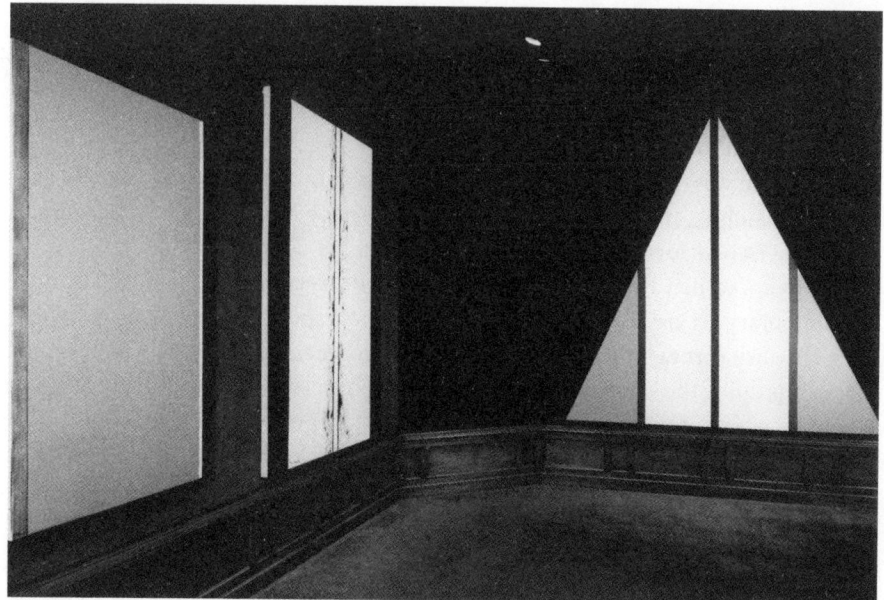

Fig. 56 Knoedler Gallery, 1969. From left: *Who's Afraid of Red, Yellow and Blue I, White Fire II, Chartres*. Photograph Paulus Leeser

Hess may have been entirely ingenuous when, alone with Murray as Fourcade commandeered Barney for a meeting, he said that the incongruity of Barney at Knoedler was driven by Barney's need for "security": he was "worried about his own immortality" and Knoedler and the people around the gallery were a "responsible group of people."[20] It could be possible that Hess didn't recognize his own stagecraft, directing the characters and blocking the scenes. Annalee recalled Barney saying "I closed the fifties with my show at French & Company, I'd like to close the sixties with my show at Knoedler's. I'd really like to see my paintings up against the velvet." But he might just as likely have said that he wanted to see his paintings up against de Kooning's.

"It was time to let people know what I've been doing," he told the critic Douglas Davis. "I feel free at Knoedler's, too. It's not an exclusive club; they show all kinds of artists. Bill de Kooning and I are there simply as painters."[21] Encouraged by Barney, Davis devoted a large portion of his article to a comparison between the two over the years. "But there is no sense of competition between them . . . 'It is a beautiful show,' [Barney] keeps saying about the de Kooning retrospective." When, immediately before de Kooning's retrospective opened in New York, Bates Lowry, the new director of MoMA, offered Barney a retrospective to be curated by the scholar William Agee, Barney instead requested Hess, who had taken up O'Hara's role in arranging de Kooning's show after the poet's death.[22] It's no surprise that all of these transactions took place in a very small petri dish: earlier, when Edy de Wilde proposed an "extensive exhibition" for the Stedilijk—where de Kooning's show marked his return to Holland after 42 years—Barney stonewalled for a year while the rest of the culture developed.

Sixteen paintings—six never before shown, four of them made in 1968 and early 1969—and the sculpture *Here III* were exhibited at Knoedler's in March.

In the window facing Fifty-Seventh Street was *White and Hot*, 1967, its orange-red and white, opaquely applied Magna paint distributed on the canvas as if it were *Anna's Light* before that painting had become pregnant with the whole world.[23] As one of the three works small enough to fit in the window, it was chosen by Fourcade for the honor because he considered it "one of the most important paintings of Newman of the last ten years," he told Joseph Pulitzer, Jr., who purchased it out of the showcase, without ever going inside to see the exhibition.[24]

But it was *Anna's Light* that left most viewers staggered—"dumbfounded." And how could it not? It was the first thing one saw when entering the gallery, the largest painting Barney had ever made, its color even more overwhelming than its size: 163 square feet of cadmium red, sweeping across 217 inches stopped by 3 inches of white on the left, and 19 inches on the right. Whereas *Whose Afraid of Red, Yellow and Blue III* was clearly an expanse of red with a zip of blue and a zip of yellow, in *Anna's Light* it seemed that a red zip had inflated itself to push everything else out of its world—a kind of inversion of "zim zum," the Lurianic concept of creation in which God contracted to make space for the world, and the inspiration for the new monumental sculpture Barney was imagining as the Knoedler show was installed. He had been after "reditude," he told Davis, "as rich and as red as possible." It was a color, *Time* said, that lingered "like a mellow afterglow" throughout the exhibition, "pure poetic"—almost erotic—"pleasure."[25]

In Rosenberg's opinion, however, Barney was "after bigger game than providing a stimulus to the spectator's retina." The "substance" manipulated by Barney was "emptiness" and his "program" was to "induce emptiness to exclaim its secret: in short, he wishes to grasp the absolute through painting, and he knows that the absolute is neither red nor blue." For Barney, "color effaces itself and becomes the hue of undifferentiated substance. One might say that it is red or yellow because it must be *something*."

"The chief characteristic of a Newman is that it is there, an entity that keeps nature at bay. Bare of qualities, it excludes emotional confusion and defines itself through the austere realization of quantity: size, proportion, multiplicity, singularity, muteness, radiance." As in the Wallace Stevens lines that Rosenberg quoted: "How clean the sun when seen in its idea, / Washed in the remotest cleanliness of a heaven / that has expelled us and our images."[26]

But to Baker, and to many others who had not been on the long journey with Barney since the 1940s, the new works seemed "more physical than metaphysical." And the surprising development that had viewers *talking* was truly radical.

The two newest paintings were formed as enormous isosceles triangles, their bases over 9 feet and their heights 8 ½ feet and 10 feet. Both were in acrylic paint, both were bisected through the longest dimension—with a tiny, but potent difference. *Jericho* was black, its single red zip just off center enough to destabilize, and yet *not* destabilize, what "should" be a most solidly planted mass. *Chartres* was not only not afraid of red, yellow and blue, it was also not afraid of fearful symmetry, channeling (but definitely not illustrating) Barney's experience at the cathedral. Sitting in the gallery, speaking to the art historian and specialist in the intersection of religion and modern art Jane Dillenberger, he described with punching fist the tremendous dynamism he had felt there: one entered and was immediately confronted with the rows of columns and light pouring in.[27]

"I called one painting Chartres because of the strong assertion of my inner structure in contrast with the outside format and because of the even light in the painting, which has for me the evenness of northern light—a light without shadows," Barney wrote in *Art News*, unusually specific and revealing about his motivation. More typically, he added, "The title *Jericho* explains itself."

> And it was when Joshua was in Jericho, that he lifted up his eyes and saw, and, behold, a man was standing opposite him . . . . and Joshua went to him, and said to him, Are you for us, or for our adversaries?. . . . And the captain of the Lord's host said to Joshua . . . *"the place upon which you stand is holy"* (emphasis added).[28]

In spite of his own unwavering affection for Barney, and his anxious reliance on Barney's feedback about his own work—he could "kneel in front of Barney with respect and admiration" and "never had a show without Barney helping me choose the paintings"[29]—Liberman considered that he had a role in *Jericho* and *Chartres*. Liberman at the time had been making triangular paintings, hung with the point facing down: "The whole idea for me was sort of an opening to sky, hope, God, whatever. And Barney said to me, 'Have you ever tried doing the triangle upside down, with the point at the top?' And I said, 'Well, Barney, it would destroy my whole meaning, because that to me becomes earth bound." But it was "logical for Barney." When Liberman first saw the original *Here I* in Barney's studio, "two sticks [planted] into a mass of plaster," there was a "prophetic quality to Barney's gesture." Liberman thought it was the "gesture of a creator of a religion," it made him think of Moses: I plant my staff *here*.[30]

Barney may have had the two paintings in his mind since the making of *Broken Obelisk* at Lippincott. "While the men were moving the faces of the pyramid for him to make a final adjustment, suddenly Newman 'saw a couple of paintings,'" Hess wrote after he visited the studio in December 1968. *Chartres* and *Jericho* were "still in progress" when Hess submitted the final text for his monograph.[31] And they were only two in a show of seventeen works. But decades later, those who saw the show recall it as the time Barney "showed all the triangles."

Barney had spent his life refuting people's easy assumptions about him, about what they *seemed* to see, about what they *thought* was meant by events. It often appeared to be the source of his greatest frustration, and yet, at the same time, it may have been his greatest pleasure. Were hot artists at the end of the '60s playing with the idea of paintings in a shape derived from their supports? Were they constructing supports far removed from the expected rectilinear shape because it was "stylish"? Were critics discoursing upon this radical development? *Jericho* and *Chartres*, Barney insisted, had "nothing to do with" their format. "They didn't fit" the format. When Baker, in September or October, saw *Anna's Light* in the studio, she also saw Barney at work on the two triangular paintings; his intent, he told her, was not the sort of deductive work that some of the younger artists were doing, but "to destroy the format."[32]

"I knew that if I conformed to the triangle I would end up with either a graphic design or an ornamental image," he said, suggesting his opinion of those who had taken that route and his distance from them. "I had to transform the shape into a new kind of totality." After all, as he would write in *Art News* in April, he had "done the so-called 'shaped canvases,' or what is more correct in my case, 'no shape' canvases, as far back as 1950."[33]

As *always*, in every aspect of his life, Barney would be contrarian. But more than that, he would go further, he would not simply not abide by rules or expectations, he would deliberately provoke and engage in direct battle. How otherwise would he assert his "Imperial Self" and avoid the "total self-abnegation" that resulted from accepting the conditions that pinned him "to a particular role."[34] Was his sense of "scale" dependent upon the expanse of his canvas? He would duplicate that sense an inch-and-a-half wide. Where nearly every observer was moved by his color, Barney would insist the work was primarily about drawing. Where nearly anybody would see a triangle, Barney insisted it was a triangle destroyed. And the amazing thing was that once he enunciated it, one had to agree: of course! That was not it at all, to paraphrase Eliot's Prufrock. John Perreault in the *Village Voice*—"Paradox is the only way to describe them and to describe the states of consciousness they evoke. The forms are not significant"—and Rosenberg had gotten it right. *That* was what distinguished the work.[35]

Shortly before the Knoedler show opened, Franz Meyer and Barney were walking on Madison Avenue when Meyer noticed "from all sides, people saying 'that's Barney Newman.'"[36]

There was buzz among three generations in the art community. For younger artists, like Brice Marden, the Knoedler show "was a big deal. You *had* to go to the show: it was Newman showing, and Newman didn't [generally] show."[37] When Rosenquist walked into the exclusive atmosphere of the somewhat pompous surroundings, "Everybody's hushed and quiet and whispering." Suddenly, "Barney yells, 'Hey, Jim come on in and see my curtains. I went over to see your curtains yesterday.'"[38] Andrew Hudson, the *Washington Post* critic, saw de Kooning walking around, explaining the paintings to a friend, and was struck by the "generosity" of the Dutch artist toward the New Yorker.[39]

People were "amazed" that he had chosen *this* gallery.[40] People wondered, "what is this?"

"The Knoedler's show made no sense at all it was totally bizarre they had brown velvet walls with wainscoting and it really [almost] destroyed the paintings."[41] Twentieth-century paintings "on maroon velvet is murder," Janis pointedly told Barney.[42] That the deep moldings and shadowed panels of the wainscoting were tolerated was particularly eyebrow-raising after Barney's sensitivities at the National Collection of Fine Arts in January 1966. On the other hand, the dark walls, the woodwork, may have reminded him of his experience in the Denon Gallery of the Louvre nearly two years after the Washington installation. Why shouldn't *Who's Afraid of Red Yellow and Blue III* have a setting comparable to *The Raft of the Medusa*? Why shouldn't *Jericho* be enveloped in the same luxury as Géricault?

Murray had a theory: by lighting the paintings and not the walls, they appeared to float. It was interesting, but perhaps not entirely a success.[43] Philip Leider in the *Times* pulled no punches: it was a "dumb room with its silly brown velvet walls eating up all the light"; it made it impossible to judge whether in the discomforting *Jericho* Barney had "overcome the most impossible melodramatic elements he could have chosen," or if it were a "crude drama defeated by rhetoric." Leider noticed something else, something that certain other observers danced around: the artist whose work was "so important to so many artists and critics is distinguishable from both the 'public' Barnett Newman, and the Barnett Newman seen" at Knoedler.

The "public" Barney of the Hess catalogue—"a kind of charming, grand-manner dignity, something like de Gaulle," whose pronouncements people cheer ("My dialogue is with Michelangelo")—was "a fine role, and everyone loves it, [but] it is not half as tough as his best paintings."

In Leider's judgment, Barney commanded the respect of "perhaps a wider spectrum of artists than any other artist living" because of his *ethic*: he had "wrenched abstraction" away from a fetishistic manipulation of formal devices "back into a sterner tradition." The Knoedler show, however, while not bad, was too long on works from 1960 to 1967 that simply didn't "exist in the same world" as *Tundra*, *Cathedra*, *Vir Heroicus Sublimis*, *Shining Forth*, the *Stations*—"to name only a few."

"Perhaps Knoedler's—lucky with de Kooning, who was ready when they were—jumped the gun," Leider suggested. "Perhaps Newman was not as ready for a one-man show as Knoedler's was to announce that they had acquired him."[44]

On the last day of the show—it was pouring rain—two paintings were vandalized, or "marred" in the words of S. I. Newhouse, who had returned for a last look. They were in a back room and the damage was unnoticed. When he saw them, Newhouse immediately phoned Barney, who rushed over. Meyer and Lillian Schapiro walked in as Barney, enormously upset, examined the damage. Against the damp chill of the day, Lillian was wearing a beautiful shawl held by a safety pin, and Barney complimented her—and Meyer was off and running. He discoursed on the history of safety pins—their significance in locating German tribes in ancient Rome, that the graves of women were marked with safety pins because their shrouds were held by safety pins. The tables had turned: Meyer talked on and on and on, Barney was desperate to be free to deal with the paintings.[45]

That Knoedler picked up so many of the administrative chores might be why Barney was able to conceive and make *Zim Zum* during the early months of 1969 while also preparing his first gallery show in ten years. On the one hand, he had already proven multiple times that it was precisely overwhelming pressure that was his muse. On the other, after the show closed at the end of April, there was a striking lull in Barney's activity. Everything— the pressure, the public relations, the bitterly cold winter days in the studio, caught up with him. During the next few weeks he made frequent visits to his cardiologist, and saw a radiologist. Many of the days in May he did not leave the apartment. The state of his health may account for his process in creating *Zim Zum*. In contrast to his enthusiastic collaboration to realize *Broken Obelisk*—detailed contract, drawings, and numerous trips to North Haven—the paper records for this work are few, and Barney made only two very short trips to Connecticut.[46]

The new Hakone Open-Air Museum did not expect to receive a new, never-before exhibited work—but they did present themselves, in their November 1968 invitation, as "the largest in the world" of museums that would show outdoor sculpture. Barney did not respond until the following February. It's not clear at what moment he imagined the form a new sculpture would take. Two facing walls of pleated steel that echoed the weight-bearing walls that he and Murray designed—under similar time-pressure—for the synagogue model in 1963, may have been knocking around in his brain over the years. It was an inspired—if surprisingly specific—evocation of the concept of zim zum: god's self-contraction to allow room for creation. Since his teasing description of *Broken Obelisk* as "personal . . . . people may think it's geometrical, but it's gone beyond that" and the explicit program of the *Lace Curtain*, he was less shy about revealing (some of) his intentions.

The show in Japan was to open August 1, and the Hakone Museum was designing the installation and catalogue. Their exceedingly polite but growing concern over the two months spent waiting for details about the work he would send—the size, the weight, the insurance valuation—was somewhat alleviated only in mid-April, when Barney telegraphed his first acknowledgment of the name. "Title is Zim Zum material is corten steel size each piece is 8 feet high 26 inches wide 13 feet 6 inches long weight 2 tons each piece insurance 100000 dollars" (830,250 dollars in 2023).[47] The reply was alarmed: "Insurance value 100000 dollars is unbearable."[48]

Zim Zum was shipped to arrive "around the 21st of July." Barney sent along detailed instructions regarding the assembly of the four sections, and, by the way, "in accordance with" their request regarding a lower insurance valuation, Barney reduced it to 75,000 dollars.[49]

SIXTY-FOUR

"NEW YORK PAINTING AND SCULPTURE: 1940–1970"

William Rubin had a mission: The Museum of Modern Art's "collection is the only perfectible collection of modern painting in the world today."[1]

In June 1967, the then 39-year-old Rubin, as consultant to the museum, was instrumental in acquiring for them a gift from Sidney Janis of a hundred works by (among others) Kandinsky, Picasso, Giacometti, Mondrian, Léger, Pollock, de Kooning, and Warhol; Alfred Barr called it "unequaled among the great gifts" received by the museum. Then, a month later, upon Barr's retirement, Rubin was named curator of painting and sculpture in a reorganization of the museum's operation.

Under Barr's leadership, large numbers of American artists had been disgruntled; MoMA was accused of being "slow" in acquiring postwar work. Whatever the merits or excuses for that history, in 1967 MoMA was still considered, in America at least, the arbiter of who and what was included in an international "canon" and Barr "faced the emergence of American art like a father who wanted sons and got daughters. He did his duty and struggled to be just" but without affection and understanding.[2] The Janis-donated works that most excited Barr were Boccioni's 1913 *Dynamism of a Football Player*, two Picassos of 1913 and 1914, and a 1914 Mondrian. Now that Barr was gone and Dorothy Miller put in charge of the permanent collection, Rubin was determined to move that "canon" forward, and in the spring of 1969 he would proclaim that intention in a major exhibition widely understood as an attempt at course correction. In this he was helped immeasurably by new tax legislation that had been under negotiation for many months, with important repercussions for museums.

The U.S. Congress had been considering a reformed tax plan that would ensure the "wealthy" could not use loopholes to avoid Federal income tax. And "wealthy" now included the Newmans, who were well above the federal government's determination that a family of four's moderate standard of living in New York would require an annual income of just over 11,000 dollars. On the table was the issue of contributions of appreciated property to charitable, educational, and religious organizations; at the moment, such contributions were deducted on tax returns at their *current* value, not the price at which they had been acquired, or the price of materials, which was usually significantly lower. Clearly, this was not only of great interest to collectors—in May, Nelson Rockefeller announced his intention to leave twenty-five "key works" to MoMA and to transfer his superlative collection of "Primitive Art" to the Metropolitan Museum—but also to artists, like Barney, whose reputations had soared with the art market. And it was of great interest, as well, to curators, like Rubin, who could parlay the impending change to reboot his museum's collection. That summer of '69, a compromise was reached in the House of Representatives that exempted gifts of "non-tangible property," such as stocks, but left artworks on the chopping block. "A lot of the art world is scurrying around trying to find a way to keep Congress from taxing donations of art to museums," Hess told Schapiro.[3] The scurrying did not succeed, and before the end of the year, before the new law went into effect, artists rushed to make donations.[4]

"The New American Painting and Sculpture: The First Generation"—the title harked back to the landmark 1958 show—as Rubin (with associate curator William Agee) planned it, would not only redress scholarly and aesthetic lapses; it would also, in one grand gesture, greatly expand the museum's permanent holdings, since only works in MoMA's collection, or promised to MoMA, would be included. Many in the "First Generation" were by now comfortable enough to be concerned not only with historical enshrinement but also with deductions from their tax bill—Barney and Annalee, after their experience with auditors, certainly were—and they were happy to recognize the win-win-win opportunity. One hundred fifty-seven works were in the show; 67 were acquired between 1941 and 1965, 90 since 1966.

As for Barney, until 1968 only *Abraham* had been in MoMA's collection. Now, "in one step, as it were," Alloway recognized in *The Nation*, "the museum has represented a key period in Newman's oeuvre which is, at the same time, a central episode in postwar painting,"[5] thus gracefully rectifying 1952.

In a gorgeous installation, *The Voice* (1950), acquired by the museum with the help of Janis in 1968, despite Muriel Newman's years-long pursuit,[6] hung next to *The Wild* (1950), promised by the Kulicke family, and donated later that year; on the wall perpendicular to it, *Onement III* (1949), promised by Joseph Slifka, hung next to *Abraham. Vir Heroicus Sublimis*, a "fractional gift" of the Hellers, was on the facing wall. *Here II*, owned by Philip Johnson, was in the show, but the promised donation never came to pass. "Acquisitions" of work by Pollock, Rothko, Still, Gottlieb, and others were in similar numbers.

Of course there was outrage, and protests "in the name of morality" over "the advisability of mixing a survey of recent, in fact still current, art with acquisition policy (and politics)" in the words (and initial fears) of Alloway.[7] The Art Workers' Coalition, a "very loosely-knit and constantly-changing group"—as described by spokesperson Lucy Lippard—of dissident artists, writers, critics, filmmakers, and museum professionals including Hans Haacke, Sol LeWitt, and Carl Andre was formed in January, with MoMA, the "Establishment beast," according to news coverage, in its sights. The AWC's "13 Point" program called for increased representation of African–American artists, discontinuation of the 1.50-dollar admission fee, and, most importantly, an open hearing on "The Museum's Relationship to Artists and to Society." MoMA's counter-offer to hold a series of smaller "committee hearings" was rejected. The AWC first appeared on the greater public's radar at the end of March, in a demonstration at MoMA's Fifty-Third Street entrance. The desired "public hearing," a marathon *"kunstklatsch,"* was held on a Monday evening in mid-April in the Chelsea auditorium at the School of Visual Arts.[8]

Even the conservative critic at the *Times*, Hilton Kramer, had to admit that the issue raised, "of the artist's moral and economic status vis-à-vis the institutions that now determine his place on the cultural scene," required serious attention. The central issue, perhaps needing rescue from some incoherent rhetoric, was a "plea to liberate art from the entanglements of bureaucracy, commerce and vested critical interests . . . from the squalid politics of careerism, commercialism, and cultural mandarinism." It was a moral issue, Kramer acknowledged, "which wiser and more experienced minds had long been content to leave totally unexamined."[9]

But not Barney. These very issues had been on his mind since his run-in with the Barnes Foundation in 1926. It was the crusade he had been waging for forty years, on behalf of himself, on behalf of the original Parsons group, on behalf of the students at Emma Lake, Smith, Liberman, Murray, Judd, Flavin, and the numbers of artists whom he encouraged and for whom he—reflecting his current status—wrote deeply felt grant and job recommendations. Identified by *Times* reporter Grace Glueck as "Dad of Cool," Barney sent in a statement to be read, but then "appeared in person (to greet well-wishers on the sidewalk)" after the meeting had adjourned.[10]

The "business of getting one's work into museums" was a problem with which he had little experience, he said, since "until two years ago, I existed in only one museum in this country." But the "overriding issue" was not getting *into* a museum, but what happened to the work after it was acquired. "This is the crux of the problem."

"In this country, under American-style capitalism," the owner of "your work has complete legal, unalterable possession of it. He can hang it upside down; he can repaint any part of it; he can, if he wishes, legally destroy it totally." Barney did not want to suggest that the "Museum" *would* do any of these things, but "in the same spirit of complete possession it can package it into any kind of theme show, group show. It can make any kind of historical package it pleases without any consideration of the artist's wishes." What Barney hoped for was that the museum would "respect the wishes of the artist," as—to a fault—Alloway had, as Hess had, "even if the artist is wrong."

Then, two months after Barney lent gravitas to the *kunstklatsch* and less than a week before Rubin's show was to open at MoMA, the Coalition attacked the museum specifically for the initiative: the Museum of Modern Art was building its collection at the expense of artists, who were being "blackmailed" into donating works "in order to guarantee themselves a place in history."

Ferber, Gottlieb, Guston, Lipton, Motherwell, Rothko, Peter Grippe, Theodore Roszak, and Mrs. Ad Reinhardt—all donors to the show—jointly signed a letter in support of Rubin: "Instead of being the victim of an ill-considered attack, we feel that you should be honored and respected by the artistic community as a strong advocate of modern American art." Hare, Pousette-Dart, and Louise Bourgeois, rounding out the twelve artist–donors, did not sign, although a postscript noted they agreed that no coercion was involved.[11]

But Barney, the high-school football star *manqué*, was not to be satisfied playing defense; he knew the way to win the game was by advancing the *offense*. Thus, when a follow-up article appeared in the *Times* its very first words were "Barnett Newman, the abstract expressionist who has often been a critic of the Museum of Modern Art, came yesterday to the defense of the museum . . . Mr. Newman said that he was 'deeply suspicious of the motives and sincerity of the Art Workers' Coalition.'"[12]

In his letter, Barney wrote that he was "shocked at the kind of attack now being made by the Art Workers' Coalition . . . particularly since I am not one of those who was 'blackmailed' into giving work . . . . The hysterical charge that the Museum blackmailed artists to give paintings is spurious because the artists had only to say No . . . The moral issue here belongs to the artist—not to the Museum." (The Coalition's precise words were "a subtle form of blackmail.")

Barney called the Coalition's charges insincere and self-serving, since, instead of congratulating Rubin for trying—in the Coalition's language—"to build for the Museum the world's major collection" of the "heroic years of Abstract Expressionism," in Barney's opinion they let "the cat out of the bag when they say that to acquire 'a larger collection . . . necessitates a larger building program which continues to divert money from acquisitions of contemporary art.'"

"They don't care whether buying their work will of itself necessitate a larger building," Barney wrote, and the *Times* reported. Unfortunately, though, the *Times* did not print the red meat.

"But above and beyond all this, is it wrong for Mr. William Rubin and the Museum to go beyond the tokenism of past years so that the artists of the Coalition together with others will be able to see *what really happened in those heroic years*, which up until now the artists of the Coalition have only seen in bits and pieces? The attack, therefore, is not an attack against the Museum but is an attack against their fellow artists . . . . [emphasis added].

"And what's all this stuff about the Coalition being concerned with what they say is 'the morality of artists.' This is truly offensive. After all such moral superiority can only be understood as careerism . . . . It is the easiest thing in the world to build a career by constantly taking care of everyone else's morality except one's own. We have had too much of that already. Let's let lie the sleeping watchdog ghosts of Ad Reinhardt and Anthony Comstock. The issue facing an artist should not be another man's morality but his own."[13]

Taxes were of no small interest to the Newmans, and not simply because of the IRS audits and penalties based on filings from the lean years. Barney explicitly hated to pay "big" amounts.[14]

As Annalee escorted him to Treitel-Gratz, or ULAE, as she hummed while Barney spoke, or sat in the background reading while he was filmed, or transported his galoshes if it were raining, or made sure his vodka glass was kept filled with a custom solution largely made up of water, and devotedly sent a very long list of friends and associates flowers, or plants, or bottles of brandy for special occasions, and their children Christmas and Chanukah gifts, most observers saw Barney's handmaiden. But there was much more going on than met their eyes.

The sums of money earned from sales were now significant, and with her business degrees, intelligence, and acumen, Annalee was managing the couple's financial health. Without a committed relationship to a gallery, flexible, price-establishing arrangements could be made with agents acting privately, like Harold Diamond or Heller, who in at least one instance acted "as a friend to both parties" with no commission to be paid by either side.[15] She supervised a significant portfolio of stocks; multiple, interest-generating accounts; and advantageously juggled loans against investments.

The amounts spent on storage, restorers, vodka and doctors, and art supplies increased geometrically; in the last four months of 1969 he spent an unprecedented 1000 dollars (over 8300 dollars in 2023) at Pearl Paint and Bocour. The accumulated bills from F. R. Tripler and Abercrombie & Fitch, limousine services, lawyers, and charge accounts at various restaurants and department stores grew larger and larger. But the couple's financial activity was not just ballooning; it became considerably more complicated, and Annalee was prepared. Over the years, Barney had artfully made gifts of twenty-three works to Annalee, including the alluring, 18-foot *Cathedra* in 1956. In 1969, as his reputation soared, works began to be strategically donated or partially donated—particularly as 1969 drew to a close—both lightening the Newmans' tax burden and distributing Barney's presence among museums, a practice Annalee continued spectacularly after she became a widow.

In 1968, the Newmans invested 50,000 dollars (437,800 dollars in 2023) with Frederick Weisman for capital contributions in Western American Investing Company; in 1969, 100,000 (830,250) dollars in Houston oil and gas drilling funds, and at least 30,000 (almost 250,000) dollars more was placed with financial managers. A Swiss bank account was discussed—other artists of Barney's generation had taken that route—but there is no evidence the idea got any farther.[16]

In May they were poised to own almost 50 percent of the shares in a former stable for police horses at 11 Spring Street.[17] In June Barney and Annalee purchased three lots in an Aspen, Colorado subdivision.[18] Since they had never visited, or expressed interest in that part of the country since 1939, when Barney applied for a teaching position, it seems likely that this, too, like the drilling fund, was a place to park money, take a tax deduction, and one day, with any luck, sell.

The Spring Street property was a project in partnership with Murray and his wife, the Judds, and Kenneth MacKenzie, an architect who worked for I. M. Pei married to Lippincott's sister. The raw floor area was 23 by 76 feet and preliminary architectural plans were drawn up, showing the Newman's second-floor living quarters as a gracious fantasy that included a library/study/music room in which there was so much space that their 7-foot grand piano seemed like a boat on the sea, abundant closet space, a commodious eat-in kitchen, wide hallways, enormous living and dining areas, and long walls for paintings. A spiral staircase led down to Barney's studios—one, 27 by 23 feet, the second 15 by 35, with lots of storage area. It also opened the floodgates to a whole new battle, a campaign that "raised issues" with entrenched city opponents as dark and conflicted as the Citizen's Budget Commission had been in 1935 when Barney took on its grandee members in *The Answer*. In the *Times* article that appeared a week after the report of the MoMA show brouhaha, it wasn't until the *second* paragraph that Barney's name came up.

"Artists Against the Expressway," one group among many to oppose Robert Moses's controversial, decades-old plan to route traffic between Brooklyn and New Jersey through lower Manhattan, held its meeting at the Whitney Museum on the evening of June 19, 1969. The Museum of Modern Art, already buffeted by negative publicity, was the planned site, but when it became clear that some trustees had serious conflicts of interest, permission was denied. Speakers against the most recent incarnation proposing a ten-lane highway across what was soon to be known as SoHo included James Marston Fitch, the highly regarded founder of the program in preservation at Columbia University's Graduate School of Architecture; the dealer Richard Feigen; and Barney, recruited for his public stature as well as his principles by Julie Finch Judd, who organized the group, created the letterhead, and mapped the population. At least six thousand artists in the affected district would be impacted, losing loft space, residences, and the small business that made up the community, announced Finch, not to mention the distinctive 19th-century cast-iron buildings.

Barney told the audience of 250 that he had been pushed out of two loft studios in lower Manhattan; now he occupied one in the Expressway's path. Among the "do-gooders who are improving the city by speeding up traffic let us not overlook that the strongest forces against artists are the art lovers." He called out David Rockefeller—chairman of the Downtown-Lower Manhattan Association, who was *also* chairman of the board of the Museum of Modern Art—as "the most vocal advocate for the Expressway."

"He should have the opportunity to declare whether he has some feeling for the artists who make the art as well as the art. He should use his good offices in our behalf rather than in our destruction."[19]

In the face of widespread opposition, and in spite of the support of the editorial page—although not the architectural critic—of the *Times*, the City Planning Commission in August abandoned the Broome Street concept. A planned meeting between Rockefeller and Barney, chuckling at the prospect, was canceled.[20]

"In today's atmosphere of apparently inexorable change, he has essentially retained his 'newness,'" Elizabeth Baker wrote in February, "as if the pace of recent history did not quite apply to him."

"In terms of sheer impact upon younger artists he stands above anyone else," Douglas Davis wrote in April.[21] Barney was respected by "perhaps a wider spectrum of artists than any other artist living," was Leider's assessment. And no question, he worked for, and earned, and enjoyed the regard. But the present could never provide the satisfaction that was absent in the past. Whether it was an unclear offense by Greenberg, a felt betrayal by Rothko, or misattributed credit for pin point carbonation "a grievance was never forgotten."

Did he *still* need to correct history, specifically the history of his first ten years as a mature artist? Did he still need to settle scores that had been long forgotten by everyone else? Barney clearly believed he did; he had "been pulling trains for a long time, particularly with my own generation" he told a critic three years earlier.[22] Although "the art writers" could not avoid his influence on the young, it was "constantly being used as an easy way out" to avoid "confronting the impact the influence of my work [had] on the men of my own generation," he complained in August in an unsent draft to a friend.[23]

"The absolute images of Rothko, Newman, Gottlieb, Still, Reinhardt can co-exist in a picture collection but not in the minds of their originators," wrote one of those "art writers." "Each is the proprietor of a sacred enigma, whose authority must exceed that of all others."[24]

At the Museum of Modern Art, that influence was "obvious to me but I don't have much hope that it will be set right."[25] He was "pleased and happy" with his section, which he shared with Rothko. "Still, Gottlieb and Reinhardt are around the corner and it seems only a blind man will not see the truth of my effect on them instead of the lies and vicious smears of Motherwell Rothko & Co," he wrote to Liberman. "But what is the use—I have little hope the story will ever be publicly corrected."[26]

In an extended essay in *Art International* that summer, Alloway communicated Barney's intentions: as the "total work increases so do the number of connections between paintings. Newman is almost alone as a painter in insisting on maintaining this web of internal correspondences in preference to the series of hectic renaissances which regular exhibitions impose of the artist's career." But Alloway would not ignore Greenberg; as he conscientiously parsed the "cluster of cross-referring signs, binding his past and future" throughout Barney's exhibition history, he also devoted too many paragraphs specifically to settling scores with the autocratic critic.[27]

If the unbalanced selection of work at Knoedler that Leider noticed had been a misjudgment, it would not have been Knoedler's. Barney was diligent to a fault—as Alloway confirmed—about curating the presentation of his work. Certainly, he was overextended and exhausted, the logistics overwhelming him and Annalee. It's hard to imagine that it could have been managed without Fourcade's and Knoedler's help. And yet, in October, despite writing to his lawyer that he had been ill and his schedule "hectic beyond words with shows, etc.," Barney had come to a decision about the gallery relationship: he did "not see how" he could "possibly agree to such a contract because I see very little in my favor."

"I realize that it is to a large extent my own fault because I myself did not have a clear view of what I should demand from Knoedler," he admitted. But "in the last few weeks, things have become clearer."[28]

What precisely had become clearer would be obvious to everyone two weeks later. In the especially anticipated "New York Painting and Sculpture: 1940–1970" at the Metropolitan Museum, Barney was enshrined as top dog of his generation in a

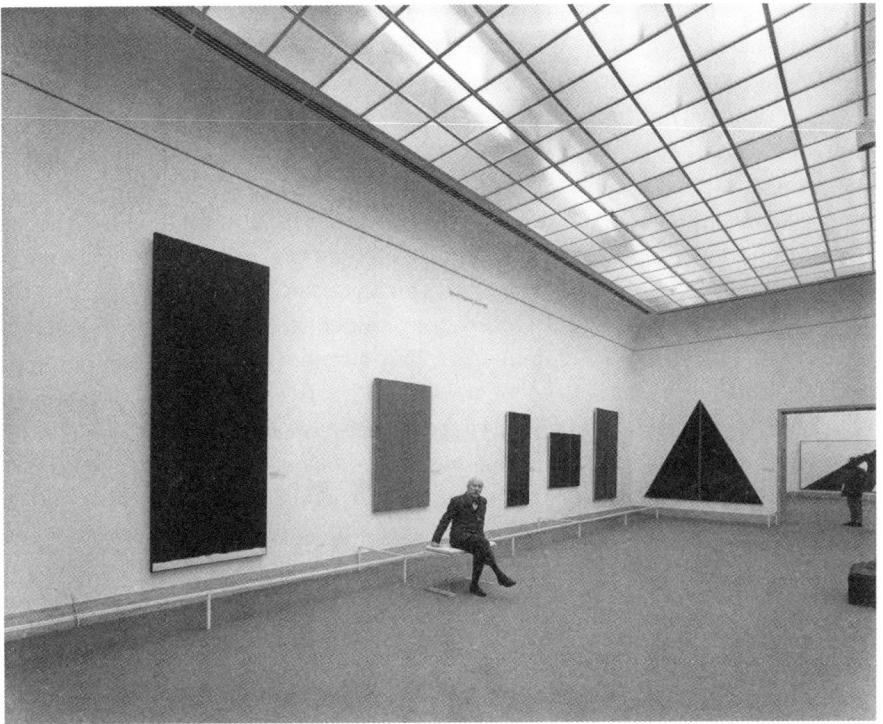

Fig. 57 Barnett Newman's room in "New York Painting and Sculpture 1940–1970" at the Metropolitan Museum of Art. From left: *Prometheus Bound, Who's Afraid of Red, Yellow and Blue I, Onement III, Covenent, Concord, Jericho.* Photograph Arnold Newman

single massive room—roughly half a basketball court—containing the breadth of his career from 1946 to 1969, both painting and sculpture. *Pagan Void, Euclidian Abyss, Onement III, Concord, Covenant, Prometheus Bound, Who's Afraid of Red, Yellow and Blue I,* the 14.5-foot *Shining Forth,* the 20-foot *Anna's Light,* the massive, triangle, *Jericho; Here I (To Marcia)* and *Here III.* And outside the museum, where he used to wander on school days, *Broken Obelisk.*

He had thirteen works—more than Pollock (nine); more than de Kooning (twelve); more than Gottlieb (eleven); more than Rothko (ten); more than Motherwell (nine); more than—and *earlier* than—Reinhardt (nine) and Still (five). Only Joseph Cornell, Jasper Johns, Ellsworth Kelly, and David Smith were more deeply represented. It didn't seem to matter that curator Geldzahler's premise—that there was *a* "New York School," that it had a unity of purpose, and that "by reason of its own achievement and the clear and indisputable effect" it had had, was the historical successor to the School of Paris—was already in dispute. Or that it was an *un*historical show, like Rubin's had been, as Alloway noted in *The Nation.* Nobody who knew "the career of Henry Geldzahler . . . could have expected a proportionate or casual presentation." Geldzahler himself did not deny a bias. "I wanted to recapitulate the experience that I had had over 15 years of looking at art," he said.[29] It was "an anthology of 43 one-man shows," in Alloway's words, a hedonistic "Versailles of avant-gardes."[30]

While critics could find their blithe excuses and legitimate complaints regarding the choices made, for the artists—both *in* and *out*—it was recorded history. As "Fifteen Americans" had been—at least in *Barney's* mind—in 1952. In Barney's mind, *that* show might as well have been "Three Americans"—Pollock, Still, and Rothko. Or, more generously, "Seven Americans"—Pollock, Still, Rothko, and Tomlin, Baziotes, Ferber, and Lippold. One wonders if he ever thought about the other eight: Joseph Glasco, Herbert Katzman, Herman Rose, and Thomas Wilfred among them.

In 1950, twenty-eight artists wrote to the president of the Metropolitan Museum of Art that "for roughly a hundred years, only advanced art has made any consequential contribution to civilization" and they had no basis to hope that the museum recognized that. Barney hand-delivered the letter, personally arranged to meet with a *Times* city editor, and was quoted by name on the front page of the newspaper. Eighteen of those artists were called "Irascible" in a *Herald Tribune* editorial, and fifteen were immortalized in a *Life* magazine photograph, fanning out from a shiny-shod Barney at its center. Now "Henry's show" at the Met contained in its center a Barnett Newman retrospective. "This batch of New York School guys . . . they *picketed* the Metropolitan" because it was so unresponsive, recalled Hopps, who had been called in to assist the overwhelmed Geldzahler. "It was *very* important for this generation."[31]

But security and happiness still seemed to elude Barney. When Betty Hess Wolff, who adored him, noted that he flourished in "an atmosphere of complete approval," she did so with indulgent affection; "nobody was as needy" as he. Now, his desperate cravings had taken a toll. The summer had been "one of the most depressing" in the art world, Barney told Liberman, recounting the situation at the Corcoran, Harithas's treatment, and the repercussions for Liberman's intended show.[32] Appropriately, it seemed to rain every day. Hess lightly reported to Schapiro that "Barney Newman has a cold," but for months others couldn't help but notice his compromised health; through much of 1969, to many of those who spent time with him, Barney appeared to be sick with one thing or another.[33] It seems to have been around this time, in the fall, that he began the nearly entirely black *Yellow Edge* in the West End Avenue apartment, hidden behind the heavy, gray-purple curtain and unseen by anyone including Annalee. When, in September, he flew to Ottawa on the eve of Rosh Hashanah to speak at the opening of Flavin's retrospective at the National Gallery of Canada, his remarks were so brief, his breathing so labored, that listeners were concerned and—in spite of requests from Flavin and the curator, Brydon Smith—Barney refused to have the tape released. He developed ringworm, and was prescribed a powerful medication by a prominent dermatologist; among its side effects—dizziness, fatigue, possible confusion, insomnia—was an extreme sensitivity to alcohol.[34]

But he didn't slow down. Even as he complained to his lawyer that he had been ill, he persisted. At a marathon dinner that began at the Russian Tea Room, Barney regaled Barbara Reise, in New York from England and soliciting Barney's feedback on the draft of her magisterial "The Stance of Barnett Newman" scheduled for *Studio*

International in February. Around 4 a.m. at the King Cole Room in the St. Regis Hotel, where the conversation had continued, he suddenly stopped to ask if Reise knew the Hasidic concept of Heaven: "An endless banquet on the Leviathan with endless conversation." In that case, Reise responded, Barney was "a walking manifestation of Heaven on Earth."[35] Later she wrote to him that when revising the article she had to expend "a tremendous amount of psychic energy trying to control my own emotions towards my own growth through awareness of your presence from taking over the tone." She "did NOT want to . . . make you into a myth, an idol, a character-larger-than-life, a sun with me as satellite."[36]

By the time of the publication party for *Memoirs of a Revolutionist* in early December, he was badly sick with what he said was flu.

SIXTY-FIVE

"AT HOME"

Over all the years when he was interviewed, and in post-factum letters in which he described the 1940s and early '50s in order to establish who did what first, Barney would repeat the description of a "primitive cultural situation," when "each lived alone in our studios" and there was a particular kind of collegiality, which he often recalled with nostalgic affection. "When I was younger . . . you could only show the work to each other, that is . . . you'd invite an artist to visit you. You'd have a nice evening and then the psychological moment that the host would decide he'd invite you into his back room to show what he had done."[1]

The idea of the artist's sanctum sanctorum, the holy of holies that he entered to summon a spiritual experience as the ancient priests did on the temple mount, was perhaps the most sustaining metaphor for Barney's vocation. No one—with the possible exceptions of Annalee (who, after she retired, would try to spend the whole day in studio), and of his last assistant, Tom Crawford, who came to Barney in August 1969—ever saw him at work in any of his studios.

If one were mystically inclined, one could read a sort of karmic resolution in the appearance of Crawford, a young man on a spiritual quest, in Barney's life during his last year. Crawford was quiet, reserved, a man who had about him the vapor of a problematic past. And indeed he had a past, but it was of a sort whose arc completed the circle of one of Barney's early imagined, partially buried, narratives for himself: the *tzadik*—a saintly and wise spiritual leader—whom he felt his father to be, and that he aspired to be himself. The 26-year-old hippy and the 64-year-old gentlemanly artist formed a profound bond, almost like father and son, spiritually guru and disciple, "kindred spirits."[2]

Originally from Kentucky, by way of upstate New York, Crawford was involved with the Catholic Worker Movement; he actually *was* a conscientious objector during the Vietnam War, and, unlike Barney's safe posture during World War II, he actually lived the consequences—three years in jail. Crawford met Jack Hunte, who was working for Frank Stella, in the East Village community where he was living, and Hunte, a frame-maker, brought him to Barney. Crawford was "very spiritual," "very, very beautiful, and very soft-spoken." His monologues—often about Jesus, Anarchism, and the Knights Templar—could seem endless. He adored Barney. And for Barney he became a kind of touchstone, a connection to his inner *tzadik*, even as he was lunching in midtown at La Grenouille and Côte Basque among the petite shaded lamps, fine linens, murals of the French coast, and society swans.

Their conversations went "on and on and on and on and on." Crawford went to the studio every day, worked until around seven, and then they would "schmooze"— often until nine or ten. Through the summer and fall of 1969 they would frequently have dinner in the studio.[3]

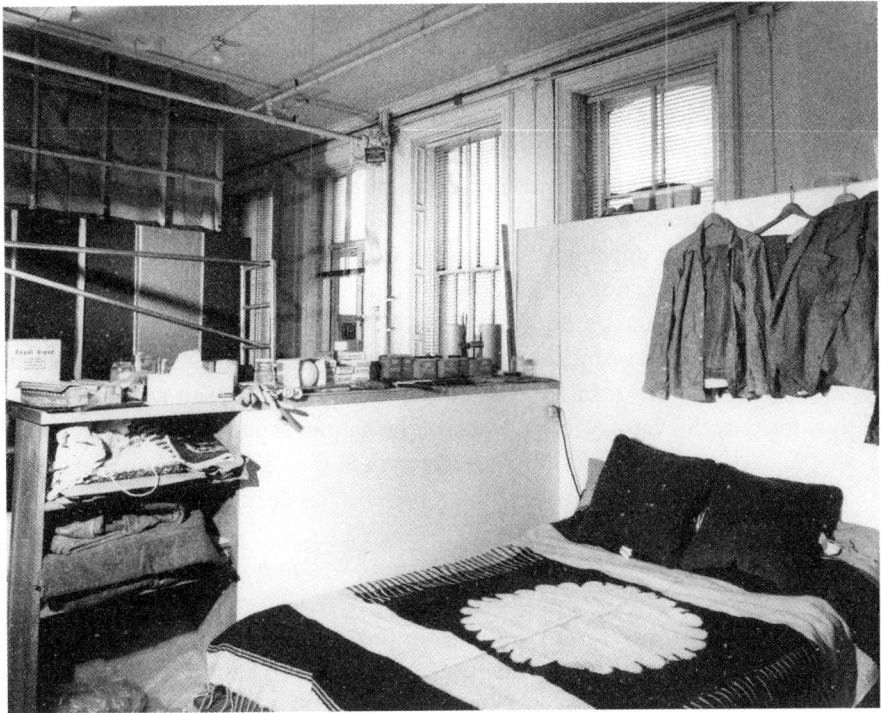

Fig. 58 The last studio, 35 White Street, 1970. Photograph Paulus Leeser

By January 1970 the studio began to serve more than ever as a refuge, more a daily routine than Barney's less regular bursts of work at Front Street or Fifty-Seventh Street. In the three floors he could spread out as never before. He went on buying splurges, purchasing prodigious amounts of paint from Bocour and specially ordered brushes—the size of house-painting brushes, but of exquisite quality—from Pearl Paint[4] and, with Crawford's assistance, prepared ambitious canvases, including a unique right triangle. Four works were completed in the first six months of the year, including a "second version" of *Be I*—the painting described by a critic in 1950 as looking like the side of a barn covered in a "rich, beautiful shade of unbroken red" that had been tragically damaged in 1958; three more were left unfinished. It was an explosion of painting unmatched since the early '50s. And there was room for something else he required. Barney had kept a cot in the Carnegie Hall studio, a geographically well-situated place to recharge while maintaining his frantic schedule. Now, on White Street, there was a fully dressed double bed on one floor, and a made-up cot on a second.

For over a decade, it was Barney who scrupulously maintained the Newmans' packed appointment diary and check-book entries; now, in January, they began to be written by Annalee, and there was intermittent commentary: "Barney did not feel well," he was "tired." Mixed in with the recurring lunches, usually at Côte Basque, with Hess and Fourcade to discuss the retrospective, with occasional concerts and evenings at the opera in Tom and Audrey Hess's box, with evenings of gallery visits and dinners with Newhouse, with regular trips to Cirker's storage facility where the deinstalled works from the Metropolitan Museum would go, were increasingly frequent visits to doctors, and—unusually for Barney—many, many days spent only between West End Avenue and White Street.

It had become much harder to keep up his public performance, although there were enough occasions when he did appear—a birthday party given by Stella Adler in his honor, Flavin's opening at the Jewish Museum and Stella's at MoMA—that observers might hardly notice a difference. But there *was* a difference. In the diary there were still diligent records of taxi rides—punctiliously noted for the IRS—but they were most often for Annalee going to the General Post Office at Thirty-Fourth Street or to banks, or to run errands for Barney. Barney himself was now more likely to travel by club car—even to Bocour—or his patrons' limousines, and more likely to shuttle back and forth to the studio than to dash west to east and up and down Manhattan. By late March there were many pages in the diary entirely empty except for the note "at home."

Home—the apartment on West End Avenue—was an odd, but not surprising, mix of no style.

One entered a gracious foyer where *Here I (To Marcia)* stood juxtaposed with the collection of entrancing crystals and geodes displayed in the most pedestrian little

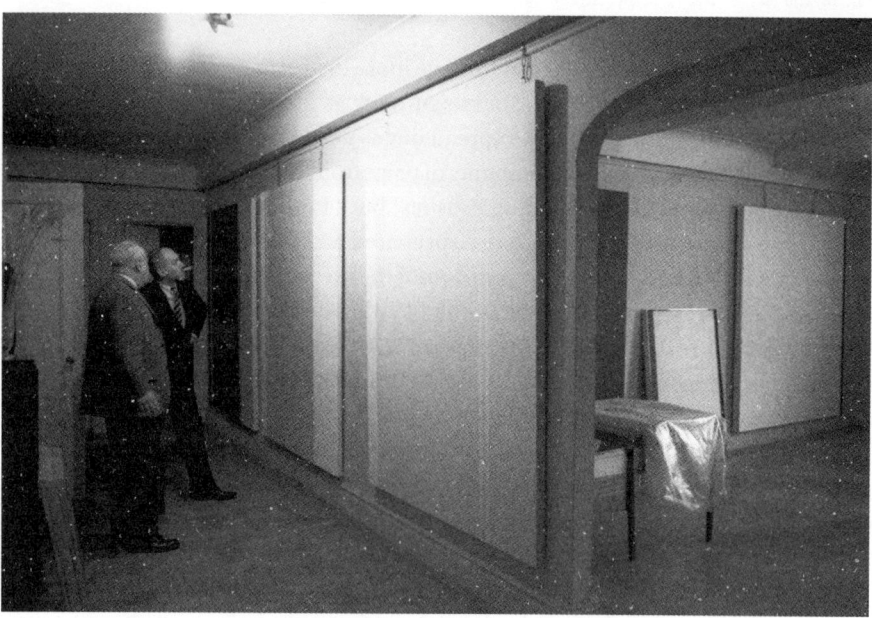

Fig. 59 Barnett Newman and Alan Solomon in the sparsely furnished apartment on West End Avenue, 1969. Hallway, from left: *Twelfth Station, Tenth Station, Ninth Station.* Through doorway: *Thirteenth Station, Right Here, Fourteenth Station.* Behind Newman is the bookcase in which his collection of geodes and crystals was displayed. Photograph Ugo Mulas

bookcase. A long and wide hallway provided a dream gallery space for Barney's
works, notwithstanding several door-
ways. Immediately off to the right as one
entered was the living room with a bank
of east-facing windows and a view of particularly beautiful ornamental brickwork
on the top floors of the building across
wide West End Avenue—a large-scale
dark and light elegantly proportioned
diamond grid. To the left was the kitchen
and what would have been a formal dining room, but which Barney had taken
over as an office. There were floor to ceiling crudely finished wood bookcases and a
simple table-desk with typical desk clutter:
papers, files, slides, slide viewers, ashtrays,
masking tape, and a few tchotchkes: glass
paperweights, an archaic pen holder, brass
candlesticks; and a cup of sharpened pen-
cils covered in Florentine marble paper
that matched the wastebasket. A ladder
leaned against the bookshelves. Earlier, the

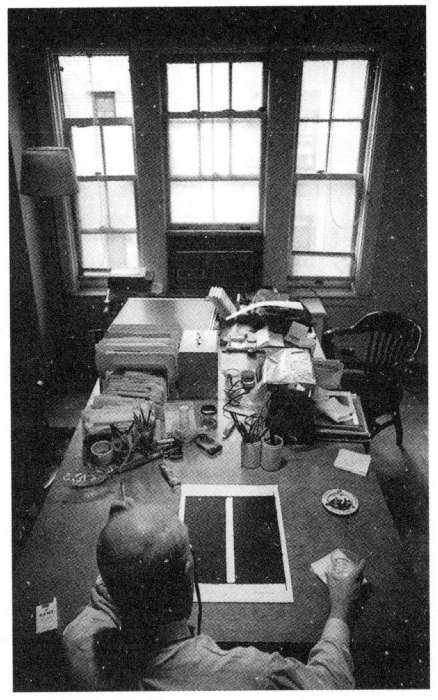

Fig. 60 Newman in his home office, 1969, with
Canto III. Photograph Ugo Mulas

grand piano had been in that space, but it had been moved into the front of the living
room. Farther down the hall were two bedrooms, one used for storage, and before the
doorway of the farther one Barney had hung the speed bag his doctor advised him to
punch for exercise.[5]

The living room had scattered anomalies: the French provincial drop-leaf side
table with a few blue and white porcelains and a Chinese lamp, was against a wall
and the larger 17th-century William and Mary gateleg table they bought from Ben
Ginsburg in 1939 was jammed into a corner, both pieces of furniture lovingly cared
for since they were in the Nineteenth Street apartment.

Other than these gestures to conventional, or refined, living, the apartment's
furnishings were sparse, austere. There were utilitarian shades on mostly curtainless
windows, a table and a few chairs, a Naugahyde sofa from an office furniture store,[6]
a couple of graceless standing lamps. "You didn't sit there and lounge around doing
nothing. You sat there with a straight back," in the "Bank of England" chairs and
discussed matters worth discussing, several visitors recalled.[7]

The point was the paintings. *Onement I, Pagan Void, The Word I, Two Edges.*
(The *Portrait of Elinor Graham* by John Graham that Barney bought in the 1940s
hung in one of the back rooms.) When Ugo Mulas photographed Barney at home
in 1965, the *Stations* were dramatically installed, but that was before they were
shown and stored.

Hester Diamond was appalled by "the state the apartment was in."[8] Large areas of ceiling paint were cracking and peeling off in great rolls. Bill Goldston came up to the apartment with Tanya Grosman to show Barney the most recent proofs of the *Notes* and was staggered: he had never seen anything like it and never forgot it. It didn't happen on farms in Oklahoma, where Goldston grew up, but it was not that unusual in early 20th-century New York apartments with their solid walls and thickly plastered interiors. Most occupants who had the funds would have scraped and repainted; but scraping and repainting would have created dust and disturbed the paintings, and they were the priority. Annalee was cautious to a fault. Barney and Grosman and Goldston sat at the chrome-and-formica kitchen table with a bottle of vodka and cigarettes.

There were those, like Barbara Rose, who found the discarded office furniture "quite a shock"; but understood the way in which Barney "loved the very well made oak office chairs"—as, just as devotedly, had Judd. It was the Newmans themselves who provided the class: Barney was "fixated on Annalee's wardrobe . . . so proud that she would have the best clothes—'Look at Annalee's legs, they're as good as Dietrich's,'" Rose recalled of her visits. Because *they* were "so elegant . . . when you went to this apartment, it had its own weird elegance."[9] The first time Alan Power was invited, he was struck by Barney "sort of standing there, shrugging his shoulders and with his monocle," strongly implying, if not saying out loud, "here we are standing alone. Standing alone and being proud to be what we are. There was a great sense of self-respect and pride in what we're doing, in what we're trying to achieve."[10]

As interior decorating philosophy, a long distance was traveled since Tony Smith advised Barney in 1941 that if he wanted to be a serious painter the first thing he had to do was "get rid of all this bourgeois Jewish furniture." Barney had gotten the message: "My work, and the work of the men I respect, took a revolutionary position against the bourgeois notion of what a painting is as an object aside from what it is as a statement," he told an interviewer in April. "Because, in the end, you couldn't even contain it in the ordinary bourgeois home."[11]

The bookcases were packed—overflowing—and Julie Finch specifically remembers how proud Barney was to tell her that he had only recently had enough money to acquire an elite sound system for their extraordinary collection of recordings. Many had been in his family since shellac 78s had been popularly available, and Barney had been haunting Sam Goody for years. They were in every format—78, 33 ⅓, HiFidelity, stereo, eight-track tape—and covered every genre: *John Barrymore reads Shakespeare*; *Hebrew Hymns, Jewish folk songs, Chassidic Melodies of the Three Festivals by the Rabbis of Modzitz, The Heritage Orchestra and Chorus's Jewish Holiday Album, The Seventh Day and Folk songs of the Shtetl by Cantor Mordecai Hershman* and *Prayers by the most renowned Cantor Koussevitzky*; *Sixty Years of Music America Loves Best* by Marian Anderson, Enrico Caruso, Horowitz, and Toscanini; *Great Voices of the Century*—Melba, Muzio, Caruso, John McCormack, Gigli, Chaliapin, Frida Leider. There were many-disk sets of the *World's Greatest Music*—Beethoven, Haydn, Brahms, and, of course, Mozart; the *Haydn Society Music for the Mature Listener*; Haydn operas and

Bach Brandenburg concertos; Burl Ives and Stravinsky and original cast albums of *Fiddler on the Roof*, and *Guys and Dolls* (in several formats) and *Hair*.

And, of course, there was jazz: Charlie Rich, Lionel Hampton, Thelonious Monk, Bill Evans, lots of Ornette Coleman, Ella Fitzgerald, Liza Minelli, The Rolling Stones, Charlie Parker, Stan Getz. His copy of *The 25-year Retrospective Concert of the Music of John Cage*, recorded in performance at Town Hall, New York, May 15, 1958, had been inscribed "for Barnett Newman—John Cage, after Emma Lake '65."

Off the master bedroom there was a little dressing room—about 9 by 5 ½ feet. This was Barney's private space, and he insisted on hanging a heavy, grayish purple wool curtain across it "so he could hide what he wanted to hide there." Annalee asked him, " 'who's going to come into your working room?' He had such a thing about secrecy and such a thing about privacy that he had that big curtain there."

"The point," Annalee remembered, was that "he didn't tell me things. And I never nagged him." It was where he kept *Yellow Edge* for himself alone, never showing it to anyone. "Perhaps he didn't like it," Annalee thought after he died, "but he didn't destroy, he didn't take it off the stretcher. He just let it hang."[12]

When Emile de Antonio came up to the apartment at the beginning of April to interview Barney for his landmark documentary *Painters Painting: New York Art Scene, 1940–1970*, he found Barney still a commanding presence. Sitting in one of the heavy oak chairs in front of a wall against which leaned the very early *Pagan Void* and *Untitled (The Break)*, Barney chain-smoked and drank whatever was the clear liquid on ice in his tall glass. But as beautiful as the tweed jacket was, the tailoring no longer fit his drooping shoulders and his sunken chest, and his breathing was irregular and distressed. It was obvious that he was physically uncomfortable.

Eight weeks earlier, Clyfford Still was featured in *Vogue*: "Those who resent Still most are frequently the very men he has influenced. Dates are bandied back and forth to prove 'who did what first,' " Katharine Kuh wrote, voicing the Still camp's response to the Motherwell imbroglio. "Whether Clyfford Still or John Doe turned out the earliest 'black painting' is of no great moment . . . . There are, indeed, very few Abstract-Expressionist painters from either the first or second generations of the movement who have not been swayed by him at one time or another."[13] Two weeks after the Still article appeared, in mid-February, Alan Solomon, 49 years old, died of a heart attack in his apartment on West End Avenue. And seven days after that, Mark Rothko, 66, committed suicide in his East Side studio. In the art community, both deaths were staggering, inconceivable blows. ("Very shocking but also very surprising. No one I have talked with had any indication," Barney telegraphed to Reise about Rothko.[14]) But then, both funerals were absorbed into Barney's routine. Solomon's was sandwiched between a visit to Liberman's studio and one to the Met. More compulsively, in the days bracketing Rothko's, for which "the art world turned out en masse,"[15] Barney went on a buying spree at Bocour and Pearl, lunched with Hess, Fourcade, and de Kooning, and attended a Whitney opening, a dinner and a party, and post-funeral tour of several gallery openings and dinner with John Coplans at Gloucester House. The next few weeks went similarly. Then, during the last week of March, the activity was mostly over.

"The defense of human dignity is the ultimate subject matter of art. And it is only in its defense that any of us will ever find strength," Barney wrote in 1946. That conviction characterized the way in which he lived for the next twenty-four years, and it continued to define his life now in the spring of 1970.

Barney rose to the occasion when de Antonio's small film crew arrived, as he had for Flavin's opening at the Jewish Museum in January, for Stella's opening at MoMA in March, and would for both Judd's opening at Castelli and Liberman's at the Corcoran later in April. De Antonio, the artist and cinematographer Ed Emshwiller, and the film's editor Mary Lampson, who was onsite recording the sound, found Barney remarkable—"intense, funny and caustic at the same time." The film was essentially in two parts: the first was weighted toward not simply an older generation of artists, but a generation who valued the goal of *authenticity*—however they applied it to themselves: Barney, de Kooning, Motherwell, Pavia. Greenberg spoke for Pollock. Interviews in the second part were with selected artists who in various ways reacted intellectually and aesthetically against what the older artists represented—among them Rauschenberg, Johns, Stella, Poons, Olitski. Even within this structure, *yet again*, Barney was at the center; his comments provided the gravitas, the moral core in the film. It was very clear to the crew that he was seriously ill—Lampson cut out the most extreme of Barney's labored breathing—and that he knew it;[16] there was the clear sense that he was talking about his legacy. If he did not say much that he hadn't said tens of times before, the few departures were heavy with intimations of both immortality and mortality.

"The beginning and the end are there at once." *That* was what he had achieved in his work, that was what his struggle had been toward.

"In the end, size doesn't count . . . . It's scale that counts. It's human scale that counts. And the only way you can achieve human scale is by the content."

Barney's portion was edited by Lampson to conclude with the artist saying those words; but the viewer was not seeing Barney smoking, drinking, fidgeting, gesturing with his extraordinarily beautiful hands. Instead, they were spoken over the camera as it panned elegiacally around "Newman's studio at his death." And then they were heard again, over an hour and more than ten interviews later, as the film drew to a close. In the end, it was human scale that counted, "and the only way you can achieve human scale is by the content."

Over the remainder of April Barney left the apartment less frequently—to see Isaiah Berlin speak at Hunter College, for a dinner for Henry Moore, to see his doctors and have x-rays taken. It could not have helped his health that there hadn't been heat in the White Street studio for many weeks—months, even. When he made the effort to go to

Washington for Liberman's Corcoran opening, which coincided with the fabulously social Corcoran Ball, he was so unwell he took his meals in the hotel room and only left for a brief visit to see the show. Back in New York his activities were mostly confined to dinners with good friends—like Rosenberg, the Diamonds, Newhouse, patrons who were in town, or Hess and Fourcade. In May, he accepted in person the Brandeis Creative Arts Award Medal for painting at an evening at the Whitney Museum, where he was extravagantly praised for the full measure of his life. "Eminent painter and sculptor of the abstract sublime; prophet, savant, ironist and warm human being; patriarch, raconteur and fearless adversary; intransigent creator whose heroic canvases split the rock of convention, opening to artists of the 1960s an empyrean of color and expansiveness; true avant-gardist whose stark and resplendent paintings are among the unadulterated joys of American life."[17] The words were nearly a perfect and parallel undoing of Reinhardt's 1954 "artist-professor and traveling-design-salesman, the Art-Digest-philosopher-poet and Bauhaus-exerciser, the avant-garde-huckster-handicraftsman and educational-shop-keeper, the holy-roller-explainer-entertainer-in-residence."

He made decisions about the placement of *Broken Obelisk* in Houston with Philip Johnson and the de Menils, about the Spring Street property with Murray and Mackenzie. He became so ill, his doctor made an extraordinary Saturday housecall.[18]

For a short time he rallied. He took over the diary log on the day he met at Stella's studio on Jones Street with members of the New York Artists Strike Against Racism, Sexism, Repression and War, which was formed—as was a nationwide strike by students—in response to the killing by National Guard troops of war protesters at Kent State University earlier in the month.[19] The same day he appeared—one of only eleven of 1500 signatories to show up in person—at an American Jewish Conference on Soviet Jewry press conference to protest the "rising tide of Soviet anti-Semitism." There was a flurry of lunches and dinners; club cars to the accountant and lawyer and doctor; there was a drive with Jasper Johns up to Philip Johnson's house in Connecticut. And for a couple of weeks, he was back in the studio.

There, S. I. Newhouse saw *Red, Yellow and Blue IV*—one of Barney's last works—just after it had been finished. "There was something that he didn't like in the red side," and he showed Newhouse how he covered that with successive layers of red paint.[20]

Robert Whitman, the cutting-edge multi-media theater artist, had a similar experience. Whitman, who owned the building at 35 White Street and lived with his family on the fourth and fifth floors, had developed a friendly routine with the older man. When Barney, sitting in his studio—always with a vodka in his hand (Whitman, like most people, assumed that after the first drink Annalee made sure the proportion of water went up and Barney collaborated in the ruse)—heard the elevator land, he would call out to Whitman. "What do you think of that red?" he asked, pointing to one of the small canvases on which Barney experimented. "I couldn't get my usual red, they didn't have it."[21] It was a social maneuver, but it was more: what impressed Whitman was that "notwithstanding the writing and the theories," Barney "was really an artist and painted. He was a *painter*." That, and one very important piece of advice that Whitman never forgot: "You just gotta outlive the bastards," Barney would repeat.

In the early summer, Richard Meier "bumped into Barney by accident" on the corner of Fifty-Ninth Street and Lexington Avenue, near Meier's office and Barney's doctor. "We spent two hours standing there talking about everything that we'd shared together." Barney appeared to have no place he had to be, and he assumed Meier didn't either. "We didn't even go into a coffee shop and sit down. We just stood on the corner talking." To Meier "it was amazing. It was amazing."[22]

Days before he died, Barney had lunch at the Gloucester House with Newhouse, whose help he solicited regarding "housing problems"—possibly referring to the stalled plans for Spring Street, or possibly to the miserable plumbing on White.[23] Around this time, Heller was eagerly pursuing an early "big white painting"—likely *The Name II*—and Barney was avoiding his entreaties.[24] Now, Newhouse was desperate to buy *Cathedra*. In March he told Barney that it was "one of a few absolute masterpieces of contemporary painting" and he "fell so profoundly in love" when he first saw it the previous year: "I'm certain that nothing ever in my life with art will be as meaningful and important as the opportunity to spend the rest of that life in the company of Cathedra."[25] But Barney was evasive: "he either had or would sell it to Edy DeWilde, and it was [possibly] at the Stedelijk. So that was out. He didn't tell me [exactly]. He just said that it wasn't for sale."

"That was my last sight of Barney, at the Gloucester House, and afterwards we parted, and I remember waving to him." The Gloucester House was very expensive, and, Newhouse recalled, "everyone was down on it because it was so expensive," but it was where Barney wanted to go, and Newhouse took him, only to be disappointed. "I remember the Gloucester House very well, and that incident with Barney because I couldn't get the painting that I wanted, and also because it was the last time I saw him. It was very meaningful.[26]

By mid-June it was Annalee who was keeping the diary again, and Annalee covering most of the bases. Together they made a visit to the Spring Street property with Meier. They went to an evening auction of antique Judaica and ritual objects and successfully bid on several small items, including a *yad*—a torah pointer—and fanciful silver spice boxes. After a Sunday evening dinner in Greenwich with the Hesses, a Monday at the studio, and dinner at Billy's with Rosenberg, Barney was so ill on Tuesday that he was coughing up blood—he hoped the source was a vocal-cord node similar to the one that had been removed in 1955[27]—and his doctor again was summoned to the apartment. Nevertheless, that night, June 30, Barney went to the opening of the Museum of Modern Art's "Information" show. In the last photograph ever taken of him, standing next to Murray, his hand assumes its reflexive position, fingers curled at monocle level in front of his torso, but strikingly it is holding neither a glass nor a cigarette.

"I think I'm in trouble," he told Annalee, as they were watching television after a simple dinner of chopped steak, tomato juice, tea with honey, and biscuits. It was

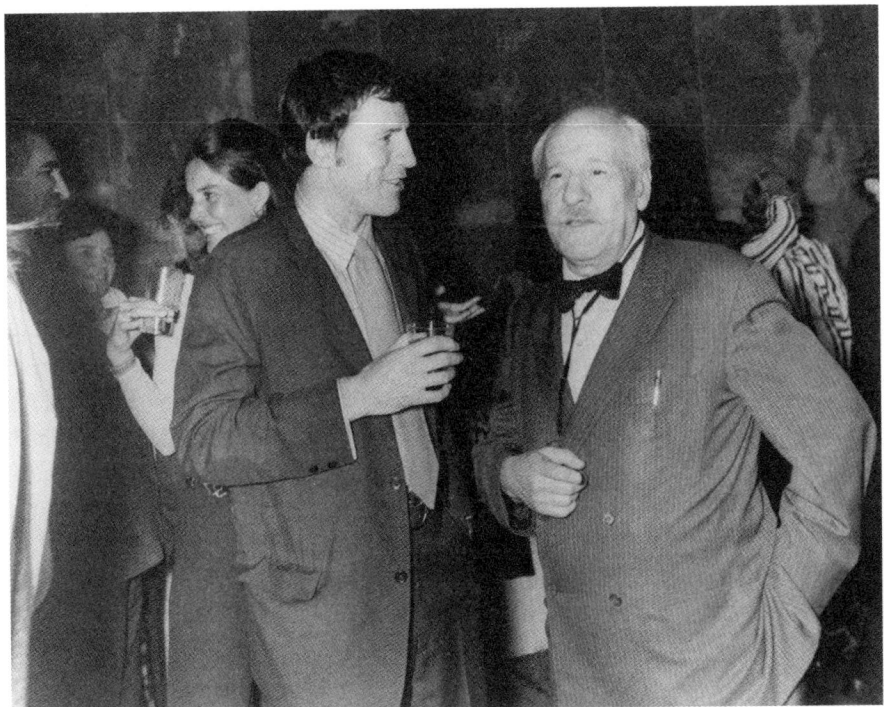

Fig. 61 The Museum of Modern Art opening party for "Information," June 30, 1970. From left: Harold and May Rosenberg, Nancy Sage, Robert Murray, Barnett Newman, a few days before his death. Photograph Manny Greenhaus Ananda Foundation N.V.

Friday night, July 3, the start of the July Fourth weekend, and they were due at the Diamonds' house on Long Island on Saturday. Then Barney lost his balance and fell to the floor. Annalee got him into bed; Dr. Feltman arranged an ambulance and a place at St. Luke's Hospital a mile directly north. In the I.C.U. Barney was in pain, but stabilized and conscious after a massive heart attack. "It was a very severe attack, wasn't it?" he asked Annalee as she said good-bye at the doctor's insistence, and then he was given morphine to enable him to sleep. Feltman drove Annalee home and returned to his patient. An hour later he called to report that Barney had died.

Three days later, as previously scheduled, *Broken Obelisk* was removed from the grounds of the Metropolitan Museum, where it had been installed for "New York Painting and Sculpture."

For a few months after Barney's death, Crawford helped Annalee clean out the studio, but he never took another regular job. He went to Japan to study aikido, "the way of harmonious spirit." The last that any of his family knew of him came from newspaper reports in 2002 when he surfaced in an unusual way. Whereas Barney had spent a day or two walking around Walden, and an afternoon with Native American earthworks in Ohio, and while Judd—during the period when Barney knew him— spent summer weeks camping in the desert with his family, Crawford for eleven years resided in a cave in the Coconino National Forest near Flagstaff, Arizona—"a philosophical choice," the local *Arizona Daily Sun* wrote.[28] When he was arrested for living on public property, he impressed a reporter by imitating perfectly the distinctive cascade of the canyon wren's call, and walked away with three books, including *Practical Taoism.* The studio on White Street had been a random detour for him; he always knew he would end up living as Native Americans historically had, likely in mountains, with no trappings of contemporary life. "Once Barnett died, all of his connections to everything just went."[29]

Barney insisted on living connected to everything. "To see the *facts* of his life properly respected so that the painter stands as a separate self without being isolated, so that he can be seen for what he is and not submerged under the jargon of fake movements, schools and styles"—*that* was the way Barney wanted to be recorded by history, "full in the presentation" of the man.[30]

Without doubt, he was, gloriously, "eminent painter and sculptor of the abstract sublime; prophet, savant, ironist and warm human being; patriarch, raconteur and fearless adversary; intransigent creator whose heroic canvases split the rock of convention, opening to artists of the 1960s an empyrean of color and expansiveness; true avant-gardist whose stark and resplendent paintings are among the unadulterated joys of American life."

But also, uncomfortably, he was righteous dispenser of harsh judgments; wily and condescending self-promoter; pompous provoker of rental and insurance agents; a manipulator of facts and a pitbull about grudges; needy and too susceptible to flattery.

Barnett Newman was an active conspirator in the creation of his own mythology—"Barney"—but he also stubbornly preserved every single particle of evidence that would debunk or undermine the inevitability of that mythology—and, not incidentally, substantiate demeaning fixations. It was only honorable, and honest: "full in the presentation."

He knew this book would be written.

One would like to imagine that as Crawford mimicked the song of the wren, he was reminded of Barney's eccentric theory categorizing birds, from most primitive to most advanced, according to the complexity of their calls. And that it was in all of Barney's complexity—not only artist, justice- and enlightenment- and truth-seeker, but also writer, civil servant, anarchist, agitator, theorist, ornithologist, philosophist, theologist, New York-ologist, son, brother, husband, and *friend*—that Barney would outlive the "bastards," whoever he thought the "bastards" were.

ACKNOWLEDGMENTS

Barnett Newman: Here is a portrait of Barnett Newman and a portrait of the vanished New York that made him; it embeds the artist in his world by following his lead—the evidence he left of how he reacted to contemporaneous events. All that flowed into Newman runs through the book and reminds readers that whatever "universal" attributes art may be thought to have, it is made in a specific time and place.

The Barnett Newman Foundation, which invited me to write this first biography of Newman (no relation to me), gave me full access to the archives collected by the artist and his wife, Annalee, and the rights to use the material, but the biography is not "authorized" in the sense that the Foundation drove the content. From beginning to end, I am responsible for the text.

For the opportunity to write this book, I thank the late Frank Stella and the late John O'Neill. I particularly thank Philip Leider for recommending me.

For brilliantly facilitating the journey, I thank John Silberman.

For gracious and reliable problem solving, Paula Pelosi and Donn Zaretsky.

For his friendship with Barney and his enormous generosity and wit in sharing his memories with me, Rob Murray.

For the astonishing and meticulously maintained archives of Newman's life and world, for expertise and consultation, support at every moment, advice, insight, and friendship I thank Heidi Colsman-Freyberger, and the staff over the years at The Barnett Newman Foundation: Monica Crozier, Marina Kastan, Dana Kautto, Shawn Roggenkamp, and the late Brigid Herold.

In the years since this book was begun, art history and the way people think about it in all manifestations has been interrogated, de-centered, re-centered, complicated, and problemitized. But artists can only make work in the culture and society in which they live, and a biographer can responsibly do nothing to alter her subject's perceptions, or the facts and circumstances of his experience. To recreate Newman's world, I was significantly helped by my own interviews with over ninety individuals who generously made their time and memories available and whose names and citations appear in the text, and by earlier interviews and estate archives held at the Archives of American Art, Smithsonian Institution in both New York and Washington, D.C.; the Getty Research Institute Research Library; the Columbia University Libraries Rare Book & Manuscript Library; the Courtauld Libraries; the Whitechapel Gallery; the Tate Library and Archive; the Museum of Modern Art Museum Archives; the Solomon R. Guggenheim Archives; the Jewish Museum; the Menil Collection Menil Archives; the Stedelijk Museum Offsite Storage Depot; the Art Students League; the New School Library; the Morgan Library & Museum; the City College of the City University of New York; the National Archives and Records Administration; and the New York City Municipal Library. I thank the librarians, archivists, and staff in those institutions for their patience and assistance. Special thanks to the Philadelphia

Museum of Art's archives and the records of Ann Temkin and Melissa Ho; their work for a Barnett Newman retrospective in 2002 was invaluable for me.

I am grateful to Anna Reinhardt of the Ad Reinhardt Foundation, who personally spent hours with me to navigate a very tangled thicket and provided especially generous access; to the late Nancy Litwin at the Adolph Gottlieb Foundation; Charles Duncan at the Richard Pousette-Dart Foundation; to Richard Shiff; Yve-Alain Bois; Ealan Wingate; Gary Schwartz; Elizabeth Goren; and the late Nan Rosenthal. And to Dodie Kazanjian, whose interviews are a remarkable resource.

The Newman family provided important genealogical information and memories. Of Barney's relatives, the late Nathan Libby, Susan Siegel, Daniel Newman, Dave and Betty Pollock, Reeva Kimble, and of Annalee's relatives, Terry Goldfarb, the late Joseph Hochstein, and Deborah Strober were particularly helpful and a pleasure to meet.

For exceptional insight into Newman's process, I thank Carol Mancusi-Ungaro; for research and assistance, I thank the extraordinary Lucy Hunter; Allyson Mehley, and Dan Friedman; for translations, Chana Pollack, Myra Mniewski, and Bakhyt Kenjeev; for the tools to manage overwhelming numbers of facts, Rita Walton; for design advice, Tina Davis.

Friends read the manuscript and provided valuable feedback. I am especially grateful to Elizabeth Baker, Louise Yelin, Charles Stuckey, and Larry Kirshbaum, and the late Walter Robinson for our conversations. The late Irving Sandler, for his ethic, historical perspective, enthusiasm, and encouragement, has been my lodestar.

Michelle Komie, Annie Miller, and Terri O'Prey at Princeton University Press have been unfailingly supportive, enthusiastic and good-humored shepherding this book to its final form; an author could ask for no more. Thank you to Elizabeth Trammell, and to Amanda Moon and Thomas LeBien for help with the text.

Finally, I have boundless gratitude for all the acquaintances and friends, and especially my Barney-beleaguered family, Bud Shulman, Sam Shulman, and Hannah Paul, who listened to stories and invocations for over fifteen years.

NOTES

ABBREVIATIONS

AAA	Archives of American Art, Smithsonian Institution	MR	Mark Rothko
		MS	Meyer Schapiro
AHB and AB	Alfred H. Barr, Jr.	RM	Robert Murray
AN	Annalee Newman	RM1	Robert Murray, personal interview, December 18, 2007
AO	Alphonso Ossorio		
B + A	Barnett and Annalee	RM2	Robert Murray, personal interview, September 8, 2008
BBN or BN	Barnett Newman		
BH	Ben Heller	RM3	Robert Murray, personal interview, December 12, 2008
BHF	B. H. Friedman		
BNFA	Barnett Newman Foundation Archives	SH	Sam Hunter
		SN	Sarah Newman
BP	Betty Parsons	SWI	Barnett Newman: *Selected Writings and Interviews*, ed. John O'Neill, New York: Knopf, 1990
CG	Clement Greenberg		
CR	Catalogue Raisonné		
CS	Clyfford Still		
DM	Dorothy Miller	TBH	Thomas B. Hess
E P-D	Evelyn Pousette-Dart	TH	Thomas Hess
HC	Holger Cahill	TBH1	Thomas B. Hess, *Barnett Newman*, New York: Walker and Co., 1969
HF	Herbert Ferber		
HR	Harold Rosenberg	TBH2	Thomas B. Hess, *Barnett Newman*, New York: The Museum of Modern Art, 1971
IS	Irving Sandler		
KO	Karlis Osis	TS	Tony Smith
		WB	William Baziotes

INTRODUCTION. "BARNEY"

1 David Sylvester, *About Modern Art*, 2nd ed., New Haven: Yale, 2001.

2 BN, unpublished 1952 review of TBH's *Abstract Painting*.

3 William Rubin, untranscribed interview with Dodie Kazanjian, Dodie Kazanjian papers, 1949–2017, bulk 1980–2017, AAA.

4 TBH, "Sketch for the Portrait of the Art Historian among Artists," *Social Research Quarterly* 45.1 (1978).

5 BN, "Football and Shakespeare," *The Answer* (Jan. 1936).

6 BN, "Response to the Reverend Thomas F. Mathews," *Revolution, Place and Symbol (Journal of the First Congress on Religion, Architecture, and the Visual Arts)*, 1969, repr. in SWI.

ONE. A GUY WHO CUTS CLASSES

1 AN, interview by John O'Neill, 1994.

2 "To Open De Witt Clinton High School Bids," *NYT* (May 10, 1903).

3 Annalee said he went to the 10th Avenue building after his freshman year. Hess has Barney at the "88th St Annex" (there was an 88th Street entrance to the 87th Street school) throughout high school. Barney might have "placed" himself there, in proximity to the Metropolitan Museum, to create a more providential story and retroactively justify his truancy.

4 TBH1.

5 Douglas Davis, notes for interview of BN, 1969.

6 BN, "In Front of the Real Thing," *Art News* 68.9 (Jan. 1970).

7 AN, interview, 1994.

8 AN, interview, 1994.

9 Registrar's records from the Art Students League; AN, interview, 1994.

10 AN, interview, 1994.

11 Nathan Libby to author, interview, July 12, 2007.

12 "Piano Workers May Strike," *NYT* (Aug. 29, 1919).

13 TH papers, 1939–1978, AAA.

14 AN, interview, 1994.

15 Libby to author, 2007.

16 Aurora Dias-Jorgensen to author, interview, July 26, 2007.

17 Howard W. Nudd, *The Official Wirt Reports to the Board of Education of New York City*, New York: Public Education Association of the City of New York, June 1916, Municipal Archives, NYC.

18 For most of this discussion of the Gary Plan, I am indebted to Raymond A. Mohl, "Schools, Politics, and Riots: The Gary Plan in New York City, 1914–1917," *Paedagogica Historica: International Journal of the History of Education* 15.1 (1975).

19 Mohl, "Schools, Politics, and Riots."

20 "Class Schedule—FROEBEL SCHOOL—1913–14," n.d., Municipal Archives, NYC.

21 *Plain Facts About the Gary Plan*, New York: Committee on Public Education, 1917, Municipal Archives, NYC.

22 "Supplementary Report, Bronx Schools," n.d., Municipal Archives, NYC; Document, n.d., Municipal Archives, NYC.

23 *Plain Facts About the Gary Plan*.

24 In its original incarnation, the plan allocated time during the day for students to have religious instruction. This incensed at least one prominent rabbi: "I am opposed because it would inevitably tend to divide our children into groups according to their religious affiliations . . . . Can you not see the unfortunate result that would ensue from the process of segregation according to creedal beliefs? I am opposed because I see in it a vehicle that might be utilized for purposes of proselytism." "Rabbi Opposes Gary Plan," *NYT* (Nov. 7, 1915).

25 Mohl, "Schools, Politics, and Riots."

26 "Teachers Examined as to Their Loyalty" and "Remove 9 Teachers from High School," *NYT* (Nov. 12 and 15, 1917).

27 For example, Henry Fairfield Osborn, Madison Grant, Maxwell Perkins, and Robert M. Yerkes.

28 AN, interview, 1994.

29 In the mid-1950s, when Barney was battling eviction from his home of 14 years, both his family's first Manhattan residence and their Bronx residence would be obliterated, the former by the construction of the East River Houses and the latter by the Cross Bronx Expressway. Barney felt his story was haunted by the ghosts of urban renewal, and particularly, Robert Moses.

30 United States Census Bureau, 1920 Census.

31 Libby to author, 2007.

32 Frances Geller Rothstein, interviews with her niece, Laura Strauss, conducted on behalf of the author, Feb. 2007.

33 "White Plains Road Business Improvement District: History," White Plains Road Business Improvement District Home Page, https://pelhamparkway.com/history.

34 The foresighted zoners of the Bronx had dedicated an extraordinary 17 percent of the land to public parks.

35 Wall text, "From The New Yorker to Shrek: The Art of William Steig," The Jewish Museum, New York City.

36 Chicken fat and cracklings.

37 Libby to author, 2007.

38 Geller Rothstein to author, interview, 2007.

39 *Jewish Communal Register: Part 1*, New York: Kehillah, Jewish Community of NYC, 1917–18.

40 "Abraham Newman," *NYT* (July 1, 1947).

41 Irving Howe and Kenneth Libo, *World of Our Fathers*, 30th anniversary ed., New York: New York UP, 2005, 16.

42 Jacob Ibn Chabib, *En Jacob: Agada of the Babylonian Talmud*, rev. and trans. S. H. Glick, New York: S. H. Glick, c.1916–21.

43 Chabib, *En Jacob: Agada of the Babylonian Talmud*.

44 Shmuel Ettinger and Marcus Pyka, "Graetz, Heinrich," vol. 8, in *Encyclopaedia Judaica*, ed. Michael Berenbaum and Fred Skolnik, 2nd ed, Detroit: Macmillan Reference USA, 2007, 26–29.

45 H. Graetz, *Popular History of the Jews*, trans. A. B. Rhine, ed. Alexander Harkavy, published with supplementary volume of recent events by Max Raisin, 3rd ed, New York: Hebrew, 1926.

46 For this discussion of these texts, I am indebted to Anne-Marie Belinfante, specialist in the Dorot Jewish Division of the New York Public Library, for her help.

47 Daniel Friedman to author, interviews, Sept. 2009.

48 *Students' Hebrew and Chaldee Dictionary to the Old Testament*, published with supplement, "Neo-Hebrew Vocabulary," comp. Alexander Harkavy, New York: Hebrew Publishing Co., 1914.

49 The essay invokes recent research into ancient civilizations, and cites the important German historian of antiquity, Eduard Meyer (d. 1930), who in his 1896 *The Origin of Judaism* had "already proven the great ideological similarities between the fables of Genesis concerning the Garden of Eden and the Greek tradition of 'A Golden Age.'"

50 *Jewish Communal Register*.

51 A schoolbook, 1919, with sketches on its endpapers signed by Barney in Hebrew, is likely the one that Annalee recalled as indicating that the 15-year-old regarded himself as an artist.

52 Myra Mniewski to author, letter, Dec. 1, 2009.

53 Isidor Margolis, *Jewish Teacher Training Schools in the United States*, New York: National Council for Torah Education of Mizrahi-Hapoel Hamizrachi, 1964.

54 *Jewish Communal Register*, 174.

55 *Tanakh, The Holy Scriptures*, 3rd ed, Jerusalem, Philadelphia: Jewish Publication Society, 1985.

56 *Tanakh, The Holy Scriptures*.

57 W. M. McCormick Blair, "Rules and Suggestions for the Contest," Washington, D.C.: Committee on Public Information, 1918.

58 Jimmy Breslin, *Damon Runyon*, New York: Dell, 1991.

TWO. BEGINNING

1 According to his birth certificate from Russia. The United States Immigration and Naturalization Service has his birthday as October 18, 1873, which is what he wrote on the ship's manifest as he came into Ellis Island, and his obituary has him as 75 in 1947. Another child, Bejla (d. 1875) was born in 1873, and there may have been a practical purpose served, in Lomza, by Abraham assuming the later birth date.

2 BN to SH, Apr. 17, 1956.

3 Reeva Kimble to author, interviews, 2011.

4 "Lomza," *Pinkas HaKehillot: Polin*, ed. Danuta Dombrovska, Abraham Wein, and Aharon Vais, 7 vols., Jerusalem: Yad Vashem, 1976–99.

5 Irving Howe and Kenneth Libo, *World of Our Fathers*, 30th anniversary ed., New York: New York UP, 2005, 6.

6 "Lomza," *Pinkas HaKehillot: Polin*.

7 Or younger. David Vital, *A People Apart: The Jews in Europe 1789–1939*, Oxford: Oxford UP, 1999, 160.

8 TBH2, 21.

9 It's hard to keep the story of Abraham, as related by Barney to Hess, and by Annalee in 1996, from unraveling. Barney told Hess that Abraham went to live with his uncle after his mother died in 1884, and then he went into the Army. Annalee places Abraham with his "uncle who was a famous rabbi" after he got out of the Army, not after his mother died. Sarah Newman's FBI file, which references Abraham, does not mention Russian Army service. It would not have been typical for a young man of Abraham's circumstances to be involuntarily conscripted. I. J. Singer, in *The Brothers Ashkenazi*, vividly describes the fears of and measures taken by Jewish families at this time: scholarly youths "maimed themselves, fasted, drank salt water, and ate lots of herring in order to ruin their health and fail the physical examination"; bribes and ransoms were arranged. "The only ones to be conscripted were the working-class youths." I. J. Singer, *The Brothers Ashkenazi*, trans. Joseph Singer, New York: Penguin 1993.

10 Howe, *World of Our Fathers*, 6–7.

11 Yohanan Petrovsky-Shtern, *Jews in the Russian Army, 1827–1917: Drafted into Modernity*, New York: Cambridge UP, 2009, 167.

12 Petrovsky-Shtern, *Jews in the Russian Army*, 175.

13 AN, interview by John O'Neill, 1994.

14 Aurora Dias-Jorgensen to author, interview, July 26, 2007.

15 Karl Marx, *The Eighteenth Brumaire of Louis Bonaparte*.

16 TH papers, 1939–1978, AAA.

17 Petrovsky-Shtern, *Jews in the Russian Army*, 177.

18 TBH1, 7.

19 Office for Metropolitan History, New York.

20 Richard Plunz, *A History of Housing in New York City: Dwelling Type and Social Change in the American Metropolis*, New York: Columbia UP, 1990, 47.

21 "Making Corlears Hook a Park," *NYT* (May 4, 1895).

22 AN, interview, 1994.

23 Hilary Ballon and Kenneth T. Jackson, eds., *Robert*

Moses and the Modern City, New York: W. W. Norton & Co., 2007. 187.

24 Harry Roskolenko, *When I Was Last on Cherry Street*, New York: Stein and Day, 1965, 2–3.

25 Howe, *World of Our Fathers*, 142.

26 Abraham Cahan, *The Education of Abraham Cahan*, ed. Leon Stein, Philadelphia: Jewish Publication Society of America, 1969, cited in Howe, *World of Our Fathers*, 219–20.

27 Howe, *World of Our Fathers*, 257.

28 Harry Roskolenko, *The Time That Was Then: The Lower East Side, 1900–14*, New York: Dial Press, 1971, 28.

29 Roskolenko, *The Time That Was Then*, 198.

30 Roskolenko, *When I Was Last on Cherry Street*, 2–3.

31 Roskolenko, *When I Was Last on Cherry Street*, 3–4.

32 Oral history interview with Aaron Siskind, Sept. 28–Oct. 2, 1982, AAA.

33 "Three Boys Drown in a Battery Slip," *NYT* (May 25, 1910).

34 David Ely Pollack, unpublished autobiography, 2006.

35 Roskolenko, *The Time That Was Then*, 67.

36 Roskolenko, *The Time That Was Then*, 48.

37 "Exploding Cauldron Kills Its Operator," *NYT* (May 11, 1909).

38 "Infant Death List Cut 50 Per Cent," *NYT* (July 25, 1909).

39 United States Census Bureau, 1910 Census.

40 "East Side Hospital Appeals for Help," *NYT* (Mar. 19, 1911).

41 Howe, *World of Our Fathers*, 149.

42 Howe, *World of Our Fathers*, 130.

43 "Big Cloak Strike Brings Out 50,000," *NYT* (July 8, 1910).

44 Jacob Riis, *How the Other Half Lives*, New York: Hill and Wang, 1957, 88–89.

45 Howe, *World of Our Fathers*, 139.

46 AN, interview, 1994.

47 1910 Census.

THREE. THE MOST INTENSE EXPERIENCES

1 New York City Business Directories; New York City Directories.

2 Irving Howe and Kenneth Libo, *World of Our Fathers*, 30th anniversary ed., New York: New York UP, 2005, 143.

3 Daniel Newman to author, interview, Mar. 10, 2009; David Pollack to author, interview, Apr. 29, 2011.

4 Howe, *World of Our Fathers*, 334–5.

5 Newman, interview, 2009; Nathan Libby to author, interview, July 12, 2007.

6 Pollack to author, 2011.

7 James Traub, *City on a Hill: Testing the American Dream at City College*, Reading, MA: Addison-Wesley Publishers, 1994, 25–8.

8 AN, interview by John O'Neill, 1994.

9 AN, interview, 1994. Barney is not in any De Witt Clinton yearbooks; on his official record at the school, "date of graduation from this high school" is blank, but there is a "DIPLOMA" stamp.

10 Originally "Adolf"; Gottlieb changed the spelling in 1933 in reaction to Hitler's election as Chancellor.

11 Barbara Reise, notes after interviewing BN, Jan. 21, 1964, Tate Archives; Adam Alexander to author, interview, Aug. 20, 2009 (Borodulin changed his name to I. J. Alexander in the late 1930s). In 1969 Barney told Hess they met at the Art Students League.

12 Will Barnet to author, interview, May 14, 2009.

13 Barnet to author, 2009.

14 Adolph Gottlieb, interview with Martin Friedman, Aug. 1962. From the archives at the Adolph and Esther Gottlieb Foundation, New York.

15 Allen Tucker, *Design and the Idea*, New York: The Arts Publishing Corp., 1930, 16; cited in *Eugene Ludens: An American Fantasist*, exhibition catalogue, ed. Susana Torruella Leval, New Paltz: SUNY/Samuel Dorsky Museum of Art, 2012.

16 Barnet to author, 2009.

17 Bob Kane to author, interview, Apr. 2, 2009.

18 The Kelekian sale took place while Barney was still in high school and Gottlieb was in Europe. In Hess's telling,

it appears that they went together, with "a whole crowd of his friends."

19 John Jones interviews with artists, Oct. 5–Nov. 12, 1965, AAA.

20 Alexander to author, 2009.

21 Alexander to author, 2009.

22 Alexander to author, 2009.

23 Abraham Cahan, *The Rise of David Levinsky: A Novel*, New York: Harper & Bros., 1917, cited in Traub, *City on a Hill*, 31.

24 Traub, *City on a Hill*, 31.

25 AN, interview, 1994.

26 BN, interview with KO, unpublished, Aug. 2, 1963.

27 Reise, notes, 1964; BN, interview with KO, 1963.

28 RM3. Newman referred to composing this symphony at Pratt Institute in 1961.

29 BN, interview with KO, 1963.

30 Reise, notes, 1964.

31 A. Rupp, letter to BBN, June 20, 1924; transcript for "Newman, B. Barnett," n.d., The College of the City of New York.

FOUR. "THE FOX KNOWS MANY THINGS"

1 TBH1, 14.

2 Edward Silverstein, letter to Barnett Newman, the Board of Examiners, Board of Education, New York, 1928.

3 Playing "musical apartments" was a common practice during these years. Most leases terminated at the same time, causing many apartments to become available; tenants were able to negotiate concessions of a couple of months of free rent, a refrigerator, or a paint job. Robert Murray recalls complaining to Barney that his landlord wouldn't paint his apartment. "What you do," Barney told him, "is move because [according to New York housing laws] then they owe you a paint job. In the early days in New York, we'd line up a mover, and as soon as we could get a mover scheduled, we'd start looking for apartments." Barney continued to try to use this strategy over the next three decades in all his real-estate dealings.

4 "Business Records," *NYT* (Sept. 9, 1931).

5 AN interviewed by Dodie Kazanjian, 1991, unpublished transcript.

6 Oral history interview with Aaron Siskind, Sept. 28–Oct. 2, 1982, AAA.

7 Adolph Gottlieb, interview with Martin Friedman, Aug. 1962. From the archives at the Adolph and Esther Gottlieb Foundation, New York.

8 William and Ethel Baziotes papers, c.1900–1992, bulk 1935–1980, AAA.

9 Avis Berman, *Rebels on Eighth Street: Juliana Force and the Whitney Museum of American Art*, New York: Atheneum, 1990, 335, 340, cited in Lindsay Pollock, *The Girl with the Gallery*, New York: Public Affairs, 2006, 187.

10 U.S., FBI, Sarah Newman, Name Check, Bureau File 123–5493, Dec. 3, 1950. Obtained under the Freedom of Information Act.

11 U.S., FBI, Sarah Newman; SN, letter to BBN, July 21, 1936.

12 Borodulin, recalling these years, always saw Gottlieb painting, but did not think of Barney as an artist. When Borodulin later had a falling out with both, it was about abstract art, which he abjured.

32 Howe, *World of Our Fathers*, 284.

33 Meyer Liben, "CCNY—A Memoir," *Commentary* (Sept. 1965), 65, cited in Howe, *World of Our Fathers*, 285.

34 Howe, *World of Our Fathers*, 282.

35 Howe, *World of Our Fathers*, 283-6.

36 BN, transcript of lecture at Hunter College, Nov. 16, 1962.

37 Carmen Herrera to author, interview, Oct. 19, 2010.

38 Frank McCourt, *Teacher Man: A Memoir*, New York: Scribner, 2005.

39 Oral history interview with Aaron Siskind, Sept. 28–Oct. 2, 1982. AAA; Carl Giarenza, *Aaron Siskind, Pleasures and Terrors*, Boston: Little Brown, 1982, 8, cited in Martin Gasser, Princeton seminar paper, Sept. 28, 1988.

40 Reise, notes, 1964.

41 *Jewish Daily Bulletin*, Mar. 2, 1929.

42 *The Home News*, n.d.

43 SWI.

44 Robert Musil, *The Man without Qualities*, New York: Vintage, 1996, 55.

13 Alexander Borodulin, letter to BN, Aug. 9, 1936.

14 Alexander Borodulin, letter to BBN, Sept. 18, 1936.

15 Lewis Mumford, *The Culture of Cities*, New York: Harcourt, Brace, and Co., 1938, 480, cited in Daniel R. Schwarz, *Broadway Boogie Woogie: Damon Runyon and the Making of New York Culture*, New York: Palgrave Macmillan, 2003, 68.

16 Ann Douglas, *Terrible Honesty*, New York: Farrar, Straus and Giroux, 1995, 20.

17 Schwarz, *Broadway Boogie Woogie*, 128-9.

18 Carl Carmer, quote from 1945 appears in "March 12, 1933: The First Fireside Chat," New York, Museum of Broadcast Television. Exhibition Series: MBC Flashback.

19 Schwarz, *Broadway Boogie Woogie*, 111.

20 Jimmy Breslin, *Damon Runyon*, New York: Dell, 1991, 229.

21 Breslin, *Damon Runyon*, 4.

22 Damon Runyon, *Trials and Other Tribulations*, Philadelphia: J. B. Lippincott, 1947, 282, cited in Schwarz, *Broadway Boogie Woogie*, 113.

23 Runyon, *Trials and Other Tribulations*, 69.

24 Laurence Bergreen, *As Thousands Cheer: The Life of Irving Berlin*, New York: Viking 1990, 313.

25 Douglas, *Terrible Honesty*, 20. David M. Kennedy, *Freedom from Fear: America in Depression and War, 1929–1945*, New York: Oxford UP, 1999, 22–3, cited in Schwarz, *Broadway Boogie Woogie*, 71.

26 Michael Emery, "Newspapers," *Encyclopedia of New York City*, ed. Kenneth T. Jackson, New Haven: Yale UP, 1995, 813; Schwarz, *Broadway Boogie Woogie*, 21–2.

27 Schwarz, *Broadway Boogie Woogie*, 69.

28 Thomas S. Buechner, director, Brooklyn Museum, letter to *NYT*, 1966, cited in Christopher Gray, "Streetscapes: Park Row; Black and White and Red All Over," *NYT* (May 6, 2012).

29 *The Palm Beach Post* (Feb. 26, 1931).

30 BN, "Deadly Weapons," Sept. 1936, unpublished.

31 Beth S. Wenger, *New York Jews and the Great Depression: Uncertain Promise*, New Haven: Yale UP, 1996, 3.

32 For documentation, see Wenger, *New York Jews*, 214, n. 4.

33 *Fortune* (Feb. 1936).

34 "35,000 Jam Streets Outside the Garden," *NYT* (Mar. 28, 1933).

35 "Other Faiths Join In: Crowd Overflowing the Garden Hears Leaders Assail Persecution," *NYT* (Mar. 28, 1933).

36 "Rabbis Denounce Hitler in Sermons," *NYT* (Mar. 26, 1933).

37 Henry McBride, "Attraction in the Galleries," *New York Sun* (Dec. 21, 1935).

38 Jean Margolies, interview with Beth Wenger, New Haven, Aug. 27, 1991, cited in Wenger, *New York Jews*, 22.

39 Wenger, *New York Jews*, 22–23. See Wenger's extensive footnotes for further reading on discrimination against Jews in the 1930s.

40 BN, letter to Dr. William J. McGrath, License Chairman, Board of Examiners, Board of Education, June 17, 1939.

41 Wenger, *New York Jews*, 27, 23.

FIVE. THE CIVIL SERVICE MAN

1 Gerald Benjamin, "Civil Service," *Encyclopedia of New York City*, ed. Kenneth T. Jackson, New Haven: Yale UP, 1995, 237.

2 Burton Hendricks, "The Jewish Invasion of New York," *McClure's* (Mar. 1913), cited in Irving Howe and Kenneth Libo, *World of Our Fathers*, 30th anniversary ed., New York: New York UP, 2005, 166.

3 "City Leaders Unite to Control Budget and Combat Waste," *NYT* (June 13, 1932).

4 Adolph Gottlieb, letter to BN, July 17, 1933.

5 Leaflet, reprinted in New York Committee to Aid Victims of German Fascism, "Nazi Letter 812 No. XI," Oct. 1933.

6 BNFA.

7 A. J. Liebling, "Two Aesthetes Offer Selves as Candidates to Provide Own Ticket for Intellectuals," *New York World-Telegram* (Nov. 4, 1933).

8 Newman v. Reinhardt 3 A.D.2d 909 (1957), Supreme Court of New York.

9 Commissioner, *Annual Report of the Board of Elections in New York City*, 31 Chambers St., New York: City Hall Library, 1933.

10 "Mayor Walker Resigns; Will Put Case to People; He Denounces Roosevelt," *The Baltimore Sun* (Sept. 2, 1932).

11 "Farley Declares He Is for McKee," *NYT* (Nov. 3, 1933).

12 "Voting Disorderly: Thugs Invade Polls," *NYT* (Nov. 8, 1933).

13 Lindsay Pollock, *The Girl with the Gallery*, New York: Public Affairs, 2006, 171–83. The venue, Nelson Rockefeller's involvement, and the decision by artists to allow their work to be shown or to withdraw, were colored by the shocking, middle-of-the-night destruction of Diego Rivera's Rockefeller Center mural two weeks earlier.

SIX. MISS GREENHOUSE

1 AN, interview by John O'Neill, 1994.

2 Joseph Hochstein to author, interview, Nov. 3, 2009.

3 Betty Greenhouse, letter to AN, Aug. 10, 1937.

4 Joseph Hochstein, personal communication, Aug. 2009.

5 Anuta Greenhouse, letter to B + A, Aug. 11, 1942.

6 The contest was one continued with Barney. Hess makes much of Barney's preference for Corneille, that he admired "the stark rhetoric of the older poet to the more subtle (and to most people, more profound) lyricism of *Phedre* or *Berenice*." Hess's interpretation was that "the typical Corneillian hero is usually locked in a dilemma very similar to Newman's as a young man. Should the hero be loyal to himself, to his own love, or to a larger social force." He remembered Barney reciting Corneille "in the sonorous voice and with the wide gestures of the classic actors." On the other hand, B. H. Friedman recalls Barney "declaiming" Racine—especially a memorable occasion in the late 1950s on the Long Island Railroad when he got "into the aisle and recite[d] . . . marching back and forth in the car doing Racine." BHF to author, interview, Jan. 15, 2007.

7 Personal communications between Annalee Greenhouse and Leah Hochstein, Aug.–Sept. 1932.

8 BN, letter to Annalee Greenhouse, Aug. 25, 1935.

SEVEN. THE SEARCH

1 Edward Alden Jewell, "A Novel of the Tragedy and Romance of Van Gogh" (review of *Lust for Life*, by Irving Stone), *NYT* (Sept. 30, 1934).

2 Edward Alden Jewell, "African Negro Art on Exhibition Here," *NYT* (Mar. 19, 1935).

3 *Fortune* 18.6 (1938).

4 BN, *The First Man Was an Artist*, manuscript, 1947, SWI.

5 BN, "Interview with Kathleen Shorthall of *Life*," 1959, conducted for research of article Dorothy Seiberling, "Baffling U.S. Art: What It Is About," *Life* (Nov. 9, 1959).

6 Barbara Reise, notes after interviewing BN, Jan. 21, 1964, Tate Archives.

7 Karlen Mooradian, *The Many Worlds of Arshile Gorky*, illustrated ed., Chicago: Gilgamesh, 1980.

8 AN, notes in the Sam Hunter Files, n.d.

9 Adam Alexander to author, interview, Aug. 20, 2009.

10 AN, interview by John O'Neill, 1994.

11 TBH1, 15.

12 Albert Taub, letter of recommendation for Barnett Newman, May 5, 1938.

13 Edna Nahshon, *Yiddish Proletarian Theatre: The Art and Politics of the Artef, 1925–1940*, Westport, CT: Greenwood, 1998.

14 Edna Nahshon, Professor of Hebrew at the Jewish Theological Seminary, personal conversation, June 2009.

15 *Vanguard* (May–June 1935).

16 BN, letter to Annalee Greenhouse, Aug. 22, 1935.

17 BN, letter to Annalee Greenhouse, Aug. 23, 1935.

18 BN, letter to Annalee Greenhouse, Aug. 28, 1935.

EIGHT. THE ANSWER

1 "Bricklayers Pay," Citizens' Budget Commission, New York, c.1932–35.

2 BN, letter to Annalee Greenhouse, Dec. 27, 1935.

3 "City Art Gallery Opened by Mayor," NYT (Jan. 7, 1936); "A Municipal Adventure: Mayor's Committee Opens Its Gallery—Academy Portraits—Paintings by Women," NYT (Jan. 12, 1936).

4 "New System Urged in Teachers' Tests," NYT (Jan. 6, 1936).

5 BN, letter to Alexander Borodulin, May 16, 1938.

6 Mildred Adams, "New York Comes of Age as a Capital of Art," NYT (Feb. 2, 1936).

7 Will Barnet to author, interview, May 14, 2009.

8 Adolph Gottlieb, interview with Martin Friedman, Aug. 1962. From the archives at the Adolph and Esther Gottlieb Foundation, New York.

9 Oral history interview with Aaron Siskind, Sept. 28–Oct. 2, 1982, AAA.

10 BN, interview with KO, unpublished, Aug. 2, 1963.

11 BN, The First Man Was an Artist, manuscript, 1947, SWI. "Rashi" (1040–1105) was the acronymic name of Shlomo ben Yitzhaki, a rabbi and author of revered canonical Torah commentary.

12 Daniel Newman to author, interview, Mar. 10, 2009.

NINE. MARRIAGE

1 AN, interview by John O'Neill, 1994.

2 Alexander Borodulin to BBN, Sept. 18, 1936.

3 AN, interview, 1994.

4 AN interviewed by Dodie Kazanjian, 1991, unpublished transcript.

5 BNFA.

6 AN, interview, 1991.

7 AN, interview, 1991.

8 BN, letter to Alexander Borodulin, courtesy Adam Alexander, Aug. 28, 1936.

9 SN, letter to BBN, July 18, 1936; AN, notes.

10 AN, interview with Ann Temkin, Nov. 6, 1997, Philadelphia Museum of Art, Library and Archives Repository.

11 BN, letter to Alexander Borodulin, Aug. 28, 1936.

12 AN, letter to the Greenhouse family, July 10, 1936, trans. Myra Mniewski.

13 AN, letter to the Greenhouse family, July 14, 1936, trans. Myra Mniewski.

14 BN, letter to Samuel and A. (?) Greenhouse, July 1936, trans. Myra Mniewski.

15 SN, letters to BBN, July 13, 15, 18, 21, 1936.

16 SN to BBN, July 15, 1936.

17 SN to BBN, July 21, 1936.

18 Alfred Leslie to author, interview, Dec. 13, 2012.

19 Files of the Civil Service Commission, Washington, D.C., 1950.

20 Civil Service Commission, 1950.

21 Aurora Dias-Jorgensen to author, interview, July 26, 2007.

22 SN, letter to AN, Sept. 6, 1943.

23 SN, letter to B + A, Nov. 25, 1942.

24 TH papers, 1939–1978, AAA.

25 "N.Y. Shows Interesting This Summer: Critic Discovers Many Fine Things on Display There," The Washington Post (Aug. 16, 1936).

26 "1936 and 1937 were watershed years in the history of American avant-garde art," according to Irving Sandler, "witnessing the eclipse of the then hegemonic Social Realism and the first concerted bid for recognition by American modernist artists."

27 Adolph Gottlieb, interview with Martin Friedman, Aug. 1962. From the archives at the Adolph and Esther Gottlieb Foundation, New York.

28 AN, interview, 1994.

29 Tom Nagai, postcard to BN, Apr. 12, 1937.

TEN. MERIT

1 "Recalls Changes on 42th Street: Fifty Years Has Transformed It into Busy Commercial Thoroughfare," NYT (Jan. 4, 1931).

2 Alexander Herzen, letter to Giuseppe Mazzini, quoted in Isaiah Berlin, Russian Thinkers, New York: Penguin, 1978, 82.

3 SN, letter to BBN, Aug. 16, 1937.

4 "Business Records," NYT (Apr. 21, 1937).

5 BN, letter to Alexander Borodulin, Aug. 11, 1937.

6 TH papers, 1939–1978, AAA.

7 BN, letter to Dr. Paul Klapper, Oct. 16, 1937.

8 In 1930 the all-women Hunter College and City College Brooklyn location merged to become Brooklyn College, not City College New York (CCNY).

9 Quoting Benton as an authority at this moment was an interesting choice. Barney's own crowd would have been aware of the older artist's declined and dishonored stature, his conservative aesthetics, anti-intellectualism, and public homophobia. But Barney correctly assumed the name alone was sufficient endorsement for the audience he was trying to reach. In its item about the qualifying exam, the Times called Benton "the American mural painter" and made no value judgment.

10 "Art Teachers' Test Is Termed Too Hard," NYT (Sept. 19, 1938).

11 Max Weber, letter to BN, Nov. 29, 1938.

12 "Can They Draw?" Art Digest (Dec. 15, 1938); "Can They Draw? Yes," Newsweek (Dec. 12, 1938); "They're Not Good Enough?" Home News, n.d.; "Some Current Shows," The Sun (Dec. 5, 1938).

13 It seems to have made at least one more appearance in March 1940 as Country Studio by B. Barnett Newman in the Art Teachers Association Exhibition at the Uptown Gallery, 259 West End Avenue.

ELEVEN. DIGNITY

1 Alexander Borodulin, letter to BN, May 17, 1938.

2 BN, letters to AN, July 18, 19, 20, 1938; "Rally Marks Date of Spanish Revolt," *NYT* (July 20, 1938).

3 James Waterman Wise, "An Open Letter to My Fellow-Jews," New York: The American League for Peace and Democracy, August 1938. The American League for Peace and Democracy, a Communist-dominated group of artists, writers and intellectuals that published Wise's "Open Letter" was, at precisely this moment, both enmeshed in mainstream politics and activities, with a claimed membership of 4,000,000 and the endorsement of the U.S. Solicitor General, *and* being investigated in the House Committee on un-American activities. By August 1939, when the Nazi–Soviet Pact "required the CPUSA [Communist Party of the USA] to abandon its support for an anti-Nazi foreign policy and attack Roosevelt as a warmonger for his continued support for the beleaguered democracies of Europe," the League was dissolved.

4 Leon Trotsky, "Art and Politics," *Partisan Review* (Aug.–Sept. 1938).

5 Cherie Burns, *The Great Hurricane: 1938*, New York: Grove/Atlantic, 2005.

6 "The Museum of Modern Art," *Fortune* 18.6 (1938).

7 Oral history interview with Bernard Braddon and Sidney Paul Schectman, Oct. 9, 1981, AAA.

8 William and Ethel Baziotes papers, c.1900–1992, bulk 1935–1980, AAA.

9 Samuel Greenhouse, letter to F. E. Shannon, Feb. 17, 1940.

10 BN, letter to Mr. Albert Rosenzweig, June 22, 1944.

11 Greenhouse, letter to Shannon, Feb. 17, 1940.

12 Hester Diamond to author, interview, Aug. 3, 2006.

13 BHF, *Art-World Details*, unpublished manuscript.

14 BN, interview with Joanna Magloff, c. 1963.

15 BN, letter to Robert Motherwell, Dec. 1, 1965.

16 Larry Poons to author, interview, June 17, 2010.

17 SN, letter to BN, July 21, 1936.

18 Abraham Newman, letter to B + A, Aug. 22, 1940.

19 CG papers, 1928–1995, the Getty Research Institute, Los Angeles.

20 CG papers.

21 Joseph Lipsky, Associate Attorney, Division of Law, University of the State of New York, State Education Dept., letter to BN, May 12, 1939.

22 "Lift Teacher Tests for Indian Schools: New Requirements Emphasize the Hardships and Demand Respect for the Primitive," *NYT* (Dec. 4, 1938).

23 U.S. Civil Service Commission, letter to BN, July 5, 1939.

24 "Lift Teacher Tests for Indian Schools."

25 Langston Hughes, *Before and Beyond*, New York: Citadel, 1992, 284.

26 William H. Rueckhert, *Encounters with Kenneth Burke*, Urbana and Chicago: University of Illinois, 1994, 122, cited in Garth Pauley, "Criticism in Context: Kenneth Burke's 'The Rhetoric of Hitler's 'Battle.' " *KB Journal* 6.1 (Fall 2009).

27 Pauley, "Criticism in Context."

28 Barney, as the president of the Fine Art Substitutes Association—which he had organized around the time of the show at A.C.A. (which he called "a national sensation")—had gotten himself an appearance on the "Let Your Hair Down Hour" (WINS radio) at the end of July, where he lobbied for the dissolution of the Board of Examiners: "They have deprived the children and the schools of the city of some of the best teaching ability, they have degraded the morale of hundreds of teachers" and created a "staff of sharecropper . . . teachers."

29 BN, letter to AN, Aug. 9, 1939.

30 Annalee's statement speaks for itself. In 1968 Barney told Hess that he "stopped making pictures around 1939–1940, and everything he did afterward was aimed at the purpose of starting to paint again." On another occasion he told Hess, "When I gave up painting, I had been doing what you might call a form of 'American Expressionism.' It was flat painting. Milton Avery was meaningful as an example. The pictures looked a little like Hockneys. I used a felt-tip brush, the kind you loaded with pastel powder." Barney told interviewers about a drawing of a cast of the Belvedere Torso which was an assignment at the Art Students League. The vanished *Studio in the Country* from the "Can We Draw?" show, and drawings made for the art teacher's licensing exam shown to John Sloan, are the only pre-1944 works whose existence is verifiable. The purchase of 48 sticks of NuPastel on December 28, 1938, would substantiate the body of work he told Hess about, which has no other documentation, either contemporary (letters, notes, listings) or subsequent (interviews with Annalee or others). Accordingly, Barney "gave up painting" within one year of beginning. The earliest extant works date from 1944, and in a 1966 interview the artist spoke of those as his "early things."

31 BN to AN, Aug. 2, 1939.

32 BN to AN, Aug. 5, 1939.

33 BN to AN, Aug. 5, 1939.

34 "Moses Is Upheld on City Hall Park Plan; Art Board Overrules Curran's Objections," *NYT* (Feb. 18, 1939).

35 BN, "New York," manuscript, c. 1939, SWI.

TWELVE. THE STANCE

1 "Would Fight for Poland: Jewish Group Here Also Offers Every Other Aid Possible," *NYT* (Aug. 30, 1939).

2 AN, letter to Anuta and Samuel Greenhouse, Aug. 27, 1939.

3 SN, letter to B + A, Sept. 1, 1939.

4 Leah Hochstein, letter to AN, Sept. 1, 1939.

5 Betty Greenhouse, letter to AN, Aug. 30, 1939.

6 "Poles' resistance Is Held Stiffening . . . German Mobility in Crossing Difficult Terrain Has Been Outstanding Feature," *NYT* (Sept. 13, 1939).

7 "Lwow Is Menaced," *NYT* (Sept. 13, 1939).

8 The Popular Front was created at the time of the Communist Party World Congress in 1935 to involve artists and writers in the class struggle.

9 "17 Members Bolt Artists' Conference: Charge Organization Backs Stalinist 'Line' and Can 'Only Damage' Free Art," *NYT* (Apr. 17, 1940).

10 Catalogue Statement, First Annual Exhibition, Mar. 1941. Federation of Modern Painters and Sculptors records, 1940–1975, AAA.

11 "No Blackout for Art" statement, 1942, Federation of Modern Painters and Sculptors records, cited in James Breslin, *Mark Rothko, A Biography*, Chicago: University of Chicago Press, 1993.

12 Barney, introducing Dan Flavin on the occasion of Flavin's 1969 opening at the National Gallery of Canada, shared the stage with Terry McGowan, Illuminating Engineer at General Electric. The information in this paragraph comes from McGowan's presentation.

13 New York World's Fair pamphlet.

14 "World's Fair Provides a Building for Contemporary American Art; Reverses Earlier Decision After Months of Controversy Among Artists' Groups," *NYT* (Apr. 12, 1938).

15 "The People Speak," *Art Digest* (Sept. 1, 1939).

16 James Johnson Sweeney, "Thoughts Before the World's Fair," *Parnassus* 11.3 (Mar. 1939).

17 "Art at N.Y. Fair," *Art Digest* (Dec. 1, 1938).

18 Peyton Boswell, "The Project Comes Through," *Art Digest* (June 1, 1940).

19 Boswell, "The Project Comes Through."

20 Edward Alden Jewell, "Fair's Art Display Gains New Work," *NYT* (June 21, 1940); "Conrow Portrait in Allied Artists' Show," *Art Digest* (June 1, 1940).

21 Sweeney, "Thoughts Before the World's Fair."

22 BN, interview with Joanna Magloff, c.1963.

23 Donald Paneth interview, 1952, in William and Ethel Baziotes papers, c. 1900–1992, bulk 1935–1980, AAA.

24 CG, "Avant-Garde and Kitsch," *Partisan Review* 6.5 (1939).

25 "Italian Masters" was an extraordinary show to be at MoMA, and it broke all previous attendance records, including those for the 1936 van Gogh exhibition and special events for the opening of the new building. Dorothy Miller,

assistant curator of painting and sculpture, specifically threw down the gauntlet to contemporary, if not necessarily American, artists: "it was decided that a group of distinguished modern painters and sculptors should be shown in the illustrious company of the Italian masters . . . . Imaginary contests between the heroes of antiquity and their modern counterparts have always had a certain fascination. Here, within the Museum of Modern Art, some such trial of strength may actually take place, for the Museum, believing in the power and quality of the modern artist, has not hesitated to accept the challenge."

26 BN, "In Front of the Real Thing," *Art News* 68.9 (Jan. 1970); repr. in SWI.

27 BN, "The Ides of Art: The Attitudes of 10 Artists on Their Art and Contemporaneousness," *The Tiger's Eye* 1.2 (Dec. 1947), repr. in SWI.

28 BN, letter to John Stephan, n.d., c.1947.

29 TH papers, 1939–1978, AAA.

30 Edward Alden Jewell, "John Sloan and the World of Art," *NYT* (Oct. 8, 1939).

31 BN, letter to John Sloan, Mar. 30, 1940.

32 Victor D'Amico, Foreword, "Exhibition by Children . . . Federal Art Gallery, Dec. 22–Jan. 10, 1939," Federal Art Project, Works Progress Administration.

33 BN, handwritten statement, June 1940.

34 BN, "The Anglo-Saxon Tradition in Art Criticism," manuscript, c. 1944–5; "The Plasmic Image," manuscript, c. 1945; "The Sublime Is Now," *The Tiger's Eye* 1.3 (Mar. 1948). All in SWI.

35 TBH2, 27.

36 BH to author, interview, Nov. 7, 2006.

37 BN, "The Plasmic Image"; "The First Man Was an Artist," *The Tiger's Eye* 1.1 (Oct. 1947), SWI.

THIRTEEN. OBJECTOR

1 "Our Cooperative House," brochure.

2 BN, letter to Marian Anderson, Mar. 27, 1940. The Daughters of the American Revolution were a powerful group of politically conservative women who in 1939 prevented Anderson from singing to an integrated audience in Constitution Hall. Irving Howe later wrote that "The day *Native Son* appeared, American culture was changed forever."

3 BN, letter to George Backer, Mar. 30, 1940.

4 BN, letter to director, WQXR Radio Station, Apr. 29, 1940.

5 BN, letter to Ralph Ingersoll, June 1, 1940.

6 Alexander Borodulin, letter to BN, June 18, 1940.

7 BN, letter to Alexander Borodulin, June 25, 1940.

8 A disputatious form of Talmudic study practiced by the more sharp-witted scholars and pupils, using subtle logical and legalistic reasoning; one purpose was to keep the study intellectually challenging and free from complacency.

9 Alexander Borodulin, letter to BN, July 1, 1940.

10 Jessie Wallace Hughan, "If We Should Be Invaded: Facing a Fantastic Hypothesis," pamphlet, New York: War

Registers League, Apr. 1940.

11 BN, letter to the Rev. John Haynes Holmes, Community Church of New York, July 30, 1940.

12 BN, letter to the Selective Service System, Jan. 16, 1942; Helen T. Fitzsimmons, Chief Clerk, Selective Service System, letter to BBN, Jan. 21, 1942.

13 TH papers, 1939–1978, AAA.

14 AN interviewed by Dodie Kazanjian, 1991, unpublished transcript.

15 Carmen Herrera to author, interview, Oct. 19, 2010.

16 BN, letter of Feb. 15, 1941.

17 AN, interview by John O'Neill, 1994.

18 Barbara Reise, notes after interviewing BN, Jan. 21, 1964, Tate Archives.

19 Draft of letter about zoo education, n.d.

20 Undated draft, 1941.

21 Lee E. Cooper, "Uprooted Thousands Starting Trek from Site for Stuyvesant Town," *NYT* (Mar. 3, 1945).

22 Tom Robbins to author, interview, Apr. 2009.

23 List of "Damages incurred by Barnett Newman, April 27, 1952."

FOURTEEN. POLEMICS

1 *Art News*, Dec. 28, 1940.

2 *Life* magazine editorial, Feb. 17, 1941.

3 AHB and Georges Hugnet, "Introduction," *Fantastic Art, Dada, Surrealism*, New York: The Museum of Modern Art, 1937.

4 MS, "The Nature of Abstract Art," *Marxist Quarterly* (Jan.–Mar. 1937), repr. in MS, *Modern Art: 19th and 20th Centuries, Selected Papers*, New York: George Braziller, 1978, 187.

5 Hans Hofmann, address at Riverside Museum, Feb. 16, 1941.

6 Hofmann, address at Riverside Museum.

7 IS papers, 1909–2007, bulk 1950–2000, the Getty Research Institute, Los Angeles.

8 BN, "Surrealism and the War," unpublished, SWI.

9 CG, "Surrealist Painting," *The Nation* (Aug. 12 and 19, 1944).

10 BN, "Surrealism and the War."

11 BN, "The True Revolution Is Anarchist!," foreword to *Memoirs of a Revolutionist* by Peter Kropotkin, New York: Horizon Press, 1968.

12 The jingoistic essay addressed Isolationism versus Internationalism—something Barney would do the following year, with a radically different thrust. Luce urged his readers to "accept wholeheartedly our duty and our opportunity as the most powerful and vital nation in the world and in consequence to exert upon the world the full impact of our influence, for such purposes as we see fit and by such means as we see fit."

13 AN to Greenhouses, n.d.

14 Samuel Melvin Kootz, *Modern American Painters*, New York: Brewer & Warden, Inc., 1930.

15 Samuel M. Kootz, "America Uber Alles," *NYT* (Dec. 20, 1931).

16 Edward Alden Jewell, "The Problem of Seeing," *NYT* (Aug. 10, 1941).

17 Edward Alden Jewell, "Challenge and Answer," *NYT* (Aug. 31, 1941).

FIFTEEN. WHAT ABOUT ISOLATIONIST ART?

1 TH papers, 1939–1978, AAA.

2 BN, interview with Joanna Magloff, c. 1963.

3 IS papers, 1909–2007, bulk 1950–2000, the Getty Research Institute, Los Angeles.

4 Barbara Reise, notes after interviewing BN, Jan. 21, 1964, Tate Archives.

5 BN, interview with Magloff, c. 1963.

6 Oral history interview with Esther Dick Gottlieb, Oct. 22, 1981, AAA.

7 Adolph Gottlieb interviewed by John Jones, Nov. 3, 1965. From the archives at the Adolph and Esther Gottlieb Foundation, New York.

8 Esther Dick Gottlieb, interview, 1981.

9 Untitled document in BNFA.

10 BN, interview with Magloff, c.1963.

11 W. J. Enright, "War Works a Swift Readjustment of Business," *NYT* (Feb. 1, 1942).

12 U.S., FBI, Sarah Newman, Name Check, Bureau File 123–5493, Dec. 3, 1950. Obtained under the Freedom of Information Act.

13 Henry R. Luce, "The American Century," *Life* (Feb. 17, 1941).

14 BN, interview with Magloff, c.1963.

15 Unsigned draft of letter to AHB, Feb. 28, 1942.

16 Adolph Gottlieb, interview, 1965.

17 The Jewish Rosenberg had fled from Paris to Manhattan in 1940; he continued to use stationery with the Paris and London, as well as New York, addresses.

18 BN to Rosenberg, Mar. 17, 1942, trans. author.

19 BN to Rosenberg, June 13, 1943.

SIXTEEN. WHAT DID YOU DO DURING THE WAR?

1 BN, interview with Joanna Magloff, c. 1963.

2 Jeanne Bultman to author, interview, Mar. 17, 2007.

3 James E. B. Breslin Research Archive on Mark Rothko, the Getty Research Institute, Los Angeles.

4 Oral history interview with David Hare, Jan. 17, 1968, AAA.

5 Jackson Pollock to Charles Pollock, Apr. 11, 1944, Morgan Library.

6 Steven Naifeh and Gregory White Smith, *Jackson Pollock: An American Saga*, New York: C. N. Potter, 1989, 363.

7 James Breslin, *Mark Rothko, a Biography*, Chicago: The University of Chicago Press, 1993, 153.

8 Edith Sachar Carson interviewed by Walter Hopps, quoted in Breslin, *Mark Rothko*.

9 Musa Mayer, *Night Studio: A Memoir of Philip Guston*, New York: Knopf, 1988, 37.

10 Mark Stevens and Annalyn Swan, *de Kooning: An American Master*, New York: Knopf, 2004, 176.

11 Oral history interview with Jack Tworkov, Aug. 17, 1962, AAA.

12 Michael Brenson, *David Smith: The Art and Life of a Transformational Sculptor*, New York: Farrar, Straus and Giroux, 2022.

13 CS, in *Clyfford Still*, San Francisco: San Francisco Museum of Modern Art, 1976, 109.

14 Alice Goldfarb Marquis, *Art Czar: The Rise and Fall of Clement Greenberg*, Boston: MFA Publications, 2006, 76–78.

15 Phong Bui, "A Conversation with Philip Pavia," *The Brooklyn Rail* (Apr. 17, 2009).

16 Oral history interview with AO, Nov. 19, 1968, AAA.

17 IS papers, 1909–2007, bulk 1950–2000, the Getty Research Institute, Los Angeles.

18 "Reed Studio Bldg. Had Interesting and Happy History," *Gloucester Daily Times* (July 28, 1949).

19 No title, *NYT* (June 27, 1942).

20 Emile Rabinovitch to "Chere Tante, cher oncle et chers cousins et cousines," Nov. 21, 1942, trans. author.

21 AN interviewed by Dodie Kazanjian, 1991, unpublished transcript.

22 BN to TH, TH papers, 1939–1978, AAA.

23 So named by Stephen Birmingham in *Our Crowd*, New York: Harper & Row, 1967.

24 RM to author, email, Nov. 5, 2012, and others.

25 BN, "The Impact of Pearl Harbor on Barnett Newman," n.d., unpublished.

26 Edward Alden Jewell, "Gallery Premiere Assists Red Cross," *NYT* (Oct. 21, 1942).

27 Frederick Kiesler, quoted in Jewell, "Gallery Premiere Assists Red Cross."

28 BN, "The Impact of Pearl Harbor on Barnett Newman."

29 BN, interview with Magloff, c. 1963.

30 IS papers, 1909–2007, bulk 1950–2000, the Getty Research Institute, Los Angeles.

31 Mira Schor, ed., *The Extreme of the Middle: Writings of Jack Tworkov*, New Haven: Yale UP, 2009, xii.

32 "The Future of the A B C Crap," typescript.

33 BN, interview with Magloff, c. 1963.

34 Sanford Hirsch, Executive Director, Adolph and Esther Gottlieb Foundation.

35 AN, interview, 1991.

36 Buffie Johnson to James Breslin, quoted in Breslin, *Mark Rothko*, 169.

37 Stevens and Swann, *de Kooning*, 345.

38 Adolph Gottlieb, interview with Martin Friedman, Aug. 1962. From the archives at the Adolph and Esther Gottlieb Foundation, New York.

39 RM and Jonathan Holstein to author, interview, Oct. 16, 2010; Sanford Hirsch to author, interview, Oct. 2009.

40 Oral history interview with Esther Dick Gottlieb, Oct. 22, 1981, AAA.

41 Edward Alden Jewell, *NYT* (Dec. 6 and 20, 1942).

42 Edward Alden Jewell, "New Artists Group Opens First Show," *NYT* (Jan. 19, 1943), and "Whitney, Metropolitan Merge," *NYT* (Jan. 24, 1943).

43 Samuel Grafton, "I'd Rather Be Right," *New York Post* (Dec. 29, 1942).

44 SN to B + A, Jan. 26, 1943.

45 Edward Alden Jewell, "Paintings Shown by Nine Artists," *NYT* (Feb. 17, 1943).

46 Edward Alden Jewell, "Modern Painters Open Show Today," *NYT* (June 2, 1943).

47 Edward Alden Jewell, "End-of-the-Season Melange," *NYT* (June 6, 1943).

48 Edward Alden Jewell, "'Globalism' Pops into View," *NYT* (June 13, 1943).

49 Barney shamelessly worked the moment: on the same day the letter was published in the *Times* he wrote his chiding letter to the dealer Rosenberg ("For Mr. Jewell considers the work of Adolph Gottlieb . . . of sufficient importance"), and another to the editor of the *New York World-Telegram* to castigate the critic Emily Genauer's "disgraceful," "vindictive," and "vulgar" show of "incompetence."

50 In the late 1950s Barney told Irving Sandler that Gottlieb was the "instigator of [the] need for new subject matter idea . . . he was agitated by [the] need for new subject matter," and wrote the "programmatic part"; Barney wrote the "preamble." Gottlieb's drafts have not been found, and the sentence that was cut by Jewell does not appear in Rothko's: "The appreciation of art is a true marriage of minds. And in art, as in marriage, lack of consummation is ground for annulment."

51 Edward Alden Jewell, "'Globalism,'" *NYT* (June 27, 1943).

52 Bonnie Clearwater, curator of the Mark Rothko Foundation, compared the language of the drafts in "Shared Myths: Reconsideration of Rothko's and Gottlieb's Letter to *The New York Times*," *Archives of American Art Journal* 24.1 (1984).

53 AN, note on file.

54 "Nazis Speed Massacres of Jews," *NYT* (June 5, 1943).

55 Dr. C. J. Thatcher to Samuel Greenhouse, copy to BN, Nov. 9, 1943.

56 AN, interview by John O'Neill, 1994.

57 BN to Albert Rosenzweig, June 22, 1944.

58 BN to Albert Rosenzweig, July 22, 1944.

59 A year later, Barr was named "Director of Research in Painting and Sculpture," and, in February 1947, "Director of Museum Collections." Many staff member insisted on reporting to him.

60 Undated and unpublished.

SEVENTEEN. BETTY PARSONS

1 Lee Hall, conversations with BP, cited in Lee Hall, *Betty Parsons: Artist, Dealer, Collector*, New York: H. N. Abrams, 1991.

2 Gerald Silk, oral history interview with BP, June 11, 1981, AAA.

3 BN, "Adolph Gottlieb," Wakefield Gallery, Feb. 7–19, 1944.

4 Hall, *Betty Parsons: Artist, Dealer, Collector*.

5 Howard Devree, "From a Reviewer's Notebook," *NYT* (Feb. 13, 1944); Edward Alden Jewell, "By Our Modernists," *NYT* (Feb. 27, 1944); Henry McBride, "Attractions in the Galleries," *The New York Sun* (Feb. 11, 1944).

6 B. B. Newman to Henry McBride, 14 Feb. 1944.

7 Oral history interview with Esther Dick Gottlieb, Oct. 22, 1981, AAA. The idea of the *Luftmensch* dates from early 20th-century Zionism, but the description that so perfectly applies to Barney was written by Greenberg in his 1943 review of Maurice Samuel's *The World of Sholom Aleichem*: "that most typical phenomenon of recent Jewish life, the Luftmensch, the man who lives in, by, and on air, the fixer, the promoter, the go-between, the man who always has a deal on hand and never a vocation."

8 "Culture of Americas Shown at Exhibition," *NYT* (Feb. 26, 1944).

9 BN to Harry L. Shapiro, Apr. 20, 1944, American Museum of Natural History, Dept. of Anthropology correspondence with Barnett Newman and Betty Parsons, 1944–1946; AAA.

10 BN, "Pre-Columbian Stone Sculpture," SWI.

11 BP, interview, 1981.

12 IS papers, 1909–2007, bulk 1950–2000, the Getty Research Institute, Los Angeles.

13 *NYT* (Jan. 30, 1942).

14 Russell Lynes, *Good Old Modern*, New York: Atheneum, 1973, 333.

15 The Museum of Modern Art's involvement with Latin America requires, and has received, much study. The large body of literature on this subject cannot be summarized here.

16 Written in response to Barr's demotion to Advisory Director. Unpublished.

17 BN, "Pre-Columbian Stone Sculpture."

18 When Siskind returned to Gloucester in the summer, and went out on Bass Rocks—where previously he

hadn't seen "anything . . . it was all full of these images. And I am sure that I was able to see those images because of my experience with photographing" the sculpture at Wakefield. Oral history interview with Aaron Siskind, Sept. 28–Oct. 2, 1982, AAA.

19 BN to Shapiro, Apr. 20, 1944.

20 Harry Shapiro to BN, Apr. 22, 1944.

21 BN to Harry Shapiro, May 21, 1944, American Museum of Natural History, Dept. of Anthropology correspondence.

22 Harry Shapiro to BN, May 22, 1944.

23 Lester Markel to BN, May 24, 1944.

24 BN, draft, BNFA.

25 Letters between BN and Harry Shapiro, Aug. 1, 3, 15, 17, 1944, American Museum of Natural History, Dept. of Anthropology.

26 Paul Cummings, oral history interview with HR, Dec. 17, 1970–Jan. 28, 1973, AAA.

27 BN, "The Problem of Subject Matter," SWI.

28 There are echoes of CG's "Towards a Newer La-ocoon," published in *Partisan Review*, July–Aug. 1940, although Newman never mentions it.

29 BN, "The Problem of Subject Matter."

30 BN, "The Problem of Subject Matter."

31 Siskind, interview, 1982.

32 *DYN* 6 (Nov. 1944).

33 "The New Image," quoted in Amy Winter, *Wolfgang Paalen: Artist and Theorist of the Avant-Garde*, Westport, CT: Praeger, 2003, 111.

34 Winter, *Wolfgang Paalen*, xxvi.

35 Barbara Reise, notes after interviewing BN, Jan. 21, 1964, and Apr. 14, 1965, Tate Archives.

36 Janis's book listed Graham, Krasner, Gyorgy Kepes, Motherwell, and de Kooning with other "abstract painters," and Gottlieb, Mark Tobey, Herbert Bayer, Roth-ko, Gorky ("long an abstract painter"), and Pollock among the "surrealist painters." Hans Hofmann, whom Janis had placed in the abstract section, was at the time painting "still lifes and interiors and landscapes" and told Janis "you know I'm really not an abstract painter." Of Rothko and Gottlieb, Janis wrote, "Both artists are known as abstract painters, but they are represented here" by works in which "surrealist overtones prevail." Sidney Janis, *Abstract and Surrealist Art*, New York: Reynal & Hitchcock, 1944.

37 BN, "La Forgue," unpublished, 1944.

38 BN, "La Forgue."

EIGHTEEN. THE BRETON OF AMERICAN PAINTING

1 Oral history interview with Esther Dick Gottlieb, Oct. 22, 1981, AAA.

2 Lee Hall, *Betty Parsons: Artist, Dealer, Collector*, New York: H. N. Abrams, 1991.

3 "An art gallery should be an active agent impelling the aesthetic education of the people—not a marketplace." Barney scribbled "Unless it teaches lessons in philosophy, the philosophy of art, it is no better, as a cultural institution, than the gaudy showrooms of Dobnox's Millinery establishment. Too often is art, for most of the galleries, mere merchandise."

4 Barney's early drawings cannot be dated precisely with any certainty. "Newman dated only twenty-six of the eighty-three extant drawings. Subsequent to the artist's death, Annalee Newman collected all the drawings (some still in the sketch pads on which they were drawn) and brought them into systematic order." Brenda Richardson, *Barnett Newman, The Complete Drawings, 1944–1969*, Baltimore: The Baltimore Museum of Art, 1979.

5 Ornithological illustrations provided inspiration for other early works. See, for instance, the photographs of fossil turkey bones (plate 25) in the October 1945 issue in his library of *The Auk*, a journal of ornithology that Barney subscribed to 1942 through 1945, which shows a spurred form remarkably like the one in *Genetic Moment*, 1947.

6 Richardson, *Barnett Newman*, 158.

7 Richardson, *Barnett Newman*.

8 S. I. Newhouse to author, interview, Feb. 13, 2007.

9 TS to IS, 1966, IS papers, 1909–2007, bulk 1950–2000, the Getty Research Institute, Los Angeles.

10 Irving Sandler, *The Triumph of American Painting*, New York: Harper & Row 1976, 79.

11 Paul Cummings, oral history interview with Buffie Johnson, Nov. 22, 1977–Jan. 23, 1978, AAA.

12 Howard Putzel, Introduction to exhibition "A Problem for Critics," May 1945.

13 BN, "The Plasmic Image," SWI.

14 IS papers.

15 Avery was "a problem" that he had to work out, Barney told Irving Sandler. "How do you treat him? Mark and Adolph sat at his feet."

16 Abe Rappaport to Mr. and Mrs. Greenhouse, May 31, 1945.

17 BN, "Surrealism and the War," unpublished, SWI.

18 BN, notes for an interview, n.d., BNFA.

19 BN, "Response to the Reverend Thomas F. Mathews," *Revolution, Place and Symbol (Journal of the First Congress on Religion, Architecture, and the Visual Arts)*, 1969; repr. in SWI.

20 BN, "Response to the Reverend Thomas F. Mathews."

21 Alfred Leslie to author, interview, Dec. 13, 2012.

22 Jewish slave laborers were tattooed at the Auschwitz camp.

23 BN, "Painting and Prose"/"Frankenstein," SWI.

24 AN to the Greenhouses, July 6, 1945.

25 MR to B + A, July 31, 1945.

26 Gottlieb to B + A, Sept. 1, 1945.

27 Ethel Baziotes to author, interview, Jan. 28, 2009.

28 Nick Carone to author, interview, Oct. 16, 2008.

29 Jeanne Bultman to author, interview, Mar. 17, 2007.

30 MR to B + A, July 31, 1945.

31 TH papers, 1939–1978, AAA.

32 BN to IS, IS papers.

33 Robert Storr, "A Man of Parts," *Tony Smith: Architect, Painter, Sculptor*, New York: MoMA, 1998.

34 IS papers.

35 AN to the Greenhouses, Aug. 10, 1945; Bob Kane to author, interview, Apr. 2, 2009.

36 BBN to Jewell, n.d., possibly never sent.

37 BN, interview with Joanna Magloff, c.1963.

38 Gottlieb to B + A, Sept. 1, 1945.

39 BBN to Mr. Hickok, the Trustees of the Sailors' Snug Harbor, Dec. 17, 1945.

40 Esther Gottlieb, interview, 1981.

41 AN to Barbara Rose, Barbara Rose papers, 1940–

1993, bulk 1960–1985, the Getty Research Institute, Los Angeles.

42 Ethel Baziotes to author, 2009.

NINETEEN. THE PLASMIC IMAGE

1 AN, interview by John O'Neill, 1994.

2 "Ioannus Magus": "John the Sorcerer" or "John the Magician" (a pseudonym Graham used); "Servus Dei": "Servant of God"; "Ex ungue leonem" is a common idiom: "from a claw, [you can judge] a lion," or less literally, "from a part, you can understand the whole"; "Qui bene castigat bene amat" is the inversion of an idiom: "he who loves well, punishes well"; Graham may have miswritten, and intended the proper meaning, or playfully, he may have intended the inversion: "he who punishes well, loves well"; "L'art est comme le supplice du pal ça commence bien mais ça finit mal": "art is like impalement it starts well but ends badly."

3 Eila Kokkinen, "John Graham During the 1940s," *Arts* (Nov. 1976).

4 Harry Rand, "John Graham," *Sum Qui Sum*, exhibition catalogue, New York: Allan Stone Gallery, 2005.

5 John Graham, *System and Dialectics of Art*, New York and Paris: Delphic Studios, 1937, 95–96.

6 BN, "The First Man Was an Artist," SWI.

7 Graham, *System and Dialectics*, 97.

8 BN, "The Plasmic Image," SWI.

9 Graham, *System and Dialectics*, 97–100.

10 RM to author, email, Nov. 5, 2012.

11 BN to Sidney Janis, Apr. 9, 1955.

12 Graham, *System and Dialectics*, 101.

13 Graham, *System and Dialectics*, 93, 96.

14 BN, "Adolph Gottlieb," SWI.

15 BN, interview with Joanna Magloff, c. 1963.

16 BN, "The Plasmic Image." Unless otherwise noted, all quotations come from this text.

17 BN, "The First Man Was an Artist."

18 AN interviewed by Dodie Kazanjian, 1991, unpublished transcript.

19 "The Anglo-Saxon Tradition in Art Criticism," SWI.

TWENTY. THE TERROR

1 The dating of Barney's early, unexhibited, works is often questioned. The doodles on the Guggenheim sheet are evidence for 1946 as a date for several works. The dates when Barney titled the works are not firmly established.

2 BN, "The Ideographic Picture," SWI.

3 Ralph Linton and Paul S. Wingert, *Arts of the South Seas*, New York: The Museum of Modern Art, 1946, and BN manuscript. This correspondence was noted in Barbara Marie Reise, "'Primitivism' in the Writings of Barnett B. Newman: A Study in the Ideological Background of Abstract Expressionism," master's thesis, Columbia University, New York, 1965, on deposit at BNFA, 21.

4 Reise, "'Primitivism' in the Writings of Barnett B. Newman."

5 Newman, "Art of the South Seas," SWI, originally published in Spanish as "Las formas artisticas del Pacifico," in *Ambos Mundos*, June 1946.

6 "A Conversation: Barnett Newman and Thomas B. Hess," The Solomon R. Guggenheim Museum, May 1, 1966. In 1969, *Studio International* considered publishing for the first time an English translation of the article; Barney asked them to "emphasize its historical value in my Life as a painter—that in this article I obviously repudiate Surrealist dogmas and question their influence, an influence that has been made much of by art historians in discussing the 40's in connection with my work."

7 Lee Hall, *Betty Parsons: Artist, Dealer, Collector*, New York: H. N. Abrams, 1991, 75, 77.

8 AN interviewed by Dodie Kazanjian, 1991, unpublished transcript.

9 Luis J. Navascués to BN, July 31, 1946.

10 Charles Seliger diary, July 5, 1970, Morgan Library.

11 Carmen Herrera to author, interview, Oct. 19, 2010.

12 Oral history interview with Jack Tworkov, Aug. 17, 1962, AAA.

13 Oral history interview with Esther Dick Gottlieb, Oct. 22, 1981, AAA.

14 Oral history interview with Philip Pavia, Jan. 19, 1965, AAA.

15 Oral history interview with Buffie Johnson, Nov. 13, 1982, AAA.

16 I am indebted to Melissa Ho's notes in the Philadelphia Museum Archives.

17 Esther Gottlieb, interview, 1981.

18 SN to BN, Aug. 1946.

19 MR to BN, Aug. 10, 1946.

20 "A Conversation: Barnett Newman and Thomas B. Hess."

21 *NYT* (July 1, 1947).

22 I am grateful to Myra Mniewski and Chana Pollack for translating and interpreting this letter. In April, The Anglo-American Committee of Inquiry had issued a report that reversed much of the 1939 White Paper, urged the relaxing of restrictions on Jewish land purchases and the admission of 100,000 more Jews into Palestine. The entire report and a lengthy editorial appeared in a Zionist journal to which Abraham subscribed, and which found its way into Barney's hands as well. Five weeks before Abraham's letter, one million American Zionists, among them Abraham, voted for delegates to the 22nd World Zionist Congress, scheduled to be held in Jerusalem in August, but now postponed to December in Basel. News reports of continuing slaughter of Jews in Poland, staggering numbers of refugees from camps who were refused entry to Palestine and other countries and were without any place to go, humanitarian zeal and nationalistic fervor contributed to the urgency. Palestine was a powder keg. In June there were waves of violence, and on July 22, 1946, the headquarters of the British military command in the King David Hotel in Jerusalem was blown up by the Zionist

paramilitary organization, Irgun (and denounced by the Jewish National Council). This is the context of Abraham's letter, and his confidence in Barney's sentient reception.

TWENTY-ONE. ONLY THE PURE IDEA

1 Lee Hall, conversations with Betty Parsons, cited in Lee Hall, *Betty Parsons: Artist, Dealer, Collector*, New York: H. N. Abrams, 1991.

2 Will Barnet to author, interview, May 14, 2009.

3 Leo G. Mazow, review of Elizabeth Hutchinson, *The Indian Craze: Primitivism, Modernism, and Transculturation in American Art, 1890–1915*, in *The Art Bulletin* 95.1 (Mar. 2013).

4 Oral history interview with Peter Busa, Sept. 5, 1965, AAA.

5 Busa, interview, 1965.

6 Barnet to author, 2009.

7 Cited in Steven Naifeh and Gregory White Smith, *Jackson Pollock: An American Saga*, New York: C. N. Potter, 1989, 281, 337.

8 The internal bisection noted by Barney was an aspect of Northwest Coast art discussed at length as early as 1927 by Franz Boas in *Primitive Art* (Oslo: H. Aschehoug & Co.) and more recently, in 1941, by Frederic H. Douglas and Rene d'Harnoncourt, who attributed it to a "tendency toward realism" in *Indian Art of the United States* (New York: The Museum of Modern Art). In 1965 Barney told Barbara Reise that he had read Boas "at some point" (the edition of *Primitive Art* in his library was from 1955), and that he was "sufficiently acquainted" with Douglas and d'Harnoncourt's interpretation to "remember it in total almost 20 years later as a tremendously funny one." Barbara Reise, notes after interviewing BN, Apr. 14, 1965, Tate Archives.

9 BN, interview with Joanna Magloff, c. 1963.

10 Katharine Kuh papers, 1875–1994, bulk 1930–1994, AAA.

11 BN, "Northwest Coast Indian Painting," 1946, SWI.

12 RM1.

13 AN, interview with Ann Temkin, June 17, 1998, Philadelphia Museum of Art, Library and Archives Repository.

14 TH papers, 1939–1978, AAA.

15 AN, interview by John O'Neill, 1994.

16 *NYT* (Oct. 6, 1946).

17 The magazine was *Possibilities*, which Motherwell edited with social/art critic Harold Rosenberg, Pierre Chareau, and John Cage, and which only existed for one issue, Winter 1947–48. "Naturally the deadly political situation exerts an enormous pressure," Motherwell and Rosenberg wrote on the title page.

18 Luis J. Navascués to John Lehman, Nov. 16, 1946.

19 Oral history interview with Jack Tworkov, Aug. 17, 1962, AAA.

20 TH papers.

21 Howard Devree, "A Reviewer's Notes," *NYT* (Dec. 8, 1946).

22 Elsa Maxwell, "Betty Parsons' Christmas Show," *New York Post* (Dec. 20, 1946).

23 Margaret Lynne Ausfeld, "Circus Girl Arrested: A History of the *Advancing American Art* Collection,

23 Renee Rabinovitch, letters to AN, 1946.

24 BP to BN, Aug. 13 and 30, 1946.

1946–48," *Advancing American Art: Politics and Aesthetics in the State Department Exhibition, 1946–48*, exhibition catalogue, Montgomery, AL: Montgomery Museum of Fine Arts, 1984, cited in Irving Sandler and Amy Newman, *Defining Modern Art: Selected Writings of Alfred H. Barr, Jr.*, New York: H. N. Abrams, 1986.

24 Hall, *Betty Parsons: Artist, Dealer, Collector*, 83.

25 BN, "The Ideographic Picture," SWI.

26 Packing slip from Joseph Mayer Co., Union Square; invoices and delivery slips from John Boyle Canvas; Fezandie & Sperrle, Inc ("pure artists dry colors").

27 In the late spring of 1947, less than a year after the Parsons Gallery had opened, Guggenheim returned to Europe. The night before she left for Venice she had dinner at the Newmans' apartment. Several of the American artists—including Pollock, Still, and Rothko—whom she had shown alongside the European Surrealists had become friends of Barney's. When Guggenheim closed Art of This Century, he told Betty, they "want to be in your gallery." Rothko and Still made the move; Pollock turned out to be a harder sell.

28 AN, interview, 1994.

29 Edward Alden Jewell, "New Phase in Art Noted at Display," *NYT* (Jan. 23, 1947); Maude Kemper Riley, *MKR's Art Outlook* 1.29 (Jan. 27, 1947).

30 BN, interview with Magloff. c. 1963.

31 IS papers, 1909–2007, bulk 1950–2000, the Getty Research Institute, Los Angeles.

32 Barney wrote a disquisition, complete with schematic drawing, on the ginseng root to charm Annalee after one of their first dates, and to explain his use of it in a 1934 poem.

33 TS to IS, IS papers.

34 Oral history interview with HF, Apr. 22, 1968–Jan. 6, 1969, AAA.

35 TS to IS, IS papers.

36 CS to BP, Apr. 1947, Betty Parsons Gallery records and personal papers, 1916–1991, bulk 1946–1983, AAA.

37 Martin Gasser, "Barnett Newman: Another Photographic Footnote," Princeton seminar paper, Sept. 28, 1988, on deposit at BNFA; oral history interview with Aaron Siskind, Sept. 28–Oct. 2, 1982, AAA.

38 John Bernard Myers interview with Barbara Rose, Barbara Rose papers, 1962–c. 1969, AAA.

39 TS, letter to AN, May 17, 1971.

40 Motherwell to Kazanjian, Dodie Kazanjian papers, 1949–2017, bulk 1980–2017, AAA.

41 HF, interview, 1968–1969.

42 BN, "Interview with Kathleen Shorthall of *Life*," 1959, conducted for research of article Dorothy Seiberling, "Baffling U.S. Art: What It Is About," *Life* (November 9, 1959); AN interview, 1994.

43 AN interviewed by Dodie Kazanjian, 1991, unpublished transcript. Pollock had a contract with Guggenheim, guaranteeing him a $300 monthly stipend, which Guggenheim felt should be transferred to his new representative.

The financial burden was eventually mitigated through a revised arrangement.

44 James Breslin, *Mark Rothko, A Biography*, Chicago: The University of Chicago Press, 1993, 222.

TWENTY-TWO. THE FIRST MAN WAS AN ARTIST

1 MR to BN, June 24, 1947.

2 BNFA. Sales and Commissions Daybook, Betty Parsons Gallery records and personal papers, 1916–1991, bulk 1946–1983. Archives of American Art, Smithsonian Institution.

3 Gottlieb to B + A, Sept. 5, 1947.

4 Barney preserved the May 15, 1948 Yiddish edition of *Der Tog*, with its four-inch banner headline announcing the U.N. vote.

5 Gottlieb to B + A, Sept. 5, 1947.

6 The story of Abraham and Isaac, of trust and duty and sacrifice, was burned into Barney's mind as the paradigm of father and son relationship. In the early 1960s, after Barney had acquired the grand master status that perfectly jibed with his dignified and dapper physical presentation, a young Larry Poons arranged a lunch with Poons's father. The elder Poons, a New York businessman, was not happy with his son's choice to be an artist. A reconciliation was no longer the issue, both men had drawn lines in the sand. But Larry thought Barney would impress his father as a model of how consequential an artist could be. They ate in the upstairs dining room at Sweet's, the legendary Fulton Fish Market restaurant that was Barney's favorite haunt. What stood out in Larry Poons's memory was Barney "going on to my father about Abraham. About killing his son." Almost killing his son. Presumably, Barney had the story right. Larry Poons to author, interview, June 17, 2010.

7 Of the many observances secular Jews could pick and choose from, honoring a deceased parent was the hardest to give up. "Don't forget if I die to say Kadish," Jack Tworkov's father wrote on the back of a drawing of him.

8 "Meganthropus" had been excavated 1936–37 in Java by paleontologist G.G.R. von Koenigswald. The "Java Giant" was initially touted in newspapers as the "missing link," the oldest and biggest human ancestor. A previous investigation by Koenigswald discovered the source of the mysterious "dragon's teeth" sold in Chinese apothecaries; they came from a genus of giant apes. In the fall of 1946 the bones of Meganthropus and the teeth of the giant ape, brought to the Museum of Natural History in New York for study, received renewed press coverage. The *NYT* articles of 1946, while referring to the giant teeth, said nothing about "dragons"; Barney knew the reference from earlier coverage, created the "metaphor," and took great dramatic license, getting several facts wrong. In 1964 he told Barbara Reise that he "used" the news story "as a take-off point."

TWENTY-THREE. ONEMENT

1 BN interviewed by David Sylvester, Mar. 3, 1967.

2 BN, transcription from audiotape, April or May 1970, of *Painters Painting: New York Art Scene, 1940–1970*, Emile de Antonio, documentary film, 1972.

3 TH papers, 1939–1978, AAA.

4 "Exhibition of Sculptures, Paintings, Drawings" by Alberto Giacometti, January 19 to February 14, 1948, with a catalogue essay by Jean-Paul Sartre; Franz Meyer,

45 CS to MR. James E. B. Breslin Research Archive on Mark Rothko. The Getty Research Institute, Los Angeles.

46 MR to BN, June 24, 1947.

47 Breslin, *Mark Rothko*, 222.

9 "Rashi" (1040–1105) was the acronymic name of Shlomo ben Yitzhaki, a rabbi and author of revered canonical Torah commentary. This is an example of how Barney loved to drop learned Jewish references into his entirely secular discourse: "What? You aren't conversant with Rashi?" he seemed to needle the readers of the journal *Tiger's Eye*, "and that his genius, which I'm invoking here, was how he could reveal in the most profound ideas the plain meaning?"

10 BN, "The First Man Was an Artist," manuscript, 1947, SWI.

11 BN, interview with Joanna Magloff, c. 1963.

12 "A Conversation: Barnett Newman and Thomas B. Hess," The Solomon R. Guggenheim Museum, May 1, 1966.

13 David Anfam, "The Tiger's Eye. New Haven," in *The Burlington Magazine* 144,1190 (May 2002).

14 BN to Ruth and John Stephan, Aug. 25, 1947.

15 BN to Mr. and Mrs. John Stephan, June 21, 1959.

16 AN interviewed by Dodie Kazanjian, 1991, unpublished transcript.

17 BN to Ruth and John Stephan, Aug. 31, 1947, *Tiger's Eye* papers, Beinecke Rare Book and Manuscript Collection, Yale University, New Haven.

18 It is unclear exactly when Barney's paintings received the titles under which we know them today. By the time of his show at Bennington College in 1958, the titles were firmly established. In the cases of works published or exhibited before then three options exist—a proper name, a descriptive title, or a number—but many of the pre-1958 paintings, sometimes appearing in informal photographs, had never been exhibited or published before the Bennington show. From later comments by Barney, and from lists of potential names that he made during the late '40s and early '50s, it can be inferred that he had names in mind, even if the works were subsequently exhibited, as in the Parsons shows of 1950 and 1951, with numbers.

19 CG, "Review of Exhibitions of Hedda Sterne and Adolph Gottlieb," *The Nation* (Dec. 6, 1947).

20 BN, response to CG, 1947, SWI.

21 *Club Without Walls: Selections from the Journals of Philip Pavia*, ed. Natalie Edgar, New York: Midmarch Arts Press, 2007.

22 BN, "The New Sense of Fate," manuscript, c. 1947–1948, SWI.

23 BN, "The Ideographic Picture," SWI.

24 BN, response to CG.

"Giacometti et Newman," in *Alberto Giacometti: Sculptures, peintures, dessin*, Paris: Museé d'Art Moderne de la Ville de Paris, 1991.

5 Quoted in Hub Crehan, *Art News* (Apr. 1959).

6 "Here we have our two heroes and which side to choose?" Reinhardt wrote Barney, sending him "Hemingway Joins Uproar Over Wright," a newspaper article about a building by Frank Lloyd Wright planned for the Grand

Canal. "Fire or water? Progress or romance? Apollo or Dionysius? The city of God and the light of reason and the cold white peaks of art?" Ad Reinhardt to BN, Mar. 24, 1954. Used by permission, © Anna Reinhardt/ARS, New York.

7 Reise described the one "he lived with" for a year as "dark bottle green w/ orange stripe down center (in heavy impasto)." Barbara Reise, notes after interviewing BN, Jan. 21, 1964, Tate Archives. No extant painting fits that description, but the darker brown used in *End of Silence*—which was exhibited in January 1950—contains more greenish pigment than that of *Onement I*. Although Hess referred to Number One, it is clear from the details he provided the painting under discussion was *Onement II*: "Tony Smith bought it from Betty Parsons, and later gave it to [the Wadsworth Atheneum in] Hartford." TH papers.

8 Harold Cohen, introduction to "Barnett Newman Talks to David Sylvester," BBC radio broadcast, Nov. 17, 1965, transcript in the Getty Research Institute, Los Angeles.

9 David Sylvester, *About Modern Art*, 2nd ed., New Haven: Yale UP, 2001.

10 Interviewed about Pollock in 1959, Barney compared the painters' "fight against ritual," and empty forms to that of Hemingway and Faulkner challenging "formal, empty," and "polished" American literature in the manner of William Dean Howells. BN, "Interview with Kathleen Shorthall of *Life*," 1959, conducted for research of article Dorothy Seiberling, "Baffling U.S. Art: What It Is About," *Life* (November 9, 1959).

11 BN, transcription from audiotape, April or May 1970.

12 HR, *Barnett Newman*, New York: H. N. Abrams, 1978.

13 Douglas Davis, notes for interview of BN, 1969.

14 Since giving *Pagan Void* to her in December 1947, Barney regularly made such presents to Annalee; they must have had faith in the work's future value, but at this early stage even Barney could not have imagined that the gifts would have any tax benefit.

15 BN interviewed by Sylvester, 1967.

16 "The Object and the Image," in *The Tiger's Eye* (Mar. 3, 1948), repr. in SWI.

17 For this and other reasons I do not agree with the precise chronology that the early drawings have been given.

18 See the description of the paint application in *Be I*, 1949, with which Barney guaranteed that the expanse of red color and the thin stripe of white would exist on precisely the same plane, in Carol Mancusi-Ungaro, "The Paintings of Barnett Newman: 'Involved Intuition on the Highest Level' ", in Richard Shiff, Carol Mancusi-Ungaro, and Heidi Colsman-Freyberger, *Barnett Newman: A Catalogue Raisonné*, New Haven: Yale UP; New York: Barnett Newman Foundation, 2004, 139, n. 44.

19 BN to John and Ruth Stephan, May 12, 1959.

20 BN to Mr. & Mrs. John Stephan, June 21, 1959.

TWENTY-FOUR. EMBATTLED

1 Howard Devree, "Art from Germany on View in Capital," *NYT* (Mar. 17, 1948). The paintings came from the so-called "202" collection of paintings discovered in Bavarian salt mines, including 15 by Rembrandt, Rubens's *Andromeda*, a panel by Castagno, and works by Giotto, Masaccio, Caravaggio, van Eyck, van der Weyden, and Cranach.

2 "Movies to Oust Ten Cited for Contempt of Congress," *NYT* (Nov. 26, 1947).

3 Aline B. Louchheim, "Classic or Modern? Museum Agreement Brings to the Fore the Slippery Question of Cleavage," *NYT* (Feb. 1, 1948).

4 *NYT* (Mar. 28, 1948).

5 *NYT* (Mar. 28, 1948).

6 To which, it is said, Motherwell responded, "You mean that you're going to do it with that little painting?" Hess identified the work under discussion as a little orange painting with "green and grey horizontal stripes"; it might possibly have been *Galaxy*, which has, since its first exhibition, at Bennington in 1958 (ex-catalogue), been hung vertically. TH papers, 1939–1978, AAA.

7 BNFA. HF papers, 1932–1987, AAA.

8 "Critics Denounced by Artists' Group," *NYT* (May 6, 1948).

9 "Controversial Art to be Sold to Bidders Under Guise of U.S. War Surplus Property," *NYT* (May 18, 1948). The art had been intended for embassies at the tour's end.

10 BN, "Arshile Gorky: Poet and Immolator," 1948, SWI.

11 Clay Spohn papers, c. 1862–1985, bulk 1890–1985, AAA.

12 CS to MR, March 23, 1948, James E. B. Breslin Research Archive on Mark Rothko, the Getty Research Institute, Los Angeles.

13 CG, "The Situation at the Moment," *Partisan Review* (Jan. 1948), repr. in *Clement Greenberg: The Collected Essays and Criticism*, ed. John O'Brian, vol. 2, *Arrogant Purpose, 1945–1949*, Chicago: The University of Chicago Press, 1988.

14 Karlen Mooradian, *The Many Worlds of Arshile Gorky*, Chicago: Gilgamesh Press Limited, 1980.

15 BN, "Arshile Gorky: Poet and Immolator."

16 Donald Paneth interview, 1952, in William and Ethel Baziotes papers, c. 1900–1992, bulk 1935–1980, AAA.

17 WB to Chris Baziotes, Nov. 10, 1948, William and Ethel Baziotes papers.

18 CS to BN, Dec. 11, 1948.

19 Oral history interview with Fritz Bultman, Jan. 6, 1968, AAA.

20 Julie Haifley, oral history interview with Grace Hartigan, May 10, 1979, AAA.

21 Steven Naifeh and Gregory White Smith, *Jackson Pollock: An American Saga*, New York: C. N. Potter, 1989, 557.

22 Naifeh and Smith, *Jackson Pollock*, 557.

23 CG, "Review of an Exhibition of Willem de Kooning," *The Nation* (Apr. 24, 1948).

24 Mark Stevens and Annalyn Swan, *de Kooning: An American Master*, New York: Knopf, 2004, 251.

25 Pat Passlof, quoted in Stevens and Swann, *de Kooning*, 268.

26 Ibram Lassaw, quoted in Stevens and Swann, *de Kooning*, 269.

27 Bultman, interview, 1968.

28 WB to Chris Baziotes, Dec. 6, 1948, William and Ethel Baziotes papers.

29 Robert Goodnough, "Artists' Sessions at Studio 35 (1950)," *Modern Artists in America, First Series*, New York: Wittenborn Schultz, 1952, 16.

30 Yvonne Thomas to author, interview, Mar. 21, 2007.

31 "Wonders of City Graphically Told," *NYT* (Aug. 22, 1948).

32 BNFA.

33 Ethel Baziotes to author, interview, Jan. 28, 2009.

34 In later years, a few of the paintings' titles—for instance *White Fire, Black Fire, The Way, The Gate*—were derived from Jewish mystical concepts, just as some were based in Talmudic Judaism (*Abraham, Covenant, Joshua*); classical mythology (*Achilles, Ulysses, Dionysius, Prometheus Bound*); and his favorite Mozart opera (*Queen of the Night*). Sometime around 1947–50, Barney made a list of possible titles for paintings that also included New Testament references—"Transfiguration," "The Deposition," as well as astronomic—"Nebulae," "Galactic," "Solstice, Crespusular," "Astral"; ancient Egyptian—"Phoenix," "Sun Rites"; and the more generic "The Awakening" and "Exaltation." He liked to show off his erudition.

35 *The Menorah Journal*, founded in 1915, was a wide-ranging forum of viewpoints "devoted first and last to bringing out the values of Jewish culture and ideals, of Hebraism and of Judaism."

36 John Slawson, "The Quest for Jewish Identity in America," *Journal of Jewish Communal Service* 40 (Fall 1963), cited in Susan A. Glenn, "The Vogue of Jewish Self-Hatred in Post-World War II America," *Jewish Social Studies* New Series 2.3 (Spring–Summer 2006), 95–136.

37 Glenn, "The Vogue of Jewish Self-Hatred," 107.

38 HR, "Jewish Identity in a Free Society: On Current Efforts to Enforce 'Total Commitment,'" *Commentary* (June 9, 1950). Barney kept the issue of the *Contemporary Jewish Record* from 1944 in which Greenberg, participating in "Under Forty: A Symposium on American Literature and the Younger Generation of American Jews," rebelled against the "suffocatingly middle-class behavior" of American Jews.

39 See Glenn, "The Vogue of Jewish Self-Hatred."

40 HR, "Jewish Identity in a Free Society."

41 Mira Schor, ed., *The Extreme of the Middle: Writings of Jack Tworkov*, New Haven: Yale UP, 2009.

42 CG, "Self-Hatred and Jewish Chauvinism: Some Reflections on 'Positive Jewishness,'" *Commentary* (Nov. 10, 1950).

43 Geoffrey Dorfman, ed., *Out of the Picture: Milton Resnick and the New York School*, New York: Midmarch Arts Press, 2002, 66.

44 CG, "Self-Hatred and Jewish Chauvinism."

45 IS to author, interview, Sept. 18, 2006.

46 The passage he quoted in his catalogue statement was incomplete enough to be a misrepresentation (*Barnett Newman: The Stations of the Cross: Lema Sabachthani*, exhibition catalogue, New York: Solomon R. Guggenheim Museum, 1966). Barney counted on there being a wall between those who paid attention to art and those who knew enough Mishnaic theology to challenge his contraband usage, which, among other impressive effects he expected it would have, also announced in a far-from-neutral climate, "I am not a self-hating Jew."

47 Barney aimed to tease Hess, an assimilated Jew.

48 BN to Hans van Weeren-Griek, Jan. 18, 1965.

49 Robert Goodnough, interview with BN, late 1950s.

TWENTY-FIVE. THE SUBLIME

1 Carol Mancusi-Ungaro, in Ann Temkin, *Barnett Newman*, exhibition catalogue, Philadelphia: Philadelphia Museum of Art, 2002, 139 n. 23.

2 Egg tempera did not yellow, as oil did. "When I painted 'The Voice,' in 1950, it was just before plastic paints were introduced as an artist's medium. The best known medium, therefore, with which to paint white was egg tempera. . . . egg tempera is one of the best and oldest vehicles for painting." Oil and egg tempera were also the materials of the 1948 *Two Edges*, but without the same brilliant effect. Carol Mancusi-Ungaro's "The Paintings of Barnett Newman: 'Involved Intuition on the Highest Level,'" in Richard Shiff, Carol Mancusi-Ungaro, and Heidi Colsman-Freyberger, *Barnett Newman: A Catalogue Raisonné*, New Haven: Yale UP; New York: Barnett Newman Foundation, 2004, is the best source regarding Newman's use of materials.

3 The 26 works in Pollock's January 1949 show at Parsons were all painted in 1948.

4 Jermayne MacAgy, foreword, catalogue for Third Annual Exhibition of Painting at the California Palace of the Legion of Honor, San Francisco, Dec. 1, 1948–Jan. 16, 1949.

5 Times and Herald Squares: centers of newspaper publishing. At the end of 1947 *Mona Lisa's Mustache: A Dissection of Modern Art*, New York: Knopf, represented

the nadir of, in Greenberg's words, "vulgarity . . . violent and banal simple-mindedness." Written by the successful society architect and designer T. H. Robsjohn-Gibbings, the book was widely discussed in the first half of 1948 when avant-garde art was under attack.

6 Barney maintained that Pissarro was underrated due to anti-Semitism. AN, interview with Ann Temkin, Philadelphia Museum of Art, Library and Archives Repository.

7 CG, "The Crisis of the Easel Picture," *Partisan Review* (Apr. 1948).

8 CG, review of an exhibition of William de Kooning, *The Nation* (Apr. 24, 1948).

9 HR, "The Herd of Independent Minds: Has the Avant-Garde Its Own Mass Culture?," *Commentary* 6.3 (Sept. 1948).

10 BN, interview with KO, unpublished, August 2, 1963. Both references occurred before Barney had seen a major sculpture by the Italian artist. It was only in 1964 that the Vatican's *Pietà* traveled to New York to be displayed at the World's Fair, where it could be viewed from a moving sidewalk. Barney continued through his life to fall back on the enduringly popular image of Michelangelo as a model of the convention-defying, entirely self-assured, insistently personal artist—for 400 years "divine"; no other standard would suffice. His understanding was stubbornly thin, focused on ambition rather than the master's ability to

transcend frustrations and compromises with patrons and politics and stunningly blind to libido. No factual information would alter his conviction.

11 Lincoln Kirstein, "The State of Modern Painting," *Harper's Magazine* (Oct. 1948).

12 Modern Art Shackled to Communism: Speech of Hon. George A. Dondero of Michigan in the United States House of Representatives, Tuesday, Aug. 16, 1949, U.S. Congress, *Congressional Record*, 81st Cong., 1st sess., vol. 95.

13 CG, "The Present Prospects of American Painting and Sculpture," *Horizon* (Oct. 1947).

14 "A *Life* Round Table on Modern Art," *Life* (Oct. 11, 1948).

15 Robert Goldwater was the editor, with contributions from Jacques Barzun, Alfred Frankenstein, Clement Greenberg, George Heard Hamilton, H. W. Janson, Lionel Trilling, and museum men Alfred H. Barr, Jr., John I. H. Baur, Holger Cahill, Lloyd Goodrich, Douglas MacAgy, and James Thrall Soby.

16 "A *Life* Round Table on Modern Art."

17 *Clyfford Still*, ed. John P. O'Neill, New York: The Metropolitan Museum of Art, 1979, 186.

18 CS to BP, Sept. 17, 1948, Betty Parsons Gallery records and personal papers, 1916–1991, bulk 1946–1983, AAA.

19 AN interviewed by Dodie Kazanjian, 1991, unpublished transcript; additional interview tape in Dodie Kazanjian papers, 1949–2017, bulk 1980–2017, AAA. AN, interview with Ann Temkin.

20 Mary Abbot to author, interview, Jan. 30, 2010.

21 Yvonne Thomas to author, interview, Mar. 21, 2007.

22 BN to MR, draft, n.d.

23 AN, interview, 1991.

24 BN, "Interview with Kathleen Shorthall of *Life*,"

1959, conducted for research of article Dorothy Seiberling, "Baffling U.S. Art: What It Is About," *Life* (Nov. 9, 1959).

25 Additional interview tape, Kazanjian papers.

26 "Jackson Pollock: An Artists' Symposium," *Art News* (Apr. and May 1967).

27 AN, interview, 1991.

28 Presumably, if Barney objected, that would have arisen in the 1959 correspondence that catalogued his decade-old grievances against Stephan.

29 HR, "Barnett Newman: 'A Man of Controversy, and Spiritual Grandeur,'" *Vogue* (Feb. 1, 1963); BN, transcription from audiotape, April or May 1970, of *Painters Painting: New York Art Scene, 1940–1970*, Emile de Antonio, documentary film, 1972.

30 TBH2.

31 In every case when a tapered vertical appears in an early work, the form tapers from top to bottom, and in all later reproductions that is how *The Two Edges* appears. The importance that Barney attributed to the magazine page as a permanent record was the "first cause" in his lawsuit against Ad Reinhardt five and a half years later.

32 William Rubin, untranscribed interview with Dodie Kazanjian, Kazanjian papers.

33 For a comprehensive discussion of the title *Onement* see Richard Shiff, "To Create Oneself: II. A New Way of Drawing," Richard Shiff, Carol Mancusi-Ungaro, and Heidi Colsman-Freyberger, *Barnett Newman: A Catalogue Raisonné*, New Haven: Yale UP; New York: Barnett Newman Foundation, 2004. The importance of a "signature" was not lost on the artists. Shortly before Ad Reinhardt's January 1952 show at Parsons, "Mark and Barney" advised him not to show a 12-foot painting Reinhardt was rushing to finish because "its [*sic*] different from the rest of the work."

TWENTY-SIX. SUBJECTS OF THE ARTIST

1 AN notes in the Sam Hunter Files, n.d.

2 Mary Abbot to author, interview, Jan. 30, 2010; Yvonne Thomas to author, interview, Mar. 21, 2007.

3 *Life* (Feb. 21, 1949).

4 BN to IS, IS papers, 1909–2007, bulk 1950–2000, the Getty Research Institute, Los Angeles.

5 BN to IS, IS papers.

6 BN to IS, IS papers.

7 Additional interview tape in Dodie Kazanjian papers, 1949–2017, bulk 1980–2017, AAA.

8 AN notes in the Sam Hunter Files.

9 Jack Tworkov to IS, IS papers.

10 Thomas to author, 2007.

11 Abbot to author, 2010.

12 Thomas to author, 2007.

13 Yvonne Thomas, James E. B. Breslin Research Archive on Mark Rothko, the Getty Research Institute, Los Angeles.

14 Thomas to author, 2007.

15 Un-aired portion of interview conducted by Lane Slate in preparation for *Contemporary American Painters* series broadcast by CBS Television, Mar. 10, 1963.

16 RM to author, interview, Oct. 16, 2010.

17 Alfred Leslie to author, interview, Dec. 13, 2012.

18 TH papers, 1939–1978, AAA. TBH, "Sketch for the Portrait of the Art Historian among Artists," *Social Research Quarterly* 45.1 (1978).

19 Thomas to author, 2007.

20 Musa Mayer, *Night Studio: A Memoir of Philip Guston*, New York, Knopf, 1988, 66.

21 Oral history interview with Conrad Marca-Relli, June 10, 1965, AAA.

22 BN to IS, IS papers.

23 Mary Fuller, "An Ad Reinhardt Monologue," *Artforum* (Oct. 1970).

24 Ad Reinhardt to Rita Reinhardt, May 1954. Used by permission, © Anna Reinhardt/ARS, New York. Courtesy the Ad Reinhardt Foundation.

25 Bradley Tomlin to BN, Dec. 5, 1949.

26 WB to Chris Baziotes, Feb. 23, 1949, William and Ethel Baziotes papers, c. 1900–1992, bulk 1935–1980, AAA.

27 Modern Art Shackled to Communism: Speech of Hon. George A. Dondero of Michigan in the United States House of Representatives, Tuesday, Aug. 16, 1949, U.S. Congress, *Congressional Record*, 81st Cong., 1st sess., vol. 95.

28 Aline Louchheim, "The State and Art," *NYT* (Sept. 4, 1949).

29 Marca-Relli, interview, 1965.

30 John Bernard Myers papers, c. 1940s–1987, bulk 1970–1987, AAA.

31 "The philistinism that feels itself confirmed by this sort of art journalism"—*Life*, *Art News*, *Art Digest*, *Harper's*, *Atlantic Monthly*—"is, I am afraid, more dangerous to culture than is generally realized." CG, "A Symposium: The State of American Art," *Magazine of Art* (Mar. 1949). See also CG, "The New York Market for American Art," *The Nation* (June 11, 1949) regarding "the Luce magazines." Both repr. in *Clement Greenberg: The Collected Essays and Criticism*, ed. John O'Brian, vol. 2, *Arrogant Purpose, 1945–1949*, Chicago: The University of Chicago Press, 1988.

32 Not quite: Boston's "Milestones of American Painting in our Century" contained works by a mixed bag of 50 artists, only four of whom were postwar, with an equal number of pre–World War I and self-taught artists.

TWENTY-SEVEN. MAN IS PRESENT

1 E P-D to author, interview, Nov. 19, 2013.

2 E P-D to author, 2013.

3 Oral history interview with Sidney Janis, Mar. 21–Sept. 26, 1972, AAA.

4 Newman v. Reinhardt 3 A.D.2d 909 (1957), Supreme Court of New York.

5 CG, "The Situation at the Moment," *Partisan Review* (Jan. 1948), cited in *Clement Greenberg: The Collected Essays and Criticism*, ed. John O'Brian, vol. 2, *Arrogant Purpose, 1945–1949*, Chicago: The University of Chicago Press, 1988.

6 Geoffrey Dorfman, ed., *Out of the Picture: Milton Resnick and the New York School*, New York: Midmarch Arts Press, 2002, 68.

7 CS to BN, Aug. 16, 1949.

8 Jack Tworkov, transcript of unpublished interview with Jessie Gifford, Nov. 1976, cited in Mira Schor, ed., *The Extreme of the Middle: Writings of Jack Tworkov*, New Haven: Yale UP, 2009. Although Tworkov said "it could have been 1948," it must have been 1949: invoices for painting material support the later date.

9 TBH1 and TBH2.

10 *NYT* (Oct. 15, 1939).

11 AN to "Dorothy," unsent postcard, Sept. 5, 1949.

12 Two years earlier, Barney had written an unpublished review of the Spanish artist's first postwar show at Pierre Matisse Gallery to support his "Ideographic" picture manifesto, and he initiated a brief correspondence.

13 B + A to Tony and Jane Smith from Marietta, Ohio, Sept. 7, 1949.

14 Ohio Historical Society.

TWENTY-EIGHT. "A SHOW AT THE BETTY PARSONS GALLERY"

1 Robert Motherwell to BN from Reno, Nov. 12, 1949.

2 Frank O'Hara, "Art New York," film interview with BN, 1964.

3 O'Hara, "Art New York."

4 These titles were given at a later date.

5 BP to AN, Nov. 16, 1949, Betty Parsons Gallery records and personal papers, 1916–1991, bulk 1946–1983, AAA.

6 Motherwell to BN, Nov. 12, 1949.

7 Bradley Walker Tomlin to BN, Dec. 14, 1949.

33 *Life* (Feb. 21, 1949).

34 *Life* (Aug. 8, 1949).

35 Milton Resnick and Ad Reinhardt, "'Attack': 1961, The Club," printed in Geoffrey Dorfman, ed., *Out of the Picture: Milton Resnick and the New York School*, New York: Midmarch Arts Press, 2002, 250.

36 Oral history interview with Fritz Bultman, January 6, 1968, AAA. Robert Motherwell, "Reflections on Painting Now," in *The Collected Writings of Robert Motherwell*, ed. Stephanie Terenzio, Berkeley: University of California Press, 1999.

37 Since 1940 Soby had held several roles at MoMA, including director of the Department of Painting and Sculpture.

38 James Thrall Soby, "Does Our Art Impress Europe?," *The Saturday Review* (Aug. 6, 1949).

39 Motherwell, "Reflections on Painting Now."

15 Barbara Reise, notes after interviewing BN, Jan. 21, 1964, Tate Archives.

16 "All the clamor over space" meant for Barney de Kooning's statement a few months earlier at the Subjects of the Artist School that "The subject matter in the abstract is space. [The artist] fills it with an attitude. The attitude never comes from himself alone. One is with a group or movement because you cannot help it." BN, "Ohio: 1949," unpublished manuscript, SWI, and HR in "The Intrasubjectives," exhibition catalogue, 1949, which appeared just as the Newmans returned to New York, before Barney's essay was written.

17 BN, "Ohio: 1949."

18 TBH2.

19 Quentin Anderson, *The Imperial Self: An Essay in American Literary and Cultural History*, New York: Knopf, 1971.

20 It was the "ideological outlook" of the makers—the Hopewell and Adena peoples and Barney—that could be analogized, not a "relationship" derived from "origin." To explain this further to Barbara Reise while they were drinking vodka, he said that simply because the beverage was consumed by both Russians and native Mexicans ("as tequila")—the former with caviar and lemon, the latter with salt—on that basis one could not say that native Mexicans were Russian.

21 BN to John Stephan, postcard, Aug. 1949.

22 Helen Carlson, "Diversity of Style and Media," *The New York Sun* (Oct. 14, 1949).

23 Samuel M. Kootz and HR, in "The Intrasubjectives," exhibition catalogue, 1949.

24 William B. Siegel, M.D., to BN, Sept. 13, 1949.

8 CS to BN, Aug. 16, 1949.

9 Amy Lee to BP, Jan. 27, 1950, Betty Parsons Gallery records and personal papers.

10 Betty Parsons Gallery to BN, May 17, 1950.

11 E P-D to author, interview, Nov. 19, 2013.

12 IS, *A Sweeper-Up After Artists*, New York: Thames & Hudson, 2003, 24.

13 Martin Gasser, "Barnett Newman: Another Photographic Footnote," Princeton seminar paper, Sept. 28, 1988, on deposit at BNFA.

14 Betty Parsons Gallery to BN, May 17, 1950.

15 What goes around comes around. In the summer of 1955, while he was teaching in Boulder, Colorado, a vertical painting of Rothko's was hung in an exhibition horizontally. "I phoned the hanger about his error," Rothko told Ferber. "Oh, it was no error . . . I thought it filled the space better." Rothko swore "by the bones of Titian" that this was true. MR to HF, July 11, 1955, HF papers, 1932–1987, AAA.

16 Betty Parsons Gallery records and personal papers.

17 Stuart Preston, "Chiefly Modern: Three New Group Shows," *NYT* (June 4, 1950).

18 It is peculiarly coincidental that Siskind didn't photograph it.

19 Emily Genauer, "Barnett Newman Exhibit," *New York Herald Tribune* (Jan. 26, 1950).

20 Aline B. Louchheim, "By Extreme Modernists," *NYT* (Jan. 29, 1950).

21 Judith Kaye Reed, "Newman's Flat Areas," *Art Digest* 24.9 (Feb. 1, 1950).

22 "Space Impelled," *Time* (Feb. 20, 1950).

23 TBH, "Barnett Newman," *Art News* (March 1950).

24 Nicolas Calas, draft for "It Is Not as It Was," for *It Is*, n.d., with BN's handwritten correction.

25 Yve-Alain Bois, "On Two Paintings by Barnett Newman," *October* 108 (Spring 2004), by permission of the Barnett Newman Foundation. In a 1967 obituary of Reinhardt, Hess wrote "an all-black painting" was included in Barney's "first show": TBH, "Ad (Adolph Dietrich Friedrich) Reinhardt," *Art News* (Oct. 1967). Barney thanked Hess for the notice: "Now that there is all this rewriting of history, the facts are most important. It will interest you then in connection with my black painting, your mention of it has been noticed by friends of my work": BN to TH, Nov. 4, 1967. It is not impossible that, 17 years after the fact, Hess may have misremembered, abetted by Barney's insistence, whether *Abraham* appeared in the January solo show or the group show four months later. In his 1971 monograph Hess called the black-on-black "an extraordinary invention," a "powerful and fresh experience" (TBH2, 60). Is it possible to believe that not only did Hess not "get" the "powerful and fresh experience" in 1950, he couldn't even see it?

26 O'Hara, "Art New York"; RM2.

27 BN draft, n.d., filed "letters to dealers Rothko-Reinhardt"; an edited version of this draft was sent to Sidney Janis, Apr. 9, 1955.

28 Barbara Reise, notes after interviewing BN, Jan. 21, 1964, Tate Archives.

29 AN, interview by John O'Neill, 1994.

30 Will Barnet to author, interview, May 14, 2009.

31 Oral history interview with Jack Tworkov, Aug. 17, 1962, AAA.

32 Nick Carone to author, interview, Oct. 16, 2008.

33 Dore Ashton to author, interview, Apr. 16, 2008.

34 TBH1.

35 TH papers, 1939–1978, AAA.

36 Annie Cohen-Solal, *Leo and His Circle: The Life of Leo Castelli*, New York: Knopf, 2010.

37 Musa Mayer, *Night Studio: A Memoir of Philip Guston*, New York: Knopf, 1988, 204.

38 AN, interview, 1994.

39 BN interviewed by David Sylvester, Mar. 3, 1967.

40 Cohen-Solal, *Leo and His Circle*.

41 *Club Without Walls: Selections from the Journals of Philip Pavia*, ed. Natalie Edgar, New York: Midmarch Arts Press, 2007, 72.

42 Tworkov, interview, 1962.

43 Geoffrey Dorfman, ed., *Out of the Picture: Milton Resnick and the New York School*, New York: Midmarch Arts Press, 2002, 68.

44 BN in a letter to Peyton Boswell, "Too Many Words—Rebuttal," *Art Digest* (Mar. 15, 1950).

45 Robert Motherwell to BN, Jan. 30, 1950.

46 Bradley Walker Tomlin to BN, Jan. 30, 1950.

47 CS to BN, Feb. 28, 1950; CS to BN, Apr. 17, 1950.

48 Tworkov, interview, 1962.

49 "The famous 'pot of paint flung at the canvas' [*sic*] would apply here with a nicety," *Art Digest* reported; Rothko is "definitely in a period of transition," said Devree, pulling his punches in *NYT*.

50 Genauer, "Barnett Newman Exhibit"; TBH, "Barnett Newman"; Reed, "Newman's Flat Area." If one stared closely at *Be I*, TBH said, "the rectangular canvas itself appeared wildly distorted. It is quite like what happens to a hen when its beak is put on the ground and a chalk line is drawn away from it in the floor."

51 TH papers.

52 Louchheim, "By Extreme Modernists." Peyton Boswell in the February *Art Digest* mocked Louchheim's review for its employment of "meaningless jargon to give profundity to some shallow abstract painting that honestly claims only decorative value." He had no intention, he said, of "singling out Barnett Newman." Gallantly, Barney wrote Boswell to defend Louchheim: "It seems to me very shabby journalism for you to use your feelings about a painter's work as a weapon of spite against a critic expressing her free feelings—a right you claim for yourself. I advisedly call it shabby journalism, because to hit below the belt as you did cannot be called yellow journalism—it's just plain yellow." He asked if it were Boswell who vandalized his work in the exhibition. BN, "Too Many Words—Rebuttal."

53 Tony Smith missed the Friday evening programs. In the fall he and his fellow faculty members at the New York University school of art education, Robert Iglehart and Hale Woodruff, privately took over the loft, renamed it, and the evenings continued until Apr. 1950.

54 Dorfman, ed., *Out of the Picture*, 68.

55 Reise, notes.

56 Dorfman, ed., *Out of the Picture*, 68.

57 IS papers, 1909–2007, bulk 1950–2000, the Getty Research Institute, Los Angeles.

58 BN, "Speech at Studio 35," Jan. 27, 1950.

59 IS to author in conversation over several occasions.

60 BN, interview with KO, unpublished, Aug. 2, 1963.

61 TBH2.

62 The movie—showing exactly at the time that "Fifteen Americans," from which Barney felt egregiously excluded, was on at MoMA—contained staggering visual drama. In an excruciating long take hundreds of reindeer topple and roll down a cliff to their deaths; in another, a small army of mounted Laplanders hunting with enormous, spread-winged eagles perched on T-shaped platforms are vividly silhouetted against the sky. Another long take watches the eagles catch and tear apart a pack of wolves. The film ends with a death-dealing avalanche. These terror-filled pri-

mal events were not what Barney talked about. Many years later he explained to Robert Murray—unlike what he told Hess about the imagined color—that it was the idea of being in a "whiteout," a horizonless, featureless landscape—emphasized by the famous curved screen of the Rivoli "film palace" where he saw it—with no markers to allow one to navigate that overwhelmed him. A feature in the *Times* that dwelled on the "frozen tundra" and the hardships suffered during the film's making may have alerted Barney to it and influenced his response.

TWENTY-NINE. "THE BIGGEST SCANDAL IN N.Y. ART WORLD"

1 "53 Living American Artists. Photographed by Herbert Matter in the Manner of the Seventeenth-Century Painter Teniers," *Vogue* (Feb. 1, 1950).

2 Eleanor Pollock, "New York at the Half-Century," *Cue* (Dec. 17, 1949).

3 Hans Noë to author, interview, June 21, 2008.

4 Among others, Tony Louvis, Mary Abbot, Robert Murray.

5 Tony Louvis to author, interview, Aug. 2009.

6 "Cities: Medieval or Modern," NBC, Aug. 1950.

7 Louvis to author, 2009.

8 "It was always an event going with Barney to somewhere. There was preparation, and 'shall we do this, shall we do that?' He would never approach anything directly. There was always a sort of preamble and a buildup and a planning. You would never just go to Tony Smith's or go to whatever destination. You'd make an arrangement and then maybe you'd alter it, and maybe you should see it in better light. And maybe you might at that stage of the day not be in such a good mood. Incredible preambles. The whole thing was almost a parody of rabbinical preparations for things." John Kasmin to author, interview, July 31, 2008.

9 Noë to author, 2008.

10 AN interviewed by Dodie Kazanjian, 1991, unpublished transcript.

11 MR to BN, Apr. 17, 1950.

12 BP to BN, Feb. 1950.

13 CS to MR, Mar. 13, 1950.

14 CS to BN, May 24, 1950.

15 BN to MR, draft, n.d.

16 CS to BN, May 4, 1950; the letter was misaddressed, and arrived later in the month.

17 CS to BN, May 10, 1950.

18 Still continued to look to Barney for corroboration; in agitated letters through the summer Still dismissed all of Western tradition—from Titian, Rubens, and Velázquez to Impressionism, Cézanne, and Picasso—critics and the larger art audience. Regarding his vision for the future, "I am sure you are with me in this," he wrote, and lobbied for a summer-session teaching position for Barney. CS to BN, July 10 and 18, 1950.

19 CS to BN, July 31, 1950.

20 Baziotes, Janice Biala, Louise Bourgeois, James Brooks, de Kooning, Jimmy Ernst, Ferber, Gottlieb, Peter Grippe, Hare, Hofmann, Weldon Kees, Ibram Lassaw, Norman Lewis, Richard Lippold, Seymour Lipton, Motherwell, Pousette-Dart, Reinhardt, Ralph Rosenborg, Stamos, Hedda Sterne, David Smith, Tomlin, and Barney.

63 "Discover the Magic of Magna," Bocour Artist Colors brochure saved by Barney, in BNFA.

64 IS interview with Ad Reinhardt, Oct. 15, 1958, IS papers.

65 For a discussion of Barney's epic saga of "pervasive anxiety over the issue of *Abraham*'s 'priority'" see Bois, "On Two Paintings by Barnett Newman," by permission of The Barnett Newman Foundation.

66 BN in O'Hara, "Art New York."

21 "I think quite possibly the symposium was more valuable to me than to anybody else," Barr wrote to Motherwell afterward. For the edited transcription that is the record of the meeting, see Robert Goodnough, "Artists' Sessions at Studio 35 (1950)," *Modern Artists in America, First Series*, New York: Wittenborn Schultz, 1952.

22 Robert Goodnough to AHB, Apr. 19, 1950, AHB papers, the Museum of Modern Art Archives, New York.

23 Goodnough, "Artists' Sessions at Studio 35 (1950)."

24 BN to MR, draft, n.d.

25 BN draft, Apr. 26, 1950.

26 "LIFE obtained from the country's museums and art schools the names of 450 artists from 38 states, all under the age of 36, and asked the artists to send in examples of their work . . . From the 450, LIFE selected 19 which it considered representative of the best young painting being done in the country today." *Life* reproduced all 19—Stamos and Hedda Sterne were included—and the Met exhibited those works "along with others from LIFE's collection which the museum considers outstanding." "19 Young Americans," *Life*, Mar. 20, 1950.

27 It was this union, formed in 1947, whose members "consider themselves 'professional' or commercial artists and business men," that Reinhardt brought up toward the end of the Studio 35 sessions.

28 Aline B. Louchheim, "Attention to the American Artist," *NYT* (Jan. 1, 1950).

29 BN to MR, draft, n.d.

30 BHF, "'The Irascibles': A Split Second in Art History," *Arts Magazine* (Sept. 1978). The participation of Pollock and de Kooning is a telling indication of the importance the artists gave to group solidarity. Both had been chosen to be among the seven artists representing the United States at the Venice Biennale opening two weeks later. It would have been difficult to make the case that they had been embargoed.

31 The ongoing irritant that was left unspoken was the Met's unspent Hearn Fund, which was established early in the century specifically for the purchase of work by living American artists. This was a bitter affront to all living artists, but especially, to the group that wrote the letter, a sign that the museum lacked the backbone to declare its policy: juries conveniently avoided commitment and responsibility to any position. According to Ferber, "the artists of both the Betty Parsons and the Kootz galleries . . . had decided earlier on never to submit their work to juries." Oral history interview with HF, Apr. 22, 1968–Jan. 6, 1969, AAA.

32 BHF, "'The Irascibles.'"

33 Charles Poore, *NYT* (May 21, 1950).

34 "18 Painters Boycott Metropolitan; Charge 'Hostility to Advanced Art,'" *NYT* (May 22, 1950). The ten sculptors were counted separately.

35 WB to Chris Baziotes, May 23, 1950, William and Ethel Baziotes papers, c. 1900–1992, bulk 1935–1980, AAA.

36 "The Irascible Eighteen," *New York Herald Tribune* (May 23, 1950).

37 Drafts and approvals are in Gottlieb's files in BNFA. Cited in BHF, "'The Irascibles.'"

38 "75 Painters Deny Museum Is Hostile," *NYT* (July 4, 1950).

39 Stuart Preston, "Three New Group Shows," *NYT* (June 4, 1950).

40 MS, "The Introduction of Modern Art in America: The Armory Show," "written in 1950 and its substance presented in a lecture at Bennington College in the winter of 1950–51," in *Modern Art: 19th and 20th Centuries, Selected Papers*, New York: George Braziller, 1978.

41 Samuel Kootz to BN, June 16, 1950.

42 BN to MR, draft, n.d.

43 BP to CS, June 29, 1950, Betty Parsons Gallery records and personal papers, 1916–1991, bulk 1946–1983, AAA.

44 BN to MR, draft, n.d.

45 MR to BN, Aug. 7, 1950.

46 Their work was largely sniffed at by the European critical community. See CG, "The European View of American Art," *The Nation* (Nov. 25, 1950) and James Johnson Sweeney's notes, published in *The Brooklyn Rail* (May 2014).

47 BN to MR, draft, n.d.

48 110 Wall Street was on Front Street, one block west of the East River, a 20-foot wide, four-story walk-up from the previous century in the shadow of the 1930 massive "wedding cake" hulk of 120 Wall Street—the only skyscraper on the downtown waterfront.

49 BN to MR, draft, n.d.

THIRTY. IRASCIBLES

1 Avis Berman, oral history interview with DM, May 14, 1981, AAA.

2 BN, interview with KO, unpublished, Aug. 2, 1963.

3 BN, interview with KO, 1963.

4 BN, interview with KO, 1963.

5 RM, Menil colloquium, Apr. 2015.

6 BN, interview with KO, 1963.

7 Hedda Sterne papers, 1939–1977, AAA.

8 BN, interview with KO, 1963.

9 BN, interview with KO, 1963.

10 In future years, when he would see his paintings hanging outside the studio, the recollection of the psychic exertion "evoked situations where the emotion became for me uncontrollable," "unnerved" him, were "overwhelming," brought on "tears." BN, interview with KO, 1963.

11 BN, interview with KO, 1963.

12 Oral history interview with HF, Apr. 22, 1968–Jan. 6, 1969, AAA.

13 BN, draft, 1953.

14 IS papers, 1909–2007, bulk 1950–2000, the Getty Research Institute, Los Angeles.

15 IS papers. Barney's account of the randomness of the inclusions is almost certainly accurate, but it leaves out at least one intentional exclusion. Lee Krasner, with reason, never got over the fact that when Barney phoned Springs to alert Pollock to the sitting, she answered the phone. "Let me speak to Jackson," he said, never thinking to invite her.

16 *The Titan: Story of Michelangelo*, Flaherty's recutting of the 1938 Curt Oertel film, *Michelangelo: Life of a Titan*, ran for months on West 57th Street and won that year's Academy Award for best documentary.

17 CS to BN, Apr. 16, 1951.

18 IS papers; Sterne papers; BHF, "'The Irascibles': A Split Second in Art History," *Arts Magazine* (Sept. 1978) reported, with no source given, that Leen told them to arrange themselves.

19 AN, interview with Ann Temkin, Nov. 6, 1997, Philadelphia Museum of Art, Library and Archives Repository.

20 It was a funny choice of words, when, eight years later, Barney described the negotiations around the photograph to Irving Sandler: "When Life magazine decided to do [the] article I became central." IS papers.

21 As late as 1958—four years after their irreparable rift—Reinhardt told Sandler, that, regarding the "myth" that it was Motherwell, Baziotes, and the Surrealists who invented Abstract Expressionism, "I can't stand artists' baloney. No one talks about Barney Newman, yet he was so central for Rothko and Still." Notice, he continued, "in that famous photograph of the Irascibles that Newman is right in the center. The picture is true. Artists like Hedda Sterne and myself were way in the back." IS interview with Ad Reinhardt, Oct. 15, 1958, IS papers.

22 "The Metropolitan and Modern Art," *Life* (Jan. 15, 1951).

23 Reinhardt, interview, 1958.

24 Years later Motherwell wrote, "My friend Barnett Newman asserts that I arranged 'The School of New York' exhibition in California in 1951. The truth is that a dealer, Frank Perls, arranged it on his own, and after he had done so, asked me to write a preface, which I did, and thereupon invented the phrase." Robert Motherwell, "Letters to the Editor," *Art International* (Oct. 1967).

25 Luis J. Navascués to BN, Feb. 9, 1951.

26 Curated by Andrew Ritchie, director of the Department of Painting and Sculpture, it included over 100 works by over 80 artists from 1913—the year of the Armory Show—to 1951, with all of the artists from the Studio 35 sessions except Bourgeois, Biala, Sterne, Kees, Rosenberg, Goodnough, Gottlieb, Hare, and Barney.

27 Michel Seuphor, trans. Francine du Plessix and Florence Weinstein, "Paris New York 1951," *Modern Artists in America, First Series*, New York: Wittenborn Schultz, 1952; French original in *Art d'aujourd'hui*, 1952.

28 Pati Garske (Still's future wife) to BP on behalf of CS, Dec. 19, 1948, Betty Parsons Gallery records and personal papers, 1916–1991, bulk 1946–1983, AAA.

29 CS to BN, Feb. 28, 1950.

30 CS to Betty Freeman, May 2, 1963, Betty Freeman papers, 1951–1969, AAA.

31 CS to BN, July 18, 1950.

32 CS to BN, Apr. 16, 1951.

33 CS to MR, Apr. 29, 1951, James E. B. Breslin Research Archive on Mark Rothko, the Getty Research Institute, Los Angeles.

34 CS to MR, May 10, 1951, James E. B. Breslin Research Archive.

35 BN to AN, June 10, 1953, and AN note on postcard.

36 CS to DM, Aug. 7, 1953; CS to DM, n.d., but referring to Aug. 7, 1953; CS to DM, Aug. 9, 1953, DM papers, 1853–2013, bulk 1920–1996, AAA.

37 CS to DM, Mar. 5, 1954, HC papers, 1910–1993, bulk 1910–1960, AAA.

38 CS to BN, Dec. 31, 1954.

39 CS to MR, May 10, 1951.

40 DM, interview, 1981.

41 Robert Goodnough, "Artists' Sessions at Studio 35 (1950)," *Modern Artists in America, First Series*, New York: Wittenborn Schultz, 1952.

42 Mark Stevens and Annalyn Swan, *de Kooning: An American Master*, New York: Knopf, 2004.

43 Stevens and Swan, *de Kooning*.

44 Nick Carone to author, interview, Oct. 16, 2008. The invitational show was such a success that it was picked up, starting in January 1953, by Eleanor Ward's Stable Gallery on 58th Street, and held as a regular event for several years. Barney was invited by the artists' committee to be in the third—where his absence was noted in the *Art Digest*'s review—and fifth, but declined. In March 1957 he was invited "as a former exhibitor in the ARTIST'S ANNUAL" to elect a committee for the sixth. His name had incorrectly appeared on the list of participants in the previous five—a good indication that he had not fallen quite as far off the radar as some liked to claim.

THIRTY-ONE. COMPELLED

1 Opinions are divided on the medium. Barney seems to have told Hess that it was enamel but contemporary conservation analysis indicates oil.

2 BN, quoted in *Time* (Feb. 20, 1950).

3 Aline B. Louchheim, "By Extreme Modernists," *NYT* (Jan. 29, 1950).

4 BN, interview with KO, unpublished, Aug. 2, 1963.

5 BN, "The First Man Was an Artist," *The Tiger's Eye* 1.1 (Oct. 1947), repr. in SWI.

6 See Armin Zweite, *Barnett Newman: Paintings, Sculptures, Works on Paper*, Ostfildern-Ruit: Hatje Cantz, 1999.

7 Franz Meyer, "Giacometti et Newman," in *Alberto Giacometti: Sculptures, peintures, dessin*, Paris: Museé d'Art Moderne de la Ville de Paris, 1991.

8 BHF to author, Jan. 15, 2007.

9 Douglas Davis, notes for interview of BN, 1969.

10 BN, interview with KO, 1963.

11 Andrew Hudson, "The Case for 'Exporting' Nation's Avant Garde Art": Interview with Andrew Hudson, *Washington Post* (Mar. 27, 1966).

12 E. C. Goossen, "The Big Canvas," *Art International* (Feb. 1958). William Rubin clarified the assertion by specifying the groundbreaking quality of Goossen's "Big Canvas": it distinguished itself "not so much by actual size as by the projection into that size, for the first time in the history of art, of an intimate and personal style with no scale referent tied to the world of objects." William Rubin, "Jackson Pollock and the Modern Tradition, Part I," *Artforum* 5.6 (Feb. 1967).

13 Liberman interviewed by Kazanjian, n.d. (1988), Dodie Kazanjian and Calvin Tomkins research materials on Alexander Liberman, 1927–1999, AAA.

14 It cannot be overstated how differently these works were experienced in the 20-foot-wide studio in which they were made, or Parsons's gallery, or Heller's living room, from the way they are seen today in the caverns of contemporary museums.

15 In 1950, the highly saturated colors of Eastman Kodak's new motion picture negative film vividly changed the look of movies; and the June 1952 release of the revolutionary, visually staggering "This Is Cinerama," radically changed the feel of movies by subsuming audiences into an enormous field of peripheral vision. This was something that Barney himself acknowledged when, years later, he stood in front of David's *Coronation of Napoleon* in the Louvre: "Talk about a wide screen! . . . we just can't see it with unspoiled, premovie eyes anymore." Also in 1951, startling his New York audience, Georges Balanchine took the transgressive step of disgarding referential costumes to present the first so-called "black and white" ballet—shifting the concept of the art from (distracting) story-telling to a focus on the movement, sculpture, and music of the dance.

16 BN interviewed by David Sylvester, Mar. 3, 1967.

17 BN, draft of response to HR.

18 The uniquely applied death sentence was and is still widely considered driven by anti-Semitism, notwithstanding the Judaism of the judge who pronounced it. Retaining the scars of vulnerability, subject to any new implications of vulnerability, anxious to recede from the public radar, American Jews urgently followed this and the news from Israel. For an incisive discussion of media attention to the Rosenberg case see Maurice Berger, "Of Cold Wars and Curators," in *How Art Becomes History*, New York: Harper Collins, 1992.

19 *NYT* (Friday, Apr. 6, 1951).

20 Popular sentiment was overwhelmingly in MacArthur's court on the day he was fired, but later (after Truman's memoirs were serialized in *Life*) Barney wrote, "I have the greatest admiration for Truman's courage [sic] dismissal of Mac[Arthur] However this question of authority has no relation with the merit of Mac[Arthur's] ideas. I have always maintained it was unfortunate that political considerations forced Truman not to agree with Mac[Arthur]." BN, draft in response to HR.

21 Hanson W. Baldwin, "The Magic of MacArthur," *NYT* (Apr. 23, 1951).

22 Stuart Preston, "Diverse New Shows," *NYT* (Apr. 29, 1951).

23 Aline B. Louchheim, "Abstraction: Camera Versus Brush," *NYT* (May 6, 1951).

24 Belle Krasne, "The Bar Vertical on Fields Horizontal," *Art Digest* (May 1951).

25 TH, "Barnet [sic] Newmann [sic]," *Art News* (Summer 1951).

26 Oral history interview with Robert Scull, June 15–28, 1972, AAA.

27 BN, statement, 1950, SWI.

28 Emily Genauer, "Art and Artists: Super-Realistic Old and Nearly Blank Modern Art Both 'Fool the Eye,'" *New York Herald Tribune* (May 6, 1951).

29 BN, interview with Joanna Magloff, c.1963.

30 Ann Temkin, "Barnett Newman on Exhibition," in *Barnett Newman*, exhibition catalogue, Philadelphia: Philadelphia Museum of Art, 2002.

31 Stuart Preston, "Chiefly Abstract," *NYT* (Apr. 8, 1951).

32 Stuart Preston, "Varied Art Shown in Galleries Here," *NYT* (May 18, 1951).

33 Preston, "Diverse New Shows."

34 CG, "Feeling Is All," *Partisan Review* (Jan.–Feb. 1952).

35 Genauer, "Art and Artists: Super-Realistic Old and Nearly Blank Modern Art."

36 Martin Gasser, "Barnett Newman: Another Photographic Footnote," Princeton seminar paper, Sept. 28, 1988, on deposit at BNFA.

37 AN, interview by John O'Neill, 1994.

38 Buffie Johnson to BN, May 7, 1951.

39 BP to CS, May 11, 1951, Betty Parsons Gallery records and personal papers, 1916–1991, bulk 1946–1983, AAA.

40 CS to MR, May 10, 1951, James E. B. Breslin Research Archive on Mark Rothko, the Getty Research Institute, Los Angeles.

41 CS to MR, May 10, 1951. Nevertheless, when he returned to New York in July, Still happily reported to Edward Dugmore that he "got some material rolling on the public relations side in a most unusual quarter." CS to Edward Dugmore, July 30, 1951, Edward Dugmore papers, 1937–1993, AAA.

42 CS to MR, May 10, 1951.

43 Carlyle Burrows, *New York Herald Tribune* (Apr. 8, 1951); Preston, "Chiefly Abstract"; M. C., *Art Digest* (Apr. 15, 1951); Dorothy Adlow, *The Christian Science Monitor* (Apr. 28, 1951).

44 Mira Schor, ed., *The Extreme of the Middle: Writings of Jack Tworkov*, New Haven: Yale UP, 2009, 190–92.

45 CS to Katharine Kuh, October 22, 1965 (also cited in James Breslin, *Mark Rothko, A Biography*, Chicago: The University of Chicago Press, 1993, 622 n. 46). Katharine Kuh papers, 1875–1994, bulk 1930–1994, AAA.

46 BP to CS, May 11, 1951.

47 Betty Parsons Gallery to Anne Fuller for *Look* magazine (May 10, 1951).

48 Anita Colby, "Recipe for Well-Dressed Beauty," *Look* (Sept. 11, 1951).

49 Leonard R. Harris, director of public relations at Prentice-Hall, to Victor Whitehorn of Whitehorn & Cowin, Sept. 11, 1951.

50 RM1.

51 E.g., BN to Alan Power, Sept. 1959, draft.

THIRTY-TWO. AMBIGUOUS MEN

1 BN, interview with KO, unpublished, Aug. 2, 1963.

2 TH, *Abstract Painting: Background and American Phase*, New York: The Viking Press, 1951, 146.

3 Ad Reinhardt to BN, June 26, 1951. Used by permission, © Anna Reinhardt/ARS, New York.

4 CS to BP, May 5, 1951, Betty Parsons Gallery records and personal papers, 1916–1991, bulk 1946–1983, AAA.

5 CS to Ed Dugmore from Cooper Square, New York City, July 30, 1951, Edward Dugmore papers, 1937–1993, AAA.

6 CS to Ed Dugmore, July 30, 1951.

7 Ad Reinhardt to Rita Salomon, Dec. 26, 1951. Used by permission, © Anna Reinhardt/ARS, New York. Courtesy the Ad Reinhardt Foundation.

8 CS to Mrs. Edith Dugmore from Cooper Square, Sept. 7, 1951, Edward Dugmore papers.

9 CS to BN, n.d., between Sept. and mid-Dec. 1951.

10 Aline B. Louchheim, "Betty Parsons: Her Gallery, Her Influence," *Vogue* (Oct. 1951).

11 BP, "Interview over WNYC, Art Festival," Oct. 16, 1951, Betty Parsons Gallery records and personal papers.

12 Liberman interviewed by Kazanjian, Jan. 1989, Dodie Kazanjian and Calvin Tomkins research materials on Alexander Liberman, 1927–1999, AAA.

13 Louchheim, "Betty Parsons."

14 Calvin Tomkins, "A Keeper of the Treasure," *The New Yorker* (June 9, 1975).

15 Lee Hall, *Betty Parsons: Artist, Dealer, Collector*, New York: H. N. Abrams, 1991, 102.

16 Still later claimed he left Parsons in late 1950, but that Parsons, Newman, and Rothko had "worked over-time" to keep it "top secret." CS to DM, Jan. 12, 1954. Parsons's gallery records show that Still was using her as his agent until at least July 1951.

17 The participants in this meeting vary in different versions. Ossorio told Irving Sandler that the group consisted of Pollock, Rothko, Still, Newman, Tomlin, Ferber, and himself. Their complaint was that "work was going out and not selling. [Parsons] was not treating them seriously but was involved with spreading creative spirit." AO to IS, IS papers, 1909–2007, bulk 1950–2000, the Getty Research Institute, Los Angeles. Very likely, there was more than a single, dramatic meeting.

18 See TBH2.

19 Barney may have thrown in Baur's book, the first in the Library of Congress series on American Civilization published by Harvard, on his own initiative. He called it a "doughy Tip Top loaf of art writing . . . the first official story of the official museum version of official American art." BN, unpublished draft. A third development in the nascent historicizing of the creative moment was the diligent studio visits by painter/art historian William Seitz for his Princeton dissertation—the first on the new art. Barney, who would have expected his friends to recommend him to Seitz, was, again, not included.

20 CS to B + A, Jan. 5, 1952.

21 TH, *Abstract Painting*.

22 Helen Frankenthaler to Barbara Rose, Barbara Rose papers, 1962–c. 1969, AAA.

23 John Bernard Myers papers, c. 1940s–1987, bulk 1970–1987, AAA.

24 Annalee notes in BNFA.

25 See the *Partisan Review* Archives, Howard Gotlieb Center, Boston University.

26 Hester Diamond to author, interview, Aug. 3, 2006.

27 BN, "Interview with Kathleen Shorthall of *Life*," 1959, conducted for research of article Dorothy Seiberling, "Baffling U.S. Art: What It Is About," *Life* (Nov. 9, 1959).

28 Steven Naifeh and Gregory White Smith, *Jackson Pollock: An American Saga*, New York: C. N. Potter, 1989, 664–65, confirmed by Raphael Gribitz.

29 AN, interview by John O'Neill, 1994.

30 Tony Smith to B + A, June 8, 1953, and other notes.

31 Jeanne Bultman to author, interview, Mar. 17, 2007.

32 Elizabeth McFadden to BN, Nov. 21, 1951.

33 BN to Jane Smith, Feb. 2, 1952, Tony Smith Estate.

34 Ad Reinhardt to BN, June 26, 1951. Used by permission, © Anna Reinhardt/ARS, New York.

35 Ad Reinhardt to Rita Salomon, n.d., summer 1951. Used by permission, © Anna Reinhardt/ARS, New York. Courtesy the Ad Reinhardt Foundation.

36 Ad Reinhardt to Rita Salomon, Jan. 9, 1952. Used by permission, © Anna Reinhardt/ARS, New York. Courtesy the Ad Reinhardt Foundation. Although marriage, in postwar America, had become fodder for mass consumption caricature, with the two most enduring and entertaining couples, Ralph and Alice Kramden of *The Honeymooners*, and Lucy and Ricky Ricardo of *I Love Lucy*, colonizing

THIRTY-THREE. "FIFTEEN AMERICANS"

1 Dodie Kazanjian and Calvin Tomkins, *Alex: The Life of Alexander Liberman*, New York: Knopf, 1993, 170.

2 BN to TH, Oct. 7, 1965, repr. in SWI.

3 Ad Reinhardt to Rita Salomon, Dec. 1951. Used by permission, © Anna Reinhardt/ARS, New York. Courtesy the Ad Reinhardt Foundation.

4 Ad Reinhardt to Rita Salomon n.d., Jan 1952. Used by permission, © Anna Reinhardt/ARS, New York. Courtesy the Ad Reinhardt Foundation.

5 Stuart Preston, "Modern Pioneers," *NYT* (Jan. 27, 1952).

6 CG, "Feeling Is All," *Partisan Review* (Jan.–Feb. 1952).

7 DM to BP, Jan. 22, 1952, Betty Parsons Gallery records and personal papers, 1916–1991, bulk 1946–1983, AAA.

8 Gerald Silk, oral history interview with BP, June 11, 1981, AAA.

9 Tworkov encapsulated the self-defeating ambivalence that was rampant: Rothko both "accused Betty Parsons of maladroit handling of publicity and praised her bitterly by saying over and over again, 'Betty you are no salesman.'" Mira Schor, ed., *The Extreme of the Middle: Writings of Jack Tworkov*, New Haven: Yale UP, 2009.

10 Virginia Wright to author, interview, May 29, 2008.

11 Janis press release quoted in John Elderfeld, *De Kooning: A Retrospective*, New York: The Museum of Modern Art, 2011.

12 Mark Stevens and Annalyn Swan, *de Kooning: An American Master*, New York: Knopf, 2004, 319.

13 Wright to author, 2008.

14 Friedel Dzubas to IS, Apr. 26, 1957, IS papers, 1909–2007, bulk 1950–2000, the Getty Research Institute, Los Angeles.

television the previous fall, the lengthy article Barney recommended to Reinhardt was dead serious: The wife problem is an "important factor when corporations pick their executives. Is she stabilizing? Integrated? Does she love her husband's job? . . . With a remarkable uniformity of phrasing, corporation officials all over the country sketch the ideal . . . she is a wife who 1) is highly adaptable, 2) is highly gregarious, 3) realizes her husband belongs to the corporation." The current generation of wives, not yet "grown older and more cantankerous," was viewed by executives as giving "us so much less trouble than the older ones." The list of rules included don't gossip, "don't turn up at the office" (or studio), don't "get tight," and "be attractive."

37 AN, "Reminiscence about why Barney was the witness at the marriage of Reinhardt and Rita," in BNFA.

38 Robert Jay Wolff, "The Dilemma of American Avant-Garde Painting," second draft of Harvard lecture, 1961, Robert Jay Wolff papers, 1926–1969, AAA.

39 Howard Devree, "By Contemporaries," *NYT* (Dec. 2, 1951).

40 Carlyle Burrows, *New York Herald Tribune* (Dec. 2, 1951).

41 CS to DM and HC, Dec. 22, 1951, DM papers, 1853–2013, bulk 1920–1996, AAA.

42 CS to B + A, Dec. 23, 1951.

43 CS to DM and HC, Dec. 27, 1951, DM papers.

44 CS to B + A, Jan. 5, 1952.

15 See TBH2, 88–89, for a concise discussion of the distinction between the "downtown" group—of which he was a prominent and forceful advocate—and the "uptown" artists.

16 CS to Edward Dugmore, Mar. 19, 1952, Edward Dugmore papers, 1937–1993, AAA.

17 CS to BN, Feb. 28, 1950.

18 Avis Berman, oral history interview with DM, May 14, 1981, AAA.

19 Steven Naifeh and Gregory White Smith, *Jackson Pollock: An American Saga*, New York: C. N. Potter, 1989, 680.

20 DM to Dr. Max Gruenwald, Jan. 15, 1952, HF papers, 1932–1987, AAA.

21 Lynn Zelevansky, "Dorothy Miller's 'Americans,' 1942–63," in *The Museum of Modern Art at Mid-Century: At Home and Abroad*, New York, The Museum of Modern Art, 1994, 71.

22 BN to Dore Ashton, Nov. 23, 1959, draft, not sent.

23 DM to David Anfam, Nov. 7, 1978, DM papers, 1853–2013, bulk 1920–1996, AAA.

24 Zelevansky, "Dorothy Miller's 'Americans.'"

25 Lynn Zelevansky to author, interview, July 19, 2010.

26 Zelevansky, "Dorothy Miller's 'Americans.'"

27 A. L. Chanin, "The World of Art," *The Compass* (Apr. 13, 1952).

28 James Breslin, *Mark Rothko, A Biography*, Chicago: The University of Chicago Press, 1993.

29 DM, interview, 1981.

30 Maud Morgan, *Maud's Journey: A Life from Art*, Berkeley: New Earth, 1995.

31 At the time of Pollock's last show at Parsons, Janis and his wife, Harriet, concluded that he was a "charlatan."

They were so dismissive that Wright, working at the gallery, "didn't even bother to walk across the hall" to see the show. "And then the next year, Pollock was in the Sidney Janis Gallery." Wright, interview, 2008.

THIRTY-FOUR. AESTHETICS AND ORNITHOLOGY

1 BNFA.

2 TH papers, 1939–1978. "The Shield of Achilles" was the title and subject of a bitter poem by W. H. Auden in 1952, and the title of a 1955 collection of his work.

3 Pierre Garai to BN, Apr. 24, 1952.

4 BN, interview with KO, unpublished, Aug. 2, 1963.

5 BN, "Editor's Letters," *Art News* (Nov. 1965). In TBH2, Hess repeated this: "Still's mighty black wall of a painting, which dominated his room at The Museum of Modern Art's 'Fifteen Americans' show in 1952, seems a response to the equally majestic assertion of Newman's *Cathedra*."

6 During meticulous restoration at the Stedelijk Museum after it had been horribly vandalized in 1997, it became apparent that there were up to six very thin layers of paint on the cotton duck.

7 CG diary, CG papers, 1928–1995, the Getty Research Institute, Los Angeles.

8 AO to BN, July 23, 1952.

9 "Museum Revamps Art Show Judging," *New York World* (June 30, 1952).

10 CS to DM and HC, July 5, 1952, DM papers, 1853–2013, bulk 1920–1996, AAA.

11 BP to BN, July 7, 1952.

12 Ad Reinhardt to BN, July 16, 1952. Used by permission, © Anna Reinhardt/ARS, New York.

13 William Seligson to BN, June 5, 1952; BN to Walter Cronan, June 26, 1952.

14 BN, interview with KO, 1963.

15 Hub Crehan, *Art News* (Apr. 1959).

16 RM1.

17 TS to B + A, Feb. 25, 1954.

18 BN, interview with KO, 1963.

19 RM to author, email, Nov. 5, 2012.

20 TBH2, 76.

21 Morris Dickstein, *Double Agent: The Critic and Society*, New York and Oxford: Oxford UP, 1992, 89.

THIRTY-FIVE. L'ERRANCE (WANDERING)

1 Robert Jay Wolff, "The Dilemma of American Avant-Garde Painting," second draft of Harvard lecture, 1961, 2, 6–7, Robert Jay Wolff papers, 1926–1969, AAA.

2 CS to AO, Dec. 18, 1953, Betty Freeman papers, 1951–1969, AAA.

3 BH to author, interview, Dec. 12, 2011.

4 Liberman interviewed by Kazanjian, Jan. 1989, Dodie Kazanjian and Calvin Tomkins research materials on Alexander Liberman, 1927–1999, AAA.

5 Dodie Kazanjian and Calvin Tomkins, *Alex: The Life of Alexander Liberman*, New York: Knopf, 1993, 231–32.

6 Alan Power to author, interview, Mar. 25, 2007.

7 John Kasmin to author, interview, July 31, 2008.

8 BN, interview with Joanna Magloff. c. 1963.

9 RM1.

10 Playbill, Oct. 24, 1953.

32 BP to CS, Dec. 16, 1953, Betty Parsons Gallery records and personal papers.

33 Wright to author, 2008.

34 Breslin, *Mark Rothko*.

22 DM papers.

23 CS to DM, Apr. 19, 1952, DM papers.

24 MR to Lloyd Goodrich, Dec. 20, 1952, Betty Parsons Gallery records and personal papers, 1916–1991, bulk 1946–1983, AAA.

25 *Uninterrupted Flux: Hedda Sterne, A Retrospective*, exhibition catalogue, Champaign, IL: Krannert Art Museum and Kinkead Pavilion, 2006.

26 I am grateful to Jonathan Holstein for pointing out the resemblance.

27 Priscilla Morgan to author, interview, Feb. 16, 2009.

28 Roland Crampton to BN, Aug. 17, 1952.

29 MR to HF, Aug. 19, 1952, HF papers, 1932–1987, AAA.

30 MR to HF, Sept. 2, 1952, HF papers.

31 Ralph Wickiser to BN, Aug. 7, 1952.

32 Woodstock notes, BNFA.

33 BN, draft; the audio record of Barney's remarks differs from both his draft and his collated, corrected, final statement; all in BNFA.

34 WNYC, Oct. 31, 1952.

35 Among others, to Ellsworth Kelly and Agnes Martin. Kelly to author, interview, Apr. 22, 2009.

36 AN, interview with Ann Temkin, Nov. 6, 1997, Philadelphia Museum of Art, Library and Archives Repository.

37 All quotations are from the original article as it appeared in the December 1952 number of *Art News*. The essay was revised for later publication in anthologies.

38 CS to HR, Dec. 14, 1952, and CS to Jackson Pollock, Dec. 14, 1952, Jackson Pollock and Lee Krasner papers, c. 1914–1984, bulk 1942–1984, AAA.

39 Ad Reinhardt to IS, Oct. 15, 1958, IS papers, 1909–2007, bulk 1950–2000, the Getty Research Institute, Los Angeles.

11 AN, "Reminiscence about why Barney was the witness at the marriage of Reinhardt and Rita," in BNFA.

12 E P-D to author, interview, Nov. 19, 2013.

13 In the 1960s, when he had become established, he told Annalee the time was right. "Oh, Barney!" she said, surprised at his naïveté about the facts of life, "I'm too old!" There is no question that Barney was naïve, or troubled, or intentionally clueless about things sexual. His own sexuality was carefully unexpressed. There are simply no stories about flirtations or escapades.

14 Deborah Strober to author, interview, June 18, 2009.

15 TBH, "Abstract Art in America (L'Art Abstrait aux Etates-Unis)," in *United States Lines, Paris Review* (June 1953).

16 BN to AN, June 10, 1953.

17 BN to AO, June 18, 1953.

18 B. H. Friedman, soon to become a great friend of Barney's, speculated that Barney may have "felt dimin-

ished by his representation" in Ossorio's collection, which had by that time a number of Pollocks—including the ten-foot *Lavender Mist*—numerous Dubuffets, and several large pieces by Still, and that Still, who had recently spent time at Ossorio's 80-acre estate, may have been rubbing this in during the car trip. BHF to author, interview, Jan. 15, 2007.

19 BN to AO, June 22, 1953.

20 CS to HC and DM, July 28, 1953, HC papers, 1910–1993, bulk 1910–1960, AAA.

21 CS to AO, Aug. 21, 1953, Betty Freeman papers.

22 CS to DM, Aug. 7, 1953, DM papers, 1853–2013, bulk 1920–1996, AAA.

23 CS to DM, Aug. 9, 1953, DM papers.

24 Howard Devree, "Modern Highlights: Museum Opens Fivefold Summer Display," *NYT* (June 28, 1953).

25 In 2015, MoMA deaccessioned and sold *Poplars at Giverny* for $16.2 million to "benefit the acquisitions fund." The painting was "an example of an Impressionist style that precedes the starting point of the museum's painting collection."

26 Dan Morris, "Why Hush Monet, Artist Asks Modern Museum," *New York Daily Mirror* (July 6, 1953).

27 BN to William A. M. Burden, July 20, 1953.

THIRTY-SIX. INDIGNATION

1 TBH, "Reinhardt: The Position and Perils of Purity," *Art News* (Dec. 1953).

2 BN to Hub Crehan, draft, Feb. 2, 1954; a slightly revised version appeared in *Art Digest* (Feb. 15, 1954).

3 BN, "The Sublime Is Now," *The Tiger's Eye* (Dec. 1948).

4 Ad Reinhardt to BN. Used by permission, © Anna Reinhardt/ARS, New York.

5 Ad Reinhardt, "The Artist in Search of An Academy, Part Two: Who Are the Artists?," *The College Art Journal* (Summer 1954), College Art Association. Edited version of Reinhardt's 1953 Woodstock talk.

6 Oral history interview with HF, Apr. 22, 1968–Jan. 6, 1969, AAA.

7 HF to BN, Aug. 10, 1964; letters between BN and HF, including Apr. 1, 1954, and July 27, 1964; canceled checks.

8 BN to Frankfurter and BN to Hess, Apr. 10, 1954. Frankfurter did not want "another article on museums and museum roles," Hess relayed to Barney. Hess himself was far more congenial; he wrote that his own feeling was that Frankfurter shied away from a discussion of the personalities (Barr, Miller, Sweeney) and hoped he and Barney could find a "formula" to treat the subject in a "general way." "I would enjoy discussing the situation with you, and, in fact, seeing you again," Hess concluded, suggesting lunch. TBH to BN, Apr. 28, 1954.

9 "Noted Painting Is Acquired Here," *NYT* (Mar. 25, 1954); Howard Devree, "Guggenheim Displays New Acquisitions with 'Clock Maker' in Place of Honor," *NYT* (Mar. 31, 1954).

10 BN to James Johnson Sweeney, May 3, 1954.

11 BN to Sweeney, May 3, 1954.

12 Inquisition-style Senate hearings derived from Senator Joseph McCarthy's hunt for Communists in the U.S.

13 Ad Reinhardt to Rita Reinhardt, letters of May 1954. Used by permission, © Anna Reinhardt/ARS, New York. Courtesy the Ad Reinhardt Foundation.

28 Ad Reinhardt to Leonard Sand, July 8, 1955. Used by permission, © Anna Reinhardt/ARS, New York. Courtesy the Ad Reinhardt Foundation.

29 Ad Reinhardt to Ambrose Doskow, Rosenman Goldmark Colin & Kaye, Jan. 26, 1955. Used by permission, © Anna Reinhardt/ARS, New York. Courtesy the Ad Reinhardt Foundation.

30 He did not care for the "artist-professor" identification much either, but, ironically, at this very moment was applying for the job at New York University that Baziotes had left for Hunter College.

31 "Symposium: Is the French Avant Garde Overrated?," *Art Digest* (Sept. 1953).

32 Ad Reinhardt to Rita Reinhardt, Aug. 25, 1953. Used by permission, © Anna Reinhardt/ARS, New York. Courtesy the Ad Reinhardt Foundation.

33 TH, "The New York Salon," *Art News* (Feb. 1954).

34 James Fitzsimmons, "Stable Group Sets a Smart Pace," *Art Digest* (Feb. 1, 1954).

35 CS to DM, Nov. 3, 1953, DM papers.

36 CS to DM, Jan. 12, 1954. DM papers.

37 CS to DM, Mar. 5, 1954, HC papers.

14 U.S., FBI, Sarah Newman, Name Check, Bureau File 123–5493, December 3, 1950. Obtained under the Freedom of Information Act.

15 CS to B + A, June 28, 1954.

16 The baroque maneuvers by Still during the summer can be reconstructed through records available in various archives. Astonishingly, carbon copies of a number were left—or intentionally placed—in the glove compartment of Still's car when it was quixotically bought by Barney in March 1955. Still was so righteous, or delusional, about his manipulation, that he must have wanted Barney to be aware of it almost a year later. There was in the car also a page of diaristic writing dated "Aug. 5, 1954," in which Still viciously condemned Reinhardt and by implication, Barney.

17 CS to DM and HC, June 30, 1954, DM papers, 1853–2013, bulk 1920–1996, AAA.

18 CS to AO, June 19, 1954, Betty Freeman papers, 1951–1969, AAA. CS to DM and HC, Aug. 11, 1954, DM papers.

19 CS to DM and HC, Mar. 5, 1954, HC papers, 1910–1993, bulk 1910–1960, AAA.

20 CS to DM and HC, June 14, 1954, DM papers.

21 Robert J. Wolff to Dean William R. Gaede, undated draft, Dec. 1954, Robert Jay Wolff papers, 1926–1969, AAA.

22 Ad Reinhardt to Rita Reinhardt, May 1954. Used by permission, © Anna Reinhardt/ARS, New York. Courtesy the Ad Reinhardt Foundation.

23 CS to BN, June 28, 1954, and July 20, 1954.

24 Calvin Tomkins, "A Keeper of the Treasure," *The New Yorker* (June 9, 1975).

25 "Quentin Reynolds Wins Libel Action," *NYT* (June 29, 1954). The suit stemmed from a 1949 column in which Pegler retaliated against Reynolds for writing, in a review of a biography of Heywood Broun, that Pegler was "morally guilty of homicide" in the death of Broun.

26 BN to Joseph Delman, Whitehorn & Cowin, July 25, 1954.

27 AN, interview by John O'Neill, 1994.

28 Yiddish: a dull, inconsequential person. A few years later, dignity restored, Barney would tell a young artist friend visiting from Canada to make sure to pack a sports jacket for engaging with the public: "We don't want to look like a couple of shmos."

29 Robert Jay Wolff, "The Dilemma of American Avant-Garde Painting," second draft of Harvard lecture, 1961, Robert Jay Wolff papers, 1926–1969, AAA.

30 BN to Delman, July 25, 1954.

31 CS to BN, July 20, 1954.

32 Ad Reinhardt to B + A, July 22, 1954; Ad Reinhardt to B + A, August 31, 1954. Used by permission, ©Anna Reinhardt/ARS, New York.

33 Ad Reinhardt to TS, end of Aug. 1954. Used by permission, © Anna Reinhardt/ARS, New York.

34 Sometime later, Rothko told Alfred Jensen that Reinhardt "has appropriated many of my esthetic concepts and he's also taken a lot from Barney Newman. Newman fathered Ad for years when Ad was literally a nursling of Papa Newman. The thanks we get for all this is a vituperous attack from Ad's vicious pen." James Breslin, *Mark Rothko, A Biography*, Chicago: The University of Chicago Press, 1993, 343, 622, n. 38.

35 Ad Reinhardt to TS, Aug. 1954. Used by permission, © Anna Reinhardt/ARS, New York.

36 Ad Reinhardt to BP, October 8, 1954 BNFA. Used by permission, © Anna Reinhardt/ARS, New York.

37 Used by permission, © Anna Reinhardt/ARS, New York. Courtesy the Ad Reinhardt Foundation, Oral History Project.

38 "The Horse Professor," *Time* (Sept. 13, 1954).

39 BHF, *Jackson Pollock: Energy Made Visible*, New York: McGraw-Hill, 1972, 224.

40 Alfred Leslie to author, interview Dec. 13, 2012.

41 BN to Joseph Delman, Whitehorn & Cowin, Dec. 28, 1954.

42 BN to Sidney Janis, Oct. 25, 1954, possibly not sent.

43 BN to Delman, Dec. 28, 1954.

44 BN to CS, Nov. 18, 1954.

45 CS to William R. Gaede, Dec. 7, 1954.

46 CS to AO, Dec. 1954, Betty Freeman papers.

47 CS to B + A, Dec. 24, 1954.

48 CS to BN, Dec. 31, 1954.

49 CS to AO, Jan. 30 and Mar. 15, 1955, copies in Betty Freeman papers.

THIRTY-SEVEN. THE BLACKEST PERIOD

1 Luis J. Navascués to BN, Jan. 10, 1955.

2 TH papers, 1939–1978, AAA. Without corroborating evidence in Barney's extensive archives, it's not impossible that he thought of doing some of these and then embellished the drama when Hess was writing his monograph.

3 Discreet Reality Corp. to Tenants of Premises 341 and 343 East 19th Street, Nov. 15, 1954; Theodore J. Gruber to BN, Jan. 11, 1955.

4 Ad Reinhardt to Ambrose Doskow, Rosenman Goldmark Colin & Kaye, Jan. 26, 1955. Used by permission, © Anna Reinhardt/ARS, New York. Courtesy the Ad Reinhardt Foundation.

5 Newman v. Reinhardt et al, Supreme Court, State of N.Y., Record on Appeal at 16–17.

6 BN to BP, draft, n.d., spring 1955, probably never sent.

7 "It was our good fortune to witness the most unpredictable of ballets, a dance of dedicated ferocity, the grave elaboration of a magic rite . . . hodgepodge of paint tubes by the hundreds . . . brushes as long as halberds . . . spilt oil cans." Michel Tapié, "Mathieu Paints a Picture," *Art News* (Feb. 1955).

8 "Art: The Fox of Paris," *Time* (Mar. 7, 1955).

9 Bile corroded Barney's "wit." Mocking the Frenchman's art was not enough; Barney was accusing him of cowardice. The World War II Battle of Sedan, in which the French defenders collapsed, was a crushing defeat for the Allies.

10 BN to editor, *Time*, Mar. 5, 1955.

11 CS to Sam Kootz, Mar. 9, 1955.

12 BN to Sam Kootz, Mar. 10, 1955.

13 BN to Joan E. Gibson, *Time*, Mar. 11, 1955.

14 BN to Sidney Janis, Apr. 9, 1955.

15 CS to Sidney Janis, Apr. 4, 1955.

16 CS to AO, Mar. 15, 1955, Betty Freeman papers, 1951–1969, AAA.

17 Because of the copy to Ossorio, some scholars have assumed that Still circulated the letter more widely.

18 CS to AO, Apr. 30, 1955, Betty Freeman papers.

19 CS to Jackson Pollock, Apr. 30, 1955, Jackson Pollock and Lee Krasner papers, c. 1914–1984, bulk 1942–1984, AAA.

20 CG, "'American-Type' Painting," *Partisan Review* (Spring 1955).

21 CS to CG, Apr. 12, 1955, CG papers, 1937–1983, AAA.

22 CG to CS, Apr. 15, 1955, CG papers.

23 CS to CG, Apr. 18, 1955, CG papers.

24 CS to BN, Apr. 20, 1955.

25 BHF, "Introduction," *Jackson Pollock: Energy Made Visible*, New York: McGraw-Hill, 1972.

26 BN to Jackson Pollock, Apr. 25, 1955, possibly not sent.

27 This was big news in the second half of 1955, with national attention. Most of the support came from state Republicans, although a number of Republican officials had been linked to a harness-racing scandal two years earlier.

28 BN to Averill Harriman, Apr. 26, 1955.

29 Press Release, Thursday, Apr. 28, 1955.

30 Allen Murray Myers, Esq., "Report on present status of Temple properties at 341–343 East 19th Street, New York City," n.d.

31 BN to Constance F. Burr, July 20, 1955.

32 Doris Elenkoff, Central Manhattan Medical Group, to BN, July 1, 1970; numerous large checks to Dr. Irwin Mandel, summer 1955.

33 AN interviewed by Dodie Kazanjian, 1991, unpublished transcript.

34 BN to Whitney, draft, Aug. 1955.

35 In one version this was followed by "your hyperopiadic chicken review . . . the fact that I dared review your

book, your refusal to print my Mathieu letter, etc." Barney may have been thin-skinned, but there was a history of Hess's heartless mockery. See chapter 28, note 51.

36 BN to TBH, Aug. 8, 1955.

37 *Euclidian Abyss* is documented in Jan. 1947; *Death of Euclid*, a less confident painting, was almost certainly done earlier, although not documented until 1948.

38 BN to CG, Aug. 9, 1955.

39 TBH to Paul Steiner, Chanticleer Press, Aug. 15, 1955, TH papers.

40 TBH to BN, Aug. 30, 1955.

41 TBH2, 109.

42 Whitehorn & Cowin, various correspondence, Oct. through Nov. 1955.

43 Myers, "Report on present status of Temple properties."

44 BN to Joseph D. McGoldrick, Oct. 25, 1955.

45 "Malicious" was a code word, a charge which could set the stage for a lawsuit.

46 BN to TBH, draft, Nov. 26, 1955.

THIRTY-EIGHT. "NEWMAN INTERESTS US MUCH MORE"

1 Greenberg, Clement, "Ten Years," Dec. 19, 1955–Jan. 14, 1956, Betty Parsons Gallery.

2 Art Students League *News* (Dec. 1955).

3 A. L. Chanin, *The Nation* (Jan. 7, 1956).

4 BN to BP, Dec. 1, 1955, with drafts.

5 Chanin, *The Nation*.

6 Stuart Preston, "Year-End Exhibitions," *NYT* (Dec. 25, 1955).

7 The 21 were: Robert Goodnough, Felix Pasilis, Milton Resnick, Wolf Kahn, Nell Blaine, Joan Mitchell, Ernest Briggs, Fairfield Porter, Gandy Brodie, Robert Rauschenberg, Larry Rivers, Friedebald Dzubas, Leland Bell, Stephan Pace, Robert De Niro, Helen Frankenthaler, Hyde Solomon, Elaine de Kooning, Seymour Remenick, Miles Forst, Michael Goldberg.

8 Friedman, scion of the Uris real-estate family who was working in the family business, always thought of himself as primarily a writer, and eventually left Uris to pursue writing full time. In 1954 he wrote a well-received article, "The New Baroque," in *Art Digest* about the tendency found in the works in MoMA's "Fifteen Americans."

9 BHF, diary, Feb. 5, 1956.

10 BHF, diary, Nov. 28, 1955, and BH in *Reconsidering Barnett Newman*, ed. Melissa Ho, Philadelphia: Philadelphia Museum of Art, 2005, 12.

11 BHF, diary, Nov. 28, 1955.

12 BH to author, interview, Nov. 7, 2006.

13 BHF to author, interview, Jan. 15, 2007.

14 BH to author, 2006.

15 William Rayner, "Betty Knows," in *Betty Parsons Retrospective*, exhibition catalogue, Montclair, NJ: Montclair Art Museum, 1974.

16 BHF to author, 2007.

17 BH to author, 2006.

18 Invoices June 10, 1957, BNFA; BH to author, interview, Nov. 7, 2006, and Dec. 12, 2011.

19 BH to author, 2006.

20 Tony and Jane Smith would purchase *Onement II* during 1956 as well—for $500—less than it was listed for in Barney's 1951 exhibition.

21 BN, "Interview with Kathleen Shorthall of *Life*," 1959, conducted for research of article Dorothy Seiberling, "Baffling U.S. Art: What It Is About," *Life* (Nov. 9, 1959); AN interview by David Peretz in Steven Naifeh and Gregory White Smith, *Jackson Pollock: An American Saga*, New York: C. N. Potter, 1989.

22 Dore Ashton, "Modern Problems: Educators, Museum Officials, Critics Discuss Controversial Issues," *NYT* (Feb. 5, 1956).

23 AN interviewed by Dodie Kazanjian, 1991, unpublished transcript.

24 CS to BN, Feb. 16, 1956.

25 For the rest of her life Annalee regretted that she wasn't better prepared. She felt she "had let Barney down," that she "hadn't paid that much attention." She was acting chairman, running the secretarial department at Bryant and working at City College. "Barney needed someone who could devote herself to him a hundred percent." And, she admitted several decades later, that her heart wasn't in it. "I didn't want Barney to do it" she told Dodie Kazanjian in 1991.

26 Victor Whitehorn to BN, Feb. 21, 1956.

27 BN to Joseph Delman, Whitehorn & Cowin, Apr. 14, 1956.

28 Ambrose Doskow to Joseph C. Sloane, Bryn Mawr College, Apr. 17, 1956.

29 Reinhardt to Ambrose Doskow, n.d., Apr. 1956. Used by permission, © Anna Reinhardt/ARS, New York. Courtesy the Ad Reinhardt Foundation.

30 SH to author, email, Oct. 15, 2006; BN to SH, Apr. 17, 1956.

31 BN to SH, Apr. 17, 1956.

32 BN to SH, May 20, 1956.

33 BN to SH, Apr. 21, 1956.

THIRTY-NINE. LOSSES

1 He "never got over it," according to Annalee.

2 Dorothy Gees Seckler, "Gallery Notes," *Art in America* 44 (Spring 1956). *Art in America* was about to redefine itself with an infusion of money and new advisors—itself an indication of a cultural transformation.

3 TBH, *Art News* (Summer 1956).

4 Sara Siegel, Temple Secretary, to BN, Aug. 15, 1956.

5 HR, "Everyman a Professional," *Art News* (Nov. 1956). The misspelling of Barney's name was consistent with executive editor Hess's needling attitude to Barney. Rosenberg and Hess were especially close colleagues and friends at this time.

6 Editorial, "An Artist Confined," *Life* (Feb. 6, 1956); Editorial, "Life and the Crazy Artist," *Art News* (Mar. 1956); Editorial, "Artists at Liberty," *Life* (Feb. 6, 1956); HR, letter to the editor, *Life* (Feb. 27, 1956). "American painting has never been so uninhibited and experimental, pushing the frontiers of technique in every direction, from abstraction to realism." "Such a ferment will doubtless prove good for art in time. More noticeable just now is how much bad painting it encourages . . . . Our art critics are overpraising the most rubbishy novelties," *Life*'s editorial stated, and cited out of context, unattributed, quotes from *Art News*, including one from Rosenberg.

7 "The Truman Memoirs: Part IV: The Recall of Gen. MacArthur," *Life* (Feb. 13, 1956).

8 "Mr. Molotov's emergence as the leading figure in the guidance of Soviet art and culture underlined the importance of that field in the eyes of the Kremlin leaders [because it] includes many phases of the party's propaganda work." Barney saved this article with his comments on it and on Rosenberg attached to it.

9 BN to Alex and Tatiana Liberman, Nov. 21, 1956, Alexander Liberman papers, c. 1912–2003, AAA.

10 TBH, "Recommended for November," *Art News* (Nov. 1956).

11 BN, drafts of response to HR.

12 TBH, "U.S. Painting: Some Recent Directions," *Art News Annual* (1956).

13 Mark Stevens and Annalyn Swan, *de Kooning: An American Master*, New York: Knopf, 2004.

14 BN to Willem de Kooning, Dec. 1956.

FORTY. TURNING POINT

1 BN to Willian A. M. Burden, Jan. 17, 1957.

2 BN to AHB, Jan. 28, 1957.

3 Barney was indeed almost alone in valuing Pissarro at this time. The first draft of his letter to Barr noted that he felt "no direct connection between my work" and the work of Pissarro, Monet, or Cézanne, but was interested in overcoming "the art theories of British art critics" and simply wanted to see "Pissarro have his day 'in Court.'"

4 BN to Helen Frankenthaler, Feb. 15, 1957.

5 Lawrence Alloway to TH, Feb. 12, 1957, TH papers, 1939–1978, AAA.

6 Porter A. McCray to Harris K. Prior, Feb. 25, 1957, the Museum of Modern Art Archives, New York.

7 CS to AO, Mar. 11, 1957, James E. B. Breslin Research Archive on Mark Rothko, the Getty Research Institute, Los Angeles.

8 Christian Geelhaar, "Collecting Post-War American Art in Basel," 1988, typescript.

9 Geelhaar, "Collecting Post-War American Art."

10 Michel Seuphor to BN, Mar. 8, 1957.

11 Janice Van Horne, *A Complicated Marriage: My Life with Clement Greenberg*, Berkeley: Counterpoint, 2013.

12 Francis V. O'Connor, oral history interview with Stanton Loomis Catlin, July 1–Sept. 14, 1989, AAA.

13 Catlin, travel and transportation expenses, Feb. 11–Apr. 26, 1957, Stanton Loomis Catlin papers, Benson Latin American Collection, University of Texas Libraries, the University of Texas at Austin; Stanton L. Catlin to BN, May 31, 1957.

14 The story brings to mind another occasion, when Friedman and Barney were discussing out-of-context tall buildings. Looking up at the skyline, Barney remarked, "Uuhhh, a lot of phalluses up there." BHF to author, interview, Jan. 15, 2007.

15 Kelly's first show with Parsons, in May, opened the same day as a Kline show at Janis, across the hall. Stepping off the elevator, one looked into Janis, which was too packed to enter. Looking the other way, into Parsons, there was an empty gallery. The legendary curator, Walter Hopps, later told Kelly, "I think I was the only one that ever saw your show. [Because] I couldn't get into Janis." Parsons saw an affinity with Barney's work, Kelly agreed with Barney that it was something else entirely. But Barney, ever after on alert for any confusion about intentions, remained sour on Kelly even after Barney became a benevolent uncle to so many others in that generation. Ellsworth Kelly to author, interview, Apr. 22, 2009

16 BN to BP, Dec. 1956.

17 Liberman interviewed by Kazanjian, Jan. 1989, Dodie Kazanjian and Calvin Tomkins research materials on Alexander Liberman, 1927–1999, AAA.

15 BN to BH, confirmation of telegram, n.d.

16 Stanton Catlin, draft, Jan.–Mar. 1963, Stanton Loomis Catlin papers.

17 AN interviewed by Dodie Kazanjian, 1991, unpublished transcript.

18 Elaine de Kooning, "Pure Paints a Picture," *Art News* (Summer 1957).

19 BH to BN, May 24, 1957.

20 Dan Flavin to Jeanne Siegel, "Around Barnett Newman," *Art News* (Oct. 1970).

21 BN to Catlin, Aug. 28, 1957, and drafts.

22 Jerrold Lanes, "Reflections on Post-Cubist Painting," *Arts* (May 1959).

23 Harold Cohen, introduction to "Barnett Newman Talks to David Sylvester," BBC radio broadcast, Nov. 17, 1965, transcript in the Getty Research Institute, Los Angeles.

24 Catlin to BN, June 21, 1957.

25 "A Conversation: Barnett Newman and Thomas B. Hess," The Solomon R. Guggenheim Museum, May 1, 1966.

26 AN to William F. Smith, General Adjustment Bureau, Inc., Feb. 15, 1958.

27 Frank Getlein, "Kidding the Id in Minneapolis," *New Republic* (Aug. 26, 1957).

28 Catlin to BN, Sept. 13, 1957.

29 BN, letter to the editor, *New Republic* (Oct. 28, 1957).

30 BN to TBH, Oct. 31, 1957.

31 TBH to BN, Nov. 1, 1957.

32 BN to Ethel Schwabacher, Nov. 22, 1957, cited in Yve-Alain Bois, "On Two Paintings by Barnett Newman," *October* 108 (Spring 2004), by permission of the Barnett Newman Foundation.

FORTY-ONE. "MENSCH. TIMES TEN"

1 TBH2.

2 TBH2.

3 BN, interview with KO, unpublished, Aug. 2, 1963.

4 AN interviewed by Dodie Kazanjian, 1991, unpublished transcript.

5 Pierre Garai, undated manuscript.

6 TH papers, 1939–1978, AAA. While the personal details of Mensch are derived from Barney, the description of his transformation owes something to the antics of the French Mathieu.

7 Janice Van Horne, *A Complicated Marriage: My Life with Clement Greenberg*, Berkeley: Counterpoint, 2013.

8 Dodie Kazanjian and Calvin Tomkins, *Alex: The Life of Alexander Liberman*, New York: Knopf, 1993.

9 BHF to author, interview, Jan. 15, 2007.

10 BH to author, interview, Nov. 7, 2006.

11 "Home for Moderns," *Time* (Nov. 25, 1957).

12 AN to Yve-Alain Bois; check to Charles E. Frankenback, Nov. 29, 1957.

13 AN, interview, 1991.

14 When Greenberg and his wife visited Barney two weeks into his hospitalization, they found him weak but provocative. When Annalee left the room, Jenny recalled, Barney "launched into an analysis" of nurses' breasts and how they stimulated him. If this indeed happened it would be an unusual, if not unique, exchange. Stories about Barney leaving the room or uncomfortably changing the subject when talk of sexual matters arose, are the norm. Van Horne, *A Complicated Marriage*.

15 CS to BN, Dec. 7, 1957.

16 BH to author, 2006.

17 Gordon Washburn to BN, Dec. 17, 1957.

18 Dore Ashton, "International Exhibition Discussed by Carnegie Head," *NYT* (Aug. 17, 1958).

19 Lynn Zelevansky, "Dorothy Miller's 'Americans,' 1942–63," in *The Museum of Modern Art at Mid-Century: At Home and Abroad*, New York: The Museum of Modern Art, 1994.

20 Porter McCray to BH, Dec. 16, 1957.

21 DM papers, the Museum of Modern Art Archives, New York. The International Council at MoMA had an arrangement: if Willem Sandberg, the great director of the Stedelijk Museum in Amsterdam were interested in exhibiting works, and MoMA could get them to the Holland–America Line, the Dutch government would foot the bill for transport.

22 This refers to the game of Bridge.

23 *NYT* (Jan. 13, 1958).

24 "Art from U.S. to Be Exhibited at Brussels Fair," *NYT* (Jan. 22, 1958).

25 Robert M. Coates, "The Art Galleries," *The New Yorker* (Dec. 27, 1958).

26 TBH, "Editorial: Innocents to Brussels," *Art News* (Mar. 1958).

27 Coates, "The Art Galleries."

28 Howard Taubman, "Brussels: American Mistakes and Lessons," *NYT* (June 1, 1958).

29 Ashton, "International Exhibition Discussed by Carnegie Head."

30 Barney did not like Lipton personally and was particularly angry because he was a "medical professional"—a dentist—present at Reynal's and "paid no attention" when Barney had his heart attack.

FORTY-TWO. "THE NEW AMERICAN PAINTING"

1 CG diary, CG papers, 1928–1995, the Getty Research Institute, Los Angeles; Lynn Zelevansky, "Dorothy Miller's 'Americans,' 1942–63," in *The Museum of Modern Art at Mid-Century: At Home and Abroad*, New York: The Museum of Modern Art, 1994; Ellsworth Kelly to author, interview, Apr. 22, 2009.

2 For the Museum of Modern Art's different approaches concerning the shows it sent abroad and the shows exhibited in New York, see Zelevansky, *The Museum of Modern Art at Mid-Century*.

3 Jean Volkmer to BN, Mar. 17, 1958, Betty Parsons Gallery records and personal papers, 1916–1991, bulk 1946–1983, AAA; DM papers, the Museum of Modern Art Archives, New York, Mar. 13, 1958.

4 Volkmer to BN, Mar. 17, 1958.

5 Patent application, June 24, 1958, BNFA.

6 Mark Stevens and Annalyn Swan, *de Kooning: An American Master*, New York: Knopf, 2004.

7 Statement in *The New American Painting: As Shown in Eight European Countries, 1958–1959*, exhibition catalogue, New York: The Museum of Modern Art / The International Council, 1959.

8 Christian Geelhaar, "Collecting Post-War American Art in Basel," 1988, typescript.

9 "The pressure behind Johns's images seems low . . . the visual intellect is still weak." TBH, "In Praise of Folly," *Art News* (Mar. 1959).

10 Stuart Preston, *NYT* (Jan. 25, 1958).

11 Zelevansky, "Dorothy Miller's 'Americans.' "

12 Howard Devree, "Chiefly Abstract," *NYT* (Mar. 9, 1958).

13 Jon Schueler, *The Sound of Sleat: A Painter's Life*, ed. Magda Salvesan and Diane Cousineau, New York: Picador, 1999, 34.

14 Reviewing contemporary art shows at the Whitney and MoMA in the Mar. 1959 *Art News*, Hess wrote that Johns's work lacked the "energy" required to burst "the skin of the banal image" and "flood the collective subconscious with revelation. It is an apparently impossible goal. There have been some far more successful attempts than Johns's . . . . And someone, I suppose, is bound to succeed sooner or later. Perhaps Johns. And perhaps, all along, Barnett Newman has been there before him." TBH, "In Praise of Folly." Barney was on Hess's mind, if not in the shows being reviewed, and the critic was making the effort to come to terms with his work. I am grateful to Elizabeth C. Baker for bringing this article to my attention.

15 When Hess published the comment, he changed it to read "instant psychoanalysis," but the notes of his interview with Barney records the former. TH papers, 1939–1978, AAA.

16 Ann Temkin, "Barnett Newman on Exhibition," in *Barnett Newman*, exhibition catalogue, Philadelphia: Philadelphia Museum of Art, 2002, 51.

17 The exhibition brochure lists 18 paintings—all by this time had titles—including loans from the Miller Company (Mr. & Mrs. Burton Tremaine) and Heller. Once again, photographs of the installation give an incomplete picture. *Dionysius* and *Galaxy* were not on the checklist, but appear in photographs.

18 CG papers.

19 AN, interview by John O'Neill, 1994.

20 BN to CG, Apr. 13, 1958.

21 CG to BN, Apr. 16, 1958.

22 CG, "Barnett Newman, First Retrospective Exhibition," exhibition catalogue, Bennington College, May 1958.

23 BN to Eugene Goossen, Apr. 17, 1958. Barney and Vandivert became friends in the late 1930s in Chilmark through Benton or Parsons. The Vandiverts, who lived on East 10th Street, gave frequent parties, introducing Barney to their large circle of friends, "trying to make him famous," as Vandivert's daughter recalled Barney jokingly told her. Susan Vandivert to author, interview, Apr. 30, 2015.

24 Lawrence Alloway, "The Reputation of Barnett Newman," BBC broadcast, Nov. 8, 1962.

25 Lawrence Alloway to BN, May 24, 1959.

26 Lawrence Alloway, "The New American Painting," *Art International* (Mar.–Apr. 1959).

27 BHF to E. J. Power, May 13, 1958.

28 J. Peter Cochrane to BP, Dec. 22, 1958, Betty Parsons Gallery records and personal papers.

29 BHF to author, interview, Jan. 15, 2007.

30 BN to Howard Nemerov, May 14, 1958.

31 BN to Howard Nemerov, June 8, 1958.

32 BN to Nemerov, June 8, 1958.

33 CG, "Painting and Sculpture in Prairie Canada Today," in *Clement Greenberg: The Collected Essays and Criticism*, ed. John O'Brian, vol. 4, *Modernism with a Vengeance, 1957–1969*, Chicago: The University of Chicago Press, 1995.

34 E. C. Goossen, "The Philosophic Line of B. Newman," *Art News* (Summer 1958).

FORTY-THREE. THE LEMA SABACHTHANI AND THE GLORY

1 BN to BH, Aug. 1, 1958.

2 BN to BH, July 25, 1958.

3 BHF diary, July 25, 1958.

4 BHF diary, Aug. 8 and 19, 1958.

5 Kleinman (a neighbor) to author, interview, Aug. 10, 2007.

6 BHF diary, Aug. 19, 1958.

7 TBH2, 94.

8 Barbara Reise, notes after interviewing BN, Jan. 21, 1964, Tate Archives.

9 BH to author, interview, Dec. 12, 2011.

10 "A Conversation: Barnett Newman and Thomas B. Hess," The Solomon R. Guggenheim Museum, May 1, 1966.

11 BH to author, 2011.

12 BN, interview with KO, unpublished, Aug. 2, 1963.

13 Here, again, Barney's words lead to some ambiguity. If he weren't thinking that he had a series, specifically the *Stations of the Cross*, in December 1961, when he exhibited the first 78-by-60-inch black-and-white canvas as *Station* and allowed it to be reproduced as *The Series, I*—completely atypical title references in his oeuvre—what was he thinking? In the unedited portion of a television interview in 1966, Barney privately acknowledged that "after I did those first two"—1958—"I realized I was going to do a series." BN interviewed by Alan Solomon, Mar. 20, 1966.

14 BN to Anthony Smith, Sept. 7, 1962. Barney used "Lama" and "Lema" interchangeably. Smith had suggested *Resurrection* as a title for *Be II*, a fifteenth painting that Barney hung with the others, to invoke "the only painting in its class: Piero della Francesca's Resurrection." But Smith himself had to acknowledge it was too symbolic and sentimental a name for Barney.

15 Barbara Rose to author, interview, Oct. 10, 2008.

16 When he checked the story with Schapiro in 1969, Hess related, "he smiled and said, if that's the way Barney remembers it, that's the way to write it." TBH, "Sketch for the Portrait of the Art Historian among Artists," *Social Research Quarterly* 45.1 (1978).

17 Maurice Tuchman to author, interview, Jan. 10, 2011.

18 BH to BN, Sept. 12, 1958; DM to BN, Dec. 3, 1958.

19 Hilton Kramer, "Report on the Carnegie International," *Arts* (Jan. 1959). There were 494 artists in the greatly expanded "Bicentennial" Pittsburgh exhibition.

20 May Wilson to BN, Dec. 1, 1958.

21 Lawrence Alloway to BN, Mar. 24, 1959.

22 "10 Americans to Watch in 1959," *Pageant* 14.8 (Feb. 1959).

23 Dore Ashton, "Art: Lecture by Rothko—Painter Dissociates Himself From the 'Abstract Expressionist' Movement," *NYT* (Oct. 31, 1958).

24 BN to Dore Ashton, Nov. 1, 1958, unsent.

25 BN to BH, Nov. 3, 1958, unsent.

26 Herbert Crehan, "Rothko's Wall of Light," *Art Digest* 29.5 (Nov. 1, 1954).

27 BN to Barney Rosset and Donald Allen, Nov. 30, 1958.

28 BN to W. McNeil Lowry, Nov. 20, 1958.

29 Arnold Rüdlinger to DM, Oct. 28, 1958, DM papers, the Museum of Modern Art Archives; Christian Geelhaar, "Collecting Post-War American Art in Basel," 1988, typescript.

30 BN to Arnold Rüdlinger, Dec. 19, 1958.

31 BN to Hans Theler, Dec. 28, 1958.

32 Arnold Rüdlinger to BN, Jan. 7, 1959.

33 BN to Arnold Rüdlinger, Jan. 11, 1959.

34 BN to Arnold Rüdlinger, Jan. 31, 1959.

35 BN to Hans Theler, Feb. 19, 1959.

36 BN to Spencer Samuels, Feb. 28, 1959.

37 Nevertheless, both Barney and Annalee filed claims against the Judd Cab Corporation for "personal injuries sustained" in the cab—Barney's diagnosed as "traumatic injury to tongue." The suit dragged on for 17 months, requiring proof of the length of time each was confined to bed; it finally was settled the following June for $800 ($8376.69 in 2023). The lawyers received 40%.

38 BHF diary, Feb. 6, 1959; Raymond J. Hagan, Executive Secretary to Police Commissioner to BN, Feb. 3, 1959.

39 Jonathan Holstein to author, interview, Oct. 16, 2010.

FORTY-FOUR. FRENCH & COMPANY

1 Martica Sawin, "New York Letter," *Art International* (May–June 1959).

2 BN to Yolanda LeWitter, Feb. 9, 1959. Barney would shortly claim to the Stephans that the title of the work was

Genesis, which they demanded be changed to *The Break* in 1948 for the purposes of *Tiger's Eye*, but in his initial correspondence with French he referred to it as *The Break*. At the close of the show, Barney had the painting returned to him, not to the Stephans.

3 BN to Yolanda LeWitter, Mar. 15, 1959.

4 Dr. Julius G. Neumann to BN, Apr. 6, 1959.

5 BN to Spencer Samuels, Feb. 23, 1959.

6 H. C. [Hubert Crehan], "Barnett Newman," *Art News* (Apr. 1959); Sawin, "New York Letter."

7 Consignment sheet from BN to French & Company, Dec. 15, 1959.

8 George Franklin to author, interview, Aug. 26, 2010.

9 Franklin to author, 2010.

10 CG, interviewed by Dodie Kazanjian, 1989, Alexander Liberman papers, c. 1912–2003, AAA.

11 BN to Tax Bureau, Department of Taxation and Finance, State of New York, Dec. 5, 1960.

12 Barney turned his IRS problems into one of his anecdotes. Every year, he said, they were audited because they never showed any income; every penny that Annalee made was accounted for by deductions. Every year it was the same agent who audited them. After about the tenth year of this routine, the agent said to him, "Mr. Newman, can I speak with you in private for a moment?" and took him aside. "You know, you've been doing this for so many years and it isn't working, why don't you try something else?"

13 Emily Genauer, "Now Come 'Inaction' Painters," *New York Herald Tribune* (Mar. 15, 1959).

14 Later, Alloway would credit Barney's predilection for curating his oeuvre himself, unaided—so that "provenance convey[ed] significance"—to an aesthetic strategy, to maintain a "web of internal correspondences in preference to the series of hectic renaissances which regular exhibitions impose o[n an] artist's career." Lawrence Alloway, "Notes on Barnett Newman," *Art International* (Summer 1969). At least equally important, it was a strategy to maintain the mythic narrative.

15 Dore Ashton, "Art: A Change in Style," *NYT* (Mar. 12, 1959).

16 Dore Ashton, "Regards sur la saison New-Yorkaise," *Cimaise* (Summer 1959).

17 H. C. [Hubert Crehan], "Barnett Newman."

18 "Picture of a Painter," *Newsweek* (Mar. 16, 1959).

19 TBH, "In Praise of Folly," *Art News* (Mar. 1959).

20 H. Rumbold, letter, *Art News* (May 1959).

21 BN to Alan Power, Sept. 4, 1959, unsent.

22 BN, letter, *Art News* (Summer 1959).

23 Jerrold Lanes, "Reflections on Post-Cubist Painting," *Arts* (May 1959).

24 Regina Bogat to author, interview, Sept. 23, 2008.

25 Will Barnet to BN, Apr. 29, 1959.

FORTY-FIVE. "A MAN AND HIS WORK"

1 Arthur McKay to BN, Feb. 11, 1959.

2 BN to Arthur McKay, Feb. 21, 1959.

3 BN to Alan Power, Sept. 1, 1959, unsent draft.

4 Will Barnet to author, interview, May 14, 2009.

5 Barnet to author, 2009.

6 Bob Kane to author, interview, Apr. 2, 2009.

7 Alex Liberman interviewed by Kazanjian, Jan. 1989,

26 Oral history interview with Henry Geldzahler, Jan. 27, 1970, AAA.

27 *Arts* (Apr. 1959).

28 "Six American Abstract Painters: Motherwell, Newman, Okada, Rothko, Tobey and Youngerman," Kimura Gallery, Tokyo, Apr. 4–30, 1959. Some accounts of the time inaccurately reported that the Kimura had purchased the painting.

29 "Moments of Vision," at the Rome–New York Art Foundation, was curated by Herbert Read, July–Nov. 1959; II Documenta '59: Kunst nach 1945.

30 AHB to Leo Castelli, Apr. 9, 1965; gallery invoice to DM, Mar. 20 1959, Betty Parsons Gallery records and personal papers, 1916–1991, bulk 1946–1983, AAA; Betsy Jones to Philip Johnson, Nov. 21. 1961, MoMA Collectors Records. MoMA came close to being the first museum to acquire a Newman, initiating the process before the Basel Kunstmuseum.

31 At a Hunter College talk in 1962, a woman on the dais with Barney reached over to a pitcher to pour herself a glass of water, only to find it filled with vodka. RM1.

32 Alex Liberman interviewed by Kazanjian, Jan. 1989, Dodie Kazanjian and Calvin Tomkins research materials on Alexander Liberman, 1927–1999, AAA.

33 Alan Power to BN, May 5, 1949.

34 Alan Power to author, interview, Mar. 25, 2007.

35 Alan Power to BN, n.d., 1959.

36 Power to author, 2007.

37 The following year, E. J. Power did purchase *By Twos* and *Eve*.

38 BN to J Stephan, May 17, 1959.

39 See chapter 23.

40 Another unhealed abscess may have been the Stephans' purchase of Still's large black painting from "Fifteen Americans"—the most "Newmanesque" of Still's works. There are echoes of Barney's repurchase of *Untitled 1, 1950* from Ossorio in 1953.

41 BN to John and Ruth Stephan, June 21, 1959.

42 Spencer Samuels to BN, and Spencer Samuels to John Green (Hecht, Hadfield, Farbach), June 18, 1959.

43 Andrew Hudson to author, interview, Apr. 19, 2010.

44 CG to BN, July 21, 1959.

45 BN to CG, Sept. 13, 1959, draft.

46 CG to BN, Oct. 3, 1959.

47 Because of Fishburne's health and relocation out of New York, *The Promise* remained unrestored when Barney had it delivered to Greenberg the following year. "It requires some care: a new stretcher and some in-painting. *The Promise* means I always keep mine." BN to CG, June 21, 1960. Greenberg was not unhappy.

48 BN to CG, Sept. 13, 1959, draft.

49 BN to Alan Power, Sept. 4, 1959, unsent.

Dodie Kazanjian and Calvin Tomkins research materials on Alexander Liberman, 1927–1999, AAA.

8 BN to Alan Power, Sept. 4, 1959, unsent.

9 BN to Power, Sept. 4, 1959; RM to author, interview, Oct. 16, 2010.

10 BN to Power, Sept. 4, 1959.

11 Roy Kiyooka, quoted in John O'Brian, "Where the

Hell Is Saskatchewan, and Who Is Emma Lake?" in *The Flat Side of the Landscape: The Emma Lake Artists' Workshops*, Saskatoon, Canada: Mendel Art Gallery, 1989.

12 O'Brian, "Where the Hell Is Saskatchewan?"

13 That struck fear in the men. When, the following day, the wife of one of the artists showed up for lunch, the husband made her stand outside in the rain, afraid to let her in. It provoked another "lecture": "Jesus, you don't keep the babes out," Barney admonished them. "Without the babes, we wouldn't exist!" RM1.

14 RM1.

15 RM to author, 2010.

16 BN to Power, Sept. 1, 1959.

17 RM1.

18 BN to Power, Sept. 4, 1959.

19 RM1.

20 Dan Wakefield, *New York in the 50s*, New York: Houghton Mifflin, 1992.

21 "8 New York Painters," *Vogue*, Oct. 15, 1959. Liberman would say that he granted *Vogue's* extraordinary platform—whenever he could—"out of an artistic admiration and fervor" to bring "a just recognition to people who in my opinion were ignored or bypassed" (Liberman, interview, 1989). Later, Barney said to him, "Alex, you know, I travel through America and they recognize me in barber shops!" because of the article in *Vogue*. When Liberman's photographs of artists in their studios were set to be shown at the Museum of Modern Art at the end of November, Barney persuaded Parsons to set a date—April 1960—for Liberman's first show of paintings and cutouts (Dodie Kazanjian and Calvin Tomkins, *Alex: The Life of Alexander Liberman*, New York: Knopf, 1993, 222).

22 Still may have made more than one version of this work, or he may have somewhat repainted it. See *1956-J No.2 (PH 1074)* in *Clyfford Still*, ed. John P. O'Neill, New York: The Metropolitan Museum of Art, 1979.

23 Dorothy Seiberling, "Baffling U.S. Art: What It Is About," *Life* (Nov. 9, 1959); Dorothy Seiberling, "The Varied Art of Four Pioneers: Analogies with Nature Help Explain Abstract-Expressionist Work," *Life* (Nov. 16, 1959).

24 *Time* (Nov. 9, 1959).

25 *Clyfford Still*, ed. O'Neill, 195.

26 Pollock's *Blue Poles*, on loan from Heller, was hung as a place-holder.

27 BHF, "The Most Expensive Restaurant Ever Built," *Evergreen Review* (Nov.–Dec. 1959).

28 BN to BHF, Sept. 29, 1959. The Museum of Modern Art "selected" for the decor *La Tête Blanche* by Etienne Hajdú, and Philip Johnson, formerly director of the museum's Department of Architecture, chose the interior accoutrements, down to the cutlery, leading Friedman to write, "you are at a good design show at the Museum of Modern Art."

29 "Picture of a Painter," *Newsweek* (Mar. 16, 1959).

30 John Kasmin to author, interview, July 31, 2008.

31 Kasmin to author, 2008.

32 BN to editor, *Life* magazine, Nov. 23, 1959, draft not sent.

33 BN to AB, Nov. 23, 1959, draft not sent.

34 BN to Dore Ashton, Nov. 23, 1959, draft not sent.

35 BN to Dorothy Seiberling, Nov. 25, 1959, drafts not sent.

36 Dorothy Gees Seckler, unpublished text from interview transcript for "Frontiers of Space," *Art News* (Summer 1962).

37 John Canaday, "Happy New Year: Thoughts on Critics and Certain Painters as the Season Opens," *NYT* (Sept 6, 1959).

38 John Canaday, "Art: No Happy New Year?," *NYT* (Sept. 20, 1959).

39 Canaday, "Happy New Year."

40 Selected by Peter Selz, 104 varyingly representational paintings and sculptures by 23 artists were intended to represent "effigies of the disquiet man," the "uniqueness of man as he confronts his fate."

41 John Canaday, "Evolution of a Public: The Audience Created for Modern Art May in Turn Be on the Point of Redirecting That Art," *NYT* (Jan. 31, 1960). Cited in Lynn Zelevansky, "Dorothy Miller's 'Americans,' 1942–63," in *The Museum of Modern Art at Mid-Century: At Home and Abroad*, New York: The Museum of Modern Art, 1994.

42 AHB, "Tastemaking," *NYT* (Sept. 25, 1960).

43 "A Letter to the New York Times," *NYT* (Feb. 26, 1961).

44 "Art Critic Censured," *NYT* (Feb. 11, 1961).

45 AN, interview by John O'Neill, 1994.

46 Barnett Newman, "Embattled Lamb," *Art News* (Sept. 1962).

47 *Mishbucha*, "family" in Yiddish; with Rosenberg and Schapiro Barney was able to deploy and deflect witticisms and puns in Yiddish as well as English.

FORTY-SIX. "NEWMAN STANDARD TIME"

1 Betty Parsons Gallery records and personal papers, 1916–1991, bulk 1946–1983, AAA.

2 Waldo Rasmussen to Hanseatische Assekuranz, Jan. 29, 1963.

3 Caroline Keck to Porter McCray, Jan. 11, 1960.

4 BN to Porter McCray, Feb. 18, 1960, and draft.

5 After a "year of consultation and research" by Barney and the conservator Riportella, the painting was able to be saved. For the extraordinary history of damage to and restoration of *Cathedra* see E. Bracht, I. Glanzer, L. Wijnberg, J. Van Adrichem, "The Restoration of Barnett Newman's *Cathedra*," in *Barnett Newman: Cathedra*, exhibition catalogue, Amsterdam: Stedelijk Museum, 2001.

6 BN to K. W. Putnam, Albert R. Lee & Company, June 11, 1961.

7 Brenda Richardson, *Barnett Newman: The Complete Drawings, 1944–1969*, Baltimore: The Baltimore Museum of Art, 1979, 158.

8 Everett Ellin to BN, Aug. 15, 1960.

9 Everett Ellin to BN, Dec. 30, 1960.

10 BHF diary, Feb. 5, 1960.

11 *Saturday Review*, Apr. 23, 1960.

12 RM1; materials invoices; Job Lot, Apr. 29, 1960.

13 BN, interview with KO, unpublished, Aug. 2, 1963.

14 *Elmer Gantry*, released in July and "packing 'em in," was so shocking and so controversial that United Artists

basically gave the movie a unique NC-16 rating before any official ratings system was instituted. Bosley Crowther, "The Big Money; Public Going for Raw Films This Summer," *NYT* (Sept. 4, 1960).

15 BN to Joseph J. Pircaro, Departmental Marine Surveyor, General Adjustment Bureau, Inc., June 16, 1966, unsent draft.

16 BNFA.

17 John Kasmin to author, interview, July 31, 2008.

18 RM1.

19 Holstein, a photographer, and scholar—one of the first to recognize and support the extraordinary creative quality of American quilts—became in New York a close friend of Murray's and through Murray a member of Barney's circle.

20 Kasmin to author, 2008.

21 After Barney moved uptown, no one who met with him avoided the fare—or the inexplicable New Orleans wallpaper—at Greengrass, "The Sturgeon King": the glamorous and elegant dealer, Irving Blum; the future chairman of Condé Nast, S. I. Newhouse; director of the Basel Kunstmuseum, Franz Meyer; Maurice Tuchman; John Kasmin.

22 RM1.

23 Donald Gratz to Dodie Kazanjian, Dodie Kazanjian papers, 1949–2017, bulk 1980–2017, AAA.

24 BHF diary, Feb. 5, 1960.

25 Andrew Hudson to author, interview, Apr. 19, 2010.

26 RM1.

27 Saul Steinberg to Jeanne Siegel, "Around Barnett Newman," *Art News* (Oct. 1971).

28 Alex Liberman interviewed by Kazanjian, Jan. 1989, Dodie Kazanjian and Calvin Tomkins research materials on Alexander Liberman, 1927–1999, AAA.

29 RM1.

30 "That was one of the things that Barney projected. He would relate to you as a peer and not as an older artist," said the painter Larry Poons—who as a young unknown had been invited to a large party on West End Avenue after writing a fan letter inspired by the French & Co. show. "That was the beautiful thing about him." Siegel, "Around Barnett Newman," and Larry Poons, interview, June 17, 2010.

31 RM1 and RM2.

32 RM1.

33 RM1.

34 Liberman, interview, 1989.

35 Francine Du Plessix Gray, "Living with Cleve," *Cleve Gray: Man and Nature 1975–2004*, New York: Neuberger Museum of Art, 2007.

36 Hudson to author, 2010.

37 RM1.

38 RM1.

39 RM1.

40 RM1.

41 Kasmin to author, 2008.

42 "A Red Tower Replacing Carnegie Hall," *Life* (Sept. 9, 1957).

FORTY-SEVEN. AUTHENTICITY

1 Kenneth Sawyer in the *Evergreen Review*, quoted in John Brooks, "Profiles: Why Fight it? (Sidney Janis)," *The New Yorker* (Nov. 12, 1960).

2 Brooks, "Profiles: Why Fight it?"

3 HR, "Literary Form and Social Hallucination," *Partisan Review* (Fall 1960).

4 Milton Resnick and Ad Reinhardt, "'Attack': 1961, The Club," printed in Geoffrey Dorfman, ed., *Out of the Picture: Milton Resnick and the New York School*, New York: Midmarch Arts Press, 2002.

5 Regina Bogat to author, interview, Sept. 23, 2008.

6 This sentence appeared in CG, *Art and Culture*, Boston: Beacon Press, 1961, as "The Late Thirties in New York"; it was an extensive revision of the 1957 essay, "New York Painting Only Yesterday" from *Art News* (Summer 1957).

7 In the minds of the emerging conceptual, minimal, and Pop artists, on the other hand, such concerns were significantly absent, or, if present at all, were addressed with a very different irony.

8 Bogat to author, 2008.

9 Robert Rosenblum, "The Abstract Sublime," *Art News* (Feb. 1961).

10 John Boyle invoice, Oct. 31, 1960.

11 BN, interview with KO, unpublished, Aug. 2, 1963.

12 The other reason was his eviction phobia. Landlords, for Barney, were like the nightmare homunculus in a Fuseli painting.

13 BN, interview with KO, 1963.

14 BN to MS, Nov. 8, 1960, MS papers, 1923–1991, Columbia University Rare Book & Manuscript Library.

15 BN to Lawrence Alloway, Dec. 29, 1960; Lawrence Alloway, "Against Picasso," *Art International* 4.8 (1960).

16 "I cannot agree enough with you concerning the importance of keeping things confidential," Barney responded in a draft, possibly never sent, "since I am certain [you] have enough to do, without the added pressure from competing artists and their collector and critic friends etc, should your interest in me get around." BN to James Elliot, Aug. 17, 1960.

17 Everett Ellin to BN, July 8 and Aug. 15, 1960. LACMA had been part of the Los Angeles Museum of History, Science and Art since 1910. Only in 1961 was it established as an independent entity. It relocated to Wilshire Boulevard in 1965.

18 Lawrence Alloway to BN, Jan. 26, 1961.

19 Lawrence Rubin to BN, Jan. 8, 1960, Jan. 17, 1961, Jan. 21, 1961. William Rubin was teaching at Sarah Lawrence and the City University of New York; his dissertation at Columbia University was on modern ecclesiastic art.

20 BN to Lawrence Rubin, Sept. 16, 1960; Lawrence Rubin to BN, Sept. 26, 1960.

21 Lawrence Rubin to BN, Jan. 21, 1961.

22 BN to Lawrence Rubin, drafts, Jan. 1960–Mar. 1961, possibly none sent.

23 BN to Lawrence Rubin, draft, n.d.

24 BN, telegram to Lawrence Rubin, n.d., Apr. 1961.

25 John Canaday, "Is Less more, and When for Whom?," *NYT* (Jan. 22, 1961).

FORTY-EIGHT. "MR. NEWMAN, WHY DO YOU PAINT?"

1 Cleve Gray and Francine du Plessix Gray interviewed by Ann Temkin, July 2000, Philadelphia Museum of Art, Library and Archives Repository.

2 TS to BN, Dec. 17, 1960.

3 Barbara Marcus to BN, Mar. 26, 1961; BN to Barbara Marcus, Apr. 12, 1961.

4 BN to Marcus, Apr. 12, 1961.

5 Marcus to BN, Mar. 26, 1961.

6 Barbara Marcus to BN, Apr. 26, 1962.

7 BN to Barbara Marcus, Dec. 31, 1961.

8 Barbara Marcus to BN, Sept. 5, 1961.

9 RM3.

10 Cleve Gray papers, 1933–2005, AAA.

11 This chronology is based on Annalee's dating. For an insurance policy taken in Jan. 1961, two—not four—of the future *Stations* are listed.

12 Chuck Ginnever, invoice, Apr. 27, 1961.

13 BN, "Preface to 18 Cantos," 1964.

14 Robert Rosenblum, "The Abstract Sublime," *Art News* (Feb. 1961).

15 Rosenblum to B + A, Nov. 18, 1959. Robert Rosenblum, "Unité et Divergences de la Peinture Américaine," *Aujourd'hui: Art et Architecture* (July 1958).

16 Rosenblum, "The Abstract Sublime."

17 Although they had known each other for over a decade, in the early 1960s, provoked by conversations around the protest to the *NYT*, Schapiro shared with Barney various writings, like the 1956 "Leonardo and Freud: An Art-Historical Study," and the January 1961 "Mr. Berenson's Values," a review of a biography in which Schapiro highlights Berenson's very complicated existence as a "new world" Jew and the place of culture in it. MS, "Mr. Berenson's Values," *Encounter* (Jan. 1961).

18 Erwin Panofsky, letter to J. Canaday, Sept. 17, 1959, in Erwin Panofsky, *Korrespondenz 1957 bis 1961*, ed.

26 BN to BH, Jan. 18, 1961.

by Dieter Wuttke, Wiesbaden: Harrassowitz, 2008; cited in Pietro Conte, "The Panofsky-Newman Controversy," *Aisthesis. Pratiche, linguaggi e saperi dell'estetico* 8.2 (Nov. 2015), 87–97, https://doi.org/10.13128/Aisthesis-17567.

19 Erwin Panofsky to MS, Mar, 7, 1946, MS papers, 1923–1991, Columbia University Rare Book & Manuscript Library.

20 MS to BN, from Jerusalem, Apr. 27, 1961.

21 Erwin Panofsky to MS, Mar. 16, 1961, MS papers.

22 BN, letter to the editor, *Art News* (May 1961). The words in square brackets were cut in the published letter.

23 Erwin Panofsky, letter to the editor, *Art News* (Sept. 1961).

24 When Schapiro had an opportunity, about 18 months later, to remind Barney that, while they may have been having fun, Panofsky was no fool, he did so in no uncertain terms. Congratulating Barney on a hagiographic article by Rosenberg that recounted this episode, he wrote, "I have only one correction . . . . To say that Panofsky is a critic is like saying that Harold Rosenberg is a public relations man. How much more interesting it would have been to say that Panofsky is a great iconologist who has solved many puzzles in Renaissance imagery by an unrivalled skill in philological decipherment of pictures, and holds the chair in this subject at the Princeton Institute for Advanced Study! This would not have lessened the merit of your letters and it would have, as they say, enhanced Harold's reputation for know-what." MS to BN, Feb. 28, 1963.

25 *Potestas audendi*: the prideful assumption by a painter of the power to create; cited by Horace, at the beginning of *Ars Poetica*.

26 BN, letter to the editor, *Art News* (Sept. 1961).

FORTY-NINE. PROMETHEUS BOUND

1 Oral history interview with Robert Scull, June 15–28, 1972, AAA.

2 There were tax considerations for both the buyer and the seller to this protocol. Even before he began to make money, the Newmans were diligent about tax—if not spending—management. Annalee, after all, was not simply a "teacher of stenography," as many recall her; she had a graduate degree in business.

3 Ernst Beyeler to author, interview, July 23, 2006.

4 Scull file, BNFA; Calvin Tomkins, "Man Who Is Happening Now," *The New Yorker* (Nov. 26, 1966).

5 Scull, interview, 1972.

6 James Rosenquist to author, interview, May 5, 2010.

7 Ernst Beyeler to BN, June 20 and July 1, 1961.

8 Ernst Beyeler to BN, Aug. 10, 1961.

9 Ironically, and unfortunately, these lessons were lost in the Scull household: a food fight among the Sculls' young sons resulted in a gob of butter hitting the exqui-

sitely vulnerable *White Fire II*. Judith E. Stein, *Eye of the Sixties: Richard Bellamy and the Transformation of Modern Art*, New York: Farrar, Straus and Giroux, 2016, 207.

10 Scull, interview, 1972.

11 Robert Scull to BN, Apr. 10, 1962.

12 Robert Scull to Gordon B. Washburn, July 28, 1961.

13 Robert Scull to Gordon B. Washburn, Aug. 18, 1961, with handwritten addition to BN.

14 Barbara Marcus to BN, Sept. 5, 1961.

15 BN to John C. Warner, Sept. 6, 1961.

16 James M. Bovard to BN, Sept. 20, 1961.

17 Betsy Jones to AB, memo, May 10, 1961, and AB to Mrs. David Meltzer, May 16, 1961, AHB papers, the Museum of Modern Art Archives, New York.

18 BH to author, interview, Nov. 7, 2006.

19 AHB papers.

20 BH to author, 2006.

21 Robert Fulford, "American Revolution," *Toronto Daily Star* (Oct. 14, 1961).

FIFTY. PRIORITY

1 BN, interview with KO, unpublished, Aug. 2, 1963.

2 BN diary, July 24, 1961.

3 BN, interview with KO, 1963. Hess, TBH2, mistakenly said that the painting was done in a second Carnegie Hall studio, but that one was not rented until 1963.

4 Credit to Barbara Rose for her insight about Barney's works and the Jewish prayer shawls worn by men.

5 BN, interview with KO, 1963.

6 The suave, Czechoslovakia-born, Harvard-educated Messer had been director of the American Federation of Arts and, since 1956, director of the Institute of Contemporary Arts in Boston. Sweeney resigned six months earlier, shortly after the opening of the radical Frank Lloyd Wright building, because of "differences in his 'ideals' and those of the museum's board of trustees." Sanka Knox, "Guggenheim Picks Museum Director," *NYT* (Jan. 31, 1961).

7 BN to H. H. Arnason, July 31, 1961.

8 H. H. Arnason to BN, Aug. 8, 1961.

9 Lawrence Fellows, "Eichmann in the Dock," *NYT* (Apr. 30, 1961).

10 David Sylvester to MS, Nov. 19, 1961, MS papers, 1923–1991, Columbia University Rare Book & Manuscript Library.

11 Guggenheim Museum, receipt of delivery, Aug. 29, 1961.

12 Sylvia Sleigh to author, interview, Nov. 15, 2006.

13 "Day In, Day Out," *Time* (Oct. 20, 1961).

14 Everett Ellin to BN, Sept. 30, 1961, and telegram, Oct. 31, 1961.

15 Everett Ellin to BN, Nov. 4, 1961. Weisman was a backer of Ellin's gallery. Oral history interview with Everett Ellin, Apr. 27–28, 2004, AAA.

16 Ellin to BN, Nov. 4, 1961.

17 *Clyfford Still*, ed. John P. O'Neill, New York: The Metropolitan Museum of Art, 1979, 197.

18 Ellin to BN, Oct. 31, 1961.

19 Patricia Still to CG, May 16, 1961, CG papers, 1937–1983, AAA.

20 Claire Loeb, radio interview with Fred and Marcia Weisman for KPFK, Ann Temkin/Newman files, Philadelphia Museum of Art, Library and Archives Repository.

21 *Cathedra* was not chosen because of its size. Both the coveted *Cathedra* and Toronto's rejected *Day One* remained in "the collection of Annalee Newman" until *Day One* was purchased by the Whitney Museum in 1967 and *Cathedra* by the Stedelijk Museum in Amsterdam in 1975. Barney preferred to have a work in a museum to cash in his hand.

22 Betty Freeman to BN, Oct. 19, 1961.

23 Karen Reagon (William Rubin's ex-wife) to BN, Oct. 18, 1961.

24 BN to H. H. Arnason, Oct. 16, 1961.

25 Arnason to BN, Aug. 8, 1961.

26 Jack Kroll, "American Painting and the Convertible Spiral," *Art News* (Nov. 1961).

27 Kroll, "American Painting."

28 BN to Fred Weisman, Dec. 13, 1961.

29 Allan Kaprow to BN, May 17 and Dec. 16, 1961; "Impurity," *Art News* (Jan. 1963).

30 IS, *A Sweeper-Up After Artists*, New York: Thames & Hudson, 2003, 285.

31 BH to author, interview, Nov. 7, 2006.

32 IS to author, interview, Oct. 18, 2006.

33 Lucy R. Lippard, "New York Letter," *Art International* (Summer 1966).

34 Jan van der Marck, quoted in Amy Newman, *Challenging Art*: Artforum *1962–1974*, New York: Soho Press, 2000.

35 SH to BN, Dec. 6, 1961.

36 Chuck Close, quoted in Newman, *Challenging Art*.

37 Samuel Wagstaff, Jr., *Continuity and Change: 45 American Abstract Painters and Sculptors*, exhibition catalogue, Hartford, CT: Wadsworth Atheneum, 1962.

38 Sam Wagstaff to BN, Mar. 12, 1962, and n.d.

39 BN, interview with KO, 1963.

40 "How They Got That Way," *Time* (Apr. 13, 1962).

41 In the next few years, even more successful, even more financially well-off, he pursued a refund of $1.60 that he felt Swissair owed him, and made an insurance claim of $28.34 for a hat and an umbrella, both of which disappeared on separate occasions during a trip to Brazil.

42 Dorothy Gees Seckler, unpublished text from interview transcript for "Frontiers of Space," *Art News* (Summer 1962).

43 Seckler, interview transcript.

44 Dorothy Gees Seckler, "Frontiers of Space," *Art in America* (Summer 1962); manuscript; interview transcript.

45 "Remnant," which can mean simply a leftover part when the main parts are gone, is also a specifically textile and frugal tailor's term: the piece of a milled bolt of fabric that remains when the bulk is sold. A talented clothing maker would know how to cut the fabric to minimize waste—just as Barney earlier had drawn patterns for most efficiently cutting his lengths of cotton duck from Boyle. It was a word so embedded in Barney's consciousness that it would easily roll off his tongue even in a context where the more painter-like "area" might be expected, and it very likely also carried for him a connotation of embarrassing, impoverished contrivance. Nothing is more luxurious, full of possibility, to a tailor than an uncut bolt of cloth.

Barney very carefully went over the complete transcript and Seckler's edited manuscript. Originally he made the distinction between "area" and "remnant" explicit: "I feel that the thing I have to contend with is the area that is in front of me. Now I know that the sense of how a thing is made is perhaps irrelevant. That is, 'everything goes.' Or, you can make a painting and decide that only a third of it is your painting. Or you can make a thing irrespective of the actual piece of canvas and take out your section and say, 'this is my work.' But this to me is cropping" (taking a slap at some color field painters). "I feel that I have to grapple with the exact area that is in front of me. When I am through what I hope that I have achieved is that every single inch on that canvas is inevitable so that if you cut a piece off what is left is a remnant." Seckler, interview transcript.

46 Seckler, "Frontiers of Space."

FIFTY-ONE. WEST COAST

1 AN, interview with Ann Temkin, Nov. 26, 1997, Philadelphia Museum of Art, Library and Archives Repository.

2 BN to Marcia Weisman, Nov. 5, 1960.

3 Museum of Modern Art, press release, July 3, 1961; Robert M. Coates, "The Art Galleries: Innovations," *The New Yorker* (Oct. 21, 1961).

4 Jonathan Holstein and RM to author, interview, Oct. 16, 2010.

5 RM to author, 2010.

6 Years after Barney's death, Murray and Annalee were able to find those molds, shrunken, dried, curled up, useless. But astonishingly, stored with them were the pieces of the plaster original. The reconstruction is now at the Menil Collection in Houston.

7 BN to Cleve and Francine Gray, Feb. 14, 1962, draft; Beverly Crest Hotel bills, Feb. 21–24, 1962.

8 BN to Weismans, Mar. 4, 1962, draft; BN to TH, Oct. 7, 1965.

9 BN to Betty and Stanley Freeman, Mar. 5, 1962, draft.

10 Larry Bell to author, interview, Nov. 14, 2011; Betty Wolff to author, interview, Dec. 2007.

11 Gerald Nordland, "Art—The New Yorkers Are Coming!," *Frontier* (Nov. 1960), cited in Catherine Grenier, ed., *Los Angeles, 1955–1985: Birth of an Art Capital*, exhibition catalogue, Paris: Centre Pompidou, 2006.

12 Musa Mayer, *Night Studio: A Memoir of Philip Guston*, New York: Knopf, 1988.

13 BHF diary, Mar. 1, 1962.

14 Allan Kaprow, "Impurity," *Art News* (Jan. 1963).

15 Cleve Gray to BN, Dec. 5, 1962.

16 Dorothy Gees Seckler, unpublished text from interview transcript for "Frontiers of Space," *Art News* (Summer 1962), 6.

17 Charles Kaprelian, interviewed by Lucy Hunter, Dec. 11, 2011.

18 James Van Dyk to BN, May 4, 1962.

19 Bryan Robertson, "O Pioneers!," *The Listener* (May 10, 1962).

20 John Kasmin to author, interview, July 31, 2008.

21 *The Listener* (July 5, 1962).

22 BN to M. Ashley, editor, *The Listener*, July 5, 1962.

23 BN to Stefan P. Munsing, July 8, 1962.

24 HR to BN, Oct. 24, 1962.

25 BN to HR, Nov. 12, 1962.

26 BN to TH, Nov. 8, 1962, published in *Art News* (Dec. 1962).

27 SH to BN, Mar. 29, 1962.

28 SH to BN, May 23, 1962.

29 BN to SH, May 24, 1962.

30 BN to SH, June 7, 1962.

31 SH to BN, Aug. 21, 1962.

32 Emily Genauer, "Art Tackled and Thrown," *New York Herald Tribune* (June 10, 1962).

33 Mayer, *Night Studio*.

34 Budd Hopkins, "Franz Kline's Color Abstractions," *Artforum* (Summer 1979).

35 Mark Stevens and Annalyn Swan, *de Kooning: An American Master*, New York: Knopf, 2004, 437.

36 TBH to MS, Oct. 15, 1962, MS papers, 1923–1991, Columbia University Rare Book & Manuscript Library.

37 James Breslin, *Mark Rothko, A Biography*, Chicago: The University of Chicago Press, 1993, 424–25.

38 Leon Mnuchin to Avel B. Silverman, Esq., Sept. 14, 1962.

39 Fred Weisman to BN, Nov. 15, 1962.

40 List of Cooperative Apartments for Sale prepared for Barnett Newman, Oct. 18, 1962.

FIFTY-TWO. "THE REPUTATION OF BARNETT NEWMAN"

1 TH to MS, Aug. 30, 1962, TH papers, 1939–1978, AAA. "I'm a long ball hitter," Barney told Murray at the time of the show, employing another macho sports metaphor, "de Kooning a fast infield hitter. We're in the same league. It's not Reinhardt's game." RM, notebook entry, Nov. 30, 1962.

2 Claire Loeb, radio interview with Fred and Marcia Weisman for KPFK, Ann Temkin/Newman files, Philadelphia Museum of Art, Library and Archives Repository.

3 "Something New Is Cooking," *Life* (June 15, 1962).

4 RM3.

5 IS, *A Sweeper-Up After Artists*, New York: Thames & Hudson, 2003, 242.

6 Ann Temkin, phone conversations with Allan Stone, May 22 and Oct. 3, 2001, Temkin/Newman files, Philadelphia Museum of Art, Library and Archives Repository.

7 Hess, TH2, makes much of Barney's predilection for the number 18—*chai* in Hebrew, connoting life.

8 BN to D. Matt, Oct. 22, 1962.

9 Temkin, phone conversations with Stone, 2001.

10 Lawrence S Levine to Bill Matt, D. Matt, Inc., Oct. 25, 1962.

11 BN diary, Aug. 1961.

12 Barbara Kulicke, conversation with the author, Jan.

20, 2010. Robert Kulicke told Yve-Alain Bois a variation on this story: he said Barney gave him the "first right of refusal" and he bought it for $5000.

13 See Mark Stevens and Annalyn Swan, *de Kooning: An American Master*, New York: Knopf, 2004, 439–41, 454–55.

14 Temkin, phone conversations with Stone, 2001.

15 Allan Stone, *Newman / De Kooning*, exhibition catalogue, Oct. 23–Nov. 17, 1962, New York: The Gallery, 1962.

16 Michael Fried, "New York Letter," *Art International* (Dec. 20, 1962).

17 Temkin, phone conversations with Stone, 2001.

18 TBH, "Reviews and Previews," *Art News* (Dec. 1962).

19 IS, "In the Art Galleries," *New York Post* (Nov. 4, 1962).

20 TBH, "Reviews and Previews." "New Realists" included Americans Johns, Larry Rivers, Robert Indiana, Warhol, Jim Dine, George Segal, Roy Lichtenstein, Claes Oldenburg, Rosenquist, Peter Agostini, and Thiebaud, along with Europeans Arman, Daniel Spoerri, and others.

21 TBH, "Reviews and Previews."

22 "Introducing the Generation, A Foldout Gallery: Young Leaders of the Big Breakthrough, a Red-Hot Hundred," *Life* (Sept. 14, 1962).

23 Lee Hall, *Betty Parsons: Artist, Dealer, Collector*, New York: H. N. Abrams, 1991, 127–28.

24 Oral history interview with Sidney Janis, Mar. 21–Sept. 26, 1972, AAA.

25 Julie Haifley, oral history interview with Grace Hartigan, May 10, 1979, AAA.

26 Stevens and Swan, *de Kooning*, 455, 435–36.

27 James Breslin, *Mark Rothko, A Biography*, Chicago: The University of Chicago Press, 1993, 426.

28 Dorothy Gees Seckler, "Frontiers of Space," *Art in America* (Summer 1962). Five out of six captions contained wrong information, either the date, title, or owner, and many of the corrections Barney indicated on the galley proofs were not made. BN to Jean Lipman, July 9, 1962.

29 Seckler, "Frontiers of Space."

30 BN, transcript of lecture at Hunter College, Nov. 16, 1962.

31 Seckler, unpublished text from interview transcript for "Frontiers of Space."

32 RM, "Barney at Hunter College," notes made at lecture, Nov. 16, 1962.

33 BN, transcript of lecture.

34 Lawrence Alloway, "The Reputation of Barnett Newman," BBC broadcast, Nov. 8, 1962.

35 Sylvia Sleigh to author, interview, Nov. 15, 2006.

36 Alloway worked closely with Barney on the text. An early draft outline lists "misunderstanding[s]," "myths," and paths "rejected" and "refused," i.e., "Misunderstanding by other artists of Newman's radical art which in its moral stance is critical of anything less than itself." Lawrence Alloway, "Memorandum," Aug. 27, 1962, and Lawrence Alloway to BN, Aug. 31, 1962.

37 James Fitzsimmons to Lawrence Alloway, Sept. 15, 1962, copy sent to BN. Although Fitzsimmons was enthusiastic, these articles never appeared. Barney was happy to refer to and quote from his early writings, but, not for the last time, willing publishers had trouble prying them from his vault.

38 Alloway, "The Reputation of Barnett Newman."

39 Rosenberg, Harold, "Action Painting: A Decade of Distortion," *Art News* (Dec. 1962).

40 Murray, Robert, "Barney at Hunter College."

FIFTY-THREE. BLACK AND WHITE

1 TH to WB, Jan. 31, 1963, TH papers, 1939–1978, AAA.

2 TH to MS, Jan. 21, 1963, TH papers.

3 Allan Kaprow, "Impurity," *Art News* (Jan. 1963).

4 Frank O'Hara, "Art Chronicle," *Kulchur* 3.9 (Spring 1963).

5 Liberman had recently been promoted to editorial director.

6 MS to BN, Feb. 28, 1963.

7 Brice Marden to author, interview, June 16, 2010.

8 HR, "Barnett Newman, A Man of Controversy, and Spiritual Grandeur," *Vogue* (Feb. 15, 1963).

9 CS to Betty Freeman, May 2, 1963, Betty Freeman papers, 1951–1969, AAA.

10 CS to Betty Freeman, Sept. 10, 1963, Betty Freeman papers.

11 CS to Freeman, Sept. 10, 1963.

12 Lawrence Alloway, "The American Sublime," *Living Arts Magazine* (June 1963).

13 CS to Betty Freeman, Nov. 1, 1963, Betty Freeman papers.

14 HR to BN, Jan. 31, 1963.

15 BN to HR, Feb. 2, 1963, draft.

16 "We"—the abstract expressionists—"took the plumbing out of painting," Barney told B. H. Friedman shortly after the broadcast aired. "They"—Rauschenberg, Dine, Wesselmann, etcetera—"are putting it back." BHF diary, Mar. 30, 1963.

17 See chapter 45.

18 Barnett Newman interviewed by Lane Slate, recorded as part of the *Contemporary American Painters* series and broadcast by CBS television on Mar. 10, 1963; BN, notes on drafts of interview, Feb.–Mar. 1963.

19 TBH to MS, Jan. 13, 1963, MS papers, 1923–1991, Columbia University Rare Book & Manuscript Library.

20 BN to Alex and Tatiana Liberman, Aug. 8, 1967.

21 Lee Hall, interview with Lawrence Alloway, quoted in Lee Hall, *Betty Parsons: Artist Dealer, Collector*, New York: H. N. Abrams, 1991, 130.

22 "The Art of Today" section of "Response," Apr. 20, 1963, with Hess, Rosenberg, Guston, Smith, and Gray; interviews with psychologist Karlis Osis and with Joanna Magloff, a West Coast artist, for a planned, but never realized, article in *Artforum*.

23 MS to BN, July 8, 1963.

24 The Solomon Guggenheim Museum loan receipt, Oct. 16, 1963.

25 AN interviewed by Dodie Kazanjian, 1991, unpublished transcript.

26 SH to BN, Oct. 24, 1963.

27 TBH to MS, Apr. 2, 1963, MS papers.

28 BN to Fred Weisman, July 19, 1963.

29 TH to MS, Jan. 21, 1963.

30 Edward Massie, M.D. to BN, June 19, 1963.

31 BN to Alan Bowness, July 19, 1963.

32 AN, interview, 1991.

33 Alfred Leslie to author, interview, Dec. 13, 2012.

34 Hester Diamond to author, interview, Aug. 3, 2006.

35 History would prove that Barney had dodged a bullet. Although with Annalee as a shield, that bullet would never have hit its mark.

36 Diamond to author, 2006; Elizabeth Baker to author, interview, Nov. 6, 2008.

37 Diamond to author, 2006.

38 Born in 1917 in Latvia, Osis was the president of the Parapsychology Foundation in New York. He devoted much of his professional research to deathbed experiences.

39 Carlo Beuf, "Divine Genius," *NYT* (July 21, 1963).

40 Charles Poore, "The Artist's Mortal Road Toward Immortality," *NYT* (Aug. 1, 1963).

41 BN, interview with KO, unpublished, Aug. 2, 1963.

FIFTY-FOUR. STATEMENTS

1 John Marion, quoted in Cleve Gray, "The Portfolio Collector," *Art in America* (June 1965).

2 William Goldston to author, interview, Apr. 9, 2010.

3 Zigmunds Priede to author, interview, Apr. 21, 2010.

4 BN, "Preface to 18 Cantos," 1964.

5 Priede to author, Apr. 21, 2010.

6 Richard Meier to author, interview, Nov. 2007.

7 The previous year, Pei had sent Barney copies of an article describing his design for the strikingly sculptural, cast concrete Everson Museum of Art in Syracuse, New York, and Barney followed up by inviting Pei to his studio.

8 BN to TS, Sept. 5, 1950.

9 "The Hebrew Myths," discussed by Robert Graves and Raphael Patai, brochure, The Poetry Center, YM-YWHA, May 15, 1963.

10 Hana Volavkova, *The Synagogue Treasures of Bohemia and Moravia*, Prague: Sfinx, 1949.

11 "Congregation Shearith Israel, The Spanish and Portuguese Synagogue."

12 RM2.

13 *Tanakh, The Holy Scriptures*, 3rd ed., Jerusalem, Philadelphia: Jewish Publication Society, 1985.

14 RM to author, interview, Oct. 16, 2010.

15 BN, in Richard Meier, *Recent American Synagogue Architecture*, exhibition catalogue, New York: The Jewish Museum, 1963.

16 BN, handwritten draft of the catalogue statement.

17 RM1.

18 Doloris Holmes, oral history interview with Lee Krasner, 1972, AAA.

19 Lee Krasner, quoted in Jeanne Siegel, "Around Barnett Newman," *Art News* (Oct. 1971).

20 Sylvia Sleigh to author, interview, Nov. 15, 2006.

21 Joanna (Magloff) Koss, conversation with author, June 22, 2016.

22 Gratz was not outfitted to make anything "super-size." Donald Gratz to Dodie Kazanjian, Dodie Kazanjian papers, 1949–2017, bulk 1980–2017, AAA.

23 "The Aloof Abstractionist," *Time* (Nov. 29, 1963).

24 Koss, conversation with author, 2016.

25 Leonard Horowitz, "Black and White," *Village Voice* (Dec. 1963).

26 Dorothy Gees Seckler, unpublished text from interview transcript for "Frontiers of Space," *Art News* (Summer 1962).

FIFTY-FIVE. EUROPE

1 MS to BN, June 13, 1964.

2 BN to Lawrence Alloway, May 24, 1964.

3 Philip Johnson, the pavilion's designer, commissioned ten artists to make 20-by-20-foot works that would circle the exterior wall of the "theaterama."

4 BN to Alex Liberman, May 20, 1964.

5 AN to Anna Greenhouse, May 20, 1964; Alan Power to author, Mar. 25, 2007.

6 The Catholic diocese was dissolved in the 16th century.

7 Power to author, 2007.

8 BN to Alloway, May 24, 1964; ticket stubs and programs; Clive Barnes, *NYT* (May 19, 1964).

9 BNFA.

10 Motherwell and Frankenthaler attended their wedding at Westminster Abbey in October; Barney and Annalee, although invited, did not.

11 William Turnbull to IS, n.d., IS papers, 1909–2007, bulk 1950–2000, the Getty Research Institute, Los Angeles.

12 "During the 1950s American painting introduced, among other things, the concept of the large painting into British art," read an essay in the catalogue. The "other things" were: "a new conception of space in painting and with it a new conception of the spectator's relationship to a painting"; the idea that paintings "can be the record of a sequence of actions" and not copies of "previous planning (painting from sketches), but as direct execution on the canvas itself" something that committed the artist "ethically"; and making the work "something existing in its own right." Roger Coleman, Introduction, *Situation*, exhibition catalogue, London: Royal Society of British Artists Galleries, 1960. This small group of artists was not associated with the radical political critique of capitalism of the Situationist International, 1957–72.

13 Bryan Robertson, Newman obituary, *The Times* (Aug. 11, 1970).

14 John Kasmin to author, interview, July 31, 2008.

15 BN to Alan Bowness, July 19 and Dec. 21, 1963.

16 Barney created an invoice for $85,000—an astonishing price for the time—with a discount that brought it to $50,000.

17 Power to author, 2007.

18 Clyde Farnsworth, "Tate Gallery Shows 310 Works Ranging from Matisse to Pop," *NYT* (Apr. 21, 1964).

19 BN to Rene and E. J. Power, July 24, 1964, draft.

20 BN to Alloway, May 24, 1964; Power to author, 2007.

21 BN to Alan Bowness, May 9, 1964.

22 BN to Liberman, May 20, 1964.

23 BN to Alloway, May 24, 1964.

24 BN to Alan Bowness and Lawrence Gowing, May 26, 1964, Tate Archives; BN to insurance company, 1966, unsent draft.

25 BN to Arnold Rüdlinger, June 10, 1964. *Joshua* was also shown at the Kunsthalle, but lent by Harriet Mnuchin.

26 Before the war, Schmidt had famously acquired "degenerate art" removed from German museums.

27 Helga Huber to author, interview, July 23, 2006.

28 BH to author, interview, Nov. 7, 2006; Hester Diamond to author, interview, Aug. 3, 2006; Ernst Beyeler to author, interview, July 23, 2006.

29 Jane Dillenger, notes, Apr. 12, 1969. There is indeed a narthex, but it is shallow.

30 AN to Anna Greenhouse, May 28, 1964; Charles Delloye to AN, Feb. 27, 1972.

31 Robert Alden, "The 'Pieta' Arrives Here, Ever So Gently," *NYT* (Apr. 14, 1964).

32 Alan Solomon, "Report on the American Participation in the XXXII Venice Biennale 1964," Alan R. Solomon papers, 1907–1970, bulk 1944–1970, AAA.

33 MS to BN, June 13, 1964.

34 "Vanity Fair: The New York Art Scene," *Newsweek* (Jan. 4, 1965).

35 Lawrence Rubin to CG, June 15, 1964.

36 *Avanti Roma* (June 21, 1964), Alan R. Solomon papers.

37 *Gazzettino di Venezia* (July 8 1964).

38 "Vanity Fair: The New York Art Scene."

39 Francis K. Lloyd to BN, Feb. 27, 1964.

40 R. W. Apple, Jr., "Gallery Opening Marked by Chaos," *NYT* (Nov. 13, 1963).

41 "USA Artist: Barnett Newman," 1966.

42 BN to John Kasmin, Feb. 29, 1964.

43 BN calculations, June 23, 1964.

44 Virginia Wright to author, interview, May 29, 2008.

45 Walter Hopps to Ann Temkin, n.d., Philadelphia Museum of Art, Library and Archives Repository.

46 Thomas Messer to author, interview, Mar. 16, 2007.

47 Lawrence Alloway to BN, July 2, 1964.

48 AN to Rene and E. J. Power, Nov. 3, 1964.

49 His old friend Navascués prepared a very basic outline of the 14 commemorated events and their history as pilgrimage, and an annotated bibliography.

FIFTY-SIX. "QUESTIONABLE HISTORICAL FACTS"

1 Ann Faber, "U.W. Art Symposium Nearly Resembles Vegetarian Dinner," *Seattle Post-Intelligencer* (Oct. 2, 1964).

2 Virginia Wright to BN, Sept. 11, 1964.

3 Faber, "U.W. Art Symposium."

4 "Symposium, Problems and Issues in Art Today," transcript, University of Washington, Oct. 1, 1964.

5 John Hinterberger, "Quo Vadis, Art? (Panel Did Not Seem Too Sure)," *The Seattle Times* (Oct. 2, 1964).

6 Bagley Wright, Virginia's husband, was a real-estate developer, patron, and philanthropist. Together, they are credited with creating an international arts and cultural hub in a former backwater—beginning with the 1962 "Century 21 Exposition," for which Wright developed Seattle's iconic Space Needle.

7 Paul Cummings, oral history interview with HR, Dec. 17, 1970–Jan. 28, 1973, AAA.

8 Virginia Wright to BN, Sept. 26, 1964; AN to E. J. Power, Nov. 3, 1964.

9 BN to Art McKay, Oct. 23, 1964, draft.

10 AN to Power, Nov. 3, 1964.

11 RM to author, interview, Oct. 26, 2011.

12 Frank O'Hara, "Art New York," film interview with BN, 1964.

13 When, in the spring of 1965, Alfred Jarry's nihilistically irreverent capriccio, "The Passion Considered as an Uphill Bicycle Race," appeared in translation in the Grove Press edition of *The Selected Works of Alfred Jarry*, Barney saved a copy for either reference or moral support of his own artistic license.

14 "Vanity Fair: The New York Art Scene," *Newsweek* (Jan. 4, 1965).

15 Lawrence Alloway, "Barnett Newman," *Artforum* (June 1965).

16 Van Weeren-Griek responded that the debate was held precisely to make the point that there was no such identity in art: "The origin of a contemporary artist has nothing to do with his work," and that the title was chosen by the panelists Dore Ashton, Paul Brach, Arthur Cohen, and Peter Selz to make that very point. Hans Van Weeren-Griek to BN, Jan. 22, 1965.

17 Murray confirms that Barney tipped $10 or $20 at every warehouse visit.

18 B. Barnett Newman, Affidavit, State of New York, County of New York, 1967.

19 "Vanity Fair: The New York Art Scene."

20 Allan Kaprow, "Should the Artist Be a Man of the World?" *Art News* (Oct. 1964).

21 Green and Barney worked "hand in glove" on the show, with Barney choosing the artists. Sam Green to Heidi Colsman-Freyberger, May 2002.

22 BN to Walter Hopps, May 23, 1965.

23 BN to Walter Hopps, May 27, 1965. This was the period when Sarah Newman was working for the Voice of America at the Vietnam desk. To be fair, all of the artists involved seemed as blithely unconcerned about participating. But of them only Barney was subsidized for a month, and debriefed after. Four years later, in 1969, the situation was very different: well over half the international artists withdrew in protest.

24 According to Annalee, it was the same issue that underlay his rage at Reinhardt: being grouped with the formalist "abstractionists"—Albers, Diller, Bolotowsky— and not that he was identified as "the avant-garde-huckster-handicraftsman and educational-shop-keeper, the holy-roller-explainer-entertainer-in-residence." AN, interview by John O'Neill, 1994.

25 BN to Hopps, May 23, 1965.

26 Grace Glueck, "Art Notes: Seven for Sao Paulo," *NYT* (May 23, 1965).

27 BN to Hopps, May 27, 1965.

28 BN interviewed by David Sylvester, Apr. 1965, rev. Nov. 1965; "Barnett Newman Talks to David Sylvester," BBC radio broadcast, Nov. 17, 1965; transcript in the Getty Research Institute, Los Angeles.

29 Walter Hopps to Ann Temkin, n.d., Philadelphia Museum of Art, Library and Archives Repository.

30 Clifton Daniel to BN, June 11, 1965; BN to Arthur Ochs Sulzberger, July 13, 1965; BN to Walter Hopps, July 15, 1965; Leon Mnuchin to Arthur Ochs Sulzberger, July 29, 1965.

31 James C. Goodale to Mnuchin & Moss, Aug. 9, 1965; Grace Glueck, "Art Notes: Demurrer," *NYT* (Oct. 17, 1965).

32 Michael Fried, "Modernist Painting and Formal Criticism," *American Scholar* (Autumn 1964).

33 "Why should a younger critic be anxious to 1) disallow the possibility that a 'metaphysics of despair' can go hand in hand with 'making the best paintings of which [Pollock] was capable,' 2) seek to drive a wedge into what had hitherto been a rather universal consensus that the forties and fifties, for the New York School, were indeed dominated by a sense of 'angst,' of 'crisis,' . . . and 3) establish the primacy of 'formal' intelligence, and this indeed for a period when evidence indicates a distinct-

ly secondary interest in formal matter, and a distinctly primary interest in 'subjects of the artist'?" asked Philip Leider in "New York School the First Generation," *Artforum* (Sept. 1965).

34 Neil A. Levine, interview with BN, "The New York School Question," *Art News* (Sept. 1965).

35 Robert Irwin to author, interview, Nov. 15, 2011.

36 Walter Hopps interviewed by Kazanjian, n.d., Dodie Kazanjian and Calvin Tomkins research materials on Alexander Liberman, 1927–1999, AAA.

37 Philip Leider, "Art: Sao Paulo," *Frontier* (Nov. 1965).

38 AN, interview, 1991; Alan Solomon to Philip Leider, quoted in Leider, "Art: Sao Paulo."

39 Barbara Rose, "The Primacy of Color," *Art International* (May 1964).

40 Frank Stella to author, interview, Dec. 1, 2010.

41 Donald Judd, "Black and White," *Arts Magazine* (Mar. 1964).

42 Larry Bell to author, interview, Nov. 14, 2011.

43 Barbara Rose to author, interview, Oct. 10, 2008.

44 Peter Bart, "Los Angeles Prepares for Museum Opening," *NYT* (Mar. 29, 1965).

45 Bengston, Bell, and Irwin were represented by Ferus Gallery, begun in 1957 by Hopps and the artist Ed Kienholz. By 1965, Hopps had moved to the museum.

46 Alan Solomon, "Making Like Competition in L.A.," *NYT* (July 11, 1965).

47 Maurice Tuchman to author, interview, Jan. 12, 2011.

48 Maurice Tuchman to MS, Aug. 27, 1964, MS papers, 1923–1991, Columbia University Rare Book & Manuscript Library.

49 BN to Maurice Tuchman, Jan. 15, 1965.

50 BN to Maurice Tuchman, Mar. 17, 1965.

51 BN to Tuchman, Jan. 15, 1965.

52 Tuchman remembered the last differently, specifically recalling a discussion about the excerpts at Barney Greengrass. Maurice Tuchman to BN, Apr. 30, 1965.

53 BN to Maurice Tuchman, Apr. 16, 1965. There was "a grain of truth" in that, Tuchman felt, about at least a couple of the paintings. But he did not have the staff or time to do the kind of "detective work" that Barney had. Tuchman to author, 2011.

FIFTY-SEVEN. SÃO PAULO

1 BN to Walter Hopps, Aug. 13, 1965.

2 Walter Hopps, "United States Exhibit, Sao Paulo Bienal," *Art in America* (June 1965).

3 BN to Walter Hopps, Aug. 13 and 14, 1965.

4 The catalogue described the exhibition as presenting "samples of the work." "Obviously," Barney countered, the show could not be "taken very seriously if the work is described as samples." Were Gorky's *Betrothal* or Pollock's *Number 1, 1949* "samples" or "treasure?"

5 Neil A. Levine, interview with BN, "The New York School Question," *Art News* (Sept. 1965).

6 Mrs. Clyfford Still to TBH, Sept. 14, 1965, BNFA. This is the letter itself, which differs slightly from the published version.

7 BN to editor of *Art News* (TBH), Oct. 7, 1965; Mrs. Still to TBH, Sept. 14, 1965; both letters were published in *Art News* (Nov. 1965).

8 CS to Katharine Kuh, Oct. 22, 1965. Katharine Kuh papers, 1875–1994, bulk 1930–1994, AAA.

9 Samuel S. Daily to BN, Aug. 27, 1965. Both Irwin and Bell believed that funding was made available for all of the artists to attend the opening receptions, but that "Barney used up all of the plane fares." Robert Irwin to author, interview, Nov. 15, 2011; Larry Bell to author, interview, Nov. 14, 2011.

10 U.S. Department of State briefing, Aug. 20, 1965.

11 Irwin to author, 2011, and others.

12 Walter Hopps to Ann Temkin, n.d., Philadelphia Museum of Art, Library and Archives Repository.

13 Roberta Gratz to author, interview, Dec. 19, 2006.

14 Dagny Corcoran to author, interview, Dec. 11, 2011; S. I. Newhouse to author, interview, Feb. 13, 2007.

15 "U.S. Art Exhibit Arrives in Brazil," *NYT* (Aug. 30, 1965).

16 Irwin to author, 2011; Larry Poons to author, interview, June 17, 2010.

17 Lucy Lippard, "The Third Stream: Constructed Paintings and Painted Structures," *Art Voices* (Spring 1965). It is revealing of his eminence that at exactly the same time Barney was being acknowledged as a hero to artists of an entirely different stripe. It was the "contention" of the young British artist Harold Cohen, whose discussion of Barney would share the BBC program in November with David Sylvester's interview, that Barney, "more than any other painter in this century" isolated the "symbolic nature of the act" of the "whole painting process," and made it "the central symbolism" of the work. Harold Cohen to BN, Nov. 8, 1965.

18 Philip Leider, "Art: Sao Paulo," *Frontier* (Nov. 1965).

19 Leider, "Art: Sao Paulo."

20 BN to Walter Hopps, June 12, 1965, draft, possibly unsent.

21 "I had been accused—especially by New York people—that I was a part of something called 'The Cool School.'" Irwin to author, 2011.

22 Albert V. Boerner, field message to USIA Washington, Oct. 22, 1964.

23 Lois Bingham to Walter Hopps, June 1, 1965, copied to BN.

24 *Handel*: Yiddish for the satisfying back and forth of doing business.

25 BN to Bela Zempleny, program officer, Department of State, June 24, 1965.

26 Bela Zempleny to BN, June 29, 1965.

27 Bela Zempleny to BN, Nov. 1, 1965; BN to Raymond Kohn, Mar. 5, 1966; Edna W. Snyder to BN, Apr. 16, 1966.

28 Corcoran to author, Dec. 11, 2011.

29 BN, interview recording, São Paulo, BNFA.

30 Baker would later become the long-time editor of *Art in America*.

31 Elizabeth Baker to author, interview, Nov. 6, 2008; caricature of BN at BNFA.

32 Alfred V. Boerner, "VIII São Paulo Bienal (Project 65–216), U.S. Information Service," Nov. 4, 1965, BNFA.

33 "Art: The Market," *Time* (Oct. 22, 1965).

34 Robert Motherwell to BN, Nov. 24, 1965.

FIFTY-EIGHT. STATIONS OF THE CROSS

1 John Canaday, "Art: With Pretty Thorough Execution," *NYT* (Apr. 23, 1966).

2 Phylacteries, called by Jews tefillin, are small leather boxes containing handwritten Torah texts, connected by black leather straps. Orthodox Jewish men wrap the straps around their arms and their heads to symbolize the commandment to fix God's words "as symbols on your hands and bind them on your foreheads" during morning prayers (Deuteronomy 11:18).

3 That Barney would so pointedly address a Christian religious subject may have found encouragement in the publication of his friend William Rubin's book, *Modern Sacred Art and the Church of Assy*, in 1961, around the time he first named the *Stations*. See Kenneth C. Lindsay, "William S. Rubin, Modern Sacred Art and the Church of Assy," *The Art Bulletin* 45 (1963).

4 On one of his trips, he may have seen (or intentionally avoided) the Phillips Collection's "Rothko Room"—a dedicated permanent space that had opened in 1960 explicitly to honor "the artist's objective of an exclusive dominion over space and spectator that he desired for his work." Phillips Collection, 2018 wall label text.

5 Val Lewton to author, interview, Sept. 7, 2012.

6 Hans Ulrich Obrist, "Walter Hopps," *A Brief History of Curating*, Zurich: Imprint, 2008.

7 Robert Irwin to author, interview, Nov. 15, 2011; Larry Bell to author, interview, Nov. 14, 2011.

8 Obrist, "Walter Hopps."

9 "USA Artists: Barnett Newman," WNET, broadcast July 10, 1966.

10 Franz Meyer to author, interview, July 22, 2006.

11 BN to Jean Leering, director, Stedelijk Van Abbemuseum, Eindhoven, Oct. 11, 1966. In 1969, Alloway wrote that Barney had first considered hanging all of the *Stations* in the High Gallery, but elected "sequence over impact" because the result was "too intense"—not to mention unworkably crowded. Lawrence Alloway, "Notes on Barnett Newman," *Art International* (Summer 1969). Sarah Newman considered the relationships developed in the *Cantos*, where the "fullest meaning" emerged when seen in sequence, to be a dry run for the *Stations* installation. Aurora Dias-Jorgensen, interview, July 26, 2007.

12 Peter Engel to Johan Enschedé en Zonen, Haarlem, Holland, Mar. 29, 1966, Guggenheim Archives.

13 J. Leering to BN, Mar. 3, 1966; BN to Leering, Oct. 11, 1966.

14 James Rosenquist, *Painting Below Zero: Notes on a Life in Art*, New York: Knopf, 2009, 154–55.

15 For some, at least, he succeeded: Franz Meyer called the *Stations* the "Sistine Chapel of modern art" because he found its "immediateness" communicated a "spiritual reality" that no other contemporary painter achieved. Franz Meyer, *Barnett Newman: The Stations of the Cross: Lema Sabachthani*, Düsseldorf: Richter Verlag, 2003; Meyer to author, 2006.

16 See Sarah K. Rich, "The Proper Name of Newman's Zip," *Reconsidering Barnett Newman*, ed. Melissa Ho, Philadelphia: The Philadelphia Museum of Art, 2005.

17 BN to Alene Tallmey, interview transcript for a one-paragraph note in *Vogue* (Apr. 15, 1966); BN to Alan Solomon, unedited interview, Mar. 20, 1966, Alan R. Solomon papers, 1907–1970, bulk 1944–1970, AAA.

18 BN, "Interview with Emile de Antonio," SWI. "It meant more than I can say to have seen the range of Barney's work—from the first 'zip' painting (the tiny acorn from which mighty oaks grew) to the last great, heroic black and white series," Virginia Wright wrote in a holiday letter to Barney and Annalee, after a Nov. 1964 visit to the studio (Virginia Wright to B + A). Hopps, too, heard Barney use the term around the time of the São Paulo Bienal, when he was being informal, not speaking seriously about his work. Walter Hopps to Ann Temkin, n.d., Philadelphia Museum of Art, Library and Archives Repository.

19 BN, interview with Solomon, 1966.

20 Damon Runyon, "No Justice: Monologue of a Horse Player (transcribed from life)," cited in Daniel R. Schwarz, *Broadway Boogie Woogie: Damon Runyon and the Making of New York Culture*, New York: Palgrave Macmillan, 2003, 83.

21 BN, statement in *Barnett Newman: The Stations of the Cross: Lema Sabachthani*, exhibition catalogue, New York: Solomon R. Guggenheim Museum, 1966. *Pirkei Avot* is a commentary on the Torah's ethics. *Mishnah* is the first codification of Jewish law.

22 "USA Artists: Barnett Newman."

23 Lawrence Alloway to Herbert Matter, Jan. 25, 1966, the Solomon R. Guggenheim Archives.

24 Lawrence Alloway to BN, Jan. 4, 1966.

25 Lawrence Alloway to Thomas Messer, memo, Jan. 28, 1966, the Solomon R. Guggenheim Archives.

26 Oral history interview with Everett Ellin, Apr. 27–28, 2004, AAA; Lawrence Alloway to Thomas Messer, memo, Dec. 8, 1965, the Solomon R. Guggenheim Archives.

27 Charlotte Curtis, "'Where to?' Asked the Cab Drivers—and So Did the Riders," *NYT* (Apr. 20, 1966).

28 "Painting: Of a Different Stripe," *Time* (Apr. 29, 1966); "Unanswerable Question," *Newsweek* (May 9, 1966).

29 Charlotte Willard, "In the Galleries," *New York Post* (May 1, 1966).

30 Larry Poons to author, interview, June 17, 2010; Barbara Rose to author, interview, Oct. 10, 2008.

31 Andrew Decker, oral history interview with Thomas M. Messer, Oct. 1994–Jan. 1995, AAA.

32 Lawrence Alloway to BN, July 2, 1964; Thomas Messer to BN, Dec. 9, 1965.

35 BN to Robert Motherwell, Dec. 1, 1965.

36 BN to David Gibbs, Dec. 19, 1959, draft.

37 BHF diary, Mar. 8, 1969.

38 Hilton Kramer, "U.S. Art From Sao Paulo on View in Washington," *NYT* (Jan. 29, 1966).

33 Thomas Messer to author, interview, Mar. 16, 2007.

34 Katharine Kuh, oral history interview, Mar. 18, 1982–Mar. 24, 1983, AAA.

35 Max Kozloff, *Art International* (June 1963).

36 Max Kozloff, "Art," *The Nation* (May 1966); BN to Carey McWilliams, June 8 and July 8, 1966.

37 Dan Flavin to BN, Jan. 16, 1967.

38 MS, notes, n.d. (in response to Canaday and Kozloff letters), MS papers, 1923–1991, Columbia University Rare Book & Manuscript Library.

39 BH to Mrs. Bliss Parkinson, BN, Tom Messer, John I. H. Baur, Robert Sarnoff, MS, Vera List, May 10, 1966. Barney shared with Schapiro, Hess, and Heller all of the correspondence to and from *The Nation* and *NYT*.

40 Josh Greenfeld, "Sort of the Svengali of Pop," *NYT Sunday Magazine*, May 8, 1966.

41 BN to Arthur Ochs Sulzberger, May 28, 1966. See Mark Godfrey, *Abstraction and the Holocaust*, New Haven and London: Yale UP, 2007 for a discussion of the *Stations of the Cross* installation in the context of the Holocaust and memory.

42 BN to MS, Sept. 2, 1966, MS papers.

43 Wilder Green, Rene d'Harnoncourt, Sheila Clarke, Thomas Flink, Alicia Legg, David Vance, memos and letters, June 13 through Aug. 11, 1967.

44 BHF to author, interview, Jan. 15, 2007.

45 Evan Turner to BN May 11, June 22, Sept. 1, 1966. As late as the end of 1969, when the important German collector Dr. Peter Ludwig tried to acquire them for permanent exhibition at Cologne's Wallraff-Richartz Museum,

Barney avoided responding, hoping for something better (Karl E. Jollenbeck to BN, Dec. 17, 1969, and May 12, 1970). "Oh no. Not Europe," he told Annalee, "I'm an American," but he was also allergic to provincial museums; he wanted his works "in the capitals of the world." Dodie Kazanjian, "Keeper of the Flame," *Vogue* (July 1991). In 1986 Annalee arranged for the series to enter the collection of the National Gallery of Art in Washington.

46 Later, in the Louvre, Barney noticed the Rothschild coat of arms painted in the upper right of Ingres's portrait of the Baroness de Rothschild. "It's like Whistler's butterfly—a collage. Ingres is the only man, with Whistler, who can stamp on a symbol as if it were outside the picture," he told the French art critic Pierre Schneider. "I try to do it when I sign my paintings." Pierre Schneider, "Through the Louvre with Barnett Newman," *Art News* (Summer 1969).

47 BN, statement in *Barnett Newman, The Stations of the Cross: Lema Sabachthani*.

48 Allene Talmey interview, Feb. 7, 1966, transcript in BNFA.

49 BN, statement, *Barnett Newman, The Stations of the Cross: Lema Sabachthani*.

50 Merrill Brockway, transcript, May 1967, for *Art of the Sixties*, "produced under the supervision and control of WCBS-TV news," BNFA; "Biltwell Clothing Company, Manufacturers of Custom Clothing for Men and Young Men," read the letterhead Barney continued to use in the late 1920s.

FIFTY-NINE. WHO'S AFRAID

1 Julie Finch to author, interview, Nov. 20, 2008.

2 "Social Note," *Village Voice* (Feb. 10, 1966).

3 Alex Liberman interviewed by Kazanjian, Jan. 1989, Dodie Kazanjian and Calvin Tomkins research materials on Alexander Liberman, 1927–1999, AAA.

4 Several years later, Newhouse purchased *Outcry*, and had it on his wall until his death.

5 S. I. Newhouse to author, interview, Feb. 13, 2007; S. I. Newhouse to BN, June 13 and Aug. 12, 1966.

6 Dodie Kazanjian and Calvin Tomkins, *Alex: The Life of Alexander Liberman*, New York: Knopf, 1993, 280.

7 Nadine Bertin to author, interview, Mar. 6, 2007.

8 Newhouse to author, 2007.

9 Arthur D. Dooley to Samuel Newhouse, Feb. 16, 1968; S. I. Newhouse, Jr. to Arthur D. Dooley, Feb. 20, 1968.

10 Andrew Hudson, "Newman Brings Grandeur to Town," *The Washington Post* (Jan. 30, 1966). In the Barney-approved text of the interview, the artist appears as something of a humorless, defensive score-settler. Too bad. Hudson remembers the interview itself as a boisterous, spirits-infused hours-long session. Andrew Hudson to author, interview, Apr. 19, 2010.

11 Andrew Hudson, "Newman Brings Grandeur to Town," and "The Case for 'Exporting' Nation's Avant-Garde Art," *The Washington Post* (Mar. 27, 1966).

12 As it turned out, neither selection was shown in Venice. At the end of February, the sponsoring agency, the National Collection of Fine Arts, canceled the agreement

with the Guggenheim, and Henry Geldzahler, on leave from the Metropolitan Museum, took over the exhibition.

13 Hilton Kramer, "'Systemic Painting': An Art for Critics," *NYT* (Oct. 11, 1966).

14 Lawrence Alloway, "Introduction," *Systemic Painting*, New York: The Solomon R. Guggenheim Museum, 1966.

15 "A Conversation: Barnett Newman and Thomas B. Hess," The Solomon R. Guggenheim Museum, May 1, 1966.

16 BN to MS, Sept. 2, 1966, original draft of altered letter.

17 Merrill Brockway, transcript, May 1967, for *Art of the Sixties*, "produced under the supervision and control of WCBS-TV news," BNFA.

18 BN, "Statement," *Art Now: New York*, 1969, repr. in SWI. At some point someone added to the title the parenthetical "To Jasper Johns." There is no documentation that it was Barney, and it was not exhibited with those words attached during his lifetime.

19 Shown in *Art of the Sixties*, "produced under the supervision and control of WCBS-TV news," broadcast July 2, 1967.

20 "USA Artists: Barnett Newman," WNET, broadcast July 10, 1966; BN, open letter to William A. M. Burden, President of the Museum of Modern Art, July 3, 1953; BN to James Johnson Sweeney, May 3, 1954.

21 AN interviewed by Dodie Kazanjian, 1991, unpublished transcript.

22 Alex Liberman interviewed by Kazanjian, n.d. (1988), Dodie Kazanjian and Calvin Tomkins research materials on Alexander Liberman, 1927–1999, AAA.

23 Frank O'Hara to BN, July 15, 1966.

24 Brad Gooch, *City Poet: The Life and Times of Frank O'Hara*, New York: Knopf, 1993, 5; Hester Diamond, interview, Aug. 3, 2006; Joanne Stern to author. If there had been such a vow, it must have been made after Barney's heart attack, the day after he visited the widow, Lee Krasner Pollock.

25 BN to MS, Sept. 2, 1966, MS papers, 1923–1991, Columbia University Rare Book & Manuscript Library.

26 Dore Ashton, "Art," *Arts & Architecture* (June 1966).

27 Barbara Rose, "Reinhardt: 'Art Related to Nothing,'" *Vogue* (Nov. 1, 1966).

28 BN to Barbara Rose, Oct. 25, 1966, unsent draft.

29 BN, draft submitted to lawyers for a letter to Hunter, n.d.

30 BN, draft of complaint to Sam Hunter, n.d.

31 Barbara Reise to B + A, Nov. 10, 1966.

32 "USA Artists: Barnett Newman"; TBH2, 73.

33 Milton Freidman, Deputy Commissioner General, USIA, to Alan Solomon, Dec. 9, 1966.

34 According to Rubin, in "Preface," *Ad Reinhardt*, New York: Rizzoli, 1991, he had "joined" the Museum of Modern Art in 1966, at which time he was organizing the important show, "Dada, Surrealism and Their Heritage." He officially assumed his position as a curator in July 1967.

35 BN to William Rubin, Dec. 31, 1966, and AN's later annotations.

36 BN to William Rubin, Feb. 4, 1967.

37 David Bourdon, "Art's Master of the Minimal," *Life* (Feb. 3, 1967).

38 BN to Rubin, Feb. 4, 1967; Annette Michaelson, "An Art Scholar's Loft: The New York Apartment of William Rubin," *Vogue* (Mar. 15, 1967).

39 Lucy R. Lippard, "New York Letter," *Art International* (Summer 1966).

40 Barney was not mentioned in the catalogue, as other artists were; according to Hunter, Reinhardt requested deletions from the catalogue of the names of artists whom Lippard had mentioned. Richard Marlin to BN, Feb. 20, 1967.

41 Hess, an advocate of Reinhardt and his work, acknowledged as much: Reinhardt "couldn't resist a few needles and jabs which typically, he knew, only Newman would understand. Thus for the opening quotation in his retrospective catalogue at the Jewish Museum (1967), he chose to cite" the words. TH papers, 1939–1978, AAA.

42 BNFA, draft, n.d., late Dec. 1966.

43 Sam Hunter, to Richard Marlin, Mnuchin, Moss & Marlin, Jan. 12, 1967.

44 In Reinhardt's opinion there was a pronounced non-legal effect. He wrote to Bryan Robertson at the Whitechapel to ask why the curator had cut him off: "Who came between us? Sam Hunter, Marlborough, Betty Parsons? Motherwell, Newman, Greenberg, Alloway? Somebody knife me?" Ad Reinhardt to Bryan Robertson, Mar. 28, 1967, Whitechapel Archives. Used by permission, © Anna Reinhardt/ARS, New York.

45 *Nox* (beware) should have been *noctem* for this use, but Barney wanted to play on "Knox." I am grateful to Heidi Colsman-Freyberger and, through her, Richard Gerberding for unraveling this.

SIXTY. "THE URGE TO BE EXALTED"

1 Photographs in Alan R. Solomon papers, 1907–1970, bulk 1944–1970, AAA.

2 Alan Solomon, "The Americans at Expo 67," draft, Alan R. Solomon papers.

3 AN interviewed by Dodie Kazanjian, 1991, unpublished transcript.

4 "Contemporary Art and the Church: The Point of Intersection," Washington Cathedral symposium, June 13, 1967.

5 BN, "The Art Survey," at "Contemporary Art and the Church: The Point of Intersection."

6 The Electric Circus was an East Village nightspot where patrons could (per a press release) "play games, dress as you like, dance, sit, think, tune in and turn on" amidst music, light shows, and a variety of performance.

7 Thomas F. Mathews and Barnett Newman, remarks at First International Congress on Religion, Architecture, and the Visual Arts, New York and Montreal, Aug. 26– Sept. 4, 1967, *Revolution, Place and Symbol (Journal of the First Congress on Religion, Architecture, and the Visual Arts)*, 1969.

8 Hillel E. Silverman to BN, Nov. 24, 1967.

9 S. I. Newhouse to author, interview, Feb. 13, 2007.

10 BN to James Fitzsimmons, Aug. 18, 1967.

11 BN, "Letters to the Editor," *Art International* (Sept. 1967); letters between James Fitzsimmons and BN, Aug. 18 and 24, Oct. 16 and 30, 1967.

12 Motherwell, "Letters to the Editor," *Art International* (Oct. 1967).

13 Meanwhile, Barney wrote to Still—after a decade's silence—to alert him to "Bob's filthy smear" against them both. "Bob thinks that by bumping our heads together he will be the winner. He is the only one besides Reinhardt who has recklessly taken it upon himself constantly to discuss other artists in public . . . . he needs shutting up. I would like it if you would let me hear from you." BN to CS, Nov. 1, 1967. Several months later, Still made his own overture to Motherwell. "I do not know of any way to deal with Newman's paranoid visciousness [*sic*]." CS to Robert Motherwell, Dec. 16, 1968, the Dedalus Foundation.

14 See chapter 37. BN, "Letters to the Editor," *Art International* (Nov. 1967).

15 TBH, "Ad (Adolph Dietrich Friedrich) Reinhardt," *Art News* (Oct. 1967); BN to TBH, Nov. 4, 1967. Hess added that Reinhardt "helped to hang" Barney's first Betty Parsons show, which was never mentioned by anyone before Barney brought it up during the "putsch" of 1967. Even at the time of the 1956 trial, when the 1950 show was discussed, Barney did not suggest that Reinhardt helped to hang it. In the later notes Hess made of conversations with Barney for his 1969 monograph, Hess specifically states "Pollock had helped him hang his second show—so had Reinhardt." TH papers, 1939–1978, AAA.

16 BN and Robert Motherwell, "Letters to the Editor," and James Fitzsimmons, "Editor reply," *Art International* (Jan. 1968). See also David Hare, "Communication," *Art News* (Dec. 1967) for further discussion of Motherwell's "startling assumption . . . that fame should be retroactive."

17 Betty Wolff to author, interview, Dec. 2007.

18 BN tax files.

19 Alan Solomon, "The *New* New York Art Scene: Who Makes It?" *Vogue* (Aug. 1, 1967).

20 Wolff to author, 2007. One result of Barney's neediness was that he was adopted into the very close family circle. Both at intimate birthdays, Thanksgivings, and Christmases, and at huge, "drop dead New Years parties"— the Newmans were always included at Tom and Audrey's Beekman Place townhouse or their well-staffed Greenwich

manor, or Betty's stately Mamaroneck spread. For the Jewish holidays, they were at the Hellers' table.

21 Sheila Clarke to Wilder Green, memo, June 28, 1967, Museum of Modern Art internal memo.

22 BN to Jan van der Marck, June 23, 1967.

23 BN to Tatiana and Alex Liberman, Aug. 8, 1967.

24 BN to Libermans, Aug. 8, 1967.

25 "Rosc Aim Frustrated Says Haughey," *The Irish Times* (Nov. 13, 1968).

26 Ada Louise Huxtable, "Downtown New York Begins to Undergo Radical Transformation," *NYT* (Mar. 27, 1967).

27 BN to Libermans, Aug. 8, 1967.

28 BN to Percy Uris, Sept. 9, 1967.

29 BN to Ann Wolensky, Oct. 16, 1967.

30 BN to Libermans, Aug. 8, 1967.

SIXTY-ONE. *BROKEN OBELISK*

1 Merrill Brockway, transcript, May 1967, for *Art of the Sixties*, "produced under the supervision and control of WCBS-TV news," BNFA.

2 BN to Tatiana and Alex Liberman, Aug. 8, 1967; BN to Waldo Rasmussen, Oct. 7, 1967.

3 Jonathan Lippincott, *Large Scale: Fabricating Sculpture in the 1960s and 1970s*, Princeton: Princeton Architectural Press, 2010.

4 Unprecedented in New York; earlier in the year, Philadelphia mounted a smaller show.

5 Grace Glueck, "Art Notes: Sculpfest," *NYT* (June 25, 1967).

6 Andrew Hudson, "Scale as Content: Bladen, Newman, Smith at the Corcoran," *Artforum* (Dec. 1967).

7 BN, "Letters," *Artforum* (Mar. 1968).

8 "Master of the Monumentalists," *Time* (Oct. 13, 1967).

9 I am grateful to Dan Friedman for pointing this out.

10 This was not atypical for the time; Barney was similarly otherwise occupied on a Saturday in mid-April when Martin Luther King, Jr., Benjamin Spock, and Harry Belafonte led over 100,000 protesting the war in Vietnam through Central Park to a massive rally at the United Nations. He could hardly have been unaware as he zigzagged back and forth from West to East, to the Frick museum, to lunch at the Russian Tea Room, to an opening at Andre Emmerich Gallery, to drinks at Schrafft's, to dinner at Max's Kansas City. But in New York, as E. B. White noted, it is uniquely possible for an individual to be insulated "against all enormous and violent and wonderful events that are taking place every minute."

11 BN to Alan Solomon, unedited interview, Mar. 20, 1966, Alan R. Solomon papers, 1907–1970, bulk 1944–1970, AAA.

12 "To Uphold Our Own Honor . . . : Leading Americans Speak Out Against Arab Threat to Destroy Israel," *NYT* (June 7, 1967).

13 BN to Moshe Decter, June 27, 1967. A second statement indeed appeared—not with Barney's questions, but with his signature among a much longer list of names, including Rothko, Greenberg, and Motherwell—in *The New York Review of Books* in December.

14 "Soviet Said to Press Anti-Jewish Drive," *NYT* (Aug. 13, 1967).

15 BNFA, n.d. An alternative version in Annalee's hand is identified "At Moshe Dicter's [*sic*] press conference."

16 Everywhere, in New York at least, were tales of Jews as heroes. "In the city's parks, restaurants, bars, on the street—wherever Jews congregated—the war was the number one topic of conversation." Sylvan Fox, "City's Jews Speak of Renewed Pride," *NYT* (June 8, 1967).

17 TBH2, 122; correspondence between the Menil Collection and Lippincott confirm that Barney himself "physically worked" on this edge. Paul Winkler to Donald Lippincott, May 7, 1982; Donald Lippincott to Paul Winkler, July 29, 1982, Menil Archives, object files.

18 Sanka Knox, "Two Stabiles May Stay Put After Move to Harlem," *NYT* (Sept. 2, 1967).

19 Lucy R. Lippard, "Beauty and the Bureaucracy," *The Hudson Review* 20.4 (Winter 1967–68).

20 Waldo Rasmussen to BN, Sept. 29, 1967.

21 Lucy Lippard to BN, Oct. 1967; Lippard, "Beauty and the Bureaucracy."

22 TBH, "Editorial: New Man in Town," *Art News* (Nov. 1967).

23 Evan Turner to BN, Oct. 9, 1967.

SIXTY-TWO. "FOR IMPASSIONED CRITICISM"

1 BN to TH, Nov. 27, 1967.

2 Pierre Schneider, "Through the Louvre with Barnett Newman," *Art News* (Summer 1969).

3 BN to TH, Nov. 27, 1967.

4 Barney told Schneider that he supposed the "noble savage" was justified, since it was his first visit to the Louvre; had they gone to the Metropolitan, the tone would have been different. Schneider's book, *Louvre Dialogues*,

was published in 1971; Barney's episode was first published in *Art News* in the summer 1969 issue. Later references to the museum visit place them in 1968, during another trip Barney made to Paris. In fact, they occurred on Nov. 24 and 26, 1967. Although comments made by Hess are responsible for the mistake, Hess himself was the recipient of the 1967 letter in which Barney described the visits: BN to TH, Nov. 27, 1967.

5 Schneider, "Through the Louvre with Barnett Newman."

6 BN to J. Leering, May 5, 1968.

7 Doris Lilly, "More Discos Are Coming," *New York Post* (June 11, 1968); Nadine Bertin Stearns to Doris Lilly, June 18, 1968.

8 BN to Fürgen Harten, June 1, 1968; BN to Jean Leering, June 3, 1967; BN to Arnold Bode, June 3, 1968.

9 Pierre Schneider to BN, Aug. 23, 1967.

10 "In New York in the late 1940s and the early '50s, there was a moment of passionate criticism that came from Greenberg, Hess, Rosenberg. Hess and Rosenberg still continue," Barney intended to say in his talk, conveniently forgetting what he thought—and said—of the last two at the earlier time. Inconveniently, Greenberg, in "Complaints of an Art Critic," published in *Artforum* the previous October, seemed to move closer to what Barney urged, forcing Barney to revise his Paris presentation. And when Greenberg's review of "Rosc" appeared, Barney sent urgent telegrams to try to alter the Baudelaire text for publication in the May issue of PREUVES: "Greenberg has suddenly appeared with a Baudelairian article in the April Art Forum." BN to Pierre Schneider, Apr. 4, 1968.

11 The relevance of Abbé Du Bos was courtesy of Liberman, and in the sentences about Baudelaire, Barney was indebted to Schapiro, who had been working on a presentation about the poet and Delacroix at the same time that Barney was preparing his own. Neither was credited. BN to Alex Liberman, Jan. 14, 1968; BN to MS, Nov. 30, 1967, and Jan. 15, 1968, MS papers, 1923–1991, Columbia University Rare Book & Manuscript Library; "The November 30th Meeting," *The PSA Bulletin* (Dec. 1967).

12 BN, "For Impassioned Criticism," *Art News* (Summer 1968).

13 William Rubin, untranscribed interview with Dodie Kazanjin, Dodie Kazanjian papers, 1949–2017, bulk 1980–2017, AAA.

14 Ben Raeburn to BN, Sept. 26, 1963, and Mar. 24, 1964.

15 BN, "The True Revolution Is Anarchist!", foreword to Peter Kropotkin, *Memoirs of a Revolutionist*, New York: Horizon Press, 1968.

16 Grace Glueck, "Art Notes: Chicago, Go Home," *NYT* (Sept. 15, 1968).

17 Norman Mark, "An Art protest Turns into a Chicago Bonus: 'Richard J. Daley' Looks Like One of the Season's Liveliest Shows," *Chicago Daily News* (Sept. 14, 1968).

18 Barbara Reise to BN, Mar. 19, 1968.

19 Brice Marden to author, interview, June 16, 2010.

20 TBH2, 123.

21 TBH2, 123.

22 BN to Ron Wolin, Dec. 7, 1968.

23 His "fellow-Aquarian," Alan Power, and Barney would joke about "nutty Aquarians." Alan Power to BN, Feb. 11, 1968, and Jan. 12, 1969.

24 TH papers, 1939–1978, AAA.

25 Aurora Dias-Jorgensen, interview, July 26, 2007.

26 TH papers.

27 Barney had the print he made for List destroyed and reprinted the plate on bigger paper. He continued to alter that and another large etching made at the same time, creating different states, and plate 13 of the *Notes*, until shortly before his death. Donn H. Steward, precis of studio log, Aug. 1971.

28 BN to John and Dominique de Menil, Aug. 26, 1969.

29 John de Menil to TBH, Nov. 19, 1967.

30 Dominique de Menil, handwritten notes, Oct. 12, 1995, the Menil Collection, Menil Archives. Jean de Menil (as he signed his letters) told Barney at a March 4, 1969, dinner for de Kooning that he planned to buy the piece. The time-frame, memorialized in a May 27 letter to Barney, complicates this story, which Annalee told Dominique de Menil decades later.

31 "City Seek Services of Famous Sculptor," *Houston Post* (Aug. 21, 1969).

32 BN to John de Menil, June 8, 1969.

33 Eventually, with the de Menils' support, what is now known as the Rothko Chapel was designed and built by Howard Barnstone and Eugene Aubry in Houston (its original architect was Philip Johnson, but he and Rothko had a falling out) to house fourteen paintings the patrons had commissioned in 1964, and *Broken Obelisk* came to rest just outside in its own reflecting pool when the building opened in 1971.

34 Jerry M. Flint, "Negro May Oppose Cavanagh in Detroit's Mayoral Campaign," *NYT* (May 30, 1969).

35 Gertrude Kasle to BN, Gertrude Kasle Gallery records, 1949–1999, bulk 1964–1983, AAA.

36 Adelyn D. Breeskin to BN, Apr. 30, 1968.

37 Grace Glueck, "Action," *NYT* (July 20, 1969).

38 "In Conversation: James Harithas with Raphael Rubinstein," *The Brooklyn Rail* (June 7, 2008).

39 Paul Richard, "Corcoran: People Crisis," *The Washington Post* (July 29, 1969).

40 Meryle Secrest, "An Era Ends: Corcoran Gallery Obelisk Removed by Creator," *The Washington Post* (July 11, 1969).

41 Glueck, "Action."

42 BN to Alex Liberman, Sept. 9, 1969.

SIXTY-THREE. KNOEDLER

1 They didn't, but the Virginia Wright Fund did present it to the University of Washington, Seattle in 1970.

2 Robert Whitman to author, interview, May 15, 2010.

3 AN, notes on expenses for the studio, n.d., BNFA; HR, interview with Willem de Kooning, 1972.

4 TBH, "Notes on Newman's 'Notes,'" *Print Collector's Newsletter* (Jan.–Feb. 1972).

5 Correspondence between BN and Knoedler Gallery, and BN and Jesse D. Wolff, June 1968 through Oct. 1969.

6 TBH had been instrumental in bringing together de Kooning and Fourcade, and likely was in this case as well.

7 Elizabeth C. Baker, "Barnett Newman in a New Light," *Art News* (Feb. 1969).

8 Harry Malcolmson, "Vancouver Still Has the Country's Leading Municipal Art Gallery," *Toronto Daily Star* (Feb. 22, 1969).

9 Bates Lowry to BN, Feb. 18, 1969.

10 Xavier Fourcade to Michael Compton, Mar. 7, 1969.

11 The foundation was established by O'Hara's sister, brother, and friends to assist the publication of young poets.

12 BHF diary, Jan. 26, 1969.

13 Schneider, possibly with Barney's collaboration, was very unhappy with *Art News*'s edits, which he had not approved.

14 TBH1, 41, 43.

15 BN to Jack Klein, Feb. 14, 1969.

16 Mark Stevens and Annalyn Swan, *de Kooning: An American Master*, New York: Knopf, 2004, 489–91.

17 The early anchor of the street as a commercial art center, the building had recently been sold to IBM.

18 Jane Dillenberger, interview with BN at Knoedler, Apr. 12, 1969.

19 Jonathan Holstein to author, interview, Oct. 16, 2010.

20 RM to author, interview, Oct. 16, 2010.

21 Douglas M. Davis, "After 10 Years, a One-Man Show by Mr. Newman," *The National Observer* (Apr. 14, 1969).

22 Lowry to BN, Feb. 18, 1969.

23 Although the hues are very similar, the medium of *Anna's Light* is acrylic.

24 Joseph Pulitzer, Jr., to Roland Balay, Apr. 30, 1969; Xavier Fourcade to Joseph Pulitzer, Jr., May 2, 1969, Knoedler archives.

25 "Art in New York," *Time* (Apr. 11, 1969).

26 HR, "The Art World: Icon Maker," *The New Yorker* (Apr. 19, 1969).

27 Dillenberger, interview with BN, 1969.

28 Joshua 5: 13–15, quoted in BN, "*Chartres* and *Jericho*," *Art News* (Apr. 1969). In a convoluted footnote to Barney's *Art News* statement, Hess invoked the city's walls "tumbling down" (quoting not the Torah but the popular song) rather than adversaries and holy ground. He added that during Barney's visit to the Louvre in 1967—Hess mistakenly, without Barney's contradiction, repeatedly places it in 1965—he was particularly impressed with the *Raft of the Medusa* by Géricault ("Jericho") and suggests that the artist was "subconscious[ly]" influenced by its composi-

tion and protagonist. Barney also withheld any objection to what seems a trivialization.

29 Liberman interviewed by Kazanjian, Jan. 1989, Dodie Kazanjian and Calvin Tomkins research materials on Alexander Liberman, 1927–1999, AAA.

30 Liberman interviewed by Kazanjian, untranscribed interview notes, n.d., Dodie Kazanjian and Calvin Tomkins research materials on Alexander Liberman.

31 TBH1.

32 Baker, "Barnett Newman in a New Light."

33 BN, "*Chartres* and *Jericho*." He was referring to *The Wild*.

34 See chapter 27.

35 John Perreault, "Art: Back Indoors," *Village Voice* (Apr. 4, 1969).

36 Franz Meyer to author, interview, July 22, 2006.

37 Brice Marden to author, interview, June 16, 2010.

38 James Rosenquist to author, interview, May 5, 2010.

39 Andrew Hudson to author, interview, Apr. 19, 2010.

40 Whitman to author, 2010.

41 Marden to author, 2010.

42 Sidney Janis to BN, Apr. 18, 1969.

43 RM3.

44 Leider, Philip, "The Artist Is Unexplained," *NYT* (Apr. 6, 1969).

45 S. I. Newhouse to author, interview, Feb. 13, 2007.

46 BN diary.

47 BN to Kiyoshi Makita, Apr. 1969. Barney wanted the sculpture to be 12 feet high and 22 ½ feet long—too large for the shipping container to Japan. In the early 1990s, Annalee had Lippincott make the full-size work as originally conceived.

48 Hakone Museum to BN, May 12, 1969.

49 BN to Toyooki Tanaka, June 23, 1969.

SIXTY-FOUR. "NEW YORK PAINTING AND SCULPTURE: 1940–1970"

1 Grace Glueck, "Museum Chooses Head for Division," *NYT* (July 11, 1967).

2 Lawrence Alloway, "Art," *The Nation* (June 30, 1969).

3 TBH to MS, Aug. 19, 1969, MS papers, 1923–1991, Columbia University Rare Book & Manuscript Library.

4 Grace Glueck, "Whitney Displaying Year's Acquisitions," *NYT* (June 10, 1970).

5 Alloway, "Art."

6 Muriel Kallis Newman to BP, n.d., after Jan. 10, 1968, Betty Parsons Gallery records and personal papers, 1916–1991, bulk 1946–1983, AAA.

7 Alloway, "Art."

8 Grace Glueck, "Art Notes: 'J'accuse, Baby! She Cried," *NYT* (Apr. 20, 1969).

9 Hilton Kramer, "Artists and the Problem of 'Relevance,'" *NYT* (May 4, 1969).

10 Glueck, "Art Notes: 'J'accuse, Baby! She Cried."

11 Grace Glueck, "Modern Museum's Policy on Artists' Gifts Assailed," *NYT* (June 12, 1969).

12 "Artist Defends Modern Museum in a Dispute Over Soliciting Art," *NYT* (June 13, 1969).

13 BN, "To Whom It May Concern," June 11, 1969. Comstock (1844–1915) was secretary of the New York Society for the Suppression of Vice.

14 AN interviewed by Dodie Kazanjian, 1991, unpublished transcript.

15 BH to AN and Robert Rowan, Jan. 22, 1969.

16 Jaime C. del Amo to BN, July 29, 1968. On their 1969 and 1970 tax returns, Annalee under "occupation" listed "oil, gas, paintings, retired teacher."

17 Correspondence May 26, 1969; Oct. 27, 1969; May 22, 1970.

18 J. R. Schwartz, Mid-Valley Land Company, correspondence with AN re Aspen Mesa Estates, June 20, 1969; Aug. 30, 1969; Sept. 8, 1969.

19 Grace Glueck, "Artists Assail Downtown Expressway," *NYT* (June 20, 1969).

20 Julie Finch to author, interview, Nov. 20, 2008.

21 Douglas Davis, *The National Observer* (Apr. 14, 1969).

22 Andrew Hudson, "The Case for 'Exporting' Nation's Avant-Garde Art," *The Washington Post* (Mar. 27, 1966).

23 BN to John Dillenberger, Aug. 28, 1969, unsent draft.

24 HR, "The Art World: Rothko," *The New Yorker* (Mar. 28, 1970).

25 BN to Dillenberger, Aug. 28, 1969.

26 BN to Alex and Tatiana Liberman, Aug. 9, 1969.

27 Lawrence Alloway, "Notes on Barnett Newman," *Art International* (Summer 1969).

28 BN to Jesse D. Wolff, Oct. 4, 1969.

29 Oral history interview with Henry Geldzahler, Jan. 27, 1970, AAA.

30 Lawrence Alloway, "Art," *The Nation* (Nov. 24, 1969).

31 Kazanjian interview with Walter Hopps, n.d., Dodie Kazanjian papers, 1949–2017, bulk 1980–2017, AAA.

32 BN to Libermans, Aug. 9, 1969.

33 Douglas Davis; Thomas B. Hess; doctors' appointments and prescriptions.

SIXTY-FIVE. "AT HOME"

1 Merrill Brockway, transcript, May 1967, for *Art of the Sixties*, "produced under the supervision and control of WCBS-TV news," BNFA.

2 Laurie Reinstein to author, interview, Sept. 22, 2008.

3 Reinstein to author, 2008.

4 Brice Marden to author, interview, June 16, 2010.

5 RM3. I am grateful to Thomas Campbell Jackson for a tour of this apartment.

6 AN interviewed by Dodie Kazanjian, 1991, unpublished transcript.

7 Alan Power to author, interview, Mar. 25, 2007; Hester Diamond to author, interview, Aug. 3, 2006; and others.

8 Diamond to author, 2006.

9 Barbara Rose to author, interview, Oct. 10, 2008.

10 Power to author, 2007.

11 BN, in *Painters Painting: New York Art Scene, 1940–1970*, Emile de Antonio, documentary film, 1972.

12 AN, interview, 1991.

13 Katharine Kuh, "Clyfford Still: Potent Force, A Major Influence in American Painting," *Vogue* (Feb. 1, 1970).

14 BN to Barbara Reise, Mar. 11, 1970.

15 HR, "The Art World: Rothko," *The New Yorker* (Mar. 28, 1970).

16 Mary Lampson to author, interview, Jan. 9, 2018.

17 "Brandeis Lauds Two Generations in Arts Awards," *NYT* (May 18, 1970).

34 Orentreich Medical Group, RX, Oct. 17, 1969.

35 Barbara Reise to Mel Bochner, Oct. 9, 1969, Tate Archives.

36 Barbara Reise, to B + A, Jan. 3, 1970. Organized by Reise, the Feb. 1970 *Studio International* featured, in addition to her exhaustive discussion, a reprint of Barney's own "*Chartres* and *Jericho*"; the first English publication of his 1946 "Art of the South Seas"; and the first publication of Judd's 1964 article, originally written for the German magazine *Das Kunstwerk*, which began: "It's not so rash to say that Newman is the best painter in this country . . . one of the world's best artists—and the best make a short list."

18 BN diary, May 23, 1970.

19 Barney drafted language in support of the general art strike on May 22, calling the "symbolic closing" of museums a "catalytic gesture" of solidarity. But others wanted to go farther, and a sub-group, the "Emergency Cultural Government Committee" agreed to a walk out of the government-sponsored exhibition at the Venice Biennial. Once again, Barney found himself protesting the protest, which, he assessed, had evolved into "pledge[s] of allegiance to a 'New Government.'" BN to Irving Petlin, June 18, 1970.

20 S. I. Newhouse to author, interview, Feb. 13, 2007.

21 After Barney's death, Annalee marked these trials so they would not be mistaken for paintings.

22 Richard Meier to author, interview, Nov. 2007.

23 BN to S. I. Newhouse, July 1, 1970.

24 BH to BN, Aug. 13, 1969, and Apr. 21, 1970.

25 S. I. Newhouse to BN, Mar. 2, 1970.

26 Newhouse to author, 2007.

27 BN diary, July 1, 1970; Doris Elenkoff to BN, July 1, 1970.

28 Larry Hendricks, "Mount Elden Cave Dweller Evicted," *Arizona Daily Sun* (Sept. 9, 2003).

29 Reinstein to author, 2008.

30 BN to SH, Apr. 17, 1956.

INDEX

Note: Page numbers in italic type indicate illustrations. Barnett Newman's life and work are distributed among several main entries beginning with "Newman, Barnett": architecture project for a synagogue; art and the art world; drawings; insults and wrongs felt and addressed by; life; paintings; prints; sculpture; statements and theories about art; studios; watercolors; writings.

67 Gallery, 159, 162
343 East Nineteenth Street, *119*
460 Park Avenue Gallery, 149

Abahu, Rabbi, 20
Abbot, Mary, 240
Abel, Lionel, 202, 222, 542
Abercrombie & Fitch, 211, 224, 425, 475, 530, 600
Abetz, Otto, 296
Abraham and Isaac (biblical figures), 3, 99, 199, 412, 632n6[ch22]
Abraham Newman & Son, 40, 41, 45–46, 72, 75, 79–80, 87, 321, 446
abstract art/abstraction: American artists' use of, 190, 204, 267; architectural uses of, 276; Barr on, 121; controversy and criticism of, 67, 95, 190, 218, 244, 433–35, 472, 538; expressionist, 161; geometric, 123, 161; Greenberg and, 116, 346–48, 516; Hess's book on, 294–96; Monet and, 364; Newman's conception of, 174, 176, 177, 180, 188, 191–92, 240, 288, 398; Pop art vs., 486–87, 490, 541; in "primitive" art, 160, 191; purist, 116, 126, 161, 177; Schapiro on, 122. *See also* Abstract Expressionism; modernism/modern art
Abstract Expressionism, 4, 136, 145, 241, 265, 297, 310, 314, 318, 343, 346–48, 360, 378–79, 383, 392, 399, 412, 421, 429, 433, 448, 457, 463, 484, 487–88, 490, 495, 519, 524–25, 527, 532, 536, 555, 599, 611, 625n30, 639n21, 656n16. *See also* New York City: art scene in; New York School
"Abstract Expressionist and Other Modern Paintings, Drawings and Sculptures" (auction), 513–14
"Abstract Painting and Sculpture in America" (exhibition, 1951), 279, 639n26
Académie de la Grande Chaumière, Paris, 32
A.C.A. Gallery, 91–92
action painting, 317–18, 378, 475, 490
Adams, Henry, 240
Adler, Stella, 608
Adorno, Theodor, 227, 572
"Advancing American Art" (exhibition, 1946–1947), 190, 219
Aeschylus, *The Choephori* and *The Eumenides*, 470
"Aesthetics and the Artist" (symposium, 1952), 313–16
"African Negro Art" (exhibition, 1935), 66
Agee, William, 590, 597
Agnew gallery, 37
Agon, S. Y., 567
Albaum, Phillip, 68
Albers, Josef, 334, 383, 658n24
Albright Art Gallery, Buffalo, New York (later Albright-Knox Gallery), 389, 430, 494, 534, 557, 561

Alexander, Brooke, 98
Alexander II, Tsar, 23–25
Alexander III, Tsar, 23, 24, 25
Allah, 542
Allan Stone Gallery, 484–86, 490, 491, 500, 540, 589. *See also* Stone, Allan
Allen, A. A., 118
Allen, Donald, 413
Allen, Gracie, 183
Allen, Hervey, *Anthony Adverse*, 54
Alloway, Lawrence, 98, 254, 378, 403–4, 411, 421, *442*, 444, 451, 470, 489–90, 493, 495, 505–7, 508, 510, 514–15, 520, 538–39, 541–42, 544–45, 549, 550–53, 559, 560, 597–98, 602–4, 650n14, 656n36[ch52], 660n11, 662n44; "The American Sublime," 493
Ambos Mundos (magazine), 180, 186
American Abstract Artists, 67, 108, 122, 143
"American Abstract Expressionists and Imagists" (exhibition, 1961), 468, 470–72, 521, *plate 15*
American art: artists and World War II military service, 135–37; Betty Parsons Gallery and, 359; criticisms of mid-century, 190, 217–20, 222–24, 232–34, 238, 242–45, 269–71, 429, 433–35, 639n46; Greenberg and, 346–48; international exposure of (1958 and after), 392, 398–99, 451, 466–67, 512–13, 532–33, 657n12[ch55]; and masculinity, 137; mid-century transformations in, 121–34, 156–58, 160, 162–63, 168–69, 191–92, 202–4, 213, 217, 230–31, 235, 244–45, 250, 255, 262, 293, 302, 316–17, 412, 417, 429, 448, 462, 612; museums' treatment of contemporary, 218, 233; Newman's criticism of, 130–31; post–Ab Ex world of, 360–61, 361, 377–81, 388–89, 391, 393, 397, 399–400, 412, 423, 428, 449, 454, 463, 486–87, 519–21, 612. *See also* Newman, Barnett, art and the art world: and the history of mid-century works
American Artist (magazine), 218
American Artists' Congress, 75, 83, 96, 105–6, 217
American Artists Professional League, 108
American Christian Committee for Refugees, 217
American Embassy, 481
American Express, 390
American Jewish Conference on Soviet Jewry, 613
American League for Peace and Democracy, 94, 625n3[ch11]
American Locomotive Company, 136
American Museum of Natural History, 150–51, 153–54, 159, 187, 189, 199, 632n8[ch22]
American Pavilion, Venice, 332
"Americans 1942" (exhibition, 1942), 127, 132, 143
American Scene painting, 128, 131

"American Vanguard Art for Paris Exhibition" (exhibition, 1951), 302–3

"American Water Colors, Drawings, and Prints" (exhibition 1952), 309

"America Paints—2nd Exhibition" (exhibition, 1950), 275

Am Haoretz, 229, 520

"Amlash Sculpture" (exhibition, 1963), 495

Anarchism, 2, 4, 10, 31, 56, 67, 69, 76, 114, 235, 522, 574, 576, 606

Anderson, Marian, 112, 610

Anderson, Quentin, 249

Andre, Carl, 597

Andre Emmerich Gallery, 663n10

Andre's (restaurant), 321

A. Newman (business), 31

Annie Get Your Gun (musical), 182

The Answer (newspaper), 54–55, 71–75, 73, 79, 89, 93, 365

anti-Semitism, 9, 13, 23, 46–49, 54–55, 57, 93, 227, 388, 538, 546, 575, 578, 613, 640n18

Apollinaire, Guillaume, 178

A. P. Smith Manufacturing Company, 168

aquatint, 579

Arbus, Diane, 404

Architectural Forum (magazine), 388

architecture: Newman's appreciation of and visits to, 104, 247, 262, 320, 356, 388, 422, 440, 501, 507, 511; Newman's project for a synagogue, 2, 334, 495, 501–5, 595

Ardon-Bronstein, Mordecai, 223

Arendt, Hannah, 227

Argent Galleries, 275

Arizona Daily Sun (newspaper), 616

Armory Show (1913), 108, 149, 270

Army Signal Laboratory, Eatontown, New Jersey, 128, 144

Arnason, H. H., 468–72, 474, 485, 521

Arnoldi, Charles, 479

Arp, Jean, 238

"Arshile Gorky, Willem de Kooning, Barnett Newman" (exhibition, 1969), 588

art. *See* American art; modernism/modern art; Newman, Barnett, art and the art world

art criticism, 158, 177–78, 202, 219, 223, 267, 295–96, 317–18, 433–35, 524, 563, 572–73. *See also* Newman, Barnett, art and the art world: critics' and artists' reception of

Art d'aujourd'hui (magazine), 283

Art Digest (magazine), 92, 218, 219, 253, 326, 327, 329, 347, 637n52, 640n44

Artef Theatre, 68–69

Artforum (magazine), 473, 481, 520, 525, 528, 566, 577, 664n10[ch62]

Art Gallery of Toronto, Ontario, Canada, 466–67, 470

Art Gallery of Vancouver, British Columbia, Canada, 586

Arthur Tooth Gallery, London, 452

Art in America (magazine), 370, 475, 481, 482, 528, 646n2[ch39], 659n30

"Art in Progress" (exhibition, 1944), 155

Art Institute of Chicago, 203, 340, 413, 576

Art International (magazine), 451, 481, 485, 488, 490, 526, 560–61, 564, 602

Artists Against the Expressway, 601

Artist's Bill of Rights, 317

artists' colonies, 78–80

Artists Equity Association, 268

"Artists for Victory" (exhibition, 1942), 143

The Artists Gallery, 133, 136

Artists Union, 156

Art News (magazine), 2, 121, 186, 224, 253, 254, 259, 288, 290, 293, 304, 308, 317, 327, 331–32, 337, 343–44, 354, 357, 367, 370–72, 378–81, 384, 392, 399, 405, 419–20, 425, 426, 434, 457, 459–60, 465, 481, 490, 491, 495, 506, 528–30, 535, 536, 561, 576, 586, 587, 592, 593, 648n14[ch42], 665n13[ch63], 665n28[ch63]

Art News Annual, 356, 360

"Art New York" (television show), 519

"The Art of Assemblage" (exhibition, 1962), 477

Art of This Century gallery, 139–40, 157, 159, 162, 180, 183, 192, 223, 560, 631n27. *See also* Guggenheim, Peggy

Arts & Architecture (magazine), 419

Art School, Perkins Cove, Maine, 79

"Art Since 1960" (exhibition, 1962), 473–74

Arts Magazine, 367, 421, 426, 486, 512, 525, 557

"Arts of the South Seas" (exhibition, 1946), 180

Art Students League, 11, 32–33, 41–43, 81, 83, 110, 129, 168, 173, 223, 240, 277, 359, 425, 447, 625n30

Art Teaching Project, 43, 80

Art Workers' Coalition, 597–99

Asher, Elise, 407

Ashton, Dore, 255, 412, 419, 420, 432, 434–35, 553

As Thousands Cheer (musical), 45

Atlantic Monthly (magazine), 232

"Attack" (artists' session, 1961), 448–49

Aubry, Eugene, Rothko Chapel, Houston, 664n33

Auden, W. H., 96

audience. *See* viewers

Audubon Center, 336

Audubon Nature Camp, 99, 160–61

Auer, Leopold, 11

Austin, Darrel, 127

automobiles, Newman and: Buick, 497; Chevrolet Master Deluxe Sport Coupe, 120, *120*, 156, 224, 337; Harvey limousine, 553; Jaguar Mark IV sedan, 282, 323–24, 341, 356, 364, 370, 644n16; Jaguar Mark V sedan, 385, 391, 407, 464; Lincoln Continental, 464; Thunderbird, 464

Avery, Milton, 41, 42, 75, 105, 159, 162, 163, 182, 201, 216, 219, 270, 625n30, 629n15; *Pink Umbrella*, 198

Ayer, A. J. "Freddie," 507

Azuma Kabuki Dancers and Musicians, 321

Babbitt, Irving, 54

Backer, George, 113

Baker, Elizabeth (Betsy), 535, 586, 591, 593, 601, 659n30

Balanchine, George, 232, 640n15

Baldwin, Carl, 409

Ball, Lucille, 322

Balzac, Honoré de, 80, 388

Bampton, Rose, 117

Barbizon School, 347

Barnes, Albert C., 337, 362; *The Art of Painting*, 38–39

Barnes Foundation, Merion, Pennsylvania, 38–39, 337, 598

Barnet, Will, 33, 75, 187–88, 270, 408, 424–25

"Barnett Newman (American painter)" (television interview), 518–19

Barnett Newman v. Ad Reinhardt and College Art Association, 2, 56, 300, 334–36, 338–39, 341–42, 356, 364–67, 369, 377, 381, 449, 555

Barney Greengrass (store and café), 440, 462, 506, 527, 549, 652n21[ch46]

Barnstone, Harold, Rothko Chapel, Houston, 664n33

Baro, Gene, 560

Barr, Alfred, 38, 39, 59, 83, 121, 148, 152, 182, 195, 239, 264, 265, 266, 268, 272, 283, 299, 300, 303, 304, 316, 337, 368, 376–77, 392, 397, 404, 410, 421, 432, 434, 466, 491, 561, 596, 638n21

Barrymore, John, 241

Bartók, Béla, 35

baseball, 2, 3, 5, 44, 211, 214, 320, 324, 363, 422, 445, 468, 477, 504–5, 526, 655n1[ch52]

Basel Kunstverein, 414

Bataille, Georges, 201

Bateson, Gregory, 233

Baudelaire, Charles, 572–73, 576, 664n10[ch62], 664n11[ch62]

Bauhaus, 111, 239, 325, 326, 329, 334, 373, 385, 524, 551

"Bauhaus 1919–1928" (exhibition, 1938–39), 111

Baur, John, 546; *American Art of the Twentieth Century* (with Lloyd Goodrich), 480; *Revolution and Tradition: Modern American Art*, 295, 641n19

Bavarian Academy of Art, 137

Baziotes, Ethel, 166, 167, 172, 183, 225

Baziotes, William, 42, 96, 108, 122, 136, 139, 141, 162, 166, 183, 219, 221, 223–26, 234, 238, 241–43, 246, 250, 257, 261, 262, 269, 275, *278*, 279, 302–3, 305, 353, 392, *429*, 448, 491, 496, 561, 604, 638n20, 639n21, 644n30; *The Dwarf*, 234

BBC. *See* British Broadcasting Corporation

Bearden, Romare, 579

Beaton, Cecil, 291

beauty, 111, 155, 176, 204, 206, 213, 232

Beck, Rosemary, 240

Beckett, Samuel, 388

Beeren, Wim, 440

Belafonte, Harry, 663n10

Bell, Alexander Graham, 566

Bell, Clive, 155, 177–78

Bell, Larry, 479, 522, 525, 526, 532, 659n9, 659n45

Bell, Leland, 646n7

Bellini, Giovanni, 107

Belmont racetrack, 341, 350–52, 446

Belvedere Torso, 625n30

Benchley, Robert, 149

Bengston, Billy Al, 479, 522, 659n45

Bennington College, Bennington, Vermont, 306, 317, 400–404, 415, 417–18, 454, 470, 489, 632n9[ch22], 633n6[ch24]

Benton, Thomas Hart, 91, 131, 261, 295, 299, 624n9[ch10], 649n23[ch42]

Ben-Zion (né Ben-Zion Weinman), 48

Berenson, Bernard, 653n17[ch48]

Berkson, Bill, 518, *550*

Berlin, Irving, 45

Berlin, Isaiah, 41, 612

Berman, Avis, 305

Bernays, Edward, 106

Bernini, Gianlorenzo, *Costanza Buonarelli*, 108

Bernstein, Leonard, 446

Bertin, Nadine, 549, 571–72

The Best Years of Our Lives (film), 183

Beth Israel Hospital, 135

Betsy (painting chimpanzee), 433, 434

Bettelheim, Bruno, 227

Betty Parsons Gallery, 182, 189–92, 194, 203, 215, 222–24, 239, 246–47, 250, 252–53, 270, 272, 275, 280, 286, 288–91, 293–94, 300, 302, 306, 309, 319, 327–28, 329, 340, 359, 361–62, 375, 404, 405, 431, 438, 487, 493, 495, 504, 555, 598, 632n9[ch22], 633n7[ch23], 641n16, 641n17, 647n15[ch39], 662n15. *See also* Parsons, Betty

beverage-carbonating invention, 96–97, *97*

Beyeler, Ernst, 440, 462–63

Bhagavad Gita, 225

Biala, Janice, 183, 638n20, 639n26

"The BIG Drawing" (exhibition, 1969), 587

The Big Sleep (film), 183

Billy's (restaurant), 506, 614

Biltwell Clothing Company, 31, 53

Biltwell Garment Inc., 87

Bingham, Lois, 533

Birdland (jazz club), 470

birdwatching. *See* ornithology/birdwatching

"Black and White" (exhibition, 1963), 495, 506, 525

Black Mountain College, 221, 272

Blackmur, R. P., *The Good European*, 201

Black Sun Press, 198

Blackwood, Caroline, 506

Bladen, Ronald, 565, 569

Blaine, Nell, 646n7

Blake, Peter, 411

Blake, William, 574

Blinken, Donald, 433–34

Block, Allan, 202

Blomowicz, Yudl, 22

The Blood-Horse (magazine), 337

Bloom, Hyman, 127, 296

Bloomingdale's, 425

Blue Note (record label), 36

Blum, Irving, 471, 652n21[ch46]

Blume, Peter, 116

Board of Examiners, 40, 90–93, 110, 625n28

Boas, Franz, 43, 101, 631n8

Boas, George, 233, 313–15

Boccioni, Umberto, *Dynamism of a Football Player*, 596

Bocour, Leonard, and his paint business, 230, 260, 385–86, 408, 562, 600, 607, 608, 611

Bogat, Regina, 449

Bolotowsky, Ilya, 48, 334, 658n24

Bolshoi Ballet, 544

Bonnard, Pierre, 132, 344

Borges, Jorge Luis, 202

Born Yesterday (play), 182

Borodulin, Alex, 32–34, 36, *37*, 43, 54, 56, 57, 59, 68–69, 77, 78, 87, 93, 113–14, 168, 277, 621n10[ch3], 622n12

Borodulin, Lazer, 34

Boswell, Peyton, 107–8, 637n52

botany, 41, 118, 160
Botticelli, Sandro, *The Birth of Venus*, 108
Bouché, René, 241
Bourdon, David, 555
Bourgeois, Louise, 365, 598, 638n20, 639n26
Bovard, James M., 466
Bowness, Alan, 509
boxing, 363, 450, 462, 468, 507. *See also* Stillman's Gym
Brach, Paul, 389, 408, 473
Bramante, Donato, 344
Brancusi, Constantin, 149, 507
Brandeis Creative Arts Award Medal, 613
Brando, Marlon, 446
Brandt, Mortimer, 157, 159, 181. *See also* Mortimer Brandt
    Gallery
Braque, Georges, 122, 132
Brazil, 217, 522, 530–35. *See also* São Paulo Bienale
Breeskin, Adelyn, 583
Breinin, Raymond, 127
Breton, André, 94, 156, 159, 178, 204
Breuer, Marcel, 501, 504
Breughel, Pieter, the Elder, 95
Briggs, Ernest, 646n7
Bright, Dolly, 586
British Broadcasting Corporation (BBC), 378, 480–81,
    489–90, 659n17
British Mandate, 221
Broadway Is My Beat (radio show), 415
Brockway, Merrill, 562
Brodie, Gandy, 238, 646n7
Bronx, New York, 13–15, 20–21
Brooklyn Botanical Gardens, 116
Brooklyn Bridge, 443
Brooklyn College, 111, 287, 319, 333, 334, 339; Department
    of Design, 198
Brooklyn Heights Press (newspaper), 369
Brooklyn Jewish Center School, 96
Brooklyn Museum, 154, 187
Brooklyn Naval Yard, 41, 128, 136
Brooks, James, 81, 137, 183, 255, *278*, 383, *429*, 434,
    638n20; *Flight*, 81–82
Brooks, Rupert, 34
Brooks, Van Wyck, 201–2
Broome Street, 601
Broun, Heywood, 43, 45, 644n25[ch36]
Brown, Byron, 183
Brown, James, 441
Bruce, David, 507
Bruce, Evangeline, 507
Bruce, Lenny, 420
Brussels World's Fair, 392–93, 400
Bryant, William Cullen, 46
Bryant High School, 224, 646n25
Buber, Martin, *Hasidism*, 225
Buchanan, Scott, 36
"buckeye" painting, 347–49, 355
Buddhism, 225
Buick, 497
Bultman, Fritz, 135, 166, 167, 223, 224, 322, *411*
Bultman, Jeanne, 167, 322, 390
Burden, William A. M., 324–26, 376
Bureau of Ships, 137

Burke, Edmund, 457
Burke, Kenneth, 101, 233
Burleigh, Henry Thacker, 441
Burlin, Paul, 219, 222
The Burning of the Sanjo Palace (scroll painting), 37
Burns, George, 183
Burr, Constance F., 352
Burrow, Trigant, *The Neuroses of Man*, 249–50
Burrows, Carlyle, 300
Busa, Peter, 187

Cabaret Voltaire, Zurich, 238
Cadmus, Paul, 131
Cage, John, 182, 238, 239, 526, 611, 631n17
Cahan, Abraham, 34
Cahill, Holger, 107, 132, 303
Calas, Nicolas, 254, 411
Calder, Alexander, 33, 182; *La Grande Vitesse*, 581
California Palace of the Legion of Honor, San Francisco,
    197, 230
California School of Fine Arts, San Francisco, 198
Calouste Gulbenkian Foundation, 509
Camino gallery, 449
Campbell, Joseph, 201
The Campus (newspaper), 34
Canaday, John, 433–35, 438, 450, 452, 458, 482, 484, 486,
    487, 538, 545–46, 550, 553, 559; *The Embattled Critic:
    Views on Modern Art*, 435, 546
capitalism, 2, 95, 218, 296, 319, 360, 373
Capitol movie theater, 11
Capote, Truman, 369
Caravaggio, 107
Carlson, Helen, 250
Carnegie Hall, 33, 63, 101, 117, 276, 445–46, 483, 501
Carnegie Institute, 391, 465–66
Carnegie International. *See* Pittsburgh (Carnegie)
    International
Carone, Nick, 166, 167, 255, 283
Carré, Louis, 272
Caruso, Enrico, 446
Cashman, Samuel, 127
Caso, Alfonso, 157
Cassatt, Mary, 33
Castelli, Leo, 282–83, 303, 399, 431, 462, 512, 546, 549
Castelli Gallery, 491, 541, 612
Catholicism, 57, 93
Catholic Worker Movement, 606
Catholic World (newspaper), 57
Catlin, Stanton, 379–85, 521
Cavallon, Giorgio, 204
CBC. *See* Citizens' Budget Commission
CBS (television network), 492, 494, 496, 567
Cedar Bar, 205, 239, 242, 255–56, 350
Central Ohio Railroad, 248
Central Park Obelisk (Cleopatra's Needle), 443, 567
Centre National d'Art Contemporain, Paris, 587
"The Century 21 Exposition" (Seattle World's Fair, 1962),
    466, 473–75, 481
Century Club, 515
Cézanne, Paul, 33, 81, 108, 123, 132, 152, 325, 346, 376,
    513, 549, 571; *The Clock Maker (The Man with Folded
    Arms)*, 332

Chagall, Marc, 243, 276, 547
Chamberlain, John, 463
Chamberlain, Neville, 95
Chambers, Whittaker, 222
Chambord (restaurant), 301
Chanin, A. L., 305
Chapin, Francis, 127
Chaplin, Charlie, "The Count," 238
Chardin, Jean-Baptiste, 95, 108
Chareau, Pierre, 631n17
Charles Egan Gallery, 183, 222, 223–24, 239, 275, 319.
    See also Egan, Charlie
Charleston (dance), 375, 390, 511
Chartres Cathedral, 511
Chasen's (restaurant), 478
Cheaper by the Dozen (film), 281
Chermayeff, Serge, 334
Cherry, Herman, 241
Cherry Street, Lower East Side, 27–30, 29
Chevrolet Master Deluxe Sport Coupe, 120, 120, 156,
    224, 337
Childs, Lucinda, 555
Chilmark, Massachusetts, 87–88, 88, 94–95,
    649n23[ch42]
Chinese restaurants, 183, 321, 425, 440, 443, 502, 506
Christ Cella (restaurant), 571
Christianity, 225. See also Jesus; Passion of Christ
Christmas Art Sale for Peace, 578
Chrysler, Walter, 153
Ciechanowicz, Moszk-Herszk, 22
Cimabue, La Maestà, 570–71
Cimaise (magazine), 419
Cirker's storage facility, 608
Citizens' Budget Commission (CBC), 53–54, 72, 74–75,
    80, 86, 101–2
City College (CCNY), 31–38, 67, 128, 225, 646n25;
    School of Education, 68
City Hall Park, 102, 103, 446
City Planning Commission, 601
civil service, 43, 53, 72–73, 79, 80, 86–87, 89–90,
    102, 113
Cizek, Franz, 109
Claremont Park, 15
Clark, Tom, 217, 242–43
classicism and the classical, 205
Cloakmakers Strike, 30
Close, Chuck, 474
clothing industry, 28, 30–32, 53, 68, 86
The Club, 205, 241–44, 256–57, 271, 275, 279, 282, 294,
    374, 399, 410–11, 448–49, 473, 482, 493, 514
Coates, Robert, 477
Coca-Cola, 531
Coconino National Forest, Flagstaff, Arizona, 616
coffee, 211, 310, 363, 419, 534, 563
Coggeshall, Calvert, 359
Cohen, Bernard, 508, 510
Cohen, Fan, 78, 253
Cohen, Harold, 98, 212, 506, 508, 510, 659n17
Cohen, Morris Raphael, 36, 227
Cohn, Bob, 518
Cohn, Roy, 332, 550
Colby, Anita, 291

Cole, Nat King, 183
Coleman, Ornette, 428, 470, 611
Coleman, Roger, 657n12[ch55]
Coleridge, Samuel Taylor, 54
College Art Association, 333–35, 341, 352, 364–67, 421
College Art Journal, 331, 333–34, 339, 365–66
College of Regina, University Art Department, Saska-
    toon, Saskatchewan, Canada, 424
color: Hofmann and, 122–23; Newman and, 214, 230,
    252, 258, 289, 348, 382, 473, 475–76, 479, 499, 519,
    552, 562, 591; Pollock and, 317. See also Color Field
    painting
Color Field painting, 399, 487, 654n45
Columbia University, 409–10; Graduate School of Archi-
    tecture, 601; Research Project, 82
Commentary (magazine), 227, 231
Commission on Quasi-Judicial Action of Administrative
    Agencies, 110
Communist Party/Communism, 31, 33, 47, 56, 64, 102,
    105, 217–19, 242–43, 262, 270–71, 287, 329, 332, 383,
    576, 625n3[ch11]
The Community Church of New York, 115
Como, Perry, 183
The Compass (newspaper), 305
Comstock, Anthony, 599
Condé Nast, 301, 320, 549, 571
Congdon, William, 322, 359
Congregation B'nai Israel, New Jersey, 276, 304, 502
Congregation Shearith Israel, 503, 504
Congregation Zichron Moshe, 417
Congress of Industrial Organizations (CIO), 94
Conrad Hilton Hotel, Chicago, 578
conscientious objector status, 115, 135, 263, 606
Constable, Rosalind, 150
constructivism, 551
Consumers' Cooperative Cafeteria, 85–86, 91, 112
"Contemporary Art and the Church: The Point of Inter-
    section" (conference, 1967), 558–59
Contemporary Art Council, Seattle Art Museum,
    517, 585
Contemporary Jewish Record (magazine), 634n38
"Continuity and Change: 45 American Abstract Painters
    and Sculptors" (exhibition, 1962), 474
Cooper Union, 101, 109, 223, 262
Coplans, John, 612
Corcoran, Dagny, 531–32
Corcoran Ball, 613
Corcoran Gallery of Art, Washington, D.C., 562, 565,
    569, 583–84, 604, 612, 613
Corneille, Pierre, 64, 225, 623n6[ch6]
Cornell, Joseph, 159, 238, 239, 376, 551, 603
Cornell University, 118, 124, 160, 501
Corot, Jean-Baptiste-Camille, 427
"Corruption in the Arts" (panel, 1961), 449
La Côte Basque (restaurant), 571, 606, 607
Coughlin, Charles, 46, 129
Courbet, Gustave, 33, 108, 438, 571, 573
Cousins, Norman, 90
Covarrubias, Miguel, 157
Crampton, Rollin, 313, 327, 329–31
Cranbrook-Life Exhibition (1940), 115–16
Craven, Thomas, 130, 132, 243, 295, 299

Crawford, Tom, 99, 606–7, 615–16
Crehan, Hub, 413, 419–20, 550
cricket, 507
Cromwell, Oliver, 416
Crosby, Bing, 183
Crotona Park, 13–14
Crown Cork & Seal, 97, 148, 497
Crowninshield, Frank, 153
cry/outcry/*geshray*, as theme in Newman's life and
    work, 5, 66–67, 80, 147, 165, 199–200, 213, 284, 329,
    345, 407, 409, 439, 512, 520, 543, 548
Cubism, 123, 139, 187, 232, 346–47, 398, 401, 410, 476
"Cubism and Abstract Art" (exhibition, 1936), 83, 121
Cue (magazine), 261–62
Cunningham, Merce, 377
Curry, John, 116, 131

Dada, 238, 285, 315, 363, *411*, 547
"Dada, Surrealism, and Their Heritage" (exhibition,
    1968), 576, 662n34
Daley, Richard J., 576–78
Dalton School, 272
Daniel, Clifton, 524
Daughters of the American Revolution (D.A.R.), 112,
    626n2[ch13]
David, Jacques-Louis, *The Coronation of Napoleon*, 640n15
Davis, Douglas, 590, 591, 601
Davis, Emma Lu, 127
Davis, Richard, 379
Davis, Stuart, 132, 162, 183, 219, 304, 374, 492
Dead Sea Scrolls, 542
de Antonio, Emile, *Painters Painting: New York Art
    Scene, 1940–1970*, 611, 612
De Chirico, Giorgio, 132
DeFeo, Jay, 431
Degas, Edgar, 33, 95, 108, 253
de Kooning, Elaine, 136, 224, 239, 241, 257, 303, 390,
    646n7; "Pure Paints a Picture," 380–81, 554
de Kooning, Willem, 2, 136, 141, 183, 190, 196, 201, 204,
    216, 221, 223–24, 228, 231, 233, 238–39, 241, 245, 250,
    255–57, 261, 267, 272, 273, 275, 277, *278*, 279–80, 282,
    294–96, 299, 303, 305, 317–18, 319, 337, 346, 361, 370,
    373–74, 378, 379, 398, 410, 430, 434, 440, 448, 449,
    450, 452, 455, 463, 466, 473, 478, 481, 483–87, 497,
    513, 514, 521, 529, 585, 589–91, 593–94, 596, 603,
    611, 612, 636n16[ch27], 638n20, 638n30, 655n1[ch52],
    664n6[ch63]; *Painting, 1948*, 234; *Pink Angel*, 442;
    Wah Kee Spare Ribs, 263; *Woman I*, 311, 589
Delacroix, Eugène, 573; *The Death of Sardanapalus*, 570
De La Mare, Walter, 34
Delloye, Charles, 462
Democratic National Convention (Chicago, 1968), 576–77
demonstrations/protests/riots, 10–13, 23, 30, 48, 55, 64,
    69, 515, 528, 576–77, 581
Dempsey, Jack, 45, 462
De Niro, Robert, 646n7
Denman, John, 517
Denny, Robyn, 411, 508
Depression, 40, 46, 49, 64, 99, 106, 141
Derain, André, 108, 132
Despiau, Charles, 108
De Stijl, 239

Detroit, Michigan, 581, 588
Devree, Howard, 150, 191, 300
De Witt Clinton High School, 9–11, *10*, 13, 32, 57
Diamond, Harold, 497, 589, 600, 613, 615
Diamond, Hester, 497, 505, 610, 613, 615
Dickinson, Emily, 34
Diebenkorn, Richard, 392
Dietrich, Marlene, 610
DiFalco, S. Samuel, 365
dignity, Newman's concern with, 76, 83, 86, 89, 90, 91,
    97, 109, 112, 120, 139, 147, 159, 180, 198, 200, 205, 245,
    291, 327, 334, 341, 464, 474, 589, 612
Dillenberger, Jane, 592
Diller, Burgoyne, 334, 658n24
Dine, Jim, 399, 509, 563, 656n16; *Green Shower*, 513
di Suvero, Mark, 463
"Doc" Perry's drug store, 45
Documenta, Kassel, Germany, 418, 421, 423, 436, 571–72
Dondero, George A., 242–44, 270
Doskow, Ambrose, 367
Dotremont, Philippe, 452
Douglas, Frederic H., 631n8
Douglas, William O., 568
Dow, Arthur Wesley, *Composition*, 187
Downtown Gallery, 183, 304
Downtown-Lower Manhattan Association, 601
Dr. Leon Pinsker Camp, 15
Du Bos, Abbé, 573, 664n11[ch62]
Dubuffet, Jean, 516, 644n18[ch35]
Duchamp, Marcel, 139, 233, 315, 325, 374; *Box-in-a-
    Suitcase*, 140
Dufferin, Sheridan 5th Marquess of, 506, 507,
    657n10[ch55]
Dufy, Raoul, 80
Dugmore, Edward, 303
Duncan, Isadora, 446
Durand-Ruel Gallery, 159
Dwan Gallery, Los Angeles, 478
Dykes Lumber, 385
DYN (magazine), 156–57, 187
Dzubas, Friedel, 137, 303, 320, 399, 646n7

Eakins, Thomas, 285
earthworks, Native American, 248–49, 258, 499
Easel Project, 43
East End Temple, 341, 352, 356, 369, 370
Eastman Kodak, 71
East New York Vocational High School, 88, 96
East River waterfront, 27–28, 46, 119, 284, 310, 369, 446
École des Beaux Arts, Paris, 56
Educational Alliance, 33
Edwards, I.E.S., *The Pyramids of Egypt*, 443
Egan, Charlie, 195, 256, 303. *See also* Charles Egan Gallery
Egypt, 372, 567–69
Egyptian art, 204–5
Ehrlich, Bill, 98
Eichmann, Adolf, 455, 469
Einstein, Albert, 107
Eisenhower, Dwight D., 338, 389, 392
Electric Circus (nightspot), 165, 559
El Greco, 37
Eliot, T. S., 34, 38, 54, 154, 166, 419, 593

Ellin, Everett, 437, 450–52, 456, 470–72, 478, 495, 497, 505, 513, 544, 550
Ellington, Duke, 520
Elliot, James, 451, 477–78, 505
Elmer Gantry (film), 439, 651n14[ch46]
Emerson, Ralph Waldo, 78
Emma Lake workshop, 424–27, 442, 518, 524, 530, 598
emotion, in art, 204, 213, 258, 274, 284, 286–87, 290, 450, 475, 479
Emshwiller, Ed, 612
Ernst, Jimmy, 122, *278*, 638n20
Ernst, Max, 164
Esquire (magazine), "Upper and Lower Bohemia," 377
etching, 578–79, 586
Euclid, 354
Evans, Bill, 41, 428, 611
Everett, Roxanne, 565
Evergreen Review (journal), 404, 413, 430
Existentialism, 227, 412
Expo 58 (Brussels), 392–93, 400
Expo 67 (Montreal), 551, 553, 554, 558–60, 572, 586

"Fantastic Art, Dada, Surrealism" (exhibition, 1936), 83
Farley, James, 56
El Faro (restaurant), 506
Farrar, Straus & Co., 182
Father of the Bride (film), 281
Faulkner, William, 633n10[ch23]
Federal Art Project, 81, 107, 110
Federal Bureau of Investigation (FBI), 82
Federation of Modern Painters and Sculptors, 106, 108, 127, 132, 133, 143–46, 173
Feeley, Paul, 320, 400, 404, 553
Feigen, Richard, 576–77, 601
Felker, Clay, 377
Feltman (doctor), 615
Ferber, Herbert, 193–96, 198, 247, 265, 276, 293, 304, 305, 309, 311, 313, 319, 331–32, 502, 598, 604, 638n20, 638n31, 641n17
Ferreira y Moyers, Maria Emilia, 156
Ferren, John, 241, 434
Ferus Gallery, Los Angeles, 478, 659n45
Fharaddin, Princess, 153
Fields, W. C., 480
Fiene, Ernest, 116
"Fifteen Americans" (exhibition, 1952), 302–11, 313, 325, 370, 387, 400, 418, 431, 471, 474, 490, 588, 589, 604, 637n62, 646n8, 650n40
"54–64 Painting and Sculpture of a Decade" (exhibition, 1964), 509–10
"Fifty Years of Modern Art" (exhibition, 1958), 392–93
film industry and movies, 217–18, 222, 320–21, 392, 640n15
Finch, Julie, 600–601, 610
Fine Art Substitutes Association, 625n28
Fiorello! (musical), 446
First Municipal Art Exhibition (1934), 59
"First Papers of Surrealism" (exhibition, 1942), 139
Fish, Hamilton, 129
Fishburne, S. J., 422–23, 650n47
Fitch, James Marston, 601

Fitzsimmons, James, 327, 490, 560–61
Five-Cent Fare Party, 56
Five Spot Café, 428, 440, 470
Flaherty, Robert, 277
Flaubert, Gustave, 80
Flavin, Dan, 98, 381, 546, 562, 567, 569, 598, 604, 608, 612
Flavin, Sonia, 567
Flushing Meadow Park, 507
Flynn, Edward Joseph, 129
Fogg Museum, Cambridge, Massachusetts, 243, 524
football, 5, 9, 36, 598
Force, Juliana, 42, 59, 219
Ford, Ford Madox (né Hueffer), 34
Ford, Gordon Onslow, 122
Ford, Whitey, 470
Ford Foundation, 413
form: aesthetics based on, 38, 121–22; in the clothing business, 68; criticism of preoccupation with, 38, 109, 141, 145, 157, 176–78, 232, 284, 522–25, 534; expressive of ideas/thoughts, 176, 196, 257; Hofmann and, 122–23; "primitive" art and, 66. *See also* formalism
formalism, 124, 145, 157, 177, 232, 383, 489, 522–25, 552, 658n24
Forst, Miles, 646n7
Forster, E. M., 54
Fortune (magazine), 46–48, 95, 135; "The Great International Art Market," 361, 371
"Forty American Moderns" (exhibition, 1944), 162–63
Fosse, Bob, 542
Fourcade, Xavier, 562, 586, 589–91, 602, 607, 611, 613, 664n6[ch63]
Four Minute Men, 20
Four Seasons (restaurant), 412, 430–31, 452, 651n28
"Fourteen Americans" (exhibition, 1946), 268
Fourth Guggenheim International Award Exhibition (1964), 514
Francis, Sam, 378–79, *429*
Frank, Joseph, "Spatial Form in Modern Literature," 166
Frankenstein, Alfred, 233
Frankenthaler, Helen, 290, 311, 319, 370, 377–78, *442*, 498, 506–7, *508*, 546, 558, 646n7, 657n10[ch55]
Frankfurter, Alfred, 121, 124, 186, 299, 332, 644n8
Franklin, George, 410, 418, 443, 452, 510
Franklin and Marshall College, 186
Frank O'Hara Foundation, 587, 664n11[ch63]
Freeman, Betty, 345, 471, 478, 492–93
French & Company Gallery, 215, 409, 415, 417–23, *418*, 426, 430, 431, 437, 452, 525, 586, 589–90, 652n30
Freud, Sigmund, 19, 126, 316
Frick Museum, 663n10
Fried, Michael, 485, 486, 524; "Art and Objecthood," 566
Friedman, Abby, 363, 389, *390*, 404
Friedman, B. H. (Bob), 98, 285, 361–63, 388–89, *390*, 404, 407, 408, 412, 415, 430–31, 468, 501, 547, 564, 623n6[ch6], 643n18[ch35], 646n8, 651n28, 656n16; "Whisper," 441
Friedrich, Heiner, 547
Frontier (magazine), 437
Frost, Rosamund, 186
F. R. Tripler & Co., 530, 600
Fry, Roger, 35, 123, 177–78, 325, 524, 571

Fuller, Buckminster, 255, 519; American Pavilion, Expo 67, Montreal, 558, *plate 18*
Fulton Fish Market, 44, 443

Gage & Tollner (restaurant), 321, 462
Galerie Lawrence, Paris, 451
Galerie Raymond Creuze, 379
Gamelan Orchestra and Dancers of Bali, 321
Garai, Pierre, 225, 387
Garbo, Greta, 149
Garfield, John, 96
Garske, Pat. *See* Still, Pat
Gary Plan riots, 11–13
Gas House district, 119
Gastor, Theodore, 542–44
Gatch, Lee, 296, 337
Gauguin, Paul, 33, 108, 354, 361
Geldzahler, Henry, 421, 505, 580, 603–4, 661n12
Gelusil, 224, 247
Genauer, Emily, 267, 269, 288, 289, 299, 420, 545, 628n49
Genesis, Book of, 3, 199, 200, 215, 490, 542–43
Genet, Jean, 202
Gentlemen's Quarterly (magazine), 364, 400
Géricault, Théodore, *The Raft of the Medusa*, 570–71, 594, 665n28[ch63]
Gerson, Otto, 496
geshray (outcry). *See* cry/outcry/*geshray*
Getlein, Frank, 383–84
Getz, Stan, 428
Giacometti, Alberto, 149, 211, 243, 285, 596; *La clairiere*, 285; *La foret*, 285; *Grande Figure*, 211; *La place*, 285
Gibbs, David, 450, 452, 505, 507
G. I. Bill, 262, 361
Gibson, Charles Dana, 446
Gibson, Joan E., 343
Gilda (film), 183
Gilman, Charlotte, 70–71
Gimbels, 425
Ginsberg, Allen, 377; "Howl," 441
Ginsburg, Cora and Benjamin, 87, 184, 225, 609
Giuffre, Jimmy, 428
Glamour (magazine), 491
Glarner, Fritz, 239
Glasco, Joseph, 604
Glazer, Nathan, 227
Glinn, Burt, 377
Gloucester, Massachusetts, 137, 142, 147, 154
Gloucester House (restaurant), 506, 567, 612, 614
Glueck, Grace, 523–25, 588, 598
Gnagy, Jon, 219
Gnostic Christianity, 225
Goebbels, Paul Joseph, 530
Gogh, Vincent van, 66, 108, 132, 253, 376
Goldberg, Michael, 646n7
Golden Anniversary Exposition, Grand Central Palace, 225
Goldsmith Brothers, 260, 385
Goldston, Bill, 498, 610
Goldwater, Barry, 508
Goldwater, Robert, 233, 365

Goldwyn, Samuel, 331
golf, 341
Goode, Joe, 479
Goodman, Paul, 201, 574–75
Goodman, Percival, 276, 502, 504
Goodnough, Robert, 241, 262, 265, 267, 478, 639n26, 646n7
Goodrich, Lloyd, and John I. H. Baur, *American Art of the Twentieth Century*, 480
Goossen, Eugene, 286, 400, 404, 426; "The Philosophic Line of B. Newman," 405–6
Gorky, Arshile, 122, 183, 201, 220–22, 230, 250, 264, 272, 294, 296, 303, 352, 354, 361, 374, 384, 442, 448, 472, 514, 561; *Untitled*, 472
Gottlieb, Adolph, 32–34, 36–38, 37, 40–43, 48, 54, 66, 75–76, 83, 96, 100, 105–6, 126–27, 132–33, 136, 137, 140, 143–47, 149–50, 156, 157, 159–60, 162, 167, 171, 173, 177, 179, 183, 192, 198, 201, 203, 206, 216, 219, 228, 235, 239, 241, 245, 250, 257, 265, 268, 270, 274–77, 278, 279, 294, 302, 309, 311, 346, 392, 400, 408, 410, 434, 448, 466, 487, 496, 502, 514, 529, 545, 568, 597, 598, 602, 603, 621n10[ch3]; 622n12, 628n50, 638n20, 639n26; *Pictograph #4*, 126; *Rape of Persephone*, 144–46, 173; *Vigil*, 234
Gottlieb, Esther, 140–41, 143, 171, 183, 198
Government War Training Program, 128
Gowing, Lawrence, 509
Graetz, Heinrich, *Popular History of the Jews*, 17
Graham, John, 33, 66, 96, 132, 153, 159, 173–75, 183, 218; *Portrait of Elinor Graham*, 173, 609; *System and Dialectics of Art*, 173–75
Gramercy Park, 444
grand piano, 112, 119, 189, 307, 600, 609
Grant, Forest, 91
Gratz, Donald, 441, 531, *531*, 565
Graves, Morris, 127, 162, 250, 517
Graves, Robert, 503
Gray, Cleve, 98, 444, 450, 454, 456, 478, 479, 505
Gray, Francine du Plessix, 444, 450, 454
Great Atlantic Hurricane (1944), 156
Greater New York Racing Association, 351
Great Hurricane of 1938, 95, 102
Greek art and culture, 34, 204–6, 213, 232
Greeley, Horace, 46
Green, Sam, 521–22, 658n21
Greenberg, Clement, 99–100, 108, 123, 136, 192, 203–4, 223–24, 227–28, 231, 244, 246, 264, 275, 279, 289, 290, 295, 299, 301–3, 306, 308, 311, 317, 319–20, 321, 326, 341, 346–52, 354–55, 359, 364, 370, 371, 379–80, 384–85, 388, 389, 391, 397, 399–401, 404–5, 407, 411, 415, 417, 418, 422–23, 449, 481, 487–90, 516, 521–22, 524, 525, 527, 549, 573, 589, 602, 612, 628n7, 634n38, 648n14[ch41], 662n44, 664n10[ch62]; "After Abstract Expressionism," 485, 488; "'American-Type' Painting," 346–48, 405, 471; *Art and Culture*, 471; "Avant-garde and Kitsch," 378; "Complaints of an Art Critic," 664n10[ch62]; "The Situation at the Moment," 220; "Towards a Newer Laocoon," 116, 628n18[ch17]
Greenberg, Jenny, 648n14[ch41]
Greene, Balcomb, 294, 296
Greenhouse, Annalee. *See* Newman, Annalee

Greenhouse, Anuta, 63, 78, 105, 185
Greenhouse, Leah. *See* Hochstein, Leah
Greenhouse, Nathan, 63, 554
Greenhouse, Samuel, 63, 78, 96–98, 118, 147–48, 180, 185, 206
Greenhouse patent lawsuit, 96, 113, 118, 147–48, 150, 157, 497
La Grenouille (restaurant), 549, 571, 606
Gribitz, Joel, 298
Grippe, Peter, 598, 638n20
Gronowicz, Yenta Vigdorovna, 25
Grooms, Red, 399
Grosman, Tatyana, 498, 500–501, 505, 515, 579, 610
Group Theatre, 43
Grover Cleveland High School Annex, 43, 62–63, 68, 77, 96, 253
Grünewald, Matthias, *Isenheim Altarpiece*, 510–12, 570
Guggenheim, Harry, 514, 545
Guggenheim, Peggy, 139–40, 162, 180, 183, 193, 223, 233, 350, 355, 432, 560, 587, 631n27, 631n43; *Out of This Century*, 243. *See also* Art of This Century gallery
Guggenheim Fellowship, 40, 89
Guggenheim International Award Exhibition (1964), 495
Guggenheim Museum (formerly Museum of Non-Objective Painting), 95, 161, 201, 323, 332, 337, 438, 445, 452, 455, 468–72, 482–83, 487, 489, 514–15, 518, 521, 538–42, *540*, 544–45, 550–51, 559, 654n6, 661n12
Guillain, Robert, 383
Guinness, Serena Belinda (Lindy) Rosemary, 507, 657n10[ch55]
Gurdjieff, George, 167
Guston, Philip, 135, 255, 256, 302, 376, 383, *429*, 448, 466, 478, 479, 482–83, 487, 497, 514, 598
Guys and Dolls (musical), 321, 356, 611

Haacke, Hans, 597
Haftmann, Werner, 514
Hahn Brothers, 572
Hahn–Duveen trial, 44
Hahn Warehouse, 422, 518
Hair (musical), 5, 164–65, 578, 611
Hajdú, Etienne, *La Tête Blanche*, 651n28
Hakone Open-Air Museum, Japan, 587, 595
Hale, Nathan, 102
Hale, Robert, 186, 269, 270
Hall, Jim, 441
Hallmark, 243
Halpert, Edith, 59, 183, 304
Hals, Frans, 107
Ham (space-traveling chimpanzee), 455
Hamilton, Richard, 508
Hammarskjold, Dag, 338
Hammond Aircraft, 136
Hampton, Lionel, 428, 611
Hansa gallery, 449
happenings, 399, 428, 549
Hare, David, 135, 139, 162, 234–35, 240–43, 265, *266*, 275, 353, 434, 598, 638n20, 639n26
Harithas, James, 561, 583–84, 604
Harkavy, Alexander, 17
Harnoncourt, Rene d', 152, 304–5, 337, 513, 561, 631n8

Harper's (magazine), 232
Harper's Bazaar (magazine), 555
Harriman, Averell, 350–51, 356
Harris, Louis, 48
Harry N. Abrams (publisher), 367
Harry Rothman (clothing store), 425
Hart, Lorenz, "Zip," 542
Hart, Moss, 45
Hartigan, Grace, 223, 337, 377, 392, 478, 487
Hasidism, 17, 26, 165, 225–26, 337, 605
Haskalah, 16–17, 23
Hattis, Phyllis, 555
Hawkins, Coleman, 440
Hayter, Stanley William, 122, 159
Hearn, Lafcadio, 54
Hearn Fund, 638n31
Hearst, William Randolph, 46
Hearst corporations, 334
Hearst newspapers, 190
Hebrew language, 16–18, 184
Heckscher, August, 338, 569
Hegel, G.W.F., 54, 122, 166
Heggen, Thomas, *Mr. Roberts*, 182–83
Heller, Ben, 111, 115, 229, 319, 362–64, 376, 379, 380, 381, 384–85, 388–89, 391–92, 397, 399, 400, 404, 407, 409–10, 412, 414, 416, 421, 431, 432, 434–37, 439, 450, 452–53, 462, 464, 466, 470, 473, 495, 505, 546, 588, 597, 600, 614, 648n17[ch42], 663n20[ch60]
Heller, Judy, 363, 384, 404, 439, 597, 663n20[ch60]
Hemingway, Ernest, 211–12, 632n6[ch23], 633n10[ch23]
Henri, Robert, 32, 33
"Henri Matisse" (exhibition, 1951), 308
Henry Street Settlement, 27, 81
Heraclitus, 150, 174
Herbert, David, 361, 441
Herrera, Carmen, 36, 183
Hersey, John: *Hiroshima*, 183; *The Wall*, 281
Herzen, Alexander, 86
Herzl, Theodor, 542
Herzliya Hebrew Teachers' College, 63
Hess, Audrey, 571, 608, 614, 663n20[ch60]
Hess, Thomas, 2, 4, 10, 17, 20, 25, 33, 40, 56, 65, 88, 115, 122, 138, 186, 211, 212, 224, 228–29, 237, 241, 247, 249, 254, 255, 257, 259, 279, 288, 290, 292, 294–96, 299, 303, 307, 308, 310–11, 314, 323, 326, 327, 329, 332, 341, 342, 354–58, 368, 370, 374, 375, 378, 380–81, 384–85, 388, 392, 399, 405, 408, 410, 419–20, 434–35, 439, 449, 450, 458–60, 464–65, 482–84, 486–87, 491, 495–96, 505, 516, *517*, 523, 535, 538, 541–43, 545, 552, 561, 562, 569, 571, 572, 576, 578, 579, 586–90, 592, 594, 597, 598, 607–8, 611, 613, 614, 623n6[ch6], 625n30, 633n6[ch24], 633n7[ch23], 634n47, 637n15, 637n50, 643n5[ch34], 644n8, 646n5[ch39], 648n14[ch42], 662n15, 662n41, 663n20[ch60], 664n6[ch63], 664n10[ch62], 665n28[ch63]; *Abstract Painting*, 228, 294–96, 329, 354, 356–58, 490; *American Painting, a Modern History*, 356; *Barnett Newman*, 588–89; "Re-inhardt: the Position and Perils of Purity," 381; "U.S. Painting: Some Recent Directions," 360–61, 377
High School of Music and Art, 68
High School of Needle Trades, 141
Hill, Ricardo, 154

Hiroshima bombing, 183, 205
Hirsch, Joseph, 127
Hiss, Alger, 222
Hitchcock, Alfred, *Notorious*, 183
Hitler, Adolf, 48, 95, 101, 105, 113, 115, 128–30, 135, 139, 140, 621n10[ch3]; *Mein Kampf*, 101
Hochstein, Joe, 96
Hochstein, Leah (née Greenhouse), 63–64, 77–78, 96, 105, 162
Hochstein, Philip, 63, 77–78, 90, 162
Hockney, David, 625n30
Hoffer, Eric, 518
Hofmann, Hans, 96, 122–23, 137, 162, 166, 167, 182, 190, 192, 195, 250, 275, 354, 359–61, 383, 400, 466, 472, 492, 514, 553, 638n20; *In the Wake of the Hurricane*, 474
Hofmann, Miz, 167, 322
Hollywood. *See* film industry and movies
Holocaust, 123, 138, 163–64, 227, 228, 263, 315, 333, 469–70
Holstein, Jonathan, 440, 454, 478, *502*, 506, 524, 585, 589, 652n19[ch46]
Holty, Carl, 183, 219, 222, 449
Holtzman, Harry, 239, 299, 313, 334
The Home News (newspaper), 38
Homer, *Iliad*, 308
The Honeymooners (television show), 642n36
Hooch, Pieter de, 294
Hook, Sidney, 101
Hoover, Herbert, 124
Hope, Bob, 183
Hope, Henry R., 365–66
Hopper, Dennis, 549
Hopper, Edward, 116
Hopps, Walter, 515, 522–26, 528, 530–33, 539, 542, 583, 604, 647n15[ch39], 659n45, 660n18
Horace, 63
Hord, Donal, 127
Horizon Press, 574
Horkheimer, Max, 227
Horn & Hardart, 246
Horney, Karen, 101
horse-racing, 337, 341, 478, 507
Hotel Brevoort, 75
Hotel Holland, 85
Hotel Statler, Boston, 78
Hotel Traymore, Atlantic City, New Jersey, 305
Houdini, Harry, 34
Houghton Mifflin Literary Fellowship, 77, 86, 89–90
House Un-American Activities Committee, 218, 222, 242, 332–33
Houston Museum of Fine Arts, 588
Howard, Charles, 127
Howard Johnson's, 367–68
Howe, Irving, 16, 20, 26, 36, 574, 626n2[ch13]
Howells, William Dean, 633n10[ch23]
Hoyland, John, 411, 508
Huber, Carlo, 440, 511
Huber, Helga, 511
Hudson, Andrew, 441, 593, 661n10
The Hudson Review (magazine), 569
Huelsenbeck, Richard, 238
Hughes, Howard, 107

Hughes, Langston, 101
Hunt, Richard Morris, 45
Hunte, Jack, 606
Hunter, Sam, 367–68, 376, 473–74, 481–82, 496, 516, *517*, 554, 556, 662n44; "Jackson Pollock: The Maze and the Minotaur," 367–68
Hunter College, 62, 64, 81, 488, 490, 612, 644n30
Huxley, Aldous, 233
Huxtable, Ada Louise, 489, 563

The Iceman Cometh (play), 182
"The Ideographic Picture" (exhibition, 1947), 191–92
Ideographic Pictures/Painters, 191–93, 198, 206, 219
Iglehart, Robert, 234, 637n53
I Love Lucy (television show), 322, 642n36
Impressionism, 123, 154–56, 182, 232, 324–25, 332, 347, 401, 410, 476, 644n25[ch35]
"Indian Art of the United States" (exhibition, 1941), 187
Indian Arts and Crafts Board, U.S. Department of the Interior, 187
Indian Boarding Schools, 187
Indian sand painting, 238
Indian Space painters, 187–88
influenza, 21
"Information" (exhibition, 1970), 614, *615*
Ingersoll, Ralph, 113
Ingres, Jean-Auguste-Dominique, 571, 661n46
Instead (magazine), 222
Institute of Contemporary Art, Boston (formerly Institute of Modern Art), 218, 233, 244, 558
Institute of Contemporary Art, London, 393, 403
Institute of Religion, Texas Medical Center, Houston, 581
Internal Revenue Service (IRS), 562, 571, 585, 599, 608. *See also* taxes
International Association of Art Critics, 434–35
International Congress on Religion, Architecture and the Visual Arts, 547, 563, 568
"International Exhibition of the New Realists" (1962), 486–87, 491
Internationalism, 627n12[ch14]
International Ladies' Garment Workers' Union, 31
"International Painting since 1950" (exhibition, 1964), 510
"Intrasubjectives" (exhibition, 1949), 219, 245, 250
Iolas, Alexander, 255
Irascibles, 55, 270–71, 275–80, *278*, 283, 292, 309, 312, 604, 639n21
IRS. *See* Internal Revenue Service
Irwin, Robert, 479, 522, 532, 539, 659n9, 659n21, 659n45
Isaiah, Book of, 503–4
Isherwood, Christopher, *The Berlin Stories*, 182
isolationism, 128–32, 145, 147, 163, 179, 627n12[ch14]
Israel, 198, 221, 287, 372, 567–69
It Is (journal), 254
It's a Wonderful Life (film), 183

Jackson, Harry (né Harry Aaron Shapiro), 137
Jaffe, Jacob, 29
Jaguar Mark IV sedan, 282, 323–24, 341, 356, 364, 370, 644n16
Jaguar Mark V sedan, 385, 391, 407, 464

James, Henry, 3, 54, 180, 201, 515
James, William, *The Varieties of Religious Experience*, 76
James Graham and Sons gallery, 587
Janis, Carroll, 409, 580
Janis, Harriet, 642n31[ch33]
Janis, Sidney, 282, 283, 316, 328, 338, 341, 344–45, 351, 448, 463, 496, 497, 561, 594, 596, 597, 642n31[ch33]; *Abstract and Surreal Art in America*, 126, 157, 628n18[ch17]
Janis Gallery, 275, 302–3, 306, 311, 316, 319, 324, 327–28, 338, 344, 362, 484–87, 491, 495, 506, 517, 554, 647n15[ch39]
Jarry, Alfred, "The Passion Considered as an Uphill Bicycle Race," 658n13
jazz, 428, 511, 611
Jefferson Diner, 224
Jesus, 308, 543, 546, 547, 606. *See also* Passion of Christ
Jeu de Paume, Paris, 570
Jewell, Edward Alden, 110, 124–25, 133–34, 143–46, 150, 153, 159, 163, 168, 173, 179, 191, 192, 206, 628n50; *Impressionists and Their Contemporaries*, 158
Jewish Daily Bulletin (newspaper), 38
Jewish Daily Forward (newspaper), 11
Jewish Museum, 229, 392, 445, 481, 491, 495, 501, 525, 541, 545, 554, 556, 579, 608, 612, 662n41
Jewish People's Fraternal Order, 217
Jewish Theological Seminary, 198
Jews and Judaism: allegedly allied with Communism, 243; and education, 12–13; education prized by, 32, 57; Greenberg and, 99–100; immigrant Jews' relationship to, 15–16; on the Lower East Side, 27–30; mid-century cultural debates among, 227–28; Newman and, 9, 11, 15–20, 48–49, 93–94, 99, 138–39, 165, 184–85, 199, 221, 225–29, 237, 287, 417, 499, 501–5, 520, 538, 542, 546, 559, 567–68, 570, 575, 578, 605, 613–14, 632n9[ch22], 634n34, 634n38, 634n46, 651n47, 663n20[ch60]; in New York, 27–30, 46, 53, 663n16[ch61]; obligations of, 199, 221, 632n7[ch22]; persecution of, in Nazi Germany, 96; in Poland, 22–23; political positions and advocacy of, 93–94; Rosenberg and, 651n47; in Russia, 22–23; Schapiro and, 651n47; "self-hatred" of, 227–29; and World War II, 138–39. *See also* anti-Semitism; Holocaust
Job Lot, 226, 438, 579, 585
Jockey Club of America, 341, 351, 356
John Boyle and Company, 191, 272, 385, 470
John F. Kennedy International Airport, 507
Johns, Jasper, 361, 393, 399, 431, 463, 478, 487, 491, 498, 501, 513–14, 603, 612, 613, 648n14[ch42], 661n18; *1st Etchings*, 579; *Gray Numbers*, 513; *Large Target Construction*, 509; *Map*, 558; *Painting with Two Balls*, 513; *Target with Four Faces*, 399; *Three Flags*, 513
Johnson, Buffie, 162, 166, 167, 183, 290, 312
Johnson, Philip, 399, 421, 503–4, 567, 569, 580, 583, 597, 613, 651n28, 657n3[ch55], 664n33; Glass House, New Canaan, Connecticut, 567, 613
Johnson, Ray, 411
Johnson, Samuel, 54
Jones, Bobby, 45
Jones, James, *From Here to Eternity*, 281
Jonson, Ben, "The Noble Nature," 314

Joyce, James, 166, 570; *Finnegan's Wake*, 440, 484; *Ulysses*, 419
Judd, Donald, 98, 410, 522, 525–26, 532, 598, 600, 610, 612, 616, 666n36
Julien Levy Gallery, 183
Jungian theory, 187

Kabbalah, 16–17, 26, 192, 225–29, 262, 294, 296, 363, 499, 504, 542. *See also* Lurianic Kabbalah
Kadish, Reuben, 187
Kahn, Louis, 501, 504
Kahn, Wolf, 646n7
Kaldis, Aristodimos, 204, 224
Kandinsky, Wassily, 161, 182, 187, 596
Kane, Bob, 33
Kanovitz, Howard, 588
Kant, Immanuel, 109, 231, 457
Kaprow, Allan, 399, 428, 472, 479, 491, 521
Kasle, Gertrude, 500, 582
Kasmin, John, 98, 431, 440–41, 495, 506, 507, 509–10, 514, 638n8, 652n21[ch46]
Katzman, Herbert, 604
Kauffman, Craig, 479
Kaye, Danny, 183
Kazin, Alfred, 574
Keck, Caroline, 436
Kees, Weldon, 247, 270, 638n20, 639n26
Kelekian collection sale, 33, 621n18
Keleman, Pal, 153
Kelly, Ellsworth, 361, 375, 392, 431, 514, 516, 551, 586, 603, 647n15[ch39]
Kennedy, John F., 454, 484, 486, 491–92, 506
Kennedy, Robert, 586
Kennedy, Stephen, 415
Kent, Rockwell, 332
Kent State University student protestor killings, 613
Kenyon Review (magazine), 314
Khrushchev, Nikita, 484
Kienholz, Ed, 659n45
Kierkegaard, Søren, 164, 260, 412
Kiesler, Frederick, 139–40, 238
Kimura Gallery, Japan, 421
King, Martin Luther, Jr., 568, 574, 578–81, 663n10
King Cole Bar, St. Regis Hotel, 571, 605
Kirstein, Lincoln, 232
Kitaj, R. B., 508
Klee, Paul, 140
Klein, Jack, 585
Kline, Franz, 136, 183, 190, 204, 223, 239, 241, 255–56, 275, 294, 302–3, 361, 376, 379, 410, 413, 429, 430, 448, 463, 466, 478, 482–83, 514, 561, 647n15[ch39]
Knights Templar, 606
Knoedler Gallery, New York, 41, 562, 571, 586–95, 602, 664n6[ch63]
Knoedler Gallery, Paris, 570, 572
Koenigswald, G.G.R. von, 632n8[ch22]
Koestler, Arthur, 164
Kohn, Gabriel, 516
Kootz, Sam, 124–25, 183, 192, 194–95, 219, 242, 245, 250, 265, 271–72, 282, 343
Kootz Gallery, 192, 222, 224, 257, 275, 342, 474–75

Kozloff, Max, 409, 545, 553

Kramer, Hilton, 541, 597–98

Krasner, Lenore (Lee), 98, 132, 196, 277, 288, 290, 297–98, 303, 319, 349, 363–64, 369n15, 370, 389, *390*, 397, 441, 450, 474, 496, 505, 513, 536

Kriesberg, Irving, 304

Kristallnacht, 96

Kropotkin, Peter, 5, 10, 54, 586; *Memoirs of a Revolutionist*, 574–75, 605

Kubler, George, 457

Kufeld, Yankel "Jack," 48

Kuh, Katherine, 188, 203, 530, 545, 611

Kuhn, Walt, 132

Kulicke, Barbara, 485

Kulicke, Robert, 437, 450, 485, 597, 655n12[ch52]

Kunitz, Stanley, 407

Kuniyoshi, Yasuo, 43, 81, 217, 243, 304; *Circus Girl Resting*, 190

Kunsthalle, Basel, 378, 379, 398, 413–14, 510

Kunsthalle, Bern, 378

Kunsthaus, Zurich, 352

Kunstmuseum, Basel, 414

Das Kunstwerk (magazine), 525, 666n36

The Lady Vanishes (film), 427

La Farge, John, 483

La Fontaine, Jean de, 80

La Forgue, Jules, 178; "Physiological Origin of Impressionism," 154–55, 158

LaGuardia, Fiorello, 56–57, 59, 68, 77–78, 89, 91, 446

LaGuardia Airport, 82

Lam, Wifredo, 182

Lampson, Mary, 612

Landis, James M., 146

Lanes, Jerrold, 420–21, 426

Langer, Susanne, 314, 316

Laredo, Jaime, 408

Lassaw, Ibram, 183, 194, 224, 638n20

Latin, 2, 35, 457–61

Latin America, 151–52

"The Latin-American Collection of the Museum of Modern Art" (exhibition, 1943), 152

Laughton, Charles, 397

The Lavender (magazine), 35

Lavski, Boruch-Szmul, 23–24

Lavski, Hinda, 24

Lavski, Samuel-Meir, 23

Lawrence, D. H., 420

Lawrence, Jacob, 304

Lawrence, Jane, 168

Lazzari, Pietro, 190, 192

Leakey, Louis, *Adam's Ancestors*, 66

Lebrun, Rico, 127, 299

Lee, Amy, 252

Leen, Nina, "The Irascibles," 277–80, *278*, 429, 604

Leering, Jean, 561, 567, 570, 571–72

Léger, Fernand, 132, 183, 224, 302, 509, 596

Leider, Philip, 525, 594, 601, 658n33[ch56]

lema sabachthani. See cry/outcry/*geshray*; Newman, Barnett, paintings: *The Stations of the Cross: Lema Sabachthani*; Passion of Christ

Lenin, Vladimir, 54

Leonardo da Vinci, 19, 107; *Mona Lisa*, 571

Leopold Wilhelm, Archduke, 261

Lerner, Max, 101

Leslie, Alfred, 81, 98, 165, 241, 496

Leval, Beatrice, *442*

Levine, Neil, 528–29

Levy, Julien. *See* Julien Levy Gallery, 239

Lewis, Norman, 299, 638n20

Lewitin, Landes, 204

LeWitt, Sol, 441, 597; "Paragraphs on Conceptual Art," 566

Libby, Nathan, 15, 128

Liberman, Alexander, 261, 286, 293, 301, 320, 372, 375–76, 385, 388, 421, 429, 438, 439, 441–42, 444, 454, 495, 505–7, 510, 549, *550*, 551, 555, 562, 564, 571, 582, 583, 592, 598, 602, 604, 611–13, 651n21, 656n5, 664n11[ch62]; Barnett Newman and *Onement VI*, 491, *plate 16*; Barnett Newman and *Who's Afraid of Red, Yellow and Blue III*, 587, *plate 20*; Lunch at the Libermans, *442*

Liberman, Tatiana (née du Plessix), 320, 372, 375, 444, 506–7, 571

Lichtenstein, Roy, 514, 541, 551; *Big Modern Painting*, 558, *plate 18*

Lieberman, William, 498

Liebling, A. J., 56

Life (magazine), 45, 55, 67, 115, 129, 132, 164, 219, 220–21, 233–34, 238, 244, 246, 261, 267–69, 276–79, 293, 299, 304, 314, 327, 371, 378, 429–32, 446, 448–49, 474, 484, 487, 491, 494, 555, 604, 638n26, 646n6[ch39]

Lilly, Doris, 571

Lincoln Center, 392, 578–79

Lincoln Continental, 464

Lindbergh, Charles, 129

Lindbergh baby kidnapping, 44

Lindsay, John, 565

Lindy's (restaurant), 506

Lipchitz, Jacques, 509

Lipkind, Maria, 225

Lipkind, Norman, 369

Lipkind, William, 36, 87, 88, 100, 225, 369

Lippard, Lucy, 473, 532, 554, 556, 569, 597, 662n40

Lippincott, Donald, 565, 569, *582*, 600

Lippincott Incorporated, 565, 568–69, 578, 581–84, 665n47

Lippmann, Walter, 45, 542

Lippold, Richard, 265, 299, 604, 638n20

Lipton, Seymour, 194, 293, 393, 598, 638n20, 648n30

List, Vera, 546, 578–79, 664n27

lithography, 456, 495, 498–501, *499*

Litvaks, 26

Lloyd, Frank, 497, 513–14

Lochhead, Ken, 424, 427

Lomza, Poland, 16, 17, 22–26, 105

London, trip to, 507–12

London Gazette (newspaper), 37

Long, Huey, 182

Longinus, 54, 457

Look (magazine), 291

Lord, Francile, 388, 389

Lord, Sheridan, 388, 389, *390*

Lord and Taylor, 425

Los Angeles County Museum of Art, 451, 470, 516, 526–29, 652n17[ch47]

Los Angeles Times (newspaper), 452

Louchheim, Aline, 243, 258, 268, 288, 637n52; "Betty Parsons: Her Gallery, Her Influence," 293

Louis, Morris, 423, 487, 513

Louvis, Tony, 98, 262–63, 288

Louvre, Paris, 32, 64, 570–71, 594, 661n46, 663n4[ch62]

Lowell, Amy, 34

Lowenthal, Jesse, 36–37, 42, 183

Lowry, Bates, 590

Lowry, W. McNeil, 413

Luce, Henry, 121, 124, 129, 233, 270, 276, 627n12[ch14]

Luce publishing company, 46–47, 361, 470

Ludwig, Peter, 661n45

Lundeberg, Helen, 127

Lurianic Kabbalah, 591

Lynes, Russell, 377

MacArthur, Douglas, 286–87, 333, 371–74, 640n20

MacKenzie, Kenneth, 600, 613

Macmillan Company, 153

MacNeice, Louis, 96

Madison Square Garden, 48, 54, 93, 462

Madison Square Hotel, 442

Magazine of Art, 233

Magna, 230, 247, 260, 284, 408, 479, 553, 591

Magnum, 403

Magritte, René, 570

Mailer, Norman, 262, 369, 406, 428; *The Naked and the Dead*, 281

Maillol, Aristide, 80, 108

Malamud, Bernard, *The Fixer*, 573

Malevich, Kazimir, 67, 254, 346, 398, 402, 419, 551; *White on White*, 288

Malraux, André, 279

Manet, Édouard, 33, 573

"The Man from Uncle" (television show), 519

Manhattan Expressway, 446

"Manifesto: Towards a Free Revolutionary Art" (Breton and Rivera, possibly drafted by Trotsky), 94

Mann, Thomas, 101

Mansfield, Katherine, 54

Mantegna, Andrea, *St. Sebastian*, 570

Mantle, Mickey, 445, 470

Marca-Relli, Conrad, 137, 190, 224, 241, 243–44, 282, 392

Marck, Ingeborg van der, 567

Marck, Jan van der, 473, 505, 562, 567

Marcus, Barbara (Sprafkin), 454–55, 465

Marden, Brice, 593

Margo, Boris, 159, 190, 192, 359

Margulis, Max, 36, 225

Marie Harriman Gallery, 41, 108

Marin, John, 261

Maris, Roger, 445, 452, 470

Maritain, Jacques, 164

Mark, Grant, 303–4

Markel, Lester, 153

Marlborough Gallery, London, 452, 497, 513, 589, 662n44

Marlborough Gallery, New York, 513

Marsh, Reginald, 131

Martin, Fletcher, 116, 127, 131

Marx, Karl, 25, 54, 56

Masaccio, *Crucifixion*, 108

Masaryk, Jan, 101

masculinity, 44, 211, 310, 380, 419–20

Masefield, John, 34

Massie, Edward, 501

Masson, André, 572

Master, Philip, 198, *455*, 529

Matheson, Hugh, 337

Mathews, Thomas F., 559

Mathieu, Georges, 342–44, 346, 350, 375, 428, 516

Matisse, Henri, 33, 80, 133, 163, 187, 231, 314, 361, 405, 509

Matisse, Patricia (later Matta), 240

Matta, Roberto, 162, 182, 296, 472, 560

Matter, Herbert, 211, 261, 268, 544

Maupassant, Guy de, 80, 211

Max's Kansas City (restaurant), 566, 567, 663n10

Maxwell, Elsa, 190–91

McBride, Henry, 42, 48, 150, 299

McCarthy, Charlie (ventriloquist's dummy), 381

McCarthy, Joseph, 270, 332–33, 335

McClure's (magazine), 53

McCray, Porter, 392, 436

McFadden, Elizabeth "Sitty," 298

"McHale's Navy" (television show), 519

McKay, Arthur, 424, 426

McKee, Joseph V., 56–57, 59, 89

McLaughlin, John, 479

McMillen Gallery, 132

McShine, Kynaston, 501

McWilliams, Carey, 545

Meadmore, Clement, 445

Medellin, Octavio, 127

Medina, Harold, 369–70

Medomak, Maine, 116

Meganthropus, 632n8[ch22]

Meier, James, 502

Meier, Richard, 98, 501, 501–3, *502*, 505, 614

"Méliès Magic" (film), 238

Mencken, H. L., 445

Mendelsohn, Eric, 504

Menil, Christophe de, 580

Menil, Dominique de, 580, 613, 664n33

Menil, John de, 580–81, 613, 664n30, 664n33

Menorah Journal, 226, 634n35

Menuhin, Yehudi, 151

Mercury Galleries, 95

Merrick, David, 571

Merrild, Knud, 127

Merrill, Robert, 305

Merton, Thomas, 202

Messer, Thomas, 455, 468, 515, 518, 539, 544–46, 550–51, 654n6

Metropolitan Museum of Art, 10, 33, 37, 59, 143, 153, 154, 159, 217–18, 232, 253, 267–71, 276, 279, 309, 434, 587, 588, 596, 602–4, 608, 611, 615, 638n26, 638n31

Metropolitan Opera, 117, 151, 276, 392, 544

Mexican and Central American Hall, American Museum of Natural History, 150–51

Mexican revolution, 160

Meyer, Franz, 211, 511, 593, 652n21[ch46], 660n15

Michael's Pub, 549

Michelangelo, 107, 231–32, 497, 541, 552, 565, 571, 594; *Pièta*, 512; Sistine Chapel ceiling, 566

Michigan National Guard, 581

Midtown Galleries, 149

Mies van der Rohe, Ludwig: Colonnade Apartments, Newark, New Jersey, 320, 440, 501; Pavilion Apartments, Newark, New Jersey, 440, 501; Seagram Building, New York City, 320, 569

Milhaud, Darius, 233

Miller, Arthur, *The Death of a Salesman*, 261

Miller, Dorothy, 127, 132, 273, 281, 282, 294, 300, 302–7, 309, 311, 325, 327, 333, 397, 400, 404, 408, 410, 431, 471, 490, 596, 626n25

Miller Company, 648n17[ch42]

Milo Bar-Bell company, 34

Minneapolis Institute of Arts, 379–84

Minor, Robert, 56

Miró, Joan, 122, 133, 231, 248, 376, 398, 636n12[ch27]

Mishnah, 225, 544

Mitchel, John Purroy, 12

Mitchell, Joan, 122, 383, 413, 646n7

Mnuchin, Leon, 491, 495, 524

Moderna Museet, Stockholm, 495

"Modern Art and Mass Culture" (conference, 1962), 482–83

Modern Art Foundry, 477, 500

"Modern Art from USA" (exhibition, 1955), 352, 379

Modern Artists in America, First Series (Robert Motherwell and Ad Reinhardt), 212, 237

modernism/modern art: crisis of, 231, 276; criticisms of, 34, 144, 218–19, 232–34, 242–44, 269–71; political significance of, 338; promotion of, 137. *See also* abstract art/abstraction

The Modern Monthly (magazine), 114

Modigliani, Amedeo, 108, 132

Moe, Henry Allen, 90

Molotov, Vyacheslav, 281, 324, 372–73, 646n6[ch39], 647n8[ch39]

MoMA. *See* Museum of Modern Art

Mondrian, Piet, 67, 126, 161, 177, 193, 231, 249, 258, 301, 329, 346, 347, 398, 401, 402, 419, 523, 524, 549, 551, 596

Monet, Claude, 33, 123, 155, 182, 231, 295, 346, 361, 376–77, 405, 427, 432, 438; *Poplars at Giverny*, 324, 644n25[ch35]; *Water Lilies*, 376

Monk, Thelonious, 428, 611

monocle, 3, 119, 381, 389, 394, 397, 429, 449, 468, 478, 482, 491, 535, 549, 552, 570, 584, 587, 610, 614

Monroe, Marilyn, 446

Montebello, Philippe de, 588

Montross Gallery, 48

Moore, Archie, 462, 468

Moore, Henry, 508, 612

Moore, Marianne, 202

More, Thomas, 505

Morgan, Maud, 203, 306, 359

Morley, Grace, 281

Morley, Malcolm, 98

Morris, George L. K., 219, 313, 334

Morris, Robert, "Notes on Sculpture, Part 3," 566

Morsbroich Museum, Leverkusen, Germany, 451

Mortimer Brandt Gallery, 157, 159, 162, 183. *See also* Brandt, Mortimer

Moses (biblical figure), 19

Moses, Ed, 437

Moses, Robert, 102, 369, 563, 601, 620n29

Motherwell, Robert, 98, 122, 135, 139, 156, 162, 183–84, 187, 189, 192, 195, 201, 203, 216, 218, 223, 228, 234–35, 238, 241–43, 245, 248, 250, 252, 257, 265, 266, 268, 271, 275–77, 278, 279, 282–83, 294, 303, 309, 313, 314, 319, 331, 334, 336, 346, 353–54, 361, 373, 379, 386, 392, 442, 448, 466, 479, 482, 487, 497, 498, 502, 505–7, 513, 514, 518, 529, 536, 546, 558, 559–61, 577, 589, 598, 602, 603, 611, 612, 631n17, 633n6[ch24], 638n20, 639n21, 639n24, 657n10[ch55], 662n13, 662n44; *Modern Artists in America, First Series* (with Ad Reinhardt), 212, 237; "The Modern Painter's World," 156–57; "The Place of the Spiritual in a World of Property," 156–57; School of New York," 219–20

movies. *See* film industry and movies

Mozart, Wolfgang Amadeus, 65, 168, 241, 273, 285–86, 610; *The Magic Flute*, 225, 364; *Queen of the Night*, 634n34

Mr. Blandings Builds His Dreamhouse, 224–25

Mr. Peanut, 381

Mt. Sinai Hospital, 391

Mumford, Lewis, 43

Munich Agreement, 95

Municipal Art Commission, Houston, 580–81

Municipal Art Gallery, 74, 83

Murch, Walter, 190, 246, 293

Murray, John Middleton, 420

Murray, Robert, 98, 188, 240, 310, 424, 426–28, 435, 438, 440, 442–45, 450, 452, 454–56, 477–78, 501–6, 502, 510, 518–19, 562, 565–66, 569, 585, 590, 594, 595, 598, 600, 613, 614, 615, 638n62, 652n19[ch46], 655n6[ch51], 658n17; *Megan's Red*, 582

Museum of Contemporary Art, Chicago, 562

Museum of Fine Arts, Boston, 37

Museum of Modern Art (MoMA), 39, 66, 80, 83, 95, 108, 111, 121, 123, 127–28, 131, 132, 143, 148, 151–52, 155, 158, 161, 177, 180, 182, 187, 192, 218, 219, 232–34, 244, 265, 268, 270, 273, 279, 285, 303–4, 308, 314–16, 324–26, 332, 337–39, 351–52, 362, 370, 376, 379, 383, 389, 391–93, 397, 399, 403, 412, 418, 421, 431, 432, 434, 438, 452, 466, 470, 477, 482–83, 491, 498, 530, 547, 553, 562, 563, 576, 580, 587, 589, 590, 596–99, 601–2, 608, 612, 614, 626n25, 636n37, 637n62, 644n25[ch35], 648n14[ch42], 648n21[ch41], 651n21, 662n34; International Program, 392, 436

Museum of Non-Objective Painting. *See* Guggenheim Museum

music, Newman and: childhood exposure to, 11; Christmas carols, 441; classical music and opera, 65, 112–13, 168, 241, 273, 276, 305, 446; jazz, 428, 440–41, 470, 511; musicals, 5, 164–65, 542; piano playing, 35, 112, 119, 189, 263, 463, 463, 525; record collection, 610–11; record store excursions, 321, 428, 440–41; symphony composition, 35, 189, 456; writings on, 34, 112

Musil, Robert, 39

Mussolini, Benito, 95, 114

Myers, John Bernard, 195, 244, 296

Myerson, Bess, 182
mysticism, 172, 226, 227, 262, 499, 634n34
mythology and mythic painting, 126–27, 133, 168–69, 201

Nagai, Tom, 83
Nagel, Ernest, 101
Naiman, Golda-Leja (née Lavski), 23–24
Naiman, Guta (aunt), 11, 21–22, 24
Naiman, Josef (uncle), 23–24
Naiman, Lejzer-Herzk (grandfather), 23–24
Naiman, Lejzor (great-grandfather), 22
Nakian, Reuben, 183, 204
Namuth, Hans, 277; Barnett Newman and Betty Parsons with *The Wild*, 284–85, *285*; Barnett Newman in his Front Street studio, *310*; Barnett Newman with Jackson Pollock and Tony Smith at the Betty Parsons Gallery for Newman's 1951 show, 297, *297*
Nancy-Université, France, 64
Napoleon, 22
Nasser, Gamal Abdel, 567
The Nation (magazine), 192, 203, 223–24, 270, 359, 360, 404–5, 545–46, 553, 597, 603
National Academy of Design, 42
National Association of Audubon Societies, 116
National Collection of Fine Arts, Washington, D.C., 539, 549, 583, 594, 661n12
National Council of Churches, 547
National Endowment for the Arts, 565, 580–81
National Gallery, Ottawa, Ontario, Canada, 427
National Gallery, Washington, D.C., 217
National Gallery of Art, Washington, D.C., 661n45
National Gallery of Canada, Ottawa, Ontario, 604
National Hebrew School of the Bronx, 18
nationalism, 130, 160, 227, 531
National Museum of Racing, Saratoga, New York, 356
National Theatre of Greece, 321
Native American art, 187–88. *See also* earthworks, Native American; Indian sand painting
nature: art in relation to, 116, 212, 315, 424, 427, 523, 591; as source of terror/mystery, 180–81, 191
Navascués, Luis J., 152, 159–60, 183, 185–86, 189, 279, 341, 658n49
Nazis, 48, 86–87, 92, 95, 138, 163, 625n3[ch11]
NBC (television network), 482
Nemerov, Howard, 404–5, 417, 420
neo-Dada, 431
neo-plasticism, 67, 140, 314, 334
Neumann, Julius G., 417
"The New American Painting" (exhibition, 1958–1959), 392, 397–99, 401, 404, 408, 411–13, 421, 508
"The New American Painting and Sculpture: The First Generation" (exhibition, 1969), 587, 596–98, 602, 603
New Bauhaus, Chicago, 168
"The New Decade: 35 American Painters and Sculptors" (exhibition, 1955), 352–54, 357, 588
Newhouse, S. I., 98, 513, 549–50, 554, 560, 571, 578, 586, 594, 608, 613, 614, 652n21[ch46], 661n4
"New Image Painting" (panel), 473
"New Images of Man" (exhibition, 1959), 434, 651n40
New Left, 575

"New London Situation" (exhibition, 1961), 508
Newman, Abraham (father), 11, 13, 15–18, 22–27, 30–32, 40, 41, 53, 75, 77, 78, 80, 88, 97–99, 113, 117, 138, 147, 164, 184–85, 198–99, 206, 221, 226, 260, 519, 621n9[ch2]
Newman, Annalee (née Greenhouse): appearance of, 65, 389, 425, 571–72, 610; assistance given to Barney in his causes and work, 132, 154, 224, 239, 264, 277, 391, 397, 408, 412, 418, 452, 496, 514, 518, 530, 535, 574, 582, 599–600, 606, 607–8; and Barney's death, 614–15; childlessness of, 141, 322, 643n13[ch35]; comments on Barney, his work, and the art world, 61–62, 67, 77, 101, 117, 177, 182, 228, 290, 317, 383, 400, 480, 495, 590, 611, 658n24; courtship and marriage of, 63–65, 69–71, 75, 77–81, *79*, 85, 96, 105, 224, 225, 574; dancing of, 375, 390, 511; family of, affected by World War II, 116, 128, 138; and family relationships, 41, 77, 226–27; finances managed by, 599–600; health of, 85, 196, 247; income of, 198, 446–47; ministrations to Barney for his health, 397, 408, 421, 425, 427, 496, 518, 613, 614; paintings given as gifts to, 213, 386, 600, 633n14[ch23], 654n21; personality/character of, 375, 599; photographs of, *50*, *61*, *88*, *120*, *322*, *390*, *403*, *440*, *442*, *455*; posthumous oversight of Barney's work by, 178, 193, 214, 254, 260, 387, 600, 615, 629n4, 655n6[ch51], 661n45, 665n47, 666n21; and the Reinhardt lawsuit, 364–65, 646n25; Reinhardt painting given to, 321, 336; rivalry with Sarah Newman, 80; socializing of, 162, 183, 241, 263, 277, 292, 297–300, 311–12, 316, 319–21, 335, 375, 525; teaching career of, 62–63, 88, 96, 100–102, 196, 224, 496, 517, 646n25; and World War II, 128; youth and education of, 62–64, 67, 96, 488
Newman, Anna (née Steinberg) (mother), 11, 13–15, 22, 25–27, 32, 41, 78, 98, 113, 198, 251, 263, 370, *455*, 456, 529, 536, 554
Newman, Arnold, 377
Newman, Barnett, architecture project for a synagogue, 2, 334, 495, 501–5, 595
Newman, Barnett, art and the art world: and the history of mid-century painting, 1, 223, 260, 280, 353–55, 384, 400, 406, 412–13, 417, 427, 431–33, 446, 474, 490, 527–30, 534, 552–53, 554–56, 560–61, 599, 602, 606, 611 (*see also* Newman, Barnett, statements and theories about art: on mid-century directions in art); art and artists admired/ignored/deplored by, 67, 123, 130–32, 139–40, 148, 176–77, 557, 561, 604 (*see also* contemporary art promoted by); art as a calling for, 1, 3–4, 76, 212; artistic training of, 11, 32–33, 41; art works owned by, 146, 153, 173, 198; avoidance of artist subculture, 40, 43, 48, 67, 76; contemporary art and artists championed by, 132–34, 149–50, 155–56, 159, 162–63, 168–69, 179, 182, 186, 191–92, 195–96, 201, 206, 213, 216, 259, 267–71, 376, 604, 639n21 (*see also* art and artists admired/ignored/deplored by); critics' and artists' reception of, 1, 2, 4, 195, 203–4, 212–13, 250, 253–58, 262, 264, 272, 287–91, 294, 298, 301–2, 308, 318–19, 323, 326–27, 329–30, 336–37, 338–39, 346–52, 354–57, 360–62, 370–71, 379, 382–83, 393, 399–401, 403–6, 410–11, 419–21, 441, 454, 457, 464–67, 471–74, 486–95, 506, 513, 520–22, 528–38, 545–47, 549, 551–53, 555–56,

Newman, Barnett (*continued*)
561, 586, 588–89, 591–94, 637n52, 648n14[ch42], 656n36[ch52], 659n17, 666n36; early, abandoned or non-existent, practice of art, 92, 101, 624n13[ch10], 625n30; exhibition of works by, 190, 192, 203, 212, 214, 215, 250, 252–58, 286–91, 359, 361–62, 379–84, 392, 397–404, 415, 417–23, *418*, 426, 436, 465–66, 468–75, 481, 484–86, 495–96, 500–506, 509–10, 515, 518, 520, 528–36, 539–40, 544, 547, 551–52, 554, *555*, 558, 562, 563, 570–72, 577, 580, 586–95, *590*, 602–4, *603*, 632n9[ch22], 633n6[ch24], 633n7[ch23], 662n15; gallery-related work of, 149–54, 159, 162, 182, 186–87, 189, 191–92, 195, 263–64, 272, 293; influence and legacy of Newman, 1, 167, 356, 359, 382, 441–42, 465, 469, 472–73, 486, 488, 491, 521–26, 528, 532, 545, 551, 553, 556, 564, 586, 601–3, 612–13; Jewish heritage as influence on Newman in, 20; mentorship provided by, 525; mother's influence on, 11; protection, preservation, restoration, and conservation of works, 382–83, 397, 418, 422–23, 436, 510, 518, 532, 539, 558, 572, 651n5; sales of work by, 203, 253, 364, 376, 381, 385, 410, 414–15, 437, 447, 451–52, 462, 466, 471, 491, 495, 509, 513–14, 520–21, 536, 549, 562, 567, 580–81, 585, 591, 597, 600, 614, 646n20, 654n21, 661n4, 664n30; self-conscious creation of himself as an artist, 2, 3–4, 76–77, 82–83, 100, 101, 109, 120, 139, 147, 162, 171–72, 175, 184, 191, 200–203, 206–7, 211–14, 237, 625n30; viewers' response to the works of, 1, 213, 249, 284, 288, 382, 401, 439, 445, 453, 489, 499–500, 541, 569, 640n14. *See also* American art

Newman, Barnett, drawings: on acetate, 563; doodles, 160–61, *161*, 180, 193, 334, 565, 566, 579, 630n1[ch20]; earliest surviving, 157, 160–62, *161*, 171, 629n4; for *Frank O'Hara / In Memory of My Feelings*, 563; given to Rosenberg on his birthday, 494; ornithology and botany notebooks as a source for, 118, 160, 629n5; return to, in 1960, 437; sketch of *Broken Obelisk*, 566–67; *Sketch of Rothko*, 474; statements on, 475–76, 488; for a synagogue, 2, 334, 501–5; ten-year hiatus in, 215; *Untitled* (1945), *181*; *Untitled* (1960), *437*; *The Void*, 485

Newman, Barnett, insults and wrongs felt and addressed by: artists' rights over their work, 598–99; art sales, 414–15; attacks on/slights of his integrity or his work, 256–57, 338, 428, 480–81, 510–12, 520, 532–34, 546, 554–55, 602; Belmont racetrack, 350–51; Betty Parsons, 375; Canaday, 433–35, 546; civil service, 72–75, 86–87; coop workers' status, 85–86; Ford Foundation, 413; Frankenthaler, 377; Glueck, 523–24; Greenberg, 347, 354–55, 423; Greenhouse patent lawsuit, 96–98, *97*, 118, 147, 147–48; Har-ithas's resignation from Corcoran, 583–84; Hess and *Art News*, 294–96, 355, 357–58, 419–20, 425; Hopps, 522–24, 528; Hunter, 554; insurance claims made by, 383–84, 436, 439, 474–75, 511–12, 572, 654n41; Irwin, 532; Jewell, 144–46; Kline, 413; landlord disputes, 85, 307, 352–54, 356–57, 407, 585, 614, 620n29; lawsuits involving or threatened by, 2, 56, 75, 85, 91, 96–98, 110, 113, 118–19, 147–48, 157, 291, 300, 307–8, 310, 331–32, 334–36, 338–39, 341–42, 351–52, 356–57, 364–67, 377, 415, 422, 439, 485, 497, 511–12, 524,

554–56, 562, 585, 649n37 (see also *Barnett Newman v. Ad Reinhardt and College Art Association*); Lippard, 554; MacArthur, 287, 371–72; misinterpretation of his work, 329–30, 347, 353–55, 431–33, 520, 522–24, 528–29, 560–61, 592–93, 613 (*see also* Newman, Barnett, statements and theories about art: on the reception of his art); modern American art debased and derided, 95, 130–34, 143–46, 219, 267–71, 268, 309, 324–26, 343–44, 465–66, 604, 628n49; Motherwell, 353–54, 559–61, 602, 662n13; on multiple fronts, 307, 341, 439, 520; Panofsky, 457–61; petty monetary claims made by, 332, 654n41; public mockery of, 546; refusal to forget, 601–2; Reinhardt, 2, 300, 334–36, 338–39, 341–42, 356, 365–67, 369, 377, 381, 449, 554–55, 599, 662n13, 662n15; Rose, 554; Rosenberg, 371–74; Rothko, 305, 344–45, 350, 412–13, 417, 602; São Paulo Bienale, 533–34; "Stances" taken by Newman, 111, 115, 123, 146, 158, 175, 206, 249, 292, 416, 604; the Stephans, 422, 650n40; Still, 417, 470–71; Tate exhibition, 510–12; taxi cab accident, 415–16; teaching, 42, 49, 88–93, 100–102, 110–12, 625n28; urban issues, 46, 71, 357, 446, 601; Willem de Kooning, 374; William Rubin, 555. *See also* Newman, Barnett, art and the art world: and the history of mid-century works; Newman, Barnett, life: moralizing/righteous tendencies of

Newman, Barnett, life: ancestors of, 16, 17, 22–23; appearance of, 3, 9, 15, 36, 37, 43, 49, 112, 167, 174, 224, 240, 253, 269, 277, 278, 284–85, 293, 305–6, 377, 381, 389, 397, 419–20, 429, 478, 491, 518, 530, 531, 535, 550, 552, 587; as artist-citizen, 67, 168, 314–15, 325, 332, 553, 555, 567–68, 573; attitudes about/behaviors toward women, 70–71, 81, 98, 141–42, 188, 240, 299, 454–55, 504–5, 536–37, 643n13[ch35], 648n14[ch41], 651n13[ch45]; bar mitzvah of, 9, 18–20, 503; birthday of, 3, 196, 207, 211–12, 237, 246, 257, 298, 364, 456, 537, 549, 587, 608; and books, 34, 120, 225–26, 610; Bronx childhood neighborhood of, 14–15, 21; courtship and marriage of, 41, *50*, 69–71, 75, 77–81, 79, 85, 96, 224, 225, 425, 427, 574; and dancing, 241, 506, 507, *508*, 511, 549; death of, 615; destruction of family houses, 620n29; drinking habit of, 116, 224, 241, 274, 329, 334, 337, 363, 370, 397, 421, 426, 438, 440–41, 444–45, 484, 496, 499, 502, 506, 517, 524, 525, 535, 604, 610, 611, 613, 650n31; education of, 9–11, 31–38; employment in the family business, 31, 40, 41, 68, 87–88; family of, affected by World War II, 138, 146; father figures for, 98; fictional representations of, 387–88; finances of, 85, 91, 117, 171, 198, 224, 252–53, 300, 321, 322, 329, 333, 337, 341, 381, 437, 446–47, 452, 466, 474, 478, 483, 514, 521, 596, 599–600, 653n2[ch49], 658n17; and food, 15; friendships of, 32–37, 43, 83, 98–99, 149–50, 159, 168, 173, 183–86, 189, 262, 297–300, 305, 311, 320, 370, 375–76, 380, 385, 388–89, 424–25, 427–28, 435, 441–45, 464–65, 497, 527, 589, 606, 613 (*see also* socializing of); gallery-related work of, 246, 309, 438, 495; government career of, 332–33; health and heart attacks of, 184, 196, 235, 247, 271, 305, 334, 353, 387, 390–91, 397, 406–9, 421, 423, 456, 482, 496–97, 501, 506,

518, 535, 553–55, 573, 595, 604–5, 607–8, 611–15, 648n14[ch41], 648n30 (*see also* drinking habit of; smoking habit of); interests and hobbies of, 40–41; Jewish heritage of, 2, 9, 11, 15–20, 48–49, 93–94, 99, 138–39, 165, 184–85, 199, 221, 225–29, 237, 287, 417, 499, 501–5, 520, 538, 542, 546, 559, 567–68, 570, 575, 578, 605, 613–14, 632n9[ch22], 634n34, 634n38, 634n46, 651n47, 663n20[ch60]); love for New York City, ii, 43–44, 102–4, 142, 262–63, 292, 320–21, 362–63, 369, 422, 439–41, 443, 445–47, 462, 470, 501, 554, 563–64; mayoral campaign of, 2, 3, 45, 55–59, 55, 74, 77–78, 89, 365, 446, 549; mentorship provided by, 98–99, 240, 262–63, 439, 454–55, 464, 645n34[ch36], 647n15[ch39]; moralizing/righteous tendencies of, 54, 85, 86, 88–89, 127–28, 137, 173, 240, 307, 329–30, 332, 334–35, 341–45, 350–58, 374–75, 377, 412–16, 422–23, 480–81, 485, 520, 528, 555, 585 (*see also* Newman, Barnett, insults and wrongs felt and addressed by); and music, 11, 65, 112–13, 119, 168, 189, 241, 263, 273, 276, 305, 321, 428, 440–41, 446, 456, 463, 463, 470, 511, 525, 542, 609–11; name of, 1, 3; parents of, 2, 11, 22–23; personality/character of, 2, 3, 13, 32, 83, 111, 195, 224, 240, 262, 274, 320–21, 329, 379, 388, 416, 421–22, 425, 438, 439–40, 480, 492, 508, 532, 588, 605, 612, 638n8 (*see also* appearance of; moralizing/righteous tendencies of; Newman, Barnett, insults and wrongs felt and addressed by); philosophical reflections and statements of, 1, 66–67, 76, 139, 160, 164, 171, 174, 175, 201, 428, 490, 494, 503–4, 543–44, 547–48, 559, 576 (*see also* Newman, Barnett, statements and theories about art); photographs of, ii, 6, 12, 21, 37, 50, 88, 107, 120, 208, 225, 253, 254, 266, 278, 284–85, 285, 297, 310, 322, 330, 390, 394, 403, 411, 426, 429, 440, 442, 455, 463, 499, 502, 508, 517, 531, 549, 550, 582, 587, 603, 608, 615, plate 16, plate 20; politics of, 2, 4–5, 10, 31, 69, 86, 93 (*see also* mayoral campaign of); relationship with his sister, Sarah, 80–82, 85, 105, 144; and religion, 76, 82, 175, 225, 320, 450, 519, 541, 547, 558–59, 592, 660n3 (*see also* Jewish heritage of); residences of, 14–15, 26–30, 44, 82, 85, 96, 112, 118–20, 119, 307, 331–32, 341, 352–53, 356–57, 364, 367, 369–70, 407–8, 483, 600–601, 608–10, 608, 609, 614, 620n29; sexuality of, 643n13[ch35]; sleeping habits and night owl tendencies, 93, 234–35, 263, 300, 321, 337, 367, 425, 535; smoking habit of, 116, 225, 278, 389, 397, 496, 526, 552, 553, 610, 611; socializing of, 162, 167, 183, 196, 225, 241, 263, 277, 292, 297–300, 311–12, 316, 319–21, 335, 375, 385, 388, 390, 407, 411, 439–45, 450, 462–63, 478, 505–9, 511, 517–18, 525–26, 549–50, 555, 561–62, 571, 580, 604–5, 607–8, 611–14, 631n27, 649n23[ch42] (*see also* friendships of); and sports, 2, 3, 5, 9, 15, 36, 44, 211, 214, 320, 324, 350, 363, 422, 445, 450, 462, 468, 477, 504–5, 507, 526, 598, 655n1[ch52]; summer vacations of, 78–81, 83, 87–88, 94, 105, 137, 147, 154, 166–68, 184–86, 247–49, 313, 336, 356, 383, 424; tax audits experienced by, 419, 562, 571, 585, 597, 650n12; teaching aspirations and career of, 40–43, 49, 68, 74–75, 77, 88–91, 96, 100, 109–11, 117, 157, 198, 238, 246, 272, 287, 333, 335, 350, 424–27, 479–80, 574, 644n30 (*see also* mentorship provided by); World's Fair press credentials, 107; and

World War II, 114–16, 126, 128–32, 135, 138–40, 146, 164, 171; youth of, 9–21, 27–30

Newman, Barnett, paintings: *Abraham* (plate 6), 98, 230, 246, 247, 252, 253–54, 260, 272, 284, 363, 380, 382–83, 384, 386, 397–98, 404, 418, 421, 519, 554–55, 597, 634n34, 637n25; *Achilles*, 307–8, 418, 470, 510, 634n34; *Adam*, 289, 291–92, 308, 330, 364, 381, 397–98, 404, 410, 432, 452; *Anna's Light*, 98, 536, 586, 591, 593, 603; *Argos*, 252; *Be* (later called *Be I*), 111, 246, 247, 252, 253, 262, 418, 479, 607, 633n18[ch23], 637n50; *Be II* (previously called *Resurrection*), 479, 485, 539–41, 649n14; *The Beginning*, 418; *Black Fire*, 510, 634n34; *Broken Obelisk* (plate 19), 664n30, 664n33; *By Twos*, 246, 451; *Cathedra* (plate 12), 301, 308–9, 363, 410, 418, 421, 423, 430, 436, 470–71, 518, 525, 533, 571–72, 594, 600, 614, 643n5[ch34], 651n5, 654n21; *Chartres*, 587, 590, 592–93, 666n36; *Concord*, 246, 247, 253, 397–98, 404, 603; *Covenant*, 246, 253, 254, 418, 603, 634n34; dating of, 193, 214–15, 236–37, 292, 308, 384–87, 637n25; *Day Before One*, 310, 410, 415, 421, 511; *Day One*, 289, 310, 418, 466–67, 470, 479, 654n21; *Death of Euclid*, 201, 212, 214, 355, 474, 646n37; *Dionysius* (plate 9), 246, 254, 421, 436, 634n34, 648n17[ch42]; *End of Silence*, 111, 212, 214, 246, 253, 633n7[ch23]; *L'Errance* (plate 13), 322–23, 418, 462, 491; *Euclidian Abyss* (*Black with Yellow*), 193, 194, 203, 215, 417, 418, 603; *Eve*, 289, 291, 330, 446, 536–37; *Galaxy*, 633n6[ch24], 648n17[ch42]; *The Gate*, 386, 418, 562, 570, 585, 634n34; *Gea* (plate 1), 192–93, 474, 576; *Genesis—The Break* (plate 2), 180, 201, 215, 422, 611, 649n2[ch44]; *Genetic Moment*, 193, 212; *Here, Here, Here*, 111; *Horizon Light*, 252, 253, 254, 330, 359, 362, 397–98, 424, 442, 474; *Jericho*, 591–94, 603, 666n36; *Joshua*, 289, 491, 524, 634n34, 665n28[ch63]; materials of, 230, 247, 252, 284, 382, 562; *Moment*, 212; *The Moment I*, 479; *The Name I*, 246; *The Name II*, 284, 614; *No. 7*, 359; *Noon-Light*, 495, 509–12; *Not There—Here*, 111, 479; *Now II*, 553, 562; *Onement*, 380, 382, 463; *Onement I* (plate 4), 206–7, 211–15, 230, 237, 260, 386, 418, 609, 633n7[ch23]; *Onement II*, 214, 250, 418, 633n7[ch23], 646n20; *Onement III*, 214, 253, 254, 418, 597, 603; *Onement IV*, 230, 246, 418, 506; *Onement V*, 421; *Onement VI* (plate 15), 322–23, 470–74, 491, 587; *Outcry*, 407, 408, 479, 527, 549, 661n4; *Pagan Void* (plate 3), 162, 180, 193, 408, 603, 609, 611, 633n14[ch23]; *Primordial Light*, 386, 408, 418, 495, 509–10, 514; *Profile of Light*, 535, 570, 572; *Prometheus Bound*, 307, 418, 423, 451, 462, 603, 634n34; *The Promise*, 246, 253, 254, 262, 422–23, 650n47; *Queen of the Night*, 364, 381, 634n34; *Queen of the Night II*, 553, 562; *Red, Yellow and Blue IV*, 613; *Right Here*, 111, 386, 495, 570, 608; *Shimmer Bright*, 587–88; *Shining Forth (To George)*, 468, 469, 495, 497, 506, 525, 594, 603; *The Stations of the Cross: Lema Sabachthani*, 2, 228, 408–9, 437–39, 445, 456, 468, 495, 515, 518–20, 538–51, 540, 553, 556, 562, 563, 594, 608, 634n46, 649n13, 660n11, 661n45; "study" for *Vir Heroicus Sublimis*, 289, 391; *The Third*, 479, 485, 495, 528; *The Three*, 509–10; titles of, 259, 485, 519, 632n9[ch22], 634n34; *Treble*, 456; *Tundra*, 253, 259, 418, 418, 421, 452, 536, 594; *Two Edges*, 201,

Newman, Barnett, paintings (*continued*)
212, 214, 235–37, *236*, 254, 609; *Ulysses*, 307, 510,
634n34; *Untitled* (1945), 193; *Untitled (The Break)*,
611; *Untitled 1, 1948*, 214; *Untitled 1, 1950*, 650n40;
Untitled 2, 1948 (plate 5), 214; *Untitled 3, 1950*, 289;
Untitled 4, 1950, 289; *Untitled I, 1949*, 246; *Uriel* (plate
14), 385–86, *418*, 485, 509; vandalization of, 257, 382,
594–95, 643n6[ch34]; *Vir Heroicus Sublimis* (plate
11), 111, 286–89, 291–92, *297*, 363, 372, 380, 382–83,
405, 408, 418, 419, 452–53, 457–62, 525, 532–33, 594,
597, 640n12; *The Voice* (plate 7), 230, 284, 289, 418,
506, 514, 597; *Voice of Fire* (plate 18), 558, 572, 586;
The Way, 111, 495, 634n34; *The Way I*, 408; *White
and Hot*, 591; *White Fire*, 491, 634n34; *White Fire
I*, 386, 507; *White Fire II*, 456, 462, 465, 473, *590*,
653n9[ch49]; *White Fire III*, 507, 540; *White Fire
IV*, 586–88; *Who's Afraid of Red, Yellow and Blue I*,
552–54, *590*, 603, 661n18; *Who's Afraid of Red, Yellow
and Blue II*, 553, 562, 572; *Who's Afraid of Red, Yellow
and Blue III* (plate 20), 553, 587, 591, 594; *The Wild*
(plate 10), 284–85, *285*, 289, 485, 597; *The Word
I*, 212, 609; *The Word II*, 386, 408, 549; working
methods of, 273–75, 355, 438–39, 475, 492, 494, 606,
654n45; *Yellow Edge*, 450, 604, 611; *Yellow Painting*
(plate 8), 246, 252, 253, 262, 479
Newman, Barnett, prints: *Cantos* portfolio, 498–500,
515, 518, 528, 531, 579, *609*, 660n11; etchings, 578;
lithographs, 456; *Notes*, 579, 610, 664n27
Newman, Barnett, sculpture: *Broken Obelisk* (plate 19),
495, 564–70, 573, 577–78, 580–85, *582*, 588, 592, 595,
603, 613, 615, 663n17[ch61]; *Here I*, 285–86, *286*, 289,
312, 363, 477–78, 501, 547, 577, 592, 655n6[ch51];
Here I (To Marcia), 477, 530, 532, 603, 608; *Here II*,
530–32, 531, *533*, 539–40, 565, 567, 569, 577, 580, 597;
Here III, 551, 552, 566–67, 577, 591, 603; *Lace Curtain
for Mayor Daley*, 577–78, *577*, 595; *Zim Zum*, 587,
591, 595, 665n47
Newman, Barnett, statements and theories about art: on
art as a brand/product, 259, 284, 318, 337, 450, 474,
516, 542, 548; on art criticism/scholarship, 155, 158,
177–78, 202, 267, 295–96, 313–16, 332, 453, 516–17,
529, 563, 572–73, 664n10[ch62]; on art history,
108, 155, 204, 205, 231–32, 376–77, 476, 497, 571;
on artistic creation, 181, 199–200, 211–12, 248–49,
259, 273–74, 284, 287, 315, 372–74, 398, 438, 450,
456, 475–76, 488–89, 519, 654n45; criticisms of the
misuses/misdirections of art, 38, 88–89, 123, 126–28,
143–44, 148, 157–58, 176, 179, 219, 315, 324–26, 332,
344–45, 353–54, 362, 368, 373, 397, 431–32, 455, 516,
557, 629n3; on drawing, 475–76, 488; general theories and principles, 3, 174–76, 313–16; on lithography,
500; on the meaning and purpose of art, 1, 2, 18, 33,
38, 66–67, 76, 88–89, 94–95, 123, 128, 140, 159–60,
166, 177, 181, 193, 201, 251, 284, 426–27, 475–76, 480,
489, 494, 519, 523, 531, 534, 538–39, 552, 556, 559,
574, 610, 612; on mid-century directions in art, 83,
108–11, 126–28, 130–33, 139, 140, 143–44, 158,
163–64, 177, 202–4, 213, 221–22, 232, 266–67, 282,
330–31, 519, 528–29, 656n16 (*see also* Newman,
Barnett, art and the art world: and the history of
mid-century works); motivations and meanings of
individual works, 568, 578, 581, 595; ornithology

metaphor in, 314–16; on political significance of art,
2, 56, 94–95, 110–11, 296, 319, 373, 531, 572–74; on
the primacy of the artist over the art, 10, 66–67, 76,
108–9, 166, 196, 235, 265–66, 288, 516, 525, 542, 559,
571, 573; on the reception of his work, 323–24, 362,
372–73, 383–84, 402, 431–33, 469, 494–95, 497,
522–25, 528, 558, 561, 590, 612 (*see also* Newman,
Barnett, art and the art world: and the history of
mid-century works; Newman, Barnett, insults and
wrongs felt and addressed by: misinterpretations of
his work); on the role of ideas/thought in art,
38, 150, 160, 168, 174, 176–77, 180, 191, 206, 288,
556; on self-evident/concrete/immediate quality
of art, 195, 211, 232, 235, 248, 267, 284, 285, 288, 331,
475, 489, 494, 499, 552. *See also* Newman, Barnett,
writings
Newman, Barnett, studios: 110 Wall Street, 272–73, *274*,
275, 284, 289, 301, 307–10, 356, 639n48; 114 Fourth
Avenue, 190; 304 East Nineteenth Street, 230; Carnegie Hall, 446, 450, 468, 501, 521, 564, 607; Front
Street, 28, 211, 310, *310*, *311*, 321, *330*, 361, 363, 379, 397,
408, 410, 419, 455, 468, 477, 483, 502, 505, 509, 521,
534, 552, 562, 563–64, 571–72, 585–86; as a sacred,
dedicated space, 273–75, 310, 427, 438–39, 444, 559,
562, 574, 606; search for his first, 171; visits to, 273,
285, 289, 301, 308–9, 363, 379, 397, 410, 444–45,
468–69, 471, 477, 509, 515, 586, 592; West End apartment, 521, 604, 611; White Street, 578, 585–86, 589,
606–7, *607*, 612, 616
Newman, Barnett, watercolors: *Studio in the Country*, 92,
624n9[ch10], 625n30
Newman, Barnett, writings: "The Anglo-Saxon Tradition
in Art Criticism," 155, 177–78; *The Answer*, 72–74;
"Are We Servants?," 74; "Arshile Gorky: Poet and
Immolator," 221–22; "Artists Prefer Schoolteachers," 140, 141–43; "The Art of the South Seas," 189,
666n36; on the Barnes Foundation, 38; catalogue
essay on Gottlieb, 149–50; "Deadly Weapons" (on
automobiles), 46, 71; Ferber exhibition catalogue
essay, 196; "The First Man Was an Artist," 163,
199–200, 202, 542, 548, 574; "Free as the Seas,"
73; "The Future of the A B C Crap," 140; Hofmann
exhibition catalogue essay, 195; "The Ideographic
Picture" exhibition catalogue essay, 191, 206, 556–57,
559; "Introduction," for Kropotkin's *Memoirs of a
Revolutionist*, 574–75; "It Must Be Destroyed!: The
TRUE Story of the Citizens' Budget Commission,
Inc.," 74; "The Literature of the Jewish People,"
17–18, 542; "Milton Avery," 163; "monologues,"
158; "The Museum of Modern Art—A Failure,"
148, 152; "The New Sense of Fate," 204–6, 213–14,
230; on Newspaper Row, 46; on New York, 102–4;
"Ohio, 1949," 250–51; "On Modern Art: Inquiry and
Confirmation," 155; "The Painting of Tamayo and
Gottlieb," 160, 163, 192; "The Plasmic Image," 145,
155, 163, 175–79; poetry, 34–35, 140; Pre-Columbian
Stone Sculpture exhibition catalogue essay, 151;
"The Problem of Subject Matter," 155, 231; "Problems of the Teachers," 101; publication of, 490, 574,
656n37[ch52]; review of paintings by Roger Fry, 35;
review of Thomas Hess's *Abstract Painting*, 295–96;
rhetoric of, 16, 20, 46, 100–102, 132, 295; "Rhymes

for a Bombed Out Nursery," "Lullaby," 165–66; "Rhymes for a Bombed Out Nursery," "Prayer," 169–71; sonnet for Annalee, 69–71; Stamos exhibition catalogue essay, 195; "Story of Communism, or 'Hope' by An Anarchist," 60–61, 141; style of, 34–35; "The Sublime Is Now," 230–32; "Surrealism and the War," 164; "Teachers' Exams—What Is Wrong?," 74–75; "To Archie Upon The Occasion Of His Prolegomena," 61; "To Joseph on the Occasion of His Seventh Birthday," 116; "To a young poet age 4," 117, 221–22; "What About Isolationist Art?," 128–32, 143, 270. See also Newman, Barnett, statements and theories about art

Newman, Elie (uncle), 117

Newman, Ethel (sister-in-law), 455

Newman, George (brother), 11, 12, 13, 15, 27, 40, 41, 77, 80, 90, 128, 451, 455–56, 455, 462, 469

Newman, Gertrude "Goldie" (sister), 11, 12, 13, 27, 80, 113, 198, 455, 456, 529

Newman, Menkes & Tikotsky, 31

Newman, Morris (uncle), 28, 30–31

Newman, Muriel Kallis Steinberg, 506, 514, 597

Newman, Sarah (sister): as an artist, 43, 76, 80–82, 91, 92, 122, 144, 171; on Barney's work, 660n11; college education of, 488; in the family business, 80, 87; and family relationships, 25, 99, 113, 198, 529; government career of, 82, 128, 171, 287, 658n23; government investigations of, 332–33; personality/character of, 81, 82; photographs of, 12, 455; relationship with Barney, 80–82, 85, 105, 144, 157, 184, 263, 456; rivalry with Annalee, 80; teaching jobs of, 43, 80, 91; and World War II, 128, 137, 147; youth of, 11

New Republic (magazine), 383–84

New School for Social Research, 75, 101, 122, 128, 579

Newspaper Row, 45–46

newspapers, 44–46

Newsweek (magazine), 92, 419, 434, 512, 513, 519–21, 536, 544, 577

"New Talent 1950" (exhibition), 264–65

New Tenement Law, 27

New World Writing, 367

"New York 13" (exhibition, 1969), 586

New York Artists Strike Against Racism, Sexism, Repression and War, 613

New York Central Supply, 272, 386

New York City: art scene in, 183, 194–96, 214, 217, 220, 222–24, 241–44, 246, 265–72, 280, 282–83, 289, 292–93, 299, 303–4, 311, 367, 388, 398, 424, 428–29, 429, 512, 526, 562, 638n30 (see also New York School; Studio 35; Subjects of the Artist School); Cleopatra's Needle (Obelisk), Central Park, 443, 567; Cue magazine on twentieth-century changes in, 261–62; influenza epidemic in, 21; Jews in, 27–30, 46, 53, 663n16[ch61]; Lower East Side, 26–30, 36; mid-century cultural growth of, 182–83; Newman's love for, 3, 43–44, 102–4, 142, 262–63, 292, 320–21, 362–63, 369, 422, 439–41, 443, 445–47, 462, 470, 501, 554, 563–64; public education system in, 11–13; "Sculpture in Environment" program, 565; World's Fair (1939), 106–8, 120, 125; World's Fair (1964), 507, 512. See also Bronx, New York

New York City Ballet, 232

New York Committee to Aid Victims of German Fascism, 55

New York Daily Mirror (newspaper), 325

New Yorker (magazine), 211, 219, 277, 291, 392, 404, 430, 448, 477

New York Herald Tribune (newspaper), 45, 153, 269–70, 275, 300, 338, 446, 545, 604

New York International Exposition of Science, Art, and Industries (1918), 20–21

New York Mirror (newspaper), 446

"New York Painting and Sculpture: 1940–1970" (exhibition, 1969), 587, 588, 602–4, 603, 615

New York Post (newspaper), 45, 92, 93, 113, 144, 269, 309, 486, 545, 569

New York School, 81, 137, 194, 219–20, 245, 276, 361, 409–10, 429, 451, 478, 525, 529, 560, 587, 603–4, 639n24, 658n33[ch56]; downtown arm of, 204–5, 223, 255, 283, 413, 448–49, 473, 478. See also Abstract Expressionism; New York City: art scene in

"New York School: The First Generation" (exhibition, 1965), 526–29

New York State Commissioner of Education, 100

New York State Department of Law, 75

New York State Pavilion, Flushing Meadow Park, 507, 657n3[ch55]

New York Sun (newspaper), 45, 150, 250

New York Supreme Court, 352, 357

New York Teacher (magazine), 91

New York Times (newspaper), 44, 45, 48, 57, 66, 75, 91, 93, 95, 96, 100, 105, 124, 132, 133, 138, 150, 153, 163, 168, 184, 189, 219, 239, 253, 257, 267–69, 287, 294, 300, 301, 309, 324, 332, 360, 364, 367, 372, 399, 412, 419, 433–34, 446, 456, 469, 486, 522–24, 533, 536–38, 546, 553, 568, 584, 588, 594, 597–99, 601, 604, 632n8[ch22], 638n62

New York Times Magazine, 140, 153, 574

New York Tribune building, 45

New York University, 67, 96, 195, 234, 246, 637n53, 644n30; Institute of Fine Arts, 379

New York Wednesday Answer (newspaper). See The Answer

New York World-Telegram (newspaper), 45, 55–56, 55, 74, 219, 253, 269, 628n49

New York Yankees, 282, 422, 445. See also Yankee Stadium

Nicholas I, Tsar, 22, 24

Nicholas II, Tsar, 24

Niebuhr, Reinhold, 101

Niemeyer, Oscar, 217, 532, 535

Nierendorf Gallery, 157, 183

Nietzsche, Friedrich, 109; The Birth of Tragedy, 214

"19 Young Americans" (exhibition, 1950), 267–68, 638n26

Ninth Street Show (1951), 282–83, 289, 319. See also Stable Gallery

Nixon, Richard, 454

Noë, Hans, 98, 262–63, 288, 503, 506

Noguchi, Isamu, 261, 551

Noland, Kenneth, 423, 487, 509, 513–14, 551

Nonagon gallery, 449

North American Committee to Aid Spanish Democracy, 94

Northwest Coast Indian art, 157, 160, 187–89, 455, 631n8
Nye, Gerald Prentice, 129

O'Brien, John P., 48, 56, 59, 89
Odets, Clifford, 43
Oedipus myth, 126, 206, 214, 227
L'Oeil (magazine), 491
Oelrichs, Blanche Marie Louise (pen name: Michael Strange), 241
Oelrichs, Dorothy Haydel "Dumpy," 182, 190
Office of Indian Affairs, U.S. Department of the Interior, 188
Office of Strategic Service (OSS), 82, 128, 333
Ogunquit, Maine, 78–81, 79, 83, 105
O'Hara, Frank, 253, 303, 377, 491, 518–19, 553, 563
Ohio, vacation trip to, 247–49. See also earthworks, Native American
Okada, Kenzo, 411, 425
Oklahoma! (musical), 182
Oldenburg, Claes, 399, 492, 513–14, 576–77; Ghost Toaster, 513; Giant Soft Fan, 558; Soft Typewriter, 513
Old Peking (restaurant), 502
Olitski, Jules, 487, 612
Olmsted, Frederick Law, 408
Olsen, Fred, 298, 362
"Open Letter to Roland Redmond, President of the Metropolitan Museum of Art," 269
Opportunity Gallery, 42
Order of the Sons of Zion, 15
originality, 231, 292, 401, 561. See also Newman, Barnett, art and the art world: and the history of mid-century painting
ornithology/birdwatching, 41, 116, 118, 160, 314–16, 336, 454, 573, 616, 629n5
Orozco, José Clemente, 75, 160
Orwell, George, Animal Farm, 182
Osis, Karlis, 497, 656n38[ch53]
Osman, Prince, 153
Ossorio, Alfonso, 136, 159, 190, 298, 303, 308, 312, 323–24, 339–40, 345, 346, 349–50, 359, 379, 641n17, 643n18[ch35], 650n40
Otto, Rudolf, The Idea of the Holy, 225
"Our Country and Our Culture" (symposium), 311
outcry. See cry/outcry/geshray

Paalen, Wolfgang, 156–57, 187
Paasche spray gun, 230
Pace, Stephan, 646n7
pacifism, 5, 114–15, 128
Paderewski, Jan, 446
Pageant (magazine), 411
Painters Painting (film), 542
"Paintings After 1945 in New York" (exhibition, 1967), 570
Palestine, 221, 567, 630n22[ch20]
Pal Joey (musical), 542
Panofsky, Erwin, 2, 35, 457–61, 549, 653n24
Paolozzi, Edward, 506, 508
Paris Brest (restaurant), 506, 518
Paris Herald Tribune (newspaper), 332
Parke-Bernet Galleries, 514, 536, 544
Parker, Charlie "Yardbird," 262, 428, 611

Parker, Raymond, 434, 478
Parkinson, Elizabeth Bliss, 546
Parsons, Betty, 149–51, 153, 158–59, 162–63, 181–82, 183, 186–87, 189–91, 195–98, 234, 242, 246, 247, 252, 264, 271–72, 280, 285–86, 285, 290–94, 300–303, 306–7, 309, 316, 319–20, 321, 322, 327–28, 336, 341–42, 359–60, 361, 375, 397, 402, 404, 415, 422, 436, 441, 454, 474, 495, 505, 520, 631n27, 642n9, 649n23[ch42], 651n21, 662n44. See also Betty Parsons Gallery
Parsons School of Design, 42
Partisan Review (magazine), 43, 94, 116, 220, 231, 233, 253, 289, 294, 296, 301, 303, 311, 320, 346, 348, 356, 358, 375, 448
Pasadena Art Museum, 479
Pasilis, Felix, 646n7
Pasmore, Victor, 506, 508
Passion of Christ, 438, 495, 542–43, 545, 548. See also Newman, Barnett, paintings: The Stations of the Cross: Lema Sabachthani
Passover, 226, 228, 240, 305, 439, 494, 559
Patai, Raphael, 503
Pathé Frères, "A Detective's Tours of the World," 238
Pavia, Philip, 136, 183, 204, 256, 434, 612
Payton, Benjamin, 547
Pearl Harbor attack, 117, 126, 128–30, 132, 139
Pearl Paint, 600, 607, 611
Peck, Priscilla, 320
Pegler, Westbrook, 45, 334, 644n25[ch36]
Pei, I. M., 501, 600, 657n7[ch54]
Pelé, 532, 534
Pelham Bay Park, 15
Penn, Irving, 277, 549; "8 New York Painters," 429, 429
Pennsylvania Turnpike, 247
Peridot Gallery, 285
"The Perils of Pauline" (film), 475
Perls, Frank, 279, 529, 639n24
Perreault, John, 593
Pétain, Philippe, 114
Petit Palais, Paris, 570
Philadelphia Museum, 547, 569
philistinism, 131, 174, 178, 229, 291, 295, 314, 345, 573, 636n31
Phillips, Duncan, 153
Phillips Collection, Washington, D.C., 660n3
philosophy, 36, 62. See also Newman, Barnett, life: philosophical reflections and statements of
Picasso, Pablo, 33, 75, 80, 108, 122, 123, 132, 133, 163, 164, 174, 187, 202, 231, 361, 398, 405, 451, 472, 509, 516, 563, 596
Piero della Francesca, 344
Pierre Matisse Gallery, 211, 285, 636n12[ch27]
Pinkas Synagogue, Prague, 503
Pinza, Ezio, 117
Piraikon Theatron, 470
Pirkei Avot, 228, 543–44
Pissarro, Camille, 33, 123, 231, 295, 325, 346, 376–77, 427, 647n3[ch40]
Pittsburgh (Carnegie) International (exhibition), 357, 391, 393, 403, 410, 465–66, 472, 514
Planter's Peanut Corporation, 71
"plasmic," 175–77
plastic quality, in art, 68, 108, 122–23, 126, 133, 176

Plato, 54, 109

Platt, Charles, 517

Plaut, James S., 218–19, 233

Plaza Hotel, 375; Oak Room, 550

PM (newspaper), 113, 283

Poetry (magazine), 37

Poland: Jews in, 16, 17, 22–26; in World War II, 105

polio, 41, 71

politics. *See* Anarchism; Communist Party/Communism; Newman, Barnett, life: mayoral campaign of; Newman, Barnett, life: politics of; Newman, Barnett, statements and theories about art: on political significance of art

Pollack, Harry, 128

Pollock, Charles, 135

Pollock, Jackson, 2, 38, 122, 132, 135, 162, 183, 187, 192, 195–96, 223, 228, 230, 233, 235, 239, 242–44, 246, 247, 250, 259, 262–63, 268, 271, 272, 273, 275, 277, *278*, 279, 282, 285, 286, 288, 290, 291, 293–94, 296–306, *297*, 311–12, 316–18, 319, 321, 324, 327, 336, 337, 338, 346, 347, 349–50, 359–64, 367–68, 370, 374, 376, 378, 383, 384, 389, 390, 397, 400, 410, 430, 440, 448, 449, 457, 466, 472, 478, 491, 513–14, 529, 533, 537, 551, 553, 560–61, 589, 596, 597, 603–4, 612, 631n27, 631n43, 633n10[ch23], 638n30, 641n17, 642n31[ch33], 644n18[ch35]; *Autumn Rhythm*, 289; *Blue Poles*, 311, 317, 362, 431, 452; *Cathedral*, 234; *Lavender Mist*, 644n18[ch35]; *Night Dance*, 359–60; *Number 1*, 286; *Number 2, 1949*, 472, *plate 15*; *One*, 452

Poons, Larry, 99, 463, 505, 522, 525, 532, 549, 555, 558, 612, 632n6[ch22], 652n30

Pop art, 378, 463, 484, 486–87, 490, 516, 533, 541, 550

Pope, Alexander, 54

Popular Front, 75, 105

Popular Science Monthly (magazine), 117

Porter, Fairfield, 122, 646n7

Portland Art Museum, Oregon, 514

"The Portrait and the Modern Artist" (exhibition, 1943), 149

Portuguese Synagogue, Amsterdam, 504, 570

Poses Institute of Fine Arts, Brandeis University, Waltham, Massachusetts, 473, 481–83, 495, 496

Possibilities (magazine), 631n17

Post, George B., 14

"Post-Abstract Painting 1950: France, America" (exhibition), 272

Post-Impressionism, 325

The Postman Always Rings Twice (film), 183

"Post-Painterly Abstraction" (exhibition, 1964), 516

Pound, Ezra, 34, 371–72

Pousette-Dart, Evelyn, 225, 322

Pousette-Dart, Richard, 162, 201, 216, 225, 276, *278*, 293, 359, 598, 638n20

Power, Alan, 98, 421–22, 440, 454, 481, 507, 509–10, 610

Power, E. J. (Ted), 378, 404, 421–22, 451, 481, 507, 540

Powers, John, 586

Pratt Institute, 88, 412, 456, 499

"Pre-Columbian Stone Sculpture" (exhibition, 1943), 150–54

Presley, Elvis, 473

Preston, Stuart, 253, 264, 267, 268, 270, 272, 284, 289, 301, 399

Priede, Zigmunds, 498–99, *499*

"Primary Structures" (exhibition, 1966), 501, 545

"primitive" art, 66, 151, 157, 176–77, 180, 189, 202, 203, 596

printmaking. *See* aquatint; etching; lithography; silk-screen printing

privacy, Newman's concern with, 342, 377, 415, 450, 463, 575, 611

"Problems and Issues in Art Today" (symposium, 1964), 516–18

Produce Exchange building, 446

Prohibition, 31, 34, 45, 61

Prokofiev, Sergei, 218

protests. *See* demonstrations/protests/riots

Proust, Marcel, 166

Provincetown, Massachusetts, 166–68, 184–86, 198, 244–45, 272

Psalm 22, 543

Psalm 24, 476

Public Works of Art Project, 42

Pulitzer, Joseph, 46

Pulitzer, Joseph, Jr., 591

Pulitzer, Ralph, Jr., 153

Pulitzer Building, 45, 72

Pulitzer Prize, 404

pure thought/idea, as basis of art, 160, 191, 206, 288, 289, 556

Purism, 232, 398, 410

Putzel, Howard, 162–63, 167, 168, 171, 183

Quakers, 129

Queens College, 88–89

Rabbi Stephen Wise Free Synagogue, 78

Rabinovitch, Renee, 164, 185

racetracks, 2, 274, 334, 341, 350–52, 446, 478, 507, 535, 554

Racine, Jean, 64, 441, 623n6[ch6]

radio, 44, 183, 270

Raeburn, Ben, 574, 576

Rahv, Philip, 320

Raisin, Max, 17

Raphael, *Madonna of the Chair*, 108

Rappaport, Abe, 164

Rashi (Shlomo ben Yitzhaki), 76, 199, 624n11[ch8], 632n9[ch22]

Rasmussen, Waldo, 569

Ratner's (restaurant), 321

Rattner, Abraham, 299

Rauschenberg, Robert, 289, 361, 399–400, 431, 491, 498, 501, 512–14, 521, 536, 558, 612, 646n7, 656n16; *Bed*, 399, 513; *Canyon*, 513; *Monogram*, 509; *Odalisk*, 399; *Rebus*, 399; "Statue of Liberty" happening, 549; *Tracer*, 513

Raynor, William, 454

RCA Building, 59

Read, Herbert, 89, 114, 155, 243, 249

"Recent American Synagogue Architecture" (exhibition, 1963), 501–5

Red Channels: The Report of Communist Influence in Radio and Television, 270

Red Cross, 128

Redding, Otis, 441

Redmond, Roland, 269, 309

Redon, Odilon, 80, 108

"Red Skelton Hour" (television show), 519

Reed Studios, Gloucester, Massachusetts, 137

Regina Five, 427

regionalism, 131, 143, 157–58

Reid, Norman, 512

Reinhardt, Ad, 2, 56, 137, 162, 186, 190, 192, 198, 203, 224, 228, 239, 241, 246, 250, 257, 260, 265, 268–71, 275–77, *278*, 279–82, 283, 292–93, 298–302, 304, 309, 316, 319, 321–22, *322*, 325–35, 338–42, 344, 347, 351, 352, 356–57, 360–62, 365–67, 372–73, 375, 377–81, 383, 386–87, 392, 410, 413, 449, 463, 483, 510–11, 550, 551, 553–56, 559, 561, 599, 602, 603, 613, 632n6[ch23], 638n20, 639n21, 645n34[ch36], 655n1[ch52], 658n24, 662n13, 662n15, 662n40, 662n41, 662n44; "The Artist in Search of an Academy," 326–27, 331, 333–34, 338–39, 366–67; "Founding Fathers Follyday," 331; *Modern Artists in America, First Series* (with Robert Motherwell), 212, 237; "Museum Racing Form," 299; "A Nosegay for the Art-Schmeckers," 304; "A Portend of the Artist as a Yhung Mandala," 367. See also *Barnett Newman v. Ad Reinhardt and College Art Association*

Reinhardt, Rita (formerly Salomon, née Ziprkowski), 292, 299–301, 316, 321–22, *322*, 327, 331, 335, 542, 598

Reis, Bernard, 497

Reise, Barbara, 193, 212, 408, 554, 577, 604–5, 611, 632n8[ch22], 633n7[ch23], 666n36; "The Stance of Barnett Newman," 604–5

religion, Newman and, 76, 82, 175, 225, 320, 450, 519, 541, 547, 575–59, 592, 660n3. *See also* Jews and Judaism

Rembrandt van Rijn, 107, 361, 523, 570

Remenick, Seymour, 646n7

Renoir, Pierre-Auguste, 33

Resnick, Milton, 137, 190, 228, 244, 258, 448–49, 646n7

Reuben's (restaurant), 450, 506

La Revista Belga (magazine), 152, 154, 155, 180, 206

Rexroth, Kenneth, 202

Reynal, Jeanne, 230, 241, 390, 397, 407, *411*, 442, 474, 497, 505, 648n30

Reynolds, Quentin, 334, 644n25[ch36]

Ribicoff, Abraham, 578

Rich, Daniel Catton, 433

"Richard J. Daley" (exhibition, 1968), 577

Richardson, Brenda, 161, 437

Richardson, Henry Hobson, 438

Riis, Jacob, 26; *How the Other Half Lives*, 30

Riley, Maude Kemper, 192–93

Riley, Orrin, 510

Rinaldi, Giulio, 462, 468

riots. *See* demonstrations/protests/riots

Riportella, 651n5

risk, for artist, 112, 139, 145, 287, 318, 447–50

Ritchie, Andrew C., 233, 300, 639n26; *Abstract Painting and Sculpture in America*, 490

ritual, Newman's concern with, 139, 175, 188, 199, 310, 320

Ritz Towers, 321

Rivera, Diego, 59, 94, 160

Rivers, Larry, 377, 463, 465, 478, 498, 505, 513, 536, 551, 646n7

Riverside Museum, 122–23, 143, 162

Rivoli Theatre, 638n62

Robbins, Tom, 317

Robertson, Bryan, 393, 480–81, 508–9, 662n44

Robeson, Paul, 96

Rockefeller, David, 601

Rockefeller, John D., 13

Rockefeller, Nelson, 59, 152, 362, 571, 596

Rollins, Sonny, 428

Roosevelt, Franklin Delano, 331, 625n3[ch11]

Roosevelt, Mrs. Theodore, Jr., 153

Roosevelt, Sara, 132

Rosand, David, 288

Rosati, James, 204

"Rosc—the poetry of vision" (exhibition, 1967), 562–63, 570, 664n10[ch62]

Rose, Barbara, 410, 526, 554, 555, 610

Rose, Billy, 153

Rose, Herman, 604

Rose Art Museum, Brandeis University, Waltham, Massachusetts, 473–74

Rosenberg, David, 449

Rosenberg, Harold, 4, 81, 212–13, 218, 227, 236, 250, 317–19, 333, 347, 370–74, 377, 378, 399–400, 405, 434–35, 449, 450, 481, 489–94, 496, 505, 516–18, *517*, 523, 542, 572, 574, 591, 593, 613, 614, *615*, 631n17, 639n26, 646n5[ch39], 651n47, 664n10[ch62]; "The American Action Painters," 317–18; "Barnett Newman, 'A Man of Controversy, and Spiritual Grandeur'", 491–93, 587; "The Herd of Independent Minds: Has the Avant-Garde Its Own Mass Culture?," 231; "Literary Form and Social Hallucination," 448

Rosenberg, Julius and Ethel, 287, 640n18

Rosenberg, May, *615*

Rosenberg, Paul, and Rosenberg Gallery, 132–34, 159, 163

Rosenblum, Robert, 457, 653n24

Rosenborg, Ralph, 638n20

Rosenman Goldmark Colin & Kaye, 341, 352

Rosenquist, James, 463, 558, 577, 593; *F-111*, 445, 541

Rosh Hashanah, 199, 336, 604

Roskolenko, Harry, 28

Rosset, Barney, 413

Roszak, Theodore, 598

Roth, Henry, 26

Rothko, Kate, 322

Rothko, Mark (né Marcus Rothkowitz), 42, 48, 75, 83, 95–96, 100, 105–6, 109, 122, 126–27, 133, 135, 140, 143–46, 149, 156, 159, 162, 167, 168, 171, 173, 178, 179, 182, 184, 186, 190, 192, 196–98, 201, 203, 206, 216, 220, 225, 228, 230, 234–35, 240, 241, 246, 250, 252–54, 257–58, 262–64, 267–68, 271–72, 274–77, *278*, 280–82, 287, 289, 290–94, 300–306, 309, 311, 313, 318–19, 322, 324, 327, 330, 332, 333, 336, 339–41, 344–46, 348–51, 353–55, 357, 359–61, 364, 370, 373, 375–76, 378–81, 386, 389, 393, 397, 410, 412–14, 417, 421, 430, 432, 442, 448, 452, 457, 463, 466, 470, 472, 483, 487–88, 490, 493, 497, 506, 513–14, 521, 534, 545, 556, 560–61, 589, 597, 598, 602, 603–4, 611, 628n50, 631n27, 637n15, 639n21, 641n17, 642n9,

645n34[ch36], 660n3, 664n33; *No. 26*, 359; *The Omen of the Eagle*, 126; *Scribble Book*, 109; *The Syrian Bull*, 144–46, 159, 173

Rothko, Mary Alice ("Mell") (née Beistle), 156, 162, 167, 225, 258, 277, 292, 417

Rothko Chapel, Houston, 534, 664n33

Rothstein, Oscar, 14

Rouault, Georges, 80, 108, 132

round table discussions, 233

Rousseau, Henri, 302

Rubin, Lawrence, 450, 451–52, 463, 513

Rubin, William, 2, 4, 237, 409, 451, 462, 495, 505, 555, 574, 580, 596–99, 603, 640n12, 652n19[ch47], 662n34; *Modern Sacred Art and the Church of Assy*, 660n3

Rubinstein, Helena, 544

Rüdlinger, Arnold, 378–79, 391, 398–99, 410, 413–15, 421, 506, 510–11, 514, 561, 570

Rüdlinger, Pia, 511

Runyon, Damon, 43, 44, 321, 326, 352, 543

Ruskin, John, 178

Russell, Bertrand, 54

Russell, Lillian, 321

Russia, Jews in, 22–25

Russian Tea Room, 447, 462, 483, 506, 571, 604, 663n10

Ruth, Babe, 45, 445

Saarinen, Aline, 432–33

Sachar, Edith, 83, 100, 135, 146

Sage, Kay, 496

Sage, Nancy, *615*

Saint-Exupéry, Antoine de, 96

Saint-Gaudens, Augustus, 483

Salomon, Rita. *See* Reinhardt, Rita

Salsedo, Andrea, 31

Samaras, Lucas, 410

Sam Goody record stores, 321, 428, 440–41, 610

Samuel, Herbert, 47

Sandberg, Willem, 473, 648n21[ch41]

Sander, Joop, 283

Sandler, Irving, 168, 192, 434, 450, 472–73, 484, 486, 624n26, 628n50, 639n21, 641n17

San Francisco Museum of Art, 196, 233

San Francisco Museum of Modern Art, 281

São Paulo Bienale, 391, 522–24, 526, 528–36, 549, 550

Saratoga, New York, 356, 383, 402

Sargent, John Singer, *Madame X*, 313

Sarnoff, Robert, 546

Saroyan, William, 542

Sartre, Jean-Paul, 227, 296, 314; *Age of Reason*, 201

Saturday Review of Literature (magazine), 38, 245, 438

Savoy Mansion, 55, 57

"Scale as Content" (exhibition, 1967), 565

Schanker, Louis, 48, 159

Schapiro, Lillian, 594

Schapiro, Meyer, 4, 19, 105, 121–22, 222, 234, 238, 241, 264–65, 270–71, 275, 279, 402, 409–11, 435, 458–60, 470, 483–84, 491, 492, 495–96, 507, 525, 527, 545–47, 553, 554, 568, 594–95, 597, 604, 651n47, 653n17[ch48], 653n24, 664n11[ch62]; "Leonardo and

Freud: An Art-Historical Study," 451; "The Social Bases of Art," 75

Schapiro, Mimi, 408

Schewe, Theodore E., *Trijugated Tragedy*, 145

Schlegell, William von, 33

Schlumberger Ltd., 580

Schmidt, Georg, 511, 657n26[ch55]

Schnabel, Day, 293

Schnakenberg, Henry, 153, 182

Schneider, Pierre, 570–72, 661n46, 665n13[ch63]; "Through the Louvre with Barnett Newman," 587

Schoenberg, Arnold, 233

Scholem, Gershom, *Zohar*, 225–26

"The School of New York" (exhibition, 1951), 279

School of Paris, 160, 245, 603

School of Visual Arts, 597

Schopenhauer, Arthur, 154, 542

Schrafft's (restaurant), 506, 663n10

Schubert brothers, 542

Schust, Dick, 288

Schwabacher, Ethel, 384, 407

Scripps Howard, 45

Scull, Ethel, 450, 462–63, 472–73, 491, 536, 586, 653n9[ch49]

Scull, Robert, 288, 445, 450, 462–65, 472–73, 486, 491, 536, 586, 653n9[ch49]

"Sculpture by Painters" (exhibition, 1949), 285

"Sculpture by Painters" (exhibition, 1951), 285

"Sculpture Downtown" (Detroit, 1969), 581

Seagram Building, 569, 583

Seattle Art Museum, 517, 585

Seattle-First National Bank, 585

Secession Gallery, 42

Seckler, Dorothy, 370, 475, 487–89

Second Coming (journal), 451

Segal, George, 399

Seiberling, Dorothy, 276, 430, 432–33

Seitz, William, 477, 482, 641n19; "Monet and Abstract Painting," 364

Sekula, Sonia, 246, 250

Seliger, Charles, 183

Seligmann, Kurt, 243, 560

Selz, Peter, 651n40

Senate Foreign Relations Committee, 262

Sepeshy, Zoltan, 116

Serkin, Rudolf, 408

Serpent Mound, Ohio, 248

Seuphor, Michel, 279–80, 379

Sewanee Review (magazine), 166

Shahn, Ben, 299, 304, 313, 332

shaped canvases, 593

Shapiro, Harry, 151, 153, 154, 189

Shas Society, 23

Shaull, R., 547

Shaw, George Bernard, 64

Shaw, Irwin, *The Young Lions*, 281

Sherry Netherland (restaurant), 506

Shostakovich, Dmitri, 218

Shulman, Max, *The Zebra Derby*, 183

Siegel, "Burrie," 128

Sievan, Maurice, 159

silk-screen printing, 117

Sills, Thomas, 241, *322*, 390, *411*, 442, 474

Silver Shirts, 46

Silvestri, Gianni, *322*

Sinai Temple, Los Angeles, 559

Sinatra, Frank, 183

Singer, Arnold, 456

Singer, I. J., 621n9[ch2]

Siporin, Mitchel, 127

Siskind, Aaron, 33, 36–37, 42, 73, 76, 83, 87, 153, 156, 182, 195, 225, 253, 256, 289–90, 628n18[ch17]; Artists' Sessions at Studio 35, *266*; Barnett Newman's first show at Betty Parsons Gallery, January 1950, *254*

Siskind, Sonia, 83, 87, *88*, 225

Sisley, Alfred, 325

Sitkowitz, Israel, 506

"Situation" (exhibition, 1960), 508, 657n12[ch55]

"Six Peintres Americains" (exhibition, 1967), 570

"Sixteen Americans" (exhibition, 1959), 431, 434

"Sixty Painters for 1960" (exhibition, 1960), 468

S. Klein's (department store), 224

Slate, Lane, 494–95, 546

Sleigh, Sylvia, *442*, 444, 470, 506, 507

Slifka, Joseph, 597

Sloan, John, 32, 33, 41, 112, 173, 261, 269, 625n30; *Gist of Art*, 110

Slobodkina, Esphyr, 190

Smith, Al, 48, 56

Smith, Brydon, 604

Smith, David, 136, 141, 182, 194, 313, 377, 411, 497, 514, 546, 551, 553, 565, 603, 638n20

Smith, Duncan, 11

Smith, Jane, 271, 297–98, 322, 364, 646n20

Smith, Leon Polk, 551

Smith, Richard, 393, 411, *440*, 508

Smith, Tony, 119, 135, 165, 167–68, 183, 184, 189, 194–95, 234, 239, 248, 262–63, 271, 288, 297–98, *297*, 310, 316–17, 319, 322, 332, 336, 364, 389, 400, 409–10, 417, 418, 422, *440*, 450, 454, 478, 484, 501–5, 565–66, 569, 598, 610, 633n7[ch23], 637n53, 646n20, 649n14

Smithson, Robert, 568; "Towards the Development of an Air Terminal Site," 566

Smithsonian American Art Museum. *See* National Collection of Fine Arts, Washington, D.C.

Smithsonian Institution, 583

Soby, James Thrall, 245, 299, 636n37

Socialism, 15, 31, 56, 57, 64

Soglow, Otto, 33, 36, *37*, 277

SoHo, 446, 601

Solman, Joseph, 48

Solomon, Alan, 481, 501–2, *502*, 505, 512, 526, 532, 542, 546, 551–52, 554, 558, 561–62, 567, *608*, 611; "The *New* New York Art Scene: Who Makes It?," 562

Solomon, Hyde, 646n7

Sonnabend, Ileanna, 256

Sophocles, *Electra*, 470

Southern Christian Leadership Conference, 580

Soutine, Chaim, 310

Soviet Union, 105, 222, 372, 392, 469–70, 486, 567–68, 613

Soyer, Raphael, 81

space: metaphorical/existential sense of, 184; and Native American art, 187–88; Newman and, 181, 184, 249, 251, 476, 545, 552; Rosenberg on, 250

Spagna, Vincent, 144

Spalding, 71

Spanish Civil War, 93–94

Spector, Jack, 409

Spender, Stephen, 202, 572

Spinoza, Baruch, 3, 34, 54, 259, 570

Spock, Benjamin, 663n10

Spohn, Clay, 220

Spring, Bob, 477

Springs, Long Island, New York, 184, 196, 223, 230, 268, 298, 316–17, 364, 370, 389, *390*, 403, 485, 553

Spruce, Everett, 127

Stable Gallery, 327, 640n44; Annual Exhibitions, 319. *See also* Ninth Street Show

Stafford, Jo, 183

Stalin, Joseph, 225, 589

Stamos, Theodoros, 42, *120*, 150, 159, 184, 192, 195, 201, 216, 246, 250, 261, 262, 272, 275, *278*, 280, 293, 296, 388, *429*, 463, 514, 638n20, 638n26; *Sounds in the Rock*, 234

Stanley, Jim, 585

State Commission on Quasi-Judicial Action of Administrative Agencies, 114

State Rent Administration, 356

Stedelijk Museum, Amsterdam, 440, 473, 562, 585, 587, 589, 590–91, 614, 648n21[ch41], 654n21

Stedelijk van Abbemuseum, Eindhoven, Netherlands, 561, 570

Steig, William, 15

Steinberg, Mendel Zurkowicz, 25

Steinberg, Saul, 182, 277, 441

Steinberg's (restaurant), 543

Stella, Frank, 431, 472, 501, 522, 525–26, 542, 555, 558, 606, 608, 612, 613; *Jasper's Dilemma*, 509

Stella, Rebecca, 526

Stendhal, 63, 211, 573

Stengel, Casey, 477

Stephan, John, 159, 189, 201–2, 213, 215–16, 230, 236, 417, 422, 650n40

Stephan, Ruth, 201, 215–16, 230, 417, 422, 650n40

Stern, Isaac, 446

Sterne, Hedda, 159, 182, 190, 246, 265, *266*, 275, 277–79, *278*, 302, 312, 638n20, 638n26, 639n21, 639n26; *Portrait of Annalee Newman*, 312–13, *312*; *Portrait of Barnett Newman*, 312, *312*

Stevens, Mark, 283

Stevens, Wallace, 591

Steward, Donn, 579

St. George's Episcopal Church, 441

Stieglitz, Alfred, 222

Still, Clyfford, 136, 162, 183–84, 186, 192, 195–98, 201, 203, 212, 216, 220, 223, 224, 228, 230, 234, 235, 241, 246, 247, 252, 257, 260, 264, 267–68, 271, 274, 275, 277, *278*, 279–83, 287, 290–96, 300–301, 303–6, 308, 309, 311, 318–19, 321–25, 327–28, 333, 335–37, 339–41, 344–50, 354–55, 357, 360, 364–65, 375, 376, 379–81, 385, 386, 389–91, 397, 417, 422, 430, 432–33, 450, 457, 470–71, 472, 475, 478, 483, 488, 491, 492–94, 506, 514, 521, 527, 529–30, 534, 550, 556, 557, 560–61, 597,

602, 603–4, 611, 631n27, 638n18, 639n21, 641n16, 641n17, 643n5[ch34], 644n16, 644n18[ch35], 650n40, 662n13; *1956-J No. 2 (PH 1074)*, 430; *Red and Black*, 390

Still, Pat (née Garske), 336, 364, 417, 471, 529

Stillman's Gym, 44, 282, 292, 320, 363, 443

St. Luke's, 615

St. Moritz Hotel, 425

St. Nicholas Arena, 450

Stone, Allan, 484–86, 489, 505. *See also* Allan Stone Gallery

Stone, Irving, *Lust for Life*, 66

The Stranger (film), 183

St. Regis Hotel, 571, 605

Strength (magazine), 34

St. Rose's Home for Incurable Cancer, 29

Stroud, Peter, 508

Stuart, Gilbert, 108

Student Mobilization Committee to End the War in Vietnam, 578

Students for a Democratic Society, 576

Studio 35, 258, 262–63, 637n53; Artists' Sessions, 265–68, *266*, 282, 298–99, 638n20, 638n21, 639n26

Studio International (magazine), 604–5, 666n36

Stuyvesant High School, 32, 37, 42

Stuyvesant Liquors, 329

Stuyvesant Town, 119

Subjects of the Artist School, 202, 234–35, 237–41, 246, 353. *See also* Studio 35

the sublime, 175, 230–32, 280, 286, 320, 457, 492–94, 580

Suez Canal, 372

suicide, 70–71; Rothko's, 611

"Suites: Recent Prints" (exhibition, 1968), 579

Sullivan, Cornelius J., 108

Sullivan, John S., 45

Sullivan, Louis, 422

Sullivan, Mrs. Cornelius J., 149

Sulzberger, Arthur Ochs, 524, 546

Surrealism, 121–24, 126–27, 139–40, 156–57, 164, 173, 180, 187, 239, 314, 373, 410, 630n1[ch20], 639n21

Swan, Annalynn, 283

Sweeney, James Johnson, 219, 332, 468, 654n6

Sweet's (restaurant), 44, 320, 443, 454, 509, 632n6[ch22]

Swissair, 654n41

Swiss National Insurance Company, 413

Sylvester, David, 1, 3, 280, 393, 470, 523, 562, 659n17

"Systemic Painting" (exhibition, 1966), 551, 554

Syverson, Terry, 506, 585

Szeemann, Harald, 506

Talmud, 16–17, 25, 98, 416, 443, 530, 536, 626n8[ch13], 634n34

Tamayo, Rufino, 160, 182, 183

Tammany Hall, 12

Tanach, 542

Tanager gallery, 449

Tanenbaum, Marc, 547

Tapié, Michel, 343, 375, 378

Tarkington, Booth, 13

Tate Gallery, London, 393, 404, 508, 509–10, 587

Tavern on the Green, 506

taxes: on art donations, 596–97, 600; audits of the Newmans' tax returns, 419, 562, 571, 585, 597, 650n12

Taylor, Francis Henry, 232, 269, 270, 309

Tchaikovsky, Pyotr, 35

Tchelitchew, Pavel, 164, 299

teacher's licensing examinations, 42, 48–49, 74–75, 77, 84, 89–92, 100, 110, 625n30

Teachers Union, 91

television, 219, 263, 270, 332–33, 392

The Ten, 42, 48, 67, 76, 95–96

Teniers, David, 261

terror, Newman's concern with, 126, 139, 160, 166, 175, 177, 180–81, 184, 205, 259, 274, 284, 287, 373, 438, 455, 457, 491, 496, 534, 548

Theatre Troupe, 40, 68–69, 79

Theler, Hans, 413–15

Thiebaud, Wayne, 484

Third American Writers Congress of the League of American Writers, 101

Third Liberty Loan, 20

Thomas, Norman, 129, 568

Thomas, Yvonne, 224, 240–41

Thoreau, Henry David, 78, 425

"Three American Painters: Kenneth Noland, Jules Olitski, Frank Stella" (exhibition, 1965), 524

Thunderbird, 464

Thurn, Ernest, 137

Tibor de Nagy Gallery, 296, 377, 390, 513

The Tiger's Eye (magazine), 189, 199, 201–2, 206, 213–16, 230, 235–37, 246, 249, 280, 330, 523

Tillim, Sidney, 486

Time (magazine), 219, 222, 254, 257, 270, 276, 293, 337, 341–44, 350, 389–90, 434, 448, 470, 474, 494, 497, 506, 536, 544, 566, 577, 591

time, experienced through art, 249

Time-Life Publications, 150

Tintoretto, 37

Titian, 95; *Pope Paul III*, 108

Tobey, Mark, 162, 183, 233, 250, 393, 512

Der Tog (newspaper), 34, 45, 221

Tolstoy, Leo, 41, 54, 63

Tomlin, Bradley, 201, 216, 219, 222, 239, 242, 246, 250, 252, 257, 271, 275–76, *278*, 293, 302, 305, 360, 370, 376, 472, 527, 561, 604, 638n20, 641n17; *Number 10*, 472

Toptani, Gulda, 153

Torah, 18–19, 23, 185, 199, 225, 503–4

Toronto Daily Star (newspaper), 466

Toscanini, Arturo, 90

totem poles, 188, 198, 248

Toulouse-Lautrec, Henri de, 108, 173

Touro Synagogue, Newport, Rhode Island, 502, 504

"Toward a New Abstraction" (exhibition, 1963), 501

Town Hall, 75

Toynbee, Arnold, 233

tragedy and the tragic, 26, 66–67, 98, 145, 146, 160, 175, 189, 191, 200, 205–6, 213, 221, 260, 519, 548

Transcendentalists, 78

trans/formation (journal), 299

Treitel-Gratz (fabricators), 506, 531, *531*, 552, 565, 599

Tremaine, Burton, 648n17[ch42]

Tremaine, Emily Hall, 203, 648n17[ch42]

tribal art. *See* "primitive" art

Triesel, Helen, 321
Trotsky, Leon, 94, 225
Truman, Harry, 190, 217, 286–87, 371–72, 640n20
Tschacbasov, Nahum, 48
Tuchman, Maurice, 409–10, 526–27, 652n21[ch46], 659n53
Tucker, Allen, 33
Tuffy, 478
Turgenev, Ivan, 211; *The Life of a Sportsman*, 454
Turnbull, William, 378, 411, 506, 508
Turner, Evan, 547, 569
Turner, J. M. W., 457
Twain, Mark, 45
"Twelve Americans" (exhibition, 1956), 370, 431
"Twelve Angry Men" (television show), 336
"Twenty Centuries of Mexican Art" (exhibition, 1940), 151–52
Twenty-Sixth Street Armory, 505
Tworkov, Jack, 136, 140, 183, 189–90, 227, 228, 239, 247, 255–56, 290, 294, 303, 337, 347, *411*, *429*, 632n7[ch22], 642n9

Uccello, Paolo, *Battle of San Romano*, 570
Ugo Mulas in New York: The New Art Scene, 551
ULAE. *See* Universal Limited Art Editions
the unconscious, 122, 123, 173
"Under the Auspices of The Museum of Modern Art" (exhibition, 1957), 376
unions, 31, 85–86
United Auto Workers, 581
United Nations, 567, 569, 663n10; headquarters, 182, 217
United States. *See* American art
Universal Limited Art Editions (ULAE), 498–501, 515, 579, 586
University in Exile, 75
University of Akron, 64
University of Bridgeport, Connecticut, 574
University of California, 333
University of Iowa, 135
University of Pennsylvania, 479; Institute of Contemporary Art, 522
University of Washington, Seattle, 517, 664n1
Uris (corporation), 388, 564
"USA Artists: Barnett Newman" (television show), 546, 552–53
U.S. Army, 332–33, 581
U.S. Army Air Corps, 82
U.S. Army Air Force, 82
U.S. Civil Service Commission, 53, 86, 100
U.S. Congress, 217, 233, 242–43, 596–97
U.S. Department of Justice, 148
U.S. Department of State, 190, 219, 245, 262, 404, 533, 535–36
U.S. Department of the Army, 217
U.S. Department of the Interior, 187, 188
U.S. Department of War, 82, 144
"Useful Household Objects Under $5" (exhibition, 1938), 111
U.S. Government Committee on Public Information, 20
U.S. Information Agency (USIA), 287, 468, 512, 522, 530, 532–33, 551, 558
U.S. Library of Congress, 243, 641n19
U.S. National Guard, 613

Valentin, Curt, 513
Valentine Dudensing gallery, 41, 126
Valley of the Eagles (film), 259, 637n62
Van Cortlandt Park, 15
Vandivert, William, 403, 417, 470, 649n23[ch42]; Barnett and Annalee Newman, 1958, *403*; Barnett Newman in his Front Street studio with *Adam*, *Eve*, and *Horizon Light*, *330*
Van Dyk, James, 480
Vanguard (journal), 69
"Vanguard American Painting" (exhibition, 1962), 468
Vannovskii, Petr, 24–26
Van Weeren-Griek, Hans, 229, 520, 658n16
Varnedoe, Kirk, 588
Vasarely, Victor, 419
Vcharian, Gabiel, 547
Venice Biennale, 233, 272, 391, 393, 400, 412, 430, 512–13, 516, 550–51, 638n30, 661n12, 666n19
Verdi, Giuseppe, *Don Carlos*, 305
Vermeer, Johannes, 320; *The Milkmaid*, 107
Veronese, Paolo, *The Wedding Feast at Cana*, 570
Vicente, Esteban, 376
Vietnam War, 522, 543, 558, 569, 606, 613, 663n10
viewers: and Native American earthworks, 249; and Newman's works, 1, 213, 249, 284, 288, 382, 401, 439, 445, 453, 489, 499–500, 541, 569, 640n14; and Rosenquist's *F-111*, 541; and Surrealist works, 140
Village Gate, 428
The Village Voice (newspaper), 593
Virginia Wright Fund, 664n1
Vogue (magazine), 39, 261, 277, 291, 293, 320, 429, 491–93, 549, 554, 555, 562, 587, 611, 651n21; "8 New York Painters," *429*
Voice of America, 82, 287, 332, 658n23
Volozhyn Yeshiva, 16, 23
Voltaire, 54
Vytlacil, Vaclav, 137

Wadsworth Atheneum, Hartford, Connecticut, 474, 495, 633n7[ch23]
Wagner, Richard, 65
Wagner, Robert, 48, 338, 446
Wagstaff, Samuel, 474, 495, 496
Wah Kee (restaurant), 263, 506
The Wakefield Bookshop, 149, 150–51, 153, 159
Wakeman, Frederic, *The Hucksters*, 182
Walden Pond, 78
Waldorf Cafeteria, 183, 204, 234, 241, 246
Walker, Jimmy, 56–57
Walker Art Center, Minneapolis, 383, 468
Wallace, George, 576
Wall Street Journal (newspaper), 577
Wanamaker's, 71, 187
Ward, Eleanor, 640n44
Warhol, Andy, 2, 479, 492, 549, 586, 596; *Jackie Kennedy*, 509
Warner, John C., 465–66
Warren, Robert Penn, 568; *All the King's Men*, 182
War Resisters League, 115
Washburn, Gordon, 391, 393, 404, 410, 465–66

Washington Gallery of Modern Art, Washington, D.C., 583

Washington Irving Evening High School, 88, 117, 137, 157, 198, 287

Washington Post (newspaper), 441, 549, 550, 584, 593

Waugh, Evelyn, *Brideshead Revisited*, 182

Weber, Max, 91–92, 132, 133

Weil, Gotshal & Manges, 572

Weinstein, Florence, 240

Weisman, Fred, 437, 470–73, 477–78, 483, 491, 495, 496, 600

Weisman, Marcia, 437, 470–73, 477–78, 491, 495, 559

Wesselmann, Tom, 656n16

West Coast art and artists, 183, 250, 437, 473, 478–79, 514, 526

Western American Investing Company, 600

Wharton, Edith, 54

"What About Jewish Art?" (panel, 1965), 520

Wheeler, Burton Kendall, 129

Wheeler, Steve, 187

Whelan, Charles, 547

Whistler, James McNeill, 253, 393, 542, 661n46

White, E. B., 44, 663n10

Whitehead, Alfred North, 314

Whitehorn & Cowin, 341

White Horse Tavern, 355

Whitelaw Reid Mansion, 139

Whitman, Robert, 613

Whitney, Gertrude, 130–32

Whitney, John Hay "Jock," 341, 351

Whitney, Mrs. Cornelius V., 153

Whitney Museum of American Art, 59, 217–18, 219, 267–68, 270, 337, 338, 352–54, 356, 357, 480, 495, 544, 601, 611, 613, 648n14[ch42]; Annual Exhibitions, 95, 233, 268, 275, 311, 421, 509, 588

Wilde, Edy de, 440, 590, 614

Wildenstein Gallery, 37, 41, 144, 146, 304

Wilder, Nicholas, 500

Wilfred, Thomas, 604

Willard, Marian, 250

Williams, Hope, 182

Williams, Tennessee, 410

Winchell, Walter, 45, 314, 325–26, 352

Wingert, Paul, 187

Winlock, Herbert, 59

Winthrop, Granville, 153

Wise, James Waterman, 93–94

Wise, Stephen S., 48, 54, 78, 138

Witness for the Prosecution (film), 397

Wittkower, Rudolf and Margot, *Born Under Saturn*, 497

WNET (television network), 544, 546

WNYC (radio station), 95, 149, 293, 316

Wolff, Betty, 562, 604, 663n20[ch60]

Wolff, Jesse, 586

Wolff, Robert, 319, 333, 334

Wolfson, Victor, 192

Wollheim, Richard, 507

women: blamed for corruption in art, 449; Newman's attitudes about/behaviors toward, 70–71, 81, 98, 141–42, 188, 240, 299, 454–55, 504–5, 536–37, 643n13[ch35], 648n14[ch41], 651n13[ch45]; New

York School artists and, 205; at Subject of the Artist School, 238, 240; in synagogues, 504–5

Wood, Grant, 130–32

Woodruff, Hale, 234, 637n53

Woodstock Artists Association, 313–16, 326, 329, 331

Woolf, Virginia, 54

Woolworth Building, 443

"Word and Image" (exhibition, 1965), 541

Works Progress Administration (WPA), 42, 67, 80, 86, 96, 108, 110–11, 126, 158, 329, 517. *See also* Federal Art Project

World Jewish Congress, 138

World's Fair (New York, 1939), 106–8, 120, 125

World's Fair (New York, 1964), 507, 512

World's Fair (Seattle, 1962), 466, 473–75, 481

World War I, 13, 18

World War II, 95, 97, 105–6, 113–16, 126, 128–32, 135–40, 146, 163–64, 168, 171, 179, 217

Worringer, Wilhelm, 166

Wouk, Herman, *The Caine Mutiny*, 281

WPA. *See* Works Progress Administration

WQXR (radio station), 113

Wright, Bagley, 473, 658n6

Wright, Frank Lloyd, 168, 233, 263, 504, 539, 574, 632n6[ch23], 654n6

Wright, Richard, *Native Son*, 112, 626n2[ch13]

Wright, Virginia, 302–3, 306, 473, 514, 517–18, 585, 642n31[ch33], 658n6, 660n18. *See also* Virginia Wright Fund

Wright's Tavern, Concord, Massachusetts, 78

WRVR (radio station), 482

Wyeth, Andrew, 533

Yaddo artists' colony, 402–3

Yale University, 217

Yamin, Alice, 87, 225

Yamin, Leo, 36, 87, 225

Yankee Stadium, 292, 470, 477. *See also* New York Yankees

Yeats, W. B., 34

Yiddish language, 2, 4, 16–18, 25, 68, 80, 97, 221, 321, 482, 511, 579, 651n47

Yizkor (Remember) prayer, 199

Yom Kippur, 199, 211

"You Are an Artist" (television show), 219

Young, Brigham, 129

Young, Mahonri, 129, 588

"Younger American Painters" (exhibition, 1954), 337

"Young Painters in the U.S. and in France" (exhibition, 1950), 275

Zarnower, Teresa, 180

Zeckendorf, William, 263

Zelevansky, Lynn, 305

Zerbe, Karl, 218

Zionism, 11, 13, 15–18, 24, 26, 185, 225–28, 287, 542, 567–68, 630n22[ch20]

zips, 206, 211, 247, 253, 256, 286, 289, 308, 417, 456, 479, 541–42, 591, 592, 660n18

Zorach, William, 81

Zukofsky, Louis, 36–37

PHOTO CREDITS